MEDICAL ABBREVIATIONS:

55,000 Conveniences at the Expense of Communication and Safety

16th Edition

Neil M Davis, MS, PharmD, FASHP

Professor Emeritus, Temple University
School of Pharmacy, Philadelphia, PA,
Editor Emeritus, Hospital Pharmacy

published by

Neil M Davis Associates, T/A MedAbbrev.com
605 Louis Drive, Suite 508B
Warminster PA 18974-2830

Phone (215) 442-7430
  (9 AM-4 PM EST, Mon-Fri)
FAX (215) 442-7432
E-mail ev@medabbrev.com
Secure Website www.medabbrev.com

First edition, 1983, titled, "1700 Medical Abbreviations:
   Conveniences at the Expense of Communications and Safety"
Second edition, 1985, titled, "Medical Abbreviations: 2300
   Conveniences at the Expense of Communication and Safety"
Third edition, 1987, titled, "Medical Abbreviations: 4200 ..."
Fourth edition, 1988, titled, "Medical Abbreviations: 5500 ..."
Fifth edition, 1990, titled, "Medical Abbreviations: 7000 ..."
Sixth edition, 1993, titled, "Medical Abbreviations: 8600 ..."
Seventh edition, 1995, titled, "Medical Abbreviations: 10,000 ..."
Eighth edition, 1997, titled, "Medical Abbreviations: 12,000 ..."
Ninth edition, 1999, titled, "Medical Abbreviations: 14,000 ..."
Tenth edition, 2001, titled, "Medical Abbreviations: 15,000 ..."
Eleventh edition, 2003, titled, "Medical Abbreviations: 24,000 ..."
Twelfth edition, 2005, titled, "Medical Abbreviations: 26,000 ..."
Thirteenth edition, 2007, titled, "Medical Abbreviations: 28,000 ..."
Fourteenth edition, 2009, titled, "Medical Abbreviations: 30,000 ..."
Fifteenth edition, 2011, titled, "Medical Abbreviations: 32,000 ..."
Sixteenth edition, 2020, titled, "Medical Abbreviations: 55,000 ..."

Library of Congress Control Number 2001012345

ISBN 978-0-931431-00-5

Warning: The user must exercise care in that the meaning shown in this book may not be the one intended by the writer of the medical abbreviation. When there is doubt, the writer must be contacted for clarification.

Printed in the USA.

Contents

Dedication

This book is dedicated to Julie, my wife, for her support, patience, assistance, and love.

Acknowledgments

The assistance of Evelyn Canizares, Greg Hammond, Absolute Service Inc., The Advisor Expert Panel, Ann Sandt Kishbaugh, Robin Miller, and Rachael Miller is gratefully acknowledged.

I would like to express my deep appreciation for the many contributions received from readers for their suggested additions and corrections. Please continue to send these to—

Dr. Neil M Davis
605 Louis Drive, Suite 508B
Warminster PA 18974

Phone (215) 442 7430
E-mail   neil@medabbrev.com
Secure Website www.medabbrev.com

Preface

The Internet Version (medabbrev.com):
Why Use It and How to Access It

Along with the purchase of each book, the book owner, at no extra cost, is entitled to a single-user license for access to the Internet version of this 16th edition. This license is valid for 12 months from the date of the initial log-in. Chrome, Internet Explorer 11, Edge Safari, FireFox, and modern Android and IOS Devices are supported.

Features of the Internet Version

- Updated weekly with about 30 entries (suggestions from users are welcomed and will be incorporated).
- Can instantly search for the meanings of abbreviations and acronyms.
- Has a reverse-search feature, for example, looking for all the abbreviations that contain the word "laparoscopic."
- Can search for cross-referenced generic and brand names of drugs.
- Click any word or drug name and be connected to the Wikipedia definition/monograph.
- Can search through the listings of symbols and lists.
- Quick access to a "Do Not Use" list of dangerous abbreviations, an explanation as to why they are dangerous, and suggested alternatives to be used. Facilities that obtain multi-user licenses may substitute their own "Do Not Use" list, which they can control and update.
- Can read the full-text of the introductory chapters of the book.
- Can add it to your WiFi-enabled devices at no extra cost.

Instructions for the Initial One-time Log-in

- Access the Website at *www.medabbrev.com*
- Click the **Register** button.
- You must agree to the Single-User License Agreement which is presented.
- You will be asked for the 8-letter access code that appears on the front inside cover of the book. This will be the only time you are asked for this code.
- At this point just follow the directions.
- Note your sign-in name and your self-assigned password. This name/password will only permit one access at a time, so keep this information confidential to ensure you do not get locked out of the site.

Searching for the Meaning of an Abbreviation on the Internet Version

- Use upper OR lower case letters as the search engine is NOT case sensitive.
- Use normal upper OR lower case letters as the search engine is NOT sensitive to whether the letters are **bold-face** or *italicized*.
- Superscripts and subscripts are to be entered as regular text.
- DO NOT enter periods, commas, hyphens, or spaces (enter afib, not a fib).
- For other details, just follow the simple instructions shown on the Website. The Internet version of the book is essentially the same as the print version except for the fact that it is searchable and is updated weekly with about 30 new entries.

Multi-user Site Licenses are Available

A copy of the Multi-User Site License agreement and its price list is available by email (ev@medabbrev.com), by clicking the "Submit Suggestions" button on *www.medabbrev.com* where you can type a request to receive it or by calling 215 442 7430. A no-cost, 3-week trial is available.

Extending or Purchasing Internet Access

A 12-month purchase or extension of the Internet version is available.

Additions, Corrections, and Suggestions are Welcomed

Please send them via any means shown below:

Neil M Davis

605 Louis Drive, Suite 508B
Warminster PA 18974-2830

FAX 215 442 7432
Email neil@medabbrev.com
Secure website www.medabbrev.com

Thank you for your help in the past.

Have You Used the medabbrev.com website Version of This Book?

- It is instantaneously searchable for the meanings of abbreviations
- It is reverse searchable (search for all the abbreviations containing a particular word)
- Each week, about 30 new entries are added

See the preface (page vii) for access instructions. A one-year, single-user access is included in the purchase price of the book. Also one-year subscriptions (no book) are available for purchase.

Multi-User Site Licenses for medabbrev.com are Available for Your Intranet

Medical facilities can substitute their own "Do Not Use" list of dangerous abbreviations for the one present. The ability also exists to list abbreviations that are unique to your region and/or organization which would normally not appear in any national list. These lists would be controlled by the facility or company. A no-cost, 3-week trial and pricing information are available by calling 215 442 7430 or via an e-mail request to ev@medabbrev.com

Chapter 1
Introduction/Warning

The book contains 55,000 entries. Listed are possible meanings of abbreviations, acronyms, slang, and symbols, as well as drug trade names and their generic name. The listings have been compiled to assist health professions, student, and all those who must understand health-related communications.

WARNING

Abbreviations are a convenience, a time saver, a space saver, a way of fitting a word or phrase into a restricted space on a form or computer, and a way of avoiding the possibility of misspelling words. However, a price can be paid for their use. Abbreviations are sometimes not understood. They can be misread, or are interpreted incorrectly. Their use lengthens the time needed to train individuals in the health fields, wastes the time of healthcare workers in tracking down their meaning, at times delays the patient's care, and occasionally results in patient harm.

The publication of this list of abbreviations is not an endorsement of their legitimacy. It is not a guarantee that the intended meaning has been correctly captured, nor is it an indication that the abbreviation is commonly used. The person who uses an abbreviation must take responsibility for making sure that it is properly interpreted. When an uncommon or ambiguous abbreviation is used and it may not be understood correctly, it should be defined by the writer. Where uncertainty exists, the one who wrote the abbreviation must be contacted for clarification.

There are three types of what are generally termed as abbreviations:

- Acronyms: Lettered abbreviations which are pronounced as a word (e.g., AIDS)
- Initialism: First letter of each word is used and it is *not* pronounced as a word (e.g., HIV)
- Brief Form: A shortened form of a word (e.g., exam)

There are many variations in how an abbreviation can be expressed. Anterior-posterior has been written as AP, A.P., ap, a.p., and A/P. Since there are few standards and those who use abbreviations do not necessarily follow these standards, this book only shows anterior-posterior as AP. This is done to make it easier to find the meaning of an abbreviation as all the meanings of AP are listed together.

When an abbreviation is made up of a series of abbreviations, it may not be listed as such. In such instances, the meaning may be determined by looking up each set of abbreviations.

Lower case letters are used when firm custom dictates as in Ag, Na, mCi, etc. The first letter of brand names are capitalized, whereas nonproprietary names appear in lower case.

The abbreviation ACT is listed as meaning doxorubicin, cyclophosphamide, and paclitaxil. The reason for this apparent disparity is that the official generic names (United States Adopted Names) are shown rather than the brand names Adriamycin and Taxol. In the case of LSD, the official name, lysergide, is given, as well as the chemical name, lysergic acid diethylamide. The Latin derivations for older medical and pharmaceutical abbreviations (*TID, ter in die*, three times daily) may be found in *Remington*.[1]

Some abbreviations which have been encountered or that have been suggested for addition to the book have not been added. Some were obscene or completely insensitive. Slang and drug name abbreviations are shown for informational purposes only and should not be used.

Abbreviations for medical facility names create problems as they are usually not recognized by the readers in other geographic areas. A clue to the fact that one is dealing with such an abbreviation is when it ends with MC, for Medical Center; HS, for Health System; MH, for Memorial Hospital; CH, for Community Hospital; UH, for University Hospital; and H, for Hospital.

The use of abbreviations are not uniform across the country, and usage tends to cluster. Sometimes physicians just make up their own abbreviations. Sometimes a physician-in-training will pick up and use abbreviations used by residents or attendings where they train. Sometimes group practices will start to use certain abbreviations. Sometimes hospitals might have banned certain abbreviations, so you might not see them used at one hospital, while at another hospital they are used. Usage will also vary by specialty.

Form designers and computer programmers should be sensitive to the fact that unrealistic restriction of space for entering data can cause users to create abbreviations which will be unfamiliar to future readers.

As in the medical and other scientific literature, organism and plant names, and non-English words and abbreviations are expressed in italics in this book and Internet version, however in the medical transcription field, these are expressed in normal typeface.[2] It also should be noted that in computerized health records, *italics*, boldface type, superscripts, and subscripts are expressed in normal typeface.

If a meaning for an abbreviation with an ending of an S can not be found, look for that abbreviation without the S. SAEs (serious adverse events) would not be found, but SAE (serious adverse event) is listed.

When an abbreviation cannot be found in this book or when the listed meaning(s) do not make sense, there is a possibility that the abbreviation has been misread. As an example, a reader could not find the meaning of HHTS. On closer examination it really was +HTS, not HHTS. Also EWT could not be identified because it was really ENT.

Some common French and Spanish abbreviations are listed in the book. Because of language structure differences, these abbreviations are often reversed, as in the case of HIV, which in Spanish and French is abbreviated as VIH.

You are entitled to a no-cost, one-year access to our website (see the Preface, page vii). If you cannot find a meaning for an abbreviation, check medabbrev.com as 30 new entries are added each week. We offer a service of searching for the meanings you cannot find. Send us at, ev@medabbrev.com, the abbreviation you cannot find and the context in which it is used and we will search for it and we get back to you.

Chapter 3 presents a list of 275 of the most commonly used abbreviations. The purpose of this list is to serve as a primer for whose entering a health-related field.

Chapter 7 contains a cross-referenced list of 5,300 generic and brand drug names. The list contains names of commonly prescribed, new drugs, and recently discontinued drugs. Brand names have their first letter capitalized whereas generic names are in lower case. This list will enable readers to obtain the generic name for brand name products or brand names for generic names. It will also serve as a spelling check.

Coded drug names and abbreviations for drug names are found in the chapter on abbreviations (Chapter 4). Abbreviated drug names should not be used as they pose a safety risk.

Avoid using abbreviations when naming a diagnosis and/or operative procedures. These are critical points of information, and their meanings must be clear to assure accurate communication for patient care, reimbursement, statistical purposes, and medicolegal documentation.

Even though an abbreviation meaning is identified in the body of an article for publication, avoid using this abbreviation in the title and abstract. Unidentified abbreviations may not be understood as only titles and abstracts are what will appear in PubMed and elsewhere.

The Council of Biology Editors (CBE), in their 1983 edition of the *CBE Style Manual* listed about 600 abbreviations gathered from 15 internationally recognized authorities and organizations.[3] The majority of these symbols and abbreviations tend to be more scientifically oriented than those which would appear in medical records. In the few situations where the CBE abbreviations differ from what is presented in this book, the CBE abbreviation has been placed in parentheses after the meaning. As is the practice in the United States, mL has been used rather than ml and the spelling of liter, meter, etc. is used rather than litre and metre, even though ml, litre, and metre are listed in the *CBE Style Manual*. A current edition of the *CBE Style Manual* was published in 2006.[4]

Only a few of the acronyms and abbreviations for the major cardiologic trials, such as, TIMI- Thrombosis In Myocardial Infarction (trial), have been included in this book. For a list of 4,200 of these acronyms and abbreviations, consult reference number 5.

For a more complete list of abbreviations used for cancer chemotherapy protocols see the appendix of the reference book/web-version, Drug Facts and Comparisons.[6]

On the *positive side*, the use of abbreviations:
- Saves time for the writer
- Saves space
- Lessens the possibility of misspellings
- Allows for fitting information into restricted space provided on a form or computer

On the *negative side*, will uncontrolled use of abbreviations result in:
- Not understood communication?
- Puzzling documentation?
- An increase in the time necessary to train health personnel
- Delays in initiating treatment?
- Patient harm?

Over the years certain abbreviations are no longer used because of changes and/or advancements. These obsolete abbreviations are not removed from this book because old records are reviewed for auditing, research, and medicolegal sleuthing. Secondly, some physicians are slow to let go of out-of-date terminology or abbreviations and will likely use early-learned abbreviations out of habit, perhaps for a lifetime. Since the purpose of the book is to help readers decipher whatever it is that they are reading, then there is no logic to restricting abbreviations to only the latest, greatest, and newest of things; the book/web version is needed to help decipher the not-so-new and not-so-great and oldest of abbreviations as well.

An examination of the abbreviations, acronyms, symbols, and their meanings is a testimonial to the problems and dangers associated with uncontrolled use of undefined abbreviations.

References

1. Hendrickson R, ed. Remington's The Science and Practice of Pharmacy, 21st ed. Phila., PA: Lippincott Williams and Wilkins, 2006.

2. Sims L. The Book of Style for Medical Transcription, 3rd ed. 2008. Association for Healthcare Documentation Integrity. Modesta, CA.

3. CBE Style Manual, 5th ed. Bethesda, MD: Council of Biology Editors; 1983.

4. Council of Science Editors, Style Manual Committee, Science style and format: the CSE manual for authors, editors, and publishers. 7th ed. Reston (VA): The Council; 2006.

5. Cheng TO, Julian D. Acronyms of cardiologic trials-2002. Int J Cardiol 2003;91:261–351.

6. Facts and Comparisons, St. Louis, Wolters Kluwer Health (factsandcomparisons.com)

Additions, Corrections, and Suggestions are Welcomed

Please send them via any means shown below:

Neil M Davis

605 Louis Drive, Suite 508B

Warminster PA 18974-2830

FAX 215 442 7432

Email neil@medabbrev.com

Secure website www.medabbrev.com

Thank you for your help in the past.

Have You Used the medabbrev.com website Version of This Book?

- It is instantaneously searchable for the meanings of abbreviations
- It is reverse searchable (search for all the abbreviations containing a particular word)
- Each week, about 30 new entries are added

See the preface (page vii) for access instructions. A one-year, single-user access is included in the purchase price of the book. Also one-year subscriptions (no book) are available for purchase.

Multi-User Site Licenses for medabbrev.com are Available for Your Intranet

Medical facilities can substitute their own "Do Not Use" list of dangerous abbreviations for the one present. The ability also exists to list abbreviations that are unique to your region and/or organization which would normally not appear in any national list. These lists would be controlled by the facility or company. A no-cost, 3-week trial and pricing information are available by calling 215 442 7430 or via an e-mail request to ev@medabbrev.com

Chapter 2

Dangerous, Contradictory, and/or Ambiguous Abbreviations

Many inherent problems associated with abbreviations contribute to or cause errors. Reports of such errors have been published routinely (see Table 1).[1-5]

Healthcare organizations are directed by the Joint Commission to formulate a "Do Not Use" list of dangerous abbreviations which should NOT be used. An example of such a list, which has been adopted from the Institute of Safe Medication Practice Inc. (ISMP) list, is shown as Table 2.

Table 1. Examples of Abbreviations That Have Been Misread or Misinterpreted

(1) "HCT250 mg" was intended to mean hydrocortisone 250 mg but was interpreted as hydrochlorothiazide 50 mg (HCTZ50 mg).

(2) Flucytosine was improperly abbreviated as 5 FU, causing it to be read as fluorouracil. Flucytosine is abbreviated 5 FC and fluorouracil is 5 FU.

(3) Floxuridine was improperly abbreviated as 5 FU, causing it to be read as fluorouracil. Floxuridine is abbreviated FUDR and fluorouracil is 5 FU.

(4) MTX was thought to be mechlorethamine. MTX is methotrexate and mechlorethamine is abbreviated HN2.

(5) **The abbreviation "U" for unit is the most dangerous one in the book, having caused numerous ten-fold insulin and heparin overdoses. The word unit should never be abbreviated.** The handwritten U for unit has been mistaken for a zero, causing tenfold errors. The handwritten U has also been read as the number four, six, and as "cc."

(6) OD, meant to signify once daily, has caused Lugol's solution to be given in the right eye.

(7) OJ meant to signify orange juice, looked like OS and caused saturated solution of potassium iodide to be given in the left eye.

(8) IVP, meant to signify intravenous push (Lasix 20 mg IVP), caused a patient to be given an intravenous pyelogram which is the usual meaning of this abbreviation.

(9) Na Warfarin (sodium warfarin) was read as "No Warfarin."

(10) The abbreviation "s̄" for "without" has been thought to mean "with" (c̄).

(11) The order for PT, intended to signify a laboratory test order for prothrombin time, resulted in the ordering of a physical therapy consultation.

(12) The abbreviation "TAB," meant to signify Triple Antibiotic (a coined name for a hospital sterile topical antibiotic mixture), caused patients to have their wounds irrigated with a diet soda. At another facility, with the same set of circumstances, they did not have TAB®, so they used Diet Shasta.®

(13) A slash mark (/) has been mistaken for a one, causing a patient to receive a 100 unit overdose of NPH insulin when the slash was used to separate an order for two insulin doses: 6 units regular insulin/20 units NPH insulin

(14) Vidarabine, an antiviral agent, was ordered as ara-A; however, ara-C, which is cytarabine, an antineoplastic agent, was given.

(15) On several occasions, pediatric strength diphtheria-tetanus toxoids (DT) have been confused with adult strength tetanus-diphtheria toxoids (Td).

(16) DTP is commonly understood to refer to diphtheria-tetanus-pertussis vaccine, but in some hospitals it is also used as shorthand for a sedative cocktail of Demerol, Thorazine, and Phenergan. Several cases have occurred where a child was vaccinated rather than given the sedative mixture.

5

(17) What does the abbreviation MR mean? Some will guess measles-rubella vaccine (M-R-Vax II, Merck), while others will assume mumps-rubella vaccine (Biavax II, Merck).

(18) The abbreviation TIW (three times a week) was thought to mean Tuesday and Wednesday when the I was read as a slash mark. Due to confirmation bias (you see what you know), this uncommon abbreviation is seen as the more commonly used TID (three times a day).

(19) PCA, meant to be procainamide, was interpreted as patient-controlled analgesia.

(20) PGE$_1$ (alprostadil, Caverject) was read as P6 E1 (Alcon's ophthalmic 6% pilocarpine and 1% epinephrine solution).

(21) A nurse transcribed an oral order for the antibiotic aztreonam as AZT, which was subsequently thought to be the antiviral drug zidovudine.

(22) An order for TAC 0.1%, intended to mean triamcinolone cream, was interpreted as tetracaine, Adrenalin, and cocaine solution.

(23) An order for SPA (salt poor albumin) was overlooked because it was not recognized as a drug order.

(24) Therapy was delayed and considerable professional time was wasted when an order for "Bactrim SS q 12 h on S/S" had to be clarified (Bactrim Single Strength every 12 hours on Saturday and Sunday).

(25) A physician wrote an order stating "may take own supply of EPO". The physician meant evening primrose oil, not Epogen (epoetin alfa).

(26) 4-MP was recommended to treat ethylene glycol poisoning. The medical resident mistakenly interpreted this as 6-MP (6-mercaptopurine). 4-MP is fomepizole (4 methylpyrazole) and 6-MP is mercaptopurine (6-mercaptopurine).

(27) An order for lomustine stated it was to be given at "hs". This was misinterpreted as to mean every night. After continuous administration, toxicity resulted in the patient's death. The drug is normally given once every 6 weeks. State complete orders such as "HS × 1 dose today," "HS nightly," or "HS nightly PRN for sleep."

(28) The directions for an order for Cortisporin Otic Solution indicated "Three drops in ® ear TID." The patient was given the drops in the rear rather than the right ear.

(29) There have been mix-ups between IL-2 and IL-11 when IL-2 is expressed as IL-II (Roman numeral 2). The II has been read as "IL eleven," and vice versa. IL-2 (interleukin 2) is aldesleukin (Proleukin) and IL-11 is oprelvekin (Neumega).

(30) A drug was ordered "Q 10 h." It was read as QID (four times daily). Drugs should not be ordered at unusual hourly intervals such as every 10, 18, or 36 hours, as this has resulted in a host of errors. Standard times are every 2, 3, 4, 6, 8, or 12 hours; once, twice, three, or four times daily; every other day, or Monday, Wednesday, and Friday and once weekly.

(31) 6 IU was read 61 units instead of the intended 6 international units.

(32) A dose of phenytoin was modified and expressed as mg/Kg/d. The d was read as "dose" rather than the intended "day" resulting in 3 extra doses being given.

(33) An order appeared as "If no BM in PM, give MOM in AM p.r.n."

(34) Sometimes ambiguous abbreviations cause financial losses to health providers. For example, an insurance provider may pay less for an office visit for mental retardation than it does for mitral regurgitation. This can happen if the coder is faced with the abbreviation MR.

(35) The abbreviation for "q PM" has been read as 9 PM (a one time dose at 9 PM) rather than every night.

(36) An order was written in a hospital, "Cortisporin 3 drops, AS bid." There was a question about the meaning of AS, but since the patient was scheduled for a colonoscopy it was decided that the meaning was "anal sphincter", so the drug was administered rectally rather than in the left ear as intended. When the patient was asked to roll over for their medicine, I suppose they could have protested that there was nothing wrong with their rectum, but then again, maybe this was part of a complex preparation for their colonoscopy!

(37) A liver transplant patient on readmission had an order handwritten, "MMF 1000 mg PO BID (mycophenolate mofetil)." Mycophenolate mofetil is the immunosuppressive agent CellCept which has been abbreviated MMF. The order was misread as 1000 mg twice daily MWF (Monday, Wednesday, and Friday). Several doses of this critical drug were omitted before the error was discovered.

(38) A prescription was written for PTU. PTU normally means propylthiouracil, however Purinethol was dispensed in error causing a fatality. Purinethol is never abbreviated PTU.

The error probably occurred because both propylthiouracil and Purinethol are available in 50 mg tablets and sit side-by-side on the pharmacy shelf. The prescriber contributed to the error by using nonstandard terminology, an abbreviation.

(39) A nurse mistaken administered Chloral Hydrate Syrup intravenously. This syrup is intended for oral administration only. This was done because the label contained the legend C IV. This was interpreted as intravenous when in fact, C IV stands for a class 4 controlled substance. All controlled substances are indicated as Roman numerals, I, II, III, IV, V. Even though 99.99% of nurses know that drugs in screw-capped bottles, labeled "syrup" are not intended for intravenous administration, it would pay to change C IV to C4 on drug company labels.

(40) After performing spinal surgery a surgeon kept his ICU patients NPO (nothing by mouth), until they had flatus and good **b**owel **s**ounds. His order was: "Strict NPO. Check BS Q2H." The patient had "blood sugar" laboratory tests drawn Q2H!

(41) An order was written for lidocaine 1% s̄ EPINEPHrine. It was misinterpreted as lidocaine 1% with EPINEPHrine. s̄ is a Latin-derived abbreviation for "without" which is rarely used. "Lidocaine 1%" is a safer way to express this order.

(42) There have been mix-ups between DTap and Tdap. DTaP is diphtheria and tetanus toxoids and acellular pertussis vaccine (DAPTACEL and TRIPEDIA, and INFANRIX). It is meant for active *immunization* of pediatric patients 6 weeks through 6 years of age. Tdap is tetanus toxoid, reduced diphtheria toxoid, and acellular pertussis vaccine (BOOSTRIX and ADACEL). It is meant to be used as *booster* shots for older children, adolescents, and adults.

(43) An infant died when she received 5 mg of morphine instead of the handwritten prescribed ".5 mg" dose when the naked decimal point was not seen. This can easily occur if the decimal point happens to fall on a line, or falls on part of a letter from the line above, or when working from poor copies of an original order. Always place a zero in front of a naked decimal (0.5 mg, not .5 mg).

(44) An order was written for Colchicine 1.0 mg IV now. The decimal point was not seen and 10 mg was administered. The patient died. This can easily occur if the decimal point happens to fall on a line, or falls on part of a letter from the line above, or when working from poor copies of an original order. Use 1 mg, not 1.0 mg. A trailing zero can correctly be used where precision is being expressed, such as in reporting a laboratory value, but never in expressing a drug dose or strength.

(45) The pharmacy received an order for a diltiazem drip. No rate of administration was listed, so the pharmacist entered "125 mg UD" in computer rate field. UD is an old-time Latin abbreviation for as directed (*ut dictum*). The nurse did not know the classical meaning of UD and interpreted as meaning unit dose. The nurse then proceeded to give the diltiazem at 125 mg/hr and ran the entire dose over one hour (the rate should have been 5 mg/hr). The nurse then asked for another diltiazem drip and also ran that one over 1 hour. The patient expired. As in many errors, it was not just one thing that caused the error. One of the many factors in causing this error was the use of an ancient abbreviation which should no longer be used.

(46) An order was writtern, "PT TO SEE PT WHEN PT WNL" which was translated as " Patient to see physical therapy when prothrombin is within normal limits" This did not cause an error, but did slow things down!

(47) In an emergency department, at physician asked the nurse to get the drug TXA. The nurse thought he said TNK. She brought the physician TNKase. The potential mistake was discovered and an error did not occur. TXA is tranexmaic acid injection (Cykiokapron) and TNK is tenecteplase injection (TNKase).

(48) ANIN could not be identified. It turned out to be a typo for two words, an in.

(49) ONJ could be identified. It turned out to be a typo for word, on.

(50) An order for tPA (alteplase [Activase]) was thought to be TPA (total parental alimentation) causing delay in initiating critical therapy.

The author would appreciate receiving other examples of abbreviations that have been misinterpreted causing error or delays so that this section can be expanded. E-mail them to neil@medabbrev.com

A prescription could be written with directions as follows: "OD OD OD," to mean one drop in the right eye once daily!

Abbreviations should not be used for drug names as they are particularly dangerous. As previously illustrated, there is the possibility that the writer may, through mental error, confuse two abbreviations and use the wrong one. Similarly, the reader may attribute the wrong meaning to an abbreviation. To further confound the problem, some drug name abbreviations have multiple meanings (see ATR, CPM, CPZ, DXM, FLU, GEM, IBC, KET, NITRO, PIT, PBZ and TMZ in Table 3). The abbreviation AC has been used for three different cancer chemotherapy combinations to mean Adriamycin and either cyclophosphamide, carmustine, or cisplatin.

Medical writers, editors, and health professionals can prevent the coining and use of these ambiguous abbreviations. To avoid the introduction of contradictory or ambiguous abbreviations, before coining a new abbreviation, one must do some research. Check this book and Medline to see other possible meanings that already exist for the planned abbreviation. Secondly, rethink if there is really a need to develop an abbreviation for the term.

Beside causing medication errors and incorrect interpretation of medical records, abbreviations can create problems because treatment is delayed while a health professional seeks clarification for the meaning of the abbreviation used. Abbreviations should not be used to designate drugs. The establishment of abbreviations for drug combinations is an ongoing problem and should require facility/organizational approvals.

Certain meanings of abbreviations in the book are followed by a warning, "this is a dangerous abbreviation." This warning could be placed after many abbreviations, but was reserved for situations where errors have been published because these abbreviations were used or where the meaning is critical and not likely to be known. If no alternative abbreviation is suggested, then the term should be spelled out rather than abbreviated. Such warning statements should also appear after every abbreviation for a drug or drug combination.

References

1. Davis NM, Cohen MR. Medication errors: causes and prevention. Warminster, PA: Neil M Davis Associates; 1983.
2. Cohen MR. Medication error reports. Hosp Pharm (appears monthly from 1975 to the present).
3. Cohen MR. Medication errors. Nursing 2011 (appears monthly, starting in Nursing 77, to the present).
4. Davis NM. Med Errors. Am J Nursing (appears monthly from 1994 to 1995).
5. Cohen MR. Medication Errors. American Pharmacists Assoc. Wash. DC, 2011.

Table 2. Dangerous Abbreviations and Dosage Designations (A "Do Not Use" List)

Problem Term	Intended Meaning	Reason for Problem(s)	Suggested Remedy
AU	both ears	Read as OU (both eyes) or not understood	Use "both ears"
cc for expressing liquid measurements	cubic centimeter (same as milliliter [mL])	Read as u (unit) or 00	Use "mL"
D/C	discharge	Interpreted as discontinue medications resulting in premature discontinuance of current medication	Use "discharge"

Table 2. Dangerous Abbreviations and Dosage Designations (A "Do Not Use" List) (*continued*)

Problem Term	Intended Meaning	Reason for Problem(s)	Suggested Remedy
IN	intranasal	Read as IV or IM or heard as IM	Write "intranasal" "nasally" or use "NAS" if limited by computer space allotted
IU	International unit	Misread as IV (intravenous); The I is read as a one (6 IU is read as 61 units)	Use "units" rather than international units, or spell out international units, using a lowercase i
OD	once daily	Interpreted as right eye	Write "once daily"
OJ	Orange juice	Read as OS (left eye) or OD (right eye)	Use "orange juice"
QOD	every other day	Interpreted as meaning "every once a day" or read as q.i.d. (four times daily)	Write "every other day"
QD	once daily	Read or interpreted as q.i.d. (four times daily)	Write "once daily"
qn	every night	Read as every hour	Write "once daily at night"
q HS	every night	Read as every hour	Use "once daily at night"
µg	microgram	When handwritten, misread as mg	Use "mcg"
sq or sub q	subcutaneous	The q is read as every or 9	Use "subcut"
ss	sliding scale or 1/2	Read as the numbers 55 and 1/2	Spell out "sliding scale" or "1/2"
T/d (with a dot over the T)	one per day	Interpreted as t.i.d. (three times daily)	Use "one per day"
T1D	type 1 diabetes (mellitus)	Read as TID (three times daily)	Use DM-1
T1DM	type 1 diabetes (mellitus)	Read as TIDM (three times daily with meals)	Use DM-1
TIW	three times a week	Interpreted as T/W (Tuesday & Wednesday); as twice a week; as t.i.d. (three times daily)	Write "three times a week"
U	unit	When handwritten, read as 0, 4, 6, or cc	Use "unit"
Apothecary system of measure (grains, minims, and drams)	Units of measure	Not understood or misunderstood	Use the metric system (mg, g, mL)

Table 2. Dangerous Abbreviations and Dosage Designations (A "Do Not Use" List) (*continued*)

Problem Term	Intended Meaning	Reason for Problem(s)	Suggested Remedy
Chemical symbols	Drug names or laboratory tests	Not understood or misunderstood	Use full name except for Na, Ca, O$_2$, K, Cl, KCl and HCl
Such as MgSO$_4$	magnesium sulfate	Not understood or misunderstood, may be read as morphine sulfate	Spell out magnesium sulfate
Uncommon Latin words or phrases such as		Not understood or misunderstood	Use
per os	By mouth		by mouth, orally, or PO
ss	1/2		1/2 or one half
UD	As directed		as directed
Lettered abbreviations for drug names or drug protocols	Drug names or drug protocols	Not understood or misunderstood	Use generic and trade name(s); Follow policy for use of protocol names in your facility.
/ (a slash mark)	with, and, or per	Read as one when followed by a number	Use "and", "with" or "per"
Roman numerals	Numbers	Not understood or misunderstood (iv read as intravenous rather than 4; iii, X, L and C, not understood)	Use Arabic numerals (4, 3, 10, 50, 100, etc.)
> and <	"greater than" or "less than"	Not understood or the meaning is reversed	Use "greater than" or "less than"
Drug name and dosage not separated by a space	Inderal 40 mg	Inderal40 mg misread as Inderal 140 mg	Always leave a space between a drug name, dose, and unit of measure
Trailing zeros; 1.0 mg	1 mg	When handwritten decimal point is not seen, read as 10 mg causing a tenfold overdose	Omit the zero, write 1 mg (see note below)
Naked decimal point; .5 mL	0.5 mL	When handwritten decimal point is not seen, read as 5 mL causing a tenfold overdose	Add a zero, 0.5 mL
Abbreviated drug names	A drug name	Misinterpreted or not recognized	Use generic or brand name
Slang	communication	Can be offensive and/or insensitive	Do Not Use slang in verbal or written communications

Note **Exception:** A **trailing zero** may be used where required to demonstrate the level of precision of the value being reported, such as for laboratory results, imaging studies that report size of lesions, or catheter/tube sizes. It should **NOT** be used in medication orders or other medication-related documentation.

Health practitioners, authors, and editors must do due diligence in creating an abbreviation or they may cause situations similar to the ones shown below. Doing a search for the proposed abbreviation on medabbrev.com, would be a good beginning. Another possibility is not to abbreviate the phrase.

ABP	=	ambulatory blood pressure
		arterial blood pressure
ACU	=	acute receiving unit
		ambulatory care unit
ADVT	=	acute deep venous ischemia
		asymptomatic deep venous thrombosis
AMI	=	amifostine
		amitriptyline
		acute mesenteric ischemia
		acute myocardial infarction
APC	=	advanced pancreatic cancer
		advanced prostate cancer
AQoL	=	Acne Quality of Life
		Assessment of Quality of Life
		Asthma-related Quality of Life
		Australian Quality of Life
ATR	=	atropine
		atracurium
AZT	=	zidovudine
		azathioprine
BCa	=	bladder cancer
		breast cancer
BO	=	bowel open
		bowel obstruction
BPM	=	beats per minute
		breaths per minute
BR	=	bright red
		brown
BSS	=	Bernard-Soupier syndrome
		Brown-Séquard syndrome
		Brooke-Spieler syndrome
		Berardinelli-Seip syndrome
		blood stasis syndrome

CAS	=	carotid artery stenosis
		cerebral arteriosclerosis
		coronary artery stenosis
CBS	=	Charles Bonnet syndrome
		chronic brain syndrome
		corticobasal syndrome
CFIs	=	chemotherapy-free intervals
		contraceptive-free intervals
CIA	=	chemotherapy-induced amenorrhea
		chemotherapy-induced anemia
		chemotherapy-induced alopecia
CLD	=	chronic liver disease
		chronic lung disease
CLOF	=	clofarabine
		clofazimine
CPM	=	cyclophosphamide
		chlorpheniramine maleate
CPZ	=	chlorpromazine
		Compazine
CRS	=	Chinese restaurant syndrome
		congenital rubella syndrome
		cytokine-release syndrome
CZP	=	carbamazepine
		certolizumab pegol
		clonazepam
DDS	=	Denys-Drash syndrome
		dialysis disequilibrium syndrome
		dopamine dysregulation syndrome
DNR	=	daunorubicin
		did not respond
		do not report
		do not resuscitate
DOG	=	delay of gratification
		delusions of grandeur

DS	=	Down syndrome Dravet syndrome	HD	=	Hansen disease Hodgkin disease Huntington disease
DW	=	dextrose in water distilled water deionized water	HO	=	hand orthosis hip orthosis
DXM	=	dexamethasone dextromethorphan	HPW	=	healthy pregrant women hypertensive pregnant women
ED	=	eating disorder(s) elbow disarticulation emotional disorder erectile dysfunction	HTx	=	hand transplantation heart transplantation
			IA	=	intra-amniotic intra-arterial intra-articular
EIH	=	enviromentally-induced hyperthermia exercise-induced hypertension exercise-induced hyperthermia exercise-induced hypoxemia	IAD	=	incontinent associated dermatits intractable atopic dermatitis
EOP	=	early-onset Parkinsonism early-onset pneumonia early-onset preeclampsia early-onset psychosis	IAI	=	Intra-abdominal infection Intra-abdominal injury
			IBC	=	invasive bladder cancer invasive breast cancer
ERT	=	enzyme replacement therapy estrogen replacement therapy	ICA	=	internal carotid artery intracranial abscess intracranial aneurysm
ESLD	=	end-stage liver disease end-stage lung disease	IHHD	=	in-hospital hemodialysis intensive home hemodialysis
FEC	=	fluorouracil, epirubicin, and cyclophosphamide fluorouracil, etoposide, and cisplatin	I & D	=	incision and drainage irrigation and debridement
FSW	=	female sex worker field service worker	IPCU	=	inpatient palliative care unit intensive pediatric care unit intensive psychiatric care unit
GCT	=	germ cell tumor giant cell tumor granulosa cell tumor	IRDM	=	insulin-required diabetes mellitus insulin resistant diabetes mellitus
GD	=	Graves disease Gaucher disease	IT	=	intrathecal intratracheal intratumoral
GEM	=	gemfibrozil gemicitabine			
HAO	=	hand osteoarthritis hip osteoarthritis	JVC	=	John Cunningham virus Jamestown Canyon virus
HCC	=	hepatocellular carcinoma Hurthle cell carcinoma	KET	=	ketamine ketoconazole

KS	=	Kawasaki syndrome
		Klinefelter syndrome
		Korsakoff syndrome
LAM	=	laminectomy
		laparoscopic-assisted myomectomy
		laser-assisted myringotomy
LAPC	=	locally-advanced pancreatic cancer
		locally-advanced prostatic cancer
LAS	=	lacric acidosis syndrome
		laxative abuse syndrome
		lymphadenopathy syndrome
LF	=	left foot
		little finger
		long finger
LFD	=	lactose-free diet
		low-fat diet
		low-fiber diet
LHSH	=	long-handled shoe horn
		long-handled shower head
LKT	=	laparoscopic kidney transplantation
		liver-kidney transplantation
LL	=	left leg
		left lung
		lower lid
		lower limb
		lower lip
LNE	=	lymph node enlargement
		lymph node excision
LNU	=	learned nonuse (splint)
		lower and upper (heard as L & U)
LT	=	liver transplantation
		Lung transplantation
LTFU	=	long-term to follow-up
		loss to follow-up
Ltx	=	liver transplant
		lung transplant

LVO	=	left ventricular opacification
		left ventricular output
		left ventricular overactivity
MBC	=	male breast cancer
		metastatic breast cancer
MFS	=	Marfan syndrome
		Miller-Fisher syndrome
		monofixation syndrome
MIGS	=	micro-invasive glaucoma surgery
		minimally invasive glaucoma surgery
		minimally invasive gynecological surgery
Mon	=	Monday
		month
MP	=	melphalan; prednisone
		mitoxantrone; prednisone
MPM	=	malignant peritoneal mesothelioma
		malignant pleural mesothelioma
MS	=	morphine sulfate
		multiple sclerosis
		mitral stenosis
		musculoskeletal
		medical student
		minimal support
		muscle strength
		mental status
		milk shake
		mitral sound
		morning stiffness
MTD	=	maximum tolerated dose
		minimum toxic dose
MTZ	=	mirtazapine
		mitoxantrone
MV	=	mechanical ventilation
		manual ventilation
NABS	=	no active bowel sounds
		normoactive bowel sounds
NAF	=	Native-American female
		Negro-American female
		normal adult female

NBM	=	no bowel movement normal bowel movement nothing by mouth
NE	=	no effect no enlargement not evaluated
NITRO	=	nitroglycerin sodium nitroprusside
NOAC	=	Novel (New or Non-vitamin K antagonist) Oral Anticoagulant(s); also defined as Novel or New No Oral Anticoagulant(s) or No Anticoagulant(s)
NSAE	=	neurosensory adverse events nonserious adverse events
OHS	=	obesity hypoventilation syndrome ocular histoplasmosis syndrome ocular hypoperfusion syndrome
OLB	=	open-liver biopsy open-lung biopsy
OPC	=	operable pancreatic carcinoma oropharynx cancer oropharyngeal candidiasis
PAA	=	popliteal arterry aneurysm pulmonary artery aneurysm
PBL	=	primary breast lymphoma primary brain lymphoma
PBZ	=	phenylbutazone pyribenzamine phenoxybenzamine
PCS	=	pelvic congestion syndrome post cholecystectomy syndrome postconcussion syndrome
PCU	=	palliative care unit primary care unit progressive care unit protective care unit
PD	=	Paget disease panic disorder Parkinson disease personality disorder Peyroine disease

PHTN	=	portal hypertension prehypertension pulmonary hypertension
Pit	=	Pitocin Pitressin
PLB	=	percutaneous liver biopsy percutaneous lung biopsy
PMS	=	Phelan-McDermid syndrome postmenopausal syndrome postconcussion syndrome
PNUS	=	perineal ultrasound peripheral nerve ultrasound prenatal ultrasound
PORT	=	postoperative radiotherapy postoperative respiratory therapy prostate-only radiotherapy
pTBI	=	pediatric traumatic brain injury penetrating traumatic brain injury
PUO	=	pruritus of unknown origin pyrexia of unknown origin
PVO	=	peripheral vascular occlusion portal vein occlusion pulmonary venous occlusion
RM	=	radical mastectomy reduction mammoplasty
RS	=	Reiter syndrome Rett syndrome Reye syndrome Richter syndrome Rumination syndrome Raynaud disease (syndrome)
RTI	=	reproductive tract infection respiratory tract infection
RWW	=	raw wastewater reclaimed wastewater
S & S	=	swish and spit swish and swallow
SA	=	suicide alert suicide attempt

SAD = social anxiety disorder
seasonal affective disorder

SCAD = spontaneous cervial artery dissection
spontaneous coronary artery dissection
stable coronary artery disease

SCCL = solitary cerebral cysticercal lesion
squamous cell cancer-like
squamous cell carcinoma of the larynx
squamous cell carcinoma of the lung
squamous cell carcinoma of the lip

SCCP = squamous cell carcinoma of the penis
small cell carcinoma of the prostate

SDBP = seated, standing, or supine diastolic blood pressure

SDRT = single-dose radiotherapy
seasonal affective disorder

SDS = Schwann-Diamond Syndrome
somatropin deficiency syndrome
sudden death syndrome

SGAs = second generation antihistamines
second generation antipsychotics

SJS = Schwartz-Jampel syndrome
Stevens-Johnson syndrome
Sawyer-James syndrome

SMS = scalded mouth syndrome
Smith-Magenis syndrome
stiff-man syndrome

SOBT = salivary occult blood test
stool occult blood test

SS = serotonin syndrome
Sézary syndrome
Sjögren syndrome
Sweet syndrome

SSE = saline solution enema
soapsuds enema

SSS = scalded skin syndrome
sick sinus syndrome

STF = special tube feeding
standard tube feeding

TAC = tetracaine, Adrenalin, and cocaine solution
triamcinolone cream

TBA = thyroid biochemical abnormalities
to be absorbed
to be added
to be administered
to be admitted
to be announced
to be arranged
to be assessed
total body (surface) area
traditional birth attendant

T/E = testosterone to epitestosterone (ratio)
testosterone to estrogen (ratio)
trunk-to-extremity skinfold thickness (index)

TICU = thoracic intensive care unit
transplant intensive care unit
trauma intensive care unit

TMZ = temazepam
temozolomide

TRZ = thioridazine
trastuzumab
trazodone
triazolam

TS = Tay-Sachs (disease)
Tourette syndrome
Turner syndrome

TSCC = thymic squamous cell carcinoma
tongue squamous cell carcinoma
tonsillar squamous cell carcinoma

tubal = tubal ligation
tubal pregnancy

Table 3. Examples of Abbreviations That Have Contradictory or Ambiguous Meanings (*continued*)

Tx	=	therapist therapy traction transcription transfer transfuse transplant transplantation treatment
VAC	=	etoposide (VePesid), cytarabine (ara-C, and carboplatin, vincristine, dactinomycin vincristine, doxorubicin)
VAD	=	vincristine, doxorubicin, (Adriamycin) and dexamethasone vincristine, doxorubicin (Adriamycin) and dactinomycin
VAP	=	vincristine, Adriamycin, and prednisone vincristine, Adriamycin, and procarbazine vincristine, actinomycin D, and Platinol AQ vincristine, asparaginase, and prednisone
WBRT	=	whole-brain radiotherapy whole-breast radiotherapy
WS	=	Waardenburg syndrome Werner syndrome West syndrome Williams syndrome

Chapter 3

Medical Abbreviation Primer

When first entering a medically-related field, one must learn the language in order to function. Part of learning this language is to learn the meaning of the abbreviations, acronyms, and symbols in use. This chapter is intended to introduce newcomers to this commonly used medically-related shorthand.

The determination of which abbreviations (refers also to acronyms and symbols) are most commonly used is based on the selection by the author with the consultation of experts in various health-related fields. The categorizing of the abbreviations is arbitrary, but is intended to represent the most common use, as the abbreviations could have been placed in many different categories.

This list could have been expanded to include many hundreds-more commonly used abbreviations, but then the list would have been too long to serve as a primer. The absence of an abbreviation from this listing does not mean it is not in common use. Each area of practice and specialty could have added their own commonly used abbreviations.

A few of the abbreviations below have more than one meaning listed. This was done when several meanings are in common use. Many abbreviations have more than one meaning and they must be viewed in their clinical context to arrive at their intended meaning. See Chapter 4 of this book for additional meanings for the abbreviations listed below.

In practice, there are inconsistencies as to how abbreviations are written. They may appear in all capital letters, lower case, or in capital letters and lower case. They may or may not have periods after each letter.

The readers are urged to read Chapter 2, Dangerous, Contradictory, and/or Ambiguous Abbreviations.

Two Hundred and Seventy-Five Commonly Used Medical Abbreviations Arranged by Category—a Primer

Physical Examination, History Portion of the Medical Record, and Discharge Summary

C/O	complains of		ROS	review of systems
CC	chief complaint(s)		SH	social history
CTA	clear to auscultation		Tx	treatment
Dx	diagnosis		CV	cardiovascular
F/U	follow-up		GI	gastrointestinal
FH	family history		GU	genitourinary
H/O	history of		EENT	ears, eyes, nose, and throat
HPI	history of present illness		HEENT	head, ears, eyes, nose, and throat
Hx	history		Ob/Gyn	obstetrics and gynecology
PE	physical examination		Peds	pediatrics
	pelvic examination		UCD	usual childhood diseases
	pulmonary embolism		A & P	auscultation and percussion
PH/SH	personal and social history		ADL	activities of daily living
PI	present illness		CN III	third cranial nerve (there are
PMH	past medical history			CN I to XII)

RCM	right costal margin (there is also a LCM)	OU	both eyes
RUQ	right upper quadrant (also there is RLQ, LUQ, and LLQ)	PERRLA	pupils equal, round, reactive to light and accommodation
TM	tympanic membrane	IOP	intraocular pressure
AAO X 3	alert, awake, and oriented to time, place, and person	ROM	range of motion
		VS	vital signs
BM	bowel movement	P	pulse
BP	blood pressure	T	temperature
CVAT	costovertebral angle tenderness	RR	respiratory rate; recovery room
DTR	deep tendon reflex	HR	heart rate
EOMI	extraocular muscles intact	RRR	regular rate and rhythm (heart)
HJR	hepatojugular reflux	WDWNWM	well developed, well nourished, white male (also there are abbreviations for females and other races [WF = white female; AAF = African-American female]
JVD	jugular venous distention		
IBW	ideal body weight		
LBW	lean body weight		
BSA	body surface area		
LMP	last menstrual period		
NAD	no apparent distress no apparent disease	YO	year old
		DOB	date of birth
		+	positive; present; plus
NC/AT	normocephalic, atraumatic	−	negative; absent; minus
NKA	no known allergies	c̄	with
NKDA	no known drug allergies	õ	negative; without
OD	right eye	W/O	without
OS	left eye		

Diseases and Symptoms

AD	Alzheimer disease	SOB	shortness of breath
AIDS	acquired immunodeficiency syndrome	URI	upper respiratory infection
		TB	tuberculosis
HIV	human immuno-deficiency virus	CVA	cerebrovascular accident; costovertebral angle
AMI	acute myocardial infarction		
MI	myocardial infarction	DVT	deep vein thrombosis
CHF	congestive heart failure	NV	nausea and vomiting
ACS	acute coronary syndrome	NVD	nausea, vomiting, and diarrhea
HT	hypertension (also HTN) height	PONV	neck vein distention postoperative nausea and vomiting
DM	diabetes mellitus		
AODM	adult onset diabetes mellitus	PUD	peptic ulcer disease
IDDM	insulin dependent diabetes mellitus	GERD	gastroesophageal reflux disease
		RA	rheumatoid arthritis
NIDDM	noninsulin-dependent diabetes mellitus	OA	osteoarthritis
		SLE	systemic lupus erythematosus
PD	Parkinson disease	TIA	transient ischemic attack
AOM	acute otitis media	HA	headache
Ca	cancer	BPH	benign prostatic hypertrophy (hyperplasia)
COAD	chronic obstructive airway disease		
COPD	chronic obstructive pulmonary disease	UTI	urinary tract infection
		STD	sexually transmitted disease
DOE	dyspnea on exertion	MVA	motor vehicle accident

Clinical Laboratory

ANA	antinuclear antibody	AST	aspartate aminotransferase
Alb	albumin	BG	blood glucose; blood gases
ALT	alanine aminotransferase	BS	blood sugar
LFT	liver function test		bowel sounds
aPTT	activated partial thromboplastin time		breath sounds
		BUN	blood urea nitrogen

CK-MB	creatine kinase, MB fraction	Mg	Magnesium (also Mg^{++})
CO_2	carbon dioxide	Na	Sodium (also Na^+)
CPK	creatinine phosphokinase	OGTT	oral glucose tolerance test
CrCl	creatinine clearance	PSA	prostate-specific antigen
SCr	serum creatinine	UA	urinalysis
C & S	culture and sensitivity	VDRL	Venereal Disease Research
ESR	erythrocyte sedimentation rate		Laboratory (test for syphilis)
Gluc	glucose	CBC	complete blood count
FBS	fasting blood sugar	Diff	differential (blood count)
HbA_{1c}	glycosylated hemoglobin	Eos	eosinophil
CHOL	cholesterol	Fe	iron
HDL	high-density lipoprotein	Hct	hematocrit
LDL	low-density lipoprotein	Hgb	hemoglobin
LDH	lactic dehydrogenase	H&H	hemoglobin and hematocrit
Trig	triglycerides	Plt	platelets
INR	international normalized ratio	MCV	mean corpuscular volume
DB	direct bilirubin	RBC	red blood cell (count)
TB	total bilirubin	Segs	segmented neutrophils
TP	total protein	WBC	white blood cell (count)
Ca	Calcium (also Ca^{++})	ABG	arterial blood gases
Cl	Chloride (also Cl^-)	WNL	within normal limits
K	Potassium (also K^+)		

Other Diagnostic Tests, Procedures, and Treatments

ECG	electrocardiogram	CT	computer tomography
EEG	electroencephalogram	IVP	intravenous pyelogram
FEV_1	forced expiratory volume in one second	MRI	magnetic resonance imaging
		PET	positron emission tomography
IPPB	intermittent positive-pressure breathing	US	ultrasound
		CABG	coronary artery bypass graft
PFT	pulmonary function tests	PCTA	percutaneous transluminal
PEEP	positive end-expiratory pressure		coronary angioplasty
MUGA	multigated (radionuclide) angiogram	PT	physical therapy
		D & C	dilatation and curettage

Physicians' Orders and Prescriptions

ASAP	as soon as possible	tab	tablet
OOB	out of bed	inj	injection
BRP	bathroom privileges	i	one
CPR	cardiopulmonary resuscitation	ii	two
DNR	do not resuscitate	q	*every (as in q 6 hours)*
DAW	dispense as written	h	hour(s)
DC or D/C	discharge	BID	*twice daily*
	discontinue	TID	*three times daily*
I/O	intake and output	QID	*four times daily*
LD	loading dose	QAM	every morning
NAS	no salt added	QPM	every evening
NPO	nothing by mouth	AC	*before meals*
PO	by mouth; postoperative	PC	*after meals*
IM	intramuscular	HS	*bedtime*
IV	intravenous	NR	*no refills (prescriptions)*
SC	subcutaneous	PRN	*as required; whenever*
SQ	subcutaneous (subcut preferred)		*necessary*
PICC	percutaneous indwelling central catheter	MRx1	*may repeat one time*
		Rx	*prescription*
IVPB	intravenous piggyback		*pharmacy*
NGT	nasogastric tube	OTC	over-the-counter (no prescription
cap	capsule		required)

Stat	*immediately*	TO	telephone order
TKO	to keep (vein) open	VO	verbal order

Drug Names and Chemicals

APAP	acetaminophen	MgSO$_4$	magnesium sulfate
ASA	aspirin	MOM	milk of magnesia
5D/W	dextrose 5% injection (in water)	NaCl	sodium chloride
Dig	digoxin	NS	normal saline (0.9% sodium
ETOH	alcohol (ethyl alcohol)		chloride; same as NSS)
FeSO$_4$	ferrous sulfate	NSS	normal saline solution (0.9%
H$_2$O	water (or H2O)		sodium chloride)
H$_2$O$_2$	hydrogen peroxide	O$_2$	oxygen
HCl	hydrochloride (when following a	PCN	penicillin
	drug name, as in thiamine HCl	tPA	tissue plasminogen activator
	[thiamine hydrochloride])	IVF	intravenous fluids
	hydrochloric acid (when it appears	TPN	total parenteral nutrition
	separately [not as part of a drug	lytes	electrolytes (sodium, potassium,
	name])		chloride, etc.)
KCl	potassium chloride		

Drug Classes

ABx	antibiotic(s)	OC	oral contraceptive
COX-2 I	cyclooxygenase-2 inhibitor	PPI	proton pump inhibitor
MAOI	monoamine oxidase inhibitor	SSRI	selective serotonin reuptake
NSAID	nonsteroidal anti-inflammatory		inhibitor
	drug	TCA	tricyclic antidepressant

Units of Measure

cm	centimeter (2.54 cm = 1 inch)	mEq	milliequivalent
g	gram (28.35 g = 1 ounce)	mg	milligram (1,000 mg = 1 gram [g])
kg	kilogram (1 kg = 2.2 pounds)	mL	milliliter (1,000 mL = 1 liter [L])
L	liter (1 L = 1,000 mL = 1 quart	mmHg	millimeters of mercury
	plus about 2 ounces)	°C	degrees Centigrade (Celsius)
lb	pound (1 lb = 0.454 Kg)	°F	degrees Fahrenheit
mcg	microgram (1,000 mcg		
	= 1 milligram [mg])		

Hospital Locations

CCU	cardiac care unit	OB	obstetrics
DR	delivery room	OR	operating room
ED	emergency department	PACU	postanesthesia care unit
ER	emergency room (same as ED)	PICU	pediatric intensive care unit
ICU	intensive care unit		pulmonary intensive care unit
L & D	labor and delivery	RD	radiology department
LDR	labor, delivery, and recovery	SICU	surgical intensive care
MICU	medical intensive care unit		unit
NICU	neonatal intensive care unit		

Miscellaneous

APRN	Advanced Practice Registered	MAR	medication administration
	Nurse		record
ARNP	Advanced Registered Nurse	MD	Doctor of Medicine
	Practitioner	PA	Physician Assistant
CNS	Clinical Nurse Specialist	PharmD	Doctor of Pharmacy
DO	Doctor of Osteopathy	RPh	Registered Pharmacist
LPN	Licensed Practical Nurse	RN	Registered Nurse
MA	Medical Assistant		

Chapter 4

Lettered and Numbered Abbreviations, Acronyms, and Slang

This chapter starts with numbers, abbreviations which start with a number or numbers, and Roman numerals. It is followed by lettered abbreviations and acronyms.

The letter-by-letter (dictionary) system of alphabetizing is used ("*ad lib*" is listed under ADL).

When an abbreviation ending with an S can not be found, check for the abbreviation without the S as it may be the plural form of one that is listed.

Brand names (proprietary names) have their first letter capitalized, whereas nonproprietary (generic) names are in lower-case letters.

Although shown for informational purposes, drug names should not be abbreviated as the meaning may not be known to the reader or interpreted as intended.

Slang is presented for informational purposes only and should not be used.

The listing of symbols and Greek letters can be found in Chapter 5.

Some of the meanings shown are very specialized or new and will not be understood by the majority of health professionals. These very specialized abbreviations are presented for informational purposes and their use in healthcare documentation should be done with assurance that they will be understood. See WARNING in chapter 1.

Number(s) or Begins with Number(s)

½ and ½	half Dakin solution and half glycerin
½ NSS	sodium chloride 0.45% (½ normal saline solution)
1°	first degree
	primary
1:1	one-to-one (individual session with staff)
100	one hundred (1×10^2)
1,000	one thousand (1×10^3)
1,500	fifteen hundred
	Health Insurance Claim Form HCFA 1500
10,000	ten thousand (1×10^4)
100,000	one hundred thousand (1×10^5)
1,000,000	one million (1×10^6)
10,000,000	ten million (1×10^7)
100,000,000	one hundred million (1×10^8)
1,000,000,000	one billion (1×10^9)
17K	17-ketosteroids
$_1O_2$	singlet oxygen
1-TU	1 tuberculin unit
2°	second degree
	secondary
2/2	secondary to

222	aspirin, caffeine, and codeine (8 mg) tablets (Canada)
24°	twenty-four hours (24 hr is safer as the ° is seen as zero)
24 h U-PRO	24 hour urine protein (exception)
25(OH)D	25-hydroxyvitamin D
282	aspirin, caffeine, codeine, and meprobamate (Canada)
2-CDA	cladribine (Leustatin; chlorodeoxyadenosine)
2D	two-dimensional
2X2	gauze dressing folded 2″ by 2″
24/7	24 hours a day, 7 days a week
3°	tertiary third degree
356h	Application to Market a New Drug, Biologic or an Antibiotic Drug for Human Use (FDA form number)
3D	three-dimensional
3D-CT	3-dimensional computed tomography
3MP	Magnetic Mini-Mover Procedure
3TC	lamivudine (Epivir)
3V	3-vessel
3×	three times
4	for (as in TI4 "therapeutic interchange for. . .") four
420	Marijuana
4-AP	4-aminopyridine (Ampyra)
4D-CT	four-dimensional computed tomography
4WW	four-wheel walker
4×4	gauze dressing folded 4″ by 4″
5 + 2	5 days of cytarabine and 2 days of daunorubicin, leukemia therapy
5-ASA	mesalamine (Asacol; Rowasa)
5FU	fluorouracil
5S's	Sort, Set-In-Order, Shine, Standardize and Sustain (steps to make the work environment Lean)
5-TU	5 tuberculin units
5YSR	5-year survival rate(s)
642	propoxyphene tablets (Canada)
6MP	mercaptopurine (Purinenthol)
7/24	7 days a week, 24 hours a day
7 + 3	7 days of cytarabine and 3 days of daunorubicin, leukemia therapy
7's	Serial 7's; a mental status examination (starting with 100, count backward by 7's)
777	Ortho Novum 777® (a triphasic oral contraceptive)

Roman Numerals (should not be used because they are not universally understood)

i	one
ii	two
iii	three
iv	four (a dangerous expression as it is read as intravenous, use 4; for additional meanings see the letters IV)
v	five (for additional meaning see the letter V)
vi	six
vii	seven
viii	eight
ix	nine
x	ten (for additional meanings see the letter X)
xi	eleven
xii	twelve
xx	twenty
XL	forty (for additional meanings see the letters XL)
L	fifty (for additional meanings see the letter L)
C	hundred (for additional meanings see the letter C)
M	thousand (for additional meanings see the letter M)

A

A	abolish
	Acanthamoeba (a genus of ameba)
	accommodation
	Acinetobacter
	active
	acute
	adenosine (also referred to as Ado)
	age
	alanine
	alert
	alive
	Alpha (Phonetic Alphabet A; pronounced AL-FAH)
	ambulatory
	angioplasty
	anterior
	anxiety
	apical
	arterial
	artery
	Asian
	assessment
	assist
	assistance
	atrial
	atrium
	auscultation
	awake
A+	blood type A positive (A positive is preferred)
A−	blood type A negative (A negative is preferred)
A′	ankle
@	at
(A)	assist
(a)	axillary temperature
a	anterior
ā	anterior before
A0×3	see AO×3
A0×4	see AO×4
A_1	aortic first heart sound
A_2	aortic second sound
A250	5% albumin 250 mL
A1000	5% albumin 1000 mL
A&0	see A&O
AA	accelerated approval (FDA)
	acetic acid
	achievement age
	active assistive
	acute appendicitis
	acute asthma
	affected area
	affirmative action
	African American
	African American (Afro-American)
	alcohol abuse
	Alcoholics Anonymous
	alopecia areata
	alpha angle
	alveolar-arterial gradient
	amino acid
	anaplastic astrocytoma
	androgenetic alopecia
	anti-aerobic
	antiarrhythmic agent
	aortic aneurysm
	aplastic anemia
	arachidonic acid
	arm ankle (pulse ratio)
	ascending aorta
	ascorbic acid (vitamin C)
	audiologic assessment
	Australia antigen
	authorized absence
	automobile accident
	cytarabine (ara-C) and doxorubicin (Adriamycin)
aa	of each
A&A	abuterol and ipratropium bromide (Atrovent) (this combination is available as Combivent Aerosol and DuoNeb inhalation solution)
	aid and attendance
	arthroscopy and arthrotomy
	awake and aware
a.a.	See AA
A-a	alveolar arterial (gradient)
a/A	arterial-alveolar (gradient)
A/A	Albuterol/Atrovent
	awake and alert
A+A	(see A&A)
AAA	abdominal aortic aneurysm
	abdominal aortic aneurysmectomy (aneurysm)
	acetabular anteversion angle
	acute anxiety attack
	animal-assisted activities
	apply to affected area
	Area Agencies on Aging
	aromatic amino acids
	arterio-arterial anastomosis
A&AA	active and active assistive
AAA's	see AAA
AAAASF	American Association for Accreditation of Ambulatory Surgery Facilities

AAAD	acute type A aortic dissection	AADC	aromatic L-amino acid decarboxylase
AAAE	amino acid activating enzyme		
AAAHC	Accreditation Association of Ambulatory Health Care	aadD	see gene website, www.ncbi.nlm.nih.gov/gene
AAAL	arthritis-attributable activity limitation	AADHD	adult attention-deficit/hyperactivity disorder
AABB	American Association of Blood Banks	AADL	advanced activities of daily living anterior atlantodental ligament
AABR	automated auditory brainstem response	[A-a]Do₂	alveolar-arterial oxygen tension gradient
AABS	adulthood antisocial behavioral syndrome	AADs	antiarrhythmic drugs
		AADSM	American Academy of Dental Sleep Medicine
AAC	Adrenalin, atropine, and cocaine advanced adrenocortical cancer antimicrobial agent-associated colitis augmentative and alternative communication	AADT	annual average daily traffic (volume)
		AAE	active assistance exercise acute allergic encephalitis acute asthma exacerbation
AACA	abuse against children and adolescents azygos anterior cerebral artery	AAECS	amino acid enriched cardioplegic solution
		A/AEX	active assistive exercise
aacA	aminoglycoside N (6')-acetyltransferase (gene)	AAF	African-American female altered auditory feedback
aacA-aphD	bifunctional aminoglycoside modifying enzyme AacA-AphD (gene)	AAFB	alcohol acid-fast bacilli
		AAFO	active ankle-foot orthoses
AACD	aging-associated cognitive decline	AAFP	American Academy of Family Physicians
AACG	acute-angle closure glaucoma		
AACLR	arthroscopic anterior cruciate ligament reconstruction	AAGSV	anterior accessory great saphenous vein
AACN	advanced automatic crash notification American Association of Colleges of Nursing American Association of Critical-Care Nurses	AAH	acute alcoholic hepatitis atypical adenomatous hyperplasia
		AAHL	age-associated hearing loss Australian Animal Health Laboratory
AACP	American Academy of Chiropractic Physicians American Association of Colleges of Pharmacy American Association of Community Psychiatrists	AAI	acute alcohol intoxication adrenaline (epinephrine) auto-injector Adult Attachment Interview allergic airway inflammation aortic augmentation index arm-ankle index atlantoaxial instability atrial demand-inhibited (pacemaker)
AACS	abdominal aortic calcification score acetoacetyl-CoA synthetase		
AACVPR	American Association of Cardiovascular and Pulmonary Rehabilitation (guidelines)	AAIN	American Association of Industrial Nurses as an inpatient
		AAION	arteritic anterior ischemic optic neuropathy
AAD	acid-ash diet acute aortic dissection anti-arrhythmic drug(s) antibiotic-associated diarrhea atlantoaxial dislocation autoimmune Addison disease	aaIPI	age-adjusted International Prognostic Index (predicts autologous stem cell transplantation outcome for patients with relapsed or primary refractory diffuse large B-cell lymphoma)
A₁AD	alpha₁-antitrypsin deficiency		
AADA	Abbreviated Antibiotic Drug Application	AAIR	age adjusted incidence rate

AAIs	animal-assisted interventions
AAIS	anterior acute ischemic stroke
	anterior ankle impingement syndrome
AAJ	atlanto-axial joint
AAJT	Abdominal Aortic Junctional Tourniquet
AAK	atlantoaxial kyphosisv
AAL	Ambient Assisted Living
	anterior axillary line
AALC	African American Leadership Coalition
aALL	adult acute lymphoblastic leukemia
AALNC	Legal Nurse Consultant
	American Association of Legal Nurse Consultants
AAM	African-American male
	amino acid mixture
AAMA	American Academy of Medical Acupuncturists
	American Association of Medical Assistants
	N-acetyl-L-alanine-N′-methyl-amide
AAMI	age-associated memory impairment
	Association for the Advancement of Medical Instrumentation
AAMS	acute aseptic meningitis syndrome
AAMT	American Association for Medical Transcription (now ADHI)
AAN	AIDS-(acquired immunodeficiency syndrome) associated neutropenia
	American Academy of Neurology (guidelines)
	analgesic abuse nephropathy
	analgesic-associated nephropathy
	aristolochic acid nephropathy
	attending's admission notes
AANA	American Association of Nurse Anesthetists
Aand	A and (a keyboard-entry error)
A and D	see A&D
A and O	alert and oriented
A and P	see A&P
AANEM	American Association of Neuromuscular & Electrodiagnostic Medicine
AAO	age at onset
	alert, awake, & oriented
AA&O	alert, awake and oriented
AAO2	alert, awake, and oriented to name and place
AAO3	alert, awake, and oriented to name, place, and time

AAO4	alert, awake and oriented to person, place, time, and situation
A/A/O	awake, alert, and oriented
AAO×2	alert, awake and oriented to person and place
AAO×3	alert, awake and oriented to person, place, and time
AA&O×4	alert, awake and oriented to person, place, time, and situation
	alert, awake, and oriented to person, place, time, and objects (watch, pen, book)
AAO×4	alert, awake and oriented to person, place, time, and situation
AAO×1	alert, awake, and oriented to person
AAOC	antacid of choice
AAOCA	anomalous aortic origin of a coronary artery
AAOS	American Academy of Orthopaedic Surgeons (guidelines)
AAP	acute anterior poliomyelitis
	American Academy of Pediatrics (guidelines)
	assessment adjustment pass
AAPC	American Academy of Professional Coders
	antibiotic-associated pseudomembranous colitis
	average annual percentage change
AAPCC	American Association of Poison Control Centers
AAPMC	antibiotic-associated pseudomembranous colitis
a/ApO2	arterial-alveolar oxygen tension ratio
AAPSA	age-adjusted prostate-specific antigen
AAQ	Acceptance and Action Questionnaire
AAR	alternating atrial rhythm
	antigen-antiglobulin reaction
	area at risk
	aspartate aminotransferase and alanine aminotransferase ratio
	automated anesthesia record
AARC	American Association for Respiratory Care (guidelines)
AARD	atlantoaxial rotatory dislocation
AARF	atlantoaxial rotatory fixation (subluxation; dislocation)
AARO	as a result of
AAROM	active-assistive range of motion

AARP	American Association of Retired Persons
AART	active antiretroviral therapy
AAS	acute abdominal series
	admit after surgery
	alkylating agent score
	allergic Aspergillus sinusitis
	anabolic androgenic steroid
	Ann Arbor stage (Hodgkin disease staging system)
	aortic arch syndrome
	Associate's Degree, Applied Science
	atlantoaxis subluxation
	atomic absorption spectroscopy
	atypical absence seizure
AASA	alpha-aminoadipic acid semialdehyde
	anterior sector acetabular angle
AASCRN	amino acid screen
AASD	acute anterior shoulder dislocations
	antidepressant-associated sexual dysfunction
aASD	artificial atrial septal defect
AASH	adrenal androgen-stimulating hormone
AASI	Ambulatory Arterial Stiffness Index
AASLD	American Association for the Study of Liver Diseases (guidelines)
AASM	American Academy of Sleep Medicine (scoring criteria; practice parameters)
AAST	American Association for the Surgery of Trauma (trauma grading)
AAST-OIS	American Association for the Surgery of Trauma - Organ Injury Scale
AASV	antibody-associated systemic vasculitis
AAT	Aachen Aphasia Test
	activity as tolerated
	alpha-antitrypsin
	androgen ablation therapy
	animal-assisted therapy
	at all times
	atrial demand-triggered (pacemaker)
	atypical antibody titer
	automatic atrial tachycardia
A₁AT	alpha1-antitrypsin
aatA	aspartate aminotransferase; see gene website www.ncbi .nlm.nih.gov/gene
A1ATD	alpha-1-antitrypsin deficiency

A₁AT-Pi	alpha1-antitrypsin (phenotyping)
AAV2	adeno-associated virus 2
AAV	ANCA (anti-neutrophil cytoplasm antibody)-associated vasculitis
	anterior accessory vein
AAVD	American Academy of Veterinary Dermatology
	brentuximab vedotin, (Adcetris), doxorubicin (Adriamycin), vinblastine, and dacarbazine
AAV-GAD	glumatic acid decarboxylase (gene viral transfer with the) adeno-associated virus
AAVR	acupuncture-associated vasovagal response (symptoms)
	adeno-associated virus receptor
AAVV	accumulated alveolar ventilatory volume
AAWD	antiandrogen withdrawal
AB	abortion
	Ace® bandage
	aggressive behavior
	antibiotic
	antibody
	Aphasia Battery
	apical beat
	armboard
	attentional blink
	products meeting bioequivalence requirements for generic pharmaceuticals
Aβ	beta-amyloid peptide
A/B	acid-base ratio
	apnea/bradycardia
A > B	air greater than bone (conduction)
A&B	apnea and bradycardia
	assault and battery
AB−	AB negative blood type (AB negative preferred)
AB+	AB positive blood type (AB positive preferred)
AB15	California's End of Life Option Act
AB42	beta amyloid 42 (a peptide whose elevated presences in the cerebrospinal fluid of still-healthy adults may signal an increased risk of developing Alzheimer disease)
Ab1	primary antibody
Ab2	secondary antibody
ABA	applied behavioral analysis
ABAO	acute basilar artery occlusion
ABAs	aluminum-based adjuvants
ABAS-II	Adaptive Behavior Assessment System Second Edition (scores)

ABBI	Advanced Breast Biopsy Instrumentation
Abbr	abbreviated as
	abbreviate(d)
ABC	abacavir (Ziagen)
	abbreviated blood count
	Aberrant Behavior Checklist
	absolute band counts
	absolute basophil count
	Activities-specific Balance Confidence (scale)
	activity-based costing
	advanced breast cancer
	airway, breathing, and circulation
	all but code (resuscitation order)
	aneurysmal bone cyst
	antigen-binding capacity
	apnea, bradycardia, and cyanosis
	applesauce, bananas, and cereal (diet)
	argon-beam coagulator
	Aristotle Basic Complexity (Score)
	artificial beta cells
	aspiration, biopsy and cytology
	automated blood count (no differential)
	automatic brightness control (radiology)
	avidin-biotin complex
ABC's	the basic organized approach
ABCD	amphotericin B cholesteryl sulfate complex (Amphotec; amphotericin B colloid dispersion)
	asymmetry, border irregularities, color variation, , and diameter (a mnemonic to assist in the evaluation of potential melanomas [also see ABCDE])
	automated blood count (differential done manually)
AbcD2	see gene website www.ncbi.nlm.nih.gov/gene
ABCDE	a mnemonic to assist in the evaluation of potential melanomas; Asymmetry, Border irregularities, Color variation, Diameter larger than a pencil eraser, and Evolving (any change in size, shape, or color)
	botulism toxoid pentavalent
ABCDE bundle	Awakening and Breathing coordination of daily sedation and ventilator removal

	trials; Choice of sedative or analgesic exposure; Delirium monitoring and management; and Early mobility and exercise (a multifaceted, interprofessional intervention that is associated with reduced ventilator and delirium days as well as increased likelihood of mobility in intensive care)
ABCD score	age, blood pressure, clinical features, duration of symptoms (prognostic score for short term risk of stroke after transient ischemic attack)
ABCS	Active Bacterial Core Surveillance (CDC)
ABCs	abstinence, fidelity ("Being faithful"), or condom use (ABCs of HIV prevention)
	Active Bacterial Core surveillance
	A_{ic}level (glycosylate hemoglobin A_{ic}, Blood pressure, and Cholesterol level (ABCs of diabetes care)
	airway, breathing and circulation stabilization (ABCs of resuscitation)
	aneurysmal bone cysts
AbCT	abdominal computed tomography
ABCT	Alcohol Behavioral Couple Therapy
ABD	after bronchodilator
	autoimmune bullous diseases (a rarely seen group of diseases, of which pemphigus and bullous pemphigoid are the major groups)
	automated border detection
	type of plain gauze dressing
Abd	abdomen
	abdominal
	abduction
	abductor
A/B/D	apnea/bradycardia/desaturation
abd/add	abduction and adduction
ABDCT	atrial bolus dynamic computer tomography
ABD GR	abdominal girth
ABDL	acute bile duct ligation
ABDM	acellular breast dermal matrices
	anterior belly of the digastric muscle
ABD PB	abductor pollicis brevis

Abd/pel	abdomin/pelvis
ABD PL	abductor pollicis longus
abdom	abdomen
	abdominal
ABDR	Alaska Birth Defects Registry
	human leukocyte antigens
	(HLA) A, B, and DR
ABDs	autoimmune bullous diseases
ABDSM	American Board of Dental Sleep
	Medicine
ABDV	doxorubicin (adriamycin),
	bleomycin, dacarbazine, and
	vinblastine
ABE	actual base excess
	acute bacterial endocarditis
	acute bilirubin encephalopathy
	adult basic education
	average bioequivalence
	botulism equine trivalent
	antitoxin
ABECB	acute bacterial exacerbations of
	chronic bronchitis
ABEP	auditory brain stem-evoked
	potentials
ABER	abduction and external rotation
Abeta	amyloid-beta
a-beta42	beta-amyloid 42
ABF	aortic blood flow
	aortobifemoral (bypass)
	aortobronchial fistula
ABFB	aortobifemoral bypass
abfB	arabinofuranosidase; see gene
	website; www.ncbi.nlm.nih
	.gov/gene
ABG	air/bone gap
	aortoiliac bypass graft
	arterial blood gases
	axiobuccogingival
ABGA	anti-basal ganglia antibody
	arterial blood gas analysis
ABGs	air-bone gaps
	arterial blood gases
ABH	Ativan, Benadryl, and Haldol
ABHR	alcohol-based hand rub
ABHRs	alcohol-based hand rubs
ABI	acquired brain injury
	acute brain injury
	ankle brachial index
	(ankle-to-arm systolic blood
	pressure ratio)
	ankle-brachial index
	anoxic brain injury
	atherothrombotic brain infarction
	auditory brainstem implant
ABI's	see ABI
ABI and PVR	ankle-brachial index and pulse
	volume recording
ABID	antibody identification

A Big	atrial bigeminy
ABIM	American Board of Internal
	Medicine
ABIM-CE	American Board of Internal
	Medicine Certification
	Examination
ABI PVR	ankle-brachial index and pulse
	volume recording
ABIS	Amputee Body Image Scale
ABK	aphakic bullous keratopathy
abl	ablation; abdominal
ABL	abetalipoproteinemia
	acute basophilic leukemia
	acute blood loss
	allograft bound lymphocytes
	axiobuccolingual
aBLA	abbreviated Biological License
	Application
ABLA	acute blood loss anemia
ABL anemia	acute blood loss anemia
ABLATE	American Breast Laser Ablation
	Therapy Evaluation
ABLB	alternate binaural loudness
	balance
ABLC	amphotericin B lipid complex
	(Abelcet)
ab-LCFA	ascending branch of the lateral
	circumflex femoral artery
ab lib	may have mean ad lib (as desired)
ABLS	Advanced Burn Life Support
	(a national standardized
	educational program)
ABLs	apical bone levels
ABLV	Australian bat Lyssavirus
ABMACN	anterior branch of medial
	antebrachial cutaneous nerve
ABMD	anterior basement membrane
	(corneal) dystrophy
aBMD	areal bone mineral density
ABML	argument-based machine learning
A/B Mods	apnea/bradycardia moderate
	stimulation
ABMR	antibody-mediated rejection
ABMS	acute bacterial maxillary sinusitis
	autologous bone marrow support
A/B MS	apnea/bradycardia mild
	stimulation
ABMT	autologous bone marrow
	transplantation
ABN	abnormal
	abnormality(ies)
	Advance Beneficiary Notice
ABNC	active but nonculturable
abnC	see gene website www.ncbi.nlm
	.nih.gov/gene
abnl bld	abnormal bleeding
ABNM	American Board of Nuclear
	Medicine

abnml	abnormal	
abnor.	abnormal	
ABNs	abnormalities	
ABO	absent bed occupant	
	blood group system (A, AB, B, and O)	
abol	abolish	
ABO/Rh	determination of blood type grouping (A,B, AB, O) and the RH factor (positive or negative)	
abortn	abortion	
ABP	ambulatory blood pressure	
	androgen-binding protein	
	arterial blood pressure	
ABPA	allergic bronchopulmonary aspergillosis	
ABPB	axillary brachial plexus block	
ABPE	atypical benign partial epilepsy	
ABPI	ankle-brachial pressure index	
	Association of the British Pharmaceutical Industry	
ABPM	allergic bronchopulmonary mycosis	
	ambulatory blood pressure monitoring	
ABPN	American Board of Psychiatry and Neurology	
ABPP	American Board of Professional Psychology	
ABQAURP	American Board of Quality Assurance and Utilization Review Physicians	
ABR	absolute bed rest	
	angiographic binary restenosis (percentage of patients with a follow-up percent diameter stenosis of greater or equal to 50% determined by quantitative coronary angioplasty)	
	antibacterial resistance	
	antibody response unit	
	auditory brain-stem response	
ABRA	see gene website, www.ncbi.nlm.nih.gov/gene	
ABRS	acute bacterial rhinosinusitis	
	Advocacy Behaviour Rating Scale	
ABRT	activity-based rehabilitative therapies	
	activity-based restorative therapy	
AbS	antibiotic stewardship	
ABS	absent	
	absorbed	
	absorption	
	Accu-Chek® blood sugar (blood glucose monitoring meter and test strips)	

	active bowel sounds
	acute brain syndrome
	admitting blood sugar
	Alterman-Bishop stent
	amniotic band syndrome
	Antenatal Bartter syndrome
	antibody screen
	at bedside
ABSA	adjusted body surface area
absc	abscess
ABSC	antibody screening
ABSH	asymmetrical basal septal hypertrophy
ABSS	Anderson Behavioral State Scale
A/B SS	apnea/bradycardia self-stimulation
ABSSI	acute bacterial skin and skin-structure infection
ABSSSI	acute bacterial skin and skin structure infections
ABT	aminopyrine breath test
	antibiotic therapy
	autologous blood therapy
ABTA	advanced biliary tract adenocarcinoma
ABTS	2,2'-azino-bis(3-ethylbenzothiazoline-6-sulphonic acid (an assay to determine antioxidant activity)
ABTX	alpha-bungarotoxin
ABTx	antibiotic therapy
ABU	Adult Burns Unit
ABUS	automated whole breast ultrasound
ABVD	doxorubicin (Adriamycin), bleomycin, vinblastine, and dacarbazine (DTIC)
ABVE	doxorubicin (Adriamycin), bleomycin, vincristine, and etoposide
ABVE-PC	doxorubicin (Adriamycin), bleomycin, vincristine, etoposide prednisone, and cyclophosphamide
ABW	actual body weight
	adjusted body weight
ABx	antibiotic
ABxs	antibiotics
aby	Abyssi
ABY	Affibody molecules
AC	abdominal circumference
	acceleration capacity (heart)
	acetate
	acromioclavicular
	activated charcoal
	acute

adjuvant chemotherapy
African Caribbean
air conditioned
air conduction
anchored catheter
annual checkup
antecubital
anterior chamber
anticoagulant
anticoagulation
anticonvulsant
arm circumference
assist control
autologous cell
axillary crutches
before meals
doxorubicin (Adriamycin) and
   cyclophosphamide

Ac — actinium
a.c. — before meals
A.C. — see AC
A-C — Astler-Coller (stages of
   colorectal cancer)
a/c — acute on chronic
A/C — acute to chronic
   anterior chamber of the eye
   assist/control
A&C — alert and cooperative
AC1 — adenylate cyclase 1 (brain); see
   gene website; www.ncbi.nlm
   .nih.gov/gene
A1C — glycosylated hemoglobin A_{1C}
5-AC — azacitidine (Vidaza)
9AC — rubitecan
   (9-aminocamptothecin)
ACA — accommodation convergence
   accommodation (ratio)
   acrodermatitis chronica
      atrophicans
   acyclovir
   adenocarcinoma
   adrenal cortical adenoma
   Affordable Care Act
   against clinical advice
   aminocaproic acid (Amicar)
   anterior cerebral artery
   anterior communicating artery
   anticanalicular antibodies
AC/A — accommodative convergence/
   accommodation ratio
ACABS — acute community-acquired
   bacterial sinusitis
AcAc — acetoacetate
ACAD — anterior circulation arterial
   dissection
AC and HS — before meals and at bedtime
ACAP — atypical community-acquired
   pneumonia

Acapella — a device producing high-
   frequency oscillations and
   positive expiratory pressure to
   promote bronchial secretion
   clearance
ACAS — acute community-acquired
   sinusitis
   asymptomatic carotid artery
   study
ACAT — acyl coenzyme A: cholesterol
   acyltransferase
ACATs — acyl-coenzyme A: cholesterol
   acyltransferases
ACB — alveolar-capillary block
   antibody-coated bacteria
   aortocoronary bypass
   before breakfast
AcB — assist with bath
AC & BC — air and bone conduction
ACBD — accessory common bile duct
   acute complicated type B aortic
   dissection
ACBE — air contrast barium enema
ACBG — aortocoronary bypass graft
AC-BPPV — anterior canal benign
   paroxysmal positional
   vertigo
ACBS — aortocoronary bypass surgery
   Asthma Call-back Survey
ACBT — active cycle of breathing
   techniques
ACC — acalculous cholecystitis
   accident
   accommodation
   accuracy
   acetyl-CoA carboxylase
   acinar cell carcinoma
   adenoid cystic carcinomas
   administrative control center
   adrenocortical carcinoma
   advanced colorectal cancer
   ambulatory care center
   American College of Cardiology
   (guidelines)
   amylase creatinine clearance
   anterior cingulate cortex
   anterior cortical cataract
   automated cell count
ACCA — Acute Cardiovascular Care
   Association
ACCAHA — American College of
   Cardiology and the American
   Heart Association
ACC/AHA — American College of Cardiology/
   American Heart Association
   (clinical practice guidelines for
   the prevention of cardiovascular disease)

ACC/AHA/HRS	American College of Cardiology/ American Heart Association/ Heart Rhythm Society (guidelines)
A-CCC	Advanced Certification in Continuity of Care
accD	acetylCoA carboxylase, beta (carboxyltransferase) subunit; see gene website www.ncbi .nlm.nih.gov/gene
ACCE	Academic Clinical Coordinator Educator
Accels	accelerations
ACCF	American College of Cardiology Foundation (guidelines) anterior cervical corpectomy and fusion
ACCF/AHA	American College of Cardiology Foundation/American Heart Association (Guidelines)
AcCh	acetylcholine
ACCh	acute calculous cholecystitis
ACCHA	may have meant AChA (anterior choroidal artery)
AC chemotherapy	doxorubicin (Adriamycin) and cyclophosphamide chemotherapy
Acc Junct	accelerated junctional (rhythm)
AC&CL	acetest and clinitest
ACCM	American College of Critical Care Medicine
ACCME	Accreditation Council for Continuing Medical Education
ACC-NCDR	American College of Cardiology- National Cardiovascular Data Registry
AcCoA	acetyl-coenzyme A
accom	accommodative
ACCP	American College of Chest Physicians
ACCR	amylase creatinine clearance ratio
ACCs	adrenocortical carcinomas
ACCT	computed tomography attenuation correction
ACCU	acute coronary care unit
Accu-Check	Accu-Chek® (blood glucose monitoring meter and test strips)
accuchk	Accu Chek®
accy	accessory
AcCy	N-acetylcysteine
ACD	absolute cardiac dullness absorbent cover dressing acid-citrate-dextrose advanced cervical dilation allergic contact dermatitis alveolar capillary dysplasia

	anemia of chronic disease anterior cervical diskectomy anterior chamber depth anterior chamber diameter anterior chest diameter before dinner average cost per day dactinomycin (actinomycin D; Cosmegen)
ACDA	anticoagulant citrate dextrose solution A (anhydrous citric acid [38 mM {millimoles}], dextrose monohydrate [136 mM], and trisodium citrate [107 mM] dihydrate solution)
ACDB	anticoagulant citrate dextrose solution B (anhydrous citric acid [23 mM {millimoles}], dextrose monohydrate [136 mM], and trisodium citrate [65 mM] dihydrate solution)
ACDC	antibody complement- dependent cytolysis
AC-DC	bisexual (slang)
ACDDS	Alcoholism/Chemical Dependency Detoxification Service
ACDF	anterior cervical decompression and fusion
ACD&F	anterior cervical diskectomy and fusion
ACDFI	anterior cervical diskectomy with fusion and instrumentation
ACDFP	anterior cervical diskectomy, fusion, and plate placement
ACDFs	adult children from dysfunctional families
ACDG	anterior chamber depth (numeric) grade
AcDH	acetaldehyde
ACDH	acetaldehyde dehydrogenase (gene/protein)
ACDIS	Association of Clinical Documentation Improvement Specialists
ACDK	acquired cystic disease of the kidney
ACDP	ancient conserved domain protein (a gene family)
ACDs	anticonvulsant drugs
ACE	acute care of the elderly (nursing unit) adrenocortical extract adverse childhood experience adverse clinical event

	aerosol-cloud enhancer
	angiotensin-converting enzyme
	antegrade colonic enema
	antegrade continence enema
	anterior center-edge (angle)
	doxorubicin (Adriamycin), cyclophosphamide, and etoposide
A.C.E.	see ACE
aceB	malate synthase; see gene website www.ncbi.nlm.nih.gov/gene
ACED	Assessment of Capacity for Everyday Decision-Making
ACEI	angiotensin-converting enzyme inhibitor
ACE levels	angiotensin-converting enzyme levels
ACELS	may have meant ACEIs (angiotensin converting enzyme inhibitors)
ACEP	American College of Emergency Physicians (policy statements and guidelines)
ACES	acute critical emergency service Agitation and Calmness Evaluation Scale
ACEs	adverse childhood experiences angiotensin I-converting enzymes attenuation coefficient estimates
ACET	air-conduction estimated from tympanometry antepartum continuous epidural therapy
Acetab	acetabular
Ace wrap	elastic bandage wrap
ACF	aberrant crypt focus accessory clinical findings acute care facility advance care planning antecubital fossa anterior cervical fusion
ACFA	accessory colonization factor A
acfD	accessory colonization factor AcfD-like protein (gene)
ACFD	adiabatic-connection fluctuation-dissipation (theorem)
AC followed by D	doxorubicin and cyclophosphamide followed by docetaxel
ACFS	acro-cardio-facial syndrome
ACG	accelerography angiocardiography
ACGF	activated carbon-coated glass fiber
ACGH	array comparative genomic hybridization

ACGME	Accreditation Council for Graduate Medical Education
ACGs	adjusted clinical groups
ACh	acetylcholine
ACH	adrenal cortical hormone aftercoming head arm girth, chest depth, and hip width
ACHA	air-conduction hearing aid
AChA	anterior choroidal artery
ACHBLF	acute-on-chronic hepatitis B liver failure
AChBP	acetylcholine binding protein
ACHD	adult congenital heart disease
AChE	acetylcholinesterase
ACHE	American College of Healthcare Executives
AChEIs	acetylcholinesterase inhibitors
ACHES	abdominal pain, chest pain, headache, eye problems, and severe leg pains (early danger signs of oral contraceptive adverse effects)
ACHF	acute congestive heart failure Advanced Certification in Heart Failure (Joint Commission's standardized performance measures for disease specific care) advanced chronic heart failure advanced congestive heart failure
A-CHF	anthracycline(s) (such as doxorubicin and idarubicin)-induced clinical heart failure
ACHFOP	Advanced Certification in Heart Failure Outpatient (Joint Commission's standardized performance measures for disease specific care)
ACHIs	acetyl cholinesterase inhibitors
ACHPN	Advanced Certified Hospice and Palliative Nurse
AChR	acetylcholine receptor anti-acetylcholine receptor
ACHRF	acute on chronic hypercapnic respiratory failure
ACHRN	Advanced Certified Hyperbaric Registered Nurse
AC&HS	before meals and at bedtime
ACI	acceleration index acute cerebral ischemia adrenal cortical insufficiency aftercare instructions anabolic-catabolic index anemia of chronic illness autologous chondrocyte implantation

ACIC	aciclovir (acyclovir)
	adenomas containing invasive carcinoma
ACID PHOS	acid phosphatase (prostatic acid phosphatase)
ACIF	anterior cervical interbody fusion
acin	acinarization (opacification of acini [a cluster of cells that resembles a many-lobed berry, such as a raspberry] in the pancreatic parenchyma by contrast)
ACIN	anal canal intraepithelial neoplasia
ACIOL	anterior chamber intraocular lens
ACIP	Advisory Committee on Immunization Practices (of the Centers for Disease Control and Prevention)
ACIS	automated cellular imaging system
ACJ	acromioclavicular joint
AC joint	acromioclavicular joint
A/CK	Accu-Chek® (blood glucose monitoring meter and test strips)
ACKD	acquired cystic kidney disease
	advanced chronic kidney disease
	anemia of chronic kidney disease
ACKI	acute-on-chronic kidney injury
ACL	accessory collateral ligament (hand)
	Allen Cognitive Level
	American cutaneous leishmaniasis
	anterior cruciate ligament (knee)
	single-bundle (hamstring autograft) anterior cruciate ligament (reconstruction)
aCL	anticardiolipin (antibody)
ACLA	aclarubicin
ACLCT	acute calcific longus colli tendinitis
ACLD	anterior cruciate ligament deficiency
	atypical cutaneous lymphoproliferative disorder
ACLE	acute cautaneous lupus erythematosus
ACLF	acute-on-chronic liver failure
	adult congregate living facility
ACLN	anterior cervical lymph nodes
ACLR	anterior cruciate ligament reconstruction
	anterior cruciate ligament repair

ACLS	advanced cardiac (cardiopulmonary) life support
	Allen Cognitive Level Screen
ACLs	atypical cribriform lesions
ACLU	American Civil Liberties Union
ACM	alternative/complementary medicine
	Arnold-Chiari malformation
ACM Ab	anticentromere antibody
ACMC	alternating consecutive maximum contractions
ACMD	adult children with mental disorder
	anterior cartilage meniscus distance
	atypical chronic myelocytic disorder
ACMDs	antenatal common mental disorders
ACME	accumulation of a concocted myriad of events
	arginine catabolic mobile element
	Automated Classification of Medical Entities
ACMG	American College of Medical Genetics and Genomics
ACMI	American College of Medical Informatics
aCML	atypical chronic myeloid leukemia
ACMT	American College of Medical Toxicology
ACMV	assist-controlled mechanical ventilation
ACN	acetonitrile
	acute conditioned neurosis
ACNB	abnormal condition of new born
ACNES	anterior cutaneous nerve entrapment syndrome
ACNHs	adrenocortical nodular hyperplasias
ACNO	acetonitrile oxide
	Assistant Chief Nursing Officer
ACNP	Acute Care Nurse Practitioner
ACNP-BC	Acute Care Nurse Practitioner, Board Certified
ACNPC	Adult Acute Care Nurse Practitioner Certification
ACNS	American Clinical Neurophysiology Society (guidelines)
	autonomic cardiac nervous system
ACNs	anthocyanins
ACNT	Patient account number assigned by the provider. (Medicare)
ACNU	nimustine HCl

ACO	Accountable Care Organization (established by the Patient Protection and Affordable Care Act. 2010)
	anterior capsilar opacification
	asthma and COPD (chronic obstructive pulmonary disease) overlap
ACOA	Adult Children of Alcoholics
ACoA	anterior communicating artery
aCOD	acetaldehyde dehydrogenase; see gene website www.ncbi .nlm.nih.gov/gene
ACOG	American College of Obstetricians and Gynecologists
ACOL	acolbifene
ACOM	anterior communicating (artery and or aneurysm)
	automated cardiac output measurement
A COMM A	anterior communicating artery
ACON	ACON Laboratories, Inc. provides diabetes care, clinical chemistry including urinalysis, and immunoassay diagnostic and healthcare products.
ACOPDE	acute chronic obstructive pulmonary disease exacerbations
ACOPIA	inability to cope
ACOR	ant colony optimization reordering (algorithm)
	Association of Cancer Online Resources
acoR	see gene website www.ncbi.nlm .nih.gov/gene
ACOS	asthma and COPD (chronic obstructive pulmonary disease) overlap syndrome
ACOS-OG	American College of Surgeons Oncology Group
ACP	accessory conduction pathway
	acid phosphatase
	adamantinomatous craniopharyngioma
	adenocarcinoma of the prostate
	advance care planning
	ambulatory care program
	American College of Physicians
	anesthesia-care provider
	anterior cervical plate
	antrochoanal polyp
	Australian College of Pediatrics
ACPA	anticitrullinated protein autoantibody
	anticytoplasmic antibodies

ACPAs	anti-citrullinated protein antibodies
AC-PC line	anterior commissure-posterior commissure line
ACPD	ambulatory continuous peritoneal dialysis
ACPF	calcium phosphate fluoride (Dentistry)
	casein phosphopeptide-amorphous calcium phosphate fluoride (tooth paste)
ACPH	air changes per hour
AC-PH	acid phosphatase
ACPM	American College of Preventive Medicine
ACPO	acute colonic pseudo-obstruction
ACPP	adrenocorticopolypeptide
ACPP PF	acid phosphatase prostatic fluid
ACPPD	average cost per patient day
ACPR	adequate clinical and parasitological response
ACPS	anterior cervical plate stabilization
ACPT	acid phosphatase, testicular, see gene website, www.ncbi.nlm .nih.gov/gene
ACQ	acquired
	Areas of Change Questionnaire
ACQ-5	asthma control questionnaire (5-item symptom and activity verson)
ACQ-6	6-item Asthma Control Questionnaire
ACR	acute cellular rejection
	adenomatosis of the colon and rectum
	albumin to creatinine ratio
	American College of Radiology
	American College of Rheumatology
	anterior chamber reformation
	anticonstipation regimen
ACR20	American College of Rheumatology rating scale (20% or more improvement)
acrB	see gene website www.ncbi.nlm .nih.gov/gene
ACRC	advanced colorectal cancer
ACRD	acquired cystic renal disease
ACRES	amplification created restriction enzyme site
ACRF	acute-on-chronic renal failure
	acute-on-chronic respiratory failure
acrF	see gene website; www.ncbi .nlm.nih.gov
ACRI	arterial catheter-related infection

ACRM	American Congress of Rehabilitation Medicine (criteria)
ACRN	AIDS-Certified Registered Nurse
ACRO	a prefix denoting a relation to extremities, top, or to an extreme
	acrolein
	acromegaly
	American College of Radiation Oncology
ACROM	active cervical (spine) range of motion
ACRO-QOL	acromegaly quality of life
ACRS	acute cardiorenal syndrome
ACS	abdominal compartment syndrome
	Acute Care Services
	Acute Chest Syndrome (a radiodensity on chest radiograph accompanied by fever and/or respiratory symptoms; a life-threatening complication of sickle cell disease)
	acute confusional state
	acute coronary syndrome
	American Cancer Society
	anodal-closing sound
	anterior compartment syndrome
	automated corneal shaper
	before supper
Acs	Anticoagulants
ACSA	anatomical cross sectional area
ACSC	ambulatory care-sensitive condition(s) (used to identify individuals for targeting of interventions to reduce preventable hospital admissions)
ACSF	anterior cervical spine fixation
	artificial cerebrospinal fluid
ACSH	ambulatory care-sensitive hospitalizations
ACSL	automatic computerized solvent litholysis
ACSM	American College of Sports Medicine (guidelines)
ACS NSQIP	American College of Surgeons National Surgical Quality Improvement Program
ACST	acute carotid stent thrombosis
ACST-1	Asymptomatic Carotid Surgery Trial 1
ACST-2	Asymptomatic Carotid Surgery Trial 2
ACSUS	AIDS (acquired immunodeficiency syndrome) Costs and Service Utilization

	Survey (sponsored by the US Agency for Health Care Policy & Research)
	atypical squamous cells of undetermined significance
ACSVBG	aortocoronary saphenous vein bypass graft
ACSW	Academy of Certified Social Workers
ACT	acceptance and commitment therapy
	activated clotting time
	active
	activity
	aggressive comfort treatment
	allergen challenge test
	anticoagulant therapy
	artemisinin-based combination therapy
	artemisinin-combination therapy (artesunate and amodiaquine [Coarsucam])
	assertive community treatment (program)
	asthma control test
	doxorubicin (adriamycin), cyclophosphamide, and paclitaxel
act	actuation
aCT	adjuvant chemotherapy
Acta2	actin, alpha 2, smooth muscle, aorta (gene/protein)
ACTA	see gene website, www.ncbi.nlm.nih.gov/gene
ACTC	see gene website, www.ncbi.nlm.nih.gov/gene
ACT-D	dactinomycin
Act Ex	active exercise
ACTG	AIDS Clinical Trial Group
ACTH	corticotropin (adrenocorticotropic hormone)
ACTHP	doxorubicin (Adriamycin), cyclophosphamide, paclitaxel (Taxol), trastuzumab (Herceptin), and pertuzumab (Perjeta) (a regimen used for the treatment of breast cancer)
ACTN1	actinin, alpha 1
ACTN2	actinin, alpha 2
ACT-Post	activated clotting time post-filter
ACT-Pre	activated clotting time pre-filter
ACTSEB	anterior chamber tube shunt encircling band
ACTZ	Acetazolamide
ACU	ambulatory care unit
ACUP	adenocarcinoma of unknown primary (origin)

ACUS	atypical cells of undetermined significance
acute hepatitis panel	go to Tables and Lists Button; Laboratory Panels
ACUV	air-contrast ultrasound venography
ACV	acyclovir (Zovirax)
	amifostine, cisplatin, and vinblastine
	anterior chamber volume
	assist control ventilation
	atrial/carotid/ventricular
A-C-V	A wave, C wave, and V wave
ACVBP	doxorubicin (Adriamycin), cyclophosphamide, vindesine, bleomycin, and prednisone
ACVC	autonomic cardiovascular control
ACVD	acute cardiovascular disease
	atherosclerotic cardiovascular disease
ACVF	autocovariance function
ACVP	doxorubicin (Adriamycin), cyclophosphamide, vincristine, and prednisone
ACVRL1	activin A receptor like type 1 (gene)
ACVS	acute cerebrovascular syndrome
	American College of Veterinary Surgeons
ACVs	articular cartilage vesicles
ACW	anterior chest wall
	apply to chest wall
ACWE	active contour without edge
ACx	auditory cortex
acyl-CoA	acyl coenzyme A
ACZ	acetazolamide
AD	accident dispensary
	adjustment
	admitting diagnosis
	advanced dementia
	advanced directive (this document allows an individual to instruct physicians and health care providers about the kind of health care they want and don't want if they are unable to tell themselves; also known as a living will)
	air dyne
	alcohol dependence
	alternating days (this is a dangerous abbreviation)
	Alzheimer disease
	androgen deprivation
	antidepressant
	aortic dissection
	assistive device

	atopic dermatitis
	autistic disorder
	autonomic dysreflexia
	axillary dissection
	axis deviation
	doxoribicin (Adriamycin) and dacarbazine (a cancer chemo-therapy regimen)
	Internet addiction disorder
	right ear
A+D	see A&D
A&D	admission and discharge
	alcohol and drug
	ascending and descending
	vitamins A and D
A.D.	see AD
A/D	see AD
ADA	adalimumab (Humira)
	adenosine deaminase
	airdyne arms (cardiac rehab)
	American Dental Association
	American Diabetes Association
	Americans with Disabilities Act
	anterior descending artery
	awareness during anesthesia
adad1	see gene website, www.ncbi.nlm.nih.gov/gene
adad2	see gene website, www.ncbi.nlm.nih.gov/gene
ADA Diet	American Diabetes Association diet
adADT	the acetylated metabolite of deacylated amidantel (triben-dimidine's active metabolite)
ADAF	active duty Air Force
ADaM	Analysis Data Model
ADAM	a disintegrin and metalloproteinases (a family of multidomain transmem-brane and secreted proteins)
	adjustment disorder with anxious mood
	Androgen Deficiency in Aging Men (questionnaire/symptom scale)
ADAMTS	A Distintegrin And Metalloprotease with Thrombospondin (there is at least 20 types)
ADAMTS13	A Distintegrin And Metalloprotease with Thrombospondin type 13 motif (von Willebrand factor cleavage protease)
adamts1 (also 2-10)	see gene website, www.ncbi.nlm.nih.gov/gene
ADAP	adhesion and degranulation promoting adapter protein

	AIDS (Acquired Immunodeficiency Syndrome) Drug Assistance Program
ADAPT	average deviation about the probability threshold (curve)
ADAS	Alzheimer Disease Assessment Scale
ADA SCID	adenosine deaminase severe combined immune deficiency
ADAS-COG	Alzheimer Disease Assessment Scale-Cognitive Subscale
ADAT	advance diet as tolerated
ADAU	adolescent drug abuse unit
Adavan	may have meant the drug, Ativan
ADB	airdyne both (cardiac rehab)
	alfaxalone-dexmedetomidine-butorphanol (veterinary sedation)
	amorous disinhibited behavior
ADC	Aid to Dependent Children
	AIDS (acquired immune deficiency syndrome) dementia complex
	analog-to-digital converter (radiology)
	antibody-drug conjugate (a targeted drug delivery system composed of an antibody linked to an active cytotoxic drug)
	anxiety disorder clinic
	apparent diffusion coefficient (radiology)
	automated dispensing cabinet
	average daily census
	average daily consumption
Ad Ca	adenocarcinoma
ADCA	autosomal dominant cerebellar ataxia
AdCC	adenoid cystic carcinoma
ADCC	antibody-dependent cellular cytotoxicity
	autosomal dominant congenital cataract
ADCD	axial diagnostic criterion for depression
adcD	see gene website www.ncbi.nlm.nih.gov/gene
ADCF	acantholytic dermatosis of the crural folds
	acute decompensated cardiac failure
	animal-derived component free
ADCHF	acutely decompensated chronic heart failure
ADCOMS	Alzheimer disease Composite Score

adCORD	autosomal dominant cone-rod dystrophy (an inherited, progressive retinal disorder with genetic and phenotypic heterogeneity)
adcR	see gene website; www.ncbi.nlm.nih.gov
ADCs	antibody-drug conjugates (targeted drug delivery system composed of an antibody linked to an active cytotoxic drug)
ADCT	area-detector computed tomography
ADC VAAN DIML	mnemonic for formatting physician orders: Admit, Diagnosis, Condition, Vitals, Activity, Allergies, Nursing procedures, Diet, Ins and outs, Medication, Labs
ADD	adduction
	alcohol-induced dose dumping
	annual disability density
	arrest in dilation/descent
	attention-deficit disorder
	average daily dose
ADDH	attention-deficit disorder with hyperactivity
ADDHF	may have meant ADHF (acute decompensated heart failure)
ADDL	additional
ADDLs	amyloid-derived diffusable ligands
ADDM	adjustment disorder with depressed mood
ADDs	AIDS (acquired immune deficiency syndrome)-defining diseases
ADDT	auditory description decision task
ADDU	alcohol and drug dependence unit
ADE	acute disseminated encephalitis
	adverse drug event
ADEK	fat-soluble vitamins A,D,E, and K
ADEM	acute disseminating encephalomyelitis
ADEN	adenoids
Adeno CA	adenocarcinoma
ADEPT	antibody-directed enzyme prodrug therapy
adeq	adequate
ADFH	autosomal dominant familial hypercholesterolemia
ADFS	autosomal dominant febrile seizures
ADFT	atrial defibrillation threshold
ADFU	agar diffusion for fungus

ADG	atrial diastolic gallop	Adj D/O	adjustment disorder
	axiodistogingival	ADJS	Adjustments
ADH	antidiuretic hormone	ADK	adenosine kinase
	atypical ductal hyperplasia	ADKPD	May have meant ADPKD
ADHA	alcohol dehydrogenase; see		(autosomal dominant poly-
	gene website www.ncbi.nlm		cystic kidney disease)
	.nih.gov/gene	ADL	activities of daily living
	American Dental Hygienists'		airdyne legs (cardiac rehab)
	Association	ADL's	activities of daily living
ADHC	adult day health care	ADLD	autosomal dominant
	see gene website, www.ncbi		leukodystrophy
	.nlm.nih.gov/gene	ADLG	average duration of life gained
ADHD	attention-deficit hyperactivity	ad lib	as desired
	disorder		at liberty
ADHD-RS-IV	attention-deficit/hyperactivity	ad-lib	see ad lib
	disorder Rating Scale IV	ADLs	activities of daily living
ADHF	acute decompensated heart failure	aDLT	adjuvant transfusion of donor
ADHFpEF	acute decompensated heart		lymphocytes
	failure with preserved	ADM	abductor digiti minimi
	ejection fraction		abductor digiti minimi (muscle)
ADHFrEF	acute decompensated heart		acceptance of disability modified
	failure with reduced ejection		acellular dermal matrix
	fraction		administered (dose)
ad hoc	formed for or concerned with		admission
	one specific purpose: an ad		adrenomedullin
	hoc compensation committee		doxorubicin (Adriamycin)
ADHR	autosomal dominant	A1DM	gestational diabetes in pregnancy
	hypophosphatemic rickets	ADM.	See ADM
ADHS	Adult Dental Health Survey	ADMA	asymmetric dimethylarginine
ADHs	alcohol dehydrogenases		asymmetrical dimethyl-L-arginine
adhT	alcohol dehydrogenase; see	adm dx	admission diagnosis
	gene website www.ncbi.nlm	ADME	absorption, distribution,
	.nih.gov/gene		metabolism, and excretion
ADI	acceptable daily intake	ADMET	adsorption, distribution,
	acute diaphragmatic injury		metabolism, excretion and
	AIDS (acquired immunodeficiency		toxicity
	syndrome) - defining illness	admin	administer
	allowable (acceptable) daily		administers
	intake		administration
	axiodistoincisal	ADMP	active-duty military personnel
A-DIC	doxorubicin and dacarbazine	ADMs	automated dispensing machines
ADIET	angle-dependent integral	ADMT	androgen deprivation
	equation theory		monotherapy
ADIM	abdominal drawing-in maneuver	Adna	ancient deoxyribonucleic acid
ADIP	afadin dilute domain-interacting	ADNA	aortic depressor nerve activity
	protein; see gene website	ADNFLE	autosomal dominant nocturnal
	www.ncbi.nlm.nih.gov/gene		frontal epilepsy
ADIPs	adipocytes	Ado	adenosine (also referred to as A)
ADIs	acceptable daily intakes	ADO	Amplatzer duct occluder
	AIDS-(acquired immunodeficiency		axiodisto-occlusal
	syndrome) defining illnesses	ADOA	Autosomal-dominant optic
ADIS C/P	Anxiety Disorders interview		atrophy
	Schedule: Child and Parent	Ad-OAP	doxorubicin, vincristine,
	Versions		cytarabine, and prednisone
ADJ	adjusted	ADOC	Adriamycin (doxorubicin),
ADJ BW	adjusted birthweight		cisplatin (DDP), vincristine
AdjBW	adjusted body weight		(Ovcovin), and cyclophos-
Adj Dis	adjustment disorder		phamide

ADOD	Alzheimer disease and other dementias
ADOL	adolescent
AdOM	adhesive otitis media
ADOM	Alcohol and Drug Outcome Measure
ADON	Assistant Director of Nursing
ADOS	Autism Diagnosis Observation Schedule (score)
AdP	adductor pollicis
ADP	adenosine diphosphate
	arterial demand pacing
adpA	see gene website www.ncbi.nlm.nih.gov/gene
ADPAC	aggressive digital papillary adenocarcinoma
ADPC	active distance to palmar crease
ADPCKD	autosomal dominant polycystic kidney disease (also ADPKD)
ADPDK	autosomal dominant polycystic disease of the kidney
ADPI	afadin DIL domain-interacting protein; see gene website www.ncbi.nlm.nih.gov/gene
ADPKD	autosomal dominant polycystic kidney disease
ADPLD	autosomal dominant polycystic liver disease
ADPV	anomaly of drainage of pulmonary vein
ADQ	abductor digiti quinti
	adequate
ADR	acute dystonic reaction
	additional document(s) request
	adverse drug reaction
	alternative dispute resolution
	doxorubicin (Adriamycin)
ADRB2	beta 2-adrenergic receptor
ADRC	adipose derived regenerative cells
	Alzheimer Disease Research Center
ADRD	Alzheimer disease and related disorders
ADRIA	doxorubicin (Adriamycin)
ADRs	adverse drug reactions
ADRS	Alzheimer Disease Rating Scale
ADRV	adult diarrhea rotavirus
ADS	admission day surgery
	anatomical dead space
	anonymous donor's sperm
	antibody deficiency syndrome
ADs	advanced directive(s) (living wills)
ADSA	Attention-Deficit Scales for Adults
	autosomal dominant sensory ataxia

	axisymmetric drop shape analysis
ADSCHF	acute decompensated systolic congestive heart failure
ADSCs	adipose-derived stem cells
AdSD	adductor spasmodic dysphonia
ADSD	autosomal-dominant striatal degeneration
ADSEP	administrative separation (the military involuntarily separation of service personnel through the administrative [non-judicial] process)
ADSHF	acute decompensated systolic heart failure
ADSCHF	acute decompensated systolic congestive heart failure
Adsol®	a red blood cell preservative solution
ADSS	adenylosuccinate synthase; see gene website; www.ncbi.nlm.nih.gov/gene
ADSSs	antimicrobial decision support systems
ADSU	ambulatory diagnostic surgery unit
ADT	admission, discharge, and transfer
	alternate-day therapy
	androgen deprivation treatment (therapy)
	antiarrhythmic drug therapy
	anticipate discharge tomorrow
	any damn thing (a placebo) (slang)
	Auditory Discrimination Test
ADTP	Adolescent Day Treatment Program
	Alcohol-Dependence Treatment Program
ADTR	Academy of Dance Therapists, Registered
ADTU	admission discharge transition unit
	adolescent (psychiatric) day treatment unit
	ambulatory diagnostic and treatment unit
ADU	automated dispensing unit
ADULT	acro-dermato-ungual-lacrimal-tooth (syndrome)
ADV₄	adenovirus vaccine, type 4, live, oral
ADV₇	adenovirus vaccine, type 7, live, oral
ADV	advance
adv	adventitious sounds (wheezes and rhonchi)
advd	advanced

Adv Dir	advanced directive (this document allows an individual to instruct physicians and health care providers about the kind of health care they want and don't want if they are unable to tell themselves; also known as a living will)
AdvSM	advanced systemic mastocytosis
ADVT	acute deep venous thrombosis
	asymptomatic deep venous thrombosis
ADW	active duty women
	Aged and Disabled Waiver
	assault with a deadly weapon
A5D5W	alcohol 5%, dextrose 5% in water for injection
ADWG	average daily weight gain
ADX	audiological diagnostic
ADx™	urine drug screen for six drugs of abuse
AE	above elbow (amputation)
	accident and emergency (department)
	acute exacerbation
	adaptive equipment
	adaptive equipment (such as wheelchairs and walkers)
	adverse event
	aerobic exercise
	air entry
	androgen excess
	anoxic encephalopathy
	antiembolitic
	arm ergometer
	aryepiglottic (fold)
A&E	Accident and Emergency (department)
A/E	adaptive equipment
	air exchange
AEA	above-elbow amputation
	anandamide
	anti-endomysium antibody
AEAP	as early as possible
AEB	as evidenced by
	atrial ectopic beat
AEBA	acute exacerbations of bronchial asthma
AEC	Absolute eosinophil count
	at earliest convenience
	automatic exposure control (radiology)
AECB	acute exacerbations of chronic bronchitis
AECG	ambulatory electrocardiogram
AECHF	acute exacerbation of congestive heart failure
AECOPD	acute exacerbation of chronic obstructive pulmonary disease
AED	accident and emergency department
	alcohol mixed energy drinks
	antiepileptic drug
	automated (automatic) external defibrillator
AED's	antiepileptic drugs
AEDD	anterior extradural defects
AEDF	absent end-diastolic flow (umbilical-artery Doppler ultrasonography)
AEDH	acute epidural hematoma
AEDP	assisted end-diastolic pressure
	automated external defibrillator pacemaker
AEDs	antiepileptic drugs
AEDV	absent end-diastolic velocity
AEE	asthma-exacerbation episodes
aEEG	amplitude-integrated electroencephalography
AEEU	admission entrance and evaluation unit
AEF	aortoesophageal fistula
AEFI	adverse events following immunization
AEG	air encephalogram
	Alcohol Education Group
AEH	atypical endometrial hyperplasia
AEIOU TIPS	mnemonic for the diagnosis of coma: Alcohol, Encepha-lopathy, Insulin, Opiates, Uremia, Trauma, Infection, Psychiatric, and Syncope
AELBM	after each loose bowel movement
AEM	active electrode monitor
	alternative equipment maintenance
	ambulatory electrogram monitor
	antiepileptic medication
AEN	acute esophageal necrosis
	anterior ethmoidal nerve
	apoptosis enhancing nuclease
AEO	acute external otitis
	apraxia of eyelid opening
aeon	a word meaning an immeasurably or indefinitely long period of time
AEON	androstenone (5alpha-androst-16-en-3-one)
AEP	auditory evoked potential
AEPs	auditory evoked potentials
AEq	age equivalent
AER	absolute excess risk
	acoustic evoked response
	aerosol

	albumin excretion rate
	auditory evoked response
AERA	Eustachian Tube Balloon Dilation System (Acclarent, Menlo Park, CA)
AERD	aspirin-exacerbated respiratory disease
Aer. M.	aerosol mask
AERO	aerosol
AERP	atrial effective refractory period(s)
	auditory event-related potential(s)
AERS	adverse event reporting system
Aer. T.	aerosol tent
AES	adult emergency service
	anti-embolic stockings
	Apathy Evaluation Scale
AEs	adverse events
AESI	adverse event of special interest
AET	alternating esotropia
	atrial ectopic tachycardia
AEU	Allergic Effector Unit
	alternative exon usage
	Spanish Association of Urology
AEV	avian erythroblastosis virus
AEWS	Accident Emergency Warning Systems
AF	acid-fast
	acoustical feedback
	amaurosis fugal
	Amaurosis fugax (a painless temporary loss of vision in one or both eyes)
	amniotic fluid
	anteflexed
	anterior fontanel open and flat
	antifibrinogen
	aortofemoral
	ascitic fluid
	atrial fibrillation
A/F	see AF
AFA	Adaptive Fractal Analysis
	ankyloblepharon filiform adnatum
	arm-fat area
	atrial fibrillation ablation
	HapMap populations of African ancestry
AfA	African American
AF-AFI	atrial fibrillation and atrial flutter
AFAIS	atrial fibrillation-associated ischemic stroke
AFAP1	actin filament-associated protein 1; see gene website www.ncbi .nlm.nih.gov/gene
AFAT	Antifat Attitudes Test
AFB	acid-fast bacilli
AFB₁	aflatoxin B1
AFBG	aortofemoral bypass graft
AFBI	Agri-food and Biosciences Institute (Northern Ireland, UK)
AFBY	aortofemoral bypass (graft)
AFC	adult foster care
	air filled cushions
	alveolar fluid clearance
	antral follicle count
AFCC	amniotic fluid cellular content
AFCH	Adult Family Care Home (Florida)
AFD	Anderson-Fabry disease
AFDC	Aid to Families with Dependent Children
AFE	amniotic fluid embolization
	autofluorescence endoscopy
AFEB	afebrile
AFEU	ante partum fetal evaluation unit
AFF	atypical femur fracture
AFFIRM	Atrial Fibrillation Follow-up Investigation of Rhythm Management trial
AF/FL	atrial fibrillation/atrial flutter
AFFs	atypical femoral fractures
aFGF	acidic fibroblast growth factor
AFH	adult family home
	angiomatoid fibrous histiocytoma
	anterior facial height
AFI	acute febrile illness
	amniotic fluid index
A Fib	atrial fibrillation
A Fib RVR	atrial fibrillation and rapid ventricular response
AFib RVR	atrial fibrillation with rapid ventricular response
AFID	Armed Forces Institute of Dentistry
AFIP	Armed Forces Institute of Pathology
AFIS	amniotic fluid infection syndrome
	Automated Fingerprint Identification System
AFIV	may have meant AFIB (atrial fibrillation)
AFIX	Assessment, Feedback, Incentives, and eXchange (A quality improvement program conducted by Centers for Disease Control and Prevention's immunization program awardees to support Vaccines for Children providers in their jurisdiction)
AFKO	ankle-foot-knee orthosis
AFL	air/fluid level
	atrial flutter
AFLD	alcohol fatty liver disease

AFLP	acute fatty liver of pregnancy	
	amplified fragment length polymorphism	
AFLs	ablative fractionated lasers	
AFLT	Aggie Figures Learning Test	
AfLT	antifungal (catheter) lock therapy	
AFlt	atrial flutter	
AFLTR	atrial flutter	
A Flu	atrial flutter	
a flutter	atrial flutter	
AFM	active fetal movement	
	acute flaccid myelitis	
	acute *Plasmodium falciparum* malaria	
	aerosol face mask	
	atomic force microscopy	
	doxorubicin (Adriamycin), fluorouracil, and methotrexate	
AFM × 2	double-aerosol face mask	
AFMYOYO	adios, my friend, you're on your own (polite form)(slang)	
AFND	Allele Frequencies Net Database	
AFO	airflow obstruction	
	ameloblastic fibro-odontoma	
	ankle-fixation orthotic	
	ankle-foot orthosis	
AFOD	alive and free of disease	
AFOF	anterior fontanel open and flat	
AFOI	awake fiberoptic intubation	
AFOM	additive freeform optics manufacturing	
	analytical figures of merit	
AFOP	acute fibrinous and organizing pneumonia	
AFOS	anterior fontanelle open and soft	
AFOSF	anterior fontanelle open, soft, and flat	
AFP	acute flaccid paralysis	
	alpha-fetoprotein	
	anterior faucial pillar	
	ascending frontal parietal	
AFQT	Armed Forces Qualification Test	
AFRD	acute febrile respiratory disease	
AFRIMS	Armed Forces Research Institute of Medical Sciences	
Afro	of <u>Afr</u>ican descent	
AFRRI	Armed Forces Radiological Research Institute	
AFRS	allergic fungal rhinosinusitis	
AF RVR	atrial fibrillation and rapid ventricular response	
AFRVR	atrial fibrillation with rapid ventricular response	
AFS	Accreditation with Follow-up Survey (The Joint Commission)	
	admit following surgery	
	allergic fungal sinusitis	

	amputation-free survival	
	Assessment Flow Sheet	
	atomic fluorescence spectometry	
AFSF	anterior fontanelle soft and flat	
AFSOF	anterior fontanelle soft, open, and flat	
	anterior, fontanelle, soft, open, flat (pediatrics)	
AFSS	Atrial Fibrillation Severity Scale (University of Toronto)	
AFT	arrived to find	
Aft/Dis	aftercare/discharge	
after	has been expressed as p., the letter P with a line above, and post; p. and the letter P with a line above may not be understood	
AFTL	anterior talofibular ligament	
AFTN	autonomously functioning thyroid nodule	
AFTs	autonomic function tests	
AFTT	adult failure to thrive	
	avulsion fracture of the tibial tubercle	
AFU	alpha-L-fucosidase	
AFV	amniotic fluid volume	
AFVSS	afebrile, vital signs stable	
AF with RVR	atrial fibrillation with rapid ventricular response	
AFX	air-fluid exchange	
	atypical fibroxanthoma	
AG	abdominal girth	
	adrenogenital	
	aminoglycoside	
	Amsler grid	
	anaplastic glioma	
	anion gap	
	antigen	
	antigravity	
	atrial gallop	
A/G	albumin to globulin ratio	
Ag	silver	
AGA	accelerated growth area	
	acute gonococcal arthritis	
	androgenetic alopecia	
	appropriate for gestational age	
	average gestational age	
AG acidosis	anion gap acidosis	
AGACNP	Adult-Gerontology Acute Care Nurse Practitioner	
Agama	the genus name of a group of small, long-tailed, insectivorous Old World lizards	
AGap	anion gap	
AGAS	accelerated graft atherosclerosis	
AGB	aboveground biomass	
AG/BL	aminoglycoside/beta-lactam	
AGBM	adolescent gay and bisexual males	
aGBM	adult glioblastoma	

AGBM-Ab	antiglomerular basement membrane antibody	AGPT1	angiopoietin-1 (gene/protein)
AGC	absolute granulocyte count	AGPT2	angiopoietin-2 (gene/protein)
	advanced gastric cancer	AGR	assessory gene regulator
	atypical glandular cells	AGR2	see gene website; www.ncbi .nlm.nih.gov/gene
	automatic gain control (radiology)	A/G ratio	albumin to globulin ratio
AgCC	agenesis of the corpus callosum	AgRP	agouti-related protein
AGCUS	atypical glandular cells of undetermined significance	AGRT	absence of gross residual tumor
AGD	agar gel diffusion	AGS	adrenogenital syndrome
A1GDM	gestational diabetes mellitus treated with diet modification		Aicardi-Goutières syndrome Alagille syndrome American Geriatric Society (guidelines)
A2GDM	gestational diabetes mellitus treated with insulin	AGS NOS	atypical glandular cells, not otherwise specified
AGE	acute gastroenteritis advanced glycation end product(s)	AGSV	angiographic stroke volume
	angle of greatest extension	AG SYND	adrenogenital syndrome
	anterior gastroenterostomy arterial gas embolism	AGT	alanine-glyoxylate aminotransferase angiotensinogen
AGECAT	automatic geriatric examination for computer-assisted taxonomy	AGTT	abnormal glucose tolerance test
		AGU	aspartylglycosaminuria
AGEP	acute generalized exanthematous pustulosis	AGUS	atypical glandular cells of uncertain significance
		AGV	Ahmed glaucoma valve
AGF	angle of greatest flexion	AGVHD	acute graft-versus-host disease
aGFR	abbreviated Modification of Diet in Renal Disease glomerular filtration rate	AGVI	Ahmed glaucoma valve implantation
		AGW	angled-tipped guidewire anogenital wart(s)
AGG	agammaglobulinemia	AGYW	adolescent girls and young women
aggl	agglutination	AgZ	silver-coated zeolite
aggl.	alpha-glucosidase inhibitor	AH	abdominal hysterectomy
aggreg	aggregation		abductor hallucis
AgHBs	hepatitis Bs antigen		Acculturated Hispanic
AGHD	adult growth hormone deficiency		airplane headache
AGIB	acute gastrointestinal bleeding		alcoholic hepatitis
agit	agitation		amenorrhea and hirsutism
AGL	acute granulocytic leukemia		amenorrhea-hyperprolactinemia
A GLACTO-LK	alpha galactoside leukocytes		antihyaluronidase
AGLT	acidified glycerol lysis test		aqueous humor
AglT	adventurous gliding motility protein; see gene website www.ncbi.nlm.nih.gov/gene		auditory hallucinations
		A&H	accident and health (insurance)
		A/H	apnea and hypopneas
AGMA	anion-gap metabolic acidosis	AHA	acetohydroxamic acid (Lithostat®)
Ag-MA	mesoporous silver-melamine		
aGMR	adjusted geometric mean ratio		acquired hemolytic anemia
AGMR	anterior glide medial rotation		American Heart Association (guidelines)
AGN	acute glomerulonephritis		
AGNA	antiglial nuclear antibody		American Hospital Association
AGNB	aerobic gram-negative bacilli		autoimmune hemolytic anemia
AgNO₃	silver nitrate	AHAC	adult human articular chondrocytes
AgNORs	argyrophilic nucleolar organizer regions (staining)		atypical hyperadrenocorticism (veterinary)
AgNP	silver nanoparticles		
AgNWs	silver nanowires	AHAs	alpha hydroxy acids
AgON	silver hyponitrite	AHase	antihyaluronidase
AGP	ambulatory glucose profile	AHBc	hepatitis B core antibody
AGPT	agar-gel precipitation test		

AHC	acute hemorrhagic conjunctivitis	AHFSO	Air Force Historical Studies Office
	acute hemorrhagic cystitis		
	Adolescent Health Center	AHFTC	Advanced Heart Failure
	alternating hemiplegia of		Transplant Cardiology
	childhood		(fellowship program)
	Ambulatory Health Care	AHG	antihemophilic globulin
	avoidable hospitalization	AHHD	arteriosclerotic hypertensive
	conditions		heart disease
AHCA	Agency for Healthcare	AHI	apnea-hypopnea index
	Administration	AHIA	may have meant AIHA
	American Healthcare Association		(autoimmune hemolytic
AHCD	acquired (non-Wilsonian)		anemia)
	hepatocerebral degeneration	AHIMA	American Health Information
AHCPR	Agency for Health Care Policy		Management Association
	and Research	AHIP	Academy of Health Information
AHCs	academic health centers		Professionals
AHD	acellular human dermis		America's Health Insurance
	acromiohumeral distance		Plans (a national political ad-
	acute hemodialysis		vocacy and trade association)
	advance health directives	AHIQA	American Health Information
	Agis Health Database		Quality Assurance (provides
	alien-hand syndrome		software to improve quality
	antecedent hematological		of patient registration data
	disorder		[ahisoftware.com])
	arteriosclerotic heart disease	AHJ	artificial hip joint
	autoimmune hemolytic disease	AHL	apparent half-life
AHDF	adult human dermal fibroblasts	AHM	ambulatory Holter monitoring
AHDH	may have meant ADHD	AHMO	anterior horizontal mandibular
	(attention deficit hyperactivity		osteotomy
	disorder)	AHN	adenomatous hyperplastic nodule
AHDI	Association for Healthcare		Assistant Head Nurse
	Documentation Integrity	AHO	a history of
AHE	acute hemorrhagic		Albright Hereditary
	encephalomyelitis		Osteodystrophy
	amygdalo-hippocampectomy		Aquaphor healing ointment
AHEC	Area Health Education Center	AHP	acute hemoperfusion
A-HEFT	African-American Heart Failure		acute hemorrhagic pancreatitis
	Trial		acute hepatic panel (see
AHEI	Alternative Healthy Eating Index		Laboratory Panels, Chapter 6)
AHER	active hip external rotation		American Herbal Pharmacopeia
AHF	antihemophilic factor		and Therapeutic Compendium
	Argentine hemorrhagic fever	AHPB	adjusted historic payment base
	(Junin virus) vaccine	AhpF	alkyl hydroperoxide reductase,
AHFM	antihemophilic factor (human),		Fisomer
	method M, (monoclonal	AHQ	Asthma Health Questionnaire
	purified)	AHR	acute humoral rejection
AHFR	aqueous humor flow rate		adjusted hazard ratios
AHFREF	acute heart failure with reduced		airway hyperresponsiveness
	ejection fraction	AHRE	atrial high-rate event
AHFS	acute heart failure syndrome(s)	AHRF	acute hypercapnic respiratory
	American Hospital Formulary		failure
	Service (a drug information		acute hypoxemic respiratory
	text book)		failure
AHFSC-GEIS	Armed Forces Health	AHRI	Armauer Hansen Research
	Surveillance Center, Division		Institute (Addis Ababa,
	of Global Emerging Infec-		Ethiopia)
	tions Surveillance and Re-	AhRI	aryl hydrocarbon receptor
	sponse System Operations		antagonist

AHRP	Alliance for Human Research Protection
AHRQ	Agency for Healthcare Research and Quality
AHS	active holistic surveillance
	adaptive hand skills
	allopurinol hypersensitivity syndrome
	Alpers-Huttenlocher syndrome
	American Headache Society
	anticonvulsant hypersensitivity syndrome
AHSA	Assistant Health Services Administrator
AHSD	may have meant ASHD (arteriosclerotic heart disease)
AHSG	alpha$_2$-Heremans Schmid glycoprotein
AHSP	alpha hemoglobin stabilizing protein
AHST	autologous hematopoietic stem cell transplantation
AHT	alternating hypertropia
	antihyaluronidase titer
	autoantibodies to human thyroglobulin
AHTG	antihuman thymocyte globulin
aHTN	antihypertensive
AHTN	Tonalide® (7-acetyl-1,1,3,4,4,6-hexamethyltetrahydronaph-thalene)
AHTR	acute hemolytic transfusion reaction
aHUS	atypical hemolytic uremic syndrome
AHV-1	anatid herpesvirus 1
AH/VH	auditory and visual hallucinations
AHVH	auditory hallucinations, visual hallucinations
AHX	aminohexanoic acid
AHZ	Apotheek Haagse Ziekenhuizen, Hague, Netherlands (Hospital Pharmacy at the Hague)
AI	accidentally incurred
	accomodative insufficiency
	allelic imbalance
	allergy index
	American Indian
	aortic insufficiency
	apical impulse
	apnea index
	aromatase inhibitor
	artificial insemination
	artificial intelligence
A/I	allergy and immunology
	allergy/immunology

A & I	Allergy and Immunology (department)
	auscultation and inspection
AIA	Accommodation Independence Assessment
	allergen-induced asthma
	allyl isopropyl acetamide
	anti-insulin antibody
	aspirin-induced asthma
AIAA	aromatase inhibitor-associated arthralgia
AI-Ab	anti-insulin antibody
AIAN	American Indian and Alaska Native
AI/AN	American Indian/Alaska Native
AIAP	azathioprine-induced acute pancreatitis
aIAT	autobiographical Implicit Association Test
AI-B	testis-specific ATPase inhibitor-like protein (gene)
AIBD	autoimmune bulls diseases
AIBF	anterior interbody fusion
AIBG	antibiotic-impregnated bone graft
AIBP	adolipoprotein A-1 binding protine; see gene website; www.ncbi.nlm.nih.gov/gene
AIBW	adjusted ideal body weight
AIC	amount in controversy
AICA	anterior inferior cerebellar artery anterior inferior communicating artery
AICBG	anterior interbody cervical bone graft
AICD	activation-induced cell death alcohol-induced ciliary dysfunction automatic implantable cardioverter/defibrillator
aicd	may have meant acid
AICDs	automatic implantable cardioverter-defibrillators
aicds	may have meant acids
AICG	autologous iliac crest graft
AICH	acute intracerebral hemorrhage acute intracranial hypertension
AICI	acute incomplete cerebral ischemia
AICID	autoimmune/chronic inflammatory diseases
aicid	may have meant acid
AICM	anti-inflammatory controller medication
AICP	acute ischemic chest pain androgen-independent carcinoma of the prostate
AICS	acute ischemic coronary syndromes

AICU	adult intensive care unit
	aspirin-intolerant chronic urticaria
AICV	antibiotic-induced candidal vaginitis
AID	absolute iron deficiency
	aid-in-dying
	aortoiliac disease
	artificial insemination donor
	automated infusion device
	automatic implantable defibrillator
AIDC	automatic identification and data capture
AIDET	Acknowledge, Introduce, Duration, Explanation, and Thank You (a system to better communicate with patients)
AIDH	artificial insemination donor husband
AIDKS	acquired immune deficiency syndrome with Kaposi's sarcoma
AIDL	activities instrumental of daily life
AIDM	steroid-induced diabetes mellitus
AIDP	acute inflammatory demyelinating polyradiculo-neuropathy
AIDS	acquired immunodeficiency syndrome
AIDS-KS	acquired immunodeficiency syndrome-positive Kaposi's sarcoma
AIDT	may have meant AITD (autoimmune thyroid disease[s])
AIE	acute inclusion body encephalitis
	assume intervention effective
AIEC	adherent-invasive Escherichia coli
AIED	autoimmune inner-ear Disease
AIEOP	Italian Association of Pediatric Hematology and Oncology (cancer study group)
AIF	aortic-iliac-femoral
AIFA	Italian Medicines Agency (Agenzia Italiana del Farmaco)
AIFF	Audio Interchange File Formant
AIFP	acute idiopathic facial paralysis
	arthroscopically-implantable force probe
AIGA	acquired idiopathic generalized anhidrosis
AIgA	aggragated immunoglobulin A
AIGHL	anterior band of the inferior glenhumeral ligament

AIH	amelogenesis Imperfecta (hereditary enamel defect diseases)
	artificial insemination with husband's sperm
	asymptomatic incidentally hyperprolactinemia
	autoimmune hepatitis
AIHA	autoimmune hemolytic anemia
AIHD	acquired immune hemolytic disease
AIHI	autoimmune hemolytic anemia (Romance languages)
AII	angiotensin II
AIIA	Angiotensin II antagonist
AIIRs	airborne infection isolation rooms
AIIS	anterior inferior iliac spine
AILD	angioimmunoblastic lymphadenopathy with dysproteinemia
AILT	angioimmunoblastic T-cell lymphoma
AIM	Annals of Internal Medicine
	anti-inflammatory medication
AIMA	angular integral mostly analytical
	Australasian Integrative Medicine Association
	automated iterative moving averaging
AIMAH	ACTH (adrenocorticotropic hormone)- independent mac-ronodular adrenal hyperplasia
AIMS	Abnormal Involuntary Movement Scale
	Arthritis Impact Measurement Scales
AIMSS	aromatase inhibitor-induced musculoskeletal syndrome
AIN	acute interstitial nephritis
	American Institute of Nutrition
	anal intraepithelial neoplasia
	anterior interosseous nerve
AIN1	anal intraepithelial neoplasia grade 1
AIN2	anal intraepithelial neoplasia grade 2
AIN3	anal intraepithelial neoplasia grade 3
AIN/PIN/M/U/R	anterior interosseous nerve, posterior interosseous nerve, median nerve, ulnar nerve, radial nerve
AINS	anti-inflammatory nonsteroidal
AIO	all-in-one (lipid emulsion, protein, carbohydrate, and electrolytes combined total parenteral nutrition)

AIOD	aortoiliac occlusive disease
AION	anterior ischemic optic neuropathy
AIP	acute infectious polyneuritis
	acute intermittent porphyria
	acute interstitial pneumonia
	asymptomatic inflammatory prostatitis
	autoimmune pancreatitis
AIPC	androgen-independent prostate cancer
AIPD	alcohol-induced psychotic disorder
	autoimmune progesterone dermatitis
AIPH	acute idiopathic pulmonary hemorrhage
AIPPs	Amputee Independent Prosthesis Properties
AIQ	5-aminoisoquinolinone
	anterior-inferior quadrant
	Aspects of Identity Questionnaire
AIR	accelerated idioventricular rhythm
	acetylcholine-induced relaxation
	acute inpatient rehabilitation
	acute insulin response
	autoimmune retinopathy
AIRE	autoimmune regulator (gene)
AIR(g)	acute insulin response to glucose
AIRR	acute infusion-related reaction
AIRVO 2	a device that features a humidifier with integrated flow source that delivers high flows of air/oxygen
AIS	Abbreviated Injury Score
	acute ischemic stroke
	adenocarcinoma in situ
	adolescent idiopathic scoliosis
	anti-insulin serum
	ASIA (American Spinal Injury Association) Impairment Scale
AIs	aromatase inhibitors
AISA	acquired idiopathic sideroblastic anemia
AIS A	ASIA (American Spinal Injury Association) Impairment Scale -Complete–No preservation of any motor and/or sensory function below the zone of injury
AIS B	ASIA (American Spinal Injury Association) Impairment Scale –Incomplete; Preserved sensation
AIS C	ASIA (American Spinal Injury Association) Impairment Scale –Incomplete; Preserved motor (nonfunctional)

AISD	actual-ideal self-discrepancy
	antidepressant-induced sexual dysfunction
AIS D	ASIA (American Sapinal Injury Association) Impairment Scale –Incomplete; Preserved motor (functional)
AIS E	ASIA (American Spinal Injury Association) Impairment Scale –Complete Recovery
AIS/ISS	Abbreviated Injury Scale/Injury Severity Score
AISs	antibiotic-impregnated shunts
AIS TLKW	acute ischemic stroke, time last known well (the amount of time since the patient was last known to be well before a stroke)
AIT	acute intensive treatment
	adoptive immunotherapy
	Advanced Individual Training (Army)
	amiodarone-induced thyrotoxicosis
	auditory integration therapy
	autoimmune thyroiditis
AITD	autoimmune thyroid disease
AITFL	anterior inferior tibiofibular ligament
AITL	angioimmunoblastic T-cell lymphoma
AITN	acute interstitial tubular nephritis
AITP	autoimmune thrombocytopenia purpura
AIU	absolute iodine uptake
	adolescent inpatient unit
AIVC	absence of the inferior vena cava
AIVR	accelerated idioventricular rhythm
AIW	abdominal imaging window
	acute inferior wall
	alcohol intervention worker
	Alice in Wonderland (syndrome)
	Analytic Information Warehouse
AIWS	Alice in Wonderland Syndrome (a rare perceptual disorder characterized by an erroneous perception of the body or the surrounding space)
AJ	ankle jerk
AJA	ajulemic acid (a synthetic analogue of tetrahydrocannabinol)
AjBW	adjusted body weight
AJCC	American Joint Committee on Cancer
AjD	adjustment disorder
AjD-A	adjustment disorder with anxiety

AJFAT	Ankle Joint Functional Assessment Tool
AJN	American Journal of Nursing
AJO	apple juice only
AJOT	American Journal of Occupational Therapy
AJR	abnormal jugular reflex accelerated junctional rhythm
AK	above-knee (amputation) actinic keratosis Alaska artificial kidney
AK1	adenylate kinase 1; see gene website, www.ncbi.nlm.nih .gov/gene
AKA	above-knee amputation alcoholic ketoacidosis all known allergies
a.k.a.	also known as
AKAs	above-knee amputations
AKC	atopic keratoconjunctivitis
AKD	atypical Kawasaki disease
AKDHC	Arizona Kidney Disease & Hypertension Centers
AKE	active knee extension
AKF	altered kidney function The Danish Institute of Governmental Research
AKG	alpha-ketoglutaric acid
AKI	acute kidney injury
AKI-D	acute kidney injury requiring dialysis
AKIN	Acute Kidney Injury Network (staging system)
Akin	procedure consists of a closing lateral wedge osteotomy of proximal phalanx combined with excision of medial eminence
AKI-on-CKD	acute kidney injury on chronic kidney disease
AKL	anterior knee laxity
AKN	acne keloidalis nuchae
AKP	anterior knee pain
AKPS	Anterior Knee Pain Scale Australian-modified Karnofsky Performance Status
AKR	aldo-keto reductase
Akr	see gene website, www.ncbi.nlm .nih.gov/gene
AKS	alcoholic Korsakoff syndrome arthroscopic knee surgery
AKT	a serine/threonine-specific protein kinase [also known as protein kinase b (PKB)]
Akt	see gene website www.ncbi.nlm .nih.gov/gene
AKU	artificial kidney unit

Al	aluminum
AL	acute leukemia Alabama anterior lip argon laser artemether-lumefantrine (antimalaria drug combination; [Riamet; Coartem]) arterial line assisted living attachment level (dental) axial length left ear
AL1	amino lipid 1 (phosphatidylglycerol)
AL2	amino lipids 2 (phosphatidylethanolamine) Amplatz Left 2-curve size (thrombectomy device)
Ala	alanine
ALA	adrenalin (epinephrine), lidocaine, and amethocaine (tetracaine) alpha-linolenic acid alpha-lipoic acid amebic liver abcess aminolevulinic acid aminolevulinic acid HCl oral (Gleolan) aminolevulinic acid (Levulan) antileukotriene agent antilymphocyte antibody as long as
ALAC	antibiotic-loaded acrylic cement
ALAD	abnormal left axis deviation
ALA-GLN	alanyl-glutamine
ALALS	acute lateral ankle ligamentous sprain
AL amyloidosis	immunoglobulin Amyloid Light-chain amyloidosis (a rare disease characterized by mis-folded amyloid protein deposits in tissues and vital organs)
ALAN	artificial light at night
ALA-PDT	aminolevulinic acid photodynamic therapy
ALARA	as low as reasonably achievable
ALAS1	5'-aminolevulinate (delta-aminolevulinate) synthase 1 (gene/protein)
ALAS2	5'-aminolevulinate synthase 2 ((gene/protein)
ALAT	alanine aminotransferase (also ALT; SGPT)
ALAX	apical long axis
ALB	albumin albuterol anterior lenticular bevel

ALBUMS — aldehyde linker-based ultrasensitive mismatch scanning
ALC — absolute lymphocte count
acetyl-L-carnitine
acute lethal catatonia
alcohol
alcoholic liver cirrhosis
allogeneic lymphocyte cytotoxicity
alternate level of care
Alternate Lifestyle Checklist
axiolinguocervical
ALCA — anomalous left coronary artery
ALCAPA — anomalous origin of the left coronary artery from the pulmonary artery
ALCAR — acetyl L-carnitine
ALCAT1 — acyl-CoA lysocardiolipin acyltransferase 1
ALCAT — antigen leukocyte cellular antibody test
ALCD — acute left-sided colonic diverticulitis
alcD — see gene website www.ncbi.nlm.nih.gov/gene
a-LCFA — ascending branch of the lateral circumflex femoral artery
alchol — alcholol
ALCL — anaplastic large-cell lymphoma
alco — alcohol
ALC R — alcohol rub
ALCs — absolute lymphocyte counts
adult Leydig cells
assisted living communities
ALCS — anterior lamina cribrosa surface
ALD — adrenoleukodystrophy
alcoholic liver disease
aldolase
Alzheimer-like dementia
ALDF — anterior lumbar diskectomy and fusion
ALDH — aldehyde dehydrogenase
ALDO — aldosterone
ALDOST — aldosterone
ALDs — alcoholic liver diseases
Alzheimer-like dementias
AMC (Academic Medical Center) Linear Disability Scale
assistive listening devices
aldS — alpha-acetolactate synthase; see gene website, www.ncbi.nlm.nih.gov/gene
ALDT — anterolateral drawer test
ALE — activation-likelihood estimation
acute liver failure
arterial line filter
assisted living facility

ALFA — Assessment of Language-Related Functional Activities
ALFF — amplitude of low-frequency fluctuations
ALFT — abnormal liver function tests
ALG — antilymphoblast globulin
antilymphocyte globulin
ALGB — adjustable laparoscopic gastric banding
algia — a word and suffix meaning pain or painful
Algo® — newborn hearing screening device
ALH — atypical lobular hyperplasia
ALHA — accessory (aberrant) left hepatic artery
ALHE — angiolymphoid hyperplasia with eosinophilia
ALI — Abbott Laboratories, Inc.
acute limb ischemia
acute lung injury
argon laser iridotomy
ALIF — anterior lumbar interbody fusion
A-line — arterial catheter
arterial line
aterial line
horizontal artifact from a bedside lung ultrasound indicating a normal lung surface (no interstitial edema)
ALJ — administrative law judge
ALK1 — activin receptor-like kinase 1
ALK — alkaline
anaplastic lymphoma receptor tyrosine kinase; see gene website www.ncbi.nlm.nih.gov/gene
anterior lamellar keratoplasty
automated lamellar keratoplasy
ALK+ — anaplastic lymphoma kinase-positive
alka phos — alkaline phosphatase (usually expressed as ALK PHOS)
alkM — alkane 1-monooxygenase; see gene website www.ncbi.nlm.nih.gov/gene
ALK ISO — alkaline phosphatase isoenzymes
ALK+ NSCLC — anaplastic lymphoma kinase-positive metastatic nonsmall cell lung cancer
ALK-P — alkaline phosphatase
ALK PHOS — alkaline phosphatase
ALKPHOS ISO — alkaline phosphatase isoenzyme
ALL — acute lymphoblastic leukemia
acute lymphocytic leukemia
allergy
anterolateral ligament

ALLD	arthroscopic lumbar laser diskectomy
ALLHAT	Antihypertensive and Lipid-lowering Treatment to Prevent Heart Attach Trial
ALLI	acute lower limb ischemia
ALLO	allogeneic
Allo-BMT	allogenic bone marrow transplantation
AlloDerm	acellular dermal matrix processed from human allograft skin (Life-Cell, Branchburg, N.J)
Allo-HCT	allogeneic hematropoietic cell transplant
allo-HSCT	allogeneic hematopoietic stem cell transplantation
alloSCT	allogeneic stem cell transplantation
ALLs	acute lymphoblastic leukemias
ALM	acral lentiginous melanoma alveolar lining material autoclave-killed *Leishmania major*
ALMI	anterolateral myocardial infarction
ALN	anterior lower neck anterior lymph node axillary lymph nodes
ALND	axillary lymph node dissection
ALNM	axillary lymph node metastasis
ALO	apraxia of eyelid opening axiolinguo-occlusal
ALOC	altered level of consciousness
ALOD	adjacent-level ossification development
Al(OH)₃	aluminum hydroxide
ALOS	average length of stay
ALP	alkaline phosphatase Alupent argon laser photocoagulation arterial line pressure
ALPACA	Advanced perihilar CholangiocarcinomA (study) Altered Partitions Across Community Architectures (a method for comparing two genome-scale networks derived from different phenotypic states to identify condition-specific modules)
ALPE	acute renal failure with severe loin pain induced by anaerobic exercise
Alpha	Phonetic Alphabet for A; pronounced AL-FAH
alpha1 AGP	alpha-1-acid glycoprotein
alpha-1 glob	alpha-1 globulin
alpha-PVP	alpha-pyrrolidinopentiophenone (flakka)
alpha-syn	alpha-synuclein
ALPPS	associating liver partition and portal vein ligation for staged hepatectomy (two-staged hepatectomy procedure)
ALPS	autoimmune lymphoproliferative syndrome
ALPSA	anterior labroligamentous periosteal sleeve avulsion
ALPZ	alprazolam (Xanax)
ALR	adductor leg raise administrative license revocation anatomical liver resection
ALRI	acute lower-respiratory-tract infection anterolateral rotary instability
ALS	acid-labile subunit acute lateral sclerosis advanced life skills advanced life support amyotrophic lateral sclerosis antilymphocyte serum
ALSFRS-R	Amyotrophic Lateral Sclerosis Functional Rating Scale, Revised
ALSG	Australian Leukemia Study Group
Alsius	The Alsius CoolGard 3000® thermal regulation catheter system
ALSOB	alcohol-like substance on breath
ALSPAC	Avon Longitudinal Study of Parents and Children
ALT	alanine aminotransferase (same as alanine transferase) alteration alterative alternate anterolateral thigh antibiodic lock technique (catheter infection prevention) antimicrobial lock therapy argon laser trabeculoplasty autolymphocyte therapy
2 *alt*	every other day (this is a dangerous abbreviation)
ALT/AST	alanine aminotransferase: aspartate aminotransferase ratio
ALTB	acute laryngotracheobronchitis
alt dieb	every other day (this is a dangerous Latin abbreviation which will not be understood)

ALTE	acute (aberrant, apparent) life threatening event
ALTEs	apparent life-threatening events
ALTF	anterolateral thigh flap
ALT FF	anterolateral thigh free flap
ALT flap	anterolateral thigh flap
al thor	every other hour (this is a dangerous abbreviation)
AltI	Altiarchaeales
ALTP	argon laser trabeculoplasty
ALTR	adverse local tissue reaction
ALUP	Alupent
ALv	attachment level (dental)
ALVAD	abdominal left ventricular assist device
ALVAL	aseptic lymphocytic vasculitis-associated lesion(s)
ALWMI	anterolateral wall myocardial infarct
ALX	Ablynx (a Belgian biopharmaceutical company's [Ablynx.com] nomenclature for their investigation drugs, such as, ALX-0171)
	alloxan (a toxic glucose analogue, which selectively destroys insulin-producing cells in the pancreas when administered to rodents and other animals)
ALZ	Alzheimer disease
ALZH	Alzheimer disease
AM2	adrenomedullin 2 (gene)
AM	adult male
	aerosol mask
	amalgam
	anovulatory menstruation
	anterior midpapillary
	morning or before noon (a.m.)
	myopic astigmatism
Am	americium
a.m.	*ante meridiem* - morning (a.m.)
	morning or before noon
AMA	advanced maternal age
	against medical advise. This implies the patient was seen and his/her discharge is being addressed by a care provider and the patient signs a form that he/she is leaving against medical advice. Check to see if this conforms to your facility's definition. (see LWBS and LWBT)
	American Medical Association
	antimitochondrial antibody
A.M.A.	see AMA

AMAA	Alternate Medicine Awareness Association
AMAC	adults molested as children
AMACR	alpha-methylacyl-CoA racemase (a positive markers of malignancy)
AMAD	activity median aerodynamic diameter
	morning admission
AM/ADM	morning admission
AMAG	adrenal medullary autograft
AMAL	amalgam
AMAN	acute motor axonal neuropathy
AMAP	American Medical Accreditation Program
	as much as possible
Amask	aerosol mask
A-MAT	amorphous material
AMAT	anti-malignant antibody test
	Arm Motor Ability Test
AMAT S/E	Arm Motor Ability Test for shoulder/elbow
AMAT W/H	Arm Motor Ability Test for wrist/hand
Am B	amphotericin B
AMB	ambulate
	ambulatory
	amphotericin B (Fungizone)
	as manifested by
AMBDs	autoimmune mucocutaneous blistering diseases
AMBER	advanced multiple beam equalization radiography
AMBI	acute multiple brain infarcts
AMBR	ambrisentan (Letairis)
AMBS	ambulates
AMBU	artificial-respiration device consisting of a bag that is squeezed by hand
ambul	ambulalation
	ambulate
	ambulatory
AM Care	brushing teeth, washing face and hands
AMC	anesthesia monitored care
	arm muscle circumference
	arthrogryposis multiplex congenita
AMCC	automated multi-channel chemistry (laboratory tests)
AMCD	Aerospace Medical Certification Division (of the Federal Aviation Administration)
aMCI	amnestic mild cognitive impairment
AM cortisol	8:00 a.m. blood level of the hormone cortisol

AM/CR	amylase to creatinine ratio
AMCs	academic medical centers
AMD	age-related macular degeneration
	arm motion detection
	arthroscopic microdiskectomy
	axiomesiodistal
	dactinomycin (actinomycin D; Cosmegen)
	methyldopa (alpha methyldopa)
AMDA	The Society for Post-Acute and Long-Term Care Medicine (formerly known as The American Medical Directors Association)
amd DR	admitting doctor
AMDP	anti-dorsalizing morphogenic protein (gene)
AMDR	acceptable macronutrient distribution range
AME	acute metabolic encephalopathy
	adenomyoepithelioma
	agreed medical examination
	alternariol monomethylether
	anthrax meningoencephalitis
	apparent mineralocorticoid excess (syndrome)
	Aviation Medical Examiner
AmED	alcohol mixed with energy drinks
AMED	Allied and Complementary Medicine Database
aMED	alternate Mediterranean diet
AMegL	acute megokaryoblastic leukemia
AMESLAN	American sign language
Amet	see gene website; www.ncbi .nlm.nih.gov
AMF	aerobic metabolism facilitator
	amifostine (Ethyol)
	amonafide
	any medical floor (as in transfer to any medical floor)
	autocrine motility factor
AMFC	adaptive multifocal fundus camera
AMFS	acral myxoinflammatory fibroblastic sarcoma
AMFs	alternating magnetic fields
	alternating magnetic frequencies
AMG	acoustic myography
	aminoglycoside
	axiomesiogingival
	Federal Republic of German's equivalent to United States Food, Drug, and Cosmetic Act
AMGA	American Medical Group Association

AMH	antimüllerian hormone
AMHS	morning and bedtime
AMI	acute mesenteric ischemia
	acute myocardial infarction
	amifostine (Ethyol)
	amitriptyline
	axiomesioincisal
AMIA	American Medical Informatics Association
AMIO	amiodarone (Cardarone)
AMIOD	amiodarone (Cordarone)
AMIS	anterior minimally invasive surgery (hip arthroplasty)
AMJ	Aronia melanocarpa juice
	Australasian Medical Journal
AMK	amikacin sulfate injection
AMKL	acute megakaryocytic leukemia
AML	acute myelogenous leukemia
	angiomyolipoma
	anterior mitral leaflet
AML-CR	acute myeloid leukemia in complete remission
AM-LM	artemether-lumefantrine (Coartem)
AML-MRC	acute myeloid leukemia with myelodysplasia-related changes
amlodipine	may have meant amlodipine (Norvasc)
amlopidine	may have meant amlodipine
AMLOS	arithmetic mean length of stay
AMLR	auditory midlatency response
	Marketing Authorization Application (French)
AMLs	acute myeloid leukemias
	angiomyolipomas
AMM	agnogenic myeloid metaplasia
AMML	acute myelomonocytic leukemia
AMMOL	acute myelomonoblastic leukemia
AMN	acute macular neuroretinopathy
	adrenomyeloneuropathy
AMNH	American Museum of Natural History (specimens)
amnio	amniocentesis
AmniSure ROM Plus®	a test kit that detects both alpha-fetoprotein and Insulin-like growth factor-binding protein 1 using a monoclonal/polyclonal antibody approach to diagnose premature rupture of membranes
AMN SC	amniotic fluid scan
amoA	ammonia monooxygenase subunit A; see gene website www.ncbi.nlm.nih.gov/gene

AMOL	acute monoblastic leukemia
AMON	acute monosymptomatic optic neuritis
	alert portable telemedical monitor
AMOVA	analysis of molecular variance
AMOX	amoxicillin
amoxicillan	may have meant amoxicillin
AMP	Accreditation Manager Plus (The Joint Commission software)
	adenosine monophosphate
	ampere
	amphetamine
	ampicillin
	ampul
	amputation
	antipressure mattress
AMPA	alpha-amino-3-hydroxy-5-methyl-4-isoxazoleproprionic acid (subtype of glutamate receptors)
AM-PAC	Activity Measure of Post-Acute Care (self-reported function of basic mobility, daily activities, and applied cognition)
ampC	beta-lactamase/D-alanine carboxypeptidase; see gene website www.ncbi.nlm.nih .gov/gene
AMPD	adenosine monophosphate deaminase
	Alternative Model for Personality Disorders
AMPH	amphetamines
ampho	amphotropic
ampho B	amphotericin-B
AMPK	AMP (adenosine monophosphate)-activated protein kinase (gene/protein)
AMPLPE	Allergies, Medications, Past medical history, Last meal, Events leading to admission (used for history and physical examination)
AMPPE	acute multifocal placoid pigment epitheliopathy
A-M pr	Austin-Moore prosthesis
AMPS	Assessment of Motor and Process Skills
AMPT	metyrosine (alphamethylpara tyrosine)
AMQ	amodiaquine (Flavoquine [France])
	artesunate-mefloquine (Coarsucam [France])
	Asthma Management Questionnaire

AMR	acoustic muscle reflex
	alternating motion rates
	amrubicin
	antibody mediated rejection
	antimicrobial resistance
AMRD	amplitude modulation rate discrimination (audiology)
	may have meant ARMD (age-related macular degeneration)
AMRI	anterior medial rotary instability
AMRs	antibody-mediated rejections
AMS	accelerator mass spectometry
	acute mountain sickness
	adult male sling (for male urinary incontinence)
	aggravated in military service
	altered mental status
	amylase
	antimicrobial stewardship
	aseptic meningitis syndrome
	atypical mole syndrome
	auditory memory span
AMSAN	acute motor sensory axonal neuropathy
AMSE	acute medical status emergency
	Autism Mental Status Exam
	average mean square error
Amsel criteria	clinical diagnosis of bacterial vaginosis if 3 of the 4 criteria are positive: homogeneous discharge, pH 4.8 or higher, presence of clue cells, and amine odor with the application of potassium hydroxide to the discharge.
amsF	see gene website; www.ncbi .nlm.nih.gov
AMSIT	Appearance, Mood, Sensorium, Intelligence, and Thought process (a portion of the mental status examination)
AMSN	Academy of Medical-Surgical Nurses
AMT-10	10-point Abbreviated Mental Test
AMT-4	4-point Abbreviated Mental Test
AMT	abbreviated mental test
	Adolph's Meat Tenderizer
	air medical transport
	allogeneic (bone) marrow transplant
	alpha-methyltryptamine
	aminopterin
	amniotic membrane transplantation
	amount
	anterior mediastinal tracheostomy
	anteromedial thigh
	Autobiographical Memory Test

AM&T   adenoidectomy with myringotomy and tympanostomy tube insertion

AMTL   antemortem tooth loss
anterior medial temporal lobe
anterior medial temporal lobectomy

AMTS   Abbreviated Mental Test Score

AMTSL   active management of the third stage of labor

AMU   accessory-muscle use
acquired megalourethra
atomic mass units (radiology)

AM-ULA   Activities Measure of Upper Limb Amputees

AMV   alveolar minute ventilation
assisted mechanical ventilation

AMVL   anterior mitral valve leaflet length

AMW   apparent molecular weight
average molecular weight

AMWs   auxiliary midwives

AMX   amoxicillin
see gene website; www.ncbi.nlm.nih.gov/gene

AMX/CLV   amoxicillin/clavulanate potassium (Augmentin)

AMY   amylase

AMY/CR   amylase/creatinine ratio

AMZ   Amitraz (an insecticide)
amoxicillin
anteromedialization

AN   acoustic neuromas
Alaska Native
amyl nitrate
anorexia nervosa
anticipatory nausea
antigen
Associate Nurse
avascular necrosis

ANA   American Nurses Association
anastrozole (Arimidex)
antinuclear antibody

ana2   anastral spindle 2 (gene)

−ANA   negative antinuclear antibody

+ANA   positive antinuclear antibody

ANA SWAB   anaerobic swab

ANAC   Association of Nurses in AIDS (acquired immunodeficiency syndrome) Care

ANAD   anorexia nervosa and associated disorders

ANADA   Abbreviated New Animal Drug Application

ANAG   acute narrow angle glaucoma

ANA positive   antinuclear antibody positive

ANAs   antinuclear antibodies

anasarca   a word meaning generalized massive edema

ANB angle   a measurement of the anterior-posterior relationship of the maxilla with the mandible (dentistry; oral maxillofacial surgery)

AnBI   anoxic brain injury

AnBX   Aspergillus niger ASKU28

ANC   absolute neutrophil count
antenatal care
antenatal course

ANCA   antineutrophil cytoplasmic antibody

ANCAs   antineutrophil cytoplasmic antibodies

ANCA vasculitis   anti-neutrophilic cytoplasmic antibody (ANCA) associated vasculitis

ANCC   American Nurses Credentialing Center

anch   anchored

ANCN   absolute neutrophil count nadir

ANCOVA   analysis of covariance

ANCs   absolute neutrophil counts
antenatal clinics

AND   Academy of Nutrition and Dietetics
allow nature death (this is a dangerous abbreviation as it may be overlooked)
anterior nasal discharge
Associate's Degree in Nursing
axillary node dissection

ANDA   Abbreviated New Drug Application

ANDV   Andes virus

ANED   alive, no evidence of disease

anes   anesthesia

anesth   anesthesiologist
anesthetia
anesthetic

ANF   antinuclear factor
atrial natriuretic factor

ANFH   avascular necrosis of the femoral head

ANFLD   may have meant NAFLD (nonalcoholic fatty liver disease)

ANG   angiogram
angiotensin

Ang-2   angiopoietin-2

AnGap   anion gap

ANG II   angiotensin II

ANGIO   angiogram

Angios   angiocardiograms

ANGPTL3   angiopoietin like 3 (gene/protein)
angiopoietin like 3 (gene)
angiopoietin-like protein 3

ANGPTL4	angiopoietin-like protein 4	ANPR	advanced notice of proposed rule making
ANH	acute normovolemic hemodilution		Advanced Notice of Proposed Rulemaking
	artificial nutrition and hydration		
	assisted nutrition and hydration	ANR	anorexia nervosa-restricting
anhedonia	a word meaning loss of pleasure in response to rewarding stimuli (normally pleasurable acts)	ANS	answer
			anterior nasal spine (cephalometric landmark)
			approximate number sense
aNHL	aggressive non-Hodgkin lymphoma		autonomic nervous system
		AnsA	L-asparaginase
ANI	asymptomatic neurocognitive impairment	ANSA-RLN	ansa cervicalis to recurrent laryngeal nerve
anicteric	a word meaning not accompanied or characterized by jaundice	ANSD	auditory neuropathy spectrum disorder
		ANSER	Aggregate Neurobehavioral Student Health and Education Review
ANIN	absolute number of involved nodes		
anin	may have been a typing error intended to be "an in" as in "an in vivo study" or "an in-depth analysis."	ANSI	American National Standards Institute
		ANST	after negative skin test
			androstenedione
ANISO	anisocytosis	ant	anterior
ANK	ankle	ANT	anterior
	appointment not kept		anthrax vaccine, not otherwise specified
ANKA	an isolate of Plasmodium berghei		enpheptin (2-amino-5-nitrothiazol)
ankyl	ankylosis; ankylosing	ANTₐ	anthrax vaccine, absorbed
	Prefix for bent; crooked; in the form of a loop; adhesion; stiffness	ANT AX	anterior axillary (line, fold, incision, pillar, etc.)
		ANTBx	antibiotic
ANL	acceptable noise level	*ante*	before
ANLL	acute nonlymphoblastic leukemia	ANTI A:AGT	anti–blood group A antiglobulin test
ANM	Assistant Nurse Manager	Anti bx	antibiotic
ANMAT	Administratión Nacional de Medicamentos, Alimentos y Tecnologia Médica (Argentina)	anti-CCP	anti-cyclic citrullinated peptide
		anti-coag	anticoagulant
		anticoag	anticoagulation
		anticoags	anticoagulants
	Argentina Regulatory Agency	anti-D	anti-D immune globulin
ANMDARE	anti-N-methyl-D-aspartate receptor encephalitis	anti-GAD	antibodies to glutamic acid decarboxylase
ANN	artificial neural network(s)	anti-GBM	anti-glomerular basement membrane
	axillary node-negative		
ANNA	artificial neural network analysis	anti-Hbe	antibody to hepatitis B e antigen (HBeAg)
ANO5	anoctamin 5 (gene; recessive mutations implicated in causing muscular dystrophy and gnathodiaphyseal dysplasia)	anti-HBc	antibody to hepatitis B core antigen (HBcAg)
		anti-HBs	antibody to hepatitis B surface antigen (HBsAg)
ANOC	Annual Notice of Changes (Medicare Part D)	anti-HCV	antibodies to hepatitis C virus
			hepatitis C virus antibodies
ANOVA	analysis of variance	antiHTN	anti-hypertensive (drugs)
ANOX3	alert and oriented to person, place, and time	anti-La	one of the hallmark autoantibodies in primary Sjögren syndrome
ANP	Adult Nurse Practitioner		
	atrial natriuretic peptide	anti-NMDAR	anti-N-methyl-d-aspartate receptor
	(anaritide acetate)		
	axillary node–positive		

anti-PF4	anti-plalelett factor 4	A-O	atlanto-occipital (joint)
antiPLT	antiplatelet	A/O	alert and oriented
anti-PM/Scl ab	anti-polymyositis/scleroderma antibodies	A&O	alert and oriented
anti-RNP	antibodies to ribonucleoprotein	A&O ×1	alert, awake, and oriented to person
anti-Ro(52/60)	one of the hallmark autoantibodies in primary Sjögren syndrome	A&O ×2	alert and oriented to person and place
anti-Scl70	anti-topoisomerase I	A & O ×3	see A&O
Anti-Sm	antigens for the Sm proteins (first found in a systemic lupus erythematosus patient, Stephanie Smith)	A&O×1	awake and oriented to person
		A&O×1	alert, awake, and oriented to person
anti-Sm	anti-*Schistosoma mansoni* (antibody)	A&O×2	awake and oriented to person and place
anti-SSA	anti-Sjögren syndrome-related antigen A	A&O×3	alert and oriented to person, place, and time
anti-Tg	antithyroglobulin (antibodies)	A&O×4	awake and oriented to person, place, time, and date
anti-TNF	anti- tumor necrosis factor	AO2	atelosteogenesis type 2
anti-TPO	anti-thyroid peroxidase (antibodies)	AOA	American Osteopathic Association
anti-Xa	antifactor activated clotting factor X (a measure of low-molecular weight heparins' and other anticoagulants' activity)		anaplastic oligoastrocytoma
		AOAA	aminooxoacetic acid
		AOAP	as often as possible
		AOAs	adult offspring of alcoholics
ant panhypopit	anterior panhypopituitarism	AO ASIF	Association for Osteosynthesis/ Association for the Study of Internal Fixation
ant sag D	anterior sagittal diameter		
ANTU	alpha naphthylthiourea		
ANTX	anatoxin-a	AO-ASIF	Arbeitsgemeinschaft für Osteosynthesefragen/ Association for the Study of Internal Fixation (classifica-tion) ("Arbeitsgemeinschaft für Osteosynthesefragen" means Association of the Study of Internal Fixation)
ant- Xa	an assay to measure/momitor plasma heparin and low mo-lecular weight heparin levels (anti-factor Xa)		
ANUG	acute necrotizing ulcerative gingivitis		
ANV	acute nausea and vomiting	AOB	accessory olfactory bulb
ANVISA	National Health Surveillance Agency (Brazil)		alcohol on breath
		AOBC	aortic occlusion balloon catheter
ANW	active-not-walking	AOBL	anemia of blood loss
ANX	anxiety	AOBS	acute organic brain syndrome
	anxious	AOC	abridged ocular chart
ANXA8	Annexin A8		acute on chronic (to categorize the chronicity of emergency conditions)
ANZDATA	Australia and New Zealand Dialysis and Transplant Registry		
			advanced ovarian cancer
AO	abdominal obesity		alteration of consciousness
	acridine orange (stain)		amoxicillin, omeprazole, and clarithromycin
	Agent Orange		
	Alveolar osteitis (also known as dry socket)		anode opening contraction
			antacid of choice
	anaplastic oligodendroglioma		area of concern
	anterior oblique	AOCCHF	acute on chronic congestive heart failure
	aorta		
	aortic opening	AOCD	anemia of chronic disease
	aortography	AOCDHF	acute-on-chronic diastolic heart failure
	artery occlusion		
	axio-occlusal	AOCKD	acute-on-chronic kidney disease
	plate, screw (orthopedics)	AoCKI	acute-on-chronic kidney injury

AOCL	anodal opening clonus
AOCLF	acute-on-chronic liver failure
AOCN	Advanced Oncology Certified Nurse
AOCNS	Advanced Oncology Certified Clinical Nurse Specialist
AOCRF	acute-on-chronic respiratory failure
AoCSHF	acute-on-chronic systolic heart failure
AOD	acute aortic dissection
	adult-onset diabetes
	alcohol and (and/or) other drugs
	alcohol and other drugs
	alleged onset date
	angle-opening distance
	arterial occlusive disease
	Assistant-Officer-of-the-Day
	atlanto-occipital dislocation
	atlantooccipital dissociation
AODA	alcohol and other drug abuse
AoDL	activities of daily living
AODM	adult-onset diabetes mellitus
AOE	acute otitis externa
A of 1	assistance of one
A of 2	assistance of two
AOFAS	American Orthopaedic Foot and Ankle Society (clinical rating scale)
AOG	age of gestation
AOH	alternariol (a mycotoxin produced by Alternaria spp. Soyasaponin)
AOI	apnea of infancy
	area of induration
AOID	adult-onset immunodeficiency
	anterior ocular inflammatory disease
	aortoiliac occlusive disease
ao-il	aorta-iliac
AOIVM	angiographically occult intracranial vascular malformation
AOK	A German health insurance company (Allgemeine Ortskrankenkasse)
	all is okay (slang)
A-OK	perfectly all right
AOL	augmentation of labor
AOLC	acridine-orange leukocyte cytospin
AOLD	automated open lumbar diskectomy
AOM	acute otitis media
	alternatives of management
AOMI	acute and old myocardial infarction combined
AONAD	alert, oriented, and no acute distress
A on C	acute on chronic
AONE	Arnadottir OT-ADL Neurobehavioral Evaluation (a standardized assessment that links performance in activities of daily living to neurobehavioral impairments)
A-ONE	The Arnadóttir OT (occupational therapy)-ADL (activities of daily living) Neurobehavioral Evaluation (a standardized assessment that links performance in ADL to neurobehavioral impairments)
AOO	age-of-onset
	anodal opening odor
	continuous arterial asynchronous pacing
AO/OTA	Association for Osteosynthesis/ Orthopaedic Trauma Association (fracture classification)
AOP	adverse outcome pathways
	anemia of prematurity
	anodal opening picture
	aortic pressure
	apnea of prematurity
AOPKD	may have meant ADPKD (autosomal dominant polycystic kidney disease)
aOR	adjusted odds ratio
AOR	Alvarado Orthopedic Research
	at own risk
	auditory oculogyric reflex
AORC	arthritis and other rheumatic conditions
AORD	arthritis and other rheumatic diseases
AORI	Anderson Orthopaedic Research Institute (classification)
AORN	Association of Operating Room Nurses (guidelines)
AORT REGURG	aortic regurgitation
AORT STEN	aortic stenosis
aortobifem	aortobifemoral bypass
AOS	ambulatory outpatient surgery
	anode opening sound
	antibiotic order sheet
	aortic ostial stenoses
	arrived on scene
	awake onset stroke (stroke developing while awake)
AOSC	acute obstructive suppurative cholangiotomy
AOSD	adult-onset Still's disease
AOSN	all other systems negative
AOT	add-on-test
	assisted outpatient treatment

AOTA	American Occupational Therapy Association
AOTB	alcohol on the breath
AOTe	anodal opening tetanus
AOUP	Azienda Ospedaliero-Universitaria Pisana (Pisa University Hospital, Italy)
AoV	ampulla of Vater
	angularis oculi vein
	aortic valve
AoVR	aortic valve replacement
AOW	absolute organ weight
	Army of Women (Dr. Susan Love Research Foundation's offers a website registration process for women to register online to receive information about opportunities for participation in research studies [www.actwithlove.org])
	onset of independent walking
A/O×3	awake and oriented to person, place, and time
A+O×3	awake and oriented to person, place, and time
AOX	antioxidant(s)
AO×1	awake and oriented to person
AO×2	awake and oriented to person and place
AO×3	awake and oriented to person, place, and time
AO×4	awake and oriented to person, place, time, and date
AP	abdomen-pelvis
	abdominal pain
	abdominoperineal
	accessory pathway
	acute pancreatitis
	Advanced Practitioner
	aerosol pentamidine
	alkaline phosphatase
	angina pectoris
	ankle pump
	antepartum
	anterior-posterior (x-ray)
	antibiotic prophylaxis
	aortopulmonary
	apical periodontitis
	apical pulse
	appendectomy
	appendicitis
	arterial pressure
	arthritis panel (see Laboratory Panels)
	artificial pancreas
	atrial pacing

	attending physician
	doxorubicin (Adriamycin); cisplatin (Platinol)
A & P	anterior and posterior
	active and present
	assessment and plans
	auscultation and percussion See A&P
A/P	abdomen/pelvis
	accounts payable
	ascites/plasma ratio
	assessment/plan
A-P	see AP
A P	see AP
$A_2 > P_2$	second aortic sound greater than second pulmonic sound
APA	aldosterone-producing adenoma
	American Psychiatric Association
	anticipatory postural adjustment
	antiphospholipid antibody
APAA	anterior parietal artery aneurysm
APAC	acute primary angle closure
APACHE	Acute Physiology and Chronic Health Evaluation
APACHE II	Acute Physiology and Chronic Health Evaluation (12 routine physiological measurements)
A-pacing	apical pacing
APAD	anterior-posterior abdominal diameter
Apaf-1	apoptosis peptidase activating factor-1; see gene website www.ncbi.nlm.nih.gov/gene
APAG	antipseudomonal aminoglycosidic penicillin
APAH	Associated pulmonary arterial hypertension
APAP	acetaminophen (N acetyl-para-aminophenol; Tylenol; paracetamol) This abbreviation should not be used on pharmacy labels; use acetaminophen.
	automatic positive airway pressure
	auto-titrating positive airway pressure
APAs	aldosterone producing adenomas
	anticipatory postural adjustments
	antiphospholipid antibodies
APA syndrome	antiphospholipid antibody syndrome
APB	abductor pollicis brevis
	atrial premature beat
APBA	aminophenylboronic acid

APBI	accelerated partial breast irradiation
APBSCT	autologous peripheral blood stem cell transplantation
APC	absolute phagocyte count
	activated protein C
	acute pharyngoconjunctiivitis (fever)
	adenoidal-pharyngeal-conjunctival
	adenomatous polyposis of the colon and rectum
	Advance Practice Clinician
	advanced prostate cancer
	Ambulatory Payment Classification
	annual percentage change
	antigen-presenting cell
	argon plasma coagulator
	aspirin, phenacetin, and caffeine (no longer marketed in the US)
	asymptomatic prostate cancer
	atrial premature contraction
	autologous packed cells
APCa	advanced pancreas cancer
APCA	African Palliative Care Association
APCA POS	African Palliative Care Association Palliative Outcome Scale
aPCC	activated prothrombin complex concentrate
APCD	adult polycystic disease
APCE	affinity probe capillary electrophoresis
APCIs	atrial peptide clearance inhibitors
APCKD	adult polycystic kidney disease
APCOG	anteroposterior center of gravity
APCR	activated protein C resistance
APCS	see gene website, www.ncbi.nlm.nih.gov/gene
AP CT	abdominopelvic computed tomography
APCT	alternating prism cover test
AP-CD/LD	Accordion Pill, a gastric-retention oral delivery platform based on folded multilayer films of carbidopa and levodopa
AP-CT	abdominal and pelvic computer tomography
APD	acid peptic disease
	action potential duration
	afferent pupillary defect
	anterior-posterior diameter
	antisocial personality disorder
	atrial premature depolarization
	auditory processing disorder

	automated peritoneal dialysis
	pamidronate disodium (aminohydroxypropylidene diphosphate)
APDC	Anxiety and Panic Disorder Clinic
APDL	activities parallel to daily living
	Ansys parametric design language
AP-DRGs	all-patient diagnosis-related groups
APDT	acellular pertussis vaccine with diphtheria and tetanus toxoids
aPDT	antimicrobial photodynamic therapy
APE	absolute prediction error
	acute psychotic episode
	acute pulmonary edema
	doxorubicin (Adriamycin), cisplatin (Platinol-AQ), and etoposide)
APECED	autoimmune polyendocrinopathy-candidiasis-ectodermal dystrophy
ApEn	approximate entropy
APER	abdominoperineal excision of the rectum
APEX	APEX nuclease (multifunctional DNA repair enzyme); see gene website www.ncbi.nlm.nih.gov/gene
apex	the extremity of a conic or pyramidal structure
APF	atlantoaxial plate fixation
aPFC	anterior prefrontal cortex
APFI	Adolescents& Psychosocial Functioning Inventory
APFT	Army Physical Fitness Test
APG	ambulatory patient group
	Apgar (score)
Apgar	appearance (color), pulse (heart rate), grimace (reflex irritability), activity (muscle tone), and respiration (score reflecting condition of newborn)
Apgars	appearance (color), pulse (heart rate), grimace (reflex irritability), activity (muscle tone), and respiration (scores reflecting condition of newborn)
APH	adult psychiatric hospital
	alcohol-positive history
	antepartum hemorrhage
aph	apheresis
APhA	American Pharmacists Association
APHA	American Public Health Association

APHAB	Abbreviated Profile of Hearing Aid Benefit
APHIS	Animal and Plant Health Inspection Service
APHON	Association of Pediatric Hematology Oncology Nursing
APHOS	alkaline phosphatase
API	active pharmaceutical ingredient
	apnea-hypoxnea Index
	Asian-Pacific Islander
APIC	Association for Professionals in Infection Control and Epidemiology
APIE	assessment, plan, implementation, evaluation (process)
APIS	Acute Pain Intensity Scale
APIVR	artificial pacemaker-induced ventricular rhythm
APKD	adult polycystic kidney disease
	adult-onset polycystic kidney disease
APL	abductor pollicis longus
	accelerated painless labor
	acute promyelocytic leukemia
	anterior pituitary-like (hormone)
	chorionic gonadotropin
AP & L	anteroposterior and lateral
APLA	antiphospholipid antibody
aPLAb	antiphospholipid antibodies
APLAs	antiphospholipid antibodies
APLAS	antiphospholipid antibody syndrome
APLD	automated percutaneous lumbar diskectomy
APLIS	anatomic pathology laboratory information system
APLS	antiphospholipid syndrome
APL syndrome	antiphospholipid syndrome
APM	auditory perceptual motor
APME	acute postinfectious measles encephalitis
APMHNP	Adult Psychiatric & Mental Health Nurse Practitioner
APML	acute promyelocytic leukemia
APMPPE	acute posterior multifocal placoid pigment epitheliopathy
APMS	acute pain management service
APMs	Alternative Payment Models
APMT	adductor pollicis muscle thickness (a method for evaluation of muscle loss and, consequently, malnutrition in adult and elderly patients)
APN	acquired pendular nystagmus
	acute panautonomic neuropathy
	acute pyelonephritis
	Adiponectin
	Advanced Practice Nurse

APNA	American Psychiatric Nurses Association
apneic	a word meaning- pertaining to or relating to the cessation of breathing
APNG	Advanced Practice Nurse in Genetics
APNO	all purpose nipple ointment (equal parts ofmupirocin 2% ointment and betameth-asone 0.1% ointment, plus miconazole powder [2%]; formulas may vary)
APNP	Advanced Pediatric Nurse Practitioner
APO	adverse patient occurrence doxorubicin (Adriamycin), prednisone, and vincristine (Oncovin)
apo	apolipoprotein
apo A	apolipoprotein A
APO(a)	apolipoprotein (A)
apoA-I	apolipoprotein A-I
apoB	apolipoprotein B
apoC	apolipoprotein C
APOC3	apolipoprotein C3 (gene/protein)
APOE	apolipoprotein E; see gene website www.ncbi.nlm.nih .gov/gene
APOE4	apolipoprotein E4
APOL1	apolipoprotein L1 (gene/protein)
APOLT	auxiliary partial orthotopic liver transplantation
APOPPS	adjustable postoperative protective prosthetic socket
APOWW	Apprehension by Peace Officer Without Warrant (patients brought in against their will by law enforcement agencies)
APP	Advanced Practice Provider(s) alternating pressure pad amyloid precursor protein appetite assume pain present
ApP	apical pulse
app	application
APPA	anterior pelvic plane axes Asia Pacific Pediatric Association
aPPD	aglycone protopanaxadiol
APPD	anterior-posterior pelvic diameter
APPE	Advanced Pharmacy Practice Experience
APPG	aqueous procaine penicillin G (dangerous terminology; since it is for intramuscular use only; write as penicillin G procaine)

APPI	atmospheric pressure photoionization		American Psychological Society antiphospholipid syndrome
appl	application	APSAC	anistreplase (anisoylated plasminogen streptokinase activator complex)
APPLA	another planned permanent living arrangement		
appr.	approximate	AP scan	abdomen/pelvis scan
approp	appropriate	APSD	Alzheimer presenile dementia
APPROX	approximate approximately	APSE	Acyrthosiphon pisum secondary endosymbiont (bacteriophage)
apprx	approximately	APSI	anterior-posterior stability index
apps	applications	APSO	Asia Pacific Stroke Organization
APPT	acute peritraumatic pulmonary thrombus		asymmetrical pedicle subtraction osteotomy
appt	appointment	APSP	assisted peak systolic pressure
APPTs	may have meant aPTTs (activated partial thrombo-plastin times)	APS-POQ	American Pain Society Patient Outcome Questionnaire
APPX	anterior-posterior pelvic x-ray	APSS	Associated Professional Sleep Societies
	appendex approximately	APSW	Association of Psychiatric Social Work (United Kingdom)
	approximation	APT	anterior pelvic tilt
APPY	appendectomy		antiplatelet therapy
AP & R	apical and radial (pulses)	apt	see gene website www.ncbi.nlm .nih.gov/gene
APR	abdominoperineal resection acute radiation proctitis anatomical programmed radiography average payment rate	APTa	adenine phosphoribosyltransferase; see gene website, www.ncbi .nlm.nih.gov/gene
Apr	April	APTA	American Physical Therapy Association
aprA	see gene website; www.ncbi .nlm.nih.gov	APTS	3-aminopropyltriethoxysilane
APRC	active plasma renin concentration	aPTT	activated partial thromboplastin time
	active post-resuscitation care	aPTTs	activated partial thromboplastin times
APR DRG	all-patient refined diagnosis-related groups	APTUS®	multidirectional angle-stable plate system (orthopedics)
A&P repair	anterior and posterior vaginal wall repair	APU	ambulatory procedure unit antepartum unit
A/P repair	anterior and posterior vaginal wall repair	APUD	amine precursor uptake and decarboxylation
AP repair	anterior and/or posterior vaginal wall repair	A-1 pulley	first annular pulley
APRN	Advanced Practice Registered Nurse	APV	amprenavir (Agenerase) appendicovesicosutomy approximate priming volume (amount of fluid needed to prime an IV access device)
aprox	approximately		
aPRP	activated platelet-rich plasma autologous platelet-rich plasma		
APRPD	anterior-posterior renal pelvic diameter	APVC	partial anomalous pulmonary venous connection
APRT	abdominopelvic radiotherapy	APVcmv	adaptive pressure ventilation/ controlled mandatory ventilation
APRV	airway pressure release ventilation		
APS	acute pain service Acute Physiology Scoring (system) adult protective services Adult Protective Services Adult Psychiatric Service	APVD	anomalous posterior vitreous detachment anomalous pulmonary venous drainage arterial peripheral vascular disease

APVP	atrial pace ventricular pace		at risk
APVR	aortic pulmonary valve replacement		aural rehabilitation autorefractor
APVS	atrial pace ventricular sense		auto-refractor
APW	aortopulmonary window		axial rotation
APX	approximately	A&R	adenoidectomy with radium
	ascorbate peroxidase; see gene		advised and released
	website www.ncbi.nlm.nih	A-R	apical-radial (pulses)
	.gov/gene	A/R	accounts receivable
AQ	accomplishment quotient		antireflective (coating)
	amodiaquine		apical/radial
aq	aqueous (watery)	AR2	Amplatz Right 2-curve size
	water		(thrombectomy device)
AQC	Alternative Quality Contract	ARA	Action Research Arm (test)
AQCs	Alternative Quality Contracts		adenosine regulating agent
aq dest	distilled water	Ara	arabinose
AQI	Air Quality Index	ara-A	vidarabine (Vira-A)
	Anesthesia Quality Institute	ara-AC	fazarabine
AQLQ-J	Asthma Quality of Life	ara-C	cytarabine (Cytosar-U)
	Questionnaire—Juniper	ARAD	abnormal right axis deviation
AQLQ-M	Asthma Quality of Life	ARAP	atherosclerotic renal-artery plaque
	Questionnaire—Marks	AR/AS	allergic rhinitis associated with
AQOL	acne quality of life		allergic sensitization
AQoL	Assessment of Quality of Life	ARAS	ascending reticular activating
	Asthma-related Quality of Life		system
	Australian Quality of Life		atherosclerotic renal-artery
AQP	aquaporin (gene/protein; there		stenosis
	are at least 7 aquaporin	ARB	angiotensin II receptor blocker
	subtypes)		antibiotic-resistant bacteria
AQP2	aquaporin-2		any reliable brand
AQP4	aquaporin-4	ARBC	allogeneic red-blood cell
AQP4 IgG	aquaporin-4 immunoglobulin G	ARB-CCB	angiotensin ii receptor blocker/
AQPs	aquaporins (genes/proteins;		calcium-channel blocker
	there are at least 7 aquaporin		(combination; Azor, Exforge,
	subtypes)		Twynsta)
AQR	ain't quite right (slang)	aRBCs	aged red blood cells
	Air Quality Standards	ARBD	alcohol-related birth defects
	anthraquinone-2-sodium		alcohol-related brain damage
	sulfonate	ARBF	adaptive recursive band-pass
Aquad	atrial quadrageminy		filtrations
Ar	argon	ARBOR	arthropod-borne virus
AR	absolute risk	ARBOW	artificial rupture of bag of water
	Achilles reflex	ARBs	angiotensin II receptor blockers
	acoustic reflex	ARC	abnormal retinal correspondence
	active resistance		adult residential care
	acute rehabilitation		aged residential care
	acute rejection		(United Kingdom)
	airway resistance		AIDS-related complex
	alcohol related		Alcohol Rehabilitation Center
	allergic rhinitis		American Red Cross
	androgen receptor		anomalous retinal correspondence
	ankle reflex		autologous red cells
	aortic regurgitation	ARCBS	American Red Cross Blood
	aortic (valve) regurgitation		Services
	apoptotic rate	ARCC	autosomal recessive congenital
	Argyll Robertson (pupil)		cataract
	Arkansas	ARCD	acquired renal cystic disease
	assisted respiration		age-related cognitive decline

Arch	Achieves
ARCOS	Automation of Reports and Consolidated Orders System (for controlled substances)
ARCP	Annual Review of Competence ge (United Kingdom)
Arcp	armadillo repeat containing 1 gene see gene website www.ncbi.nlm.nih.gov/gene
ARCR	arthroscopic rotator cuff repair
arcus	a word meaning an arch; a general term to designate an anatomical structure having a curved or bowline outline
ARCUS	trAnsRadial perCUtaneouS coronary intervention on upper extremity function (study)
ARD	acute radiation dermatitis acute respiratory disease adult respiratory distress alcohol-related dementia aphakic retinal detachment
ardC	antirrestriction protein (gene)
ARDMS	American Registry of Diagnostic Medical Sonographers
ARDS	acute respiratory distress syndrome adult respiratory distress syndrome
ARDSnet	a mechanical ventilation protocol for acute respiratory distress syndrome
ARDSNET	Acute Respiratory Distress Syndrome Network www.ardsnet.org
ARE	active-resistive exercises
AREDF	absent or reverse end-diastolic flow (in the umbilical artery)
A/REDF	absent or reversed end-diastolic flow (umbilical-artery Doppler ultrasonography)
AREDS	Age-Related Eye Disease Study
AREDS 2	Age-Related Eye Disease Study 2
AREDS 3	Age-Related Eye Disease Study 3
AREDS formula	Age-Related Eye Disease Study formula; (vitamins A, C, and E; copper and zinc)
AREG	amphiregulin
AREN	American Rehabilitation Educational Network
AREP	autosomal-recessive early-onset parkinsonism
AREs	active regulatory elements (genetic variants) adverse radiation effects antioxidant response elements

ARES	may have meant Aris® (a permanent, synthetic, midurethral support sling for implantation using the transobturator technique)
ARF	acute renal failure acute respiratory failure acute rheumatic fever amylase-rich food (flour)
ARfD	acute reference dose (an estimate of a daily oral exposure for an acute duration (24 hours or less) to the human population that is likely to be without an appreciable risk of deleterious effects during a lifetime)
ARFF	at risk for falling
ARFI	acoustic radiation force impulse (imaging)
ARFID	avoidant/restrictive food intake disorder Avoidant/Restrictive Food Intake Disorder (previously known as selective eating disorder)
ARG	alkaline reflux gastritis arginine
ARGNB	antibiotic-resistant gram-negative bacilli
ARH	autosomal recessive hypercholesterolemia
ARHL	age-related hearing loss
ARHNC	advanced resected head and neck cancer
ARI	acute renal insufficiency acute respiratory illness acute respiratory infection aldose reductase inhibitor arousal index
ARIA	Allergic Rhinitis and its Impact on Asthma (guidelines)
ARIA-E	amyloid-related imaging abnormality - edema
ARIA-H	amyloid-related imaging abnormality - hemosiderin deposition
ARIES	automatic retinal image quality assessment system automatic retinal interest evaluation system Avastin Regimens: Investigation of Effectiveness and Safety (study)
ARIF	arthroscopic reduction and internal fixation
ARIMA	autoregressive integrated moving average (model)

A

ARIs	activation-recovery intervals
	acute respiratory infections
Aris®	a permanent, synthetic, midurethral support sling for implantation using the transobturator technique
ARISCAT	Assess Respiratory Risk in Surgical Patients in Catalonia (score)
arith	arithmetic
ARJP	autosomal recessive juvenile parkinsonism
ARK	see gene website, www.ncbi.nlm.nih.gov/gene
ARKs	AMPK (AMP [adenosine monophosphate]-activated protein kinase)-related kinases
ARL	acquired immunodeficiency syndrome (AIDS) - related lymphoma
	average remaining lifetime
ARLD	alcohol-related liver disease
ARM	acid reduction medication
	anorectal malformations
	anorectal manometry
	anxiety reaction, mild
	artificial rupture of membranes
armA	16S rRNA methyltransferase conferring resistance to all aminoglycosides (gene)
ARMA	autoregressive moving average
ARMD	adverse reaction to metal debris
	adverse reactions to metal debris (as in metal-on-metal hip implants)
	age-related macular degeneration
ARMHS	Australian Rural Mental Health Study
ARMS	alveolar rhabdomyosarcoma
	amplification refractory mutation system
	at-risk mental state
ARN	acute retinal necrosis
ARNA	American Radiological Nurses Association
ARND	alcohol-related neurodevelopmental disorder
ARNIs	angiotensin-receptor neprilysin inhibitors
ARNP	Advanced Registered Nurse Practitioner
ARO	ankle-repositioning orthosis
aroB	see gene website, www.ncbi.nlm.nih.gov/gene
AROBF	a return of bowel function

ArOH	Compounds in which an OH (alcohol) group is attached directly to an aromatic ring are designated ArOH and called phenols
AROM	active range of motion
	artifical rupture of membranes
ARP	absolute refractory period
	acute radiation proctitis
	alcohol rehabilitation program
	arthritis panel
ARPAE	acoustic resolution photoacoustic endoscopy
ARPC	androgen-resistant prostate cancer
ARPDK	autosomal recessive polycystic disease of the kidney
ARPE	amylase-rich pleural effusion
ARPF	anterior release posterior fusion
ARPKD	autosomal recessive polycystic kidney disease
ARPN	Advanced Practice Registered Nurse
ARPs	alcohol-related problems
ARPT	acid reflux provocation test
ARR	absolute risk reduction
	Academy of Radiology Research
	aldosterone/renin ratio
	annualized relapse rate
	anterior rectal resection
	arrive
aRR	adjusted rate ratio
ARRA	American Recovery and Reinvestment Act (2009)
ARRA-HITECH	American Recovery and Reinvestment/Health Information Technology for Economic and Clinical Health Act (2009)
arrhy	arrhythmia(s)
ARROM	active resistive range of motion
ARROW	antiresonant reflecting optical waveguide
ARRS	American Roentgen Ray Society
ARRT	American Registry of Radiologic Technologists
ARS	acute radiation sickness
	acute radiation syndrome
	antirabies serum
arsD	see gene website, www.ncbi.nlm.nih.gov/gene
ART	Accredited Record Technician (for newer title, see RHIT)
	Achilles (tendon) reflex test
	acoustic reflex threshold(s)
	adjuvant radiation therapy
	androgen replacement therapy

anesthesia release time (patient-on-table until release for surgical preparation)

antiretroviral therapy

arterial

articulatory (technique)

assessment, review, and treatment

assisted reproductive technology

automated reagin test (for syphilis)

arterio   arteriogram

ARTG   Australian Register of Therapeutic Goods

arth   arthritis

ARTH   Arthrobacter

arthr   arthritis

arthritis panel   go to Tables and Lists Button; Laboratory Panels

arthro   arthrogram

ARTIC   articulation

ARTIs   acute respiratory tract infections

ART line   arterial line

ART R Fe   right femoral artery

ArtT   art therapy

ARU   acute receiving unit
acute rehabilitation unit
alcohol rehabilitation unit

ARUP   Associated Regional and University Pathologists (Salt Lake City, Utah)

ARV   AIDS-related virus
antiretroviral

ARVC   arrhythmogenic right ventricular cardiomyopathy

ARVC/D   arrhythmogenic right ventricular cardiomyopathy/dysplasia

ARVD   arrhythmogenic right ventricular dysplasia
atherosclerotic renovascular disease

ARVI   acute respiratory viral infections

ARVMB   anomalous right ventricular muscle bundles

ARVs   antiretroviral drugs

ARVT   antiretroviral therapy

ARW   Accredited Rehabilitation Worker

ARWY   airway

ARX   aristaless-related homeobox; see gene website, www.ncbi .nlm.nih.gov/gene

A's   as in 5 A's- ask, advise, assess, assist, and arrange follow-up (developed for smoking counseling)

As   arsenic

AS   activated sleep
active surveillance
alpha-synuclein
American Samoa
anabolic steroid
anal sphincter
androgen suppression
Angleman syndrome
ankylosing spondylitis
anterior synechia
anxiety sensitivity
aortic stenosis
artesunate (an antimalarial agent)
Asperger syndrome
atherosclerosis
atropine sulfate
AutoSuture®
doctor called through answering service
left ear

A/S   see AS

AsA   ascorbic acid

ASA   American Society of Anesthesiologists
American Statistical Association
angiosarcoma
argininosuccinate
as soon as
aspirin (acetylsalicylic acid)
atrial septal aneurysm

ASA 81   aspirin tablets 81 milligrams (baby aspirin)

ASA I   American Society of Anesthesiologists' Classification. Healthy patient with localized pathological process

ASA II   American Society of Anesthesiologists' Classification. A patient with mild to moderate systemic disease

ASA III   American Society of Anesthesiologists' Classification. A patient with severe systemic disease limiting activity but not incapacitating

ASA IV   American Society of Anesthesiologists' Classification. A patient with incapacitating systemic disease

ASA V   American Society of Anesthesiologists' Classification. Moribund patient who is not expected to live without the operation

ASA VI	American Society of Anesthesiologists' classification. Declared brain-dead patient whose organs are being removed for donor purposes
5-ASA	mesalamine (5-aminosalicylic acid) (this is a dangerous abbreviation as it is mistaken for five aspirin tablets)
ASAA	acquired severe aplastic anemia
ASACL	American Society of Anesthesiologists Classification
ASAD	arthroscopic subacromial decompression
ASA + ERDP	aspirin and extended-release dipyridamole (Aggrenox)
aSAH	aneurysmal subarachnoid hemorrhage
AS/AI	aortic stenosis/aortic insufficiency
ASAM PPC-2	Patient Placement Criteria published by the American Society of Addiction Medicine, Second Edition
ASAP	Alcohol and Substance Abuse Program
	as soon as possible
	atypical small acinar proliferation
ASAPS	The American Society for Aesthetic Plastic Surgery
AS-AQ	artesunate-amodiaquine
ASAR	abdominosacral amputations of the rectum
	aortic stenosis with aortic regurgitation
AS/AR	aortic stenosis with aortic regurgitation
ASAS	Assessment of SpondyloArthritis international Society
ASAT	abdominal subcutaneous adipose tissue
	aspartate aminotransferase (also ALT; SGOT)
ASB	anesthesia standby
	anterior skull base
	asymptomatic bacteriuria
ASBMR	activity-specific birth month ratio
	American Society of Bone and Mineral Research
ASBMS	American Society for Metabolic & Bariatric Surgery
ASBO	adhesive small-bowel obstruction
ASBs	artificially sweetened beverages

A's & B's	apnea and bradycardia
ASC	abdominal sacrocolpopexy
	active symptom control
	adult stem cell
	altered state of consciousness
	ambulatory surgery center
	anterior subcapsular cataract
	antimony sulfur colloid
	apocrine skin carcinoma
	ascorbic acid (vitamin C)
	asymptomatic carotid stenosis
ascA	acetyl-CoA synthetase (gene)
ASCA	antisaccharomyces cerevisiae
ASCAD	atherosclerotic coronary artery disease
Asc Ao	ascending aorta
ASCBD	may have meant ASCVD (atherosclerotic cardiovascular disease)
ASCCC	advanced squamous cell cervical carcinoma
ASCCHN	advanced squamous cell carcinoma of the head and neck
ASCCP	American Society for Colposcopy and Cervical Pathology (guidelines)
ASCD	atherosclerotic coronary disease
ASC-H	atypical squamous cells of high-grade (cell classification in Papanicolaou test)
ASCHF	aortic stenosis and congestive heart failure
ASCI	acute spinal cord injury
ASCID	atypical squamous cells indefinite for dysplasia
ASCIs	antigen-specific cancer immunotherapeutic (agents)
ASCO	American Society of Clinical Oncology
ASCOT	Anglo-Scandinavian Cardiac Outcomes Trial
ASCP	abdominal sacral colpopexy
	American Society for Clinical Pathology
	American Society of Consultant Pharmacists
	antegrade selective cerebral perfusion
	anterosuperior calcaneal process
ASCQR	Ambulatory Surgical Center Quality Reporting
ASCR	autologous stem cell rescue
ASCRD	may have meant ASCVD (arteriosclerotic cardiovascular disease)
ASCs	adipose stem cells
	adipose-derived stem cells
ASCS	autologous stem cell support

ASCT	allogenic stem cell transplantation		adults sepsis events
	autologous stem cell		amorphous selenium
	transplantation	ASED	autologous serum eye drops
ASCUD	May have been misread for	ASEP	asymmetric simple exclusion
	ASCVD (arteriosclerotic		process
	cardiovascular disease)	ASEPT®	a pleural drainage system
ASCUS	atypical squamous cells of	ASER	American Society of Emergency
	undetermined significance		Radiology
ASC-US	atypical squamous cells of	ASES	American Shoulder and Elbow
	undetermined significance		Score
	(cell classification in		American Shoulder and Elbow
	Papanicolaou test)		Surgeons
ASCUS-H	atypical squamous cells of	ASEX	Arizona Sexual Experiences
	undetermined significance,		(sexual dysfunction scale)
	favors high-grade squamous	ASF	anterior spinal fusion
	intraepithelial lesions		asymmetric screen film (radiology)
ASCUS-L	atypical squamous cells of		auditory spatial facilitation
	undetermined significance,	ASFA	Adoption and Safe Families Act
	favors low-grade squamous	ASFR	age-specific fertility rate
	intraepithelial lesions	ASFS	anterior segment fibrosis
ASCVD	arteriosclerotic cardiovascular		syndrome
	disease	ASG	assignment
ASCVR	arteriosclerotic cardiovascular		atrial septal graft
	renal disease	AsGa	arsenium-gallium (laser)
AScVS	anti-scorpion venom serum	aSGA	SsgA-like proteins are a family
ASD	acute stress disorder		of actinomycete-specific
	adjacent segment disease		regulatory proteins that
	adjacent-segment degeneration		control cell division and spore
	adult spinal deformity		maturation in streptomycetes
	aldosterone secretion defect	ASGE	American Society for Gastroin-
	amorphous solid dispersion		testinal Endoscopy (guidelines)
	androstenedione	ASGUS	atypical squamous glandular
	annual summary dose (ionizing		cells of undetermined
	radiation)		significance
	atrial septal defect	ASH	American Society of
	autism spectrum disorder(s)		Hematology (guidelines)
ASD I	atrial septal defect, primum		asymmetric septal hypertrophy
ASD II	atrial septal defect, secundum	AsH	hypermetropic astigmatism
ASDA	American Sleep Disorders	ASHA NOMS	American Speech-Language
	Association (criteria)		Hearing Association National
ASDAS	Ankylosing Spondylitis Disease		Outcomes Measurement
	Activity Score		System
ASDC	Association of Sleep Disorders	Ash Catheter	Ash Split Cath (a dual-lumen
	Centers		tunneled hemodialysis
ASDf	female children with autism		catheter with a single
	spectrum disorders		double-D transcutaneous
ASDH	acute subdural hematoma		portion connecting to multi-
ASD/PFO	atrial septal defect, patent		holed cylindrical tips in a
	foramen ovale		central vein; named after
ASDPs	antisocial personality disorders		Dr. Stephen Ash)
ASDs	amorphous solid dispersions	ASHD	arteriosclerotic heart disease
	atrial septal defects	ASHE	American Society for
	autism spectrum disorders		Healthcare Engineering
ASD/VSD	atrial septal defect and	ASHF	acute systolic heart failure
	ventricular septal defect		antigen-specific helper factor
ASDz	adjacent segment disease	aSHF	anterior second heart field
ASE	abstinence symptom evaluation	ASHP	American Society of
	acute stress erosion		Health-Systems Pharmacists

ASHRAE	American Society of Heating, Refrigerating and Air-Conditioning Engineers (humidity level recommendations)
Ash Split Cath	a dual-lumen tunneled hemodialysis catheter with a single double-D transcutaneous portion connecting to multi-holed cylindrical tips in a central vein; named after Dr. Stephen Ash
ASHT	American Society of Hand Therapists
ASI	active specific immunotherapy
	Addiction Severity Index
	anterior supine intermuscular (approach)
	Anxiety Sensitivity Index
	Anxiety Status Inventory
	Arterial Stiffness Index
aSi	amorphous silicon
ASIA A	American Spinal Injury Association (Score) A (Complete–No preservation of any motor and/or sensory function below the zone of injury)
ASIA B	American Spinal Injury Association (Score) B (Incomplete–Preserved sensation)
ASIA C	American Spinal Injury Association (Score) C (Incomplete–Preserved motor [nonfunctional])
ASIA D	American Spinal Injury Association (Score) D (Incomplete–Preserved motor [functional])
ASIA E	American Spinal Injury Association (Score) E (Complete Recovery)
ASICs	acid-sensing ion channels
ASID	anxiogenic stressor-induced depression
	Australasian Society for Infectious Diseases
ASIF	anterior spinal instrumentation and fusion
ASIH	absent, sick in hospital
ASILs	abnormal signal intensity lesions
ASIMC	absent, sick in medical center
ASIR	adaptive statistical iterative reconstruction
	age-standardized incidence rates

ASIS	anterior superior iliac spine
ASI-TLKW	Acute ischemic stroke, time last known well (the amount of time since the patient was last known to be well before a stroke)
ASK	antistreptokinase
ASK™	Applied Semantic Knowledge
ASKase	antistreptokinase
ASL	American Sign Language
	antistreptolysin (titer)
ASLD	argininosuccinate lyase deficiency
ASLO	antistreptolysin-O
ASL-PWI	arterial spin labelling perfusion-weighted imaging
ASLR	active straight leg raise (test)
ASLV	avian sarcoma and leukosis virus (Rous virus)
ASM	atrial systolic murmur
AsM	myopic astigmatism
ASMA	antismooth-muscle antibody
ASMC	airway smooth muscle cells
ASMD	acid sphingomyelinase deficiency (also known as Niemann-Pick disease Type B)
	see gene website, www.ncbi.nlm.nih.gov/gene
	atonic sclerotic muscle dystrophy
ASMI	anteroseptal myocardial infarction
ASMR	age-standardized mortality rate(s)
	autonomous Sensory Meridian Response (a perceptual phenomenon in which specific auditory and/or visual stimuli consistently elicit tingling sensations on the neck, scalp, and shoulders, as well as a positive and relaxed emotional state)
ASMS	American Society for Mohs Surgery (criteria)
ASMT	see gene website, www.ncbi.nlm.nih.gov/gene
Asn	asparagine
ASN	Associate's of Science in Nursing
as needed	When searching for how a word or phrase is abbreviated, click "Word Search" above the Search box; as needed, has been abbreviated as PRN (as the occasion arises).
ASNHL	acute sensorineural hearing loss
	asymmetrical sensorineural hearing loss
	autoimmune sensorineural hearing loss
ASO	accessory sinus ostia
	administrative services only (contract)

	AIDS (acquired immundeficiency syndrome) service organization(s)
	aldicarb sulfoxide
	allele-specific oligodeoxynucleotide (probes)
	Amplatzer Septal Occluder
	antisense oligonucleotides (e.g. nusinersen [Spinraza])
	antistreptolysin-O titer
	arterial switch operation
	arteriosclerosis obliterans
	asthma and COPD (chronic obstructive pulmonary disease)
	automatic stop order
As₂O₃	arsenic trioxide (Trisenox)
ASO/ATRA	arsenic trioxide injection and all-trans retinoid acid (tretinoin) capsules
ASOC	advanced-stage ovarian cancer
ASOD	anterior segment ocular dysgenesis
ASOM	acute suppurative otitis media
ASOs	antisense oligonucleotides (e.g. nusinersen [Spinraza])
ASOT	antistreptolysin-O titer
ASOTP	Affiliate Sex Offender Treatment Provider
ASP	acute suppurative parotitis
	acute symmetric polyarthritis
	adjacent segment pathology
	Antimicrobial Stewardship Program
	antisocial personality
	application service provider
	asparaginase
	aspartic acid
	aspiration
aspA	see gene website www.ncbi.nlm.nih.gov/gene
ASPAN	American Society of PeriAnesthesia Nurses (guideline)
AspAT	aspartate aminotransferase
ASPD	antisocial personality disorder
aspD	aspartate aminotransferase; see gene website www.ncbi.nlm.nih.gov/gene
ASPDV	anterior superior pancreaticoduodenal vein
ASPECTS	Alberta Stroke Program Early Computer Tomography Score
ASPEN	American Society for Parenteral and Enteral Nutrition (Guidelines)
ASPN	asporin; see gene website www.ncbi.nlm.nih.gov/gene
ASPPA	Athlete's Self Perception of Physical Abilities

ASPs	after-school programs
	antimicrobial stewardship programs
ASPS	alveolar soft part sarcoma
ASPSCR1	alveolar soft part sarcoma critical region 1
ASPVD	arteriosclerotic peripheral vascular disease
ASQ	Ages and Stages Questionnaire
	anterior-superior quadrant
ASQ3	Ages and Stages Questionnaire 3rd edition
ASQ:SE	Ages and Stages Questionnaire– Social Emotional
ASQ-SE	Ages and Stages Questionnaires: Social Emotional (a first level screening tool that is designed to identify children who may be at risk for social or emotional difficulties)
ASR	age-standardized rates
	aldosterone secretion rate
	articular surface replacement
	automatic speech recognition
ASRA	Alcohol Severity Rating Scale
ASRD	alcohol and substance-abuse related diagnoses
	aspirin-sensitive respiratory disease
ASRM	American Society for Reproductive Medicine (Infertility with endometriosis score/staging)
ASRS	ADHD (attention-deficit/ hyperactivity disorder) Self-Report Scale
	Autism Spectrum Rating Scale
ASRT	acoustic stapedial reflex threshold
AS's	positive form of abbreviations beginning with AS (see AS) see AS
ASS	anterior superior supine
	aspirin (some European countries)
	assessment
ASSC	acute splenic sequestration crisis
	automatic sleep stage classification
ASSD	antisynthetase syndrome (a condition characterized by myositis, arthritis, interstitial lung disease, Raynaud phenomenon and the presence of autoantibodies targeting aminoacyl trans- fer RNA [ribonucleic acid] synthetases)
	average symmetric surface distance

ASSH	American Society for Surgery of the Hand
ASSIST	Approaches and Study Skills Inventory for Students
assmt	assessment
Assoc	associated
ASSRs	auditory steady-state responses
ASST	assessment
	autologous serum skin test
asst	assistant
asst liv	assisted living
AST	allergy skin test
	androgen suppression therapy
	antimicrobial susceptibility testing
	Anxiety Sweats Tremor (Scale)
	Aphasia Screening Test
	aspartate aminotransferase (SGOT)
	astemizole
	astigmatism
AST/ALT	aspartate aminotransferase to alanine aminotransferase ratio
AstdVe	assisted ventilation
ASTH	asthenopia
ASTI	acute soft tissue injury
ASTIG	astigmatism
ASTL	see gene website, www.genecards.org
ASTM	American Society for Testing and Materials
	augmented soft tissue mobilization
AS TOL	as tolerated
ASTP	Alcohol Skills Training Program (a motivational enhance-ment and skills training approach, in reducing alcohol consumption by and negative consequences in students sanctioned for violations of campus alcohol policies)
ASTRO	American Society for Therapeutic Radiation and Oncology
	astrocytoma
ASTVD	May have been misheard for ASCVD (arteriosclerotic cardiovascular disease)
Astym®	(A-stim) treatment is a rehabili-tation program that is designed to stimulate the regenerative healing process of the body
ASTZ	antistreptozyme test
ASU	ambulatory surgical unit
ASV	adaptive servoventilation
	antisnake venom

As(V)	dissolved arsenate
ASVD	arteriosclerotic vessel disease
ASVP	atrial sense ventricular pace
ASVT	axillo-subclavian vein thrombosis
ASV titration	adaptive servoventilation titration
ASW	African Ancestry in southwest USA (population samples of HapMap [a catalog of common genetic variants that occur in human beings])
ASWA	abnormal slow wave activity
ASx	asymptomatic
ASXL1	additional sex combs like 1, transcriptional regulator (gene)
ASYM	asymmetric(al)
asymm	asymmetric
	asymmetry
A symptoms	absence of systemic symptoms of fever, night sweats, and weight loss which can be associated with both Hodgkin lymphoma and non-Hodgkin lymphoma
ASYS	Anesthesia Synchronization Software
asys	asystole(s)
ASz	antecedents of schizophrenia
A&T	adenoids and tonsils
At	astatine
AT	abdominothoracic
	Achilles tendinopathy
	Achilles tendon
	activity therapy (therapist)
	Addiction Therapist
	anaerobic threshold
	Anderson tube
	antithrombin
	applanation tonometry
	artificial tears
	ataxia-telangiectasia
	atraumatic
	atrial tachycardia
AT3	antithrombin III
AT 10	dihydrotachysterol (Hytakerol; DHT®)
ATA	American Thyroid Association (practice guidelines)
	antithyroid antibodies
	antitopoisomerase antibodies
	atmosphere absolute
	authority to administer
ATACH	Antihypertensive Treatment in Acute Cerebral Hemorrhage (trial)
a tach	atrial tachycardia
A-Tachy	atrial tachycardia

ATaF anterior talofibular

ATAF Arabidopsis transcription
activation factor; see gene
website www.ncbi.nlm.nih
.gov/gene
atrial tachycardia/atrial flutter

AT/AF atrial tachycardia and/or atrial
fibrillation

ATAQ Asthma Therapy Assessment
Questionnaire

ATAQ-IPF Asthma Therapy Assessment
Questionnaire-Idiopathic
Pulmonary Fibrosis

ATB antibiotic
aquatic therapy bar
atypical tuberculosis

ATBF African tick-bite fever

ATBs antibiotics

ATBX antibiotic(s)

ATC acute toxic class
aerosol treatment chamber
alcoholism therapy classes
all-terrain cycle
anaplastic thyroid carcinoma
antituberculous chemoprophylaxis
around the clock
around-the-clock
Arthritis Treatment Center
Athletic Trainer, Certified

ATCA atherosclerotic-targeting
contrast agent

ATCC American Type Culture Collection

ATCCS acute traumatic central cord
syndrome

ATCh acetylthiocholine

ATCH may have meant ACTH
(adrenocorticotropic hormone)

ATCP amorphous tricalcium phosphate

ATD anthropometric test device
anticipated time of discharge
antithyroid drug(s)
aqueous tear deficiency
asphyxiating thoracic dystrophy
autoimmune thyroid disease

ATDs assistive technology devices

ATE adipose tissue extraction

ATEC Autism Treatment Evaluation
Checklist

AT-EI assistive technology and
environmental interventions

Atel Atelectasis

ATEM analytical transmission electron
microscopy

ATEs arterial thromboembolic events

ATF Alcohol, Tobacco, and Firearms
(Bureau)
anterior talofibular (ligament)
arrive to find

At Fib atrial fibrillation

ATFL anterior talofibular ligament

ATFP arcus tendineus fascia pelvis
(ligament)

AT III FUN antithrombin III functional

AtFx activating transcription factor x;
see gene website www.ncbi
.nlm.nih.gov/gene

ATG antithymocyte globulin

ATH adenotonsillar hypertrophy

athero atherosclerosis

ATHN American Thrombosis and
Hemostasis Network

ATHR angina threshold heart rate

ATI Abdominal Trauma Index
acute traumatic ischemia
angiotensin II type 1

AT III antithrombin III

ATIN acute tubulointerstitial nephritis

ATK above-the-knee
see gene website, www.ncbi
.nlm.nih.gov/gene

ATL Achilles tendon lengthening
adult T-cell leukemia
anterior temporal lobectomy
anterior tricuspid leaflet
antitension line
atypical lymphocytes

ATLA arcus tendineus elevator ani
(ligament)

atlE see gene website www.ncbi.nlm
.nih.gov/gene

ATLF anthrax toxin lethal factor

ATLL adult T-cell leukemia lymphoma

ATLP anterior thoracolumbar locking
(implant) plate

ATLS acute tumor lysis syndrome
advanced trauma life support

ATM acute transverse myelitis
ataxia telangiectasia mutated
(gene)
atmosphere

At ma atrial milliamp

ATME adequate treatment-month
equivalents

ATMs adipose tissue macrophages

ATN acute tubular necrosis
amyloid, tau, and neurode-
generation (biomarkers tied to
prediction of memory decline)

ATNC atraumatic normocephalic

aTNM autopsy staging of cancer

ATNR asymmetrical tonic neck reflex

ATO arsenic trioxide (Trisenox)

ATOD alcohol, tobacco, and other
drug(s)

ATOD-C Alcohol, Tobacco and Other
Drugs, Certified

ATOS	3-dimensional optical scanner
	arterial thoracic outlet syndrome
Atos	an international information technology services company providing an electronic medical records system
ATP	ability to pay
	according-to-protocol
	addiction treatment program
	adenosine triphosphate
	anterior tonsillar pillar
	antitachycardia pacemaker
	antitachycardia pacing
	at his point
	autoimmune thrombocytopenia purpura
ATPA	anterior transpetrosal approach
ATPAP	auto-titrating positive airway pressure
ATP III	Adult Treatment Panel III
ATPase	adenosine triphosphatase
ATPS	ambient temperature & pressure, saturated with water vapor
ATR	Achilles tendon reflex
	anterior temporal lobe resection
	atracurium (Tracrium)
	atrial
	atropine
	attenuated total reflection
AT2R	angiotensin II receptor, type 2 (gene; also known as Tagtr2)
ATRA	all-*trans* retinoic acid (tretinoin-Vesanoid®)
ATRA-ATO	all-*trans* retinoic acid (retinoic acid)-arsenic trioxide (combination therapy)
atr fib	atrial fibrillation
atrial fib	atrial fibrillation
atrial tach	atrial tachycardia
ATRO	atropine
ATRP	atom transfer radical polymerization
ATRT	atypical teratoid/rhabdoid tumor
AT/RT	atypical teratoid/rhabdoid tumor
ATRX	acute transfusion reaction
ATS	Activity Tolerance Scale
	American Thoracic Society (guidelines)
	antimony trisulfide
	antitetanic serum (tetanus antitoxin)
	anxiety tension state
	arthroscopy
	Australasian Triage Scale
ATS1	Andersen-Tawil syndrome see gene website www.ncbi.nlm .nih.gov/gene
ATS-Amod	artesunate/amodiaquine (antimalarial combination)
ATSDR	Agency for Toxic Substances and Disease Registry
ATS/ERS	American Thoracic Society/ European Respiratory Society
ATSI	Aboriginal and Torres Straight Islander
ATSO	admit to (the) service of
ATSO4	atropine sulfate
ATSP	asked to see patient
ATST	atorvastatin (Lipitor)
ATT	alternating triple therapy
	antitetanus toxoid
	arginine tolerance test
	at the time
attestation	A word meaning the act of showing or evidence showing that something is true. A healthcare organization must demonstrate (attestation) meaningful use in order to be eligible for payments from the federal government under either the Medicare or Medicaid Electronic Health Records incentive program.
ATTN	attending
	attention
aTTP	acquired thrombotic thrombocytopenic purpura
ATTP	alpha tocopherol transfer protein (gene)
ATT PHYS	attending physician
ATTR	transthyretin-related amyloidosis
ATTR-CM	transthyretin amyloid cardiomyopathy
ATU	alcohol treatment unit
ATUE	abbreviated therapeutic use exemption
ATUS	American Time Use Survey (US Bureau of Labor Statistics)
ATUs	Authorization for Uses (France)
ATV	all-terrain vehicle
	atazanavir (Reyataz)
at. Wt	atomic weight
ATX	atelectasis
	atomoxetine HCl (Strattera)
atyp	atypical
ATYP	atypical gland suspicious for adenocarcinoma
	atypical glands suspicious for cancer
ATZ	anal transitional zone
AU	allergenic (allergy) units

	arbitrary units
	both ears (each ear). This is a DANGEROUS abbreviation that should NOT be used. It appears on the MedAbbrev and other "Do Not Use List", as it has been read as both eyes (OU) or not understood. Use "both ears."
Au	gold
A/U	at umbilicus
198$_{Au}$	radioactive gold
A.U.	see AU
AUA	average ultrasound age
AUA score	American Urological Association—pertains to benign prostatic hypertrophy symptoms
AUASI	American Urological Association Symptom Index
AUASS	American Urological Association Symptom Score
AUB	abnormal uterine bleeding
AUB-A	abnormal uterine bleeding related to uterine adenomyosis
AUB-C	abnormal uterine bleeding related to coagulopathy
AUB-E	abnormal uterine bleeding related to endometrial causes
AUB/HMB	abnormal uterine bleeding/ heavy menstrual bleeding
AUB/HUB	abnormal uterine bleeding/ heavy uterine bleeding
AUB-I	iatrogenic abnormal uterine bleeding
Aubl.	an abbreviation for the name Jean Baptiste Christophore Fusée Aublet, a French pharmacist, botanist and explorer, is used to indicate this individual as the author when citing a botanical name
AUB-L	leiomyoma-related abnormal uterine bleeding
AUB-LSM	abnormal uterine bleeding caused by (uterine) leiomyomas
AUB-M	abnormal uterine bleeding related to malignancy and hyperplasia
AuBMT	autologous bone marrow transplant
AUB-N	abnormal uterine bleeding not yet classified
AUB-O	abnormal uterine bleeding related to ovulatory dysfunction

AUB-P	abnormal uterine bleeding caused by endometrial polyps
AUC	analytical ultracentrifugation appropriate-use criteria area under the curve
AUCt	area under the curve to last time point
AUD	alcohol use disorder amplifiable units of DNA (deoxyribonucleic acid) arthritis of unknown diagnosis auditory Doctor of Audiology
Au D	Doctor of Audiology
AUD COMP	auditory comprehension
AUD D	Doctor of Audiology
aud hallu	auditory hallucinations
audio	audiological
AUDIT	Alcohol Use Disorders Identification Test
AUDIT-C	Alcohol Use Disorders Identification Test for alcohol consumption
AUEC	area under the effect curve
AUF	undifferentiated fever
AUFs	undifferentiated fevers
AUG	acute ulcerative gingivitis
aug	augmentation
Aug	August
AUG	Augustine; an International Society of Blood Transfusion (ISBT) blood group
AUGIB	acute upper gastrointestinal bleeding
AUGS	American Urogynecologic Society
AUIC	area under the inhibitory curve
AUL	acute undifferentiated leukemia
AUM	ambulatory urodynamic monitoring
AuNPs	gold nanoparticles
AUO	German Association of Urologic Oncology
AUP	alcohol use problems
AuP	gold porphyrin
Au@PDA NPs	polydopamine-coated gold nanoparticles
AUR	acute urinary retention Antimicrobial Use and Resistance
AUROC	area under the receiver operating characteristic curve
AUS	acute urethral syndrome artificial urinary sphincter auscultation
ausc	auscultation
AUSCAN	Australian/ Canadian Osteoarthritis Hand Index

AuSCT	autologous stem cell transplantation
AUS/FLU	atypic of undetermined significance/follicular lesion of undermined significance
AUSS	abdominal uterosacral suspension
AutD	autistic disorder
auth	author authority authorization authorized
AUTO	autologous automatic
auto diff	automated differential count (neutrophils, lymphocytes, monocytes, eosinophils, and basophils)
AutoF	autofluorescence
AutoPap	automated reading of Papanicolaou smears
AutoPAP	automatically titrating positive airway pressure
auto-PEEP	self-performed positive end-expiratory pressure breathing
autoSCT	autologous stem cell transplantation
AUTO SP	automatic speech
AUX	auxillin; see gene website www.ncbi.nlm.nih.gov/gene
AV	acne vulgaris anteverted anticipatory vomiting aortic valve arteriovenous atrioventricular auditory visual auriculoventricular
A:V	arterial-venous (ratio in fundi)
A-V	see AV
AVA	anthrax vaccine, adsorbed aortic valve area aortic valve atresia arteriovenous anastomosis
AVA-EE	aortic valve area epicardial echocardiography
AVAF	anteverted, anteflexed (position)
avail	available
AVAPS	average volume-assured pressure support
AVAT	assessment of the Achilles tendon
AVB	atrioventricular block Aventis Behring
A/V/B	auditory/visual/both
AvBD	avian beta-defensin
AV block	atrioventricular block

AVC	acrylic veneer crown aortic valve calcification atrioventricular conduction
AV canal	atrioventricular canal
AVCD	atrioventricular canal defects atrioventricular conduction dysfunction
AVD	aortic valve disease apparent volume of distribution arteriosclerotic vascular disease atrioventricular delay cerebrovascular accident (French, Spanish)
AV dissociation	atrioventricular dissociation
AVDO$_2$	arteriovenous oxygen difference
AVDP	asparaginase, vincristine, daunorubicin, and prednisone avoirdupois
AVDR	arteriovenous anastomoses from donor to recipient
AVE	aortic valve echocardiogram atrioventricular extrasystole
AVEA	an apparatus that delivers invasive and noninvasive mechanical ventilation for neonatal, pediatric and adult patients
AVED	ataxia with isolated vitamin E deficiency
aver	a word meaning: to affirm positively; declare average
AVF	appendicovesical fistula arteriovenous fistula augmented unipolar foot (left leg)
AV fistula	arteriovenous fistula
AVFRP	atrioventricular node functional refractory periods
AVG	arteriovenous graft
avg	average
AVGE	Aloe vera gel extract
AV graft	arteriovenous graft
AVGs	ambulatory visit groups
AVGS	autogous vein graft stent
AVH	acute viral hepatitis auditory verbal hallucination
AVHB	atrioventricular heart block
AVHS	auditory and visual hallucinations
AVHs	auditory verbal hallucinations
AVI	aortic valve implantation
avid	a word meaning showing great enthusiasm for or interest in
AVIR	aquatic victim-instead-of-rescuer (syndrome) Association of Vascular and Interventional Radiographers

AVIT	anterior vitrectomy
AVJA	atrioventricular junction ablation
AVJR	atrioventricular junctional rhythm
AVK	antivitamin K
AVL	American visceral leishmaniasis
aVL	augmented voltage unipolar left (left arm electrocardiogram lead)
AVLL	apical vertebra lateral listhesis
AVLT	auditory verbal learning test
AVM	arteriovenous malformation
AVMA	American Veterinary Medical Association
AV malformation	arteriovenous malformation
AVMs	arteriovenous malformations
AVN	arteriovenous nicking atrioventricular node avascular necrosis
AVna	atrioventricular nodal artery
AVNA	atrioventricular node ablation
AVNAT	may have meant AVNRT (atrioventricular nodal reentrant tachycardia)
AVNB	atrioventricular nodal block
AVNERP	atrioventricular node effective refractory period
AV nicking	arteriovenous nicking
AV node	atrioventricular node
AVNR	atrioventricular nodal re-entry
AVNRT	atrioventricular nodal reentrant tachycardia
AVO	Aloe vera-olive oil
A-VO$_2$	arteriovenous oxygen difference
AVOC	avocation
AVP	arginine vasopressin atrioventricular pacing Aventis Pasteur
AVPA	arginine vasopressin receptor antagonism
AV pacing	atrioventricular pacing
AVPs	Amplatzer vascular plugs
AVPU	alert, (responds to) verbal (stimuli), (responds to) painful (stimuli), unresponsive (mnemonic used by EMTs to judge patients' level of consciousness)
AVR	aortic valve replacement
aVR	augmented voltage unipolar right (right arm electrocardiogram lead)
AVRC	aortic valve ring calcification
avrD	avirulence D protein; see gene website; see gene website www.ncbi.nlm.nih.gov/gene
AVRNT	may have meant AVNRT (atrioventricular node reentrant tachycardia)
AVRP	atrioventricular refractory period
AVRT	atrioventricular reciprocating tachycardia
AVS	after visit summary aortic valve sclerosis atriovenous shunt
AVSD	atrioventricular septal defect
AV shunt	arteriovenous shunt
AVSS	afebrile, vital signs stable
AVT	arginine vasotocin atrioventricular tachycardia atypical ventricular tachycardia auditory, visual, and tactile (hallucinations)
AVU	arterial virtual unenhanced (radiology)
AV3V	anteroventral third ventricular region
AVV	atrioventricular valve
AV valve	atrioventricle valve
AVVR	atrioventricular valve regurgitation atrioventricular valve replacement
AvWS	acquired von Willebrand's syndrome
AVX	Advanced Vector eXtensions
AW	abdominal wall abdominal wall reconstruction abnormal wave airway associated with
A&W	alive and well
A/W	able to work appearing with associated with
AWA	alcohol withdrawal assessment as well as
aWAT	abdominal white adipose tissue
A waves	atrial contraction wave
AWB	autologous whole blood
AWC	approach with care
AWD	alcohol withdrawal delirium alive with disease
AWDW	assault with a deadly weapon
AWE	acetowhite epithelium
AWHONN	Association of Women's Health, Obstetric and Neonatal Nurses
AWI	anterior wall infarct
AWL	abdominal wall lift actual working length (dental)

AWMF-S3	Arbeitsgemeinschaft der Wissenschaftlichen Medizinischen Fachgesellschaften (Association of the Scientific Medical Societies in Germany), pilonidal sinus guidelines	
AWMI	anterior wall myocardial infarction	
AWO	airway obstruction	
AWOL	absent without leave	
AWP	airway pressure	
	alcohol withdrawal protocol	
	average wholesale price	
AWR	abdominal wall reconstruction	
AWRU	active wrist rotation unit	
AWS	Airway Scope	
	alcohol withdrawal seizures (syndrome)	
	axillary Web Syndrome	
AWSA	Alcohol Withdrawal Severity Assessment (scale)	
AWT	abdominal wall thickness	
	acting without thinking	
	airway wall thickness	
	androgen withdrawal therapy	
	antibiotic wait-time	
	aortic wall thickness	
AWU	alcohol withdrawal unit	
AWV	Annual Wellness Visit	
	aortic wave velocity	
AWW	angioedema without wheals	
	average weekly wage	
AX	anxiety	
	axis	
ax	axillary	
AX1	axial biparietal tradsthalamic view	
Ax1	axillary node, level 1	
AX2	axial biparietal fall view	
	axial biparietal falx view	
Ax2	axillary node, level 2	
Ax3	axillary node, level 3	
aXa	anti-factor Xa (low molecular weight heparin [LMWH] therapy and apixaban are monitored by the anti-factor Xa assay)	
ax-fem,fem.	axilla-femoral-femoral (graft)	
AXB	axillary block	
AX BI FEM	axillo-bifemoral (bypass)	
AXBIFEM	axillo-bifemoral (bypass)	
AXC	aortic cross clamp	
AxD	Alexander disease (a rare neurodegenerative disorder caused by gain of function	

	mutations in the glial fibrillary acidic protein [GFAP] gene;	
ax-fem	axillary-femorall (artery bypass)	
AXFEM	axillofemoral	
AxFG	axillofemoral bypass graft	
AXFR	axillofemoral reconstruction	
AxiaLIF	axial lumbar inter body fusion (the procedure involves implanting a short threaded rod, after the center of the disc is removed from between the last lumbar vertebra and the sacrum)	
axill	axillary	
AXIOS stent	a lumen-apposing self-expandable metallic stent designed for enteric drainage of nonadherent lumens	
AXND	axillary node dissection	
AXO	axotactin; see gene website www.ncbi.nlm.nih.gov/gene	
A×O×3	awake and oriented to person, place, and time	
AXR	abdomen x-ray	
axSpA	axial spondyloarthritis	
AxSYM®	immunodiagnostic testing equipment	
AXT	alternating exotropia	
AY	acrocyanotic (infant color)	
AYA	adolescents and young adults (ages of 15 and 39)	
AYAs	adolescents and young adults (ages of 15 and 39)	
AZ	Arizona	
AZA	azathioprine (Imuran)	
5 AZA-CdR	5-Aza-2′-deoxycitidine (decitabine; Dacogen)	
AZA-CR	azacitidine (Vidaza)	
5-AZC	azacitidine (Vidaza)	
AzdU	azidouridine	
AZE	azelastine hydrochloride (Astelin)	
azithro	azithromycin (Zithromax: Zithromax Z-Pak)	
AZM	acquisition zoom magnification	
	azithromycin (Zithromax; Z-Pak)	
AZOOR	acute zonal occult outer retinopathy	
AZQ	diaziquone	
AZT	zidovudine (azidothymidine; Retrovir)	
A-Z test	Aschheim-Zondek test (diagnostic test for pregnancy)	
α_1AGP	alpha1-acid glycoprotein	

B — bacillus
bands
beta
better
bicep
bilateral
black
bloody
bolus
boron
both
botulism (Vaccine B is botulism toxoid)
Bravo (Phonetic Alphabet for B; pronounced BRAH-VOH)
brother
Brucella (as in *B. abortus*)
buccal
See 'Plan B'

B− — blood type B negative (B negative is preferred)

B+ — blood type B positive (B positive is preferred)

B% — could be 8%

b% — could be 6%

B I — Billroth I (gastric surgery)

B II — Billroth II (gastric surgery)

b/4 — before

B_1 — thiamine HCl

B_{12} — cyanocobalamin

B_{19} — parvovirus B19

B_2 — riboflavin

B_3 — nicotinic acid

B_5 — pantothenic acid

B-52 — Haldol 5 mg and Ativan 2 mg intravenous (slang)

B_6 — pyridoxine HCl

B_7 — biotin

B_8 — adenosine phosphate

B_9 — benign
folic acid

BA — backache
Baker Act (Florida mental health act enabling involuntary commitment)
Baptist
bed alarm
benzyl alcohol
bile acid
biliary atresia
bioavailability
blood agar
blood alcohol
Boehler angel

bone age
Bourns assist
branchial artery
broken appointment
bronchial asthma
buccoaxial
butyric acid

Ba — barium

B > A — bone greater than air

B < A — bone less than air

B&A — before and after
brisk and active

B/A — See BA

BAA — beta-adrenergic agonist

BA-52A — Florida's Baker Act report form required by law enforcement officers for initiating involuntary mental health examination (form 3052a)

BAAM — Beck airway airflow monitor

BAAR — bacilles acido-alcoolo-résistants (acid fast bacilli culture)

Bab — Babinski

BA-52B — Florida's Baker Act report form required by law enforcement officers for initiating involuntary mental health examination (form 3052b)

BABA — bilateral axillo-breast approach (robotic thyroidectomy)

BAC — Bacterial Artificial Chromosome
benzalkonium chloride
blood-alcohol concentration
breast arterial calcification
bronchioloalveolar carcinoma
buccoaxiocervical

BACCA — basal cell cancer

BACE — beta-site APP (amyloid precursor protein)-cleaving enzyme

BACE1 — beta-site APP (amyloid precursor protein)-cleving enzyme 1 (beta secretase)

BACI — bovine anti-cryptosporidium immunoglobulin

BACM — blocking agent corticosteroid myopathy

BACON — bleomycin, doxorubicin, lomustine, vincristine, and mechlorethamine

BACOP — bleomycin, Adriamycin®, cyclophosphamide, vincristine, and prednisone

BACPAC — Bulk Activities Post Approval Change

BACs — bacterial artificial chromosomes

BACT — bacteria
base-activated clotting time

BAD	Benadryl, Ativan, and Decadron	BaM	barium meal
	bipolar affective disorder	BAMC	Brooke Army Medical Center
	blunt aortic disruption	BA-MDIs	breath-actuated metered-dose
BADL	basic activities of daily living		inhalers
BADS	Behavioral Assessment of the	BAMP	bone anchored maxillary
	Dysexecutive Syndrome		protraction
BAE	bronchial artery embolization	BAMS	bioaerosol mass spectrometry
BaE	barium enema	BAN	breath activated nebulizer
BaEAC	barium enema with air contrast		British Approved Name
BAEDP	balloon aortic end diastolic	Banana Bag	a yellow colored intravenous
	pressure		infusion containing a multi-
BAEP	brain stem auditory evoked		vitamin product, folic acid,
	potential		thiamine hydrochloride, and
BAER	brainstem auditory evoked		possibly magnesium sulfate in
	responses		5% dextrose or 0.9% sodium
BAERs	brain stem auditory evoked		chloride. Contents vary from
	responses		hospital to hospital. Used for
BaEV	baboon endogenous virus		alcohol patients. (slang)
BAFF	B cell activated factor	BAND	band neutrophil (stab)
BAFF-R	B-cell-activating factor receptor	B and O	belladonna and opium
BAG	buccoaxiogingival		(suppositories)
BAHA	bone-anchored hearing aids	B and P	binge and purge
BAHS	bone-anchored hearing system(s)	bands	band cells are also called band
BAI	blunt abdominal injury		neutrophils and stab cells.
	brachial-ankle index		A count of band neutrophils
	breath-actuated inhalers		is used as a measure of
	Brief Assessment Interview		inflammation
BAIDS	Joint Biological Agent	Banff	a classification system for renal
	Identification and Diagnostic		allograft rejection
	System	BANS	back, arm, neck and scalp
BAIQ	below average intelligence	BAO	basal acid output
	quotient		basilar artery occlusion
BAK cage	Bagby and Kuslich cage (an	BAOM	bilateral acute otitis media
	interbody fusion system used	BAP	balloon angioplasty
	to stabilize the spine)		blood agar plate
BAL	balance	BAP1	BRCA1 (breast cancer gene 1)
	blood-alcohol level		associated protein 1
	British antilewisite	BAPE	benign asbestos pleural effusion
	(dimercaprol)	BAPS	balance activation proprioceptive
	bronchoalveolar lavage		system
BALB	binaural alternate loudness		biomechanical ankle platform
	balance		system
BAL DIL	balloon dilation	BAPT	Baptist
Baldor hybrid	a hybrid Cannabis product with	baPWV	brachial-ankle pulse wave
	a high THC (tetrahydrocan-		velocity
	nabinol) content (content	BAR	Bernese ankle rule
	ratio 60:1,THC to CBD		biofragmentable anastomotic
	(cannabidiol) which clinically		ring
	gives this product high	Barb	barbiturate
	psychoactive effects	Barc	Barcelona
BALF	bronchoalveolar lavage fluid	BARC	Bleeding Academic Research
B-ALL	B cell acute lymphoblastic		Consortium (which
	leukemia		standardized key ischemic
BALP	bone alkaline phosphatase		endpoint definitions such as
BALT	bronchus-associated lymphoid		stent thrombosis for studies
	tissue		aimed at evaluating coronary
BAM	bony acetabular morphology		stents and other bleeding
	Brain Acoustical Monitor		complications)

BARDA | Biomedical Advanced Research and Development Authority (U.S. Department of Health and Human Services)

BARD score | Used to predict advanced fibrosis in nonalcoholic liver disease (body mass index, aspartate transaminase/alanine aminotransferase ratio, and diabetes mellitus)

BARI 2D | Bypass Angioplasty Revascularization Investigation 2 Diabetes Trial

BARN | bilateral acute retinal necrosis

BAROS | Bariatric Analysis and Reporting Outcome System

Barrx™ | a radiofrequency energy generator to control depth and uniformity of tissue ablation in the gastrointestinal tract

// bars | parallel bars

BAR Troche | Benadryl, Ativan, and Reglan troche

Barts | Saint Bartholomew's Hospital (London, United Kingdom)

BAS | balloon atrial septostomy
Barnes Akathisia Scale
behavioral activation system
bile acid sequestrants
boric acid solution
boric acid suppositories
bronchial asthma (in) status

BaS | barium swallow

BAs | bile acids

BASA | baby aspirin (81 mg chewable tablets of aspirin)

BASC | Behavior Assessment System for Children

BASDAI | Bath Ankylosing Spondylitis Disease Activity Index

basic metabolic panel | go to Tables and Lists Button; see Laboratory Panels, Chapter 6

BASIL | Bypass versus Angioplasty in Severe Ischaemia of the Leg (trial)

BASIS | Basic Achievement Skills Individual Screener

BASK | basket cells

BASMI | Bath Ankylosing Spondylitis Metrology Index

baso. | basophil

BASOs | basophilic granulocytes

BASOSTIP | basophilic stippling

BASRI | Bath Ankylosing Spondylitis Radiology Index

BaSw | barium swallow

Ba swallow | barium swallow

BAT | baroreflex activation therapy
basophil activation test
Behavioral Avoidance Test
best available therapy
blunt abdominal trauma
borreliacidal-antibody test
Brain Attack Team
brightness acuity tester

BATF | Bureau of Alcohol, Tobacco and Firearms

BATO | boronic acid adduct of technetium oxime

batt | battery

BAU | bioequivalent allergy units

BAUS | British Association of Urological Surgeons

BAV | bicuspid aortic valve

BAVMs | brain arteriovenous malformations

BAVP | balloon aortic valvuloplasty

BAVR | bioprosthetic aortic valve replacement

BAW | bronchoalveolar washing

BAX | B-cell leukemia/lymphoma 2-associated X protein; see gene website www.ncbi.nlm.nih.gov/gene

BB | baby boy
back to back
backboard
bad breath
bed bath
bed board
beta blocker(s) [acebutolol (Sectral), tenolol (Tenormin), betaxolol (Kerlone), betaxolol (Betoptic S), bisoprolol fumarate (Zebeta), acebutolol (Sectral), atenolol (Tenormin), carvedilol (Coreg), esmolol (Brevibloc)]
bilateral breast
blanket bath
blood bank
blow bottle
blue bloaters
body belts
both bones
breakthrough bleeding
breast biopsy
bronchial brushing
brush biopsy
buffer base
bulging bag (amniotic sac is found to be protruding from the cervix during a pelvic or speculum examination)

B × B | back-to-back

B&B	bismuth and bourbon
	bowel and bladder
	Box and Block (test for manual dexterity of upper extremity function)
B/B	backward bending
	bowel and bladder
B1B	beta-1 selective blocker(s) [a subclass of beta blockers that are commonly used to treat high blood pressure. Drugs in this class include atenolol (Tenormin), metoprolol (Lopressor), nebivolol (Bystolic) and bisoprolol (Zebeta, Monocor)]
B2B	beta-2 selective blocker(s)
	business-to-business
BB3	Basic Blue 3
	bombesin-like receptor 3 (gene/protein)
BBA	born before arrival
BBAS	blade and balloon atrial septostomy
BBAVF	brachiobasilic arteriovenous fistula
BBB	baseball bat beating
	blood-brain barrier
	bundle branch block
BBBB	bilateral bundle branch block
BBBD	blood-brain barrier disruption
BBBP	blood-brain barrier permeability
BBBx	bilateral breast biopsy
BBC	basal-bolus plus correction-insulin dose regimen
	bilateral breast cancer
	bilirubin binding capacity
	Brown-Buerger cystoscope
BBCS	bumps, bruises, cuts and scrapes (i.e. no serious injuries) (slang)
BBD	baby born dead
	before bronchodilator
	benign breast disease
BBE	biofield breast examination
	bleed base excess
BBF	bladder blood flow
	blood and body fluids
BBFA	both bones forearm
BBFF	both bone forearm fracture
BBFP	blood and body fluid precautions
BBG	brilliant blue G (stain)
BBH7	Block-Bonilla-Hansen 7 (culture media)
BBH	blood-bank hold
BBI	basal-bolus insulin (regimen)
	Bowman Birk inhibitor
BBIC	Bowman Birk inhibitor concentrate

BBKA	bilateral below-knee amputation
BBL	bottle blood loss
BBlocker	beta blocker(s) [acebutolol (Sectral), tenolol (Tenormin), betaxolol (Kerlone), betaxolol (Betoptic S), bisoprolol fumarate (Zebeta), acebutolol (Sectral), atenolol (Tenormin), carvedilol (Coreg), esmolol (Brevibloc)]
b-blocker	beta-adrenergic blocking agents (e.g. metoprolol, Timolol, Nadolol, etc.)
BBM	banked breast milk
BBO2	blow-by (passive delivery) oxygen
BBOW	bulging bag of water
BBP	blood-borne pathogen
	butyl benzyl phthalate
BBPE	bloodborne pathogen exposure
BBPR	bcl-2-bax protein ratio
BBPS	Boston Bowel Preparation Scale
BBPV	see BPPV (benign paroxysmal positional vertigo)
BBR	bibasilar rales
BBRA	Balanced Budget Refinement Act of 1999, USA
B2B-RMC	beat-to-beat respiratory-motion-correction
BBS	Bardet-Biedl syndrome
	benign biliary strictures
	Berg Balance Scale
	bilateral breath sounds
BBSC	Benefit and Burden Scale for Children
	bone-to-bone substitute contact
BBSE	bilateral breath sounds equal
BBSI	Brigance Basic Skills Inventory
BBT	baby's blood type
	basal body temperature
	Buteyko breathing technique
BB to MM	belly button to medial malleolus
BBVP	may have meant BPPV (benign paroxysmal positional vertigo)
BBW	black box warning (Food and Drug Administration)
B Bx	breast biopsy
BC	back care
	base curve
	basket catheter
	battered child
	bed and chair
	beta carotene
	bicycle
	birth control
	bladder cancer
	Blatt capsulodesis
	blood culture
	Blue Cross

bone conduction
Bourn control
breast cancer
buccocervical
buffalo cap (cap for intravenous line)
B/C   because
B&C   biopsy and curettage
            board and care
            breathed and cried
BCA   balloon catheter angioplasty
            basal cell atypia
            bichloracetic acid
            bicinchoninic acid
            bowel cleansing agent
            brachiocephalic artery
BCa   bladder cancer, breast cancer, bone cancer (this is a dangerous abbreviation)
BCAA   branched-chain amino acids
BC > AC   bone conduction greater than air conduction
BC < AC   bone conduction less than air conduction
BCACP   Board Certified Ambulatory Care Pharmacist
bCAM   Brief Confusion Assessment Method
BCAO   bilateral carotid artery occlusion
B. cat   *Branhamella catarrhalis*
B-CAVe   bleomycin, lomustine (CCNU), doxorubicin (Adriamycin), and vinblastine (Velban)
BCAVF   brachiocephalic arteriovenous fistula
BCB   Brilliant cresyl blue (stain)
BCBA   Board Certified Behavior Analyst
BCBR   bilateral carotid body resection
BCBS   Blue Cross Blue Shield
BCBs   blood culture bottles
BCC   basal cell carcinoma
            birth control clinic
            Burkholderia cepacia complex (a group of Gram-negative, rod-shaped
BCCa   basal cell carcinoma
BCCs   basal cell carcinomas
BCD   basal cell dysplasia
            Board Certified Diplomate in Clinical Social Work
            borderline of cardial dullness
BCd   cadmium blood levels
BCDCSW   bleomycin, cyclophosphamide, and dactinomycin
BCDH   bilateral congenital dislocated hip
BCE   basal cell epithelioma
            beneficial clinical event
            bilateral cervical exploration

BceA   bacitracin export ABC transporter ATP-binding protein; see gene website www.ncbi.nlm.nih.gov/gene
BCEA   bivariate contour ellipse area
BCEDP   breast cancer early detection program
B cell   B lymphocyte
B cells   a lymphocyte of a type produced in the Bone marrow (hence the name) and actively participating in the immune response
BCES   bilateral chest, external surface
BCETS   Board Certified Expert in Traumatic Stress
BCF   basic conditioning factor
            Baylor core formula
            branchial cleft fistula
BCFA   branched chain fatty acids
BCG   bacille Calmette-Guérin vaccine
            ballistocardiogram
            bicolor guaiac
BCGT   Brucella Coombs gel test (veterinary)
BCH   benign cephalic histiocytosis
            benign coital headache
BCHA   bone-conduction hearing aid
BCHD   bone conduction hearing device
BChE   butyrylcholinesterase
BCI   blunt carotid injury
            brain-computer interface
BCID   breast cancer at initial diagnosis
            FilmArray® Blood Culture Identification panel is a multiplex polymerase chain reaction–based rapid diagnostic test that can detect 24 sepsis-related pathogens (bacteria and yeast) and three antimicrobial resistance genes in patients with suspected sepsis
BCID-FP   Blood Culture Identification panel, Fungal Pathogen
BCIDO   bacterial clinical infectious diseases ontology
BCIE   bullous congenital ichthyosiform erythroderma
BCIR   Barnett continent intestinal reservoir
BCIS   Beck Cognitive Insight Scale
BCIs   brain-computer interfaces
BCIS-JS   British Cardiovascular Intervention Society myocardial jeopardy score
BCL   basic cycle length
            bio-chemoluminescence

Bcl2	B cell leukemia/lymphoma 2	BCPS	Board Certified Pharmacotherapy Specialist
BCL2	B cell leukemia/lymphoma 2 (gene/protein)	BCPT	Board Certified Pharmacotherapy
	(B-cell chronic lymphocytic leukemia/lymphoma) apoptosis regulator	BCQ	breast central quadrantectomy
		BCR	bicaudate ratio
Bcl-2	B-cell chronic lymphocytic leukemia/lymphoma (gene)		blood urea nitrogen/creatinine ratio
			breakpoint cluster region (gene)
BCL6	B-cell CLL/lymphoma 6 (gene/ protein)		bulbocavernosus reflex
		BCR-ABL	fusion transcripts; see gene website www.ncbi.nlm.nih .gov/gene
B/C/L	BUN,(blood urea nitrogen), creatinine, lytes (electrolytes)		
BCLC	Barcelona Clinic Liver Cancer (staging)	BCR/ABL	fusion transcripts; see gene website, www.ncbi.nlm.nih .gov/gene
BCLL	B-cell chronic lymphocytic leukemia	B/C ratio	blood urea nitrogen/creatinine ratio
BCLP	bilateral cleft lip and palate		
BCLS	basic cardiac life support	BCRC	Benefits Coordination and Recovery Center (Medicare)
BCM	below costal margin		
	birth control medication	BCRE	black cohosh root extract
	birth control method	BCRL	breast cancer-related lymphedema
	body cell mass		
BCMA	B cell maturation antigen	BCRP	breast cancer resistance protein
	bar-code medication administration	BCRS	Brief Cognitive Rate Scale
		BCRT	breast conservation followed by radiation therapy
BCME	bis (chloromethyl) ether		
BCMH	Bureau for Children with Medical Handicaps	BCS	battered child syndrome
			Biopharmaceutical Classification System (mechanistic frame-work for understanding the concept of drug absorption in terms of permeability and solubility)
BCNP	Board Certified Nuclear Pharmacist		
BCNSP	Board Certified Nutrition Support Pharmacist		
BCNU	bacteria-controlled nursing unit		
	carmustine (BiCNU; Gliadel)		body contouring surgery
BCOC	bowel care of choice		breast-conserving surgery
	bowel cathartic of choice		Budd-Chiari syndrome
BCON study	bladder (cancer) carbogen and nicotinamide (study)	BCSC	breast cancer stem cells
			Breast Cancer Surveillance Consortium (National Institutes of Health; National Cancer Institute)
BCOP	Board Certified Oncology Pharmacist		
BCOR	BCL (B-cell lymphoma 6) corepressor (gene)		
		BCSF	bone cell stimulating factor
BCP	beta-caryophyllene	BCSH	British Committee for Standards in Hematology (guidelines)
	biochemical profile		
	birth control pills	BCSS	Board Certified Sleep Specialist
	blood cell profile		bone cell stimulating substance
	carmustine (BiCNU), cyclo-phosphamide, and prednisone	BCT	Bag Carrying Test
			bladder core temperature
BCPAP	Broun continuous positive airway pressure		blunt cardiac trauma
			brachiocephalic trunk
bCPAP	bubble continuous positive airway pressure		breast-conserving therapy
			broad complex tachycardias
BCPNN	Bayesian Confidence Propogation Neural Network	betA	see gene website www.ncbi.nlm .nih.gov/gene
BCPP	Board Certified Psychiatric Pharmacist	BCTP	bi-component triton tri-n-butyl phosphate
B-CPR	bystander cardiopulmonary resuscitation	BCTQ	Boston Carpal Tunnel Questionnaire

BCTSQ	Boston Carpal Tunnel Syndrome Questionnaire (score)	BDF	bilateral distal femoral
			black divorced female
BCU	burn care unit	BDG	beta D-glucam
BCUG	bilateral cystourethrogram		bidirectional Glenn (a surgical
BCV	brachiocephalic vein		procedure, part of the
BCVA	best-corrected visual acuity		single-ventricle palliation
BCVIs	blunt cerebrovascular injuries		pathway)
BCVPP	carmustine (BCNU),	BDH	bacterial dermohypodermitis
	cyclophosphamide,		Bochdalek diaphragmatic hernia
	vinblastine, procarbazine,	BDI	Beck Depression Inventory
	and prednisone		bile duct incision
BCVPP-Bleo	carmustine (BCNU),		bile duct injury
	cyclophosphamide,	BD-IPMN	branch duct intraductal papillary
	vinblastine, procarbazine,		mucinous neoplasm
	prednisone, and bleomycin	BDI SF	Becks Depression Inventory-Short
BCW	blue-collar workers		Form
BCX	blood culture	BDK	BCKDH (branched-chain
BCXs	blood cultures		alpha-keto acid dehydrogenase)
BD	1,4-butanediol		kinase
	band neutrophil		febrile infection-related epilepsy
	base deficit		syndrome
	base down	BDL	below detectable limits
	behavior disorder		bile duct ligation
	Behçet disease	B-DLCL	diffuse large B-cell lymphoma
	bile duct	BDM	black divorced male
	biotinidase deficiency	bDMARD	biological disease modifying
	bipolar disorder(s)		antirheumatic drug
	birth date	BDNF	brain-derived neurotrophic
	birth defect		factor
	blood donor	BDOD	brain-dead organ donor
	bortezomib and dexamethasone	BDOPA	bleomycin, dacarbazine,
	Bowen disease		vincristine (oncovin®),
	brain dead		prednisone, and doxorubicin
	Breslow depth		(Adriamycin)
	bronchial drainage	BDP	beclomethasone dipropionate
	bronchodilator		(Beconase AQ; QVAR)
	buccodistal		best demonstrated practice
	Buerger disease	BDR	background diabetic retinopathy
	United Kingdom abbreviation		bile duct resection
	for twice a day		black-dot ringworm
B&D	bathing and dressing		bortezomib, dexamethasone,
B-D	Becton Dickinson and Company		and rituximab
B/D	see BD		bronchodilator response
BDA	bile duct adenoma		bulk dose regimen
BDAE	Boston Diagnostic Aphasia Examination	BDRL	may have meant VDRL (Venereal Disease Research Laboratory); a blood test
BDAS	balloon dilation atrial septostomy	BDS	bile duct stone(s)
BDBS	Bonnet-Dechaume-Blanc syndrome	BDSM	Bondage and discipline, Dominance and submission, and Sadism and masochism
BDC	Blatt dorsal capsulodesis		
	burn-dressing change	BDT	benzodithiophene
BDCM	bromodichloromethane		bronchodilator tests
BDD	body dysmorphic disorder	BDUMP	bilateral diffuse uveal
	bronchodilator drugs		melanocytic proliferation
BDE	bile duct exploration	BDUs	battle dress uniforms
	bone density examination	BDV	Borna disease virus
	boron dose enhancer	BDZ	benzodiazepine

BDZs	benzodiazepines
BE	bacterial endocarditis
	balance exercise
	barium enema
	Barrett esophagus
	base excess
	below elbow
	binge eating
	bioequivalence
	bread equivalent
	breast examination
Be	beryllium
B↓E	both lower extremities
B↑E	both upper extremities
B & E	brisk and equal
BEA	below-elbow amputation
BEAC	carmustine (BiCNU), etoposide, cytarabine (ara-C), and cyclophosphamide
BEACH	Bettering the Evaluation And Care of Health (nationally representative survey of randomly sampled family Australian physicians' activities)
BEACOPP	bleomycin, etoposide, doxorubicin (Adriamycin), cyclophosphamide, vincristine (Oncovin), procarbazine, and prednisone
BEAM	brain electrical activity mapping carmustine BCNU), etoposide, cytarabine (ara-C), and methotrexate
BEAMing	Beads, Emulsion, Amplification, and Magnetics (an ultrasensitive mutation-detection assay)
BEAR	Bourn electronic adult respirator
BEB	benign essential blepharospasm blepharospasm
BEC	bacterial endocarditis
BECS	balloon-expandable covered stent
BECs	bronchial epithelial cells
BECT	barium enema computed tomography
BECTS	benign epilepsy with central-temporal spikes
BED	binge-eating disorder biochemical evidence of disease biological effective dose biological equivalent dose
BEE	basal energy expenditure
BEecf	base excess in the extracellular fluid
BEEP	bevacizumab combined with etoposide and cisplatin

Beers Criteria	For the geriatric population, an explicit criteria identifies high-risk drugs using a list of potentially inappropriate medications that have been identified as having an unfavorable balance of risks and benefits by themselves and considering alternative treatments available
BEF	bronchoesophageal fistula
before	has been expressed as b/4, ante, a., and the letter A with a line above; all of which may not be understood
BEGA	best estimate of gestational age
BEH	behavior benign essential hypertension
behav	behavioral
Beh Sp	behavior specialist
BEI	backscattered electron images bioelectric impedance butanol-extractable iodine
BEL	blood ethanol level
Bela	belatacept (Nulojix)
BEM	Boundary Element Method
BEN	nephropathy
Bentall procedure	cardiac surgery to treat combined aortic valve and ascending aorta disease such as Marfan syndrome, involving composite graft replacement of the aortic valve, aortic root and ascending aorta, with re-implantation of the coronary arteries into the graft
BENZO	an organic chemical structural unit benzocaine
Benzos	benzodiazepines (such as diazepam [Valium], chlordiaz-epoxide [Librium], etc.,)
Benzo(s)	medications such as Xanax and Valium (benzodiazepines) primarily used for treatment of anxiety
BEO	best eye opening *Brucella epididymoorchitis*
BEP	bleomycin, etoposide, and cisplatin (Platinol) brain stem evoked potentials
BE-PEG	balanced electrolyte with polyethylene glycol
BER	basic electrical rhythm benign early repolarization Biological and Environmental Research (Department of Energy)

BERAM	boomerang-shaped extended rectus abdomens myocutaneous (flap)	BFCC-QIO	Beneficiary and Family Centered Care Quality Improvement Organization (Medicare)
BERD	bidirectional error diffusion		
	biostatistics, epidemiology, and research design	BFCNs	basal forebrain cholinergic neurons
	Birth Events Records Database	BFD	blackfoot disease
BERT	background equivalent radiation time	BFEC	benign focal epilepsy of childhood
BES	benign esophageal stricture	BFED	benign focal epileptiform discharges
	biolimus-eluting stent		binding free-energy decomposition
BEs	Biomonitoring Equivalents		
BeS	beryllium sensitization	BFEDC	benign focal epileptiform discharges
BESR	back-end speech recognition		
	back-end speech recognition	BFF	bacteria-free filtrate
BESS	Balance Error Scoring System		bilateral femur fracture
	bilateral endoscopic sinus surgery	bFGF	basic fibroblast growth factor
		BFI	Brief Fatigue Inventory
	biportal endoscopic spinal surgery	BFIE	benign familial infantile epilepsy
BEST	bio-electrical stimulation therapy	BFL	breast firm and lactating
BeST	Behavioral Shaping Therapy (program)	B-FLY	butterfly
BESTest	Balance Evaluation Systems Test	BFM	Berlin-Frankfurt-Munster (cancer study group)
beta-hCG	beta-human chorionic gonadotropin		black married female
			body fat mass
beta-OHB	beta-hydroxybutyrate		bright field microscope
BEV	beams-eye view	BFMDRS	Burke-Fahn-Marsden Dystonia Rating Scale
	bevacizumab (Avastin)		
	billion electron volts	BFNC	benign familial neonatal convulsions
	bleeding esophageal varices		
bev	beverage	BFO	Bismuth Ferric Oxide (BiFeO3)
BF	barefoot		blood flow oscillations
	biceps femoris	BFP	biologic false positive
	biofeedback		blue fluorescent protein
	black female		body fat percentage
	bone fragment	BFR	Backward Functional Reach (test)
	boyfriend		
	breakfast fed		blood filtration rate
	breast-fed		blood flow rate
	breastfeeding		body fat ratio
B & F	back and forth	B. frag	*Bacillus fragilis*
B/F	bound-to-free ratio	BF's	breastfeeds
	boyfriend	BFT	bentonite flocculation test
%BF	percentage of body fat		biofeedback training
BFA	baby for adoption	BFU$_e$	erythroid burst-forming unit
	basilic forearm	BFW	body fat weight
	bifemoral arteriogram	BG	baby girl
BfArM	German Federal Institute for Drugs and Medical Devices		basal ganglia
			blood glucose
BFAST	Blat-like Fast Accurate Search Tool (facilitates the fast and accurate mapping of short reads to Genome reference sequences)		bone graft
		B-G	Bender-Gestalt (test)
		B/G	see BG
		BG-12	dimethyl fumarate (Tecfidera)
B-fast	breakfast	BGA	Bundesgesundheitsamt (German drug regulatory agency)
BFB	biofeedback		
BFC	benign febrile convulsion	B-GALACTO	beta galactosidase

BGB	belowground biomass	BHC	Behavioral Health Care
	blood-gas barrier		benzene hexachloride
	Bürgerliches Gesetzbuch		Braxton Hicks contractions
	(German: Code of Civil Law)	B-HCC	hepatitis B-related hepatocellular
BGC	balloon guide catheter		carcinoma
	basal-ganglion calcification	bHCG	beta human chorionic
BGCS	British Gynaecological Cancer		gonadotropin
	Society	BHCN	Behavioral Health Care Network
BGCs	balloon guide catheters	BHD	Birt-Hogg-Dubé (syndrome: a
	biosynthetic gene clusters		rare hereditary autosomal
BGCT	benign glandular cell tumor		dominant condition charac-
BGDC	Bartholin gland duct cyst		terized by benign cutaneous
BGDR	background diabetic retinopathy		lesions, lung cysts, increased
BGF	blood glucose fluctuations		risk of spontaneous pneumo-
BGG	barium gallogermanate (glass)		thorax and renal cancer)
	Biomedical Genetics and		carmustine, hydroxyurea, and
	Genomics (Journal)		dacarbazine
	bovine gamma globulin	BHDS	Birt-Hogg-Dubé syndrome
	The German federal law of		(a rare hereditary autosomal
	equal treatment of disabled		dominant condition charac-
	persons (Behindertengleich-		terized by benign cutaneous
	stellungsgesetz des Bundes)		lesions, lung cysts, increased
bGG	biopsy Gleason grade		risk of spontaneous pneumo-
BGHT	glucose breath hydrogen testing		thorax and renal cancer)
BGI	Baerveldt glaucoma	B-HEXOS-	beta hexosaminidase A
	implantation	A-LK	leukocytes
BG-ICH	basal ganglia intracerebral	BHF	British Heart Foundation
	hemorrhage	BHGI	The Breast Health Global
BGK	Bhatnagar-Gross-Krook		Initiative
	(equation)	BHH	behavioral health home
BGL	blood glucose level	BHI	biosynthetic human insulin
BGlu	blood glucose		brain-heart infusion
BGM	blood glucose monitoring	BHL	bilateral hilar lymphadenopathy
bGS	biopsy Gleason score	BHLHS	borderline hypoplastic left heart
BGSU	bisexual, gay, straight, undecided		structures
BGT	Bender-Gestalt test	BHMCO	behavioral health managed care
	blood glucose testing		organization
BGTT	borderline glucose tolerance test	BHN	bridging hepatic necrosis
BGUS	biclonal gammopathies of	BHO	bilateral hip osteoarthritis
	undetermined significance	BHOB	beta-hydroxybutyrate
BGV	bleeding gastric varies	BHP	Basic Health Program
BH	behavioral health		(Affordable Care Act)
	bowel habits		boarding home placement
	Braxton Hicks (contractions)		British Herbal Pharmacopeia
	breath holding	BHR	Birmingham hip resurfacing
Bh	bohrium		bronchial hyperresponsiveness
BH1	BCL-2 (B-cell lymphoma	BHRT	bioidentical-hormone
	protein 2) homology 1		replacement therapy
BH2	BCL-2 (B-cell lymphoma	BHS	Beck Hopelessness Scale
	protein 2) homology 2		Behavioral Health Services
BH3	BCL-2 (B-cell lymphoma		beta-hemolytic streptococci
	protein 2) homology 3		breath-holding spell
BH4	tetrahydrobiopterin	BHT	behavioral health technician
BHA	butylated hydroxyanisole		borderline hypertensive
BHB	beta-hydroxybutyrate		breath hydrogen test
BHBA	beta hydroxybutyric acid		butylated hydroxytoluene
BHBC	bicyclist hit by car	BHU	basic health unit
BHBT	beta-hydroxybutyrate		behavioral health unit

BHV-1	bovine herpesvirus type 1	BIDMC	Beth Israel Deaconess Medical Center (Boston MA)
BHVI	blunt hollow viscus injury		
BHWU	Bair Hugger warming unit	BIDPC	twice daily, after meals
BI	Barthel Index	BIDS	bedtime insulin, daytime sulfonylurea
	base in		
	blader irrigation	BIDT	Brain Injury Day Treatment
	Blair incision	BIDWM	twice daily, with meals
	bleeding index (dental)	BIE	bullous ichthyosiform erythroderma
	body image		
	Boehringer Ingelheim Pharmaceuticals, Inc.	BIEST	a combination of two estrogens; estriol (E-3), and estradiol (E-2)
	bowel impaction		
	brain injury	BIF	bifocal
Bi	bismuth	BiFC	bimolecular fluorescence complementation (assay)
B/I	see BI		
BIA	bioelectrical impedance analysis	BIFEM	bifemoral bypass
	biospecific interaction analysis	bIFIs	breakthrough invasive fungal infections
BIAP	bovine intestinal alkaline phosphatase		
		BIG	botulism immune globulin
BIB	brought in by		Breast International Group
BIB®	BioEnterics® Intragastric Balloon	BIGEM	bigeminal
		BIG-IV	botulism immune globulin intraveneous (human)
BIBA	brought in by ambulance		
BIBEMS	brought in by emergency medical services	BIH	benign intracranial hypertension
			bilateral inguinal hernia
BIBF	product of Boehringer Ingelheim GmbH, such a BIBF 1120 (nintedanib [Ofev])	BIID	body integrity identity disorder
		BIISS	behaviourally-induced inadequate sleep syndrome
BiBi	bilateral hearing aids	BIL	bilateral
BIBLE	brought in by law enforcement		brother-in-law
BIBM	Bioinformatics and Biomedicine	BILAT	bilateral
	brought in by medics	BILAT SLC	bilateral short leg case
BIBP	biliointestinal bypass	BILAT SXO	bilateral salpingo-oophorectomy
	brachial intra-arterial blood pressure	Bili	bilirubin
		BILI-C	conjugated bilirubin
BIC	bone-to-implant contact	BIL MRY	bilateral myringotomy
	brain injury center	BILT	total bilirubin
BICAP	bipolar electrocoagulation therapy	BIMA	bilateral internal mammary arteries
Bicarb	bicarbonate	bimal	bimalleolar
BiCNU®	carmustine	BIMS	Brief Interview for Mental Status
BICR	blinded independent central review	BIMs	bacteriophage-immune mutant (bacteria)
BICROS	bilateral contralateral routing of signals	BIN	twice a night (this is a dangerous abbreviation)
BICU	burn intensive care unit		
BID	body image dissatisfaction	BIND	Biological Investigational New Drug
	brought in dead		
	twice daily (twice a day)	BIO	binocular indirect ophthalmoscopy
	two times a day		
b.i.d.	twice a day (BID is preferred as in some cases there is a character limitation where computer orders are to be entered)	BIOF	biofeedback
		BIOM	biomechanical
		BiomHED	biomimetic hand exotendon device
		BIOP	biological optimization
BIDAC	twice daily, before meals	bIOP	biomechanical-compensated intraocular pressure
BIDBS	twice daily blood sugar (glucose)		
BIDCC	twice daily with meals	biops	biopsy

BiOX	bismuth oxyhalide	BITA	bilateral internal thoracic artery
BIP	bleomycin, ifosfamide, and cisplatin (Platinol)	BITC	benzyl isothiocyanate
	bleomycin-induced pneumonitis	BITE	Bulimic Investigatory Test, Edinburgh (a self-rating scale for bulimia)
	brain injury program		
BIPA	Benefits Improvement and Protection Act	BiTE	bi-specific T-cell engager
	Program Benefits Improvement and Protection Act of 2000, USA	BITS	Bioness Integrated Therapy System
		BIV	bovine immunodeficiency virus
		BiV	biventricular
BiPAP	bilevel (biphasic) positive airway pressure	Bi-V	biventricular (pacing)
		BiVAD	biventricular assist device
BiPAP-S	bilevel positive airway pressure-spontaneous	BIVAL	bivalirudin (Angiomax)
		BiVent	Airway pressure release ventilation (AVRV)
BiPAP ST	bilevel positive airway pressure-spontaneous/timed	bivent	biventricular
BiPD	biparietal diameter	bivent/ICD	biventricular/implantable cardioverter-defibrillator
BIPLEDs	bilateral independent periodic lateralized epileptiform discharges	BiVICD	biventricular implantable cardioverter defibrillator
BIPP	bismuth iodoform paraffin paste	BiVP	biventricular pacing
BIPQ	Brief Illness Perception Questionnaire	Biv pacemaker	biventricular pacemaker
		BiVPM	biventricular pacemaker
BIPS	Bowel Injury Prediction Score	BiVPPM	biventricular permanent pacemaker
BIR	back internal rotation		
BIRADS	Breast Imaging Reporting and Data System (0 = incomplete, 1 = negative, 2 = benign findings, 3 = probably benign, 4 = suspicious abnormality, 5 = highly suspicious of malignancy, and 6 = known biopsy with proven malignancy)	BIW	twice a week (This is a dangerous abbreviation. It is best to spell it out.)
		BIX	biological index
		BIZ-PLT	bizarre platelets
		BJ	Bence Jones (protein)
			biceps jerk
			body jacket
			bone and joint
BI-RADS	Breast Imaging Reporting and Data System (American College of Radiology)	Björk-Shilley	a mitral valve prosthesis
		BJD	bovine Johne disease
			British Journal of Dermatology
BIRADS2	Breast Imaging Reporting and Data System, benign findings (see BIRADS)	BJE	bone and joint examination
			bones, joints, and extremities
BIRB	Biomedical Institutional Review Board	BJHS	benign joint hypermobility syndrome
BI-RFG	relative functional gain of the Barthel index	BJI	bone and joint infection
		BJLO	Benton Judgement Line Orientation (test)
BIS	behavioral inhibition system	BJM	bones, joints, and muscles
	bioimpedance spectroscopy	BJOA	basal joint osteoarthritis
	Bispectral Index	BJOT	British Journal of Occupational Therapy
BISAP	Bedside Index for Severity in Acute Pancreatitis (scoring system)	BJP	Bence Jones protein
		BJR	Bezold-Jarisch reflex
Bi-SLT	bilateral, sequential single lung transplantation	BK	backward
			balloon kyphoplasty
bisp	bispinous diameter		below knee (amputation)
BISS	Bipolar Inventory of Symptoms Scale		bradykinin
			bullous keratopathy
BIT	behavioral inattention test	Bk	berkelium
	burp in transit (gas seen in the stomach on an abdominal film) (slang)	BKAs	below-ankle amputees (amputations)

BKC	benzalkonium chloride	BLAE	benign lymphangioendothelioma
	blepharokerato-conjunctivitis	BLAST	Basic Local Alignment Search
BKD	bacterial kidney disease		Tool
BKE	background-known-exactly	blasto	blastomycosis
	(radiology)	blasts	an immature stage in cellular
	Boost Kid Essentials (dietetic		development before
	formulations)		appearance of the definitive
bkfast	breakfast		characteristics of the cells
BKFO	bent knee fall out	BLB	Boothby-Lovelace Bulbulian
bkfst	breakfast		(oxygen mask)
bkft	breakfast		bronchoscopic lung biopsy
Bkg	background	BLBCL	may have meant DLBCL (diffuse
BKI	bumped kinase inhibitor		large B-cell lymphoma)
BKN	BK (polyomavirus)-virus	BLBK	blood bank
	nephropathy (BK are the	BLBS	bilateral breath sounds
	initials of person from whom	BL = BS	bilateral equal breath sounds
	the virus was isolated)	BlCa	bladder cancer
BK	BK (polyomavirus)-virus	BLCM	Bayesian latent class models
nephropathy	nephropathy	BLCO	bilateral carotid arterial occlusion
BKO	below-knee orthosis	bl cult	blood culture
BKP	balloon kyphoplasty	B-L-D	breakfast, lunch, and dinner
BKR	bicompartmental knee	BLDC	brushless direct current (motors)
	replacement	bldg	bleeding
	bradykinin receptor B1 (gene)	bld tm	bleeding time
BKS	bradykinesia score	BLE	bilateral lower extremity
BKs	bradykinins		both lower extremities
BKTT	below-knee to toe (cast)	bleb	a large vesicle (more than 5 mm)
BKV	BK polyomavirus		containing serous or seropuru-
BKVAN	BK virus (polyomavirus)-		lent fluid
	associated nephropathy	BLED	see HAS-BLED score (used to
BK viremia	BK (polyomavirus) virus		calculate the risk of major
	(BK are the initials of person		bleeding with anticoagulation
	from whom the virus was		in atrial fibrillation (http://
	isolated)		www.globalrph.com/has-bled
BK virus	BK (polyomavirus) virus		-score.htm)
BKWC	below-knee walking cast	BLEED	ongoing Bleeding, Low blood
BKWD	backward		pressure, Elevated prothrom-
BKWP	below-knee walking plaster		bin time, Erratic mental
	(cast)		status, and unstable comorbid
BL	balloon laryngoplasty		Disease (riskfactors for
	baseline		continued gastrointestinal
	baseline (fetal heart rate)		bleeding)
	bilateral	BLEO	bleomycin sulfate
	bioluminescence	bleph	blepharitis
	bland		blepharoplasty
	blast cells	BLEs	baggy lower eyelids
	blood level	BLESS	bath, laxative, enema, shampoo,
	blood loss		and shower
	blue		Bronchiectasis and Low-Dose
	bronchial lavage		Erythromycin Study (trial)
	bupivacaine liposome inj	bLf	bovine lactoferrin
	(Exparel)	BLFHR	baseline fetal heart rate
	Burkitt lymphoma	BLG	bovine beta-lactoglobulin
bl	bleeding	BLH	bilateral hemilaminotomy
BLA	baseline assessment		bleomycin hydrolase
	Biological License Application		borderline hypertension
	blood-loss anemia	BLI	bioluminescence imaging
blad	bladder		blast lung injury

BLIC   beta-lactamase inhibitor combination

B-line   a kind of comet-tail artifact from a bedside lung ultrasound indicating subpleural interstitial

BLIP   beta-lactamase inhibiting protein

Bliss   A designer psychotropic product whose main ingredient is Mephedrone

Blk   B lymphoid kinase; see gene website; www.ncbi.nlm.nih .gov

BLL   bilateral lower lobe
blood lead level
brows, lids, and lashes

BLLE   bilateral leg edema

BLLS   bilateral leg strength
bilateral lung sounds

BLM   bilateral mastectomy
bleomycin sulfate
Bloom syndrome protein

BLN   bronchial lymph nodes

BLND   bilateral lymph node dissection

BLOB   backward loss of balance

BLOBS   bladder obstruction

BLOC   brief loss of consciousness

BLOKS   Boston Leeds Osteoarthritis Knee Score

blood pressure   blood pressure has been abbreviated as BP

BLP   blastomycosis-like pyoderma (also known as pyoderma vegetans)

BLPB   beta-lactamase-producing bacteria

BLPD   borderline personality disorder

B/L PE   bilateral pedal edema

BLPLND   bilateral pelvic lymph node dissection

BLPO   beta-lactamase-producing organism

BLQ   below the limit of qualification
both lower quadrants

BLR   bleeding log record

BLRC   Biomedical Library Review Committee
blood lactate recovery curves

BLS   basic life support
Bureau of Labor Statistics

BLSO   Basic Life Support in Obstetrics

BLST   band limited sherbet transformed

BLT   bacon, lettuce, and tomato sandwich
balanced ligamentous tension
bending, lifting, and twisting restrictions following surgery

   benign liver tumor
bilateral lung transplantation
blood-clot lysis time
brow left transverse

BIT   bleeding time

BLTR   bilamellar tarsal rotation

BLTs   benign liver tumors

BLU   bedside lung ultrasound

B.L. unit   Bessey-Lowry units

blunts   a cigar emptied of its tobacco and replaced with marijuana

BLUS   bedside lung ultrasonography

BLU-U®   Blue Light Photodynamic Therapy Illuminator (peak wavelength occurs at 417 ±5 nm and the maximum absorption peak for porphyrins occurs at 410 nm) is generally indicated to treat dermatological conditions

BLV   bovine leukemia virus

B'ly   bilaterally

BLyS   B-lymphocyte stimulator; see gene website www.ncbi.nlm .nih.gov/gene

BM   bacterial meningitis
behavior modification
betamethasone
black male
body mass
Body Master
bone marrow
bone metastases
bowel movement
brain metastases
breast milk
bronchomalacia
buccal margin
budget manager
bullous myringitis
bullying/mobbing

B2m   beta-2 microglobulin; see gene website www.ncbi.nlm.nih .gov/gene

BMA   bimalleolar angle
biomedical application
bismuth subsalicylate, metronidazole, and amoxicillin
bone marrow aspiration
British Medical Association

Bmab   bevacizumab (Avastin)

BMAB   bone marrow aspiration and biopsy

BMAC   bone marrow aspirate concentrate

BMAH   bilateral macronodular adrenal hyperplasia

BMAT   basic motor ability test(s)

BMB	bone marrow biopsy	BMIS	bone marrow iron store
	brain microbleeds	BMIs	body mass indexes
BMBCh	Bachelor of Medicine, Bachelor		brain-machine interfaces
	of Surgery, (Latin: *Medicinae*	BMIz-score	body mass index z-score
	Baccalaureus, Baccalaureus		(the optimal measure of
	Chirurgiae)		annual adiposity change in
BMBF	German Ministry of Education		elementary school children)
	and Research	BMJ	bones, muscles, joints
BMBs	bone marrow biopsies		British Medical Journal
	bone marrow-derived basophils	BMK	birthmark
BMBx	bone marrow biopsy	BML	bone marrow lesion
BMC	basement membrane complex	B-MLUS	monoclonal B-cell lymphocytosis
	bone marrow cells		of undetermined significance
	bone marrow culture	BMM	black married male
	bone mineral content		bone marrow metastases
BM2c	Boatswain's Mate 2nd Class		bone marrow micrometastases
BMChB	Bachelor of Medicine and	BMMC	bone marrow mononuclear
	Bachelor of Surgery (Latin;		T cells
	Medicinae Baccalaureus,	BMMM	bone marrow micrometastases
	Baccalaureus Chirurgiae)	BMMNC	bone marrow mononuclear cell
BMCS	balloon-mounted coronary stents	BMMs	bone marrow macrophages
BMD	Becker muscular dystrophy	B-MODE	brightness modulation
	benchmark dose	BMP	basic metabolic profile (panel)
	bipolar manic depressive		(see Laboratory Panels)
	bipolar mood disorder		bone morphogenetic protein
	bone marrow depression	BMPC	bone marrow plasmacytosis
	bone mineral density	BMPEA	beta-methylphenethylamine
	broth microdilution		(positional isomer of
BMDC	bone marrow-derived stem cells		amphetamine)
BMDI	biomedical device integration	BMPs	bone-morphogenic proteins
	(into the electronic medical	BMQ	Beliefs about Medicines
	record)		Questionnaire
	bone mineral density index	BMR	basal metabolic rate
BME	basal medium Eagle (diploid		best motor response
	cell culture)	BMRC	British Medical Research
	bimanual examination		Council
	biomedical engineering	BMRM	bilateral modified radical
	black and minority ethnic		mastectomy
	bone marrow edema	BMRS	Broberg and Morrey Rating
	brief maximal effort		System
BMEC	brain-microvascular endothelial	BMS	bare-metal stents
	cell		Bowel Management System
BMEP	bone marrow edema pattern		Bristol-Myers Squibb Company
BMES	bone marrow edema syndrome		burning mouth syndrome
BMET	biomedical equipment	BMs	bowel movements; also see BM
	technology (technician)	BM's	see BM
BMF	black married female	BMSC	bone marrow stromal cells
	buccinator myomucosal flap		bone marrow-derived stem cells
BMFDS	Burke-Marsden-Fahns dystonia	BMT	bilateral myringotomy and tubes
	rating scale		bismuth subsalicylate,
BMFS	bone marrow failure syndrome		metronidazole, and tetracycline
BMG	benign monoclonal gammopathy		bone marrow transplant
B2MG	beta-2 microglobulin	BM&T	bilateral myringotomy and tubes
BMGF	Bill & Melinda Gates	BMTH	bismuth, metronidazole,
	Foundation		tetracycline, and a histamine
BMH	bone marrow harvest		H$_2$-receptor antagonist
BMI	body mass index	BMTN	bone marrow transplant
Bmilk	breast milk		neutropenia

BMTs	basic military trainees	BNR	bladder neck retraction
	bone marrow transplantations	BNS	benign nephrosclerosis
BMTT	bilateral myringotomy with		Bing-Neil Syndrome
	tympanic tubes	BNSRP	bilateral nerve sparing robotic
BMTU	bone marrow transplant unit		prostatectomy
BMTx	bone marrow transplant	BNT	back to normal
BMTZ	betamethasone		Boston Naming Test
BMU	basic multicellular unit	BNZ	benznidazole
BMV	balloon mitral valvuloplasty	BO	Barrett oesophagus (UK and
BMW	bare-metal wire		other countries)
	biomedical waste		base out
BMX	see gene website; www.ncbi		because of
	.nlm.nih.gov/gene		behavior objective
BMY	Bristol-Meyers Squibb		body odor
BMZ	betamethasone (Celestone)		bowel obstruction
BN	battalions		bowel open
	bladder neck		bronchiolitis obliterans
	brachial neuritis		bucco-occlusal
	bulimia nervosa	B&O	belladonna & opium
BNA	borderline nuclear abnormalities		(suppositories)
	bridged nucleic acid	BOA	behavioral observation
BNa	blood sodium concentration		audiometry
BNBAS	Brazelton Neonatal Behavioral		born on arrival
	Assessment		born out of asepsis
BNC	binasal cannula	BOB	ball-on-back
	bladder neck contracture	BOC	beats of clonus
BNCT	boron neutron capture therapy		boceprevir (Victrelis)
BND	benign nodular disease	BOCF	baseline observation carried
	bladder neck descent		forward
	bloody near dead (slang)	BOD	bag over drain
	bloody nipple discharge		bilateral orbital decompression
BNDD	Bureau of Narcotics and		Board of Drugs (Sweden)
	Dangerous Drugs (forerunner		burden of disease
	to today's Drug Enforcement	BODE	body mass index, airflow
	Administration [DEA])		obstruction, dyspnea, and
BNE	but not exceeding		exercise capacity (index)
bNED	biochemical no evidence of	Bod Units	Bodansky units
	disease	BOE	bilateral otitis externa
BNF	British National Formulary	BOFS	Branchio-Oculo-Facial
BNG	benign nodular goiter		Syndrome
	Bradbury-Nielsen gate	BOFs	blowout fractures
BNHL	B-cell non-Hodgkin lymphoma	BOG	Board of Governors
BNI	Barrow Neurological Institute	BOH	Board of Health
	(pain scale)		bundle of His
	blind nasal intubation	BOHB	beta hydroxybutyrate
BNL	below normal limits	BOK	BCL-2-related ovarian killer
	breast needle localization		(gene)
Bn M	bone marrow	BOLD	bleomycin, vincristine
BNO	bladder neck obstruction		(oncovin®), lomustine, and
	bowels not open		dacarbazine
BNP	brain natriuretic peptide		blood oxygenaton level-
	B-type natriuretic peptide		dependent (response)
	(nesiritide [Natrecor])	BOLO	be on (the) look out (slang)
BNPA	binasal pharyngeal airway	BOLT	bilateral orthotopic lung
BNPEP	brain type natriuretic peptide		transplantation
BNPP	bis-(p-nitrophenyl) phosphate	BOM	benign ovarian mass
	(an esterase inhibitor)		bilateral otitis media
BNPT	brain natriuretic peptide test	BOMA	bilateral otitis media, acute

BOME	bilateral otitis media with effusion		bisphosphonate (Actonel, Boniva, Fosamax, Reclast, Zometa, etc.)
BOMP	bleomycin, vincristine (oncovin®), mitomycin, and cisplatin (Platinol)		blood pressure
			bodily pain
BoNTA	botulinum toxin type A		body powder
BoNTs	Botulinum neurotoxins		British Pharmacopeia
BOO	bladder outlet obstruction		bronchopleural
	breathing on own		bullous pemphigoid
BOOB	benzoylperoxide		bypass
BOOP	bronchiolitis obliterans-organizing pneumonia	bp	base pair(s) (genetics)
		B/P	see BP
BOP	bleeding on probing	B&P	binge and purge
BOR	best overall response (rate)	BP1	blood pressure QTL 1 (gene)
	bortezomib (Velcade)	BP-200	Bourn Infant Pressure Ventilator
	bowels open regularly	BP3	see gene website www.ncbi.nlm.nih.gov/gene
	bronchio-oto-renal (syndrome)		
BORN	State Board of Registration in Nursing	BPA	birch pollen allergy
			bisphenol A
BORospA	borreliosis (Lyme disease, Borrelia sp.) vaccine, outer surface protein A	BPAD	bipolar affective disorder
		BPAP	bilevel positive airway pressure
		BPAR	biopsy-proven acute rejection
BORR	best overall response rate	BPAS	basi-parallel anatomical scanning
BOS	base of support		
	bronchiolitis obliterans syndrome		behavioral pain assessment scale
	bundling of services		branch pulmonary artery stenosis
BOS1	bronchiolitis obliterans syndrome stage 1	BPAs	best practice alerts (advisories)
BOS2	bronchiolitis obliterans syndrome stage 2	BPb	blood lead levels
			whole blood lead concentration
BOS3	bronchiolitis obliterans syndrome stage 3	BPBPR	may have meant BRBPR (bright red blood per rectum)
BOS/CLAD	bronchiolitis obliterans syndrome, subtype of chronic lung allograft dysfunction	BPC	British Pharmaceutical Codex
		BPCF	bronchopleural cutaneous fistula
		BPCI	Bundled Payments for Care Improvement (Centers for Medicare & Medicaid Services)
BOS/RAS	bronchiolitis obliterans syndrome/restrictive allograft syndrome		
BOSS	Becker orthopedic spinal system	BPCIC	Biological Price Competition and Innovation Act
BOT	base of tongue	BPCO	broncho-pneumopathie chronique obstructive
	borderline ovarian tumors		
BOU	burning on urination	BPD	benzoporphyrin derivative
BOUGIE	bougienage		biliopancreatic diversion
BOVR	Bureau of Vocational Rehabilitation		biparietal diameter
			borderline personality disorder
BOW	bag of water		bronchopulmonary dysplasia
BOW-I	bag of water–intact	BPd	diastolic blood pressure
BOW-R	bag of water–ruptured	BPDCN	blastic plasmacytoid dendritic cell neoplasm
BP	back pain		
	bathroom privileges	BPD/DS	biliopancreatic diversion with a duodenal switch (obesity surgery)
	bed pan		
	Bell palsy		
	bench press	BPDO	bile-pancreatic duct obstruction
	benzoyl peroxide	BPE	benign prostatic enlargement
	biological parent (s)	BPEG	British Pacing and Electrophysiology Group
	bipolar		
	birthplace		

BPEI	Bascom Palmer Eye Institute (University of Miami School of Medicine; Florida)		BPPD	base-pairing probability distribution
BPEP	bipolar plasma enucleation of the prostate			basic phonological processing disabilities
bPEP	brachial pre-ejection period		bPPD	bovine purified protein derivative
BPES	blepharophimosis-ptosis-epicanthus inversus syndrome (blepharophimosis syndrome)		BppL	lower baseplate protein
			BPPP	bilateral pedal pulses present
			BPPPV	may have meant BPPV (benign paroxysmal positional vertigo)
BPF	Brazilian purpuric fever			
	bronchopleural fistula		BP,P,R,T,	blood pressure, pulse, respiration, and temperature
BP fistula	bronchopleural fistula			
BPG	bypass graft		BPPs	bradykinin-potentiating peptides
	penicillin G benzathine (Bicillin L-A; Permapen) for IM use only		BPPV	benign paroxysmal positional vertigo
BPH	benign prostatic hypertrophy		BPR	beeper
	bronchopulmonary hygiene			blood per rectum
BPHC	Bureau of Primary Health Care (The Joint Commission)			blood pressure recorder
				body position retraining (sleep medicine)
BPI	bactericidal/permeability increasing (protein)		BPRS	Brief Psychiatric Rating Scale
	bipolar disorder, Type I		BPS	bilateral partial salpingectomy
	Brief Pain Inventory			bladder pain syndrome
BPIG	bacterial polysaccharide immune globulin			blood pump speed
			BPs	bisphosphonates (Actonel, Boniva, Fosamax, Reclast, Zometa, etc.)
BPII	bipolar type II disorder			
BPIT	bolus-plus-infusion transformation			systolic blood pressure
	brief psychodynamic interpersonal therapy		BPSCT	may have meant PBSCT (peripheral blood stem cell transplantation)
BPL	benzylpenicilloylpolylysine			
	bone probing length (dental)		BPSD	behavioral and psychological symptoms of dementia
BPLA	blood pressure, left arm			
B-PLL	B-cell prolymphocytic leukemia			bronchopulmonary segmental drainage
BPLND	bilateral pelvic lymph node dissection		BPS/IC	bladder pain syndrome/interstitial cystitis
BPM	beats per minute			
	breaths per minute		BPSO	bilateral prophylactic salpingo-oophorectomy
BPN	bacitracin, polymyxin B, and neomycin sulfate		BPT	bedside percutaneous tracheostomy
BPNC	Breast Patient Navigator Certification			BioPort Corporation
BPND	binding potential with respect to non-displaceable compartment		B-PT-B	bone-patellar tendon-bone
			BPTB	bone-patellar tendon-bone (graft)
BPO	benign prostatic obstruction		BpTRU	a non-invasive, automated blood pressure monitor
	benzoyl peroxide			
	bilateral partial oophorectomy		BPU	benzoylphenylurea
BPOC	barcode point-of-care			Biopsy Pick-Up
BPOP	bizarre parosteal osteochondromatous proliferation (Nora's Lesion)			bleeding peptic ulcer
				blood perfusion unit(s)
BPP	bilateral perisylvian polymicrogyria		BPV	benign paroxysmal vertigo
				benign positional vertigo
	biophysical profile			bovine papilloma virus
BppB	see gene website www.ncbi.nlm.nih.gov/gene		BPVV	may have meant BPPV (benign paroxysmal positional vertigo)
BPPC	Basic Patient Privacy Consent(s)		BPW	biparietal width
				buffered peptone water (media)

	caudal type homeobox 2 (gene/ protein)	BRAS	bilateral renal artery stenosis
	posterior bladder wall	brash	a word meaning heartburn;
BPX-80	a centrifugal blood pump		water brash is heartburn with
BPX	brain-specific protein, X-linked;		regurgitation of sour fluid or
	see gene website www.ncbi		almost tasteless saliva into the
	.nlm.nih.gov/gene		mouth
BQ	betel quid	BRAT	bananas, rice (rice cereal),
Bq	becquerel		applesauce, and toast
BQL	below quantifiable levels		Baylor rapid autologous
BQR	brequinar sodium		transfuser
BR	bathroom		blunt thoracic abdominal trauma
	bed rest	BRATT	bananas, rice (rice cereal),
	bendamustine and rituximab		applesauce, toast, and tea diet
	Benzing retrograde	BRATY	bananas, rice (rice cereal),
	birthing room		applesauce, toast, and yogurt
	blink rate		diet
	blink reflex	Bravo	a rating or designation of B
	Bloom-Richardson (breast cancer		(as in Alpha, Bravo)
	grading for aggressive		an esophageal pH monitoring
	potential)		system
	bowel rest		Phonetic Alphabet for B;
	brachioradialis		pronounced BRAH-VOH
	breast	BRB	blood-retinal barrier
	breast reconstruction		bright red blood
	breast reduction	BRBN	blue rubber bleb nevus
	breech		syndrome
	bridge	BRBNS	Blue Rubber Bleb Nevus
	bright red		Syndrome
	brown	BRBPI	birth-related brachial plexus
Br	breath		injury
	bromide	BRBPR	bright red blood per rectum
B/R	see BR	BRBR	bright red blood per rectum
B/r	radiation-resistant (as in	BRBRP	may have meant BRBPR (bright
	Escherichia coli strain B,		red blood per rectum)
	radiation-resistant)	BRC	bladder reconstruction
BRA	bananas, rice (rice cereal), and	BrCa	breast cancer
	applesauce (diet)	BRCA1	breast cancer gene 1
	brain	BRCA2	breast cancer gene 2
BRAC 1/2	BRCA1 (breast cancer gene 1)	BRC-ABL	An onco-protein generated from
	and BRCA2 (breast cancer		the fusion of Bcr and Abl genes
	gene 2)	BRCL	blood return central line
BrAC	breath alcohol content	BRCM	below right costal margin
BRACA	see BRCA	BRCP	breast cancer resistance protein
brach	brachial	BrdU	bromodeoxyuridine
Brachy	brachytherapy	BRE	benign rolandic epilepsy
Braden Scale	for predicting pressure sore risk		brain and reproductive
Braden Score	evaluates (predicts) a patient's		organ-expressed (gene/protein)
	risk of developing a pressure	BRER	blink reflex excitability recovery
	ulcer; consists of six cate-	BRET	bioluminescence resonance
	gories: sensory perception,		energy transfer
	moisture, activity, mobility,	BRex	breathing exercise
	nutrition, and friction/shear)	b-RFA	bipolar radiofrequency ablation
BRADY	bradycardia	Br Fdg	breast-feeding
BRAF	B-Raf proto-oncogene, serine/	BRFS	biochemical relapse-free
	threonine kinase (gene)		survival
BRANCH	branch chain amino acids	BRFSS	Behavioral Risk Factor
BRAO	branch retinal artery occlusion		Surveillance System (CDC)
		BRG	baroreflex gain

Brg-1	see gene website, www.ncbi.nlm.nih.gov/gene
BR grade	Bloom-Richardson (breast cancer grading for aggressive potential)
BRI	see gene website; www.ncbi.nlm.nih.gov/gene
	see gene website; www.ncbi.nlm.nih.gov/gene
Brig Gen	Brigadier General
BRIP	blink reflex inhibition by a prepulse
BRIT1	BRCT (breast cancer 1 C-terminal) repeat inhibitor of hTERT (human telomerase repeat transcriptase) expression (gene/protein)
BRJ	brachial radialis jerk
BRK	breast tumor kinase
BRKF	breakfast
brkfst	breakfast
BRL	Buffalo rat liver (cells)
BRM	biological response modifiers
BRMs	biologic response modifiers
BRN	brown
BRO	brother
BROM	back range of motion
Bronch	bronchoscopy
BRONJ	bisphosphonate-related osteonecrosis of the jaw
BRONK	bronchoscopy
Brov	Broviac® (cuffed small diameter central venous catheter)
BRP	bathroom privileges
BRPBR	may have meant BRBPR (bright red blood per rectum)
BRPHC	borderline resectable pancreatic head cancer
BRPL	blood return peripheral line
BrPM	breaths per minute
BRPPR	may have meant BRBPR (bright red blood per rectum)
BRPR	base regulatory potential rate
BRR	Bannayan-Riley-Ruvalcaba (syndrome)
BR RAO	branch retinal artery occlusion
BRRB	bright red rectal bleeding
BRRS	Bannayan-Riley-Ruvalcaba syndrome
BrRT	breast radiotherapy
BR RVO	branch retinal vein occlusion
BRS	baroreceptor reflex sensitivity
	baroreflex sensitivity
	brain reward system
BrS	breath sounds
	Brugada syndrome
BRST-1	breast Cancer Antigen 1
BRST-2	breast Cancer Antigen 2
BRSV	bovine respiratory syncytial virus
BRTL	Bayer Reference Testing Laboratory. Berkeley CA
Brtl mouse	Brittle IV mouse was developed as a knock-in model for osteogenesis imperfecta type IV. A Gly349Cys substitution was introduced into one col1a1 allele, resulting in a phenotype representative of the disease
BRTO	balloon-occluded retrograde transvenous obliteration
BRU	basic remodeling unit (osteon)
	brucellosis (*Brucella melitensis*) vaccine
BRUE	Brief Resolved Unexplained Event (American Academy of Pediatrics)
bruit	a word meaning sound
BRVO	branch retinal vein occlusion
−BS	negative bowel sounds
+BS	positive bowel sounds
BS	bariatric surgery
	barium swallow
	bedside
	before sleep
	Behçets syndrome
	Bennett seal
	blind spot
	blood sugar
	Blue Shield
	bone scan
	bowel sounds
	Braden Scale (for predicting pressure sore risk)
	breath sounds
B's	bradycardia episodes
BS−	bowel sounds negative
BS+	positive bowel sounds
B & S	Bartholin and Skene (glands)
	bending and stooping
	Brown and Sharp (suture sizes)
B/S	see BS
BS×4	bowel sounds in all four quadrants
BSA	body surface area
	bowel sounds active
	Brief Scale of Anxiety
BSAB	Balthazar Scales of Adaptive Behavior
BSAb	broad-spectrum antibiotics
bsaB	see gene website www.ncbi.nlm.nih.gov/gene
bsAbs	bispecific antibodies
BSAER	brainstem auditory evoked responses

BSAG   bovine serum albumin-glutaraldehyde (glue)

BSAP   bone-specific alkaline phosphatase

BSAS   Bedside Shivering Assessment Scale
Bosley-Salih-Alorainy syndrome

BSB   bedside bag
body surface burned

BSBE   Bachelor of Science in Biomedical Engineering
breath sounds bilaterally equal

BSBL   block sparse Bayesian learning

BSC   basosquamous (cell) carcinoma
bedside care
bedside commode
best supportive care
biological safety cabinet
Biomedical Science Corps
body-shape change
burn scar contracture

BSCA   brain stem cavernous angioma
British Society for Contact Dermatitis, database)
British Society for Cutaneous Allergy (formerly known as the British Society for Contact Dermatitis, database)

BSCC   bedside commode chair
Bjork-Shiley convexo-concave (valves)
British Society for Clinical Cytology

BSCDVA   best spectacle corrected distance visual acuity

BSCL   Berardinelli-Seip Congenital Lipodystrophy

BSCR   birdshot chorioretinopathy

BSCT   blood stem cell transplantation

BSCTA   bone subtraction computed tomography angiography

BSCVA   best spectacle-corrected visual acuity

BSD   baby soft diet
bedside drainage
behavioral symptoms of dementia
brain stem death
bulimia-spectrum disorder

BSD license   Berkeley Source Distribution (a class of simple and very liberal licenses for computer software)

BSDs   bipolar spectrum disorders

BSE   bedside swallow evaluation
bovine spongiform encephalopathy
breast self-examination
broccoli sprout extracts

BSEC   bedside easy chair

BSepF   black separated female

BSepM   black separated male

BSER   brain stem evoked responses

BSF   black single female
busulfan (Myleran)

BSG   Bagolini striated glasses
brain stem gliomas
British Society of Gastroenterology

BSGA   beta streptococcus group A

BSGI   breast-specific gamma imaging

BSHG   British Society for Human Genetics

BSI   bloodstream infection
body substance isolation
brain stem injury
Brief Symptom Inventory

BSID-II   Bayley Scales of Infant Development

BSL   baseline
Biological Safety Level
biosafety level (i. e. BSL-1, -2, -3, -4)
blood sugar level

BSL-1   Biosafety Level 1

BS L base   breath sounds diminished, left base

BSLTx   bilateral sequential lung transplantation

BSM   black single male
blood safety module
body surface mapping

BSN   Bachelor of Science in Nursing
bowel sounds normal

BSNA   bowel sounds normal and active

BSNMT   Bachelor of Science in Nuclear Medicine Technology

BSNT   breast soft and nontender

BSNUTD   baby shots not up to date

BSO   bilateral salpingo-oophorectomy
l-buthionine sulfoximine

bSOD   bovine superoxide dismutase

BSOM   bilateral serous otitis media

BSP   body substance precautions
bone sialoprotein
Bromsulphalein®

BSPA   bowel sounds present and active

BSPM   body surface potential mapping

BSR   Bayesian shrinkage regression
bedside rails
body stereotactic radiosurgery
bowels sounds regular

BSRI   Bem Sex Role Inventory

BSRT (R)   Bachelor of Science in Radiologic Technology (Registered)

BSS	bacteriostatic saline solution (0.9% sodium chloride with benzyl chloride)		Blalock-Taussig (shunt)
			bleeding time
	Baltimore Sepsis Scale		blood transfusion
	bedside scale		blood type
	Berardinelli-Seip syndrome		bluetongue
	Bernard-Soupier syndrome		blunt trauma
	bismuth subsalicylate (the active ingredient of Pepto-Bismol)		borderline tuberculoid (leprosy)
			bowel tones
	black silk sutures		brachytherapy
	blood stasis syndrome		brain tumor
	Bristol Stool Scale		breast tumor
	Brooke-Spieler syndrome		bronchial thermoplasty
	Brown-Séquard syndrome	Bt	*Bacillus thuringiensis*
BSS®	balanced salt solution	B-T	Blalock-Taussig (shunt)
BSSE	basis set superposition error	B/T	between
BSSG	sitogluside	Bt#	bottle number
BSSLTX	bilateral sequential single-lung transplants	BTA	below the ankle
			bladder tumor antigen
BSSO	bilateral sagittal split osteotomy		bladder tumor-associated analytes
BSSRO	bilateral sagittal split-ramus osteotomy		botulinum toxin type A (Botox)
		BTAI	blunt traumatic aortic injury
BSSS	benign sporadic sleep spikes	BTAR	blunt traumatic aortic rupture
BSST	breast self-stimulation test	BTB	back to bed
BST	Beddit Sleep Tracker		beat-to-beat (variability)
	bedside testing		blue TheraBand
	bovine somatotropin		bone-patellar tendon-bone (autograft)
	brain-stem tumors		
	brief stimulus therapy		breakthrough bleeding
Bst	boost		bromthymol blue (agar)
BSTAT	Bronchoscopy Skills and Tasks Assessment Tool	bTB	bovine tuberculosis
		BTB autograft	bone-patellar tendon-bone autograft
B-strep	beta hemolytic streptococcus		
BSU	Bartholin, Skenes, urethra (glands)	BTBV	beat-to-beat variability
		BTC	behind-the-counter
	behavioral science unit		bilateral tubal cautery
BSu	blood sugar		biliary tract cancer
BSUS	bedside ultrasound		biliary tree cancer
	body surface ultrasound		bladder tumor check
BSUs	bone structural units		by the clock
BSUTD	baby shots up to date	BTCP	breakthrough cancer pain
	Base Service Unit	BTD	benign thyroid disease
BSV	between-subject variability		bortezomib, thalidomide, and dexamethasone
	binocular single vision		
	bleeding stomal varices	BTE	Baltimore Therapeutic Equipment
BSW	Bachelor of Social Work		
	bedscale weight		behind-the-ear (hearing aid)
BSX	bypass surgery		below-the-elbow
B symptoms	systemic symptoms of fever, night sweats, and weight loss which can be associated with both Hodgkin lymphoma and non-Hodgkin lymphoma		Biafine topical emulsion
			bisected, totally embedded
		BTEX	benzene, toluene, ethyl benzene, and xylene (pollutants)
		BTF	blenderized tube feeding
BT	Baker tube	BTFS	breast tumor frozen section
	bedtime	BTG	beta thromboglobulin
	behavioral therapy	B-Thal	beta thalassemia
	bituberous	BTHOOM	beats the hell out of me (better stated as 'differed diagnosis')
	bladder tumor		

BTI	biliary tract infection		Breast Test Wales
	bitubal interruption		by the way
BTJ	beetroot juice	BtW	birth weight
	Biotechnology Journal	BTW M	between meals
	bone-to-tendon junction	BTWN	between
BTK	Bruton tyrosine kinase (gene/	BTX	Botulinum toxin type A (Botox)
	protein)	BTX-A	botulinum toxin type A (Botox)
BTK3	Bullet Hole Testing Kit 3	BTZ	bortezomib (Velcade)
BTKA	bilateral total knee arthroplasty	BU	base up (prism)
BTKR	bilateral total knee replacement		below umbilicus
BTL	bilateral tubal ligation		Bethesda units (hematology)
btl	bottle		Bodansky units
BTL/BPS	bilateral tubal ligation/bilateral		burn unit
	partial saipingectomy		busulfan (Myleran)
btl fdg	bottle feeding	B/U	ratio of biliary to urinary
BTLS	basic trauma life support		excretion
BTM	beta thalassemia major	BUA	broadband ultrasound
	bilateral tympanic membranes		attenuation
	bismuth subcitrate, tetracycline,	BuBc slides	a test used to measure bilirubin
	and metronidazole		in neonatal specimens (total
	bone turnover marker(s)		bilirubin is calculated from
BTm	beta thalassemia minor		the Bu [unconjugated bili-
BTMEAL	between meals		rubin] and the Bc [bilirubin
BTMP	bleeding through menstrual pads		conjugated to glucuronic
BTMs	bone turnover markers		acid] and referred to as
BTMZ	betamethasone		neonatal bilirubin [NBIL])
BTNP	brain type (B-type) natriuretic	BUCAT	busulfan, carboplatin, and
	peptide		thiotepa
BTO	bilateral tubal occlusion	BuCy	busulfan and cyclophosphamide
BTP	basilar trunk perforator	BUD	beyond-use date
	(aneurysm)		budesonide (Rhinocort)
	beta-trace protein	BUdR	bromodeoxyuridine
	bismuth tribromophenate	BUE	bilateral upper extremities
	breakthrough pain		both upper extremities
BTPABA	bentiromide	BuE	butyrylesterase
BTPR	blunt traumatic pericardial	BUFA	baby up for adoption
	rupture	BUI	boating under the Influence
BTPS	body temperature pressure	BULB	bilateral upper lid blepharoplasty
	saturated	BUM	bumetanide
BTPV	bilateral thoracic paravertebral	BUMEL	busulphan and melphalan
	(block)	bumph	a word meaning useless or
BTR	bladder tumor recheck		tedious printed information or
BTS	Blalock-Taussig shunt		documents
BTSH	bovine thyrotropin	BUN	blood urea nitrogen
BT shunt	Blalock-Taussig shunt		bunion
BTT	bridge to transplant	BUN/Cr	blood urea nitrogen/creatinine
BTT-LVAD	bridge to transplant left		ratio
	ventricular assist device	BUO	bleeding of undetermined origin
BTU	behavior therapy unit	BUPE	buprenorphine and naloxone
	British thermal unit(s)		(Suboxone) (slang)
BTV	biological target volume	Bupi	bupivacaine (Marcaine;
	(radiology)		Sensorcaine)
	bluetongue virus	BUP/NLX	buprenorphine/naloxone
BTV-8	bluetongue virus serotype 8		(Suboxone; Burnavail)
BTW	back to work	BUQ	both upper quadrants
	behind-the-wheel	BUR	back-up rate (ventilator)
	behind-the-wheel evaluation	Burch surgery	retropubic urethropexy surgery
	between	Burd	Burdick suction

BURP	see gene website www.ncbi.nlm.nih.gov/gene
BURP maneuver	back, upward, right lateral, pressure (improves the visualization of the larynx)
burr	a word meaning a form of drill used for creating openings in bone or similar hard material
BUS	Bartholin, urethral, and Skenes glands
	bladder ultrasound
	bulbourethral sling
BUSV	Bartholin urethral Skeins vagina
BUT	biopsy urease test
	break up time
	(tear) breakup time
Butt Paste	16% Zinc Oxide ointment. Contents and strengths can vary from hospital to hospital. (Slang and a commercial product)
BV	bacterial vaginitis
	bereaved
	bereavement
	bevacizumab (Avastin)
	biological value
	blood volume
BVAD	biventricular assist device
BVAS	Birmingham Vasculitis Activity Score
BVBS	bronchovesicular breath sounds
BVCP	bilateral vocal cord paralysis
BVD	bovine viral diarrhea
BVDU	bromovinlydeoxyuridine (brivudin)
BVE	blood volume expander
BVES	blood vessel epicardial substance
BVF	biventricular failure
	bulboventricular foramen
bvFTD	behavioral variant of frontotemporal dementia
BVG	Federal Association of Geriatrics (Bundesverband Geriatrie; Germany)
Bvg	see gene website www.ncbi.nlm.nih.gov/gene
BVH	biventricular hypertrophy
BVI	blood vessel invasion
BVL	bilateral vas ligation
BVM	bag valve mask
BVMG	Bender Visual-Motor Gestalt (test)
BVO	branch vein occlusion
	brominated vegetable oil
BVP	biventricular pacing
	blood volume processed (hemodialysis)

BVR	best verbal response
	Bureau of Vocational Rehabilitation
BVRO	bilateral vertical ramus osteotomy
BVRT	Benton Visual Retention Test
BVS	bioresorbable vascular scaffold (stent)
BVT	basilica vein transportation
	bilateral ventilation tubes
BVVP	benign paroxysmal positional vertigo
BVZ	bevacizumab (Avastin)
BW	bandwidth (radiology)
	birth weight
	bite-wing (radiograph)
	bloodwork
	body water
	body weight
B & W	Black and White (milk of magnesia & aromatic cascara fluidextract)
B/W	see BW
BWA	bed-wetter admission
BWAT	Bates-Jensen Wound Assessment Tool (score)
BWC	bladder-wash cytology
BWCO	baby won't come out (needs Caesarian) (slang)
BWCS	bagged white cell study
BWD	backward
	birth weight discordance
	birth weight distribution
	body weight dissatisfaction
BWF	Blackwater fever
BWFI	bacteriostatic water for injection
BWG	Bland-White-Garland (syndrome)
BWH	Brigham and Women's Hospital (Boston MA)
BWI	burn wound infection
BWidF	black widowed female
BWidM	black widowed male
BWK	bilateral wasting kidneys
bwK	bullwinkle
BWL	behavioral weight loss
	body weight loss
BWMSs	ballast water management systems
BWR	body weight ratio
	body weight reduction
BWS	battered woman syndrome
	Beckwith-Wiedemann syndrome
	body-weight support
	Burch-Wartofsky scores
BWs	bite-wing (x-rays)
BWSE	black widow spider envenomation

BWSTT	body weight-supported treadmill training
BWT	bowel wall thickness
BWV	Brain Wave Vibration
BWX	bite-wing x-ray
Bx	behavior
	biopsy
BX BS	Blue Cross and Blue Shield
BXM	B cell crossmatch
BXO	balanitis xerotica obliterans
Bxs	biopsies
B/Y	blue/yellow
BYOD	Bring Your Own Drugs; programs that provide arrest-free, saver-use (provide needles and resuscitation standby) areas for intravenous drug users
ΦBZ	phenylbutazone
BZD	benzodiazepine
BZDZ	benzodiazepine
BZO	barium zirconate (BaZrO3) benzodiazepine(s) (such as diazepam [Valium], chlor-diazepoxide [Librium], etc.,)
BZP	benzylpiperazine (known as 1-benzylpiperazine, A2, Frenzy, Nemesis, Lovely and Lovelies)

C

C	ascorbic acid
	carbohydrate
	Catholic
	Caucasian
	Celsius
	centigrade
	cervical
	Charlie (Phonetic Alphabet C; pronounced CHAR-LEE or SHAR-LEE)
	chemotherapy
	Chlamydia
	circulator
	clubbing
	conjunctiva
	constricted
	cyanosis
	cysteine
	cytidine
	cytidine (also referred to as Cyd)
	hundred
c	with
	circa, a word from Latin, meaning around or about
C+	with contrast
c̄	with
C′	cervical spine
C#	cycle (menstrual) number cycle number
C1	A classification under the US Controlled Substances Act for substances that have a high potential for abuse, having no currently accepted medical use in treatment (e.g. heroin, LSD, marijuana, peyote, methaqualone). Also written as CI
	cyclopentolate 1% ophthalmic solution (Cyclogyl)
	first cervical nerve root
	first cervical vertebrae
	plastic explosive
C2	A classification under the US Controlled Substances Act for drugs that have a high potential for abuse which may lead to severe psychological or physical dependence. (e.g. hydromorphone, methadone, oxycodone, amphetamine, cocaine). Also written as CII
	second cervical nerve root
	second cervical vertebrae

C3	A classification under the US Controlled Substances Act for drugs that have a potential for abuse less than substances in schedules I or II and abuse may lead to moderate or low physical dependence or high psychological dependence (e.g. Tylenol with code)
	complement component 3 (an immune system protein that plays a role in the development of inflammation)
	third cervical nerve root
	third cervical vertebrae
C4	A classification under the US Controlled Substances Act drugs that have a low potential for abuse relative to substances in schedule III (e.g. alprazolam, diazepam, triazolam). Also written as CIV
	complement component 4 (an immune system protein that plays a role in the development of inflammation)
	fourth cervical nerve root
	fourth cervical vertebrae
C5	A classification under the US Controlled Substances Act; drugs that have a low potential for abuse relative to substances listed in schedule IV and consist primarily of preparations containing limited quantities of certain narcotics.
	fifth cervical nerve root
	fifth cervical vertebrae
C6	sixth cervical vertebrae
	sixth cervical vertebral nerve
C7	seventh cervical nerve root
	seventh cervical vertebrae
C8	eighth cervical nerve root
CO2	see CO2
C_p	chlamydophila pneumoniae
	chlamydophilia
C_{II}	second cranial nerve
CA	California
	cancelled appointment
	cancer antigen
	Candida albicans
	caprylic acid
	carcinoma
	cardiac amyloidosis
	cardiac arrest
	carotid artery
	catheter ablation
	celiac artery

	cellulose acetate (filter)
	Certified Acupuncturist
	chronologic age
	chronological age
	Clinic Assistant
	Cocaine Anonymous
	community-acquired
	competent authority
	compressed air
	continuous aerosol
	coracoacromial
	coracoacromial (ligament)
	coronary angioplasty
	coronary artery
CA 125	cancer antigen 125
CA199	see CA19-9
CA19-9	carbohydrate antigen 19-9, (cancer antigen 19-9; sialylated Lewis A antigen) used as a diagnostic and treatment measure for pancreatic and other cancers
CA 19-9	cancer antigen 19-9, a high amount is most commonly caused by pancreatic cancer, but it can also be caused by the other cancers and byliver, gallbladder, and pancreas infections
CA72-4	cancer antigen 74-2 (a tumor marker, monitoring metastatic or recurrent tumors of the gastrointestinal tract, lung, breast, and ovaries)
CA 72-4	cancer antigen 74-2 (a tumor marker, monitoring metastatic or recurrent tumors of the gastrointestinal tract, lung, breast, and ovaries)
CA27.29	cancer antigen 27.29, an antigen found in a blood test that is done specifically for people with breast cancer to monitor the course of the disease
CA27-29	cancer antigen 27-29, an antigen found in a blood test that is done specifically for people with breast cancer to monitor the course of the disease
C&A	Clinitest® and Acetest®
C/A	conscious, alert
C + A	children and adolescents
C+A	children and adolescents
Ca	Calcium
Ca^{++}	calcification
	calcium
$Ca2+$	calcium (calcium ion)
CAA	cerebral amyloid angiopathy
	coloanal anastamosis

	complex aortic aneurysm		colitis-associated cancer
	crystalline amino acids		Community Action Center
CAAD	carotid artery disease		computer-assisted coding
	computer-assisted anatomic		computerized autocoding
	dissection		coronary artery calcification
CA-AKI	community-acquired acute		coronary artery calcium
	kidney injury	CACB	chronic angle closure glaucoma
CAAP-1	Certified Associate Addiction	CACD	central anterior chamber depth
	Professional, level 1		central areolar choroidal
CAB	Cabotegravir		dystrophy
	catheter-associated bacteriuria	CACG	chronic angle-closure glaucoma
	cellulose acetate butyrate	CaChEIs	centrally acting cholinesterase
	combined androgen blockade		inhibitors
	complete abortion	CACI	compounding aseptic
	complete atrioventricular block		containment isolator
	Consumer Affairs Branch (FDA)		computer-assisted continuous
	coronary artery bypass		infusion
cabage	could be referring to CABG	CaCl$_2$	calcium chloride
	(coronary-artery bypass graft)	CA-cIAIs	community-acquired complicated
CABANA	Catheter Ablation versus		intra-abdominal infections
	Antiarrhythmic Drug Therapy	C. acnes	Cutibacterium (formerly
	for Atrial Fibrillation Trial (an		Propionibacterium) acnes
	international atrial fibril-	CaCO$_3$	calcium carbonate
	lation study that compares	CACP	cisplatin
	anti-arrhythmic drugs to	CACS	cancer-related anorexia/cachexia
	catheter ablation)		carotid artery calcified stenosis
cabbage	could be referring to CABG		coronary artery calcium score
	(coronary-artery bypass graft)	CAD	cadaver (kidney donor)
CABBG	see CABG (coronary-artery		calcium alginate dressing
	bypass graft)		carotid artery dissection
CABC	chondroitinase ABC		cervical artery dissection
C-ABC	chondroitinase ABC (ABC		chronic allograft dysfunction
	refers to chondroitin sulfate		computer-aided detection
	A, B and C)		computer-aided diagnosis
CaBD	cancellous bone density		computer-aided dispatch
CABE	cancer-associated benign		coronary artery disease
	epithelium		coronary atherosclerotic disease
CABG	coronary artery bypass graft	CaD	calcium and vitamin D
CABGE	see CABG (coronary-artery		(fortified milk)
	bypass graft)	CADAC	Certified Alcohol and
CABH	Could be referring to coronary-		Drug Abuse Counselor
	artery bypass graft (CABG;	CADASIL	cerebral autosomal dominant
	Cabbage)		arteriopathy with subcortical in-
CaBI	calcium bone index		farcts and leukoencephalopathy
CABL	Cardiovascular Abnormalities	CADB	clinical and administrative
	and Brain Lesions (study)		database
CABP	community-acquired bacterial	cadB	lysine/cadaverine antiporter (gene)
	pneumonia		putative lysine/cadaverine
CaBP	calcium-binding protein		transporter (gene)
CABS	coronary artery bypass surgery	CAD-CAM	computer-aided design/
	Corrigan Agitated Behavior Scale		computer-aided manufacturing
cAbs	capture antibodies		(dental crowns)
CABSI	catheter-associated bloodstream	CADD®	Computerized Ambulatory Drug
	infection		Delivery (pump)
CAC	cardioacceleratory center	CADHC	Contract Adult Day Health Care
	carotid artery calcification	CADILLAC	Controlled Abciximab and Device
	Certified Alcohol Counselor		Investigation to Lower Late An-
	chronic active colitis		gioplasty Complications (trial)

CADL	communication activities of daily living (speech/cognitive test)
CADP	computer-assisted design of prosthesis
CADRF	coronary artery disease risk factors
CADS	Candida-associated denture stomatitis
CADSIL	may have CADASIL (cerebral autosomal-dominant arteriopathy with subcortical infarcts and leukoencephalopathy)
CADT	continuous androgen deprivation therapy
CADXPL	cadaver transplant
CADz	coronary artery disease
CAE	cardiovascular adverse event
	cellulose acetate electrophoresis
	Certified Association Executive
	childhood absence epilepsy
	coronary artery ectasia
	coronary artery endarterectomy
	cyclophosphamide, doxorubicin (Adriamycin), and etoposide
CAEC	cardiac arrhythmia evaluation center
	Cook airway exchange catheter
CaEDTA	calcium disodium edetate
CAERS	Center for Food Safety and Applied Nutrition's Adverse Event Reporting System
CAEs	cardiovascular adverse events
CAEV	caprine arthritis encephalitis virus
CAF	chronic atrial fibrillation
	controlled atrial flutter/ fibrillation
	coronary artery fistula
	cyclophosphamide, doxorubicin (Adriamycin), and fluorouracil
CAFé	Cancer Patient Fracture Evaluation (study)
CAFD	changing acceleration of flow direction
CafD	cafeteria diet
CAFF	controlled atrial fibrillation/flutter
CaFL	calcaneofibular ligament
cAFL	common atrial flutter
CAFT	Clinitron® air fluidized therapy
CAG	chronic atrophic gastritis
	closed angle glaucoma
	continuous ambulatory gamma globin (infusion)
	coronary arteriography
	critical angle of Gissane
CaG	calcium gluconate
	gemcitabine and carboplatin regimen of cancer
CAGB	coronary artery bypass grafting (Romance Languages)

	S100 calcium binding protein A9 (gene)
CaGB	carcinoma of the gallbladder
CAGE	a questionnaire for alcoholism evaluation. Have you ever felt the need to Cut down your drinking? Have you ever felt Annoyed by criticism of your drinking? Have you ever felt Guilty about your drinking? Have you ever taken a drink (Eye opener) first thing in the morning?
	cerebral arterial gas embolism
	conjugative assembly genome engineering
CAGE AID	The CAGE questionnaire for alcohol abuse Adapted to Include Drugs (Have you ever felt you ought to Cut down on your drinking or drug use? Have people Annoyed you by criticizing your drinking or drug use? Have you felt bad or Guilty about your drinking or drug use? Eye Opener; Have you ever had a drink or used drugs first thing in the morning to steady your nerves or to get rid of a hangover?)
cagluconate	calcium gluconate
CAGS	Canadian Association of General Surgeons
CAGs	cancer-associated genes
CAGS and ACS	Canadian Association of General Surgeons and American College of Surgeons
CAH	chronic aggressive hepatitis
	command auditory hallucination(s)
	congenital adrenal hyperplasia
	Critical Access Hospital (a designated small facility that gives limited outpatient and in-patient hospital services to people in rural areas. They receive cost-based reimbursement)
CaHA	calcium hydroxylapatite
CAHB	chronic active hepatitis B
CAHD	chronic acquired hepatocerebral degeneration
	coronary artery heart disease
CAHPS	Consumer Assessment of Healthcare Providers and Systems
CAHPS-CC	Consumer Assessment of Healthcare Providers and Systems Cultural Competency Item Set
CAHs	critical access hospitals

CAI	carbonic anhydrase inhibitors	cALL	childhood acute lymphoblastic
	carboxyamide aminoimidazoles		leukemia
	carotid artery injury	CALLA	common acute lympho-blastic
	chronic ankle instability		leukemia antigen
	compounding aseptic isolator	CALM	cafe-au-lait macule
	computer-assisted instructions		Coordinated Anxiety Learning
CAIA	collagen antibody-induced arthritis		and Management
	computer-assisted image analysis	CALNOC	Collaborative Alliance for
'caid	Medicaid		Nursing Outcomes
cAIMP	cyclic adenosine-inosine	Cal O2Sat	calculated oxygen saturation
	monophosphate	CalPERS	California Public Employees'
CAINS	Clinical Assessment Interview		Retirement System
	for Negative Symptoms	CALR	calreticulin (gene)
CAIRO	CApecitabine, IRinotecan,	CALS	cafe-au-lait spots
	Oxaliplatin	CALs	coronary artery lesions
Ca IS	carcinoma in situ	CAM	campylobacter vaccine
CAIV	cold-adapted influenza virus		Caucasian adult male
	vaccine		cell adhesion molecules
CAJ	cavoatrial junction		child abuse management
	China Academic Journals		chorioamnionitis
	cricoarytenoid joint		complementary and alternative
CAKUT	congenital anomalies of the		medicine
	kidney and urinary tract		confusion assessment method
CAL	callus		controlled ankle motion
	chronic airflow limitation		cystic adenomatoid malformation
	clinical attachment level (dental)	CAMA	Chronic and Acute Medical
	computer-assisted learning		Assistance
	coronary artery lesions		corrected-arm-muscle area
Cal	kilocalorie (large calorie;	CAMAC	Comprehensive Accreditation
	1,000 [small] calories)		Manual for Ambulatory Care
cal	calorie (small calorie)		(The Joint Commission)
C$_{alb}$	albumin clearance	CAMBHC	Comprehensive Accreditation
calc	calculation		Manual for Behavioral Health
CALCA	calcitonin related polypeptide		Care (The Joint Commission)
	alpha (gene)	CAM boot	controlled ankle movement
CALCB	calcitonin related polypeptide		(walking) boot
	beta (gene)	CAMCAH	Comprehensive Accreditation
calcs	radiographic calcifications		Manual for Critical Ac-
cal ct	calorie count		cess Hospitals (The Joint
calculated PRA	calculated panel-reactive antibody		Commission)
CALD	chronic active liver disease	CAMCOG	Cambridge Cognitive Examination
CALDWELL	a surgical procedure to clear a	CAMD	cirrhosis, age, male sex, and
LUC	blocked or infected maxillary		diabetes mellitus (score;
	sinus that involves entering the		hepatocellular carcinoma risk
	sinus through the mouth by way		determinants)
	of an incision into the canine		Coalition Against Major Diseases
	fossa above a canine tooth,		computer-aided molecular design
	cleaning the sinus, and creating	CAMEL	CArcinoma and MELanoma
	a new and enlarged opening for	CAMF	cyclophosphamide, Adriamycin,
	drainage through the nose		methotrexate, and fluorouracil
CALGB	Cancer and Leukemia Group B	CAMH	Comprehensive Accreditation
CALI	chromophore-assisted laser		Manual for Hospitals
	inactivation	CAMICU	Confusion Assessment Method
CALIPER	Computer-Aided Lung		for the Intensive Care Unit
	Informatics for Pathology	CAM ICU	Confusion Assessment Method
	Evaluation and Rating (soft-		for the Intensive Care Unit
	ware and measurements from	CaMKII	calcium/calmodulin-dependent
	pulmonary function tests)		protein kinase II

CAMLAB	Comprehensive Accreditation Manual for Laboratory and Point-of-Care Testing (The Joint Commission)
CAMNCC	Comprehensive Accreditation Manual for Nursing Care Center (The Joint Commission)
CAMOBS	Comprehensive Accreditation Manual Office-Based Surgery (The Joint Commission)
CAMP	compound muscle action potential
	cyclophosphamide, doxorubicin (Adriamycin), methotrexate, and procarbazine
cAMP	cyclic adenosine monophosphate
CA-MRSA	community-acquired methicillin-resistant *staphylococcus aureus* community-associated methicillin-resistant *Staphylococcus aureus*
CAMs	cell adhesion molecules
CA-MSSA	community-acquired methicillin-susceptible *Staphylococcus aureus*
CAMT	congenital amegakaryocytic thrombocytopenia
CAN	anterior cervical (lymph) nodes
	cannabis
	cardiovascular autonomic neuropathy
	Certified Nursing Assistant
	chronic allograft nephropathy
	contrast-associated nephropathy
	cord around neck
CA/N	child abuse and neglect
CAN-A	Certified Nursing Assistant - Advanced
CANC	cancelled
cANCA	cytoplasmic antineutrophil cytoplasmic antibody
CANDA	computer-assisted new drug application
C1 and C2	cervical vertebrae 1 and 2
C2 and C3	cervical vertebrae 2 and 3
C3 and C4	cervical vertebrae 3 and 4
C4 and C5	cervical vertebrae 4 and 5
C5 and C6	cervical vertebrae 5 and 6
C6 and C7	cervical vertebrae 6 and 7
C and C	see C&C
CANDLE	chronic atypical neutrophilic dermatosis with lipodystrophy and elevated temperature syndrome
C and S	see C&S
CAN-KLB	*Candida albicans, Klebsiella pneumoniae* vaccine

CANOMAD	chronic ataxic neuropathy combined with ophthalmo-plegia, immunogobulin M protein, cold agglutinins, and anti-disialosyl antibodies (syndrome)
CANP	Certified Adult Nurse Practitioner
CANPC	Certified Anesthesia and Pain Management Coder (CANPC™)
CANS	central auditory nervous system complaints of the arm, neck and/or shoulders
CANTAB	Cambridge Neuropsychological Test Automated Battery
CANTOS	Canakinumab Anti-Inflammatory Thrombosis Outcomes Study
CANVAS	CANagliflozin (Invokana) cardio-Vascular Assessment Study cerebellar ataxia with neuropathy and vestibular areflexia syndrome
CANVAS-R	CANagliflozin (Invokana) cardioVascular
CAO	chronic airway (airflow) obstruction coronary artery occlusion
CAOD	coronary artery occlusive disease
Ca(OH)2	calcium hydroxide
CAOS	chronic abruption-oligohydramnios sequence computer-assisted orthopedic surgery
CaOx	calcium oxalate
CAOX4	conscious, alert/awake, and oriented to person, place, time and recent events
CAP	capecitabine (Xeloda)
	capsule
	cellulose acetate phthalate
	Certified Addiction Professional
	cervical acid phosphatase
	chemistry admission profile
	chloramphenicol
	College of American Pathologists (cancer checklist)
	community-acquired pneumonia
	compound action potentials
	cyclophosphamide, doxorubicin (Adriamycin), and cisplatin
C/A/P	chest/abdomen/pelvis (medical examination)
Ca/P	calcium to phosphorus ratio
cap	capillary
CA4P	combretastatin A4 prodrug
CAPA	Certified Ambulatory Perianesthesia Nurse

	Corrective and Preventive Action (related to FDA)	CAPTEM	capecitabine (Xeloda) and temozolomide (Temodar)
CAPB	central auditory processing battery	CaPTHUS	a scoring model for a preoperative diagnostic
	cocamidopropyl betaine		tool for distinguishing
CAPC	Center to Advance Palliative Care		single-gland from multi
capC	capsular polysaccharide		glandular disease including
	synthesis protein Cap8C; see		preoperative serum calcium
	gene website www.ncbi.nlm		and parathyroid hormone
	.nih.gov/gene		values plus ultrasound and
CAPD	central auditory processing		Sestamibi scanning
	disorder	capu	cappuccino; see gene website
	continuous ambulatory peritoneal		www.ncbi.nlm.nih.gov/gene
	dialysis	CAPWA	computerized arterial pulse
	Cornell Assessment for Pediatric		waveform analysis
	Delirium	CAQ	Certificate of Added Qualification
CAP-D	Cornell Assessment for Pediatric	CAR	cancer-associated retinopathy
	Delirium		cardiac ambulation routine
CapeOx	capecitabine and oxaliplatin		carotid artery repair
CAPG	capping protein (actin filament),		carotid artery spin labeled
	gelsolin-like; see gene website		chimeric antigen receptor
	www.ncbi.nlm.nih.gov/gene		coronary artery revascularization
CapGem	capectibine and gemcitabine		cortisol awakening response
Cap-Gem	capectibine and gemcitabine		Coxsackie adenovirus receptor
CAPIRI	capecitabine and irinotecan (also	CA-RA	common adductor-rectus
	known as ZELIRI)		abdominis
CAPLA	computer-assisted product	CARA	Comprehensive Addiction and
	license application		Recovery Act of 2016
CaPNA	capture peptide nucleic acid	CARB	carbohydrate
CAPNON	calcifying pseudo neoplasm	CARBO	Carbocaine
	of the neuraxis (a rare central		carboplatin (Paraplatin)
	nervous system lesion that is	carbs	carbohydrates
	found in both the brain and	CARCs	Claim Adjustment Reason
	the spine)		Codes (Medicare)
CAPOX	capecitabine and oxaliplatin	CARD	Cardiac Automatic Resuscitative
CAPP	Child Abuse Prevention Program		Device
	(New York, NY)	cardio	a combining prefix denoting
CAP-PIRO	Community Acquired		relationship to the heart
	Pneumonia—Predisposition	CARDS	Community Acquired Respiratory
	Infection Reaction, Organ		Distress Syndrome
	failure (prognostic scores for	CARES	Cancer Rehabilitation Evaluation
	influenza pneumonia patients)		System
CaPPS	calcium pentosan polysulfate	CARF	Commission on Accreditation of
CAPS	aspects of cognition, affective		Rehabilitation Facilities
	state, physical condition, and	CArG box	Serum response factor is a
	social factors (patient assess-		transcription factor that binds
	ment; parameters)		to a DNA cis element known
	caffeine, alcohol, pepper, and		as the CArG box, which
	spicy food (dietary		is found in the proximal
	restrictions)		regulatory regions of over
	cryopyrin-associated periodic		200 experimentally validated
	syndromes		target genes.
caps	capsules	CARM	Centre for Adverse Reactions
CAPS-SX	Clinical Administered Post-		Monitoring (New Zealand)
	traumatic Stress Disorder		Classification Association Rule
	Scale - One Week Symptom		Mining
	Version	C-arm	fluoroscopy image intensifier
Capt	Captain		(configuration arm)

CARN	Certified Addiction Registered Nurse		CaSC	carcinoma of the sigmoid colon
CARN-AP	Certified Addictions Registered Nurse - Advanced Practice		CASCC	Certified ASC Coder (CASCC™)
CAROT	CARtilage in obese knee OsteoarThritis (study)		CAS-CBT	Competence and Adherence Scale for Cognitive Behavioral Therapy
carot	carotid		CASD	cell activation and signaling-directed
CARP	Canadian Association of Retired Persons			Checklist for Autism Spectrum Disorder
	Coronary Artery Revascularization Prophylaxis (trial)		casD	CRISP RNA (crRNA) containing Cascade antiviral complex protein (gene)
	see gene website, www.ncbi.nlm.nih.gov/gene		CASH	chemotherapy-associated steatohepatitis
CARRA	Childhood Arthritis and Rheumatology Research Alliance (treatment plans)		CASHD	coronary arteriosclerotic heart disease
CARS	Childhood Autism Rating Scale		CASL	continuous arterial spin labeled
	coherent anti-Stokes Raman scattering		CASL MRI	continuous arterial spin-labeling magnetic resonance imaging
CART	classification and regression tree		CASP	Child Analytic Study Program
	cocaine and amphetamine regulated transcript			clinical adjacent segment pathology
CAR-T	chimeric antigen receptor modified T cells		CASPAR criteria	ClASsification for Psoriatic ARthritis criteria
cART	combination antiretroviral therapy		CASPO	caspofungin acetate (Cancidas)
CARTI	community-acquired respiratory tract infection(s)		CASPR	contacting associated protein-like 1 (gene/protein)
CARTO®	three-dimensional electroanatomical mapping system (Biosense Webster, Inc., USA)		CASPR2	contactin associated protein-like 2 gene/protein
			CASR	see gene website, www.ncbi.nlm.nih.gov/gene
CARTs	cardiovascular reflex tests		CaSR	calcium-sensing receptor
CARV	community-acquired respiratory virus		CASS	computer-aided sleep system
			CA-SSTIs	community-acquired skin and soft tissues infections
CAS	carotid angioplasty and stunting		CAST®	color allergy screening test
	carotid arterial stent (stenting)		CASWCM	Certified Advanced Social Work Case Manager
	carotid artery stenosis		CAT	Cardiac Arrest Team
	cephalic arch stenosis			carnitine acetyl transferase
	cerebral arteriosclerosis			catalase
	Chemical Abstracts Service			cataract
	Clinical Asthma Score			category
	collision avoidance system			Child Advocacy Team
	combined androgen suppression			Childrens Apperception Test
	computer-assisted surgery			coital alignment technique
	condomeless anal sex			combat application tourniquet
	coronary artery stenosis			complementary and alternative therapy
CASA	cancer-associated serum antigen			computed axial tomography
	Center on Addiction and Substance Abuse			critical airway (response) team
	computer-assisted semen analysis			methcatinone
			CAT2	catalase 2 (gene)
	court appointed special advocate		CatA	see gene website www.ncbi.nlm.nih.gov/gene
CA-SAI	community-acquired *Staphylococcus aureus* infections		catB	muconate and chloromuconate cycloisomerase (gene)

catC see gene website, www.ncbi.nlm.nih.gov/gene

CAT/CLAMS Cognitive Adaptive Test/Clinical Linguistic and Auditory Milestone Scale

CAT DQ Cognitive Adaptive Test Development Quotient

Cath Catholic

cath cardiac catheterizion (as in cath lab)
catheter

cathed catheterized

cath lab cardiac catheterization laboratory (department)

Catho Catholic Church

catM see gene website, www.ncbi.nlm.nih.gov/gene

CATS catecholamines

CAT SCAN computed axial tomography procedure

CATSHL camptodactyly, tall stature, and hearing loss (syndrome)

CATT card agglutination test with stained trypanosomes

CAU Caucasian
caudal

cAu colloidal gold

Cauc Caucasian

CAUD congenital anterior urethral diverticulum

CAUIT may have meant CAUTI (catheter-associated urinary tract infection)

CAUTI catheter-associated urinary tract infection

CAV-1 canine adenovirus type 1

CAV cardiac allograft vasculopathy
computer-aided ventilation
congenital absence of vagina
cyclophosphamide, doxorubicin (Adriamycin), and vincristine

CAVB complete atrioventricular block

CAVC common atrioventricular canal
complete atrioventricular canal

CAVD calcific aortic valve disease

CAVE Content Analysis of Verbatim Explanation
cyclophosphamide, doxorubicin, (Adriamycin) vincristine, and etoposide

caveat a word meaning a warning or caution

Caveat emptor Latin for "Let the buyer beware" (the buyer alone is responsible for checking the quality and suitability of goods before a purchase is made)

Cavg average steady-state concentration

CAVH continuous arteriovenous hemofiltration

CAVHD continuous arteriovenous hemodialysis

CAVI cardio-ankle vascular index

CAVM cerebral arteriovenous malformation

CAV-P-VP cyclophosphamide, doxorubicin (Adriamycin), vincristine, cisplatin, and etoposide

CAVR continuous arteriovenous rewarming

CAVS calcific valve stenosis

CAVSD complete atrioventricular septal defect

CAVU continuous arteriovenous ultrafiltration

CAW carbonaceous-activated water (Willard Water)

CAWR central airway resistance
Chinese age-weight rule (formula)
complex abdominal wall reconstruction (repair)

CAX central axis

CaxP calcium-phosphate product

Ca x P calcium times phosphorus product

CB call back
cerebellopontine
cesarean birth
chronic bronchitis
code blue
cognitive behavioural
concha (conchae) bullosa
conjugated bilirubin (direct)
(umbilical) cord blood

c/b characterized by

CB1 cannabinoid receptor, type 1

CB2 cannabinoid receptor type 2

C&B chair and bed
crown and bridge

C&B complicated by

CBA chronic bronchitis and asthma
cost-benefit analysis
County Board of Assistance

Cbag C-terminal domain of Bag-1

CBAPF Certified Board of Addiction Professionals

CBASP Cognitive Behavioral Analysis System of Psychotherapy

CBAT computer-based auditory training

cBAT calculated bioavailable testosterone

CBAVD congenital bilateral absence of the vas deferens

CBB	cord blood bank		CBEU	cytobacteriological examination of urine
	criterion-based benchmark		CBF	cerebral blood flow
CBBB	complete bundle branch block		CBFS	cerebral blood flow studies
CBBD	childhood bladder and bowel dysfunction		CBFV	cerebral blood flow velocity
CBBDQ	Childhood Bladder and Bowel Dysfunction Questionnaire		CBG	capillary blood gas
				capillary blood glucose
CBBG	Coomassie Brilliant Blue G		CBGD	corticobasal ganglionic degeneration
CBBS	clear, bilateral, breath sounds			
CBBs	cell-based biosensors		CBGM	capillary blood glucose monitor
CBC	carbenicillin		CBGS	Cambridge Baby Growth Study
	complete blood count		CBGs	census block groups
	contralateral breast cancer		CBH	collimated beam handpiece (for laser)
CBCA	catheter-based coronary angiography			
			CBHH	Community Behavioral Health Hospital (Minnesota, US)
	criterion-based clinical audits			
CBCC	cisplatin-based combination chemotherapy		CBHSQ	Center for Behavioral Health Statistics and Quality (Substance Abuse and Mental Health Services Administration)
CBCD	complete blood count with differential			
CBC D	complete blood count with differential			
CBCDA	carboplatin		CBI	Caregiver Burden Index
CBCL	Child Behavior Checklist			clinical and business intelligence
CBCPD	competency-based continuing professional development			continuous bladder irrigation
			CBIC	core biopsy imprint cytology
CBCs	complete blood counts		cbiD	see gene website www.ncbi.nlm.nih.gov/gene
CBCT	community based clinical trials			
	cone-beam computed tomography		CBIR	content-based image retrieval
CBC with D	complete blood count with differential		CBIT	Comprehensive Behavioral Intervention for Tics
			cBiT	Compendium for Biomaterial Transcriptomics (cbit. maastrichtuniversity.nl).
CBD	cannabidiol			
	chronic beryllium disease			
	closed bladder drainage		CBJ	cranberry juice
	collected bone debris		CBK	calcific band keratopathy
	common bile duct		CBK-SRT	CyberKnife (Accuray, Sunnyvale, CA)-based stereotactic radiotherapy
	cortical bone decortication			
	corticobasal degeneration			
CBDA	cannabidiolic acid		cblA	cobalamin A type
CBDCA	carboplatin (cis-diammine-1, 1-cyclobutane dicarboxylate platinum II)		CBLI	cumulative lood lead index
			CBM	China BioMedical Literature Database
				chromoblastomycosis (also known as chromomycosis)
CBDE	common bile duct exploration			
CBDI	common bile duct injury			covered by Medicare
CBDS	common bile duct stone(s)			cryopreserved bone marrow
CBD stones	common bile duct stones		CBMC	cord blood mononuclear cell
CBDT	cisplatin, carmustine (BiCNU), dacarbazine, and tamoxifen		CBMs	carbohydrate-binding modules
			CBN	chronic benign neutropenia
CBE	Changes Being Effected (FDA regulatory term)			collected by nurse
			CBO	cerebral blood oxygenation
	charting by exception		CBOCs	community-based outpatient clinics
	child birth education			
	clinical breast examination		CBP	chronic benign pain
CBEFM	Clear-blue Easy Fertility Monitor			copper-binding protein
CBER	Center for Biologics Evaluation and Research (FDA)		CBPC	Community-Based Palliative Care (certification, The Joint Commission)
CBET	Certified Biomedical Equipment Technician			

CBPI	Cytokinesis-Blocked Proliferating Index	CBT-I	cognitive behavioral therapy for insomnia
CBPP	congenital brachial plexus palsy contagious bovine pleuropneumonia		cognitive behavioral therapy for people with insomnia (American College of Physicians guidelines)
CBPS	Community Based Prevention Services	CBTRUS	Central Brain Tumor Registry of the United States
	congential bilateral perisylvian syndrome	CBTS	Carlsbad By The Sea (a skilled nursing facility)
	coronary bypass surgery		
CB1R	cannabinoid-1 receptor	CBU	cumulative breath units
CBR	carotid bodies resected	CBV	central blood volume
	clinical benefit rate		cerebral blood volume
	clinical benefit responders		cyclophosphamide, carmustine
	complete bedrest		(BiCNu), and etoposide
CBRAM	controlled partial rebreathing-anesthesia method		(VePesid)
CBRF	Child Behavior Rating Form	CBVD	cerebrovascular disease
CBRN	California Board of Registered Nursing	CBVT	cone-beam volumetric tomographic (imaging)
	chemical, biological, radiological, or nuclear (agents)	CBW	corrected body weight
			cotton bollworm
			current body weigh
CB RRR s M/R/G	cardiac beat, regular rhythm and rate without murmurs, rubs, or gallops	CBX	carbenoxolone
		Cbx	aspartate aminotransferase; see gene website www.ncbi .nlm.nih.gov/gene
CBrS	clear breath sounds		
CBRT	concomitant boost radiotherapy	cbx	crossbronx; see gene website www.ncbi.nlm.nih.gov/gene
CBS	capillary blood sugar		
	Caregiver Burden Screen	Cby	Chibby
	Catherine Bergego Scale (for neglect assessment)	CBZ	carbamazepine (Tegretol)
		CBZE	carbamazepine epoxide
	Charles Bonnet syndrome	CC	calcaneocuboid (joint)
	chronic brain syndrome		carbon copy (copy sent to)
	coarse breath sounds		cardiac catheterization
	cord blood serum		Care Coordinator
	corticobasal syndrome		Catholic
	Cruveilhier-Baumgarten syndrome		cerebral concussion
	cystathionine beta-synthase		cerebral cortex
CBSCT	cord blood stem cell transplantation		cervical cancer
			chart check (as in 24 hour CC)
CBSE	clinical bedside swallow evaluation		chest compression
			chief complaint
CBSI	catheter-associated bloodstream infection		cholangiocarcinoma
			choriocarcinoma
CBSPD	Certification Board for Sterile Processing and Distribution		chronic complainer
			chronic constipation
			circulatory collapse
CBS with Diff	may have meant CBC with Diff (complete blood count with differential)		circumcision
			clean catch (urine)
			Clinical Coordinator
CBT	carotid body tumor		clomiphene citrate (Clomid)
	cognitive behavioral therapy		Collaborative Care
	cord blood transplant		colony count
	cortical bone trajectory		comfort care
CBTC	Canadian Brain Tumor Consortium		coracoclavicular
			cord compression
CBT-E	cognitive behavioral therapy-enhanced		corpus callosum
			craniocaudad

C

	craniocervical
	creatinine clearance
	critical care
	critical condition
	cubic centimeter (for expression of liquid measurements) This is a DANGEROUS abbreviation when poorly written, that should NOT be used. It appears on the medabbrev.com and other Do Not Use Lists, as it has been read as unit (U) and 00. Use mL
	curved cutter (stapling device)
	with correction (with glasses)
	with food (usually written with lines over the CCs; this is a poor abbreviation as it is not in common use and may not be understood)
C_c	concentration of drug in the central compartment
C_1-C_7	cervical vertebra 1 through 7
C_1-C_8	cervical nerves 1 through 8
C_1.... C_{12}	cranial nerves 1 to 12
C/C	cholecystectomy and operative cholangiogram
	complete upper and lower dentures
	complications and comorbidity
	counseling and coordination of care
	see CC and C&C
C0-C2	occipitocervical spine junction
C1C2	cervical region C1C2
	cervical vertebrae 1 and 2
C1-C2	cervical vertebrae 1 and 2
C2C3	cervical region C2C3
	cervical vertebrae 2 and 3
C2-C3	cervical vertebrae 2 and 3
C3C4	cervical region C3C4
	cervical vertebrae 3 and 4
C3-C4	cervical vertebrae 3 and 4
C3-C6	subaxial spine junction
C3-C7	cervical vertebrae 3, 4, 5, 6, and 7
C4C5	cervical region C4C5
	cervical vertebrae 4 and 5
C4-C5	cervical vertebrae 4 and 5
C5C6	cervical region C5C6
	cervical vertebrae 5 and 6
C5-C6	cervical vertebrae 5 and 6
C6C7	cervical vertebrae 6 and 7
C6-C7	cervical vertebrae 6 and 7
CCII	Clinical Clerk-2nd year
CC3	third coiled-coil (domain)
C&C	cold and clammy
	confirmed and compatible

C & C	cold and clammy
CCA	calcium-channel antagonist
	Certified Coding Associate
	cholangiocarcenoma
	circumflex coronary artery
	common carotid artery
	concentrated care area
	continuous cool aerosol
	countercurrent chromatography
	critical care area
CCa	colon cancer
cCa	corrected calcium
CCAA	calcified carotid artery atheromas
CCAC	clear cell adenocarcinoma of the cervix
	Community Care Access Centre (Canada)
ccaC	see gene website www.ncbi.nlm.nih.gov/gene
CCACF	Climate Change Adaptation Conceptual Framework
CCAD	Central Cardiac Audit Database (United Kingdom)
	cervicocranial artery dissection
	chronic coronary artery disease
	common carotid artery diameter
	common carotid artery dissection
CCAH	congenital central alveolar hypoventilation (syndrome)
CCAM	congenital cystic adenomatoid malformation (of the lung)
CCAO	chronic common carotid artery occlusion
CCAP	capsule cartilage articular preservation
CCARB	Controlled Carbohydrate Assessment Registry Bank (Study)
C-CASA	Columbia Classification Algorithm for Suicide Assessment
CCAT	common carotid artery thrombosis
C-CATODSW	Certified Clinical Alcohol, Tobacco and Other Drugs Social Worker
CCAU	clear cell adenocarcinoma of the urethra
	continuing care as usual
CCAVC	complete common atrioventricular canal
CCB	calcium channel blocker(s)
	Community Care Board
	corn, callus, and bunion
	with breakfast
CCBD	Center for Cancer and Blood Disorders

	central cell binding domains		Continuity of Care Document
	continuous controllable balloon dilator		cortical collecting duct
			crossed cerebellar diaschisis
CCBH	chronic cutaneous bacterial hypersensitivity	CCDC	Certified Chemical Dependency Counselor
CCBHC	Certified Community Behavioral Health Clinics (Department of Health and Human Services)	CCDC-1	Certified Chemical Dependency Counselor, Level One
		CCDD	congenital cranial dysinnervation disorder
CCBT	Certified Cognitive Behavioral Therapist	CCDM	Culture Collection of Dairy Microorganisms
CCC	Cancer Care Center	CCDS	color-coded duplex sonography
	Cardiac Center Certification (The Joint Commission)	CCE	clubbing, cyanosis, and edema
			colon capsule endoscopy
	central corneal clouding (Grade 0+ to 4+)		countercurrent electrophoresis
			critical care echocardiography
	Certificate of Clinical Competency	C/C/E	clubbing, cyanosis, and edema
	Certified Cardiology Coder (CCC™)	CCEGD	colonoscopy with consecutive esophagogastroduodenoscopy
	child care clinic	CC-EMG	corpus cavernousum electromyography
	cholangiocellular carcinoma		
	chronic Chagas cardiomyopathy	CCEP	cortico-cortical evoked potential(s)
	circulating cancer cells		
	clinical competency committees	CCF	carotid cavernous fistula
	clinical coordinating center		cephalin cholesterol flocculation
	closed chest compressions		Cleveland Clinic Foundation
	complex chronic conditions		compound comminuted fracture
	Comprehensive Cancer Center		congestive cardiac failure
	concordance correlation coefficient		crystal-induced chemotactic factor
	continuous curvilinear capsulorrhexis	CCFA	cycloserine cefoxitin fructose agar
	Coricidin Cough and Cold (slang)	CCFE	cyclophosphamide, cisplatin, fluorouracil, and estramustine
CC & C	colony count and culture		
C/C/C	see CCC	CCFL	cold cathode fluorescent lamp
C/cc	colonies per cubic centimeter	CCFS	Composite Cerebellar Functional Score
CCC-A	Certificate of Clinical Competence in Audiology	CCFs	chronic-care facilities
CCCE	Clinical Center Coordinator Educator	CCG	Children's Cancer Group
			custom cutting guides
CCCN	Certified Continence Care Nurse	CCGPP	Council on Chiropractic Guidelines and Parameters
CCCP	carbonyl cyanide m-chlorophenylhydrazone (efflux-pump inhibitor)	CCgR	complete cytogenetic response
		CCH	chronic cluster headache
	continuous control of endotracheal tube cuff pressure		collagenase Clostridium histolyticum
CCCs	continent catheterizable channels		Collagenase Clostridium histolyticum (Xiaflex injection)
CCC-SLP	Certificate of Clinical Competence in Speech-Language Pathology		community care home
			Cook County Hospital
CCCT	clomiphene citrate challenge test	Cch	conjunctivochalasis
CCD	central core disease	CCHB	congenital complete heart block
	charge coupled device (radiology)	CCHC	see gene website, www.ncbi.nlm .nih.gov/gene
	childhood celiac disease		
	chin-chest distance	CCHD	complex congenital heart disease
	cleidocranial dysplasia		cyanotic congenital heart disease
	clinical cardiovascular disease	CCHF	Congo Crimean hemorrhagic fever
	colopocystodefecography		

CCHFV	Crimean-Congo hemorrhagic fever virus	CCM	calcium citrate malate
			cerebral cavernous malformation
CCHIE	Coastal Connect Health Information Exchange (North Carolina)		Certified Care Manager
			cervical compression myelopathy
			children's case management
CCHIP	Community Childhood Hunger Identification Project (indicators)		Comprehensive Care Medicine
			corneal confocal microscopy
			country coordinating mechanism
CCHO	consistent carbohydrate		Critical Care Medicine
cc/hr	cubic centimeters per hour (mL/hr is preferred)		cyclophosphamide, lomustine (CCNU; CeeNU), and methotrexate
CCHS	congenital central hypoventilation syndrome	CCMA	caseous calcification of the mitral annulus
CCHT	care coordination home telehealth	CCMHC	Certified Clinical Mental Health Counselor
	Certified Clinical Hemodialysis Technician	CCML	Computational Chemistry Markup Language
CCI	calculated creatinine clearance	CCMS	capture compound mass spectrometry
	Charlson's Comorbidity Index		
	chronic coronary insufficiency	CCMs	cerebral cavernous malformations
	Correct Coding Initiative	CCMSU	clean catch midstream urine
	corrected count increment	CCMU	critical care medicine unit
CCIC	Canadian Consortium for the Investigation of Cannabinoids	CCN	CMS (Centers for Medicare & Medicaid Services) Certification Number
	colon cancer-initiating cell		continuing care nursery
CCICs	colon cancer-initiating cells		cyr61, ctgf, nov (family of proteins)
ccIIV3	cell-culture inactivated influenza vaccine, trivalent (Flucelvax)		
CCIO	Chief Clinical Informatics Officer	CCND	central compartment neck dissection
	complete cranial iliac osteotomy		central compartment node dissection
CCIS	Cleveland Clinic Fecal Incontinence Score	ccnd	cyclin D (gene)
CCJ	calcaneocuboid joint	CCND1	cyclin D1 (gene)
	craniocervical junction	CCND2	cyclin D2 (gene)
CCJAP	Certified Criminal Justice Addiction Professional	CCNS	cell cycle-nonspecific
			Certified Clinical Nurse Specialist
CCJAS	Certified Criminal Justice Addiction Specialist	CCNU	lomustine (CeeNu)
		CCO	continuous cardiac output
CC Joint	calcaneocuboid joint		Corporate Compliance Officer
CCK	Cholecystokinin		corrected coronary opacification
	cholecystokinin	CCOHTA	Canadian Coordinating Office of Health Technology Assessment
cCk	classic Kaposi sarcoma		
CCK-OP	cholecystokinin octapeptide		
CCK-PZ	cholecystokinin pancreozymin	C-collar	cervical collar
CCL	cardiac catheterization laboratory	CCOP	Community Clinical Oncology Program (initiated by the National Cancer Institute)
	critical condition list		
CCl4	carbon tetrachloride	CCoV	canine coronavirus
CCLab	Combinatorial Chemistry Laboratory (software)	CCP	clinical coordinating pharmacy
			common compensatory pattern
CCL2BT	catheterisation laboratory to balloon time		cricoid pressure
			crystalloid cardioplegia
CCLE	chronic cutaneous lupus erythematosus		cyclic citrullinated peptide
		ccpA	catabolite control protein A; see gene website www.ncbi.nlm .nih.gov/gene
CCLS	Certified Child Life Specialist		
CCLs	columnar cell lesions		

CCP antibodies	anti-cyclic citrullinated peptide antibodies		Physician
			Clara Cell Secretory Protein
CCPD	continuous cycling (cyclical) peritoneal dialysis	CCS-P	Certified Coding Specialist, Physician-Based
CCPs	Corporate Compliance Programs	CCSQ	Center for Clinical Standards
CCPTN	Critical Care Pharmacotherapy Trials Network		and Quality (Centers for Medicare & Medicaid Services)
CCQ	California Child Q-set	CCSR	Center for Clinical Sciences
CCR	California Cancer Registry		Research
	cardiac catheterization recovery		childhood cataract surgical rate
	cardiocerebral resuscitation	CCSS	Childhood Cancer Survivor Study
	complete cytogenetic remission	CCSV	cell-cultured smallpox vaccine
	Continuity of Care Record	CCSVI	chronic cerebrospinal venous insufficiency
	continuous complete remission		
	conventional care regimens	CCSW	Certified Clinical Social Worker
	counterclockwise rotation	CCT	calcitriol
C_{cr}	creatinine clearance		carotid compression tomography
cCR	complete clinical remission		central corneal thickness
CCRC	Certified Clinical Research Coordinator		Certified Cardiographic Technician
	continuing care residential community		chest computed tomography
			Clomid challenge test
CCRCC	clear-cell renal cell carcinoma		closed cerebral trauma
CC-RCC	clear-cell renal-cell carcinoma		closed cranial trauma
CCRN	Certified in Critical Care Nursing		collision cell technology
	Critical Care Registered Nurse		Completed course of treatment
CCRP	Certified Clinical Research Professional		congenitally corrected transposition (of the great vessels)
	core circadian regulatory proteins		Critical Care Technician
CCRT	concurrent chemoradiotherapy		critical care time
CCRU	critical care recovery unit		critical care transport
CCRx	a prescription drug plan		crude coal tar
CCS	California Children's Services	CCt	CCT for Calorie count
	Calvin classification system (grades I-V)	CCTA	coronary computed tomographic angiography
	Canadian Cardiovascular (Angina) Society (grades I-IV)	CCTC	CellSearch Circulating Tumor Cell
	cell cycle-specific	CC-TGA	congenitally-corrected transposition of the great arteries
	central cord syndrome		
	certified coding specialist		
	cervical cancer screening	CCT in PET	crude coal tar in petroleum
	childhood cancer survivors	CCTN	Canadian Cardiac Transplant Network
	color-contrast sensitivity		
	Constipation Scoring System		coronary care-trained nurse
	Cronkhite-Canada syndrome		Italian National Advisory Toxicological Committee
CC & S	cornea, conjunctiva, and sclera		
CCSA	Canadian Cardiovascular Society Angina (score)	CCTP	Community-Based Care Transitions Program
CCSD	chronic cervical spinal disorder	CCTV	closed circuit television
CCSE	Cognitive Capacity Screening Examination	CCU	coronary care unit
			critical care unit
CCSF	Canadian Cardiovascular Society Functional (class)	CCUA	clean catch urinalysis
		CCUP	colpocystourethropexy
	carotid-cavernous sinus fistula	CCUS	carbon capture, utilization, and storage
CCSI	cross-correlation synchrony index		
			clonal cytopenias of undetermined significance
CCSK	clear cell sarcoma of the kidney		
CCSP	Certified Chiropractic Sports		critical care ultrasonography

C

CCV	cardio(vascular) and cerebrovascular		cumulative doses cycle day, referring to cycle day number of the menstrual cycle; eg.: CD#1, first day of menstruel cycle
	clathrin-coated vesicles		
	coronary collateral vessels		
	Critical Care Ventilator (Ohio)		
	critical closing volume		cyclodextran
	cyclophosphamide, irinotecan (CPT-11), and vincristine	Cd	cytarabine and daunorubicin cadmium
CCVD	cardiovascular and cerebrovascular disease		concentration of drug
		C/D	cigarettes per day
	catalytic chemical vapor deposition		cup-to-disc ratio
		C1D1	treatment cycle 1, day 1
CCVDs	cardiovascular and cerebrovascular diseases	C2D1	treatment cycle 2, day 1
		C4d	an established marker of antibody-mediated acute renal allograft rejection
CCVHD	may have meant cGVHD (chronic graft-versus-host disease)		
		C&D	curettage and desiccation
CCVTC	Certified Cardiovascular and Thoracic Surgery Coder (CCVTC™)		cystectomy and diversion
			cytoscopy and dilatation
		CDA	Certified Dental Assistant
CCW	childcare worker		chenodeoxycholic acid (chenodiol)
	counterclockwise		
CCWR	counterclockwise rotation		chloride depletion alkalosis
CCX	complications		Clinical Document Architecture (CDC)
CCY	cholecystectomy		
CCyR	complete cytogenetic response		congenital dyserythropoietic anemia
CD	cadaver donor		
	candela	CDAC	Clostridium difficile-associated colitis
	Castlemans disease		
	celiac disease	CDA4CDT	Clinical Documentation Architecture for Common Document Types (project)
	cervical dystonia		
	cesarean delivery		
	character disorder	CDAD	Clostridium difficile-associated diarrhea
	childhood disease		
	chlorproguanil-dapsone (Lapdap)	CDAI	Clinical Disease Activity Index
	chronic dialysis		Crohn Disease Activity Index
	claudication (walking) distance	CDAK	Cordis Dow Artificial Kidney
	closed drainage	CD and I	clear, dry, and intact
	Clostridium difficile	CDAP	continuous distended airway pressure
	Clusters of Differentiation (e.g. CD38)		
		CDASH	Clinical Data Acquisition Standards Harmonization
	common duct		
	communication disorders	CDB	cough and deep breath
	compact disc	C&DB	cough and deep breath
	complementarity-determining	cDBP	central diastolic blood pressure
	complicated delivery		
	conduct disorder	CDC	calculated day of confinement
	conjugate diameter		cancer detection center
	contact dermatitis		carboplatin, doxorubicin, and cyclophosphamide
	continuous drainage		
	controlled delivery (extended release drug delivery)		Centers for Disease Control and Prevention
	conventional denture		Certified Drug Counselor
	convulsive disorder		chenodeoxycholic acid (chenodiol)
	cool-down		
	cortical dysplasia		Cholesterol-dependent cytolysins
	Crohn disease		

116

chronic disseminated candidiasis
circular diagnostic catheter
Clostridium difficile colitis

CDCA   chenodeoxycholic acid (chenodiol)

CDCC   complement-dependent cellular cytotoxicity

CD2-CD350   cluster of differentiation, a protocol used for the identification of cell surface molecules present on white blood cells, providing targets for immunophenotyping of cells (cd_marker_handbook.pdf)

CDCP   Centers for Disease Control and Prevention (CDC is official abbreviation)

CDCR   conjunctivo-dacryocystorhinostomy

CdCS   Cri du Chat syndrome

CDD   Certificate of Disability for Discharge
cytidine deaminase

CDDD   cervical degenerative disk disease

cDDD   cumulative defined daily dose

cddD   aldehyde dehydrogenase (gene)

CDDN   Certified Developmental Disabilities Nurse

CDDP   cisplatin (Platinol)

CDDS   central dialysis fluid delivery system
Cornell Scale for Depression in Dementia

CDDs   community-based drug distributors
cardiac death donors

CDE   canine distemper encephalitis
Certified Diabetes Educator
common data element
common duct exploration

CDEF   Combined Dose and Exposure Factor

CDEO   Certified Documentation Expert Outpatient (CDEO®)

CDER   Center for Drug Evaluation and Research (FDA)

CDFI   color Doppler flow imaging

CDG   carbohydrate-deficient glycoprotein
congenital disorders of glycosylation

CDGE   constant denaturant gel electrophoresis

CDGP   constitutional delay of growth and puberty

CDGS   carbohydrate-deficient glycoprotein syndrome

CDH1   cadherin 1 (gene)

CDH   chronic daily headache
congenital diaphragmatic hernia
congenital dislocation of hip
congenital dysplasia of the hip

CDHD   consciousness deficit hypoactivity disorder

CDHF   Canadian Digestive Health Foundation
choline-deficient high-fat diet

CDHP   5-chloro-2 4-dihydroxypyridine

CDI   cardiac device infection
Children's Depression Inventory
clean, dry, and intact
clinical documentation improvement
Clostridium difficile infection
color Doppler imaging
conformation-dependent immunoassay
contact-dependent growth inhibition
Cotrel Duobosset Instrumentation

CDI-25   Caring Dimension Inventory

CD&I   clear, dry, and intact

C/D/I   clean, dry, and intact
clean/dry/intact

CdiA   contact-dependent inhibition of growth factor; see gene website www.ncbi.nlm.nih.gov/gene

CDIC   *Clostridium difficile*-induced colitis

CDIDs   chronic disabling inflammatory diseases

C Dif   *Clostridium difficile*

C diff   *Clostridium difficile*

C difficile   *Clostridium difficile*

CDIO   Chief Dental Informatics Officer

CDIP   chronic demyelinating inflammatory polyneuropathy

CDIP-58   Cervical Dystonia Impact Profile

CDIS   Clinical Document Improvement Specialists

CDISC   Clinical Data Interchange Standards Consortium

CDJ   choledochojejunostomy

CDK   climatic droplet keratopathy
cyclin-dependent kinase

CDK2   cyclin-depenent kinases 2

CDK3   cyclin-dependent kinase 3 (gene/protein)

CDK4/6   cyclin-dependent kinase 4/6 (gene/protein)

CDKI   cyclin-dependent kinase inhibitor

cdkl5	cyclin-dependent kinase-like 5 (gene)
CDLC	continuous double-loop closure
CDLE	chronic discoid lupus erythematosus
CDLM	contact diode laser for myringotomy
CdLS	Cornelia de Lange syndrome
CDM	charge description master
	clinical data management
	clinical development monitor
CDMA	chloride depletion metabolic alkalosis
	code-division multiple-access
CDMHP	County Designated Mental Health Professional (this name was changed to Designated Mental Health Professional (DMHP)
CDMO	contact development and manufacturing organization
CDMOs	contract development and manufacturing organizations
CDMP	Compliant Documentation Management Program
	Comprehensive Diabetes Management Program
CDMPs	cartilage-derived morphogenetic proteins
CDMS	Certified Disability Management Specialist
	clinically definite multiple sclerosis
CDN	Canadian
cDNA	complementary deoxyribonucleic acid
CDNH	chondrodermatitis nondularis helicis
CDNVGs	color-display night-vision goggles
CDO	cartilage disorder
CDOMD	chronic disabling occupational musculoskeletal disorder
CDONA/LTC	Certified Director of Nursing Administration in Long-Term Care
CDP	cancer detection program
	chemical dependence profile
	Chemical Dependency Professional
	Child Development Program
	clinical development plan
	complete decongestive physiotherapy
	computerized dynamic posturography
	crystalline degradation product
	cytidine diphosphate

C/D/P	complete blood count, differential blood count, and platelets
CDPAP	Consumer Directed Personal Assistance Program (a state-wide Medicaid program that provides an alternative way of receiving home care services, where the consumer has more control over who provides their care and how it is provided)
CDPH	California Department of Public Health
CDPP	may have meant CDDP (cisplatin [cis-diammine-dichloridoplatinum(II)])
CDQ	corrected development quotient
CDR	cancer detection rate
	Cause of Death Registry
	clinical data repository
	Clinical Dementia Rating
	cognitive dietary restraint
	commonly deleted region
	continuing disability review
	cup-to-disc ratio
	recordable compact disc
CDRH	Center for Devices and Radiological Health
CDR(H)	cup-to-disc ratio horizontal
CDRIE	cardiac device-related infective endocarditis
CDRP	Cancer Disparities Research Partnership (program)
CDRS	Certified Driver Rehabilitation Specialist
	Children's Depression Rating Scale
CDRs	complementary determining regions
CDRV	cup-to-disc ratio vertical
CDS	Chemical Dependency Specialist
	Chronic Disease Score
	clinical decision support
	closed-door seclusion
	cognitive dysfunction syndrome (veterinary)
	color Doppler sonography
	continuous dopamine stimulation
CDSA	Controlled Drugs and Substances Act (Canada)
CDSC	Communicable Disease Surveillance Centre (United Kingdom)
CDSM	chronic disease self-management
CDSPIES	congestive heart failure, drugs, spasm, pneumothorax, Infection, embolism, and secretions (differential diagnosis mnemonic)

CDSR	Cochrane Database of Systematic Reviews
CDSS	Cervical Dystonia Severity Scale
	Clinical Decision Support Systems
	computer decision-support software
CDSSs	clinical decision support systems
CDST	cost decision support tool
CDT	carbohydrate-deficient transferrin
	catheter-directed thrombolysis
	Chemical Dependency Technician
	clinical development team
	Clinical Dietetic Technician
	Clock-Drawing Test
	Clostridium difficile toxin
	complete decongestive therapy (for lymphedema)
	connecting discourse tracking (measure of speech perception)
	current dental terminology
	cystic dysplasia of the testis
	cytolethal distending toxin
CDTA	cyclohexane-1, 2-diaminetetraacetic acid
CDTM	collaborative drug therapy management
CDTS	Composite Drug Toxicity Score
CDTU	Critical Decision Treatment Unit
CDU	chemical dependence unit
	chemical dependency unit
	color-coded duplex ultrasonography
CDUS	Carotid Duplex Ultrasonography
CDV	canine distemper virus
	cardiovascular
	cyclophosphamide, doxorubicin, and vincristine
CDVA	corrected distance visual acuity
CDW	cell dry weight
	charge density wave (interactions among electrons and phonons that can also lead to supercon- ductivity and other competing or entangled phases)
	Clinical Data Warehouse (system)
CDX	chlordiazepoxide (Librim)
CDX2	caudal type homeobox 2 (gene/ protein)
cDXA	central dual-energy X-ray absorptiometry
cdyn	dynamic compliance
CDZM	cefodizime
CDZP	*chlordiazepoxide* HCl (originally marketed as Librium)
CE	California encephalitis
	capillary electrophoresis
	capsule endoscopy

	carboplatin and etoposide
	cardiac enlargement
	cardiac enzymes
	cardioesophageal
	Carpentier-Edwards (heart valve prosthesis)
	cataract extraction
	central episiotomy
	cervical examination
	chemoembolization
	chest expansion
	cholesterol ester
	community education
	conjugated estrogens
	continuing education
	contrast echocardiology
	cystic echinococcosis
C&E	consultation and examination
	cough and exercise
	curettage and electrodesiccation
C/E	see CE
Ce	cerium
CEA	carcinoembryonic antigen
	carotid endarterectomy
	center edge angle
	cost-effectiveness analysis
CeA	central amygdala
CeAD	cervical artery dissection
CEAP	Clinical Etiologic Anatomic Pathophysiologic (classification of chronic venous disease)
CEAs	cost-effectiveness analyses
CEB	calcium entry blocker
	carboplatin, etoposide, and bleomycin
CEBBS	clear, equal, bilateral breath sounds
cebo	placebo
CEBPA	CCAAT/enhancer binding protein alpha; see gene website www.ncbi.nlm.nih .gov/gene
CEBS	Certified Employee Benefit Specialist
	Chemical Effects in Biological Systems (database)
CEBV	chronic Epstein-Barr virus
CEC	capillary electrochromatography
	Cardiac Evaluation Center
	circulating endothelial cells
	Council for Exceptional Children
CECA	Childhood Experience of Care and Abuse (interview)
CECD	congenital endothelial corneal dystrophy
CEmacron	cataract extraction with
c/IOL	intraocular lens

CECS	chronic exertional compartment syndrome	CEL	cardiac exercise laboratory
	Courtauld Emotional Control Scale	CELE	celecoxib (Celebrex)
		CELF	Clinical Evaluation of Language Fundamentals
CECT	cecostomy tube		
	contrast-enhanced computed tomography	CE-LIF	capillary-electrophoresis with laser-induced fluorescence
CED	Camurati-Engelmann disease	CELIP	Claims Expansion Line-item Processing
	canine elbow dysplasia		
	cavity evaluation device	CELP	chronic erosive lichen planus
	clinically effective dose	CELs	Federally Qualified Health Center(s)
	convection-enhanced delivery		
	cystoscopy-endoscopy dilation	CELSS	controlled ecological life-support system
CEDC	Certified Emergency Department Coder (CEDC™)		
		CEM	carboplatin, etoposide, and melphalan
CEDM	contrast-enhanced digital mammography		Clinical Event Manager
			confocal endomicroscopy
CEDRD	Certified Eating Disorders Registered Dietitian	CEMC	Certified Evaluation and Management Coder (CEMC™)
CEDRN	Certified Eating Disorders Registered Nurse	CEMD	consultative examination by physician
CEDS	Certified Eating Disorders Specialist	CE-MRA	contrast-enhanced magnetic resonance angiography
CEE	Central European encephalitis	ce-MRI	contrast enhanced magnetic resonance imaging
	childhood epileptic encephalopathy	CEMS	Children's Emotional Manifestation Scale
	conjugated equine estrogen (Premarin; conjugated estrogen)	CEMs	Clinical Element Models
		CEN	Certified Emergency Nurse
cEEG	continuous electroencephalography (monitoring)		Certified (Nurse)- Emergency Room
			European Committee for Standardization
CEF	chick embryo fibroblast		
	cyclophosphamide, epirubicin, and fluorouracil	CENOG	computerized electroneuro-ophthalmogram
CEFM	continuous external fetal monitoring	CENTER-TBI	Collaborative European NeuroTrauma Effectiveness Research in Traumatic Brain Injury (study)
CEFOT	cefotaxime (Claforan)		
CEFOX	cefoxitin (Mefoxin)		
CEFTAZ	ceftazidime	centi	a hundredth
CEFUR	cefuroxime	Cenz	enzyme concentration
CEG	Clarke Error Grid (analysis)	CEO	chief executive officer
CEGA	cervical esophagogastric anastomosis	CEOP	childhood epilepsy with occipital paroxysms
	combined epidural and general anesthesia		cyclophosphamide, epirubicin, Oncovin (vincristine), and prednisolone
CEH	chronic expanding hematoma		
CEHRT	certified electronic health record technology (Centers for Medicare and Medicaid Services)	CEOT	calcifying epithelial odontogenic tumor
CEI	continuous extravascular infusion	CEP	cardiac enzyme panel
	converting enzyme inhibitor		Certified Emergency Paramedic
CEIA	capillary electrophoresis immunoassay analysis		chronic eosinophilic pneumonia
			cognitive evoked potential
CEID	cardiac electronic implantable device		congenital erythropoietic porphyria
CE/IOL	cataract extraction with intraocular lens		countercurrent electrophoresis
			cyclophosphamide, etoposide, and cisplatin (Platinol)
CEJ	cervical-enamel junction (dental)		

CEPC	circulating endothelial progenitor cells	CESA	combined endovascular and surgical approach
CEPD	cerebral embolic protection device(s)	CESB	cervical epidural steroid block
			chronic electrical stimulation of the brain
CEPE	cataract extraction by phacoemulsification	CES-D	Center for Epidemiologic Studies - Depression
CEPH	cephalic		
	cephalosporin	CESI	cervical epidural steroid injection
CEPH FLOC	cephalin flocculation	CESM	contrast-enhanced spectral mammography
CEPP (B)	cyclophosphamide, etopside, procarbazine, prednisone, and bleomycin	CET	cold-exposure test
			common extensor tendon
CEPTH	may have meant CTEPH (chronic thromboembolic pulmonary hypertension)	CETA	concentration equilibrium transport assay
		CETC	circularing epitheliel tumor cells
CER	comparative effectiveness research	CETN	Certified Enterostomal Therapy Nurse
	conditioned emotional response	CETP	cholesteryl ester transfer protein
CE&R	central episiotomy and repair	CETPH	may have meant CTEPH (chronic thromboembolic pulmonary hypertension)
CERA	continuous erythropoiesis receptor activator (methoxy polyethylene glycol-epoetin beta [Micera])		
		CETPi	cholesteryl ester transfer protein inhibitor(s)
	cortical evoked response audiometry	cETT	cuffed endotracheal tube
CERAD	Consortium to Establish a Registry for Alzheimer Disease	CEU	Utah residents with ancestry from northern and western European ancestry (populations included in HapMap - see HapMap)
CERC	Crisis Emergency and Risk Communication (training)		
CERD	chronic end-stage renal disease	CEUS	contrast-enhanced ultrasound
Cerec®	Chairside Economical Restoration of Esthetic Ceramics (dental crowns; Omnicam, Dentsply Sirona)	CEV	cyclophosphamide, etoposide, and vincristine
		CEVO	Certified Emergency Vehicle Operator
CERT	Centers for Education and Research on Theraputics	CEWA	combined ELISA (enzyme-linked immunosorbent assay)-Western blot analysis
	Community Emergency Response Teams		
	Comprehensive Error Rate Testing	CE w/IOL	cataract extraction with intraocular lens
	Computer Emergency Response Team	CEX	Clinical Evaluation Exercise
		CF	calcium leucovorin (citrovorum factor)
cert	certification		cancer-free
Cert MDT	Certified in Mechanical Diagnosis and Therapy		cardiac failure
			Caucasian female
CERULO	ceruloplasmin		cervical foley
CERV	cervical		Christmas factor
CES	cauda equina syndrome		cisplatin and fluorouracil
	central excitatory state		complement fixation
	Children's Emergency Services		contractile force
	cognitive environmental stimulation		correction factor
			count fingers
	estrogen, conjugated (conjugated estrogen substance)		cystic fibrosis
		C&F	cell and flare
			chills and fever
			condoms and foam
CE's	possessive or plural forms of CE (see CE)	C/F	clinical features
			see CF

C3F8	perfluoropropane	CFL	cadaveric fascia lata
Cf	californium		calcaneofibular ligament
CFA	common femoral artery		cisplatin, fluorouracil, and
	complete Freunds adjuvant		leucovorin calcium
	confirmatory factor analysis	CFLD	cystic fibrosis-associated liver
	contralateral foramen area		disease
	cystic fibrosis anthropathy	CFLEX	see C-Flex
CFAC	complement-fixing antibody	C-Flex	a continuous positive airway
	consumption		pressure device that provides
C-factor	cleverness factor		pressure adjustability at exha-
CFAE	complex fractionated atrial		lation (the amount the pres-
	electrogram		sure is lowered as determined
CFAP43	cilia and flagella associated		by one of three settings that
	protein 43 (gene)		can be adjust for comfort)
CFB	change from baseline	C-Flex®	a thermoplastic elastomer tubing
	complement factor B; see gene		specifically designed to meet
	website www.ncbi.nlm.nih		the demands of pharmaceu-
	.gov/gene		tical and biopharmaceuti-
CFCF	carbon fiber composite frame		cal applications for fluid
	(cage)		processing
CFCs	chlorofluorocarbons	CF-LVAD	continuous-flow left ventricular
CfCs	Conditions for Coverage		assist devices
	(Medicare)	CFLX	ciprofloxacin (Cipro)
CFD	color-flow Doppler		circumflex
	computational fluid dynamics	CFM	cerebral function monitor
CFDA	Chinese Food and Drug		close fitting mask
	Administration		complement factor H
cfDNA	cell-free deoxyribonucleic acid		craniofacial microsomia
CFDS	color flow Doppler sonography		cross-friction massage
CFE	common femoral endarterectomy		cyclophosphamide, fluorouracil,
cFE	cryptogenic focal epilepsy		and mitoxantrone
CFEA	complex fractionated	CFMH	calls for medical help
	electrogram-guided ablation	CFMP	chronic facial musculoskeletal
CFEM	Common in Fungal Extracellular		pain
	Membranes (a protein	CFNB	continuous femoral nerve block
	superfamily)	CFNP	congenital facial nerve palsy
CFF	citrated functional fibrinogen		cystic fibrosis nasal polyp
	critical fusion (flicker) frequency	CFNS	chills, fever, and night sweats
CFFT	critical flicker fusion threshold		craniofrontonasal syndrome
CFG	comfort functional goal	CFO	custom foot orthotic
	(guideline for pain tolerance)	CFP	cyan fluorescence protein
	convergent functional genomics		cystic fibrosis protein
CFH	chemical fume hood	CFPC	Certified Family Practice Coder
CFHR1	complement factor H related 1		(CFPC™)
	(gene)	CFPP	Childbirth Fear - Prior to
CFHR3	complement factor H related 3		Pregnancy (scale)
	(gene)	CFPPs	coal-fired power plants
CFI	chemotherapy-free intervals	CFPT	cyclophosphamide, fluorouracil,
	confrontation fields intact		prednisone, and tamoxifen
	The Center for the Intrepid	CFR	case-fatality rates
cfiA	metallo-beta-lactamase		*Code of Federal Regulations*
	(carbapenemase-producing		coronary flow reserve
	gene)	CFRB	critical findings read back
CFIDS	chronic fatigue immune	CFRD	cystic fibrosis-related diabetes
	dysfunction syndrome	CFRDM	cystic fibrosis-related diabetes
CFIs	chemotherapy-free intervals		mellitus
	contraceptive-free intervals	CFRLD	cystic fibrosis related liver
CFJ	Cervical facet joint		disease

CFRN	Certified Flight Registered Nurse	CG	capectibine and gemcitabine
			cardiogreen (dye)
CFRP	carbon-fiber reinforced polymer		caregiver
CFR PEEK	carbon-fiber reinforced polyetheretherketone		caregiver
			cholecystogram
CFRT	conventional fractionated radiotherapy		cholesterol granuloma
			Cockcroft-Gault (equation)
CFS	cancer family syndrome		contact guard (physical therapy)
	Child and Family Service		contact guarding
	childhood febrile seizures		contralateral groin
	chronic fatigue syndrome		control group
	Clinical Frailty Scale (scores)	CGA	clonal group A
	congenital fibrosarcoma		comprehensive geriatric assessment
	craniofacial surgery		
CFSAN	Center for Food Safety and Applied Nutrition (FDA)		contact guard assist
			corrected gestation age
CFSQ	Caregiver's Feeding Styles Questionnaire	CgA	chromogranin A
		CGAF	Consolidated Grant Applicant File (NIH)
CFT	capillary filling time		
	chronic follicular tonsillitis	CGAS	Children's Global Assessment Scale
	chronic food toxicity (i. e. obesity)		
		CGB	chronic gastrointestinal (tract) bleeding
	complement fixation test		
CFTD	congenital fiber type disproportion	CGCG	central giant-cell granuloma
		CGCR	Clinical Global Consensus Rating
CFTR	cystic fibrosis transmembrane (conductance) regulator		
		CGD	chronic glycogen deficit
	cystic fibrosis transmembrane receptor		chronic granulomatous disease
		CGE	capillary gel electrophoresis
CFTs	clot formation times		cobalt Gray equivalent
CFTX	cefotaxime sodium (Claforan)		coffee ground emesis
CFTx	Chironex fleckeri (Australian box jellyfish) toxin	CGE-LIF	capillary gel electrophoresis with laser-induced fluorescence
	lung transplant for cystic fibrosis		
CFU	colony-forming units	CGF	continuous gavage feeding (infant feeding)
	criteria for use		
CFU-E	colony-forming unit-erythroid		cumulative (primary) graft failure
CFU-G	colony-forming unit-granulocyte		
CFU-G/M	colony-forming unit-granulocyte/ macrophage	cGFR	calculated glomerular filtration rate
CFU-M	colony-forming unit-macrophage	CGG	cytosine-guanine-guanine (trinucleotide)
CFU/mL	colony-forming units per milliliter		
CFU-S	colony-forming unit-spleen	CGH	comparative genomic hybridization
CFV	common femoral vein		
CFVR	coronary flow velocity reserve	CGI	Clinical Global Impressions (scale)
CFW	calcofluor white (stain)		
	Carworth Farms Webster (mice)	CGIBD	Center for Gastrointestinal Biology and Diseases (University of North Carolina at Chapel Hill Chapel Hill, NC)
	crystalline fiber waveguide (laser)		
CFX	cefixime; cefotaxime sodium; ceftriaxone; cefuroxime; cephalexin; ciprofloxacin (this is a dangerous abbreviation; drug names should not be abbreviated)		
		CGIC	Certified Gastroenterology Coder
			Clinical Global Impression of Change
		CGIs	Clinical Global Impressions
		CGI-S	Clinical Global Impressions, Severity of Illness
	chromogenic factor X		
	circumflex coronary artery	CGI-TD	Global Impression of Change-Tardive Dyskinesia
CFZ	carfilzomib (Kyprolis)		

C

CGL	chronic granulocytic leukemia
	congenital generalized
	lipodystrophy
	with correction/with glasses
CGM	continuous glucose monitoring
	(monitor)
	cortical gray matter
CGMP	Current Good Manufacturing
	Practices
cGMP	cyclic guanosine monophosphate
CGMS	continuous glucose monitoring
	systems
C3GN	C3 (one of the 3 pathways of
	complement activation)
	glomerulonephritis
CGN	Certified Gastroenterology Nurse
	chronic glomerulonephritis
cGN	crescentic glomerulonephritis
CGP	Certification in Geriatric
	Pharmacy
	comprehensive genomic profiling
C-GRD	coffee-ground
CGRN	Certified Gastroenterology
	Registered Nurse
CGRP	calcitonin gene-related peptide
CGRP-R	calcitonin gene-related peptide
	receptor
CGRT	Center for Gut Rehabilitation
	and Transplantation
CGS	cardiogenic shock
	catgut suture
CGSC	Certified General Surgery Coder
	(CGSC™) Credential
CGTT	cortisol glucose tolerance test
cGVHD	chronic graft-versus-host disease
cGy	centigray
CH	Caribbean Hispanic
	chest
	chief
	child (children)
	chronic
	cluster headache
	concentric hypertrophy
	congenital hypothyroidism
	convalescent hospital
	crown-heal
	hospital (centre hospitalizer)
C&H	cocaine and heroin
CH4	methane
CH50	total hemolytic complement
Ch	hepatic clearance
ch[1]	Christ Church chromosone
CHA	common hepatic artery
	compound hypermetropic
	astigmatism
	congenital hypoplastic anemia
CHAA	common hepatic artery
	aneurysm

ChABC	chondroitinase ABC (ABC
	refers to chondroitin sulfate
	A, B and C)
CHAD	cyclophosphamide, altretamine,
	(hexamethylmelamine),
	doxorubicin (Adriamycin),
	and cisplatin (DDP)
CHADS2	congestive heart failure,
	hypertension (blood pres-
	sure consistently above
	140/90 mmHg or treated
	hypertension on medication),
	age equal to or greater
	than 75 years, diabetes
	mellitus, and prior Stroke,
	transient ischemic attack,
	or thromboembolism has a
	value of 2,each other item
	has a value of 1; predictive
	value scores for stroke risk in
	patients with peripheral artery
	disease as a guideline of start-
	ing anticoagulant treatment)
CHADVASC	see CHA2DS2VASc
CHADSVASc	see CHA2DS2VASc
CHADS VASc	see CHA2DS2VASc
CHADS-VASc	see CHA2DS2VASc
CHADS2VASC	CHA2DS2VASc
CHADS2-VASc	see CHA2DS2VASc
CHA2DS2VASc	Congestive heart failure (or Left
	ventricular systolic dysfunc-
	tion), Hypertension: blood
	pressure consistently above
	140/90 mmHg (or treated
	hypertension on medication),
	Age equal to or greater 75,
	Diabetes mellitus, prior
	Stroke or transient ischemic
	attack or thromboembolism,
	Vascular disease (e.g.
	peripheral artery disease,
	myocardial infarction, aortic
	plaque), Age 65-74 years, Sex
	category, female), (predictive
	value scores for stroke risk in
	patients with peripheral artery
	disease as a guideline of start-
	ing anticoagulant treatment;
	each category has a value of 1
	except for those followed by a
	2, which have a value of 2)
CHA2DS2-VASc	see CHA2DS2VASc
CHAI	Commission for Healthcare
	Audit and Inspection (United
	Kingdom)
	continuous hepatic artery
	infusion

CHAMOCA	cyclophosphamide, hydroxyurea, dactinomycin, methotrexate, vincristine, leucovorin, and doxorubicin	CHC	Certified in Healthcare Compliance
			Children's Health Center
			chronic hepatitis C
CHAMPS	Community Healthy Activities Model Program for Seniors (questionnaire)		combined hormonal contraceptive
			community health center
CHAMPUS	Civilian Health and Medical Program of the Uniformed Services		concentric hypertrophic cardiomyopathy
		CHCA	Child Health Corporation of America
CHAMPVA	Civilian Health and Medical Program - Veterans Administration	C-HCC	hepatitis C-related hepatocellular carcinoma
Chandelier sign	used to describe a patient who experiences extreme pain during a physical examination	CH₃-CCNU	semustine
		CHCM	cellular hemoglobin concentration mean
CHAP	child health associate practitioner	CHCN	Community Health Center Network (headquartered in Alameda County, California)
	cyclophosphamide, altretamine, (hexamethylmelamine), doxorubicin (Adriamycin), and cisplatin (Platinol)	CHCs	community health centers
		CHCT	caffeine-halothane contracture test
CHAPS	zwitterionic (a molecule carrying both a positive and a negative charge) detergents	cHct	central hematocrit
		cHCV	chronic hepatitis C virus (infection)
CHAQ	childhood health assessment questionnaire	CHD	canine hip dysplasia
			changed diaper
Charcot	Jean-Martin Charcot (1825-1893, his name is associated with Charcot–Marie–Tooth disease, Charcot-Bouchard aneurysms, Charcot–Leyden crystals Charcot arthropathy, Charcot neuroarthropathy, etc.)		childhood diseases
			Chinese in Metropolitan Denver, CO, USA (population samples of HapMap [a catalog of common genetic variants that occur in human beings])
			chronic hemodialysis
			common hepatic duct
CHARGE	coloboma (of eyes), hearing deficit, choanal atresia, retardation of growth, genital defects (males only), and endocardial cushion defect		congenital heart defect
			congenital heart disease
			conventional in-center hemodialysis
			coordinate home care
Charlie	Phonetic Alphabet for C,; pronounced CHAR-LEE or SHAR-LEE		coronary heart disease
		CHD 1	chromodomain helicase DNA binding protein 1 (gene/protein)
CHART	complaint, history, assessment, Rx (treatment), transport		
	continuous hyperfractionated accelerated radiotherapy	CHD-APAH	congenital heart disease associated pulmonary arterial hypertension
	Craig Handicap Assessment and Reporting Technique	CHDF	continuous hemodiafiltration
ChAT	choline acetyltransferase	CHDL	claw horn disruption lesions
chat	putative 3-phenylpropionic transport (gene)	CHDP	city health development planning (World Health Organization)
CHB	chronic hepatitis B		
	complete heart block	CHDS	Certified Healthcare Documentation Specialist
	Han Chinese from Beijing (populations included in HapMap - see HapMap)	CHE	chronic hepatic encephalopathy
CHBHA	congenital Heinz body hemolytic anemia		comprehensive health examination

CHEDDAR	Chief Complaint; History: social and physical as well as contributing factors; Examination; Details of problems and complaints; Drugs and dosage - list current meds; Assessment, diagnostic process, total impression; Return visit information or referral (format of documentation)	chemo/XRT	chemotherapy with radiation therapy
CHEF	clamped homogeneous electric field	CHEMPACK	a kit containing antidotes for an organophosphate chemical attack
ChEI	cholinesterase inhibitor	Chem Panel	A battery of tests (chemistry panel) which can vary from facility to facility. It may include chloride, carbon dioxide, potassium, sodium, phosphate, total protein, albumin, glucose, urea nitrogen, uric acid, creatinine, total bilirubin, alkaline phosphatase, lactic acid dehydrogenase, and aspartate aminotransferase.

CHEDDAR — Chief Complaint; History: social and physical as well as contributing factors; Examination; Details of problems and complaints; Drugs and dosage - list current meds; Assessment, diagnostic process, total impression; Return visit information or referral (format of documentation)

CHEF — clamped homogeneous electric field

ChEI — cholinesterase inhibitor

ChEi — cholinesterase inhibitor

CHEK2 — checkpoint kinase 2 (gene)

CHEM 20 — A battery of 20 laboratory tests consisting of sodium (Na), potassium (K), chloride (Cl), carbon dioxide (CO_2), creatinine, glucose, urea nitrogen (BUN), albumin, calcium (Ca), magnesium (Mg), inorganic phosphorus, alkaline phosphatase (ALK PHOS), alanin

Chem 7 — laboratory tests for sodium, potassium, chloride, bicarbonate or carbon dioxide, blood urea, nitrogen, creatinine, and glucose

Chem 8 — laboratory tests for sodium, potassium, chloride, bicarbonate or carbon dioxide, blood urea nitrogen, creatinine, glucose, and calcium

Chem 10 — a battery of venous blood tests; sodium, potassium, chloride, bicarbonate, blood urea nitrogen (BUN), creatinine, glucose, calcium, magnesium, and phosphorus

Chem 12 — a battery of 12 tests (chemistry panel) which can vary from facility to facility. It may include chloride, carbon dioxide, potassium, sodium, phosphate, total protein, albumin, glucose, urea nitrogen, uric acid, creatinine, total bilirubin, alkaline phos

chemdep — chemical dependency

chem dep — chemical dependence

CHEMO — chemotherapy

chemorad — chemoradiation therapy

ChemoRT — chemotherapy and radiation therapy

ChemoRx — chemotherapy

chemoTx — chemotherapy

chemo/XRT — chemotherapy with radiation therapy

CHEMPACK — a kit containing antidotes for an organophosphate chemical attack

Chem Panel — A battery of tests (chemistry panel) which can vary from facility to facility. It may include chloride, carbon dioxide, potassium, sodium, phosphate, total protein, albumin, glucose, urea nitrogen, uric acid, creatinine, total bilirubin, alkaline phosphatase, lactic acid dehydrogenase, and aspartate aminotransferase.

CHEOPS — Children's Hospital of Eastern Ontario Pain Scale

CHEP — Canadian Hypertension Education Program
cricohyoidoepiglottopexy

CHESS — chemical shift suppression

CHEST — chick embryotoxicity screening test

chest PA — posterior-anterior chest X-ray

ChEt — cholesterol esterase

CHF — chronic heart failure
congestive heart failure

CHF DD — congestive heart failure with diastolic dysfunction

CHFE — congestive heart failure exacerbation(s)

CHFN — Canadian Heart Failure Network
Certified Heart Failure Nurse

CHFpEF — chronic heart failure with preserved ejection fraction
congestive heart failure with preserved ejection fraction

CHFR — checkpoint with forkhead and ring finger domains (a protein coding gene)

CHFrEF — chronic heart failure with reduced ejection fraction
congestive heart failure with reduced ejection fraction

CHFV — combined high-frequency of ventilation

CHG — change
Chlorhexidine gluconate (Hibiclens; PerioGard)

CHHA — Certified Home Health Aide

CHI — closed head injury
Consolidated Health Informatics
creatinine-height index
crushing head injury (injuries)

CHIBLOC — closed head injury, brief loss of consciousness

C

CHIC2	cysteine-rich hydrophobic domain 2 (gene)		Chinese herb nephropathy
			Community Health Nurses
CHID	Combined Health Information Database	CHO	aldehyde (-CHO)
			carbohydrate
CHIK	Chikungunya (virus)		Chemical Hygiene Officer
CHIKV	Chikungunya virus		Chinese hamster ovary
CHILD	congenital hemidysplasia with ichthyosiform nevus and limb defects (syndrome)	-CHO	aldehyde
		C_{H2O}	free-water clearance
		CHO_a	cholera vaccine, attenuated live (oral)
CHIN	community health information network	CHOC	Children's Hospital of Orange County (CA)
CHIP	Children's Health Insurance Program		chocolate
	clonal hematopoiesis of indeterminate potential (accumulation of mutated stem cells in the bone marrow)	$CHO_{cn}LPS$	cholera vaccine, lipopolysaccharide-toxin conjugate
		$C_2 H_5 OH$	alcohol (ethyl alcohol)
	comprehensive health insurance plan	CHOD	cyclophosphamide, doxorubicin (Adriamycin), vincristine, and dexamethasone
	iproplatin (cis-dichloro,trans-dihydroxy-bis-isopropylamine platinum[IV])	CHOEP	cyclophosphamide, doxorubicin (hydroxydaunorubicin), vincristine (Oncovin), and prednisolone (CHOP) with the addition of etoposide
ChIP	chromatin immunoprecipitation		
CHIPRA	Children's Health Insurance Program Reauthorization Act of 2009		
		$CHOi_{-w}$	cholera vaccine, inactivated whole cell
CHIPS	chemotaxis inhibitory protein of Staphylococcus aureus	chol	cholesterol
		cholang	cholangiogram
	Cholinergic Pathways Hyperintensities Scale	chole	cholecystectomy
		choley tube	cholecystostomy tube
	Collaborative HIV (human immunodeficiency virus) Paediatric Study (United Kingdom and Ireland)	CHOL/TG	cholesterol/triglycerides ratio
		Choly	cholecystectomy
		CHONC	Certified Hematology and Oncology Coder (CHONC™)
CHIPs	community health improvement plans		
		chondro	chondroplasty
CHIR	Chiron Corporation	CHO_o	cholera, oral vaccine
chirp	a short, high-pitched sound	CHOP	Children's Hospital of Philadelphia
Chix	chickenpox		
CHKA	choline kinase alpha, see gene website, www.ncbi.nlm.nih.gov/gene		cyclophosphamide, doxorubicin (hydroxydaunorubicin), vincristine (Oncovin), prednisone
CHKB	choline kinase beta, see gene website, www.ncbi.nlm.nih.gov/gene	CHOPBleo	cyclophosphamide, doxorubicin (hydroxydaunorubicin), vincristine (Oncovin), prednisone, and bleomycin
chk2	checkpoint kinase 2 (gene/protein)		
CHL	conductive hearing loss	CHOP-R	cyclophosphamide, doxorubicin (hydroxydaunorubicin), vincristine (Oncovin), prednisone, and rituximab
cHL	classical Hodgkin lymphoma		
CHLC	Cooperative Human Linkage Center		
		chorio	chorioamnionitis
ChloMP	chlorambucil, mitoxantrone, and prednisolone	CHO_{tox}	cholera toxin/toxoid vaccine
		CHOW	Change of Ownership
ChlVPP	chlorambucil, vinblastine, procarbazine, and prednisone	ChOx	cholesterol oxidase
		CHP	Certification in Healthcare Privacy
CHM	complete hydatidiform mole		
ChM-I	chondromodulin-I		chronic hemodialysis patients
CHN	central hemorrhagic necrosis	ChP	Chinese Pharmacopeia
	Certified Hemodialysis Nurse		

C

CHPA	Consumer Healthcare Products Association (a trade association representing manufacturers and marketers of over-the-counter medicines and dietary supplements)
CHPB	Canadian Health Protection Branch (the equivalent of the U.S. Food and Drug Administration)
CHpEF	may have meant CHFpEF (congestive heart failure with preserved ejection fraction)
CHPI	cervical human papillomavirus infection
CHPN	Certified Hospice and Palliative Nurse
CHPV	Codman Hakim programmable valve
CHPX	chickenpox
CHR	ceiling heart rate (cardiac rehab)
	Cercaria-Hullen reaction
	clinical high risk
	clinically high risk
	complete hematologic remission
	complete hematological response
ChREBP	carbohydrate response element-binding protein
CHRF	chronic hypercapnic respiratory failure
CH/RG	Chido/Rodgers; an International Society of Blood Transfusion (ISBT) blood group
CHRN	Certified Hyperbaric Registered Nurse
ChronoHAI	circadian-based hepatic artery infusion
CHRPE	congenital hypertrophy of the retinal pigment epithelium
CHRS	congenital hereditary retinoschisis
CHS	Cannabinoid Hyperemesis Syndrome
	Chediak-Higashi syndrome
	contact hypersensitivity
CHS database	Clatit Health Services' database (Israel's largest health fund, with over 4.4 million members)
chst-1	CarboHydrate SulfoTransferase (gene)
CHT	Certified Hand Therapist
	Certified Hyperbaric Technician
	Certified Hypnotherapist
	chemotherapy
	closed head trauma
ChT	chemotherapy

CHTL	chymotrypsin-like
CHTM	commercial Haemophilus test medium
CHTN	chronic hypertension
	Cooperative Human Tissue Network (established by the National Cancer Institute)
CHU	closed head unit
CHUC	Certified Health Unit Coordinator
Chux	a brand of disposable diaper (Procter & Gamble)
CHVP	cyclophosphamide, doxorubicin (hydroxydaunorubicin), teniposide (VM26), and prednisone
CHW	community health workers
CHWG	chewing gum
CHX	chlorhexidine
CHX/T	chlorhexidine-thymol varnish (Cervitec Plus)
CHyst	Cesarean hysterectomy
CHZ	chlorzoxazone (Parafon Forte DSC)
	see gene website www.ncbi.nlm.nih.gov/gene
CI	cerebral infarction
	cesium implant
	chronic illness
	Clinical Instructor
	cochlear implant
	coitus interruptus
	colon inertia
	colonization index
	commercial insurance
	complete iridectomy
	confidence interval
	continuous infusion
	contraindications
	convergence insufficiency
	core imprint (cytology)
	coronary insufficiency
	see Cl
C I	see Cl
C/I	crown-to-implant (ratio)
	see CI
Ci	curie(s)
CI30	cumulative incidence at 30 years
CIA	calcaneal insufficiency avulsion
	chemotherapy-induced alopecia
	chemotherapy-induced amenorrhea
	chemotherapy-induced anemia
	chronic idiopathic anhidrosis
	collagen-induced arthritis
	common iliac artery
CIAA	competitive insulin autoantibodies
CIACS	cocaine-induced acute coronary syndrome

C

CIAD   Center for Food Research and Development (Centro de Investigación en Alimentación y Desarrollo, Mexico)

CIAED   collagen-induced autoimmune ear disease

cIAI   complicated intra-abdominal infections (multidrug resistance)

CIAKI   contrast-induced acute kidney injury

CI-AKI   contrast-induced acute kidney injury

CIB   Carnation Instant Breakfast®
Clock-in-the-Box (cognitive assessment; the test has two parts, first there is a page of brief instructions that the test taker is asked to commit to memory, then when they are ready, they are given a response sheet on which they try to follow the instructions to the best of their ability)
crying-induced bronchospasm
cytomegalic inclusion bodies

cibC   see gene website www.ncbi.nlm.nih.gov/gene

CIBD   Center for Inherited Blood Disorder
chronic inflammatory bowel disease

CIBH   change in bowel habit

CIBI   Clinician Interview-Based Impression (of change)

CIBIC   Clinician Interview-Based Impression of Change

CIBICplus   Clinician's Interview-Based Impression of Change with Caregiver Input

cibo   may have meant CEBO (placebo)

CIBP   chronic intractable benign pain

C-IBS   constipated predominant irritable bowel syndrome

CIC   cardioinhibitory center
Certified in Infection Control
Certified Inpatient Coder (CIC™)
chronic idiopathic constipation
circulating immune complexes
clean intermittent catheterization
completely in the canal (hearing aid)
coronary intensive care

CICA   constrained independent component analysis

CICC   chronic inflammation-induced colon cancer

CICD   caspase-independent cell death
chemical irritant contact dermatitis

CICE   combined intracapsular cataract extraction

CICI   chemotherapy-induced cognitive impairment

CICP   Countermeasures Injury Compensation Program
C-terminal propeptide of collagen type-I

CICR   calcium-induced calcium release

CICU   cardiac intensive care unit

CI-CV   Drug Enforcement Agency scheduled substances class one through five

CICVC   centrally inserted central venous catheter

CID   Center for Infectious Diseases (CDC)
Central Institute for the Deaf
cervical immobilization device
chemotherapy-induced diarrhea
clinically important difference
collision-induced dissociation
combined immunodeficiency
cytomegalic inclusion disease

CIDB   chronic inflammatory disease of the bowel

CIDNP   chemically-induced dynamic nuclear polarization

CIDP   chronic inflammatory demyelinating polyneuropathy
chronic inflammatory demyelinating polyradiculoneuropathy

CIDPN   chronic inflammatory demyelinating polyneuropathy

CIDS   cellular immunodeficiency syndrome
continuous insulin delivery system

CIDs   clinically important differences

CIE   capillary immunoelectrophoresis
cerebrovascular ischemic event(s)
chemotherapy-induced emesis
chronic intermittent ethanol
congenital ichthyosiform erythroderma
counter immunoelectrophoresis
crossed immunoelectrophoresis

CIEA   continuous infusion epidural analgesia

CIED   cardiovascular (cardiac) implantable electronic device

CIEDs   cardiovascular implanted electronic devices

CIEF	capillary isoelectric focusing
CIEP	counter immunoelectrophoresis
CIFN	chemotherapy-induced fever and neutropenia
CI 5-FU	continuous infusion of fluorouracil
CIG	cigarettes
CIGS	copper indium gallium di-selenide (compound semiconductor; solar cells)
CIH	Certified in Industrial Health
	continuous infusion haloperidol
CIHD	chronic ischemic heart disease
CIHI	Canadian Institute for Health Information
CIHR	Canadian Institutes of Health Research
CII	continuous insulin infusion
	see C2
C II	see C2
CIIA	common internal iliac artery
CIII	see C3
C III	see C3
CIIP	chronic idiopathic intestinal pseudo-obstruction
	computerized insulin infusion protocol(s)
	continuous infusion insulin pump
CIIRP	chronic idiopathic intestinal pseudoobstruction syndrome
CIIRx	Century II Bicarbonate Dialysis Machine
CIL	carbamazepine-induced lupus
CILA	cognitive impairment linked to aging
	Cookgas intubating laryngeal airway
CILC	classic invasive lobular carcinoma
CILD	chronic infiltrative lung disease
	chronic interstitial lung disease
CILV	common-inlet left ventricle
CIM	change in menses
	chemotherapy-induced mucositis
	constraint-induced movement
	convective interaction media
	corticosteroid-induced myopathy
	critical illness myopathy
CIMCU	cardiac intermediate care unit
CIMP	CpG (cytosine-phosphate-guanine) island methylator phenotype
CIMS	chemical ionization mass spectrometry
CIMT	carotid (artery) intima-media thickness
	constraint-induced movement therapy

C/IMV	continuous positive airway pressure intermittent mandatory ventilation
CIN	cervical intraepithelial neoplasia
	chemotherapy-induced neutropenia
	chromosomal (chromosome) instability
	chronic interstitial nephritis
	contrast-induced nephropathy
C_{IN}	insulin clearance
CIN1	cervical intraepithelial neoplasia grade 1
CIN2	cervical intraepithelial neoplasia grade 2
CIN3	cervical intraepithelial neoplasia grade 3
CIN3+	cervical intraepithelial neoplasia grade 3 or worse
CINAHL	Cumulative Index to Nursing and Allied Health
CINCA	chronic infantile neurologic cutaneous arthropathy
CIND	carpal instability nondissociative
	cognitive impairment, no dementia
	cognitive impairment, not demented
CINE	chemotherapy-induced nausea and emesis
	cineangiogram
CINHAL	Cumulative Index to Nursing and Allied Health Literature
CIN I	cervical intraepithelial neoplasia, grade 1
CIN II	cervical intraepithelial neoplasia, grade 2
CIN III	cervical intraepithelial neoplasia, grade 3
CINM	critical illness neuromyopathy
CINRG	Cooperative International Neuromuscular Research Group
CINT	constraint-induced movement therapy
CINV	chemotherapy-induced nausea and vomiting
CIO	chief information officer
	corticosteroid-induced osteoporosis
CIOD	chemotherapy-induced ovarian dysfunction
CIOMS	The Council for International Organization of Medical Sciences
CIP	Cardiac Injury Panel
	Certified IRB (Institutional Review Board) Professional
	chronic interstitial pneumonia
	critical illness polyneuropathy

CIPAP	may refer to CPAP (continuous positive airway pressure)
CIP-BOOP	chronic interstitial pneumonia with bronchiolitis obliterans
CIPD	chronic intermittent peritoneal dialysis
CIPMN	critical illness polyneuromyopathy
CIPN	chemotherapy-induced peripheral neuropathy
CIPO	chronic intestinal pseudo-obstruction
CIPP	Context, Input, Process and Product (Stufflebeam's evaluation model)
CIR	continent intestinal reservoir
CIRB	central institutional review board
CIRC	Circulation Improving Resuscitation Care (trial)
	circumflex
circ	circulation
	circumcision
	circumference
	circumferential
	circumflex
circa	a word from Latin, meaning around or about
CIRCC	Certified Interventional Radiology Cardiovascular Coder (CIRCC®)
CIRCI	critical illness-related corticosteroid insufficiency
circ & sen	circulation and sensation
circum	circumcision
circumf	circumference
CIREN	Crash Injury Research Engineering Network (database)
CIRF	cocaine-induced respiratory failure
CIRM	California Institute of Regenerative Medicine
cirr	Cirrhosis
CIRS	Comorbidity Illness rating scale
	Cumulative Illness Rating Scale
CIRS-G	Cumulative Illness Rating Scale-Geriatric
CIRT	carbon ion radiotherapy
	Cardiovascular Inflammation Reduction Trial
CIRV	common-inlet right ventricle
CIS	Cancer Information Service (National Cancer Institute)
	carcinoma in situ
	Clinical Information System
	clinically isolated syndrome
	Columbia Impairment Scale
	Commonwealth of Independent States
	continuous interleaved sampling
CI&S	conjunctival irritation and swelling

CISB	continuous interscalene block
CISC	clean intermittent self-catheterization
CISCA	cisplatin, cyclophosphamide, and doxorubicin (Adriamycin)
CISCOM	The Centralized Information Service for Complementary Medicine
CISD	critical incident stress debriefing (used by EMTs)
Cis-DDP	cisplatin (Platinol)
CISH	chromogen in situ hybridization
CISM	critical incident stress management (debriefing used by EMTs)
CIS-R	Clinical Interview Schedule, Revised
CISS	cold Intolerance Severity Score
	cold-induced sweating syndrome
	constructive interface in steady state (imaging)
	constructive interference in steady state
	coping Inventory for Stressful Situations
CISS-15	Convergence Insufficiency Symptom Survey (patients having difficulty pulling their eyes together)
CI-Stim	cochlear implant stimulation
CIT	chemotherapy-induced toxicities
	cold ischemia time
	constraint induced therapy (protocol)
	conventional immunosuppressive therapy
	conventional insulin therapy
	Crisis Intervention Team
CITIDS	citation identifiers (National Library of Medicine)
CITP	capillary isotachophoresis
CITR	Collaborative Islet Transplant Registry
CIU	chronic idiopathic urticaria
	crisis intervention unit
CIV	common iliac vein
	continuous intravenous (infusion)
C4 IV	see C4
C IV	see C4
CIVA	corrected intermediate visual acuity
CIVAS	centralize intravenous additives (Pharmacy) services
CIVD	Cold-induced vasodilatation
CIVI	continuous intravenous infusion
CIVIQ	chronic venous insufficiency quality of life questionnaire

CIVP	chronic inflammatory visceral pain
	common iliac venous pressure
CIWA	Clinical Institute Withdrawal Assessment for Alcohol (score)
CIWA-Ar	Clinical Institute Withdrawal Assessment for Alcohol-Revised scale
CIWAS	Clinical Institute Withdrawal Assessment for Alcohol Scale
CIX	cachexia inducing xenografts
	collagen type IX
CIXU	constant infusion excretory urogram
CJCP	Certified Joint Commission Professional
CJD	Creutzfeldt-Jakob disease
cJET	congenital junctional ectopic tachycardia
CJH	cutaneous juvenile hemangioma
CJMP	Certified Joint Commission Professional
CJMs	common Jewish mutations
CJR	centric jaw relation
CJS	chronic joint symptoms
	Criminal Justice System
CK	check
	conductive keratoplasty
	creatine kinase
	cytokeratin
CK1	cytokeratin 1
CK7	cytokeratin-7, A protein found in simple glandular epithelia, and in transitional epithelium. It is used in immunohistochemistry. Also known as keratin, keratin-7 (K7) or sarcolectin (SCL).
CK20	cytokeratin-20, a protein found in gastric and intestinal mucosa. It is used in immunohistochemistry. Also known as Keratin 20
CK+	cytokeratin-positive
CKA	cancer killing activity
	cytokine kinetics assay
CKB	China Kadoorie Biobank
CK&B	may have been misheard for CK-MB, creatine kinase MB fraction
CK-BB	creatine kinase BB band (primarily in brain)
CKC	closed kinetic chain (exercises)
	cold-knife conization
	cold knife conization (of the cervix)

CKD	chronic kidney disease (stage 1- with normal or high glomerular filtration rate (GFR) (GFR greater than 90 mL/min); stage 2- Mild CKD (GFR = 60-89 mL/min); stage 3A- Moderate CKD (GFR = 45-59 mL/min); stage 3B- Moderate CKD (GFR = 30-44 mL/min); stage 4- Severe CKD (GFR = 15-29 mL/min); stage 5- End Stage CKD (GFR less than 15 mL/min)
	cubic centimeters per kilogram per day
CKD1	chronic kidney disease stage 1 (mildest)
CKD2	chronic kidney disease stage 2
CKD3	chronic kidney disease stage 3
CKD4	chronic kidney disease stage 4
CKD5	chronic kidney disease stage 5 (most severe)
CKD EPI	Chronic Kidney Disease Epidemiology Collaboration (an equation to estimate glomerular filtration rate)
CKD MBD	chronic kidney disease with mineral and bond disorders
CKD/pre-KT	chronic kidney disease before kidney transplantation
CKDs	chronic kidney diseases
CKDT	terminal chronic kidney disease transplant chronic kidney disease (stage)
CKD-T	chronic kidney disease after transplantation
CKdV	combined Korteweg-de Vries (equation)
CKF	chronic kidney failure
C/kg	coulomb per kilogram (radiology)
CK-HMW	high molecular weight cytokeratin (this antibody labels squamous, ductal and complex epithelia, and is useful in the differentiation of benign prostate glands from prostatic adenocarcinoma and the classification of neoplastic tissue as carcinoma or epithelial origin.)
CKI	casein kinase I
	cyclin-dependent kinase inhibitor
CKiD	Chronic Kidney Disease in Children (cohort study)
CK-ISO	creatine kinase isoenzyme
cKit	a member of the subfamily of receptor tyrosine kinases

c-Kit	a member of the subfamily of receptor tyrosine kinases
CKLT	combined kidney and liver transplantation
CKMB	creatine kinase-MB (fraction)
CK MB	creatine kinase MB fraction (primarily in cardiac muscle)
CK-MB	creatine kinase MB fraction (primarily in cardiac muscle)
CKMM	creatine kinase MM fraction (primarily in skeletal muscle)
CKO	see gene website www.ncbi.nlm.nih.gov/gene
cKO	conditional knockout (mice)
CKP	chronic knee pain
CKR	chemokine receptor
CKRS	Cincinnati Knee Rating System CyberKnife radiosurgery
CKRs	chemokine receptors
CKs	cytokeratins
CKT	cadaver-donor kidney transplantation
CKVO	Commissie Klinisch Vergelijkend Onderzoek (Dutch)
CKW	clockwise
CL	call light
	central line
	chemoluminescence
	clear liquid
	cleft lip
	closed-loop
	cloudy
	confidence limits
	contact lens
	critical list
	cutaneous leishmaniasis
	cycle length
	lung compliance
C$_L$	compliance of the lungs
C-L	consultation-liaison
C&L	consult and liaison (psychiatry)
C/L	carbon per liter (as in 5 mg C/L)
	commissure to longitudinal (ratio)
	contralateral
	Cormack–Lehane (classification; classifies views obtained by direct laryngoscopy based on the structures seen)
Cl$^-$	chloride
cl	closed
CLA	clarithromycin (Biaxin)
	community living arrangements
	congenital lactic acidosis
	congenital laryngeal atresia
	conjugated linoleic acid
CLABSI	central line-associated bloodstream infection
CLAD	chronic lung allograft dysfunction

CLAD/BOS	chronic lung allograft dysfunction with bronchiolitis obliterans syndrome
CLAG	cladribine, cytarabine (ara-C), and filgrastim (granulocyte colony-stimulating factor)
CLAG-M	cladribine, cytarabine (ara-C), filgrastim (granulocyte colony-stimulating factor) and mitoxantrone
C lam	cervical laminectomy
CLAMS DQ	Clinical Linguistic and Auditory Milestone Scale Development Quotient
CLAMSS	cleavage- and ligation-associated mutation-specific sequencing
CLAP	contact laser ablation of prostate
clapt	a word meaning to fit together and make fast
CLARE	contact lens-associated acute red eye
CLAS	Cancer Linear Analogue Scale congenital localized absence of skin
CLASBI	may have meant CLABSI (central line-associated bloodstream infection)
CLASBSIs	central line-associated bloodstream infections
CLASS	computer laser-assisted surgical system
CLASS I	congestive heart failure with no limitation with ordinary activity (New York Heart Association Classification)
CLASS II	congestive heart failure with slight limitation of physical activity
CLASS III	congestive heart failure with marked limitation of physical activity
CLASS IV	congestive heart failure with inability to engage in any physical activity without symptoms
Clav	clavicle
CLB	chlorambucil (Leukeran) coccidian-like body
CLB$_{atx}$	*Clostridium botulinum* antitoxin
CLBBB	complete left bundle branch block
CLBD	cortical Lewy body disease
CLBP	chronic low back pain
CLBR	cumulative live birth rate
CLBRs	cumulative live birth rates
CLBSIs	central line-associated blood stream infections
CLBtox	*Clostridium botulinum* toxoid vaccine

CLC	closed-loop control
	Community Living Center
	cork leather and celastic (orthotic)
CL/CP	cleft lip and cleft palate
Clcr	creatinine clearance
CLD	central lung distance (radiation therapy)
	chronic lung disease
	clear liquid diet
	Clostridium difficile vaccine
Cl$_d$	dialysis clearance
cLDL-C	calculated low-density lipoprotein cholesterol
CLDP	chronic lung disease of prematurity
cldy	cloudy
CLE	centrilobular emphysema
	chronic lateral epicondylosis
	confocal laser scanning endomicroscopy
	congenital lobar emphysema
	constant-load exercise
	continuous lumbar epidural (anesthetic)
	cutaneous lupus erythematosus
CLEA	Contaminated Land Exposure Assessment (model)
	continuous labor epidural analgesia
CLED	cysteine lactose electrolyte-deficient (agar)
CLEIA	chemiluminescent enzyme immunoassay
CLEP	college level examination program
Clepsi	maybe a misspelling for Klebsiella pneumoniae, a Gram-negative organism
CLES	clinical laboratory equipment specialists
CLETZ	contoured loop excision of the transformation zone
C-LETZ	contoured loop excision of the transformation zone
CLF	cholesterol-lecithin flocculation
	clofazimine
CLG	clorgyline
CLH	chronic lobular hepatitis
CLHA	children living with HIV (human immunodeficiency virus)/AIDS (acquired immune deficiency syndrome)
	crosslinked hyaluronic acid
CLI	central lymphatic irradiation
	clomipramine
	critical leg ischemia
	critical limb ischemia

CLIA	chemiluminescent immunoassay
	Clinical Laboratory Improvement Amendments (1988)
CLIFAHDD syndrome	contractures of the limbs and face with associated respiratory distress; distal arthrogryposis; severe axial hypotonia; and severe global developmental delay
CLINDA	clindamycin (Cleocin)
C Line	central-line (a catheter placed into a large vein in the neck, chest or groin)
	central-line (a catheter placed into a large vein in the neck, chest or groin)
clinic unit	200 pounds (slang)
ClinROs	clinician-reported outcomes
Cl$_{int}$	intrinsic clearance
CLIP	call-light in place
CLIPPERS syndrome	**Chronic Lymphocytic Inflammation with Pontine Perivascular Enhancement Responsive to Steroids**; it is an inflammatory central nervous system disorder that gives rise to brainstem symptoms such as diplopia and articulatory disorders
CLIR	call-light in reach
	chemiluminescent immunoreactive renin
	cross-language information retrieval
CLKT	combined liver and kidney transplantation
CLL	chronic lymphocytic leukemia
CLLE	columnar-lined lower esophagus
CLL-IPI	chronic lymphocytic leukemia international prognostic index
clliq	clear liquid
Cl Liq	clear liquids
CLL/SLL	chronic lymphocytic leukemia/ small cell lymphoma
CLM	colorectal liver metastases
	cutaneous larva migrans
CLN	centrolobular necrosis
	cervical lymph node
	cleft lip nose
	clonazepam (Klonopin)
CLN1	neuronal ceroid lipofuscinosis type 1
CLN2	neuronal ceroid lipofuscinosis type 2
CLNC	Certified Legal Nurse Consultant
CLND	central lymph node dissection
	cleft lip nasal deformities
	completion lymph node dissection

Cl$_{NR}$ nonrenal clearance
CLO Campylobacter-like organism
close
cod liver oil
CLOF clofarabine (Clolar)
clofazimine (Lamprene)
clonazepam may have meant clonazepam
(Klonopin)
Clonopin may have meant Klonopin
(clonazepam)
CLOS closed-loop optogenetic
stimulation
CLOs Chlamydia-like organisms
CLO test Campylobacter-like organism test
Cloud 9 A mixture containing the
psychoactive drug methylene-
dioxypyrovalerone (MDPV)
Cloud Nine A mixture containing the
psychoactive drug methylene-
dioxypyrovalerone (MDPV)
CLOVES Congenital Lipomatous
syndrome Overgrowth, Vascular malfor-
mations, Epidermal nevi and
Spinal abnormalities
CLOX clock-drawing task (cognitive
impairment text)
CLP cecal ligation and puncture
cleft lip and palate
consultation-liaison psychiatry
CL & P cleft lip and palate
CL/P cleft lip with or without cleft
palate
CLPB may have meant CLBP (chronic
low back pain)
ClpB caseinolytic protease B
CLPC contact lens-induced papillary
conjunctivitis
clpC see gene website www.ncbi.nlm
.nih.gov/gene
CLPD chronic lymphoproliferative
disorder
CLPD-NK chronic lymphoproliferative
disorder(s) of NK cells
CL PSY closed psychiatry
CLPU contact lens-induced peripheral
ulceration
CLQ chloroquine phosphate (Aralen)
Claustrophobia Questionnaire
CLQT Cognitive Linguistic Quick Test
Cl$_r$ renal clearance
CLRB clinical laboratory (results) read
back
CL/RBBB complete left/right bundle
branch block
ClRed closed reduction
CLRO community leave for
reorientation
CLRs C-type lectin-like receptors

CLRT composite likelihood ratio test
continuous lateral rotation therapy
(patient positioning)
corneal light reflection test
CLS capillary leak syndrome
Child Life Specialist
community living skills
CLSC Quebec government community
clinic, first point of contact for
non-emergency medical and
social services (carrefour local
de services communautaires)
CLSD chronic lumbar spinal disorder
cranio-lenticulo-sutural dysplasia
CLSE calf-lung surfactant extract
(Infasurf)
CLSI Clinical and Laboratory Standards
Institute
CLSM confocal laser scanning
microscopy
CLT chronic lymphocytic thyroiditis
clot lysis time
complex lymphedema therapy
cool lace tent
cl$_T$ total body clearance
CLTC clathrin, heavy chain; see gene
website www.ncbi.nlm.nih
.gov/gene
CLTI chronic limb-threatening ischemia
CLU chronic leg ulcers
clusterin (gene/protein)
CLV cuff-leak volume
cutaneous leukocytoclastic
vasculitis
CLVH concentric left ventricular
hypertrophy
CLVN cool-large volume nebulizer
CL VOID clean voided specimen
CLW$_c$ Clostridium welchii type C
(Pigbel) toxoid vaccine
CLWR cell length/width ratio
CLWs contact lens wearers
CLX celecoxib (CeleBREX)
chlorhexidine
clysis hypodermoclysis
CLZ clozapine (Clozaril)
CM capreomycin (Capastat)
CarboMedics (heart valve
prosthesis)
cardiac monitor
cardiomegaly
cardiomyopathy
care management
care manager
Case Manager
Caucasian male
cavernous malformation
cerebral malaria

135

	Certified Midwife	CMC	carboxymethylcellulose
	cervical myelopathy		carpometacarpal (joint)
	Chiari malformation		Case Management Certified
	chondromalacia		Chemistry, Manufacturing, and
	chronic migraine (headache)		Controls (section)
	cochlear microphonics		chloramphenicol
	common migraine		chronic mucocutaneous
	continuous manufacturing		candidiasis
	continuous microwave		clinically meaningful change
	continuous murmur		closed mitral commissurotomy
	contrast media	CMC arthritis	carpometacarpal (joint) arthritis
	costal margin	CMCC	Chinese Medical Current Content
	cow's milk		Medical Current Contents
	culture media	CMCD	carboxymethylcellulose dressing
	cutaneous melanoma	CMCI	Chinese Medical Citation Index
	cystic mesothelioma	cMCI	converting (converted) mild
	tomorrow morning (this is a		cognitive impairment
	dangerous abbreviation)	CMCJ	carpometacarpal joint
Cm	curium	CMCJ-3	third carpometacarpal joint
cM	centimorgan (one one-hundredth	CMCJ-OA	carpometacarpal joint
	of a morgan; the unit of		osteoarthritis
	distance on a linkgage map)	CMC joint	carpometacarpal joint
	centi-Morgans	CMCN	Certified Managed Care Nurse
cm	centimeter (2.54 cm = 1 inch)	CMCT	central motor conduction time
cm1	circumflex marginal 1		creamatocrit (provides lipid and
CM-1	Chiari malformation, typr 1		caloric measure of mothers'
cm2	circumflex marginal 2		milk)
cm^2	square centimeters	CMD	congenital muscular dystrophy
cm^3	cubic centimeter		coronary microvascular
CMA	Certified Medical Assistant		dysfunction
	Certified Movement Analyst		corrected mass defect
	chromosomal microarray analysis		cytomegalic disease
	compound myopic astigmatism	CMDC	carbon monoxide diffusing
	cost-minimization analysis		capacity
	cow's milk allergy	CMDLD	coal mine dust lung disease
CMAC	Case Management Administrator,	CMDRH	Center for Medical Devices
	Certified		and Radiological Health
CMAF	centrifuged microaggregate filter		(of the Food and Drug
CMAI	Cohen-Mansfield Agitation		Administration)
	inventory	CMDSC	Certified MDS Coordinator
CMAPs	compound muscle action	CME	cervicomediastinal exploration
	potentials		(examination)
CMAr	cingulate motor area		continuing medical education
CMAS	Childhood Myositis Assessment		cystoid macular edema
	Scale	CMED	cervical microendoscopic
	cytidine monophospho-N-		diskectomy
	acetylneuraminic acid synthe-	CMEF	cervical microendoscopic
	tase; see gene website www		foraminotomy
	.ncbi.nlm.nih.gov/gene	cMEM	coherent maximum entropy on
CMAs	cell microarray		the mean
	census metropolitan areas	CMEPs	cervicomedullary motor-evoked
	(Canada)		potentials
CMAS-R	Children's Manifest Anxiety	CMER	current medical evidence of
	Scale-Revisited		record
C_{max}	maximum concentration of drug	CMET	see gene website, www.ncbi.nlm
CMB	carbolic methylene blue		.nih.gov/gene
CMBBT	cervical mucous basal body	C-MET	see gene website; www.ncbi.nlm
	temperature		.nih.gov/gene

C

CMF	chrondromyxoid fibroma
	cyclophosphamide, methotrexate and fluorouracil
CMFM	cardiac magnetic field mapping
CMFN	coated magnetofluorescent nanoparticles
CMFP	cyclophosphamide, methotrexate, fluorouracil, and prednisone
CMFT	cyclophosphamide, methotrexate, fluorouracil, and tamoxifen
CMFT	same as CMF with tamoxifen
CMFVP	cyclophosphamide, methotrexate, fluorouracil, vincristine, and prednisone
CMG	Case-Mix Group
	coarse mesh gauze
	cystometrogram
CMGM	chronic megakaryocytic granulocytic myelosis
CMGN	chronic membranous glomerulonephritis
CMGs	case-mix groups
CMH	Cochran Mantel Haenzel
	community mental health
	current medical history
cmH$_2$O	centimeters of water
CMHC	Certified Mental Health Counselor
	community mental health center
C/MHC	Community/Migrant Health Center
CMHD	Centre for Modeling Human Disease (www.cmhd.ca)
CMHN	Community Mental Health Nurse
cm H2O	centimeters of water
CMI	case mix index
	cell-mediated immunity
	Chiari I malformation type I
	clomipramine (Anafranil)
	collagen meniscus implant
	Consumer Medicine Information (Australia)
	Cornell Medical Index
CM-I	Chiari malformation Type I
CMIC	Centre for Medical Image Computing (University College London, UK)
Cmic	microbial biomass
CMID	cytomegalic inclusion disease
C$_{min}$	minimum concentration of drug
CMIO	Chief Medical Informatics Officer
CMIP	Certification Measure Information Process (The Joint Commission)
CMIR	cell-mediated immune response
CMIT	chloromethylisothiazolinone (also known as methyl-chloroisothiazolinone; a preservative found in liquid personal care products)

CMIT/MIT	chloromethylisothiazolinone and methylisothiazolinone (preservatives found in liquid personal care products)
CMJ	carpometacarpal joint
	cervicomedullary junction
	countermovement jump
CMK	congenital multicystic kidney
CML	cell-mediated lympholysis
	chronic myelogenous leukemia
	chronic myeloid leukemia
CML-5	lower second premolar
CML-BP	blastic phase chronic myeloid leukemia
CML-CP	chronic myeloid leukemia in chronic phase
CMM	Comprehensive Major Medical (insurance)
	comprehensive medication management
	continuous metabolic monitor
	cutaneous malignant melanoma
CMME	chloromethyl methyl ether
CMML	chronic myelomacrocytic leukemia
CMML-1	chronic myelomonocytic leukemia type 1
CMML-2	chronic myelomonocytic leukemia type 2
CMMM	cutaneous malignant melanoma metastases
CMMoL	chronic myelomonocytic leukemia
CMMS	Columbia Mental Maturity Scale
CMN	cephalomedullary nailing
	Certificate of Medical Necessity
	congenital melanocytic nevi
	congenital mesoblastic nephroma
CMNT	complete median nerve transection
	cyst with a mural nodule tumor
CMO	cardiac minute output
	cardiomyopathy
	cetyl myristoleate
	Chief Medical Officer
	comfort measures only (resuscitation order)
	consult made out
	contact manufacturing organization
CMO 1	corticosterone methyl oxidase type 1
CMOP	cardiomyopathy
C-MOPP	cyclophosphamide, mechlorethamine, vincristine (Oncovin), procarbazine, and prednisone
CMOS	complementary metal-oxide semiconductor

CMP	cardiomyopathy	CMS-HCC	Centers for Medicare and
	chondromalacia patellae		Medicaid Services Hierarchical
	chronic musculoskeletal pain		Condition Categories
	comprehensive (complete)	cm sq	square centimeters
	metabolic profile (see	CMSRN	Certified Medical-Surgical
	Laboratory Panels)		Registered Nurse
	cushion mouthpiece	CMSS	cutaneous melanoma-specific
CMPA	cow's milk protein allergy		survival
CMPD	chronic myeloproliferative	CMSs	congenital myasthenic
	disorder(s)		syndromes
Cmpd	compound	CMST	Chinese medical syndrome type
CMPF	cow's milk, protein-free		circulation, motion, sensation,
CM-PF	centremedian-parafascicular		and temperature
CMPI	Center for Medicine in the	CMSUA	clean midstream urinalysis
	Public Interest	CMSW	Certified Master Social Worker
	cow's milk protein intolerance	CMT	carpometatarsal (joint)
CMPR	clinically meaningful pain relief		celiomesenteric trunk
	curve multi-planar reconstruction		Certified Massage Therapist
CMPS	chronic myofascial pain syndrome		Certified Medical Transcriptionist
CMPT	cervical mucous penetration test		Certified Medication Technician
cmptr	computer		Certified Music Therapist
cmpy	crimpy (gene/protein)		cervical motion tenderness
CMR	cardiac magnetic resonance		Charot-Marie-Tooth (phenotype)
	(imaging)		(disease)
	cardiometabolic risk		Chiropractic manipulative
	cardiovascular magnetic		treatment
	resonance		choline magnesium trisalicylate
	cerebral metabolic rate		(Trilisate)
	chief medical resident		combined modality therapy
	child (1-4 years) mortality rates		congenital muscular torticollis
	chloroform-methanol residue		continuing medication and
	compressive myofascial release		treatment
	crude mortality rate		cutis marmorata telangiectasia
CMRI	cardiac magnetic resonance	CMT2B	Charcot-Marie-Tooth type 2B
	imaging	CMTC	cutis marmorata telangiectatica
CMRIT	combined modality		congenita
	radioimmunotherapy	CMT2C	type 2C Charcot-Marie-Tooth
CMRNG	chromosomally mediated		disease
	resistant *Neisseria gonorrhoeae*	CMT4C	Charcot-Marie-Tooth (disease)
CMRO	chronic multifocal recurrent		type 4C
	osteomyelitis	CMTD	Charcot-Marie-Tooth disease
CMRO$_2$	cerebral metabolic rate for oxygen		chronic multiple tic disorder
CMS	cardiometabolic syndrome	CMTS	color, motion, temperature, and
	Centers for Medicare and		sensation
	Medicaid Services (replaces	CMTX	chemotherapy treatment
	HCFA)	CMU	cardiac monitoring unit
	children's medical services	CMUA	continuous motor unit activity
	chocolate milkshake	CMUSE	cryptogenic multifocal ulcerous
	circulation, motion, sensation		stenosing enteritis
	constant moderate suction	CMV	cisplatin, methotrexate, and
	continuous motion syndrome		vinblastine
cms	centimeters (cm)		continuous mechanical
cm/s	centimeters per second		ventilation
CMSC	Certified Medical Staff		controlled mechanical
	Coordinator		ventilation
CMSE	Core Measure Solution		conventional mechanical
	Exchange®		ventilation
cm/sec	centimeters per second		cool mist vaporizer

138

	countermovement vertical jump	C_{Na}	sodium clearance
	cytomegalovirus	CNAA	Certified in Nursing
	cytomegalovirus vaccine		Administration, Advanced
CMVD	chronic mitral valvular disease	CNAG	chronic narrow angle glaucoma
	coronary microvascular	CNAP	continuous negative airway
	dysfunction		pressure
CMVECs	cerebromicrovascular endothelial	CNB	continuous nerve block
	cells		core-needle biopsy
CMVIG	cytomegalovirus immune globulin	CNC	clinical nurse coordinator
CMV IgG	cytomegalovirus		Community Nursing Center
	immunoglobulin G		Consonant-Vowel Nucleus-
CMV PCR	cytomegalovirus polymerase		Consonant (Maryland CNC
	chain reaction		word list)
CMVR	cytomegalovirus retinitis	CNCbl	cyanocobalamin
CMVS	culture midvoid specimen	CNCC	cranial neural crest cells
cmWP	centimeters of water pressure	CNCH	chondrodermatitis nodularis
CMX	crossmatch		chronica helicis
CMY	cardiomyopathy	CNCP	chronic noncancer pain
	see gene website, www.ncbi.nlm	CND	canned
	.nih.gov/gene		cannot determine
c-Myc	v-myc myelocytomatosis viral		central-neck dissection
	oncogene homolog; see gene		chronic nausea and dyspepsia
	website www.ncbi.nlm.nih	CNDC	chronic nonspecific diarrhea of
	.gov/gene		childhood
CMZL	cutaneous marginal zone	CNDM2	cerebral neuropathology of
	lymphomas		type 2 diabetes mellitus
CN	categorically needy	CNE	Certified Nurse Educator
	charge nurse		Chief Nurse Executive
	cognitively normal		chronic nervous exhaustion
	congenital nystagmus		continuing nursing education
	cranial nerve(s)		could not establish
Cn	copernicium		culture-negative endocarditis
	cyanide	CNED	continual no evidence of disease
C/N	contrast-to-noise ratio	CNEP	continuous negative extrathoracic
CN1	cranial nerve 1 (olfactory)		pressure
CN2	cranial nerve 2 (optic)	C-NES	conversion nonepileptic seizures
CN2-12	cranial nerves 2-12	CNF	cyclophosphamide, mitoxantrone
CN3	cranial nerve 3 (oculomotor)		(Novatantrone), and
CN4	cranial nerve 4 (trochlear)		fluorouracil
CN5	cranial nerve 5 (trigeminal)	CNFP	Certified Family Nurse
CN6	cranial nerve 6 (abducens)		Practitioner
CN7	cranial nerve 7 (facial)	CNG	complete, no growth
CN8	cranial nerve 8 (vestibulocochlear)	CNH	central neurogenic hypernea
CN9	cranial nerve 9 (glossopharyngeal)		community nursing home
CN10	cranial nerve 10 (vagus)		continuous normobaric hypoxia
CN11	cranial nerve 11 (accessory)		contract nursing home
CN12	cranial nerve 12(hypoglossal)	CNHC	chronodermatitis nodularis
C1N1	may have meant CIN 1		helicis chronicus
	(a low-grade abnormal		community nursing home care
	cervical intraepithelial	CN I	cranial nerve 1 (olfactory)
	neoplasia)	CN II	cranial nerve 2
CN1a	5'-nucleotidase, cytosolic IA		cranial nerve 2 (optic)
	(gene)	CN III	cranial nerve 3 (oculomotor)
CNA	Certified in Nursing	CN II-XII	cranial nerves 2 to 12
	Administration	CN IV	cranial nerve 4 (trochlear)
	Certified Nurse Aide	CN IX	cranial nerve 9 (glossopharyngeal)
	Certified Nurse Assistant	CNI	calcineurin inhibitors
	chart not available		cranial nerve injury

CNICS	CFAR (Center for AIDS Research) Network of Integrated Clinical Systems	cNPP	corrected negative predictive power
	Childhood National Immunization Coverage Survey	CNPS	cardiac nuclear probe scan
		CNR	contrast-to-noise ratio (radiology)
CNIO	Chief Nursing Informatics Officer	CNRN	Certified Neuroscience Registered Nurse
CNKI	China National Knowledge Infrastructure		Certified Neurosurgical Registered Nurse
CNL	chemonucleolysis	CNS	central nervous system
	chronic neutrophilic leukemia		Certified Nutrition Specialist
	Clinical Nurse Leader		Clinical Nurse Specialist
	Connaught Laboratories		coagulase-negative staphylococci
CNLCP	Certified Nurse Life Care Planner		congenital nephrotic syndrome
			Crigler-Najjar syndrome
CNLD	chronic neonatal lung disease	CNSC	Certified Nutrition Support Clinician
CNLSD	condensation nucleation light scattering detection	CNSD	Certified Nutrition Support Dietitian
CNM	certified nurse midwife	CNSET	calcifying nested stromal-epithelial tumor
	Clinical Nutrition Manager		
CNML	Nurse Manager and Leader Certification	CNSHA	congenital nonspherocytic hemolytic anemia
CNMP	chronic, nonmalignant pain	CNSL	central nervous system lymphoma
CNMT	Certified Nuclear Medicine Technologist	CNS-LS	Center for Neurologic Study-Lability Scale
CNN	Certified in Nephrology Nursing	CNS lymphoma	central nervous system lymphoma
	congenital nevocytic nevus	CNSN	Certified Nutrition Support Nurse
CNNA	culture-negative neutrocytic ascitis	CNS PTLD	central nervous system post-transplant lymphoprolif-
CNNF	Centro Nacional de Neurofibromatose (database) (National Center for Neuro-fibromatosis, Rio de Janeiro, RJ, Brazil)		erative disorder(s)
		CNSS	Canadian Neurological Stroke Scale
		CNSs	clinical nurse specialists
CNNP	Certified Neonatal Nurse Practitioner		conserved noncoding sequences
		CNST	central nervous system tumor(s)
	chronic nonspecific neck pain		Clinical Negligence Scheme for Trusts (United Kingdom)
CNO	Chief Nursing Officer		
	community nursing organization	CNT	could not tell
CNOP	cyclophosphamide, mitoxantrone (Novantrone), vincristine (Oncovin), and prednisone		could not test
		CNTA	combined neurosurgical and transfacial approach
CNOR	Certified Nurse, Operating Room	CNTF	ciliary neurotrophic factor
CNOs	carbon nano-onions	CNTR	controls
	chief nursing officers	CNTRL	centriolin (gene)
cNOS	constitutive nitric oxide synthase		control(s)
CNP	2′,3′-cyclic nucleotide 3′ phosphodiesterase (gene)	CNTs	computerized neuropsychological tests
	capillary nonprofusion	CNV	choroidal neovascularization
	chronic neck pain		contingent negative variation
	C-type natriuretic peptide		copy number variations
	culture negative pyelonephritis	CN V	cranial nerve 5 (trigeminal)
CNPA	chronic necrotizing pulmonary aspergillosis	CN VI	cranial nerve 6 (abducens)
		CN VII	cranial nerve 7 (facial)
CNPB	continuous negative pressure breathing	CN VIII	cranial nerve 8 (vestibulocochlear)
CNPI	Checklist for Nonverbal Pain Indicators	CNVM	choroidal neovascular membrane
		CNVs	copy number variations

CNX calnexin (gene/protein)
CN X cranial nerve 10 (vagus)
CN XI cranial nerve 11 (accessory)
CN XII cranial nerve 12(hypoglossal)
CO carbon monoxide
cardiac output
castor oil
centric occlusion
Certified Orthoptist
cervical orthosis
Colorado
Colton; an International Society
of Blood Transfusion (ISBT)
blood group
complains of
Contractual Obligation. Amount
form which the provider is
financially liable. The patient
may not be billed for this
amount. (Medicare code)
corn oil
corneal opacity
court order
Co cobalt
C/O check out
complained of
complains of
under care of
CO₂ carbon dioxide
CO₃ carbonate
⁶⁰Co radioactive isotope of cobalt
COA children of alcoholic
chronic obstructive asthma
coenzyme A
condition on admission
CoA coarctation of the aorta
COAD chronic obstructive airway
disease
COAG chronic open angle glaucoma
coag coagulation
CoAg-ELISA coproantigen enzyme-linked
immunosorbent assay
coag negative coagulase negative
coag-neg Staph coagulase-negative
Staphylococcus
coags coagulation panel (prothrombin
time , activated partial thromboplastin time, thrombin
time, and fibrinogen)
COAGSC coagulation screen
coagu coagulation
COAP cyclophosphamide, vincristine
(Oncovin), cytarabine
(ara-C), and prednisone
coapt a word meaning to fit together
and make fast
COAR coarctation
COARCT coarctation

COAT Children's Orientation and
Amnesia Test
chronic opioid analgesic therapy
coat neg coagulase negative
COB chronic obstructive bronchitis
cisplatin, vincristine (Oncovin),
and bleomycin
coordination of benefits
cobA see gene website www.ncbi.nlm
.nih.gov/gene
Coban™ self-adherent, nonadhesive
elastic wrap for securing,
compression or support
cobas® 6000 a series of clinical chemistry and
immunochemistry analyzers
cobD cobalamin biosynthesis protein;
see gene website www.ncbi
.nlm.nih.gov/gene
COBE chronic obstructive bullous
emphysema
COBGC Certified Obstetrics Gynecology
Coder (COBGC™)
COBI cobicistat (Tybost)
COBRA Consolidated Omnibus Budget
Reconciliation Act of 1985
(allows for temporarily
keeping employers or union
health coverage after em-
ployment ends or after losing
coverage as a dependent of
the covered employee)
COBS chronic organic brain syndrome
COBT chronic obstruction of biliary
tract
COC calcifying odontogenic cyst
Certified Outpatient Coder
(COC™)
chain of custody
cocaine
combination oral contraceptive
continuity of care
cocci coccidioidomycosis (valley fever)
COCCIO coccidioidomycosis
CO/CI cardiac output/cardiac index
COCM congestive cardiomyopathy
COCN Certified Ostomy Care Nurse
COCP combined (estrogen and
progestin) oral contraceptive
pill
CoCr cobalt-chromiun alloy
Co-Cr cobalt-chromium
COCs combination oral contraceptives
COD carotid occlusive disease
cataract, right eye
cause of death
chronic oxygen dependency
coefficient of oxygen delivery
condition on discharge

CODAS	chronotherapeutic oral drug absorption system
Code...	Check with your facility as the meanings shown above may vary from facility/region/country to facility/region/country
CODE 99	patient in cardiac or respiratory arrest
Code black	slang referring to a patient in cardiopulmonary arrest requiring a resuscitation team
Code Blue	medical emergency - adult patient in cardiac or pulmonary arrest
Code Brown	a patient's bed containing excrement (slang)
Code C	slang referring to a patient in cardiopulmonary arrest requiring a resuscitation team
Code Gray	combative person
Code Grey	combative person
Code Orange	hazardous material spill/release
Code Pink	infant abduction
Code Purple	child abduction
Code R	code reperfusion
Code Red	fire
CODES	Crash Outcome Data Evaluation System (National Highway Traffic Safety Administration-sponsored)
Code Silver	person with a weapon and/or a hostage situation
Code T	code trauma
Code Triage	an external disaster an internal disaster
Code White	medical emergency û pediatric
Code Yellow	a patient's bed containing urine (slang) bomb threat
codine	may have meant codeine
COD-MD	cerebro-oculardysplasia muscular dystrophy
CODO	codocytes
CODOX-M	cyclophosphamide, vincristine (Oncovin), doxorubicin, high-dose methotrexate
CODOX-M/IVAC	cyclophosphamide, vincristine (Oncovin), doxorubicin, methotrexate, ifosfamide, etoposide (VePesid), and cytarabine (AraC)
CODOX-M/IVAC+R	cyclophosphamide, vincristine (Oncovin), doxorubicin, methotrexate, ifosfamide, etoposide (VePesid), and cytarabine (AraC) plus rituximab

CODOX-MR/IVAC	cyclophosphamide, vincristine (Oncovin), doxorubicin, methotrexate, rituximab, ifosfamide, etoposide (VePesid),and cytarabine (AraC)
CODP	may be referring to chronic obstructive pulmonary disease (COPD)
COE	Centers of Excellence co-evaporation court-ordered examination
COEPS	cortically originating extrapyramidal symptoms
COER-24	24-hour controlled-onset, extended-release (dosage form)
C of C	certificate of compliance
COFN	Committee on the Fetus and Newborn (American Academy Of Pediatrics)
COFS	cerebro-oculo-facioskeletal
COG	center of gravity Central Oncology Group Children's Oncology Group cognitive function tests
COG-LTFU	Children's Oncology Group, Long-Term Follow-Up (Guidelines)
COGN	cognition
COGS	Collaborative Oncological Gene-environment Study
COGTT	cortisone-primed oral glucose tolerance test
COH	circumference of head controlled ovarian hyperstimulation
COHA	community onset, healthcare facility acquired
COHb	carboxyhemoglobin
COHgb	carboxyhemoglobin
COHN	Certified Occupational Health Nurse
COHN/CM	Certified Occupational Health Nurse/Case Manager
COHN-S	Certified Occupational Health Nurse - Specialist
COHN-s/CM	Certified Occupational Health Nurse - Specialist Case Manager
COI	conflict of interest
COINS	coinsurance
Coke	Coca-Cola® cocaine
COL	colonoscopy
Col	Colonel
COL25A1	collagen, type XXV, alpha 1 (Alzheimer disease amyloid-associated protein); see gene website www.ncbi.nlm.nih .gov/gene

COLAs cost-of-living adjustments
COLD chronic obstructive lung disease
Computer Output to Laser Disk
COLD A cold agglutin titer
COLDSPA character; onset; location; duration; severity; pattern; associated symptoms (for pain assessment)
coll collection
Collyr eye wash
col/mL colonies per milliliter
colo colon
colon colonoscopy
colp colporrhaphy
COLPO colposcopy
COLTRU *colletotrichum truncatum*
COM calcium oxalate monohydrate
center of mass
chronic otitis media
citrate of magnesia
crotchety old man (slang)
COMBO combination ultrasound with electrical stimulation
COME chronic otitis media with effusion
COMF comfortable
COMLA cyclophosphamide, vincristine (Oncovin), methotrexate, calcium leucovorin, and cytarabine (ara-C)
COMM Current Opioid Misuse Measure
COMME Committee E, a German Federal Health Agency committee for the evaluation of herbal remedies
COMP Committee on Orphan Medicinal Products (EMEA)
compensation
complications
composite
compound
compress
cyclophosphamide, vincristine (Oncovin), methotrexate, and prednisone
comp compatible
CompAC Compassionate Use Advisory Committee
ComPASS Comprehensive Pediatric and Adolescent Support Services Care Team
comprehensive metabolic pane go to Tables and Lists Button; Laboratory Panels
CompSAS complex sleep apnea syndrome
CO-MRSA community-onset methicillin-resistant *Staphylococcus aureus*
COMS clinical outcomes management system

CoMSAS Complex Mixture Safety Assessment Strategy
COMT catechol-*O*-methyl-transferase
Certified Ophthalmic Medical Technologist
COMTA Commission on Message Therapy Accreditation
CON catheter over a needle
certificate of need
conservatorship
control
CON A concanavalin A
conc concentrated
cond condition
conditional
conditioned
conditioning
conditions
conductance
conductive
conductivity
CONEP National Commission for Ethics in Research (Brazil)
CONF see gene website, www.ncbi.nlm.nih.gov/gene
Conf Conference
CONG congenital
gallon
CONJ conjunctiva
CONN tool box a Matlab-based cross-platform software for the computation, display, and analysis of functional connectivity in functional magnetic resonance imaging
CONPADRI I cyclophosphamide, vincristine, doxorubicin, and melphalan
CONPADRI II conpadri I plus high-dose methotrexate
CONPADRI III conpadri I plus intensified doxorubicin
CONS consultation
CoNS coagulase-negative staphylococci
consol consolidation
CONSORT Consolidated Standards of Reporting Trials
constip constipation
constp constipation
cont contains
continue
continuous
contusions
con't continue(d)
cont'd continued
contd continued
contra contraindication(s)
CONTRAL contralateral
contralat contralateral
CONTRX contraction(s)

CONTs	controls, as in a clinical trial control group
CONTU	contusion
CONUS	conus medullaris (slang)
CONV	conversation
conver	conversion
Conv. ex.	convergence excess
convo	conversation (slang)
ConvRx	conventional therapy
—COOH	carboxylic acid
Coombs test	a positive test indicates antibodies that act against red blood cells, due to autoimmune hemolytic anemia, chronic lymphocytic leukemia, or similar disorders
COOP	cooperation
COORD	coordinated coordination
CO-Ox	Co-oximetry
COP	center of pressure change of plaster cicatricial ocular pemphigoid *Colibacilosis porcina* vaccine colloid osmotic pressure complaint of pain cryptogenic organizing pneumonia cycophosphamide, vincristine (Oncovin), and prednisone
CoP	code of practice Communities of Practice Conditions of Participation
COP 1	copolymer 1
COPA	cuffed oropharyngeal airway
COPAdM	cyclophosphamide, vincristine (Oncovin), prednisone, doxorubicin (Adriamycin) and methotrexate
CoPAT	community-based parenteral anti-infective therapy
COPBLAM	cyclophosphamide, vincristine (Oncovin), prednisone, bleomycin, doxorubicin (Adriamycin), and procarbazine (Matulane)
COPC	Certified Ophthalmology Coder (COPC) chemicals of potential concern community-oriented primary care
COPD	chronic obstructive pulmonary disease
COPD AE	acute exacerbation of chronic obstructive pulmonary disease
COPDE	chronic obstructive pulmonary disease exacerbation
COPE	chronic obstructive pulmonary emphysema

COPM	Canadian Occupational Performance Measure
CopN	Chlamydial (pneumoniae) outer protein N
COPP	cyclophosphamide, vincristine, procarbazine, and prednisone
COPS	community outpatient service
CoPs	Conditions of Participation (Centers for Medicare & Medicaid
COPT	circumoval precipitin test
COQ2	coenzyme Q2 4-hydroxybenzoate polyprenyltransferase; see gene website www.ncbi.nlm.nih.gov/gene
COR	center of rotation coefficient of reproducibility complete oral rehabilitation conditioned orientation response coronary
CoR	custodian of records
cOR	crude odds ratio
CORA	conditioned orientation reflex audiometry
cor art	coronary artery
CORBA	Common-Object Request Broker Architecture
coRCC	may have meant ccRCC (clear cell renal cell carcinoma)
CORD	cone-rod dystrophy (an inherited, progressive retinal disorder with genetic and phenotypic heterogeneity)
CORE	cardiac or respiratory emergency
C9orf72	chromosome 9 open reading frame 72; see gene website www.ncbi.nlm.nih.gov/gene
CORF	Comprehensive Outpatient Rehabilitation Facility
CORLN	Certified Otorhinolaryngology and Head/Neck Nurse
coro	coronary
coron	coronary
CORP	cor pulmonale
Corpack	may have meant Corpak (a marketer of medical devices focused on enteral feeding)
Corpak	a marketer of medical devices focused on enteral feeding
corrCa	corrected calcium
CoRs	centers of rotation
CORT	Certified Operating Room Technician
CorVis ST	Corneal Visualization Scheimpflug Technology
CorX	a closed extracorporeal circuit

COS	cataract, left eye		Clinical Psychologist
	change of shift		closing pressure
	Chief of Staff		cold pack
	childhood-onset schizophrenia		constrictive pericarditis
	clinically observed seizure		convenience package
	controlled ovarian stimulation		cor pulmonale
	Crisis Outpatient Services		creatine phosphokinase
COSC	Certified Orthopaedic Surgery		cricopharyngeal
	Coder (COSC™)		cyclophosphamide and cisplatin
C_{osm}	osmolal clearance		(Platinol)
COSTART	Coding symbols for a thesaurus		cystopanendoscopy
	of adverse reaction terms		process capability
COT	chronic opioid therapy	cP	centipoise
	content of thought	C_p	concentration of drug plasma
	course of treatment		phosphate clearance
	court-ordered treatment	C_p	Chlamydia pneumoniae
COTA	Certified Occupational Therapy	C/P	carbohydrate-to-protein ratio
	Assistant		central-to-peripheral ratio
	colon-ovarian tumor antigen		see C&P
COtd	thermodilution cardiac output	C&P	compensation and pension
COTE	comprehensive occupational		complete and pain-free (range of
	therapy evaluation		motion)
co-treat	treatment involving more than		complete and pushing
	one professional		cystoscopy and pyelography
COTT CH	cottage cheese	CP5	capsular polysaccharides 5
COTX	cast-off, to x-ray	CP8	capsular polysaccharides 8
CoTx	concurrently treated	CPA	cardiopulmonary arrest
COU	cardiac observation unit		carotid photoangiography
	cataracts, both eyes		cerebellopontine angle
COV	coefficient of variation		chest pain alert
COW	circle of Willis		child protection agency
COWA	controlled oral word association		chronic pulmonary aspergillosis
COWAT	Controlled Oral Word Association		Collaborative Practice Agreement
	Test		color power angiography
COWS	Clinical Opioid Withdrawal Scale		conditioned play audiometry
	cold to the opposite and warm to		congenital primary aphakia
	the same		cyclophosphamide (Cytoxan)
COX	Coxsackie virus		cyproterone acetate
	cyclooxygenase		cyproterone acetate (Androcur)
	cytochrome C oxidase	CPAA	condition present at admission
COX-2	cyclo-oxygenase-2	CPAC	California Program on Access to
CP	calculation point		Care
	canaloplasty		Canadian Partnership Against
	centric position		Cancer
	cerebellopontine	cpaC	see gene website, www.ncbi
	cerebellopontine (angles)		.nlm.nih.gov/gene
	cerebral palsy	cPACNS	primary angiitis of the central
	Certified Paramedic		nervous system of childhood
	chemical peel	CPAD	cavopulmonary assist device
	chemistry profiles	cPAD	chronic Population Adjusted Dose
	chest pain	CPAF	chlorpropamide-alcohol flush
	chloroquine-primaquine	C_{PAH}	para-amino hippurate clearance
	chondromalacia patella	CPAM	congenital pulmonary airway
	chronic pain		malformation
	chronic pancreatitis	CPAN	Certified Postanesthesia Nurse
	cleft palate	CP angle	cerebellopontine angle
	clinical pathway	CPAP	continuous positive airway
	clinical plan		pressure

c-PAP	continuous positive airway pressure		cigarettes per day
CPAs	Collaborative Practice Agreements		citrate-phosphate-dextrose
			continuing professional development
	cryoprotective agents	cPd	colloidal palladium
CP assess	cardiopulmonary assessment	CPDA-1	citrate-phosphate-dextrose-adenine-one
CPAT	cerebellopontine angle tumor		
	collaborative practice assessment tool	CPDA-2	citrate-phosphate-dextrose-adenine-two
CPB	cardiopulmonary bypass	CPDD	calcium pyrophosphate deposition disease
	celiac plexus block		
	Certified Professional Biller (CPB™)	CPDG2	carboxypeptidaseG2
		CPDM	chronic proliferative dermatitis mutation
	cisplatin, cyclophosphamide, and carmustine (BiCNU)		
	competitive protein binding	cpdm	chronic proliferative dermatitis; see gene website www.ncbi .nlm.nih.gov/gene
CPBA	competitive protein-binding assay		
CPBP	cardiopulmonary bypass	CPDN	Certified Peritoneal Dialysis Nurse
CPC	cancer prevention clinic		
	cerebral palsy clinic	CPDR	Center for Prostate Disease Research (Department of Defense)
	Certified Professional Coder (CPC®)		
	cetylpyridinium chloride	CPE	cardiogenic pulmonary edema
	choroid plexus cyst		chronic pulmonary emphysema
	chronic passive congestion		Clinical Pastoral Education
	clinicopathologic conference		*Clostridium perfringens* enterotoxin
	coil planet centrifuge		
	continue plan of care		clubbing, pitting, or edema
CPC 1 (also 2-5)	Cerebral Performance Category 1 to 5 scale		complete physical examination
			continuing professional education
CPCC	Certified Professional Co-Active Coach		cytopathic effect
CPCD	Certified Professional Coder in Dermatology (CPCD™)	CPEB	cytoplasmic polyadenylation element binding (protein)
CPC-H	Certified Procedural Coder, Hospital-Based	C-PEC	containment primary engineering control
CP-CML	chronic phase chronic myeloid leukemia	CPE-C	cyclopentenylcytosine
		CPEDC	Certified Pediatrics Coder (CPEDC™)
CPCO	Certified Professional Compliance Officer - CPCO™		
		CPEFM	Clear-Plan Easy Fertility Monitor
CPCP	Cancer Prevention and Control Program	CPEO	chronic progressive external ophthalmoplegia
	chronic post-cast pain	CPEP	C-peptide
CpcPH	combined pre- and post-capillary pulmonary hypertension	CPER	chest pain emergency room
		CPET	cardiopulmonary exercise testing
CP/CPPS	chronic prostatitis/chronic pelvic pain syndrome	CPETU	chest pain evaluation and treatment unit
CPCR	cardiopulmonary-cerebral resuscitation	CPEU	chest pain evaluation unit
		CPEx	cardiopulmonary exercise (testing)
CPCS	clinical pharmacokinetics consulting service		
		CPF	cerebral perfusion pressure
CPCs	calcium phosphate cements		chlorpyrifos (an insecticide)
	circulating progenitor cells	CPFE	combined pulmonary fibrosis and emphysema
CPCU	chemistry process control unit		
CPD	cephalopelvic disproportion		context preexposure facilitation effect
	chorioretinopathy and pituitary dysfunction	CPFT	Certified Pulmonary Function Technologist
	chronic peritoneal dialysis		

CPFX	ciprofloxacin (Cipro)	Clinical Performance Measure
CPG	clinical practice guidelines	Clinical Practice Model
CPG2	carboxypeptidase G2	conditioned pain modulation
CPGN	chronic progressive	constant passive motion
	glomerulonephritis	continue present management
CPH	chronic paroxysmal hemicrania	continuous passive motion
	chronic persistent hepatitis	contralateral prophylactic
CPHI	Communication Profile for the	mastectomy
	Hearing Impaired	counts per minute
CPHM	Cox proportional hazards	cricopharyngeal myotomy
	regression models	cycles per minute
CPHQ	Certified Professional in	cyclophosphamide
	Healthcare Quality	CPMA Certified Professional Medical
CPHRM	Certified Professional in	Auditor (CPMA®)
	Healthcare Risk Management	CPmax peak serum concentration
CPhT	Certified Pharmacy Technician	CPMC copies per million cells
CPI	chronic public inebriate	CPMDI computerized pharmacokinetic
	constitutionally psychopathia	modeldriven drug infusion
	inferior	CPmin trough serum concentration
CPIC	Children's Perception of	CPMM constant passive motion machine
	Interparental Conflict (scale)	CPMP Committee for Proprietary
	Clinical Pharmacogenetics	Medicinal Products (of the
	Implementation Consortium	European Union)
	(guidelines)	CPMR cardiopulmonary and metabolic
	Community Partners in Care	rehabilitation (program)
	(study)	cerebral palsy with mental
CPID	chronic pelvic inflammatory	retardation
	disease	CPMSM Certified Professional Medical
CPIO	Chief Pharmacy Informatics	Services Management
	Officer	CPN central parenteral nutrition
CPIP	chronic pulmonary insufficiency	Certified Pediatric Nurse
	of prematurity	chronic pyelonephritis
CPIS	Clinical Pulmonary Infection	common peroneal nerve
	Score	complete parenteral nutrition
CPJ	cartilage-pannus junction	cutaneous polyarteritis nodosa
	concentrated pomegranate juice	CPNA Certified Pediatric Nurse
CPK	creatine phosphokinase (BB,	Associate
	MB, MM are isoenzymes)	CPNB continuous peripheral nerve
CPK1	calcium-dependent protein	block
	kinase 1 (gene)	CPNI common peroneal nerve injury
CPK-BB	creatine phosphokinase BB	CPNL Certified Pediatric Nurse -
	fraction	Long-Term Care
CPKD	childhood polycystic kidney	CPNP Certified Pediatric Nurse
	disease	Practitioner
CPKMB	creatine phosphokinase	CPO Chief Pharmacy Officer
	isoenzyme, muscle-brain	Chief Privacy Officer
	(marker for cardiac damage	continue present orders
	[myocardial infraction])	curved periacetabular osteotomy
CPK MB	creatine phosphokinase	CPOA Certified Paraoptometric Assistant
	isoenzyme, muscle-brain	chronic peripheral obstructive
	(marker for cardiac damage	arteriopathies
	[myocardial infraction])	CPOC cyclic path optical configuration
CPL	criminal procedure law	CPOD chronic obstructive pulmonary
CPM	cancer pain management	disease (Romance language
	central pontine myelinolysis	speaking countries)
	Certified Professional Midwife	CPOE computerized physician
	chlorpheniramine maleate	(prescriber) order entry
	chronic progressive myelopathy	cpoise centipoises

CPOM	continuous pulse oximeter monitoring		computer-based patient records
CPON	Certified Pediatric Oncology Nurse		computerized patient record
C-PORT	Cardiovascular Patient Outcomes Research Team		customary, prevailing and reasonable (charge payment method)
C-Port®	a distral coronary artery anastomosis system		tablet (French)
		CPR-1	all measures except cardiopulmonary resuscitation (check for local meanings)
CPOT	Critical-Care Pain Observation Tool	CPR-2	no extraordinary measures (to resuscitate) (check for local meanings)
CPOX	chicken pox		
CPP	cell-penetrating peptides	CPR-3	comfort measures only (check for local meanings)
	central precocious puberty		
	cerebral perfusion pressure	cPRA	calculated panel-reactive antibody
	chronic pelvic pain	CPRAM	controlled partial rebreathing anesthesia method
	complete placenta previa		
	conditioned place preference	CPRD	Clinical Practice Research Datalink (United Kingdom)
	coronary perfusion pressure		
	cryo-poor plasma	CPRE	colangiopancreatographic retrograde endoscopy
CPP-ACP	casein phosphopeptide-amorphous calcium phosphate		complete primary repair of (bladder) exstrophy
CPPB	continuous positive pressure breathing		
		CPRI	Child and Parent Resource Institute
CPPC	chronic painful physical condition		
	congenital posterior pole cataract	CP/ROMI	chest pain, rule out myocardial infarction
CPPD	calcium pyrophosphate deposition		
	calcium pyrophosphate deposition (disease)	CPRP	comprehensive pain rehabilitation program
	calcium pyrophosphate dihydrate	CPRS	Categorical Pain Relief Scale
	cisplatin		Comprehensive Psychopathological Rating Scale
CP & PD	chest percussion and postural drainage		
			computerized patient record system
CPPE	complicated parapneumonic effusion		
		CPRSOCS	Comprehensive Psychiatric Rating Scale, ObsessiveCom-pulsive Subscale
CPPM	Certified Physician Practice Manager (CPPM®)		
CPP NIBP	cerebral perfusion pressure measurements performed by noninvasive (brachial) blood pressure	CPRS-RS	Conners Parent Rating Scale-Revised: Short Form
		CPRU	cardiac procedure recovery unit
		CPS	calcium phosphosilicate
CPPP	chronic persistent post-surgical pain		carbamyl phosphate synthetase
			cardiopulmonary support
cPPP	corrected positive predictive power		Center for Prevention Services (CDC)
CPPS	chronic pelvic pain syndrome		cervical pedicle screw
CPPs	cell-penetrating peptides		chest pain syndrome
CPPS/CP	chronic pelvic pain syndrome/chronic prostatitis		child protective services
			Chinese paralytic syndrome
CPPT	concurrent patient-partner treatment		chloroquinepyrimethamine sulfadoxine
	culture-positive pulmonary tuberculosis		chronic paranoid schizophrenia
cPPT	central polypurine tract		clauses per sentence
CPPV	continuous positive pressure ventilation		clinical performance score
			clinical pharmacokinetic service
CPQ	Conners Parent Questionnaire		clinical pharmacy specialist
CPR	cardiopulmonary resuscitation		CoaguChek® Plus System
	clinical pregnancy rate		

coagulasepositive staphylococci
complex partial seizures
counts per second
cumulative probability of
success
CPs clinical pathways
contact precautions
CPS I carbamyl phosphate synthetase I
cPSA complexed prostate-specific
antigen
CPSB Chesapeake-Potomac Spina
Bifida (association)
CPSC Consumer Product Safety
Commission
CPSD carbamoyl-phosphate synthetase
1 deficiency
catheter-based peripheral
sympathetic denervation
corrected pattern standard
deviation
CPSET Care Process Self-Evaluation Tool
CPSI Chronic Prostatitis Symptom
Index
CPSN Certified Plastic Surgical Nurse
CPSP central post-stroke pain
CPSS Cincinnati Prehospital Stroke
Scale
congenital portosystemic shunts
CPST cardiopulmonary stress testing
cerebral palsy with spastic
tetraplegia
CPT camptothecin
carnitine palmitoyl transferase
chest physiotherapy
child protection team
chromoperturbation
chronic paranoid type
cognitive processing therapy
cold pressor test
Continuous Performance Test
corticosteroid pulse treatment
current perception threshold
Current Procedural Terminology
(coding system)
CPT 2013 Current Procedural Terminology
2013
CPT 2019 Current Procedural Terminology
2019
CPT11 irinotecan HCl (Camptosar)
CPT2 carnitine palmitoyltransferase 2;
see gene website www.ncbi
.nlm.nih.gov/gene
CPTA Certified Physical Therapy
Assistant
CPT/C current perception threshold,
computerized
CPT1C carnitine palmitoyltransferase
1C (gene/protein)

CPTd central-peripheral temperature
difference
CPTED chronic pulmonary
thromboembolic disease
CPTH chronic post-traumatic headache
CPT11 may have meant CPT-11
(irinotecan HCl [Camptosar])
CPTP cyclopentyltriazolopyrimidine
CPT/S chest physiotherapy and suction
CPTx continue present therapy
(treatment)
CPU children's psychiatric unit
clinical pharmacology unit
CPUE chest pain of unknown etiology
CPUM Certified Professional in
Utilization Management
CPUR Certified Professional Utilization
Review
CPV canine parvovirus
cowpox virus
cyclopropavir
CPVA circumferential pulmonary vein
ablation
CPVD cerebrovascular/peripheral
vascular disease
CPVT catecholaminergic polymorphic
ventricular tachycardia
CPX complete physical examination
CPXT cardiopulmonary exercise
test(ing)
CPZ chlorpromazine; Compazine®
(CPZ is a dangerous abbreviation as it could be either)
CQ chloroquine
C1q the first subcomponent of the C1
complex of the classical
pathway of complement
activation
CQDS cumulative quality disruption
score
CQI continuous quality improvement
CQM clinical quality measure
CR calorie restriction
capillary refill
cardiac rehabilitation
cardiorespiratory
case reports
cervical radiculopathy
chief resident
chorioretinal
clockwise rotation
closed reduction
cochlear reflectance
colon resection
complete remission
computed radiography
contact record
controlled release

	Correction and Reversals (Medicare code)	CRAO	central retinal artery occlusion
	cosmetic rhinoplasty	CRAP	cardiac responsive adriamycin protein; see gene website www.ncbi.nlm.nih.gov/gene
	cranial treatment (technique)		
	creamed		
	credentialing	CRAVF	congenital renal arteriovenous fistula
	cycloplegia retinoscopy		
Cr	chromium	CRAX	crackers
	creatinine	CRB	cervical ripening balloon
	crutch(es)		Clinical Review Board
C/R	conscious, rational		correct retinal boundaries
	consult requested	CRBBB	complete right bundle branch block
C&R	convalescence and rehabilitation		
	cystoscopy and retrograde	cRBC	cultured red blood cells
CR1	complement component (3b/4b) receptor 1: see gene website www.ncbi.nlm.nih.gov/gene	CRBIs	catheter-related bloodstream infections
		CRBL	cerebellum
		CRBP	cellular retinol-binding protein
CR_1	first cranial nerve	CR-BSI	catheter-related bloodstream infection(s)
CR-1	CRIPTO-1 (a cell surface/ secreted oncoprotein)		
		CRBSIs	catheter-related bloodstream infections
CR2	complement receptor type 2; see gene website, www.ncbi.nlm.nih.gov/gene		
		CRC	case review committee
			Certified Rehabilitation Counselor
CR3	complement receptor 3		
Cr3	trivalent chromium		Certified Risk Adjustment Coder (CRC™)
CRA	central retinal artery		
	chronic rheumatoid arthritis		child-resistant container
	cisretinoic acid (isotretinion, Accutane®)		circumferential retinal cryopexy
			clinical research center
	Clinical Research Associate		Clinical Research Coordinator
	colorectal anastomosis		colorectal cancer
	contract research assistant	CR & C	closed reduction and cast
	corticosteroid-resistant asthma	CRCA	conditional replication-competent adenovirus
	cranial		
CRAB	calcium elevation, renal insufficiency, anemia, and bone lesions (characteristic features of multiple myeloma)	CRCa	colorectal cancer
		crcA	see gene website www.ncbi.nlm.nih.gov/gene
		CRCI	cancer-related cognitive impairment(s)
	carbapenem-resistant Acinetobacter baumannii		chemotherapy-related cognitive impairment(s)
CRABP	cellular retinoic acid binding protein		
		CrCl	creatinine clearance
CRAbs	chelating recombinant antibodies	Cr CL	creatinine clearance
		$CrCl_2$	chromic chloride
CRADA	Cooperative Research and Development Agreement (with NIH)	CRCLM	colorectal liver metastases
		$CRCO_2$	cerebrovascular reactivity to carbon dioxide
CRAFFT	car, relax, alone, friends, forget, trouble (questionnaire to assess teenage risk of substance abuse)	CrCo	chromium-cobalt alloy
		CRCP	chronic rotator cuff pathology
		CrCP	critical closing pressure
		CRCS	colorectal cancer screening
CRAG	cerebral radionuclide angiography	CRCT	Cancer Research Center of Toulouse (France)
CrAg	cryptococcal antigen	cRCT	cluster randomized controlled trial
CRAMS	circulation, respiration, abdomen, motor, and speech		
		CRD	childhood rheumatic disease
CRAN	craniotomy		chronic renal disease
crani	craniotomy		chronic respiratory disease

	colorectal distension
	cone-rod dystrophy
	congenital rubella deafness
	crown-rump distance
CRDM	computed radiographic digital mammography
CRDS	cavity ring down spectroscopy
CRD-T	may have meant CRT-D (cardiac resynchronization therapy defibrillator
CRE	carbapenem-resistant Enterobacteriaceae
	cumulative radiation effect
crea	creatinine
creat	creatinine
CREC	ciprofloxacin-resistant *E. coli*
CREF	cycloplegic refraction
CRELM	screening tests for CongoCrimean, Rift Valley, Ebola, Lassa, and Marburg fevers
CREP	Cancer Risk Education Program
	crepitation
CRES	Certified Radiology Equipment Specialist
CREST	calcinosis, Raynauds disease, esophageal dysmotility, sclerodactyly, and telangiectasia
CRET	chemiluminescence resonance energy transfer
CRF	cancer-related fatigue
	cardiac risk factors
	cardiorespiratory fitness
	cardiovascular risk factors
	carfentanil
	case report form
	chronic renal failure
	chronic respiratory failure
	corneal resistance factor
	corticotrophin-releasing factor
c-RFA	cooled radiofrequency ablation
CRFs	clinical risk factors
CRFZ	closed reduction of fractured zygoma
CRG-L2	Cancer related gene-Liver 2
CrGN	crescentic glomerulonephritis
CRH	corticotropin-releasing hormone
CRh	complete remission with hematologic recovery
CrH	chronic headache
crhb	corticotropin releasing hormone b (gene)
CRHC	Certified Rheumatology Coder (CRHC™)
CRHCa	cancer-related hypercalcemia
CRI	Cardiac Risk Index
	catheter-related infection
	chronic renal insufficiency

	complete remission with incomplete hematologic recovery
	cranial rhythmic impulse
CRIB	Clinical Risk Index for Babies
CRIC	Chronic Renal Insufficiency Cohort (study)
CRIE	crossed radioimmunoelectrophoresis
	chronic right iliac fossa
	closed reduction and internal fixation
CRIM	cross-reacting immunologic material
CRIMF	closed reduction/intermaxillary fixation
CRIP1	cysteine-rich intestinal protein 1 (gene/protein)
CRIS	controlled-release infusion system
CRISP	cysteine-rich secretory protein
crisper	see CRISPR
CRISPR	clustered regularly interspaced short palindromic repeats (to customize an organism's genes)
CRISPR-Cas9	clustered regularly interspaced short palindromic repeats (CRISPR)-CRISPR-associated protein-9 nuclease (Cas9), (a viral defense system found in bacteria and archaea, that has emerged as a genome editing tool)
crit	hematocrit
CRKL	crackles
CRKP	carbapenem-resistant Klebsiella pneumoniae
CRL	cancer-related lymphedema
	Clinical Resource Leader
	Complete Response Letter (U.S. Food and Drug Administration)
	crown rump length
CRLM	colorectal liver metastases
CRM	canalith repositioning maneuver(s)
	cardiac rhythm management
	circumferential resection margins
	clinical resource manager
	continual reassessment method
	cream
	cross-reacting mutant
CRM +	cross-reacting material positive
CrmA	cytokine response modifier A
CRMD	children with retarded mental development
CRMMF	closed reduction and mandibulomaxillary fixation
CRMO	chronic recurrent multifocal osteomyelitis

CRMP4	collapsin response mediator protein 4
CRMP5	collapsin response mediator protein 5
CRMP-5	collapsin response mediator protein 5
CRMP	collapsin response mediator protein; see gene website www.ncbi.nlm.nih.gov/gene
CRMPs	collapsin response mediator proteins
CRMs	certified reference materials cis-regulatory modules coronary resistance microvessels
cRMS	cerebral rhabdomyosarcomas
CRN	Certified Radiologic Nurse colorectal neoplasia crown
CRNA	Certified Registered Nurse Anesthetist
CRNFA	Certified Registered Nurse, First Assistant
CRNH	Certified Registered Nurse in Hospice
CRNI	Certified Registered Nurse Intravenous
CRNL	Certified Registered Nurse - Long-Term Care
CRNO	Certified Registered Nurse in Ophthalmology
CRNP	Certified Registered Nurse Practitioner
CRO	cathode ray oscilloscope contract research organization(s)
CROACC	cannot rule out anything, correlate clinically (slang)
CRoC	Combat Ready Clamp
croc	croconaine
CROM	cervical range of motion chronic refractory osteomyelitis clinician-rated outcome measure Cromer; an International Society of Blood Transfusion (ISBT) blood group
CROMY	chronic refractory osteomyelitis
Crook-U	a prison ward in a hospital (slang)
CROS	contralateral routing of signals
CROW	Charcot Restraint Orthotic Walker
CRP	canalith repositioning procedure chronic relapsing pancreatitis coronary rehabilitation program corticoreticular pathway C-reactive protein
C-RP	C-reactive protein
C&RP	curettage and root planning
CRPA	C-reactive protein agglutinins
CRPC	castration-refractory prostate cancer

CRPD	chronic restrictive pulmonary disease
CRPF	chloroquine-resistant *Plasmodium falciparum*
CR-POPF	clinically relevant postoperative pancreatic fistula
CRPP	closed reduction and percutaneous pinning
CRPR	Child-Rearing Practices Report
CRPS	complex regional pain syndromes
CRPS1	complex regional pain syndrome type 1
CRPS2	complex regional pain syndrome type 2 complex regional pain syndrome type I
CRPS-I	complex regional pain syndrome type 1
CRPS-II	complex regional pain syndrome type 2
CRPT	complete response of the primary tumor
CRQ	Chronic Respiratory (Disease) Questionnaire
CRR	community rehabilitation residence
CRRC	Canadian Rheumatology Research Consortium Cardiovascular Risk Reduction Clinic
CRRN	Certified Rehabilitation Registered Nurse
CRRN-A	Certified Rehabilitation Registered Nurse - Advanced
Crrp	complement receptor-related protein; see gene website www.ncbi.nlm.nih.gov/gene
CRRT	continuous renal replacement therapy
CRS	cardiorenal syndrome (a disorder of the kidneys or the heart where an acute or long term dysfunction in one of these organs may cause an acute or long-term dysfunction of the other) care record summary Carroll Self-Rating Scale catheter-related sepsis Center for Scientific Review (NIH) Chemical Reference Substances child restraint system(s) Chinese restaurant syndrome chronic rhinosinusitis Clinical Respiratory Score cocaine-related seizure(s) colon-rectal surgery

congenital rubella syndrome
continuous running suture
corneal refractive surgery
cryoreductive surgery
cytokine release syndrome
cytokine-release syndrome
CRSBIs   may have meant CRBSIs
   (catheter-related bloodstream
   infections)
CRSD   circadian rhythm sleep disorder
CRSM   chronic rhinosinusitis mucus
CRSP   Children's Report of Sleep
   Patterns
   chronic rhinosinusitis with nasal
   polyposis
   may have meant CRPS (complex
   regional pain syndrome)
crsp   cryptorchidism with white
   spotting, deletion region (gene)
CRSP-S   Children's Report of Sleep
   Patterns—Sleepiness Scale
CRS-R   Coma Recovery Scale-Revised
CRST   calcification, Raynauds
   phenomenom, scleroderma,
   and telangiectasia
   Clinical Rating Scale for Tremor
CRT   cadaver renal transplant
   calreticulin
   capillary refill time
   Cardiac Rescue Technician
   cardiac resynchronization therapy
   cartilage roof triangle
   cathode ray tube
   central reaction time
   central retinal thickness
   Certified Rehabilitation
   Therapist
   Certified Respiratory Therapist
   chemoradiotherapy
   choice reaction time
   circuit resistance training
   cognitive remediation therapy
   controlled room temperature
   copper reduction test
   corticoreticulospinal tract
   cranial radiation therapy
crtB   phytoene synthase (gene)
CRTD   cardiac resynchronization therapy
   defibrillator
CRT D   cardiac resynchronization therapy
   defibrillator
CRT-D   cardiac resynchronization therapy
   defibrillator
   cardiac resynchronization therapy-
   defibrillator (device)
crtI   phytoene dehydrogenase; see
   gene website www.ncbi.nlm
   .nih.gov/gene

CRT-ICD   cardiac resynchronization
   therapy-implantable
   cardioverter defibrillator
CRT P   cardiac resynchronization
   therapy pacemaker
CRTP   cardiac resynchronization therapy
   pacing
   coercive-restraint therapy
   parenting
Crtp   see gene website, www.ncbi.nlm
   .nih.gov/gene
CRT-P   cardiac resynchronization
   therapy-pacemaker
   cardiac resynchronization
   therapy-pacemaker (device)
CRT pacemaker   cardiac resynchronisation
   therapy pacemaker
Cr Tr   crutch training
CRTs   case report tabulations
CRTT   Certified Respiratory Therapy
   Technician
CRTU   Clinical Research Trials Unit
CRTX   cast removed take x-ray
CRTx   chemoradiotherapy
CRU   cardiac rehabilitation unit
   catheterization recovery unit
   clinical research unit
crulls   a word meaning curly; curled
crus   a word referring to anatomical
   structures that are leg-shaped
CRV   central retinal vein
CRVF   congestive right ventricular
   failure
CRVO   central retinal vein occlusion
CRWT   colorectal wall thickening
CRx   chemotherapy
CRYO   cryoablation
   cryoprecipitate
   cryosurgery
cryo-EM   cryo-electron microscopy
CRYPTO   a prefix meaning hidden or
   concealed
   cryptococcal meningitis
   cryptococcus
CRYST   crystals
crystal   methamphetamine (slang)
CS   cardiogenic shock
   cardioplegia solution
   cat scratch
   cervical spine
   cesarean section
   Chemstrips
   chest strap
   chlorobenzylidene malononitrile
   cholesterol stone
   cigarette smoker
   Clinical Specialist
   clinical stage

clinically significant
close supervision
closing speed
conditionally susceptible
congenital syphilis
conjunctiva-sclera
conscious sedation
consciousness
consultation
consultation service
controlled substances
controlled substances (manufacture, importation, possession, use and distribution of certain drugs of potential abuse that are regulated by US government). See C1, C2, C3, C4 and C5)
cornstarch
coronary sinus
cortical screw
corticosteroid(s)
counterstrain (technique)
cranial setting
Cushing syndrome
customer service
cycloserine
o-chlorobenzylidene malononitrile

Cs   cesium

CS IV   clinical stage 4

C&S   conjunctiva and sclera

C & S   see C&S
cough and sneeze
culture and sensitivity

C/S   cervical spine
cesarean section
consultation
culture and sensitivity

C+S   see C&S

CSA   central sleep apnea
childhood sexual abuse
compressed spectral activity
controlled substance analogue
Controlled Substances Act
corticosteroid-sensitive asthma
cross-sectional area
cryosurgical ablation

CsA   cyclosporine (cyclosporin A)

CSAA   clinically suspected acute appendicitis

CSA-AKI   cardiac surgery-associated acute kidney injury

CSAC   Certified Substance Abuse Counselor

CsA-ME   cyclosporine microemulsion (Neoral)

CSAP   cryosurgical ablation of the prostate

CSAT   Center for Substance Abuse Treatment (U.S. Department of Health and Human Services)

CSB   caffeine sodium benzoate
Cheyne-Stokes breathing
Children's Services Board

CSBF   coronary sinus blood flow

CSBG   carotid-subclavian bypass graft

CSBM   complete spontaneous bowel movements

CSBO   complete small bowel obstruction

cSBP   central systolic blood pressure

CSC   car seat check
central serous chorioretinopathy
Children's Specialty Clinic
comprehensive stroke center
cornea, sclera, and conjunctiva
cryogen spray cooling
cryopreserved stem cells

C-SCA   containment segregated compounding area

CSCC   cutaneous squamous cell carcinoma

cSCC   cutaneous squamous cell carcinoma

CSCHF   chronic systolic congestive heart failure

CSCI   continuous subcutaneous infusion

CsCI   cesium chloride

Cscope   colonoscope
colonoscopy

CSCR   central serous chorioretinopathy

CSCS   Certified Strength and Conditioning Specialist

CSCs   cancer stem cells

CSD   cat scratch disease
celiac sprue disease
chronic subjective dizziness
conduction system disorder (disease)
congenital sensorineural deafness
cortical spreading depression

C S&D   cleaned, sutured, and dressed

CSDD   Center for the Study of Drug Development

CSDH   chronic subdural hematoma
combined systolic and diastolic hypertension

CSDHs   chronic subdural hematomas

csDMARDs   conventional synthetic disease-modifying antirheumatic drugs

CSDME   clinically significant diabetic macular edema

CSDPP   controlled substances diversion prevention program

CSE   combined spinal/epidurals
convulsive status epileptics

	cross-section echocardiography	CSL	chemical safety level
	cystathionine gamma-lyase	CSLD	chronic suppurative lung disease
CSEA	combined spinal-epidural anesthesia	cSLE	childhood-onset systemic lupus erythematous
C-SEC	containment secondary engineering control	CSLO	confocal scanning laser ophthalmoscopy
C sect	cesarean section	CSLU	chronic status leg ulcer
csection	cesarean section	CSM	cancer-specific mortality
C section	cesarean section		carotid sinus massage
CSED	Center for the Study of Emerging Diseases (Jerusalem,		cause-specific mortality cerebrospinal meningitis
CSed	sedentary controls		cervical spondylotic myelopathy
CSEMS	covered self-expanding metal stents		circulation, sensation, and movement
CSEP	core-stabilization exercise programs		Committee on Safety of Medicines (United Kingdom)
CSF	cerebrospinal fluid		continue same medications
	colony-stimulating factors	CSMC	Cedars-Sinai Medical Center
	coronary slow flow		(Los Angeles)
CSFA	certified Surgical First Assistant	CSME	clinically significant macular
CSFD	cerebrospinal fluid drainage		edema
CSFELP	cerebrospinal fluid electrophoresis	CSMN	chronic sensorimotor
CSFP	cerebrospinal fluid pressure		neuropathy
CSGIT	continuous-suture graft-inclusion technique	CSMS	combined symptom and medication score (a standard-
CSH	carotid sinus hypersensitivity		ized method that balances
	cavernous sinus hemangioma		both symptoms and the need
	chronic subdural hematoma		for antiallergic medication in
	combat surgical hospital(s)		an equally weighted manner)
C-Sh	chair shower	CSMT	central subfield macular thickness
CSHCN	children with special health care needs		circulation, sensation, movement, and temperature
CSHCS	Children's Special Health Care Services	CSN	Certified School Nurse cystic suppurative necrosis
CSHF	chronic systolic heart failure	CSNB	congenital stationary night
	clinical signs of heart failure		blindness
CSHQ	Children's Sleep Habits Questionaire	CSNRB	cervical selective nerve root block
CSI	chemical shift imaging	CSNRT	corrected sinus node recovery
	Computerized Severity Index		time
	continuous subcutaneous infusion	CSNS	carotid sinus nerve stimulation
		CSO	Chief Security Officer
	coronary stent implantation		Consumer Safety Officer (FDA)
	corticosteroid injection		copied standing orders
	craniospinal irradiation	CSOE	cardiac source of embolism
CsI	cesium iodide	CSOM	chronic serous otitis media
CSICU	cardiac surgery intensive care unit		chronic suppurative otitis media
CSID	congenital sucraseisomaitase deficiency	CSOS	Controlled Substance Ordering System (US Drug Enforcement Agency)
CSII	continuous subcutaneous insulin infusion	CSP	cellulose sodium phosphate cervical spine pain
CSIO	continuous subcutaneous infusion of opiates		Cesarean scar pregnancy chiral stationary phase
CSIP	cerebral spastic infantile paralysis		compounded sterile preparation cutaneous silent period
CSIR	Institute of Council of Scientific and Industrial Research	Cspg4	chondroitin sulfate proteoglycan 4 (gene/protein)

CSPGs	chondroitin sulphate proteoglycans
CSPI	Certified Specialist in Poison Information
C-SPI	Certified Specialist in Poison Information
C spine	cervical spine
CSPMP	Controlled Substances Prescription Monitoring Program (The Arizona State Board of Pharmacy)
CSPP	common spatial patterns patches
CSPP1	centrosome/spindle pole associated protein 1 (gene)
CSPT	clinical support pharmacy technician (Canada)
	combined strength and proprioception training
	computer screen photo assisted technique
	cortico-striatal-pallidal-thalamic (circuit)
CSR	central supply room
	Cheyne-Stokes respiration
	class switch recombination
	clinical statistical report
	clinical support resource
	combat stress reaction
	corrected sedimentation rate
	corrective septorhinoplasty
CSRD	childhood-onset severe retinal dystrophy
CSRS	Cervical Spine Research Society
C-SRSS	Columbia-Suicide Severity Rating Scale
CSRT	choice stepping reaction time
C-S RT	craniospinal radiotherapy
CSS	Canadian Stroke Scale (score)
	cancer-specific survival
	carotid sinus stimulation
	Central Sterile Services
	chemical sensitivity syndrome
	chewing, sucking, and swallowing
	child safety seats
	Churg-Strauss syndrome
	clinical surveillance systems
C_{ss}	concentration of drug at steady-state
CSSD	closed system sterile drainage
CSSI	Care Support and System Innovation (program)
CSSM	clinically significant stent migration
C-SSRS	Columbia-Suicide Severity Rating Scale
CSSS	coronary subclavian steal syndrome

cSSSI	complicated skin and skin-structure infections
cSSSIs	complicated skin and skin-structure infections
cSSTI	complicated skin and soft-tissue infection(s)
cSSTIs	complicated skin and soft-tissue infections
CSSU	cardiac short-stay unit
CST	caesarean section prior to labor at term
	cardiac stress test
	castration
	cavernous sinus thrombosis
	central sensory conducting time
	cerebroside sulfotransferase
	Certified Surgical Technologist
	Chester step test
	contraction stress test
	convulsive shock therapy
	corticospinal tract
	cosyntropin stimulation test
	static compliance
cSt	centistoke
C_{STAT}	static lung compliance
CSTD	closed-system (drug) transfer device
CSTE	Council of State and Territorial Epidemiologists
CSTFA	Certified Surgical Technologist First Assistant
CsTFA	cesium trifluoroacetate
CSTK	Comprehensive Stroke (performance measurement implementation guide; the Joint Commission)
CSTO	cat smarter than owner (Veterinary slang)
CSTP	Core Stabilization Training Program
CSTs	corticospinal tracts
CSU	cardiac surgery unit
	cardiac surveillance unit
	cardiovascular surgery unit
	casualty staging unit
	catheter specimen of urine
	chronic spontaneous urticarial
	cold stream unit
CSVD	cerebral small-vessel disease
CSVL	central sacral vertical line
CSVT	cerebral sinovenous thrombosis
CSW	cerebral salt-wasting (syndrome)
	Clinical Social Worker
CSWCM	Certified Social Work Case Manager
CSWD	conservative sharp wound debridement
	corticosteroid withdrawal

CSWL	clinically significant weight loss	CTABL	clear to auscultation, bilateral
	cross-situational word learning	CTA B/L	clear to auscultation bilateral
	(children are able to resolve	CTAC	computed tomography-based
	the referential ambiguity of		attenuation correction
	learning new words by track-	c-TACE	conventional transarterial
	ing co-occurrence probabili-		chemoembolization
	ties across moments in time)	CTAD	citrate-theophylline-adenosine-
CSWS	cerebral salt wasting syndrome		dipyridamole (solution for
	commercial sex workers		blood collection)
CSWSS	continuous spikewaves during	ctaD	see gene website www.ncbi.nlm
	slow sleep		.nih.gov/gene
CSX	cardiac syndrome X	CTAG	conformable thoracic aortic
CSXN	cesarean section		stent-graft (GORE TAG®
Csy	CRISPRs (clustered regularly		Thoracic Endoprothesis)
	interspaced short palindromic	CTAP	clear to auscultation and
	repeats) system yersinia		percussion
	(proteins/immune system)		computed tomography during
CT	calcitonin		arterial portography
	calf tenderness	CT AP	computed tomography
	cardiothoracic		abdominopelvic
	carpal tunnel	CTAS	Canadian Triage and Acuity Scale
	cellulose triacetate (filter)	CTAs	computed tomography
	cervical traction		angiographies
	cervicothoracic	CTAV	computed tomographic
	chemotherapy		angiography and venography
	chest tube	CTB	ceased to breathe
	Chlamydophila trachomatis		cholera toxin B
	circulation time	CTBA	computed tomograpy bronchial
	client		angiogram
	clinical trial	CTBS	chitobiase (gene)
	clotting time	cTBS	continuous theta burst stimulation
	coagulation time	CTC	Cancer Treatment Center
	coated tablet		circular tear capsulotomy
	compressed tablet		circulating tumor cells
	computed tomography		Clinical Trial Certificate
	computerized tomography		(United Kingdom's equivalent
	Connecticut		to the Investigational
	Coombs test		New Drug Application)
	corneal thickness		Common Toxicity Criteria
	corneal transplant		computed tomographic
	corrective therapy		colonography
	cytarabine and thioguanine		cubital tunnel compression
	cytoxic drug		cyclophosphamide, thiotepa,
C/T	cholecystostomy tube		and carboplatin
	compared to	CTCA	Cancer Treatment Centers of
Ct	count		America
C_t	concentration of drug in tissue	CTCAE v3.0	Common Terminology Criteria
C7-T2	cervicothoracic spine junction		for Adverse Events,
CTA	catamenia (menses)		version 3.0 (National Cancer
	clear to auscultation		Institute grading system for
	Composite tissue allograft		treatment-related toxicities)
	computed tomographic		grade 1 = mild grade 2 =
	angiography		moderate grade 3 = severe
CTAB	clear to ausculation, bilaterally		grade 4 = life-threatening
CTA B	clear to auscultation, bilaterally		or disabling grade 5 = death
	docetyl trimethylammonium		related
	bromide (a cationic surfactant)	CT CAP	computed tomography of the
C-TAB	cyanide tablet		chest, abdomen, and pelvis

c-TCD	contrast transcranial Doppler		CTGA	complete transposition of the great arteries
CTCL	cutaneous T-cell lymphoma (mycosis fungoides)			corrected transposition of the great arteries
CTCOFR	Composite Time to Complete Organ Failure Resolution		CTGF	connective tissue growth factor
CTCs	circulating tumor cells		CT guided	computer tomography guided
CTD	carboxy-terminal domain		CTH	clot to hold
	carpal tunnel decompression		CTHA	computed tomography hepatic arteriography
	chest tube drainage			
	Cognitive Test for Delirium		ctHb	total hemoglobin concentration
	Common Technical Document		CTI	cavotricuspid isthmus
	connective tissue disease			certification of terminal illness
	corneal thickness depth		cTI	cardiac troponin I
	cumulative trauma disorder		CTIBL	cancer treatment-induced bone loss
CTD-APAH	connective tissue disease-associated pulmonary arterial hypertension		CTICU	cardiothoracic intensive care unit
			CTID	chemotherapy-induced diarrhea
CTDB	cough, turn, and deep breath		CTI line	cavotricuspid isthmus line
CT & DB	cough, turn & deep breath		CTIN	chronic tubulointestinal nephritis
CTDI	computed tomography dose index		CTIS	California Teratogen Information Service
CTD-ILD	connective tissue disease related (associated) interstitial lung disease		CTJ	cervicothoracic junction
			CTK	central toxic keratopathy
ctDNA	circulating deoxyribonucleic acid		Ctk	Csk-like protein-tyrosine kinase
CTDP	Certified Training and Development Professional		CTL	cervical, thoracic, and lumbar
				chronic tonsillitis
CTDR	cervical total disk replacement			control (subjects)
CTDW	continues to do well			cytotoxic T-lymphocytes
CTE	chronic traumatic encephalopathy		C/T/L	cervical, thoracic, and lumbar
	computed tomography enterography		CT-L	chymotrypsin-like
			CTLA-4	cytotoxic T-lymphocyte-associated antigen 4
CTED	chronic thromboembolic disease			
	complete testicular epididymal dissociation		CTLC	calcific tendonitis of the longus colli (muscle)
CTEF	cartilaginous tibial eminence fracture			contact transscleral laser cyclophotocoagulation
	congenital tracheoesophageal fistula		CTLG	computed tomographic lymphography
CTEP	Cancer Therapy Evaluation Program		CTLI	canine trypsin-like immunoreactivity
	Center for Therapy Evaluation Programs (National Cancer Institute)		CTLM	computed tomography-laser mammography
			CTLSO	cervicothoraciclumbosacral orthosis
CTEPH	chronic thromboembolic pulmonary hypertension		CTM	Chlor-Trimeton
				clinical trials materials
CTET	clinical-touch embryo transfer			computed tomographic myelography
CTEV	congenital talipes equinovarus (clubfoot)			
CTF	clanging tuning fork (test)		CT/MPR	computed tomography with multiplanar reconstructions
	Colorado tick fever		CTMS	clinical trial management systems
	continuous tube feeding			
CTFESI	cervical transforaminal epidural steroid injection		CTN	calcitonin
				Certified Transcultural Nurse
CTFIS	cervical transforaminal injection of steroids			Clinical Trials Network
CTG	cardiotocography			contraction
C/TG	cholesterol to triglyceride ratio		cTn	cardiac troponin I

ctnA	component of the counting factor complex (gene)	CTPH	chronic thromboembolic pulmonary hypertension
C & T N, BLE	color and temperature normal, both lower extremities	CTPI	computed tomography perfusion imaging
cTnC	cardiac troponin C	CTPN	central total parenteral nutrition
cTnI	cardiac troponin I	CTPS	cytidine triphosphate synthase
cTNM	clinical-diagnostic staging of cancer	CTPs	cell-processed therapeutic products
CTNS	cystinosin, lysosomal cystine transporter; see gene website www.ncbi.nlm.nih.gov/gene		connective tissue progenitors consensus treatment plans
		CTQ	Childhood Trauma Questionnaire
cTns	cardiac troponins	CTR	capsular tension ring
cTnT	cardiac troponin T		carpal tunnel release
CTO	cervicothoracic orthosis		carpal tunnel repair
	chronic total (coronary) occlusion		Certified Tumor Registrar
ctO2	the sum of the concentration of hemoglobin-bound oxygen and the concentration of physically dissolved oxygen		cosmetic transdermal reconstruction
			cubital tunnel retinaculum
CTOA	cue-target onset asynchrony	CTRB	Clinical Trial Review Board
C_1 to C_9	precursor molecules of the complement system		critical tests read back
		CTRC	Cancer Therapy Research Center (University of Texas Health Science Center, San Antonio)
CTOD	crack tip opening displacement (test which evaluates fracture toughness of a cracked material)		
		CTRD	Cardiac Transplant Research Database
CTOH	common tracts of homozygosity	CTRL	chymotrypsin-like; see gene website www.ncbi.nlm.nih .gov/gene
CTO PCI	chronic total occlusion percutaneous coronary intervention percutaneous coronary intervention for chronic total occlusion	
			control(S) (group)
CTO-PCI	percutaneous coronary intervention of chronic total occlusions	CTRS	Certified Therapeutic Recreation Specialist
			Conners Teachers Rating Scale
CTOPP	Comprehensive Test of Phonological Processing	CT-RT	chemo-radiotherapy
		CTRX	ceftriaxone sodium (Rocephin)
CTO RCA	chronic total occlusion in the right coronary artery	CTS	cardiothoracic surgeon
			carpal tunnel syndrome
CTP	comprehensive treatment plan		closed-tube sampling
CTPA	cervical-thoracic pelvic angle	CTSA	Clinical Translational Science Awards (programs, NIH)
	clear to percussion and auscultation	
	computed tomography pulmonary angiogram	CT scan	computerized tomography scan (a radiographic, three-dimensional image of a body structure constructed by computer from a series of plane cross-sectional images made along an axis)
CTPD	Chinese Technology Periodical Database	
CT PE	an examination of the chest that uses a combination of high speed computed tomography imaging and an Iodine contrast to make very thin (1.5mm) and detailed pictures of the pulmonary artery and vein to detect a pulmonary embolism	
		CTSIB	Clinical Test Sensory Interaction Balance
		CTSP	called to see patient
		CTSS	closed tracheal suction system
		ctsT	see gene website www.ncbi.nlm .nih.gov/gene
CTPE	cadmium-transformed prostate epithelial (cells)	CTSU	Clinical Trial Service Unit
CTPEH	may have meant CTEPH (chronic thromboembolic pulmonary hypertension)		Clinical Trial Service Unit and Epidemiological Studies Unit
		CTSX	cathepsin X
CT PET	computed tomography/positron emission tomography	CTT	congenital trigger thumb
			cotton-thread test

C

CT/TA	Code T/Trauma Alert	CUC	Certified Urology Coder (CUC™)
CTTH	chronic tension-type headache		chronic ulcerative colitis
CTTS	Certified Tobacco Treatment		Clinical Unit Clerk
	Specialist	CUCNS	Certified Urologic Clinical
CTTs	colonic transit times		Nurse Specialist
CTU	computed tomographic urography	CUD	cause undetermined
C tube	chest tube		controlled unsterile delivery
CTV	clinical target volumes (radiation	CUDs	cannabis use disorders
	therapy)	CUFCM	Century Ultrafiltration Control
	clinical tumor volume		Machine
CT-V	cardiothoracic-vascular	CUG	cystourethrogram
	computed tomography-	Cu-IUD	copper intrauterine device
	venography	culd	a mis-typing for could
CTVs	clinical target volumes	CUL8R	see you later (slang)
CTVT	canine transmissible venereal	cult	a word meaning a religious
	tumor		movement or social group
CTW	central terminal of Wilson		with socially deviant or novel
CTX	cerebrotendinous xanthomatosis		beliefs and practices
	cervical traction		culture
	chemotherapy	cum	cumulative
	Clinical Trial Exemption	cumm	cubic millimeter (1 cubic
	contraction		centimeter [cc] = 1,000 cubic
	cotrimoxazole		millimeters [cumm; mm^3])
	C-telopeptide	cu mm	cubic millimeter
	cyclophosphamide (Cytoxan)	CUN-BAE	Clinic Universidad de Navarra -
CTXN	contraction		Body Adiposity Estimator
CTXNS-EK	cefotaxime-non-susceptible	CUNP	Certified Urologic Nurse
	Escherichia coli or Klebsiella		Practitioner
	pneumoniae	CUNV	chronic unexplained nausea and
CTXS	contractions		vomiting
CTXs	cardiotoxins	CUOG	Canadian Urologic Oncology
	ciguatoxins		Group
CTZ	chemoreceptor trigger zone	CUP	carcinoma of unknown primary
	cotrimoxazole (sulfamethoxazole		(site)
	and trimethoprin)	CUPS	carcinoma of unknown primary
CU	cause undetermined		site
	cause unknown	CUR	condom-use resistance
	chronic undifferentiated		curettage
	chronic urticaria		cystourethrorectocele
	clinical units	CURB-65	for predicting mortality in
	color unit		community-acquired
	communicates understanding		pneumonia; an index based
	convalescent unit		on confusion, uremia,
	Cuprophan (filter)		respiratory rate, pressure
Cu	copper		blood, age 65 or older
C$_u$	urea clear clearance	CURL	partial curl-ups
C/U	checkup	CURN	Certified Urologic Registered
	creatine/urea ratio		Nurse
CUA	calcific uremic arteriolopathy	curr	current
	(calciphylaxis)	CUS	carotid ultrasound
	Certified Urologic Associate		chronic undifferentiated
	clean urinalysis		schizophrenia
	cost-utility analysis		compression ultrasonography
CUB domain	a structural motif of residues		contact urticaria syndrome
	found in extracellular and		cranial ultrasound
	plasma membrane-associated	cUS	cranial ultrasound
	proteins (complement C1r/	CUSA	Cavitron ultrasonic suction
	C1s, Uegf, Bmp1)		aspirator

cusp	a word meaning a pointed end where two curves meet; a tapering projection
CUSS	Chronic Urticaria Severity Score
CUT	chronic undifferentiated type (schizophrenia)
CUTA	congenital urinary tract anomaly
cUTI	complicated urinary tract infections (multidrug resistance)
cutR	two-component system response regulator; see gene website www.ncbi.nlm.nih.gov/gene
CuTS	cubital tunnel syndrome
CV	A classification under the US Controlled Substances Act; drugs that have a low potential for abuse relative to substances listed in schedule IV and consist primarily of preparations containing limited quantities of certain narcotics.
	cardiovascular
	cardioversion
	cell volume
	cisplatin and etoposide (VePesid)
	coefficient of variation
	color vision
	common ventricle
	consonant vowel
	contrast venography
	conventional (mechanical) ventilation
	curriculum vitae
C V	see C5
C/V	cervical/vaginal
CV4	compression of the 4th ventricle (technique)
CVA	cerebrovascular accident
	costovertebral angle
	cough-variant asthma
	Customer Value Assessment (survey; The Joint Commission)
CVAAS	cold vapor atomic absorption spectrometry
cvaC	colicin V synthesis protein; see gene website www.ncbi.nlm .nih.gov/gene
CVAD	central venous access device
CV-AFS	cold vapor atomic fluorescence spectrometry
CVAH	congenital virilizing adrenal hyperplasia
CVAI	cranial vault asymmetry index
CVAP	central venous access port(s)
CVAS	cough visual analog scale

CVAs	cerebrovascular accidents
CVAT	costovertebral angle tenderness
CVA tenderness	costovertebral angle tenderness
CVA/TIA	cerebrovascular accident/ transient ischemic attack
cVAX	ventral anterior homeobox 1 (also known as VAX1) (gene)
CVB	chronic villi biopsy
	group B coxsackievirus
CVB3	coxsackievirus B3
CVB-D	cyclovirobuxine D
CVBHD	may have meant CVVHD (continuous venovenous hemodialysis)
CVC	central venous catheter
	chief visual complaint
	consonant-vowel-consonant (nonsense syllables)
CVCT	cardiovascular computed tomography
	couples-based voluntary (human immunodeficiency virus) counseling and testing
CVCU	cardiovascular care unit
CVD	cardiovascular disease
	cisplatin, vinblastine, and dacarbazine
	collagen vascular disease
CVDH	cardiovascular-disease-related hospitalizations
CVDU	chronic ventilator-dependent unit
CVE	containment ventilated enclosure
CVEB	cisplatin, vinblastine, etoposide, and bleomycin
cVEMPs	cervical vestibular-evoked myogenic potential(s)
CVENT	controlled ventilation
CVEs	cerebrovascular events
CVF	cardiovascular failure
	cardiovascular fitness
	central visual field
	cervicovaginal fluid
	cobra venom factor
	colovesical fistula
	confrontational visual fields
CVG	cochleovestibular ganglion
	coronary vein graft
	cutis verticis gyrata
CVHC	Cardiovascular Health Clinic
CVHD	carcinoid valvular heart disease
	chronic valvular heart disease
	cycles of continuous veno-venous hemodialysis
C-VHI-10	Children Voice Handicap Index-10b (questionnaire)
CVHtn	cardiovascular hypertension

CVVHF	continuous venovenous hemofiltration
CVVT	coefficient of variation of tidal volume
Cvx	cervix
CW	careful watch
	case worker
	chest wall
	clockwise
	compare with
C/W	consistent with
	crutch walking
CWA	chemical warfare agents
CWAF	Chemical Withdrawal Assessment Flowsheet
CWAL	continuous wave argon laser
CWAP	continuous wave arthroscopy pump
CWAs	chemical warfare agents
CWB	capillary whole blood
CWCN	Certified Wound Care Nurse
CWD	canal wall down
	cell wall defective
	change wet dressing
	chronic wasting disease
CWE	cotton-wool exudates
CWF	chronic wound fluid
	community water fluoridation
CWH	continuous venovenous hemofiltration
cWHD	C-terminal winged-helix domain
CWHDF	continuous venovenous hemodiafiltration
CWI	cell wall integrity
	cold-water immersion
CWL	Caldwell-Luc
	cutaneous water loss
CWM	comprehensive weight management
CWMS	color, warmth, movement, and sensation
CWO	closing wedge osteotomy
CWOCN	Certified Wound, Ostomy and Continence Nurse
CWON	Certified Wound Ostomy Nurse
CWP	centimeters of water pressure
	childbirth without pain
	chronic widespread pain
	coal workers' pneumoconiosis
	cold wet packs
cWPW	concealed Wolff-Parkinson-White syndrome
CWR	clockwise rotation
CWS	Certified Wound Care Specialist
	comfortable walking speed
	cotton-wool spots
CWT	compensated work training

CWV	closed wound vacuum
CX	cancel
	carfentanil and xylazine (veterinary)
	cervix
	chronic
	circumflex
	circumflex artery
	cylinder axis
	cystectomy
Cx	culture(s)
CXA	circumflex artery
Cx'd	cancelled
Cx Bx	cervical biopsy
CXC	C-X-C motif chemokine 11-1 (gene)
CXD	computed X-ray densitometer
CXE	Caudwell Xtreme Everest (closed circuit breathing system)
CXL	collagen crosslinking
	corneal crosslinking
CxMT	cervical motion tenderness
CXN	connection
CxP	cervical pregnancy
CXR	chest x-ray
CXRAY	chest X-ray
CXRS	Charge eXchange Recombination Spectroscopy
CXRs	chest radiographs
CXRT	chemoradiation therapy
Cxs	connexins
	contractions
CXTX	cervical traction
C282Y	a mutation in the HFE gene (hereditary hemochromatosis, a autosomal recessive disorder)
CY	calendar year
	cyclophosphamide
Cy	cysteine
C&Y	Children with Youth (program)
CYA	Children and Youth Agency
	cover your ass (slang)
CyA	cyclosporine
CyADIC	cyclophosphamide, doxorubicin (Adriamycin), and dacarbazine
CyBorD	cyclophosphamide, bortezomib, and dexamethasone
CYC	cyclophosphamide (Cytoxan)
Cyclo C	cyclocytidine HCl
Cyd	cytidine (also referred to as C)
CYF	Children, Youth and Families
CYFRA	cytokeratin fragment
CYL	cylinder
CYP	cytochrome P-450 system
CYP450	cytochrome P-450 system

CYP3A4	cytochrome P450 enzyme 3A4 (there are many cytochrome P450 enzymes, such as CYP2E1, CYP1A1, CYP2D6, etc.)
CYP2C9	cytochrome P450, family 2, subfamily C, polypeptide 9 (gene/ a highly polymorphic enzyme variant responsible for the metabolism of a wide range of clinical drugs phenytoin, warfarin, etc.])
CYP2C19	cytochrome P450, family 2, subfamily C, polypeptide 19 (gene/ a highly polymorphic enzyme variant responsible for the metabolism of a wide range of clinical drugs [amitriptyline, clopidogrel, doxepin, imipramine, trimipramine, voriconazole, citalopram, escitalopram, etc.)
CYP2D6	cytochrome P450, family 2, subfamily D, polypeptide 6 (gene/ a highly polymorphic enzyme variant responsible for the metabolism of a wide range of clinical drugs [doxepin, imipramine, fluvoxamine, nortripyline, paroxetine, tamoxifen, tramadol, trimipramine, etc.)
CYRO	cryoprecipitate
CYS	Children and Youth Services
CysC	cystatin C
CYSTA	cystathionine
cystatin E/M	see gene website, www.ncbi.nlm.nih.gov/gene
CYSTO	cystogram cystoscopy
CYT	cyclophosphamide (Cytoxan)
Cyt	cytosine
CYTA	cytotoxic agent
Cy TBI	cyclophosphamide and total body irradiation
CYVADIC	cyclophosphamide, vincristine, doxorubicin (Adriamycin), and dacarbazine (DTIC)
CYVE	high dose cytarabine and etoposide (Vespid)
CZ	central zone (prostate needle biopsy location)
CZE	capillary zone electrophoresis
CZI	crystalline zinc insulin (regular insulin)
CZP	carbamazepine (Tegretol) certolizumab pegol inj (Cinzia) clonazepam (Klonopin)
CZT	cadmium zinc telluride

D	aspartic acid daughter day dead decay Delta (Phonetic Alphabet D; pronounced DELL-TA) deltoid dependent depression dextro dextrose (glucose) diagonal diarrhea diastole dictated dilated diminished Dinamap (blood pressure monitor) diopter distal distance divorced dorsal
D+	note has been dictated/look for report
D−	note not dictated, save chart for doctor
$D_{0(2/7/00)}$	Day zero (the day treatment begins, February 7th, 2000)
D1	day 1
D_1	day one (first day of treatment) first diagonal branch (coronary artery) first dorsal (thoracic) vertebrae
D2	second dorsal (thoracic) vertebrae
D_2	ergocalciferol second diagonal branch (coronary artery)
2/d	twice a day (this is a dangerous abbreviation)
2-D	two-dimensional
D3	cholecalciferol third dorsal (thoracic) vertebrae
3-D	three-dimensional
$D-3_{+}7$	cytarabine and daunorubicin
D4	fourth dorsal (thoracic) vertebrae
4D	4 prism diopters
4-D	four-dimensional
D5	dextrose 5% injection fifth dorsal (thoracic) vertebrae
$D_{5/.45}$	dextrose 5% in 0.45% sodium chloride injection

D6	sixth dorsal (thoracic) vertebrae	DABA	Diplomate of the American Board of Anesthesiology
D7	seventh dorsal (thoracic) vertebrae	DABAT	Diplomate of the American Board of Applied Toxicology
D8	eighth dorsal (thoracic) vertebrae	dAbs	detection antibodies
D9	ninth dorsal (thoracic) vertebrae		domain antibodies
D10	tenth dorsal (thoracic) vertebrae	DAC	day activity center
D11	eleventh dorsal (thoracic) vertebrae		decitabine
D12	day 12		disabled adult child
	twelfth dorsal (thoracic) vertebrae		Division of Ambulatory Care
d12	see gene website www.ncbi.nlm .nih.gov/gene	DACA	distal anterior cerebral artery
		dACC	dorsal anterior cingulate cortex
D-15	Farnsworth panel D-15 color vision test	DACEs	drugs with anticholinergic effects
		DAC-HYP	daclizumab (Zenapax) high-yield process
D50	50% dextrose injection		
DA	darbepoetin alfa (Aranesp)	DACi	deacetylase inhibitor
	dark adaptation (test)	DACL	Depression Adjective Checklists
	Debtors Anonymous	DA-CPR	dispatcher-assistance cardiopulmonary resuscitation
	degenerative arthritis		
	delivery awareness	DACR	Dindigul Ambilikkai Cancer Registry (India)
	Dental Assistant		
	diagnostic arthroscopy	DACS	deep anterior cerebellar stimulation
	diastolic augmentation		
	direct admission		density-adjusted cell sorting
	direct agglutination	DACT	dactinomycin (Cosmegen)
	disc area	DAD	diffuse alveolar damage
	Discharge Advocate		diode array detector
	diversional activity		Disability Assessment of Dementia
	dopamine		
	drug addict		Discharge Abstract Database (Canada)
	drug aerosol		
	duodenal atresia		dispense as directed
Da	daltons		drug administration device
	Dalton(s)		father
D/A	discharge and advise	DADA2	deficiency of adenosine deaminase 2
	drug and alcohol		
D&A	drug and alcohol	DADS	distal acquired demyelinating symmetrical (neuropathy)
DAA	dead after arrival		
	direct-acting antiviral agent (such as simeprevir and sofosbuvir, paritaprevir, glecaprevir, voxilaprevir, ombitasvir, ledipasvir, daclatasvir, elbasvir, grazoprevir, velpatasvir, pibrentasvir)	DADs	photodiode array detectors
		DAE	diving air embolism
		DAEC	diffuse-adherence Entamoeba coli
		DAEM	distributed activation energy model
	dissection aortic aneurysm	DA-EPOCH-R	dose-adjusted etoposide, prednisone, vincristine (Oncovin), cyclophosphamide, doxorubicin (hydroxydaunorubicin), and rituximab
DA/A	drug/alcohol addiction		
DAAs	direct-acting antiviral agents (such as simeprevir and sofosbuvir, paritaprevir, glecaprevir, voxilaprevir, ombitasvir, ledipasvir, daclatasvir, elbasvir, grazoprevir, velpatasvir, pibrentasvir)		
		DAF	decay-accelerating factor
			delayed auditory feedback
		DAFE	Dial-A-Flow Extension®
		DAFM	double-aerosol face mask
		DAFNE	dose adjustment for normal eating
DAB	days after birth	DAFO	dynamic ankle-foot orthosis
	Deutsche Arzneibuch (German Pharmacopeia)	DAG	diacylglycerol
	diamino benzidine		dianhydrogalactitol

DAGT direct antiglobulin test
DAH diffuse alveolar hemorrhage
disordered action of the heart
DAHLC Dan Abraham Healthy Living
Center (Mayo Clinic)
DAI diffuse axonal injury
DAIDS Division of AIDS (of the
National Institute of Allergy
and Infectious Diseases,
NIH)
DAIR debridement, antibiotics and
implant retention (treatment
for surgical site prosthetic
joint infections)
DAK Deutsche Angestellten
Krankenkasse – German
Salaried Employees Health
Insurance Funds
DAL diffuse aggressive lymphomas
drug analysis laboratory
DALE disability-adjusted life
expectancy
DALK deep anterior lamellar kerato-
plasty
DALM dysplasia-associated lesion or
mass
DALY disability-adjusted life year(s)
DALYs disability-adjusted life years
DAM diacetylmonoxine
DAMA discharged against medical
advice
DAMP damage-associated molecular
pattern (protein)
deficits in attention, motor
control, and perception
DAMPA 3-(dimethylamino)-
1-propylamine
DAN diabetic autonomic neuropathy
DANA drug-induced antinuclear
antibodies
DandC dilatation and curettage
Drug Rules of Drugs and
Cosmetics (act, India)
D and E dilation and evacuation
DAO daimine oxidase (over-the-
counter digestive product for
enzyme prevention of hista-
mine imbalance)
DAo descending aorta
DAOH days alive and out of hospital
DAOM depressor anguli oris muscle
DAP 3,4-diaminopyridine
dapsone
diabetes-associated peptide
diastolic augmentation pressure
distending airway pressure
dose area product (radiology)
Draw-A-Person

daPa decapascal (a measurement of
air pressure; whereby,
1.02 mm H20 = 1.00 daPa)
dapA dihydrodipicolinate synthase;
see gene website www.ncbi
.nlm.nih.gov/gene
dapE N-succinyl-diaminopimelate
deacylase (gene)
DAPI 4',6-diamidino-2-phenylindole
(fluorescent dye binds
strongly to DNA and is used
for visualizing cell nuclei)
dapk death-associated protein kinase
(gene/protein)
DAPP-BQ Dimensional Assessment of
Personality Pathology-Basic
Questionnaire
DAPT Draw-A-Person Test
dual antiplatelet therapy
(clopidogrel [Plavix], and
aspirin)
DAR daily affective rhythm
data, action, response
dara daratumumab inj (Darzalex)
DARB darbepoetin alfa (Aranesp)
DARC Detection of Apoptosing Retinal
Cells
DARE data, action, response, and
evaluation
Database of Abstracts of
Reviews of Effects
DA-R-EPOCH dose-adjusted etoposide,
prednisone, vincristine
(Oncovin), cyclophospha-
mide, doxorubicin (hydroxy-
daunorubicin), and rituximab
DARP drug abuse rehabilitation
program
drug abuse reporting program
DARPA Defense Advanced Research
Projects Agency (US Department of Defense)
DARQ diarylquinoline
DARS Dimensional Anhedonia Rating
Scale
DART developmental and reproductive
toxicology (protocols)
D/ART depression/awareness,
recognition and treatment
DAS data acquisition system
(radiology)
day of admission surgery
developmental apraxia of speech
died at scene
disease activity score
distractive auditory stimuli
dynamometer anchoring station
DAs daily activities

DASE	dobutamine-atropine stress echocardiography	Db	dubnium
		dB	decibel
DASH	Dietary Approaches to Stop Hypertension (diet)	D2B	door-to-balloon (time)
		DBA	Diamond-Blackfan anemia
	Disabilities of the Arm, Shoulder, and Hand (questionnaire/rating)		doing business as
		dBA	decibels measured on the A-scale
DASI	Duke Activity Status Index	DB ACL	double-bundle (hamstring
DASS	Depression Anxiety Stress Scale		autograft) anterior cruciate
	dialysis access steal syndrome		ligament (reconstruction)
DAST	Drug Abuse Screening Test	D-BART	Dementia-Behavioral
DAT	daunorubicin, cytarabine, (ara-C), and thioguanine		Assessment and Response Team
	definitely abnormal tracing (electrocardiogram)	DBAS	Dysfunctional Beliefs and Attitudes about Sleep (scale)
	dementia of the Alzheimer type	DBB	deproteinized bovine bone
	diet as tolerated	DB & C	deep breathing and coughing
	diphtheria antitoxin	DBCG	Danish Breast Cancer
	direct antiglobulin test		Cooperative Group
	dual antiplatelet therapy (aspirin and clopidogrel)	DBCL	diffuse large B-cell lymphoma
		DBD	Diabetic bladder dysfunction
	duration of antimicrobial therapy		donation (after) brain death
			milolactol (dibromodulicitol)
DAT−	negative direct antiglobulin test	DBDS	Dementia Behavior Disturbance
DAT+	positive direct antiglobulin test		Scale
dATP	2′-deoxyadenosine triphosphate	DBE	deep breathing exercise
DaTscan	dopamine transporter (Isoflupane I-123) imaging (GE Healthcare)		double-balloon endoscopy
			double-balloon enteroscopy
		DBED	penicillin G benzathine (for IM use only; Bicillin L-A)
DAU	daughter		
	drug abuse urine	dBEMCL	decibel effective masking contralateral
DAUNO	daunorubicin (Cerubidine; DaunoXome)		
		D5BES	dextrose in balanced electrolyte solution
DAVA	vindesine sulfate (Eldisine; desacetyl vinblastine amide sulfate)		
		DBFaFx	double-bone forearm fracture
		DBG	dabigatran etexilate (Pradaxa)
DAVE	The Data Assessment and Verification program	D&BH	dot and blot hemorrhages
		DBH	double-bundle hamstring (tendon graft)
DAVF	dural arteriovenous fistula		
DAVM	dural arteriovenous malformation	dB HL	decibel hearing level
		dBHL	decibels hearing
DAV SEP	deviated septum	DBI	documented by initials
DAW	dispense as written	DBI®	phenformin HCl
DAWN	Drug Abuse Warning Network	DBIL	direct bilirubin
DAX	decellularized aortic xenograft	DBILI	direct bilirubin
	Driving Anger Expression Inventory	D Bili	direct bilirubin
		DBKT	Diabetes: Basic Knowledge Test
DB	database	DBL	double beta-lactam
	date of birth	db-LCFA	descending branch of the lateral circumflex femoral artery
	Decision Board		
	deep breathe	DBLCL	may have meant DLBCL (diffuse large B-cell lymphoma)
	demonstration bath		
	dermabrasion		
	diaphragmatic breathing	DBM	demineralized bone matrix
	difficulty breathing		dibenzoylmethane
	Digit Backwards (test)		donor breast milk
	direct bilirubin	DBMD	Duchenne/Becker Muscular Dystrophies
	double blind		

D

DBMT	displacement bone marrow transplantation		dendritic cells
DBN	downbeat nystagmus		Dermatochalasis (a skin excess in the upper eyelid which may
dBnHL	decibels normalized hearing level (intensity stimulus)		be associated with either an aesthetic and functional defect,
DBO	darbepoetin alfa (Aranesp)		blocking the peripheral vision)
DBP	D-binding protein		dextrocardia
	diastolic blood pressure		diagonal conjugate
	dibutyl phthalate		dichorionic (twins)
DBPC	double-blind, placebo-controlled (study)		direct Coombs (test)
			direct current
DBPCFC	double-blind, placebo-controlled food challenge		discharge
			discomfort
DBPR/ESRB	Division of Bioterrorism Preparedness and Response/		discontinue
	Epidemiology Surveillance		displacement chromatography
	and Response Branch, (Cen-		District of Columbia
	ters for Disease Control and		docetaxel and cisplatin
	Prevention)		Doctor of Chiropractic
DBPT	dacarbazine (DTIC), carmustine		dorsal compartment
	(BCNU), cisplatin (Platinol),		Dupuytren contracture
	and tamoxifen		dyskeratosis congenita
DBQ	debrisoquin	d7c	day 7 drug concentration
DBQI	Downs and Black Quality Index	D&C	dilatation and curettage
	(checklist for the assess-		direct and consensual
	ment of the methodological	D & C	see D&C
	quality of randomized and	D/C	discharge (D/C is most often
	non-randomized studies)		used to mean "discontinue,"
DBR	distributed Bragg reflector (laser)		but when seen in context is
DBS	De Barsy syndrome		understood to mean dis-
	deep brain stimulation		charge. In some institutions
	desirable body weight		the word discharge may be re-
	diminished breath sounds		quired to be spelled out rather
	dorsal blocking splint		than abbreviated to avoid
	dried blood spot		possible confusion)
	dried blood stain		discontinue (see other meaning
	dry blood spot	D+C	for D/C)
DBS IPG	deep brain stimulation	DCA	see D&C
	implantable pulse generator		deoxycholic acid
dB SL	decibel sensation level		dichloroacetate
dB SPL	decibel sound pressure level		directional coronary
DB splint	Dennis Brown splint		atherectomy
DBSs	dietary botanical supplements		disk/condyle adhesion
DBT	dialectical behavior therapy		double-cup arthroplasty
	digital breast tomosynthesis		sodium dichloroacetate
	drug benefit threshold	DCAG	double-coronary artery graft
DBV	dense breast volume	DCAPBTLS	deformities, contusions,
	diastolic blood viscosity		abrasions, and punctures/
	diluted bee venom		penetrations, burns, tender-
DBW	desired body weight		ness, lacerations, and swelling
	dry body weight		(an assessment mnemonic
DBX	demineralized bone matrix		used by EMTs)
DBZ	dibenzamine	DC-ART	disease controlling anti-
DC	daunorubicin and cytarabine		rheumatic therapy
	daycare	DCB	drug-coated balloon
	deceleration capacity (heart)	DC&B	dilation, currettage, and biopsy
	decompressive craniotomy	DCBE	double-contrast barium enema
	decrease	DCBS	Department for Community Based Services

DCBs	drug-coated balloons		docetaxel, cisplatin, and fluorouracil
DCBS/SS	Department for Community Based Services/Social Services		pentostatin (Nipent; 2' deoxycoformycin)
DCBT	double-cord-blood transplantation	DCFS	Department of Children and Family Services
DCC	day care center		
	delayed cord clamping	DCG	diagnostic cardiogram
	deleted in colorectal cancer (gene/protein)	DCH	delayed cutaneous hypersensitivity
	diabetes care clinic	DCh	Dermatochalasis (a skin excess in the upper eyelid which may be associated with either an aesthetic and functional defect, blocking the peripheral vision)
	direct current cardioversion		
DC cardioversion	direct current cardioversion		
DCCB	dihydropyridine calcium channel blocker		
DCCF	dural carotid-cavernous fistula		
DCCM	dilated congestive cardiomyopathy	DCHF	decompensated chronic heart failure
DCCs	day care centers		decompensated congestive heart failure
DCCT	Diabetes Control and Complications Trial (questionnaire)		diastolic congestive heart failure
		dCHF	diastolic congestive heart failure
DC-CV	direct current (electrical) cardioversion	D-CHF	diastolic congestive heart failure
		DCHF-DA	dichlorodihydrofluorescein diacetate
DCD	deceased (sounds like French "décédé")	DCHP	dicyclohexyl phthalate
	developmental coordination disorder	DCI	decompression illness
			delayed cerebral ischemia
	dicyandiamide		distal contractile integral
DC'd	discontinued	DCIA	deep circumflex iliac artery (flap)
DCD	donation after cardiac death		
	donation after circulatory death	DC ICD	dual-chamber implantable cardioverter defibrillator
DCDA	dichorionic-diamniotic (twins)		
DCE	delayed contrast-enhancement	DC-ICD	dual-chamber implantable cardioverter defibrillator
	designated compensable event		
	detection-controlled estimation	DCing	discharging
	distal clavicle excision		discontinuing
D&C&E	dilation, curretage, and evacuation	DC'ing	discontinuing
		DCIS	ductal carcinoma in situ
DCed	decalcified	DCIs	discharge instructions
D/Ced	discharged (D/Ced is also often used to mean "discontinued," but when seen in context is understood to mean discharged. In some institutions the word discharged may be required to be spelled out rather than abbreviated to avoid possible confusion)	DCL	damage control laparotomy
			diffuse cutaneous leishmaniasis
		DC-LAMP	dendritic cell-lysosomal-associated membrane protein
		DCLHβ	diaspirin cross-linked hemoglobin
		DCLO	diffusing capacity of the lung for carbon monoxide
		DCLV	double-chambered left ventricle
DC'ed	discontinued	DCM	dementia care mapping
DCE-MRI	dynamic contrast enhanced magnetic resonance imaging		dichloromethane
			dilated cardiomyopathy
DCEP	dexamethasone, cyclophosphamide, etoposide, and cisplatin (Platinol)	DCMHO	discharge medication handout
		DCMO	dilated cardiomyopathy
		DCMP	dilated cardiomyopathy
DCF	data collection form	DCMXT	dichloromethotrexate
	Denomination Commune Francaise (French-approved nonproprietary name)	DCN	Darvocet N
		DC negative	dendritic cells negative
		DCNU	chlorozotocin

DCNVA	distance-corrected near visual acuity		distal convoluted tubule
			dynamic contour tonometry
DCO	damage control orthopedics	D-CTIN	drug-induced chronic tubulointestinal nephritis
	death certificates only (cases known only from death certificates)	DCTM	delay computer tomographic myelography
	diffusing capacity of carbon monoxide	DCU	day care unit
		DCUS	duplex-color ultrasonography
DCOG	Dutch Childhood Oncology Group	DCVAC/PCa	dendritic cells pulsed with killed prostate cancer cell line
DCP	dichlorphenamide (Keveyis)		LNCaP (prostate cancer therapy)
DCP®	calcium phosphate, dibasic	DCVC	dual-channel virus counter
	discharge planner (plan)	DCW	direct care worker
	dynamic compression plate	DCX	doublecortin
DCPC	diode laser cyclophotocoagulation	DCYS	Department of Children and Youth Services
	Division of Cancer Prevention and Control (United States Centers for Disease Control and Prevention)	DD	D-dimer (a fibrin degradation product present in the blood after a blood clot is degraded by fibrinolysis; used to help
DCPM	daunorubicin, cytarabine, prednisolone, and mercaptopurine		diagnose thrombosis) debridement/decontamination
DCPN	direction-changing positional nystagmus		deceased donor(s) delayed diarrhea
DCPPM	dichlorprop methyl (a pesticide)		delivery date
DCR	dacryocystorhinostomy		denileukin diftitox (Ontak)
	delayed cutaneous reaction		dependent drainage
	digital contact radiography		Descemet detachment
	disease control rate		detrusor dyssynergia
	distal clavicle resection		developmental disabilities
DCRC	disseminated colorectal cancer		developmental dyslexia
DCRF	data case report forms		developmentally delayed
3DCRT	three-dimensional conformal radiation therapy		developmentally disabled dialysis dementia
DCRV	double-chambered right ventricle		diastolic dysfunction
DCS	damage-control surgery		dichorionic diamniotic (twins)
	decompression sickness		died of the disease
	discharge summary		difference-in-differences
	dorsal column stimulator		(comparing the change over
	dual chamber syringe		time in an outcome variable
DCSA	double-contrast shoulder arthrography		for the treatment group, compared to the change over time
DCSAD	Diagnostic Classification of Sleep and Arousal Disorders		for the control group) differential diagnosis
DCSD	degenerative cervical spine disease		disc diameter discharge diagnosis
dCSF-CN	distal cerebrospinal fluid-contacting neuron		Doctor of Divinity
dcSSc	diffuse cutaneous systemic sclerosis		dose-dense double dose (used by Radiology)
DCSW	Diplomate in Clinical Social Work		down drain dry dressing
DCT	daunorubicin, cytarabine, and thioguanine		dual disorder Duchenne dystrophy
	decisional conflict theory		due date
	deep chest therapy		Dupuytren Disease
	dichorionic twins		dysthymic disorder
	direct (antiglobulin) Coombs test	D & D	debridement and dressing

diarrhea and dehydration

divorced and desperate (middle aged female who visits doctor weekly just for male attention) (slang)

drilling and drainage

drop and dangle (rehabilitation program following total knee arthroplasty)

D → D	discharge to duty
D1 . . . 12	dorsal nerves 1–12
D/D	diarrhea/dehydration
D-1 . . . D-12	dorsal vertebrae 1 to 12
D1/D2	first and second diagonal branches (coronary artery)
DDA	dideoxyadenosine
DDAC	didecyl dimethyl ammonium chloride (an antiseptic/ disinfectant)
DDAH	dimethylarginine dimethylaminohydrolase
DDAP	diammine dicarboxylic acid platinum
DDC	zalcitabine (dideoxy-cytidine; Hivid)
DDCHD	duct-dependent congenital heart disease
DD CHF	diastolic dysfunction and congestive heart failure
DDCI	dopadecarboxylase inhibitor
DD-CKD	dialysis-dependent chronic kidney disease
DDCV	definitive dependence on continuous mechanical ventilation
	dodecoxycarbonylvaline (a chiral surfactant)
DDD	defined daily doses
	degenerative disk disease
	dense deposit disease
	dihydropyrimidine dehydrogenase deficiency
	Dowling-Degos disease
	fully automatic pacing
DDDI	Dula Dangerous Driving Index
DDDi	infant defined daily dose
DDDKT	may have meant DDKT (deceased donor kidney transplant)
DDD-PPM	a form of dual-chambered pacing in which the atria and the ventricles are paced; the atrium and the ventricle are sensed and paced or inhibited, depending on the native cardiac activity sensed
DDDR	pacemaker code (D = chamber paced-dual, D = chamber sensed-dual, D = response to sensing-dual, R = programmability-rate modulation)
DDDR-70	dual-chamber rate responsive pacing at 70/minute
DDDS	Division of Developmental Disabilities Services
DDE	dichlorodiphenylethylene
DDEB	dystrophic epidermolysis bullosa
DDFS	distant disease free survival
DDGB	double-dose gallbladder (test)
DDGIs	drug-drug-gene interactions
DDH	developmental dysplasia of the hip
DDHAM	decellularized, dehydrated human amniotic membrane
DDHF	decompensated diastolic heart failure
DDHT	double-dissociated hypertropia
DDI	didanosine (dideoxyinosine; Videx)
	dressing dry, intact
	drug-drug interaction
D-dimer	a fibrin degradation product present in the blood after a blood clot is degraded by fibrinolysis; used to help diagnose thrombosis
DDIR	pacemaker mode; ventricular and atrial sensing and pacing with rate
D/DIR	direct treatment method
DDIs	donor-derived infections
	drug-drug interactions
DDis	developmental disorder
DDiv	Doctor of Divinity
DDKT	deceased donor kidney transplantation
DDKTx	deceased donor kidney transplantation
DDL	Dear Doctor Letter
	dedifferentiated liposarcoma
ddI	didanosine (dideoxyinosine; Videx)
DDLS	dedifferentiated liposarcoma
DDLT	deceased-donor liver transplantation
DDM	drift-diffusion model
DDMAC	Division of Drug Marketing, Advertising and Communications (FDA)
DDMC	diabetes disease management clinic
ddMVAC	dose-dense methotrexate, vinblastine, doxorubicin (adriamycin), and cisplatin

DDNOS	dissociative disorder, not otherwise specified	DDx	differential diagnosis
DDNS	digestive disease and nutrition service	D_5E_{48}	5% Dextrose and Electrolyte 48
DDO	D-aspartate oxidase (gene/enzyme)	D_5E_{75}	5% Dextrose and Electrolyte 75
		DE	Delaware
DDP	cisplatin (Platinol)		dermal epidermal (junction)
ddPCR	droplet digital polymerase chain reaction		digitalis effect
			diminished emotionality
			disordered eating
DDPS	Detailed Descriptions of Pharmacovigilance Systems		donor eggs
		D&E	dilatation and evacuation
DDR	dead donor rule		dilation and evacuation
	direct digital radiography	D/E	dilation and evacuation
DDRA	dead despite resuscitation attempt	3-DE	three-dimensional echocardiography
DDRE	Division of Drug Risk Evaluation (FDA)	2-DE	two-dimensional echocardiography
			two-dimensional gel electrophoresis
DDRT	deceased donor renal transplantation	DEA	diethylamine
DDRT-PCR	differential display reverse transcription polymerase chain reaction	DEA#	Drug Enforcement Administration number (physician's federal narcotic number)
DDRTx	deceased donor renal transplant	DEAE	diethylaminoethyl
DDRUL	dorsal distal radioulnar ligament	DEARE	delayed effects of acute radiation exposure
DDS	4, 4-diaminodiphenyl-sulfone (dapsone)	DEB	diepoxybutane (test)
			drug-eluting balloon
	Denys-Drash Syndrome		drug-eluting bead
	dialysis disequilibrium syndrome		dystrophic epidermolysis bullosa
	Doctor of Dental Surgery		
	dopamine dysregulation syndrome	DEBs	doxorubicin-eluting beads
			drug-eluting balloons
	dose-dense chemotherapy	DEB-TACE	drug-eluting beads for transarterial chemoembolization
	double-decidual sac (sign)		
D & Ds	death and doughnuts. Slang for morbidity and mortality conferences	DEC	Data Element Catalog
			deciduous (primary teeth)
			diethylcarbamazine (Hetrazan)
DDSI	death from drug self-intoxication		Drug Evaluation and Classification (a standardized curriculum to train police officers)
	Dual Diagnosis Screening Instrument (to screen psychiatric disorders in substance users in treatment and nontreatment-seeking samples; Barcelona, Spain)		
		Dec	December
		dec	decrease(d)
		DECA	nandrolone decanoate (Deca-Durabolin)
	dual (probe) difference specimen imaging	DECAFS	Department of Children and Family Services
DDST	Denver Development Screening Test	decaliter	10 liters (10,000 mL)
		DECEL	deceleration
DDT	chlorophenothane	decels	decelerations (temporary drops in the heart rate)
	drug development tools		
DDTP	drug dependence treatment program	DECG	Doppler echocardiography
			dynamic echocholecystography
DDV	deep dorsal vein	DEcIDE	Developing Evidence to Inform Decisions about Effectiveness (centers)
DDVAP	Could be misread; see DDAVP		
DDVP	dimethyl 2,2-dichlorovinyl phosphate (Dichlorvos, an organophosphorus pesticide)	decomp	decomposition
		decort	decortication

decr	decrease(d)	DEL	delivered
DECT	dual-energy computed tomography		delivery
			deltoid
DECUB	decubitis	DELM	digital epiluminescence microscopy
decube	decubitus (ulcer)		
DED	diabetic eye disease	delt	deltoid
	died in emergency department	Delta	Phonetic Alphabet for D; pronounced DELL-TA
	dry eye disease		
DEE	daily energy expenditure	delts	deltoids
DEEDS	drugs, exercise, education, diet, and self-monitoring	DEM	drug evaluation matrix
		DEMMI	de Morton Mobility Index
DEEG	depth electroencephalogram deteriorating electroencephalogram	demo	demographics
			demonstration
		demo'd	demonstrated
DEET	diethyltoluamide	DEMP	diethyl methylphosphonate
DEF	decayed, extracted, or filled	DEMRI	dynamic enhanced magnetic resonance imaging
	defecation		
	deficiency	DE-MRI	delayed-enhancement magnetic resonance imaging
2-DEF	two-dimensional echo-derived ejection fraction		
		De Novo	from the beginning; from scratch; new; beginning again
DEFIB	defibrillate		
defic	deficiency	DENS	Drug Effects on the Nervous System (scale)
DEFT	defendant		
	driven equilibrium Fourier transform (technique)	dent	dental
			dentistry
DEG	diethylene glycol	DenV	dengue virus
deg	degree	Denver II	Denver Developmental Screening Test - second edition
degen	degenerative		
dehis	dehiscence		
DEHP	diethylhexyl phthalate	DEP	dependence
DEHSI	diffuse excessive high signal intensity		dependent
		DEPO	long-acting (depot)
Dehy	dehydrocostuslactone	depr	depression
dehy	dehydrated dehy	DEPs	diesel exhaust particles
DEI	diffraction-enhanced imaging	DEP ST SEG	depressed ST segment
DEIP	may have meant DIEP (deep inferior epigastric perforator [flap])	DEPT	Distortionless Enhancement by Polarization Transfer
		dept	department
DEJ	dentin-enamel junction	DEQ	Drug Effects Questionnaire
DEK	a gene/nuclear phosphoprotein; a transcription factor involved in mRNA (messenger ribonucleic acid) splicing, transcriptional control, cell division and differentiation	DEq	dose equivalents
		DER	disulfiram-ethanol reaction
		DERB	dual-ended readout block
		DERM	dermatology
		DERT	dietary education and resistance training
DEKA arm	a prosthetic limbs designed to give servicemen and women who have lost limbs the option of returning to active duty or otherwise function as normally as possible; designed by Dean Kamen at the DEKA Research and Development Corporation; currently called the LUKE [The Life Under Kinetic Evolution] arm)	DES	desflurane (Supreme)
			diethylstilbestrol
			diffuse esophageal spasm
			disequilibrium syndrome
			Dissociative Experience Scale
			drug-eluting stent
			dry-eye syndrome
			dysfunctional elimination syndrome (urology)
		DESAT	desaturation
		desats	desaturation (decreases in the percentage of oxygen found in the circulating blood supply)

D

desatted	desaturated		defibrotide
DESC1	see gene website, www.ncbi .nlm.nih.gov/gene		degree of freedom
			dengue fever
DESD	detrusor-external sphincter dyssynergia		depth of field
			dexfenfluramine
desD	see gene website www.ncbi.nlm .nih.gov/gene		diabetic father
			diagnostic findings
DESF	desflurane (Suprane)		diastolic filling
DESH	disproportionately enlarged subarachnoid-space hydrocephalus		dietary fiber
			dorsiflexion
			drug-free
DESI	Drug Efficacy Study Implementation		dye-free
		D&F	decayed and filled
DESIs	decision support interventions	D/F	see DF
DESS	double-echo steady state (magnetic resonance imaging)	DFA	delayed feedback audiometry
			diet for age
			difficulty falling asleep
DES to LAD	drug eluting stent to left anterior descending (artery)		direct fluorescent antibody
			distal forearm
DET	diethyltryptamine	DFAAPA	Distinguished Fellow of the American Academy of Physician Assistants
	Dionne Egress Test		
	dipyridamole echocardiography test		
		DFB	distributed feedback (laser)
DETC	dendritic epithelial T cell	DFC	drug-free communities
	diethyldithiocarbamate (a superoxide dismutase [SOD] inhibitor)	DFCI	Dana-Farber Cancer Institute
		DFD	defined formula diets
			degenerative facet disease
DETOX	detoxification	DFE	dilated fundus examination
DEV	deviation		distal femoral epiphysis
	duck embryo vaccine	DFF	DNA (deoxyribonucleic acid) fragmentation factor
DeVIC	dexamethasone, etoposide (VePesid), ifosfamide, and carboplatin		
		DFFP	Diploma of the Faculty of Family Planning (Royal College of Obstetricians and Gynaecologists, United Kingdom)
Devic disease	also known as neuromyelitis optica is an autoimmune disorder that leads to the inflammation and demyelin- ation of the optic nerve and spinal cord nerves		
		DFG	Deutsche Forschungsgemein schaft (German Research Foundations; comparable to the US NIH)
DEVR	dominant exudative vitreoretinopathy		direct forward gaze
DEX	dexamethasone	DFI	diabetic foot infection
	dexmedetomidine (Precedex)		disease-free interval
	dexrazoxane (Zinecard)		Druggan-Forsythe-Iversen (agar)
	dexter (right)		
	dexverapamil	DFib	defibrillator
Dex	blood glucose (dextrose) level monitoring	dFIB	derived fibrinogen
		dFLC	difference between involved and uninvolved FLCs [free light chains]
DEXA	dual-energy x-ray absorptiometry		
Dexes	blood glucose (dextrose) level monitoring	DFLE	disability-free life expectancy
		DFM	decreased fetal movement
DexMTZ	dexamethasone		deep finger massage
Dex's	blood glucose (dextrose) levels monitoring		deep-friction massage
		DFMC	daily fetal movement count
DF	day frequency (of voiding)	DFMO	eflornithine (difluoro- methylorithine)
	decayed and filled		
	deferred	DFMR	daily fetal movement record

DFNB	discharge final, not billed (report)	dghtr	daughter
DFO	deferoxamine (Desferal)	dghtr's	daughters
DFOM	deferoxamine (Desferal)	DGI	disseminated gonococcal infection
DFP	diastolic filling period isoflurophate (diisopropyl flurophosphate)		dynamic gait index
		DGIs	drug-gene interactions
		DGL	deglycyrrhizinated licorice
DF/PF	dorsiflexor and plantarflexor (ankle movements)	DGM	ductal glandular mastectomy
		DGME	diethylene glycol monoethyl ether (an aid in transdermal delivery systems)
DFR	diabetic floor routine		
DFRC	deglycerolized frozen red cells		
DFR I	dialysate flow rate (hemodialysis)	DGN	dorsal genital nerve German Society for Neurology
DFS	disease-free survival Division of Family Services Doppler flow studies	DGOU	German Orthopaedic and Trauma Society
		DGP	deamidated gliadin peptides
DFSP	dermatofibrosarcoma protuberans	DGPPN	German Society for Psychiatry, Psychotherapy and Neuropsychiatry
DFT	defibrillation threshold (testing)		
DFTD	Tasmanian devil facial tumor disease	DGR	duodenogastric reflux
		DGRi	duodenogastric reflux index
DFTS	digital flexor tendon sheath	DGS	DiGeorge syndrome
DFTs	defibrillation thresholds	DGs	documentation guidelines
DFTT	defibrillation threshold tests dipole flow tracer tests	DGT	decaffeinated green tea
		DGTR-1	see gene website www.ncbi.nlm .nih.gov/gene
DFU	dead fetus in uterus diabetic foot ulcer digital flexible ureteroscope	DH	delayed hypersensitivity Dental Hygienist Department of Health dermatitis herpetiformis developmental history diaphragmatic hernia
DFV	D'Aoust Fineman virus dengue fever vaccine diarrhea, fever, and vomiting Dexide face wash		
		D+H	delusions and hallucinations
DFWO	dorsiflexory wedge osteotomy	D/H	deuterium/hydrogen ratio
DFX	deferasirox (Exjade)	D-H	Dimon-Hughston (intertrochanteric osteotomy technique)
DFYS	Division of Family and Youth Services (government agency)		
		DHA	Defense Health Agency (US Department of Defense) dihydroxyacetone docosahexaenoic acid
DG	diagnosis dorsal glides downward gaze Duarte galactosemia		
		DHAC	dihydro-5-azacytidine
DGA	DiGeorge anomaly disseminated granuloma annulare	DHAD	mitoxanthrone HCl (Novantrone)
		DHANP	Diplomate of the Homeopathic Academy of Naturopathic Physicians
DGBI	Billroth-I distal gastrectomy		
DGD	differential group delays		
DGE	delayed gastric emptying	DHAP	dexamethasone, high-dose cytarabine, (ara-A) cisplatin (Platinol)
DGF	delayed graft function		
DGGE	denaturing gradient gel electrophoresis		docosahexaenoic acid-paclitaxel
DGH	district general hospital (United Kingdom)	DHA-TP	dihydroartemisinin, trimethoprim, and piperaquine
DGHAL	Doppler-guided hemorrhoidal artery ligation	DHBV	duck hepatitis B virus
		DHC	decompressive hemicraniectomy Dental Health Component digital holographic cytometry dihydrocapsaicin disc height change
DGHs	district general hospitals (United Kingdom)		
DGHT	discriminative generalized Hough transform		

dHc	dorsal hippocampus
DHCA	deep hypothermia circulatory arrest
DHCC	dihydroxycholecalciferol
DHD	daily hemodialysis
	dissociated horizontal deviation
DHE	dental health education
DHE 45®	dihydroergotamine mesylate
DHEA	dehydroepiandrosterone
DHEAS	dehydroepiandrosterone sulfate
DHES	Department of Health and Environmental Science(s)
DHF	dengue hemorrhagic fever
	diastolic heart failure
dHFpEF	decompensated heart failure with preserved ejection fraction
DHFR	dihydrofolate reductase
DHHS	Department of Health and Human Services
DHI	Dizziness Handicap Inventory
	dynamic hyperinflation
DHIC	detrusor hyperactivity with impaired contractility
DHIs	digital health interventions
DHIS 2	District Health Information Software 2
DHL	diffuse histocytic lymphoma
DHM	digital holographic microscopy
	donor human milk
DHN	dihydroxynaphthalene
DHP-1	dehydropeptidase-1
DHP	dental hygiene program
	dihydropyridine
DHPG	ganciclovir
DHPLC	denaturing high-performance liquid chromatography
DHPR	dihydropteridine reductase
DHPS	dihydopteroate synthase
DHR	delayed hypersensitivity reaction
	disk height ratio
DHS	deoxyhypusine synthase
	Department of Homeland Security
	Department of Human Services
	duration of hospital stay
	dynamic hip screw
DHSI	Depressive Health State Index
	Digestive Health Status Instrument
DHST	delayed hypersensitivity test
DHT	dihydrotachysterol (Hytakerol; DHT®)
	dihydrotestosterone
	dissociated hypertropia
	Dobhoff (Dobbhoff) tube

DHTF	Dobhoff (Dobbhoff) tube feeding
DHTR	delayed hemolytic transfusion reactions
DI	(Beck) Depression Inventory
	date of injury
	Debrix Index
	Delirium Index
	detrusor instability
	diabetes insipidus
	diagnostic imaging
	Diego; an International Society of Blood Transfusion (ISBT) blood group
	Dietetic Intern
	Disability Index
	dorsal interossei
	drug interactions
D&I	debridement and irrigation
	dry and intact
D/I	see DI
DIA	Drug Information Association
	drug-induced agranulocytosis
	drug-induced amenorrhea
D-IA	idarubicin and cytarabine
Dia	diameter
diab	diabetes
	diabetic
DIACF	displaced intra articular calcaneal fracture
diag	diagnosis
DIAIH	drug-induced autoimmune hepatitis
DIAL	Development Indicators for Assessment of Learning
DIAM	drug-induced aseptic meningitis
DIAm	diaphragm muscle
diam	diameter
DIAPPERS criteria	Delirium, Infection (urinary), Atrophic urethritis and vaginitis, Pharmaceuticals, Psychological disorders (especially depression), Excessive urine output, Restricted mobility, Stool impaction; (causes of transient incontinence)
DIAS	diastolic
DIAS BP	diastolic blood pressure
Diath SW	diathermy short wave
DIAZ	diazepam (Valium)
DIB	difficulty in breathing
	disability insurance benefits
DIBC	drug-induced blood cytopenias
DIBD	drug-induced behavioral disinhibition
DIBH	deep inspiration breath-hold

DIB-R — Diagnostic Interview for Borderlines (personality disorders) - Revised

DIBS — dead-in-bed syndrome diarrhea-predominant irritable bowel syndrome

D-IBS — diarrhea-predominant irritable bowel syndrome

DIC — dacarbazine (DTIC-Dome) diagnostic imaging center differential interference contrast disseminated intravascular coagulation drug information center

DICA — distal internal carotid artery

DICA-P — Diagnostic Interview for Children and Adolescents for Parents

DICA-PPY — Diagnostic Interview for Children and Adolescents for Parents of Preschool and Young Children

DICC — dynamic infusion cavernosometry and cavernosography

DICE — dexamethasone, ifosfamide, cisplatin, and etopside, with mesna

DICLOX — dicloxacillin (Dynapen)

DICM — diabetic induced cardiomyopathy differential interference contrast microscopy

DICOM — Digital Imaging and Communication in Medicine

DICP — demyelinated inflammatory chronic polyneuropathy

DIC panel — disseminated intravascular coagulation panel (prothrombin time, activated partial thromboplastin time, fibrinogen, D-dimer, platelet count, and factor V)

DICS — Dynamic Imaging of Coherent Sources

DICs — drug information centers

DICT — dose-intensive chemotherapy

DID — death(s) from intercurrent disease delayed ischemia deficit difference-in-differences (comparing the change over time in an outcome variable for the treatment group, compared to the change over time for the control group) dissociative identity disorder drug-induced disease

DiDi — dichorionic-diamniotic (twins)

DIE — died in emergency department drug-induced esophagitis

DIEA — deep inferior epigastric artery (flap)

dieb alt — every other day (this is a dangerous Latin abbreviation which will not be understood)

DIED — died in emergency department

DIEP — deep inferior epigastric perforator (flap)

DIF — differentiation-inducing factor

diff — differential blood count

DIFFC — dropped in for friendly chat (i. e. no medical problem) (slang)

diff-in-diff — difference-in-differences (comparing the change over time in an outcome variable for the treatment group, compared to the change over time for the control group)

DIFNG — double incision free nipple graft

DIG — digoxin (this is a dangerous abbreviation)

DIG FAST — a mnemonic of mania symptoms (Distractibility and easy frustration, Irresponsibility and erratic uninhibited behavior, Grandiosity, Flight of ideas, Activity increased with weight loss and increased libido, Sleep is decreased, and Talkativeness

dig stim — digital stimulation

DIH — died in hospital

DIHS — Division of Immigration Health Services drug-induced hypersensitivity syndrome

DIJOA — dominantly inherited juvenile optic atrophy

DIL — daughter-in-law dilute drug information leaflet drug-induced lupus

Dil — digital stimulation

dil — dilated dilation

DiLA — dialkylated amino acids based upon arginine

DILC — dose-intensity limiting criterium

DILD — diffuse infiltrative lung disease drug-induced liver disease

DILE — drug-induced lupus erythematosus

DILI — drug-induced liver injury

DILS — diffuse infiltrative lymphocytosis syndrome drug-induced lupus syndrome

dilt — diltiazem hydrochloride

DILV — double-inlet left ventricle

DIM	3,3'-diindolylmethane	DIRA	deficiency of interleukin-1
	days in milk		receptor antagonist
	diminish		drug-Induced rhabdomyolysis
D₅IMB	Ionosol MB with 5% dextrose		atlas
	injection	DIRD	drug-induced renal disease
DIMD	drug-induced movement	DIRV	double-inlet right ventricle
	disorders	DIS	daily interruption of sedation
D immitis	Dirofilaria immitis (heartworm)		Diagnostic Interview Schedule
DIMOAD	diabetes insipidus, diabetes		(questionnaire)
	mellitus, optic atrophy, and		digital imaging spectrophotometer
	deafness		dislocation
DIMS	disorders of initiating and		dissemination in space (lesion)
	maintaining sleep	dis	displacement
DIN	disease impact number	DISA	disseminated autonomy
	ductal intraepithelial neoplasia	DiSA	Dirofilaria immitis (heartworm)
DIND	delayed ischemic neurologic		somatic antigen(s)
	deficit	DISC	death-inducing signaling complex
DINK	did not keep (appointment)		disabled infectious single cycle
	(slang)		(virus)
DIO	diet-induced obesity		discharge
	dorsal interosseus		dynamic integrated stabilization
DIOS	distal ileal obstruction syndrome		chair
	distal intestinal obstruction	disc	discontinue
	syndrome	disch	discharge
DIP	desquamative interstitial	dischg	discharge
	pneumonia	DISC-IV	Diagnostic Interview Schedule
	diphtheria toxoid vaccine		for Children-Version 4
	diplopia	DISCUS	Dyskinesia Indentification
	Diprivan (propofol)		System Condensed User Scale
	drip infusion pyelogram	DISE	drug-induced sleep endoscopy
	drug-induced parkinsonism	DISH	diffuse idiopathic skeletal
	urinalysis dipstick (slang)		hyperostosis
DIP_ant	diphtheria antitoxin	DISI	dorsal intercalated segmental
DIPC	dynamic infusion		(segment) instability
	pharmacocavemosometry	DISIDA	diisopropyl iminodiacetic acid
DI PER TE	diphtheria, pertussis, and tetanus	D₅ISOM	5% Dextrose and Isolyte M
	vaccine	D₅ISOP	5% Dextrose and Isolyte P
DIPG	diffuse intrinsic pontine gliomas	DISP	dispensary
DIPI	direct intraperitoneal		dispense
	insemination		dispersion
DIPJ	distal interphalangeal joint		displacement
DIP joint	distal interphalangeal joint		disposable
Dip MDT	Diploma in Mechanical	dispo	disposition
	Diagnosis and Therapy	DISPRO	DIStance-From-the-PROtotype
DIPNECH	diffuse idiopathic pulmonary		(a multidimensional scaling
	neuroendocrine cell		approach to personality
	hyperplasia		assessment)
DIPP	Finnish Type 1 Diabetes	DISR	drug-induced skin reactions
	Prediction and Prevention	DIST	distal
	(Study)		distilled
DIPS	direct intrahepatic portosystemic	DIT	diiodotyrosine
	shunt		dissemination in time (lesion)
DIPSS	Dynamic International Prognostic		drug-induced thrombocytopenia
	Scoring System	DITMA	drug-induced thrombotic
DIR	digital infrared imaging		microangiopathy
	direct and indirect renumeration	DITP	drug-induced thrombocytopenia
	directions	DITRA	deficiency of interleukin-36
	drug-induced rhabdomyolysis		receptor antagonist

DIU	death in utero	D_L	maximal diffusing capacity
	diuretic(s)	dLAD	distal left anterior descending
DIV	double-inlet ventricle		(artery)
DIVA	differentiation of infected from	DLAR	direct low-anterior resection
	vaccinated animals	DLB	dementia with Lewy bodies
	digital intravenous angiography		direct laryngoscopy and
divertic	diverticulitis		bronchoscopy
	diverticulosis	DL&B	direct laryngoscopy and
Div ex	divergence excess		bronchoscopy
DIVP	dilute intravenous Pitocin	DLBCC	may have meant DLBCL
DIW	deionized water		(diffuse large B cell lymphoma)
Dix–Hallpike	a diagnostic maneuver used to	DLBCL	diffuse large B-cell lymphoma
test	identify benign paroxysmal	DLBD	diffuse Lewy body disease
	positional vertigo (BPPV)	DLB&E	direct laryngoscopy,
DIY	do-it-yourself		bronchoscopy and
DJ	double-J (stent)		esophagoscopy
DJD	degenerative joint disease	DLBL	diffuse large B-cell lymphoma
DJF	distal junctional failure	DLBLC	diffuse large B-cell lymphoma
	duodenojejunal flexure		(France, Spain, etc.)
DJI	Dow Jones Industrial Average	DLBP	disabling low back pain
	duodenojejunal junction	DLC	double lumen catheter
DJK	distal junctional kyphosis	DLCBCL	diffuse large cell B-cell
DJO	DJO Global, Inc., a provider of		lymphoma
	orthopedic devices	DLCBL	may have meant DLBCL
DJP	Doctor of Jurisprudence		(diffuse large B cell lymphoma)
	(a law degree)	d-LCFA	descending branch of the lateral
DJS	Dubin-Johnson syndrome		circumflex femoral artery
	Duke Jeopardy Score	DLCL	diffuse large cell lymphoma
DJ stent	double J stent	DLCN	Dutch Lipid Clinic Network
DK	dark		(diagnostic criteria for familial
	diabetic ketoacidosis		hypercholesterolemia)
	diseased kidney	DLCO	carbon monoxide diffusing
	don't know		capacity
DKA	diabetic ketoacidosis		diffusing capacity of the lungs
	didn't keep appointment		for carbon monoxide
DKB	deep knee bends	DLCOcor	diffusing capacity of the lungs
DKC	double knee to chest		for carbon monoxide, corrected
	dyskeratosis congenita		(based on hemoglobin)
DKD	diabetic kidney disease	DLCO sb	diffusing capacity of the lungs
DKE	dynamic knee-extension		for carbon monoxide, single
DKH	German Cancer Aid (Deutsche		breath
	Krebshilfe)	DL CO SS	study state carbon monoxide
DKI	diffusion kurtosis imaging		diffusing capacity
DKO	double-knockout (mice)	DLCOunc	diffusing capacity of the lungs for
D-K-S	Damus-Kaye-Stansel		carbon monoxide, uncorrected
	(operation/procedure)	dLCX	distal left circumflex artery
DKTC	double-knee to chest (stretch)	DLD	date of last drink
DL	danger list		deterministic lateral displacement
	deciliter (dL preferred)		developmental language disorder
	diagnostic laparoscopy		dihydrolipoamide
	direct laryngoscopy		dehydrogenase (gene)
	double-leg		dyslipidemia
	drug level	dLDL-C	direct measurement low-density
	dual lumen		lipoprotein cholesterol
	ductal lavage	DLE	decrement-load exercise
D/L	dextrorotatory isomer/levorotatory		discoid lupus erythematosus
	isomer ratio		disseminated lupus
dL	deciliter (100 mL)		erythematosis

DLEK	deep lamellar endothelial neoplasia	DLT	dose-limiting toxicity double-lumen tube double-lung transplant
DLES	driveline exit site		
DLEs	delusional-like experiences	DLTT	dosing least toxic time
DLF	digitalis-like factor ductal lavage fluid	DLTX	double lung transplantation
		DLU	diffused lung uptake
DLFAPA	Distinguished Life Fellow of the American Psychiatric Association	DLV	delavirdine (Rescriptor)
		DL/VA	diffusion capacity corrected for alveolar volume
DLH	dl-homocysteic acid	DLVCL	may have meant DLBCL (diffuse large B-cell lymphoma)
DLI	diverting loop ileostomy donor lymphocyte infusion driveline infections		
		DLVD	diastolic left ventricular diameter
DLIF	digoxin-like immunoreactive factors direct lumbar interbody fusion	DLW	doubly labeled water
		DLY	daily delay
DLIS	digoxin-like immunoreactive substance		discounted life years
		DM	data management dehydrated and malnourished dermatomyositis dextromethorphan diabetes mellitus diabetic mother diastolic murmur disease management distant metastases
DLK	deep lamellar keratoplasty dual leucine-zipper kinase		
DLL	decompressive lumbar laminectomy		
Dll	Distal-less; see gene website www.ncbi.nlm.nih.gov/gene		
Dll3	delta-like 3 (gene/protein)		
dLL	dorsal Lisfranc ligament		
DLMP	date of last menstrual period	DM1	myotonic dystrophy type 1
DLNG	dl-norgestrel	DM2	diabetes mellitus type 2
DLNMP	date of last normal menstrual period	DMA	Director of Medical Affairs
		DMAA	1,3 dimethylamylamine (methylhexaneamine; a recreational stimulant) distal metatarsal-articular angle
DLNs	distant lymph nodes		
dLOC	duration of loss of consciousness		
DLOs	dolichol-linked oligosaccharides		
DLP	dislocation of patella dose-length product (radiology) double-limb progression dyslipidemia; high cholesterol	D-mab	denosumab
		DMAC	disseminated *Mycobacterium avium* complex
		DMAD	disease-modifying antirheumatic drug
DLPD	diffuse lymphocytic poorly differentiated	DMAE	dimethylaminoethanol
DLPFC	dorsolateral prefrontal cortex	DMAIC	disseminated *Mycobacterium avium-intracellulare* complex
DLQI	Dermatology Life Quality Index		
D5LR	dextrose 5% in lactated Ringer injection	DMAPT	dimethylaminoparthenolide
		DMARD	disease modifying antirheumatic drug
DLROW	a test used in mental status examinations (patient is asked to spell WORLD backwards)	DMARDs	disease-modifying antirheumatic drugs
		DMAS	Drug Management and Authorization Section
DLRPN	diabetic lumbosacral radiculoplexus neuropathy		
		DMAs	data mining algorithms
DLRT	dogleg radiotherapy	DMAT	disaster medical assistance team
DLS	daily living skills digitalis-like substances double-limb support dynamic light scattering	DMATs	Disaster Medical Assistance Teams
		DMAU	dimethandrolone undecanoate (male hormonal contraceptive)
DLSC	double-lumen subclavian catheter		
DLSS	degenerative lumbosacral stenosis	dmax	depth of maximum dose
		DMB	data monitoring board
DLST	drug-induced lymphocyte stimulation test	DMBA	dimethylbenzanthracene

DMC	dactinomycin, methotrexate, and cyclophosphamide	DMHP	Designated Mental Health Professional
	data monitoring committee	DMI	desipramine (Norpramin)
	Delirium Motor Checklist		diabetic muscle infarction
	diabetes management center		diaphragmatic myocardial infarction
DMCS	Dyggve-Melchior-Clausen syndrome	DMID	diabetes mellitus type 1, insulin-dependent
D-MCT	Metacognitive Training for Depression	DM II	diabetes mellitus type 2
DMD	Descemet membrane detachment	DM Isch	diaphragmatic myocardial ischemia
	disciform macular degeneration	DMJ	Danish Medical Journal
	Doctor of Dental Medicine		Diabetes and Metabolism Journal
	drowsiness monitoring device		Diploma in Medical Jurisprudence
	Duchenne muscular dystrophy		
DMDD	disruptive mood dysregulation disorder	DMKA	diabetes mellitus ketoacidosis
dmdD	methylthioacryloyl-CoA hydratase; see gene website www.ncbi.nlm.nih.gov/gene	DML	distal motor latency
		dml	see gene website, www.ncbi.nlm.nih.gov/gene
DMD w/SRNM	disciform macular degeneration with subretinal neovascular membrane	DMM	decreased muscle mass
			destabilization of the medial meniscus
DME	diabetic macular edema	dMMR	defective deficient mismatch repair
	Director of Medical Education		
	durable medical equipment	DMN	default mode network (a set of brain regions that typically deactivate during perfor- mance of cognitive tasks)
DMEC	data-monitoring and ethics committee		
DMED	dexmedetomidine (Precedex)		dysplastic melanocytic nevus
	diabetes mellitus-induced erectile dysfunction	DMNID	diabetes mellitus type 2, non-insulin-dependent
DMEK	Descemet membrane endothelial keratoplasty	DMO	diabetic macular oedema
			dimethadone
DMEM	Dulbecco Modified Eagle Medium	DMOADs	disease-modifying osteoarthritis drugs
DMEPA	Division of Medication Error Prevention and Analysis (FDA)	DMOG	dimethyloxaloylglycine
		DMOOC	diabetes mellitus out of control
DMEPOS	durable medical equipment, prosthetics, orthotics, and supplies	DMORTs	Disaster Mortuary Operational Response Teams
		DMP	data management plan
DMERC	Durable Medical Equipment Regional Carrier		data monitoring plan
			dimethyl phthalate
DMEs	drug-metabolizing enzymes	DMPA	depot medroxyprogesterone acetate
DMETS	Division of Medication Errors and Technical Support (FDA)		
		DMPA-SC	subcutaneous depot medroxyprogesterone acetate
DMF	decayed, missing, or filled		
	dimethyl fumarate (Tecfidera)	DMPC	dimyristoylphosphatidyl choline
	distant metastases-free	DMPG	dimyristoylphosphatidyl glycerol
	Drug Master File	dMPH	dexmethylphenidate (Focalin)
DMFI	distant metastases interval	DMPK	drug metabolism and pharmacokinetics
DMFS	decayed, missing, or filled surfaces		
	distant metastasis-free survival	DMPM	diffuse malignant peritoneal mesothelioma
DMFT	decayed, missing, and filled teeth	DMPS	dimercaptopropane-sulfonic acid
DMFu	dimethyl fumarate (Tecfidera)	DMQ	dextromethorphan and quinidine (Nuedexta)
DMG	dimethylglycine		
	Department of Mental Health		Dimensions of Mastery Questionnaire
	dimethylhydrazine		
DMHg	dimethyl mercury		

DMQ-R	Drinking Motives Questionnaire, Revised	DNC	Dermatology Nurse, Certified
			determined by neurological criterion (related to death)
DMR	degenerative mitral regurgitation		did not come
D-MRI	dynamic magnetic resonance imaging		dilatation and curettage (usually written as D & C)
DMS	dimethylsulfide		dorsal nerve of the clitoris
DMSA	succimer (dimercaptosuccinic acid; Chemet)	DNCB	dinitrochlorobenzene
DMSA scan	99m technetium dimercaptosuccinic acid scintigraphy	DNCS	del Nido cardioplegia solution
		DND	dead end (gene)
			delayed neurological deficit
DMSL	distal median sensory latency		delayed neuronal death
DMSO	dimethyl sulfoxide		died a natural death
DMT	Digit Memory Test	dnDSA	*de novo* donor-specific antibodies
	dimethyltryptamine		
	disease modifying therapy	DNE	diabetes nurse educator
DMT1	diabetes mellitus type 1	DNEPTE	did not exist prior to enlistment
	divalent metal transporter 1	DNET	dysembryoplastic neuroepithelial tumor
DMT2	diabetes mellitus type 2		
DMTA	dynamic mechanical thermal analysis	DNF	deep neck flexors
		DNFB	Discharged, No Final Bill (report)
DMTS	dimethyl trisulfide	DNFC	does not follow commands
DMTs	disease modifying therapies	DNG	dienogest
DMTU	dimethylthiourea	DNH	de novo hepatitis B
DMV	disc, macula, and vessels		do-not-hospitalize
	Doctor of Veterinary Medicine	DNI	do not intubate
DMVP	discs, vessels, macula periphery		drug-nutrient interaction(s)
DMX	diathermy, massage, and exercise	DNIC	diffuse noxious inhibitory controls [currently known as conditioned pain modulation (CPM)]
DMZ	Demilitarized Zone		
DN	denuded		
	diabetic nephropathy	DNIF	duties not including flying
	dicrotic notch	DNKA	did not keep appointment
	down	DNL	de novo lipogenesis
	dysplastic nevus (nevi)	DNMT	DNA (deoxyribonucleic acid) methyltransferase
D & N	distance and near (vision)		
D/N	day-to-night ratio	DNMT3A	DNA (deoxyribonucleic acid) methyltransferase 3A
	defect-to-normal ratio		
D2N	door-to-needle (time)	DNN	did not nurse
DNA	deoxyribonucleic acid	Dno	nitric oxide diffusing capacity
	did not answer	DNOs	drunken night outs
	did not assess	DNP	2,4-Dinitrophenol (available outside of the US as Biomax, Alpha Dinitrophenol; Aldifen; Fenoxyl Carbon N; Caswell #392; Solfo Black; Nitro Cleenup; 1 Hydroxy-2, 4-Dinitrophenol; Nitrophen; Aldifen; Chemox)
	did not attend		
	does not apply		
DNA ds	deoxyribonucleic acid double stranded		
DNAi	DNA (deoxyribonucleic acid) interference		
DNAR	do not attempt resuscitation		
DNAR-CC	do not attempt resuscitation, comfort care		did not pay
			do not publish
DNase	deoxyribonuclease		Doctor of Nursing Practice
DNA ss	deoxyribonucleic acid single stranded		dorsal Nail Plate
			dorsal nerve of the penis
DNB	daunorubicin		dynamic nuclear polarization
	Diplomate of the National Board of Medical Examiners	DNPH	dinitrophenylhydrazine
		DNR	daunorubicin
DNBI	disease and nonbattle injury		did not respond

D

	digital noise reduction
	do not report
	do not resuscitate (A written order by a physician letting health care personnel know that a patient does not wish to be resuscitated in the event of a cardiac or respiratory arrest. Full care is given until the time the patient stops breathing or their heart stops beating. [check for local meaning])
	dorsal nerve root
DNRCC	do not resuscitate- comfort care (a person receives any care that eases pain and suffering, but no resuscitative measures to save or sustain life [check for local meaning])
DNR-CC	see DNRCC
DNRCCA	see DNRCC-A
DNRCC-A	do not resuscitate comfort care-arrest (a person receives all measures of medical care to sustain life up to the time of until the time he or she experiences a cardiac or respiratory arrest and then cardiopulmonary resuscitation is not initiated [check for local meaning])
DNR CCA	see DNRCC-A
DNR-CCA	see DNRCC-A
DNRDNI	do not resuscitate, do not intubate (check for local meaning)
DNR DNI	do not resuscitate, do not intubate (check for local meaning)
DNR/DNI	do not resuscitate, do not intubate (check for local meaning)
DNRI	dopamine and norepinephrine reuptake inhibitor
DNRO	do not resuscitate order
DNRP	Danish National Registry of Patients
DNR-P	do not resuscitate (directive) signed by patient (check for local meaning)
DNR-S	do not resuscitate (directive) signed by surrogate (check for local meaning)
dnrS	see gene website www.ncbi.nlm.nih.gov/gene
DNS	deviated nasal septum
	Director of Nursing Services
	do not show
	doctor did not see patient
	Doctorate, Nursing Science
	dysplastic nevus syndrome

D_5 1/4NS	dextrose 5% in 1/4 normal saline (0.225% sodium chloride) injection
D5 1/2 NS	dextrose 5% in 0.45% sodium chloride inj (NS = normal saline solution which is 0.9% sodium chloride solution)
D5NS	dextrose 5% in 0.9% sodium chloride injection
	dextrose 5% in 0.9% sodium chloride (normal saline) injection
D5 NS	dextrose 5% in 0.9% sodium chloride (normal saline) injection
D_5NS	5% dextrose in normal saline (0.9% sodium chloride) injection
DNSE	daptomycin-nonsusceptible Enterococcus
DNSTL	desmoplastic nested spindle cell tumor of liver
DNT	did not test
	dysembryoplastic neuroepithelial tumor
DNU	diabetic neuropathic ulcer(s)
	do not use
DNUA	do not use abbreviations
DNV	Det Norske Veritas (certifying organization)
DNVI	distal neurovascular intact
DNW	did not wait
DO	detrusor overactivity
	diet order
	dissolved oxygen
	distocclusal
	distraction osteogenesis
	Doctor of Osteopathy
	doctor's order
	Dombrock; an International Society of Blood Transfusion (ISBT) blood group
D/O	day(s) old
	disorder
	see DO
✓DO	check doctor's order
DO₂	oxygen delivery
D.O.	see DO
DOA	date of admission
	dead on arrival
	dilate on arrival
	dominant optic atrophy
	driver of automobile
	duration of action
DOAC	direct oral anticoagulant(s) (dabigatran [Pradaxa], rivaroxaban [Xalreto], apixaban [Eliquis])

DOACs	direct oral anticoagulants (dabigatran [Pradaxa], rivaroxaban [Xalreto], apixaban [Eliquis])
DOA-DRA	dead on arrival despite resuscitative attempts
DOAJ	directory of open access journals
DOB	dangle out of bed
	date of birth
	Dobrava hantavirus
	dobutamine
	doctor's order book
Dobbhoff (Dobhoff tube)	a weighted, small-bore, flexible nasogastric tube having several standard depth markings (There is no general agreement as to whether the correct spelling is Dobhoff or Dobbhoff, among medical dictionaries and medical writers, although "Dobbhoff" is the registered trademark of Sherwood Services AG. The tube was named after two Drs. Dobbie and Hoffmeister)
Dobhoff tube	see Dobbhoff
DOC	date of conception
	Department of Corrections
	diabetes out of control
	died of other causes
	diet of choice
	disorders of consciousness
	docetaxel (Taxotere)
	drug of choice
	Drug Optimization Clinic
DOCA	deoxycorticosterone acetate
DOCP	deoxycorticosterone pivalate
DOCS	Dimensional Obsessive-Compulsive Scale
	disorders of consciousness
	Disorders of Consciousness Scale
docs	doctors
DOD	date of death
	dead of disease
	drug overdose
DoD	Department of Defense
Δ OD 450	deviation of optical density at 450
DODD	demand oxygen delivery device
DODTR	Department of Defense Trauma Registry
DOE	date of examination
	degree of enhancement
	Department of Energy
	Design of Experiments
	disease-oriented evidence
	dyspnea on exertion
DOES	disorders of excessive somnolence
DoF	degree(s) of freedom
	depth of field
	depth of focus
doff	to take off
DOG	delay of gratification
	delusions of grandeur
DOG1	a highly-sensitive marker often included in the immuno-histochemical panel for the diagnosis of gastrointestinal stromal tumors
DOH	Department of Health
DOI	date of implant (pacemaker)
	date of injury
	digital object identifier
DO₂I	oxygen delivery index
DOJ	Department of Justice
Dok	see gene website, www.ncbi.nlm.nih.gov/gene
DOL	days of life
DOL #2	second day of life
DOLV	double-outlet left ventricle
DOM	dissolved organic matter
	Doctor of Oriental Medicine
	domiciliary
	domiciliary care
DOMS	delayed-onset muscle soreness
DON	Director of Nursing
	donepezil HCl (Aricept)
	dysthyroid optic neuropathy
DONFL	dissociated optic nerve fiber layer
DOOC	diabetes out of control
DOOR	deafness, onychodystrophy, osteodystrophy, and mental retardation (syndrome)
DOP	degenerate oligonucleotide-primed
	delta-opioid peptide (receptors)
	dopamine
DOPAC	dihydroxyphenylacetic acid
DOPL	differential optical path loss
	Division of Occupational and Professional Licensing
Dopplar	may have meant Doppler
DOPS	diffuse obstructive pulmonary syndrome
	dihydroxyphenylserine
	Director of Pharmacy Service(s)
Doptone	a hand-held, portable ultrasound tool used for fetal monitoring
DOQI	Disease Outcomes Quality Initiative; as in K/DOQI (National Kidney Foundation Kidney Disease Outcomes Quality Initiative [guidelines])

DOR date of release
diminished ovarian reserve
duration of response
DORs delta opioid receptors
diagnostic odd ratios (the ratio of
the odds of the test being positive if the subject has a disease
relative to the odds of the test
being positive if the subject
does not have the disease)
DORV double-outlet right ventricle
DORx date of treatment
DOS date of service
date of surgery
dead on scene
doctor's order sheet
DOSA day of surgery admission
DOSAK Central Tumor Registry operated
by the German-Austrian-
Swiss Association for Head
and Neck Tumors
Dosepak a customizable medication
package that improves medication adherence by present-
ing important information in
a readable format on the outer
carton and delivering pills in
a calendared blister
DOSS docusate sodium (dioctyl
sodium sulfosuccinate)
DOST direct oocyte-sperm transfer
DOT date of transcription
date of transfer
days of therapy
died on table
directly observed therapy
Directory of Occupational Titles
Doppler ophthalmic test
dotatate lutetium Lu 177 dotatate inj
(a Lu-177-labeled
somatostatin analogue
peptide [Lutathera])
DOTS directly observed treatment,
short course
Doughnut computed tomography (CT)
scanner (slang)
doula a word of Greek origin for a
trained professional who provi-
des nonmedical support before,
during, or after childbirth
DOV date of visit
distribution of ventilation
DOW days of the week
discharge order written
DOWB Days of the Week Backward
(cognitive assessment)
DOX doxepin
doxorubicin (Adriamycin)

DOXY doxycycline
doz dozen
DP days postburn
dental prosthesis
depersonalization
diastolic pressure
dietary patterns
disability pension
discharge planning
disease progression
docetaxel; cisplatin
dorsalis pedis (pulse)
D/P dialysate-to-plasma ratio
DPA Department of Public Assistance
dipropylacetic acid
D-penicillamine (penicillamine;
Cuprimine)
dual photon absorptiometry
durable power of attorney
DPAC digital papillary adenocarcinoma
ductal pancreatic adenocarcinoma
ductopapillary apocrine
carcinoma
DPACE dexamethasone, cisplatin
(Platinol), doxorubicin
(Adriamycin), cyclophosphamide, and etoposide
D-Pace a company that designs and
manufactures high perfor-
mance, negative ion sources
for particle accelerators
dexamethasone 40 mg orally
daily for 4 d and a 4-d (day)
continuous infusion of cisplatin (Platinol) 10 mg/m2/d,
doxorubicin (Adriamycin)
10 mg/m2/d, cyclophos-
phamide 400 mg/m2/d, and
etoposide (40 mg/ m2/d)
administered every 4–6 weeks
DPAH familial pulmonary (arterial)
hypertension
DPAHC durable power of attorney for
health care
DPAP diastolic pulmonary artery
pressure
DPAT as in 8-Hydroxy-2-(di-n-propyl-
amino)tetralin (8-OH-DPAT)
DPB days postburn
diffuse panbronchiolitis
dorsal penile block
DPBS Dulbecco phosphate-buffered
saline
DPC delayed primary closure
discharge planning coordinator
distal palmar crease
DPCA Diabetes Prevention and Control
Alliance

dPCA	dihedral principle component analysis			dorsal posterior mesencephalic tegmentum
DPCP	diphenylcyclopropenone (diphencyprone)		DPN	deep peroneal nerve dermatosis papulosa nigra
dPCR	digital polymerase chain reaction			diabetic peripheral neuropathy
DPD	depersonalization disorder dihydropyrimidine			diabetic polyneuropathy diprenorphine
	dihydropyrimidine dehydrogenase		DPNB	dorsal penile nerve block
DPDL	diffuse poorly differentiated lymphocytic lymphoma		DPNP	diabetic peripheral neuropathic pain
DPDS	biphenyl diselenide disconnected pancreatic duct syndrome		DPNS	deep pharyngeal neuromuscular stimulation
DPDT	diphenyl ditelluride		DPNs	diabetic peripheral neuropathies
dP/dt	rate of rise of left ventricular pressure		DPOA	durable power of attorney
			DPOAE	distortion-product otoacoustic emission
DPE	Division of Pharmacovigilance and Epidemiology (FDA)		DPOAHC	durable power of attorney for health care
DPEJ	direct percutaneous endoscopic jejunostomy		DPOA-HC	durable power of attorney for healthcare for health care
dPET	dynamic positron emission tomography		DPOC	direct peroral cholangioscopy
DPF	docetaxel, cisplatin, and fluorouracil		DPOE	distortion product otoacoustic emission
2,3-DPG	2,3-diphosphoglyceric acid		DPP	Diabetes Prevention Program
DPGN	diffuse proliferative glomerulonephritis			dorsalis pedal pulse duration of positive pressure
DPH	Department of Public Health diphenhydramine (Benadryl)		DPP4	dipeptidyl peptidase IV
			DPP-IV	dipeptidyl peptidase IV
	Doctor of Public Health phenytoin (diphenylhydantoin; Dilantin)		DPPC	colfosceril palmitate (dipalmitoylphosphatidylcholine)
DPI	days postinfection		DPPE	tesmilifene (diethyl phenylmethyl phenoxy ethanamine)
	dietary protein intake Doppler perfusion index		DPP4I	dipeptidyl peptidase-4 inhibitors (gliptins such as Januvia,
	drug package insert dry powder for inhalation			Onglyza, Nesina, and Tradjenta)
	dry-powder inhaler		DPP4i	dipeptidyl peptidase-4 inhibitors
dpi-1	protein disulfide-isomerase 1 (gene)		DPP-4 inhibitors	dipeptidyl peptidase-4 inhibitors (gliptins such as Januvia, Onglyza, Nesina, and
DPIL	dextrose (percentage), protein (grams per kilogram) Intralipid® (grams per kilogram)			Tradjenta)
			DPPM	defective parts per million
			dppm	1,1-Bis(diphenylphosphino) methane (a chelating ligand)
DPIV	digital particle image velocimetry			bis(diphenylphosphino)methane
DPJ	dislocation of prosthetic joint		DPPT	Deep Pressure and Proprioceptive Technique (a brushing tech-
DPL	diagnostic peritoneal lavage			nique and joint compressions
DPLD	diffuse parenchymal lung disease			to reduce sensory defensive-
D5PLM	dextrose 5% and Plasmalyte M® injection			ness in children) deoxypodophyllotoxin
DPM	distintegrations per minute (dpm)		DP/PT	dorsalis pedis artery and posterior tibial artery (pulses)
	Doctor of Podiatric Medicine drops per minute ductal plate malformation		DPPV	may have meant BPPV (benign paroxysmal positional vertigo)
DPMT	degenerate primer MOB (a classification for mobilization regions of bacterial plasmids) typing		DPPX	dipeptidyl-peptidase-like protein 6 (gene/protein)

DPR   Department of Professional Regulation

diagnostic procedure room

DPRB   dorsal penile ring block

DPRN   donor-positive, recipient-negative

DPS   diaphragm pacing stimulation

diaphragm pacing system

disintegration per second

distal pancreatectomy with splenectomy

dps   degrees per second

DPSI   Diabetes Problem-Solving Interview

DPSS   Department of Public Social Service

DPsy   Doctor of Psychology

DPT   Demerol, Phenergan, and Thorazine (this is a dangerous abbreviation)

diphtheria, pertussis, and tetanus (immunization)

Doctor of Physical Therapy

Driver Performance Test

dPT   dilute prothrombin time

DPTA   diethylene triamine pentaacetic acid

DPTM   direct patient tumor model

DPTPM   diphtheria, pertussis, tetanus, poliomyelitis, and measles

DPU   delayed pressure urticaria

DPUD   duodenal peptic ulcer disease

D-PUFA   deuterated (isotope-reinforced) polyunsaturated fatty acids

DPV   German/Austrian Diabetes Patienten Verlaufsdokumenation (documentation registry)

DPVSs   dilated perivascular spaces

DPW   days per week

Department of Public Welfare

DPWG   Dutch Pharmacogenetics Working Group

DPXA   dual-photon x-ray absorptiometry

DPYD   dihydropyrimidine dehydrogenase gene, (polymorphic enzyme variant responsible for the metabolism of a wide range of clinical drugs [capecitabine, fluorouracil, tegafur, etc.])

DQ   development quotients

D&Q   deep and quiet

DQ2   see gene website www.ncbi.nlm .nih.gov/gene

DQ5   Distress Questionnaire-5

DQ7   haplotype human leukocyte antigen(HLA)

DQA   Data Quality Audit

DQB   boLa class II histocompatibility antigen, DQB*0101 beta chain-like (gene)

DQE   detective quantum efficiency (radiology)

DQI   Diet Quality Index

DQM   data quality manager

DQOL   diabetes quality of life

DQOLS   Dermatology Quality of Life Scales

DQRS   Drug Quality Reporting System (FDA)

DR   delayed release

delivery room

diabetic retinopathy

diagnostic radiology

digital radiography

dining room

diurnal rhythm

drug resistant

human leukocyte antigen, type

Dr   doctor

dr   dram (see dram)

DR4   death receptors 4

DRA   Deficit Reduction Act of 2005

distal rectal adenocarcinoma

drug-related admissions

DRAF   diastolic retrograde arterial flow

Draf   an endoscopic frontal recess surgical approach

DRAM   damage-regulated autophagy modulator

Distress and Risk Assessment Method

dram   a unit of measure (one dram equals about 3.7 mL, or about 3.89 grams, and teaspoonful). This apothecary system unit of measure should never be used as it is not understood by today's health professionals. Use milliliters (mL), grams (g), or teaspoonful (5 mL)

DRAMs   drug resistance-associated mutations

DRAPE   drug-related adverse patient event

DRBA   dopamine receptor blocking agent(s)

DRBAs   dopamine receptor blocking agents

DRC   dose-response curve

dRCA   distal right coronary artery

DRD   dopa-responsive dystonia

DRD1 (also 2-5)   see gene website, www.ncbi .nlm.nih.gov/gene

DRDs   drugs-related deaths

D

DRE	digital rectal examination	DRRTP	Domiciliary Residential
	Drug Recognition Expert (for		Rehabilitation Treatment
	detection of impaired drivers)		Program ((Department of
	drug-resistant epilepsy		Veterans Affairs)
DREAM	downstream regulatory element	DRS	Delirium Rating Scale
	antagonistic modulator (gene)		designated record set
DREEM	Dundee Ready Education		Disability Rating Scale
	Environment Measurement		disease-related symptoms
DRESS	depth resolved surface coil		Duanes retraction syndrome
	spectroscopy	DRSG	dressing
DRESS	drug reaction with eosinophilia	DRSI	disease-related symptom
syndrome	and systemic symptoms		improvement
	syndrome	DRSP	drospirenone
DREZ	dorsal root entry zone		drug-resistant *Streptococcus*
DRF	dialysis-dependent renal failure		*pneumoniae*
	differential renal function	DRS-R98	Delirium Rating Scale-
	distal radius fracture		Revised-98
DRFx	distal radius fracture	DRT	drug-related thrombocytopenia
DRG	diagnosis-related groups	DrTPar	diphtheria toxoid (reduced
	dorsal root ganglia		antigen quantity for adults),
DRGE	drainage		tetanus toxoid, and acellular
DRGS	dorsal root ganglion stimulation		pertussis (reduced antigen
DRGs	diagnosis-related groups		quantity for adults) vaccine,
DRH	Division of Reproductive Health		for adult use
	(CDC)	DRUB	drug screen-blood
DRHF	decompensated right heart failure	DRUJ	distal radioulnar joint
DRI	defibrillation response interval	dRVVT	dilute Russell viper venom time
	Dietary Reference Intakes		(test)
	Disability Rating Index	dRWT	may have meant dRVVT
	Discharge Readiness Index		(dilute Russell viper venom
	dopamine reuptake inhibitor		time)
DRIL	distal revascularization internal	DRZ	dexrazoxane (Zinecard)
	ligation	DS	deep sleep
DRIP	Diagnostic Radiological Index		degenerative spondylolisthesis
	of Protection		diaphragmatic surgery
DRJ	Disaster Recovery Journal		dietary supplement
DRL	distal residual limb(s)		discharge summary
DRLs	diagnostic reference levels		disoriented
	(radiology)		distant supervision
DRM	drug-related morbidity		double strength
DRN	dorsal raphe nucleus		double-stapled (suture)
	drug-related neutropenia		Down syndrome
DRNG	may have meant drug		Dravet syndrome
DROM	dorsiflexion range of motion		drug screen
	dynamic range of motion	Ds	darmstadtium
DrotAA	drotrecogin alfa (activated)	D&S	diagnostic and surgical
	(Xigris)		dilation and suction
DRP	data review plan	D/S	5% dextrose and 0.9% sodium
	drug-related problem		chloride (saline) injection
DRPLA	dentatorubral-pallidolluysian		ratio of diastolic to systolic
	atrophy		duration
DRPN	diabetic radiculoplexus	%DS	percent diameter stenosis
	neuropathy	D5S	dextrose 5% in 0.9% sodium
DRPn	drug-resistant *Streptococcus*		chloride (saline) injection
	pneumoniae	D$_5$-1/2S	5% dextrose in 0.45% sodium
DRR	digitally reconstructed		chloride (saline) injection
	radiography	18Ds	Special Operations Forces
	drug regimen review		medics

DSA	digital subtraction angiography (angiocardiography)	DSIR	Designer of Small Interfering RNA (ribonucleic acid)
	Donor Sperm Archive	DSL	desaturated lecithin
	donor-specific antibody	DSM	Dead Sea mud
DSAEK	Descemet stripping automated endothelial keratoplasty		death and serious morbidity delayed systolic murmur
DSAP	disseminated superficial actinic porokeratosis		disease state management drink skim milk
dSAT	deep subcutaneous adipose tissue	DSM-4	Diagnostic and Statistical
DSB	drug-seeking behavior		Manual of Mental Disorders
DSBs	double-strand (DNA) breaks		4th Edition
DSC	Day Surgery Center	DSM-5	Diagnostic and Statistical
	differential scanning calorimeter		Manual of Mental Disorders
	Disease-Specific Care (Certification; The Joint Commission)	DSM IV	5th Edition Diagnostic and Statistical Manual of Mental Disorders
	Down syndrome child		4th Edition
	dynamic susceptibility contrast	DSM-IV-TR	Diagnostic and Statistical
DScD	Doctor of Science in Dentistry		Manual of Mental Disorders
DSCSA	Drug Supply Chain Security Act		4th Edition - Text Revision
DSD	degenerative spinal disease	DSM-V	Diagnostic and Statistical
	detrusor sphincter dyssynergia		Manual of Mental Disorders
	diaphanospondylodysostosis		5th Edition
	digital selenium drum (radiology)	dSMA	distal spinal muscular atrophy
	discharge summary dictated	DSMB	Data and Safety Monitoring
	disorders of sexual development		Board
	dry sterile dressing	DSMC	Data Safety and Monitoring
DSDB	direct self-destructive behavior		Committee
DSDH	double stranded, intertwined double helix	DSME	Diabetes Self Management Education
ds DNA	double-stranded deoxyribonucleic acid	DSML	Directory Service Markup Language
DSE	dobutamine stress echocardiography	DSMOs	Designated Standard Maintenance Organizations
DSEAK	see DSAEK	DSMS	Diabetes Self-Management
DSEK	Descemet stripping endothelial keratoplasty	DSMs	Support degradable starch microspheres
DSF	differential scanning fluorometry		Diagnostic and Statistical Manuals
	doxorubicin, streptozocin, and fluorouracil		dose-surface maps (radiotherapy) dural sinus malformations
DSG	deoxyspergualin	DSMT	Diabetes Self Management
	desogestrel		Training
	dressing	DSN	Dialysis Surveillance Network
DSG1	desmoglein 1 (gene)		(CDC)
DSH	deliberate self-harm	DSO	distal subungual onychomycosis
DSHEA	Dietary Supplement Health and Education Act of 1994	DSP	Dexcom Seven Plus (a continuous blood glucose monitoring
DSHF	decompensated systolic heart failure		device) diabetic sensorimotor
DSHR	delayed skin hypersensitivity reaction		polyneuropathy digital signal processor
DSHS	Department of Social and Health Services		disseminated superficial porokeratosis
DSI	deep shock insulin		distal symmetrical polyneuropathy
	Depression Status Inventory	DSPC	distearoylphosphatidyl choline
	diffusion spectrum imaging	DSPD	dangerous severe personality
	dysphonia severity index		disorder
DSIAR	double-stapled ileoanal reservoir	D-SPINE	dorsal spine

DSPN	diabetic sensorimotor polyneuropathy	DSVP	Dietary Supplement Verification Program (United States Pharmacopeia purity compliance)
	distal sensory polyneuropathy		
	distal symmetric polyneuropathy	DSW	Doctorate in Social Work
DSPS	delayed sleep phase syndrome	DSWI	deep sternal wound infection
DSRCT	desmoplastic small round cell tumor		deep surgical wound infection
		DSX	dysmetabolic syndrome X
DSRF	drainage subretinal fluid	DT	deceleration time
DSRIP	Delivery System Reform Incentive Payment (Center for Medicare and Medicaid program to provide States the opportunity to innovate and transform their Medicaid programs)		delirium tremens
			diabetic teaching
			dietary thermogenesis
			dietetic technician
			diphtheria and tetanus toxoids, adsorbed, pediatric strength
dsRNA	double-sided deoxyribonucleic acid		discharge tomorrow
			docetaxel (Taxotere)
DSRS	distal splenorenal shunt		duplicate therapy
DSS	dengue shock syndrome	D&T	diagnosis and treatment
	Department of Social Services		dictated and transcribed
	Disability Status Scale	D/T	date/time
	discharge summary sheet		due to (a phrase meaning- as a result of; caused by; ascribable to; because of)
	disease-specific survival		
	distal splenorenal shunt		
	docusate sodium (dioctyl sodium sulfosuccinate)	DT1	diabetes type 1
		DT2	diabetes type 2
	double simultaneous stimulation (a method of testing afferent visual, somatosensory, and auditory pathways for signs of unilateral brain damage)	d4T	stavudine (Zerit)
		DTA	descending thoracic aneurysm
		DTAA	descending thoracic aortic aneurysm
		DTAB	dodecyl trimethylammonium bromide (a cationic surfactant)
dSSc	diffuse systemic sclerosis		
DSSD/T	dominant sigmoid sinus with dehiscence or thinning	DTAD	drain tube attachment device
		DT's	delirium tremens
DSSLR	double, seated straight leg raise	d-tag	d-tagatose
DSSN	distal symmetric sensory neuropathy	DTaP	Diphtheria toxoid, tetanus toxoid, and acellular pertussis vaccine, adsorbed (Daptacel, Infanrix, and Tripedia for active immunization for infants and children under the age of 7 years)
DSSP	distal symmetric sensory polyneuropathy		
DSST	Digit-Symbol Substitution Test		
DST	daylight saving time		
	dexamethasone suppression test		
	digit substitution test	DTaP-IPV-HB-PRP-T	hexavalent diphtheria (D)-tetanus (T)-acellular pertussis (aP)-inactivated poliovirus (IPV)-hepatitis B (HB)-Haemophilus influenzae type b (PRP-T) vaccine (indicated for primary and booster vaccination of infants and toddlers against diphtheria, tetanus, pertussis, hepatitis B, poliomyelitis and invasive diseases caused by Haemophilus influenzae type b)
	dobutamine stress test		
	donor-specific (blood) transfusion		
	drug-susceptibility testing		
D-Stick	See D-Stix (Dextrostix)		
D-Stix	Dextrostix		
DSTO	dog smarter than owner (Veterinary slang)		
DSU	day stay unit		
	day surgery unit		
DSUH	direct suggestion under hypnosis		
D/Sum	discharge summary		
DSUR	Development Safety Update Report	DTAR	descending thoracic aneurysm repair
DSV	digital subtraction ventriculography		descending thoracic aortic rupture
	domestic and/or sexual violence		direct thoracic aortic repair

DTB	deutetrabenazine	DTO	danger to others
	distance-to-break		deodorized tincture of opium
	door-to-balloon (time)		(warning: this is *NOT*
DTBC	tubocurarine (D-tubocurarine)		paregoric)
DTBE	Division of Tuberculosis	DTOGV	dextral-transposition of great
	Elimination		vessels
DTC	day treatment center	DTP	differential time to positivity
	diabetes treatment center		(time necessary for the blood
	differentiated thyroid cancer		cultures from the central
	direct-to-consumer (advertising)		venous catheter and the pe-
	disseminated tumor cells		ripheral vein to become posi-
	diticarb (diethyldiothio-		tive, as well as other relevant
	carbamate)		patient information)
	tubocurarine (D-tubocurarine)		diphtheria, tetanus toxoids,
DTCA	direct-to-consumer advertising		pertussis (antigens unspeci-
DTCP	Donation and Transplantation		fied) vaccine
	Community of Practice		distal tingling on percussion
DTD	developmental topographical	DTP3	diphtheria, tetanus and pertussis
	disorientation		vaccine
	developmental trauma disorder	DTPa	diphtheria toxoid, tetanus
	diastrophic dysplasia		toxoid, and acellular pertus-
DTD #30	dispense 30 such doses		sise vaccine, for pediatric use
DTE	deceleration time of E wave	DTPA	pentetic acid (diethylenetriamine-
	desmoplastic trichoepithelioma		penta acetic acid)
	door-to-electrocardiogram (time)	DTPa-HIB	diphtheria toxoid, tetanus toxoid,
	Doppler tissue echocardiograph		and acellular pertussis, and
DTF	deep transverse friction		*Haemophilus influenzae*
	Dental Treatment Facility		type b conjugate vaccine
DTFM	deep transverse friction massage	DTPa-HIB-IPV	diphtheria toxoid, tetanus
DTG	dolutegravir (Tivicay)		toxoid, and acellular per-
DTGA	dental treatment under general		tussis, and *Haemophilus*
	anesthesia		*influenzae* type b conjugate,
dTGA	dextrotransposition of the great		and poliovirus inactivated
	arteries		vaccine
DTH	delayed-type hypersensitivity	DTPI	dual-time-point imaging
DTI	deep tissue injury	DTPI PET/CT	dual-time-point-imaging positron
	Department of Trade and		emission tomography/
	Industry (United Kingdom)		computed tomography
	diffusion-tensor imaging	DTP$_w$	diphtheria, tetanus toxoids,
	direct thrombin inhibitor		whole-cell pertussis vaccine
	Doppler tissue imaging	DTR	Dance Therapist, Registered
DTIC	dacarbazine (DTIC-Dome)		deep tendon reflexes
D TIME	dream time		Dietetic Technician Registered
DTIs	direct thrombin inhibitors	dtr	daughter
DTL	Dawson-Trick-Litzkow (fiber	DTR's	see DTR
	electrodes)	DTRAX	a posterior cervical expandable
	denticleless protein homolog;		cage (Providence Medical
	see gene website www.ncbi		Technology, Lafayette,
	.nlm.nih.gov/gene		California, United States)
	dominant temporal lobe	DTRS	dominant torso rotational strength
DT LVAD	destination therapy left	DTRs	deep tendon reflexes
	ventricular assist device		Dietetic Technicians, Registered
DTM	deep tissue massage		dynamic treatment regimes
	dermatophyte test medium	DTS	danger to self
DTMS	drug therapy management service		Delirium Triage Screen
dTMS	deep transcranial magnetic		digital tomosynthesis
	stimulation		donor specific transfusion
DTN	door-to-needle (time)		dopaminergic treatment state

DTs	delirium tremens	D&UE	dilation and uterine evacuation
3D TSE	three-dimensional turbo-spin echo (images)	DUF	Doppler ultrasonic flowmeter
DTSQ	Diabetes Treatment Satisfaction Questionnaire	DUH	dyschromatosis universalis hereditaria
DTT	diffusion tensor tractography	DUI	driving under the influence
	diphtheria tetanus toxoid	DUID	driving under the influence of drugs
	dithiothreitol	DUII	driving under the influence of intoxicants
	double tunnels technique		
DTTP	deoxythymidine triphosphate	DUKM	dialysate urea kinetic modeling
	differential time to positivity (time necessary for the blood cultures from the central venous catheter and the peripheral vein to become positive, as well as other relevant patient information)	DUIL	driving under the influence of liquor
		DUM	drug use monitoring
		DUN	dialysate urea nitrogen
		DUNHL	diffuse undifferentiated non-Hodgkins lymphoma
		DUO	Duotube®
D tube	a weighted, small-bore, flexible nasogastric tube having several standard depth markings	duod	duodenal
		Duo Neb®	ipratropium bromide and albuterol inhalation
D-tube	a weighted, small-bore, flexible nasogastric tube having several standard depth markings	DUP	duration of untreated psychosis
		duplex scan	a noninvasive examination that uses high-frequency sound waves (ultrasound) to capture internal images of the major arteries in the arms, legs and neck
	duodenostomy tube		
DTUS	diathermy, traction, and ultrasound		
DTV	due to void		
DTVP	Developmental Test of Visual Perception	DUR	device utilization ratio
			drug utilization review
DTwP	diphtheria and tetanus toxoids with whole-cell pertussis vaccine		duration
		DUS	digital ultrasound
			distal urethral stenosis
DTX	detoxification		Doppler ultrasound stethoscope
	docetaxel (Taxotere)		duplex ultrasonography
DU	decubitus ulcer	3DUS	three-dimensional ultrasound
	demonstrates understanding	DUSN	diffuse unilateral subacute neuroretinitis
	depleted uranium		
	developmental unit	DUT	see gene website, www.ncbi .nlm.nih.gov/gene
	diabetic urine		
	diagnosis undetermined	DUV	deep ultraviolet
	dialysis unit	DUX4	double homeobox 4; see gene website; www.ncbi.nlm.nih .gov/gene
	duodenal ulcer		
	duroxide uptake		
DUAP	dorsoulnar artery perforator (flap)	DV	data verification
			distance vision
DUB	Dubowitz (score)		domestic violence
	dysfunctional uterine bleeding		double vision
DUBI	dysfunctional urinary bladder instability	D&V	diarrhea and vomiting
			disc and vessels
dUCBT	double umbilical cord blood transplantation		ductions and versions
		D-V	dorsal-ventral
DUCL	dorsal ulnocarpal ligament	DVA	Department of Veterans Affairs
DUD	dihydrouracil dehydrogenase		developmental venous anomaly
DUDIT-C	Drug Use Disorders Identification Test consumption questions		directional vacuum-assisted (biopsy)
DUE	drug use evaluation		distance visual acuity
	dual-mode ultrasound elastography		vindesine (Eldisine; desacetyl vinblastine amide sulfate)

DVB	divinylbenzene
DVC	direct visualization of vocal cords
	dorsal vagal complex
	dorsal venous complex
D V® Cream	dienestrol vaginal cream
DVD	digital video disc
	dissociated vertical deviation
	double-vessel disease
dve	see gene website www.ncbi.nlm.nih.gov/gene
DVET	double-volume exchange transfusion
DVF	displacement vector field
	divided visual field
DVG	double vein graft
DVH	dose-volume histogram
DVI	atrioventricular sequential pacing
	digital vascular imaging
	direct visual inspection
DVID	distributed, versioned, image-oriented dataservice
DVIU	direct vision internal urethrotomy
DVLA	Driver and Vehicle Licensing Agency (United Kingdom)
DVM	Doctor of Veterinary Medicine
DVMP	disks, vessels, and macula periphery
DVO	Dachverband Osteologie (German Osteology Society) (guidelines)
	distance vision only (glasses prescription)
DVP	digital volume pulse
	divalproex (Depakote)
dVP	da Vinci (robotic) prostatectomy
DVPA	daunorubicin, vincristine, prednisone, and asparaginase
DVPX	divalproex sodium (Depakote)
DVR	darunavir (Prezista)
	Division of Vocational Rehabilitation
	dose-volume relationship
	double-valve replacement
DVSA	digital venous subtraction angiography
DVST	dural venous sinus thrombosis
DVT	deep vein thrombosis
	digital volume tomography
DVTP	deep vein thrombophlebitis
DVTPE	venous thromboembolism and pulmonary embolism
DVT/PE	venous thromboembolism and pulmonary embolism
DVT PPX	deep venous thrombosis prophylaxis
DVTS	deep venous thromboscintigram

DVU	direct vision internal urethrotomy
	discovertebral units
DVVC	direct visualization of vocal cords
DVVT	diluted viper venom time (assay)
DW	daily wear (lens)
	daily weight
	deionized water
	detention warrant
	dextrose in water
	diffusion-weighted (imaging)
	distilled water
	doing well
	double wrap
	dry weight (hemodialysis)
D/W	also see DW
	dextrose in water
	discussed with
D-W	Dandy-Walker (deformity/malformation)
	Danis-Weber (classification for ankle fractures)
D5W	5% dextrose inj (5% dextrose in water inj)
D-5-W	5% dextrose inj (5% dextrose in water inj)
D$_5$W	5% dextrose (in water) injection
D10W	10% dextrose (in water) injection
D20W	20% dextrose (in water) injection
D50W	50% dextrose (in water) injection
D70W	70% dextrose (in water) injection
5 DW	5% dextrose (in water) injection
DWA	daily weighted average
	dynamic wave arc (radiation oncology)
DWC	Diabetic Wound Certification
DWD	died with disease
DWDA	Death with Dignity Act (Oregon and Montana)
DWDL	diffuse well-differentiated lymphocytic lymphoma
DWHP	disabling wrist/hand pain
DWI	diffusion-weighted (magnetic resonance) imaging
	driving while impaired
	driving while intoxicated
DWI-ADC	diffusion-weighted with apparent diffusion coefficient measure
DWI-ASPECTS	Diffusion-weighted Imaging Alberta Stroke Program Early Computed Tomography Score
DWI/PI	diffusion-weighted imaging/perfusion imaging

D

DWM	Dandy-Walker Malformation
DWMI	deep white-matter ischemia
	diffuse white-matter injury
DWMRI	diffusion-weighted magnetic
	resonance imaging
DWO	Delft-Westland-Oostland
	(a geographic region in the
	Netherlands)
	dual-wavelength overlapping
DwO	dieters with obesity
DWO-RRS	dual-wavelength overlapping
	resonance Rayleigh scattering
DWP	Department for Work and
	Pensions (UK)
	discussed with patient
	Doppler waveform patterns
	dose-width product (dental)
DWR	deep water running
DWRT	delayed work recall test
DWSCL	daily-wear soft contact lens
DWSMB	Dean-Woodcock Sensory Motor
	Battery (measures of
	sensory-motor functioning)
DWT	discrete wavelet transform
	(a time-frequency tool,
	used in computer-aided
	signal analysis of epileptic
	electroencephalography)
DWV	Dandy-Walker variant
	(a congenital anomaly)
DWW	dynamic wall walk
Dx	diagnosis
	diagnostic evaluation
	disease
DXA	dual-energy x-ray absorptiometry
Dx'd	diagnosed
Dx'ed	diagnosed
DXD	deaf marrying deaf
Dxd	diagnosed
Dxed	diagnosed
DXG	dioxalane guanine
DxLS	diagnosis responsible for length
	of stay
DXM	dexamethasone
	dexmedetomidine (Precedex)
	dextromethorphan
DxMBB	diagnostic medial branch block
DXN	deaf marrying normal hearing
	dexamethasone
	doxorubicin
	DxN VERIS Molecular
	Diagnostics System integrates
	sample introduction, nucleic
	acid extraction, reaction
	setup, real-time polymerase
	chain reaction amplification
	and detection, and results
	interpretation into one system

DXP	diazepam (Valium)
DXR	delayed xenograft rejection
	digital X-ray radiogrammetry
	doxorubicin
DXRT	deep x-ray therapy
DXS	Dextrostix®
DXT	deep x-ray therapy
DY	dusky (infant color)
	dysprosium
D/y	diopter change per year
d/y	days per year
DYBOCS	Dimensional Yale-Brown
	Obsessive-Compulsive Scale
DYF	drag your feet (author's note:
	see you in court)
DYFS	Division of Youth and Family
	Services
DYN	dynamic
	dynorphin
dyne	a unit of force that, acting on a
	mass of one gram, increases
	its velocity by one centime-
	ter per second every second
	along the direction that it acts
DYRK1A	dual-specificity tyrosine-(Y)-
	phosphorylation regulated
	kinase 1A
Dys	dystrophinsee gene website
	www.ncbi.nlm.nih.gov/gene
dys	a prefix meaning difficult,
	impaired, abnormal, or bad
DysD	dysthymic disorder
DYSF	dysferlin; see gene website
	www.ncbi.nlm.nih.gov/gene
dysfn	dysfunction; dysfunctional
dysfnx	dysfunction; dysfunctional
dysfunc	dysfunctional; dysfunction
Dysfxn	dysfunction (dysfunctional)
dyslip	dyslipidemia
DYTRO	dynamic tone-reducing orthosis
DZ	diazepam (Valium)
	disease
	dizygotic
	dozen
DZP	diazepam
DZT	dizygotic twins
DZX	dexrazoxane (Zinecard)

E

E   East (as in the location e.g., 2E, would be second floor, East wing)
Echo (Phonetic Alphabet E; pronounced ECK-OH)
edema
effective
electronic
eloper
enema
energy
engorged
eosinophil
Escherichia
esophoria for distance
ethambutol [part of tuberculosis regimen as in RHZ (E/S)/HR]
evaluation
evening
expired
eye
methylenedioxymethamphetamine (MDMA; Ecstasy)

E′   elbow
esophoria for near

e-   electron

E₁   estrone

E₂   estradiol

E₃   estriol

4E   4 plus edema

E11   Echovirus 11
embryonic day 11 (11-day-old embryo)

E20   Enfamil 20®

EA   early amniocentesis
egg allergic
elbow aspiration
electroacoustic analysis
electroacupuncture
enteral alimentation
epidermolytic acanthoma
epidural anesthesia
episodic ataxia
esophageal atresia
European American

E/A   European-American

E&A   evaluate and advise

E → A   say E,E,E, comes out as A,A,A upon auscultation of lung showing consolidation

ea   each

EAA   electrothermal atomic absorption
epidural anaesthesia and analgesia
essential amino acids
extrinsic allergic alveolitis

EAB   elective abortion
Ethical Advisory Board

EABR   evoked auditory brainstem response

EABV   effective arterial blood volume

EAC   endometrial adenocarcinoma
erythema annulare centrifugum
esophageal adenocarcinoma
external auditory canal

EACA   aminocaproic acid (epsilon-aminocaproic acid)
esophageal adenocarcinoma

EACs   esophageal adenocarcinomas
external auditory canals

EADL   extended activities of daily living

EADM   adverse event dose modification

EADs   early after-depolarizations

EAE   experimental allergic encephalomyelitis
experimental autoimmune encephalomyelitis

EAEC   enteroaggregative *Escherichia coli*

EAF   enteroatmospheric fistula
eosinophilic angiocentric fibrosis

eAG   estimated average glucose

EAggEC   enteroaggregative *Escherichia coli*

EAH   eating in the absence of hunger

EAHF   eczema, allergy, and hay fever

EAI   East-African Indian
endometriosis-associated infertility
epinephrine auto-injector(s)
erythema ab igne
Exercise Addiction Inventory

EAL   electronic artificial larynx

EAM   electroanatomic activation mapping
external auditory meatus

eAMD   exudative age-related macular degeneration

EAN   effective atomic number
ethylammonium nitrate
experimental autoimmune neuritis

E and M   see E&M

EAP   Early Access Program (premarketing use of drug)
Employment (Employee) Assistance Programs
erythrocyte acid phosphatase
etoposide, doxorubicin (Adriamycin), and cisplatin (Platinol)

EAPG   extra-adrenal paraganglioma

EAPM   endoscope-assisted partial mastectomy

E

E-App	electronic application	EBAM	Experience Based Access Management (electronic medical records)
EAR	estimated average requirement excess absolute risk		
E/A ratio	a marker of the function of the left ventricle representing the ratio of peak velocity blood flow from gravity in early diastole (the E wave) to peak velocity flow in late diastole caused by atrial contraction (the A wave). It is calculated using echocardiography	EBAR	European Biliary Atresia Registry examiner-based assessment of reliability (scoring system)
		EBB	electron beam boosts equal breath bilaterally
		EBBS	equal bilateral breath sounds
		EBBx	endobronchial biopsy
		EBC	early (stage) breast cancer endocrine-responsive breast cancer endoscopic brush cytology esophageal balloon catheter exhaled breath condensate
EARLIES	early decelerations		
EAR OX	ear oximetry		
EART	extended abdominal radiation therapy		
EAS	external anal sphincter	EBCPGs	evidence-based clinical practice guidelines
EASA	electrochemically assisted self-assembly European Aviation Safety Agency	EBCT	electron-beam computed tomography
EASC	endoscopic ambulatory surgery center	EBCTCG	Early Breast Cancer Trialists' Collaborative Group
EASE	Estimation and Assessment of Substance Exposure (model)	EBD	endocardial border delineation endoscopic balloon dilation evidence-based decision (making) evidence-based dentistry
EASI	Eczema Area and Severity Index extra-amniotic saline infusion		
EAST	external rotation, abduction stress test	EBE	equal bilateral expansion
		EBEA	Epstein-Barr (virus) early antigen
EAT	Eating Attitudes Test ectopic atrial tachycardia epicardial adipose tissue	EBER	Epstein-Barr virus-encoded RNA (ribonucleic acid)
		EBES	endobronchial electrosurgery
EATEF	esophageal atresia with tracheoesophageal fistula	EBF	erythroblastosis fetalis exclusive breastfeeding
EA/TEF	esophageal atresia with tracheoesophageal fistula	EBG	evidence-based practice guidelines
EATL	enteropathy-associated T-cell lymphoma	EBH	evidence-based healthcare expiration breath-hold
EAU	experimental autoimmune uveitis	EBI	early brain injury European Bioinformatics Institute
EAUS	endoanal ultrasound	EBIs	evidence-based interventions
EAV	equine arteritis virus	EBL	endoscopic band ligation endoscopic brow-lift estimated blood loss
e3AVB	episodic third-degree atrioventricular block		
EAVR	early anti-viral response may have meant EVAR (endovascular aneurysm repair)	EBL-1	European bat lyssavirus 1
		EBLA	expected blood loss anemia
		EBLP	evidence-based laboratory practice
eAVR	elective aortic valve replacement	EBLs	elevated blood lead levels
EB	eosinophilic bronchitis epidermolysis bullosa Epstein-Barr (virus) Evans Blue	EBLT	endobronchial laser therapy
		EBM	evidence-based medical education evidence-based medicine expressed breast milk
EB1	end-binding protein 1	EBMD	epithelial basement membrane dystrophy
EB2	end-binding protein 2 Epstein-Barr virus protein 2		
		EBMIL	excess body mass index loss
EB3	end-binding protein 3	%EBMIL	percentage excess body mass index loss
EBA	enamel bonding agent epidermolysis bullosa acquisita expanded bed adsorption	EBMT	European Bone Marrow Transplant (registry group)

EBNA	Epstein-Barr (virus) nuclear antigen		emergency contraception
EBO	evidence-based outcomes		endocervical
eboost	electron boost		endometrial cancer
EBOS	early-onset benign occipital seizure		energy conservation
			enteric coated
EBOV	Ebola virus		Environment of Care (The Joint Commission)
EBO-Z	Ebola Zaire virus		epirubicin and cyclophosphamide
EBP	electric breast pump		*Escherichia coli*
	epidural blood patch		esophageal candidiasis
	evidence-based practice		esophageal carcinoma
EBPG/ERBP	European Best Practice Guidelines/European Renal Best Practice		ethics committee
			etopside and carboplatin
			European Community
EBPM	event-based prospective memory		extracellular
EBR	external beam radiotherapy		eye care
	eye-blink rate		eyes closed
EBRA-FCA	Ein Bild Roentgen Analyse-femoral component analysis	E_2C	estradiol cypionate
		E&C	education and counseling
EBRs	evidence-based recommendations		evacuation and curettage
EBRT	external beam radiation therapy	EC50	the concentration of a drug, antibody, or toxicant that gives half-maximal response
EBRTx	external beam radiotherapy		
EBS	empiric Bayesian screening		
	epidermolysis bullosa simplex	ECA	enteric coated aspirin (tablets)
EBSB	equal breath sounds bilaterally		Epidemiological Catchment Area
EBSL	may have meant ESBL (extended spectrum beta-lactamase)		ethacrynic acid (Edecrin)
			external carotid artery
EBT	electron beam tomography	ECAD	extracorporeal albumin dialysis
	erythromycin breath test	eCAM	electronic Compilation of Analytical Methods
EBUS	endobronchial ultrasonography (ultrasound)		
		e-CAM	electronic Compilation of Analytical Methods
	endobronchial ultrasound		
EBUS-FNA	endobronchial ultrasound-guided fine-needle aspiration	ECASA	enteric coated aspirin (tablets)
		ECAT	elemental carbon attributable to traffic
EBUS-TBNA	endobronchial ultrasound-guided transbronchial needle aspiration		
		ECAT EXACT HR	a high-resolution positron emission tomography (PET) scanner (CTI/Siemens, Knoxville, TN, USA)
EBUS-TFNA	endobronchial ultrasound-guided transbronchial fine-needle aspiration		
EBV	Epstein-Barr virus		
EBVCA	Epstein-Barr viral capsid antigen	ECBD	exploration of common bile duct
		eCBL	Escherichia coli cystathionine beta-lyase
EBVEA	Epstein-Barr virus, early antigen		
EBVNA	Epstein-Barr virus, nuclear antigen	ECBO	enterocytopathogenic bovine orphan (virus)
EBV PCR	Epstein-Barr virus polymerase chain reaction (assay)	ECBU	examen cytobacteriologique des urines (urine culture)
EBVR	Epstein-Barr virus receptor	ECC	early childhood caries
EBVS	electrothermal bipolar vessel sealing		edema, clubbing, and cyanosis
			embryonal cell cancer
EBW	estimated body weight		emergency cardiac care
EBWL	excess body weight loss		Emergency Communications Center
EBx	endometrial biopsy		
EC	ejection click		endocervical curettage
	electric cigarettes		external cardiac compression
	electrical cardioversion		extracorporeal circulation
	electrocautery	eCC	estimated creatinine clearance
	emergency center	E/C/C	edema, clubbing, and cyanosis

eCCC	extrahepatic cholangiocarcinoma	ECHMO	may have been misheard for ECMO (extracorporeal membrane oxygenation)
ECCE	extracapsular cataract extraction		
ecchy	ecchymosis	ECHO	echocardiogram
ECCO	European Crohn's and Colitis Organization (guidelines)		enterocytopathogenic human orphan (virus)
ECD	E-cadherin		etoposide, cyclophosphamide, doxorubicin (hydroxydaunomycin), and vincristine (Oncovin)
	electron capture dissociation		
	endocardial cushion defect		
	equivalent current dipole		
	Erdheim-Chester disease	Echo	Phonetic Alphabet for E; pronounced ECK-OH
	expanded criteria donors		
	extracellular domain	ECHO (2D)	echocardiogram (2-dimensional)
E-CD	E-cadherin	EChoG	electrocochleography
ECDB	encourage to cough and deep breathe	ECHO/RV	echocardiography/radionuclide ventriculography
ECDC	European Centre for Disease Prevention and Control	ECHOs	echocardiographs
		ECI	early childhood intervention
ECDPC	European Centre for Disease Prevention and Control		extracorporeal irradiation
		ECIB	extracorporeal irradiation of blood
ECDs	electronic control devices		
ECE	endothelin-converting enzyme	ECIC	external carotid and internal carotid
	extracapsular extension		
ECEMC	Grupo de Trabajo del Estudio Colaborativo Español de Malformaciones Congènitas (Spanish Collaborative Study of Congenital Malformations)		external cortex of the inferior colliculus
			extracranial to intracranial (anastamosis)
		EC-IC	extracranial-intracranial (bypass surgery)
ECEMG	evoked compound electromyography		
		ECID	European Centre for Infectious Disease
ECEP	Early Childhood Evaluation Program		
		e-Cigarette	electronic-cigarette
ECF	enterocutaneous fistula	ECIN	exposed cases impact number
	epirubicin, cisplatin, and fluorouracil	ECK1	*Escherichia coli* K1
		ECL	electrochemiluminescence
	extended care facility		enterochromaffin-like
	extracardiac Fontan (procedure)		extend of cerebral lesion
	extracellular fluid		extracapillary lesions
ECF-A	eosinophil chemotactic factors of anaphylaxis	ECLA	extracorporeal lung assist
		ECLIA	electrochemilimunescence immunoassay
EC fistula	enterocutaneous fistula		
E/C/F/TAF	Genvoya, a tablet containing elvitegravir 150 mg, cobicistat 150 mg, emtricitabine 200 mg (FTC [beta-L-2',3'-dideoxy-5-fluoro-3'-thiacytidine]), and tenofovir alafenamide 10 mg	ECLP	extracorporeal liver perfusion
		ECLS	extracorporeal life support
		ECM	endoscopic cautery marking
			erythema chronicum migrans
			esophagocardiomyotomy
			extracellular mass
			extracellular matrix
E/C/F/TDF	Stribild, a tablet containing elvitegravir 150 mg, cobicistat 150 mg, emtricitabine 200 mg (FTC [beta-L-2',3'-dideoxy-5-fluoro-3'-thiacytidine]), and tenofovir disoproxil fumarate 300 mg	ECM/BCM	extracellular mass, body cell mass ratio
		ECMO	enterocytopathogenic monkey orphan (virus)
			extracorporeal membrane oxygenation
ECFV	extracellular fluid volume	ECN	extended care nursery
ECG	electrocardiogram	ecNOS	endothelial constitutive nitric oxide synthetase
ECGE	extracorporeal gas exchange		
ECGG	electrocardiogram glove	ECNU	Endocrine Certification in Neck Ultrasound
ECHINO	echinocyte		

ECochG	electrocochleography	ECR	emergency chemical restraint
ECOG	Eastern Cooperative Oncology Group		extensor carpi radialis
		e-CR	endoscopic complete response
ECoG	electrocochleography	E/C Ratio	estriol/creatinine ratio
	electrocorticogram	ECRB	extensor carpi radialis brevis
ECOG PS	Eastern Cooperative Oncology Group Performance Score (0 = perfect health, 1 = symptomatic but completely ambulatory, 2 = symptomatic, less than 50% in bed during the day, 3 = symptomatic, greater than 50% in bed, but not bedbound, 4 = bedbound (completely disabled), and 5 = death	eCrCl	estimated creatinine clearance
		eCRF	Electronic Case Report Form
		ECRI	Emergency Care Research Institute
		ECRL	extensor carpi radialis longus
		ECRMC	El Centro Regional Medical Center
		ECRP	endoscopic retrograde cholangiopancreatography
		ECS	elective cosmetic surgery
			electrocerebral silence
			endocannabinoid system
Ecoli	*Escherichia coli*		endometrial-cancer-specific
E coli	*Escherichia coli*		extracorporeal septoplasty
ECOM	endotracheal cardiac output monitor (endotracheal bioimpedance cardiography)	EC-SPM	electrochemical-scanning probe microscopy
		ECSs	elastic compression stockings
Ecom(50)	The determination of the center-of-mass energy at which 50% of a precursor ion decomposes during collision-induced dissociation	ECSW	extracorporeal shockwave
		ECSWL	extracorporeal shockwave lithotripsy
		ECT	ecarin clotting time
			electrochemotherapy
Econ	economic(s)		electroconvulsive therapy
ECOP	EGFR (epidermal growth factor receptor)-coamplified and overexpressed protein (gene/protein)		electroshock treatment
			emission computed tomography
			energy conservation training (occupational therapy to manage fatigue)
ECOs	embryonal carcinomas of the ovaries		enhanced computed tomography
ECOS-16	Assessment of health related quality of life in osteoporosis (questionnaire)	ECTA	extracapsular tonsillectomy and adenoidectomy
		ECTb	Emory Cardiac Toolbox
ECO$_{tox}$	*Escherichia coli* (heat-labile toxin) vaccine	EC-TCPC	extracardiac conduit total cavopulmonary connection
ECP	effective conduction period	eCTD	electronic Common Technical Document
	effusive constrictive pericarditis	ecto	a prefix meaning outside
	emergency care provider	ectomy	surgical removal of something, usually from inside the body (a suffix or word)
	emergency contraceptive pills		
	eosinophil cationic protein		
	external counterpulsation		
	extracorporeal photochemotherapy	ECTR	endoscopic carpal tunnel release
	extracorporeal photopheresis	ECU	electrocautery unit
ECPB	emergency cardiopulmonary bypass		emergency care unit
			emotional care units
ECPD	external counterpressure device		environmental control unit
ECPL	endocavitary pelvic lymphadenectomy		eternal care unit (morgue) (slang)
			extensor carpi ulnaris
ECPP	extracorporeal photopheresis	ECUG	extensor carpi ulnaris groove
eCPP	estimate cerebral perfusion pressure	ECU tendinitis	extensor carpi ulnaris tendinitis
		ECV	ear-canal volume
eCPR	extracorporeal cardiopulmonary resuscitation		electrical cardioversion
			emergency center visits
eCQMs	electronic clinical quality measures (The Joint Commission)		external cephalic version (obstetrics)

ECVD	extracellular volume depletion	EDB	estimated date of birth
ECVE	extracellular volume expansion		ethylene dibromide
ECVP	extracellular volume depletion (dehydration)		extensor digitorum brevis
		EDC	effective dynamic compliance
ECVS	European College of Veterinary Surgeons		electronic data capture
			end diastolic counts
ECW	extracellular water		estimated date of conception
ECWHSP	Enhanced Coal Workers' Health Surveillance Program (CDC)		estimated date of confinement
			estramustine, docetaxel, and carboplatin
EC/WS	energy conservation/warning signs		extensor digitorum communis
ECWs	expected confidence widths	ED&C	electrodesiccation and curettage
ECX	epirubicin, cisplatin, and capecitabine (Xeloda)	EDCCV	external direct current cardioversion
ECZ	eczema	EDCF	endothelium-derived constricting factor
ED	eating disorder(s)		
	education	EDCP	eccentric dynamic compression plates
	effective dose		
	elbow disarticulation	EDCs	endocrine disrupting chemicals
	emergency department	EDCTP	European and Developing Countries Clinical Trials Partnership
	emotional disorder		
	energy density		
	energy drink(s)	EDD	Employment Development Department (State of California)
	epidural		
	erectile dysfunction		
	ethynodiol diacetate		endothelium-dependent dilation
	every day (this is a dangerous abbreviation)		esophageal detector device
			estimated due date
	exhaustion disorder		expected date of delivery
	extensive disease	EdD	Doctor of Education
	extensor digitorum	EDDP	2-ethylidene-1,5-dimethyl-3, 3-diphenylpyrrolidine (methadone's main metabolite)
E/D	see ED		
E&D	education and development		
ED50	median effective dose; a dose that produces the desired effect in 50 per cent of a test population	EDE	epidural empyema
		Edem	ER degradation enhancer, mannosidase alpha-like 1; see gene website www.ncbi .nlm.nih.gov/gene
ED95	a dose that produces the desired effect (effective dose) in 95 per cent of a test population		
		EDENT	edentulous
EDA	elbow disarticulation	EDF	elongation, derotation, and flexion
EDAC	early definitive abnormal closure	EDG	endothelial differentiation gene
	Early Detection of Alcohol Consumption (test)	EDH	epidural hematoma
			extradural hematoma
	excessive dynamic airway collapse	EDHCA	Emergency Department Health Care Assistant
EDAM	edatrexate	EDHF	endothelial-derived hyperpolarizing factor
EDAMS	encephalo-duro-arterio-myo-synangiosis		
		EDI	early detection and intervention
ED and C	electrodessication, and curettage		Early Development Instrument
EDAP	Emergency Department Approved for Pediatrics		Eating Disorders Inventory
			electrodeionization
	etoposide, dexamethasone, cytarabine, (Ara-C) and cisplatin (Platinol)		Electronic Data Interchange
			enhanced depth imaging
		EDi	electrical activity of the diaphragm
EDAS	encephalodural arterio-synangiosis		
		EDIC	Epidemiology of Diabetes Inter-ventions and Complications (Study)
EDAT	Emergency Department Alert Team		

EDIE Trial	Early Detection and Intervention Evaluation (psychosis)
EDITAR	extended-duration topical arthropod repellent
EDL	extensor digitorum longus
ED/LD	emotionally disturbed and learning disabled
EDLF	endogenous digitalis-like factors
EDLS	endogenous digitalis-like substance
EDM	early diastolic murmur
	esophageal Doppler monitor
	extensor digiti minimi
EDMD-AD	autosomal dominate Emery-Dreifuss muscular dystrophy
EDNO	endothelium-related nitric oxide
EDNOS	eating disorder not otherwise specified
	eating disorder, not otherwise specified
EDO	ejaculatory duct obstruction
	estimate the day of ovulation
eDoC	estimated date of conception
eDoc	electronic documentation system
EDP	emergency department physician
	end-diastolic pressure
EDPIV	software package for evaluating recordings of digital particle image velocimetry
EDPS	emergency department procedural sedation
EDQ	extensor digiti quinti (tendon)
EDQM	European Directorate for the Quality of Medicines & HealthCare
EDQPI	emergency department quality and performance indicator
EDQV	extensor digiti quinti five
EDR	edrophonium (Tensilon)
	escalating dose regimen
	everyday racism
	extended dynamic range
	extreme drug resistance
EDRD	Eating Disorder Registered Dietitian
EDRF	endothelium derived relaxing factor (nitric oxide)
EDRIC	estimated dose of radiation to immune cells
EDRN	Early Detection Research Network (National Cancer Institute)
EDS	Edinburgh Dysphagia Score
	Ehlers-Danlos syndrome
	estrogen deficiency syndrome
	excessive daytime somnolence
EDs	eating disorders
	endocrine disruptors

EDS HM	Ehlers Danlos syndrome (subtype) hypermobility
EDS-HT	Ehlers-Danlos syndrome, hypermobility type
EDSS	Expanded Disability Status Scale; a method of quantifying disability in multiple sclerosis and monitoring changes in the level of disability over time) *(http://www.mstrust.org .uk/atoz/edss.jsp)*
EDT	exposure duration threshold
EDTA	edetic acid (ethylenediaminetetraacetic acid)
EDTNA/ERCA	European Dialysis and Transplant Nurses Association/European Renal Care Association
EDTP	egg-derived tyrosine phosphatase; see gene website www.ncbi .nlm.nih.gov/gene
EDTR	emergency department trauma room
	endotracheal
EDTU	emergency diagnostic and treatment unit
EDU	eating disorder unit
edu	education
EDUC	education
EDV	end diastolic velocity
	end-diastolic volume
	epidermal dysplastic verruciformis
EDVi	indexed end-diastolic volume
EDW	estimated dry weight
EDX	edatrexate
	electrodiagnostic
	electrodiagnostic testing
	energy-dispersive X-ray (analysis)
EDXA	energy dispersive X-ray analysis
EDXRF	energy-dispersive x-ray fluorescence
EE	emetic episodes
	emotional exhaustion
	end to end
	energy expenditure
	eosinophilic esophagitis
	equine encephalitis
	erosive esophagitis
	esophageal endoscopy
	ethinyl estradiol
	exchange efficiency (units)
	expressed emotion
	external ear
	extrathyroid extension
E & E	eyes and ears
E/E	see EE
E/e	early diastolic transmitral/mitral annular velocity ratio

E/E'	mitral E wave to mitral tissue doppler E' wave	EES	everolimus-eluting stent
EEA	electroencephalic audiometry	EES®	erythromycin ethylsuccinate
	elemental enteral alimentation	EEsAI	Eosinophilic Esophagitis Activity Index
	end-to-end anastomosis	EET	early exercise testing
	energy expended with activity	EEUS-NA	endoscopic esophageal
	eversion endarterectomies		ultrasound-guided needle
EEC	ectrodactyly-ectodermal		aspiration
	dysplasia (cleft syndrome)	EEV	encircling endocardial
	endogenous erythroid colony		ventriculotomy
E-EC	edge-to-edge (clip)	EF	eccentric fixation
EE/CMA	ethinylestradiol/chlormadinone		ejection fraction
	acetate (Belara; not available		endurance factor
	in the US)		erythroblastosis fetalis
EECC	external ear canal cholesteatoma		executive functions
EECG	electroencephalography		extended-field (radiotherapy)
	epicardial electrogram	E/F	extension/flexion (ratio)
	esophageal electrogram	EFA	essential fatty acid
	exercise electrocardiography		estimated fetal age
EECP	enhanced external counter-pulsation	EFAD	essential fatty acid deficiency
		E faecalis	Enterococcus faecalis
EECT	external ear canal temperature	E-FAP	Emory Functional Ambulation Profile
EED	Economic Evaluation Database (UK)	eFAST	extended focused assessment
	embryonic ectoderm		sonography for trauma
	development (protein)		(the use of ultrasound as a
	erythema elevatum diutinum		sensitive and reliable tool to
EE/DRSP	ethinylestradiol/drospirenone (Yasmin)		evaluate patients presenting to the emergency department
EEE	eastern equine encephalomyelitis		with acute and sub-acute
	edema, erythema, and exudate		thoracoabdominal trauma and
	external eye examination		hypotension
EEEV	eastern equine encephalitis virus	EFAST2	an all-electronic system
EEF	enterocutaneous fistula		designed by the Department
	Intramuscular fat (gene; see		of Labor, Internal Revenue
	gene website www.ncbi.nlm		Service, and Pension Benefit
	.nih.gov/gene)		Guaranty Corporation to
EEfRT	Effort Expenditure for Rewards		simplify and expedite the
	Task (a behavioral measure of		submission, receipt, and
	cost/benefit decision-making)		processing of the Form
EEG	electroencephalogram		5500 and Form 5500-SF
EEI	energy expenditure index	EFBW	estimate fetal body weight
	esophageal eosinophilic infiltration	EFC	enzyme-fragment complementa-tion (assay)
EEL	external elastic lamina		
EELS	electron energy loss spectrometry	EFc	see gene website www.ncbi.nlm
EEM	emotional enhancement of		.nih.gov/gene
	memory	EFCS	European Federation of Cytology Societies
	excitation-emission matrix		
	external elastic membrane	EFD	episode free day
EEN	estimated energy needs	EFDA	Expanded Functions Dental
	exclusive enteral nutrition		Assistant
EENT	eyes, ears, nose, and throat	EFdA	4'-Ethynyl-2-fluoro-2'-
EEO	electroendosmosis		deoxyadenosine
	erosive external otitis	EFDs	executive function deficits
EEP	end expiratory pressure	EFE	endocardial fibroelastosis
EER	extended endocardial resection		epidemic fatal encephalopathy
	extraesophageal reflux	EFF	effacement
EERD	extraesophageal reflux disease	effac	effacement

Effu	effusion(s)
EFG	elevated fasting glucose
Efgr	epidermal growth factor receptor; see gene website www.ncbi.nlm.nih.gov/gene
EFHBM	eosinophilic fibrohistiocytic lesion of bone marrow
EFI	esophageal food impaction extended-field irradiation
EFLV	ejection fraction, left ventricular
EFM	electronic fetal monitor(ing) external fetal monitoring
EFMM	external fetal maternal monitor
EFMT	electric field mediated transfer
EFN	effusion
EFO	Experimental Factor Ontology (an application ontology driven by experimental variables including cell lines to organize and describe the diverse experimental variables and data resided in the EMBL-EBI [The European Bioinformatics Institute] resources)
EFP	extraretinal fibrovascular proliferation
EFPIA	European Federation of Pharmaceutical Industries and Associations
EFR	effective filtration rate
EFRT	extended field radiotherapy
EFRV	ejection fraction, right ventricular
EFS	event-free survival
EFT	electronic funds transfer emotion-focused therapy
EFTR	endoscopic full-thickness resection
EFV	efavirenz (Sustiva)
EFVPTC	encapsulated follicular variant of papillary thyroid cancer
EFW	estimated fetal weight
EF/WM	ejection fraction/wall motion
EFX	enrofloxacin (available for veterinary use as Baytril) etifoxine (a non-benzodiazepine anxiolytic with an anticonvulsant effect, not available in the US) Xenadrine (over-the-counter weight loss medication)
EG	ethylene glycol
E&G	excision and grafting
e.g.	for example
EGA	esophageal gastric (tube) airway esophagogastric anastomosis estimated gestational age

EGA-MS	evolved gas analysis-mass spectrometry
EGB	endoscopic grasp biopsy
EGb	extract of *Ginkgo biloba*
EGBUS	external genitalia, Bartholin, urethral, and Skene glands
EGC	early gastric carcinoma
EGCG	epigallocatechin-3-gallate
EGD	esophagogastroduodenoscopy
EGD EUS	esophagogastroduodenoscopy with endoscopic ultrasound
EGDS	esofago-gastro-duodeno-scopia (Italian for esophagogastroduodenoscopy)
EGDT	early goal-directed therapy
	esophagogastric devascularization and transection
EGE	eosinophilic gastroenteritis
EGF	epidermal growth factor
EGFR	epidermal growth factor receptors estimated glomerular filtration rate
EGFRm	mutated epidermal growth factor receptor EGFRm eliminate BG-12 dimethyl fumarate
EGG	electrogastrography
EGID	eosinophil-associated gastrointestinal disorder(s)
EGJ	esophagogastric junction
EGJOO	esophagogastric junction outflow obstruction
EGL	eosinophilic granuloma of the lung
EGM	electrogram (any record produced by changes in electric potential) electrogustometry
EGN	electrognathographic (a computerized, electronic 3-Dimensional tracking in real-time, of mandibular movement in the frontal, sagittal, and horizontal planes)
EGO	expert-guided optimization
EGP	endogenous glucose production epithelial glycoprotein; see gene website www.ncbi.nlm.nih .gov/gene
EGPA	eosinophilic granulomatosis with polyangiitis
EGR	early growth response; see gene website; www.ncbi.nlm.nih .gov/gene
EGR1	early growth response 1; see gene website; www.ncbi .nlm.nih.gov/gene
eGRF	estimated glomerular rate of filtration
EGS	ethylene glycol succinate
EGSs	external guide sequences

E

EGTA	esophageal gastric tube airway	EHOB	elevated head of bed
	ethyleneglycoltetracetic acid	EHOB®	a company that provides
EGUS	Equine Gastric Ulcer Syndrome		waffle-type products to
EGUs	electrical generating units		prevent the formation of
EGV	elvitegravir		bed sores; EHOB stood for-
	esophagogastric varices		elevate head of bed)
EH	eccentric hypertrophy	EHP	eosinophilic hepatic
	educationally handicapped		pseudotumor(s)
	Employee Health	EHPH	extrahepatic portal hypertension
	enlarged heart	EHPVO	extrahepatic portal venous
	essential hypertension		obstruction
	extramedullary hematopoiesis	EHR	electronic health records
Eh	*Entamoeba histolytica*	EHRA	European Heart Rhythm
EhaC	energy-converting hydrogenase		Association
	A subunit C; see gene website	EHRs	electronic health records
	www.ncbi.nlm.nih.gov/gene	EHRT	(knee) extension heel raise test
eHAC	equine hydroxyapatite collagen	EHRZ/4HR2	daily ethambutol, isoniazid,
EHB	elevate head of bed		rifampicin, and pyrazinamide
	extensor hallucis brevis		for 2 months, followed by
EHBA	extrahepatic biliary atresia		4 months of daily rifampcin
EHBDC	extrahepatic bile duct cancer		and isoniazid
EHBF	extrahepatic blood flow	EHS	Early Head Start (program)
EHC	enterohepatic circulation		electrical hypersensitivity
EHD	electronic home detension		employee health service
	extrahepatic (bile) duct		Englebreth-Holm-Swarm
EHDA	etidronate sodium		(tumor)
EHDP	etidronate disodium (Didronel)		exertional heat stroke
EHE	epithelioid hemangioendothelioma	EHT	electrohydrothermosation
	equivalent household expenditure		essential hypertension
EHEC	enterohemorrhagic *Escherichia*	EHTN	essential hypertension
	coli	EI	ear impression(s)
EHF	Ebola hemorrhagic fever		early intervention
	epidemic hemorrhagic fever		entry inhibitor
	extremely high frequency		environmental illness
EHG	electrohysterogram		enzyme immunoassay
EHH	episodic hypothermia with		extensor indicis
	hyperhidrosis	E/I	expiratory to inspiratory (ratio)
	esophageal hiatal hernia	E & I	endocrine and infertility
EHI	exertional heat illness	EIA	enzyme immunoassay
EHIT	endovenous heat-induced		exercise-induced asthma
	thrombus		external iliac artery
EHL	electrohydraulic lithotripsy	EIAB	extracranial-intracranial arterial
	extensor hallucis longus		bypass
EHL/EDL/	extensor hallucis longus muscle,	EIAC	enzyme-inducing anticonvulsants
FHL/FDL/	extensor digitorum longus	EIACD	enzyme-inducing anticonvulsant
GSC/TA	muscle, flexor hallucis longus		drug
	muscle, flexor digitorm	EIAD	extended-interval aminoglycoside
	longus muscle, gastrocnemius		dosing
	soleus complex muscle,	EIAEDs	enzyme-inducing antiepileptic
	tibialis anterior muscle		drugs
EHM	expressed human milk	EIAV	equine infectious anemia virus
EHMF	Enfamil Human Milk Fortifier	EIB	exercise-induced bronchospasm
EHMT1	euchromatic histone-lysine	EIC	early eschemic change(s)
	N-methyltransferase 1;		electrical impedance cardiography
	see gene website www.ncbi		endometrial intraepithelial
	.nlm.nih.gov/gene		carcinoma
EHN	ethotoin		epidermal inclusion cyst
EHO	extrahepatic obstruction		extensive intraductal component

E

EICA	extra-intracranial artery (bypass)	EJB	ectopic junctional beat
EICD	exercise-induced cardiac damage	EJD	ejaculatory dysfunction
EICF	exercise-induced cardiac fatigue		European Journal of Dermatology
eICP	estimate intracranial pressure	EJF	ejaculatory function
EICU	emergency intensive care unit	EJN	extended jaundice of newborn
eICU	electronic intensive care unit	EJP	excitatory junction potential
EID	electroimmunodiffusion	EJV	external jugular vein
	electronic infusion device	EK	Ektachem 400 (see Laboratory
EIDC	extreme intervertebral disk		Panels)
	collapse		erythrokinase
EIDs	emerging infectious diseases	EKA	endokinin A
EIEC	enteroinvasive *Escherichia coli*	eKASPER	enhanced Kentucky All Schedule
EIF	echogenic intracardiac focus		Prescription Electronic
eIF	eukaryotic initiation factor		Reporting
eif	see gene website; www.ncbi.	EKC	epidemic keratoconjunctivitis
	nlm.nih.gov/gene	EKD	end (stage) kidney disease
eIF-4E	eukaryotic initiation factor 4E	EKF	extended Kalman filter
EIH	end inspiration hold	EKG	electrocardiogram
	environmentally-induced	EKIT	exchange kinetics by inversion
	hyperthermia		transfer
	exercise-induced hypertension	E-Kit	a drug dispensing machine
	exercise-induced hyperthermia		designed for long term care
	exercise-induced hypoxemia		facilities
EIL	elective induction of labor		emergency kit
	extension in lying	EKMO	excessive knee medial opening
EIM	electric impedance myography		may have meant ECMO
	extraintestinal manifestation(s)		(extracorporeal membrane
EIMs	extraintestinal manifestations		oxygenation)
EIN	Employer Identification Number	EKO	echoencephalogram
	endometrial intraepithelial	EKOS®	a system designed for endovas-
	neoplasia		cular dissolution of arterial
eIND	Electronic Investigational New		occlusions and thrombi via
	Drug (application)		targeted drug delivery cathe-
EIOA	excessive intake of alcohol		ters that also emit ultrasound
eIOL	elective induction of labor	EKS	electrokinetic supercharging
EIOP	elevating intraocular pressure	EKs	elbow knee synostosis; see gene
EIP	Early Intervention Program		website www.ncbi.nlm.nih
	elective interruption of pregnancy		.gov/gene
	Emerging Infections Program		epidermal keratinocytes
	end-inspiratory pressure	EKY	electrokymogram
	extensor indicis proprius	EL	elliptical
EIPH	exercise-induced pulmonary		encephalitis lethargica
	hemorrhage		exercise limit
eIPV	enhanced inactivated polio		exploratory laparotomy
	vaccine	E-L	external lids
EIR	entomological inoculation rate	ELA	early life adversity
EIS	electrical impedance scanning		Establishment License
	endoscopic injection scleropathy		Application
	extension in standing	ELAD	extracorporeal liver-assist device
EISR	expanded international search	ELAFF	extended lateral arm free flap
	report	ELAM	endothelial leukocyte adhesion
EIT	electrical impedence tomography		molecule
EITB	enzyme-linked immunoelectro-	ELAMS	Electronic Laboratory Animal
	transfer blot		Monitoring System
EIV	external iliac vein	ELAP	expansive open-door
EJ	ejection		laminoplasty
	elbow jerk		exploratory laparotomy
	external jugular		eye-level arterial pressure

elap	eye lens aplasia; see gene website, www.ncbi.nlm.nih.gov/gene	ELNs	electronic laboratory notebooks
E lap	exploratory laparotomy	ELOA	Elongin A; see gene website www.ncbi.nlm.nih.gov/gene
ELAR	effective lymphatic absorption rate		epidural lysis of adhesions equine lysozyme with oleic acid
ELB	early light breakfast	ELOP	estimated length of program
	elbow	ELOS	estimated length of stay
ELBW	extremely low birth weight (less than 1000 g)	ELP	electrophoresis eruptive lingual papillitis
ELC	earlobe creases	ELPS	excessive lateral pressure
ELCA	excimer laser coronary angioplasty		syndrome
		ELR	estimated lifetime risk
ELCPM	endoscopic laser cricopharyngeal myotomy	ELS	early life stress Eaton-Lambert syndrome
ELD	end-of-life decision (s) endoscopic lumbar discectomy		Editor in the Life Sciences endolymphatic sac
ELDU	extralabel drug use		extragenital lichen sclerosus
ELEC	elective	ELSA	English Longitudinal Study of Ageing
electrolytes	salts and minerals (such as sodium chloride, potassium, calcium, and sodium bicar-	ELSD	evaporative light scattering detection
	bonate) that can conduct elec- trical impulses in the body		evaporative light scattering detector
elev	elevated	ELSI	ethical, legal, and social implications
ELF	elective low forceps endoscopic laser foraminotomy	ELSIE	Extractables and Leachables Safety Information Exchange
	epithelial lining fluid etoposide, leucovorin, and	ELSO	Extracorporeal Life Support Organization (Registry)
	fluorouracil	ELSS	emergency life support system
	extremely low frequency	ELST	endolymphatic sac tumor
ELFA	enzyme-linked fluorescent immunoassay	ELT	ectopic liver tissue endoscopic laser therapy
ELFMF	extremely low frequency magnetic fields		euglobulin lysis time
ELG	endolumenal gastroplication endoluminal graft	ELTR	European Liver Transplant Registry
ELH	endolymphatic hydrops	ELVIS™	Enzyme-Linked Virus Inducible System
ELI	endomyocardial lymphocytic infiltrates	ELVO	emergent large-vessel occlusion
ELIF	extraforaminal lumbar interbody	ELVs	exosome-like vesicles
	fusion	ELYTES	electrolyte test panel; sodium
ELIG	eligible		$(Na+)$, potassium $(K+)$,
ELIOT	electron intraoperative treatment		chloride $(Cl-)$, and bicar-
ELISA	enzyme-linked immunosorbent assay		bonate $(HCO3-$; sometimes reported as total CO2)
ELISPOT	enzyme-linked immunospot	e-lytes	electrolytes (salts and minerals
ELITT	endometrial laser intrauterine thermal therapy		[such as sodium chloride, po- tassium, calcium, and sodium
Elix	elixir		bicarbonate])
ELIZA	enzyme-linked immunosorbent assay	EM	early memory earmold
ELLIP	ellipotocytosis		ejection murmur
ELM	epiluminescent microscopy external laryngeal manipulation		ektomesenchymoma electron microscope
ELM scale-2	Early Language Milestone Scale - second edition		emergency medicine Emergency Medicine Physician(s)
ELN	electronic laboratory notebook		emmetropia
ELND	elective lymph node dissection		eosinophilia-myalgia (syndrome)

erythema migrans
erythema multiforme
erythromelalgia
esophageal manometry
estramustine (Emcyt)
Evaluation and Management
(coding system)
event memory
extensive metabolizers
external monitor
E/M evaluation and management
(guidelines; coding system)
E&M endocrine and metabolic
evaluation and management
EMA early morning awakening
endomysial antibody (antibodies)
European Medicines Agency
(European Union)
EMA-CO etoposide, methotrexate,
dactinomycin (actinomycin-D),
cyclophosphamide, and
vincristine (Oncovin)
eMAR electronic medication
administration record
EMARDD early-onset myopathy
Syndrome characterized by areflexia,
respiratory distress, and dys-
phagia (rare recessive genetic
disorder associated with mutations in the MEGF10 gene)
EMATALA may have meant EMTALA
(Emergency Medical
Treatment and Labor Act)
a 1986 federal law that
requires anyone coming to
an emergency department
to be stabilized and treated,
regardless of their insurance
status or ability to pay
EMB endometrial biopsy
endomyocardial biopsy
eosin-methylene blue (agar)
ethambutol (Myambutol)
Explanation of Medicare Benefits
emb embolism
EMBASE Excerpts Medica dataBASE
(a biomedical and pharmaco-
logical database, produced by
Elsevier)
EMBD extended modified B-distribution
(electromyography)
may have meant EBMD (estimated bone mineral density)
EMBL European Molecular Biology
Laboratory
EMBL-EBI European Molecular Biology
Laboratory-European
Bioinformatics Institute

embm embolism
EMBR electrochemical membrane
bioreactor
EmbR number of embryos required to
achieve at least one live birth
embR see gene website www.ncbi.nlm
.nih.gov/gene
EMBU Egna Minnen Beträffande
Uppfostran, (Swedish
acronym for "Own Memories
of Parental Rearing"), a
self-report questionnaire that
assesses perceived parental
rearing style in adolescents
EMBx endomyocardial biopsy
EMC encephalomyocarditis
endometrial currettage
essential mixed cryoglobulinemia
extraskeletal myxoid
chondrosarcoma
EmCa endometrial carcinoma
epithelial-myoepithelial
carcinoma
EMCO may have meant ECMO
(extracorporeal membrane
oxygenation)
EMCV encephalomyocarditis virus
EMD electromechanical dissociation
Emergency Medicine Department
EMDA electromotive drug administration
EMDAT The International Emergency
Disasters Database
EMDR eye movement desensitization
and reprocessing
EME early myoclonic encephalopathy
extreme medical emergency
EMEA European Medicines Evaluation
Agency
EMERG emergency
EMF elective midforceps
electromagnetic field(s)
electromagnetic flow
electromotive forces
endomyocardial fibrosis
erythrocyte maturation factor
evaporated milk formula
EMG electromyograph
emergency
essential monoclonal
gammopathy
EMG(GG) genioglossus electromyography
EMG/NCS electromyogram/nerve
conduction study
EMH extramedullary hematopoiesis
EMI ear mold impression
educably mentally impaired
elderly and mentally infirm
electromagnetic interference

emia	a suffix denoting the presence of a substance in the blood
EMIC	Emergency Maternal and Infant Care Program
	emergency maternity and infant care
E-MICR	electron microscopy
EMIT	enzyme-multiplied immunoassay technique (test)
EMK	emergency medical kit
EML	Essential Medicines Lists (World Health Organization)
EMLA®	eutectic mixture of local anesthetics (lidocaine and prilocaine in an emulsion base)
EMLB	erythromycin lactobionate
EMM	erythema multiforme major
EMMA	eye-movement measuring apparatus
Emmi®	Expectation Management and Medical Information (programs)
EMMV	extended mandatory minute ventilation
EMN	electromagnetic navigation
	European Myeloma Network
EMo	ear mold
EmOC	emergency obstetric care
EMOI	Electronic Medical Office Integration (emoi.org)
emot	emotion, emotions, emotional
EMP	electromolecular propulsion
	estramustine phosphate (Emcyt)
empa	empagliflozin (Jardiance)
EmPAC	a nano emulsion formulation of paclitaxel
EMPD	extramammary Paget disease
EMPI	enterprise master patient index
EMR	Eastern Mediterranean Region (WHO)
	educable mentally retarded
	electrical muscle stimulation
	electronic medical record
	emergency mechanical restraint
	empty, measure, and record
	endoscopic mucosal resection
	eye-movement recording
EMS	early morning specimen
	early morning stiffness
	electrical muscle stimulation
	emergency medical services
	Emergency Medical System (Pre-hospital)
	eosinophilia myalgia syndrome
	Extended Mallampati Score
EMs	event memories
EMSA	electrophoretic mobility shift assay

eMSN	electronic Medicare Summary Notice
EMST	expiratory muscle strength training
EMSU	early morning specimen of urine
EMT	Emergency and Military Tourniquet
	emergency medical technician
	epithelial-mesenchymal transformation
	epithelial-mesenchymal transition
	estramustine (Emcyt)
EMTA	Emergency Medical Technician, Advanced
EMTALA	Emergency Medical Treatment and Labor Act of 1986 (a federal law requiring hospital emergency departments to medically screen every patient who seeks emergency care and to stabilize or transfer those with medical emergencies, regardless of health insurance status or ability to pay)
EMTC	emergency medical trauma center
EMT-D	emergency medical technician-defibrillation
EMTLA	may have meant EMTALA (Emergency Medical Treatment and Labor Act of 1986)
EMT-P	Emergency Medical Technician, Paramedic
EMU	early morning urine
	electromagnetic unit
	epilepsy monitoring unit
EMV	equine morbilli virus
	eye, motor, verbal (grading for Glasgow Coma Scale)
EMVC	early mitral valve closure
EMW	electromagnetic waves
EMZL	extranodal marginal-zone (B-cell) lymphoma
EN	each nostril
	enema
	enteral nutrition
	erythema nodosum
E/N	eggnog
E 50% N	extension 50% of normal
ENA	extractable nuclear antigen
ENaC	epithelial sodium channel
ENB	electromagnetic navigational bronchoscopy
	esthesioneuroblastoma
ENBD	endoscopic nasobiliary drainage
en bloc	a phrase meaning; all at once; all together (organs or tissues are removed from the body in con- tinuity, without prior dissection)

ENC	encourage
enceph	encephalitis
	encephalomyelitis
	encephalopathy
eNDA	Electronic New Drug Application
endart	endarterectomy
ENDO	endodontia
	endodontics
	endoscopy
	endotracheal
Endo Bx	endometrial biopsy
EndoCAB	plasma antiendotoxin core antibody
endocr	endocrine
ENDS	electronic nicotine delivery systems
endus	as in Streptomyces endus
ENE	extra nodal extension
ENETS	European Neuroendocrine Tumor Society (guidelines)
ENF	Enfamil
ENF c Fe	Enfamil with iron
ENFD	epidermal nerve fiber density
ENG	electronystagmogram
	engorged
ENKTCL	extranodal natural killer T cell lymphoma
ENKTL	extranodal natural killer T-cell lymphoma
ENL	enlarged
	erythema nodosum leprosum
enl	enlarge; enlarged; enlargement
enlrgmt	enlargement
ENMG	electroneuromyography
ENMT	ears, nose, mouth, and throat
ENN	Elman neural network
	Emergency Nutrition Network (UK)
	Encuesta Nacional de Nutrición (National Nutritional Survey, Mexico)
	enniatin
eNO	exhaled nitric oxide
ENOG	electroneurography
eNOS	endothelial nitric oxide synthase
ENOX	enoxaparin (Lovenox)
ENP	extractable nucleoprotein
ENR	Encinitas Nursing & Rehabilitation (a skilled nursing facility)
ENRD	endoscopy-negative reflux disease
ENS	enteric nervous system
	exogenous natural surfactant
EnSite NavX	a three-dimensional mapping system that permits catheter placement inside the venous system and movement inside the heart chambers without the use of X-rays

ENSs	electroencephalographic neonatal seizures
ENSS	Spanish National Health Survey
ENT	ears, nose, throat
ENTC	ear, nose and throat clinic
entC	see gene website, www.ncbi.nlm.nih.gov/gene
entero	a combining prefix denoting relationship to the intestines
ENTIS	European Network of Teratology Information Services
ENTV	enzootic nasal tumor virus
ENU	N-ethyl-N-nitrosourea
ENUP	European Network of Uropathology
ENV	environment
env	environmental (e.g., env allergies)
ENVD	elevated new vessels on the disk
ENVE	elevated new vessels elsewhere
ENVT	environment
ENZ	enzastaurin
EO	early onset
	elbow orthosis
	embolic occlusion
	eosinophilia
	ethylene oxide
	evidence of
	external oblique (muscle)
	eyes open
e/o	evidence of
E&O	errors and omissions
	evaluation and observation
EOA	erosive osteoarthritis
	esophageal obturator airway
	examine, opinion, and advice
	external oblique aponeurosis
EOAD	early-onset Alzheimer disease
EOAE	evoked otoacoustic emissions
EOB	edge of bed
	explanation of benefits
EOC	Emergency Operations Center
	enema of choice
	epithelial ovarian cancer
EOD	early-onset disease
	end of day
	end of document
	end organ damage
	every other day (this is a dangerous abbreviation)
	extent of disease
EODWO	end-of-dose wearing off
EOE	emotional over-eating
	Equal Opportunity Employer
	extraosseous Ewings sarcoma
EoE	eosinophilic esophagitis
EOFAD	early-onset form of familial Alzheimer disease

E of I	evidence of insurability	EOS	early-onset scoliosis
EOG	electro-oculogram		early-onset sepsis
	electro-olfactogram		end of service
	Ethrane, oxygen, and gas (nitrous oxide)		end of session
			end of shift
EOGBS	early-onset group B streptococcal (sepsis)		end of study
			eosinophil
EOHs	emergency obstetric hysterectomies	eosin	eosinophil
		eosino	eosinophils
EOIT	end of initial treatment	EOSS	early-onset schizophrenia spectrum (disorders)
EOL	end-of-life		
EOLC	end-of-life-care		end of shift summation
EOLRI	end-of-life replacement indicator (pacemaker insertion)		Experiencing of Self Scale
		EOT	early-onset tinnitus
EOM	error of measurement		end of therapy
	external otitis media		end of treatment
	extraocular movement	EOTs	extra-ocular tendons
	extraocular muscles	EOU	ease of use
EOMB	explanation of Medicare benefits	EOVAP	early-onset ventilator-associated pneumonia
EOMD	early-onset mood disorders		
EOMF	external oblique myocutaneous flap	EO-VAP	early-onset ventilator-associated pneumonia
		EOW	every other week (this is a dangerous abbreviation)
EOMG	early-onset myasthenia gravis		
EOMI	extraocular movements intact	EOX	epirubicin, oxaliplatin, and capecitabine (Xeloda)
	extraocular muscles intact		
EOMS	early-onset multiple sclerosis	EP	birth parent (s)
EOMs	extraocular muscles		ectopic pregnancy
EON	ethambutol-induced optic neuropathy		electronic prescribing
			electrophysiologic
EONS	early-onset neonatal sepsis		electrophysiologist
EOO	external oculomotor ophthalmoplegia		element of performance
			elopement precaution
EOP	early-onset Parkinsonism		Emergency Physician
	early-onset pneumonia		endogenous pyrogen
	early-onset preeclampsia		English-Proficient
	early-onset psychosis		Episcopalian
	emergency operations plan (in the event of a disaster)		esophageal pressure
			etoposide and cisplatin (Platinol)
	external occipital protuberance		
EOP1	end-of-phase 1		evoked potentials
EOP2	end-of-phase 2	E/P	estriol/progesterone ratio
EOPA	early-onset pauciarticular arthritis	E&P	estrogen and progesterone
	elongated one-piece arterial (cannula)	EPA	eicosapentaenoic acid
			Environmental Protection Agency
	nudE neurodevelopment protein 1 like 1 (gene)	ePA	electronic prior authorization
		EPAB	extracorporeal pneumoperitito- neal access bubble
E-OPCAB	emergency off-pump coronary artery bypass		
		EP ablation	cardiac electrophysiology ablation
EOPD	early-onset Parkinson disease		
EOR	emergency operating room	E-Panel	electrolyte panel
	end of range	EPAP	expiratory positive airway pressure
EORA	elderly onset rheumatoid arthritis		
EORTC	European Organization for the Re- search and Treatment of Cancer	EPAT	extracorporeal pulse-activated therapy
		EPB	extensor pollicis brevis
EORTC QLQ C30	European Organization for Research and Treatment of Cancer Quality of Life Questionnaire	EPBD	endoscopic papillary balloon dilatation
		EPBx	extended prostate biopsy

E

EPC	emergency protective custody
	epilepsy partials continua
	(a syndrome of continuous
	focal jerking)
	erosive prephloric changes
	external pneumatic compression
EPCA	early prostate cancer antigen
Ep-CAM	epithelial cell adhesion molecule
EPCP	epithelial cell progenitor
EPCs	endothelial progenitor cells
	Evidence-based Practice Centers
EPCV	engineering, procurement,
	construction, and validation
EPD	electrode placement device
	equilibrium peritoneal dialysis
ePDMP	electronic-only prescription
	drug monitoring programs
	Enhanced Prescription Drug
	Monitoring Program
	(Wisconsin Department
	of Safety and Professional
	Services)
EPDS	Edinburgh Postnatal Depression
	Scale
EPE	eosinophilic pleural effusion
EPEC	enteropathogenic *Escherichia coli*
EPEG	etoposide (VePesid)
EPEs	extrapyramidal effects
EPF	endoscopic plantar fasciotomy
	Enfamil Premature Formula®
	Expanded Problem Focused
	extrapyramidal features
EPFR	early peak filling rate
	endoscopic plantar fascia release
EPG	electronic pupillography
	electropalatography
	Episodic Payment Group
EPHEMERIS	Evaluation chez la Femme
	Enceinte des Medicaments et
	de lemurs RISques, (a French
	database including prescribed
	and dispensed reimbursed
	drugs during pregnancy and
	pregnancy outcomes)
EPHI	electronic protected health
	information
EPI	echo planar imaging (radiology)
	echoplanar imaging
	epinephrine
	epirubicin (Ellence)
	epitheloid cells
	exercise pressure index
	exocrine pancreatic insufficiency
	Expanded Program of
	Immunizations, (World
	Health Organization)
	Eysenck Personality Inventory

EPIC	etoposide, prednisolone,
	ifosfamide, and cisplatin
EPID	electronic portal imaging devices
	epidural
EPIDs	electronic portal imaging devices
epiDX	epirubicin (49-epidoxorubicin;
	Ellence)
EPIG	epigastric
EPIS	epileptic postictal sleep
	episiotomy
epith	epithelial
epithel	epithelial
EPL	effective patent life
	extensor pollicis longus (tendon)
EPLBD	endoscopic papillary large
	balloon dilation
Epley	a maneuver used to treat benign
	paroxysmal positional vertigo
ePLND	extended pelvic lymph-node
	dissection
EPM	electronic pacemaker
EPME	external post-mortem examination
EPMR	electronic patient medical record
EPN	emphysematous pyelonephritis
	ependymoma
	ependymoma
	estimated protein needs
EPO	epoetin alfa (erythropoietin;
	Epogen)
	evening primrose oil
	exclusive provider organization
EPOA	enduring power of attorney
epoa	erythropoietin A (gene)
EPOC	Effective Practice and
	Organisation of Care
	(Cochrane databases)
	excess postexercise oxygen
	consumption
	excess post-exercise oxygen
	consumption
EPOCH	etoposide, prednisone, vin-
	cristine (Oncovin), cyclo-
	phosphamide, doxorubicin
	(hydroxydaunorubicin)
EPP	emergency power pack
	erythropoietic protoporphyria
	extrapleural pneumonectomy
EPPID	electronic positive patient and
	specimen identification
EPPK	epidermolytic palmoplantar
	keratoderma
EPPV	early post- marketing phase
	vigilance (Japan's system
	of spontaneous reporting of
	adverse drug reactions)
EPPY	events per patient year
EPQ	Exercise Participation
	Questionnaire

E

EPQ-R	Eysenck Personality Questionnaire-Revised	EPUB	an e-book file format with the extension .Epub that can be downloaded and read on devices like smartphones, tablets, computers, or e-readers
EPR	electron paramagnetic resonance		
	electron paramagnetic (spin) resonance		
	electronic prescription record	EPV	estimated placental volume
	electrophrenic respiration		events per variable
	emergency physical restraint	EPW	early pregnancy (body) weight
	epirubicin (Ellence)		electric power wheelchairs
	estimated protein requirement	EPY	events/person-year
	expiratory pressure relief	eq	equal
EPRI	electron paramagnetic resonance imaging	EQC	equivalent quality control
		EQ-5D	European Quality of life scale (EuroQol-5) (includes single item measures of: mobility, self-care, usual activities, pain/discomfort, and anxiety/depression)
EPRP	External Peer Review Program (Veterans Health Administration)		
EPRT	expiratory phase rise time		
EPS	Elder Protective Services		
	electrophysiologic study	EQ-5D-5L	European Quality of life scale (EuroQol-5) (includes single item measures of: mobility, self-care, usual activities, pain/discomfort, and anxiety/depression)- 5-level version
	encapsulating peritoneal sclerosis		
	expressed prostatic secretions		
	extrapulmonary shunt		
	extrapyramidal symptoms		
	extrapyramidal syndrome		
Eps	elements of performance	equip	equipment
EPSA	evoked potential signal averaging	equiv	equivalent
		ER	emergency room
EPSCCA	extrapulmonary small cell carcinoma		emotion recognition
			end range
EPSDT	Early and Periodic Screening, Diagnosis, and Treatment (Medicaid)		estrogen receptors
			extended release
			external resistance
EPSE	extrapyramidal side effects		external rotation
EPSI	Eating Pathology Symptoms Inventory	Er	erbium
		E & R	equal and reactive
	echo planar spectroscopic imaging		examination and report
		ER +	estrogen receptor-positive
EPSP	excitatory postsynaptic potential	ER −	estrogen receptor-negative
EPSS	E point septal separation	ER-a	estrogen receptor alpha (either positive or negative)
EPSTD	may have meant EPSDT (Medicaid's Early and Periodic Screening, Diagnosis and Treatment)		
		ER-b	estrogen receptor beta (either positive or negative)
		ERA	environmental risk assessment
EPSTT	may have meant EPSDT (Early and Periodic, Diagnosis, Screening and Treatment [Medicaid])		estrogen receptor assay
			evoked response audiometry
		%ERAD	eradication rates
		ERAF	early recurrence of atrial fibrillation
EP study	electrophysiologic study		
EPT	electroporation therapy		endorectal advancement flap
	endpoint temperature	ERAS	Electronic Residency Application Service
EPT®	early pregnancy test		
EPTE	existed prior to enlistment		enhanced recovery after surgery (protocols)
ePTFE	expanded polytetrafluoroethylene		
ePTFE graft	expanded polytetrafluoroethylene graft	erbB1	estrogen receptor (tyrosine kinase family) type B1
EPTS	existed prior to service	ERBB2	see gene website; www.ncbi.nlm.nih.gov/gene (also known as HER-2/neu)
EPUAP	European Pressure Ulcer Advisory Panel		

ERBD	endoscopic retrograde biliary drainage
ERbeta	estrogen receptor beta
ERBT	erythromycin breath test
ER by ICA	estrogen receptor immunocytochemistry assay
ERC	endoscopic retrograde cholangiography
	Ethics Review Committee
ERCA	European Renal Care Association
ERCB	extensor carpi radialis brevis
ERCC	excision repair cross-complementation (enzyme)
ERCC-1	excision repair cross-complementation, group 1
ERCD	elective repeat cesarean delivery
ERCP	endoscopic retrograde cholangiopancreatography
ERCS	elective repeat caesarean section
ERCT	emergency room computerized tomography
ERD	early retirement with disability
	emotion regulation difficulties
ERDs	event-related desynchronizations
ERDP	extended-release dipyridamole
ERE	external rotation in extension
EREFS	endoscopic reference score (used to determine severity of 5 endoscopic findings: edema, rings, exudates, furrows, and strictures)
EREM	extended-release epidural morphine
ERF	esophagorespiratory fistula
	extended rehabilitation facility
	external rotation in flexion
ERFC	erythrocyte rosette forming cells
ERG	electroretinogram
-ergic	a suffix meaning pertaining to or affecting of
ERH	extended right hepatectomy
ERI	elective replacement indicator
	erythropoietin resistance index
ERIC	Enterobacterial repetitive intergenic consensus
ERIC-PCR	Enterobacterial repetitive intergenic consensus sequences polymerase chain reaction
ERIG	equine-rabies immune globulin
ERI ICD	elective replacement indicator of an (automatic) implantable cardioverter-defibrillator
ERK	extracellular signal-regulated kinase
ERL	effective refractory length

ERLND	elective regional lymph node dissection
ERM	epiretinal membrane
ERMBT	erythromycin breath test
ERMedic	provides online emergency medical information storage and retrieval (ermedic.com)
ERMS	embryonal rhabdomyosarcoma
	exacerbating-remitting multiple sclerosis
ERN	entity reference number
	error-related negativity (signal)
ERNA	equilibrium radionuclide angiocardiography
ERO	effective regurgitant orifice
EROM	external range of motion
EROS	event-related optical signal
ERP	effective refractory period
	emergency room physician
	endocardial resection procedure
	endoscopic retrograde pancreatography
	end-range pain
	estrogen receptor protein
	event-related potentials
	exposure and ritual prevention
	extubation readiness protocol
ERPC	evacuation of retained products of conception
ERPF	effective renal plasma flow
ER positive	estrogen receptor positive
ERPR	estrogen receptors and progesterone receptors
ER-REBOA	Eliason-Rasmussen Resuscitative Endovascular Balloon Oclusion of the Aorta
ERRL	An extract of Delta 9-tetrahydrocannabinol, the principal psychoactive constituent of the cannabis plant
ERRLA	equal, round, reactive to light and accommodation
ERRT	Exposure, Relaxation, and Rescripting Therapy
ERS	endoscopic Raman spectroscopy
	evacuation of retained secundines (afterbirth)
	extended, rotated, side bent (position of the spine)
	Extension Rotation Syndrome (Lumbar Extension Rotation Syndrome)
ERSD	endoplasmic reticulum storage disease
	end-stage renal disease
ERSP	event related spectral perturbations
ERSPC	European Randomised Study for Screening of Prostate Cancer

E

ERSR	Electronic Regulatory Submission and Review	ESAs	erythropoietin-stimulating agents
ERSs	event-related synchronizations	ESAT	extrasystolic atrial tachycardia
ERS-TM	Event Reporting System - Transfusion Medicine	ESB	electrical stimulation of the brain endocrine screening battery endoscopic sympathetic block environmental specimen bank
ERT	enzyme replacement therapy estrogen replacement therapy external radiotherapy extubation readiness test		
		ESBC	early-stage breast cancer
		ESBI	Early Screening and Brief Intervention
ERTD	emergency room triage documentation	ESBL	extended-spectrum beta-lactamase
Ertl	An amputation osteoplasty technique promoted by Janos Ertl, Sr MD to enhance rehabilitation after transtibial amputation	ESBLE	extended-spectrum beta-lactamase-producing enterobacteriaceae
		ESBL GNR	extended spectrum beta-lactamase gram negative rod(s)
ERTs	enzyme replacement therapies error rate thresholds	ESBLKP	extended-spectrum beta-lactamase-producing *Klebsiella pneumoniae*
ERUS	endorectal ultrasound		
ERV	early revascularization expiratory reserve volume	ESBL UTI	extended spectrum beta-lactamases urinary tract infection
eRVSP	estimated right ventricular systolic pressure		
		ESBO	epoxidized soybean oil
ERVV	Erve virus	ESC	embryonic stem cells end systolic counts European Society of Cardiology (guidelines) Evidence of Standards Compliance (The Joint Commission)
e-Rx	electronic prescription		
Er:YAG	Erbium: yttrium aluminum garnet (laser)		
ERYTH	erythromycin		
ES	elastic stockings electrical stimulation electronic signature *Eleutherococcus senticosus* (Siberian Ginseng) embryonic stem (cells) emergency service endoscopic sclerotherapy endoscopic sphincterotomy end-stage end-to-side epileptic seizure(s) ever-smokers Ewings sarcoma excessive sleepiness ex-smoker extra strength		
		ESCAPE	See ESKAPE
		ESCC	epidural spinal cord compression esophageal squamous cell carcinoma
		eschar	a word meaning a necrotic tissue in the process of separating from viable tissue, produced by a thermal burn, corrosive application, or gangrene
		ESCM	embryonic stem cell-derived cardiomyocytes
		ESCOP	European Scientific Cooperative on Phytotherapy
Es	einsteinium	ESCOPD	end-stage chronic obstructive pulmonary disease
ESA	early systolic acceleration end-to-side anastomosis erythropoiesis-stimulating agents ethmoid sinus adenocarcinoma	ESCP	endosonography-guided cholangiopancreatography esophageal squamous cell papillomas European Society of Clinical Pharmacy European Society of Coloproctology
ESADDI	estimated safe and adequate daily dietary intake		
ESAgs	excretory-secretory antigens		
ESAP	evoked sensory (nerve) action potential	ESCPs	evoked spinal cord potentials
		ESCS	electrical spinal cord stimulation
ESAR	external subannular aortic ring	ESCULAP	Contrast-enhanced Ultrasound for Liver Lesion Assessment in Patients at Risk
ESAS	Edmonton System Assessment System (Scale)		

ESD	early supported discharge	ESKD	end-stage kidney disease
	Emergency Services Department	ESL	English as a second language
	endoscopic submucosal dissection	ESLB	may have meant ESBL (extended-
	esophagus, stomach, and		spectrum beta-lactamase)
	duodenum	ESLD	end-stage liver disease
ESDL	end-stage-liver-disease		end-stage lung disease
	(Romance languages)	ESLW	estimated standard liver weight
ESDM	Early Start Denver Model	ESM	ejection systolic murmur
	(for autism)		endolymphatic stromal myosis
ESDR	European Society for		ethosuximide (Zarontin)
	Dermatological Research	ESMO	European Society of Medical
	French and Spanish abbreviation		Oncology
	for end-stage renal disease	ESN	educationally subnormal
ESE	exon splice enhancer	ESN(M)	educationally subnormal-
ES EOC	early-stage epithelial ovarian		moderate
	cancer	ESN(S)	educationally subnormal-severe
ESES	electrical status epilepticus	ESO	esophagus
	during sleep		esotropia
eSET	elective single embryo transfer	ESO/D	esotropia at distance
ESF	external skeletal fixation	ESO/N	estropia at near
ESFA	European Food Safety Authority	Esoph	esophagus
ESFT	Ewing sarcoma family of tumors	ESP	endometritis, salpingitis, and
ESG	electrosympathicograph		peritonitis
	endovascular stent grafting		end-systolic pressure
ESGE	European Society of Gas-		especially
	trointestinal Endoscopy		extrasensory perception
	(guidelines)	ESPAC	European Study Group for
ESH	endoscopic saphenous (vein)		Pancreatic Cancers
	harvest	ESPD	European Society if Pediatric
ESHAP	etopside, methylprednisolone		Dermatology
	(Solu-Medrol), high-dose	espD	ESX-1 (ESAT-6 system)
	cytarabine (ara-C), and		secretion-associated protein D;
	cisplatin (Platinol)		see gene website www.ncbi
ESHD	early-stage Hodgkin Disease		.nlm.nih.gov/gene
	end-stage heart disease	ESPGHAN	The European Society for Paedia-
ESHF	end-stage heart failure		tric Gastroenterology, Hepato-
ESI	electric source imaging		logy and Nutrition (guidelines)
	electrospray ionization	ESPL1	Extra spindle pole bodies
	Emergency Severity Index		homolog 1; see gene website,
	epidural steroid injection		www.ncbi.nlm.nih.gov/gene
ESI-K	Early Screening Inventory-	ES/PNET	Ewings sarcomas and peripheral
	Kindergarden		neuroectodermal tumor
ESI-MS	electrospray ionization mass	ESPNIC	European Society of Pediatric
	spectrometry		and Neonatal Intensive Care
ESIN	elastic stable intramedullary	ESPVR	end-systolic pressure-volume
	nailing		relation
ESI-P	Early Screening inventory-	ESR	early sheath removal
	Preschool		electron spin resonance
ESI-R	Early Screening Inventory-		erythrocyte sedimentation rate
	Revised	ESRA-C	electronic self-report assessment-
ESIs	epidural steroid injections		cancer
ESKAPE	hospital antibiotic resistant	ESRB	Epidemiology Surveillance and
	pathogens (Enterococcus		Response Branch, (Centers
	faecium, Staphylocccus aureus,		for Disease Control and
	Klebsiella pneumoniae,		Prevention)
	Acinetobacter baumannii,		estrogen receptor 2 (ER beta) gene
	Pseudomonas auruginosa, and	ESR/CRP	erythrocyte sedimentation
	Enterobacter species		rate/C-reactive protein (ratio)

E

ESRD	end-stage renal disease
ESRF	end-stage renal failure
ESRI	Economic and Social Research Institute (data base, Ireland)
	electron spin resonance imaging
	extended, sidebend, rotated left
ESRL	ribonuclease, RNase A family, 9 (non-active); see gene website www.ncbi.nlm.nih.gov/gene
ESRO	European Space Research Organization
ESRP1	epithelial splicing regulatory proteins 1
ESRr	extended, sidebend, rotated right
ESRS	Extrapyramidal Symptom Rating Scale
esRVP	estimated right ventricle systolic pressure
ESS	elastic scattering spectroscopy
	emotional, spiritual, and social
	endometrial stromal sarcoma
	endoscopic sinus surgery
	English springer spaniel(s)
	epistaxis Severity Score
	Epworth Sleepiness Scale
	essential
	euthyroid sick syndrome
ES-SCLC	extensive-stage small-cell lung cancer
EST	early stent thrombosis
	Eastern Standard Time
	electroshock therapy
	electrostimulation therapy
	Emotional Stroop Task
	endodermal sinus tumor
	endoscopic sphincterotomy
	endoscopic spincterotomy
	established patient
	estimated
	exercise stress test
	expressed sequence tag
est GFR	estimated glomerular filtration rate
EStim	electrical stimulation
ESTS	extremity soft tissue sarcoma
ESTs	expressed sequence tags
ESU	electrical stimulation unit
	electrosurgical unit
ESUR	European Society of Urogenital Radiology (guidelines)
ESUS	embolic stroke of undetermined source
ESV	end-systolic volume
ESVH	endoscopic saphenous vein harvest
	extraction site ventral hernias
ESVi	Indexed end-systolic volume
ESVL	endovascular spiral vagal (stimulation) lead

ESWAL	see ESWL
ESWL	extracorporeal shock wave lithotripsy
ESWOL	may have meant ESWL (extracorporeal shock wave lithotripsy)
ESWR	early steroid withdrawal regimen
ESWT	extracorporeal shock wave therapy
ESZ	eszopiclone (Lunesta)
ET	ejection time
	embryo transfer
	endocrine therapy
	endometrial thickness
	endothelin
	endotoxin
	endotracheal
	endotracheal tube
	endurance training
	enterostomal therapy (therapist)
	epirubicin and paclitaxel (Taxol)
	esotropia
	essential thrombocythemia
	essential tremor
	Eustachian tube
	evaluation and treatment
	Ewing tumor
	exchange transfusion
	exercise treadmill
	exposure time
et	and
ET'	esotropia at near
E&T	evaluation and treatment
E(T)	intermittent esotropia at infinity
E(T')	intermittent esotropia at near
ET-1	endothelin-1
2ET	two embryo transfer
ET @ 20'	esotropia at 6 meters (infinity)
ETA	endotracheal airway
	estimated time of arrival
	etanercept (Enbrel)
	ethionamide (Trecator-SC)
	event-tree analysis
ETAAD	early onset thoracic aortic aneurysm and dissection
ETAAS	electrothermal atomic absorption spectrometry
ETAC	early treatment of the allergic child
et al	and others
ETASU	Elements To Assure Safe Use (Food and Drug Administration)
ETBD	etiology to be determined
EtBr	ethidium bromide
ETC	ecarin clotting time
	electrothermal capsulorrhaphy
	Emergency and Trauma Center

E

	emergency treatment center
	endoscopic tissue culture
	epirubicin, paclitaxel, (Taxol), and cyclophosphamide
	esophageal-tracheal Combitube
	estimated time of conception
etc	and other things; and so on; and so forth (et cetera)
ETCH-C	Evaluation Tool of Children's Handwriting-Cursive
ETCO$_2$	end-tidal carbon dioxide
ETD	electron transfer dissociation
	endoscopic transformational diskectomy
	eustachian tube dilation
	eustachian tube dysfunction
	eye-tracking dysfunction
ETDA	may have meant EDTA (ethylenediaminetetraacetic acid)
ETDH	may have meant ETOH (ethyl alcohol [alcohol])
ETDLA	esophageal-tracheal double lumen airway
ETDRS	Early Treatment Diabetic Retinopathy Study (letter chart)
ETE	end-to-end
	extrathyroidal extension
ETEA	Essential Tremor Embarrassment Assessment (score)
ETEC	enterotoxigenic *Escherichia coli*
ETF	early treament failure
	eustachian tubal function
etfL	see gene website, www.ncbi.nlm .nih.gov/gene
ETFN	empiric therapy in a febrile neutropenic (patient)
ETFT	Eustachian tube function test
ETG	Episodic Treatment Group
ETGT	equal to or greater than
ETH	elixir terpin hydrate
	ethanol
	Ethrane
ETHc̄C	elixir terpin hydrate with codeine
ETHO	ethosuximide (Zarontin)
ethol	ethology
ETI	ejective time index
	endotracheal intubation
etiol	etiology
ETKTM	every test known to man
ETL	echo train length (radiology)
	electrically tunable lens
ETLE	extratemporal lobe epilepsy
ETLT	equal to or less than
ETM	elevated T-maze (test)
	ethambutol HCl
ETMR	embryonal tumor with multilayered rosettes

ETN	erythema toxicum neonatorum
	etanercept (Enbrel)
	extent of transmural necrosis
eTNS	external trigeminal nerve stimulation
ETO	emergency treatment order(s)
	estimated time of ovulation
	etoposide (VePesid)
	eustachian tube obstruction
EtO	ethylene oxide
E to A	say EEE, comes out as AAA or AAAH upon auscultation of lung showing consolidation
E to A ratio	E/A ratio is a marker of the function of the left ventricle representing the ratio of peak velocity blood flow from gravity in early diastole (the E wave) to peak velocity flow in late diastole caused by atrial contraction (the A wave). It is calculated using echocardiography
EtOH	alcohol (ethyl alcohol)
	alcoholic
ETOHic	alcoholic
Etohism	alcoholism
ETOM	etomidate (Amidate)
ETOP	elective termination of pregnancy
ETOS	Elsom Therapeutic Optimism Scale
eTOX	electronic toxicity; a project whose objective is to predict in vivo toxicological endpoints in drug development (European Innovative Medicines Initiative)
E tox	erythema toxicum (newborn rash)
ETP	elective termination of pregnancy
	electronic transmission of prescriptions
ETPs	endogenous thrombin potentials
ETR	end-of-treatment response
	etravirine (Intelence)
ETS	early tumor shrinkage
	elevated toilet seat
	endoscopic transthoracic sympathectomy
	endotracheal suction
	end-to-side
	environmental tobacco smoke
	erythromycin topical solution
ETS®	urine drug screen for six drugs of abuse
ETST	estimated total sleep time
ETT	endotracheal tube
	endurance treadmill test
	esophageal transit time

E

	exercise tolerance test	EUS-CPN	endoscopic ultrasound-guided celiac plexus neurolysis
	exercise treadmill test (time)		
	extrathyroidal thyroxine	EUS-FNA	endoscopic ultrasonography with fine-needle aspiration
ETTH	episodic tension-type headache		
ETT-Tl	exercise treadmill test with thallium	EUTH	euthanasia
		EV	Enterobius vermicularis
ET tube	endotracheal tube		enteroviruses
ETU	emergency and trauma unit		epidermodysplasia verruciformis
	emergency treatment unit		esophageal varices
ETUs	Ebola treatment units		estramustine and vinblastine
ETV	endoscopic third ventriculostomy		etoposide and vincristine
ETX	edatrexate		eversion
ETYA	eicosatetraynoic acid	eV	electron volt (unit of radiation energy)
EU	Ehrlich units		
	endotoxin units	EV71	enterovirus-71
	equivalent units	E2V	estradiol valerate
	esophageal ulcer	EVA	Entry and Validation Application
	etiology unknown		ethylene vinyl acetate
	European Union		etoposide, vinblastine, and doxorubicin (Adriamycin)
	excretory urography		
Eu	europium	EVAAR	endovascular aortic aneurysm repair
E/U	see EU		
EUA	examine under anesthesia	EVAC	evacuation
EUBs	Euro-Brazilians	EVAc	ethylene-vinyl acetate copolymer
EUCAST	European Committee for Antimicrobial Susceptibility Testing	EVAD	extracranial vertebral artery dissection
EUCD	emotionally unstable character disorder	EVALs	poly (ethylene-co-vinyl alcohol) s
		eval	evaluate
EUD	external urinary device		evaluation
EUE	emotional under-eating		evaporation
EuE	eutopic endometrium	EVAP	early-onset ventilator associated pneumonia
EUF	epidural under fluoroscopy		
	explicit uncertainty factor		electrovaporization of the prostate
EUG	extrauterine gestation	EVAR	endovascular aneurysm repair
EUL	extra uterine life	EVB	empirical valence bond
EULAR	European League Against Rheumatism		esophageal variceal bleeding
		EVBL	endoscopic variceal band ligation
EUM	external urethral meatus	EVC	Ellis-van Creveld syndrome
EU/mL	ELISA (enzyme-linked immunosorbent assay) units per milliliter	EVD	Ebola viral disease
			external ventricular (ventriculostomy) drain
			extraventricular drain
	endotoxin units per milliliter	EV-D68	enterovirus D68
EUN	endogenous urinary nitrogen		
EUnetHTA	European Network for Health Technology Assessment	EVDAS	EudraVigilance Data Analysis System (European Medicines Agency [European Union])
EUP	Experimental Use Permit		
	extrauterine pregnancy	E2V/DNG	estradiol valerate and dienogest (Natazia)
EURL	European Reference Laboratory		
EuroSIDA	a prospective observational cohort study to assess the impact of antiretroviral drugs on the outcome of the general population of 14,000 HIV-infected patients living in Europe	EVE	endoscopic vascular examination
			endovascular embolization
			evening
		EVER	eversion
		every other day	there is no safe abbreviation for every other day, write-out, every other day
EUS	endoscopic ultrasonography		
	esophageal ultrasound	every 2 weeks	there is no safe abbreviation for every 2 weeks; write-out, every 2 weeks
	external urethral sphincter		

E

EVF	enterovesical fistula	EWG	Expert Working Group
EVG	elvitegravir (Vitekta)	EWHO	elbow-wrist-hand orthosis
	endovascular grafting	EWL	estimated weight loss
EVH	endoscopic (saphenous) vein	EWOB	equal work of breathing
	harvesting	EWS	Early Warning Score
EVI	Exposure to Violence Interview		Ewing sarcoma
EVI1	ecotropic viral integration site 1		Ewing sarcoma gene
evid	evidence	EWSCLs	extended-wear soft contact lenses
EVIS	End Video Inform System,	EWSL	may have meant ESWL (extracor-
	Olympus, Tokyo		poreal shock wave lithotripsy)
	(video-endoscopes)	EWSR1	Ewing sarcoma RNA binding
EVIs	endovascular interventions		protein 1 (gene)
EVL	endoscopic variceal ligation	EWT	erupted wisdom teeth
EVLA	endovenous laser ablation	Ex	exposure
EVLP	ex-vivo lung perfusion	ex	examined
EVLT	endovenous laser therapy		example
EVLW	extravascular lung water		excision
EVM	error vector magnitude		exercise
EVN	extraventricular neurocytoma	exac	exacerbating; exacerbated
EVO	endoscopic variceal obturation		exacerbation
	evodiamine	exam	examination
EVO2	Truview EVO2 laryngoscope	EXAMD	exudative age-related macular
evo-devo	evolutionary developmental		degeneration
	biology	ExB	excisional biopsy
EVP	episcleral venous pressure	EXC	excision
EVPI	expected value of perfect	excis	excision
	information	excl	excludex, exclusive, excluded,
EVR	endovascular repair		or excluding
EVS	electronic vessel sealing	excret	excretion
	endoscopic variceal sclerosis	ExDS	Excited Delirium Syndrome
EVSP	early vasospasm	EXE	exemestane (Aromasin)
	electrokinetic vascular streaming	EXEC 22	Executive 22 chemistry profile
	potential		(see Laboratory Panels)
EVT	endovascular therapy	EXECHO	exercise echocardiography
	endovascular thrombectomy	EXEF	exercise ejection fraction
	Expressive Vocabulary Test	EXER	exercise
EVTAR	endovascular thoracoabdominal	EX FIX	external fixator (fixation)
	aneurysm repair	ExFix	external fixator
EVUS	endovaginal ultrasound	ex-fix	external fixator (fixation)
EVV	extravascular volume	EXGBUS	external genitalia, Bartholin
EVVD	may have meant EWD		(glands), urethral (glands),
	(expressive writing disorder)		and Skene (glands)
EW	elsewhere	EXHVT	exhaled tidal volume
	extended wear (lens)	EXIT	Ex-Utero Intrapartum Treatment
EWALL	European Working Group	EXIT 25	Executive Interview (cognitive
	on Adult ALL (acute		impairment test)
	lymphoblastic leukemia)	EXL	elixir
	(study)	EXLAP	exploratory laparotomy
EWB	emotional well-being	ex-lap	exploratory laparotomy
	estrogen withdrawal bleeding	ExM	expansion microscopy
	existential well-being	EXOPH	exophthalmos
EWBH	extracorporeal whole body	ExoS	a Pseudomonas aeruginosa
	hyperthermia		secreted toxin (exoenzyme S)
EWCL	extended-wear contact lens	exoS	exoenzyme S (gene)
EWDs	Ethnic Word Descriptors	EXP	experienced
EWE	Eastern and Western encephalo-		expired
	myelitis vaccine		exploration
EWF	empyema with fistula		expose

E

exp	expiratory
expect	expectorant
expir	expiration, expiratory
EXPL	exploratory
exp lap	exploratory laparotomy
expl lap	exploratory laparotomy
explor lap	exploratory laparotomy
exr	see gene website, www.ncbi.nlm.nih.gov/gene
EXS	exfoliation syndrome
EXs	exacerbations
	exercises
	exudates
EXT	extension
	extensor (tendon)
	external
	extract
	extraction
	extremities
	extremity
Ext mon	external monitor
extn	extension
extrav	extravasation
extrem	extremity; extremities
ext rot	external rotation
EXTUB	extubation
EXU	excretory urogram
EZ	Edmonston-Zagreb (vaccine)
	ellipsoid zone
EZH2	Enhancer of Zeste homolog
EZ-HT	Edmonston-Zagreb high-titer (vaccine)
EZN	Ehrlich-Ziehl Neelsen (staining method for the diagnosis of tuberculosis)
EzPAP®	a positive airway pressure system

F

F	facial
	Fahrenheit
	fair
	false
	fasting
	father
	feces
	female
	finger
	firm
	flexion
	flow
	fluoride
	Foxtrot (Phonetic Alphabet F; pronounced FOKS-TROT)
	French
	Friday
	fundi
	fundus
	phenylalanine
	phenylalanine (also referred to as Phe)
f	Frequency
F/	full upper denture
/F	full lower denture
(F)	final
°F	degrees Fahrenheit
F =	firm and equal
F_1	offspring from the first generation
F_2	offspring from the second generation
F/2	Field of 2
F_3	Fluothane
14F	14-hour fast required
F II-F XIII	factor 2 through 13
FVII	factor VII (antihemophilic factor 7)
F VIII	factor VIII (eight; antihemophilic factor)
FA	fatty acid
	femoral acetabular
	femoral artery
	fetus active
	fibroadenoma
	first aid
	flip angle (radiology)
	fludarabine (Fludara)
	fluorescein angiogram
	fluorescent antibody
	folic acid
	folinic acid (leucovorin calcium) (this is a dangerous abbreviation)
	forearm

E

	fractional anisotropy	
	Friedreich ataxia	
	functional activities	
Fa	father	
F/A	see FA	
F&A	foot and ankle	
FAA	febrile antigen agglutination	
	folic acid antagonist	
FAAAAI	Fellow of the American Academy of Allergy, Asthma and Immunology	
FAACT	Fellow of the American Academy of Clinical Toxicology	
FAAD	Fellow American Academy of Dermatology	
FAAFP	Fellow of the American Academy of Family Physicians	
FAAH	fatty acid amide hydrolase	
FAAHI	fatty acid amide hydrolase inhibitor(s)	
FAAM	Functional Ankle Ability Measure	
FAAMT	Fellow of the American Association for Medical Transcription	
FAAN	Fellow of the American Academy of Neurology	
	Fellow of the American Academy of Nursing	
	Food Allergy and Anaphylaxis Network	
FAAP	family assessment adjustment pass	
	Fellow of the American Academy of Pediatrics	
FAAPM	Fellow, American Academy of Pain Management	
FAARC	Fellowship of the American Association for Respiratory Care	
FAASOL	formalin, acetic, and alcohol solution	
FAB	digoxin immune Fab (Digibind®)	
	fertility awareness-based (methods of contraception)	
	French-American-British Cooperative group	
	functional arm brace	
FABACs	fatty acid bile acid conjugates	
FA-BCID	FilmArray Blood Culture IDentification panel is a multiplex polymerase chain reaction–based rapid diagnostic test that can detect 24 sepsis-related pathogens	

	(bacteria and yeast) and three antimicrobial resistance genes in patients with suspected sepsis	
FABER	flexion, abduction, and external rotation	
FABERE	flexion, abduction, external rotation, and extension (test)	
FABF	femoral artery blood flow	
FABIANS	felt awful but I'm allright now syndrome (slang)	
FABIR	may have meant FABER (flexion, abduction, and external rotation)	
FABQ	Fear-Avoidance Beliefs Questionnaire	
Fabr	Fabricius	
fabR	see gene website www.ncbi.nlm.nih.gov/gene	
FABRE	may have meant FABER (flexion, abduction, and external rotation)	
FAC	ferrite ammonium citrate	
	fluorouracil, doxorubicin (Adriamycin), and cyclophosphamide	
	follows all commands	
	fractional area change	
	fractional area concentration	
	free active chlorine	
	functional aerobic capacity	
FAc	fluocinolone acetonide	
F/A/C	see FAC	
FACA	Fellow of the American College of Anaesthetists	
FACAG	Fellow of the American College of Angiology	
FACAL	Fellow of the American College of Allergists	
FACAN	Fellow of the American College of Anesthesiologists	
FACAS	Fellow of the American College of Abdominal Surgeons	
FACC	Fellow of the American College of Cardiology	
FACCP	Fellow of the American College of Chest Physicians	
FACCPC	Fellow of the American College of Clinical Pharmacology & Chemotherapy	
FACD	Fellow of the American College of Dentists	
FACE	Fatality Assessment and Control Evaluation (National Institute for Occupational Safety and Health report)	
	Fellow of American College of Endocrinology	

221

	Fellow of American College of Epidemiology	FACT-B	Functional Assessment of Cancer Therapy-Breast
	fluorophore-assisted carbohydrate electrophoresis	FACT-F	Functional Assessment of Cancer Therapy-Fatigue
FaCE	Facial Clinimetric Evaluation	FACT-G	Functional Assessment of Cancer Therapy-General
FACEM	Fellow of the American College of Emergency Medicine	FACT-L	Functional Assessment of Cancer Therapy-Lung
FACEP	Fellow of the American College of Emergency Physicians	FACT-O	Functional Assessment of Cancer Therapy - Ovarian
FACES	pain scale for assessing pain intensity	FACT-P	Functional Assessment of Cancer Therapy-Prostate
FACG	Fellow of the American College of Gastroenterology	FAD	familial Alzheimer disease Family Assessment Device
FACH	forceps to after-coming head		fetal abdominal diameter
FACHE	Fellow of the American College of Healthcare Executives		fetal activity determination flavin adenine dinucleotide
FACIT-F	Functional Assessment of Chronic Illness Therapy Fatigue Subscale	FADD	Fas-associated death domain (protein)
FACLM	Fellow of the American College of Legal Medicine	FADDIR	flexion adduction internal rotation (test)
FACN	Fellow of the American College of Nutrition	fader	audio mixer (soundboard) level or volume knob or slider
FACNM	Fellow of the American College of Nurse-Midwives	FADI	Foot and Ankle Disability Index
FACNP	Fellow of the American College of Neuropsychopharma -cology	FADIR	flexion, adduction, and internal rotation
		fadR	fatty acid metabolism regulon transcriptional regulator (gene)
FACO	Fellow of the American College of Otolaryngology	FADS	fetal akinesia deformation sequences
FACOG	Fellow of the American College of Obstetricians & Gynecologists	FAE	fatal adverse event fetal alcohol effect
FACOS	Fellow of the American College of Orthopedic Surgeons	FAEE	fatty acid ethyl ester
FACP	Fellow of the American College of Physicians	FAERS	FDA (Food and Drug Administration) Adverse Event Reporting System
FACPRM	Fellow of the American College of Preventive Medicine	FAF	frequency-altered feedback fundus autofluorescence
FACR	Fellow of the American College of Radiology	FAFSA	Free Application for Federal Student Aid
	Fellow of the American College of Rheumatology	FAGA	full-term appropriate for gestational age
FACRO	Fellow of the American College of Radiation Oncology	FAH	fumarylacetoacetase hydrolase
		FAI	femoroacetabular impingement
FACS	familial cold autoinflammatory syndrome		functional ankle instability Functional Assessment Inventory
	Fellow of the American College of Surgeons	FA/ICG	fluorescein angiogram/ indocyanine green angiography
	fluorescent-activated cell sorter	FAID	facilitated aid in dying
FACSM	Fellow of the American College of Sports Medicine	FAIR	flow-sensitive alternating inversion recovery
FACT	Flexible Assertive Community Treatment	FAIS	femoroacetabular impingement syndrome (a movement -related disorder)
	focused appendix computed tomography	FAIT	fetal alloimmune thrombocytopenia
FACT-An	Functional Assessment of Cancer Therapy-Anemia	FAK	focal adhesion kinase

222

FAL	femoral arterial line	F-ara-A	fludarabine phosphate (Fludara)
FALL	fallopian	FARS	Fatality Analysis Reporting
FALS	familial amyotrophic lateral		System
	sclerosis		Friedreich Ataxia Rating Scale
falx	a sickle-like form	FARs	floating absolute risks
FAM	family	FAS	fetal acoustic stimulator
	fluorouracil, doxorubicin		fetal alcohol syndrome
	(Adriamycin), and mitomycin		forefoot abduct shoes
	full allosteric modulators		foreign accent syndrome
FAMA	fluorescent antibody to		full analysis set
	membrane antigen	Fas	fatty acids
FAME	fatty acid methyl ester	FASAY	functional analysis of separated
	fluorouracil, doxorubicin		alleles in yeast
	(Adriamycin), and semustin	FASC	fasciculations
	(methyl CCNU)		fluorescent-activated substrate
FamHx	family history		conversion (assay)
FAMMM	familial atypical multiple mole	FASCRS	Fellow of the American Society
	melanoma		of Colon and Rectal Surgeons
FAMS	fluorouracil, doxorubicin	FASD	fetal alcohol spectrum
	(Adriamycin), mitomycin,		disorder(s)
	and streptozotocin	FASHP	Fellow of the American Society
FAMTX	fluorouracil, doxorubicin		of Health-System Pharmacists
	(Adriamycin), and	FASI	Facial Angiofibroma Severity
	methotrexate		Index
FANA	fluorescent antinuclear antibody		field-amplified sample injection
F and C	fever and chills		focal abnormal signal intensities
F and N	fluids and nutrition	FASPS	familial advanced sleep-phase
FANG	fluorescent angiography		syndrome
FANSS&M	fundus anterior, normal size and	FASS	Farmaceutiska Specialiteter i
	shape and mobile		Sverige, the Swedish national
FAO	fatty acid oxidation		formulary of drugs
	Food and Agriculture		field-amplified sample stacking
	Organization		foot and ankle severity score
FAODs	fatty acid beta-oxidation disorders	FASS/SPC	Farmaceutiska Specialiteter
FAOS	Foot and Ankle Outcome Score		i Sverige, the Swedish
FAP	Facility Admission Profile		national formulary of
	familial adenomatous polyposis		drugs; Summary of Product
	familial amyloid polyneuropathy		Characteristics
	femoral artery pressure	FAST	facial droop, arm weakness,
	fibrillating action potential		slurred speech, and time to
	functional ambulation profile		call 911 (mnemonic to help
FAPA	fetal asphyctic preconditioning		recognize and act on seeing
	flowing atmospheric-pressure		stroke symptoms)
	afterglow (a source for		fetal acoustic stimulation testing
	atmospheric-pressure,		flow-assisted short-term
	ambient desorption/ionization		fluorescent allergosorbent
	mass spectrometry)		technique
FAPA syndrome	bouts of fever, adenitis,		focused assessment with
	pharyngitis, and aphthous		sonography for trauma
	ulcers		functional assessment staging
FAPS	functional abdominal pain		test (assessment technique
	syndrome		for evaluating functional
FAQ	frequently asked question(s)		deterioration in Alzheimer
	Functional Activities		disease patients throughout
	Questionnaire		the entire course of the illness)
FAQs	frequently asked questions	Faster R-CNN	Faster Region-based
FAR	false acceptance rate		Convolutional Neural
	frontal arousal rhythm		Network

FASTHUG	daily evaluation of patients' feeding, analgesia, sedation, thromboembolic prophylaxis, elevation of the head of the bed, ulcer prophylaxis, and glucose control to assure essential aspects of care for critically ill patients are met
FAST HUG	see FASTHUG
FAT	Fetal Activity Test
	fluorescent antibody test
	focal atrial tachycardia
	food awareness training
FATSAT	fat saturation
Fat-Sat	Fat-Sat pulses are short-duration radio frequency pulses tuned to the resonance frequency of fat.
FATWO	female adnexal tumors of probable Wolffian origin
FAU	fatty acid unsaturation
	see gene website www.ncbi.nlm .nih.gov/gene
FAV	facio-auricular vertebral
FAVA	femoral anteversion angle
FAvB	food avoidance behavior
FAVD	forceps-assisted vaginal delivery
fAVG	forearm arteriovenous graft
FAW	Filipino-American women
Fax	telecopying (facsimile)
FAZ	foveal avascular zone
FB	facet block
	fasting blood (sugar)
	feedback
	fiberoptic bronchoscopy
	finger breadth
	flexible bronchoscopy
	foreign body
	Forwarding Balance (Medicare code)
	full body
F/B	followed by
	forward bending
	forward/backward
	front/back
FBA	foreign body aspiration
FBAO	foreign body airway obstruction
FBB-HKS/ADHS	The German Rating scale for attention-deficit hyperactivity disorder
FBC	full (complete) blood count
FBCOD	foreign body, cornea, right eye
FBCOS	foreign body, cornea, left eye
FBD	familial British dementia
	fibrocystic breast disease
	functional bowel disease
FBE	familial Barrett's esophagus

Fbe	see gene website www.ncbi.nlm .nih.gov/gene
FBF	forearm blood flow
	total blood flow
FBG	fasting blood glucose
	foreign-body-type granulomata
FBH	hydroxybutyric dehydrogenase
fbHCG	free beta-human chorionic gonadotropin
FBHH	familial benign hypocalciuric hypercalcemia
FBI	flossing, brushing, and irrigation
	full bony impaction
FBL	fecal blood loss
FBM	felbamate (Felbatol)
	fetal breathing motion
	foreign body, metallic
FBMs	flashbulb memories
FBN1	see gene website, www.ncbi .nlm.nih.gov/gene
FBO	for the benefit of
FBOT	fecal occult blood testing (Romance languages)
FBP	frontal bite plane (dental)
FBPR	first (office) blood pressure reading
	fresh bleeding per rectum
FBRCM	fingerbreadth below right costal margin
FBS	failed back syndrome
	fasting blood sugar
	fetal bovine serum
	foreign body sensation (eye)
FBSE	full-body skin examination
FBSS	failed back surgery syndrome
FBT	family-based treatment
	fentanyl buccal tablet
	food-borne trematode
FBU	fingers below umbilicus
FBUT	fluorescein (tear film) breakup time
FBW	fasting blood work
FC	family care
	family conference
	febrile convulsion
	female child
	fever, chills
	film coated (tablet)
	financial class
	finger clubbing
	finger counting
	flexion contractor
	flow compensation (radiology)
	flucytosine (Ancobon)
	foam cuffed (tracheal or endotrachael tube)

	Foley catheter	FCE	fluorouracil, cisplatin, and etoposide
	follows commands		
	foster care		functional capacity evaluation
	French Canadian	FCEPS	Fuel Cell Energy/Power System
	full (resuscitation) code	fceps	forceps
	functional capacity	FCFC	full code, full care
	functional class	Fc/Fc	ferrocenium/ferrocene
F&C	fever and chills	FCFD	fluorescence capillary-fill device
	foam and condom	FCFM	fibered confocal fluorescence microscopy
F/C	fever and chills		
	see FC	FCG	fasting capillary glucose
F + C	flare and cells	FCGs	family caregivers
5FC	flucytosine (this is a dangerous abbreviation as it can be seen as 5FU)	FCH	(18)F-fluorocholine
			familial combined hyperlipidemia
FCA	Federal False Claims Act		fibrosing cholestatic hepatitis
	femoral cortical allograft	FCHL	familial combined hyperlipemia
	fetal cardiac activity	FCI	flow cytometric imminophenotyping
FCAS	familial cold autoinflammatory syndrome		
		FCL	fibular collateral ligament
F. cath.	Foley catheter	F-CL	fluorouracil and calcium leucovorin
FCB	fluorescent cell barcoding		
FCBD	fibrocystic breast disease	FCM	facial choreic movements
fCBG	fasting capillary blood glucose		flow cytometry
FCBIIB	focal cortical dysplasia type IIB		Foley criteria met
FCC	familial cerebral cavernoma		functional communication measure
	familial colonic cancer		fuzzy C-mean
	family centered care		
	femoral cerebral catheter	FCMC	family centered maternity care
	follicular center cells	FCMD	Fukiyama congenital muscular dystrophy
	fracture compound comminuted		
FC2c	Fire Controlman 2nd Class	FCMN	family centered maternity nursing
FCCA	Final Comprehensive Consensus Assessment		
		fcMRI	functional connectivity magnetic resonance imaging
FCCC	fracture complete, compound, and comminuted		
		FCMS	Foix-Chavany-Marie syndrome
FCCL	follicular center cell lymphoma	FCMs	fecal corticosterone metabolites
FCCM	Fellow, American College of Critical Care Medicine		food contact materials
		FCN	Financial Control Number (Medicare)
FCCP	carbonyl cyanide p-(trifluoromethoxy) phenylhydrazone (an uncoupler of oxidative phosphorylation in mitochondria)		
		F/C/N	fever, chills, and nausea
		F/C/N/S	fever, chills, nausea, and sweating
		FCNs	Faith Community Nurses
		FCNV	fever, cough, nausea, and vomiting
	Fellow of the American College of Chest Physicians		
		F/C/N/V	fever, chills, nausea, and vomiting
	Fellow of the American College of Clinical Pharmacy		
		F/C/N/V/D	fever, chills, nausea, vomiting, and diarrhea
FCCU	family centered care unit		
FCD	feces collection device	FC-NYHA	functional capacity- according to the New York Heart Association(see NYHA)
	fibrocystic disease		
	fixed complete denture (prosthodontics)		
		FCOHb	cord blood fetal carboxyhemoglobin
	focal cortical dysplasia		
	Fuchs corneal dystrophy	FCOU	finger count, both eyes
FCDB	fibrocystic disease of the breast	FCP	formocresol pulpotomu
FCD II	focal cortical dysplasia type 2	fcps	forceps

FCPT	foveal center point thickness	FDA	Food and Drug Administration
FCQ-T	Food Cravings		fronto-dextra anterior
	Questionnaire-Trait	FDAAA	Food and Drug Administration
FCR	fear of cancer recurrence		Amendments Act of 2007
	flexor carpi radialis	FDA-CASA	Food and Drug Administration
	fractional catabolic rate	2012	Classification Algorithm for
FCRB	flexor carpi radialis brevis		Suicide Assessment 2012
Fc receptor	an antibody receptor involved	FDA Form 483	written communications issued
	in antigen recognition which		by the Food and Drug
	is located at the membrane		Administration to drug firm
	of certain immune cells		management at the conclusion
	including B lymphocytes,		of an inspection when an
	natural killer cells,		investigator(s) has observed
	macrophages, neutrophils,		any conditions that in their
	and mast cells; the name is		judgment may constitute vio-
	derived as it recognizes Fc		lations of the Food Drug and
	fragment of antibodies		Cosmetic Act and related Acts
FCRT	fetal cardiac reactivity test	FDAMA	Food and Drug Administration
	focal cranial radiation therapy		Modernization Act (1997)
FCS	familial chylomicronemia	FDAVB	first-degree atrioventricular
	syndrome (a genetic disorder		(heart) block
	characterized by severe hyper-	FDB	first-degree burn
	triglyceridemia and recurrent		flexor digitorum brevis
	pancreatitis due to a deficiency	FDBL	fecal daily blood loss
	in lipoprotein lipase)	FDC	familial dilated cardiomyopathy
	fever, chills, and sweating		Fetal Diagnostic Clinic
	fluorescence correlation		fixed-dose combination
	spectroscopy		(preparations)
F/C/S	fever, chills, and sweating	FDCA	Food, Drug, and Cosmetic Act
FCSEMS	fully covered self-expandable	FD&C Act	Food, Drug, and Cosmetic Act
	metal stent	FDCS	follicular dendritic cell sarcomas
FCSNVD	fever, chills, sweating, nausea,	FDCs	follicular dendritic cells
	vomiting, and diarrhea	FDD	focus to detector distance
FCSRT	Free and Cued Selective		(radiology)
	Reminding Test	FDE	fixed-drug eruption
FCT	fever-clearance time	FDEIA	food-dependent, exercised
	film-coated tablet		induced anaphylaxis
	fluorescein clearance test	FDF	flexor digitorum profundus
	forced choice testing		(tendon)
FCU	flexor carpi ulnaris (tendon)	FDG	feeding
FCV	feline calicivirus		fluorine-18-labeled deoxyglucose
FCx	frontal cortex		(^{18}fluorodeoxyglucose)
FCZ	fluconazole	FDGB	fall down, go boom (slang)
FD	Fabry disease	FDGPET	positron emission tomography
	familial dysautonomia		with ^{18}fluorodeoxyglucose
	Farber disease	FDG PET	positron emission tomography
	fetal demise		with ^{18}fluorodeoxyglucose
	fetal distress	FDG-PET/CT	18fluorodeoxyglucose positron
	focal distance		emission tomography/
	food diary		computed tomography
	forceps delivery	FDGS	feedings
	Forestier Disease	FDI	Facial Disability Index
	free drain		first dorsal interosseous
	full denture		food-drug interaction
	fully dilated		Functional Disability Index
	functional deficits	FDIP	fourth dorsal interosseus pedis
	functional dyspepsia		(muscle)
F & D	fixed and dilated	FDIU	fetal death in utero

FDL	flexor digitorum longus
FDLI	Food and Drug Law Institute (*a not-for-profit 501(c)(3) organization*)
FDLMP	first day of last menstrual period
FDM	feline diabetes mellitus
	fetus of diabetic mother
	fiber density mapping
	Financial decision-making
	flexor digiti minimi
FDMA	first dorsal metatarsal artery
FDMC	fracture dislocation of the mandibular condyle
FDN	FADD (Fas-associated death domain)-dominant negative
	functional dry needling
FD-OCT	Fourier domain optical coherence tomography
FDOPA	18F-fluorodihydroxyphenylalanine (a radiopharmaceutical for the diagnosis and detection of neuroendocrine tumors)
FDP	fibrin-degradation products
	fixed dental prosthesis
	fixed-dose procedure
	flexor digitorum profundus
FDPCA	fixed-dose patient-controlled analgesia
FD-PET	fluorodopa-positron emission tomography
FDPs	fixed dental prostheses
FDQB	flexor digiti quinti brevis
FDR	false discovery rate (the expected proportion of false positives among all significant hypotheses)
	first-dose reaction
FDS	flexor digitorum superficialis
	flow-diverter stent
	for duration of stay
	functional disability status
FDT	frequency-doubling technology (perimetry for visual field screening)
	fronto-dextra transversa (right frontotransverse)
	Functional Dexterity Test
FDTC	Family Drug Treatment Court
	follicular derived thyroid carcinoma
FdU	floxuridine (5-fluoro-2'-deoxyuridine; also FUDR and 5-FdU)
FDV	female-directed violence
FDVA	Florida Department of Veterans' Affairs

FE	fat embolism
	field echo (radiology)
	flexion and extension
	frequency encode (radiology)
Fe	female
	iron
F&E	fluids and electrolytes
	full and equal
FEA	finite element analysis
	flat epithelial atypia
FEB	febrile
	fetal echogenic bowel
Feb	February
FEBM	edema-free body mass
FEBT	fentanyl effervescent buccal tablet
FEC	fluorouracil, epirubicin, and cyclophosphamide
	fluorouracil, etoposide, and cisplatin
	forced expiratory capacity
FEC100	fluorouracil, epirubicin, and cyclophosphamide (the 100 refers to 100 mg/m^2 of epirubicin)
FECD	Fuchs endothelial corneal dystrophy
FECG	fetal electrocardiogram
FeCh	ferrochelatase
FECP	free erythrocyte coproporphyrin
FeCrNi	iron-chroimium-nickel alloy
FECT	fibroelastic connective tissue
FED	fish eye disease
	freestanding emergency department
Fe def	iron deficiency
FEDs	freestanding emergency departments
FEE	Far-Eastern equine encephalitis
FEEN	Spanish Foundation for Neurological Diseases
FEES	fiberoptic endoscopic evaluation of swallowing
	fiberoptic endoscopic examination of swallowing
FEESST	flexible endoscopic evaluation of swallowing with sensory testing
FEEST	Facial Expressions of Emotion: Stimuli and Tests (a test for emotion recognition)
FEF	feeling of ear fullness
	forced expiratory flow rate
FEF2575	forced expiratory flow during the middle half of the forced vital capacity

FEFxy	forced expiratory flow between two designated volume points in the forced vital capacity
FEG-SEM	field emission gun-scanning electron microscopy
FEH	focal epithelial hyperplasia (Heck disease)
FEHBP	Federal Employee Health Benefits Plan
FEHC	Family Evaluation of Hospice Care (survey)
FEL	familial erythrophagocytic lymphohistiocytosis
	free electron laser
FeLV	feline leukemia virus
FEM	femoral
	finite element method
	fluid-electrolyte malnutrition
FEMA	Federal Emergency Management Agency
fem-ax	femoro-axillary (artery bypass)
FEM-FEM	femoral femoral (bypass)
FEMG	facial electromyography
FEM-POP	femoral popliteal (bypass)
FEM-TIB	femoral tibial (bypass)
femto	prefix for units denoting a factor of 10^{-15} or 0.000,000,000,000,001
femtoliter	a volume equal to 10^{-15} liters, (one quadrillionth liter)
FEN	fluid, electrolytes, and nutrition
F/E/N	fluids, electrolytes, and nutrition
FENa	fractional extraction of sodium
FENGI	Fluids, Electrolytes, and Nutrition, gastroenterology
FENIB	familial encephalopathies with neuroserpin inclusion bodies
FeNO	fractional exhaled nitric oxide (used for diagnosis of asthma and to make treatment decisions)
FEN-PHEN	fenfluramine and phentermine
FENS	field-electrical neural stimulation
FENs	foreign-educated nurses
fent	fentanyl
FEOM	full extraocular movements
FEP	first-episode psychosis
	free erythrocyte porphyrins
	free erythrocyte protoporphorin
	functional exercise program
Fe-PILC	Iron pillared interlayered clay(s)
FER	flexion, extension, and rotation
FERGs	focal electroretinograms
Fern Test	a 'fern-like' appearance on a cervical mucus slide used to provide indirect evidence of ovulation and fertility
FERPA	Family Educational Rights and Privacy Act
FERR	serum ferritin
FES	Falls Efficacy Scale
	fat embolism syndrome
	floppy eyelid syndrome
	forced expiratory spirogram
	functional electrical stimulation
FES04	FeSO4 (ferrous sulfate)
FESEM	field emission scanning electron microscopy
FESI	field-enhanced sample injection
FES-I	Falls Efficacy Scale-International
FES-I (Ch)	Chinese version of the 16-item Falls Efficacy Scale International
FeSO$_4$	ferrous sulfate
FESR	front-end speech recognition
FESS	functional endoscopic sinus surgery
FESz	first-episode schizophrenia
FET	familial essential tremor
	fixed erythrocyte turnover
	forced expiratory time
	frozen elephant trunk (technique enables combined aortic arch and descending aortic repair)
	frozen embryo transfer
FETI	fluorescence (fluorescent) energy transfer immunoassay
FETO	fetoscopic endotracheal occlusion
FEU	fibrinogen equivalents units
FEUO	for external use only
FeUrea	fractional excretion of urea
FEV	familial exudative vitreoretinopathy
FEV$_1$	forced expiratory volume in one second
FEVAR	fenestrated endovascular aneurysm repair
FEVC	forced expiratory vital capacity
FEVER	see FEVAR
FEV1/FVC	forced expiratory volume (time)/ forced vital capacity ratio (also called Tiffeneau-Pinelli index, is a calculated ratio used in the diagnosis of obstructive and restrictive lung disease)
FEVG	Fraction d'éjection ventriculaire gauche (French; left ventricular ejection fraction)
FEVI	forced expiratory volume in 1 (first) second
FEVR	familial exudative vitreoretinopathy

FEV$_{1\%VC}$	forced expiratory volume in one second as percent of forced vital capacity		Five-Factor Model (of personality)
FF	fat free		freedom from metastases
	fecal frequency		full-face mask
	filtration fraction	FFMQ	Five-Facet Mindfulness Questionnaire
	finger-to-finger	FFN	fetal fibronectin
	five-minute format	FFNPL	flexible fiberoptic nasopharyngolaryngoscope
	flat feet		
	fluticasone furoate (Arnuity Ellipta)	FFOH	fall from own height
		FFOV	functional field of view
	force fluids	FFP	free from progression
	formula fed		fresh frozen plasma
	forward flexion	FFPE	formalin-fixed, paraffin-embedded
	foster father		
	Fox-Fordyce (disease)	FFPT	formalin-fixed, paraffin-embedded tissue
	fundus firm		
	further flexion	FFQ	food frequency questionnaire
F&F	filiform and follower	FFR	Forward Functional Reach (test)
	fixes and follows		fractional flow reserve
	flashes and floaters		freedom from relapse
F/F	face to face	FFROM	full, free range of motion
F→F	finger to finger	FFS	failure-free survival
F2F	face-to-face		fall from standing
	fit-to-flow (microfluidic adaptors)		fee-for-service
			feet-first supine
FFA	free fatty acid		Fight For Sight
	frontal fibrosing alopecia		flexible fiberoptic sigmoidoscopy
	fundus fluorescein angiogram		
	fusiform face area	FFSH	falls from standing heights
FFAF	freedom from atrial fibrillation	FFSR	failure-free survival rate
FFAT	Free Floating Anxiety Test	FFSU	Federation Francaise du Sport Universitaire (French Federation of University Sports)
FFB	flexible fiberoptic bronchoscopy		
FFCD	French Foundation for Digestive Cancerology		
		FFT	fast-Fourier transforms
FFD	fat-free diet		flicker fusion threshold
	finger-to-floor distance		free-floating thrombus
	fixed flexion deformity	FFTC	fast-Fourier Transform Convolution
	focal-film distance		
FFDM	freedom from distant metastases	FFTDWB	flat foot touchdown weight bearing
	full-field digital mammography		
ffDNA	free fetal DNA (deoxyribonucleic acid)	FFTP	first full-term pregnancy
		FF1/U	fundus firm 1 cm above umbilicus
FFDs	free-form deformations	FF2/U	fundus firm 2 cm above umbilicus
FFE	free-flow electrophoresis		
FFEs	Federally-facilitated Exchanges (Affordable Care Act)	FFU/1	fundus firm 1 cm below umbilicus
		FFU/2	fundus firm 2 cm below umbilicus
FFF	field-flow fractionation		
	freedom from (biochemical and/or clinical) failure	FF@u	fundus firm at umbilicus
		FF/UMEC/VI	fluticasone furoate/, umeclidinium, and vilanterol inhalation powder (Trelegy Ellipta)
FFG	fusiform gyrus		
FFH	focal fibrous hyperplasia (dental)		
FFI	fast food intake	FF/VI	fluticasone furoate and vilanterol (Breo Ellipta)
	fatal familial insomnia		
	Foot Function Index	FFWB	flat foot weight bearing
FFL	flexible fiberoptic laryngoscopy	FFWU	full fever work-up
FFM	fat-free mass	FFY	Federal fiscal year
	five finger movement		

FG	fasting glucose	FHA	filamentous hemagglutinin
	fibrin glue	FHB	flexor hallucis brevis
	fistulogram	FHBL	familial
	Fournier gangrene		hypobetatalipoproteinemia
	functional group	FHC	familial history of cancer
	fusiform gyrus		familial hypertrophic
FGA	functional gait assessment		cardiomyopathy
FGAPs	first-generation antipsychotic		family health center
	drugs		fetal human colon (cell line)
FGAs	first-generation antihistamines	FHCC	Federal Health Care Center
FGC	familial gigantiform cementoma		fibrolamellar hepatocellular
	female genital cutting		carcinoma
	full gold crown		follicular Hurthle cell
FGD	familial glucocorticoid		carcinoma
	deficiency	FHCIC	Fuch heterochromic iridocyclitis
	focus group discussion(s)	FHD	family history of diabetes
	functional gastrointestinal		femoral head diameter
	disorders	FHDM	family history of diabetes mellitus
FGDs	focus group discussions	FHF	Filoviral hemorrhagic fever
FGF	fibroblast growth factor		fulminant hepatic failure
FGF-12	fibroblast growth factor 12	FHH	familial hypocalciuric
FGF23	fibroblast growth factor 23		hypercalcemia
FGFR	fibroblast growth factor		fetal heart heard
	receptor (gene)	FHHD	family history of heavy drinking
FGFR2	fibroblast growth factor		Florida Hospital Heartland
	receptor 2		Division (Lake Placid, FL)
FGFs	fibroblast growth factors		frictional hyperkeratotic hand
FGID	functional gastrointestinal		dermatitis
	disorder(s)	FHI	fibrous hamartoma of infancy
FGL	fingolimod (Gilenya)		frontal horn index
Fgl-2	fibrinogen-like protein 2		Fuch heterochromic iridocyclitis
FGM	female genital mutilation	FHIT	fragile histidine triad protein
FGM/C	female genital mutilation/cutting	FHL	flexor hallucis longus
FGP	fundic gland polyps		functional hallux limitus
FGR	fetal growth restriction	FHLD	lateral herniation of the
fgr	finger		lumbar disc
FGS	FG syndrome (FG stands for the	FHM	familial hemiplegic migraine
	surnames of the first patients		fetal heart monitor
	to be described with this		fetal heart motion
	condition; also known as	FHN	family history negative
	Opitz-Kaveggia syndrome)		femoral head necrosis
	fibrogastroscopy	FHNH	fetal heart not heard
	focal glomerulosclerosis	FHO	family history of obesity
FG syndrome	FG stands for the surnames of	FHP	family history positive
	the first patients to be		forward head posture
	described with this condi-	FHR	fetal heart rate
	tion; also known as Opitz-	FHRB	fetal heart rate baseline
	Kaveggia syndrome	FHRBL	fetal heart rate baseline
FGX	fluid-gas exchange	FHRs	factor H-related proteins
FH	familial hypercholesterolemia		fetal heart rates
	family history	FHRT	(knee) flexion heel raise test
	favorable histology	FHRV	fetal heart rate variability
	fetal head	FHS	Family Health Service
	fetal heart		fetal heart sounds
	fundal height		fetal hydantoin syndrome
F/H	See FH		food hypersensitivity
FH+	family history positive	FHT	fetal heart tone
FH−	family history negative		fetal heart tracing

FHTs   family health teams
     fibrohistiocytic tumors
FHTV   fetal head and trunk volume
FHVP   free hepatic vein pressure
FHX   fluorouracil, hydroxyurea, and
     radiotherapy
FHx   family history
FI   fecal incontinence
     feeding intolerance
     fiscal intermediary
     fluorescence index
     food impaction
Fi02   See FiO2
FIA   familial intracranial aneurysms
     Family Independence Agency
       (formerly Department of
       Social Services)
FIAC   fiacitabine
FIADH   may have meant SIADH
     (syndrome of inappropriate
     antidiuretic hormone
     hypersecretion)
FIAU   fialuridine
FIB   fascia iliaca block
     fibrillation
     fibula
     focused ion-beam
FIB-4   fibrosis-4 score (a calculation
     which estimates the amount
     of scoring in the liver to
     optimize the management
     of patients with chronic
     hepatitis C virus)
FIBA   International Basketball
     Federation
fibr   Fibrillation
     fibrinogen
Fibs   fibroblasts
FIBTEM   fibrin-based thromboelastometry
     (assesses the clot firmness of
     the fibrin clot)
FICA   Federal Insurance Contributions
     Act (Social Security)
FICAT   Federative International
     Committee on Anatomical
     Terminology
Ficat   a functional radiographic bone
     evaluation rating
FICB   fascia iliaca compartment block
Fick's Law   Fick's law of diffusion; molecules
     tend to move from higher
     concentration to a lower
     concentration where the rate
     of diffusion across a membrane
     is directly proportional to the
     concentration gradient and
     inversely related to the thick-
     ness of the membrane

$FiCO_2$ fraction of inspired carbon
     dioxide
FICS   Fellow of the International
     College of Surgeons
FID   father in delivery
     flame ionization detection
     focus to isocentre distance
       (radiology)
     free induction decay
FIESTA   fast imaging employing steady-
     state acquisition (imaging)
FIF   forced inspiratory flow
FiF   Functional Intact Fibrinogen
     (test)
FIFO   first-in-first-out
     fly-in, fly-out (workers)
FIGE   field inversion gel
     electrophoresis
FIGLU   formiminoglutamic acid
FIGO   International Federation of
     Gynecology and Obstetrics
FIGS   fluorescence image-guided
     surgery
FIH   first-in-human (trial)
FIHOA   Functional Index for Hand
     Osteoarthritis
FIHP   familial isolated
     hyperparathyroidism
FII   food Insulin Index (an algorithm
     for ranking foods based
     on their insulin demand
     relative to an isoenergetic
     reference food)
FIL   father-in-law
     Filipino
     flexion in lying
FIM   functional independence measure
FIMS   flow-injection mass spectrometric
     Fédération Internationale du
     Médicine du Sport
     (International Federation
     of Sports Medicine)
FIN   flexible intramedullary nail
FINA   Federation International
     Natation Association (rules)
FIND   follow-up intervention for
     normal development
FiO_2 fraction of inspired oxygen
FIP   feline infectious peritonitis
     flatus in progress
FIPV   feline infectious peritonitis virus
FIQ   Fibromyalgia Impact
     Questionnaire
FIR   far-infrared (radiation)
     fast inversion recovery
     favorable immune response
     fetal inflammatory response
     finite impulse response

F

	flow increase rate	FKA	failed to keep appointment
	see gene website; www.ncbi		formally known as
	.nlm.nih.gov/gene	FKBP	FK-506 binding protein
FIRDA	frontal intermittent rhythmic		(tacrolimus; Prograf)
	delta activity	FKC	formalin-killed cell (vaccine)
	(electroencephalograph)	FKD	Kinetic Family Drawing
FIRES	febrile infection-related epilepsy	FKE	full knee extension
	syndrome	FKGL	Flesch-Kincaid Grade
FIRI	fasting insulin resistance index		Level (score)
Firmagon	degarelix inj	FKO 115	Klinische Forschergruppe #115
FIRS	fetal inflammatory response		(clinical research unit research
	syndrome		grant # 115, Germany)
FIS	flexion in standing	FL	fatty liver
FISH+	fluorescence in situ		femur length
	hybridization positive		fetal length
FISH	fluorescent (fluorescence) *in situ*		flerovium
	hybridization		Florida
FISH-MD	fluorescence in situ hybridization-		fluid
	Microdissection		fluorescein
FISit	flexion in sitting		fluorouracil and leucovorin
FISMP	Fellow of the Institute of Safe		flutamide and leuprolide acetate
	Medication Practices		focal laser
FISP	fast imaging with steady state		focal length
	precision		follicular lymphoma
FISS	flexion in step-standing		full liquids
FIST	Function in Sitting Test		functional limitations
FIT	fecal immunochemical test	fL	femtoliter (10^{-15} liter)
	functional inferior turbinoplasty	F/L	father-in-law
FITC	fluorescein isothiocyanate	FLA	free-living amebic (ameba)
	conjugated		frequent low amplitude
FITL	fetal intolerance to labor		low-friction arthroplasty
FITs	fecal immunochemical tests	FLACC	Face, Legs, Activity, Cry, and
FITT	frequency, intensity, type,		Consolability (pain
	and time		assessment scale)
FIT test	fecal immunochemical test	FLACS	femtosecond laser-assisted
FIUD	fetal intrauterine death		cataract surgery
FIV	feline immunodeficiency virus	FLAER	fluorescently labeled bacterial
	in vitro fertilization (French)		toxin aerolysin (a test reagent
FIVC	forced inspiratory vital capacity		for paroxysmal nocturnal
five times a day	there is no safe abbreviation for		hemoglobinuria)
	five times a day; write out,	FLAG	fludarabine, ara-C (cytarabine),
	five times a day (this is a		and G-CSF (filgrastim)
	difficult schedule to ad-	FLAIR	fluid attenuated inversion
	here to)		recovery (imaging)
FIX	factor IX (nine)	Flakka	alpha-pyrrolidinovalerophenone,
FJA	facet joint arthropathy		(alpha-PVP) a psychoactive
	first jejunal artery		substance, chemically close
FJB	facet joint block		to cathinone
FJI	facet joint injection	FLAP	5-lipoxygenase activating
	functional jejunal interposition		protein
FJN	familial juvenile nephrophthisis		fluorouracil, leucovorin,
FJP	familial juvenile polyposis		doxorubicin (Adriamycin),
FJROM	full joint range of motion		and cisplatin (Platinol)
FJS	finger joint size	FLARE	Fluorescence-Assisted
FJS-12	Forgotten Joint Score-12		Resection and Exploration
FJSI	facet joint steroid injection		(imaging system)
FJV	first jejunal vein	FLASH	fast low-angle shot
FK506	tacrolimus (Prograf)	FLAVO	flavopiridol

FLB	funny looking beat	FLOT	fluorescence laminar optical tomography
FLBS	funny looking baby syndrome (see note under FLK)		fluorouracil, leucovorin, oxaliplatin, and Taxotere (docetaxel)
FLC	follicular large cell lymphoma		
	fuzzy logic control	floz	fluid ounce (30 mL)
FLCR	free light chain ratio (components of immunoglobulins)	FLP	Falling Leaf Program
			fasting lipid profile
FLD	fatty liver disease		Functional Limitations Profile
	field		funny looking parents (should
	fluid		never be used: unusual
	flutamide and leuprolide acetate depot		facial features, is a better expression)
	full liquid diet	FLQ	Fluoroquinolone-type antibiotics
	full lower denture		such as ciprofloxacin
FLDS	Fundamentalist Church of Jesus Christ of Latter-Day Saints	FLR	foveal light reflex
		FL REST	fluid restriction
		FLS	fibroblast-like synoviocytes
Flds	flavodoxins		flashing lights and/or scotoma
FL Dtr	full lower denture		flu (influenza)-like symptoms
FLE	frontal lobe epilepsy		flu-like symptoms
FLe	fluorouracil and levamisole	FLSA	Fair Labor Standards Act
flex	flexion		Functional Living Skills Assessment
flex-ex	an elbow neurological sign to detect unilateral upper extremity non-organic paresis		
		FLT	fluorothymidine
flex sig	flexible sigmoidoscopy	FLT3	fms-like tyrosine kinase-3
flex sigmoid	flexible sigmoidoscopy	FLT-3	Feline McDonough Sarcoma-like tyrosine kinase-3
FLF	funny looking facies (see note under FLK)		
		FLT3 ITD	Fms-like tyrosine kinase 3-internal tandem duplication
FLG	filaggrin (gene)		
	funny looking grin (radiology)	FLT3-ITD	Fms-like tyrosine kinase 3-internal tandem duplication
FLGA	full-term, large for gestational age		
		FLU	fluconazole (Diflucan)
FLI-1	Friend leukemia integration site 1 (A nuclear transcription factor)		fludarabine (Fludara)
			flunisolide (Aero Bid)
			fluoxetine (Prozac)
FLIC	Functional Living Index-Cancer		fluticasone propionate (Flonase)
FLIE	Functional Living Index-Emesis		influenza
FLIM	fluorescence lifetime imaging microscopy	FLU A	influenza A virus
		FLU/BU	fludarabine-based regimens with busulfan
FLIP	functional lumen imaging probe		
FLIPI	Follicular Lymphoma International Prognostic Index	Flud	fludarabine (Fludara)
		fluid	fluidotherapy
FLK	funny looking kid (should never be used: unusual facial features, is a better expression)	Fluido®	a pressure infusion device used in to warm large volumes of fluid over a short period of time
		FLU/MEL	fludarabine-based regimens with melphalan
FLK from FLP	funny looking kid from funny looking parents (should never be used: unusual facial features, is a better expression)	FLUO	Fluothane
		fluoro	fluoroscopy
		FLUS	follicular lesion of uncertain significance
fll	flyless; see gene website www.ncbi.nlm.nih.gov/gene	FLUT	flutamide (Eulexin)
		FLV	Friend leukemia virus
FLL	focal liver lesion(s)	FLW	fasting laboratory work
FLM	fetal lung maturity	FLX	flexion
FLN	leucovorin (folinic acid)		fluoxetine (Prozac)
FLNA	filamin A; see gene website; www.ncbi.nlm.nih.gov/gene	FLZ	flurazepam (Dalmane)

F

FM	face mask	FML	familial multiple lipomatosis
	family medicine	FMLA	Family and Medical Leave
	family member(s)		Act of 1993
	fat mass	FMM	fine matrix mapping
	fetal movements		foramen magnum meningioma
	fibromyalgia (syndrome)	FMN	first malignant neoplasm
	fine motor		flavin mononucleotide
	floor manager	FMO	fluence map optimization
	fluorescent microscopy	FMOA	full-mouth odontectomy and
	follicular mucinosis		alveoloplasty
	foster mother	FMOL	femtomole (10^{-15} mole)
Fm	fermium	FMP	fasting metabolic panel
+FM	see FM		first menstrual period
F & M	firm and midline (uterus)		functional maintenance program
F/M	see FM	FMPA	full-mouth periapicals
FMA	Fugl-Meyer Assessment	FMQA	Florida Medical Quality
fmachop	fluorouracil, methotrexate,		Assurance
	cytarabine (ara-C), cyclo-	FMR	fetal movement record
	phosphamide, doxorubicin		focused medical review
	(hydroxydaunorubicin),		functional magnetic resonance
	vincristine (Oncovin),		(imaging)
	and prednisone		functional manual reaction
FMAER	frequency modulation auditory		functional mitral regurgitation
	evoked response	FMR1	fragile X mental retardation 1
FMA-LE	Fugl-Meyer Lower Extremity	FMRD	full-mouth restorative dentistry
	(motor) Assessment	fMRI	functional magnetic resonance
FMA-UE	Fugl-Meyer Upper Extremity		imaging
	(motor) Assessment	FMRP	fragile X mental retardation
FMB	fluctuating-masker benefit		protein(s)
FMC	fetal movement count	FMS	fast macula scans
	fine motor coordination		Fecal Management System
fMCG	fetal magnetocardiography		fibromyalgia syndrome
FMCSA	Federal Motor Carrier Safety		fluorouracil, mitomycin, and
	Administration		streptozocin
FMD	family medical doctor		full-mouth series
	fibromuscular dysplasia	F & MS	frontal and maxillary sinuses
	flow-mediated dilatation	FMT	fecal microbiota transplantation
	foot-and-mouth disease		floating mass transducer
	functional movement disorder		fluorescein meniscus time
FMDs	functional movement disorders		(dry-eye test)
FMDV	foot-and-mouth disease virus		functional muscle test
FME	Frühsommer-meningoenzephalitis	FMTC	familial medullary thyroid
	vaccine		carcinoma
	full-mouth extraction	FMTM	fast macular thickness maps
FMEA	failure mode and effects analysis	FMU	first morning urine
FMEN-1	familial multiple endocrine	FMV	flow-mediated vasodilation
	neoplasia, type 1		fluorouracil, semustine (methyl-
FMF	familial Mediterranean fever		CCNU), and vincristine
	fetal movement felt	FMX	full-mouth x-ray
	forced midexpiratory flow	FMZ	flumazenil (Romazicon)
FMG	fine mesh gauze	FN	facial nerve
	foreign medical graduate		false negative
FMH	family medical history		febrile neutropenia
	fetomaternal hemorrhage		femoral neck
	fibromuscular hyperplasia		finger-to-nose (test)
FM 100-hue	Farnsworth-Munsell 100-hue test		flight nurse
FmHx	family history	F&N	fluids and nutrition
FMI	fat mass index	F/N	fluids and nutrition

FNA	femoral neck anteversion	FNR	false negative rate
	fine-needle aspiration	FNS	food and nutrition services
FNa	filtered sodium		functional neuromuscular
FNAB	fine-needle aspiration biopsy		stimulation
FNAC	fine-needle aspiratory cytology	F/NS	fever and night sweats
FNAIT	fetal and neonatal alloimmune	FNSD	functional neurological
	thrombocytopenia		symptom disorder
FNAST	Finnegan Neonatal Abstinence	FNSS	Functional Needs Support
	Scoring Tool		Services
FNB	femoral nerve block	FNSs	facial nerve schwannomas
FNBMD	femoral neck bone mineral density	FNT	finger-to-nose (test)
FNC	Family Nurse Clinician	FNTC	fine-needle transhepatic
	femoral nerve catheter		cholangiography
FNCB	fine needle core biopsy	FNU	femoral nonunion
FNCJ	fine-needle catheter jejunostomy		frequency of nighttime urination
FNCLCC	Fédération Nationale des	FNW	femoral neck width
	Centres de Lutte Contre le	FNX	flunixin meglumine injection
	Cancer (French Federation		(Banamine, a nonsteroidal
	of Cancer Centers Sarcoma		anti-inflammatory agent;
	Group; grading)		Veterinary)
FND	fludarabine, mitoxantrone	FO	father of
	(Novantrone), and		fiberoptic
	dexamethasone		find out
	focal neurological deficit		finger orthosis
FNE	fear of negative evaluation		fish oil
	febrile neutropenic episode		foot orthosis
	first-night effect (polysomnograph)		foramen ovale
FNEs	Fear of Negative Evaluation Scale		foreign object
	febrile neutropenic episodes		fronto-occipital
	focal neurological episodes	F/O	see FO
	free nerve endings	FOA	fronto-orbital advancement
FNF	femoral-neck fracture	FOB	father of baby
	finger-nose-finger (test)		fecal occult blood
FNG	fibrinogen		feet out of bed
	Frascati Neutron Generator		fiberoptic bronchoscope
	free nipple grafting		foot of bed
fng	Fringe; see gene website	FOBS	Fear of Birth Scale
	www.ncbi.nlm.nih.gov/gene	FOBs	follow-on biologics
FNGI	nasolaryngoscopy-guided	FOBT	fecal occult blood test
	injection	FOC	father of child
FNH	focal nodular hyperplasia		fear of childbirth
FNHL	follicular non-Hodgkins		fluid of choice
	lymphoma		fronto-occipital circumference
FNHTR	febrile nonhemolytic transfusion	FOCF	first observation carried
	reaction		forward
FNI	Family Nurture Intervention	foci	plural of the word focus
	fine-needle injection		(a central point, as of
FNL	femoral neck length		attention or activity)
FNMTC	familial nonmedullary thyroid	FOD	fatty oxidation disorder(s)
	carcinoma		fiber orientation distribution
FNN	facial nerve neuritis		first-order decay
	fuzzy neural network		first-order difference
FNP	Family Nurse Practitioner		fish oil diet
FNP-BC	Family Nurse Practitioner-		fixing right eye
	Board Certified		florid osseous dysplasia
FNP-C	Certified Family Nurse		free of disease
	Practitioner		fronto-occipital distance
FN-PSG	full-night polysomnograms	FoD	fear of death

F

FODMAPs	fermentable oligosaccharides, disaccharides, monosaccharides and polyols (short-chain poorly absorbed carbohydrates)
FODMOPs	may have meant FODMAPs
FODs	fatty oxidation disorder(s)
FOE	functionally-oriented exercises
FoE	figure-of-eight (suture)
FOEB	feet over edge of bed
FOF	fell on floor
	fosfomycin tromethamine (Monurol)
FOG	Fluothane, oxygen and gas (nitrous oxide)
	freezing of gait
	full-on gain
FOGQ	Freezing of Gait Questionnaire
FOH	family ocular history
FOI	fiberoptic intubation
	flight of ideas
FOIA	Freedom of Information Act
FOID	fear of impending doom
FOIS	Functional Oral Intake Scale (speech therapy)
FOK	feeling-of-knowing (episodic memory procedure)
FOL	fiberoptic laryngoscopy
FOLFIRI	leucovorin, (folinic acid) fluorouracil, and irinotecan
FOLFIRINOX	leucovorin (folinic acid), fluorouracil, irinotecan, and oxaliplatin
FOLFOX	leucovorin (FOLinic acid), Fluorouracil, and OXaliplatin (a base for many chemotherapy regimens)
FOLFOXIRI	fluorouracil, leucovorin, oxaliplatin, and irinotecan
FOLFOXIRI-Bev	fluorouracil, leucovorin, oxaliplatin, and irinotecan plus bevacizumab
FOLs	fibro-osseous lesions (dentistry)
Foly	may have meant Foley catheter
FOM	father's own milk (used in place of "mother's own milk" when lactating parent is transgender male)
	floor of mouth
FOMi	fluorouracil, Oncovin, (vincristine), and mitomycin
FOMO	fear of missing out
FONSI	finding of no significant impact
Fontan Procedure	a heart operation used in children to treat complex congenital heart defects
FOO	family of origin
FOOB	fell out of bed

FOOSH	fall on outstretched hand
FOP	fasting office profile
	father of patient
	fibrodysplasia ossificans progressiva
FOPS	fiberoptic proctosigmoidoscopy
FOR	facilitated oscillatory release (technique)
f-OR	functional overreaching
Form 483	written communications issued by the Food and Drug Administration to drug firm management at the conclusion of an inspection when an investigator(s) has observed any conditions that in their judgment may constitute violations of the Food Drug and Cosmetic Act and related Acts
Form 1013	Certificate Authorizing Transport To Emergency Receiving Facility & Report Of Transportation (Georgia Department of Behavioral Health & Developmental Disabilities)
FORMIL	foreign military
FORS	FORS; an International Society of Blood Transfusion (ISBT) blood group
FOS	Fabry Outcome Survey
	fiberoptic sigmoidoscopy
	fixing left eye
	force of stream (urology)
	fosphenytoin (Cerebyx)
	fructooligosaccharides
	full of stool (slang)
	future order screen
FOSC	freestanding outpatient surgery center
FOSH	fall on outstretched hand
FOS-MSSI	Fabry Outcome Survey-Mainz Severity Score Index
FOSQ	Functional Outcomes of Sleep Questionnaire
FOSS	Functional Outcome Swallowing Scale
FOT	forced oscillation technique
	form of thought
	frontal outflow tract
FOTB	may have meant FOBT (fecal occult blood test)
FOTO	Focus On Therapeutic Outcomes, Inc. (database)
FOU	footprint of uncertainty
FOV	field of view
FOVI	field of vision intact
FOW	fenestration of oval window

F

Foxtrot	Phonetic Alphabet for F; pronounced FOKS-TROT		final printed labeling (FDA document)
FOZ	functional optical zone		flexor pollicis longus (tendon)
FP	fall precautions		forward pressure level
	false positive	FPLD	familial partil lipodystrophy
	familial porencephaly	FPLV	feline panleucopenia virus
	family planning	FPM	full passive movements
	family practice	FPN	ferroportin
	family practitioner	FPNA	first-pass nuclear angiocardiography
	family presence		
	fertility preservation	FPNP	Family Planning Nurse Practitioner
	fetoprotein		
	fibrous proliferation	FPO	fetal pulse oximetry
	flat plate	FPOR	follicle puncture for oocyte retrieval
	fluorescence polarization		
	fluticasone propionate	FPP	farnesyl pyrophosphate
	food poisoning	FPPE	Focused Professional Practice Evaluation
	foster parent		
	frozen plasma	FPR	facilitated positional release (technique)
	fundus photo(s)		
F/P	fluid/plasma (ratio)		false-positive rate
F-P	femoral popliteal		fluoroscopy programmed radiography
fpA	fibrinopeptide A		
FPAL	full term, premature, abortion, living	FPS	frames per second (radiology)
		FPs	false positives
fPap	fungiform papillae	FPS-R	Faces Pain Scale-Revised
FPB	femoral-popliteal bypass	FP-STEMI	false positive diagnosis of ST-segment elevation myocardial infarction
	flexor pollicis brevis		
FPC	familial pancreatic cancer		
	familial polyposis coli	FPT	Faux Pas Test (20 short stories containing incidents of faux pas [someone mistakenly saying something they shouldn't have] are read to the individual, who is then asked questions to determine whether or not they recognized the faux pas)
	family practice center		
FPD	feto-pelvic disproportion		
	fixed partial denture		
FPDL	flashlamp-pumped pulsed dye laser		
FPE	first-pass effect		
FPED	fibrovascular pigment epithelium detachment		Federal Poverty Threshold
			federal, provincial, and territorial (Canada)
FPEP	fall prevention exercise program		
FPF	false positive fraction		flat-panel tomography
	fibroblast pneumocyte factor		fully porous titanium
FPFs	fluorescent positive features		functional performance test
FPG	fasting plasma glucose	FPU	family participation unit
FPGN	focal proliferative glomerulonephritis	FPV	fosamprenavir (Lexiva)
		FPZ	fluphenazine
FPHC	false positive hepatitis C	FPZ-D	fluphenazine decanoate (Prolixin)
FPHL	female-pattern hair loss	FQ	fluoroquinolones
FPHPQ	Fabry-specific Pediatric Health and Pain Questionnaire		frequency
		FQHC	Federally Qualified Health Center(s)
FPHT	fosphenytoin sodium (Cerebyx)		
		FQHCs	Federally Qualified Health Centers
FPHx	family psychiatric history		
FPIA	fluorescence-polarization immunoassay	FQs	fluoroquinolones
		FR	failure rate
FPIES	food protein-induced enterocolitis syndrome		fair
			father
FPL	federal poverty level		Father (priest)
	final printed labeling		

	Federal Register
	first responder
	flow rate
	fluid removed
	fluid restriction
	fluid retention
	foam roller
	foveal reflex
	fractional
	fractional reabsorption
	frequent relapses
	Friends
	frothy
	full range
	functional restoration
F & R	force and rhythm (pulse)
F/R	fire/rescue
Fr	francium
	French (catheter/needle gauge scale; measures the outside diameter of needles and catheters
FRA	fall risk assessment
	femoral ring allograft
	fluorescent rabies antibody
FRAC	fracture
FRACS	Fellow of the Royal Australian College of Surgeons
FRACTS	fractional urines
FRAG	fragment
FRAG-X	Fragile X Syndrome
FRAIL scale	fatigue, resistance, ambulation, illnesses, and loss of weight scale
FRAME	frequency recognition algorithm for multiple exposures (radiology)
FRAP	family risk assessment program
	ferric-reducing antioxidant power (assay)
	fluorescence recovery after photobleaching
FRA score	fall risk assessment scale score
	feeding readiness assessment score
FRAX	fracture risk assessment tool from the World Health Organization
FraX	fragile X syndrome
FRC	focused rigidity casts
	frozen red cells
	functional residual capacity
FRCPC	Fellow of the Royal College of Physicians of Canada
FRCPE	Fellow of the Royal College of Physicians of Edinburgh
FRCSC	Fellow of the Royal College of Surgeons of Canada

FRCSE	Fellow of the Royal College of Surgeons of Edinburgh
FRCSI	Fellow of the Royal College of Surgeons of Ireland
FRDA	Friedreich ataxia
FRDs	firearm-related deaths
FRE	flow-related enhancement
free T4	thyroxine unbound to protein
FREQ	frequency
FRES	Flesch Reading Ease Score
FRET	fluoresence resonance energy transfer
FRF	filtration replacement fluid
FRG	Functional Related Groups
FRG1	see gene website; www.ncbi .nlm.nih.gov/gene
FRH	febrile-range hyperthermia
FRI	febrile respiratory illness
	fluorescence reflectance imaging
	Functional Rating Index
Fri	Friday
FRIDs	fall-risk-increasing drugs (e.g.; antidepressants, anxiolytics, hypnotics and sedatives, antiarrhythmics, etc.)
FRJM	full range of joint movement
FRM	full range of motion
FRN	fetal rhabdomyomatous nephroblastoma
FRNT	focus-reduction neutralization test
FRO	floor reaction orthosis
FROA	full range of affect
FROC	free-response receiver operating characteristic (analysis)
FROI	filtered region of interest
fROI	functional region of interest
FROM	full range of motion
FROMAJE	functioning, reasoning, orientation, memory, arithmetic, judgment, and emotion (mental status evaluation)
FRP	follicle regulatory protein
	functional refractory period
FRR	false rejection rate
	false-recent rate
	familial relative risk
	flexion-relaxation ratio
frr	ribosome recycling factor; see gene website www.ncbi.nlm .nih.gov/gene
FRRS	first rib resection and scalenectomy
FRS	first-rank symptoms
	flexed, rotated, side bent (position of the spine)

F

	Flexion Rotation Syndrome (Lumbar Rotation with Flexion Syndrome)		fracture, simple and complete
	Framingham risk scores		fracture, simple, and comminuted
	Functional Rating Scale	F/S/C	fever, sweating, and chills
	Functional Recovery Score	FSCC	fracture, simple, complete, and comminuted
FRSN	fluoroquinolone-resistant *Streptococcus pneumoniae*	FSCs	follicle stem cells
FRSS	forward resuscitative surgery system	FSD	female sexual dysfunction focal-skin distance fracture, simple and depressed
FRT	female reproductive tract	FSDS	Female Sexual Distress Scale
	Functional Reach Test	FSE	fast spin-echo
Fru	fructose		fetal scalp electrode
FRW	firearm-related wound(s)		floated standard errors
FrX	fragile X syndrome	FSED	fat- and sugar-enriched diet
FS	female spayed	FSEDs	freestanding emergency departments
	fetoscope		
	fibrin sealant	FSF	fibrin stabilizing factor
	fibromyalgia syndrome	FSFI	Female Sexual Function Index
	field size	FSG	fasting serum glucose
	fingerstick		focal and segmental glomerulosclerosis
	flexible sigmoidoscopy		
	fluorescein strip	FSGA	full-term, small for gestational age
	Fogo Selvagem (the endemic form of pemphigus foliaceus)	FSGF	fasting-state gastric fluid
	food stamps	FSGN	focal segmental glomerulonephritis
	foreskin		
	fractional shortenings	FSGS	focal segmental glomerulosclerosis
	free standing		
	frozen section	FSH	facioscapulohumeral
	full sternotomy		follicle-stimulating hormone
	full strength	FSHD	facioscapulohumeral muscular dystrophy
	functional status		
F & S	full and soft	FSHMD	facioscapulohumeral muscular dystrophy
F/S	see FS		
FSA	Family Services Association	FSHR	follicle stimulating hormone receptor
	Flexible Spending Account		
	Focused Standards Assessment (The Joint Commission)	FSI	foam stability index
		FSIAD	female sexual interest/arousal disorder
FSAD	female sexual arousal disorder(s)		
FSAID	Female Sexual Arousal/Interest Disorder	FSIGT	frequently-sampled intravenous glucose tolerance test
		FSIQ	Full-Scale Intelligence Quotient (part of Wechsler test)
FSALO	Fletcher suite after loading ovoids		
FSALT	Fletcher suite after loading tandem	FSIR	familial standardized incidence ratio
			Fellow of the Society of Interventional Radiology
FSAS	Florida Shock Anxiety Scale		
FSAs	Forward Sortation Areas		
FSB	fetal scalp blood	FSIS	Food Safety and Inspection Service (USDA)
	fresh stillbirth		
	full spine board	FSL	fasting serum level
FSBG	fingerstick blood glucose	FSM	Food Service Manager
FSBM	full-strength breast milk		functional status measures
FSBS	fetal scalp blood sampling	F-SM/C	fungus, smear and culture
	fingerstick blood sugar	FSME	Frühsommer-meningoencephalitis (tick-borne encephalitis)
FSC	Fatigue Symptom Checklist		
	flexible sigmoidoscopy		
	follows simple commands	FSMR	forward stepwise multiple regression
	Forensic Science Center		

FSMSO	Fellow of the American Society of Medication Safety Officers	FT	face tent
			family therapy
			fast-twitch
FSN	Family Systems Nursing		feeding tube
	FreeStyle Navigator (a continuous blood glucose monitoring device)		filling time
			finger tip
			flat-top (bifocals)
FSO	flaxseed oil		flexor tendon
	for screws only (prosthetic cups)		fluidotherapy
	frontal sinus obliteration		follow through
FSOP	French Society of Pediatric Oncology		foot (ft)
			Fourier transform (radiology)
FSP	Family Service Plan		free testosterone
	fibrin split products		full thickness
	Food Stamp Program		full-term
FSR	fractionated stereotactic radiosurgery	F/T	free-to-total ratio
		FT₃	free triiodothyronine
	fusiform skin revision	F₃T	trifluridine (Viroptic)
FSRl	flexed, sidebent, rotated left	FT₄	free thyroxine
FSRP	Framingham Stroke Risk Profile	FTA	femorotibial angle
FSRr	flexed, sidebend, rotated right		fluorescent titer antibody
FSRS	fractionated stereotactic radiosurgery		fluorescent treponemal antibody
		FTA-ABS	fluorescent treponemal antibody absorption
FSRT	fractionated stereotactic radiotherapy		
		FTAAD	familial thoracic aortic aneurysm and dissection
FSS	Fatigue Severity Scale		
	federal supply schedule (cost source)	FTAGA	Full-term average gestational age
		FTB	fingertip blood
	fetal scalp sampling	FTBD	full-term born dead
	fetal scalp stimulation	FTBI	fractionated total body irradiation
	Flinders Symptom Score		
	Forensic Science Service (United Kingdom)	FTC	emtricitabine (beta-L-2′, 3′-dideoxy-5-fluoro-3′-thiacytidine) (Emtriva)
	Freeman-Sheldon syndrome		
	French steel sound (dilated to #24FSS)		fallopian tube carcinoma
			Federal Trade Commission
	frequency-selective saturation		follicular thyroid carcinoma
	full-scale score		frames to come
	functional somatic symptoms		full to confrontation
FSSO	Fellow of the Society of Surgical Oncology	FTC/TDF	emtricitabine (Emtriva) and tenofovir disoproxil fumarate (Viread)
FSST	Four Square Step Test (a performance-based balance tool involving stepping over four single-point canes placed on the floor in a cross configuration)		
		FTD	failure to descend
			frontotemporal degeneration
			frontotemporal dementia
			full-term delivery
FST	forward surgical team(s)	FTD-MND	frontotemporal dementia-motor neuron disease
FSU	functional spinal unit		
FSV	fat-soluble vitamin(s)	FTE	failure to engraft
	fotoselective vaporization	FTEs	full-time equivalents
fSVA	frozen surrogate variable analysis	FTF	failure to fly, for attempted suicide (slang)
			finger-to-finger
FSW	feet of sea water (pressure)		free thyroxine fraction
	field service worker	FTFC	face-to-face care
FSWs	female sex workers		fourier transform flow cytometer
	focal slow waves (electroencephalograph)		full to finger counting (ophthalmology)

FTFQ	full to four quadrants (visual field testing)
FTFTN	finger-to-finger-to-nose
FTG	Foley (catheter) to gravity
	full-thickness graft
FTHUE	Functional Test for the Hemiplegic Upper Extremity
FTI	farnesyltransferase inhibitor
	force-time integral
	free testosterone index
	free thyroid index
	free thyroxine index
FT$_4$I	free thyroxine index
FTICR-MS	Fourier-transform ion cyclotron resonance-mass spectrometry
FTIP	finger tip
FTIR	Fourier transform infrared (spectroscopy)
FTIUP	full-term intrauterine pregnancy
FTKA	failed to keep appointment
FTLB	full-term living birth
FTLD	frontotemporal lobar degeneration
	frontotemporal lobar dementia
FTLFC	full-term living female child
FTLMC	full-term living male child
FTM	female-to-male (transgenders)
	female-to-male (transmission)
	fluid thioglycollate medium
FTMH	full-thickness macular hole(s)
fTmps	fluoresced transmembrane potentials
FTMS	Fourier transform mass spectrometer
FTN	finger-to-nose
	full-term nursery
FTNB	full-term newborn
FTNB AGA	full-term newborn, appropriate for gestational age
FTND	Fagerstrom Test for Nicotine Dependence
	full-term normal delivery
FTNSD	full-term, normal, spontaneous delivery
FTNVD	full-term normal vaginal delivery
FTO	full-time occlusion (eye patch)
F to N	finger-to-nose
FTOZ	frontotemporal orbitozygomatic
FTOZ1	one-piece frontotemporal orbitozygomatic
FTP	failure to progress
	frontotemporoparietal
	full-term pregnancy
FTR	failed to report
	failed to respond
	father
	for the record
FTRAM	free transverse rectus abdominis myocutaneous (flap)

FTRD	full thickness resection device
FTS	farnesyl thiosalicylic acid
	fast-track surgery
	fentanyl transdermal system
	first-trimester screening
	Food Tolerance Scores
FTSD	full-term spontaneous delivery
FTSF	fallopian tube stripping forceps
FTSG	full-thickness skin graft
FTSST	Five-Times Sit-to-Stand Test
FTSTS	Five-Time-Sit-To-Stand (test)
FTSVD	full-term spontaneous vaginal delivery
FTT	failure to thrive
	fetal tissue transplant
	Finger-Tapping Test
FTU	fingertip unit(s)
Ftube	feeding tube
FTUPLD	full-term uncomplicated pregnancy, labor, and delivery
FTUs	functional tooth units
FTV	Fortovase (saquinavir, soft gel cap)
	functional trial visit
FTW	failure to wean
	full-time wear(glasses correction)
FTX	field training exercise
	see gene website; www.ncbi .nlm.nih.gov
fTx	failed renal transplant patients
FU	Farmacopeia Ufficiale (Italian Pharmacopoeia)
	fluorouracil
	follow-up
	fraction unbound
F U	see FU
F & U	flanks and upper quadrants
F/U	follow-up
	fundus at umbilicus
F↑U	fingers above umbilicus
F↓U	fingers below umbilicus
FU12	12 month follow-up
FU4	follow-up for
F/U4	follow-up for
5-FU	fluorouracil
FUA	flat and upright (x-ray of the) abdomen
FUB	functional uterine bleeding
FUBAR	fouled up beyond all recognition (slang)
fucK	L-fuculokinase; see gene website www.ncbi.nlm.nih.gov/gene
FUCO	fractional uptake of carbon monoxide
FUD	fear, uncertainty, and doubt
	frequency, urgency, and dysuria
	full upper denture
FUDR®	floxuridine

F

FUDS	fluoroscopic urodynamic study	F/V/C/N	probably meant- fever, chills, nausea, and vomiting (F/C/N/V)
FUDs	follow-up days		
FUDtr	full upper denture		
FUE	follicular unit extraction	FVD	fever, vomiting, and diarrhea
FUFA	fluorouracil and leucovorin (folinic acid)	FVFR	filled voiding flow rate
		FVH	focal vascular headache
FU/FL	full upper denture, full lower denture	FVL	factor V-Leiden (mutation)
			femoral vein ligation
FUFOL	fluorouracil and leucovorin calcium (folinic acid)		flow volume loop
			functional visual loss
FugI	Fugl-Meyer Assessment of Motor Recovery After Stroke	FVM	fetal ventriculomegaly
			fibrovascular membrane
FUI	functional urinary incontinence	FVN	familial visceral neuropathy
FUL	federal upper limit (price list)	FVO	Falciparum Vietnam-Oak Knoll (a strain of *Plasmodium falciparum*)
FULG	fulguration		
full code status	cardiopulmonary resuscitation consisting of the possibility for defibrillation, chest compressions, and intubation		Family Violence Option
			femoral varus osteotomy
		FVP	foot venous pressure
FU/LP	full upper denture, partial lower denture	FVPTC	follicular variant of papillary thyroid cancer
5FU/LV	fluorouracil and leucovorin	FVR	feline viral rhinotracheitis
FUMIR	fluorouracil and mitomycin with external beam radiotherapy		forearm vascular resistance
		FVS	field verification simulation
		FVT	fast ventricular tachycardia
FUN	follow-up note	f/VT	respiratory frequency-to-tidal volume ratio (rapid shallow breathing index; a predictor of mechanical ventilation weaning)
FUNASA	Fundão Nacional de Sade (Brazil's national health agency)		
func	function		
funct	function functional	FVWs	flow-velocity waveforms (umbilical artery Doppler)
FUNG-C	fungus culture	FW	fetal weight
FUNG-S	fungus smear		Filipino women
FUO	fever of undetermined origin	F/W	followed with
FUOV	follow-up office visit	F waves	fibrillatory waves
FUp	follow-up		flutter waves
FUR	follow-up report	FWB	fetal well-being
fURS	flexible ureterorenoscopy		free water bolus
FU-RT	fluorouracil with radiation therapy		fresh whole blood
			full weight bearing
FUS	focused ultrasound		functional well being
	Fuchs uveitis syndrome		functional well-being
	fusion	FWBAT	full-weight bearing as tolerated
fuss	a word meaning showing unnecessary or excessive concern about something	FWBR	friends with benefits relationship
		FWCA	functional work capacity assessment
FUT	fibrinogen update test	FWD	fairly well developed
FUV	follow-up visit		forward
FV	femoral vein	FWE	A fly-wheel ergometer
F&V	fruits and vegetables	FWF	fat white female (slang)
FVA	functional visual acuity		fever without a focus
FVa	blood coagulation factor V activated		free water flush (water given via a feeding tube to provide hydration to meet patients total fluid needs)
FVBG	free vascularized bone graft		
FVC	false vocal cord(s)		free water fraction
	forced vital capacity	FWF-2D	fuzzy 2-D Weiner filter
FVCA	four-vessel cerebral angiography		

FWG	fluid weight gain	
FWH	foramen of Winslow hernia	
FWHM	full width at half maximum (radiology)	
FWIW	for what it's worth (slang)	
FWM	fetal white matter	
	four-wave mixing	
	frontal white matter	
fWP	f-wave power	
FWR	family-witnessed resusication	
	free-water reserve	
	free-weight resistance	
FWS	fetal warfarin syndrome	
FWW	front-wheeled walker	
F/X	effects	
Fx	fraction	
	fractional urine	
	fracture	
Fx's	fractures	
fXa	factor Xa (a blood clotting factor)	
fXaI	factor Xa inhibitor (rivaroxaban [Xarelto], dabigatran [Pradaxa], edoxaban [Savaysa], andapixaban [Eliquis])	
Fx-BB	fracture both bones	
Fx-dis	fracture-dislocation	
FXI	Factor XI (eleven)	
FXL	functional	
FXM	flow cytometric crossmatch	
FXN	function	
fxnal	functional	
FXNL	functional	
fxns	fractions	
FXPOI	fragile X primary ovarian insufficiency	
FXR	farnesoid X receptor	
	fracture	
FXS	fragile X syndrome	
Fx(s)	fractures	
FXTAS	fragile X-associated tremor/ataxia syndrome	
FY	Duffy; an International Society of Blood Transfusion (ISBT) blood group	
	fiscal year	
FYC	facultative yeast carrier	
FYI	for your information	
FZ	flutamide and goserelin acetate (Zoladex)	
FZRC	frozen red (blood) cells	

G

G	gain (as in audiology; G50)
	gallop
	gastrostomy
	gauss (a unit of magnetic flux density in radiology)
	gavage feeding
	gingiva
	Golf (Phonetic Alphabet G; pronounced GOLF)
	good
	grade
	grass (allergies)
	gravida
	grip
	guaiac
	guanine
	guanosine
	riboflavin (vitamin G)
g	grams (28.35 g = 1 ounce)
g%	gram percent
G−	gram-negative
G+	gram-positive
	guaiac-positive
G↑	increasing
G↓	decreasing
↑g	increasing
↓g	decreasing
G1-4	grade 1-4
G0	no pregnancies (gravida)
G1	first generation
	genotype 1
	group 1
	phase 1 of a cycle
G2	genotype 2
	group 2
G3	genotype 3
	group 3
G4	genotype 4
	group 4
G5	genotype 5
	group 5
G6	group 6
G7	group 7
G8	group 8
G9	group 9
G-11	hexachlorophene
GA	gallium arsenide
	Gamblers Anonymous
	gastric analysis
	general anesthesia
	general appearance
	geographic atrophy
	Georgia
	geriatric assessment

	gestational age
	ginger ale
	glatiramer acid (Copaxone)
	glucose/acetone
	glycated albumin
	glycyrrhetinic acid
	granuloma annulare
Ga	gallium
^{67}Ga	gallium citrate Ga 67
GA1	glutaric aciduria (academia) type 1
GAA	acid alpha-glucosidase
	glacial acetic acid
GAAS	generally accepted as safe
GAB	gestational age at birth
GABA	gamma-aminobutyric acid
GABAA	gamma-aminobutyric acid subunit A
GABAAR	gamma-aminobutyric acid subunit A receptor
GABAB	gamma-aminobutyric acid B
GABG	German Adjuvant Breast Cancer Study Group
GABHS	group A beta hemolytic streptococci
GABS	group A beta strep (hemolytic streptococci)
GAC	gastric adenocarcinoma
	granular activated carbon
GACI	generalized arterial calcification of infancy
GAD	generalized anxiety disorder
	Genetic Association Database
	glutamic acid decarboxylase
GAD55	glutamate decarboxylase
GAD65	glutamic acid decarboxylase 2 (GAD2);see gene website www.ncbi.nlm.nih.gov/gene
	glutamic acid decarboxylase 2 (gene/protein)
GAD 7	self-rating generalized anxiety disorder 7-question evaluation tool/scale
GADA	glutamic acid decarboxylase autoantibodies
GAE	granulomatous amebic encephalitis
GAEB	good air entry bilaterally
GAF	geographic adjustment factors
	Global Assessment of Functioning (scale)
GAG	glycosaminoglycan
GAGS	global acne grading system
GAGPS	glucosaminoglycan polysulfate
GAHM	genioglossus advancement and hyoid myotomy
GAHT	gender-affirming hormone therapy
GAIA	Genome Annotation and Information Analysis

Gail Score	a breast cancer risk assessment tool that calculates a woman's risk of developing breast cancer within the next five years and within her lifetime (http://www.cancer.gov /BCRISKTOOL)
GAIN	Generating Antibiotic Incentives Now (US Food and Drug Administration)
GAINS	goggle-augmented imaging and navigation system
GAL	galanthamine hydrobromide (Reminyl)
	gallon (1 gallon US = 3.8 L; 1 gallon UK = 4.5 L)
	Guardian Ad Litem (a guardian appointed by the court to represent the interests of Infants, the unborn, or incompetent persons in legal actions)
GalC	galactocerbrosidase
GALD	gated autosynchronous luminescence detector
	gestational alloimmune liver disease
G'ale	ginger ale
GALI-PUT	galactose-1-phosphate uridye transferase enzyme
GALT	galactose-1-phosphate uridyltransferase (gene)
	gut-associated lymphoid tissue
GAM	Gamma Knife
	gene-activated matrices
GAME score	Genetic And Morphological Evaluation score
gamma-GT	gamma glutamyl transferase
	gamma-glutamyl transpeptidase
GAMT	guanidinoacetate methyltransferase
GAN	giant axonal neuropathy
G and C	gemcitabine and carboplatin
GAO	General Accounting Office
GAP	glans approximation procedure
	GTPase activating protein
GAP-43	growth-associated protein-43
GAR	gonnococcal antibody reaction
GARD	graded autocatalysis replication domain
GARFT	glycinamide ribonucleotide formyl transferase
garg	gargle
GARP	Genetic Algorithm Rule-Set Prediction
GART	genotypical antiviral resistance testing
	see gene website, www.ncbi .nlm.nih.gov/gene

G

GAS	gender-affirming surgery	GBH	gamma benzene hexachloride
	general adaption syndrome		(lindane)
	ginseng-abuse syndrome	GBHD	see GVHD
	Glasgow Assessment Schedule	GBHs	glyphosate-based herbicides
	Global Assessment Scale	GBIA	Guthrie bacterial inhibition
	group A streptococcal		assay
	(*Streptococcus pyogenes*)	GBL	gamma butyrolactone
	disease vaccine	GBM	glioblastoma multiforme
	group A streptococci		glomerular basement membrane
	group A streptococcus	GBMHM	Groupe des Biologistes Molécu-
GaS	gastrocnemius-soleus muscles		laires des Hémopathies
Gas Anal F&T	gastric analysis, free and total		Malignes, (French Molecular
Gascan	gallium scan		Biology Group in Hematology)
GAST	gastrocnemius	GBMI	guilty but mentally ill
Gastroc	gastrocnemius	GBMs	glioblastoma multiformes
GAT	geriatric assessment team group	GBMT	glomerular basement membrane
	adjustment therapy		thickness
	Goldman applanation tonometry		guideline-based medical therapy
GATA2	guanine-adenine-thymine-	GBN	gabapentin
	adenine binding protein 2		ganglioneuroblastoma
	(gene)		Gaussian Bayesian networks
GATA3	GATA (guanine-adenine-		German Biobank Node (a cross-
	thymine-adenine) binding		institutional of 4 biobank
	protein 3 (gene)		[biospecimens] network)
GATB	General Aptitude Test Battery	GBNs	graphene-based nanomaterials
GAU	geriatric assessment unit	GBP	gabapentin (Neurontin)
GAVE	gastric antral vascular ectasia		gastric bypass
GAVI	Global Alliance for Vaccines		gated blood pool (imaging)
	and Immunization	GBPS	gated blood pool scan
Gaw	airway conductance	GBq	gigabecquerel (I Curie = 37 GBq)
GB	gallbladder	GBR	gamma band response (audiology)
	gastric button (feeding tube)		good blood return
	gingival bleeding		guided bone regeneration
	Ginkgo biloba		guided bone regenerative
	grab bars	GBRAS	Grade, Roughness, Breathiness,
	Guillain-Barré (syndrome)		Asthenia, Strain
G & B	good and bad	GBS	gallbladder series
GBA	ganglionic-blocking agent		gastric bypass surgery
	gingivobuccoaxial		group B streptococcal
	glucosylceramidase beta gene;(pa-		(*Streptococcus agalactiae*)
	tients with non-neuronopathic		disease vaccine
	Gaucher disease and heterozy-		group B streptococci
	gous GBA mutation carrier are		Guillain-Barré syndrome
	at increased risk for Parkinson	GBs	Glasgow-Blatchford bleeding
	disease)		score
GBACR	Greater Bay Area Cancer Registry	GBS+	group B streptococcal positive
GBAE	grit-blasted acid-etched (dental)	GBSI	group B streptococcus
GBBS	group B beta hemolytic		infection(s)
	streptococcus	GBSS	granule-bound starch synthase;
GBC	gadolinium-based contrast		see gene website www.ncbi
	gallbladder cancer		.nlm.nih.gov/gene
GBCAs	gadolinium-based contrast agents	GBT	Ginkgo biloba tablet
GBD	gallbladder disease		glucose breath test
	global burden of disease	gbt	glycine betaine transmethylase;
GBE	*Ginkgo biloba* extract		see gene website www.ncbi
GBEF	gallbladder ejection fraction		.nlm.nih.gov/gene
GBF	gastrobronchial fistula	GBUS	gallbladder and biliary (tree)
GBG	gonadal-steroid binding globulin		ultrasound

G-button	gastrostomy-button (feeding tube)	GC/FID	gas chromatography/flame ionization detection
GBV	gender-based violence	GCFs	giant cell fibromas
GBV-C	GB virus type C (also known as hepatitis G virus)	GCG	genes encoding the peptide precursors for glucagon
GBW	generalized body weakness		giant cell glioblastoma
GBX	gall bladder extraction (cholecystectomy)	GCI	General Cognitive Index
GC	Garcinia Cambogia	GCIIS	glucose control insulin infusion system
	gas chromatography	G-CIMP	glioma-CpG (cytosine-phosphate-
	gastric cancer		guanine) island methylator
	gemcitabine and carboplatin		phenotype
	genetic counselor	GCKD	glomerulocystic kidney disease
	geriatric chair (Gerichair®)	GCL	generalized congenital
	gingival curettage		lipodystrophy
	gliomatosis cerebri	GCM	giant cell myocarditis
	glucocorticoid		good central maintained
	gonococci (gonorrhea)	g/cm	grams per centimeter
	good condition	g/cm²	grams per square centimeter
	graham crackers	GCMD	generalized cardiovascular
G&C	gemcitabine and carboplatin		metabolic disease
G3C	Global Genetics and Genomics Community	GCMN	giant congenital melanocytic nevus
G−C	gram-negative cocci	GC-MS	gas chromatography-mass
G+C	gram-positive cocci		spectroscopy
GCA	gastric cardia adenocarcinoma	GCO	gas chromatography-olfactometry
	general cognitive ability		GetCheckedOnline (Web-based
	ghost cell ameloblastoma		testing for sexually transmitted
	giant-cell arteritis		and blood-borne infections,
	see gene website, www.ncbi		Vancouver, Canada)
	.nlm.nih.gov/gene	GCP	gentamicin, clindamycin, and
GC and CT	Neisseria gonorrhoeae and		polymyxin topical preparation
	Chlamydia trachomatis		Good Clinical Practice
GCarbo	gemcitabine and carboplatin regimen of cancer	GCPC	gastric cancer with peritoneal carcinomatosis
GCB	germinal center B-cell-like (lymphoma)	GCPFL	grid-controlled variable-rate pulsed fluoroscopy
	gradient compression bandaging	GCPS	Greig cephalopolysyndactyly
GCBP	gated cardiac blood pool		syndrome
GCBS	Global Collaboration for	GC-qMS	gas chromatography-quadrupole
	Blood Safety (World Health		mass spectrometry
	Organization)	GC/QTOF	gas chromatography/quadrupole
GCBs	germinal center B cells		time-of-flight mass
GCC	glassy cell carcinoma		spectrometry
	guanylyl cyclase C	GCR	gastrocolonic response
GCCT	ganglion cell complex thickness		glucocerebrosidase
	glycerol-cryopreserved corneal tissue	GCRC	General Clinical Research Center
GC&CT	Neisseria gonorrhoeae and	GCS	Glasgow Coma Scale
	Chlamydia trachomatis		glucocorticosteroid(s)
GC/CT	Neisseria gonorrhoeae and		graduated compression stockings
	Chlamydia trachomatis	GCS3	Glasgow Coma Scale 3 (score)
GCDFP	gross cystic disease fluid protein	GCS 14	Glasgow Coma Scale 14
GCE	general conditioning exercise		(14-point original scale)
	giant cell ependymoma	GCS 15	Glasgow Coma Scale 15
GCF	giant cell fibroblastoma		(15-point scale)
	grid conversion factor (radiology)	GCSE	generalized convulsive status epilepticus

G

G-CSF	filgrastim (granulocyte colony-stimulating factor)
	filgrastim (Neupogen; granulocyte colony-stimulating factor)
GCSF	filgrastim (Neupogen; granulocyte colony-stimulating factor)
GCSI	Gastroparesis Cardinal Symptom Index
GCSs	glucocorticosteroids
	graduated compression stockings
GCST	Gibson-Cooke sweat test
GCT	general care and treatment
	germ cell tumor
	giant cell tumor
	glucose challenge test
	granulosa cell tumor
GCTB	giant cell tumor of the bone
GCTs	giant cell tumors
	granulosa cell tumors
GCTT	germ-cell testicular tumor
GCTTS	giant cell tumour of tendon sheath
GCU	gonococcal urethritis
GCV	ganciclovir (Cytovene)
	great cardiac vein
GCVF	great cardiac vein flow
GCVP	gemcitabine, cyclophosphamide, vincristine, and prednisolone
GCW	glomerular capillary wall(s)
GD	gastric distension
	Gauchers disease
	gemcitabine (Gemzar) and docetaxel (Taxotere)
	gender dysphoria
	generalized delays
	gestational diabetes
	good
	gravely disabled
	Graves disease
Gd	gadolinium
GD2	disialoganglioside 2
G&D	growth and development
GDA	gastroduodenal artery
GDB	Guide Dogs for the Blind
Gd-BOPTA	gadolinium benzyloxypropionic tetra acetate
GDC	Gartner duct cysts
	Guglielmi detachable coil
GDD	glaucoma drainage devices
	gnathodiaphyseal dysplasia
G1DD	grade 1 diastolic dysfunction
G2DD	grade 2 diastolic dysfunction
G3DD	grade 3 diastolic dysfunction
G4DD	grade 4 diastolic dysfunction
Gd-DTPA	gadopentetate (Magnevist)
Gd-DTPA-BMA	gadodiamide (Omniscan)
GdE	gadolinium enhancing
GDEM	global digital elevation model

GDF11	growth differentiation factor 11; see gene website www.ncbi.nlm.nih.gov/gene
GDFA	grandfather
GDH	gangrenous diaphragmatic hernia
	glutamic dehydrogenase
GdHPD03A	gadoteridol
GDI	Gait Deviation Index
	glaucoma drainage implant(s)
	Good Death Inventory
GDJ	gastroduodenal junction
g/dL	grams per deciliter (grams per 100 mL)
GDLD	gelatinous drop-like corneal dystrophy
GDM	gestational diabetes mellitus
GDM1	gestational diabetes type 1
GDMA	glycerol dimethacrylate
GDMA1	gestational diabetes mellitus treated with diet modification
GDMA2	gestational diabetes mellitus treated with insulin
GdmCl	guanidinium hydrochloride
GD MO	grandmother
Gd-MRI	gadolinium-enhanced magnetic resonance imaging
GDMS	Glow Discharge Mass Spectrometry
GDMs	gestation diabetic mothers
GDMT	guideline-directed medical therapy
GDNF	glial cell-derived neurotrophic factor; see gene website www.ncbi.nlm.nih.gov/gene
Gd$_2$O$_2$S	gadolinium oxysulphide
GDP	gamma-detecting probe
	gel diffusion precipitin
G6DP	may have meant G6PD (glucose-6-phosphate dehydrogenase)
GDPP	gonadotropin-dependent precocious puberty
GDPs	general dental practitioners
	glucose degradation products
GDR	glucose disposal rate
	gradual dose reduction
GDS	Geriatric Depression Scale
	gestational diabetes screen
	Global Deterioration Scale
GDS-15	15-item Geriaric Depression Scale
GDT	Game of Dice Task
	gap-detection threshold
	goal-directed therapy
gDtr	truncated form of glycoprotein D
GDUFA	Generic Drug User Fee Amendments (2012)
GDV	gastric dilatation-volvulus (veterinary)

GDx®	a scanning laser polarimeter	
GE	gainfully employed	
	gastric emptying	
	gastroenteritis	
	gastroenterology	
	gastroesophageal	
	gemcitabine and erlotinib	
	General Electric	
	geometric efficiency (radiology)	
	Gerbich; an International Society of Blood Transfusion (ISBT) blood group	
	gradient echo (radiology)	
	group exercise	
Ge	germanium	
G/E	see GE	
GEA	gastroepiploic artery	
GEB	gum-elastic bougie	
GEC	galactose elimination capacity	
	gastroesophageal cancer	
GED	General Educational Development (Test)	
	General Equivalency Diploma	
GEDI	global end-diastolic volume index	
GEDSA	Global Enteral Device Supplier Association	
GEE	gait energy expenditure	
	generalized estimating equations (statistics)	
	Global Evaluation of Efficacy	
	glycine ethyl ester	
	graft-enteric erosion	
GE-EPI	gradient-echo echo-planar (imaging)	
GEF	graft-enteric fistula	
GEFS +	Generalized epilepsy with febrile seizures plus	
GEFs	gunine-nucleotide exchange factors	
GEH	generalized eruptive histiocytosis	
GEICAM	Grupo Español de Investigation en Cancer de Mama (the Spanish Group for the Investigation of Breast Cancer)	
GEJ	gastroesophageal junction	
GE junction	gastroesophageal junction	
GEK	Gmünder Ersatzkasse (a German health insurance company; merged with the BARMER Ersatzkasse to BARMER GEK)	
GEL	giant esophageal leiomyoma	
gel	gelatin	
GELF	Groupe d'Endoscopie de Langue Française study	
GEM	gemcitabine (Gemzar)	
	gemfibrozil (Lopid)	

	general equivalence mapping	
	generalized erythema multiforme	
gemba	the place where value is created; in manufacturing, the gemba is the factory floor (Japanese)	
GemCap	gemcitabine and capectibine	
GemCis	gemcitabine and cisplatin	
GEMOX	gemcitabine and oxaliplatin	
GEMS	Global Enteric Multicenter Study	
GEMs	genome-scale (metabolic) models	
GEMU	geriatric evaluation and management unit	
GemVin	gemcitabine and vinorelbine	
GEN	general	
	general anesthesia	
	genital	
GenA	Generation of Action Verbs	
gena	a word meaning cheek or lateral side of the face	
GenD	genetic doping	
GEN/ENDO	general anesthesia with endotracheal intubation	
Genl	General	
genl	general	
GENTA/P	gentamicin-peak	
GENTA/T	gentamicin-trough	
genu	a word meaning the knee or anything bent like the knee	
geo	geographic	
GEP	gastroenteropancreatic	
	gene expression profiles	
GeP	genioplasty	
GEP-NETs	gastroenteropancreatic neuroendocrine tumors	
GEQ	generic equiavalent	
GER	gastroesophageal reflux	
GERB	gastroesophageal reflux disease (Russian)	
GERD	gastroesophageal reflux disease	
gero	a prefix denoting a relationship to old age or to the aged	
Gero	Gerontologist	
	Gerontology	
GES	gastric electrical stimulation	
	gastric emptying scintigraphy	
GEST	gestational	
gest diab	gestational diabetes	
GET	gastric emptying time	
	graded exercise test	
GET 1/2	gastric emptying half-time	
GETA	general endotracheal anesthesia	
GETS	Glasgow and Edinburgh Throat Scale	
GETV	gadolinium-enhancing tumor volume	
GEU	geriatric evaluation unit	
GEV	gastroesophageal varies	

GeV	gigaelectronvolt (one billion electron volts)	GFX®	a kit for the isolation and con-centration of DNA (desoxy ribonucleic acid) fragments
GF	gastric fistula		
	girlfriend	GG	gamma globulin
	gluten free		Gastrografin (diatrizoate meglu-mine and diatrizoate sodium oral soln)
	grandfather		
G/F	girlfriend		
GFAAS	graphite furnace atomic absorption spectrometry		Gates-Glidden (dental drills)
			genioglossus
GFAP	glial fibrillary acidic protein		guaifenesin (glyceryl guaiacolate)
GF-BAO	gastric fluid, basal acid output	G=G	grips equal and good
GFCL	Goldmann fundus contact lens	GGA	generalized gradient approximation
GFD	gluten-free diet		
GFE	girlfriend experience		geranylgeranylacetone
GFFF	gravitational field-flow fractionation	Ggc	gamma-glutamyl cyclotransferase; see gene website www.ncbi .nlm.nih.gov/gene
GFI	Goodness-of-Fit Index		
	Groningen Frailty Index	GGCX	gamma-glutamyl carboxylase
	Guidance for Industry (US Food and Drug Administration)	GGD	Galli-Galli disease
		GGDP	geranylgeranyl diphosphate
GFi	inferior frontal gyrus	GGDS	global genome damage score
GFI1	growth factor independent 1; see gene website www.ncbi .nlm.nih.gov/gene	GGE	Gastrografin enema
			generalized glandular enlargement
		GG EMG	genioglossus electromyography
GFJ	grapefruit juice	GGF	great grandfather
GFL	GDNF (glial cell line-derived neurotrophic factor) family ligand	GGG	triplet of the adjacent nucleotide, glycine, in the messenger ribonucleic acid chain that codes for a specific amino acid in the synthesis of a protein molecule
GFM	good fetal movement		
GFN	genitofemoral nerve		
gFOBT	guaiac-based fecal occult blood test		
		GGH	gamma-glutamyl hydrolase
GFOC	gated fiber-optic-coupled dosimeter	GGI	57-kb gonococcal genetic island
			genomic grade index
	gliofibrillary oligodendrocytes		Gillette Gait Index
GFOP	grandfather of patient	GGM	great grandmother
GFP	green fluorscent protein	GGO	ground-glass opacity
GFR	glomerular filtration rate	GGOs	ground glass opacities
	grunting, flaring, and retractions	GGPD	Could be misread; see G6PD
GFRAA	glomerular filtration rate in an African American		geranylgeranyl prenyl diphosphate
		GGPT	geranylgeranyl protein transferase
	glomerular filtration rate stimu-lated by amino acids	GGR	geranylgeranyl reductase
			global genomic repair
GFRdopa	glomerular filtration rate stimu-lated by low-dose dopamine	GGS	glands, goiter, and stiffness
			group G streptococci
GFS	gel-forming solution	GGT	gamma-glutamyltransferase
	glaucoma filtering surgery		gamma-glutamyltranspeptidase
	gloved fingertip sampling	GGTP	gamma-glutamyltranspeptidase
GFs	growth factors	GGTs	gamma-glutamyltranspeptidases
GFTA	Goldman-Fristoe Test of Articulation	GH	general health
			genetic hemochromatosis
GFV	gastric fluid volume		gestational hypertension
	gastric fundal varices		gingival hyperplasia
GFX	a pan-protein kinase C inhibitor (bisindolylmaleimide)		glenohumeral
			good health
	gatifloxacin (Zymaxid ophthalmic solution)		group home
			growth hormone
	gemifloxacin (Factive)	G/H	grooming and hygiene

G

g/h	grams per hour	GI bleed	gastrointestinal bleed
G&H	grooming and hygiene	GIBS	gastrointestinal bleeding scintigraphy
GH$_3$	Gerovital		
GHAA	Group Health Association of America	GIBs	gastrointestinal bleeds
		GIC	general immunocompetence
GHB	gamma hydroxybutyrate (sodium oxybate; Xyrem)		Global Impression of Change
		GI 6 CaP	Gleason Index of cancer of the prostate of 6
GHb	glycosylated hemoglobin		
GHC	German Headache Consortium (study)	GICOR	The Spanish Group of Clinical Research in Radiation Oncology
GHCs	general health checkups		
GHD	growth hormone deficiency	GICU	general intensive care unit
GHDA	growth hormone deficiency (syndrome) in adults	GID	gastrointestinal distress
			gender identity disorder
GHF	glycoside hydrolase family	GIDA	Gastrointestinal Diagnostic Area
	government health funding	GIE	gastrointestinal endoscopy
GHG	greenhouse gases		global index event
GHGEs	greenhouse gas emissions	GIFD #3	colonoscope
GHI	growth hormone insufficiency	GIFT	gamete intrafallopian (tube) transfer
GHJ	glenohumeral joint		
G-H jt	glenohumeral joint	giga	a prefix designating a 1,000,000,000 (one billion)
GHK	glycyl-l-histidyl-l-lysine, a tripeptide (K is a symbol for lysine)		
		GIGT	gestational impaired glucose tolerance
GHLC	glenohumeral ligament complex	GIGU	gastrointestinal and genitourinary
GHM	gynecological health maintenance	GI/GU	gastrointestinal and genitourinary
GHPP	Genetically Handicapped Persons Program	GIH	gastrointestinal hemorrhage
			Gujarati Indians in Houston, Texas, USA (population samples of HapMap [a catalog of common genetic variants that occur in human beings])
GHP(S)	gated heart pool (scan)		
GHQ	General Health Questionnaire		
GHRF	growth hormone releasing factor		
GHRH	growth hormone releasing hormone		
		GII	group two
GHRP	Good Health Research Practice (World Health Organization)	G II	grade two
		GIII	group three
GHRP-6	growth hormone-releasing hexapeptide	G III	grade three
		GIK	glucose-insulin-potassium
GHS	given health state	GIL	gastrointestinal (tract) lymphoma
	Globally Harmonized System of Classification Labeling of Chemicals	GILD	gastrointestinal and liver diseases
		GILL	Gill; an International Society of Blood Transfusion (ISBT) blood group
	see gene website www.ncbi.nlm .nih.gov/gene		
		GILZ	glucocorticoid-induced leucine zipper
GHSG	German Hodgkin Study Group		
GHT	glaucoma hemifield test	GIM	General Internal Medicine
GHTN	gestational hypertension	GIMO	gene insertion/marker out
GHVD	may have meant GVHD (graft-versus-host disease)	GIMTO	Gruppo Italiano Trapianto di Midollo Osseo (Italian Group for Bone Marrow Transplantation) registry/procedure
GHWs	graphic health warnings		
GI	gastrointestinal		
	gingival index (dental)	GINA	Global initiative for Asthma (guidelines; was launched in 1993 in collaboration with the National Heart, Lung, and Blood Institute, National Institutes of Health, USA, and the World Health Organization)
	glycemic index		
	granuloma inguinale		
	group one		
G I	grade one		
GIA	gastrointestinal anastomosis		
GIB	gastric ileal bypass		
	gastrointestinal bleeding		

GING	gingiva	g/kg/d	grams per kilogram per day
	gingivectomy	GKRS	gamma knife radiosurgery
GINs	gastrointestinal nematodes	GKRT	gamma knife radiotherapy
GIO	glucocorticoid-induced osteoporosis	GKS	Gamma Knife surgery
		GKSRS	Gamma Knife stereotactic radiosurgery
GIOP	glucocorticoid (steroid)-induced osteoporosis	GKT	gamma-knife thalamotomy
GIP	gastric inhibitory peptide	GL	gastric lavage
	gastric inhibitory polypeptide		glaucoma
	giant cell interstitial pneumonia		glycemic load
	glucose-dependent insulinotropic polypeptide		greatest length
		GLA	gamolenic acid
GIPO	gene in position order		gingivolinguoaxial
GIPP	gonadotropin-independent precocious puberty		glucose-lowering agents
		GLAD	glenoid labrum articular disruption
GIPU	gastrointestinal procedure unit	GLB	Graham-Leach-Bliley Act of 1999
GIQLI	Gastrointestinal Quality of Life Index (Eypasch)		
GIR	glucose infusion rate	GLBT	gay, lesbian, bisexual, and transgender
GIRD	glenohumeral internal rotation deficit	GLBTQ	gay, lesbian, bisexual, transgender, or questioning one's sexual identity
GIRDCA	Gruppo Italiano Ricerca Dermatiti da Contatto e Ambientali (patch test series)		
		GLC	gas-liquid chromatography
			glaucoma
GIS	gas in stomach	GLD	Glanders (*Actinobacillus mallei*) vaccine
	gastrointestinal series		
GISA	glycopeptide intermediate-resistant *Staphylococcus aureus*		globoid cell leukodystrophy (Krabbe disease)
GISI	gastrointestinal, small intestines	GLDH	glutamate dehydrogenase
GIST	gastrointestinal stromal tumor	GLENN	Bidirectional Glenn procedure (shunt); directs superior vena cava to the pulmonary arteries to correct congenital heart devices (William W L Glenn)
GIT	gastrointestinal tract		
GITB	gastrointestinal tuberculosis		
GITS	gastrointestinal therapeutic system		
	gut-derived infectious toxic shock		
GITSG	Gastrointestinal Tumor Study Group	GLF	ground-level fall (a fall from standing position)
GITT	glucose insulin tolerance test	GLILD	granulomatous-lymphocytic interstitial lung disease
GIUS	gastrointestinal Ultrasound		
giv	given	GLIO	glioblastoma
G IV	grade four	GLL	green-light laser
GIWU	gastrointestinal work-up	GLM	general linear model
GJ	gastrojejunal	GLN	glomerulonephritis
	gastrojejunostomy	Gln	glutamine
	grapefruit juice	GLOB	Globoside; an International Society of Blood Transfusion (ISBT) blood group
G/J	see GJ		
GJA	gastrojejunal anastomosis		
GJ anastomosis	gastrojejunal anastomosis	glob	globulin
GJB2	gap junction protein beta 2 (gene; mutations related to hearing loss)	GLOC	gravity-induced loss of consciousness
		GLOM	glomerular
GJH	generalized joint hypermobility		glomerulus
GJIC	gap junction intercellular communication	GLOS	gadolinium leakage into ocular structures
GJT	gastrojejunostomy tube	GLP	Gambro Liendia Plate
GJ tube	gastrojejunal tube		Good Laboratory Practice (Principles of)
GK	Gama Knife		group-living program
G1K	greater than one thousand		

GLP-1	glucagon-like peptide-1
GLP-1A	glucagon-like peptide-1 receptor agonists (albiglutide [Tanzeum], dulaglutide [Trulicity], exenatide [Bydureon, Byetta], liraglutide [Victoza], and lixisenatide [Adlyxin])
GLP-1RA	glucagon-like peptide-1 receptor agonists (albiglutide [Tanzeum], dulaglutide [Trulicity], exenatide [Bydureon,Byetta], liraglutide [Victoza], and lixisenatide [Adlyxin])
GLR	gravity lumbar reduction
GLS	generalized least squares
GLT-1	glutamate transporter-1
GLU 5	five-hour glucose tolerance test
GLU	glucose
Glu	glutamic acid
glu	glutamate binding protein; see gene website www.ncbi.nlm .nih.gov/gene
gluB	glutamate binding protein; see gene website www.ncbi.nlm .nih.gov/gene
GLUC	glucose
glu doc	point-of-care blood glucose monitoring
glupoc	point-of-care blood glucose monitoring
GLUT1	glucose transporter 1 (also GLUT 2 to 14); see gene website www.ncbi.nlm.nih .gov/gene
glute	gluteus maximus
glutes	gluteus maximus, gluteus medius, and gluteus minimus
gluts	gluteal muscles
Glx	glutamate and glutamine
GLYCOS Hb	glycosylated hemoglobin
GM	fetal generalized body movements
	galactomannan
	gastric mucosa
	general medicine
	genetically modified
	gentamicin
	geometric mean
	gram (g)
	grand mal
	grandmother
	gray matter
	gross motor
	gut microbiota
G-M	Geiger-Müller counter
GM3	ganglioside mannoside 3
GM –	gram-negative

GM +	gram-positive
gm%	grams per 100 milliliters
g/m²	grams per square meter
GMA	grand mal attack
	grandmother
GMAWS	Glasgow Modified Alcohol Withdrawal Scale
Gmax	gluteus maximus (muscle)
	maximum growth rates
GmbH	Gesellschaft mit beschränkter Haftung (a corporation with restricted liability or a private limited liability company)
GMC	general medical clinic
	general medical condition
	General Medical Council (United Kingdom)
	geometric mean concentration
	grey matter concentration
	gross motor coordination
GM2c	Gunner's Mate 2nd Class
GMCD	grand mal convulsive disorder
GM-CSF	sargramostim (granulocyte-macrophage colony-stimulating factor; Leukine)
GMD	gray matter density
gm/dL	grams per deciliter (100 mL)
GME	gaseous microemboli
	graduate medical education
Gmed	gluteus medius (muscle)
GMeM	gluteus medius muscle
GMF	general medical floor
GMFCS	Gross Motor Function Classification System
GMFM	gross motor function measure
GMG	no real problem (gornisht mit gornisht)
GMH	germinal matrix hemorrhage
GMI	graded motor imagery
GMin	gluteus minimus (muscle)
GML	Gingival margin levels
GMLOS	geometric mean length of stay
GMLT	Groton Maze Learning Test
GMN	genome-scale metabolic network
GMOC	general medicine on call
	grandmother of child
GMOP	grandmother of patient
GMOs	genetically modified organisms
GMP	general medical panel
	Good Manufacturing Practices
	guanosine monophosphate
GMR	gallop, murmur or rub
gMRI	glymphatic magnetic resonance imaging
GMRs	geometric mean ratios
GMS	galvanic muscle stimulation
	general medical services

	general medicine and surgery	GNRI		geriatric nutritional risk index
	Gomori methenamine silver (stain)	GNRs		gold nanorods gram negative rods
gms	grams (g)	GNS		gram-negative sepsis
GM&S	general medicine and surgery			oblimersen sodium (Genasense)
GMSCs	gingiva-derived mesenchymal stem cells	GnSAF		gonadotropin surge attenuating factor
GMSPS	Glasgow Meningococcal Septicemia Prognostic Score	GNT GNYHA		Graduate Nurse Technician Greater New York Hospital
GMTs	geometric mean antibody titers			Association
GMV	glomerular membranous vesicle	GO		gemtuzumab ozogamicin
GN	glomerulonephritis			(Mylotarg)
	graduate nurse			Graves ophthalmopathy
	gram-negative			Greek Orthodox
GNA	*Galanthus nivalis* agglutinin	GOAT		Galveston Orientation and
	gram negative anaerobes			Amnesia Test
GNAS	guanine nucleotide binding protein, alpha stimulating (gene)	GOBI		growth monitoring, *o*ral rehydration, *b*reast feeding, and
GNAs	gram negative anaerobes			*I*mmunization
GNB	ganglioneuroblastoma	GOC		goals of care
	gram-negative bacilli			growth of concern
	gram-negative bacteremia	GOCS		Global Obsessive-Compulsive
GNBM	gram-negative bacillary meningitis			Scale
GNC	gram-negative cocci	GOCT		glaucoma optical coherence
GND	gram-negative diplococci			tomography
GNDS	Guy's Neurological Disability	GOD		glucose oxidase
	Scale	GODM		gestational onset diabetes mellitus
GNE	glucosamine (UDP-N-acetyl)-	GOE		Great Oxygenation Event
	2-epimerase/N-acetylman-	GOF		gain-of-function
	nosamine kinase [gene;	GOG		Gynecologic Oncology Group
	regulates and initiates biosyn-	GOJ		gastro-oesophgeal junction
	thesis of N-acetylneuraminic			(UK and other countries)
	acid (NeuAc), a precursor of	GOK		God only knows
	sialic acids])	GOLD		Global Initiative for Chronic
GNEM-FAS	GNE (gene) myopathy-			Obstructive Lung Disease
	Functional Activity Scale			(guidelines)
GNET	gastric neuroendocrine tumor	Golf		Phonetic Alphabet for G;
GNETs	gastric neuroendocrine tumors			pronounced GOLF
GNF	Genomics Institute of the	GOM		granular osmiophilic
	Novartis Research Foundation	GOMER		get out of my emergency room
GNFs	graphene nanoflakes			(slang)
GNG	gluconeogenesis	GON		gonioscopy
	go/no-go (frontal executive			gonococcal ophthalmia
	function test)			neonatorum
GNID	gram-negative intracellular			greater occipital nerve
	diplococci			greater occipital neuritis
GNL	gradient nonlinearity (radiology)	GONA		glaucomatous optic nerve atrophy
gnl	gluconolactonase (gene/protein)	GONB		greater occipital nerve block
GNM	Gaussian network model	GONIO		gonioscopy
	graphene nanomesh	GOO		gastric outlet obstruction
GNO	good neurological outcome	GOOB		pronouncing the pseudoword
	ground nut oil			goob as if pronouncing the
GNP	Geriatric Nurse Practitioner			real word good
	Gerontological Nurse Practitioner	GOPO		government-owned, privately-
GNR	gram-negative rods			operated
GnRH	gonadotropin-releasing hormone	GOR		gastro-oesophageal reflux
GnRHa	gonadotropin-releasing hormone			(United Kingdom)
	agonist			general operating room

G

GORD	gastro-oesophageal reflux disease (United Kingdom)		G4P3	gravida (number of pregnancies) 4, para (number of live births) 3
GORE	a company that produces vascular grafts, endovascular and interventional devices, surgical meshes, sutures, and staple line reinforcement materials		G4P4	gravida (number of pregnancies) 4, para (number of live births) 4
			G-P	gravida-para (pregnancies; pregnancies resulting in the livebirth of at least one child)
	goal-oriented requirements engineering		G/P	gravida/para
GORK	God only really knows (slang)		G0P0	no pregnancies, no births (over 20 weeks)
GOS	galactose oxidase and Schiff reagent (test)		G1P0	one pregnancy, no live births
			G1P1	one pregnancy; one pregnancy that went to term (see G4P3104 and GPMAL)
	General Ophthalmic Services (Scottish)			
	Glasgow Outcome Scale		g3p3	three pregnancies, 3 went to term
GOSE	Glascow Outcome Scale-Extended		G2P2	two pregnancies; two pregnancies that went to term (see G4P3104 and GPMAL)
GOS-E	Extended Glasgow Outcome Scale		GPA	gelatin particle agglutination
GOSV	Gossas virus			global program on AIDS
GOT	glucose oxidase test			grandfather
	glutamic-oxaloacetic transaminase (aspartate aminotransferase)			granulomatosis with polyangiitis (Wegener granulomatosis)
	goals of treatment		G#P#A#	gravida (number of pregnancies) para (number of live births) abortion (number of abortions)
GOV1	gastro-oesophageal varices type 1 (esophageal varices extending along lesser curvature side of stomach)			
			GPAM	glycerol-3-phosphate acyltransferase, mitochondrial (gene/protein)
GOV2	gastro-oesophageal varices type 2 (esophageal varices extending along greater curvature side of stomach)		GPAS	Global Patient Assessment Scale
			GPAs	gastroprotective agents
				general physical activities
GOX	glucose oxidation			giant pituitary adenomas
GP	gabapentin (Neurontin)			grade point averages
	gastroparesis		G6Pase	glucose-6-phosphatase
	Gemcitabine plus cisplatin (Platinol)		GPB	gram-positive bacilli
			GPC	gel permeation chromatography
	general practitioner			Geriatric Primary Care (Veterans Administration)
	globus pallidus			
	glucose polymers			giant papillary conjunctivitis
	glycoprotein			glycerophosphorylcholine
	gram-positive			G-protein coupled
	grandparent			gram-positive cocci
	gutta percha		GPCCl	gram-positive cocci in clusters
GP1	glycoprotein 1		GPCL	gas-permeable contact lens
	group one		GPCR	G protein-coupled receptors
GP2	group two		GPCRs	G protein-coupled receptors
GP3	group three		GPCs	glial progenitor cells
G4P3104	four pregnancies (gravid), 3 went to term, one premature, no abortion (or miscarriage), and 4 living children (p 5 para)		GPC/TP	glycerylphosphorylcholine to total phosphate
			GPD	glycophorin D
G2P0	gravida			granulomatous periorificial dermatitis
g2p1	gravida (number of pregnancies) 2, para (number of live births) 1		G6PD	glucose-6-phosphate dehydrogenase
G3P2	gravida (number of pregnancies) 3, para (number of live births) 2		GPDs	generalized parton distributions
				generalized periodic discharges

GPE	global perceived effect	G6PT	glucose-6-phosphate transporter
GPEDs	generalized periodic eleptiform discharges	GPT	glutamic pyruvic transaminase
GPEH	giant paraesophageal hernia		Grooved Pegboard Test (of hand function)
GPEHR	giant paraesophageal hernia repair	GPU	geriatric psychiatric unit
GPFA	generalized paroxysmal fast activity (an electroencephalographic finding in patients with symptomatic generalized epilepsy consisting of 15-25Hz bifrontally predominant generalized fast activity seen predominantly in sleep)	GPVP	good pharmacovigilance process
		GPVTS	General Practice Vocational Training Scheme (UK)
		GPx	glutathione peroxidase
		GPx-1	glutathione peroxidase-1
		GR	GameReady (cold compression)
			gastric resection
			growing rod
			growth rate
GPFX	grepafloxacin	gr	grade
GPGL	gamma probe guided lymphoscintigraphy		grain (one grain equals 64.8 mg). This apothecary system unit of measure should never be used as it is not understood by today's health professionals. Use milligrams (mg)
GPHs	glycoprotein hormones		
GPI	general paralysis of the insane glucose-6-phosphate isomerase glycoprotein IIb/IIIa receptor inhibitor(s)		
		G−R	gram-negative rods
GPi	globus pallidus interna	G+R	gram-positive rods
G-PLT	giant platelets	G/R	green/red ratio
GPMAL	gravida, para, multiple births, abortions, and live births	GRA	glucocorticoid remediable aldosteronism
GPN	General Pediatric Nurse glossopharyngeal neuralgia graduate practical nurse		granisetron (Kytril)
		GRAAL	GRAph ALigner (algorithm)
		GRAALL	Group for Research on Adult Acute Lymphoblastic Leukemia (study)
GPO	group purchasing organization		
G1PO	may have meant G1P0 (pregnant for the first time and has not yet delivered)	GRACE	Geriatric Resources for Assessment and Care of Elders
G2PO	see G2P0		
GPOEM	gastric per-oral endoscopic pyloromyotomy	GRACE score	Global Registry of Acute Coronary Events score
G-POEM	gastric peroral endoscopic myotomy	GRADE	Grades of Recommendations, Assessment, Development and Evaluation
GPOH	Gesellschaft für Pädiatrische Onkologie und Hämatologie (German Society for Pediatric Oncology and Hematology)		
		GRAFO	ground-reaction ankle foot orthosis
GPOs	general practitioners in oncology (Canada) group purchasing organizations	grain	One grain equals 64.8 mg. This apothecary system unit of measure should never be used as it is not understood by today's health professionals. Use milligrams (mg)
GPP	gingivoperiosteoplasty Good Programming Practice		
GPR	global postural re-education gram-positive rod	gran	granisetron (Kytril) granulocytes
GPRD	General Practice Research Database (United Kingdom)	GRAS	generally recognized as safe
		GRASE	Generally Recognized as Safe and Effective
GPS	Gamma Poisson Shrinker Goodpastures syndrome	GRASS	gradient recalled acquisition in a steady state
GPS™	Gravitational Platelet Separation (System)	GRAT	Gratitude, Resentment, and Appreciation Test
GPs	general practitioners glycoproteins	Grav.	gravid (pregnant)

G

gravida 6, para4-0-2-3	6 pregnancies resulting in 4-full term deliveries with 0 premature births and 2 abortions or miscarriages and 3 living children	GRV	gastric residual volume
		GRY rats	Groggy rats, a novel rat model of absence-like epilepsy
GRC	gastric remnant cancers	GS	gallstone
GRD	gastroesophageal reflux disease		gastric sleeve
GRDA	generalized rhythmic delta activity		gastrocnemius/soleus
GRD DTR	granddaughter		general surgery
GRD SON	grandson		generalized seizure
GRE	glycopeptide-resistant *Enterococcus spp*		Gleason score
			gliosarcoma
	graded resistive exercise		glucosamine sulfate
	gradient refocused echo		gluteal sets
	gradient-recalled echo		Gram stain
GReD	Genetics, Reproduction and Development Laboratory, Clermont-Ferrand, France		grip strength
		G/S	5% dextrose (glucose) and 0.9% sodium chloride (saline) injection
GRed	glutathione reductase	G & S	gait and stance
GR-FR	grandfather	GSAP	greatest single allergen present
GRFT	griffithsin (a broad-spectrum antiviral protein against several glycosylated viruses)	G-SAS	Gambling Symptom Assessment Scale
		GSC	gastrocnemius soleus complex muscles
grh	grainy head (gene)	GS-Cbl	glutathionylcobalamin
GRIN2A	glutamate receptor, ionotropic, N-methyl D-aspartate 2A (gene)	GSCF	may have meant granulocyte colony stimulating factor (G-CSF)
		GSCs	glioblastoma stem cells
GRKP	gentamicin-resistant *Klebsiella pneumoniae*	GSCU	geriatric skilled care unit
		GSD	gallstone disease
GR-MO	grandmother		German shepherd dog(s)
GRN	granules		gestational sac diameter
	green		gestodene
GRO	growth-related oncogene		globule-size distribution
GROC	Global Rating of Change (scale)		glucogen storage disease
GRP	Good Regulatory Practice	GSD-1	glycogen storage disease, type 1
	group	GSD-1b	glycogen storage disease type 1b
$Gr_1P_0AB_1$	one pregnancy, no births, and one abortion	GSD IV	glycogen storage disease IV
		GSE	genital self-examination
GRPHM	group home		gluten sensitive enteropathy
GRP/RC	Group codes and Claim Adjustment Reason Codes (Medicare)		grip strong and equal
		GSES	General Self-Efficacy Survey
GRR	gross reproduction rate	GSF	Gold Standards Framework (United Kingdom)
GRS	gender reassignment surgery		
	Genetic Risk Score		growing skull fracture
	Global Rating Scale(s)	GSH	glutathione
	GRACE (Global Registry of Acute Coronary Event) risk score	GSI	genuine stress incontinence
		GSIS	glucose-stimulated insulin secretion
GRs	glucocorticoid receptors	GSIs	gamma secretase inhibitors
GRT	gastric residence time	GSK	GlaxoSmithKline
	gene replacement therapy	GSL	goniosynechialysis
	genotypic resistance testing	GSM	genitourinary syndrome of menopause
	glandular replacement therapy		
	Graduate Respiratory Therapist		Global System of Mobile Communication
	grasp and release test		
	group-randomized trial		grey-scale median
GRTT	Graduate Respiratory Therapist Technician	GSMD	gestational sack and maternal date
		GSMs	gamma secretase modulators

G

GSN	gelsolin; see gene website www .ncbi.nlm.nih.gov/gene	GTB	gastrointestinal tract bleeding
			green TheraBand
GSO	gadolinium oxyorthosilicate	GTC	generalized tonic-clonic (seizure)
GSP	gallstone pancreatitis	GTCS	generalized tonic-clonic seizure
	general survey panel	GTCs	green tea catechins
	generalized social phobia	GTD	gestational trophoblastic disease
	Good Statistical Practice	GTDS	granisetron transdermal system
GSPN	greater superficial petrosal neurectomy		(Sancuso)
		GTE	general therapeutic exercise
GSR	galvanic skin resistance (response)		greater than or equal to
			Green tea extract
	gastrosalivary reflex	GTF	gastrostomy tube feeding
	gunshot residue		glucose tolerance factor
GSS	Genotypic-sensitivity scores		glucosyltransferase
	Gerstmann-Straüssler-Scheinker (syndrome)	GTG	gamma-glutamyltransferase; see gene website www.ncbi.nlm .nih.gov/gene
GST	glutathione S-transferase		
	gold sodium thiomalate (Myochrysine)	GTH	gonadotropic hormone
		GTIC	genetic testing in children
	Grocery Shelving Task	GTIs	genotoxic impurities
GSTM	gold sodium thiomalate (Myochrysine)	gtl	glycosyl transferase-like protein; see gene website www.ncbi .nlm.nih.gov/gene
GSUI	genuine stress urinary incontinence		
		GTM	generative topographic mapping
GS-US7	gray-scale seven-joint ultrasound score		geometric transfer matrix
			glaucomatous trabecular meshwork
GSV	greater saphenous vein		
GSW	gunshot wound	GTN	gestational trophoblastic neoplasms
GSWA	gunshot wound to abdomen		
GT	gait		glomerulo-tubulo-nephritis
	gait training		glyceryl trinitrate (name for nitroglycerin in the United Kingdom)
	gastrostomy		
	gastrotomy tube		
	gene therapy	GTO	Golgi tendon organ(s)
	genotype	GTP	gestational thrombocytopenia
	gestational thrombocytopenia		glutamyl transpeptidase
	Glanzmann thrombasthenia		green tea polyphenols
	glucose tolerance		guanosine triphosphate
	Graston Technique (instrument-assisted soft tissue mobiliza-tion that enables clinicians to address soft tissue lesions and fascial restrictions)	GTPAL	gestation, term, preterm, abortion and living
		GTPS	greater trochanteric pain syndrome
		GTPs	green tea polyphenols
	great toe	GTR	Genetic Test Registry
	greater than		granulocyte turnover rate
	greater trochanter		gross total resection
	green tea		guided tissue regeneration
	group therapy	GTS	Gilles de la Tourette syndrome
GT1	genotype 1	gtt.	drops
GT2	genotype 2	GTT	gestational trophoblastic tumor
GT3	genotype 3		getational transient thyrotoxicosis
GT4	genotype 4		
GT5	genotype 5		Global Trigger Tool (A method for harm identification and demonstrated harm reduc-tion [Institute for Healthcare Improvement])
GT6	genotype 6		
GT7	genotype 7		
GT8	genotype 8		
G/T	glycine/taurine ratio		
GTA	glutaraldehyde		glucose tolerance test

G

gtt	slow intravenous infusion (drip [Latin abbreviation for drop])	gut	intestines or bowel
GTT agar	gelatin-tellurite-taurocholate agar	GV	gentian violet
GTT2H	glucose tolerance test 2 hours (oral)		growth velocity
GTT3H	glucose tolerence test 3 hours (oral)	G V	grade five
GTTP	Group Teen Triple P (a broad-based parenting intervention program delivered for parents of teenagers who are interested in learning a variety of parenting skills; triple P = positive parenting program)	GVAX	vaccines consisting of prostate or pancreatic cancer cell lines and genetically modified to secrete granulocyte-macrophage colony-stimulating factor (GM-CSF)
gtts	drops	GVB	gastric variceal bleeding
G tube	gastrostomy tube	GVC	gestational vascular complications
G-tube	gastrostomy tube	GVD	graft vascular disease
GTV	gross tumor volume		granulovacuolar degeneration
GTW	multi-glycoside of Tripterygium wilfordii Hook. f. (a Chinese herb)	GVDH	may have meant GVHD (graft-versus-host disease)
GTX	gemcitabine, docetaxel (Taxotere), and capecitabine (Xeloda)	GVE	gastric vascular ectasia (a distinct lesion consisting of telangiectatic vessels within the superficial gastric mucosa)
GTx	granulocyte transfusions		global visual evaluation
GU	gastric ulcer	G−ve	gram-negative
	gastric upset	G+ve	gram-positive
	genitourinary	GVF	Goldmann visual fields
	gonococcal urethritis		good visual fields
G −	gram-negative	GVG	vigabatrin (gamma-vinyl GABA)
	guaiac negative	GVH	generalized visceral hypersensitivity
guaC	see gene website www.ncbi.nlm .nih.gov/gene	GVHD	graft-versus-host disease
GUAG	get-up-and-go (test)	G VI	grade six
guaiac	brown resin obtained from guaiacum trees, used as a flavoring and in varnishes, formerly used medicinally as a test for traces of blood in the feces	GVL	graft-versus leukemia
		GVM	graft verses malignancy
		GVMs	glomuvenous malformations
		GVN	gentamicin, vancomycin, and nystatin
		GVP	gemcitabine, vinorelbine, and cisplatin (Platinol)
		GVR	goiter volume reduction
			graft volume reduction
GUAR	guarantor	GVS	galvanic vestibular stimulation
GUD	genital ulcer disease		gastric vertical stapling
GUDCA	glycoursodeoxycholic acid	GVSDS	growth velocity standard deviation score
GUHD	my have meant GVHD (graft-versus-host disease)	GVT	graft-versus-tumor
GUI	genitourinary infection	GW	gestational weeks
guiac	may have meant guaiac		Gulf War
GUM	Genitourinary Medicine (clinics)	G/W	dextrose (glucose) in water
		G&W	glycerin and water (enema)
Guo	guanosine	GWA	genome-wide association
GUR	genetically unresolved		gunshot wound of the abdomen
GUS	genitourinary sphincter	GWAMA	genome-wide association meta-analysis
	genitourinary system		
GUSB	beta-glucuronidase enzyme	GWAS	genome-wide association studies
GUSS	Hugging Swallowing Screen		
GUSTO	Global Utilization of Streptokinase and TPA for Occluded Arteries	GWASs	genome-wide association studies
		GWBI	General Well-Being Index

G

GWC	gamma-well counting		
	Goldmann-Witmer coefficient		
	green waste compost	**H**	
GWD	Guinea worm disease	H	H; an International Society of
GWE	genome-wide expression		Blood Transfusion (ISBT)
	(analysis)		blood group
GWIA	Genome-Wide Interaction		*Haemophilis*
	Analysis		Haldol (haloperidol); as in
GWMFT	Graded Wolf Motor Function		vitamin H (slang)
	Test		hamstrings
GWNL	grossly within normal limits		head
GWOT	Global War on Terrorism		heart
GWS	Gulf war syndrome		height
GWT	gunshot wound of the throat		*Helicobacter*
GWTG	Get With The Guidelines		Hemovac
	(American Heart Association		heroin
	program)		high
GWTG-HF	American Heart Association's		Hispanic
	Get With The Guidelines		histidineI
	Program for heart failure		Hotel (Phonetic Alphabet H;
GWTG-Stroke	Get With The Guidelines-		pronounced HOH-TEL)
	Stroke		hour
GWX	guide wire exchange		husband
GXP	graded exercise program		hydrogen
GXT	graded exercise test		hypermetropia
Gy	gray (a gray is defined as the		hyperopia
	absorption of one joule of		hyperphoria
	radiation energy per kilogram		hypodermic
	of matter)		isoniaized [part of
GYN	gynecology		tuberculosis regimen as in
GYNE	gynecology		RHZ (E/S) /HR]
GYNONC	Gynecologic Oncology		objective angle
GYN/ONC	gynecology/oncology		trastuzumab (Herceptin)
GYO	gynecology-oncology	H′	hip
GZTS	Guilford-Zimmerman	H⁺	hydrogen icon
	Temperament Survey	Ⓗ	hypodermic injection
		H²	hiatal hernia
		H₂	hydrogen
		H20	See H2O (water)
		H24	24 hour
		3H	high, hot, and a helluva lot
		H/0	zero hours (as in 0-8 h/0-24)
		HA	headache
			hearing aid
			heart attack
			hemadsorption
			hemagglutination
			hemolytic anemia
			Hispanic American
			horizontal abduction
			hospital admission
			hospital-acquired
			hyaluronan
			hyaluronic acid
			hydroxyapatite
			hyperalimentation
			hypermetropic astigmatism
			hypothalmic amenorrhea

H/A	headache	HACP	Healthcare Accredited Certification Program
	head-to-abdomen (ratio)		
	height for age		Healthcare Accredited Certified Professional
	holding area		
HAA	haloacetic acid		hemispheric antegrade cerebral perfusion
	hepatitis-associated antigen		
HA-1A®	nebacumab		hospital-acquired conditions penalties
HAAB	hepatitis A antibody		
HAAE	high-frequency augmented acoustic environment	HACS	hyperactive child syndrome
		HAD	height-adjustable desks
HAAF	hypoglycemia-associated autonomic failure		HIV (human immunodeficiency virus)-associated dementia
HA-AKI	hospital-acquired acute kidney injury		human adjuvant disease
			hypertonic acetate dextran
HAART	highly active antiretroviral treatment	HADD	hydroxyapatite deposition disease
HAAs	haloacetic acids	HAdd	hip adduction
HAB	hospital-acquired bacteremia		horizontal adduction
HABD	hyaluronic acid binding domain	HADDS	hypotonia ataxia developmental disorder syndrome
HAbd	hip abductor (muscle)		
H Abd	horizontal abduction	HADH	the reduced form of nicotinamide-adenine dinucleotide (hybrid donors in the biochemical redox reactions)
HABF	hepatic artery blood flow		
HABP	hospital-acquired bacterial pneumonia		
	hyaluronan binding protein		
HABP2	hyaluronan binding protein 2 (gene)	HADS	Hospital Anxiety and Depression Scale
HABPs	high activity binding peptides	HAE	hearing aid evaluation
HABP/VABP	hospital-acquired and ventilator-associated bacterial pneumonia		hepatic artery embolization
			herb-related adverse event
			hereditary angioedema
HABS	Harvard Aging Brain Study	HAEC	Hirschprungs associated enterocolitis
HABs	harmful algal blooms		
	health-related attitudes and behaviors	HAF	hyperalimentation fluid
		HAGG	hyperimmune antivariola gamma globulin
hAbs	humanized antibodies		
HAC	hand-assisted colectomy	HAGHL	humeral avulsion of the glenohumeral ligament
	healthcare-associated condition		
	hearing-aid consultation	HAGL	humeral avulsion of the glenohumeral ligament
	hospital acquired condition		
	hydroxyapatite cement	HAGMA	high anion gap metabolic acidosis
HAc	acetic acid		
HA1c	glycosylated hemoglobin	HAH	high-altitude headache
HACA	human antichimeric antibodies	HAHA	human anti-human antibodies
	Hypothermia After Cardiac Arrest (trial)	HAI	healthcare-associated Infections
			hemagglutination inhibition assay
HACCP	Hazard Analysis Critical Control Point(s)		
			hepatic arterial infusion
HACE	hepatic artery chemoembolization	HAIC	hepatic arterial infusional chemotherapy
	high-altitude cerebral edema	HAIDI	hemodialysis access induced distal ischemia
HACEK group	Haemophilus parainfluenzae, H. aphrophilus, and H. paraphrophilus, Actinobacillus actinomycetemcomitans, Cardiobacterium hominis, Eikenella corrodens, and Kingella kingae		
		HAIP	hepatic artery infusion pump
		HAIR-AN	hyperandrogenism insulin resistance-acanthosis nigricans
		HAK	hyperalimentation kit
			hyperkeratotic actinic keratosis

HAL	hemorrhoidal artery ligation
	hip axis length
	hyperalimentation
HALC	hand-assisted laparoscopic colectomy
HALDN	hand-assisted laparoscopic donor nephrectomy
HALE	health-adjusted life expectancy
HALN	hand-assisted laparoscopic (radical) nephrectomy
HALNU	hand-assisted laparoscopic nephroureterectomy
HALO	halothane (Fluothane)
	hip and ankle linked orthosis
	hours after light onset
HALRI	hospital-acquired lower respiratory infections
HALS	hip abduction with lumbar stabilization
HALs	hand-assisted laparoscopic surgery
HALSR	hand-assisted laparoscopic sigmoid resection
HALT	hypo-attenuated leaflet thickening
HAM	Haldol, Ativan, and morphine
	high-alert medication(s) (medications where recurring reported errors have had serious consequences and warrant special attention)
	high-dose cytarabine (ara-C) and mitoxantrone
	HTLV-1-associated myelopathy
	human albumin microspheres
HAMA	human antimurine antibody
HAM-A	Hamilton Anxiety (scale)
HAMD	Hamilton Depression (scale)
HAMLET	human alpha-lactalbumin made lethal to tumor cells
HAMS	hamstrings
HAM/TSP	HTLV-1 (human T-lymphotropic virus type 1) associated myelopathy linked to tropical spastic paraparesis
HAN	heroin-associated nephropathy
HANA	HIV non-AIDS (human immunodeficiency virus-associated non-acquired immunodeficiency syndrome)
HANAC syndrome	hereditary angiopathy with nephropathy, aneurysms, and muscle cramps (syndrome)
HAND	handheld echocardiography
	HIV-(human immunodeficiency virus) associated neurocognative disorder(s)

H and H	Hunt and Hess scale/score (grading systems used to classify the severity of a subarachnoid hemorrhage based on the patient's clinical condition; used as a predictor of patient's prognosis/ outcome, with a higher grade correlating to lower survival rate)
HaNDL	headache and neurological deficits with cerebrospinal fluid lymphocytosis
HANE	hereditary angioneurotic edema
HANYS	Healthcare Association of New York State
HAO	hearing aid orientation
HAP	heredopathia atactica polyneuritiformis
	hospital-acquired pneumonia
	hydroxyapatite
HAp	hydroxyapatite
HAPA	Health Action Process Approach (suggests that the adoption, initiation, and maintenance of **health** behaviors must be explicitly conceived as a **process** that consists of at least a motivation phase and a volition phase)
HAPC	hospital-acquired penetration contact
HAPD	home-automated peritoneal dialysis
HAPE	high-altitude pulmonary edema
HAPI	hospital-acquired pressure injury
HaPI	Health and Psychosocial Instruments (a database of Information on behavioral measurement instruments)
HAPIs	hospital-acquired pressure injuries
haplo	haplotype
HapMap	A catalog of common genetic variants that occur in human beings. It describes what these variants are, where they occur in our DNA, and how they are distributed among people within populations and among populations in different parts of the world. (The International Haplotype Map Project) (hapmap.org)
HAPS	hepatic arterial perfusion scintigraphy
HAPTO	haptoglobin
HAPU	hospital-acquired pressure ulcers

HAQ	Headache Assessment Questionnaire	hATTR	hereditary transthyretin-related amyloidosis
	Health Assessment Questionnaire	HATU	2-(1H-7-Azabenzotriazol-1-yl)–1,1,3,3 tetramethyl uranium hexafluorophosphate (a peptide-coupling reagent)
HAQ-DI	Health Assessment Questionnaire Disability Index		
HAR	high-altitude retinopathy	HAV	hallux abducto valgus
	hyperacute rejection		hepatitis A vaccine
HARD	heartworm-associated respiratory disease		hepatitis A virus
		HAVAb	hepatitis A virus antibodies
HARDI	high-angular resolution diffusion-weighted imaging	HAV Ab-M	Hepatitis A virus – IgM
		HAVD	hand arm vein distension
HARH	high-altitude retinal hemorrhage	HAVF	higher abdominal visceral fat
HARP	hypoprebetalipoproteinemia, acanthocytes, retinitis pigmentosa, and pallidale degeneration (syndrome)	HAV-HBV	hepatitis A virus and hepatitis B virus vaccine
		HAZ	height-for-age Z-Score
HARRT	may be HAART	HAZWOPER	Hazardous Waste Operations and Emergency Response
HARS	Hamilton Anxiety (Rating) Scale	HB	heart block
	HIV-associated adipose redistribution syndrome		heart-beating (donor)
			heel-to-buttock
HART	hyperfractionated accelerated radiotherapy		hemoglobin (Hb)
			hepatitis B
HAS	Hamilton Anxiety (Rating) Scale		high calorie
	head shaft angle		hold breakfast
	headache associated with sexual activity		housebound
			House-Brackmann (Facial Grading Scale)
	Health Savings Account		hydrocodone bitartrate
	hemangiosarcoma	Hb	hemoglobin
	Holmes-Adie syndrome	H2B	histone H2B-like (gene)
	home assessment service	H/B	see HB
	hyperalimentation solution	H-B	House-Brackmann (Facial Grading Scale)
HASA	horizontal acetabular sector angle	1°HB	first degree heart block
HasA	heme acquisition system A	HB1°	first degree heart block
HASBLED score	used to calculate the risk of major bleeding with anticoagulation in atrial fibrillation	HB2°	second degree heart block
		HB3°	third degree heart block
		HBA	His Bundle ablation
HAS-BLED score	used to calculate the risk of major bleeding with anticoagulation in atrial fibrillation	HBAB	hepatitis B antibody
		Hb1Ac	glycosylated hemoglobin
hASC	human adipose-derived stem cells	HbA1c	glycosylated hemoglobin
HASCI	head and spinal cord injury	HBAC	hyperdynamic beta-adrenergic circulatory
HASCVD	hypertensive arteriosclerotic cardiovascular disease		
		HBAg	hepatitis B virus antigen
HASHD	hypertensive arteriosclerotic heart disease	HbA1c	may have meant HbA1c (glycosylated hemoglobin)
HASTE	half-Fourier acquisition single-shot turbo spin-echo	HbAS	sickle cell trait
		HBB	hand behind back
HASTI	reported assessments of symptoms score)		hospital blood bank
		HBBW	hold breakfast for blood work
HAT	head, arms, and trunk	HBC	health and beauty care
	hepatic artery thrombosis		hereditary breast cancer
	heterophile antibody titer		hit by car
	histone acetyltransferase	Hb-C	hemoglobin C
	hormone ablative therapy	Hb1c	see HbA1c
	hospital arrival time	HBcAB	hepatitis B core antibody
	human African trypanosomiasis (sleeping sickness)	HBcAg	hepatitis B core antigen

HbCO	carboxyhemoglobin	HBM	Health Belief Model
HBcore	hepatitis B core antigen		human biomonitoring
HbCV	*Haemophilus* b conjugate		human bone marrow
	vaccine		human breast milk
HBD	has been drinking	HBME-1	Hector Battifora mesothelial-1
	hydroxybutyrate dehydrogenase		human bone marrow endothelial
HBDH	hydroxybutyrate dehydrogenase		cell marker-1
hBDs	human beta defensins	HBNK	heparin-binding neurotrophic
HBE	Harris-Benedict Equation		factor
	(predicts resting energy	hBNP	human b-type natriuretic peptide
	expenditure)		(nesiritide [Natrecor])
	hepatitis B epsilon	HBO	hit by owner (owner's car)
	human bronchial epithelial		(Veterinary slang)
	(cells)		hyperbaric oxygen
	hypopharyngoscopy, bronchos-		(HBO_2 preferred)
	copy, and esophagoscopy	HBO_2	hyperbaric oxygen
HbE	hemoglobin epsilon	HbO_2	hemoglobin, oxygenated
HBeAb	hepatitis Be antibody (antigen)		hyperbaric oxygen
HBeAg	hepatitis Be antigen		(HBO_2 preferred)
HBEC	human bronchial epithelial cells	HBOC	hemoglobin-based oxygen
HBED	hydroxybenzylethylene-diamine		carrier
	diacetic acid		hereditary breast and ovarian
H Bee	honey bee (allergies)		cancer
HBEX	home-based exercise	HBOT	hyperbaric oxygen treatment/
HBF	hazardous body fluid		therapy (HBO_2T preferred)
	hepatic blood flow	HBO_2T	hyperbaric oxygen treatment
HbF	fetal hemoglobin	HBoV	human bocavirus
H-B FGS	House-Brackmann Facial	HBP	Healthy Beginnings Plus
	Grading Scale		high blood pressure
HBG	hemoglobin, gamma; see gene	HBPC	Home-Based Primary Care
	website; see gene website		(Veterans Administration)
	www.ncbi.nlm.nih.gov/gene	hbPG	hyperbranched polyglycidol
Hb/g	micrograms of hemoglobin per	HBPM	home blood pressure
	gram of feces		monitoring
HBGA	had it before, got it again (slang)	HBPV	home blood pressure variability
HBGM	home blood glucose monitoring	HBR	half-body radiation
HBGS	House-Brackmann Grading	HBr	hydrobromide
	System (Scale)	HBRs	human biting rates
HBH	hand behind head	HBRT	horseback riding therapy
	Health Belief Model	HBS	Health Behavior Scale
HBHC	hospital based home care		human body shape
HBI	Harvey-Bradshaw Index		hungry bone syndrome
	hemibody irradiation	HbS	sickle cell hemoglobin
HBID	hereditary benign intraepithelial	HBsAb	antibody to hepatitis B surface
	dyskeratosis		antigen
HBIG	hepatitis B immune globulin	HBsAg	hepatitis B surface antigen
HBIPS	hospital-based inpatient	HbSC	sickle cell hemoglobin C
	psychiatric services	HBSS	Hanks balanced salt solution
Hb Kansas	mutant hemoglobin with a low	HbSS	sickle cell anemia
	affinity for oxygen	Hb-SS	homozygous sickle cell disease
hblA	hemolysin BL binding	HBT	hydrogen breath test
	component: see gene website		hypertrophy of the base of the
	www.ncbi.nlm.nih.gov/gene		tongue
H2 blockers	histamine 2-receptor antagonists	HBUS	hepato-biliary ultrasound
	[e.g. ranitidine (Zantac),	HBV	hepatitis B vaccine
	cimetidine (Tagamet),		hepatitis B virus
	famotidine (Pepcid), etc.)]		honey-bee venom
HBLV	B-lymphotropic virus human	HB0V	human bocavirus

H

HBV-ACLF	hepatitis B-related acute-on-chronic liver failure	HCAO	hepatitis C-associated osteosclerosis
HBVig	hepatitis B virus immune globulin	HCAP	healthcare-associated pneumonia
HBVP	high biological value protein	H-CAP	altretamine (hexamethyl-melamine), cyclophosphamide, doxorubicin (Adriamycin), and cisplatin (Platinol)
HBW	high birth weight		
H/BW	heart-to-body weight (ratio)		
HC	hair count		
	hairy cell	HCAPS	see gene website, www.ncbi.nlm.nih.gov/gene
	handicapped		
	head circumference	H Caps	Hospital Consumer Assessment of Healthcare Providers and Systems (HCAHPS: a Center for Medicare and Medicaid Services standardized publicly reported survey of patients' perspectives of hospital care)
	health coaching		
	healthy controls		
	heart catheterization		
	heater/cooler		
	heel cords		
	hemicrania continua		
	Hickman catheter	HCASMC	human coronary artery smooth muscle cell(s)
	Hilar cholangiocarcinoma (Klatskin tumor)		
		HCB	hexachlorobenzene
	hip circumference	hCB-ECs	human cord blood-derived endothelial cells
	home care		
	hospital course	HC-BPPV	horizontal canal benign paroxysmal positional vertigo
	hot compress		
	housecall	HCBR	human carbonyl reductase
	Huntington chorea	HCBS	home and community-based services
	hydrocephalus		
	hydrocortisone	HCC	Hearing Coordination Center
4-HC	4-hydroperoxycyclo-phosphamide		hepatocellular carcinoma
H1C	glycosylated hemoglobin (also HbA1c and A1C)		Hurthle cell carcinoma
		HCCA	Hilar cholangiocarcinoma (Klatskin tumor
HC03	see HCO3		
H & C	hot and cold	HCCL	heavily calcified coronary lesions
H/C	see HC		
HCA	continuous heated aerosol	HCCM	hepatic colorectal cancer metastases
	health care aide		
	heterocyclic antidepressant		high-concentration contrast media
	High-Content Analysis		
	hydroxycitric acid	HCCS	holocytochrome c synthase (gene)
	hypercalcemia		
	hypercapnic acidosis	HCCs	hepatocellular carcinomas
	hypothermia circulatory arrest	HCD	health care directive
HCAB	Health Care Advisory Board		herniate cervical disk
	healthcare-associated bacteremia		high cholesterol diet
			hydrocodone
hcAb	heavy-chain antibodies		hydrocolloid dressing
HC/AC	fetus head circumference to abdominal circumference ratio	HCE	hepaticocholecystoenterostomy
			human corneal epithelial
			see gene website www.ncbi.nlm.nih.gov/gene
HCAHPS	Hospital Consumer Assessment of Healthcare Providers and Systems (survey/score; a national standardized survey instrument designed to assess the patient's perspective of hospital care for public reporting purposes)		
		HCF	health care facility
			Society for Hospital Epidemiology of America (guidelines)
		HCFA	Health Care Financing Administration
		HCFC	hydrochlorofluorocarbon
		HCFU	1-Hexylcarbamoyl-5-fluorouracil (camofur)
HCAIs	healthcare-associated infections		

hCG	beta human chorionic gonadotropinbeta
	human chorionic gonadotropin
HCGs	high-contrast gratings
hCGs	human chorionic gonadotropins
hCGt	total human chorionic gonadotrophin
HCH	Healthcare for the Homeless
	hexachlorocyclohexane
	hygroscopic condenser humidifier
HCHF diet	high-carbohydrate, high-fat (diet)
HCHG	high-carbohydrate, high-glycemic index
HCHL	hypercholesterolemia
HCHO	formaldehyde
	high carbohydrate
Hchol	hypercholesterolemia
hChP	hindbrain choroid plexus
HCHs	hexachlorocyclohexanes (pesticides)
HCHV	Health Care for Homeless Veterans (Department of Veterans Affairs)
HCI	home care instructions
	hydrochloric acid (when it appears separately [not as part of a drug name])
	hydrochloride (when part of a drug name, as in thiamine HCl [thiamine hydrochloride])
HCIS	Healthcare Information System
HCIs	healthcare-associated infections
Hcit	homocitrulline (a carbamylation-derived product that has been identified as a biomarker of morbidity and mortality in patients with chronic kidney disease)
HCKD	hereditary cystic kidney disease
HCL	hairy cell leukemia
	hydrogel contact lens
H/CL	heart-to-contralateral lung (ratio)
HCLF	high carbohydrate, low fiber (diet)
HCLG	high-carbohydrate, low-glycemic index
HCLP	high carbohydrate, low protein (diet)
HCLs	hard contact lenses
HCLV	hairy cell leukemia variant
HCM	health care maintenance
	heterogeneous cation-exchange membrane
	hypercalcemia of malignancy
	hypertrophic cardiomyopathy

HCMA	Hypertrophic Cardiomyopathy Association
HCMC	Hennepin County Medical Center (Minneapolis MN)
	Ho Chi Minh City (Vietnam)
HCMP	hypertrophic cardiomyopathy
HCMV	human cytomegalovirus
HCN	Hürthle cell neoplasm
	hyperpolarization-activated cyclic nucleotide-gated ion channels
HCn	hydrogen cyanide
HCO	health care organization(s)
HCO$_2$	formate
HCO$_3$	bicarbonate
HCOM	may have meant HOCM (hypertrophic obstructive cardiomyopathy)
hCoV	human coronavirus
HCP	handicapped
	healthcare personnel
	healthcare provider
	healthcare proxy
	hearing conservation programs
	hereditary coporphyria
	hexachlorophene
	home chemotherapy program
	hospital chemistry profile
	Human Connectome Project
	hydrocephalus
HCPA	Hospital de Clinicas de Porto Alegre (Porto Alegre, Brazil)
hcpA	HP1-like protein (gene/protein)
HCPCS	Healthcare Common Procedural Coding System
HCPOA	healthcare power of attorney
HCPT	10-hydroxycamptothecin
HCQ	hydroxychloroquine (Plaquenil)
HCR	health care review
hCRF	human corticotrophin-releasing factor (Xerecept)
HCRP	hospital corneal retrieval program
hCRP	human complement regulatory protein
	human c-reactive protein
HCRT	hypocretin (orexin) neuropeptide precursor; see gene website www.ncbi.nlm.nih.gov/gene
HCS	hazard communication standard
	healthcare surrogate
	heel-cord stretches
	high content screening
	human chorionic somatomammotropin
HCs	healthy controls
17-HCS	17-hydroxycorticosteroids
HCSE	horse chestnut seed extract
HCSMA	hereditary canine spinal muscular atrophy

HCSP	heterotopic cesarean scar pregnancy	HCY	homocysteine
		HCYS	homocysteine
HCSS	hypersensitive carotid sinus syndrome	HCZ	head circumference-for-age Z-Score
HCST	Health Canada Surveillance Tool (to assess adherence of dietary intakes with Canada's Food Guide)	HD	haloperidol decanoate
			Hansen disease
			hazardous drug
			hearing distance
	hematopoietic cell signal transducer (gene)		heart disease
			Heller-Dor (procedure)
HCT	head computerized (axial) tomography		heloma durum
			hemodialysis
	hematocrit		herniated disk
	hematopoietic cell transplantation		high definition
			high dose
	histamine challenge test		hip disarticulation
	home care teams		Hirschsprung disease
	human chorionic thyrotropin		Hodgkin disease
	hydrochlorothiazide (this is a dangerous abbreviation)		hospital day
			hospital discharge
	hydrocortisone		house dust
HCTC	Hürthle cell thyroid carcinoma		Huntington disease
Hctc/Hctv	capillary to venous hematocrit ratio	HD1	early-stage Huntington disease
		HD2	histone deacetylase type 2
HCTCI	hematopoietic cell transplantation comorbidity index		late-stage Huntington disease
			second-order harmonic distortion
HCTI	Horney-Coolidge Tridimensional Inventory (57-item personality measure based on the theory of Karen Horney)	HD3	histone deacetylase 3; see gene website www.ncbi.nlm.nih .gov/gene
		HD4	histone deacetylase 4 gene
HCTU	home cervical traction unit		4-hour hemodialysis
HCTV	high-cellularity tumor volume	H&D	Hurter and Driffield (curve)
Hctv	venous hematocrit	H63D	HFE gene mutation (a hemo-chromatosis gene mutation)
HCTZ	hydrochlorothiazide (this is a dangerous abbreviation)	HDA	heteroduplex analysis
HCU	hand-carried ultrasound		high-dose arm
	hand-held cardiac ultrasound	HDAC	high-dose cytarabine (ara-C)
	healthcare utilization		histone deacetylase
HCUP	Healthcare Cost and Utilization Project	HDAC2	histone deacetylase 2
		HDAd	helper-dependent adenoviral
HCV	hepatitis C vaccine	HD-ara-C	high-dose cytarabine (ara-C)
	hepatitis C virus	HDBQ	Hilton Drinking Behavior Questionnaire
HCVA	high-contrast visual acuity		
HCVAb	hepatitis C virus antibody	HD-Bu	high-dose busulfan
HCV Ab	hepatitis C antibody	HDC	habilitative day care
HCV-Ab	hepatitis C antibody		high-dose chemotherapy
HCVAD	hyperfractionated cyclophos-phamide, vincristine, doxorubicin (Adriamycin), and dexamethasone		histamine dihydrochloride
			hydrodynamic chromatography
		HD&C	hysteroscopy dilation and curettage
HCVD	hypertensive cardiovascular disease	HDC-ASCS	high-dose chemotherapy with autologous stem cell support
HcWAP	HcToll3 (toll-like receptors from the freshwater pearl mussel Hyriopsis cumingii) regulated expression of whey acidic protein	HD catheter	hemodialysis catheter
		HDCC	high-dose combination chemotherapy
		HD-CCV	high-dose cyclophosphamide, irinotecan (CPT-11), and vincristine
HCWs	health-care workers		

HD-CPA	high-dose cyclophosphamide	HDO	deuterium protium oxide, a form
HDCPT	high-dose cyclophosphamide		of heavy water
	therapy		high definition oscillometry
HDC-SCR	high-dose chemotherapy with		hydrodeoxygenation
	stem-cell rescue	HdO	hand orthosis
HDCT	high-dose chemotherapy	HD-OCT	high-definition optical coherence
HDCV	rabies virus vaccine, human		tomography
	diploid (human diploid cell	HDP	high-density polyethylene
	vaccine)		hydroxymethyline diphosphonate
HDD-CKD	hemodialysis dependent-chronic		hypertensive disorders of
	kidney disease		pregnancy
HDE	humanitarian device exemption	HDPA	high-dose pulse administration
	(FDA)	HDPAA	heparin-dependent platelet-
H/D-Ex	hydrogen/deuterium amide		associated antibody
	exchange (mass spectrometry)	HDPC	hand piece
HD-Ex	hydrogen/deuterium amide	HDPE	high-density polythylene
	exchange (mass spectrometry)	HDR	head-down rest
HDF	hemodiafiltration		heparin dose response
HDFN	hemolytic disease for the fetus		high dose rate
	and newborn		high-dose rituximab
HDG	hydrogel (dressing)		husband to delivery room
HDGC	hereditary diffuse gastric cancer	HDRA	histoculture drug response assay
HDGF	hepatoma-derived growth factor	HDRB	high-dose rate brachytherapy
HDH	high-density humidity	HDRP	Healthcare Delivery Research
HDI	high-definition image		Program
HDIs	herb-drug interactions	HDRS	Hamilton Depression Rating
	histone deacetylase inhibitors		Scale
HDIT	high-dose immunosuppressive	HDRT	high-dose radiotherapy
	therapy	HDRW	hearing distance for watch to be
HDK	high-dose ketoconazole		heard in right ear
HDL	high-density lipoprotein	HDS	Hamilton Depression (Rating)
HDL-C	high-density lipoprotein		Scale
	cholesterol		Healthcare Documentation
	high-density lipoprotein-		Specialist
	cholesterol		hemodynamically stable
HDLP	histone deacetylase-like protein		herniated disk syndrome
HDL-P	high-density lipoprotein-		Hester Davis Scale (for fall risk
	particle		assessment)
HDLW	hearing distance for watch to be		HIV (human immunodeficiency
	heard in left ear		virus) Dementia Scale
HDM	home-delivered meals		Hospital Discharge Summary
	house dust mite	HDs	healthy donors
HDMEC	human dermal microvascular	HDSCR	health deviation self-care
	endothelial cells		requisite
HDMP	high-dose methylprednisolone	HDS-R	Hasegawa Dementia
HD-MTX	high-dose methotrexate		Scale-Revised
HD-MTX-CF	high-dose methotrexate and leu-	HDSS	high dead-space syringes
	covorin (citrovorum factor)	HDSSI	high dose sliding scale insulin
HD-MTX/LV	high-dose methotrexate and		(suggested for patients with
	leucovorin		infections or those receiving
HD MWF	hemodialysis Monday,		therapy with high dose
	Wednesday, and Friday		corticosteroids)
HDN	hemolytic disease of the	HDT	habilitative day treatment
	newborn		hearing distraction test
	heparin dosing nomogram	HD-tACS	high-density transcranial alter-
	high-density nebulizer		nating current stimulation
HDNS	Hodgkin disease, nodular	HD TTS	hemodialysis Tuesday, Thursday,
	sclerosis		and Saturday

H

HDU	hemodialysis unit	HED	high-energy diet
	high-dependency unit (an intensive care unit)	HEDIS	Healthcare Effectiveness Data and Information Set (quality measures)
HDV	hepatitis D virus		
HDW	hearing distance (with) watch	hEDS	hypermobile Ehlers-Danlos syndrome
HDX	hydrogen/deuterium exchange		
HDX MS	hydrogen/deuterium exchange mass spectrometry	HEEADSSS	Home, Education/Employment, Eating, Activities, Drugs, Sexuality, Suicidal ideation and Safety (a psychosocial interview framework)
HDYF	how do you feel		
HE	hard events		
	hard exudate		
	health education	HEELP	see HELLP
	health educator	HEENMT	head, eyes, ears, nose, mouth and throat
	hearing evaluation		
	hemoglobin electrophoresis	HEENT	head, eyes, ears, nose, and throat
	hepatic encephalopathy		
He	helium	HEET	hypothermia, environmental, exposure, and trauma (garment)
H/E	however		
H&E	hematoxylin and eosin		
	hemorrhage and exudate	HEF	hepatic extraction fraction
	heredity and environment	heff peff	pronunciation of the abbreviation HFpEF (heart failure with preserved ejection fraction) (slang)
HE4	human epididymis protein 4, a tumor marker		
HEA	health		
HEADSS	Home, Education, Activities, Drug use and abuse, Sexual behavior, and Suicidality and depression (interview instrument)	HeFH	heterozygous familial hypercholesterolemia
		HeFPEF	heart failure with preserved ejection fraction
		HeFREF	heart failure with reduced ejection fraction
HEADSSS	may have meant HEEADSSS (Home, Education/Employment, Eating, Activities, Drugs, Sexuality, Suicidal ideation and Safety [a psychosocial interview framework])	HEG	hyperemesis gravidarum
		HEH	hepatic epithelioid hemangioendothelioma
		HEHE	hepatic epithelioid hemangioendothelioma
HEAD-US	Hemophilia Early Arthropathy Detection with Ultrasound (protocol to detect abnormalities in joints without history of hemarthrosis and clinically asymptomatic joints of people with hemophilia)	HEHP	high energy/high protein (diet/meals)
		HEI-2005	Healthy Eating Index-2005
		HEICS	Hospital Emergency Incident Command System
		HEK	human embryonic kidney
		HEL	*Helicobacter pylori* vaccine
			human embryonic lung
HEAR	hospital emergency ambulance radio	HeLa	Henrietta Lacks tumor cells
		HELLP Syndrome	hemolysis, elevated liver enzymes, and low platelet count
HEART score	History, ECG (electrocardiogram), Age, Risk factors, and Troponin (score)		
		HELP	high energy/low protein (diet/meals)
HEAT	human erythrocyte agglutination test		Hospital Elder Life Program
			see HELLP
HEB	hydrophilic emollient base	HELPP	see HELLP
HEC	Health Education Center	HEM	hypertensive emergency
	high emetogenic chemotherapy	Hem	Hematology
	hyperinsulinemic-euglycemic clamp	HEMA	hydroxyethylmethacrylate
		HEMC	hydroxyethyl methylcellulose
HeCOG	Hellenic Cooperative Oncology Group	hemC	hydroxymethylbilane synthase (gene)

heme	a prosthetic group that consists of iron contained in a porphyrin. Heme is a component of hemoglobin.	hepato	liver; liver-related
		hep B	hepatitis B
			hepatitis B vaccine
		hep C	hepatitis C
Heme+	presence of blood or a hemoglobin component	hep cap	heparin cap
		Hepcon	point-of-care monitor- heparin concentration and protamine dose calculation (Medtronic, Minneapolis, MN)
HEME/ONC	Hematology/Oncology		
HEMI	hemiplegia		
hemi	hemiparesis		
hemoc	hematology/oncology		
HEMOG	may have meant HemOnc (Hematology Oncology Department or Physician)	HEPEF	may have meant HFpEF (heart failure with a preserved ejection fraction)
		hep gtt	intravenous heparin infusion (gtt is Latin for drop)
hemol	hemolysis		
HemOnc	Hematology Oncology (department; physician)	hep lock	heparin lock (an intravenous catheter with a needless connection, filled with a small amount of heparin to prevent clotting
Hem/Onc	Hematology/Oncology		
hemonc	hematology/oncology		
HEMOSID	hemosiderin	Heppl	may have meant Hepple stages of osteochondral lesions of the talus as determined by magnetic resonance imaging
HemosIL® AcuStar HIT-Ab- (PF4-H)	a chemiluminescent immunoassay for heparin-induced thrombocytopenia antibodies		
HEMPAS	hereditary erythrocytic multinuclearity with positive acidified serum test	Hepple	Hepple stages of osteochondral lesions of the talus as determined by magnetic resonance imaging
HEMS	helicopter emergency medical services	HEPR	see gene website, www.ncbi.nlm.nih.gov/gene
HEN	hemorrhages, exudates, and nicking	heprin	may have meant heparin
		HePTFE	expanded polytetrafluoroethylene bonded with heparin
	home enteral nutrition		
	Hospital Engagement Network (The Joint Commission)	Hep Xa UFH	heparin Level Anti-Xa, unfractionated (test)
He-Ne	helium-neon (laser)	HER	electronic health record
HENMT1	HEN (Hua Enhancer 1 Homolog 1) methyltransferase 1		external hip rotation
		HER2	human epidermal growth-factor receptor 2
HENT	head, ears, nose, and throat	HERD	high-emotion regulation difficulties
hENT1	human equilibrative nucleoside transporter 1		
		hERG	human ether-a-go-go-related gene
HEOM	hierarchy equation of motion	HER2/neu	human epidermal growth factor receptor 2 (a proto-oncogene; a protein that appears on the surface of some breast cancer cells)(also known as HER2)
HEP	hemoglobin electrophoresis		
	hemorrhage, exudates and papilledema		
	heparin		
	hepatic	HeRO™	Hemodialysis Reliable Outflow (subcutaneously implanted device)
	hepatoerythropoietic porphyria		
	hepatoma		
	histamine equivalent prick	HERP	human exposure (dose)/rodent potency (dose)
	home exercise program		
hep	hepatitis	HERV-H	human endogenous retrovirus H
HEp2	human laryngeal epithelial carcinoma cell line	Herz	a cardiovascular journal; German word meaning heart
HEPA	hamster egg penetration assay	HES	hetastarch (hydroxyethyl starch; Hespan)
	high-efficiency particulate air (filter)		
			Hospital Episode Statistics (United Kingdom)
HepA	hepatitis A vaccine		
hep A	hepatitis A		hypereosinophilic syndrome

H

HEs	hypertensive emergencies		HFdEF	heart failure with depressed ejection fraction
hESC	human embryonic stem cells		HFE	hemochromatosis
hESC-RPE	human embryonic stemcell-derived retinal pigment epithelial cells		HFeEF	may have meant HFdEF (heart failure with depressed ejection fraction)
hESCs	human embryonic stem cells			may have meant HFpEF (heart failure with preserved ejection fraction)
HETF	home enteral tube feeding			
HEU	HIV (human immunodeficiency virus) -exposed, but uninfected			may have meant HFrEF (heart failure with reduced ejection fraction)
HEV	hepatitis E vaccine hepatitis E virus high-endothelial venule		HFEF	high frequency emphasis filtering (radiology)
Hex	altretamine (hexamethyl-melamine; Hexalen)		HFEPF	may have meant HFpEF (heart failure with preserved ejection fraction)
Hexa-CAF	altretamine (hexamethyl-melamine), cyclophosphamide, methotrexate (amethopterin), and fluorouracil			
			HFFD	high-fructose and high-fat diet
HF	Hageman factor		HFFY	Health Facts For You (as in HFFY#!077)
	hard feces			
	hay fever		hFH	heterozygous familial hypercholesterolemia
	head of fetus			
	healthy families		HFHC	high fat, high cholesterol (diet)
	heart failure		HFHD	high-flux hemodialysis
	hemorrhagic fever		HFHL	high-frequence hearing loss
	high frequency		HFI	hereditary fructose intolerance
	high-flex		HFIP	hexafluoro-isopropranolol
	hip fracture		HFJV	high-frequency jet ventilation
	Hispanic female		HFLT	hemosiderotic fibrolipomatous tumor
	hot flashes			
	house formula		H flu	*Haemophilus influenzae*
	hypofractionated (radiation therapy)		HFM	hand-foot-and-mouth (disease) (often caused by coxsackievirus A16) hemifacial microsomia
Hf	hafnium			
HFA	health facility administrator high-functioning autism hydrofluoroalkane-134a			
			HFMD	hand-foot-and-mouth disease (often caused by coxsackievirus A16)
HFABP	heart-type fatty acid-binding protein		HFMEA	Healthcare-Failure-Mode-Effects-Analysis
H-FABP	heart-type fatty acid-binding protein		HFmEF	heart failure with midrange ejection fraction (left ventricle ejection fraction 40-49%)
HFACS	Human Factors Analysis and Classification System			
HFAP	Healthcare Facilities Accreditation Program (American Osteopathic Association)		HFmrEF	heart failure with mid-range ejection fraction (borderline; left ventricular ejection fraction between 40 and 50%.)
HFAS	hereditary flat adenoma syndrome			
HFB	high-frequency band			
HFbEF	heart failure with borderline ejection fraction		HFMSE	Hammersmith Functional Motor Scale-Expanded
HFC	hydrofluorocarbon		HFNC	high-flow nasal cannula
HFCB	horizontal flow clean bench		HFNEF	heart failure with normal ejection fraction
HFCC	high-frequency chest compression			
HFCS	high-fructose corn syrup		HFNO	high-flow nasal oxygen
HFCs	hydrofluorocarbons		HFO	high-frequency oscillation
HFD	high-fiber diet high-forceps delivery high-frequency discharges		HFO2	histone H4 (gene)
			HfO$_2$	hafnium oxide (known as hafnia)

HFOD	high fermentable oligosaccharides, disaccharides, monosaccharides, and polyol diet	HG	handgrasp
			handgrip
HFOV	high-frequency oscillatory ventilation		Harris-Galante (cups used in hip replacements; types I or II)
HFP	hepatic function panel (see Laboratory Panels)		hemoglobin
			hyperemesis gravidarum
	heterochromatic flicker photometry	Hg	mercury
		HGA	high-grade astrocytomas
		HgA1c	glycosylated hemoglobin
	Hoffa fat pad	HG-ACIN	high-grade anal canal intraepithelial neoplasia
HFpEF	heart failure with preserved ejection fraction		
HFpEP	may have meant heart HFpEF (failure with preserved ejection fraction)	HGAIN	high-grade anal intraepithelial neoplasia
		HGAP	Hierarchical Genome-Assembly Process
HFpER	may have meant HFpEF (heart failure with preserved ejection fraction)	Hgb	hemoglobin
		Hgb A1c	glycosylated hemoglobin
		Hgb ELECT	hemoglobin electrophoresis
HFPF	high-frequency pressure fluctuations	HgbF	fetal hemoglobin
		HgbS	sickle cell hemoglobin
HFPPV	high-frequency positive pressure ventilation	HgbSC	sickle-cell hemoglobin type C
		HgbSS	homozygous sickle hemoglobin
HFprEF	may have meant heart failure with preserved ejection fraction (HFpEF)	HGC	Human Genetics Commission (UK)
		HGD	high-grade dysplasia
HFPTA	high-frequency pure-tone average	HG-DCIS	high-grade ductal carcinoma *in situ*
HFR	hemorrhagic fever with renal syndrome vaccine	HGDI	Hunter Gaston Diversity Index
		Hgdk dis	Hodgkin disease
HFrEF	heart failure with reduced ejection fraction	HGE	human granulocytic ehrlichiosis
		HGES	handgrasp equal and strong
HFrHF	may have meant HFrEF (heart failure with reduced ejection fraction [less than 50%])	HGF	hepatocyte growth factor
			hereditary gingival fibromatosis
		Hgfa	hepatocyte growth factor a (gene/protein)
HFRS	hemorrhagic fever with renal syndrome	HGFA	hepatocyte growth factor activator
HFRT	hypergractionated radiotherapy	HGG	high-grade glioma
HFS	hand-foot skin (reaction)		human gamma globulin
	hand-foot syndrome		hypogammaglobulinemia
	head-first supine	HGH	human growth hormone
	hemifacial spasm	HGI	Human Genome Initiative
	hot flash score	HGIL	high-grade intraepithelial lesion(s)
HFs	hair follicles	HGL	high glycemic loan
HFSH	human follicle-stimulating hormone		high-grade lesion
			see gene website, www.ncbi.nlm.nih.gov/gene
HFSNHL	high-frequency sensorineural hearing loss		
HFSRT	hypofractionated stereotactic radiotherapy	HGLA	hepatobiliary laboratory abnormalities
HFST	hearing-for-speech test	HGM	high-gamma modulation
HFT	hands-free technique		home glucose monitoring
	high frequency tympanometry	HGMA	high-grade molecular abnormality
HFUPR	hourly fetal urine production rate	HGN	hypogastric nerve
HFUS	high-frequency ultrasound	HGNC	HUGO Gene Nomenclature Committee
HFV	high-frequency ventilation		
	high-fruit/vegetable (diet)		HUGO (Human Genome Organization) Gene Nomenclature Committee
HFX RT	hyperfractionated radiation therapy		

H

HGO	hepatic glucose output	HH5	Holstein Friesian Lethal
	hip guidance orthosis		Haplotype 5
HGP	Human Genome Project	H&H	hemoglobin and hematocrit
HGPIN	high-grade prostatic		Hunt and Hess scale/score
	intraepithelial neoplasia		(grading systems used to
HGPRT	hypoxanthine-guanine		classify the severity of a sub-
	phosphoribosyl-transferase		arachnoid hemorrhage based
HGPS	Hutchinson-Gilford Progeria		on thepatient's clinical con-
	Syndrome		dition; used as a predictor of
hGR	human glucocorticoid receptor		patient's prognosis/outcome,
	(gene)		with a higher grade correlat-
HGS	hand-grip strength		ing to lower survivalrate)
	human genome sequence	H+H	hemoglobin and hematocrit
HG-SAs	high-grade serrated adenomas	H/H	hemoglobin/hematocrit
HGSC	high-grade serous (ovarian)	h/h	holohemispheric
	carcinoma	HHA	hand-held assist
HGSIL	high-grade squamous		health hazard appraisal
	intraepithelial lesion		hereditary hemolytic anemia
HGSOC	high-grade serous ovarian		home health agency
	cancer		home health aid
HGSS	high-grade stromal sarcoma	HHABN	Home Health Beneficiary Notice
HGT	height		of Noncoverage
	horizontal gene transfer	HHAC	handheld ultrasound-measured
HGT1	high-grade T1 (bladder cancer)		fetal abdominal circumference
HGT2	High-affinity Glucose	HHAE	hiatal hernias after
	Transporter (putative) (gene)		esophagectomy
HGTA	Federal Act on Human Genetic	HH Assist	hand held assist
	Testing (Switzerland)	HHb	deoxyhemoglobin
HG-TAs	high-grade tubular adenomas	hHb6	human hair basic keratin gene
Hg TOC	mercury-total organic carbon	HHC	hereditary hemochromatosis
	(complexes)		home health care
Hg-TOC	mercury-total organic carbon	HHCA	home health care agency
	(complexes)		hypothermic hypokalemic
HGUC	high-grade urothelial carcinoma		cardioplegic arrest
HGUS	high-grade undifferentiated	HHcy	hyperhomocysteinemia
	uterine sarcomas	HHD	Doctor of Holistic Health
HGV	hepatitis G vaccine		handheld dynamometer
	hepatitis G virus		home hemodialysis
HH	hand hygiene		household distance (physical
	hard of hearing		therapy goal of mobility)
	head hood		hypertensive heart disease
	heart healthy	HHE	4-hydroxyhexenal
	heated humidity		hand-held echocardiography
	hepatic hydrothorax		(apparatus)
	hereditary hemochromatosis		Health Hazard Evaluation
	hiatal hernia		heel horn erosion
	home health		hemiconvulsion-hemiplegia-
	homonymous hemiopia		epilepsy (syndrome)
	household		human haplotype E
	hyperhidrosis	HHFM	high-humidity face mask
	hyperhomocystinemia	HHFNC	humidified high-flow nasal
	hypoeninemic hypoaldosteronism		cannula
	hypogonadotropic hypogonadism	HHG	high-order harmonic generation
hh2	hedgehog homolog 2 (gene)		hypogonadotropic
Hh3	hemopoietic histocompatibility		hypogonadism
	3 (gene)	HHH	hypermethionemia,
hH3	histone H3 (gene)		hyperammonemia, and
hH4	human histamine 4 (receptor)		homocitrolinemia (syndrome)

HHHA	homemaker home health aide
H/HHA	Homemaker and/or Home Health Aide (Veterans Administration)
HHHFNC	heated, humidified, high-flow, nasal cannula
HHHQ	Health Habits and History Questionnaire (Block-National Cancer Institute)
HHHT	hepatic hereditary hemorrhagic telangiectasia
HHI	Healthier Hospitals Initiative Hirschman-Herfindahl Index
HHIE-S	hearing handicap inventory for the elderly-short form
hHK-1	human hemokinin-1
HHK	hybrid histidine kinase
HHL	hereditary hearing loss hippuryl-histidyl-leucine historical height loss
hhl	see gene website, www.ncbi.nlm.nih.gov/gene
HHM	high-humidity mask humoral hypercalcemia of malignancy Hypoglycemia-Hyperglycemia Minimizer System (Animas Corp.)
HHN	hand-held nebulizer
HHNC	hyperosmolar hyperglycemic nonketotic coma
HHNK	hyperglycemic hyperosmolar nonketotic (coma)
HHNKC	hyperglycemia hypersmolar non-ketotic coma
HHNKS	hyperglycemic hyperosmolar nonketotic state
HHNS	hyperosmolar-hyperglycemic nonketotic syndrome
HHOs	hand hygiene opportunities
HHOT	hand-hygiene observation team hand-hygiene observation tool
HHPPS	home health prospective payment system
HHPT	home-health physical therapy hook of hamate pull test
HHRF	histopathological high risk features Human Healthcare and Research Foundation (Mumbai, India)
HHRG	Home Health Resource Group (reimbursement categories for home health)
HHRN	Homeless and Housing Resource Network (Substance Abuse and Mental Health Services Administration)

HHS	handheld shower Harris hip score Health and Human Service (US Department of) hyperosmolar hyperglycemic state Hypothenar Hammer syndrome
HHSH	head-to-head single stranded helix
HHSN	(US Department of) Health and Human Service Number
HHT	hepatic hydrothorax hereditary hemorrhagic telangiectasia
HHT1	hereditary hemorrhagic telangiectasia type 1
HHT2	hereditary hemorrhagic telangiectasia type 2
HHTC	high-humidity trach collar
HHTM	high-humidity trach mask
HHTS	high-humidity tracheostomy shield
HHU	handheld ultrasound
HHUS	handheld ultrasound
HHV6	human herpesvirus type 6
HHV7	human herpesvirus type 7
HHV8	human herpesvirus type 8
HHVG	human herpes virus G
HI	*Haemophilus influenzae* Hawaii head injury health insurance hearing impaired hemagglutination inhibition homicidal ideation hospital insurance human insulin hypomelanosis of Ito hypoxic-ischemic hypopnea index
Hi5	HIV positive ("V" being the Roman numeral for 5) (slang)
H/I	hyperactivity and impulsivity hypoxia and ischemia
HIA	hemagglutination inhibition antibody
5-HIAA	5-hydroxyindoleacetic acid
HIAA	hydroxyindoleacetic acid
HIAO	hypothalamic injury associated obesity
HIAP	human intracisternal A-type particle hyperactivity/inattention problems
HiAP	Health in All Policies
hiAP	human intestinal alkaline phosphatase
hIAPP	human islet amyloid polypeptide

HINN	Hospital-issued Notice of Non-coverage
HINT	Harris Infant Neuromotor Test
	Hearing in Noise Test
HINTS	Health Information National Trends Surveys (National Cancer Institute)
HIO	health insuring organization
	hepatic iron overload
HIP	health insurance plan
HIPA	heparin-induced platelet aggregation
HIPAA	Health Insurance Portability and Accountability Act of 1996
HIPC	hormone-independent prostate cancer
HIPEC	hyperthermic intraperitoneal chemotherapy
HIPJ	hallux interphalangeal joint
Hippa	Health Insurance Portability and Accountability Act of 1996 (HIPAA)
HIPPAA	may have meant HIPAA (Health Insurance Portability and Accountability Act of 1996)
HIPPS	Health Insurance Prospective Payment System
hi-pro	high-protein
HIR	head injury routine
HIRE	HealthCore Integrated Research Environment
HIRZ	high intermediate risk zone
HIS	Bundle of His
	Hanover Intensive Score
	Health Intention Scale
	high-intermittent suction
	histidine
	Home Incapacity Scale
	hospital (healthcare) information system
HISA	Home Improvement and Structural Alterations (grant)
His-MenCY-TT	hib-meningococcal (bivalent) conjugate vaccine (MenHibrix)
HISMS	How I See Myself Scale
HISN	heparin-induced skin necrosis
Hisp	Hispanic
HISQUI19	Hearing Implant Sound Quality Index (questionnaire)
HISS	hypertropic idiopathic subaortic stenosis
HIST	histamine
HISTO	histoplasmin skin test
	histoplasmosis
histopath	histopathologic
	histopathology

HIT	health information technology
	heparin-induced thrombocytopenia
	high-intensity training
	histamine inhalation test
	home infusion therapy
HIT-6	Headache Impact Test
HIT-ab	heparin-induced thrombocytopenia antibodies
HITOC	hyperthermic intrathoracic chemotherapy
HiTOP	Hierarchical Taxonomy of Psychopathology
HITS	high-intensity transient signals
HITTS	heparin-induced thrombotic thrombocytopenia syndrome
HIU	head injury unit
HIV	human immunodeficiency virus
HIV-1	human immunodeficiency virus type 1
HIV-2	human immunodeficiency virus type 2
HIVAN	human immunodeficiency virus-associated nephropathy
HIVAT	home intravenous antibiotic therapy
HIVD	herniated intervertebral disk
HIV-D	human immunodeficiency virus-related dementia
HIVF	home intravenous fluids
HIV-G	human immunodeficiency disease-associated gingivitis
HIVICK	human-immunodeficiency-disease-associated immune complex kidney (disease)
hi-vit	high-vitamin
HIVMP	high-dose intravenous methylprednisolone
HIVN	human immunodeficiency virus nephropathy
HIX	humification index
HIZ	high-intensity zone(s)
HJB	Howell-Jolly bodies
HJHS	Hemophilia Joint Health Score
HJR	hepatojugular reflux
HK	hand-to-knee
	heel-to-knee
	hexokinase
hK6	human kallikrein 6
HKAFO	hip-knee-ankle-foot orthosis
HKAO	hip-knee-ankle orthosis
HKB	Haken-Kelso-Bunz (mathematical formula model)
	heat-killed bacteria
hkb	huckebein; see gene website www.ncbi.nlm.nih.gov/gene
HKD	hyperkinetic disorder
HKFO	hip-knee-foot orthosis

H

HKMN   Hickman (catheter)
HKO   hip-knee orthosis
HKPs   housekeeping proteins
HKS   heel-knee-shin (test)
HKT   heterotopic kidney transplant
HL   hairline
   half-life
   hallux limitus
   haloperidol
   harelip
   hearing level
   hearing loss
   heavy lifting
   hemilaryngectomy
   heparin lock
   hepatic lipase
   Hickman line
   Hodgkin lymphoma
   hyperlipidemia
H&L   heart and lung
HL7   Health Level Seven International (standards for health information) (www.hl7.org)
HLA   horizontal long-axis
   human leukocyte antigen
HLA-A   human leucocyte antigen A
HLA-ABDR   human leukocyte antigens A, B, and DR
HLAB   major histocompatibility complex, class I, B (HLA-B); see gene website www.ncbi .nlm.nih.gov/gene
HLA-B   human leukocyte antigen B, gene (polymorphic enzyme variant responsible for the metabolism of awide range of clinical drugs [abacavir, allopurinol, carbamazepine, phenytoin, etc.,]) HLA-B
HLAB27   human leukocyte antigen B27 (has been suggested to be important in the pathogenesis of ankylosing spondylitis) human leukocyte antigen-B27
HLA B27   human leukocyte antigen B27 (has been suggested to be important in the pathogenesis of ankylosing spondylitis)
HLA-B27   human leukocyte antigen-B27
HLA-C   human leucocyte antigen C
HLA-D   human leucocyte antigen D
HLA-DR   human leukocyte antigen, type DR
HLA-G   human leukocyte antigen G
HLA negative   heart, lungs, and abdomen negative
HLB   head, limbs, and body
HLCs   human landing catches

HLD   haloperidol decanoate (Haldol)
   herniated lumbar disk
   high lipid disorder
   high-level disinfection
   hyperlipidemia
HLDA   Human Leukocyte Differentiation Antigens (workshop)
HLDP   hypoglossia-limb deficiency phenotype
HLES   hypertensive lower esophageal sphincter
HLF   human lung fibroblast
Hlf   hepatic leukaemia factor
hLF   human lactoferrin
HLGD   high-level gait disorder
HLGR   high-level gentamicin resistance
HLGT   High Level Group Term
HLH   helix-loop-helix
   hemophagocytic lymphohistiocytosis
   human luteinizing hormone
HLHS   hypoplastic left heart syndrome
HLI   head-lice infestation
HLIV   heparin lock intravenous
HLK   heart, liver, and kidneys
HLL   horizontal lid laxity
   hyperechoic lung lesions
HLM   heart-lung machine
   hemosiderin-laden macrophages
H/L medicine   heterophil to lymphocyte ratio
HLN   hand-assisted laparoscopic nephrectomy
HLNH   high-level nursing home
HLOC   health locus of control
   higher level of care
HLOS   hypertensive lower oesophageal sphincter (United Kingdom and other countries)
HLP   hyperlipidemia (hyperlipoproteinemia)
   hyperlipoproteinemia
HLPA   high-intensity light physical activity
HLPD   hepato-ligamento-pancreatoduodenectomy
HLPs   harmful legal products
   healthy living programs
   histone-like proteins
HLRCC   hereditary leiomyomatosis renal cell cancer
hLS   human lung surfactant
HLSL   heel slides
HLT   heart-lung transplantation (transplant)
   High Level Term
Hlth   health
HLTR   heart-lung transplant recipient(s)

HLTV-1	human T cell leukemia virus type 1	HMGCR	3-hydroxy-3-methylglutaryl-CoA (coenzyme A) reductase (gene; is the rate-controlling enzyme of the metabolic pathway that produces cholesterol and other isoprenoids)
HLV	herpes-like virus hypoplastic left ventricle		
HM	hand motion head movement health maintenance heart murmur heavily muscled heloma molle hepatomegaly Hispanic male Holter monitor home human milk human semisynthetic insulin humidity mask	HMH	hepatic mesenchymal hamartoma
		HMI	healed myocardial infarction history of medical illness
		HMII	HeartMate® 2, a left ventricular assist device (www.thoratec.com)
		HM II	HeartMate® 2, a left ventricular assist device (www.thoratec.com)
		HM III	HeartMate® 3, a left ventricular assist device (www.thoratec.com)
HM2	HeartMate II; left ventricular assist device	HMIR	human malaria infectious reservoir
HM3	HeartMate 3 (a left ventricular assist device; Abbott Laboratories, Lake Forest, Il)	HMIS	hospital medical information system
		HMK	homemaking
H&M	hematemesis and melena	HM & LP	hand motion and light perception
HMA	hemorrhages and microaneurysms heteroduplex mobility assay hypomethylating agent	HMM	altretamine (hexamethyl-melamine; Hexalen)
		HMN	hypoglossal motor nucleus
HMB	beta-hydroxy-beta methylbutyrate (a leucine metabolite) heavy menstrual bleeding homatropine methylbromide hypersensitivity to mosquito bites	HMO	Health Maintenance Organization human milk oligosaccharides hypothetical mean organism
		HMOA	hindrance modulated orientational anisotropy
		HMOPOS	Health Maintenance Organization Point-of-Service
HMBA	hexamethylene bisacetamide	HMP	hand breast pump health maintenance plan hereditary metabolic profile hexose monophosphate hot moist packs
HMC-1	human mast cell-1		
HMD	hyaline membrane disease		
HMDP	hydroxymethyline diphosphonate		
HME	heat and moisture exchanger heat, massage, and exercise hereditary multiple exostoses home medical equipment hot melt extrusion human monocytic ehrlichiosis	HMPAO	hexylmethylpropylene amineoxine
		HMPC	Committee on Herbal Medicinal Products (EMEA) Home Management Plan of Care
		HMPCC	hydroxymethylpentylcyclohexene carboxaldehyde (a fragrance ingredient; Lyral)
HMECs	Human Mammary Epithelial Cells	HMPS	hereditary mixed polyposis syndrome
HMEF	heat moisture exchanging filter	HMPs	herbal medicinal products
HMETSC	heavy metal screen	hMPV	human metapneumovirus
HMF	human milk fortifiers	HMR	histocytic medullary reticulosis Hoechst Marion Roussel
HMFD	may have meant HFMD (hand, foot and mouth disease)	¹H-MRS	proton magnetic resonance spectroscopy
HMG	human menopausal gonadotropin	HMS	Hunter-MacDonald syndrome hyper-reactive malarial splenomegaly hypodermic morphine sulfate (this is a dangerous abbreviation)
HMGB1	high-mobility group box 1 (chromosomal protein)		
HMG-CoA	hydroxymethyl glutaryl coenzyme A		

H

HMS®	medrysone	HNKH	hyperglycemic nonketotic hypertonicity
hMSCs	human mesenchymal stem cells		
HMSE	Headache Management Self-Efficacy Scale	HNKS	hyperosmolar nonketotic syndrome
HMSN I	hereditary motor and sensory neuropathy type I	HNL	histiocytic necrotizing lymphadenitis (Kikuchi-Fujimoto disease)
HMSR	high medical-social risk		
HMSS	hyperactive malarial splenomegaly syndrome	HNLN	hospitalization no longer necessary
hmt	hydroxymethyltransferase; see gene website www.ncbi.nlm.nih.gov/gene	HNMM	mucosal melanomas of the head and neck
		¹H-NMR	proton nuclear magnetic resonance (spectroscopy)
HMV	home mechanical ventillation		
HMWCK	high molecular weight cytokeratin	HNN	hybrid neural network
		HNNE	Hammersmith Neonatal Neurological Examination
HMWK	high-molecular weight kininogen	HNO	Hals-Nasen-Ohren Heilkunde (throat, nose and ear medicine [German])
HMX	heat massage exercise		
HM XVE	HeartMate XVE, a pulsatile left ventricular assist device		
			nitroxyl
H2N2	Asian influenza virus	HNP	herniated nucleus pulposus
H5N1	avian influenza A virus	HNPCC	heredity nonpolyposis colorectal cancer
HN	head and neck		
	head nurse	HNPP	hereditary neuropathy with liability to pressure palsies
	high nitrogen		
	home nursing	HNRNA	heterogeneous nuclear ribonucleic acid
	hyponatremia		
H&N	head and neck	HNS	0.45% sodium chloride injection (half-normal saline)
H/N	head and neck		
HN2	mechlorethamine HCl		head and neck surgery
H1N1	Spanish Influenza virus		head, neck, and shaft
H3N2	Hong Kong influenza virus		Nance-Horan syndrome; see gene website www.ncbi.nlm.nih.gov/gene
HNA	high nucleic acid		
	hostile (aortic) neck anatomy		
	human neutrophil antigens	HNSCC	squamous cell carcinoma of the head and neck
HNa	hyponatremia		
HNBP	high-normal blood pressure	HNSN	home, no services needed
HNC	head and neck cancer	HNT	hantaan (hantavirus) vaccine
	Holistic Nurse, Certified	HNV	has not voided
	human neutrophil collagenase	HNWG	has not worn glasses
	hyperosmolar nonketotic coma	HO	hand orthosis
HNCa	head and neck cancer		handout
HNCCG	Head and Neck Cancer Cooperative Group		heme oxygenase
			Hemotology-Oncology
HND	high-nutrient-density (diet)		heterotropic ossification
HNE	human neutrophil elastase		hip orthosis
HNF	hepatocyte nuclear factor(s)		house officer
Hnh	see gene website www.ncbi.nlm.nih.gov/gene		humeral orthosis
		Ho	holmium
HNI	hospitalization not indicated	HO-1	heme oxygenase-1
HNK-1	beta-1,3-glucuronyltransferase 1 (human natural killer-1); see gene website www.ncbi.nlm.nih.gov/gene	+HO	Hemocult positive
		H/O	history of
		H2O	water
		H2O2	hydrogen peroxide
HNKDC	hyperosomolar nonketotic diabetic coma	HOA	hand osteoarthritis
			hip osteoarthritis
HNKDS	hyperosmolar nonketotic diabetic state		hypertrophic osteoarthropathy
		HOB	head of bed

HOBE	head-of-bed elevation
HOBUPSOB	head of bed up for shortness of breath
HOC	Health Officer Certificate
	higher-order, correlations
HOCC	human ovarian carcinoma cell
HOCM	high-osmolality contrast media
	hypertrophic obstructive cardiomyopathy
HOCOM	may have meant HOCM (hypertrophic obstructive cardiomyopathy)
HOCUM	may have meant hypertrophic obstructive cardiomyopathy (HOCM)
HOD	heroin overdose
HoFH	homozygous familial hypercholesterolemia
HOG	halothane, oxygen, and gas (nitrous oxide)
	Hoosier Oncology Group
HOH	hand-over-hand (rehabilitation term)
	hard of hearing
	head of household
HOHA	hospital onset, healthcare facility acquired
Hohn catheter	a silver impregnated cuff central line
HOI	history of immunizations
	hospital onset of infection
hokum	a word meaning pretentious nonsense
HoLAP	holmium laser ablation of the prostate
HoLEP	holmium-laser enucleation of the prostate
HOM	high-osmolar contrast media
HOMA	homeostasis model assessment
	homeostatic assessment model algorithm (index)
HOMA-IR	Homeostasis Model Assessment of Insulin Resistance
HOMCs	human omentum-derived mesothelial cells
HOME	Home Observation for Measurement of the Environment
HOMS	Hematology/Oncology Medical Specialists
HOMU	history of medication use
HONC	Hooked on Nicotine Checklist
	hyperosmolar, nonketotic coma
Honda	hypertensive obese non-compliant diabetic adult (slang)
HONK	hyperosmolar nonketotic
honks	sounds similar to a goose's honk
HoNOS	Health of the Nation Outcome Scales

HOOS	Hip Dysfunction and Osteoarthritis Outcome Score
HOOS-PS	Hip Dysfunction and Osteoarthritis Outcome Score- Physical Function Shortform
HOP	hourly output
	hypokalemic
HOPD	hospital outpatient department
HOPI	history of present illness
Hopkins-25	Hopkins Symptom Checklist-25
HO PPX	heterotrophic ossification prophylaxis
HOPS	homotypic fusion and vacuole protein sorting
HOR	higher-order repeat
HORF	high-output renal failure
horiz	horizontal
Horiz Abd	horizontal abduction
Horiz Add	may have meant Horiz Abd (horizontal abduction)
HORS	Hemiballism/Hemichorea Outcome Rating Score
HOS	Health Outcomes Survey
	Holt-Oram syndrome
	hybrid orthosis system
	hypoosmotic swelling
hosp	hospital
HOT	home oxygen therapy
Hotel	Phonetic Alphabet for H; pronounced HOH-TEL
HOTH	how often this happens
HoTN	hypotension
HOTR	human oxytocin receptor
HOVT	visual acuity testing protocol that limits responses to four letters (H, O, T, or V)
HOW	hours of work
HOWR	hospice observation without resuscitation
Ho:YAG	holmium: yttrium-aluminum-garnet
HP	Harvard pump
	heel pad
	Helicobacter pylori
	hemipelvectomy
	hemiplegia
	herbal products
	high-protein (supplement)
	home program
	hot packs
	house physician
	hydrogen peroxide
	hydrophilic petrolatum
	hypersensitivity pneumonitis
	hypertrophic pachymeningitis

Hp	*Helicobacter pylori*	HPFB	Health Products and Food
H&P	history and physical		Branch (Canada)
H/P	see HP	HPFH	hereditary persistence of fetal
H+P	history and physical		hemoglobin
HPA	hybridization protection assay	HPG	human pituitary gonadotropin
	hypothalamic-pituitary-adrenal	2hPG	2-h post-challenge glucose
	(axis)	HPH	Hashimoto-Pritzker histiocytosis
HPAEPAD	high-pH anion exchange	HPI	history of present illness
	chromatography coupled	HPIMS	high-performance ion mobility
	with pulsed amperometric		spectrometry
	detection	HPIN	high-grade prostatic
HPAI	highly pathogenic avian influenza		intraepithelial neoplasia
	A virus	HPIP	history, physical, impression,
HPAP	high peak airway pressure		and plan
hPAP	hereditary pulmonary alveolar	HPJ	Hoffman, Pons, and Janer
	proteinosis		(parasite testing)
	human placental alkaline	HPK	hyperkeratosis
	phosphatase	HPL	human placenta lactogen
HPAT	home parenteral antibiotic		hyperlipidemia
	therapy		hyperplexia
HPB	Health Protection Branch	HPLC	high-performance (pressure)
	(the Canadian equivalent		liquid chromatography
	of the U.S. Food and Drug	HPLD	hyperlipidemia
	Administration)	HPLP II	Health-Promoting Lifestyle
HPBL	human peripheral blood		Profile-II
	lymphocyte(s)	HPM	hemiplegic migraine
HPC	hemangiopericytoma	HPMA	*N*-(2-Hydroxypropyl)methacryl-
	hematopoietic progenitor cell		amide (used as a carrier for
	hereditary prostate cancer		low molecular weight chemo-
	history of present condition		therapeutic agents to enhance
	(complaint)		therapeutic efficacy and limit
HPCE	high-performance capillary		side effects)
	electrophoresis	HPMC	high-performance membrane
HPCT	hematopoietic progenitor cell		chromatography
	transplantation		hydroxypropyl methylcellulose
	hospital palliative care team	HPMG	hard palate mucosal graft
HPD	hearing protection device	HPMRS	hyperphosphatasia with mental
	high-protein diet		retardation syndrome
	histrionic personality disorder	HPMS	high pressure mass spectrometry
	home peritoneal dialysis	HPMV	Deferred Action for Childhood
	hours post dose		Arrivals
HpD	hematoporphyrin derivative	HPN	home parenteral nutrition
HP&D	hemoprofile and differential	HPNI	hemodialysis prognostic
HPDP	health promotion and disease		nutrition index
	prevention	HPNS	high-pressure nervous syndrome
HPE	hemorrhage, papilledema,	HPO	hydrophilic ointment
	exudate		hypertrophic pulmonary
	history and physical		osteoarthropathy
	examination	HPOA	hypertrophic pulmonary
	holoprosencephaly		osteoarthropathy
HPET	*Helicobacter pylori* eradication	HPOT	hippotherapy vocational therapy
	therapy		that uses horse movement
	human prostate epithelial	HPP	human pancreatic polypeptide
	tumor (cells)		hyperkalemia periodic paralysis
HPeV	human parechovirus		hypophosphatasia
HPeVs	human parechoviruses	2HPP	2-hour postprandial (blood
HPF	high-power field		sugar)
	hours post fertilization	2HPPBS	2-hour postprandial blood sugar

HPPD	4-hydroxyphenylpyruvate dioxygenase (gene/enzyme)
	hallucinogen persisting perception disorder
	hours per patient day
HPpEF	may have meant HFpEF (heart failure with preserved ejection fraction)
HPPM	hyperplastic persistent pupillary membrane
HPPV	high-frequency positive pressure ventilation
HPRC	hereditary papillary renal carcinoma
hPRL	prolactin, human
HPRO	knee prosthesis
Hprt	hypoxanthine guanine phosphoribosyl transferase; see gene website www.ncbi.nlm.nih.gov/gene
HPS	hantavirus pulmonary syndrome
	heel pad stiffness
	Helicobacter pylori serology
	hepatopulmonary syndrome
	hypertrophic pyloric stenosis
HpSA	*Helicobacter pylori* stool antigen
HPSEC	high-performance size exclusion chromatography
HPSP	Health Professions Scholarship Program
	phosphoserine phosphatase; see gene website www.ncbi.nlm.nih.gov/gene
HPT	heparin protamine titration
	histamine provocation test
	home pregnancy test
	hyperparathyroidism
9HPT	9-hole Peg Test
HPTD	highly permeable transparent dressing
hPTH	human parathyroid hormone
	human parathyroid hormone I$_{34}$ (teriparatide)
HPTM	home prothrombin time monitoring
HPTN	HIV (human immunodeficiency virus) Prevention Trials Network
HPTT	heat pain tolerance thresholds
HPTX	hemopneumothorax
HPU	Helicobacter pylori urease
HPV	Human papillomavirus
	Human papillomavirus vaccine
	Human parovirus
	hypoxic pulmonary vasoconstriction
HPV4	human papillomavirus vaccine, quadrivalent (Gardasil)

HPV9	human papillomavirus vaccine, quadrivalent (Gardasil 9)
HPV16	human papillomavirus 16
HPVAS	Heft-Parker visual analog scale
HP VAS	Heft-Parker visual analog scale
HPVG	hepatic portal venous gas
HPW	healthy pregnant women
	hypertensive pregnant women
HPX	hyperekplexia
	hypoxia
HPx	hepatectomy
	hydroperoxide
Hpx	hemopexin (gene/protein)
H pylori	*Helicobacter pylori*
H pylori	Helicobacter pylori
HPZ	high-pressure zone
HQ	hazard quotient
	hydroquinone
HQC	hydroquinone cream
HQL	health-related quality of life
HR	hallux rigidus
	handrail
	Harrington rod
	hazard ratio
	health related
	health rider (cardiac rehab)
	heart rate
	hemorrhagic retinopathy
	histamine release
	hospital record
	hour
	human resources
H & R	hysterectomy and radiation
Hr −2	minus two hours (two hours prior to treatment)
Hr 0	zero hour (when treatment starts)
HRA	high-right atrium
	hip resurfacing arthroplasty
	histamine releasing activity
H2RA	histamine$_2$-receptor antagonist
HRAD	hyper-reactive airway disease
HR-ALL	high-risk acute lymphoblastic leukemia
HRAM	high-resolution accurate-mass (mass spectrometer)
HRAS	Harvey rat sarcoma viral oncogene homolog (gene)
H2RAs	histamine 2-receptor antagonists [e.g. ranitidine (Zantac), cimetidine (Tagamet), famotidine (Pepcid), etc.)]
HR-BD	high risk for bipolar disorder
HRC	Human Rights Committee
HRCT	high-resolution computed tomography

HRD	hazard ratios of death
	homologous recombinant deficiency
	human retroviral disease
	hypertension renal disease
	hypoparathyroidism, retardation, and dysmorphism (syndrome)
HRE	high-resolution electrocardiography
HRECG	high-resolution electrocardiography
HR-ECUS	high-resolution epicardial ultrasonography
href	Hypertext REFerence (HTML [hypertext markup language] code used to create a link to another page)
HREM	high-resolution episcopic microscopy
	high-resolution esophageal manometry
HRET	Health Research and Educational Trust
	heel-rise endurance test
HRF	Harris return flow
	health-related facility
	histamine-releasing factor
	hypertensive renal failure
	hypoxic respiratory failure
HRG	heregulin
	high-risk group
	histidine-rich glycoprotein
HRGs	high-risk groups
hrHPV	high-risk human papillomavirus
HR-HPV	high-risk human papillomavirus
HRHS	hypoplastic right heart syndrome
HRHs	high-risk heterosexuals
HRI	HMG-CoA (3-hydroxy-3-methylglutaryl-coenzyme A) reductase inhibitors
HRIF	high-risk infant follow-up
	histamine inhibitory releasing factor
HRIG	human rabies immune globulin
HRIM	high-resolution impedance manometry
HRL	head rotated left
HRLA	human reovirus-like agent
HRLM	high-resolution light microscopy
hRLX-2	synthetic human relaxin
hrly	hourly
HRM	high resolution manometry
	human resources management
HRMPC	hormone-refractory metastatic prostate cancer
HRMS	high-resolution mass spectrometry

HRMT	human resting muscle (myofascial) tone
HRN	hepatic (cytochrome P450) reductase null (mice)
hRN	human rennin
HRNB	Halstead-Reitan Neuropsychological Battery
HR-NMIBC	high-risk non-muscle-invasive bladder cancer
HROB	high-risk obstetrics
HR-OCT	high-resolution optical coherence tomography
HROs	high-reliabiity organizations
HRP	high-risk pregnancy
	horseradish peroxidase
HRP-2	histidine-rich protein-2
HRPC	hormone-refractory prostate cancer
HRpEF	may have meant HFmrEF (heart failure with mid-range ejection fraction)
hRPT	human renal proximal tubule
hrpT	type III secretion protein (gene)
HRQL	health-related quality of life
HRQOL	health-related quality of life
HRR	Hardy Rand and Rittler (Color Vision Test)
	head rotated right
	heart rate recovery
	heart rate regular
	heart rate reserve
HRRC	High Risk Referral Clinic
	Human Research Review Committee
HRrEF	may have meant HFrEf (heart failure with reduced ejection fraction)
HRRP	Hospital Readmission Reduction Program
HRRR	heart regular rate and rhythm
HRRT	high-resolution research tomograph
HRS	Haw River syndrome
	Health and Retirement Study (Institute for Social Research, Univ. of Michigan, Ann Arbor, MI)
	hepatorenal syndrome
	Hodgkin-Reed-Sternberg (cells)
hrs	hours
HRS2	hepatorenal syndrome type 2
Hrs2	mouse minor satellite DNA 2 (gene)
HRSA	Health Resources and Services Administration (US Department of Health and Human Resources)

HRSD	Hamilton Rating Scale for Depression		hippocampal sclerosis
HRSEM	high-resolution scanning electron microscopy		house staff
			Hurler syndrome (also MPS 1)
			hysteroscopy
HRST	heat, reddening, swelling, or tenderness	Hs	hassium
		H&S	hearing and speech
	heavy resistance strength training		hemorrhage and shock
HRSV	human respiratory syncytial virus		hysterectomy and sterilization
HRT	heart rate	H → S	heel-to-shin
	heart rate turbulence	H/S	see HS
	Heidelberg retina tomograph	H2S	hydrogen sulfide
	heparin response test	HSA	Health Services Administration (Administrator)
	high-risk transfer		
	hormone replacement therapy		Health Systems Agency
	hyperfractioned radiation therapy		human serum albumin
HRTEM	high-resolution transmission electron microscopy		hypersomnia-sleep apnea
		HSAN	hereditary sensory and autonomic neuropathy (types I-IV)
HRT/HRTT	hold red top/hold red top tube		
HRT-RCM	Heidelberg Retinal Tomograph with Rostock Corneal Module	HSAR	household secondary attack rate
		HSAT	high and sustained (rhGAA [recombinant human acid alpha-glucosidase] IgG [immunoglubulin G]) antibody titers
HRTS	high-rise toilet seat		
HRU	health resource utilization		
HRUS	high-resolution ultrasonography		
HRV	heart rate variability		
	heterogeneous resistance to vancomycin		home sleep apnea test (testing)
		HSB	hospital scatter bed
	human rhinovirus		husband
hrVFSE	high-resolution radiographic videofluoroscopic swallowing examination	HSBG	heel-stick blood gas
		HSBS	evening blood sugar
		HSC	hematopoietic stem cell
HRVO	hemicentral retinal vein occlusions		hepatic stellate cells
		HSCC	hypopharyngeal squamous cell carcinoma
HRZ	high risk zone		
	hyporeflective zone	HSCL	Hopkins Symptom Check List
HRZE	isoniazid, rifampicin, pyrazinamide, and ethambutol [regimen for tuberculosis])	HSCP	highly calcium-sensitive pool
		HSCR	Hirschsprung disease
		hsCRP	high-sensitivity C-reactive protein
HS	bedtime (must specify if a dose is to be given one time or every night)	hs-CRP	high-sensitivity C-reactive protein
		HSCSS	hypersensitive carotid sinus syndrome
		HSCT	hematopoietic stem cell transplant
	half-strength		
	hamstring sets	HSD	Honestly Significant Difference (test) (Turkey)
	hamstrings		
	handsewn (suture)		hypoactive sexual desire (disorder)
	Harmonic scalpel		
	Hartmans solution (lactated Ringer's)	HSDD	hypoactive sexual desire disorder
		HSDI	high-speed digital imaging
	heart size	HSE	herpes simplex encephalitis
	heart sounds		human skin equivalent
	heavy smoker		hypertonic saline-epinephrine
	heel slides	HSEES	Hazardous Substances Emergency Events Surveillance
	heel spur		
	heel stick	HSES	hemorrhagic shock and encephalopathy
	hemorrhagic shock		
	hereditary spherocytosis	HSF	high spatial frequencies
	herpes simplex		high-saturated-fat
	hidradenitis suppurativa		hypertrophic scar fibroblasts
	high school		

H

HSF-1	heat shock factor 1	HSPP	hemorrhagic stroke during
HSG	herpes simplex genitalis		pregnancy and puerperium
	hysterosalpingogram		Hutchinson Smoking Prevention
HSGYV	heat, steam, gum, yawn,		Project
	and Valsalva maneuver	hSPP	human signal peptide peptidase
	(for otitis media)	HSQ	Health Status Questionnaire
HSH	harmonic scalpel	HSR	heated serum reagin
	hemorrhoidectomy		hypersensitivity reaction
	hypomagnesemia with		hypofractionated stereotactic
	secondary hypocalcemia		radiotherapy
HSHHC	Healthy Sleep Habits, Happy	H/S ratio	heart-to-skull ratio
	Child (a book by Marc	HSRC	Human Subjects Review
	Weissbluth)		Committee
H-SIL	high-grade squamous	HSS	half-strength saline solution
	intraepithelial lesions		(0.45% sodium chloride
HSJ	hepatic schistosomiasis		injection)
	japonica		Hospital Surgical Service
HSK	herpes simplex keratitis		hypertonic saline solution
	hyperkeratotic seborrheic		(3%, 5% or 7.5% sodium
	keratosis		chloride injection) (This is a
HSL	herpes simplex labialis		dangerous abbreviation)
	hormone sensitive lipase	hssB	hssA/2C/7E family protein
HSLC	Headache Specific Locus of		(gene)
	Control (Scale)	hSSB1	human single-strand DNA
	hepatic stem-like cells		(deoxyribonucleic
HSLC-DV	Headache-Specific Locus		acid)-binding protein 1
	of Control (Scale)-Dutch	HSSE	high soap suds enema
	Version	HS-SPECT	high-speed single-photon
HSLF	high-sugar/low-fiber		emission computed
HSM	hepatosplenomegaly		tomography
	holosystolic murmur	HS-SPME	headspace-solid-phase
hs-meg	hepatosplenomegaly		microextraction
HSMN	hereditary sensory motor	H/S syndrome	Hurler-Scheie syndrome
	neuropathy	HST	home sleep testing
HSN	Hansen-Street nail		horseshoe tear (retina)
	head-shaking nystagmus		hospital support teams
	heart sounds normal		hospital support team(s)
	hereditary sensory neuropathies	HSTCL	hepatosplenic T-cell lymphoma
	hereditary sensory neuropathy	HS-tk	herpes simplex thymidine kinase
HSO	heavy silicone oil	HSTL	hepatosplenic T cell lymphoma
HSOs	health service organizations	hsTnT	high-sensitivity troponin T
	human service organizations	hsUHR-OCT	high-speed ultra-high-resolution
HSP	heat shock protein		optical coherence
	Henoch-Schönlein purpura		Tomography
	hereditary spastic paraparesis	HSV	herpes simplex virus
	hereditary spastic paraplegia		highly selective vagotomy
	human subject protection	HSV-1	herpes simplex virus type 1
	hypersensitivity pneumonitis		herpes simplex virus type 1
	hysterosalpingography		vaccine
HSPC	hydrogenated soy phosphatidyl	HSV-2	herpes simplex virus type 2
	choline	HSV6	herpes simplex virus type 6
HSPE	high-strength pancreatic	HSV12	herpes simplex virus types 1,
	enzymes		2 vaccine
HSPEF	may have meant HFPEF (heart	HSVD	hypertensive small vessel disease
	failure with preserved [left	HSVE	herpes simplex virus encephalitis
	ventricular] ejection fraction)	HSVI	herpes simplex virus type 1
HSPN	Henoch-Schönlein purpura	HSVPCR	herpes simplex virus polymerase
	nephritis		chain reaction

HSV PCR	herpes simplex virus polymerase chain reaction	HTCZ	may be HCTZ
HSV SEM	herpes simplex virus (disease) clinical manifestations isolated to the skin eye and mouth	HTDS	high-throughput drug screening
		HTE	highly treatment experienced (patients)
HSW	Health and Safety at Work (Act, United Kingdom) Heshouwu (Polygonum multiflorum Thunb) a herbal medicine heterosexual women human solid waste	hTERT	human telomerase reverse transcriptase
		HTF	house tube feeding
		hTf	human transferring
		HTG	hypertriglyceridemia
		HTGL	hepatic triglyceride lipase
		HTGP	hypertriglyceridemic-induced pancreatitis
HSZ	high signal zones	HTH	see gene website, www.ncbi.nlm .nih.gov/gene
HT	hammertoe head trauma healing time Health Technician hearing test heart heart transplant height heparin trap(hep-trap; heparin lock; a venous access device) high temperature hormonotherapy Hubbard tank hypermetropia hypertension hyperthermia hyperthyroid hyperthyroidism hypertropia	HTHD	hard thoracic herniated discs
		HTHD	hypertensive hemodialysis (patient)
		HTI	Hemoclot® Thrombin Inhibitor (assay)
		HT-IMMS	Hadamard transform ion mobility mass spectrometry
		HTK	heel-to-knee (test) histidine-tryptophan-ketoglutarate (Bretschneider solution)
		HTL	hearing threshold level honey-thick liquid (diet consistency) human T-cell leukemia human thymic leukemia
		HTLA	high-titer, low-avidity (antibodies) human T lymphocyte antigen
HT-1	hereditary tyrosinemia type 1	HTLV 1	human T-cell lymphotrophic virus type 1
H&T	hospitalization and treatment		
H/T	heel and toe (walking)	HTLV III	human T-cell lymphotrophic virus type III
H(T)	intermittent hypertropia		
HTA	Health Technology Assessment (Program) hydrothermal ablation hypertension (French)	HTM	Haemophilus test medium high threshold mechanoceptors
		hTM	human tropomyosin
		HTML	hypertext markup language
ht aer	heated aerosol	HTN	hypertension
HTAi	Health Technology Assessment International	HTNB	hypertension with brachydactyly (syndrome)
		HtnHD	hypertensive heart disease
HTAP	hypertriglyceridemia induced acute pancreatitis	HTNs	hyperfunctioning thyroid nodules hypertensives
HTAT	human tetanus antitoxin	HTNV	Hantaan virus
HT autograft	hamstring tendon autograft	HTO	high tibial osteotomy
HTB	hot tub bath	HTP	House-Tree-Person-test
HTBF	high-throughput blood fractionation	5-HTP	serotonin (5-hydroxytryptophan)
		hTPH	human tryptophan hydroxylase (gene)
HTBZ	dihydrotetrabenazine		
HTC	heated tracheostomy collar high-throughput (protein) crystallization hypertensive crisis	HTPN	home total parenteral nutrition
		HTR	hard tissue replacement
		HTRG	hypertriglyceridemia
HTCVD	hypertensive cardiovascular disease	hTRT	human telomerase reverse transcriptase

HTS	head traumatic syndrome	HUK	human urinary kallikrein
	heel-to-shin (test)	HUM	heat, ultrasound, and massage
	Hematest® stools	HUM7030	human insulin, regular 30 units/
	high-throughput screening		mL with human insulin
	hypertrophic scarring		isophane suspension 70 units/
HTSCA	human tumor stem cell assay		mL (Humulin® 70/30 insulin)
HtSDS	height standard deviation score	HUMARA	human androgen receptor assay
H-TSH	human thyroid-stimulating	humid	humidified
	hormone	HUM L	human insulin zinc suspension
HTSI	Healthcare Technology Safety		(Humulin® L Insulin)
	Institute (Association for the	HUM N	human insulin isophane suspen-
	Advancement of Medical		sion (Humulin® N Insulin)
	Instrumentation)	HUM R	human insulin, regular
HTT	hand thrust test		(Humulin® R Insulin)
	hyalinizing trabecular tumor	HUN	hydroureteronephrosis
HTTC	Hemophilia and Thrombosis	HUP	Hospital of the University of
	Treatment Center		Pennsylvania
HTTP	Hypertext Transfer Protocol		human umbilical (cord) plasma
HTU	home telemedicine unit	hUP	human uridine phosphorylase
HTV	herpes-type virus	HUR	hydroxyurea
HTVD	hypertensive vascular disease	HUS	head ultrasound
HTW	hip to waist (ratio)		hemolytic uremic syndrome
	hostility toward women		Hospital Unit Secretary
	hot tap water		husband
HTX	hemothorax	husb	husband
HTx	hand transplantation	HUSC	Hospital Unit Service
HTy	hydroxytyrosol (an antioxidant		Coordinator
	found in olive leaf and oil)	HuSIS	Human-Surrogate Interaction
Hty	hypersprouty (gene)		Space (consists of a dedicated
HTZ	heterozygote(s)		physical space, structures,
	heterozygous		and components designed
HU	head unit		specifically for carrying out
	hydroxyurea		controlled studies related to
	hypertensive urgencies		human-surrogate interactions)
Hu	Hounsfield units	HUSs	hemolytic uremic syndromes
HUAEC	human umbilical endothelial cells	HUSTTP	hemolytic uremic syndrome and
HuB	see gene website, www.ncbi.nlm		thrombotic thrombocytopenic
	.nih.gov/gene		purpura
HUC	hospital unit coordinator	HUT	head-upright tilt (test)
HUCBC	human umbilical cord blood		hyperplasia of usual type
	cells	HUTT	head-up tilt-table testing
hUC-MSCs	human umbilical cord	HUV	human umbilical vein
	mesenchymal stem cells	HUVEC	human umbilical vein
HUD	humanitarian use device (FDA		endothelial cells
	designation)	HUVS	hypocomplementemic urticarial
HUD-VASH	Housing and Urban Development-		vasculitis syndrome
	Department of Veterans Affairs	HV	hallux valgus
	Supportive Housing		Hantavirus
HUF	human uterine fibroblast		has voided
HuGe	*Human Genome* Epidemiology		healthy volunteer(s)
	Navigator		Hemovac®
HUGO	Human Genome Organization		hepatic vein
HUH	Humana Hospital		herpesvirus
HUI	Health Utilities Index		home visit
HUI2	Health Utilities Index Mark 2		hypervariable
HUI3	Health Utilities Index Mark 3		hyperventilation
HUIFM	human leukocyte interferon	H&V	hemigastrecomoty and vagotomy
	meloy	HVA	homovanillic acid

H

HVAC	heating, ventilating, and air conditioning	HVY	heavy
			heavy-intensity exercise
HVAD	hemodialysis vascular access dysfunction		human virus Y (a fictitious virus describing human
HVAD®	HeartWare ventricular assist device (a small implantable centrifugal blood pump)		T-lymphotropic virus in terms of neurological outcomes)
HVB	hepatits B virus	HW	hemiwalker
HVBP	Hospital Value-Based Purchasing (Centers for Medicare & Medicaid Services)		heparin well
			homework
			housewife
HVC	hepatitis virus type	HWA	Health Workforce Australia
HVD	hypertensive vascular disease		(closed in 2014 and the essential functions were transferred
HVDO	hypovitaminosis D osteopathy		to the Department of Health)
HVE	high-voltage electrophoresis		husband-to-wife assault
HVES	high-voltage electrical stimulation		hypoferritinemia without
HVF	Humphrey visual field		anemia
HVFA	Humphrey visual field analyzer	HWB	hot water bottle
HVFD	homonymous visual field defects	HWC	high waist circumference
		HWD	Hardy-Weinberg disequilibrium
HVGS	high-voltage galvanic stimulation	HWE	hot water epilepsy
HVHs	high-volume hospitals (as defined by each study)	HWFE	housewife
		HWG	has worn glasses
HVI	high-voltage ICD (implantable cardioverter-defibrillator)	HWH	halfway house
		HWI	hazardous waste incinerator
	hollow viscus injury		hookworm infection
HVII	hypervariable segment II		hot water immersion
hVISA	heterogeneous vancomycin-intermediate Staphylococcus aureus	HWM	hand-wrist maturation
		HWO	tracer wash out from the heart
		HWP	home walking program
HVL	half-value layer		hot wet pack
	hippocampal volume loss	HWPG	has worn prescription glasses
HVLA	high-velocity, low-amplitude (spinal manipulation)	HWR	hand washing plus rubbing with an alcohol-based solution
HVLP	high-volume low-pressure (tracheal tube cuff)		hardware
			Health, Work, and Retirement
HVLT	Hopkins Verbal Learning Test-Revised		(longitudinal study)
HVMA	herpesvirus Macaca arctoides	HWs	health workers
HVN	hyperventilation-induced nystagmus		Hispanic whites
		HWWS	handwashing with soap
HVOD	hepatic veno-occlusive disease	HWWS syndrome	Herlyn-Werner-Wunderlich syndrome (a congenital
HVOO	hepatic venous outflow obstruction		anomaly of the urogenital tract, typically character-
HVOR	horizontal vestibulo-ocular reflex		ized by uterus didelphys, obstructed hemivagina, and
HVOTO	hepatic venous outflow tract obstruction		ipsilateral renal agenesis)
		Hx	history
HVP	hollow viscus perforation		hospitalization
	hospital value-based purchasing	HXM	altretamine (hexamethylmelamine;
HVPC	high-voltage pulsed current		Hexalen)
HVPG	hepatic venous pressure gradient	Hx & Px	history and physical
HVR	hypoxic ventilatory response		(examination)
HVS	hyperventilation syndrome	Hy	hypermetropia
HVS-TK	herpes simplex virus thymidine kinase	hyal	hyaluronidase
		HyCoSy	hysterosalpingo-contrast
HVT	high tidal volume		sonography
	turkey herpesvirus	hydro	hydrocephalus

H

HYDRO	hydronephrosis	HYPT	hyperventilation provocation test
	hydrotherapy	HYs	healthy years of life
hydrops	a word meaning accumulation of clear, watery fluid or edema	hys	hysteroscopy
		hyst	hysterectomy
HYG	hygiene	hyster	hysterectomy
HYHA	may have mean NYHA (New York Heart Association [classification of heart disease])	hysto	the prefix histo (tissue)
		HYVET	Hypertension in the Very Elderly Trial
HYK	hyperketonemia	HZ	herpes zoster
HYN	hyponychium	Hz	Hertz
HYP	hyperkalemic	HZD	herpes zoster dermatitis
HYPER	above	HZE	Herpes zoster encephalitis (particles)
	higher than		high-charge and energy (particles; high [H] atomic number [Z] and energy [E])
Hyper Al	hyperalimentation		
hyperbili	hyperbilirubinemia		
hyperCa	hypercalcemia		
hyperchol	hypercholesterolemia	HZO	herpes zoster ophthalmicus
hypercoag	hyper coagulation	HZ/su	herpes zoster subunit (zoster vaccine recombinant, adjuvanted inj; Shingrix)
HyperCVAD	hyperfractionated cyclophos-phamide, vincristine, Adriamycin (doxorubicin), and dexamethasone		
		HZV	herpes zoster (shingles) vaccine herpes zoster virus
HyperCVAD/MA	hyperfractionated cyclophos-phamide, vincristine, doxorubicin (Adriamycin), and dexamethasone fol-lowed by methotrexate and cytarabine (ara-C)		
hyperK	hyperkalemia		
hyperMg	hypermagnesemia		
hyperNa	hypernatremia		
hyperOsm	hyperosmolality		
hyperphos	hyperphosphatemia		
HyperPTH	hyperparathyroidism		
HYPER T & A	hypertrophic tonsils and adenoids		
hyperTG	hypertriglyceridemia		
hyperTN	hypertension		
HYPO	below		
	hypodermic injection		
	lower than		
hypoCa	hypocalcemia		
HYPOFx	hypo-fraction		
hypoK	hypokalemia		
hypokin	hypokinesia		
hypoMg	hypomagnesemia		
hypoNa	hyponatremia		
hyponat	hyponatremia		
hypoOsm	hypo-osmolality		
hypophos	hypophosphatemic?		
hypopit	hypopituitarism		
HypoPT	hypoparathyroidism		
HypoT	hypothermia		
	hypothyroidism		
HypoT4	below the normal total thyroxine (T4) level		
hypoTN	hypotension		
HYPOX	hypophysectomy		

I

I	impression
	incisal
	incontinent
	independent
	India (Phonetic Alphabet I; pronounced IN-DEE-AH)
	initial
	inspiration
	intact (bag of waters)
	intake
	intermediate
	intrinsics
	iodine
	iris
	isoleucine
	one
(I)	independent
(I)	independent
I_2	iodine
I 10	the tablet imprint for Ibuprofen 800 mg
I^{131}	radioactive iodine
I-131	iodine 131
I-3+7	idarubicin and cytarabine
IA	ideational apraxia
	idiopathic anaphylaxis
	incidental appendectomy
	incurred accidentally
	indigenous Australian(s)
	initial assessment
	Internet addiction
	interoceptive awareness (an ability to accurately perceive interoceptive processes, which comprise receiving, processing, and integrating body-relevant signals together with external stimuli)
	intra articular (this could be a dangerous abbreviation as it may be interpreted as intra-amniotic or intra-arterial)
	intra-amniotic (this could be a dangerous abbreviation as it may be interpreted as intra-arterial or intra-articular)
	intra-arterial (this could be a dangerous abbreviation as it may be interpreted as intra-amniotic or intra-articular)
	invasive aspergillosis
	Iowa
I&A	irrigation and aspiration
I/A	irrigation and aspiration see IA

IAA	ileoanal anastomosis
	insulin autoantibodies
	interrupted aortic arch
	intra-abdominal abcess
	intra-abdominal adiposity
	intra-arterial angiography
IAAA	inflammatory abdominal aortic aneurysms
IAAT	intra-abdominal adipose tissue
IAB	incomplete abortion
	induced abortion
	intermittent androgen blockade
	International Association of Biomedical Gerontology
IABC	intra-aortic balloon counterpulsation
IABCP	intra-aortic balloon counterpulsation
IABG	intra-arterial blood gas monitoring system
IABP	intra-aortic balloon pump(ing)
	intra-arterial blood pressure
IAC	internal auditory canal
	intra-arterial chemotherapy
	isolated adrenal cell
IACC	intraarterial cytoreductive chemotherapy
IAC-CPR	interposed abdominal compressions–cardiopulmonary resuscitation
IACD	implantable automatic cardioverter-defibrillator
	interatrial conduction delay
IACD-10	International Classification of Diseases
IACET	International Association for Continuing Education and Training
IACG	intermittent angle-closure glaucoma
IACNS	isolated angiitis of central nervous system
IACP	intra-aortic counterpulsation
IACs	influenza assessment centers (Canada)
	inhaled anticholinergics
	intracranial artery calcifications
IACUC	Institutional Animal Care and Use Committee
IAD	implantable atrial defibrillator
	incontinence-associated dermatitis
	inflammatory airway disease (veterinary)
	inflammatory articular disease
	intermittent androgen deprivation
	intractable atopic dermatitis
	intraoperative autologous (blood) donation

IADHS	inappropriate antidiuretic hormone syndrome	IAP	independent adjudicating panel intermittent acute porphyria intra-abdominal pressure intracarotid amobarbital procedure intrapartum antibiotic prophylaxis
IADL	independent activities of daily living Instrumental Activities of Daily Living		
IADLs	instrumental activities of daily living	IAPB	International Agency for the Prevention of Blindness
IADP	intrathecal analgesic delivery pump	IA/PIU	Internet addiction/pathological Internet use
IADSA	intra-arterial digital subtraction angiography	IAPP	ileoanal pouch procedure islet amyloid polypeptide
IADT	intermittent androgen deprivation therapy	IAQ	indoor air quality
IAEA	International Atomic Energy Agency	IARC	International Agency for Research on Cancer idiopathic acute recurrent pancreatitis inverse Argyll Robertson pupil
IAEDF	may have meant IAEDP (International Association of Eating Disorders Professionals)		
IAEDP	International Association of Eating Disorders Professionals	IART	intra-atrial reentrant tachycardia
		IAS	idiopathic ankylosing spondylitis intermittent androgen suppression internal anal sphincter International Antiviral Society Interpersonal Adjective Scales
IAEDV	intermittent absent end diastolic velocity		
IAET	International Association for Enterostomal Therapy (Standards of Care Dermal Wounds: Pressure Ulcers)– see WOCN		
		IASA	internal anal sphincter achalasia
		IASD	interatrial septal defect
		IASDA	may have meant IADSA (intra-arterial digital subtraction arteriography)
IAF	intra-abdominal fat		
IAG	indolyl-3-acryloylglycine		
IAGT	indirect antiglobulin test	IASI	intra-articular steroid injection
IAHA	immune adherence hemagglutination	IASP	International Association for the Study of Pain
IAHC	intra-arterial hepatic chemotherapy	IASTM	Instrument Assisted Soft Tissue Mobilization (physical therapy)
IAHCSMM	International Association of Healthcare Central Service Materiel Management	IAT	immunoaugmentive therapy Implicit Association Test indirect antiglobulin test insertional Achilles tendinopathy intracarotid amobarbital test intraoperative autologous transfusion
IAHD	idiopathic acquired hemolytic disease		
IAHE	Italian Association of Health Economics (guidelines)		
IAI	intra-abdominal infection intra-abdominal injury intra-amniotic infection		
		IATC	intraarticular
		IATN	International Alliance of Translational Neuroscience
IALD	instrumental activities of daily living	IATPA	intra-arterial tissue plasminogen activator
IAM	internal auditory meatus	IATT	intra-arterial thrombolytic therapy
IAN	indinavir (Crixivan) -associated nephrolithiasis inferior alveolar nerve intern's admission note	IAU	implementation as usual intervention as usual
		IAV	infraclavicular axillary vein intermittent assist ventilation
IANB	inferior alveolar nerve block		
I and D	irrigation and debridement	IAVR	inadequate virologic response
I and R	insertion and removal	IAW	I agree with in agreement with Indian American women
IAO	immediately after onset inferior anterior oblique infrarenal aortic occlusion		
		IAWs	ion-acoustic waves

290

IB	ileal bypass	IB-IVUS	integrated backscatter
	instant breakfast		intravascular ultrasound
	insulin receptor binding test	IBM	ideal body mass
	investigator's brochure		impaired bed mobility
	isolation bed		inclusion-body myositis
IB1A	interferon beta-1a (Avonex)	IBMI	initial body mass index
Iba1	ionized calcium-binding adaptor	IBMIR	instant blood-mediated
	molecule 1		inflammatory reaction
IBAM	idiopathic bile acid malabsorption	IBMTR	International Bone Marrow
IBBB	intra-blood-brain barrier		Transplant Registry
IBBBB	incomplete bilateral bundle	IBNR	incurred but not reported
	branch block	IBOW	intact bag of waters
IBC	inflammatory breast cancer	IBP	ibuprofen
	Institutional Biosafety		inflammatory back pain
	Committee		intrableb pigmentation
	invasive bladder cancer		isobutylparaben
	invasive breast cancer	IBPB	interscalene brachial plexus
	iron binding capacity		block
IBCLC	International Board-Certified	IBPS	Insall-Burstein posterior stabilizer
	Lactation Consultant	IBR	immediate breast reconstruction
IBCs	intervascular bridging cells		infectious bovine rhinotracheitis
	intracellular bacterial communities	IBRS	Inpatient Behavior Rating Scale
IBCT	incorrect blood component	IBS	irritable bowel syndrome
	transfused	ibsC	see gene website www.ncbi.nlm
	inlay butterfly cartilage		.nih.gov/gene
	tympanoplasty	IBS-C	irritable bowel syndrome,
	Integrative Behavioral Couple		constipation predominant
	Therapy (based in part on	ibsD	see gene website www.ncbi.nlm
	traditional behavioral couple		.nih.gov/gene
	therapy but expands both the	IBS-D	Irritable Bowel Syndrome -
	conceptualization of couple		Diarrhea Type
	distress and of intervention)	IBSM	induced blood-stage malaria
IBD	infectious bursal disease		Internet-delivered behavioral
	inflammatory bowel disease		stress management
	isosulfan blue dye	IBT	immune-based therapy
IBD7	inflammatory bowel disease 7		ink blot test (Rorschach test)
	(gene)		interblinking time
IBDa	inflammatory bowel	IBTR	intrabreast-tumor recurrence
	disease-related arthritis		ipsilateral breast tumor recurrence
IBDQ	Inflammatory Bowel Disease	IBU	ibuprofen
	Questionnaire	ibuprofen	may have meant ibuprofen
IBE	incomplete bladder emptying	IBUS	International Breast Ultrasound
	individual bioequivalence		School (guideline)
IBF	ipsilateral breast failure	IBV	infectious bronchitis virus
IBG	iliac bone graft	IBW	ideal body weight
IBH	insect bite hypersensitivity	IC	between meals
IBH-4	human breast cancer cell lines		ileocecal
	(also 6, 7, etc.)		iliac crest
IBHC	integrated behavioral health care		immune complex
	iterative beam-hardening		immunocompromised
	correction		incipient cataract (grade 11 to 41)
IBI	intermittent bladder irrigation		incomplete
ibid	at the same place		indirect calorimetry
IBiG	Institute of Biology and Genetics		indirect Coombs (test)
	(University of Genoa, Italy)		individual contact
IBILI	indirect bilirubin		individual counseling
IBIS-II	International Breast (Cancer)		infant certification
	Intervention Study II		infection control

	informed consent	ICAO	internal carotid artery occlusion
	initial certification	ICARE	International Cancer Alliance
	inspiratory capacity		for Research and Education
	intensive care	iCare	a device to measure intraocular
	intercostal		pressure (tonometry)
	intercourse		an electronic medical record
	intermediate care		system
	intermittent catheterization	ICARS	International Cooperative Ataxia
	intermittent claudication		Rating Scale
	interstitial changes	ICAS	intermediate coronary artery
	interstitial cystitis		syndrome
	intracerebral		internal carotid artery stenosis
	intracranial	ICAST-C	ISPCAN (International Society
	intraincisional		for the Prevention of
	ion chromatography		Child Abuse and Neglect)
	irinotecan and carboplatin		Child Abuse Screening
	irritable colon		Tool-children version
I&C	incision and curettage	ICA stenosis	internal carotid artery stenosis
I/C	imipenem-cilastatin (Primaxin)	iCAST™	a balloon expandable covered
I3C	indole-3-carbinol		stent
IC$_{50}$	half maximal inhibitory	ICAST-P	ISPCAN (International Society
	concentration		for the Prevention of Child
IC10	the concentration of drug		Abuse and Neglect) Child
	needed to inhibit 10% of		Abuse Screening Tool-Parent
	a specific biological or		version
	biochemical function	ICAT	infant cardiac arrest tray
IC50	the concentration of drug		isotope-coded affinity tag
	needed to inhibit 50% of	ICB	intracranial bleeding
	a specific biological or	ICBG	iliac crest bone graft
	biochemical function	ICBL	immune cell binding ligand
IC90	the concentration of drug needed	ICBN	International Code of Botanical
	to inhibit 90% of a specific		Nomenclature
	biological or biochemical	IC/BP	interstitial cystitis/bladder pain
	function		syndrome
ICA	ileocolic anastomosis	ICBT	intercostobronchial trunk
	independent component analysis	ICC	idiopathic chronic cough
	intermediate care area		immunocytochemistry
	internal carotid artery		Indian childhood cirrhosis
	intracranial abscess		Infection Control Committee
	intracranial aneurysm		interstitial cells of Cajal
	invasive coronary angiography		intraclass correlation coefficient
	islet-cell antibody		intracluster correlation coefficient
	Isolated congenital anosmia		invasive cervical carcinoma
iCa	ionized calcium		islet cell carcinoma
ICAAC	Interscience Conference on	ICCC	intraclass correlation coefficient
	Antimicrobial Agents and	iCCC	intrahepatic cholangiocarcinomas
	Chemotherapy	ICCC-3	International Classification of
ICAD	intrecranial atherosclerotic		Childhood Cancers, 3rd Edition
	disease	ICCD	intensified charge-coupled device
ICaL	L-type Calcium(2+) current	ICCE	intracapsular cataract extraction
iCal	a personal calendar application	ICC-MY	myenteric interstitial cells of
	made by Apple		Cajal
ICAM-1	intercellular adhesion molecule-1	ICCP	Integrated Care Certification
ICAM	intracellular adhesion molecule		Program (The Joint
ICAMA	Interstate Compact on Adoption		Commission)
	and Medical Assistance		International Campaign for
ICANN	International Corporation for		Cures of Spinal Cord Injury
	Assigned Names and Numbers		Paralysis (guidelines)

ICCs	intraclass correlation coefficients
ICCU	intensive coronary care unit
	intermediate coronary care unit
ICD	implantable cardioverter-defibrillator
	impulse control disorders
	indigocarmine dye
	informed consent document
	instantaneous cardiac death
	intercusp distance (dental)
	irritant contact dermatitis
	isocitrate dehydrogenase
ICD-9	International Classification of Diseases, 9th Revision
ICD-10	International Classification of Diseases and Related Health Problems, 10th revision
ICD-11	International Classification of Diseases and Related Health Problems, eleventh revision
ICDA	International Classification of Disease, Adapted
ICDB	incomplete database
ICDC	implantable cardioverter defibrillator catheter
ICD 9 CM	International Statistical Classification of Diseases, 9th Revision, Clinical Modification
ICD-CRT	implantable cardioverter defibrillator-cardiac resynchronization therapy
ICDD	International Center for Diffraction Data (database)
ICDE	International Conference on Data Engineering
icdE	isocitrate dehydrogenase; e14 prophage attachment site; tellurite reductase (gene)
iCDI	initial Clostridium difficile infection
ICDO	International Classification of Diseases for Oncology
ICD-10-PCS	International Statistical Classification of Diseases, Tenth Revision, Procedure Coding Classification System
ICDSC	Intensive Care Delirium Screening Checklist
ICDU	image-directed color doppler ultrasound
ICE	ice, compression, and elevation
	ifosfamide, carboplatin, and etoposide
	Immigration and Customs Enforcement
	individual career exploration
	interleukin-1 alpha converting enzyme

	interleukin-1 beta converting enzyme
	intracardiac echocardiography
	intracortical electroencephalography
ice	crystal methamphetamine (slang)
+ice	add ice
	plus ice
ICECI	International Classification of External Causes of Injuries
icEEG	intracranial electroencephalography
ICEF	intracardiac echogenic focus (foci)
ICER	incremental cost-effectiveness ratio
	Institute for Clinical and Economic Review (www.icer-review.org)
ICERs	incremental cost-effectiveness ratios
ICES	ice, compression, elevation, and support
	intracranial electrical stimulation
ICF	intermediate care facility
	International Classification of Functioning, Disability, and Health
	intracellular fluid
ICF-IID	intermediate care facilities for individuals with intellectual disabilities
ICG	impedence cardiography
	indocyanine green
ICGA	indocyanine green angiography
ICH	immunocompromised host
	International Conference on Harmonization (of Technical Requirements for Registration of Pharmaceuticals for Human Use)
	intracerebral hemorrhage
	intracranial hemorrhage
ICHD-II	International Classification of Headache Disorders 2nd Edition
ICHT	immuno-chemotherapy
ICI	immune checkpoint inhibitor
	intracavernosal injection
	intracranial injury
ICIQ-SF	International Consultation on Incontinence Questionnaire
ICISG	International cancer Information Service Group
ICIT	intensified conventional insulin therapy
iCJD	iatrogenic Creutzfeldt-Jakob disease

ICK	inhibitor cystine knot (peptides)	ICPC	International Classification of Primary Care
	intestinal cell kinase		
ick factor	a person finding a procedure, proposal, or other suggestion being inherently disgusting or distasteful		Interstate Compact on the Placement of Children
		ICPC-2	International Classification of Primary Care, 2nd revision
ICL	intracorneal lens	ICPD	International Conference on Population and Development (1994; United Nations)
	isocitrate lyase		
ICLBBB	incomplete left bundle branch block		
		iCPET	invasive cardiopulmonary exercise testing
ICLE	intracapsular lens extraction		
ICM	implantable cardiac monitor(s)	ICPI	immune checkpoint inhibitors
	inner cell mass	ICP/MS	inductively-coupled plasma- mass spectrometry
	intensive care management		
	intercostal margin	ICP-OES	inductively coupled plasma (coupled with) optical emission spectroscopy
	intercostal muscle		
	intracerebral cavernous malformations		
			inductively-coupled plasma– optical emission spectrometry
	Intracycle Monitoring (The Joint Commission)		
		ICPP	intubated continuous positive pressure
	ischemic cardiomyopathy		
ICMD	internal coordinate molecular dynamics	ICPs	intracranial pressures
		ICR	insulin to carbohydrate ratio
	International Consortium on Mammographic Density		intercaudate nucleus ratio
			intercostal retractions
	intracerebral microdialysis		intrastromal corneal ring
ICMJE	International Committee of Medical Journal Editors	ICRA	infection control risk assessment
		ICRBBB	incomplete right bundle branch block
ICMMO	Institute of Molecular Chemistry and Materials of Orsay		
		ICRC	International Committee of the Red Cross
icmO	see gene website www.ncbi.nlm.nih.gov/gene		
		ICRF-159	razoxane
ICMP	ischemic cardiomyopathy	ICRP	International Commission on Radiological Protection
ICMs	intracerebral cavernous malformations		
		ICRS	International Cartilage Repair Society (knee cartilage injury rating scale)
iCMY	ischemic cardiomyopathy		
ICN	infection control nurse		
	intensive care nursery		intrastromal corneal ring segments
	Internal Control Number (Medicare)		
		ICRU	International Commission on Radiation Units and Measurements
ICN2	neonatal intensive care unit level II		
		ICS	ileocecal sphincter
ICNB	intercostal nerve block		inhaled corticosteroid(s)
	International Code of Nomenclature of Bacteria		intercostal space
			International Continence Society (guidelines/staging)
Icon-FES	Iconographical Falls Efficacy Scale Icon		
			intraoperative cell salvage
ICOS	inducible T-cell costimulatory	icsbp	interferon consensus sequence binding protein
ICP	inductively coupled plasma		
	infantile cerebral palsy	ICSC	idiopathic central serous choroidopathy
	intercostal position (for chest lead)		
	intermittent catheterization program	ICS-CERT	Industrial Control Systems Cyber Emergency Response Team (US Dept of Homeland Security)
	intracranial pressure		
	intrahepatic cholestasis of pregnancy		
ICPA	Integrated Care Program Alignment (The Joint Commission)	ICSD	International Classification of Sleep Disorders

ICSH	interstitial cell-stimulating hormone
ICSI	intracytoplasmic sperm injection
ICSN	International Cancer Screening Network (a voluntary consortium of countries that have active population-based cancer screening programs and active efforts to evaluate and improve the processes and outcomes from cancer screening)
ICSR	Individual Case Safety Reports
	intercostal space retractions
ICSRA	intercompartmental supraretinacular artery
ICSs	inhaled corticosteroids
icSSC	incremental change in state-spanning coactivity
ICT	icterus
	immunochromatographic test
	indirect Coombs' test
	induction chemotherapy
	inflammation of connective tissue
	intensive conventional therapy
	intermittent cervical traction
	intracranial temperature
	intracranial tumor
	intracutaneous test
	iron chelation therapy
	islet cell transplant
ictal	a word meaning relating to or caused by a stroke or seizure
ICTM-CJK	International Classification of Traditional Medicine, China, Japan and Korea Version
ICTO	idiopathic carpal tarsal osteolysis
ICTP	C-terminal telopeptide of type I collagen
ICTRP	International Clinical Trials Registry Platform (World Health Organization)
ICTX	intermittent cervical traction
ICTx	intensive chemotherapy
ICU	intensive care unit
ICUD-EAU	International Consultation on Urological Diseases-European Association of Urology Consultation on Bladder Cancer (recommendations)
ICUR	Incremental Cost-Utility Ratio
ICUS	idiopathic cytopenia of undetermined significance
	intracoronary ultrasound
ICUs	intensive care units
ICV	ileocecal valve
	intracerebroventricular
ICVA	intracranial vertebral artery
	ischemic cerebrovascular accident
IC valve	ileocolic valve
ICVD	ischemic cerebrovascular diseases
ICVH	ischemic cerebrovascular headache
ICVR	intermediate cardiovascular risk
ICW	in connection with
	intact canal wall
	intercellular water
ID	Idaho
	identification
	identify
	idiotype
	ifosfamide, mesna uroprotection, and doxorubicin
	immunodiffusion
	incision and debridement
	incision and drainage
	induction delivery
	infectious disease
	infectious disease (physician or department)
	initial diagnosis
	initial dose
	intellectual disability
	internal derangement
	intradermal
	iron deficiency
id	the same
I D	see ID
I&D	incision and debridement
	incision and drainage
	irrigation and debridement
I+D	see I&D
I/D	see ID
IDA	idarubicin (Idamycin)
	iron deficiency anemia
IDAC	I-domain antigenic-peptide conjugate(s)
	Institute of Development, Aging, and Cancer (Japan)
	intermediate-dose cytarabine
IDAM	infant of drug abusing mother
IDAST	identification and antimicrobial susceptibility testing
IDB	incomplete database
IDC	idiopathic dilated cardiomyopathy
	invasive ductal cancer
IDCA	initial detection and candidate analysis
IDCa	intraductal carcinomas

IDCC	hI-con1 (Iconic)-dependent cell-mediated cytotoxicity intraductal cholangiocarcinoma	IDEAL Clinic	The Improving Diet, Energy and Activity for Life (The Obesity Institute at Children's National Health System)
IDCF	immunodiffusion complement fixation	IDeg	Insulin degludec inj (Tresiba)
IDCM	idiopathic dilated cardiomyopathy ischemic dilated cardiomyopathy	IDEM	intradural extramedullary *the same*
IDCP	idiopathic duct-centric pancreatitis	IDEO	Intrepid Dynamic Exoskeletal Orthosis
IDC-P	intraductal carcinoma of the prostate	IDET	intradiskal electrothermal therapy
IDD	inflammatory demyelinating disorder insulin-dependent diabetes intellectual and developmental disabilities interictal dysphoric disorder intervertebral disk disease iodine-deficiency disorders	IDF	infant driven feeding International Diabetes Federation ischemic digital loss Israel Defense Forces
		IDFC	immature dead female child
		IDG	interdisciplinary group
		ID-GDM	insulin-dependent gestational diabetes mellitus
I/DD	intellectual and developmental disabilities	IDH	intradialytic hypotension intramural duodenal hematoma isocitric dehydrogenase
IDDD	Interview for Deterioration in Daily life in Dementia intrathecal drug delivery device	IDH1	isocitrate dehydrogenase 1; see gene website www.ncbi.nlm.nih.gov/gene
IDDI	interictal dysphoric disorder inventory International Drug Development Institute (Belgium)	IDH2	isocitrate dehydrogenase 2; see gene website www.ncbi.nlm.nih.gov/gene
		IDI	Interpersonal Dependency Inventory intrathecal drug infusion
IDDM	insulin-dependent diabetes mellitus		
IDDM1	insulin-dependent diabetes mellitus 1; see gene website, www.ncbi.nlm.nih.gov/gene	IDIC	isodicentric chromosome
		IDIS	Iowa Drug Information System
		IDK	internal derangement of knee
IDDM2	insulin-dependent diabetes mellitus 2; see gene website, www.ncbi.nlm.nih.gov/gene	IDL	intermediate-density lipoprotein isodose line
		IDLE	indolent lesions of epithelial of origin
IDDM11	insulin dependent diabetes mellitus 11 (gene)	IDLH	immediately dangerous to life or health
IDDMII	may have meant IDDM11 (insulin dependent diabetes mellitus 11 gene)	IDLS	iterative double least square
		IDLs	instrument detection limits
IDDS	implantable drug delivery system intrathecal drug delivery systems	IDM	infant of a diabetic mother intermediate diastolic murmur
		IDMC	immature dead male child Independent Data Monitoring Committee
IDDs	intellectual and developmental disabilities	IDMM	infectious diseases specialists/ medical microbiologists may have meant IDDM (insulin-dependent diabetes mellitus)
IDDSI	International Dysphagia Diet Standardization Initiative		
IDDT	Insulin Dependent Diabetes Trust (United Kingdom) integrated dual disorders treatment		
		IDMn	low-iron (iron-deficient) diet supplemented with manganese
IDE	insulin degrading enzyme Investigational Device Exemption	IDMP	International Drug Monitoring Program
IDEA	Individuals with Disabilities Education Act	IDMS	isotope dilution mass spectrometry

IDN	inferior dental nerve
	integrated delivery network
	interdigital neuroma
	intradialytic nutrition
	isosorbide dinitrate
IDNA	iron-deficient, not anemic
ID-NAT	individual donation nucleic acid (amplification) testing
IDO	idiopathic detrusor overactivity
	indoleamine 2,3-dioxygenase-1
IDOM	initial distant organ metastasis
IDP	initiate discharge planning
	inosine diphosphate
IDPA	idiopathic dilatation of the pulmonary artery
IDPm	isocitrate dehydrogenase 2 (NADP+), mitochondrial; see gene website www.ncbi .nlm.nih.gov/gene
IDPN	intradialytic parenteral nutrition
IDR	idarubicin
	idiosyncratic drug reaction
	intradermal reaction
ID reaction	a pruritic, eczematous dermatitis associated with, but usually distant to, another inflammatory or infectious skin lesion (id has its origins in Greek, meaning father-son; a dermatophytosis causing a secondary allergic skin dermatitis)
IDS	infant-directed speech
	infectious disease service
	integrated delivery system
	intradermal smears
I&D's	see I&D
IDSA	Infectious Disease Society of America (guidelines)
IDSA/ATS	Infectious Diseases Society of America/American Thoracic Society (prognostic scores for influenza pneumonia patients)
IDSC	Investigational Drug Steering Committee (National Cancer Institute)
iDSC-MRI	intraoperative dynamic susceptibility contrast magnetic resonance imaging
IDSS	internal decompression of spinal stenosis
iDSs	integrated delivery systems
IDS-SR	Inventory of Depressive Symptomology, self-report version
IDSV	indicator dilation stroke volume
IDT	intensive diabetes treatment
	interdisciplinary team
	intradermal test

IDTF	independent diagnostic testing facility
ID-TLR	ischemia-driven target lesion revascularization
IDTP	immunodiffusion tube precipitin
IDTU	Intoxicated Driver Testing Unit
IDU	idoxuridine
	infectious disease unit
	injecting drug user
IDV	indinavir (Crixivan)
	intermittent demand ventilation
IDVA	intervertebral disk volumetric analysis
IDVC	indwelling venous catheter
IDVU	may have meant IVDU (intravenous drug user)
IDW	intradialytic weight
IDWG	interdialytic weight gain
iDXA	dual-energy X-ray absorptiometry scanner (Lunar iDXA, General Electric Healthcare)
IE	ifosfamide, and etoposide with mesna
	immunoelectrophoresis
	induced emesis
	infectious enteritis
	infective endocarditis
	initial evaluation
	inner ear
	internal/external (rotation)
	international unit (European abbreviation)
I/E	inspiration versus time spent in expiration (ratio)
	inspiratory to expiratory ratio
I:E	inspiratory to expiratory ratio
i.e.	that is
IEA	inferior epigastric artery
	interictal epileptiform activity
	International Epidemiological Association
IEC	independent ethics committee
	inpatient exercise center
	intradiskal electrothermal coagulation
	intraepidermal carcinoma
IECFs	incidental extra-cardiac findings
IED	immune-enhancing diet
	improvised explosive device
	interictal epileptic discharge
	intermittent explosive disorder
IEDB	immune epitope database
IeDEA	International Epidemiology Databases to Evaluate AIDS (an international research consortium established by the National Institute of Allergy and Infectious Diseases to

	provide resources for globally diverse HIV/AIDS [human immunodeficiency virus/ acquired immunodeficiency syndrome] data)
IEE	idiopathic eosinophilic esophagitis
	image-enhanced endoscopy
IEED	involuntary emotional expression disorder
IEEE	Institute of Electrical and Electronics Engineers
IEEG	intracranial electroencephalogram
IEF	isoelectric focusing
IEGR	factor Xa cleavage site
IEH	involuntary emergency hospitalization
IEI	idiopathic environmental intolerance
IEL	internal elastic lamina
	intestinal-intraepithelial lymphocyte
iELISA	invertase enzyme-linked immunosorbent assay
IELs	intraepithelial lymphocytes
IELT	Intravaginal Ejaculatory Latency Time
IEM	immune electron microscopy
	inborn errors of metabolism
	inherited erythromelalgia
iEMG	integrated electromyography
IEMR	integrated electronic medical records
IEN	intraepithelial neoplasia
IENFD	intraepidermal nerve fiber density
IEP	idiopathic eosinophilic pneumonia
	immunoelectrophoresis
	Individualized Education Plan
IEPA	immunoelectrophoresis analysis
IEQ	illness effects questionnaire
I:Eratio	inspiratory to expiratory time ratio
IES	Impact of Event Scale
IES-R	Impact of Event Scale-Revised
IET	infantile estropia
IEX	ion exchange
IF	idiopathic flushing
	ifosfamide (Ifex)
	iliofemoral
	immunofluorescence
	impaired fecundity
	incidental findings
	index finger
	injury factor
	interferon

	interfrontal
	intermaxillary fixation
	internal fixation
	intestinal failure
	intrinsic factor
	involved field (radiotherapy)
IFA	immunofluorescent assay
	imported fire ants
	indirect fluorescent antibody
	iron and folic acid
IFALD	intestinal failure-associated liver disease
IFAT	immunofluorescence antibody test (technique)
IFBS	irrational Food Beliefs Scale
IFC	indwelling Foley catheter
	interferential current
	intravital flow cytometry
IFCC	International Federation of Clinical Chemistry (units)
IFCN	International Federation of Clinical Neurophysiology (standards)
IFD	invasive fungal diseases
IFDs	invasive fungal diseases
IFDVT	iliofemoral deep vein thrombosis
IFE	immunofixation electrophoresis
	in-flight emergency
	intravenous fat emulsion (Intralipid; Liposyn)
IFF	if and only if
	inner fracture face
IFG	impaired fasting glucose
	inferior frontal gyrus
IFGT	impaired fasting glucose tolerance
IFH	inflammatory fibrous hyperplasia
IFI	invasive fungal infection
IFIS	International Fitness Scale
	intraoperative floppy-iris syndrome
IFIs	invasive fungal infections
iFISH	interphase fluorescence in situ hybridization
IFL	indolent follicular lymphoma
	irinotecan, fluorouracil, and leucovorin
IFM	Intergroupe Francophone du Mylélome (myeloma French-speaking group)
	internal fetal monitoring
IFN	interferon
IFN α	interferon alpha 1
IFNB	interferon beta-1 b (Betaseron)
IFO	ifosfamide (Ifex)
	in front of

iFOB	immunological fecal occult blood (test)
iFOBT	immunochemical fecal occult blood tests
IFOP	infrared fiber-optic probe
IFOS	ifosfamide (Ifex)
IFOX	Iressa (gefitinib), fluorouracil, oxaliplatin, and leucovorin
IFP	inflammatory fibroid polyps
IFPAC	International Forum on Process Analytical Chemistry
IFPMA	International Federation of Pharmaceutical Manufacturers Associations
iFR	instantaneous wave-free ratio
IFRT	involved-field radiotherapy
IFSAC	Inventory of Functional Status After Childbirth
IFSE	internal fetal scalp electrode
IFSO	International Federation for the Surgery of Obesity and Metabolic Disorders
IFSP	individualized family service plan
IFT	intraflagellar transport see gene website, www.ncbi.nlm.nih.gov/gene
IFTA	interstitial fibrosis and tubular atrophy
IFU	inclusion forming units indications for use instructions for use
IFUB	may have meant IUFD (intrauterine fetal death)
IFVA	influenza A virus intraoperative fluorescence vascular angiography
IFVB	influenza B virus
IFX	infliximab (Remicade)
IG	image-guided immunoglobulin
Ig	immunoglobulin
IGA	internet gaming addiction
IgA	immunoglobulin A
IgAD	immunoglobulin A deficiency
IgAN	immunoglobulin A nephropathy
IGAP	inferior gluteal artery perforator (flap)
IgA tTG	immunoglobulin tissue transglutaminase
IGB	intragastric balloon
IGBs	intragastric balloons
iGBS	invasive group B streptococcus
IGC	Impairment Group Code(s) intermediate glucose control
IGCCC	International Germ Cell Consensus Classification
IGCME	Irvine Gass cystoid macular edema

IGCS	inpatient geriatric consultation services
IGD	intermediate-grade dysplasia Internet gaming disorder
IgD	immunoglobulin D
IG-DCIS	intermediate-grade ductal carcinoma *in situ*
IGDE	idiopathic gait disorders of the elderly
IGDM	infant of gestational diabetic mother
IGE	idiopathic generalized epilepsy impaired gas exchange
IgE	immunoglobulin E
IGF1	insulin-like growth factor 1
IGFA	indocyanine-green fundus angiography
IGF-BP3	insulin-like growth factor binding protein 3
IGFBP-3	insulin-like growth factor-binding protein 3
IG-FESS	image-guided funduscopic nasal surgery
IGF1R	insulin-like growth factor 1 receptor insulin-like growth factor 1 receptor (gene)
IGFR	insulin-like growth factor receptor
IgG	immunoglobulin G
igG1	immunoglobulin G subclass 1
igG2	immunoglobulin G subclass 2
igG3	immunoglobulin G subclass 3
igG4	immunoglobulin G subclass 4
IgG4-RD	immunoglobulin G4-related disease
IgG4-SC	immunoglobulin G4-related sclerosing cholangitis
IGHL	inferior glenohumeral ligament
IGHV	immunoglobulin heavy chain variable domain (gene)
IGHy	human immunoglobulin 10% with recombinant human hyaluronidase (HyQvia)
IGI	image guided implant image guided implantology
IGIB	Institute of Genomics & Integrative Biology
IGIM	immune globulin intramuscular
IGIV	immune globulin intravenous
Igl	immunoglobulin lambda chain complex; see gene website www.ncbi.nlm.nih.gov/gene
IGlar	Insulin glargine inj (Lantus)
iGlar	insulin glargine
IgM	immunoglobulin M
IgM-MGUS	immunoglobulin M monoclonal gammopathy of undetermined significance

IGN	ilioinguinal nerve	IHC	idiopathic hypercalciuria
	image-guided navigation		immobilization hypercalcemia
	immunotactoid glomerulopathy		immunohistochemical
	imprinted gene network		immunohistochemical analysis
	inert gas narcosis		immunohistochemistry
IGP	interstitial glycoprotein		inner hair cell (in cochlea)
IGR	inert gas rebreathing	IHCA	in-hospital cardiac arrest
	intrauterine growth retardation	IHCP	idiopathic hypertrophic cranial
IGRA	Interferon-gamma release assay(s)		pachymeningitis
IGRT	image guided radiation therapy		Institute for Health and
IGS	image-guided surgery		Consumer Protection (Joint
IGT	immune gestational		Research Centre, European
	thrombocytopenia		Commission)
	immunoprophylaxis by gene		intrahepatic cholestasis of
	transfer		pregnancy
	impaired glucose tolerance	IHD	intermittent hemodialysis
	Iowa Gambling Task (a measure		intraheptic duct (ule)
	of decision-making under		ischemic heart disease
	ambiguity (i.e., uncertain risk	IHDN	integrated health delivery network
	contingencies)	IHDS	International HIV (human
IGTN	impaired glucose tolerance and		immunodeficiency virus)
	neuropathy		Dementia Scale
	ingrown toenail	IHES	idiopathic hyperesinophilic
IGTT	impaired glucose tolerance test		syndrome
	intraperitoneal glucose	IHFF	is here for follow-up
	tolerance test	iHFF	irradiated human fetal fibroblast
	intravenous glucose tolerance test	IHFFU	is here for follow-up
IGUR	intrauterine growth retardation	IHFs	isolated hip fractures
	(IUGR)	IHGK	immortalized human gingival
IGV1	isolated gastric varices in the		keratinocytes
	fundus of the stomach	IHH	idiopathic hypogonadotrophic
IGV2	isolated gastric varices type 2		hypogonadism
	(gastric varices elsewhere	IHHD	individualized hypoenergetic-
	in the stomach, not in the		hypolipidemic diet
	fundus)		in-hospital hemodialysis
IGVA	image-guided vascular access		intensive home hemodialysis
IgVH	immunoglobulin heavy-chain		(equal to or greater than
	variable-region mutated		16 hours per week)
	gene (a marker for progno-		ischemic and hypertensive heart
	sis in patients with chronic		disease
	lymphocytic leukemia)	IHHE	infantile hepatic
IgX	immunoglobulin X		hemangioendothelioma
IH	indirect hemagglutination	IHHS	idiopathic hyperkinetic heart
	infantile hemangioma		syndrome
	infectious hepatitis	IHI	Institute for Healthcare
	inguinal hernia		Improvement
	inhaled	IHN	infectious hematopoietic necrosis
	in-house		intractable hiccups and nausea
	intradialytic hypotension	IHNs	integrated health networks
IHA	immune hemolytic anemia	IHNV	infectious hematopoietic
	indirect hemagglutination		necrosis virus
	infusion hepatic arteriography	IHO	idiopathic hypertrophic
	intrahepatic arterial		osteoarthropathy
IHAC	interhemispheric arachnoid cyst	IHP	idiopathic hypertrophic
IHBD	intrahepatic bile duct		pachymeningitis
IHBDD	intrahepatic bile duct		idiopathic hypoparathyroidism
	dilatation (Caroli disease		inferior hypogastric plexus
	and syndrome)		isolated hepatic perfusion

IHPH	intrahepatic portal hypertension
IHPS	infantile hypertrophic pyloric stenosis
IHR	inguinal hernia repair
	intrinsic heart rate
IHS	Idiopathic Headache Score
	Indian Health Service
	integrated healthcare system
	International Headache Society (criteria)
IHs	infantile hemangiomas
	iris hamartomas
IHSA	iodinated human serum albumin
IHSF	idiopathic hypercalciuria in calcium stone-forming patients
IHSS	idiopathic hypertrophic subaortic stenosis
	in-home supportive services
IHT	insulin hypoglycemia test
IHTC	intrahepatic triglyceride content
IHTSDC	International Health Terminology Standard Organisation
IHTT	interhemispheric transfer time
IHU	inpatient hospice unit
IHV	inactivated hantavirus vaccine
	isocapnic hyperventilation
IHW	inner heel wedge
II	image intensifier (radiology)
	internal iliac (artery)
	two
ii	two
IIA	internal iliac artery
IIAC	idiopathic infantile arterial calcification
IIB	phase, class, stage, group, etc. 2 B
II bars	parallel bars
IIC	invisible-in-the canal
IICP	increased intracranial pressure
IICU	infant intensive care unit
	intermediate intensive care unit
IID	infectious intestinal disease
IIDD	idiopathic inflammatory demyelinating diseases
IIEF	International Index of Erectile Function
IIEF-5	International Index of Erectile Function (5 questions)
IIEF-EF	erectile function scores on the International Index of Erectile Function
IIF	indirect immunofluorescence
IIH	idiopathic infantile hypercalcemia
	idiopathic intracranial hypertension
	iodine-induced hyperthyroidism
IIHT	iodide-induced hyperthyroidism
III	three

iii	three
IIIA	grade 3A
	stage 3A
IIM	idiopathic inflammatory myopathies
	intracortical interaction mapping
IINB	iliohypogastric ilioinguinal nerve block
I/IND	indirect treatment method
IIP	idiopathic interstitial pneumonitis
IIPF	idiopathic interstitial pulmonary fibrosis
IIQ	Incontinence Impact Questionnaire
IIS	idiopathic infantile scoliosis
	immunization information system
IISs	immunization information systems
	interictal spikes
IITs	investigator-initiated trials
iITx	isolated intestinal transplant
IIV	inactivated influenza vaccine
	Intraindividual variability
IIV4	quadrivalent inactivated influenza vaccine
IIV3	trivalent inactivated influenza vaccine
IJ	ileojejunal
	internal jugular
I&J	insight and judgment
I/J	see IJ
IJC	internal jugular catheter
IJ CVC	internal jugular central venous catheter
IJD	inflammatory joint disease
IJDDC	International Journal of Diabetes in Developing Countries
IJ DVT	internal jugular deep venous thromboses
IJO	idiopathic juvenile osteoporosis
IJP	internal jugular pressure
IJPC	International Journal of Pharmaceutical Compounding
IJR	idiojunctional rhythm
IJRT	idiopathic juxtafoveal retinal telangiectasia
IJs	infective juveniles
IJT	idiojunctional tachycardia
	idiopathic juxtafoveal telangiectasia
IJV	internal jugular vein
IK	immobilized knee
	interstitial keratitis
IKDC	International Knee Documentation Committee (evaluation; score; form)

IKS	International Knee Society (score)	Ileo	Ileum
IKV	Issyk-Kul virus	ILESI	interlaminar epidural steroid injection
IL	Illinois	ILF	indicated low forceps
	immature lungs	ILFC	immature living female child
	interleukin (1, 2, etc.)	ILG	isoliquiritigenin
	intralesional	ILH	islets of Langerhans
	Intralipid®	ILHP	ipsilateral hemidiaphragmatic paresis
IL-11	oprelvekin (Neumega; interleukin-11)	ILI	influenza-like illness
IL-17	interleukin 17		isolated limb infusion
IL-2	aldesleukin (Proleukin; interleukin-2)	iliac	a word meaning pertaining to the lateral, flaring portion of the hip bone
IL5	interleukin 5 (gene/protein)		
IL6	interleukin-6	ILIF	interlaminar lumbar instrumental fusion
ILA	iliolumbar artery		
	individual learning activity	ILIs	influenza-like illnesses
	inferior lateral angle		isolated limb infusions
	insulin-like activity	ILK	intralesional Kenalog
ILAC	interlobar arterial collaterals	ILM	internal limiting membrane
	international Laboratory Accreditation Cooperation	ILMA	intubating laryngeal mask airway
ILAEC	Intersocietal Commission for Accreditation of Echocardio- graphy Laboratories	ILMC	immature living male child
		ILMF	infiltrative lymphocytic mural folliculitis
ILB	incidental Lewy body	ILMI	inferolateral myocardial infarct
IL28B	interleukin 28B (a cytokine); see gene website www.ncbi .nlm.nih.gov/gene	ILMP	internal limiting membrane peeling
		ILND	inguinal lymph node dissection
ILBBB	incomplete left bundle branch block	ILP	independent living program
			interstitial laser photocoagulation
ILBW	infant, low birth weight (less than 2,500 g)		isolated limb perfusion
ILC	interstitial laser coagulation	ILQTS	idiopathic long QT (interval) syndrome
	invasive lobular cancer	ILR	implantable loop recorder
il cond	ileal conduit	IL4R	interleukin 4 receptor (gene/protein)
ILCOR	International Liaison Committee on Resuscitation		
ILC2s	type 2 innate lymphoid cells	IL6R	interleukin 6 receptor (gene/protein)
ILD	immature lung disease	ILRT	intralumenal radiotherapy
	implantable loop device		involved-lesion radiation therapy
	indentation load deflection		isolated locally recurrent tumors
	interlaminar distance in flexion	ILS	increased life span
	intermediate density lipoproteins		independent living skills
	interstitial lung disease		intralabyrinthine schwannomas
	ischemic leg disease		intralaminar screws
ILDA	incremental linear discriminant analysis		intralesional steroidintralesional steroid
	independent living donor advocate	ILs	interleukins
			ionic liquids
ILE	infantile lobar emphysema	ILSMs	Interim Life Safety Measures (The Joint Commission)
	injectable lipid emulsion		
	intravenous lipid emulsion (Intralipid; Liposyn)	ILT	interstitial laser therapy
	involutional lateral entropion	ILVEN	inflammatory linear verrucal epidermal nevus
Ile	isoleucine		
ILEA	intermittent labor epidural analgesia		inflammatory linear verrucous epidermal nevi

ILVNC	isolated left ventricular noncompaction	IMDN	immature denuded
		IMDs	inherited metabolic disorders
ILWS	International Workshop on Leucocyte Differentiation Antigens	IME	important medical event
			independent medical examination (evaluation)
ILY	intermedilysin	IMED	a brand of infusion pumps
I'ly	independently		IMED Mobility is a provider
IM	ice massage		of new and used wheelchair
	imatinib mesylate (Gleevec)		accessible vans, Home
	infant mortality		Mobility Access and Bruno
	infectious mononucleosis		Stairlifts with locations in
	intermediate metabolizer(s)		Minnesota, South Dakota,
	intermetatarsal		Iowa, Nebraska, and Arkansas
	internal margin (for radiotherapy)	IMF	idiopathic myelofibrosis
	internal medicine		ifosfamide, mesna
	intramuscular		uroprotection, methotrexate,
	intramedullary		and fluorouracil
IMA	inferior mesenteric artery		immobilization mandibular
	internal mammary artery		fracture
IMAC	ifosfamide, mesna uroprotection, doxorubicin (Adriamycin), and cisplatin		inframammary fold
			intermaxillary fixation
		IM-FSIGT	insulin-modified frequently-sampled intravenous glucose tolerance test
	immobilized metal affinity chromatography		
IMAE	internal maxillary artery embolization	IMG	internal medicine group
		IMGN	idiopathic membranous glomerulonephritis
IMAG	internal mammary artery graft		
IMAO	monoamine oxidase inhibitors (Romance languages)	IMGU	insulin-mediated glucose uptake
		IMH	idiopathic myocardial hypertrophy
IMAO-A	monoamine oxidase inhibitor(s) A		
IMAO-B	monoamine oxidase inhibitor(s) B		intramural hematoma
IMARD	immunomodulating antirheumatic drugs	IMHO	in my humble opinion (slang)
			International Medical Health Organization
IMAT	intensity-modulated arc therapy		
IMAX	internal maxillary artery	IMHS	intramedullary hip screw
IMB	intermenstrual bleeding	IMH test	indirect microhemagglutination test
	intramenstrual bleeding		
IMBP	immobilized mismatch binding protein	IMI	imipramine
			impending myocardial infarction
IMBs	intensity-modulated beams		
IMC	intermediate care		inferior myocardial infarction
	intermittent catheterization		intramuscular injection
	intramedullary catheter	131I-MIBG	iodine131-metaiodobenzyl-guanidine (iobenguane 131I)
IMCI	Integrated Management of Childhood Illness		
		IMID	immune-mediated inflammatory diseases
IMCN	intermediate care nursery		
IMCO2	inspired minimum carbon dioxide (the smallest value sensed during inspiration)	IMiD	immunomodulatory drug
		IMIDs	immune-mediated inflammatory diseases
			immunomodulatory drugs (e.g., thalidomide, pomalidomide, and lenalidomide for treatment of multiple myeloma)
IMCP	interactive multimedia computer program		
IMCU	intermediate care unit		
IMDC	International Metastatic Renal Cell Carcinoma Database Consortium		
		IMIED	immune-mediated inner ear disease
IMDH	inosine monophosphate dehydrogenase	IMIG	intramuscular immunoglobulin
		IMJ	incudomalleal joint
	isopropymalate dehydrogenase	IMLC	incomplete mitral leaflet closure

IMM	immune modulating nutrition (immunonutrition)		left ventricle and displaces it into the ascending aorta, unloading the left ventricle and increasing forward flow.
	immunizations		
	irreversible morbidity or mortality	impl	implant
IMMC	interdigestive migrating motor complex	IMPN	intraductal mucinous papillary neoplasm
imm gran	immature granulocytes	importuning	a word meaning to make improper advances toward a person; to press or beset with solicitations; demand with urgency or persistence
immod	immobilization, immobilized, and immodile		
IMMPACT	Initiative on Methods, Measurement, and Pain Assessment in Clinical Trials (recommendations)		
		IMPR	implantation rate
IMMS	ion mobility mass spectrometry	IMPS	intensity-modulated photocurrent spectroscopy
IMMs	immunomodulators	IMPs	integral membrane proteins
immune	immunization	IMPT	intensity-modulated proton therapy
immuno	a prefix for immune and immunity	IMPX	impaction
IMN	idiopathic membranous nephropathy	IMQ	Infant/Child Monitoring Questionnaires
	internal mammary (lymph) node	IMR	infant mortality rate
	intramedullary nail		ischemic mitral regurgitation
IM nail(s)	intramedullary nail(s)	IMRA	immunoradiometric assay
IMO	immunomodulatory oligonucleotide	IMRaD	introduction, methods, results, and discussion (format)
	infantile malignant osteopetrosis	iMRI	intraoperative magnetic resonance imaging
IMOC	integrated model of care	IMRIS	A company which makes magnetic resonance or multi-slice computer tomography scanners for use in the operating room to provide intra-operative images.
iMOC	intermolecular complementation		
IMP	impacted		
	important		
	impression		
	improved		
	inosine monophoshate	IM rod	intramedullary rod
imp	impaired	IMRS	intensity-modulated radiosurgery
IMPAC®	National Oncology Database (aggregated tumor registries)		
		IMRT	intensity modulated radiation therapy
IMPALA	International Multidisciplinary Program to Address Lung Health and TB in Africa	IMS	immunosuppressants
			incident management system
			incurred in military service
Impella 2.5®	A percutaneously placed ventricular-assist device that is used in high-risk coronary interventional procedures to provide hemodynamic support. It aspirates up to 2.5 liters/min of blood from the left ventricle and displaces it into the ascending aorta, unloading the left ventricle and increasing forward flow.		Internal Medicine Specialist (Hospitalist)
			ion mobility spectrometry
		Ims	involuntary movements
		IMSCT	intramedullary spinal cord tumor
		IMSS	Mexican Institute for Social Security (Instituto Mexicano del Seguro Social)
Impella 5®	A percutaneously placed ventricular-assist device that is used in high-risk coronary interventional procedures to provide hemodynamic support. It aspirates up to 5 liters/min of blood from the	IMT	Inflammatory myofibroblastic tumor
			inspiratory muscle training
			intimal medial thickness
		iMTA	Institute for Medical Technology Assessment (Netherlands)
		IMU	intermediate medicine unit

ImUS	immediate-use (steam) sterilization
ImUSS	immediate-use steam sterilization
IMV	inferior mesenteric vein
	intermittent mandatory ventilation
	intermittent mechanical ventilation
	invasive mechanical ventilation
IMVP-16	ifosfamide, mesna uroprotection, methotrexate, and etoposide
IMWG	International Myeloma Working Group (diagnostic criteria)
IN	Indian; an International Society of Blood Transfusion (ISBT) blood group
	Indiana
	insulin (it is dangerous to use abbreviations for insulin therapy)
	intranasal (This is a DANGEROUS abbreviation that should NOT be used. It appears on the medabbrev. com and other Do Not Use Lists, as it has been read as intravenous (IV); spell out "intranasal")
In	indium
in	inch
INAD	in no apparent distress
	infantile neuroaxonal dystrophy
	Investigational New Animal Drug
inadeq	inadequate
INB	intercostal nerve blockade
inbox notifications	electronic health records asynchronous alerts related to test results, referral responses, medication refill requests, and messages
INC	incisal
	incision
	incomplete
	incontinent
	increase
	inside-the-needle catheter
Inc	inclusion membrane proteins
INCAT-ONLS	Inflammatory Neuropathy Cause and Treatment-Overall Neuropathy Limitation Scale
INCC	Institut National du Cancer du Canada
IncD	inclusion membrane protein expression in Chlamydia trachomatis
INCIs	intranuclear cytoplasmic inclusions
INCL	infantile neuronal ceroid lipofuscinosis
INCMNSZ	Instituto Nacional de Ciencias Médicas y Nutrition (Mexico)
incont	incontinence
	incontinent
INCPH	idiopathic noncirrhotic portal hypertension
incr	increase
	increment
Inc Spir	incentive spirometer
INCSs	intranasal corticosteroids
incus	the middle of the three diminutive bones of the ear
IND	incision and drainage
	independent
	indinavir (Crixivan)
	induced
	Investigational New Drug (application)
INDA	Investigational New Drug Application
INDEP	independent
India	Phonetic Alphabet for I; pronounced IN-DEE-AH
INDIGO	interstitial laser ablation of the prostate
INDM	infant of nondiabetic mother
INDO	indomethacin
INDP	immunization with neurally derived peptides
INDS	initial debulking surgery
^{111}In-DTPA	indium pentetate
INE	infantile necrotizing encephalomyelopathy
INEO	internet nutrition education opportunity
IN/EV	inversion/eversion
INEX	inexperienced
INF	infant
	infarction
	infected
	infection
	inferior
	influenza virus vaccine, not otherwise specified
	information
	infused
	infusion
	intravenous nutritional fluid
INF$_a$	influenza virus, attenuated live vaccine
INFC	infected
	infection
INFD	intraepidermal nerve fiber density
INFi	influenza virus inactivated vaccine
iNFL	indolent nonfollicular lymphoma

inflam	inflammation	INPC	International Neuroblastoma
	inflammatory		Pathology Classification
Info	information	iNPH	idiopathic normal pressure
INFs	influenza viron vaccine,		hydrocephalus
	split viron	INPP5A	inositol polyphosphate
INFs-AB3	influenza virus inactivated		5-phosphatase
	vaccine, split virion, types A	inpt	inpatient
	and B, trivalent	INQ	inferior nasal quadrant
INF_w	influenza viron vaccine,	INR	integrated neuromuscular
	whole viron		release (technique)
INFXN	infection(s)		international normalized
inf urog	infusion urogram		ratio (for anticoagulant
infx	infection		monitoring)
ING	inguinal	INRG	International Neuroblastoma
✓ing	checking		Risk Group (database)
ING3	inhibitor of growth family,	INRs	international normalized ratios
	member 3 (gene/protein)	INS	idiopathic nephrotic syndrome
INH	inhalation		inspection
	isoniazid (isonicotinic acid		insurance
	hydrazide)		intranasal corticosteroids
INH/RPT-3	a 3-month regimen of once	ins and outs	inputs and outputs
	weekly rifapentine and	INSERM	National Institute of Health and
	isoniazid (for prevention of		Medical Research (France)
	latent tuberculosis infection	insitu	in the natural or normal place
	progression to active disease)		(in situ)
iNHL	indolent non-Hodgkin	in situ	in the natural or normal place
	lymphoma	InsJ	IS150 transposase A (gene)
iNHL-FL	indolent non-Hodgkin	insp	inspiration
	lymphomas- follicular		inspiratory
	lymphoma	INSS	International Neuroblastoma
inhal	inhalation		Staging System
inhib	inhibition	INST	instrumental delivery
inhl	inhalation	INSTI	intergrade strand transfer
INI	intranuclear inclusion		inhibitor
INIT	Integrative Network Inference	instr	instruct
	for Tissues		instruction
inj	injection		instrument(s)
	injury	insuff	insufficiency
INJs	injections	insulin gtt	insulin drip (infusion)
INK	injury not known	INT	intermittent needle therapy
	intranasal ketamine		internal
iNKT	invariant natural killer T (cell)	int	intake
INL	inner nuclear layer	INTERMACS	Interagency Registry for
	isolated neck-lift (procedure)		Mechanically Assisted
INM	inner nuclear membrane		Circulatory Support
	Institute of Neuroscience and	INTERP	interpretation
	Medicine (Germany)	Interv	intervention
	intraoperative neurological	Int Med	internal medicine
	monitoring	Int mon	internal monitor
INN	International Nonproprietary	intol	intolerance
	Name	intox	intoxication; intoxicated
INO	inhaled nitrous oxide	intra	a prefix meaning within, into,
	internuclear ophthalmoplegia		or during
Ino	inosine	intraop	intraoperative
INOCA	ischemia and no obstructive	intra op	during surgery
	coronary artery (disease)	intra-op	during surgery
INOP	internodal ophthalmoplegia	intro	introduction
iNOS	inducible nitric oxide synthase	int rot	internal rotation

inttrx	intermittent traction		intraocular lens
intub	intubation		intraocular lymphoma
INTVW	interview	IOLAB	a subsidiary company of Bausch
inu	inulin		& Lomb Inc., maker of
INV	inversion		ophthalmic-related products
	Invirase (saquinavir,	IOLI	intraocular lens implantation
	hard gel cap)	IOLM	intraoperative lymphatic
INVC	invasive cardiology		mapping
inver	inversion	IOLT	intraocular lens thickness
invol	involuntary	IOM	Institute of Medicine
INVOS	in vivo optical spectroscopy		intraoperative monitor(ing)
INX	infliximab (Remicade)	ioMRI	intra-operative magnetic
INZ	isoniazid		resonance imaging
IO	inferior oblique	ION	internuclear ophthalmoplegia
	initial opening		ischemic optic neuropathy
	inoperable	IONB	ileal orthotopic neobladder
	internal oblique (muscle)	IONIS	indirect optic nerve injury
	intestinal obstruction		syndrome
	intraocular pressure	IONM	intraoperative neuromonitoring
	intra-Ommaya	IONs	ischemic optic neuropathies
	intraoperative	IONTO	iontophoresis
	intraosseous	IOOA	inferior oblique overaction
I&O	intake and output	IOP	intensive outpatient program
I/O	intake and output		intraocular pressure
IOA	intact on admission		intraosseous puncture
IOB	infraorbital (nerve) block		iontophoresis
	insulin-on-board	IOPA	intramural periodical
IOC	intern on call		(radiograph)
	intraoperative cholangiogram		intraoperative periarticular
IOCG	intraoperative cholangiogram		(injection)
IOC-MC	International Olympic Committee	IOPC	intraductal oncocytic papillary
	Medical Commission		carcinoma
IOD	implant-supported overdenture	IOPD	infantile onset Pompe disease
	interorbital distance	IOPI	Iowa Oral Performance
IODM	infant of diabetic mother		Instrument (measures strength
IOE	intraoperative endoscopy		and endurance of lip, cheek,
IOF	International Osteoporosis		tongue strength, and tongue
	Foundation		muscles)
	intraocular fluid	IOPO	intracavity optical parametric
IOFB	intraocular foreign body		oscillator
IOFNA	intraoperative fine needle	IOPP	interdisciplinary outpatient pain
	aspiration		program
IOFS	intraoperative flexible	IOPs	intraocular pressures
	sigmoidoscopy	ioPTH	intraoperative parathyroid
	intraoperative frozen section		hormone (measurements/
IoFS	Impact on Family Scale		monitoring)
IOG	Improving Outcomes Guidance	IOR	ideas of reference
	inferior occipital gyrus		immature oocyte retrieval
	intraosseous ganglion		inferior oblique recession
IOGC	intraosseous ganglion cyst		inhibition of return
IOH	idiopathic orthostatic		initial orthodontic records
	hypotension	IO-RB	intraocular retinoblastoma
IO-HDRBT	intraoperative high-dose-rate	IORT	intraoperative radiation therapy
	brachytherapy	IOS	intraoperative sonography
IOI	idiopathic orbital inflammation	I&Os	intakes and outputs
	intraosseous infusion	I&O's	intakes and outputs
IOL	induction of labor	I/Os	inputs/outputs
	interosseous ligament	I/O's	intakes and outputs

IOSH	Institute for Occupational Safety and Health	IPAQ	International Physical Activity Questionnaire
IOSLL	interosseous scapholunate ligament	IPAS	International Pregnancy Advisory Services
IOT	intraocular tension		intrapancreatic accessory spleen
	involuntary outpatient treatment		
IOTA	International Ovarian Tumour Analysis	I-PASS	a framework and way of standardizing the patient hand-off process (Illness severity;
IOTEE	intraoperative transesophageal echocardiography		P: Patient summary; A: Action items; S: Situation awareness
IOTT	intensification-of-treatment trigger (criteria)		and contingency planning; S: Synthesis by receiver)
IOUS	intraocular ultrasound		
	intra-operative ultrasound	IPB	infrapopliteal bypass
IOV	initial office visit	IPBB	may have meant IPPB
IP	ice pack		(intermittent positive-pressure
	ideal protein		breathing)
	iliopsoas	IpbB	IPB-dihydrodiol dehydrogenase
	in plaster		(gene)
	incubation period	IPC	indirect pulp cavity
	individualized plan		indwelling pleural catheter
	infection preventionist		intermittent pneumatic
	Infrapatellar		compression (boots)
	infundibulopelvic		intrapartum colonization
	inpatient		intraperitoneal chemotherapy
	interpersonal therapy	IP&C	Infection Prevention and
	interphalangeal		Control
	interstitial pneumonia	IPCD	idiopathic paroxysmal cerebral
	intestinal permeability		dysrhythmia
	intraperitoneal		infantile polycystic disease
	invasive procedures	IPCK	infantile polycystic kidney
	inverted (inverting) papilloma		(disease)
	investigational product	IPCM	inferior pharyngeal constrictor
I/P	iris/pupil		muscle
IP3	inositol triphosphate	IPCR	inpatient cardiac rehabilitation
IPA	independent practice association	IPCS	International Program on
	interpleural analgesia		Chemical Safety
	invasive pulmonary aspergillosis	IPCs	insulin-producing cells
	isopropanol (isopropyl alcohol)	IPCT	intraperitoneal chemotherapy
IPAA	ileal pouch-anal anastomosis	IPCU	inpatient palliative care unit
IPAB	Independent Payment Advisory Board		intensive pediatric care unit
			intensive psychiatric care unit
IPAC	infection prevention and control	IPCV	idiopathic polypoidal choroidal
IPACK	local anesthetic infiltration		vasculopathy
	between the popliteal artery		inferior petroclival vein
	and capsule of the knee	IPD	idiopathic Parkinson disease
iPACK-HD	inhibit the progression of arterial		immediate pigment darkening
	calcification with vitamin K		inflammatory pelvic disease
	in hemodialysis patients		intermittent peritoneal dialysis
iPad	a line of tablet computers,		interpupillary distance
	developed and marketed by		interspinous process
	Apple Inc		decompression
IPAF	interstitial pneumonia with		invasive pneumococcal disease
	autoimmune features	IPDA	inferior pancreaticoduodenal
IPAH	idiopathic pulmonary arterial		artery
	hypertension	ipdA	dihydrolipoamide dehydroge-
IPAP	inspiratory positive airway		nase; see gene website www
	pressure		.ncbi.nlm.nih.gov/gene

IPE	initial psychiatric evaluation	IPMT	intraductal papillary mucinous tumor
iPEP	interfering peptide		isolated pharmacomechanical thrombolysis
iPET	interim positron emission tomography	IPN	infantile periarteritis nodosa
IPEX	immunodysregulation, polyendocrinopathy, enteropathy, X-linked (syndrome)		infected pancreatic necrosis
			intern's progress note
			interstitial pneumonia
IPF	idiopathic pulmonary fibrosis	IPNB	intraductal papillary neoplasm of the bile duct
	interstitial pulmonary fibrosis	IPNM	intraductal papillary mucinous neoplasm
IPFD	intrapartum fetal distress		
IPFP	infrapatellar fat pad	IPO	inferior posterior oblique
IPG	immobilized pH gradient		intestinal pseudo-obstruction
	impedance plethysmography	IPOC	interdisciplinary plan of care
	implantable pulse generator	IPOF	immediate postoperative fitting
	individually polymerized grass		
IPGTT	intraperitoneal glucose tolerance test	IPOI	intraprostatic ozone injection
		IPOM	intraperitoneal onlay mesh
IPH	idiopathic pulmonary hemosiderosis	IPOP	immediate postoperative prosthesis
	interphalangeal	IPOS	ideal Post-Operative Shoe (Bird and Cronin)
	intraparenchymal hemorrhage		
	intraperitoneal hemorrhage	IPP	infantile perineal protrusion
IPHC	intraperitoneal hyperthermic chemotherapy		inflatable penile prosthesis
			intrapleural pressure
IPHEP	independent progressive home exercise program		intravesical prostatic protrusion
			involvement of patient and population
IPHP	intraperitoneal hyperthermic chemotherapy		isolated pelvic perfusion
			isopropylparaben
IPI	idiopathic pituitary insufficiency	IPPA	inspection, palpation, percussion, and auscultation
	International Prognostic Index (used for risk stratification of patients with lymphomas)		
		IPPB	intermittent positive-pressure breathing
IPJ	interphalangeal joint	IP-PDT	intraperitoneal photodynamic therapy
IP joint	interphalangeal joint		
IPK	intractable plantar keratosis	IPPE	initial preventive physical examination
IPL	inner plexiform layer		
	intense pulsed light	IPPF	immediate postoperative prosthetic fitting
IP ligament	infundibulopelvic ligament		
IPL/MGX	intense pulsed light and meibomian gland expression (therapy)	iPPG	imaging photoplethysmogram
		IPPI	interruption of pregnancy for psychiatric indication
IPM	interventional pain management	IPPP	infantile perianal pyramidal protrusion
	intranodal-palisaded myofibroblastoma		
		IPPR	inpatient pulmonary rehabilitation
	intrauterine pressure monitor	iPPROM	iatrogenic preterm prelabor rupture of fetal membranes
IPMA	intraductal papillary mucinous adenoma		
IPMC	intraductal papillary mutinous carcinoma	IPPS	Inpatient Prospective Payment System (Medicare)
IPMI	inferoposterior myocardial infarct	IPPV	intermittent positive pressure ventilation
IPMM	may have meant IPMN (intraductal papillary mucinous neoplasm)	IPR	inpatient rehab
		IPRG	Interdisciplinary Pharmacogenomics Review Group (FDA)
IPMN	intraductal papillary mucinous neoplasm		
IPMs	integral projection models		

iPRO™	a continuous glucose monitoring system		IPV	inactivated poliovirus vaccine intimate partner violence intrapulmonary percussive ventilation
IPS	idiopathic pneumonia syndrome infundibular pulmonic stenosis initial prognostic score intermittent photic stimulation intraparietal sulcus		IPVC	interpolated premature ventricular contraction
iPS	induced pluripotent stem (cells)		IPW	interphalangeal width
IPSA	inverse-planning simulated annealing (algorithm)		IQ	intelligence quotient
iPSA	initial prostate-specific antigen		IQCP	Individualized Quality Control Plan (Centers for Medicare & Medicaid Services)
iPSC	induced pluripotent stem cell		IQP	intraquartile range (statistical term)
IPSCs	islet-producing stem cells			
IPSF	immediate postsurgical fitting		IQR	Inpatient Quality Reporting (program) interquartile range (statistical term)
IPSID	immunoproliferative small intestinal disease			
ipsilat	ipsilateral			
IPSP	inhibitory postsynaptic potential		IQVIA	I (IMS Holdings, Inc) and Q (Quintiles corp) merged companies, via (moving forward); an American multi-national company serving the combined industries of health information technologies and clinical research
IPSS	inferior petrosal sinus sampling International Prognostic Scoring System International Prostate Symptom Score			
IPSS-R	International Prognostic Scoring System, Revised			
IPSSWM	International Prognostic Scoring System for Waldenström macroglobulinemia		IQWiG	German Institute for Quality and Efficiency in Health Care
IPST	intraprocedural stent thrombosis		IR	immediate-release (tablets) immunoreactive inferior rectus (muscle) infrared inpatient rehabilitation insulin resistance internal reduction internal resistance internal rotation interventional radiology intraoral radiography (dental) inversion recovery (radiology)
IPSY	intermediate psychiatry			
IPT	insulin pump therapy intended primary treatment intermittent pelvic traction interpersonal psychotherapy			
IPTA	independent prior to admission International Pediatric Transplant Association intrapericardial triamcinolone acetate			
iPTA	in vitro platelet toxicity assay		I&R	insertion and removal
IPTB	indicated preterm birth		I/R	ischemia/reperfusion (injury)
IPTc	intermittent preventive treatment of malaria in children		Ir	iridium
			IRA	ileorectal anastomosis Individual Retirement Account infarct-related artery
iPTH	parathyroid hormone by radioimmunoassay			
IPTi	intermittent preventive treatment of malaria in infants		IRAAF	intraoperative radiofrequency ablation for chronic atrial fibrillation
IPTi-SP	intermittent preventive treatment of malaria in infants with sulfadoxine-pyrimethamine (Fansidar)		IRAD	International Registry of Acute Aortic Dissection
			IRA-EEA	ileorectal anastomoses with end-to-end anastomosis
IPTp	intermittent preventive treat-ment of malaria in pregnancy		irAEs	immune-related adverse events
IPTWs	inverse probability treatment weights		IRAF	immediate recurrence of atrial fibrillation
IPTX	intermittent pelvic traction		IRAP	interleukin-1 receptor antagonist protein
IPU	interim platelet unit isoproturon (a herbicide)		IRB	Institutional Review Board

IRBA	Armed Forces Biomedical Research Institute (France)	IRIS	immune reconstitution inflammatory syndrome
	Institutional Review Board approval	IRIV	immunopotentiating reconstituted influenza virosomes
IRBBB	incomplete right bundle branch block	IRL	infrared light inspiratory resistive loading
IRBC	immature red blood cell irradiated red blood cells	IRLS	International Restless Leg Syndrome (Study Group Rating Scale)
iRBCs	*Plasmodium falciparum*-infected red blood cells	IRLSSG	International Restless Leg Syndrome (Study Group Rating Scale)
IRBP	implantable rotary blood pump interphotoreceptor retinoid-binding protein	IRM	magnetic resonance imaging (French)
IRC	indirect radionuclide cystography	IRMA	immediate response mobile analysis (blood analysis system)
	infrared coagulation Institutional Review Committee (Board)		immunoradiometric assay intraretinal microvascular abnormalities
IRCU	intensive respiratory care unit	IRMP	intraoperative relaxed muscle positioning
IRD	immune renal disease(s)		
IRDA	intermittent rhythmic delta activity	IRMS	isotope-ratio mass spectrometry
IRDM	insulin-requiring diabetes mellitus	IRN	iterated rippled noise
		IRNR	impaired recall but normal recognition
	insulin-resistant diabetes mellitus	IRNS	intercostal repetitive nerve stimulation
IR drain	interventional radiology drain	I-RODS	Inflammatory Rasch-built Overall Disability Scale
IR-DRGs	International Refined Diagnosis Related Groups		
IRDS	idiopathic respiratory distress syndrome	IROM	internal range of motion
		IROS	ipsilateral routing of signals
	infant respiratory distress syndrome	IROX	irinotecan and oxaliplatin
IRE	internal rotation in extension	IRP	intellectual property rights
IRED	infrared emission detection	IRPD	infrared photodissociation
iReg	regular insulin	IRR	incidence rate ratio
IR/ER	internal/external rotation		infection-related resorption (dental)
IRF	impaired renal function		
	improvement in renal function		inferior rectus recession
	inpatient rehabilitation facilities		infrared radiation
	internal rotation in flexion		intrarenal reflux
	intraretinal fluid		irregular rate and rhythm
IRFE	infrared fluorescence endoscopy	IRRC	Institutional Research Review Committee
IRF-PAI	Inpatient Rehabilitation Facility Patient Assessment Instrument		
		irreg	irregular irregulary
IRGN	infection-related glomerulonephritis	IRRG	insulin release rate in response to glucose
IRGO	isocentric reciprocating gait orthosis	IRR HYDRO	irreversible hydrocolloid
		irrig	irrigation
IRH	intraretinal hemorrhage	IRRR	image-rich radiology reports
IRI	immunoreactive insulin		insulin receptor-related receptor
	irinotecan (Camptosar)	IRRs	incidence rate ratios
	ischemic reperfusion injury	IRRT	intermittent renal replacement therapy
IRIF	intraoral Kirschner wire fixation		
	ionizing radiation-induced foci	IRS	Information and Referral Society
IRIR	impaired recall and impaired recognition		insulin receptor substrate insulin-resistance syndrome

IRSB	intravenous regional sympathetic block
IRSG	Intergroup Rhabdomyosarcoma Study Group
IRT	immunoreactive trypsin
	incident response team
IRTP	individual real-time PCR (polymerase chain reaction)
IRTS	Intensive Residential Treatment Program
IRTs	initial response times
IRU	intensive rehabilitation unit
IRV	inspiratory reserve volume
	inverse ratio ventilation
IRVAN	idiopathic retinal vasculitis, aneurysms, and neuroretinitis
IRZ	intermediate risk zone
IS	iliosacral
	in situ
	incentive spirometer
	induced sputum
	infant star ventilator
	infarct size
	Information Services (Department)
	intercostal space
	inventory of systems
	ipecac syrup
	ischemic stroke
	isthmus spondylolisthesis
I2S	iduronate-2-sulfatase
I-S	Ionescu-Shiley (prosthetic heart valve)
I&S	intact and symmetrical
I's & O's	inputs and outputs
	intake and output
I/S	instruct/supervise
ISA	ileosigmoid anastomosis
	Incest Survivors Anonymous
	intrinsic sympathomimetic activity
	isavuconazonium (Cresemba)
ISAAC	International Study of Asthma and Allergies in Childhood (questionnaire; protocol)
ISAC	Immuno Solid-phase Allergen Chip
ISADH	inappropriate secretion of antidiuretic hormone
ISAM	infant of subtance abusing mother
Is and Os	inputs and outputs
I's and O's	inputs and outputs
	intake and output
ISAT	International Subarachnoid Aneurysm Trial
ISB	inappropriate sexual behaviors
	incentive spirometry breathing
	interscalene block

	interscalene (brachial plexus) block
	isosulfan blue
ISBN	International Standard Book Number
ISBP	Interscalene brachial plexus
ISBPB	interscalene brachial plexus block
ISBT	International Society of Blood Transfusion
ISC	carcinoma *in situ* (also CIS)
	indwelling subclavian catheter
	infant servo-control
	infant skin control
	intermittent self-catheterization
	intermittent straight catheterization
	isolette servo-control
ISCC	invasive squamous cell carcinoma
	invasive squamous cervical carcinoma
ISCD	International Society for Clinical Densitometry
ISCEV	International Society for Clinical Electrophysiology of Vision (guidelines)
ISCH	idiopathic spinal cord herniation
ISCM	intramedullary spinal cord metastases
I/SCN	urinary iodine/thiocyanate ratio
ISCO	International Standard Classification of Occupations
ISCOM	immunostimulating complex
ISCP	infection surveillance and control program
ISCs	irreversible sickle cells
ISCU	infant special care unit
ISD	inhibited sexual desire
	initial sleep disturbance
	intrinsic (urethral) sphincter deficiency
	isosorbide dinitrate (Isordil)
ISDA	item-specific deficit approach
IsdA	iron-regulated surface determinant A (a Staphylococcus aureus surface protein)
iSDHs	isolated subdural hematomas
ISDN	isosorbide dinitrate (Isordil)
ISE	Integrated Safety Summary
	internal scalp electrode
	ion-sensitive electrode
ISEL	*in situ* end labeling
ISF	Insulin Sensitivity Factor
	interstitial fluid
ISFET	ion-selective field effect transistor
ISG	immune serum globulin (immune globulin)

ISH	isolated systolic hypertension	IS/OS	inner and outer segment
IsHD	ischemic heart disease	Is&Os	inputs and outputs
ISHH	*in situ* hybridization histochemistry	I's/O's	inputs and outputs
		ISOs	isoenzymes
ISHLT	International Society for Heart and Lung Transplantation	ISP	Individual Service Plan
			inferior spermatic plexus
ISHT	isolated systolic hypertension		interspace
ISI	Insomnia Severity Index		intracellular sigma peptide
	Insulin Sensitivity Index	ISPP	individualized sleep promotion plan
	International Sensitivity Index		
ISIA	International Serum Industry Association	ISQ	as before; continue on (*in status quo*)
ISIF	*in situ* immunofluorescence	ISQ	implant stability quotient
ISJ	incudostapedial joint		*In Status Quo* (no change)
ISK	inflamed seborrheic keratosis	ISQua	International Society for Quality in Health Care
	isokinetic		
ISKD	intramedullary skeletal kinetic distractor	ISR	*in situ* reconstruction
			injection site reaction
ISL	isolated stork-lift (procedure)		in-stent restenosis
ISLD	in-stent luminal diameter		integrated secretory response
ISLM	ipsilateral supraclavicular lymph node metastasis	ISRCTN	International Standard Randomized Controlled Trial Number
ISLs	interspinous ligaments		
ISM	illness self-management	IS-RRCEA	*in situ* ring-stripping retrograde carotid endarterectomy
	image scanning microscopy		
	in situ microparticles	ISRs	injection site reactions
	Isthmian	ISRT	Interval Shuttle-Running Test
ISMA	infantile spinal muscular atrophy		involved site radiotherapy
		IS10S	10% invert sugar in 0.9% sodium chloride (saline) injection
ISMN	isosorbide mononitrate		
ISMO®	isosorbide mononitrate		
ISMP	Institute for Safe Medication Practices	ISS	idiopathic short stature
			Individual Self-Rating Scale
ISNA	iron-sufficient, not anemic		Injury Severity Score
ISNCSCI	International Standards for Neurological Classification of Spinal Cord Injury (developed by the American Spinal Injury Association)		Inova Health System Sedation Scale
			insulin sliding scale
			Integrated Summary of Safety
			International Staging System (for multiple myeloma)
ISO	International Organization for Standardization		irritable stomach syndrome
	isocenter		ischial spine sign
	isodose	ISSc	limited systemic sclerosis
	isoenzyme	ISSHL	idiopathic sudden sensorineural hearing loss
	isoflurane (Forane)		
	isolette	ISSI-2	Insulin Secretion-Sensitivity Index-2
	isoproterenol		
I/S/O	input stage output (regulation of diuretic dosing based on 24-hour intake and output)	ISSM	International Society for Sexual Medicine
		ISSP	Infant Support Services Program
ISOE	isoetharine	ISSSTE	The Institute of Social Security and Services for Civil Servants (*Instituto de seguridad y Servicios Sociales de los Trabajadores del Estado*) (Mexico)
ISOF	isoflurane (Forane)		
ISOK	isokinetic		
isol	isolution		
ISOLS	International Society of Limb Salvage (classifuction)		
ISOM	inner stripe of the outer medulla	ISSVD	International Society for the Study of Vulvovaginal Disease
	isometric		

ISSVG	may have meant ISSVD (International Society for the Study of Vulvovaginal Disease)
ISSWM	International (Prognostic) Scoring System for Waldenström macroglobulinemia
IST	immunosuppressive therapy
	inappropriate sinus tachycardia
	injection sclerotherapy
	insulin sensitivity test
	insulin shock therapy
ISTAT	mortality and census data base of the Italian Central Institute of Statistics
iSTAT®	a handheld and test cartridge blood analysis system which can test for cardiac markers, blood gases, chemistries and electrolytes, lactate, coagulation, and hematology
iStent®	trabecular microbypass stent
ISTH	International Society on Thrombosis and Hemostasis (guidelines)
ISTM	instrument-assisted soft-tissue mobilization
I-STOP PMP	Internet System for Tracking Over-Prescribing (act); Prescription Monitoring Program
iSTS	independent sit-to-stand
ISU	intermediate surgical unit
ISUIA	International Study of Unruptured Intracranial Aneurysms
ISUOG	International Society of Ultrasound in Obstetrics and Gynaecology (guidelines)
ISV	internal spermatic vein
	intersegmental vessel(s)
	intrasubject variability
IS10W	10% invert sugar injection (in water)
ISW	interstitial water
ISWI	incisional surgical wound infection
IT	iliotibial
	incentive therapy
	individual therapy
	inferior turbinate
	inferior-temporal
	information technology
	inspiratory time
	intensive therapy
	intermittent traction
	interpreted
	intertrochanteric
	intertuberous

	intrathecal, intra-tracheal, intra-tumor, intra-tympanic, and inhalation therapy (This is a DANGEROUS abbreviation that should NOT be used to apply to routes of administration. It appears on the medabbrev.com and other Do Not Use Lists.) Spell out intrathecal, intra-tracheal, intra-tumor, intra-tympanic, and inhalation therapy
	immature-to-total (as in immature-to-total neutrophil ratio)
I/T	intensity/time
	see IT
ITA	individual treatment assessment
	inferior temporal artery
	intensive treatment area
	itasetron
ITAC	intestinal-type adenocarcinoma
ITADE	ipsilateral, thoracoabdominal horizontal, dermofat (flap)
ITAG	internal thoracic artery graft
ITAL	intrathoracic artificial lung
ITB	iliotibial band
	initial tumor burden
	intrathecal baclofen
IT band	iliotibial band
ITBC	intraluminal typical bronchial carcinoid
ITBFS	iliotibial band friction syndrome
ITBP	intrathecal baclofen pump
ITBR	inverted-T breast reduction
ITBS	iliotibial band syndrome
	Iowa Tests of Basic Skills
ITBW	inability to bear weight
ITC	Incontinence Treatment Center
	indirect treatment comparison
	inferior temporal cortex
	in-the-canal (hearing aid)
	isothermal titration calorimetry
ITCd	intercalated cell mass, dorsal subregion
ITCG	inferior turbinate composite graft
IT chemo	intrathecal chemotherapy (this a dangerous abbreviation as IT can be mistaken for IV [intravenous]; spell out intrathecal)
ITCP	idiopathic thrombocytopenic purpura
ITCs	isolated tumor cells
ITCU	intensive thoracic cardiovascular unit
ITCv	intercalated cell mass, ventral subregion

ITCZ	itraconazole (Sporanox)	ITQ	inferior temporal quadrant
ITD	impedence threshold device	ITR	isotretinoin (Accutane)
ITDD	intrathecal drug delivery	ITRA	itraconazole (Sporanox)
ITDS	interval debulking surgery	IT ratio	immature-to-total neutrophil ratio
ITE	insufficient therapeutic effect	ITS	intelligent testing strategies
	in-the-ear (hearing aid)		internal transcribed spacer
ITF	inpatient treatment facility		intratympanic steroids
ITFF	intertrochanteric femoral		iontophoretic transdermal system
	fracture		isometric trunk stabilization
ITFS	iliotibial tract friction syndrome	ITSA	an evaluation methodology
ITGCN	intratubular germ cell neoplasia		in which a single treatment
ITGV	intrathoracic gas volume		unit's outcome is studied over
ITH	inferior turbinate hypertrophy		time and the intervention
	intratumoral hemorrhage		is expected to "interrupt"
I/Time	inspiratory time		the level and/or trend of the
IT INJs	intrathecal injections (this is a		outcome, subsequent to its
	dangerous abbreviation as		introduction
	it also stand for intrathecal,	ITSCU	infant-toddler special care unit
	intra-tracheal, intra-tumor, or	ITST	intertrochanteric-subtrochanteric
	intra-tympanic injection	ITT	identical twins (raised) together
ITIS	infrared thermal image scanner		incremental treadmill test
it is	intertrial intervals		insulin tolerance test
ITL	immediate threat to life		intention-to-treat (analysis)
ITM	Institute of Tropical Medicine	iTTP	idiopathic thrombotic
	(Antwerp, Belgium)		thrombocytopenic purpura
ITMNs	insecticide-treated mosquito	IT-tPA	intrathecal tissue plasminogen
	nets		activator
IT MTX	intrathecal methotrexate (it is	ITU	infant-toddler unit
	dangerous to abbreviate this		intensive therapy unit
	critical procedure with an		intensive treatment unit
	expression which could be	ITV	Insertion torque value
	misinterpreted)	ITVAD	indwelling transcutaneous
IT-MTX	intrathecal methotrexate (it is		vascular access device
	dangerous to abbreviate this	ITX	immunotoxin(s)
	critical procedure with an	ITx	intestinal transplant
	expression which could be	Itx	intestinal transplantation
	misinterpreted)	ITZ	itraconazole (Sporanox)
ITN	idiopathic trigeminal neuralgia	IU	inpatient unit
	irinotecan (Camptosar)		internal urethrotomy
ITNs	insecticide-treated nets		international unit (This is a
	(bednets)		DANGEROUS abbreviation
ITOC	intratracheal oxygen catheter		that should NOT be used. It
ITOP	intentional termination of		appears on the medabbrev.
	pregnancy		com and other Do Not Use
ITOU	intensive therapy observation unit		Lists, as it has been read
ITP	idiopathic thrombocytopenic		as intravenous (IV) or the I
	purpura		is read as a one (6 IU read
	immune thrombocytopenia		as 61 units); use "units" or
	immune thrombocytopenia		"International Units.")
	purpura	IUAI	insertive unprotected anal
	interim treatment plan		intercourse
	intrathecal (pain) pump		intrauterine artificial
	Isotachophoresis		insemination
ITPA	Illinois Test of Psycholinguistic	IUBT	intrauterine blood transfusion
	Ability	IUC	intrauterine catheter
ITPN	intraductal tubulopapillary	IUCD	intrauterine contraceptive device
	neoplasm (of the pancreas)	IUCP	my have meant IUPC
IT pump	intrathecal pump		(intrauterine pressure catheter)

IUD	intrauterine death	IVA	in vitro activation
	intrauterine device		Intervir-A
IUDE	intrauterine drug exposure		invasive adenocarcinomas
IUDF	intrauterine fetal death	IV ABx	intravenous antibiotics
IUDR	idoxuridine (Herplex)	IVAC	ifosfamide, etoposide (VePesid),
IUE	in utero electroporation		and cytarabine (AraC)
IUFB	intrauterine foreign body		incisional vacuum-assisted
IUFD	intrauterine fetal death (demise)		closure
	intrauterine fetal distress	iVAC	infection-related ventilator-
IUFT	intrauterine fetal transfusion		associated complication
IUG	intrauterine gestation	IVAD	implantable vascular access
IUGR	intrauterine growth retardation		device
	(restriction)		implantable venous access
IUH	unilateral hydrocephalus		device
IUI	intrauterine insemination	IVAE	*in vitro* acrosome exocytosis
IUI/COH	intrauterine insemination	IVAP	implantable venous access port
	with controlled ovarian	iVAPS	intelligent volume-assured
	hyperstimulation		pressure support
IU/L	international units per liter	IVAS	interactive visual analog scale
IULN	institutional upper limit of		intravenous analgesia and
	normal		sedation
IU/mL	international units per milliliter	IVAs	idiopathic ventricular
IUMR	intrauterine myelomeningocele		arrhythmias
	repair	IVaS	intravascular stenting
IUO	inflammation of unknown	iVAS	intravascular ventricular assist
	origin		system
IUP	intrauterine pregnancy	IVAT	intravenous antibiotic therapy
IUPAC	International Union of Pure	IVBAT	intravascular bronchoalveolar
	and Applied Chemistry		tumor
	(nomenclature)	IVBPs	intravenous bisphosphonates
IUPAT	intrauterine pregnancy at term	IVC	inferior vena cava
IUPB	infected units per billion		inspiratory vital capacity
IUPC	intrauterine pressure catheter		intravenous chemotherapy
IUPD	intrauterine pregnancy delivered		intravenous cholangiogram
IUP,TBCS	intrauterine pregnancy, term		intraventricular catheter
	birth, cesarean section		intraventricular conduction
IUP,TBLC	intrauterine pregnancy, term	IVCB	(umbilical) cord blood injected
	birth, living child		intravenously
IUR	intrauterine retardation	IVCCM	in-vivo corneal confocal
IURG	intrauterine growth retardation		microscopy
	(appears in some non-English	IVCD	intraventricular conduction delay
	languages)	IVCF	inferior vena cava filter
IUS	intrauterine system	IVC filter	inferior vena cava filter
IUSS	immediate-use steam	IVCI	intravenous continuous infusion
	sterilization	IVCON	intravenous contrast (radiology)
IUT	intersection-union test	IVCP	inferior vena cava pressure
	intrauterine transfusion	IVCS	intravenous conscious sedation
IUTD	immunizations up to date	IVCV	inferior venacavography
IUTP	intrauterine term pregnancy	IVD	*in vitro* diagnostic
IUTs	intrauterine transfusions		instrumental vaginal delivery
IUV	in utero ventilation		intervertebral disk
IV	four		intravenous drip
	interview		ischemic vascular dementia
	intravenous	IVDA	intravenous drug abuse
	invasive	IVDK	Information Network of
	inversion		Departments of Dermatology
	symbol for class 4 controlled		(Göttingen University)
	substances		(http://www.ivdk.org)

IVDMIAs	*in vitro* diagnostic multivariate index assays	IVIF	in vivo fertilization
IVDSA	intravenous digital subtraction angiography	IVIG	intravenous immunoglobulin
		IVIgG	intravenous immunoglobulin G
IVDU	intravenous drug user	IVIS	in vivo imaging system
IVE	ifosfamide?, etoposide (VP-16), and epirubicin regimen	IVIS®	an imaging system designed to improve quantitative outcomes of in vivo imaging
	immersive visualization environment	IVJC	intervertebral joint complex
	in vivo expression	IVK	intravitreal injection of triamcinolone acetonide (Kenalog) (also IVTA)
	Influenza vaccine effectiveness		
IVED	interventricular ejection delay	IVL	intravascular lymphomatosis
	intraventricular electrical dyssynchrony		intravenous lock
		IVLBCL	intravascular large B-cell lymphoma
IVELT	intravaginal ejaculation latency time		
		IVLBW	infant of very low birth weight (less than 1,500 g)
IVET	*in vivo* expression technology		
IVF	*in vitro* fertilization	IVLE	intravenous lipid emulsions
	intervertebral foramina	IVM	*in vitro* maturation
	intravenous fluid(s)		intravenous vasoactive medication
	intraventricular fibrinolysis		ivermectin
IVFA	intravenous fluorescein angiography	IVMF	Institute for Veterans and Military Families
IVFBT	*in vitro* fertilization boosted tree (model)	IVMP	intravenously administered methylprednisolone
IVFD	*in vitro* fertilization with donor spermatozoa	IVNA	in vivo neutron activation (analysis to measure several total body elements such as calcium, sodium, and phosphorus)
IVFE	intravenous fat emulsion (preferred abbreviation is ILE [injectable lipid emulsion] as IVFE could be confused with IVFe [intravenous iron])		
		iVNA	integrated vagus nerve activity
		IVNC	isolated (left) ventricular noncompaction
IVFe	intravenous iron		isolated ventricular noncompaction
IVF-ET	*in vitro* fertilization-embryo transfer		
		IVNs	intravenous narcotics
IV fluids	intravenous fluids	IVO	intraoral vertical osteotomy
IVFs	*in vitro* fertilizations	IVOR	as in the minimally invasive Ivor Lewis esophagectomy (a transhiatal approach by laparotomy, a two incision surgery utilizing both laparotomy and right thoracotomy)
	intravenous fluids		
IVFT	intravenous fetal transfusion		
IVGG	intravenous gamma globulin		
IVGR	may have meant IUGR (intrauterine growth retardation)		
		IVOX	intravascular oxygenator (oxygenation)
IVGTT	intravenous glucose tolerance test		
IVH	intravenous hyperalimentation	IVP	intravenous push (this is a dangerous meaning as it is read as intravenous pyelogram)
	intraventricular hemorrhage		
IVHV	immunoglobulin heavy chain variable domain (gene)		intravenous pyelogram
IVI	intravitreal injection	IVPB	intravenous piggyback
IVID	intravenous iron dextran (INFeD; DexFerrum)	IVPF	isovolume pressure flow
		IVPM	in vitro pharmacodynamic model
iViewGT	an amorphous silicon electronic portal imaging device used to validate for pre-treatment verification of clinical intensity modulated radiation therapy treatment plans (Elekta Instrument AB Stockholm)	IVPP	Institute of Vertebrate Paleontology and Paleoanthropology (Chinese Academy of Sciences)
			intravesical prostatic protrusions, (so-called median lobes)

IVPT	in vitro permeation test (used to characterize the bioavailability of compounds applied on the skin)
IVPU	intravenous push
IV push	medication given directly intravenously (IV) into a vein, intravenous tubing (set), or catheter using a needle and syringe (warning: potassium chloride should NOT be given IV push; recheck IV push orders for other drugs to make sure they are correct)
IVR	idioventricular rhythm
	in vivo recovery (a calculated measure of pharmacokinetics; it is the percentage of therapeutic polypeptide or protein given via intravenous injection detectable in the circulation a short time after administration)
	interactive voice-response (system)
	intravaginal ring
	intravenous retrograde
	intravenous rider (this is a dangerous abbreviation as it has been read as IVP-intravenous push)
	isovolumic relaxation (time)
IVRA	intravenous regional anesthesia
IVRAP	intravenous retrograde access port
IVRG	intravenous retrograde
IV-RNV	intravenous radionuclide venography
IVRO	intraoral vertical ramus osteotomy
IVRS	interactive voice response system
IVRT	isovolumic relation time
IVS	intraventricular septum
	irritable voiding syndrome
IV's	four's
	intravenous medications
IvsB	see gene website, www.ncbi.nlm.nih.gov/gene
IVSD	intraventricular septal defect
IVSE	interventricular septal excursion
IVSM	interventricular septal mass
	intravenous SoluMedrol (methylprednisolone)
	intravulvosubmucosally (Veterinary)
IVSO	intraoral vertical segmental osteotomy
IVSP	in vitro synthesized protein
IVSS	intravenous Soluset®

IVST	interventricular septum thickness
IVT	iintraventricular
	intravenous thrombolysis
	intravenous transfusion
IVTA	intravitreal injection of triamcinolone acetonide
IV-tPA	intravenous tissue plasminogen activator (Alteplase Recombinant Inj [Activase])
IVTTT	intravenous tolbutamide tolerance test
IVU	interventional unit
	intravenous urography (urogram)
IVUC	intravenous ultrasound catheter
IVUD	may have meant IVDU (intravenous drug user)
IVUS	intravascular ultrasound
IVVD	intravenous volume depletion
IVVMI	may have meant IWMI (inferior wall myocardial infarct)
IW	inferior wall
	inspiratory wheeze
IWB	Index of Well-Being
	internalized weight bias
IWB-EA	immediate weight-bearing and early ambulation
IWCLL	International Workshop on Chronic Lymphocytic Leukemia (guidelines/criteria)
IWD	individual with a disability
IWG	International Working Group (diagnostic criteria)
IWG-MRT	International Working Group for Myelofibrosis Research and Treatment
IWI	inferior wall infarction
IWL	insensible water loss
	involuntary weight loss
IWM	invasive wound mucormycosis
IWMDs	inverse-variance weighted mean differences
IWMI	inferior wall myocardial infarct
IWML	idiopathic white matter lesion
iWOB	imposed work of breathing
IWP	Indo-West Pacific (region)
	Inhibitor(s) of Wnt production (Wnt is a linguistic blend of words int and Wg and stands for "Wingless-related integration site" Wnt pathway's clinical importance has been demonstrated by mutations that lead to various diseases, including breast and prostate cancer, glioblastoma, type II diabetes and others)
	isolated whey protein

IWRS	Interactive Web Response System (a computer systems which randomizes)
IWS	Index of Work Satisfaction
IW STEM	inferior wall ST-segment elevation myocardial infarction
IWT	ice-water test
	impacted wisdom teeth
ix	nine
Ixa	ixabepilone
IXT	intermittent exotropia
IY	Incredible Years® (a parenting program has been disseminated across the United Kingdom to prevent child disruptive behavioral problems)
	Iyengar yoga
IZ	immunizations
	infarct zone
	innervation zone
IZS	intravenous zinc supplementation
IZs	innervations zones

J

J	Jaeger measure of near vision with 20/20 about equal to J1
	jejunostomy
	Jewish
	joint
	joule
J	joules
	juice
	Juliett (Phonetic Alphabet for J; pronounced JEW-LEE-ETT)
J 1-16	Jaeger near acuity notation (1 to 16 scale)
JA	Jaccoud arthropathy
	Japanese American(s)
	joint aspiration
	juvenile arthritis
JAAD	Journal of the American Academy of Dermatology
JACCOL	Jaundice, Anemia, Clubbing, Cyanosis, Oedema (edema) and lymphadenopathy
JACHO	may have meant JCAHO (Joint Commission on Accreditation of Healthcare Organizations [this name has been changed to JC, Joint Commission])
Jack	jacknife position
JACO	see JCAHO
JADAS	juvenile arthritis disease activity score
JADER	Japanese Adverse Drug Event Report
JAE	juvenile absence epilepsy
JAFAR	Juvenile Arthritis Functional Assessment Report
JAHCO	may have meant JCAHO (Joint Commission on Accreditation of Healthcare Organizations [this name has been changed to JC, Joint Commission])
JAK	janus activated kinase
JAK2	Janus kinase 2; see gene website www.ncbi.nlm.nih.gov/gene
JAK2V617F	a mutation of the Janus kinase 2 (JAK2) gene/protein seen in patients with myeloprolifera-tive neoplasms
JAMA	*Journal of the American Medical Association*
JAMG	juvenile autoimmune myasthenia gravis
JAN	Japanese Accepted Name
Jan	January
JAR	junior assistant resident

JARAN	junior assistant resident admission note	JDMS	juvenile dermatomyositis
JAS	Japan Atherosclerosis Society (guideline)	JE	Japanese encephalitis
	juvenile-onset ankylosing spondylitis	JEB	junctional epidermolysis bullosa junctional escape beat
JATD	Jeune asphyxiating thoracic dystrophy	JE-CV	Japanese encephalitis chimeric virus vaccine (Imojev, Sanofi Pasteur, France)
JBD	jugular bulb diverticulum Juvenile bipolar disorder	JEJ	jejunum
JBE	Japanese B encephalitis	JEN	Japanese encephalitis vaccine
JBH	just being honest (slang)	JER	junctional escape rhythm
JBS	Johanson Blizzard syndrome	JET	jejunal extension tube junctional ectopic tachycardia
JC	John Cunningham (virus) Joint Commission (www.jointcommission.org) junior clinicians (medical students)	Je T'aime	French: I Love You (slang)
		JETT	Junctional Emergency Treatment Tool
		JEV	Japanese encephalitis virus
jc	juice	JE-VC	Inactivated, Vero cell culture-derived Japanese encephalitis vaccine (Ixiaro)
JCA	juvenile chronic arthritis		
JCAHO	Joint Commission on Accreditation of Health-care Organizations (this has been changed to JC, Joint Commission)	JF	joint fluid
		JFK	JFK (John F. Kennedy, Johnson Rehabilitation Institute, Center for Head Injuries, 2048 Oak Tree Rd, Edison, NJ 08820) modified Coma Recovery Scale (CRS-R)
JCC	Jackson cross cylinder (astigmatism test)		
jce	juice	JFS	Jewish Family Service
JCI	Joint Commission International	JFT	jugular foramen tumor
J/cm^2	joules per square centimeter	JGCT	juvenile granulosa cell tumor
JCO	*Journal of Clinical Oncology* Juvenile Court Order	JGI	jejunogastric intussusception
		JH	joint hypermobility
JCOG	Japanese Clinical Oncology Group	JHEQ	Japanese Orthopaedic Association Hip Disease Evaluation Questionnaire
JCP	juvenile cobalamin deficiency	JHH	Johns Hopkins Hospital Journal of Human Hypertension
JCQ	Job Content Questionnaire		
JCR	Joint Commission Resources	JHHLM	Johns Hopkins Highest Level of Mobility (a standardized scale of mobility used in hospitals to communicate a patient's mobility status across providers)
JCT	junction		
JCV	Jamestown Canyon virus John Cunningham virus		
JC Virus	Jamestown Canyon virus		
JD	Doctor of Jurisprudence (a law degree) jaundice	JHR	Jarisch-Herxheimer reaction
		JHS	joint hypermobility syndrome
		JI	jejunoileal
JDA	Japan Dietetic Association Japanese Dermatological Association	JIA	juvenile idiopathic arthritis
		JIB	jejunoileal bypass
		JIC	just in case
JDC	Job Demand-Control juvenile drug courts	JIP	Journal of Infection Prevention
		JIP1	JNK (c-Jun N-terminal kinase)-interacting protein-1
JDCS	Job Demand-Control-Support		
JDD	Journal of Drugs in Dermatology	JIS	juvenile idiopathic scoliosis
JDG	jugulodigastric	JIT	just-in-time
JDGMNT	judgment	JITAI	Just-in-Time Adaptive Intervention(an emerg-ing technology-driven behavior-change intervention type and capitalize on data that is collected via mobile
JDGMT	judgment		
JDLR	Just doesn't look right (something is wrong, but no diagnosis has been made yet) (slang)		
JDM	juvenile diabetes mellitus		

J

	sensing technology (e.g., smartphones) to trigger appropriate support in real-life)	JODM	juvenile-onset diabetes mellitus
		JOF	juvenile ossifying fibroma
JJ	jaw jerk	JOLs	judgments of learning
	joint jack	JOMAC	judgment, orientation, memory, abstraction, and calculation
J & J	Johnson & Johnson Health Care Systems, Inc.	JOMACI	judgment, orientation, memory, abstraction, and calculation intact
JJ stent	double J stent		
JK	Kidd; an International Society of Blood Transfusion (ISBT) blood group	JOR	jaw-opening reflex
		JORRP	juvenile-onset recurrent respiratory papillomatosis
Jka	a Kidd blood group	JP	Jackson-Pratt (drain)
Jkb	a Kidd blood group		Jobst pump
JL4	Judkins Left 4-curve size (catheter)		joint protection
		JPA	joint position awareness
JLD	just like dad; an explanation for a child's unusual facial features (slang)		juvenile pilocytic astrocytoma
		JPB	junctional premature beats
		JP BS	Jackson-Pratt to bulb suction
JLIS	Jessner lymphocytic infiltration of the skin	JPC	junctional premature contraction
		JP drain	Jackson-Pratt drain
JLO	Judgement of Line Orientation (test)	JPEG	Joint Photographic Experts Group (image compression technology)
JLP	juvenile laryngeal papillomatosis		
JLT	joint line tenderness	J PEG	jejunal tube inserted via percutaneous endoscopic gastrostomy
JLV	Joint Legacy Viewer (Veterans Health Administration)		
JM	joint mobilization	JPOF	juvenile psammomatoid ossifying fibroma
JM-9	iproplatin		
JMC	Jansen metaphyseal chondrodysplasia	J Pouch	ileo-anal anastomosis-reservoir
		J-Pouch	ileo-anal anastomosis-reservoir
JMCs	junctional membrane complexes	JPS	joint position sense
JME	juvenile myoclonic epilepsy		juvenile polyposis syndrome
JMG	juvenile myasthenia gravis	JPT	Japanese from Tokyo (populations included in HapMap - see HapMap) Japanese in Tokyo, Japan (from HapMap [A catalog of common genetic variants that occur in human beings])
JMH	John Milton Hagen; an International Society of Blood Transfusion (ISBT) blood group		
JMI	Jones Medical Inc.		
JMML	juvenile myelomonocytic leukemia		
		JPV	J paramyxovirus
JMS	junior medical student		juvenile pemphigus vulgaris
JNA	juvenile nasopharyngeal angiofibroma	JQ1	a selective inhibitor against the transcriptional regulators, bromodomain and extra-terminal family of proteins (named after Jun Qi who synthesized the compound)
JNB	jaundice of newborn		
JNCL	juvenile-onset neuronal ceroid lipofuscinosis		
JND	just noticeable difference		
JNR	Just not right (something is wrong but no diagnosis has been made) (slang)	JQL	JIRA (a truncation of Gojira, the Japanese name for Godzilla, [Atlassian Software Company]) Query Language
JNT	joint		
JNVD	jugular neck vein distention	JQPS	The Joint Commission Journal on Quality and Patient Safety
Jo1	histidyl tRNA (transfer ribonucleic acid) synthetase		
JOAG	juvenile-onset open-angle glaucoma	JR	JR; an International Society of Blood Transfusion (ISBT) blood group
JOAS	Japanese Orthopedic Association Score		junctional rhythm

J

JR4	Judkins Right 4-curve size (catheter)		JWC	Jinghua Weikang Capsule (for the treatment of chronic gastritis)
JRA	juvenile rheumatoid arthritis			Journal of Wound Care
JRAAA	juxtarenal abdominal aortic aneurysm		JWH	one of the John W. Huffman (JWH) research group at Clemson University's 450 synthesized cannabi- noids, such as JWH-018
JRAN	junior resident admission note			
Jr BF	junior baby food			
JRC	joint replacement center		JWH-018	one of the John W. Huffman (JWH) research group at Clemson University's 450 synthesized cannabinoids
JRP	juvenile recurrent parotitis			
JRS	Jankovic Rating Scale joint repositioning sense			
JS	Joubert syndrome		Jx	joint
JSF	Japanese spotted fever		JXG	juvenile xanthogranuloma
JSN	joint space narrowing		JXN	junction junctional
JSPE	Jefferson Scale of Physician Empathy			
JSRV	jaagsiekte sheep retrovirus			
J stent	see DJ stent			
JSW	joint space width			
JT	jejunostomy tube joint junctional tachycardia			
JTC	jumping to conclusions			
JTF	jejunostomy tube feeding			
JTH	Jebsen Test of Hand (Function)			
JTJ	jaw-to-jaw (position)			
JTP	joint projection			
JTPA	Job Training Partnership Act			
JTPS	juvenile tropical pancreatitis syndrome			
JTs	jugular tubercles jumping translocations			
JTTR	Joint Theater Trauma Registry The Joint Theater Trauma Registry			
J tube	jejunostomy tube			
jug	jugular vein			
Jul	July			
Juliett	Phonetic Alphabet for J; pronounced JEW-LEE-ETT			
Jun	June			
junc	junction			
junct	junction			
JUV	juvenile			
JV	jugular vein			
JVC	jugular venous catheter			
JVD	jugular venous distention			
JVHL	Joint Venture Hospital Laboratories			
JVI	jugular-valve incompetence			
JVP	jugular venous pressure jugular venous pulsation jugular venous pulse			
JVPT	jugular venous pulse tracing			
JVR	jugular venous reflux			
JVT	jugular vein thrombosis			
JW	Jehovah's Witness			

K

K	cornea
	kelvin
	keratometry (diagnostic instrument for measuring the curvature of the anterior surface of the cornea; a tear osmolarity measurement)
	ketamine (Ketalar; Vitamin K, Special K and Super K)
	Kilo (Phonetic Alphabet K; pronounced KEY-LOH)
	kilodalton
	Kosher
	lysine
	potassium
	thousand
	vitamin K
K′	knee
K+	potassium
K_1	phytonadione (METHYTON)
K2	a variety of herbal mixtures that produce experiences similar to marijuana
K_2	menatetrenone
K_3	menadione
K_4	menadiol sodium diphosphate
510(k)	Medical Device Premarket Notification
KA	kainic acid
	kala-azar
	keratoacanthoma
	ketoacidosis
Ka	first order absorption constant in hr.$^{-1}$
KAB	knowledge, attitude, and behavior
K-ABC	Kaufman Assessment Battery for Children
KABINS	knowledge, attitude, behavior, and improvement in nutritional status
KACT	kaolin-activated clotting time
KAD	knee alignment device
KAdd	knee adduction
KAFO	knee-ankle-foot orthosis
KAH	kidney after heart (transplants)
Kaizen	Good Change (Japanese)
KAL	kidney after lung (transplants)
KAL1	Kallmann syndrome 1; see gene website, www.ncbi.nlm.nih .gov/gene
KAM	knee adduction moment

Kangaroo care	a technique practiced on newborns, usually preterm infants, where the infant is held, skin-to-skin, with an adult
KAO	keep artery open
	knee-ankle orthosis
KAP	knowledge, attitudes and practices (questionnaire)
Kappa	tenth letter of the Greek alphabet
Kappa statistic	Precision, as it pertains to agreement between observers (interobserver agreement; intended to give a quantitative measure of the magnitude of agreement between observers)
KAS	Katz Adjustment Scale
KASH	knowledge, abilities, skills, and habits
KASPER	Kentucky All Schedule Prescription Electronic Reporting (law)
kat	katal
K-A units	King-Armstrong units
KB	ketone bodies
	knee-bearing
Kb	kilobase (genetics; 1,000 base pairs)
KBD	Kashin-Beck disease
KBG	a rare genetic disease (syndrome) whose name was derived from the initials of the affected patients in the original report. Characterized by a distinct facial phenotype, macrodontia, short stature, developmental delay, and/or mental retardation
KBM	kindness-based meditation
kBq	kilobecquerel
kBq/kg	kilobecquerel per kilogram
KC	kangaroo care
	keratinocyte carcinoma
	keratoconjunctivitis
	keratoconus
	kinship care
	knees-to-chest
	Korean conflict
K/C	potassium-creatinine ratio
kcal	kilocalorie
kcal/dL	kilocalories per deciliter (100 mL)
kcal/kg/day	kilocalories per kilogram of body weight per day (also known KKD)
kcal/oz	kilocalories per ounce (30 mL)
kcals	kilocalories

KCCQ	Kansas City Cardiomyopathy Questionnaire	KDR	kinase domain receptor; see gene website www.ncbi.nlm.nih.gov/gene
KCCT	kaolin cephalin clotting time		
KChIPs	potassium channel-interacting proteins	KDRI	Kidney Donor Risk Index (to evaluate the donor quality of deceased donor kidneys)
kCi	kilocurie		
KCl	potassium chloride	KDT	ketogenic dietary therapies
KCN	keratoconus		Korotkoff (sound) delay time
Kcnj10	potassium inwardly-rectifying channel, subfamily J, member 10 (gene; also known as Kir4.1)	KDU	Kidney Dialysis Unit
		K Dur	see K-Dur (potassium chloride tablets)
		K-Dur	A brand of potassium chloride tablets
KCO	carbon monoxide diffusion constant	KdV	Korteweg-de Vries (equation)
		KE	first order elimination rate constant in hr.$^{-1}$
	potassium channel opener		
KCOT	keratocystic odontogenic tumor	KED	Kendrick extrication device
KCP	Kaposi sarcoma-associated herpesvirus-complement (KSHV) control protein Kielin/chordin-like protein; see gene website www.ncbi.nlm.nih.gov/gene		kinetic energy discrimination
		KEEP	Kidney Early Evaluation Program (National Kidney Foundation)
		KEL	Kell; an International Society of Blood Transfusion (ISBT) blood group
KCS	keratoconjunctivitis sicca		
KCZ	ketoconazole (Nizoral)	k_{el}	elimination rate constant
KD	Kawasaki disease	KELS	Kohlman Evaluation of Living Skills
	Keto Diastix®		
	ketogenic diet	KEO	Kuromoji (Lindera umbellata) essential oil
	kidney donors		
	knee disarticulation	keo	effect-compartment equilibration rate-constant
	knowledge deficit		
kd	kilodalton	Kep	redistribution rate constant (percentage decline in activity per minute)
K-D	King-Devick Test®		
KDA	known drug allergies		
kDa	kiloDalton		
KDB	Kahook Dual Blade	KESS	Knowles-Eccersley-Scott-Symptom Questionnaire (constipation scores)
	ketamine-dexmedetomidine-butorphanol (veterinary sedation)		
		KET	ketamine (Ketalar)
	kidney disease burden		ketoconazole (Nizoral)
KDC	brand name of infant warmer		ketones
KDIGO	Kidney Disease: Improving Global Outcomes (an independent organization with the mission to improve care and outcomes of patients with kidney disease worldwide through the development and coordination of clinical practice guidelines)	KETO	ketoconazole (Nizoral)
		17 Keto	17 ketosteroids
		keV	kilo-electron volts
		KEVD	Krupin eye valve with disc
		KF	kidney function
		KFA	kinetic fibrinogen assay
		KFAB	kidney-fixing antibodies
		KFAO	knee-foot-ankle orthosis
KDOQI	Kidney Disease Outcome Quality Initiative	KFD	Kikuchi-Fujimoto disease
			Kyasanur Forrest disease
		KFE	knee flexion and extension
KDPI	Kidney Donor Profile Index (for the assessment of deceased donor kidney quality)	KF-NAP	Kessler Foundation Neglect Assessment Process
		KFO	kieferorthopädie (orthodontic)
KDQ	Kidney Disease Questionnaire	KFR	Kayser-Fleischer ring
KDQOL	Kidney Disease Quality of Life	KFS	Klippel-Feil syndrome
KDQOL-SF	Kidney Disease Quality of Life Instrument-Short Form	KFSD	keratosis follicularis spinulosa decalvans

K

KFT	kidney function test
kg	kilogram (1 kg = 2.2 pounds)
K-G	Kimray-Greenfield (filter)
KGC	Keflin, gentamicin, and carbenicillin
KGF	keratinocyte growth factor
kgm	kilogram (1 kg = 2.2 pounds)
kg/m2	kilograms per meter square
kg/m^2	kilograms per square meter
KGR	kinetic growth rate (degree of hypertrophy at initial volume assessment divided by number of weeks elapsed after a portal vein embolization)
17-KGS	17-ketogenic steroids
kg/sq m	kilograms per square meter
KGy	kiloGray
K24H	potassium, urine 24-hour
Khat	A flowering plant containing a monoamine alkaloid called cathinone, an amphetamine-like stimulant.
KHC	kinesin heavy chain
KHE	kaposiform hemangioendothelioma
KHF	Korean hemorrhagic fever
KHK	ketohexokinase gene (fructokinase) ketohexokinase (fructokinase)
KHQ	King's Health Questionnaire
kHz	kilohertz
KI	karyopyknotic index knee immobilizer potassium iodide
Ki67	a key prognostic molecule for invasive breast cancer
Ki-67	is a nuclear protein marker to determine the growth fraction of a given cell population such as carcinomas of the prostate, brain, breast, pancrease, nephroblastoma, etc.
KICS	KSHV (Kaposi Sarcoma Herpesvirus) inflammatory cytokine syndrome
kICS	k-Space image correlation spectroscopy
KID	keratitis, ichthyosis, and deafness (syndrome) kidney
KIDGO	may have meant KDIGO
KiKK	Kinderkrebs in der Umgebung von Kernkraftwerken (a study of children less than 5 years old, diagnosed with cancer during 1980-2003 while residing near nuclear power stations in western Germany)

KILEN	Consumer Association for Medicines and Health (Sweden; an adverse drug reaction reporting system)
killojoule	may have meant kilojoule (KJ)
Kilo	Phonetic Alphabet for K; pronounced KEY-LOH
kilo	kilogram thousand
kilos	kilograms (1 kilogram = approximately 2.2 US pounds)
KIM-1	kidney injury molecule 1
KIN	kinetic
KINARM	kinesiological instrument for normal and altered reaching movements (a robotic exoskeleton)
KIR	knee internal rotation
Kir4.1	inward rectifier-type potassium channel 4.1 (gene; also known as Kcnj10)
KISS	saturated solution of potassium iodide
KIT	a cytokine receptor expressed on the surface of hematopoietic stem cells as well as other cell types (also known as C-kit receptor and CD117) Kahn Intelligence Test
KIU	kallikrein inhibitor units
KiVa	an antibullying program (developed in the University of Turku, Finland)
Kiva®	Vertebral Compression Fracture Treatment System
Kiwi OmniCup	a fetal vacuum extraction device
KJ	kilojoule knee jerk
KJR	knee jerk reflex
KK	knee kick knock-knee
KKD	kilocalories per kilogram of body weight per day (kcal/kg/day)
KKOV	Kasokero virus
KKS	kallikrein-kinin system
K&L	Kellgren and Lawrence (scale for osteoarthritis assessment)
KL6	Krebs von den Lungen 6 (a sialylated carbohydrate antigen)
KLB	klebsiella vaccine
KL-BET	Kleihauer-Betke
KLC	keratosis lichenoides chronica Kinesin light chains
Kleb	*Klebsiella*
Klepsi	Klebsiella pneumoniae, a Gram-negative organism
KLF	Krüppel-like factor

K

KLF12	Krüppel-like factor 12
KLH	keyhole limpet hemocyanin
K-Lor®	potassium chloride tablets
KLOSG	Kellgren and Lawrence osteoarthritis severity grade
KLS	kidneys, liver, and spleen
	Kleine-Levin syndrome
KLT	King laryngeal tube (airway)
KM	kanamycin
km	kilometer (1000 meters; approximately 0.62 miles)
K/M	threshold pyrogenic dose divided by the dose of the drug in units/kilogram/hour (the formula for calculating an endotoxin limit in pharmaceuticals)
KMB	ketamine-midazolam-bupivacaine
KMC	Kangaroo mother care (includes thermal care through continuous skin-to-skin contact, support for exclusive breastfeeding or other appropriate feeding, and early recognition/response to illness)
	kinetic Monte Carlo (a broad class of algorithms that solve problems through the use of random numbers)
KMCM	kangaroo mother care method
KMnO₄	potassium permanganate
KMO	Kaiser-Meyer-Olkin (measure of statistical sampling adequacy)
KMP	Kasabach-Merritt phenomenon
KMV	killed measles vaccine
KN	knee
	Knops; an International Society of Blood Transfusion (ISBT) blood group
KNa	sodium-activated potassium currents
KNb	potassium diniobium
KND	Kassena-Nankana district (Ghana)
	kneading
	Korean native ducks
KNO	keep needle open
Knoa	Software for end-user experience and performance management solutions
KNSA	Kron Nutritive Sucking Apparatus
KNV	corneal (korneal) neovascularization
KO	keep open
	knee orthosis
	knocked out
KOA	knee osteoarthritis
KODA	kid of deaf adult
KOH	potassium hydroxide
KOL	key opinion leader

KOOS	Knee Injury and Osteoarthritis Outcome Score
KOP	kappa-opioid peptide (receptors)
	Knowledge of Psychosis (assessment instrument)
KOR	keep open rate
KOSCHI	King's Outcome Scale for Closed Head Injury
KOT	keratocystic odontogenic tumor
KP	hot pack
	Kaiser Permanente (integrated healthcare delivery model)
	keratoprecipitate
	kinetic perimetry
	knee pain
	kyphoplasty
kPa	kilopascal
	kilopascals
K-pad	a pad which provides either topical heat or cooling by means and circulating heated or cooled water; intended to reduce pain and/or inflammation
kPa/mm/Hg	kilopascals per millimeter of mercury
KPC	Klebsiella pneumoniae carbapenemase
KPCA	Kernel Principal Component Analysis
KPD	kidney paired donation
KPE	Kelman phacoemulsification
KPHOS	K-Phos (potassium phosphate monobasic)
KPI	Kunitz Protease Inhibitor
KPIs	key performance indicators
KPM	kilopounds per minute
KPMAS	Kaiser Permanente Mid-Atlantic States
KPro	keratoprosthesis
KPS	Karnofsky performance status (scores) (scale)
KPT	keratoplasty
KPTT	kaolin partial thromboplastin time
KQI	key quality indicators
Kr	krypton
Kras	v-Ki-ras2 Kirsten rat sarcoma viral oncogene homolog; see gene website www.ncbi.nlm.nih.gov/gene
KRD	carfilzomib (Kyprolis), lenalidomide (Revlimid), and dexamethasone
	ketosis-resistant diabetes
Krea-Cl	creatinine clearance (German)
KRIs	Key Risk Indicators
K-rod	Küntscher rod
KRS	Kufor-Rakeb syndrome
KRT	kidney replacement therapy

krt	keratin (also known as cytokeratin); see gene website www.ncbi.nlm.nih.gov/gene	KTO	potassium titanate
		KTP	potassium-titanyl-phosphate (laser)
Kru	residual renal urea clearance	KTPI	kidney transplantation provision of information (required by dialysis providers)
kRU	kilo-relative units		
KS	Kansas		
	Kaposis sarcoma	KTR	kidney transplant recipients
	Kawasaki syndrome	Ktrans	kinetic parameters transfer constant
	keratitis sicca		
	kidney stone	KTRV	Keterah virus
	Klinefelter syndrome	KTS	Klippel-Trenaunary syndrome
	Korsakoff syndrome	KTU	kidney transplant unit
17-KS	17-ketogenic steroids		known to us
	17-ketosteroids	KTV	key target volume
KSA	knowledge, skills, and abilities	Kt/V(urea)	the product of the urea clearance and the duration of the dialysis session normalized to the volume of distribution of urea
K-SADS	Kiddie Schedule For Affective Disorders and Schizophrenia		
KSE	knee sling exercises		
KS-F	Knee Society function (score)	KTWS	Klippel-Trenaunay-Weber syndrome
KSHV	Kaposi sarcoma-associated herpesvirus		
		KTx	kidney transplantation
KSI	killed-and-serious-injury	KTxp	kidney transplantation
KS/OI	Kaposi sarcoma and opportunitic infections	KTZ	ketoconazole (Nizoral)
		KUB	kidney ultrasound biopsy
KSP	Karolinska Scales of Personality		kidney(s), ureter(s), and bladder
KSPT	Kauffman Speech Praxsis Test	K/uL	thousand per cubic milliliter
KSR	potassium chloride sustained release (tablets)	kU/L	Radioallergosorbent test reports of immunoglobulin E made against specific foods in units known as kilounits (1,000 units) per liter
KSS	Karolinska Sleepiness Scale		
	Kearns-Sayre syndrome		
	knee society score		
KSW	Kimmelstiel-Wilson disease	KUNV	Kunjin Virus
	knife stab wound	Kup	potassium uptake protein; see gene website www.ncbi.nlm.nih.gov/gene
KT	kidney transplant		
	Kinesio (Kinesiology) tape (lifts the skin to create a small space between the muscle and dermis layers taking the pressure off swelling or injured muscles, allowing smooth muscle movement and making space for drainage and blood flow)		
		KUS	kidney(s), ureter(s), and spleen
		kV	kilovolt
		KVAs	vitamin K antagonists
		KVFD	Kelvin-Voigt Fractional Derivative
		KVO	keep vein open
		KVP	kilovolt peak
		KW	Keith-Wagener (ophthalmoscopic finding, graded I-IV)
	known to		
KTA	knowledge-to-action (a conceptual framework intended to help those concerned with knowledge translation deliver sustainable, evidence-based interventions)		kilowatt
			Kimmelstiel-Wilson
		KWB	Keith, Wagener, Barker
		KWIC	keywork in context
		K wire	Kirschner wires (stainless steel pin with a drill tip used mainly in orthopedics and plastic surgery)
KTC	knee-to-chest		
KTH	Royal Institute of Technology (Kungliga Tekniska hogskolan; a university in Stockholm, Sweden)	K-wire	Kirschner wire
		KWNP	Kernohan-Woltman notch phenomenon
		K/X	ketamine and xylazine
KTM	ketamine	KXRF	K-shell X-ray Fluorescence
	ketorolac tromethamine	KY	Kentucky
	Korean Traditional Medicines	KynA	kynurenic acid

K

kyph	kyphectomy
	kyphoplasty
	kyphosis
kypho	kyphoplasty
	kyphosis
Kypho-IORT	kyphoplasty combined with
	intraoperative radiotherapy
kypho-orthosis	a combination of kyphosis and
	scoliosis

L	fifty
	lateral
	left (this is a dangerous
	abbreviation; spell out "left"
	to avoid surgical, treatment,
	and diagnosis-related errors)
	Lente insulin (this is a
	dangerous abbreviation, since
	there is also a Lantus insulin
	available)
	leucine
	levorotatory
	Lima (Phonetic Alphabet for L;
	pronounced LEE-MAH)
	lingual
	Listeria
	liter (1 L = 1,000 mL = 1 quart
	plus about 2 ounces)
	liver
	low
	lumbar
	lung
L	*Laribacter*
L1	first language
	first lumbar nerve root
	first lumbar vertebrae
L1-2	lumbar spine, between first
	and second vertebrae
	(the disk space)
L2	second language
	second lumbar nerve root
	second lumbar vertebrae
L3	third lumbar nerve root
	third lumbar vertebrae
L4	fourth lumbar nerve root
	fourth lumbar vertebrae
L5	fifth lumbar nerve root
	fifth lumbar vertebrae
LA	lactic acid
	language age
	laryngeal amyloid
	laser acupuncture
	latex agglutination
	Latin American
	left arm
	left atrial
	left atrium
	leukoaraiosis
	(a radiologic finding)
	light adaptation
	linguoaxial
	linoleic acid
	lives alone
	local anesthesia
	local anesthetic

	long acting	LAc	Licensed Acupuncturist
	Louisiana	LACA	left atrial catheter ablation
	lupus anticoagulant		locally advanced cervical
	lymphadenectomy		adenocarcinoma
La	lanthanum	LACC	locally advanced cervical
L&A	light and accommodation		carcinoma
L+A	light and accommodation	LACE	listening and communication
	living and active		enhancement
L/A	length for age	LACI	lacunar circulation infarct
	see LA		lipoprotein-associated
L>R	left greater than right		coagulation inhibitor
LAA	large artery atherosclerosis	LACN	lateral antebrachial cutaneous
	left atrial appendage		nerve
LAA	left atrial pressure, a wave	lacr	lacrimal
LAAC	left atrial appendage closure	lacR	lactose phosphotransferase
	long-acting anticholinergic(s)		system repressor; see gene
laaC	see gene website www.ncbi.nlm		website www.ncbi.nlm.nih
	.nih.gov/gene		.gov/gene
LAA clip	left atrial appendage clip	LACR	laparoscopically-assisted colon
	(Atriclip)		resection
LAACs	long-acting anticholinergics		laser-assisted cartilage reshaping
LAAE	low-frequency augmented	LACS	laser-assisted capsular shrinkage
	acoustic environment	LACT-ART	lactate arterial
LAAL	left anterior axillary line	LACV	La Crosse virus
	left atrial appendage lipomas		(mosquito-borne virus, a
LAAM	levomethadyl acetate (l-alpha		major cause of pediatric
	acetylmeth-adol, Orlaam)		encephalitis in the USA)
LAAO	left atrial appendage occlusion	LAD	laser anesthesia device
LAAS	large artery atherosclerosis		left anterior descending
LAAs	leukemia-associated antigens		(coronary artery)
LAAT	left atrial appendage thrombus		left atrial diameter
LAB	laboratory		left atrial dimension
	left abdomen (LAb)		left axis deviation
LABA	laser-assisted balloon angioplasty		leukocyte adhesion deficiency
	long-acting beta 2-agonist		ligament augmentation device
LABBB	left anterior bundle branch block		Long axis distraction
LABC	lateral antebrachial cutaneous		lymphadenopathy
	nerve	LADA	latent autoimmune diabetes in
	locally advanced breast cancer		adults
LABD	linear immunoglobulin (Ig)		left anterior descending
	A bullous dermatosis		(coronary) artery
LABE	low-angle backscattered	LADCA	left anterior descending
	electron		coronary artery
LABG	may have meant LAGB	LADD	left anterior descending diagonal
	(laparoscopic adjustable	LAD DES	left anterior descending artery
	gastric banding)		drug-eluting stent
LaBP	laser-assisted bioprinting	LAD-DES	left anterior descending artery
LABR	laparascopic-assisted bowel		drug-eluting stent
	resection	LADDs	lifetime average daily doses
labs	clinical laboratory tests	LADG	laparoscopy-assisted distal
LAC	laceration		gastrectomy
	lactobacillus acidophilus vaccine	LAD-MIN	left axis deviation minimal
	laparoscopic-assisted colectomy	LAD PCI	left anterior descending artery
	left antecubital		percutaneous coronary
	left atrial catheter		intervention
	locally advanced cancer	LAD-PCI	left anterior descending artery
	long arm cast		percutaneous coronary
	lupus anticoagulant		intervention

LADPG	laparoscopically assisted distal partial gastrectomy	LALP	Liver Alkaline Phosphatase
LADs	lamina-associated domains	LALT	larynx-associated lymphoid tissue
ladS	Lost Adherence Senso; see gene website www.ncbi.nlm.nih .gov/gene		low air loss therapy (mattress)
LAE	left atrial enlargement long above elbow	LAM	lactational anovulatory method (birth control) laminectomy laminogram
LAEC	locally advanced esophageal cancer		laparoscopic-assisted myomectomy
LAEI	large artery elasticity index		laser-assisted myringotomy
l'ly	L-lysine		Latin-American male
LAeq	equivalent continuous A-weighted sound pressure level (an index for noise)		lymphangioleiomyomatosis (a rare disease seen mostly in young women caused by
LAEs	liver-associated enzymes		abnormal proliferation of
LAF	laminar air flow Latin-American female low animal fat		smooth muscle-like cells (LAM cells) in the lungs and extrapulmonary sites)
	lymphocyte-activating factor	lam✓	laminectomy check
LAFB	left anterior fascicular block	LAMA	laser-assisted microanastomosis
LAFD	Los Angeles Fire Department		long-acting muscarinic
LAFF	lateral arm free flap		antagonist
LAFM	locally acquired *Plasmodium falciparum* malaria	LAMB	mucocutaneous lentigines, atrial myxoma, and blue nevus
LAFR	laminar airflow room		(syndrome)
LafV	see gene website; www.ncbi .nlm.nih.gov/gene	L-AMB	liposomal amphotericin B
		Lambda	eleventh letter of the Greek
LAFW	laminar airflow workbench		alphabet
LAG	lymphangiogram	LAMI	low- and middle-income
LAGB	laparoscopic adjustable gastric banding	LAMMA	laser microprobe mass analysis
		LAMN	low-grade appendiceal
LAH	left anterior hemiblock		mucinous neoplasm
	left atrial hypertrophy	LAMP	Low Activities of Daily Living
LAHB	left anterior hemiblock		Monitoring Program
LAHNC	locally advanced squamous cell head and neck cancer	LAMS	Longitudinal Assessment of Manic Symptoms (study)
LAHS	lymphoma-associated hemophagocytic syndrome		Los Angeles Motor Scale lumen-apposing metal stent
LAI	left atrial isomerism long-acting injectable	LAMs	leukemia-associated macrophages
LAIAs	long-acting insulin analogues	LAN	LAN; an International Society
LA-ICGA	laser-assisted indocyanine green angiography		of Blood Transfusion (ISBT) blood group
LAIT	latex agglutination inhibition test		lymphadenopathy
LAIV	live, attenuated influenza vaccine	LANC	long arm navicular cast
LAIV4	live, attenuated influenza vaccine (quadrivalent)	L1 and L2	lumbar vertebrae 1 and 2
		L2 and L3	lumbar vertebrae 2 and 3
		L3 and L4	lumbar vertebrae 3 and 4
LAK	lymphokine-activated killer	L4 and L5	lumbar vertebrae 4 and 5
LAL	laser-assisted liposuction	L5 and S1	lumbar vertebra 5 and
	left atrial (appendage) ligation		sacral vertebrae 1
	left axillary line	lang	language
	limulus amebocyte lysate (used as a quality control test for endotoxin [pyrogens])	LA-NSCLC	locally-advanced nonsmall-cell lung cancer
		LAO	left anterior oblique
	lysosomal acid lipase		long-acting opioid(s)
LALD	lysosomal acid lipase deficiency	LAOMs	local anesthetic-opioid mixtures
LALLS	low-angle laser light scattering	lap	laparoscopic

LAP	laparoscopy
	laparotomy
	latency associated peptide
	left abdominal pain
	left atrial pressure
	leucine amino peptidase
	leukocyte alkaline phosphatase
	lower abdominal pain
LAPA	locally-advanced pancreatic adenocarcinoma
lap appy	laparoscopic appendectomy
lap band	a minimally invasive surgical procedure (laparoscopy) with a silicone gastric band placed around the top of the upper part of the stomach
Lap-Band®	laparoscopic-adjustable gastric banding
lap BSO	laparoscopic bilateral salpingo-oophorectomy
LAPC	locally advanced pancreatic cancer
LapChole	laparoscopic cholecystectomy
lap choley	laparoscopic cholecystectomy
LAPEC	laparoscopic-assisted percutaneous endoscopic cecostomy
LAPMs	long acting and permanent methods (of contraception)
LAPMS	long arm posterior molded splint
LAP Nissen	laparoscopy, surgical, esophagogastric fundoplasty
LAPS	Laboratory Acute Physiology Score
LAPs	low-acuity procedures
LAPW	left atrial posterior wall
LAQ	long arc quad
LAQs	Leader Affect Questionnaires
LAR	laryngeal adductor reflex
	left arm, reclining
	long-acting release
	low anterior resection
LARC	locally advanced rectal cancer
LARCs	long-acting reversible contraceptives
LARIAT™ Procedure	in patients who are unable to take anticoagulants for atrial fibrillation, a suture delivery device places and tightens a loop stitch around the base of heart's left atrial appendage, permanently sealing it off from the rest of the heart and blocking stroke-causing blood clots from traveling to the brain
LARM	left arm
LARS	laparoscopic antireflux surgery

LARSI	lumbar anterior-root stimulator implants
LAS	lactic acidosis syndrome
	lateral ankle sprain
	laxative abuse syndrome
	left arm, sitting
	leucine acetylsalicylate
	ligamentous articular strain
	long arm splint
	low-amplitude signal
	lung allocation score (a score that to balance wait list mortality and posttransplant survival)
	lymphadenopathy syndrome
	lymphangioscintigraphy
	lysine acetylsalicylate
LASA	Linear Analogue Self-Assessment (scales)
	lipid-associated sialic acid
	look-alike, sound-alike
LASCC	locally advanced squamous cell carcinoma
LASCCHN	locally advanced squamous cell carcinoma of the head and neck
LASD	Los Angeles County Sherriff's Department
LASEC	left atrial spontaneous echo contrast
LASER	light amplification by stimulated emission of radiation
LASGB	laparoscopic adjustable silicone gastric banding
LASH	left anterosuperior hemiblock
LASIK	laser *in situ* keratomileusis
LASO	left anterior superior oblique
L-ASP	asparaginase (Elspar)
LAST	left anterior small thoracotomy
LASV	Lassa virus
LASW	Licensed Advanced Social Worker
LAT	lateral
	latex agglutination test
	left anterior thigh
	lidocaine, epinephrine, (Adrenalin) and tetracaine
	living apart together (relationship)
LATCH	literature attached to chart
LATH	Large Animal Teaching Hospital
LaTME	laparoscopic total mesorectal excision
La-TME	laparoscopic total mesorectum excision
lat.men.	lateral meniscectomy
Lats	latissimus dorsi
LATS	long-acting thyroid stimulator

L

	long biceps tendon
	low back tenderness
	low back trouble
LBTs	lanthanide-binding tags
LBV	left brachial vein
	low biological value
LBVO	left brachial vein occlusion
LBVS	ligand-based virtual screening
LBW	lean body weight
	low birth weight
	(less than 2,500 g)
LBWI	low birth weight infant
LC	Lactation Consultant
	laparoscopic cholecystectomy
	Laënnecs cirrhosis
	left circumflex
	leisure counseling
	lethal concentration
	level of consciousness
	levocarnitine (Carnitor)
	ligneous conjunctivitis
	liquid chromatography
	living children
	low calorie
	low cholesterol
	lung cancer
	lymphocele
L&C	lids and conjunctivae
L/C	levodopa and carbidopa
3LC	triple-lumen catheter
	see LC
LC1	laryngeal clefts type 1
LC 1	see LC1
	lateral compression (pelvic
	fracture) type 1 (impaction
	fracture at the sacrum)
LC2	laryngeal clefts type 2
	lateral compression (pelvic
	fracture) type 2 (fracture that
	extends through the posterior
	iliac wing at the level of the
	sacroiliac joint)
LC50	median lethal concentration
LCA	latent class analysis
	(a statistical tool)
	Leber congenital amaurosis
	left circumflex artery
	left coronary artery
	leukocyte common antigen
	life cycle assessment
	light contact assist
LCAB	late course accelerated boost
	(external beam radiotherapy)
	left coronary artery branch
LCAD	long-chain acyl-coenzyme
	A dehydrogenase
LCADL	London Chest Activity of Daily
	Living

LCAH	life-care at home
	lipoid congenital adrenal
	hyperplasia
LCAL	large-cell anaplastic lymphoma
	lifetime cumulative attachment
	loss (dental)
LCaP	localized prostate cancer
LCAR	l-carnitine
LCAT	lecithin cholesterol
	acyltransferase
LCB	left costal border
LCBDE	laparoscopic common bile duct
	exploration
LCBI	laboratory-confirmed
	bloodstream infection
LCC	left coronary cusp
	left cranial-caudal
	(mammogram view)
LCCA	left circumflex coronary artery
	left common carotid artery
	leukocytoclastic angiitis
LCCE	Lamaze-Certified Childbirth
	Educator
LCCK	Legacy Constrained Condylar
	Knee
LCCM	low-concentration contrast
	media
LCCS	low cervical cesarean section
LCCV	leukocytoclastic vasculitis
LCD	coal tar solution
	(*liquor carbonis detergens*)
	laryngeal closure duration
	last covered day (hospital
	utilization review)
	lattice corneal dystrophy
	liquid crystal display (radiology)
	Local Coverage Determination
	localized collagen dystrophy
	low contrast detail (radiology)
	low-calcium diet
LCDC	Laboratory Centre for Disease
	Control (Canada)
LCDCP	low-contact dynamic
	compression plate
LCDD	light chain deposition disease
LCDE	laparoscopic common duct
	exploration
LCDH	left-sided congenital
	diaphragmatic hernia
LCDs	local coverage
	determinations
	Local Coverage Determinations
	(Medicare)
LCE	laparoscopic cholecystectomy
	lateral center-edge (angle)
	left carotid endarterectomy
	leukocyte esterase
	levodopa/carbidopa/entacapone

L

LCEA	lung carcinoma expressed antigens	LCMN	large congenital melanocytic nevi
L CEA	lung carcinoma expressed antigens	LCMP	low carbohydrate, moderate protein (diet)
LC-EI-MS	liquid chromatography-electron impact-mass spectometry	LC-MS-MS	liquid chromatography coupled to tandem mass spectrometry
LCF	late clinical failure	LCMV	lymphocytic choriomeningitis virus
	left circumflex		
	lipid cholesterol fractionation	LCN	lidocaine
	lipoprotein cholesterol fractionation	LCNB	large-core needle biopsy
		LCNEC	large cell neuroendocrine carcinoma
LCFA	lateral circumflex femoral artery		
	long-chain fatty acid	LCO	low cardiac output
LC-FAODs	long chain fatty acid oxidation disorders	LCOS	low cardiac output syndrome
		LCP	late-career physician
LCFAs	Long-chain fatty acids		left chest port
LCFM	left circumflex marginal		Leishmaniasis Control Program
LCFV	left common femoral vein		locking compression plate
LCGC	Chromatographyonline. com, a global resource for peer-reviewed technical information on the field of chromatography and the separation sciences		long, closed, posterior (cervix)
		LCPC	Licensed Clinical Professional Counselor
		LCPD	Legg-Calvé-Perthes disease
		LCPs	late-career physicians
		LCPT	Licensed Clinical Pastoral Therapists
	local cerebral glucose content	LCPUFAs	long-chain polyunsaturated fatty acids
LCGU	local cerebral glucose utilization		
LCH	Langerhans' cell histiocytosis	LCPV	left common pulmonary vein
	lobular capillary hemangioma	LCQ	Leicester cough questionnaire
	local city hospital	LC-Q/TOF	liquid chromatography -quadrupole/time of flight (mass spectrometry analysis)
LCHAD	long-chain 3-hydroxyacle-CoA dehydrogenase		
LCHADD	long-chain 3-hydroxyacyl-CoA dehydrogenase deficiency	LCR	cerebrospinal fluid (French)
			laryngeal chemoreflexes
LCHG	low-carbohydrate, high-glycemic index		late cortical response
			late cutaneous reaction
LCI	lung clearance index		ligase chain reaction
LCIA	left common iliac artery		locus control region
	life cycle impact assessment		low contrast resolution
LCIG	levodopa-carbidopa intestinal gel (Duopa, AbbVie)	LCRS	Living Conditions Rating Scale
		LCRs	low-copy repeats
LCINS	lung cancer in never-smokers	LCS	laparoscopic colorectal surgery
LCIS	lobular cancer in situ		Leydig cell stimulation
LCIV	left iliac common vein		lids, conjunctiva and sclera
LCL	lateral collateral ligament		low constant suction
	localized cutaneous leishmaniasis		low continuous suction
			lumbar (spinal) canal stenosis
	lymphoblastoid cell line		lung cancer screening
LCLC	large-cell lung carcinoma		Lung Cancer Subscale
	lateral collateral ligament complex	LCSB	Liaison Committee for Specialty Boards sponsored by The American Medical Association's Council on Medical Education, in conjunction with the American Board of Medical Specialties
LCLF	low-cholesterol, low-fat (diet)		
LCLG	low-carbohydrate, low-glycemic index		
LCM	laser-capture microdissection		
	left costal margin		
	lower costal margin		
	lymphocytic choriomeningitis		
LCMI	left ventricular mass index		low-calorie sweetened beverage

L

LCSC	liver cancer stem cell		lumbar drain (drainage)
	lung cancer stem cell		Lyme disease
LCSCs	lung cancer stem cells	L&D	labor and delivery
LCSD	left cardiac sympathetic	L+D	labor and delivery
	denervation	L/D	labor and delivery
LCSG	left cardiac sympathetic		light to dark (ratio)
	ganglionectomy		loss/damage
	lost child support group	LD-1	lactic dehydrogenase 1
LCSS	Lung Cancer Symptom Score	LD-5	lactic dehydrogenase 5
lcSSc	limited cutaneous systemic	LD$_{50}$	median lethal dose
	sclerosis	LDA	laser-Doppler anemometry
LCSW	Licensed Clinical Social Worker		limit of detection amount
	low continuous wall suction		linear discriminant analysis
LCSW-C	Licensed Certified Social		lines, drains, and airways
	Worker – Clinical		low-density areas
LCT	long-chain triglyceride		low-dose aspirin
	low cervical transverse		low-dose arm
	lymphocytotoxicity		low-dose aspirin
LCTA	lungs clear to auscultation	L/D/A	lines, drains, and airways
LCTAB	lungs clear to auscultation,	LDAC	low-dose cytarabine (ara-C)
	bilaterally	LDASA	low-dose aspirin
LCTCS	low cervical transverse cesarean	LDB	Legionnaires disease bacterium
	section	LD-B	liposomal doxorubicin and
LCTD	low-calcium test diet		bortezomib
LCTs	Leydig cell tumors	LDCOC	low-dose combination oral
	liver chemistry tests		contraceptive
	long-chain triacylglycerols	LD-CT	low-dose (spiral) computed
LCV	leucovorin		tomography
	leukocytoclastic vasculitis	LDD	laser disk decompression
	low cervical vertical		Lee and Desu D (test)
LCVA	left-hemispheric cerebrovascular		Lhermitte-Duclos disease
	accident		light-dark discrimination
	low-contrast visual acuity		lumbar disk disease
LCVAT	left costovertebral angle	LDDD	lumbar degenerative disk
	tenderness		disease
LCWS	low continuous wall suction	LDDS	local dentist
LCX	left circumflex coronary artery	LDEA	left deviation of electrical axis
LCx	left circumflex artery	LDEI	large-dose extended-interval
LD	laboratory department		(dosing)
	lactic dehydrogenase	L-Dex	lymphedema index
	(formerly LDH)	LDF	laser-Doppler flowmetry
	laser Doppler		left dorsal frontal
	last dose	LDG	laparoscopic distal gastrectomy
	latissimus dorsi	LDH	lactic dehydrogenase
	Leadership (standard)		low dose heparin
	learning disability		lumbar disk herniation
	learning disorder	LDIH	left direct inguinal hernia
	left deltoid	LDIR	low-dose of ionizing radiation
	Legionnaires disease	LDISS	Learning Disability
	lethal dose		Intensive Support Service
	levodopa		(United Kingdom)
	Licensed Dietician	LDI-TOF-MS	laser desorption/ionization time-
	liver disease		of-flight-mass spectrometer
	living donor	LDK	low-dose ketoconazole
	loading dose	LDKT	living (live) donor kidney
	long dwell		transplantation
	low density	LDL	limitation of daily life
	low dosage		low-density lipoprotein

LDL-C	low-density lipoprotein cholesterol	LDT	laboratory-developed test
			left dorsotransverse
LDLp	low-density lipoprotein particles	LD-T	lactic dehydrogenase total
		LDTs	laboratory-developed tests
	low-density lipophorins (insects)	LDUB	long double upright brace
		LDUH	low-dose unfractionated heparin
LDLR	low-density lipoprotein receptor	LDV	laser Doppler velocimetry
			laser Doppler vibrometry
LDLT	living donor liver transplantation	LDX	lisdexamfetamine dimesylate (Vyvanse)
LDLTx	living donor liver transplantation	LE	labor epidural
			late entry
LDM	lorazepam, dexamethasone, and metoclopramide		lateral epicondylitis (tennis elbow)
			left ear
	low-dose metronomic chemotherapy		left eye
			lens extraction
LDMRT	low-dose mediastinal radiation therapy		leptin
			leukocyte esterase
LDN	laparoscopic donor nephrectomy		Lewis; an International Society of Blood Transfusion (ISBT) blood group
	Licensed Dietitian Nutritionist		
	living-donor nephrectomy		
	low-dose naltrexone (ReVia)		limbic encephalitis
LDNF	lung-derived neurotrophic factor		live embryo
LDO	Licensed Dispensing Optician		local excision
l-dopa	levodopa		lower extremities
LDP	laparascopic distal pancreatechtomy		lupus erythematosus
			lymphedema
LD-PCR	limiting dilution polymerase chain reaction	LEA	linoleoylethanolamide
			lower extremity amputation
LDPM	laser Doppler perfusion monitoring		lumbar epidural anesthesia
		LEAD	lower extremity arterial disease
LDQA	laboratory-developed quadruplex assay	LE's	see LE
LDR	labor, delivery, and recovery	LEAN system	The core idea of LEAN is to maximize customer value while minimizing waste; creating more value for customers with fewer resources
	length-to-diameter ratio		
	long-duration response		
	lumbar disc replacement		
LDR-BT	low-dose rate (prostate) brachytherapy	LEAP	Lower Extremity Amputation Prevention (program)
LDR/P	labor, delivery, recovery, and postpartum	LEARN	Lifestyle, Exercise, Attitudes, Relationships, Nutrition
LDRT	live donor renal transplantation	LEAS	Lower-Extremity Activity Scale
LD-RT	low-dose radiotherapy	LEB	lower extremity bypass
LDS	Language Development Survey		lumbar epidural block
	locked-door seclusion	LEC	lateral entorhinal cortex
	lumbar degenerative spondylolisthesis		lens epithelial cell
LDSS	low dead-space syringes	LECA	left external carotid artery
LDSSI	low-dose sliding scale insulin (suggested starting point for thin and elderly patients, or those being initiated on total parenteral nutrition)	LECBD	laparoscopic exploration of the common bile duct
		LE-CEMRA	lower extremity contrast-enhanced magnetic resonance angiography
LD SSI	low-dose sliding scale insulin (suggested starting point for thin and elderly patients, or those being initiated on total parenteral nutrition)	LECS	laparoscopic and endoscopic cooperating surgery
		LED	light emitting diode
			liposomal encapsulated doxorubicin (Doxil)

	lowest effective dose	LEMG	laryngeal electromyography
	lupus erythematosus disseminatus	LEMON	Look externally, Evaluate, Mallampati scoring, Obstruction, Neck mobility (a mnemonic for evaluation difficult laryngoscopy)
LEDIF	light emitting diode-induced fluorescence		
LEDVT	lower extremity deep vein thrombosis	LEMS	Lambert-Eaton myasthenic syndrome
LEE	last eye examination		
	lower extremity edema		Lower Extremity Motor Score
LEED	low energy electron diffraction	LEN	lenalidomide (Revlimid)
	low-energy electron diffraction	LENI	lower extremity noninvasive (vascular studies)
LE edema	lower extremity edema		
LEEP	loop electrosurgical excision procedure	LENT-SOMA	Late Effect of Normal Tissue – Subjective Objective Management Analytic (toxicity table)
LEEPs	loop electrosurgical excision procedures		
LEF	leflunomide (Arava)	LEO	law enforcement officer
	lower extremity fracture		see gene website, www.ncbi. nlm.nih.gov/gene
LeFort fractures	are fractures of the midface, which collectively involve separation of all or a portion of the midface from the skull base. The Le Fort classification system attempts to distinguish according to the plane of injury.		
		LEOD	lens extraction, right eye
		LEOI	lower extremity overuse injury
		LEOS	lens extraction, left eye
		LEP	leptospirosis
			limited English proficiency
			liposome-encapsulated paclitaxel
			lower esophageal pressure
LeFort osteotomy	upper jaw surgery that involves sectioning and repositioning the maxilla, or upper jaw, to correct its abnormal position		lower extremity pain
			lower-extremity performance
		LEP2	leptospirosis 2
		LE prep	lupus erythematosus preparation
LeFort fractures	are fractures of the midface, which collectively involve separation of all or a portion of the midface from the skull base. The Le Fort classification system attempts to distinguish according to the plane of injury.	LEPs	laser-evoked potentials
		LER	low endotoxin recovery
		LERD	low-emotion regulation difficulties
		LERS	Lumbar Extension With Rotation Syndrome
		L-ERX	leukoerythroblastic reaction
		LES	local excitatory state
LEFS	Lower Extremity Functional Scale		lower esophageal sphincter
			lumbar epidural steroids
LEFT	lower extremity functional test		Lumbar Extension Syndrome
LEG	Legionella bacteria		lupus erythematosus systemic
LEH	liposome-encapsulated hemoglobin	Lesb	Lesbian
		LESEP	lower extremity somatosensory evoked potential
LEHPZ	lower esophageal high pressure zone	LESG	Late Effects Study Group
		LESI	lumbar epidural steroid injection
LEI	lower extremity injury	LESP	lower esophageal sphincter pressure
LEIA	larval exsheathment inhibition assay		
		LESS	laparoendoscopic single-site surgery
	left external iliac artery		
LEJ	ligation of the esophagogastric junction	LESS-RH	laparoendoscopic single-site radical hysterectomy
LEL	low-energy laser	LESVH	left endoscopic saphenous vein harvest
LELCC	lymphoepithelioma-like cholangiocarcinoma		
		LET	a topical anesthetic solution containing lidocaine, epinephrine, and tetracaine
LELs	lymphoepithelial lesions		
LEM	lateral eye movements		
	light electron microscope		lateral elbow tendinopathy

L

left esotropia
leukocyte esterase test
lidocaine, epinephrine and
   tetracaine gel
linear energy transfer
lupus erythematosus tumidis
LETM   longitudinally extensive
   transverse myelitis
LETs   liver enzyme tests
LETZ   loop excision of the
   transformation zone
LEU   leucine
leuk   leukemia
   leukocyte
leuk est   leukocyte esterase (a urine test
   to look for white blood cells
   and other signs of infection)
leuko   a prefix meaning white;
   denoting relationship to
   leukocytes
leuks   leukocytes
LEV   levamisole (Ergamisol)
   levator muscle
   levetiracetam (Keppra)
LEVA   levamisole (Ergamisol)
LEVD   lower extremity venous disease
Level 1®   a pressure infusion device used
   in to warm large volumes of
   fluid over a short period of
   time
LEVF   left ventricular ejective fraction
   (Romance languages)
LEVO   Levophed (norepinephrine inj)
levo   levorotation; rotating a
   plane of polarized light
   counterclockwise (to the left)
Lex   Lewis X (a glycosidic antigen
   implicated in tumor
   progression and metastases)
LEX   life expectancy
LEXT   lumbar extensor exercise
   intervention
LF   lacrimal fluid
   laparoscopic fundoplications
   Lassa fever
   Latin female
   left foot
   left frontal
   Life Fitness (personal training
   equipment)
   little finger
   living female
   long finger
   long finger or little finger
   low fat
   low forceps
   low frequency
   lymphatic filariasis

L/F   Latin female
LFA   left femoral artery
   left forearm
   left fronto-anterior
   leukocyte function-associated
   antigen
   low-friction arthroplasty
   lumbar facet arthropathy
   lymphocyte function-associated
   antigen
LFA-1   leukocyte function-associated
   antigen-1
LFAB   lipid formulations of
   amphotericin B
LFB   low-frequency band
LFC   lateral femoral condyle
   LeFort colpocleisis
   living female child
   low-fat and cholesterol
LFCN   lateral femoral
   cutaneous nerve
LFCS   low-flap cesarean section
LFD   lactose-free diet
   low FODMAP (fermentable
   oligosaccharides,
   disaccharides,
   monosaccharides, and
   polyol) diet
   low-fat diet
   low-fiber diet
   low-forceps delivery
   lunate fossa depression
LFDEP   may have meant LVEDP (left
   ventricular end-diastolic
   pressure)
LFEM   left femoral
LFF   liver fat fraction
   low frequency fatigue
   low frequency fluctuations
LFGNR   lactose fermenting
   gram-negative rod
LFH   ligamentum flavum hypertrophy
   lower face height
LFI   local-field irradiation
LFJ   laparoscopic feeding
   jejunostomy
   lumbar facet joint
LFL   left frontolateral
LFLC   low fat, low cholesterol
   lung fibrosis and lung cancer
LFLG   low-flow and low-gradient
   (aortic stenosis)
LF/LGAS   low-flow/low-flow/low-gradient
   aortic stenosis
LFM   lateral force microscopy
LFN   lateral femur nail
LFNC   low fat, no cholesterol (diet)
   low-flow nasal cannula

LFO	low-frequency oscillations	LGFD	looks good from the doorway.
LFOD	low fermentable oligosaccharides,		Slang for a patient who
	disaccharides,		complains but looks fine.
	monosaccharides, and	LGG	low-grade gliomas
	polyol diet	L-GG	*Lactobacillus rhamnosus*
LFOs	low-frequency oscillations		strain GG
LFP	left frontoposterior	LGH	Lancaster General Hospital
	Low Fowler position		lower gastrointestinal
LFPN	large-fiber peripheral		hemorrhage
	neuropathy	LGHP	large group health plan
LFPs	latent fingerprints		low glycemic (index)
LFRS	Lumbar Flexion With Rotation		high-protein (diet)
	Syndrome	LGI	lower gastrointestinal (series)
LFS	leukemia-free survival	LGI1	leucine-rich, glioma inactivated
	Li-Fraumeni syndrome		1 (gene)
	liver function series	LGIB	lower gastrointestinal bleeding
LFT	latex flocculation test	LGIL	low-grade intraepithelial
	left fronto-transverse		lesion(s)
	liver function tests	LGIOS	low-grade intraosseous-type
	low-flap transverse		osteosarcoma
LFTs	liver function tests	LGIT	lower gastrointestinal tract
LFU	limit flocculation unit		low-glycemic index treatment
	lost to follow-up	LGL	large granular lymphocyte
LFV	left femoral vein		low glycemic load
	leg fluid volume		low-grade lymphoma(s)
	low flow velocities		Lown-Ganong-Levine
LG	large		(syndrome)
	laryngectomy	LGLL	large granular lymphocytic
	left gluteal		leukemia
	linguogingival	LGLS	Lown-Ganong-Levine syndrome
	lymphography	LGM	left gluteus medius (maximus)
lg1	liguleless 1 (gene)	LGMD2L	limb-girdle muscular dystrophy
L-G	Lich-Gregoire		Type 2L
	(ureteroneocystostomy)	LGN	lateral geniculate leaflet
LGA	large for gestational age		lobular glomerulonephritis
	left gastric artery	LGNB	lactose-fermenting
	localized granuloma annulare		gram-negative bacilli
LGAS	low-gradient aortic stenosis	LGNET	low grade neuroendocrine
LGAs	Local Government Areas		carcinoma
LGB	lesbian, gay, and bisexual	LG-NHL	low-grade non-Hodgkins
LGBP/LC	laparoscopic gastric bypass		lymphoma
	with simultaneous	LGR	see gene website, www.ncbi
	cholecystectomy		.nlm.nih.gov/gene
LGBT	lesbian, gay, bisexual and	LGS	Lennox-Gastaut syndrome
	transsexual		low-Gomco suction
LGBTQ	lesbian, gay, bisexual,	LG-SAs	low-grade serrated adenomas
	transgender, or questioning	LGSIL	low-grade squamous
	one's sexual identity		intraepithelial lesion
LGBTQI	lesbian, gay, bisexual,	LGSOC	low-grade serous ovarian
	transgender, queer, or intersex		carcinoma
LGCM	latent growth curve modeling	LGSW	Licenses Graduate Social
LGCP	laparoscopic greater curve		Worker
	plication	LGT	lower genital tract
LGD	low-grade dysplasia		low-grade temperature
LG-DCIS	low-grade ductal carcinoma	lgtA	lacto-N-neotetraose biosytheseis
	in situ		glycosyl transferase; see gene
LGE	late gadolinium enhancement		website www.ncbi.nlm.nih
LGEA	long-gap esophageal atresia		.gov/gene

L

LG TAs	low-grade tubular adenomas	LHV	lay health volunteer(s)
LG-TAs	low-grade tubular adenomas		left hepatic vein
lgth	length		lower heating value
LGV	left gastric vein	LHW	lay health worker
	lymphogranuloma venerum	LHWs	lay health worker(s)
LH	laparoscopic hysterectomy	LI	lactose intolerance
	learning handicap		lamellar ichthyosis
	left hand		large intestine
	left handed		laser iridotomy
	left hemisphere		learning impaired
	left hyperphoria		linear interpolator (radiology)
	long handled		linguoincisal
	luteinizing hormone		liver involvement
	lymphoid hyperplasia	Li	lithium
L58H	a variant of transthyretin-related	LIA	laser interference acuity
	amyloidosis		latex immunoturbidimetric assay
L/h	liters per hour		left iliac artery
LHA	left hepatic artery	LIAC	a mobile linear accelerator
LHAd	dorsal region of the lateral		dedicated to intraoperative
	hypothalamic area		radiation therapy
LHB	long head of the biceps	LiAc	lithium acetate
LHBT	lactulose hydrogen breath testing	LIAS	lipoic acid synthetase
	long head of the biceps tendon	LIB	left in bottle
LHC	left heart catheterization		local in breast
	light-harvesting complex	LIC	left iliac crest
LHCJ	left heart catheterization,		left internal carotid
	Judkins approach		leisure interest class
LHD	laparoscopic Heller-Dor		lung insufflation capacity
	(myotomy)	LICA	left internal carotid artery
	left hepatic duct	LICD	lower intestinal Crohn disease
	left-hand dominant	LICM	left intercostal margin
LHDs	local health departments	Li_2CO_3	lithium carbonate
LHE	lateral humeral epicondylitis	$LiCO_3$	lithium carbonate (the proper
	light-harvesting efficiency		designation is Li_2CO_3)
LHEs	lay health educators	Licox®	a brain tissue partial pressure
LHF	left heart failure		oxygen monitor
LHG	left hand grip	LICS	left intercostal space
LHH	left homonymous hemianopsia	LICSW	Licensed Independent Clinical
LHI	Labor Health Institute		Social Worker
LHL	left hemisphere lesions	LID	L-DOPA (Levodopa)-induced
	left hepatic lobe		dyskinesia
LHM	laparoscopic Heller myotomy		levodopa-induced dyskinesia
	liver hanging maneuver	LIDAR	Laser Imaging Detection and
LHON	Leber hereditary optic neuropathy		Ranging
LHP	left hemiparesis	LiDAR	light detection and ranging
LHR	legal health record	LIDC	Lung Image Database Consortium
	leukocyte histamine release	LIDD	lumbar intervertebral disk
	long-handled reacher		disorder(s)
	(occupational therapy)	Lido	lidocaine
LHRH	luteinizing hormone-releasing	LIF	laser-induced fluorescence
	hormone		left iliac fossa
LHRH-A	luteinizing hormone-releasing		left index finger
	hormone analogue		leukemia-inhibiting factor
LHRT	leukocyte histamine release test		liver (migration) inhibitory factor
LHS	left hand side	LIFE	laser-induced fluorescence
	long-handled sponge		emission
LHSH	long-handled shoe horn		lung imaging fluorescence
LHT	left hypertropia		endoscopy

L

L IF MP	left index finger metacarpal joint		barrier is implanted using
LIFT	ligation of intersphincteric		a laparoscopic approach
	fistula tract	LIO	laser-indirect ophthalmoscope
LIG	ligament		left inferior oblique (muscle)
	lymphocyte immune globulin	LIOU	laparoscopic intraoperative
LIGHTS	phototherapy lights		ultrasound
lights		LIP	licensed independent
LIH	laparoscopic inguinal		practitioner
	herniorrhaphy		lithium-induced polydipsia
	last image hold (radiology)		lymphocytic interstitial
	left inguinal hernia		pneumonia
LIHA	low impulsiveness, high anxiety	LIPA	Light-intensity physical activity
LIHD	left intrahepatic (bile) duct		lipase A; see gene website
LIHR	laparoscopic inguinal hernia		www.ncbi.nlm.nih.gov/gene
	repair	LiPA assay	Versant Hepatitis C virus
	laparoscopic incisional hernia		genotype assay
	repair	LipoRV	liposomal rabies vaccine
	left inguinal hernia repair	LIPV	left inferior pulmonary vein
LIIA	left internal iliac artery	LIQ	liquid
LIID	latanoprost-induced iris darkening		liquor
LIJ	left internal jugular		lower inner quadrant
LILA	low impulsiveness, low anxiety	LIQs	liquids
LILACS	Latin American and Caribbean	LIR	laser-induced retinopathy
	Literature on Health Sciences		left iliac region
LILT	low-intensity laser therapy		left inferior rectus
LIM	limited toxicology screening	LIR-1	leucocyte immunoglobulin-like
LIMA	left internal mammary		receptor-1
	artery (graft)	LI-RADS	Liver Imaging Reporting and
Lima	Phonetic Alphabet for L;		Data System (a system for
	pronounced LEE-MAH		interpreting and reporting
LIMA-LAD	left internal mammary artery to		of imaging features on
	left anterior descending (graft)		multidetector computed
LIMA to LAD	left internal mammary artery		tomography and magnetic
	to the left anterior descending		resonance studies in patients
	artery (coronary artery		at risk for hepatocellular
	bypass graft)		carcinoma)
LIMDU	limited duty	LIRZ	low intermediate risk zone
LIMS	laboratory information	LIS	late-onset idiopathic scoliosis
	management system(s)		lateral internal sphincterotomy
LIN	liquid nitrogen		left intercostal space
	lobular intraepithelial neoplasia		local index of significance
LINAC	linear accelerator		locked-in syndrome
LINCL	late-infantile neuronal ceroid		low intermittent suction
	lipofuscinosis		lung injury score
LINDI	lithium-induced nephrogenic	LISO	left inferior superior oblique
	diabetes insipidus	LISS	less invasive stabilization system
LING	lingual		low ionic strength saline
LINQ	Lung Information Needs	LISW	Licensed Independent Social
	Questionnaire		Worker
linX	short chain dehydrogenase;	LISW-S	Supervising Licensed
	see gene website www.ncbi		Independent Social Worker
	.nlm.nih.gov/gene	LIT	literature
LINX®	a reflux management system		liver injury test
	(Torax Medical, St. Paul,		low-intensity (resistence) training
	MN, USA) that by use	LITA	left internal thoracic artery
	of a magnetic device	lites	may have meant lytes [electrolyte
	designed to augment the		test panel; sodium (Na+),
	lower esophageal sphincter		potassium (K+), chloride

L

LITETAR	(Cl−), and bicarbonate (HCO3−; sometimes reported as total CO2)]
	low intensity thermally evoked tail avoidance response
LITH	lithotomy
LITHO	lithotripsy
LITS	light and intermittent smokers
LITT	laser interstitial thermal therapy
	laser-induced thermotherapy
LIV	left innominate vein
	lowest instrumented vertebra
LIVB	live birth
LIVC	left inferior vena cava
LIVCD	local intraventricular conduction delay (disturbances)
L-IVP	limited intravenous pyelogram
LIVPRO	liver profile (see Laboratory Panels)
LIWC	Linguistic Inquiry Word Count
LIWS	low intermittent wall suction
LIZ	lower inner zone (breast)
LJ	left jugular
	lockable joints
LJL	lateral joint line
LJM	limited joint mobility
LK	lamellar keratoplasty
	left kidney
LKA	Lazare-Klerman-Armour (Personality Inventory)
LKB	Lyman-Kutcher-Birman (model for estimating the tumor control probability and normal tissue complication probability)
LKD	living kidney donation (donor)
LKDT	living kidney donor transplantation
LKM-3	liver-kidney microsomal antibodies type 3
LKM1	liver-kidney microsome type 1 (gene/antibody)
LKN	last known normal (time in patients suspected with acute stroke)
LKN-1	leukotactin-1
LKO	liver-specific knockout (mice)
LKR	lysine ketoglutarate reductase; see gene website www.ncbi.nlm.nih.gov/gene
LKRD	living kidney related donation(s)
LKS	Landau-Kleffner syndrome
	liver, kidneys, spleen
	Lysholm knee scores
LKSB	liver, kidneys, spleen, and bladder
LKSNP	liver, kidneys, and spleen not palpable

LKT	laparoscopic kidney transplantation
	leukotoxin
	liver-kidney transplantation (combined)
LKW	left kidney weight
LKWT	last known well time
LL	large lymphocyte
	left lateral
	left leg
	left lower
	left lung
	leg lowering
	lepromatous leprosy
	lid lag
	long leg (brace or cast)
	lower lid
	lower limb
	lower lip
	lower lobe
	lumbar laminectomy
	lumbar length
	lumbar lordosis
	lymphoblastic lymphoma
	lymphocytic leukemia
LL2	limb lead two
L&L	lids and lashes
L₁...L₅	lumbar nerve 1 through 5
	lumbar vertebra 1 through 5
L1L2	lumbar vertebrae 1 and 2
L1-L2	first & second lumbar vertebrae
	lumbar vertebrae 1 and 2
L2-L3	lumbar vertebrae 2 and 3
L3-L4	lumbar vertebrae 3 and 4
L4-L5	lumbar vertebrae 4 and 5
LLA	left lower arm
	lids, lashes, and adnexa
	limulus lysate assay
LLAP	Legionella-like amebal pathogen
LLAs	lipid-lowering agents
LLAT	left lateral
LLB	last living breath
	left lateral bending
	left lateral border
	long leg brace
LLBCD	left lower border of cardiac dullness
LLC	laparoscopic laser cholecystectomy
	Lewis lung carcinoma
	limited liability corporation
	long leg cast
	lower lateral cartilage (nasal)
LLCHH	localized Langerhans' cell histiocytosis
LLD	late-life depression
	left lateral decubitus

	left length discrepancy	LLR	large local reaction
	lower (limb) length difference		left lateral rectus
	lower limit of detection		left lumbar region
LLDP	left lateral decubitus (sleeping)	LLRE	lower lid, right eye
	position	LLRP	left lateral recumbent position
LLDSP	left lateral decubitus sleeping	LLRT	low-load resistance training
	position	LLS	lazy leukocyte syndrome
LLE	left lower extremity	LLSB	left lower sternal border
	liquid-liquid extraction	LLSD	laser light scattering detector
	little league elbow	LLSE	lower left sternal edge
	local linear embedding	LLT	left lateral thigh
	lower limb edema		lipid-lowering therapy
LLETZ	large loop excision of the		lowest level term
	transformation zone	ll	parallel bars
L-LETZ	large loop excision of the	LLTT	lower-limb tension test(s)
	transformation zone	LLU	Loma Linda University
LLF	lower lung field	LLV	low-level viremia (defined as
LLFG	long leg fiberglas (cast)		a human immunodeficiency
LLFP	lower lung field pneumonia		virus viral load between the
LLFTB	lower lung field tuberculosis		lower limits of detection
LLG	left lateral gaze		(20-75 copies/mL) and 1000)
LL-GXT	low-level graded exercise test	LLWC	long leg walking cast
LLI	leg-length inequality	LLX	left lower extremity
	long leg immobilizer	LLY	Eli Lilly and Company
	lower limb injuriy		years of life lost (Romance
LLIF	lateral lumbar interbody fusion		languages)
LLINs	long-lasting insecticidal bednets	LLy	lymphoblastic lymphoma
	long-lasting insecticidal nets	llz	see gene website www.ncbi
LLITN	long-lasting insecticide-treated		.nlm.nih.gov/gene
	nets	LM	landmarks
LLL	late-lumen loss		lateral meniscus
	left lower leg		left main (coronary artery)
	left lower lid		left message
	left lower lobe (lung)		lentigo maligna
LLLE	lower lid left eye		light microscopy
LLLNR	left lower lobe, no rales		linguomesial
LLL PNA	left lower lobe pneumonia		living male
LLLT	low-level laser therapy		lower midline
LLM	leg lean mass		lung metastases
	lipid-lowering medication		lymphatic malformation
LLN	lower limit of normal		left main (coronary artery)
LLO	Legionella-like organism		disease
LLOD	lower lid, right eye	L/M	Latin male
	lower limit of detection		left message
LLOQ	lower limit of quantitation		liters per minute
LLOS	lower lid, left eye		see LM
LLOV	Lloviu virus	Lm1	lymphomyeloid antigen 1;
LLP	Limited Liability Partnership		see gene website www.ncbi
	long leg plaster		.nlm.nih.gov/gene
LLPA	lifespan leisure physical activity	LMA	laryngeal mask airway
	low-intensity light physical		left mentoanterior
	activity		liver membrane autoantibody
LLPDD	late luteal phase dysphoric	LMA-AI	intubating laryngeal mask
	disorder		airway assisted intubation
LLPS	low-load prolonged stress	LMA	laryngeal mask airway for
LLPV	left lower pulmonary vein	bronchoscopy	fiberoptic bronchoscopy
LLQ	left lower quadrant (abdomen)	LMAC	light-to-moderate alcohol
	lower limit of quantitation		consumption

LMAM	left message on answering machine	LMR	left medial rectus
		LMRM	left modified radical mastectomy
LMAO	laughing my ass off (slang)		
Lmax	maximum lesion count during (actinic keratosis) treatment	LMRP	Local Medical Review Policy
		LMRPs	local medical review policies
LMB	Laurence-Moon-Biedl syndrome	LMRTs	lateral meniscus root tears
	left main bronchus	LMS	lateral mass screw
LMBB	Laurance-Moon-Bardet-Biedl (syndrome)		lateral medullary syndrome
			leiomyosarcomas
LMC	living male child	LMSB	left main stem bronchus
LMCA	left main coronary artery	LMSF	localized management of the sinus floor
	left middle cerebral artery		
LMCAT	left middle cerebral artery thrombosis	LM/SL	lymphatic mapping and sentinel lymphadenectomy
LMCL	left midclavicular line	LMST	leptomeningeal metastasis in solid tumors
LMD	Langer mesomelic dysplasia		
	local medical doctor	LMSW	Licensed Master Social Worker
	low molecular weight dextran	LMT	lateral meniscal tear
	lumbar microdiskectomy		left main trunk
LME	left mediolateral episiotomy		left mentotransverse
LMEE	left middle ear exploration		Letter Memory Test
LMF	left middle finger		Licensed Massage Therapist
	melphalan (L-PAM), metho-trexate, and fluorouracil		light moving touch
		LMTCB	left message to call back
LMFT	Licensed Marriage and Family Therapist	LMTD	left main trunk disease
		LMTRC	left message to return call
LMHC	Licensed Mental Health Counselor	LMTX	leucomethylthioninium salts
		LMV	lamivudine (Epivir)
LMHP	Licensed Mental Health Practitioner	LMW	low molecular weight
		LMWD	low molecular weight dextran
LMHPE	Licenses Mental Health Professional, Eligible	LMWH	low molecular weight heparins
		LMWID	low-molecular-weight iron dextran inj (INFeD)
LMI	large multivalent immunogen		
	lateral mass index	LMX	leader-member exchange (theory)
	lean mass index	LN	latent nystagmus
L/mim/m2	liters per minute per square meter		left nostril (nare)
L/min	liters per minute		lymph nodes
LMK	let me know (slang)	LN$_2$	liquid nitrogen
LML	left medial lateral	LNA	alpha-linolenic acid
	left middle lobe		low nucleic acid
LMLE	left mediolateral episiotomy	LNB	lymph node biopsy
LMLO	left medial-lateral oblique (mammogram view)	LNBx	lymph node biopsy
		LNC	Legal Nurse Consultant
LMM	lentigo maligna melanoma	LNCaP	lymph node carcinoma of the prostate
LMN	letter of medical necessity		
	lower motor neuron	LNCC	Legal Nurse Consultant, Certified
LMNA	see gene website www.ncbi .nlm.nih.gov/gene		
		LNCs	lymph node cells
LMNL	lower motor neuron lesion	LND	lateral neck dissection
LMOM	left message on (answering) machine		light-near dissociation
			living non-directed (donors)
LMOR	left message on recorder		lonidamine
LMP	last menstrual period		low-nutrient-density (diet)
	left mentoposterior		lymph node dissection
	low malignant potential	LNE	lymph node enlargement
LMP1	latent membrane protein 1		lymph node excision
LMPC	Laser Microdissection and Pressure Catapulting	LNEC	laryngeal neuroendocrine carcinoma

LNF	laparoscopic Nissen fundoplication		level of consciousness
			local
LNG	levonorgestrel		localization
LNG-IUS	levonorgestrel-releasing intrauterine system		loss of consciousness
		LOCA	late onset cerebellar ataxia
LNH	linfoma no hodgkin (Spanish: non-Hodgkin lymphoma)	LOCF	last-observation-carried-forward (used for inputting data missing due to dropouts in longitudinal clinical trials)
	lymphoid nodular hyperplasia		
	lymphome non hodgkinien (French: non-Hodgkin lymphoma)		
		LOCM	low-osmolality contrast media
		LOCQ	Locus of Control Questionnaire
LNL	Laboratori Nazionali di Legnaro (Italy)	LOCS	Lens Opacities Classification System (score)
	linear, non-linear, linear (model)	locum	someone (physician, clergyman, etc.) who substitutes temporarily for another member of the same profession
LNM	Lansinoh for Nursing Mothers (ointment used for sore nipples)		
		Locum tenens	a Latin phrase that means "to hold the place of, to substitute for"(health professionals who temporarily fulfills the duties of another or when a hospital or region is short staffed or underserved)
	lymph node metastases		
LNMC	lymph node mononuclear cells		
LNMP	last normal menstrual period		
LNNB	Luria-Nebraska Neuropsychological Battery		
LNOK	legal next of kin		
LNP	lipid nanoparticle	LOD	late-onset disease
LNR	lymph node ratio		limit of detection
LNRKT	living nonrelated kidney transplantation		line of duty
			logarithm of adds
LNS	lymph node sampling		
LNT	late neurological toxicity	LOE	lack of efficacy
LNU	laparoscopic nephroureterectomy		left otitis externa
			level of evidence
	learned non-use	LoEF	low ejection fraction
LNW	lyse-no-wash	LOEL	lowest-observed-effect level
LO	lateral oblique (x-ray view)	LOF	lack of function
	linguo-occlusal		leaking of fluids
	liquid oxygen		leave on floor
	lumbar orthosis		loss of fit
5-LO	5-lipoxygenase		loss-of-function
LOA	late-onset agammaglobulinemia	LOFD	low outlet forceps delivery
	leave of absence	Lofstrand	a brand of heavy duty adjustable aluminum forearm crutches
	left occiput anterior		
	Letter of Agreement	LOG	Logmar chart
	level of alertness	LoG	Laplacian of Gaussian (filter)
	long-acting opioid	log	logarithm any base
	looseness of associations	log_e	logarithm base 3 (natural)
	lumbar osteoarthritis	log_2	logarithm base 2
	lysis of adhesions	log_{10}	logarithm base 10
LOAD	late-onset Alzheimer disease	logMAR	logarythm of the minimum angle of resolution
LOAEL	lowest observed adverse effect level		
		logy	a suffix meaning- the science and/or study of
LOB	loss of balance		
LOb	lower-body obese		a word meaning sluggish; groggy
LOBF	line of best fit		
LOC	lab-on-a-chip	LOH	loss of heterozygosity
	laxative of choice	LOHF	late-onset hepatic failure
	level of care	LOHP	oxaliplatin (Eloxatin)
	level of comfort	LOI	level of injury
	level of concern		level of intervention

345

	Leyton Obsessional Inventory	LOTN	Lady of the night (Cestrum
	loss of imprinting		nocturnum [a plant])
LOIH	left oblique inguinal hernia	LOU	level of understanding
LOINC	Logical Observation Identifiers	LOV	last office visit
	Names and Codes		length of ventilation
LOL	laughing out loud (slang)		loss of vision
	left occipitolateral	LOVA	loss of visual acuity
	little old lady (slang)	LOVT	low tidal volume ventilation
LOLINAD	little old lady in no apparent	Low T	low testosterone
	distress	LOX	lipid oxidation
LOM	left otitis media		lysyl oxidase
	limitation of motion	LOXO-101	larotrectinib (Vitrakvi)
	little old man	LOZ	lozenge
	little old man (slang)	LP	lamina propria
	low-osmolar (contrast) media		laparoscopic pyeloplasty
LOMN	letter of medical necessity		lash ptosis
LOMS	late-onset multiple sclerosis		late potentials
LOMSA	left otitis media, suppurative,		Licensed Psychologist
	acute		light perception
LOMSC	left otitis media, suppurative,		linguopulpal
	chronic		lipid panel (see Laboratory
LoNa	low sodium		Panels)
long	longitudinal		lipoprotein
LOO	length of operation		low protein
LOOCV	leave-one-out cross-validation		lumbar puncture
LOP	laparoscopic orchiopexy	L&P	lidocane and prilocaine
	leave on pass	L/P	lactate-pyruvate ratio
	left occiput posterior		lidocane/prilocaine
	level of pain	L1780P	a variant of the BRCA1 (Breast
	limb occlusion pressure		Cancer Gene 1) gene
LOPD	late-onset Parkinson disease	L5%P	lidocaine 5% patch (Lidoderm)
	late-onset Pompe disease	LP5	Life-Pak 5
LOPS	loss of protective sensation	LPA	left pulmonary artery
LOQ	limit(s) of quantitation		lysophosphatidic acid
	lower outer quadrant	LPA%	left pulmonary artery oxygen
LOR	loss of resistance		saturation
LORD	late-onset retinal degeneration	Lp(a)	lipoprotein (a)
LORETA	low-resolution electromagnetic	L-PAM	melphalan (Alkeran)
	tomography	LPB	ipoblastoma
LORS-I	Level of Rehabilitation Scale-I		lumbar plexus block
LOS	large offspring syndrome	LPC	laser photocoagulation
	length of stay		leukocyte-depleted packed cells
	limits of stability (test)		Licensed Professional
	line-of-sight		Counselor
	loss of sight	LPCA	left posterior communicating
	lower oesophageal sphincter		artery
	(United Kingdom and other		long posterior ciliary artery
	countries)	LPCC	Licensed Professional Certified
	low-output syndrome		Counselor
lo-SES	lower socioeconomic status	LPC-L	lymphoplasmacytoid lymphoma
LOT	laser optical tweezers	Lpmacron-cP	light perception with projection
	left occiput transverse	LPD	leiomyomatosis peritonealis
	Licensed Occupational		disseminata
	Therapist		low potassium dextran
	Life Orientation Test		low-protein diet
	(questionnaire/score)		luteal phase defect
	questionnaire		luteal phase deficiency
LOTA	last on-treatment assessment		lymphoproliferative disease

LPDA	left posterior descending artery	LPM	latent primary malignancy
LPDs	lateralized periodic discharges		liters per minute
	lymphoproliferative disorders	LPME	liquid-phase microextraction
LPEP	left pre-ejection period	LPMSE	leave prior to medical screening
LPF	late parasitological failure		examination
	liver plasma flow		leave prior to medical service
	low-power field	LPN	laparosopic partial nephrectomy
	lymphocytosis-promoting factor		Licensed Practical Nurse
LPFB	left posterior fascicular block	LPO	left posterior oblique
LPFL	lateral patellofemoral ligament		light perception only
LPFVT	left posterior fascicular	LPP	lichen planopilaris
	ventricular tachycardia	LPPC	left posterior parietal cortex
LPF-VT	left posterior fascicular		leukocyte-poor packed cells
	ventricular tachycardia	LPPH	late postpartum hemorrhage
LPG	lipophosphoglycan	Lp-PLA2	lipoprotein-associated
	liquefied petroleum gas		phospholipase A2
LPGs	laboratory practice guidelines	LPR	laryngopharyngeal reflux
LPH	left posterior hemiblock		leprosy (Hansens disease) vaccine
	lumbar puncture headache	LPRD	laryngopharyngeal reflux disease
LPHA	local public health agency	LPS	last Papanicolaou smear
LPHAs	local public health agencies		latency to persistent sleep
LPHB	left posterior hemiblock		lipopolysaccharide
LPHD	lymphocyte-predominant	lpsB	lipopolysaccharide core biosyn-
	Hodgkin disease		thesis mannosyltransferase;
LPHL	lymphocyte-predominant		see gene website www.ncbi
	Hodgkin lymphoma		.nlm.nih.gov/gene
LPHS	loin pain-hematuria syndrome	LPSDT	laryngopharyngeal sensory
LPI	laser peripheral iridectomy		discrimination testing
	last patient in	LP SHUNT	lumboperitoneal shunt
	leukotriene pathway inhibitor	LPSO	left posterior superior oblique
	lysinuric protein intolerance	LPmacron-sP	light perception without
LPICA	left posterior internal carotid		projection
	artery	LPT	Language Processing Test
LPIH	left-posterior-inferior hemiblock		late preterm (infants born at
LPIT	lumbar puncture and intrathecal		34 to 36 weeks' gestation)
	(chemotherapy or other agents)		leave prior to triage
LPK	Lewis polycystic kidney (rat[s])		leptospirosis (Leptospira-
	liver pyruvate kinase		*Leptospires* sp.) vaccine
LPL	laparoscopic pelvic		Licensed Physical Therapist
	lymphadenectomy		low-pain threshold
	left posterolateral	LPTMS	Laboratoire de Physique
	lipoprotein lipase		Théorique et Modèles
	lymphoplasmacytic lymphoma		Statistiques (Laboratory of
LplA	lipoid acid ligase A		Theoretical Physics Models
LPLC	low-pressure liquid		and Statistics)
	chromatography	LPTN	Licensed Psychiatric Technical
LPLK	lichen planus-like keratosis		Nurse
LPLND	laparoscopic pelvic lymph	LPUP	loss of primary unassisted patency
	node dissection	LPV	left portal vein
	lateral pelvic lymph node		left pulmonary vein
	dissection		lopinavir
lPLND	limited pelvic lymph node	LPV/r	lopinavir and ritonavir
	dissection	LPV/RTV	lopinavir/ritonavir
LPLs	lamina propria lymphocytes	LPx	lipid peroxidation
	lysophospholipids	LPZ	lateral peripheral zone (prostate
LPL/WM	lymphoplasmacytic		needle biopsy location)
	lymphoma/Waldenström	LQ	lower quartile
	macroglobulinemia	LQA	limit of quantitation amount

L

LQT	long QT (interval)	LRGB	laparoscopic Roux-en-Y gastric bypass
LQT1	a specific type of long QT (interval) syndrome. There are 10 types	L&IR gtt	Levophed and Regitine drip (infusion)
LQTS	long QT (interval) syndrome	LRH	laparoscopic radical hysterectomy
LR	labor room	LRHC	laparoscopic right hemicolectomy
	lactated Ringers (injection)		
	laser resection	LRHT	living-related hepatic transplantation
	late response		
	lateral rectus (muscle)	LRI	limbal relaxing incision
	left-right		lower respiratory infection
	light reflex	LRINEC	Laboratory Risk Indicator for Necrotizing Fasciitis (score)
	likelihood ratios		
	local recurrence	LRINEC	Laboratory Risk Indicator for Necrotizing Fasciitis (score; a tool for distinguishing necrotizing fasciitis from other soft tissue infections)
Lr	lawrencium		
L&R	left and right		
L → R	left to right		
L/R	left/right		
LR1A	labor room 1A		
LRA	left radial artery	LRIT	logistic regression with an interaction term
	left renal artery		
LRAD	least restrictive assistive device	LRKT	living-related kidney transplantation
LRAP	leucine-rich amelogenin peptide (a product of alternative splicing of the amelogenin gene)		
		LRK TX	living related kidney transplant
		LRLT	living-related liver transplantation
LRB	late rectal bleeding		
LRb	leptin receptor	LRM	left radical mastectomy
LRBA	lipopolysaccharide-responsive and beige-like anchor (gene/protein)		local regional metastases
		LRMP	last regular menstrual period
		LRN	laparoscopic radical nephrectomy
LRBC	locally recurrent breast cancer	LRNC	lipid-rich necrotic-core
LRC	licensed relative care (foster care homes)	LRND	left radical neck dissection
		LRNY	laparoscopic Roux-en-Y (procedure)
	locoregional control		
	lower rib cage	LRNYGB	laparoscopic Roux-en-Y gastric bypass
LRCP	Licentiate of the Royal College of Physicians		
		LRO	long range objective
LRCS	Licentiate of the Royal College of Surgeons	LROM	limited range of motion
		Lrot	left rotation
LRCx	lower respiratory (tract) culture	LROU	lateral rectus, both eyes
LRD	least restrictive device	LRP	laparoscopic radical prostatectomy
	least restrictive diet		
	limb reduction defects		lipoprotein receptor-related protein
	living renal donor		
	living-related donor		lung-resistance protein
LRDKT	living related donor kidney transplant	LRP1	low density lipoprotein receptor-related protein 1; see gene website www.ncbi.nlm.nih.gov/gene
LRDRT	living-relate donor transplantation		
LRDRTx	living-relate donor transplantation	LRP4	low-density lipoprotein receptor-related protein 4
LRDT	living-related donor transplant	LRPLND	laparoscopic retroperitoneal lymph node dissection
LRE	localization-related epilepsy		
LREH	low-renin essential hypertension	LRPN	lumbosacral radiculoplexus neuropathy
LRF	left rectus femoris		
	left ring finger	LRPRBC	leucocytes-reduced packed red blood cells
	local-regional failure		
LRFS	local recurrence-free survival	LRPV	lower right pulmonary vein

LRPV SCORE	logistic regression probability value (logistic regression to predict probability of brain dysfunction; a neurocognitive assessment of pilots)		loose stool
			low salt
			lumbosacral
			lung sounds
			Lynch syndrome (is characterized
LRQ	lower right quadrant		by germline abnormalities in
LRR	light reflection rheography		mismatch repair genes, leading
	local recurrence rates		to predisposition to multiple
	locoregional recurrences		cancers)
LRRH	low-Renin Renal Hypertension	L&S	ligation and stripping
LRRK2	leucine-rich repeat kinase 2 gene		liver and spleen
LRRT	locoregional radiotherapy	L/S	lecithin-sphingomyelin ratio
LRRTx	living-related renal transplantation		lumbar spine
			lumbosacral
LRS	lactated Ringers solution	L5-S1	lumbar fifth vertebra to sacral
	learned nonuse (splint)		first vertebra (where the lumbar
LRSG	laparoscopic reoperative sleeve gastrectomy		and sacral spines join)
			lumbar vertebra 5 and sacral
LRSP	long-range surface plasmon		vertebrae 1
LRT	Lateral Reach Test	L7/S1	lumbosacral (junction)
	likelihood ratio test	LSA	left sacrum anterior
	living renal transplant		left subclavian artery
	local radiation therapy		lichen sclerosus et atrophicus
	lower respiratory tract		lipid-bound sialic acid
lrtA	light repressed protein A-like protein; see gene website www.ncbi.nlm.nih.gov/gene		lymphosarcoma
		LS & A	lichen sclerosis et atrophicus
		LSAD	legal/statistical area description
LRTC	long-range temporal correlations	LSAs	low-sedating antihistamines
	lower respiratory tract colonization	LSB	left scapular border
			left sternal border
LRTD	living relative transplant donor		local standby
	lower respiratory tract disease		lumbar spinal block
LRTI	ligament reconstruction with tendon interposition		lumbar sympathetic block
		LSBE	long-segment Barrett esophagus
	lower respiratory tract infection	LSBP	lateralized single-bundle patellar (tendon graft)
	lower respiratory tract infection(s)	LS BPS	laparoscopic bilateral partial salpingectomy
LRTT	lateralized reaction-time task	LSC	laser scanning cytometry
	locoregional tumor treatment		last sexual contact
LRU	laparoscopic nephroureterectomy		late systolic click
			least significant change
	lipase releasing units		left subclavian (artery) (vein)
LRV	left renal vein		leukemia stem cells
	log reduction value		lichen simplex chronicus
LRW	LAL (*Limulus* amebocyte lysate) reagent water		liquid scintillation counting
			lung sounds clear
LRYGB	laparoscopic Roux-en-Y gastric bypass	LSCA	left scapuloanterior
			left subclavian artery
LRZ	lorazepam (Ativan)	LSCC	laryngeal squamous cell carcinoma
LS	left side		
	legally separated	LSCCB	limited-state small-cell cancer of the bladder
	Leighs syndrome		
	levator scapula	LSCD	limbal stem cell deficiency
	lichen sclerosus	LSCM	laser scanning confocal microscopy
	liver scan		
	liver stiffness	L-scope	laparoscope
	liver-spleen	LSCP	left scapuloposterior

L

LSCS	lower segment cesarean section	LSNA	lumbar sympathetic nerve activity
LSCTA	lung sounds clear to auscultation		
LS CTA	lung sounds, clear to auscultation	LSO	left salpingo-oophorectomy
			left superior oblique
LSCTAB	lung sounds clear to auscultation, bilateral		lumbosacral orthosis
		LSP	left sacrum posterior
LSCV	left superior caval vein		liver-specific (membrane) lipoprotein
LSD	least significant difference		
	low-salt diet	LS-PAF	long-standing persistent atrial fibrillation
	lumbosacral derangement		
	lysergic acid diethylamide (lysergide)	L–Spar	Elspar (asparaginase)
		L spine	lumbar spine
	lysosomal storage disorder	LSPO	left superior posterior oblique
LSD1	lysine-specific demethylase 1	LSPV	left superior pulmonary vein
LSE	left sternal edge	LSQ	Life Situation Questionnaire
	local side effects	LSR	laser skin resurfacing
LSEA	lichen sclerosus et atrophicus		left superior rectus
L/sec	liters per second	L/Sratio	lecithin/sphingomyelin ratio
LSed	level of sedation	LSRL	lumbosacral root lesion(s)
LSetA	lichen sclerosus et atrophicus	LSS	Level of Sitting Scale
LSF	line spread function (radiology)		Lewis-Sumner syndrome (see MADSAM)
	low spatial frequencies		
	low-saturated fat		limb-sparing surgery
LSFA	low-saturated fatty acid (diet)		liver-spleen scan
LSG	laparoscopic sleeve gastrectomy		lumbar spinal stenosis
	of lymphoscintigraphy	LS scan	liver-spleen scan
LSH	laparoscopic supracervical hysterectomy	LSSI	Lipp Stress Symptoms Inventory
		LSSS	large, simple safety study
	leishmaniasis vaccine		Liverpool Seizure Severity Scale
	lutein-stimulating hormone		
LSHF	low-sugar/high-fiber	LST	left sacrum transverse
LSHR	laparoscopic suprapubic hernia repair		left scapulotransverse
			leishmanin skin test
LSHS-R	Launay-Slade Hallucinations Scale-revised	LSTAT	life support for trauma and transport
		LSTC	laparoscopic subtotal cholecystectomy
LSI	levonorgestrel subdermal implant		
			laparoscopic tubal coagulation
LSIL	low-grade squamous intraepithelial lesion	LsTG	laparoscopic subtotal gastrectomy
LSIs	lifesaving interventions	LSTL	laparoscopic tubal ligation
	life-sustaining interventions	LSTM	lean soft tissue mass
	limb symmetry Indices	L's & T's	lines and tubes
LSK	liver, spleen, and kidneys	LSU	life support unit
LSKM	liver-spleen-kidney-megalgia		lipasemic units
LSL	left sacrolateral	LSV	left subclavian vein
	left short leg (brace)		lesser saphenous vein
LSLF	low sodium, low fat (diet)	LSVC	left superior vena cava
LSLT	left single lung transplant	LSVD	may have meant LVSD (left ventricular systolic dysfunction)
LSM	laser scanning microscope		
	late systolic murmur		
	least squares mean	LSVT® Big	Lee Silverman Voice Treatment (method for improving physical/occupational activities in individuals with Parkinson and other diseases)
	limited sampling model		
	liver stiffness measurements		
	liver, spleen masses		
LSMFT	liposclerosing myxofibrous tumor		
		LSVT® Loud	Lee Silverman Voice Treatment (method for improving voice
LSMT	life-sustaining medical treatment		

L

	and speech in individuals with Parkinson and other disease)	LTCBDE	laparoscopic transcystic common bile duct exploration
LSW	left-side weakness	LTCCS	low transverse cervical cesarean section
	Licensed Social Worker	LTCD	low transverse cesarean delivery
LT	laboratory technician	LTCF	long-term care facility
	lactate threshold	LTCH	inpatient long term care hospital
	left		(average length of stay
	left thigh		greater than 25 days)
	left triceps	LTCHs	long-term care hospitals
	less than	LTC-IC	long-term culture-initiating cells
	leukotrienes	LTCL	lateral talocalcaneal ligament
	Levin tube	Lt Col	Lieutenant Colonel
	light	LTCR	long-term complete remission(s)
	light touch	LTCS	low-transverse cesarean section
	liver transplantation	LTCVC	long-term tunnelled central venous catheter
	locomotor training		
	long term	LT CVC	landmark technique central venous catheter (placement)
	low transverse		
	lower trapezius (muscle)	LTD	largest tumor dimension
	lumbar traction		leg transfer device
	lung transplantation		line, tube and drain (incident)
	lunotriquetral		lipid tear deficiency
	lymphotoxin		long-term depression
L&T	lettuce and tomato		long-term disability
L/T	long term	LTD$_4$	leukotriene D$_4$
LT3	liothyronine sodium (Cytomel)	LTE	less than effective
LT4	levothyroxine		less than or equal to
LTA	laryngeal tracheal anesthesia		life-threatening event
	laryngotracheal applicator		longterm exposure
	lateral thoracic arteries	LTE$_4$	leukotriene E$_4$
	local tracheal anesthesia	LTEC	laryngotracheo-esophageal cleft
LTAC	intralesional triamcinolone acetonide		long term extended care facilities
	long-term acute care	LtEc	Lumbricus terrestris
LTACHs	long-term acute care hospitals		(the earthworm source of
LTAD	long-term androgen deprivation		a high-molecular-weight
LTAH	leukotriene A4 hydrolase		extracellular hemoglobin
LTAS	left transatrial septal		[erythrocruorin]; has potential
LTB	laparoscopic tubal banding		use as a blood substitute
	laryngotracheobronchitis		because of its resistant to
	London tuberculosis Register		oxidation and aggregation
LTB1	may have meant LTBI (latent tuberculosis infection)		during storage)
		LTED	long-term estrogen deprivation
LTB$_4$	leukotriene B$_4$	LTF	lost to follow-up
LTBI	latent tuberculosis infection	LTFU	long-term follow-up
LTBR	lateral temporal bone resection		loss to follow-up
	lymphotoxin beta receptor (gene)	LTG	lamotrigine (Lamictal)
			long term goal(s)
LTC	Lapra-Ty (suture) clip		long-term goal
	left to count		low-tension glaucoma
	long thick closed	L-TGA	left-transposition of great arteries
	long-term care		
LTC$_4$	leukotriene C$_4$	Lt Gen	Lieutenant General
LTC-101	long-term care form-101	LTGV	long-term glycemic variability
LTCA	lateral talocalcaneal angle	LTH	left total hip (arthroplasty)
	longterm chronoamperometry		lingual tonsil hypertrophy
LTCBC	long-term cord blood cultures		luteotropic hormone

LTHA	Lifetime History of Aggression (questionnaire)	LTPFS	long-term progression-free survivors
L-THA	left total hip arthroplasty	LTR	laryngotracheal reconstruction
LTHR	lactate threshold heart rate		long terminal repeats
	left total hip replacement (it is safer to spell out "left")		lower trunk rotation
LTI	latent tuberculosis infection	LTRA	leukotriene receptor antagonist (e.g. montelukast [Singulair])
	long transverse incision		leukotriene receptors antagonists
LTi	lymphoid tissue-inducer (cells)	LTRI	life threatening respiratory illness(es)
LTIF	lateral transpsoas interbody fusion		may have meant LRTI (lower respiratory tract infection[s])
LTIL	lunotriquetral interosseous ligament		
LTIOL	lunotriquetral interosseous (ligament)	LTS	laparoscopic tubal sterilization
			laryngotracheal separation
LTK	laser thermal keratoplasty		laryngotracheal stenosis
	left total knee (arthroplasty)		long-term survivors
LTKA	left total knee arthroplasty		low-temperature sterilization
LTKR	left total knee replacement (it is safer to spell out "left")	LTSA	long-term sickness absence
		LTSP	long-term stationary phase
LTL	laparoscopic tubal ligation		luteinized thecomas associated with sclerosing peritonitis
	left temporal lobectomy		
	leukocyte telomere length	LTSR	latency time of the swallowing reflex
LTLD	lyso-thermosensitive liposomal doxorubicin		
		LTSS	long-term services and supports
LTLs	leukocyte telomere lengths	LTT	lactose tolerance test
LTM	long-term memory		lymphocyte transformation test
	long-term monitoring	LT-TCPC	lateral tunnel-total cavopulmonary connection
L-TME	laparoscopic total mesorectum excision		
		LTUI	low transverse uterine incision
LTNP	long-term nonprogressors (HIV infections)	LTUM	long-term evaluation of the uncertainty in measurement
LTNs	light-triggered nanotheranostics (the integrated combination of target-specific diagnostics and delivery of therapeutics based on nanotechnology platforms)	LTV	long-term variability
			long-term ventilation
			Luche tumor virus
		LTV 0	long-term variability–absent
		LTV+	long-term variability–average to moderate
LTOC	longest single time-off cardioplegia	LTVC	long-term venous catheter
		LTVW	longterm ventilation weaning
LTOLE	long-term open-label extension (allows continued prescribing of unlicensed drugs after a randomized trial)	LTWN	long-term low-level white noise
		LTx	liver transplant
			lung transplantation
LTOs	long-term outcomes	LTZ	letrozole (Femara)
LTOT	long-term oxygen therapy	LU	left upper
LTP	laparoscopic transcapsular prostatectomy		left ureteral
	laser trabeculoplasty		living unit
	lateral tibial plateau		Lutheran
	lateral trochanteric pain		Lutheran; an International Society of Blood Transfusion (ISBT) blood group
	lipid transfer protein (gene/protein)		
		L & U	lower and upper
	long-term plan	LUA	left upper arm
	long-term potentiation	LUBE	lower-upper bound estimation
Ltp	liver transport protein (gene/protein)		lubricant and lubricant-like debris/contamination
LTPA	leisure-time physical activity		lubricating; lubricant

LUC	luciferase	LuTX	lung transplantation	

LUC — luciferase
LUCAS — Lund University Cardiopulmonary Assist System
LUCAS-2 — Lund University Cardiopulmonary Assist System 2
LUCL — lateral ulnar collateral ligament
LUD — left uterine displacement
LUDKT — living unrelated donor kidney transplantations
LUE — left upper extremity
LuesI — primary syphilis
LuesII — secondary syphilis
LuesIII — tertiary syphilis
LUFF — lateral upper arm free flap (reconstruction of pharyngeal defect)
LUG — levator-urethral gap
LUH — left uterine horn
LUKT — living-unrelated kidney transplantation
LUL — left upper lid
left upper lobe (lung)
LUM — laparascopic-ultraminilaparotomic myomectomy
LUMA — luminometric methylation assay
Lum Lam — lumbar laminectomy
lump — lumpectomy
LUNA — laparoscopic uterosacral nerve ablation
LUOB — left upper outer buttock
LUOQ — left upper outer quadrant
LUP — loop unfolding protein; see gene website www.ncbi.nlm.nih .gov/gene
LUPA — low-utilization payment amount (Medicare)
LUPV — left upper pulmonary vein
LUQ — left upper quadrant
LURD — living-unrelated donor
LURKT — living-unrelated kidney transplantation
LURT — living-unrelated renal transplantation
LURTx — living unrelated renal transplantation
LUS — laparoscopic ultrasonography
laryngeal ultrasound
lower uterine segment
lung ultrasound
LUSB — left upper scapular border
left upper sternal border
LUST — lower uterine segment transverse
LUT — look up table (radiology)
lower urinary tract
LUTD — lower urinary tract dysfunction
LUTO — lower urinary tract obstruction
LUTS — lower urinary tract symptoms
LUTT — lower urinary tract tumor

LuTX — lung transplantation
LUW — lungworm vaccine
LUX — left upper extremity
LV — leave
left ventricle
left ventricular
leucovorin
live virus
Lv — livermorium
LVA — left ventricular aneurysm
LVAD — left ventricular assist device
L-VAM — leuprolide acetate, vinblastine, doxorubicin (Adriamycin), and mitomycin
LV Angio — left ventricular angiogram
LVAO — large visceral artery occlusion
LVAo — left ventricle aorta
LVAP — late-onset ventilator associated pneumonia
LVAS — large vestibular aqueduct syndrome
left ventricular assist system
LVAT — left ventricular activation time
LVATS — lobectomy by video-assisted thoracoscopic surgery
LVATs — may have meant LVADs (left ventricular assist devices)
LVBP — left ventricle bypass pump
LVBr — left ventricular branch (of the right coronary artery)
LVC — laser vision correction
low viscosity cement
low vision clinic
LVCR — left ventricular circumferential strain
LV CR — left ventricular circumferential strain
LVD — left ventricular dimension
left ventricular dysfunction
LVDD — left ventricular diastolic dysfunction
LVDd — left ventricular end-diastolic diameter
LVDEP — may have meant LVEDP (left ventricular end diastolic pressure)
LVDF — left ventricular diastolic function
LVDP — left ventricular diastolic pressure
LVDs — left ventricular systolic diameter
LVDT — linear variable differential transformer
LVDV — left ventricular diastolic volume
LVE — left ventricular enlargement
LVEDD — left ventricular end diastolic diameter
LVEDDI — left ventricular end-diastolic diameter (dimension) index

L

LVEDP	left ventricular end-diastolic pressure	LVMTCO	left voice mail (for patient) to call office
LVEDV	left ventricular end-diastolic volume	LVN	Licensed Visiting Nurse Licensed Vocational Nurse
LVEF	left ventricular ejection fraction	LVNC	left ventricular noncompaction
LVEH	left ventricular excentric hypertrophy	LVO	large vessel occlusion left ventricular opacification
LVEMB	left ventricular endomyocardial biopsy		left ventricular output left ventricular overactivity
LVEN	linear verrucous epidermal nevi	LVOF	linear variable optical filter
LVEP	left ventricular end pressure lung volume expansion protocol	LVOR	linear vestibulo-ocular reflex
LVESD	left ventricular end-systolic dimension	LVOT	left ventricular outflow tract
		LVOTO	left ventricular outflow tract obstruction
LVESV	left-ventricular end-systolic volumes	LVOT-TVI	left ventricular outflow tract time-velocity integral
LVESVI	left ventricular end-systolic volume index	LVP	large volume parenteral large-volume paracentesis
LVET	left ventricular ejection time		left ventricular pressure
LVF	left ventricular failure		lopinavir
	left ventricular function	LVPW	left ventricular posterior wall
	left visual field		ventricular posterior wall diameter
LVFP	left ventricular filling pressure	LVPWd	left ventricular posterior wall
LVFU	leucovorin and fluorouracil		thickness in diastole
LVFWR	left ventricular free wall rupture	LVQ	learning vector quantization
LVFX	levofloxacin (Levaquin)	LVR	laparoscopic ventral rectopexy
LVFx	left ventricular function		leucovorin
LVG	left ventriculogram		lung volume recruitment
	left ventrogluteal	LVRS	lung-volume reduction surgery
LVGLS	left ventricular global longitudinal strain	LVRT	liver-volume replaced by tumor
		LVS	laryngeal videostroboscopy
LVgram	left ventricular angiogram		left ventricular strain
LVH	left ventricular hypertrophy	LVSD	left ventricular systolic
LVHR	laparoscopic ventral hernia repair		dysfunction
LVHs	low-volume hospitals (as defined by each study)	LVS EMI	left ventricular subendocardial myocardial ischemia
LVI	lymphovascular invasion	LVSF	left ventricular shortening
LVID	left ventricular internal diameter		fraction
LVIDd	left ventricle internal diameter at end-diastole		left ventricular systolic function
		LVSG	laparoscopic vertical sleeve
LVIDs	left ventricle internal dimension systole		gastrectomy
		LVSI	lymphovascular space
LVIM	may have meant LVMI (left ventricular mass index)		involvement (invasion) lymph-vascular space invasion
LVIS	low-profile visualized intraluminal support (device; self-expanding braided stent for stent assisted coiling of intracranial aneurysms)	LVSP	left ventricular systolic pressure
		LVST	left cervical vagosympathetic trunk
		LVSW	left ventricular stroke work
		LVSWI	left ventricular stroke work index
LVL	large volume leukapheresis	LVT	Leapfrog volume threshold
	left vastus lateralis		levetiracetam (Keppra)
LV lead	left ventricle pacemaker lead		Licensed Veterinary Technician
LVM	left ventricular mass		low tidal volume
	left voice message	LV thrombus	left ventricular thrombus
LVMI	left ventricular mass index	LVTs	Leapfrog volume thresholds
LVMM	left ventricular muscle mass	IVUS	intravascular ultrasound
LVMR	laparoscopic ventral mesh rectopexy	LVV	left ventricular volume live varicella vaccine

L

LVVM	left message voicemail	LWTC	left without treatment completed
LVVT	left ventricle (originated) ventricular tachycardia	LX	larynx local irradiation lornoxicam (Xefo; available outside the United states) lower extremity
LVW	left ventricular wall		
LVWI	left ventricular work index		
LVWMA	left ventricular wall motion abnormality	LX 2	human hepatic stellate cells
		LXC	laxative of choice
LVWMI	left ventricular wall motion index	LXR	liver X receptor
LVWT	left ventricular wall thickness	lxr	see gene website www.ncbi .nlm.nih.gov/gene
LVX	levofloxacin		
LW	lacerating wound	LXT	left exotropia
	Landersteiner-Wiener; an International Society of Blood Transfusion (ISBT) blood group	LY	an inhibitor of phosphatidyli-nositol 3-kinase
		LYCD	live yeast cell derivative
		LyE	lymphedema
L & W	Lee and White (coagulation) living and well	LYEL	lost years of expected life
		LYFT	Life-Years from Transplantation
LWAQ	Living with Asthma Questionnaire	LYG	lymphomatoid granulomatosis
		LYM	Lyme disease vaccine lymphocytes
LWAT	limitation or withdrawal of active treatment	LYMPH	lymphatic
		lymphs	lymphocytes
LWBD	left without being discharged	LyP	lymphomatoid papulosis
LWBS	left without being seen. This implies the patient was registered but not triaged or assessed. Check to see if this conforms to your facility's definition (see LWBT and AMA)	LYPv	lymphoid tyrosine phosphatase
		LYS	large yellow soft (stools) life-years saved lysine
		lysis	a word meaning destruction
		lytes	electrolyte test panel; sodium (Na+), potassium (K+), chloride (Cl−), and bicarbonate (HCO3−; sometimes reported as total CO2)
LWBT	left without being treated. Patients who have been seen and triaged, but are waiting to be evaluated further; they leave without being further treated - their absence is without notification. Check to see if this conforms to your facility's definition. (see LWBS and AMA)		
		LZ	landing zone
		LZM	lysozyme
LWC	leave without consent		
LWCT	Lee-White clotting time left without completing treatment		
LWD	Leri-Weill dyschondrosteosis		
LWF	limited midcarpal arthrodesis		
LWIs	lateral-wedge insoles		
LWK	Luhya in Webuye, Kenya (population samples of HapMap [a catalog of common genetic variants that occur in human beings])		
LWMH	see LMWH		
LWOBS	left (leave) without being seen		
LWOP	leave without pay		
LWOT	left without treatment		
LWP	large whirlpool		
LWR	laparoscopic wedge resection		
LWS	Late Whiplash Syndrome low wall suction		

L

M

M   M sign - patient just utters "Mmmm" (slang)
male
manual
marital
married
masked (audiology)
mass
medial
memory
mesial
meta
meter (m)
methionine
Mike (Phonetic Alphabet for M; pronounced MIKE)
mild
million
minimum
moderate
molar
Monday
monocytes
mother
motor
mouth
murmur
muscle
Mycobacterium
Mycoplasma
myopia
myopic
thousand

3M   mitomycin, mitoxantrone, and methotrexate

M_1 first mitral sound

M_2 second mitral sound

M_3 third mitral sound

m^2 square meters (body surface)

M0   nonmetastatic

M1   left mastoid
Mallampati score 1 (classes 3 or 4 are associated with more difficult intubation as well as a higher incidence of sleep apnea)
tropicamide 1% ophthalmic solution (Mydriacyl)

M2   Mallampati score 2 (classes 3 or 4 are associated with more difficult intubation as well as a higher incidence of sleep apnea)
right mastoid

M-2   vincristine, carmustine, cyclophosphamide, melphalan, and prednisone

M3   Mallampati score 3 (classes 3 or 4 are associated with more difficult intubation as well as a higher incidence of sleep apnea)
third molar

M-3   medical student 3rd year

M-3+7   mitoxantrone and cytarabine

M4   Mallampati score 4 (classes 3 or 4 are associated with more difficult intubation as well as a higher incidence of sleep apnea)

M-4   medical student 4th year

M42   The medical necessity form must be personally signed by the attention physician. (Medicare)

M200   volociximab

MA   machine
Marketing Authorization (EU)
Massachusetts
Master of Arts
mean arterial (blood pressure)
medical assistance
medical assistant
medical authorization
Medicare Advantage (insurance)
megestrol acetate
menstrual age
mental age
metabolic acidosis
meter-angle
methamphetamine
Mexican American
microalbuminuria
microaneurysms
Miller-Abbott (tube)
milliamps
monoclonal antibodies
motorcycle accident

mA   milliamp [milliampere] (1 ampere [= 1,000 milliamperes)
milliamperage (radiology)

M/A   mood and/or affect

MA01   If you do not agree with what we approved for these services, you may appeal our decision. (Medicare code)

MA02   If you do not agree with this determination. (Medicare code)

MA-1   Bennett volume ventilator

MA18   The claim information is also being forwarded to the patient's supplemental insurer. (Medicare code)

MA59	Alert: The patient overpaid you for these services. You must issue the patient a refund within 30 days for the difference between his/her payment and the total amount shown as patient responsibility on this notice. (Medicare code)	
MA67	Correction to a prior claim. (Medicare code)	
MA72	Alert: The patient overpaid you for these assigned services. You must issue the patient a refund within 30 days for the difference between his/her payment to you and the total of the amount shown as patient responsibility and as paid on this notice. (Medicare code)	
MA101	A Skilled Nursing Facility (SNF) is responsible for payment of outside providers who furnish these services/ supplies to residents. (Medicare code)	
MA112	Missing/incomplete/invalid group practice information. (Medicare code)	
MA130	Your claim contains incomplete and/or invalid information, and no appeal rights are afforded because the claim is unprocessable. Please submit a new claim with the complete/correct information. (Medicare code)	
MAA	macroaggregates of albumin malaria-associated anemia Marketing Authorization Application (European Union)	
MAAAP	macroaggregated albumin arterial perfusion	
MAAP	Micro-computer Accident Analysis Package (software) mucosal advancement flap anoplasty	
MAARI	medically attended acute respiratory illness	
MAAS	Mindfulness Attention Awareness Scale Motor Activity Assessment Scale	
MAB	Massachusetts Biologic Laboratories maximum androgen blockade Mycobacterium abscessus	

mAb	monoclonal antibody
MABC	Movement Assessment Battery for Children
MABI	mindfulness- and acceptance-based interventions
MABIS	multiatlas-based image segmentation (a radiology algorithm involving animal irradiation organ at risk delineation)
MABM	mandibular alveolar bone mass
MABP	mean arterial blood pressure
mAbs	monoclonal antibodies
MAC	Macintosh laryngoscope blade macrocytic erythrocytes macrophage macula maximal allowable concentration medial arterial calcification Medicare Appeals Council membrane attack complex Mental Adjustment to Cancer (scale) methotrexate, dactinomycin (Actinomycin D), and cyclophosphamide microcystic adnexal carcinoma mid-arm circumference minimum alveolar concentration mitral annular calcification mitral annular calcium monitored anesthesia care multi-access catheter *Mycobacterium avium* complex
M2A capsule	mouth-to-anus capsule (a wireless endoscopy system)
MACC	methotrexate, doxorubicin, (Adriamycin) cyclophosphamide, and lomustine (Cee Nu)
MACCC	Master Arts, Certified Clinical Competence
MACCE	major adverse cardiac and cerebrovascular event
MACE	major adverse cardiac (cardiovascular) event(s) Malon antegrade continence enema Malone antegrade colonic enema
MACI	Master of Arts in Clinical Investigation
MAC-IC	Monitored Anesthesia Care-intracranial
MAC infection	Mycobacterium avium complex infection

M

MACIS	Metastases, Age, Completeness of Resection, Invasion, and Size (cancer staging system)	MAEEW	moves all extremities equally well
MACOP-B	methotrexate, doxorubicin, (Adriamycin) cyclophospha-mide, vincristine (Oncovin), prednisone, and bleomycin with leucovorin rescue	MAES	moves all extremities slowly
		Maestro system	a pacemaker-like device that uses electrical impulses to control appetite to produce weight lose
		MAEW	moves all extremities well
MACP	Manipulation Association of Chartered Physiotherapists	MAEX4	moves all 4 extremities
		MAF	malignant ascites fluid
	Master of Arts in Counseling Psychology		metabolic activity factor
			Mexican-American female
	Member, American College of Physicians	MAFAs	movement-associated fetal (heart rate) accelerations
MACRA	Medicare Access and CHIP (Children's Health Insurance Program) Reauthorization Act of 2015	MAFE	malaria-attributable fraction of fever episodes
		MAF-GFI	Multidimensional Assessment of Fatigue-Global Fatigue Index
MAC-RB	Monitored Anesthesia Care-retrobulbar	MAFO	molded ankle/foot orthosis
		MAFP	maternal alpha-fetoprotein
MACRO	macrocytes	MAG	medication administration guideline (record)
MACS	magnetic activated cell sorting		
MACs	malignancy-associated changes		myelin-associated glycoprotein (antibodies)
MACTAR	McMaster-Toronto Arthritis Patient Reference (Disability Questionnaire)	mag	magnesium (Mg)
		MAG-3	mercaptoacetyltriglycine (chelated with radioactive technetium-99m for diagnostic kidney imaging)
MAD	major affective disorder		
	mandibular advancement device		
	mind altering drugs		
	moderate atopic dermatitis	mag cit	magnesium citrate
	mucosal atomization device	mag citrate	magnesium citrate
	multiple-ascending doses	MAGEC	MAGnetic Expansion Control (system of percutaneously expandable magnetically-controlled rods)
Mad2	mitotic arrest defective protein 2		
MAdCAM-1	mucosal addressin cell adhesion molecule-1		
		MAGIC	mouth and genital ulcers with inflamed cartilage (syndrome)
MADD	Mothers Against Drunk Driving		
	multiple acyl-coenzyme A dehydrogenase deficiency	MAGMA	Magnetic Resonance Materials in Physics, Biology and Medicine (Official Journal of the European Society for Magnetic Resonance in Medicine and Biology)
MADIT-II	Multicenter Automatic Defibrillator Implantation Trial II		
MADL	mobility activities of daily living		
		mag oxide	magnesium oxide
MADM	mosaic analysis with double markers	MAGP	meatal advancement glandulophaleoplasty
	multiple-attribute decision making	MAGP-1	microfibril-associated glycoprotein 1
MADRS	Montgomery-Åsburg Depression Rating Scale	mag phos	magnesium phosphate
		MAGPI	meatal advancement and glanuloplasty
MADSAM	multifocal acquired demyelinating sensory and motor (neuropathy)	MagSO4	magnesium sulfate (more commonly abbreviated MgSO4)
MAE	medical air evacuation		
	modifications and adaptive equipment	mag sulf	magnesium sulfate
		mag sulfate	magnesium sulfate
	moves all extremities	MAHA	macroangiopathic hemolytic anemia
MAEE	moves all extremities equally		

M

MAHS	malignancy-associated hemophagocytic syndrome	malnut	malnutrition
MAI	maximal aggregation index	MAL-PDT	methyl aminolevulinic acid photodynamic therapy
	Medication Appropriateness Index	MALS	median arcuate ligament syndrome
	minor acute illness		multiangle light scattering
	multiphoton autofluorescence imaging	MALT	mucosa-associated lymphoid tissue
	Mycobacterium avium-intracellulare	MALToma	lymphoma of mucosa-associated lymphoid tissue
MAIC	*Mycobacterium avium-intracellulare* complex	MAM	mammogram Mexican-American male
MAID	medical aid in dying		monitored administration of medication
	mesna, doxorubicin (Adriamycin), ifosfamide, and dacarbazine	MAM-36	Manual Ability Measure-36
		MAMC	Madigan Army Medical Center
	monofocal acute inflammatory demyelinating (lesions)		mid-arm muscle circumference
		Mammo	mammography
MAIF	mitral-aortic intervalvular fibrosa	MAMP	methamphetamine milliampere
MAI infection	Mycobacterium avium-intracellulare infection	m-AMSA	amsacrine
		MAMTT	minimal active muscle tendon tension
maint	maintenance		
MAIR	metabolic acidosis-induced retinopathy	MAMX	Mexican American born in Mexico
MAIS	Maximum Abbreviated Injury Scale	MAN	malignancy associated neutropenia
			malignant acanthosis nigricans
Maj	Major		manual
maj	major		massive aspiration of newborn
Maj Gen	Major General	MAND	McCarron Assessment of Neuromuscular Development
MAK	male germ cell-associated kinase; see gene website, www.ncbi.nlm.nih.gov/gene		
		Mand	mandibular
		Mandy	powder or crystalline form of methylenedioxy-methylamphetamine (MDMA; Ecstasy)
Mako protocol	minimally invasive robotic bone-sparing unicompartmental knee arthroplasty		
		MANE	Morrow Assessment of Nausea and Emesis
MAL	malaria vaccine		
	malignant	MANEC	mixed adenoneuroendocrine carcinoma
	methyl aminolevulinate		
	midaxillary line	MANIP	manipulation
	Motor Activity Log	manitol	may have meant mannitol
MALA	metformin-associated lactic acidosis	MANOVA	multivariate analysis of variance
mALB	micro albumin	MAO	maximum acid output
MALDI	matrix-assisted laser desorption ionization	MAO-A	monoamine oxidase type A
		MAO-B	monoamine oxidase type B
MALDI-TOF MS	matrix-assisted laser desorption ionization-time of flight mass spectrometry	MAOD	maximal accumulated oxygen deficit
		MAOI	monoamine oxidase inhibitor
MALF	multi-atlas likelihood fusion	MAOIs	monoamine oxidase inhibitors
malF	maltose transporter membrane protein (gene/protein)	MAOP	methyl aminolevulinate Mid-Atlantic Oncology Program
MALG	Minnesota antilymphoblast globulin	MAP	magnesium, ammonium, and phosphate (Struvite stones)
malig	malignant		malignant atrophic papulosis
MALL	massive all-layer liposuction		mean airway pressure
mall	malleolus		

mean arterial pressure
Medical Assistance Program
Medicare Allowable Payment
megaloblastic anemia of
    pregnancy
Miller Assessment for
    Preschoolers (test for
    developmental delays)
mitogen-activated protein
mitomycin, doxorubicin
    (Adriamycin), and cisplatin
    (Platinol)
morning after pill (oral
    contraceptives)
muscle-action potential
Mycobacterium avium
    subspecies *paratuberculosis*
MYH-associated polyposis

map	see gene website www.ncbi.nlm.nih.gov/gene
mAPAP	micronized acetaminophen
MAPCA	major aortopulmonary collateral artery
MAPCAs	major aortopulmonary collateral arteries
MAPCs	multipotent adult progenitor cells
MA-PD	Medicare Part C prescription drug plan
MAPE	mean absolute percentage error
MAPI	Millon Adolescent Personality Inventory
MAPK	mitogen-activated protein kinase
MAPKAP-K2	mitogen-activated protein kinase-activated protein kinase 2
MAPS	Make a Picture Story
MAPs	Mindful Awareness Practices
MAPT	mapping using accumulated probe trajectories
	microtubule-associated protein tau; see gene website, www.ncbi.nlm.nih.gov/gene
M-A-QoLQII	Moorehead-Ardelt Quality of Life Questionnaire II
MAR	marital
	medication administration record
	melanoma-associated retinopathy
	mineral apposition rates
Mar	March
MARD	mean absolute relative difference
MARE	manual active-resistive exercise
MARF	modified apically repositioned flap (dental)
marg	marginal

MARS	Molecular Adsorbent Recirculating System (removes protein-bound and water-soluble toxins with albumin dialysis to improve environment for hepatic regeneration and clinical recovery)
	Moss Attention Rating Scale
MARSA	methicillin-aminoglycoside-resistant *Staphylococcus aureus*
MARSALA	Mutated Allele Revealed by Sequencing with Aneuploidy and Linkage Analyses
MARSI	medical adhesive-related skin injury
marsup	marsupialization (a surgical technique of cutting a slit into an abscess or cyst and suturing the edges of the slit to form a continuous surface from the exterior surface to the interior surface of the cyst or abscess. Sutured in this fashion, the site remains open and can drain freely.)
MART-1	melanoma antigen recognized by T-cells
MARV	Marburg virus
MAS	Modified Ashworth Scale
	mobile arm support
mAs	milliampere seconds
MASA	mutant allele-specific amplification
MASC	mammary analogue secretory carcinoma
	Multidimensional Anxiety Scale for Children
MASD	moisture-associated skin damage
MASDA^{SM}	Multiple-Allele-Specific Diagnostic Assay
MASER	microwave amplification (application) by stimulated emission of radiation
MASH	mobile Army surgical hospital
MASH POT	mashed potatoes
mass	massage
mass spec	mass spectrometry
MAST	mastectomy
	medical antishock trousers
	Michigan Alcoholism Screening Test
	military antishock trousers
MAT	manual arts therapy
	maternal
	maternity
	mature

	medication administration team		medulloblastoma
	medication-assisted treatment		mesiobuccal
	metabolic activation therapy		methylene blue
	microscopic agglutination test		mouth breathing
	Miller Analogies Test		myocardial bands
	Miller-Abbott tube	M/B	mother/baby
	Monocyte Activation Test (a test	MB+	Malloy Body(ies) positive
	for presence of pyrogens in	MBA	Master of Business
	pharmaceutical products)		Administration
	multifocal atrial tachycardia		Maxwell-Brancheau
matA	see gene website, www.ncbi		Arthroereisis (subtalar
	.nlm.nih.gov/gene		implant)
MaterniT21™	noninvasive prenatal test to	M-BACOD	methotrexate (high-dose),
	detect Trisomy 21, the most		bleomycin, doxorubicin
	common cause of Down		(Adriamycin),
	syndrome		cyclophosphamide,
MATGF	maternal grandfather		vincristine (Oncovin),
MATGM	maternal grandmother		and dexamethasone with
MATHS	muscle pain, allergy, tachycardia		leucovorin rescue
	and tiredness, and headache	2-MBAD	2-methylbutyryl-CoA
	syndrome		dehydrogenase
MATS	Meningococcal antigen typing	MBB	medial branch block
	system		midline-blocked boost
MATTB	the Manufacturers Assistance		(radiation therapy)
	and Technical Training	MBBCh	Bachelor of Medicine and
	Branch (FDA)		Bachelor of Surgery
MAU	microalbuminuria	MB BCh	Bachelor of Medicine, Bachelor
MAUDE	Manufacturer and User Facility		of Surgery (Latin: Medicinae
	Device Experience (FDA)		Baccalaureus, Baccalaureus
maunt	maternal aunt		Chirurgiae)
MAUS	Mexican American born in the	MBBS	Bachelor of Medicine, Bachelor
	United States		of Surgery
MAVD	mixed aortic valve disease	MBBs	medial branch blocks
MAVR	mitral and aortic valve	MBC	male breast cancer
	replacement		maximum bladder capacity
MAWL	maximum acceptable weight		maximum breathing capacity
	of lift		metastatic breast cancer
MAWM	middle aged, white male		methotrexate, bleomycin, and
Mawp	mean airway pressure		cisplatin
MAWS	Michigan Alcohol Withdrawal		minimal bactericidal
	Severity (score)		concentration
MAX	maximum		mucinous breast carcinoma
max	maxillary	MBCA	membranous basal cell adenoma
MAX A	maximum assistance (assist)	MBChB	Bachelor of Medicine and
max @	maximum assistance		Bachelor of Surgery
MAXCONT	maximum contrast method	MB-CK	a creatinine kinase isoenzyme
MaxED	maximum effective dose	MBCT	Mindfulness-Based Cognitive
MAxL	midaxillary line		Therapy
May	May	MBD	mammographic breast density
MAYO	mayonnaise		Marchiafava-Bignami disease
Maze Procedure	surgery performed to treat		metabolic bone disease
	atrial fibrillation by making		metastatic bone disease
	a number of incisions on		methyl-binding domain
	the left and right atrium to		methylene blue dye
	form scar tissue		minimal brain damage
MB	Mallory body		minimal brain dysfunction
	mandible	MBE	may be elevated
	Medical Board		medium below elbow

M-BESS	Modified Balance Error Scoring System	MBq	megabecquerels
MBEST	Modulus Blipped Echo-planar Single pulse Technique	MBR	major breakpoint region
			Medical Birth Registry
MBF	meat-base formula	MBS	modified barium swallow
	myocardial blood flow	mBSE	murine bovine spongiform encephalopathy
MBFC	medial brachial fascial compartment	MBSR	mindfulness-based stress reduction
MBG	myocardial blush grade	MBSS	modified barium-swallow study
MBGNs	mesoporous bioactive glass nanoparticles	MBT	2-mercaptobenzothiazole
			maternal blood type
MBHI	Millon Behavioral Health Inventory		mother's blood type
			multiple blunt trauma
MBI	methylene blue installation	MBTS	modified Blalock-Taussig shunt
	Mini Battery of Achievement	MBU	mother and baby unit
	Modified Barthel Index		(a psychiatric unit for
	molecular breast imaging		women and their infants)
MBIs	mindfulness-based interventions	MBUs	mother and baby units
MBL	Mannan-binding lectin	MBV	microvascular blood volume
	mannose-binding lectin	MBW	multiple-breath (inert gas)
	marginal bone loss		washout
	menstrual blood loss	MC	male child
	metallo-beta-lactamases		male circumcision
MBL-D	Mannan-binding lectin (deficiency)		male, castrated
			manual cues
MBM	mind-body medicine		Medicare
	mother's breast milk		medium-chain (triglycerides)
MBMD	macular Bruch membrane defects		melanosis coli
			metacarpal
	Millon Behavioral Medicine Diagnostic (inventory)		metatarso - cuneiform
			microcalcifications (breast)
mBMD	mandibular bone mineral density		mini-laparotomy cholecystectomy
	metacarpal bone mineral density		miscarriage
MBN	medial branch neurotomy		mitoxantrone and cytarabine
MBNb	mushroom-body neuroblast		MitraClip (minimally invasive
MBNW	multiple-breath nitrogen		catheter-based mitral valve
	washout		repair procedure)
MBO	malignant bowel obstruction		mitral commissurotomy
	mesiobuccal occulsion		mixed cellularity
MBO2	coiled-coil protein required		mixed cryoglobulinemia
	for normal flagellar motility		molluscum contagiosum
	(gene)		monochorionic (twin)
MbO2	oxymyoglobin		monocomponent highly purified
MBOs	multivalent binding oligomers		pork insulin
MBOT	mucinous borderline ovarian		*Moraxella catarrhalis*
	tumors		mouth care
MBP	malignant brachial plexopathy		multicenter (study)
	mannan-binding protein		myocarditis
	mannose-binding protein	Mc	moscovium
	mechanical bowel preparation	mC	millicoulomb
	medullary bone pain	M + C	morphine and cocaine
	mesiobuccopulpal	MC3	third metacarpal
	myelin basic protein	MCA	Medicines Control Agency
MBPM	Medicare Benefit Policy Manual		(United Kingdom)
MBPS	morning blood pressure surge		megestrol, cyclophosphamide,
Mbps	megabit (one million bits) per second		and doxorubicin (Adriamycin)

metacarpal amputation
micrometastases clonogenic assay
middle cerebral aneurysm
middle cerebral artery
monoclonal antibodies
motorcycle accident
multichannel analyzer
multiple congenital anomalies

2-MCA	2-methyl citric acid
MCA aneurysm	middle cerebral artery aneurysm
McAb	monoclonal antibody (antibodies)
McAbs	monoclonal antibodies
MCAD	medium-chain acyl-CoA dehydrogenase
MCADD	medium chain acyl-coenzyme A dehydrogenase deficiency
MCAF	monocyte chemoattractant and activity factor
MCAID	Medicaid
MCAL	California's Medicaid Health Insurance
MCAO	middle cerebral artery occlusion
MCAP	middle cerebral artery pressure
MCAR	missing at random (incomplete data)
	missing completely at random (incomplete data)
MCARE	Medicare
MCART	Medical Countermeasures to Radiologic Threats (consortium)
McAS	McCune-Albright syndrome
MCA stroke	middle cerebral artery stroke
MCAT	Medical College Admission Test
MCAVI	methotrexate, carboplatin, and vinblastine
MCB	Medicines Control Board (United Kingdom's equivalent to the United States Food and Drug Administration)
	midcycle bleeding
	middle chamber bubbling
MCBDD	National Center On Birth Defects and Developmental Disabilities
McB pt	McBurney point
MCBS	Medicare Current Beneficiary Survey
MCC	meningococcal serogroup C conjugate
	Merkel cell carcinoma
	microcrystalline cellulose
	midstream clean-catch
	motorcycle crash
	multiple (two or more) chronic conditions
	mutated in colorectal cancers (gene/protein)

MCCD	manual chest compression-decompression (maneuver)
	Medical Certification of Cause of Death
MccD	see gene website www.ncbi.nlm.nih.gov/gene
MCCM	moderate-concentration contrast media
MCCN	Mayo Clinical Care Network
MCCs	Merkel cell carcinomas
	multiciliated cells
	multiple chronic conditions
MCCU	mobile coronary care unit
MCD	macular corneal dystrophy
	malformation of cortical development
	mean cell diameter
	Medicaid
	microvascular coronary dysfunction
	minimal-change disease
	multicentric Castleman disease
	multicystic dysplasia
	multiple consecutive discharges (pacemaker related)
MCDA	minimum constantly detectable amount
	monochorionic-diamnionic (twins)
	multiple criteria decision analysis
MCDK	multicystic dysplasia of the kidney
MCDT	mast cell degranulation test
MCE	major coronary event
	microcystic edema
	myocardial contrast echocardiography
mcEq	microEquivalent
MCF	maximum clot firmness
	multicentric foci
MCF10A	Michigan Cancer Foundation human mammary epithelial cell line 10A (a widely used in vitro model for studying normal breast cell function and transformation)
MCF-7	Michigan Cancer Foundation-7 (a breast cancer cell line)
MCFA	medium-chain fatty acid
MCFAP	medial circumflex femoral artery perforator (flaps)
MCG	magnetocardiogram
	magnetocardiography
mcg	microgram (1,000 mcg = 1 milligram)
mcg/dL	micrograms per deciliter (micrograms per 100 mL)
mcg/g	micrograms per gram

M

mCGH	metaphasic comparative genomic hybridization		midclavicular line
	microarray comparative genomic hybridization		midcostal line
			modified chest lead
			most comfortable level
mcg/h	micrograms per hour	mcL	microliter (1 millionth of a liter; 1 thousandth of a milliliter
mcg/kg/min	micrograms per kilogram per minute		
		MCLL	most comfortable listening level
mcg/L	micrograms per liter	MCLNS	mucocutaneous lymph node syndrome
mcgm	microgram (mcg preferred)		
mcg/min	micrograms per minute	MCLs	mantle cell lymphomas
mcg/mL	micrograms per milliliter		medial collateral ligaments
MCGN	minimal-change glomerular nephritis		most comfortable levels
		MCM	medical countermeasures
mcgs	micrograms (mcg preferred)		minichromosome maintenance
MCH	mean corpuscular hemoglobin	MCMA	monochorionic-monoamniotic twins
	microfibrillar collagen hemostat		
	muscle contraction headache	MC/MA	monochorionic-monoamniotic twins
MCHAT	Modified Checklist for Autism in Toddlers		
		MCMI	Millon Clinical Multiaxial Inventory
MCHC	mean corpuscular hemoglobin concentration		
		mcmol	micromoles (one millionth [10^{-6}] of a mole)
MCHFR	may have meant MTHFR (methylenetetrahydrofolate reductase gene)		
		MCN	minimal change nephropathy
		MCNS	minimal change nephrotic syndrome
MCHL	medial head of the coracohumeral ligament		
		mCNV	myopic choroidal neovascularization
MCHS	Mayo Clinic Health Systems		
MCI	mass-casualty incident	MCO	managed care organization
	methylchloroisothiazolinone (a preservative found in liquid personal care products)		mupirocin calcium ointment (Bactroban Nasal)
		Mco2	carbon dioxide excretion
	mild cognitive impairment	MCOT	mobile cardiac outpatient telemetry
	modified cognitive interviewing		
mCi	millicuries	mcousin	maternal cousin
MCID	minimum clinically important difference(s)	MCP	mean carotid pressure
			metacarpophalangeal joint
MCI/MI	as mixture of methylchloroisothiazolinone and methylisothiazolinone (preservatives found in liquid personal care products)		metoclopramide (Reglan)
			monocyte chemotactic protein
			Monthly Capitation Payment
		MCP1	first metacarpophalangeal joint
		MCP2	macrophage cationic peptide 2 (gene/biomaker)
mCIMT	modified constraint-induced movement therapy		
			second metacarpophalangeal joint
mcIU	micro international unit(s)	mCPAP	mask continuous positive airway pressure
mcIU/mL	micro-international units per milliliter		
		MCPD	monochloropropanediol
MCJ	metatarsocuneiform joint	MCPF	mediastinoscope-controlled parasternal fenestration
	midcarpal joint		
	mucocutaneous junction	MCPIP1	monocyte chemoattractant protein-induced protein 1
	see gene website www.ncbi.nlm.nih.gov/gene		
		MCPJ	metacarpophalangeal joint
mckat	microkatal (one millionth [10^{-6}] of a katal)	MCP joint	metacarpophalangeal joint
		mcPP	meta-chlorophenylpiperazine (a psychoactive street substitute for ecstasy)
MCKD2	medullary cystic kidney disease type 2		
MCL	mantle cell lymphoma	mcpS	methyl-accepting chemotaxis protein; see gene website www.ncbi.nlm.nih.gov/gene
	maximum comfort level		
	medial collateral ligament		

M

MCQ	multiple-choice question(s)	MCTZ	methyclothiazide (Enduron)
MCQ-30	Metacognitions Questionnaire	MCU	micturating cystourethrogram
MCR	Mayo Clinic Rochester	MCUG	micturating cystourethrogram
	Medicare	MCUs	memory care units
	metabolic clearance rate	MCV	mean corpuscular volume
	minor cluster region		measles antigen-containing
	myocardial revascularization		vaccines
MC=R	moderately constricted and	mcV	microvolt
	equally reactive	MCV4	quadrivalent meningococcal
MCRC	metastatic colorectal cancer		conjugate vaccine
MCRF	medical care referral form	MCVRI	minimal coronary vascular
MCRI	medication compounding-		resistance index
	related infections	MCX	Mixed-mode Cation-eXchange
mCRP	monomeric isoform of	MCx	motor cortex
	C-reactive protein	MCYLS	marginal cost per year of life
mCRPC	metastatic castration-resistant		saved
	prostate cancer	MCyR	major cytogenetic response
MCS	manufacturer cannot supply	MD	macula degeneration
	maternal cigarette smoking		Madelung disease (a rare lipid
	mechanical circulatory support		metabolic disorder of adipose
	mental component summary		tissue overgrowth, which
	microculture and sensitivity		has been reported to be
	minimally conscious state		related to alcohol abuse [also
	moderate constant suction		known as benign symmetric
	motor cortex stimulation		lipomatosis])
	multiple chemical sensitivity		maintenance dialysis
	myocardial contractile state		maintenance dose
MCs	mast cells		major depression
MC&S	microscopy, culture, and		mammary ductoscopy
	sensitivity		mammary dysplasia
MCSA	minimal cross-sectional area		mammographic density
MCSCs	melanocyte stem cells		manic depression
MCSD	mechanical circulatory support		Maryland
	device		mean deviation
	minimal clinically significant		medical doctor
	difference		mediodorsal
M-CSF	macrophage colony-stimulating		Mediterranean Diet
	factor		Ménière disease
MC-SR	moderately constricted and		mental deficiency
	slightly reactive		mesiodistal
MCST	microcystic stromal tumor		metastatic disease
MCT	manual cervical traction		microdialysis
	mean circulation time		moderate dose
	medial canthal tendon		monochorionic-diamnionic
	medium chain triglyceride		(twins)
	medullary carcinoma of the		movement disorder
	thyroid		multiple dose
	microwave coagulation therapy		muscular dystrophy
	monochorionic twin		myocardial damage
	multislice computed tomography	Md	mendelevium
MCT1	monocarboxylate transporter 1	MD1	myotonic dystrophy type 1
MCTB	medical contact-to-balloon	md2	see gene website www.ncbi.nlm
	(interval)		.nih.gov/gene
mCTC	microcomputed tomography	MD-50®	diatrizoate sodium injection 50%
	colonography	MDA	3,4-methylenedioxyamphetamine
MCTD	mixed connective tissue disease		Magen David Adom (Israeli
mCTSIB	Modified Clinical Test of Sensory		national ambulance service)
	Interaction on Balance		malondialdehyde

M

	manual dilation of the anus	MDDS		medical device data systems (Food and Drug Administration)
	mass drug administrations (diethylcarbamazine plus albendazole to stop transmission of filariasis)	MDE		major depressive episode
		MDEC		Matrigel-derived endothelial cells
	Medical Devises Agency (United Kingdom)	MDF		myocardial depressant factor
	Medical Doctor of Anesthesiology	MDG4		Millennium Development Goal 4
	methylenedianiline (a common industrial chemical with health and product safety concerns)	MDGF		macrophage-derived growth factor
		MDGs		Millenium Development Goals
		MDH		malate dehydrogenase; see gene website www.ncbi.nlm.nih .gov/gene
	micrometastases detection assay			
	motor discriminative acuity			medullary dorsal horn
	Multichannel Discrete Analyzer			multiple drug hypersensitivity
	Muscular Dystrophy Association	MDHAQ		Multidimensional Health Assessment Questionnaire
mda5	melanoma differentiation associated gene 5 (gene/protein)			
		MDI		manic-depressive illness
				Mental Development Index
MDA LDL	malondialdehyde conjugated low-density lipoprotein			mental developmental index
				metered-dose inhaler
MDAC	multiple-dose activated charcoal			methylenedioxyindenes
MDACC	MD Anderson Cancer Center			multi-directional instability
MDADI	MD Anderson Dysphagia Inventory			multiple daily insulin
		MDIA		Mental Development Index, Adjusted
MDAS	Memorial Delirium Assessment Scale			
		MDII		multiple daily insulin injection
MDASI - BT	M. D. Anderson Symptom Inventory - Brain Tumor Module	MDIS		metered-dose inhaler-spacer (device)
		MDiv		Master of Divinity
MDB	Mallory-Denk-bodies	MDJ		mesencephalo-diencephalic junction
	medulloblastoma; see gene website; www.ncbi.nlm.nih .gov/gene			
		MDL		method detection limit
				microdirect laryngoscopy
MDC	Major Diagnostic Category			minimum description length
	medial dorsal cutaneous (nerve)	mDLB		mild dementia with Lewy bodies
	minimal detectable change			
MDCM	mildly dilated congestive cardiomyopathy	MDLFC		mid-dorsolateral prefrontal cortex
MDCO	medial displacement calcaneal osteotomy	MDM2		an oncogenic homologue protein
		MDM		medical decision making
MDCT	multidetector-row computed tomography			mid-diastolic murmur
				minor determinant mix (of penicillin)
MDCTA	multidetector computed tomographic angiography			
		MDMA		methylenedioxy-methamphetamine (ecstasy)
MDCW	Medicare waiver			
MDD	major depressive disorder	MDMX		an oncogenic homologue protein
	manic-depressive disorder	MDNT		midnight
	Medical Device Directive (EU)	MDO		mentally disordered offender
MDDD	minor depression/dysthymic disorder	MDOT		modified directly observed therapy
MDDM	mood disorder with depressive manifestations	MDP		methylene diphosphonate
		MDPH		Michigan Department of Public Health
MDDR	Major Depressive Disorder, Recurrent			
		MDPI		maximum daily permissible intake
	MDL (Master Drug List) drug data report (database)			

MDPs	Markov decision processes
MDPV	methylenedioxypyrovalerone (also knows as Mtv, MDPK, Magic, Super Code and Peevee)
MDQ	Mood Disorders Questionnaire
MDR	Medical Device Reporting (regulation)
	minimum daily requirement
	multi-dimensionality reduction
	multidisciplinary rounding
	multidrug resistance
MD=R	moderately dilated and equally reactive
MDR-1	multidrug resistance gene
mdrA	see gene website www.ncbi.nlm .nih.gov/gene
MDRD	Modification of Diet in Renal Disease
MDRD-eGFR	Modification of Diet in Renal Disease estimated glomerular filtration rate
MDRD GFR	Modification of Diet in Renal Disease (estimated) glomerular filtration rate
MDRE	multiple-drug-resistant enterococci
MDREF	multidrug resistant enteric fever
MDRGN	multidrug-resistant gram-negative (bacteria)
MDRI	mean duration of recent infection
MDRO	multidrug-resistant organism
MDROs	multidrug-resistant organisms
MDRPs	multidrug resistant pathogens
MDRPU	medical device related pressure ulcers
MDRS	Mattis Dementia Rating Scale
MDRS I/P	Mattis Dementia Rating Scale - Initiation/Preservation subscale
MDRSP	multidrug resistant *Streptococcus pneumoniae*
MDRT	Multi-Directional Reach Test
	multiple-drug rescue therapy
MDR-TB	multidrug-resistant tuberculosis
MDR UTI	multidrug-resistant urinary tract infection
MDS	maternal deprivation syndrome
	Mediterranean diet score
	Miller-Dieker syndrome
	Minimum Data Set
	multidimensional scaling
	myelodysplastic syndromes
MDs	medical devices
	medical doctors
MDSC	myeloid-derived suppressor cells

MDSCs	myeloid-derived suppressor cells
MDS-EB	myelodysplastic syndrome with excess blasts
MDS/MPN	myelodysplastic syndrome and myeloproliferative neoplasms overlapping diseases
MD-SR	moderately dilated and slightly reactive
MDS/RAEB	myelodysplastic syndrome with refractory anemia with excess blasts
MDSs	myelodysplastic syndromes
MDSSI	moderate dose sliding scale insulin (suggested starting point for average patient)
	multiple disabilities with severe sensory impairment
MDSU	medical day stay unit
MDT	maggot debridement therapy
	Mechanical Diagnosis and Therapy
	motion detection threshold
	multidisciplinary team
	multidrug therapy
MDTB	multidisciplinary tumor board
MDTM	multidisciplinary team meeting
MDTP	multidisciplinary treatment plan
MDTS®	Metered Dose Transdermal Spray System
MDU	maintenance dialysis unit
	microvascular Doppler ultrasonography
MDUO	myocardial disease of unknown origin
MDV	Marek's disease virus
	multiple dose vial
MDW	monocyte distribution width
MDX	X-linked muscular dystrophy
MDX mice	a strain of mice that is used as a disease model for human muscular dystrophy
MDY	month, date, and year
ME	macular edema
	Maine
	manic episode
	medical events
	medical evidence
	medical examiner
	mestranol
	Methodist
	microemulsion
	middle ear
	mistaken entry
	muscle energy (technique)
	myalgic encephalomyelitis
M&E	Mecholyl and Eserine
	mucositis and enteritis

M

M/E	metabloic/endocrine	MEDAC	multiple endocrine deficiency
	monitor and evaluate		Addison's disease
	myeloid-erythroid (ratio)		(autoimmune) candidiasis
MEA	malt extract agar	MEDB	musculus extensor digitorum
	measles virus vaccine		brevis
	microwave endometrial	MEDCO	Medcosonolator
	ablation	MedDiet	Mediterranean diet
MEAD	Medicaid for Employed Adults	MedDRA	Medical Dictionary for
	with Disabilities		Regulatory Activities
MEA-I	multiple endocrine	MEDEX	medication administration record
	adenomatosis type I	MeDi	Mediterranean diet
MEAs	microelectrode arrays	MEDIC	Medicare Drug Integrity
MEAT	middle ear adenomatous tumor		Contractor
MEB	Medical Evaluation Board		multiecho data image
	methylene blue		combination
MEC	meconium	Medigap	Medicare Supplement Insurance
	medical eligibility criteria	Mediport	a reservoir compartment that has
	middle ear canal(s)		a silicone bubble for needle
	minimum effective		insertion, with an attached
	concentration		plastic tube (the catheter).
	mitoxantrone, etoposide, and	MEDL	microendoscopic decompressive
	cytarabine		laminotomy
	moderately emetogenic	MEDLARS	Medical Literature Analysis and
	chemotherapy		Retrieval System
mecA	penicillin binding protein 2	MEDLINE	National Library of Medicine
	prime; see gene website		medical database
	www.ncbi.nlm.nih.gov/gene	MED NEC	medically necessary
MeCCNU	semustine	Med Onc	medical oncologist (oncology)
ME/CFS	myalgic encephalomyelitis/	MedOnc ITE	Medical Oncology In-Training
	chronic fatigue syndrome		Examination
MECG	maternal electrocardiogram	MedPAC	Medicare Payment Advisory
Mech	mechanical		Commission
mech soft	mechanical soft	MedPAR	Medical Provider Analysis
MeCP	semustine (methyl CCNU)		Review File
	cyclophosphamide, and	MedRec	medication reconciliation
	prednisone	med rec	medical reconciliation
MECP2	methyl CpG (cytosine-guanine		medical record(s)
	dinucleotide) binding protein 2	MEDS	medications
	(gene/protein)	Med-Surg	Medical/Surgical (nursing unit)
MECs	measured environmental	Med/Surg	Medical/Surgical (nursing unit)
	concentrations	medsurg	Medical/Surgical (nursing unit)
MED	male erectile dysfunction	med surg	medical-surgical unit
	maximal (maximum) economic	MEE	maintenance energy expenditure
	dose		measured energy expenditure
	medial		middle ear effusion
	median erythrocyte diameter	MEED	median effective radiation dose
	medical		medium energy electron
	medication		diffraction
	medicine	MEE/OC	middle ear exploration
	medium		with ossicular chain
	medulloblastoma		reconstruction
	micro-endoscopic discectomy	MEF	maximum expired flow rate
	minimal erythema dose		middle ear fluid
	minimum effective dose	Mef	mefloquine (Lariam)
	monocular elevation deficiency	MEF-2	myocyte enhancer factor-2
	morphine equivalent dose	MEFR	mid expiratory flow rate
	multiple epiphyseal dysplasia	MEFV	maximum expiratory
MEd	Master of Education		flow-volume

MEG	magnetoencephalogram	MEMS/NEMS	micro/nanoelectromechanical
	magnetoencephalography		systems
megabase pairs	a million base pairs (a unit	MEN	medically-enhanced normality
	consisting of two nucleobases		meningeal
	bound to each other by		meninges
	hydrogen bonds)		meningitis
Meg-CSF	megakaryocytic colony-		meningococcal (*Neisseria*
	stimulating factor		*meningitidis*) (serogroups
MEGX	monoethylglycinexylidide		unspecified) vaccine
MeHg	methylmercury	MEN1	see gene website, www.ncbi
MEI	magnetic endoscope imaging		.nlm.nih.gov/gene
	medical economic index	MEN2	see gene website, www.ncbi
MEIA	microparticle enzyme		.nlm.nih.gov/gene
	immunoassay	MEN2A	multiple endocrine neoplasia
MEKC	micellar electrokinetic		type 2A
	chromatography	MenACWY-	meningococcal conjugate vaccine,
MEL	maximum exposure limit	CRM	quadrivalent (Menveo)
	melatonin	MenACWY-D	meningococcal conjugate vaccine,
	melphalan (Alkeran)		quadrivalent (Menactra)
MEL140	melphalan 140 mg/m^2	MEN2B	multiple endocrine neoplasia
	(a conditioning regimen		type 2B
	administered to newly	MenB	serogroup B meningococcal
	diagnosed patients with		vaccine
	multiple myeloma undergoing	MenB-4C	serogroup B meningococcal
	autologous stem cell		vaccine (Bexsero)
	transplantation)	MenB-FHbp	serogroup B meningococcal
MEL200	melphalan 200 mg/m^2		vaccine (Trumenba)
	(a conditioning regimen	ME-NBI	magnifying endoscopy with
	administered to newly		narrow band imaging
	diagnosed patients with	MEN$_{cn-AC}$	meningococcal (*Neisseria*
	multiple myeloma undergoing		*meningitidis*) serogroups A, C
	autologous stem cell		conjugate vaccine
	transplantation)	MEN$_{cn-B}$	meningococcal (*Neisseria*
MELAS	mytochondrial,		*meningitidis*) serogroup B
	encephalomyopathy, lactic		conjugate vaccine
	acidosis, and stroke-like	MEND	multifunctional envelope-type
	episodes (syndrome)		nano device
MEL B	melarsoprol (Arsobal)	MEN(II)	multiple endocrine neoplasia
MELD	Model for End-Stage Liver		(type II)
	Disease (score)	MeNO	nitromethane
MELDNa	Model for End-Stage Liver	meno	menopausal
	Disease and Serum Sodium	MENPs	magneto-electric nanoparticles
	(scoring system)	MEN$_{ps}$	meningococcal (*Neisseria*
MELD score	Model for End-Stage Liver		*meningitidis*) polysaccharide
	Disease score		vaccine, not otherwise
MELF	microcystic, elongated, and		specified
	fragmented (pattern)	MEN$_{ps-ACYW}$	meningococcal (*Neisseria*
MELP	modified endoscopic Lothrop		*meningitidis*) serogroups A,
	procedure		C, Y, W-135 polysaccharide
MEM	memory		vaccine
	monocular estimate method	MEN$_{ps-B}$	meningococcal (*Neisseria*
	(near retinoscopy)		*meningitidis*) serogroup B
MEMB	modified eosin-methylene blue		polysaccharide vaccine
	(agar)	MENS	microcurrent electrical
MEMG	masseter (muscle)		neuromuscular stimulation
	electromyographic events		mini-electrical nerve stimulator
MEMS	microelectromechanical	MEO	malignant external otitis
	systems		Medical Examiner's Office

M

mEOC	mucinous epithelial ovarian carcinoma
MeOH	methyl alcohol
MEOS	microsomal ethanol oxidizing system
MEP	maximal expiratory pressure
	meperidine
	motor-evoked potential
	multimodality-evoked potential
MEPA	Medication Error Prevention Analysis (FDA)
MEPI	Mayo Elbow Performance Index
MEPM	meropenem (Merrem)
MEPN	myxopapillary ependymoma
MEPS	Mayo Elbow Performance Score
	Medical Expenditure Panel Survey
MEQ	Mystical Experience Questionnaire
mEq	milliequivalent
mEq/24H	millequivalents per 24 hours
mEq/L	milliequivalents per liter
mEq/liter	milliequivalents per liter
MEQs	morphine equivalents
MER	medical evidence of record
	methanol-extracted residue (of phenol-treated BCG)
	milk ejection reflex
M/Eratio	myeloid/erythroid ratio
MERC	Medical Education Research Certificate (program)
MERCI Retriever	a medical device designed to treat ischemic strokes (Mechanical Embolus Removal in Cerebral Ischemia)
merF	see gene website www.ncbi.nlm .nih.gov/gene
MERFF	may have meant MERRF (myoclonic epilepsy with ragged-red fibers)
Meridia (W)	sibutramine monohydrate (W)
MERP	Medication Error Reporting and Prevention (of the National Coordinating Council)
merP	mercury transport protein periplasmic component; see gene website www.ncbi.nlm .nih.gov/gene
MERPs	medical emergency response plans
MERRF	myoclonic epilepsy and ragged red fibers
MERS	Middle East Respiratory Syndrome (coronavirus)
	mild encephalitis/ encephalopathy with a reversible splenial lesion
MERSA	see MRSA

MERS-CoV	Middle Eastern respiratory syndrome-coronavirus
MERS-TM	Medical Event Reporting System - Transfusion Medicine
MERT	medical emergency response team
MES	maximal electroshock
	mesial
	microembolic signals
	monopolar electrocautery scissors
	myoelectric signals
MESA	microsurgical epididymal sperm aspiration
	Multi-Ethnic Study of Atherosclerosis
MESCC	metastatic epidural spinal cord compression
MeSH	Medical Subject Headings of the National Library of Medicine
Mesna	a chemotherapeutic agent (2-mercaptoethane sulfonate sodium).
meso	mesothelioma
MESS	Mangled Extremity Severe Score
MEST	mesodermal specific transcript (gene)
MET	medical emergency team
	medical emergency treatment
	mesenchymal-epithelial transition
	metabolic
	metabolic equivalent task
	metabolic equivalent test
	metamyelocytes
	metastasis
	metronidazole
	muscle energy technique
meT	methyltestosterone
META	metamyelocytes
metab	metabolic
	metabolism
MetAP1	methionine amino peptidase 1
MetAP2	methionine amino peptidase 2
Metavir	meta-analysis of Histological Data in Viral Hepatitis (score which provides a model for interpreting a liver biopsy for the degree of fibrosis)
metB	cystathionine gamma-synthase (gene/protein)
METC	Medical Ethics Committee (Institutional Review Board)
metC	cystathionine beta-lyase (gene)
METD	minimal effective therapeutic doses
	minimum external transverse diameter

MetD	metabolic disturbances	M & F	male and female
metD	DL-methionine transporter	M/F	male-female ratio
	subunit (gene)	Mf4	macrophage 4
	metastatic disease	MFA	malaise, fatigue, and anorexia
MeTeOR	Meniscal Tear in Osteoarthritis		Master of Fine Arts
	Research (trial)	MFAC	middle fossa arachnoid cyst
METH	methamphetamine		multiple fruit-flavored alcoholic
	methicillin		drinks in a can
MetHb	methemoglobin	MFAT	multifocal atrial tachycardia
	methemoglobinemia	MFB	mammary myofibroblastoma
methyl CCNU	semustine		metallic foreign body
methyl G	mitroguazone dihydrochloride		multiple-frequency bioimpedance
	(Zyrkamine)	MFC	medial femoral condyle
methyl GAG	mitroguazone dihydrochloride		multifocal choroiditis
	(Zyrkamine)	MfC	*Medicines for Children*
methylpred-	(Medrol)	MFCP	mobile floating carotid plaque
nisolone		MFCU	Medicaid Fraud Control Unit
METRO	MElanocytic tumor and	MFD	Memory for Designs
	TRichOblastoma		midforceps delivery
metropolol	may have meant metoprolol		milk-free diet
METRx	micro-endoscopic excision		multiple fractions per day
	utilizing tubular retractors	MFEM	maximal forced expiratory
METS	metabolic equivalents (multiples		maneuver
	of resting oxygen uptake)	mf-ERG	multifocal-electroretinogram
	metastases	MFES	Modified Falls Efficacy Scale
MetS	metabolic syndrome	MFFS	Medicare fee-for-service
met synd	metabolic syndrome		monostatic fixed focus scanner
METT	maximum exercise tolerance test		myelofibrosis-free survival
	modified endotracheal tube	M-FFS	Medicare Fee-for-Service
METZ	see METS	MFFs	muscle fiber fragments
MEUs	mobile eye units	MFFT	Matching Familiar Figures Test
MEV	mouse encephalomyelitis virus	mfgr	manufacturer
MeV	million electron volts	MFH	malignant fibrous histiocytoma
MEWDS	multifocal evanescent white dot		Medical Foster Home (Veterans
	syndrome		Administration abbreviation)
	multiple evanescent white dot	MFI	mean fluorescent intensity
	syndrome		Multidimensional Fatigue
MEWS	malaria epidemic early warning		Inventory
	system	MFIP	Minnesota Family Investment
	Modified Early Warning Score		Program
MEX	Mexican	MFIQ	Mandibular Function
MF	Malassezia folliculitis		Impairment Questionnaire
	Malassezia furfur	MFISH	multicolor fluorescence in situ
	masculinity/femininity		hybridization
	meat-free	MFK	mass fluctuation kinetics
	median frequency	MFL	meniscofemoral ligament
	(anasthesia-depth monitor)		menstrual fluid loss
	mesial facial		modified facelift
	methotrexate and fluorouracil	MFM	Maternal Fetal Clinic
	midcavity forceps		maternal fetal medicine
	middle finger		multifidus muscle
	midforceps	MF/MC	multifocal and multicentric
	mother and father	MFMU	Maternal-Fetal Medicine Unit
	multifidus		(of the Eunice Kennedy
	multifocal		Shriver National Institute
	mycosis fungoides		of Child Health and Human
	myelofibrosis		Development Network)
	myocardial fibrosis	MFN2	mitofusin 2 (gene)

MFNS	mometasone furcate nasal spray (Nasonex)	MGd	motexafin gadolinium (Xcytrin)
		MGDF	megakaryocyte growth and development factor
MFPP	myofascial pelvic pain		
MFPS	myofascial pain syndrome	mg/dL	milligrams per deciliter (milligrams per 100 mL)
MFR	mid-forceps rotation		
	myocardial flow reserve	MGE	medial ganglionic eminence
	myofascial release		mobile genetic element
Mfr	manufacturer	MGF	macrophage growth factor
MFS	Marfan syndrome		mast cell growth factor
	maternal-fetal surgery		maternal grandfather
	Medical Fee Schedule	MGFA	Myasthenia Gravis Foundation of America
	mestastases free survival		
	Miller-Fisher syndrome	MGG	May-Grünwald-Giemsa (stain)
	mitral first sound	mg/g	milligrams per gram
	Modified Flemons Score	mggf	maternal great grandfather
	monofixation syndrome	MGGM	maternal great grandmother
MFT	muscle function test	mggm	maternal great grandmother
MFU	medical followup	MGH	Massachusetts General Hospital
MFVNS	middle fossa vestibular nerve section	mg/24h	milligrams per 24 hours
		mg/h	milligrams per hour
MFVPT	Motor Free Visual Perception Test	MGHL	middle glenohumeral ligament
		mg/hr	milligrams per hour
MFVR	minimal forearm vascular resistance	MGH-S	Massachusetts General Hospital clinical staging method
MG	malignant glioma	MgHz	may have meant MHz (megahertz)
	mammography		
	Marcus Gunn	MGIB	major gastrointestinal bleeding
	Michaelis-Gutmann (bodies)	MGIs	mobilizable genomic islands
	myasthenia gravis	MGIT	mycobacteria growth indicator (incubator) tube
Mg	magnesium		
mg	milligram (1,000 mg = 1 g [gram])	mg/kg	milligram per kilogram
		mg/kg/d	milligram per kilogram per day
mG	milligauss	mg/kg/hr	milligram per kilogram per hour
M&G	myringotomy and grommets	mgl	milligrams of iodine
M/G	murmur or gallop	mGlu5	metabotropic glutamate receptor subtype 5
Mg++	magnesium		
Mg2+	magnesium ion	MGM	maternal grandmother
mg%	milligram percent (the number of milligrams of a substance in 100 milliliters of solution [e.g., blood, urine])		milligram (mg is correct)
		mg/m2	milligram per square meter
		MGMA	Medical Group Management Association
	milligrams per 100 milliliters	mg/mL	milligrams per milliliter
µg	microgram (1/1000 of a milligram) (This is a dangerous abbreviation when hand written, as it is read as mg. Use mcg)	mgmnt	management
		mgms	milligrams (mg preferred)
		Mgmt	management
		MGN	membranous glomerulonephritis
		MGNT	malignant glioneuronal tumor
MGA	minimum glottal area	MGNTs	malignant glioneuronal tumors
	Myasthenia Gravis Association	MGO	methylglyoxal
mgaunt	maternal great aunt	MgO	magnesium oxide
MGB	mini-gastric bypass	MGOH	modified graft-over-host
MGBG	mitoguazone (Zyrkamine)	MgOH	magnesium hydroxide
MgCl₂	magnesium chloride	MG/OL	molecular genetics/oncology laboratory
MGCT	malignant glandular cell tumor		
MGD	mammography-detected breast cancer	MgOx	magnesium oxide
		MGP	Marcus Gunn pupil
	meibomian gland dysfunction		maternal grandparents
	multi glandular disease		matrix Gla-protein

	medical group practice	MHA	main hepatic artery
	monoclonal gammopathy		Master of Hospital Administration
MgP	magnesium phosphate		Mental Health Assistant
	magnesium pidolate		methotrexate, hydrocortisone,
MGPN	may have meant		and cytarabine (ara-C)
	membranoproliferazive		microangiopathic hemolytic
	glomerulonephritis (MPGN)		anemia
MGPS	Multi-item Gamma Poisson		microhemagglutination
	Shrinker		migraine headache
mGPS	modified Glasgow prognostic	MHA-TP	microhemagglutination-
	score		*Treponema pallidum*
MGR	murmurs, gallops, or rubs	MHB	maximum hospital benefits
M/G/R	murmurs, gallops, and rubs		Medicare Hospice Benefit
MGRS	masculine gender role stress	MHb	methemoglobin
	Multicentre Growth Reference	MHBSS	modified Hank balanced salt
	Study (World Health		solution
	Organization)	MHC	major histocompatibility complex
MGS	magnetic guidance system		mental health center (clinic)
	malignant glandular schwannoma		mental health counselor
	Meckel-Gruber syndrome	M/hct	microhematocrit
MgS04	see MgSO4	MHD	10-hydroxycarbazepine
MGSD	mean gestational sac diameter		(oxcarbazepine metabolite)
MgSO4	magnesium sulfate. This is a		maintenance hemodialysis
	DANGEROUS abbreviation		maximum heart distance
	that should **NOT** be used. It		(radiation therapy)
	appears on the MedAbbrev	MHDs	mental health disorders
	and other "Do Not Use Lists,"	MHE	minimal hepatic encephalopathy
	as it has been read as	MHFTR	may have meant MTHFR
	morphine sulfate or not		(methylene tetrahydrofolate
	understood. Use "magnesium		reductase)
	sulfate."	mHg	millimeters of mercury
MGT	management	MHH	mental health hold
MGTD	no growth to date	M/H/H	melena, hematochezia, and
mgtt	minidrop (60 minidrops equals		hematemesis
	one mL)	MHI	Mental Health Index
mguncle	maternal great uncle		(information)
MGUS	monoclonal gammopathy of		mild head injury
	undetermined significance	MHICM	Mental Health Intensive Case
MGVs	mean gray values		Management (US Veterans
MGW	multiple gunshot wound		Affair)
MGW enema	magnesium sulfate, glycerin,	MHID	Mental Health/Intellectual
	and water enema		Disabilities
MGX	meibomian gland expression	MHIP	mental health inpatient
M-GXT	multistage graded exercise test	MHIV	microsurgical high-inguinal
mGy	milligray (1 gray equals		varicocelectomy
	1,000 milligrays; a gray is	MHL	maximum heart length
	defined as the absorption of		(radiation therapy)
	one joule of radiation energy		mesenchymal hamartoma of the
	per kilogram of matter)		liver
MH	macular hemorrhage	MHLW	Ministry of Health, Labor, and
	macular hole		Welfare (Japan)
	malignant hyperthermia	MH/MR	mental health and mental
	marital history		retardation
	medical history	MHN	major hepatic necrosis
	menstrual history		massive hepatic necrosis
	mental health		mental health nurse
	mobile home	MHO	medical house officer
	moist heat		medication handout

M

373

MHP	moist heat packs	MIBC	muscle-invasive bladder cancer
MHPE	Master in Health Professions Education	MIBE	measles inclusion body encephalitis
MHR	maximum heart rate	MIBG	iodine-131-meta-iodoben-
MHRA	Medicines and Healthcare products Regulatory Agency (United Kingdom)		zylguanidine injection (AdreView; iobenguane) a radioisotope used in a
MHRI	Mental Health Research Institute		scintiscan imaging test to
MHS	major histocompatibility system		find or confirm the presence
	malignant hyperthermia		of pheochromocytoma and
	susceptible		neuroblastoma
	mental health services	MIBI	technetium Tc99m sestamibi
	monomethyl hydrogen sulfate		(a myocardial perfusion
	multihospital system		agent; Cardiolite)
MHsFHF	malarial hepatitis-stimulating	MIBK	methylisobutylketone
	fulminant-hepatic failure	MIC	major histocompatibility
MHSI	medical hyperspectral imaging		complex (MHC) class I
MHT	malignant hypertension		chain-related proteins
	mental health team		maternal and infant care
	Mental Health Technician		medical intensive care
MHTAP	microhemagglutination assay		methacholine inhalation
	for antibody to *Treponema*		challenge
	pallidum		microcytic erythrocytes
MHTFR	may have meant MTHFR		microscope
	(methylenetetrahydrofolate		minimum inhibitory
	reductase (gene)		concentration
MHtn	malignant hypertension	MIC-1	macrophage inhibitory
MHV	mechanical heart valves		cytokine-1
	middle hepatic vein	MIC7 (also 12)	see gene website, www.ncbi
MHW	medial heel wedge		.nlm.nih.gov/gene
	mental health worker	MICA	mentally ill chemical abuser
MHX	methohexital sodium	MICAR	Mortality Medical Indexing,
MHx	medical history		Classification, and Retrieval
MHxR	medical history review	MICD	mechanical irritant contact
MHz	megahertz		dermatitis
MI	membrane intact	MICE	mesna, ifosfamide, carboplatin,
	mental illness		and etoposide
	mental institution	MIC-KEY	gastrostomy feeding tubes
	mesial incisal	MICN	Mobile Intensive Care Nurse
	methylisothiazolinone (a	MICP	microbial-induced calcite (calcium
	preservative found in liquid		carbonate) precipitation
	personal care products)		minimally invasive cosmetic
	Michigan		procedure(s)
	mitral insufficiency	MICR	methacholine inhalation chal-
	myocardial infarction		lenge response
M I	Mallampati score 1 (classes 3	Micra®	a transcatheter pacing system;
	or 4 are associated with more		a minaturized completely
	difficult intubation as well as		self-contained pacemaker,
	a higher incidence of sleep		implanted directly in the heart
	apnea		without leads (Medtronic,
M/I	mortality to incidence ratio		Minneapolis MN)
MIA	malnutrition, inflammation, and	MICRO	microcytes
	atherosclerosis (syndrome)	micro-CT	microcomputer tomography
	medically indigent adult	MicroDISC	a provider of the off-the-shelf
	minimally-invasive anesthesia		and custom rugged and com-
	missing in action		mercial computers, cameras,
MIAVR	minimally invasive aortic valve		computers, frame grabbers,
	replacement		systems, and lenses

microdisc — microdiscectomy; a minimally invasive surgical procedure to remove portions of a herniated disc to relieve pressure on the spinal nerve column

MICROG — microgram (mcg is preferred)

microgray — 1,000,000 micrograys equals 1 gray (a gray [Gy] is unit of absorbed radiation equal to the dose of one joule of energy absorbed per kilogram of matter; also equals 100 rads)

micromet — micrometastasis

micron — micrometer (is one-millionth of a meter); one-thousandth of a millimeter. One 25-thousandth of an inch

microV — microvolt

MICS — microincision cataract surgery
minimally invasive cardiac surgery

MICU — medical intensive care unit
mobile intensive care unit

MID — mesioincisodistal
microvillus inclusion disease
mild iron deficiency
minimal ineffective dose
minimally important difference
multi-infarct dementia

mid — middle

MIDAS — migraine disability assessment scale

MIDCAB — minimally invasive direct coronary artery bypass (surgery)

MIDD — maternally inherited diabetes and deafness

MIDEPIS — midline episiotomy

MIDI — myocardial infarction during intercourse

Mid I — middle insomnia

MIDLF — midline lumbar fusion

MIDLIF — may have meant MIDLF (midline lumbar fusion)

mid noc — midnight

MIE — maximim inspiratory effort
meconium ileus equivalent (cystic fibrosis)
medical improvement expected
minimally invasive esophagectomy

MI-E — mechanical insufflation-exsufflation
mechanical insufflator-exsufflator

MIEA-TRCHA — Medicare Improvement and Extension Act of 2006 under Division B, Title I of the Tax Relief and Health Care Act of 2006

MIED — methotrexate, ifosfamide, etoposide, and dexamethasone

Mied — moderate intermittent explosive disorder

MIEI — medication-induced esophageal injury

MIF — Merthiolate, iodine, and formalin
mifepristone (RU 486; Mifeprex)
migration inhibitory factor

MIF 50%VC — midinspiratory flow at 50% of vital capacity

Mifflin St Jeor — a formula for calculating the resting metabolic rate

mIFL — modified irinotecan, fluorouracil, and leucovorin

MIFR — midinspiratory flow rate

MIFS — myxoinflammatory fibroblastic sarcoma

MIG — measles immune globulin

Miga — Mitoguardin (gene)

mIgA — monomeric immunoglobulin A

MIGB — metaiodobenzylguanidine ([123] I metaiodobenzylguanidine imaging)
methylisogermabullone

MIGET — multiple inert gas elimination technique

MIGS — maximum isometric grip strength
micro-invasive glaucoma surgery
minimally invasive glaucoma surgery
minimally invasive gynecological surgery

MIH — medication-induced headache
migraine with interparoxysmal headache
myointimal hyperplasia

MII — multichannel intraluminal impedence

M II — Mallampati score 2 classes 3 or 4 are associated with more difficult intubation as well as a higher incidence of sleep apnea)

M III — Mallampati score 3 (classes 3 or 4 are associated with more difficult intubation as well as a higher incidence of sleep apnea)

M

Mike	Phonetic Alphabet for M; pronounced MIKE	MINOCA	myocardial infarction with non-obstructive coronary arteries
mikes	micrograms (slang)		
MIL	medically induced labor	mins	minutes
	mesial incisal lingual (surface)	MIO	minimum identifiable odor
	military		monocular indirect
	mother-in-law		ophthalmoscopy
MILD	minimally invasive lumbar decompression	MIOL	multifocal intraocular lens
		MIOM	multimodal intraoperative
milF	see gene website www.ncbi.nlm.nih.gov/gene		(neuro)monitoring
		MIP	macrophage inflammatory
mililiter	may have meant milliliter (one thousandth of a liter; approximately 30 mL = 1 once)		protein
			maximum inspiratory pressure
			maximum-intensity projection (radiology)
mililter	see milliliter (ml)		mean intrathoracic pressure
Million	Million Visual Analogue Scale (measures patient's level of pain and disability)		mean intravascular pressure
			medical improvement possible
			metacarpointerphalangeal
MILS	maternally inherited Leigh syndrome		Michigan Biologic Products Institute
			minimally invasive parathyroidectomy
MIMCU	medical intermediate care unit		
MIME	mitoguazone, ifosfamide, methotrexate, and etoposide with mesna	MIPI	MCL (mantle cell lymphoma) International Prognostic Index
		M-IPMN	main duct (pancreatic duct-involved) intraductal papillary mucinous neoplasm
MIMR	Maternal-Infant Mortality Review		
MIN	mammary intraepithelial neoplasia		
	melanocytic intraepidermal neoplasia	MIPO	minimally invasive plate osteosynthesis
	mineral	MIPP	maximum-intensity pixel projection (images for MRI)
	minimum		
	minor	MIPPA	Medicare Improvements for Patients and Providers Act of 2008
min	minimal		
	minute(s)		
MIN A	minimal assistance (assist)		
min. @	minimum assistance	MiPPV	minimally-invasive positive-pressure ventilator
MINDS	Minnesota Detoxification Scale		
MINE	medical improvement not expected	MIPS	Merit-Based Incentive Payment System
	Medical Information Network of Europe	MIPs	molecularly imprinted polymers
		MIRD	medical internal radiation dose
	mesna, ifosfamide, mitoxantrone (Novantrone), and etoposide	MIRM	Mycoplasma pneumoniae-induced rash and mucositis
MINI	Mini International Neuropsychiatric Interview	miRNA	micro ribonucleic acid
		MIRP	myocardial infarction rehabilitation program
mini-BAL	mini-bronchoalveolar lavage (a blind, non bronchoscopic procedure, used to obtain samples from the lower respiratory tract from patients on mechanical ventilation)		
		MIRPE	minimally invasive repair of pectus excavatum
		MIRS	Medical Improvement Review Standard
		MIRSA	see MRSA
mini-CEX	mini-Clinical Evaluation Exercise (a method to assess the clinical competencies of trainees)	MIRU-VNTR	mycobacterial interspersed repetitive units containing variable number of tandem repeats
Mini Neb	a small compact, lightweight compressor nebulizer system	MIS	management information systems
MinIP	minimum intensity projection (radiology)		melanoma *in situ*

M

	minimally invasive surgery	MIU	million international units
	mitral insufficiency		minor injury unit
	moderate intermittent suction	mIU	milli-international unit
MIS 2	minimally invasive surgery with		(one-thousandth of an
	2-incision technique (total hip		International unit)
	arthroplsty)	MIUL	milli-international units per liter
MISA	mentally ill and substance abusing	mIU/L	milli-international units per liter
MISC	miscarriage	mIU/mL	milli-international units per
	miscellaneous		milliliter
M Isch	myocardial ischemia	MIUs	minor injury units
MISH	multiple *in situ* hybridization	MIV	murine leukemia virus
MISI	Matsuda Insulin Sensitivity Index	M IV	Mallampati score 4 (classes 3
	Muscle Insulin Sensitivity Index		or 4 are associated with more
M-ISI	Michigan Incontinence		difficult intubation as well as
	Symptom Index (score)		a higher incidence of sleep
MISO	misonidazole		apnea)
MISP	minimally invasive simple	MIVA	mivacurium (Mivacron)
	prostatectomy	MIVE	maximum isometric voluntary
	Minimum Initial Services		extension
	Package	MIVF	maintenance intravenous fluids
	mitotic spindle positioning (gene)		maximal isometric voluntary
MISS	minimally invasive spine surgery		force
	Modified Injury Severity Score		maximum isometric voluntary
	(Scale)		flexion
	Mothers in Sympathy and	MIW	mental inquest warrant
	Support (related to stillbirths)	mix mon	mixed monitor
MIST	metabolites in safety testing	MJ	marijuana
	minimally invasive skin		megajoule
	tightening	mJ	millijoules
	minimally-invasive surfactant	MJA	Medical Journal of Australia
	therapy	MJD	Machado-Joseph Disease
	modified incremental step test	MJHS	Metropolitan Jewish Health
MIS TLIF	minimally invasive surgery-		System (Brooklyn NY)
	transforaminal lumbar	MJL	medial joint line
	interbody fusion	MJP	marijuana paraphernalia
MIT	meconium in trachea		multiple juvenile polyps
	methylisothiazolinone	MJS	medial joint space
	(a preservative found in liquid	MJT	Mead Johnson tube
	personal care products)	MK	microbial keratitis
	miracidia immobilization test	μkat	microkatal (micro-moles/sec)
	mono-iodotyrosine	MK2	mitogen-activated protein kinase-
	multiple injection therapy		activated protein kinase 2
	(of insulin)	MKAB	may keep at bedside
MITO-C	mitomycin (Mutamycin)	MKB	married, keeping baby
MITOX	mitoxantrone (Novantrone)	MK-CSF	megakaryocyte colony-
mitR	myocyte enhancer factor-2		stimulating factor
	interacting transcriptional	MKD	medial knee displacement
	repressor; see gene website		mevalonate Kinase Deficiency
	www.ncbi.nlm.nih.gov/gene		mevalonate kinase deficiency
MitraClip	minimally invasive catheter-		(also known as the
	based mitral valve repair		hyperimmunoglobulinemia
	procedure		D syndrome)
MITs	medical imaging technologists	MKI	mitotic-karyorrhectic index
	microscopically intra-thyroid	MKK	Maasai in Kinyawa, Kenya
	tumors		(population samples of
	minimally invasive therapies		HapMap [a catalog of
MITT	microbiological intent-to-treat		common genetic variants that
	modified intent-to-treat		occur in human beings])

M

MKM	Mehrkoordinaten Manipulator		melioidosis (*Pseudomonas*
	microgram per kilogram per		*pseudomallei*) vaccine
	minute		metachromatic leukodystrophy
MKP	melanoma of known primary		microlumbar diskectomy
	(site)		microsurgical lumbar
MKS	Meckel-Gruber syndrome		diskectomy
	(also known MGS)		minimal lethal dose
	Mounier-Kuhn syndrome		minimal luminal diameter
MKs	megakaryocytes	MLDA	Mutational Load Distribution
ML	malignant lymphoma		Analysis
	mediolateral	MLDA-21	minimum legal drinking age 21
	middle lobe	MLDT	Manual Lymph Drainage
	midline		Therapist
	milliliter (one thousandth	MLE	major line extension
	of a liter; approximately		maximum likelihood estimation
	30 mL = 1 once) (preferred		medial lower eyelid
	abbreviation is mL)		midline (medial) episiotomy
	mucosal leishmaniasis	MLEE	multilocus enzyme
mL	milliliter (one thousandth of a		electrophoresis
	liter; approximately 30 mL =	MLF	median longitudinal fasciculus
	1 once)		microdroplets of lung fluid
ml	milliliter (one thousandth of a	MLFS	Medicis Lip Fullness Scale
	liter; approximately 30 mL =		morphologic leukemia free state
	1 once) (preferred abbrevia-	MLFs	mouse lung fibroblasts
	tion is mL)	MLH1	mismatch repair gene; see gene
M/L	monocyte to lymphocyte (ratio)		website www.ncbi.nlm.nih
	mother-in-law		.gov/gene
ML1	mediolateral 1 (coronary artery	MLHFQ	Minnesota Living With Heart
	branch)		Failure Questionnaire
MLA	medical laboratory assay	mL/hr	milliliters per hour
	mento-laeva anterior	MLI	measles-like illness
MLAC	minimum local analgesic		Molecular Libraries Initiative
	concentration		(NIH)
MLAD	midsegment left anterior		multilevel intervention
	descending (artery)		multiple lacunar infarcts
	minimum (effective) local	MLIF	monocyte locomotion inhibitory
	anesthetic dose		factor
MLAP	mean left atrial pressure	MLK	mixed lineage kinase
MLB	microlaryngobronchoscopy		montelukast sodium (Singulair)
	microlaryngoscopy and	mL/kg/hr	milliliters per kilogram per hour
	bronchoscopy	MLL	mixed-lineage leukemia
	multilayer bandaging		Morel-Lavallée lesion
MLBW	moderately low birth weight	MLL5	mixed-lineage leukemia 5 (gene)
MLC	metastatic liver cancer	MLM	mixed linear model
	minimal lethal concentration		see gene website www.ncbi.nlm
	mixed lymphocyte culture		.nih.gov/gene
	multileaf collimator	mL/min	milliliters per minute
	multilevel care	MLN	manifest latent nystagmus
	multilumen catheter		mediastinal lymph node
	myelomonocytic leukemia,		melanoma vaccine
	chronic		mesenteric lymph node
MLCCC	multilayer coil countercurrent	MLND	mediastinal lymph node
	chromatography		dissection
MLCOG	mediolateral center of gravity	MLNS	minimal lesions nephrotic
MLCX	middle part of the left		syndrome
	circumflex artery		mucocutaneous lymph node
MLD	manual lymph drainage		syndrome (Kawasaki
	masking level difference		syndrome)

M

MLO	medial linkage orthosis	MLV	monitored live voice
	medial-lateral oblique	MLWHF	Minnesota Living with Heart
	(mammogram view)		Failure (questionnaire)
	mesiolinguo-occlusal	MM	major medical (insurance)
MLP	mento-laeva posterior		malignant melanoma
	mesiolinguopulpal		malignant mesothelioma
	midlevel provider		Marshall-Marchetti
MLPA	multiple ligation probe		medial malleolus
	amplification		medial meniscus
MLPJ	mechanical loosening of		medical marijuana
	prosthetic joint		Medication Management
MLPN	Medical Licensed Practical		(standard, The Joint
	Nurse		Commission)
MLPP	maximum loose-packed position		member months
MLPs	mid-level providers		meningococcic meningitis
mLPS-RH	minilaparoscopic radical		mercaptopurine and methotrexate
	hysterectomy		methadone maintenance
MLPT	moderate-to-late preterm		micrometastases
MLR	medical loss ration		millimeter (mm)
	(US Affordable Care Act)		mindfulness meditation
	middle latency response		mismatch (ing)
	mixed lymphocyte reaction		mist mask
	multiple logistic regression		monochorionic-monoamniotic
MLRA	multiple linear regression		twins
	analysis		morbidity and mortality
mlrB	see gene website; www.ncbi		motor meal
	.nlm.nih.gov		mucous membrane
MLS	macrolides, lincosamides, and		multiple myeloma
	streptogramins		muscle movement
	Maroteaux-Lamy syndrome		muscularis mucosae
	maximum likely-hood		myelomeningocele
	(likelihood) score	mM	millimolar
	mediastinal B-cell lymphoma	mm	millimeter
	with sclerosis	mm^2	square millimeter
	midline shift	mm^3	cubic millimeter
mLs	milliliters (mL preferred)	M&M	milk and molasses
mL/s	milliliter per second		morbidity and mortality
mL's	milliliters (mL preferred)		(conference)
MLSA	multilocus sequence analysis	M/M	male/male
MLSI	medial-lateral stability index		monocyte/macrophage (lineage)
MLSMR	Molecular Libraries Small		the ratio between the maximum
	Molecule Repository (NIH)		and minimum
MLST	multi-locus sequence typing	MMA	maxillomandibular advancement
MLT	melatonin		methyl methacrylate
	mento-laeva transversa		methylmalonic acid
	microbial limit testing		methylmalonic aciduria (cobala-
mLTBR	modified lateral temporal bone		min deficiency)
	resection		middle meningeal artery
MLTC	Managed Long Term Care		Mixed Martial Arts
mltC	membrane-bound lytic murein		multimodal analgesia
	transglycosylase (gene)	mmac	methylmalonic aciduria and
MLTC-1	mouse Leydig tumour cell line		homocystinuria type c-like
MLU	mean length of utterance		protein; see gene website
MLUS	mean length of utterance		www.ncbi.nlm.nih.gov/gene
	modified lung ultrasound	MMACHC	methylmalonic aciduria
MLUs	mean length of utterances		(cobalamin deficiency) cblC
MLU-W	mean length of utterance in words		type, with homocystinuria
MLUw	mean length of utterance in words		(gene)

M

MMAE	monomethyl auristatin E	MMFI	modified mechanical fragility index (red blood cell susceptibility to mechanically induced hemolysis)
MMAR	Medical Marijuana Access Regulations (Canada)		
MMAS-8	Morisky Medication Adherence Scale-8		multimodality fusion imaging (the simultaneous visualization of spatially aligned and juxtaposed medical images obtained by two or more image modalities)
MMB	medial branch block		
	medullomyoblastoma		
	mouth-to-mouth breathing		
M/M/B	medetomidine, midazolam, and butorphanol	MMFR	maximal mid-expiratory flow rate
MMBC	mixed mucinous breast carcinoma	MMG	magnetomyography
			mammography
	multifocal and multicentric breast cancer		mechanomyography
		MMH	Milligan-Morgan hemorrhoidectomy
MMC	maxillomandibular complex		
	Medicaid Managed Care	MMHg	monomethyl mercury
	migrating motor complex	mmHg	millimeters of mercury
	mild memory complaints	mm/Hg	millimeters of mercury
	minimum microbicidal concentration	mm/H$_2$O	millimeters of water
		mm/hr	millimeters per hour
	Mismatch Correction	MMI	maximal medical improvement
	mitomycin (mitomycin C)	mMiDAS	modified migraine disability assessment scale
	mixed-microbial-culture		
	modified Mallampati test	MMIHS	megacystis microcolon intestinal hypoperistalsis syndrome
	Montefiore Medical Center (Bronx NY)		
		MMII	second meiotic metaphase
	Mother's Milk Cooperative	MMIS	malignant melanoma in situ
	mucosal mast cell	MMIs	multiple mini-interviews
	myelomeningocele	MMK	Marshall-Marchetti-Krantz (cystourethropexy)
	myoelectrical migrating complex		
mMCC	metastatic Merkel cell carcinoma	MML	minimal masking level (audiology)
MMCP	mumps, measles, chickenpox	mM/L	millimoles per liter
MMCR	Müller muscle-conjunctival resection (a technique to correct upper eyelid ptosis)	MMM	medical management of miscarriage
			metastic malignant melanoma
MMCT	mitocyn C trabeculectomy		mitoxantrone, methotrexate, and mitomycin
MMD	malignant metastatic disease		
	moyamoya disease		mucous membrane moist
	mucus membranes dry		myelofibrosis with myeloid metaplasia
	myotonic muscular dystrophy		
MMDA	3-methoxy-4,5-methylenedioxyamphetamine (a psychedelic drug)	MMMA	methylmalonic acuduria; see gene website www.ncbi.nlm.nih.gov/gene
	mean micronutrient density adequacy	mMMP-9	mutant matrix metalloproteinase-9
mm/dd/yy	month date, year, as in 02/15/12	mMMSE	modified version of the mini mental status examination
mMDL	median motor distal latency		
MME	membrane metalloendopeptidase	MMMT	malignant mixed mesodermal tumor
	morphine milligram equivalents		metastatic mixed müllerian tumor
MMECT	multiple monitor electroconvulsive therapy	MMN	may or may not (be)
			mismatch negativity
MMEFR	maximal mid-expiratory flow rate		multifocal motor neuropathy
MMF	maxillomandibular fixation		multiple micronutrients
	mean maximum flow	MMNB	may or may not be
	mismatch field	MMNCB	multifocal motor neuropathy with conduction blocks
	mycophenolate mofetil (CellCept)		
		MMO	maximum mouth opening

M

MMOA	maxillary mandibular odontectomy alveolectomy
mmol	millimole
mmol/L	millimoles per liter
μmol	micromole
MMORPGs	massively multiplayer online role-playing games
MMP	matrix metalloproteinase
MMP-8	matrix metallproteinase-8
MMP-9	matrix metallproteinase-9
MMP	mitochondrial myopathy
	mucous membrane pemphigoid
	multiple medical problems
	multiplexed molecular profiling (system)
MMPI	matrix metalloproteinase inhibitor
	Minnesota Multiphasic Personality Inventory
MMPI-A	Minnesota Multiphasic Personality Inventory - Adolescent version
MMPI-D	Minnesota Multiphasic Personality Inventory-Depression Scale
MMPN	methylmercaptopurine nucleotide(s)
mMPN	miniaturized most probable number
6-MMPR	6-methylmercaptopurine riboside
MMPs	membership medical practices
MMPW	mean matched population weight
MMR	major molecular response
	maternal mortality ratio
	measles, mumps, and rubella
	measles, mumps, and rubella vaccine
	menometrorrhagia
	midline malignant reticulosis
	mild mental retardation
	mismatch repair
MMRA	medial meniscal posterior root avulsion
mmrA	see gene website www.ncbi.nlm.nih.gov/gene
mMRC	Modified Medical Research Council (dyspnea scale)
MMRD	mismatch repair-deficient
	mismatched related donor
MMRE	multifrequency magnetic resonance elastography
MMRISK	a mnemonic for judging who is at high risk for melanomas; greater than 3 atypical moles, moles that are many in number, red hair and/or freckles, inability to tan, severe sunburn before age 14, kindred (family history of melanoma)
MMRM	Mixed-effects Models Repeated Measures (analysis)

MMRP	mismatch repair protein(s)
	mismatch repair-proficient
MMR-P	mismatch repair proficient
MMRS	Metropolitan Medical Response System
MMRTs	medial meniscus root tears
MMRV	measles virus, mumps virus, rubella virus and varicella virus vaccine
	measles, mumps, rubella, and varicella vaccine
MMR-VAR	measles virus, mumps virus, rubella virus and varicella virus vaccine
MMS	Medication Management Standards
	Mini-Mental State (examination)
	modified Mallampati score
	Mohs micrographic surgery
mm/s	millimeters per second
MMSAs	metropolitan and micropolitan statistical areas
mMSC	mouse mesenchymal stem cells
MMSE	Mini-Mental State Examination
MMSI	Modified Masood Scoring Index
MMSP	multiplex methylation-specific PCR (polymerase chain reaction)
MMT	malignant mesenchymal tumors
	manual muscle test(ing) grading (http://scottsevinsky.com/pt/mmt.html)
	meal-tolerance test
	medial meniscal tear
	methadone maintenance treatment
	Mini Mental Test
	mixed müllerian tumors
	Modified Mallampati Test
MMT 5/5	manual muscle test; the subject completes range of motion against gravity with maximal resistance
MMTP	Methadone Maintenance Treatment Program
MMTS	micrometastases
	methyl methanethiosulfonate
MMTV	malignant mesothelioma of the tunica vaginalis
	monomorphic ventricular tachycardia
	mouse mammary tumor virus
MMTx	MetaMap Transfer (program)
MMU	medication management and use
	mobile medical unit
mmu	millimass units
MMUD	mismatch unrelated donor
MMURD	mismatched unrelated donor
MMV	mandatory minute volume

M

MMVR	mechanical mitral value replacement	MNMCB	motor neuropathy with multifocal conduction block
MMVT	monomorphic ventricular tachycardia	MNNB	Monas-Nitz Neuropsychological Battery
mMVTx	modified multivisceral	MNNs	memristive neural networks
MMW	Munich Medical Weekly (Muncherer Medizinische Wochenschrift)		metastatic neck nodes
		MNO	magnitude of negative outcome
		MnO	manganese oxide
MMWR	*Morbidity and Mortality Weekly Report*	MnP2	mandibular second premolar
		MnPc	manganese phthalocyanine
MMx	multimatrix; a tablet formulation designed to begin dissolution in the terminal ileum	MN PMP	Minnesota Prescription Monitoring Program
		MNPRT	mixed neutron and photon radiotherapy
MN	Master of Nursing	MNR	marrow neutrophil reserve
	Master's Degree in Nursing	MN-RETs	micronucleated reticulocytes
	midnight	MNS	masculinity norms salience
	Minnesota		mean nocturnal saturation
	mononuclear		mediastinal nodal sterilization
Mn	manganese		Melnick Needles syndrome
M&N	morning and night		midnight snacks
	Mydriacyl and Neo-Synephrine		MNS; an International Society of Blood Transfusion (ISBT) blood group
M/N	midnight		
MNAR	missing not at random (incomplete data)		
		MNSc	Master of Nursing Science
MNB	mouth-to-nose breathing	MnSOD	manganese superoxide dismutase
MNBB	median nerve branch block	Mn SSEPS	median-nerve somatosensory-evoked potentials
M NBI	magnifying endoscopy with narrow band imaging		
		MNT	medical nutrition therapy
MNC	malnourished child (children)	MnT	manganese accumulation in teeth
	malnourished controls	MNTB	medial nucleus of the trapezoid body
	monomicrobial necrotizing cellulitis		
		mNT-BBAVF	modified nontransposed bra-chiobasilic arteriovenous fistula
	mononuclear leukocytes		
MNCD	malingered neurocognitive dysfunction	MNV	murine norovirus
		MNV-1	murine norovirus-1
mNCD	mild neurocognitive disorder	MNX	meniscectomy
MNCH	maternal, newborn, and child health	MNZ	metronidazole
		MO	medial oblique (x-ray view)
MNCV	motor nerve conduction velocity		medication overdose
MND	minor neurological dysfunction		menhaden oil
	modified neck dissection		mesio-occlusal
	motor neuron disease		mineral oil
MNE	micronucleated erythrocytes		Missouri
	Minimum Norm Estimates		monocyte
	monosymptomatic nocturnal enuresis		months old
			morbidly obese
MNF	myelinated nerve fibers		morning of
MnF2	manganese fluoride		mother
MNG	multinodular goiter		multiple organisms
MNGIE	mitochondrial neurogasteroin-testinal encephalomyopathy (syndrome)		myositis ossificans
			molybdenum
mngmt	management	mo	month
mngt	management		month (this is a dangerous abbreviation as it might not be understood or interpreted as Monday; spell-out- month or Monday)
MNH	maternal and newborn health		
MnH	manganese accumulation in hair		
MNL	mononuclear leukocyte		
MNM	mononeuritis multiplex		

M/O	morning of
MO2	oxygen metabolism
MOA	mechanism of action
	metronidazole, omeprazole, and amoxicillin
	mixed oligoastrocytoma
	mode of action
MoAb	monoclonal antibody
MOAC	metal oxide affinity chromatography
moaC	molybdopterin biosynthesis, protein C (gene)
MOAD	Mother of All Databases
MOAHI	mixed obstructive apnea and hypopnea index
MOAI	may have meant MAOI (monamine oxidase inhibitor)
	mixed obstructive (sleep) apnea index
MOAS	Modified Overt Aggression Scale
MOB	main olfactory bulb
	medical office building
	mobility
	mobilization
	mother of baby
mobE	see gene website; www.ncbi .nlm.nih.gov
Mobitz block	a second-degree atrioventricular block (one or more [but not all] of the atrial impulses fail to conduct to the ventricles due to impaired conduction)
MOB-PT	mitomycin, vincristine (Oncovin), bleomycin, and cisplatin (Platinol)
Mobs	mobilizations
mOBS	modified Oxford bone score
MOC	Maintenance of Certification
	medial olivocochlear
	Medical Officer on Call
	metronidazole, omeprazole, and clarithromycin
	mother of child
MoCA	Montreal Cognitive Assessment (to measure cognitive impairment)
MOCHA	markers of coagulation and hemostatic activation
	Men of Color Health Awareness (project)
	Modeling of Congenital Hearts Alliance
	Models of Child Health Appraised (project)
MOCI	Maudsley Obsessive-Compulsive Inventory
MOCT	macular optical coherence tomography

MOD	magneto-optical disc (radiology)
	maturity onset diabetes
	medical officer of the day
	mesio-occlusal-distal
	method of delivery
	mode of death
	moderate
	moment of death
	multiorgan dysfunction
MOD A	moderate assistance (assist)
modA	molybdate transporter subunit; see gene website www.ncbi .nlm.nih.gov/gene
mod @	moderate assistance (PM & R)
MODEMS	Musculoskeletal Outcomes Data Evaluation and Management Scale
Mod I	modified independence (able to move on own but with modification (such as with an assistive device, decrease speed, etc.)
Mod. I	modified independence (able to move on own but with modification (such as with an assistive device, decrease speed, etc.)
MODI	modified independent (e.g., a patient who is independent, but requires a walker)
MoDi	monochorionic-diamniotic (twins)
Mo/Di	monochorionic-diamniotic (twins)
MODM	mature-onset diabetes mellitus
Mod-MPI	myocardial performance index
MODS	microscopic-observation drug-susceptibility assay
	multiple-organ dysfunction syndrome
mod-sev	moderate to severe
mod/sev	moderate to severe
MODY	maturity-onset diabetes of the young
MOE	movement of extremities
MOEMs	micro-opto-electro-mechanical systems
MOF	mesial occlusal facial
	methotrexate, vincristine (Oncovin), and fluorouracil
	methoxyflurane (Penthrane)
	multiple-organ failure
MOFS	multiple-organ failure syndrome
MOG	myelin-oligodendrocyte glygoprotein
Moga	mogamulizumab- kpkc inj (Poteligeo)
mOGC	metastatic oesophago-gastric cancer

M

MOG IgG	myelin oligodendrocyte glyco-protein immunoglobulin G
MOG-IgG	myelin oligodendrocyte glyco-protein immunoglobulin G
MOH	medication overuse headache
MoH	Ministry of Health (Canada)
MOHOST	Model of Human Occupation Screening Tool
Mohs	Mohs technique; serial excision and microscopic examination of skin cancers
MOHSW	Liberian Ministry of Health and Social Welfare
MOI	mechanism of injury
	multiplicity of infection
MoICU	mobile intensive care unit
MOID	Mammalian Orthologous Intron Database
MOJAC	mood orientation, judgement, affect, and content
MOL	method of limits
MOLLI	modified Look-Locker inversion (recovery imaging)
Mollies	powder or crystalline form of methylenedioxy-methylam-phetamine (MDMA; Ecstasy)
Molly	powder or crystalline form of methylenedioxy-methylam-phetamine (MDMA; Ecstasy)
MOLST	medical orders for life-sustaining treatment
MOM	milk of magnesia
	mother
	mother's own milk
	mucoid otitis media
MoM	multiples of the median
	metal-on-metal (arthroplasty)
MoMo	monochorionic-monoamniotic twins
Mo/Mo	molybdenum/molybdenum (anode target/filter combina-tions used in mammography)
	monochorionic-monoamniotic twins
MOMO syndrome	macrosomia, obesity, macrocephaly, and ocular abnormalities syndrome
MOMP	major outer membrane protein
MON	maximum observation nursery monitor
Mon	Monday
MONA	morphine, oxygen, nitroglycerin, and aspirin
MONO	infectious mononucleosis
	monocyte
	monospot
MonoDi	monochorionic-diamniotic (twins)
mono mono	monochorionic, monoamniotic

MONOS	monocytes
mons	an anatomic term for an eleva-tion or eminence
	months
mons pubis	the rounded fleshy prominence over the symphysis pubis in the female
MONT	montelukast (Singulair)
monthly	There is no widely acceptable, recognized abbreviation for monthly or once a month, write it out.
Monti	tubularized bladder flap (Monti procedure)
MOON	Multicenter Orthopaedic Out-comes Network
MOOSE guidelines	Meta-analysis of observational studies in epidemiology guidelines
MOP	medical outpatient
	mother of patient
	mu-opioid peptide (receptors)
8 MOP	methoxsalen (Oxsorlen)
MOPD II	Majewski osteodysplastic pri-mordial dwarfism type II
MOPP	mechlorethamine, vincristine (Oncovin), procarbazine, and prednisone
MOPU	medical outpatient unit
MOPV	monovalent oral poliovirus vaccine
moPV1	monovalent oral type 1 poliovirus vaccine
MOR	morphine
	mortality odds ratio
	mu opioid receptor
mOR	matched odds ratio
MoRFs	molecular recognition features
Mo/Rh	molybdenum/rhodium (anode target/filter combinations used in mammography)
morn	morning
Moro orange	a blood orange, an anthocyanin-rich promoted for weight management and in the pre-vention of obesity
Moro reflex	a reflex reaction of infants upon being startled (as by a loud noise or a bright light) that is characterized by extension of the arms and legs away from the body and to the side and then by drawing them together as if in an embrace
MOS	Medical Outcome Study
	mirror optical system
mOS	median overall survival
Mosc	Moscow

MOSD	multiple organ system dysfunction
MOSES	Multidimensional Observation Scale for Elderly Subjects
MOSF	multiple-organ system failure
MOSFET	metal oxide semiconductor field-effect transistor (dosimeter)
mOsm	Milliosmole (one thousandth of an osmole)
mOsm/kg	milliosmol per kilogram
mOsmol	milliosmole
MOSsf-20	Medical Outcomes Study, short form 20 items
MOSsf-36	Medical Outcomes Study, short form, 36 items
MOT	motility examination
MOTA	Method Other Than Acceleration
MOTS	mucosal oral therapeutic system
MOTT	Mycobacteria other than tubercle
MOU	medical oncology unit
	memorandum of understanding
MOUS	multiple occurrences of unexplained symptoms
MOV	minimum obstructive volume
	multiple oral vitamin
MOW	Meals on Wheels
MOX	moxifloxacin (Avelox)
MOXFQ	Manchester-Oxford Foot Questionnaire
MOY	months of the year
MOYB	Months of the Year Backward (cognitive assessment)
MP	malignant pyoderma
	Mallampati
	mastopexy
	melphalan and prednisone
	menstrual period
	mercaptopurine (Purinethol)
	metacarpal phalangeal joint
	methylprednisolone
	military police
	mitoxantrone; prednisone
	moist pack
	monitor pattern
	monophasic
	motor potential
	mouthpiece
	multipurpose
	muscularis propria
	myocardial perfusion
4 MP	methylpyrazole (fomepizole; Antizol)
6-MP	mercaptopurine (Purenthol)
M & P	Millipore and phase
M/P	maternal/paternal
M:P	milk to plasma ration (related to breast feeding concentrations of drug)

MPA	main pulmonary artery
	Master of Public Administration
	Medical Products Agency (Sweden)
	Medicinal Products Agency (Switzerland)
	medroxyprogesterone acetate
	microscopic polyangiitis
MPa	megapascal
MPAC	Memorial Pain Assessment Card
MPACT	Metastatic Pancreatic Adenocarcinoma Clinical Trial
MPA/E2C	medroxyprogesterone acetate; estradiol cypionate (Lunelle)
MPAF	maximum per amplicon frequency
	multiphoton autofluorescence
MPAG	mycophenolic acid glucuronide
MPAL	mixed-phenotype acute leukemia
MPAP	mean pulmonary artery pressure
MPAQ	McGill Pain Assessment Questionnaire
MPAS	Masters of Physician Assistant Studies
MPAs	minor physical anomalies
MPAT	mate preference towards altruistic traits
	modified plate agglutination test
MPB	male-pattern baldness
	mephobarbital
MPBFV	mean pulmonary-blood-flow velocity
MPBNS	modified Peyronie bladder neck suspension
MPC	meperidine, promethazine, and chlorpromazine
	mucopurulent cervicitis
MPCA	multiway principal component analysis
mPCa	metastatic prostate cancer
MPCC	Medical Policy Coordinating Committee
MPCM	maculopapular cutaneous mastocytosis
	middle pharyngeal constrictor muscle
MPCN	microscopically positive and culturally negative
MPCP	magnetic resonance cholangiopancreatography
M-PCR	multiplex polymerase chain reaction
MPCU	medical progressive care unit
MPD	maximum permissable dose
	methylphenidate (Ritalin)
	moisture permeable dressing
	multiple personality disorder
	myeloproliferative disorder

M

	myofascial pain dysfunction (syndrome)		Milk-product intolerance
mPD	minimal peripheral dose		myocardial performance index
mPDA	metastatic pancreatic ductal adenocarcinoma		myocardial perfusion imaging
		MPIF-1	myeloid progenitor inhibitory factor-1
MPDPS	multiparous desires permanent sterilization	MPIP	Medicaid Provider Incentive Program
MPDS	molecular property diagnostic suite		Melanoma Patients' Information Page
	multipurpose (contact lens) disinfecting solution(s)		Moderately Premature Infant Project
	myofascial pain dysfunction syndrome	MPJ	metacarpophalangeal joint
MPDs	myeloproliferative disorders	MP joint	metacarpal phalangeal joint
MPE	malignant pleural effusion	MPK	milligram per kilogram
	massive pulmonary embolism	MPL	maximum permissable level
	mean prediction error		mesiopulpolingual
	multiphoton excitation	MPL®	monophosphoryl lipid A
	myxopapillary ependymoma	MPLC	medium pressure liquid chromatography
	myxopapillary function		
MPEC	multipolar electrocoagulation	MPM	malignant peritoneal mesothelioma
MPEG	methoxypolyethylene glycol		
MPER	membrane-proximal external region		malignant pleural mesothelioma
			Mortality Prediction Model
MPF	methotrexate, cisplatin (Platinol), and fluorouracil	mpMRI	multiparametric magnetic resonance imaging
	methylparaben free	MPN	monthly progress note
MPFC	medial prefrontal cortex		most probable number
MPFL	medial patellofemoral ligament		multiple primary neoplasms
m-PFL	methotrexate, cisplatin (Platinol), fluorouracil, and leucovorin		myeloproliferative neoplasm
		MP-NAT	minipool nucleic acid (amplification) testing
MPFS	Medicare Physician Fee Schedule		
MPG	mean pressure gradient	MPNST	malignant peripheral nerve sheath tumor
MPGN	membranoproliferative glomerulonephritis	MPO	male-pattern obesity
			myeloperoxidase
MPGR	multiplanar gradient recalled	MPOA	medial preoptic area
MPH	massive pulmonary hemorrhage	MPO-ANCA	myeloperoxidase anti-neutrophil cytoplasmic antibodies
	Master of Public Health		
	methylphenidate (Ritalin)	MPOC-20	The Measure of Processes of Care 20 (questionnaire)
	miles per hour		
MPHD	multiple pituitary hormone deficiencies	MPOD	macular pigment optical density
		MPP	massive periretinal proliferation
MPHFR	may have meant MTHFR (methylenetetrahydrofolate reductase; see gene website www.ncbi.nlm.nih.gov/gene		maximum pressure picture
			multiple presentation phenotype
		MPPA	medial parapatellar arthrotomy
			Methamphetamine Production Prevention Act of 2008
MPHL	male-pattern hair loss		
MPHR	maximal predicted heart rate	mPpa	mean pulmonary artery pressure
MPI	Mannheim Peritonitis Index (intended to provide early prognostic evaluation of abdominal sepsis desiring to select high? risk patients for more aggressive therapeutic procedures and to provide objective classification of the severity of disease)	mPpa-Q	mean pulmonary artery pressure-cardiac output
		MPPH syndrome	developmental brain disorder characterized by megalencephaly, polymicrogyria, polydactyly, and hydrocephalus
		MPPs	multipoint progenitors (cells)
	manufacturer's package insert	MPPT	methylprednisolone pulse therapy
	master patient index	MPPV	minimally-invasive positive-pressure ventilator
	Maudsley Personality Inventory		

M

MPQ	McGill Pain Questionnaire
MPR	massive periretinal retraction
	medication possession ratio
	multiplanar reconstruction
MP-RAGE	magnetization prepared rapid
	acquisition gradient-echo
MPS	Maternal Perinatal Scale
	mean particle size
	microcurrent point stimulation
	mononuclear phagocyte system
	mucopolysaccharidosis
	multiphasic screening
	myofascial pain syndrome
MPS-1	mucopolysaccharidosis I
MPS-II	mucopolysaccharidosis II
	(Hunter syndrome)
mPSL	methylprednisolone
MPSS	massively parallel signature
	sequencing
	methylprednisolone sodium
	succinate
MPSV4	meningococcal polysaccharide
	vaccine (Quadravalent)
MPS VII	mucopolysaccharidosis type VII
MPT	Master of Physical Therapy
	melphalan, prednisone, and
	thalidomide
	moderate preterm (infants born
	at 32 to 33 weeks' gestation)
	multiple parameter telemetry
MPTA	medial proximal tibial angle
	posterior tympanotomy
	approach
MPTJ	may have meant MTPJ (meta-
	tarsophalangeal joint)
MPTRD	motor, pain, touch, and reflex
	deficit
MPTT	malignant proliferating trichi-
	lemmal tumor
MPU	maternal pediatric unit
	medical progressive unit
MPV	mean platelet volume
MPVV	mean portal vein velocity
MPXV	monkeypox virus
MPZ	midperipheral zone (prostate
	needle biopsy location)
MQ	mefloquine (Lariam)
	memory quotient
MQIIP	Monitored Quality Improvement
	Impact Program
MQOL	McGill Quality of Life
	Questionnaire
MQS III	Medication Quantification Scale
	version 3 (an instrument
	with clinical and research
	applications for quantifying
	medication regimen use in
	chronic pain populations)

MQSA	Mammography Quality Stan-
	dards Act (enacted by the
	United States Congress to
	regulate the quality of care
	in mammography; officially
	effective in 1994, extended
	in 2004 to continue through
	2007)
MQTFL	medial quadriceps tendon femo-
	ral ligament
MR	Maddox rod
	magnetic resonance
	manifest refraction
	may repeat
	mean ranking
	measles-rubella
	medial rectus
	medical record
	mental retardation
	milliroentgen
	mitral regurgitation
	moderate resistance
M&R	measure and record
M/R	minocycline and rifampicin
MR#	medical records number
MR − 1	may repeat once
MR × 1	may repeat times one (once)
MRA	magnetic resonance angiography
	main renal artery
	medical record administrator
	medical research associate
	midright atrium
	multivariate regression analysis
MRABT	Mobile Robotic Assistive
	Balance Trainer
mrad	millirad
MRADL	Manchester Respiratory Activities
	of Daily Living (physical
	disability questionnaire;
	Manchester, UK)
	mobility related activities of
	daily living
MRADLs	mobility-related activities of
	daily living
MRAN	medical resident admitting note
MRAP	mean right atrial pressure
MRAS	main renal artery stenosis
MRAV	magnetic resonance angiography
	and venography
MRB	mineralocorticoid receptor
	blocker
	see gene website, www.ncbi
	.nlm.nih.gov/gene
MRC	Master of Rehabilitation
	Counseling
	Medical Research Council (UK)
MRCA	magnetic resonance coronary
	angiography

M

MRCC	metastatic renal cell carcinoma	MRE	magnetic resonance elastography
MRCG	Malaria Research and Control Program (University of California)		manual resistance exercise
			most recent episode
MR-CHOP	methotrexate 2 g/m2(day1), rituximab 375 mg/m2(day1), cyclophosphamide 750 mg/m2(day3), doxorubicin 50 mg/m2(day3), vincristine 1.4 mg/m2(day3), prednisolone 100 mg(day1-5).	MREF	Medical Research and Evaluation Facility
		mREE	measured resting energy expenditure
		mRem	millirem
		MREP	Medicare Remit Easy Print software
MRC-NPS	Medical Research Council Neurological Performance Score	MR-EPT	magnetic resonance - electrical properties tomography
MRCNS	methicillin-resistant coagulase-negative staphylococci	MRFC	mouse rosette-forming cells
		MR FIT	Multiple Risk Factor Intervention Trial
MRCP	magnetic resonance cholangiopancreatography	MRG	mortality reference group
			murmurs, rubs, and gallops
	Member of the Royal College of Physicians	M/R/G	murmurs, rubs, and gallops
	mental retardation, cerebral palsy	mRGCs	melanopsin-expressing retinal ganglion cells
MR/CP	mental retardation, cerebral palsy	MRgFUS	magnetic resonance-guided focused ultrasound
MRCPs	movement-related cortical potentials	MRgHIFU	magnetic resonance-guided high-intensity focused ultrasound
MRCS	Member of the Royal College of Surgeons	MRgLITT	magnetic resonance-guided laser interstitial thermotherapy
MRCT	multiregional clinical trials		magnetic resonance-guided laser-induced thermotherapy
MRD	margin reflex distance		
	matched related donor(s)	MRGS	movement-related gamma synchronization
	Medical Records Department		
	Minimal Record of Disability	MRGs	metal resistance genes
	minimal residual disease	MRH	Maddox rod hyperphoria
MRD1	marginal reflex distance 1		multicentric reticulohistiocytoses
MRDA	mental retardation, deafness and ankylosis (syndrome)	MRHD	maximum recommended human dose
mrdA	penicillin-binding protein 2, transpeptidase involved in peptidoglycan synthesis (gene)	MRHT	modified rhyme hearing test
		MRI	magnetic resonance imaging
			mean rate index
		MRI/A	magnetic resonance imaging and angiography
MRDD	Maize rough dwarf disease		
	maximum recommended daily dose	MRIB	magnetic resonance imaging of the breast
	Mental Retardation and Development Disabilities	MRICU	Medical Respiratory Intensive Care Unit
MR/DD	mental retardation and developmental delays	MR/ID	mentally retarded/intellectual disabled
MRDL	maximum residual disinfectant level (the highest level of a disinfectant allowed in drinking water)	M & R I & O	measure and record input and output
		MRI-PDFF	magnetic resonance imaging (estimated) proton-density fat fraction
MRDM	malnutrition-related diabetes mellitus	MRIs	magnetic resonance imagings
MRDO	multidrug-resistant organisms (Romance languages)	MRJ	marijuana
		MRK	Merck & Co., Inc.
MRDSA	magnetic resonance digital subtraction angiography	MRKH	Mayer-Rokitansky-Kuster-Hauser (syndrome)

M

MRKHS	Mayer-Rokitansky-Küster-Hauser syndrome	MRSCN	coagulase-negative methicillin resistant staphylococci
MRL	magnetic resonance lymphography	MRSD	maximum rate of systolic distension
	maximum residue level (s)		maximum recommended starting dose
	minimal response level		methadone-related sexual dysfunction
	moderate rubra lochia		
MRLT	mesalamine-related lung toxicity		
MRLVD	maximum residue limits of veterinary drugs	MRSE	methicillin-resistant *Staphylococcus epidermidis*
MRM	magnetic resonance microimaging	MRSOPA	maneuvers performed during neonatal resuscitation
	modified radical mastectomy		when there is ineffective
MRMT	Minnesota Rate of Manipulation Test		ventilation; **M**: Mask adjustment.,**R**: Reposition
MRMT-1	metastasizing rat's mammary tumor (cells) number 1		airway. (try again), **S**: Suction mouth and nose. **O**: Open
MRN	magnetic resonance neurography		mouth. (try again), **P**: Pressure increase, **A**: Airway alternative.
	malignant renal neoplasm	MRSS	methicillin-resistant
	medical record number		*Staphylococcus* species
	medical resident's note		modified Rodnan skin-thickness score
mRNA	messenger ribonucleic acid		
MRND	modified radical neck dissection	MRSSA	may have meant MRSA (methicillin-resistant
MRO	multidrug resistant organism(s)		Staphylococcus aureus)
MROC	male reproductive organ cancers		
	Mastectomy Reconstruction Outcomes Consortium (study)	MRT	magnetic resonance tomography
MRONJ	medication-related osteonecrosis of the jaw		malignant rhabdoid tumor
			mean response time
MROP	manual removal of placenta		mitochondrial replacement therapy
MROU	medial rectus, both eyes		modified rhyme test
MRP	multidrug resistance-associated protein		myofascial release therapy
MRPC	magnetic resonance cholangiopancreatography	MRTA	magnetic resonance tomographic angiography
mRPC	mouse retinal progenitor cell	MRTI	magnetic resonance thermal imaging
MRPN	medical resident progress note		
MRPs	medication-related problems	mRT-LAMP	multiplex reverse transcription loop-mediated isothermal
MRR	medial rectus recession		amplification (assay)
	medical record review	MR/TR	mitral and tricuspid regurgitation
	Medication Reconcilliation Record	MR-TRUS	magnetic resonance-transrectal ultrasound
MRS	macular raster scan		
	magnetic resonance spectro-scopic imaging	MRU	magnetic resonance urography
			medical resource utilization
	magnetic resonance spectroscopy	M/R/U	routine and microscopy urinalysis
	Melkersson-Rosenthal syndrome		
	mental retardation syndrome	MRV	magnetic resonance venography
	methicillin-resistant *Staphylococcus aureus*	MRV®	mixed respiratory vaccine
mRS	modified Rankin scale	MRVC	magnetic resonance voiding cystography
MRSA	methicillin-resistant *Staphylococcus aureus*	MRX	*Moraxella catarrhalis* vaccine
MRSAB	methicillin-resistant *Staphylococcus aureus* *bacteremia*	MRx	manifest refraction
		MRx1	may repeat one time
		MS	male spayed
MRSA PCR	methicillin-resistant Staphylococcus aureus polymerase chain reaction		mass spectroscopy
			Master of Science
			median sternotomy

	medical student	MSAT	mass screening and treatment
	medical/surgical		(malaria)
	mental status		metronomic scheduling of
	milk shake		anticancer treatment
	minimal support		Minnesota Sedation Assessment
	Mississippi		Tool
	mitral sounds		motion style acupuncture
	mitral stenosis		treatment
	moderately susceptible	Msat	micro satellite(s)
	modified shock index	MSB	mainstem bronchus
	morning stiffness		maximal sterile barrier
	morphine sulfate (this is a	MSBOS	maximum surgical blood order
	dangerous abbreviation)		schedule
	motile sperm	MSBP	mean systolic blood pressure
	motility study		Munchausen syndrome by proxy
	motion sickness	MSC	major symptom complex
	multiple sclerosis		Medical Service Corps
	muscle spasm		mesenchymal stomal cells
	muscle strength		midsystolic click
	musculoskeletal		MS Contin®
3MS	Modified Mini-Mental Status	MSCA	McCarthy Scales of Children's
	(examination)		Abilities
MS04	see MSO4	MSCC	malignant spinal cord
MS1	medical student year 1		compression
MS2	medical student year 2		midstream clean-catch
MS3	medical student year 3		(urine culture)
MS4	fourth-year medical student	MSCCC	Master Sciences, Certified
MS III	third-year medical student		Clinical Competence
M & S	microculture and sensitivity	MSCN	medial sural cutaneous nerve
ms	microsecond	MSCP	mitochondrial solute carrier
	milliseconds		protein; see gene website
m/s	meters per second		www.ncbi.nlm.nih.gov/gene
MSA	Medical Savings Accounts	MSCRAMMs	microbial surface component
	membrane-stabilizing activity		reacting with adhesive matrix
	methane sulfonic acid		molecules
	metropolitan statistical area	MSCs	mesenchymal stem cells
	microsomal autoantibodies	MSCT	multislice computed
	multiple system atrophy		tomography
	multistage activation	MSCU	medical special care unit
MSAC	Medical Services Advisory	MSCWP	musculoskeletal chest wall pain
	Committee (Australia)	MSD	male sexual dysfunction
MSA-C	multiple system atrophy		mean (gestational) sac diameter
	subtype C		microsurgical diskectomy
MSAD	multiple scan average dose		midsleep disturbance
	(radiology)		musculoskeletal disorder(s)
MSAF	meconium-stained amniotic fluid	MSDBP	mean sitting diastolic blood
MSAFP	maternal serum alpha-fetoprotein		pressure
MSAP	mean systemic arterial pressure	MS-DBB	medial septum and diagonal
MSAp	multiple system atrophy		band of Broca
	is a neurodegenerative	mSDL	median sensory distal latency
	disorder characterized by	MS-DRG	Medicare Severity-adjusted
	autonomic dysfunction with		Diagnosis-Related Group
	parkinsonism symptoms	MSDRG(s)	Medicare Severity Diagnosis-
MSA-P	multiple system atrophy-		related Group(s)
	parkinsonian type	MS-DRGs	Medicare Severity-adjusted
MSAS	Mandel Social Adjustment Scale		Diagnosis-Related Groups
MSAS-SF	Memorial Symptom Assessment	MSDS	material safety data sheet
	Scale – short form	MSDs	musculoskeletal disorders

M

MSE	mean squared error	MSI-H	high microsatellite instability
	Mental Status Examination	MSI-L	low microsatellite instability
	multiscale entropy	MSIP	Multiple Sclerosis Impact Profile
msec	milliseconds	MSIR®	morphine sulfate immediate
m/sec	meters per second		release tablets
MSEL	myasthenic syndrome of	MSIS	Multiple Severity of Illness
	Eaton-Lambert		System
MSER	mean systolic ejection rate	MSIV	fourth-year medical student
	Mental Status Examination		microsurgical subinguinal
	Record		varicocelectomy
MSET	Modified Six Elements Test	MSJ	manubriosternal joint
mSET	mandating single-embryo transfer		Mifflin-St.-Jeor (equation;
MSF	meconium-stained fluid		predicts resting energy
	Mediterranean spotted fever		expenditure)
	megakaryocyte stimulating factor	MSK	medullary sponge kidney
	Médicins Sans Frontières		musculoskeletal
	(Doctors Without Borders)	MSKCC	Memorial Sloan-Kettering
MSFA	maxillary sinus floor		Cancer Center
	augmentation	MSKUS	musculoskeletal ultrasound
MSG	massage	MSL	maximum step length (test)
	methysergide (Sansert)		midsternal line
	monosodium glutamate		multiple symmetrical lipomatosis
MSGO4	may have meant MgSO4	MSLA	morphine sulfate long acting (this
	(magnesium sulfate)		is dangerous abbreviation)
MSGT	malignant salivary gland tumor	MSLP	Master of Speech-Language
MSH	melanocyte-stimulating		Pathology
	hormone	MSLT	multiple sleep latency test
MSH2	methyl-directed mismatch repair	MSM	magnetic starch microspheres
	protein (mutS) homolog 2;		maxillary sinus mucocele
	see gene website www.ncbi		men who have sex with men
	.nlm.nih.gov/gene		methsuximide (Celontin)
MSH6	mismatch repair gene; see gene		methylsulfonylmethane
	website www.ncbi.nlm.nih		midsystolic murmur
	.gov/gene	mSMART	Mayo Stratification of Myeloma
MSHA	mannose-sensitive		and Risk-Adapted Therapy
	hemagglutinin	MSMO	men who have sex with men only
	Master of Science in Health	MSMW	men who have sex with men and
	Administration		women
MSHQ	Mount Sinai Hospital	MSN	Master of Science in Nursing
	Questionnaire		Medicare Summary Notice
MSHS	marijuana third-hand smoke	MSNA	muscle sympathetic nerve activity
	Migrant and Seasonal Head	MSNE	myoclonic status in nonprogres-
	Start (programs)		sive encephalopathy
	Mount Sinai Health System	MS non-ON	multiple sclerosis without a
	(New York, NY)		history of optic neuritis
MSHs	melanocyte-stimulating	MSO	managed services organization
	hormones		mental status, oriented
MSI	magnetic source imaging		mentally stable and oriented
	mass sociogenic illness		most significant other
	microsatellite instability	MSO4	morphine sulfate. This is a
	multiple subcortical infarction		**DANGEROUS** abbreviation
	musculoskeletal impairment		that should **NOT** be used. It
MSIA	mass spectrometric		appears on the MedAbbrev
	immunoassay		and other "Do Not Use
MSICS	manual sutureless small-incision		Lists," as it has been read
	extracapsular cataract surgery		as magnesium sulfate or not
MSICU	medical surgical intensive care		understood. Use "morphine
	unit		sulfate."

MSOD	multiple system organ dysfunction		MSS	Marital Satisfaction Scale
				maternal serum screening
MSOF	multisystem organ failure			mean sac size
MSOH	Master of Science in Occupational Health			microsatellite stable
				minor surgery suite
MSOM	men who have sex with only men		MSSA	methicillin sensitive staphylococcus aureus
MS-ON	multiple sclerosis with a history of optic neuritis			methicillin-susceptible *Staphylococcus aureus*
MSOT	multispectral optoacoustic tomography		MSS-CR	mean sac size and crown-rump length
MSP	Medicare Secondary Payer		MSSE	Multiple Sclerosis Self-Efficacy (Scale)
	Medoff sliding plate			
	multiple sexual partners			multiple self-healing squamous epithelioma
	musculoskeletal pain			
MSPB	medicare spending per beneficiary		MSSI	Mainz Severity Score Index (a disease Severity Scoring System validated for quantifying the disease burden of Fabry disease)
MSPC	multivariate statistical process control			
MS-PCR	methylation-specific polymerase chain reaction			
MSPH	Master of Science in Public Health			maternal separation and social isolation
MSPI	milk soy protein intolerance		MSSO	Maintenance and Support Services Organization
M spike	a zone of increased concen- tration of a monoclonal immunoglobulin when seen by serum protein electropho- resis; a frequent finding in the general population and typi- cally is pathognomonic of an asymptomatic, premalignant condition (low risk) called monoclonal gammopathy of undetermined significance (MGUS)		MSSP	Maternal Support Services Program
				Medicare Shared Savings Program
			MSSR	multiple sclerosis surveillance registry
			MSSS	Multiple Sclerosis Severity Score
			MSSU	midstream specimen of urine
			MSSW	magnetostatic surface waves
			MST	maladies sexuellement transmissibles (French for sexually transmitted diseases)
MSPN	medical student progress notes			mean survival time
MSPQ	Modified Somatic Perception Questionnaire			median survival time
				mental stress test
MSPT	metachronous second primary tumor			military sexual trauma
				modified Schirmer test
	motor speed and precision test			Montenegro skin test
MSPU	medical short procedure unit			multiple subpial transection
MSQ	Mental Status Questionnaire		MSTA®	mumps skin test antigen
	meters squared		MSTI	multiple soft tissue injuries
	Migraine-Specific Quality of Life Questionnaire		MSTR	method-specific trimester range
MSR	muscle stretch reflexes		MSTS	American Musculoskeletal Tumor Society (functional rating system)
MSRA	methionine sulfoxide reductase A (gene)			
MSRD	multiple sclerosis and related disorders		MSTU	mobile stroke treatment unit
MSRE	methylation-sensitive restriction enzyme		MSU	maple-syrup urine
				medication set up
MSRPP	Multidimensional Scale for Rating Psychiatric Patients			midstream urine
				monosodium urate
MSRS	minimalist-style running shoes		MSUD	maple-syrup urine disease
MSRS-R	Multiple Sclerosis Rating Scale Revised		MSUS	musculoskeletal ultrasound
			MSUs	midstream specimens of urine

M

MSUV	maximal standardized uptake value
mSv	millisievert (radiation unit)
MSVD	Mount Sinai Visiting Doctors (program)
MSW	Master of Social Work
	multiple stab wounds
mSWAT	modified Severity-Weighted Assessment Tool
MSWL	modified shock-wave lithotripsy (modified HM3 lithotripter)
MSWM	MatriStem Wound Matrix (porcine urinary bladder derived extracellular matrix)
	municipal solid waste management
MSWS	Medical Social Worker Student
MT	empty
	macular target
	maggot therapy
	maintenance therapy
	malaria therapy
	malignant teratoma
	manual therapy
	Medical Technologist
	Medical Transcriptionist
	metatarsal
	methadone
	middle turbinate
	midtarsal (joint)
	mindfulness training
	mini-trampoline
	mirror therapy (rehabilitation program)
	monitor technician
	Montana
	mucosal thickening
	muscle tone
	muscles and tendons
	music therapy (Therapist)
	myringotomy tube(s)
Mt	meitnerium
M&T	myringotomy with tube insertion
M & T	*Monilia* and *Trichomonas*
M/T	masses of tenderness
	myringotomy with tubes
MTA	Medical Technical Assistant
	metatarsal adduction
	mineral trioxide aggregate
	molecularly targeted agent
	multi-targeted antifolate, pemetrexed disodium (Alimta)
4-MTA	4-methylthioamphetamine
MTA1	metastasis-associated protein 1
MTAC	mass transfer area coefficient
MTAD	tympanic membrane of the right ear
MT/AK	music therapy/ audiokinetics
MTAS	tympanic membrane of the left ear
MT(ASCP)	Registered Medical Technologist (American Society of Clinical Pathologists)
MTase	methyltransferase
MTAU	tympanic membranes of both ears
MTB	molecular tumor board
	Mycobacterium tuberculosis
MTBC	Music Therapist-Board Certified
	Mycobacterium tuberculosis complex
MTBE	methyl tert-butyl ether
mTBI	mild traumatic brain injury
MTB PCR	polymerase chain reaction testing for the detection of Mycobacterium tuberculosis
MTC	magnetization transfer contrast
	magnetization transfer contrast (radiology)
	medullary thyroid carcinoma
	metoclopramide
	mitomycin (Mutamycin)
	Multi-tiered Co-Pay Programs
MTCD	mixed connective tissue disease (as seen in French, Spanish, etc.)
MTCSA	mid-thigh muscle cross-sectional area
MTCT	mother-to-child transmission
MTD	maximum tolerated dose
	metastatic trophoblastic disease
	methadone
	minimum toxic dose
	Monroe tidal drainage
	Mycobacterium tuberculosis direct (test)
MTDDA	Minnesota Test for Differential Diagnosis of Aphasia
MTDI	maximum tolerable daily intake
MTDM	Medication Therapy Disease Management (program)
mtDNA	mitochondrial deoxyribonucleic acid
MTDT	*Mycobacterium* tuberculosis direct test
MTE	Medical Team Evaluation
	multiple trace elements
MTE-4®	trace metal elements injection (there was also a #5, #6, and #7) (no longer marketed)
MTEE	micro-transesophageal echocar-diographic (probe)
MTET	modified treadmill exercise testing

M

MTF	male-to-female (transmission)	mTLIF	minimally invasive transforam-
	medical treatment facility		inal lumbar interbody fusion
	modulation transfer function	MTLP	metallothionein-like protein(s)
	modulation transfer function	MTLV	midtidal lung volume
	(radiology)	MTM	medication therapy management
MTFHR	may have meant MTHFR		modified Thayer-Martin
	(methylenetetrahydrofolate		medium
	reductase)		mouth-to-mouth (resuscitation)
MTFL	multitask feature learning		myotubular myopathy
MTG	middle temporal gyrus (gyri)	MTMT	maximal tolerated medical
	midthigh girth		therapy
MTH	methamphetamine	mTNBC	metastatic triple-negative breast
MTHER	may have meant MTHFR		cancer
	(methylenetetrahydrofolate	MTNX	methylnaltrexone
	reductase; see gene website	M1 to M7	categories of acute nonlympho-
	www.ncbi.nlm.nih.gov/gene		blastic leukemia
MTHFR	methylenetetrahydrofolate	mTOR	mammalian target of rapamycin
	reductase; see gene website		(gene/protein)
	www.ncbi.nlm.nih.gov/gene	mTORC1	multi-component mechanistic
MTHHR	may have meant MTHFR		target of rapamycin
	(methylenetetrahydrofolate		complex 1
	reductase)	mTOT	mitochondrial target of
MTHR	maximum theoretical heart rate		thiazolidinediones (e.g.
MTHRF	may have meant MTHFR		rosiglitazone [Avandia],
	(methylenetetrahydrofolate		pioglitazone [Actos])
	reductase)	MTP	massive transfusion protocol
MTHs	metatarsal heads		master treatment plan
mths	months		medial tibial plateau
MTI	magnetization transfer imaging		median time to progression
	malignant teratoma intermediate		medical termination of
mTICI	modified Treatment in Cerebral		pregnancy
	Infarction (revascularization		metatarsophalangeal
	treatment outcomes scale/		microsomal triglyceride transfer
	score)		protein
mTICI 0	modified thrombolysis in	MTPJ	metatarsophalangeal joint
	cerebral infarction, grade 0	MTP joint	metatarsophalangeal joint
	(no perfusion)	MTR	magnetization transfer ratio
mTICI 1	modified thrombolysis in		microtubal reanastomosis
	cerebral infarction, grade 1		mother
mTICI 2a	modified thrombolysis in	MTR-ō	no masses, tenderness, or
	cerebral infarction, grade 2a		rebound
mTICI 2B	modified thrombolysis in	MTrPs	myofascial trigger points
	cerebral infarction, grade 2b	MTRS	Licensed Master Therapeutic
mTICI 3	modified thrombolysis in		Recreation Specialist
	cerebral infarction grade 3	MTS	May-Thurner syndrome
MTJ	midtarsal joint		mesial temporal sclerosis
	muscle-to-tendon junction		Muir-Torre syndrome
MT joint	midtarsal joint	MTSO	medical transcription service
MTL	medial temporal lobe		provider
	mediastinal tuberculous	MTSS	medial tibial stress syndrome
	lymphadenitis	mTSS	menstrual toxic shock syndrome
	Metropolitan Life (Insurance		modified total Sharp score
	Company) Table (for		van der Heijde-modified total
	desirable weight)		Sharp score
MTLE	medial (mesial) temporal-lobe	MTST	maximal treadmill stress test
	epilepsy	MTT	mamillothalamic tract
MTLE-HS	mesial temporal lobe epilepsy		mean transit time
	with hippocampal sclerosis		methylthiotetrazole

M

MTT assay   4, 5-Dimethyl-2-thiazolyl)-2, 5-diphenyl-2H-tetrazolium bromide assay (The MTT system is a means of measuring the activity of living cells via mitochondrial dehydrogenases)

mttB   putative trimethylamine methyltransferase protein (gene)

MTU   malignant teratoma undifferentiated methylthiouracil

MTV   metabolic tumor volume

MTw   motion wracker wireless

MTWA   microvolt T-wave alterans

MTX   methotrexate

MTX-LPDs   methotrexate-associated lymphoproliferative disorders

MTZ   mirtazapine (Remeron) mitoxantrone (Novantrone)

MU   million units monitor unit Murphy unit

mU   milliunits

MUA   manipulation under anesthesia

MUAC   middle upper arm circumference

MUAP   motor unit action potential

MUC   mucin mucosal ulcerative colitis

mUC   metastatic urothelial carcinoma

MUC5AC   mucin 5AC, oligomeric mucus/ gel-forming (gene/protein)

Mucor   Mucorales (saprophytic aerobic fungi that have a special predilection for the nasal sinuses and lung)

MUCP   maximum urethral closure pressure

MUD   matched unrelated donor(s)

MUD   match unrelated donor

   allo-HSCT   allogeneic hematopoietic stem cell transplantation

MUD BMT   matched unrelated donor bone marrow transplants

MUDDLES   miosis, urination, diarrhea, diaphoresis, lacrimation, excitation of central nervous system, salivation, and consciousness disturbance (symptoms of organophosphorus anticholinesterase insecticide, and organophosphate intoxication)

MUD PBSCT   matched unrelated donor peripheral blood stem cell transplantation

MUDPILES   methanol; uremia; diabetic ketoacidosis; paraldehyde; isoniazid, iron or inborn errors of metabolism; lactic acid; ethylene glycol; salicylates (checklist of possible causes of anion gap metabolic acidosis)

MudPIT   multidimensional protein identification technology

MUDs   marijuana-use disorders

MUE   medication use evaluation

MUFA   monounsaturated fatty acid

MuFTI   transform type spectrometer to apply an aperture synthesis technique to millimeter and submillimeter waves)

MUG   microgram (mcg is preferred)

MUGA   multigated acquisition (scan; a nuclear medicine test designed to evaluate the function of the right and left ventricles of the heart)

MUGAs   multiple gated acquisitions

MUGs   mitosis with unreplicated genomes

MUGUS   may have meant MGUS (monoclonal gammopathy of undetermined significance) or mucus

MUGX   multiple gated acquisition exercise

MUHH   Marie Unna hereditary hypotrichosis

MUI   mixed urinary incontinence

MULE   microcomputer upper limb exerciser

multip   multiparous (having had 2 or more pregnancies which resulted in variable fetuses)

MuLV   murine leukemia virus

MUM   mumps virus vaccine

MU/min   monitor units per minute (a measure of machine output from a clinical accelerator for radiation therapy such as a linear accelerator or an orthovoltage unit)

mU/min   milliunits per minute (1,000 mU = 1 unit)

muncle   maternal uncle

MUNE   motor unit estimates

MUNSH   Memorial University of Newfoundland Scale of Happiness

MUO   metastasis of unknown origin

MUP   melanoma of unknown primary (origin)

M

MUPAT	multiple-site perineal applicator technique
MUPIT	Martinez Universal Perineal Interstitial Template
MUPS	medically unexplained physical symptoms
MUPs	major urinary proteins (mouse)
	motor unit (action) potentials
	motor unit potentials
MUR	Medicines Use Review (UK)
M/U/R/Ax	median nerve, ulnar nerve, radial nerve, axillary nerve
MURCS	müllerian duct aplasia, renal aplasia, and cervicothoracic somite dysplasia (association)
MURD	matched unrelated donor
murP	see gene website www.ncbi.nlm .nih.gov/gene
MUS	midurethral sling
MuSC	muscle stem cells
musc/skel	muscular and skeletal
MUSE®	Medicated Urethral System for Erection (alprostadil urethral suppository)
MuSK	muscle-specific tyrosine kinase
mus-lig	musculoligamentous
MUT	methylmalonyl CoA mutase; see gene website www.ncbi.nlm .nih.gov/gene
mut	mutation
MUTYH	mutY homolog; see gene website; see gene website www.ncbi.nlm.nih.gov/gene
MUU	mouse uterine units
MV	manual ventilation
	mechanical ventilation
	megavolts
	mesenteric vasculitis
	minute volume
	mitoxantrone and etoposide
	mitral valve
	mixed venous
	multivesicular
mV	millivolts
M/V	mass/volume ratio
MVA	malignant ventricular arrhythmias
	manual vacuum aspiration
	mitral valve area
	modified vaccina ankara
	motor vehicle accident
M-VAC	methotrexate, vinblastine doxorubicin (Adriamycin), and cisplatin
MVAS	Million Visual Analogue Scale (measures patient's level of pain and disability)
MVAs	motor vehicle accidents

MVB	methotrexate and vinblastine
	mixed venous blood
MVC	maraviroc (Selzentry)
	maximal voluntary contraction
	Microvascular Compression Syndrome
	motor vehicle collision (crash)
MVc	mitral valve closure
MVCAD	multivessel coronary artery disease
MV-CBCT	mega-voltage cone-beam computed tomography
MVD	Marburg virus disease
	microvascular decompression
	microvessel density
	mitral valve disease
	multivessel disease
MVE	mitral valve (leaflet) excursion
	Murray Valley encephalitis
MVEV	Murray Valley Encephalitis Virus
MVFF	microvascular free-flap (reconstructive surgery)
MV Grad	mitral valve gradient
MVH	mouse vasa homolog; see gene website www.ncbi.nlm.nih .gov/gene
MVHs	medium-volume hospitals (as defined by each study)
MVI®	brand name for parenteral multivitamins
MVI 12®	brand name for parenteral multivitamins
MVI	malignant vascular injury
	misoprostol vaginal insert (available in the European Union as Misodel)
	multiple vitamin injection
	multivitamin
MVIC	maximum voluntary isometric contractions
MVID	microvillus inclusion disease
MVIE	maximum voluntary isometric exertion
MV IE	mitral valve infective endocarditis
MVIF	maximal voluntary isometric force
MVIT	maintenance venom immunotherapy
	multivitamin
MVITM	multivitamin with minerals
MVL	mean viral load
	Mediterranean visceral leishmaniasis
	mid-vertical line
	multivesicular liposomes
MVLs	mitral valve leaflets
MVM	multivitamin and multimineral

mvmt	movement	MWA	mean wave amplitude
MVN	medial vestibular nucleus		microwave ablation
MVO	mixed venous oxygen saturation		migraine with aura
MVO2	myocardial oxygen consumption	MWB	minimal weight bearing
MVOHCM	midventricular obstructive	MWC	major wound complications
	hypertrophic cardiomyopathy		manual wheelchair
MVP	maximum vertical pocket	MWCO	molecular weight cutoff
	(sonographic evaluation of	MWD	maximum walking distance
	amniotic fluid volume)		microwave diathermy
	mean venous pressure	6MWD	6-minute walking distance
	mitomycin, vinblastine, and	MWE	myocardial work efficiency
	cisplatin (Platinol)	MWF	Monday, Wednesday, and Friday
	mitral valve prolapse	M-W-F	Monday-Wednesday-Friday
MVPA	moderate-to-vigorous physical	M/W/F	Monday, Wednesday, and Friday
	activity	MWF HD	Monday, Wednesday, and Friday
MVPP	mechlorethamine, vinblastine,		hemodialysis
	procarbazine, and prednisone	MWFS	Monday, Wednesday, Friday,
MVPS	mitral valve prolapse syndrome		and Saturday (this is a
MVPT-3	Motor-Free Visual Perception		dangerous abbreviation)
	Test-3rd edition	MWh	megawatt-hour
MVR	massive vitreous retraction	MWI	Medical Walk-In (Clinic)
	micro-vitreoretinal (blade)	MWL	massive weight loss
	mitral valve regurgitation	MWM	mobilization with movement
	mitral valve replacement	MWO	may write orders
MVRA	missionary/volunteer/research/	MWOA	migraine without aura
	aid workers	MWP	manual wheelchair propulsion
MVRe	mitral valve repair	MWS	maximum walking speed
MVRI	mixed vaccine respiratory		Mickety-Wilson syndrome
	infections		Muckle-Wells syndrome
MVS	mitral valve stenosis	MWT	maintenance of wakefulness test
	motor, vascular, and sensory		Mallory-Weiss tear
	Multichannel Verification		malpositioned wisdom teeth
	System		maximal walking time
MVT	misoprostol vagina tablet	6-MWT	6-minute walk test
	(Cytotec)	MWTP	municipal wastewater treatment
	monomorphic ventricular		plants
	tachycardia	MWV	Medicare (Annual) Wellness
	movement		Visit
	multiform ventricular	MX	macromolecular X-ray
	tachycardia	Mx	mammography
	multivisceral transplant		manifest refraction
	multivitamin		mastectomy
MVTx	multivisceral transplant		maxilla
MVU	mitral valve unit		movement
	Montevideo units		myringotomy
MVUs	microvascular units	MxA	myxovirus resistance protein A
	Montevideo units (obstetrics)	mXELIRI	modified capecitabine (Xeloda)
MVV	maximum ventilatory volume		and irinotecan
	maximum voluntary ventilation	MXL	Mexican ancestry in Los
	mixed vespid venom		Angeles, California (from
MV/VS	mechanical ventilation and/or		HapMap [A catalog of
	vasopressor support		common genetic variants that
MVW	multiplayer virtual world		occur in human beings])
MVX	see gene website, www.ncbi	MXR	metformin extended-release
	.nlm.nih.gov/gene		(Glucophage XR)
6MW	6-minute walk (test)	MXT	mitoxantrone HCl injection
12MW	12-minute walk (test)	MxV	Mexico virus
mW	milliwatt	My	myopia

MYC	see gene website, www.ncbi.nlm.nih.gov/gene
MYCN gene	V-Myc Avian Myelocytomatosis Viral Oncogene Neuroblastoma Derived Homolog
MYD	mydriatic
Myd88	myeloid differentiation primary response gene 88
myelo	myelocytes
	myelogram
MyG	myasthenia gravis
MYH	myosin heavy chain; see gene website www.ncbi.nlm.nih.gov/gene
My HealthEVe	email/web service the Veterans Administration
Mynx	a vascular closure device; is an extravascular vascular closure device designed to minimize the discomfort commonly associated with closing the small hole in the artery following catheterization procedure
MYO	make-your-own (cigarettes)
MYOP	myopia
Myoview®	technetium Tc 99m tetrofosmin
MYR	myringotomy
MYS	medium yellow soft (stools)
MZ	monozygotic
Mz	magnetization vector (radiology)
m/z	mass-to-charge ratio
MZBCL	marginal zone B-cell lymphoma
MZDI	Modified Zung Depression Index
MZL	marginal zone lymphoma
MZT	monozygotic twins

N

N	asparagine
	nausea
	negative
	Negro
	Neisseria
	nerve
	neutrophil
	never
	newton
	night
	nipple
	nitrogen
	no
	nodes
	nonalcoholic
	none
	normal
	North (as in the location 2N, would be second floor, North wing)
	not
	notified
	noun
	November (Phonetic Alphabet for N; pronounced NO-VEM-BER)
	NPH insulin (it is dangerous to use abbreviations for insulin therapy)
	number
	size of sample
0.1N	tenth-normal
5'-N	5'-nucleotidase
N1	study night 1
N 2.5	phenylephrine HCl 2.5% ophthalmic solution (Neo-Synephrine)
N₂	nitrogen
n-3	omega-3
N-9	nonoxynol 9
N20	may have meant N2O (nitrous oxide)
N77	Missing/incomplete/invalid designated provider number. (Medicare code)
N365	This procedure code is not payable. It is for reporting/information purposes only. (Medicare code)
NI.... N XII	first through twelfth cranial nerves
NA	Narcotics Anonymous Native American Negro adult

M

	new admission	NAC	acetylcysteine (N-acetylcysteine; Mucomyst)
	nicotinic acid		nasal allergen challenge
	no answer		neoadjuvant chemotherapy
	nonadherence		nipple-areola complex
	nonalcoholic		no acute changes
	norethindrone acetate		no anesthesia complications
	normal axis	nAc	anacardic acid
	not admitted	N-AC	acetylcysteine (also known as N-acetylcysteine)
	not applicable		
	not available	NAC1	NAC (nucleus accumbens-associated protein) domain-containing protein 21/22; see gene website www.ncbi .nlm.nih.gov/gene
	nurse aide		
	Nurse Anesthetist		
	nurse's aid		
	Nursing Assistant		
N & A	normal and active		
N/A	see NA	NACD	no anatomical cause of death
Na+	sodium	NACE	net adverse clinical event
NAA	N-acetylaspartate	nACh	nicotinic acetylcholine
	National Average Allowance (federal physician office visit cost guide)	nAChR	nicotinic acetylcholine receptor
		NACI	National Advisory Committee on Immunization
			sodium chloride (salt)
	neutron activation analysis		
	no apparent abnormalities	NACID	North American Climate Integration and Diagnostics (This website describes a climate database that was developed to facilitate the study of environmental impacts on terrestrial ecosystems in North America. The site was established to describe the database, track progress, and share ideas about climate integration and diagnostics.)
	nucleic acid amplification		
NAAA	neo-adjuvant androgen ablation		
NAAC	no apparent anesthesia complications		
NAACCR	North American Association of Central Cancer Registries		
NAA/Cr	N-acetylaspartate/creatine ratio		
NAAD	neo-adjuvant androgen deprivation (therapy)		
NaAsO2	sodium arsenite		
NAAT	nucleic acid amplification techniques (testing)	NACID-NDEP1	North American Climate Integration and Diagnostics - Nitrogen Deposition Version 1
NAATPT	not available at the present time		
NAB	neocortical amyloid-beta	NaClO	sodium hypochlorite
	Neuropsychological Assessment Battery	NaCMC	sodium carboxymethyl cellulose
		NACOR	National Anesthesia Clinical Outcomes Registry (Anesthesia Quality Institute)
	not at bedside		
nab	nanoparticle albumin-bound		
Nab-P	nanoparticles albumin-bound paclitaxel	NACRT	neoadjuvant chemoradiotherapy
nab-P+G	nab-paclitaxel (Abraxane) and gemcitabine	NACS	Neurologic and Adaptive Capacity Score
nab-P + G	nab-paclitaxel (Abraxane) and gemcitabine	NACT	neoadjuvant chemotherapy
		NAD	nicotinamide adenine dinucleotide
nAb-PTX	nanoparticle albumin-bound paclitaxel (Abraxane)		no active disease
NABS	no active bowel sounds		no acute distress
	normoactive bowel sounds		no apparent distress
Nabs	neutralizing antibodies		no appreciable disease
NABT	normal-appearing brain tissue		normal axis deviation
NABTC	North American Brain Tumor Consortium		nothing abnormal detected
NABX	needle aspiration biopsy	na1D	see gene website, www.ncbi .nlm.nih.gov/gene

NADA	New Animal Drug Application
NADCs	non-AIDS-defining cancers
NADE	New Animal Drug Evaluation
nadh	see gene website, www.ncbi .nlm.nih.gov/gene
nadir	a word meaning the lowest point
NADN	nicotinamide adenosine dinucleotide nucleotidase
	no acute distress noted
NADP	nicotinamide adenine dinucleotide phosphate
NADPH	nicotinamide adenine dinucleotide phosphate
NADSIC	no apparent disease seen in chest
NaE	exchangeable sodium
NAEB	nonasthmatic eosinophilic bronchitis
NA-EEEV	North American eastern equine encephalitis virus
NAEO	no acute events overnight
NAEON	no acute events overnight
NAEPP	National Asthma Education and Prevention Program (guidelines)
NAET	Nambudripad allergy elimination technique
NAF	nafcillin
	Native-American female
	Negro adult female
	nipple aspirate fluid
	normal adult female
	Notice of Adverse Findings (FDA post-audit letter)
NaF	sodium fluoride
NaFeEDTA	sodium iron (III) ethylenediaminetetraacetic acid (sodium iron edetic acid)
NaFI	see NaF (sodium fluoride)
NAFLD	nonalcoholic fatty liver disease
NAG	N-acetyl-beta-d-glucosaminidase
	narrow angle glaucoma
NAGA	N-acetylgalactosaminidase; see gene website www.ncbi .nlm.nih.gov/gene
NAGLU	N-acetylglucosaminidase (gene/protein)
NAGMA	Normal Anion Gap Metabolic Acidosis
NAGS	N-acetylglutamate synthase
NAHC	National Association for Home Care & Hospice
NaHCO₃	sodium bicarbonate
NAHI	nonaccidental head injury
NAHS	nonarthritic Hip Score
NaHS	sodium hydrosulfide

NAI	no action indicated
	no acute inflammation
	nonaccidental injury
	Nuremberg Aging Inventory
NaI	sodium iodide
NAICA	no acute intracranial abnormalities
NAICP	nonalcoholic idiopathic chronic pancreatitis
NAID	nonanemic iron deficiency
NaIO3	sodium iodate
NAION	nonarteritic anterior ischemic optic neuropathy
NAIP	NLR family (NOD [nucleotide-binding oligomerization domain]-like receptors) apoptosis inhibitory protein (gene/protein)
NAIS	neoaortoiliac system
	neonatal arterial ischemic stroke
	nuclear activation-based imaging spectroscopy
NAIs	neuraminidase inhibitors
NAIT	neonatal alloimmune thrombocytopenia
Nak	Numb-associated kinase; see gene website www.ncbi.nlm .nih.gov/gene
	sodium/potassium pump (Na+/K+-ATPase)
NAL	nasal angiocentric lymphoma
NALC	N-acetyl-L-cysteine
NALC-NaOH	N-acetyl-L-cysteine-sodium hydroxide
NALD	neonatal adrenoleukodystrophy
NALFD	may have meant NAFLD (nonalcoholic fatty liver disease)
NAM	nail-apparatus melanoma
	National Academy of Medicine (formally the Institute of Medicine)
	Native-American male
	nicotinamide
	no abnormal masses
	normal adult male
naMCI	non-amnestic mild cognitive impairment
NAMCS	National Ambulatory Medical Care Survey
NAMI	National Alliance for Mental Illness
NAMs	negative allosteric modulators
	non-Asian males
Na⁹⁹ᵐ TcO₄-	sodium pertechnetate Tc 99m
NAN	National Alert Network (of the National Coordinating Council for Medication Error

	Reporting and Prevention [NCC MERP])
NANB	non-A, non-B (hepatitis) (hepatitis C)
NANBH	non-A, non-B hepatitis (hepatitis C)
NANC	nonadrenergic, noncholinergic
NAND	nandrolone
NANDA	North American Nursing Diagnosis Association (taxonomy)
N and V	nausea and vomiting
NaNP	sodium nitroprusside
NANSAIDs	nonaspirin, nonsteroidal anti-inflammatory drugs
NANT	New Approaches to Neuroblastoma Therapy (consortium)
NAO	nasal airway obstruction
NaOCl	sodium hypochlorite
NAOE	natural antioxidant extract (an extract of Spinacea oleracea [spinach])
NaOH	sodium hydroxide
NAOMC	nothing abnormal on microscopic colposcopy
NAP	narrative, assessment, and plan
	no apparent pathology
	nosocomial acquired pneumonia
	nursing assistive personnel
Nap1	nucleosome assembly protein 1; see gene website www.ncbi .nlm.nih.gov/gene
NAPA	N-acetyl procainamide
NAPD	no active pulmonary disease
NaPent	Pentothal Sodium
Na Phos	sodium phosphate
NaPO4	sodium phosphate (a generic term for a variety of salts of sodium and phosphate)
naproxen sodium	Aleve (over-the-counter)
NAPSRx	National Association of Pharma-ceutical Sales Representatives
NAR	nasal airflow resistance
	no action required
	no adverse reaction
	nonambulatory restraint
	not at risk
	Nursing and Rehabilitation
	nursing assessment record
NARC	narcotic(s)
Narcam	may have meant Narcan (nalox-one hydrochloride injection)
narco	narcotic
NARCO-SS	Neurological, Airway, Respiratory, Cardiovascular, Other categories and Surgical Severity

narcs	narcotic law enforcement agents (slang)
	narcotics (slang)
NARD	noninflammatory autoimmune rheumatic disease(s)
NaRI	noradrenaline reuptake inhibitor
NARMS	National Antimicrobial Resistance Monitoring System
NARP	neurogenic muscle weakness (neuropathy), ataxia and retinitis pigmentosa (syndrome)
NARS	see gene website www.ncbi.nlm .nih.gov/gene
NART	National Adult Reading Test (United Kingdom)
NAS	nasal
	Neonatal Abstinence Syndrome
	new active substance
	no abnormality seen
	no added salt
NASA	National Aeronautics and Space Administration
NASBA	nucleic-acid sequencing based amplification
NASCET	North American Symptomatic Carotid Endarterectomy Trial
NaSCN	sodium thiocyanate
nasD	nitrite reductase; see gene website www.ncbi.nlm.nih .gov/gene
Nasdaq	National Association of Securities Dealers Automated Quotations
NASH	nonalcoholic steatohepatitis
NaSH	National Surveillance System for Healthcare Workers (CDC)
NASID	may have meant NSAID (nonsteroidal anti-inflammatory drug)
NAS-NRC	National Academy of Sciences – National Research Council
NASPE	North American Society for Pacing and Electrophysiology
NaSSA	noradrenergic and specific serotonergic antidepresssant
NASTI	necrotizing acute soft-tissue infection
NASTT	nonspecific abnormality of ST segment and T wave
NAT	N-acetyltransferase
	no action taken
	no acute trauma
	nonaccidental trauma
	nonspecific abnormality of T wave
	nucleic acid test (testing)

N

NATP	neonatal alloimmune thrombocytopenia	NBAS	Neonatal Behavioral Assessment Scale
	neonatal alloimmune thrombocytopenic purpura	NBB	N-butylscopolammonium bromide (Buscopan Injection)
natural flavors	flavoring constituents derived from a spice, fruit or fruit juice, vegetable or vegetable juice, edible yeast, herb, bark, bud, root, leaf or similar plant material, meat, seafood, poultry, eggs, dairy products, or fermentation products, whose significant function in food is flavoring rather than nutritional		needle breast biopsy
			newborn blood
			night blindness b
		NB-BAL	nonbronchoscopic-bronchoalveolar lavage
		NBC	newborn center
			nonbed care
			nuclear, biological and chemical
NAUC	normalized area under the curve	n-BCA	n-butyl cyanoacrylate (glue/patch/embolization)
NAUTI	nosocomially-associated urinary tract infections	NBCC	National Breast Cancer Coalition
NAV	nerve, artery, vein (heart catheterization procedure-related)	NBCCS	nevoid basal cell carcinoma syndrome (also known as Gorlin syndrome)
NaV	sodium voltage-gated channel		
nav	navicular	NBD	nasobiliary drainage
NAVA	neurally adjusted ventilatory assist		neurologic bladder dysfunction
			no brain damage
	neutrally adjusted ventilator assistance	nbDMARDs	nonbiologic disease-modifying antirheumatic drugs
nAVB	no atrioventricular block	NBE	near-band-edge (diffraction emission)
Nav Bronch	navigational bronchoscopy		
NAVR	native aortic valve regurgitation	NBF	not breast fed
NavX EnSite	a three-dimensional mapping system that permits catheter placement inside the venous system and movement inside the heart chambers without the use of X-rays	NBG	no bacterial growth
			normalized background
		nbg	see gene website, www.ncbi.nlm.nih.gov/gene
		NBG Code	North American Society for Pacing and Electrophysiology and British Pacing and Electrophysiology Group (NASPE/BPEG) Generic Pacemaker Code
NAW	nasal antral window		
NAWCO	National Alliance of Wound Care and Ostomy		
NAWM	normal-appearing white matter		
NAWS	National Agricultural Workers Survey	NBH	new bag (bottle) hung
		NBHH	newborn helpful hints
NaY	sodium yttrium	NBHS	newborn hearing screening
nay	a word to express a negative answer or vote	NBI	narrow-band imaging
			no bone injury
NB	nail bed	NBIA	neurodegeneration with brain iron accumulation (syndromes)
	nail biting		
	nasal breathing	NBICU	newborn intensive care unit
	navigational bronchoscopy	NBIH	a temporary pacing electrode catheter, bipolar (named after Newark Beth Israel Hospital where the C. R. Bard, Inc product was partially developed)
	needle biopsy		
	nerve biopsy		
	nerve block		
	neuroblastomas		
	newborn		
	nitrogen balance		
	no better		National Battery Ingestion Hotline (phone 202-625-3333)
	note well		
NBAL	net muscle protein balance	nBiPAP	nasal bilevel (biphasic) positive airway pressure
	nitrogen balance		

NBIs	nosocomial bloodstream infections	NBTIs	novel bacterial topoisomerase inhibitors
NBL/OM	neuroblastoma and opsoclonus-myoclonus	NBTNF	newborn, term, normal female
NBM	no bowel movement	NBTNM	newborn, term, normal, male
	normal bone marrow	NBTS	National Blood Transfusion Service
	normal bowel movement	NBUVB	narrow-band ultraviolet B
	nothing by mouth	NB-UVB	narrowband ultraviolet B
NBME	National Board of Medical Examiners	NBVV	non-bleeding visible vessel
		NBW	normal birth weight (2,500–3,999 g)
NBMU	Neuropsychiatry and Behavioral Medicine Unit	NBx	needle biopsy
NBN	narrow-band noise	NBY	not back yet
	newborn nursery	NC	nasal cannula
	nibrin (gene)		neck circumference
NBNB	nonbloody, nonbilious		Negro child
NB/NB	nonbloody, nonbilious		neurologic check
nb/nb	homozygous normoblastosis (mice)		no change
NBO	nonbacterial osteitis		no charge
	normobaric oxygen (therapy)		no complaints
NBOMes	N-benzyl-oxy-methy derivatives (potent class of illicit synthetic stimulants; also known as 2C phenylethylamines and N bomb)		noncontributory
			normocephalic
			North Carolina
			nose clamp
			nose clips
			not classified
NBOS	narrow base of support		not completed
NBOs	neurofibromatosis bright objects		not cultured
NBP	needle biopsy of prostate		nuclear color (lens)
	no bone pathology	9 NC	rubitecan (9-nitrocamptothecin)
	noninvasive blood pressure	N/C	see NC
NBQC	narrow base quad cane	NCA	neurocirculatory asthenia
NBQT regimen	nonbismuth quadruple therapy (standard dose: twice daily rabeprazole 20 mg, amoxicillin 1 g, metronidazole 500 mg, and clarithromycin 500 mg for 7 days; therapy for Helicobacter pylori infections)		no congenital abnormalities
			normal coronary arteries
			nurse-controlled analgesia
		NCAD	without (non) coronary artery disease
		NCAM	neuronal cell adhesion molecule
NBR	no blood return	N/CAN	nasal cannula
NBRM	negative binomial regression model	NCAP	nasal continuous airway pressure
NBS	newborn screen (serum thyroxine and phenylketonuria)		noncalcificatied coronary artery plaque
	Nijmegen breakage syndrome	NCAS	zinostatin (neocarzinostatin)
	no bacteria seen	NCAT	normocephalic, atraumatic
	normal bowel sounds	NC/AT	normocephalic, atraumatic
Nbs	Nanobodies	NCB	natural childbirth
NBSCU	newborn special care unit		net clinical benefit
NBSP	nonbreaking space (a HyperText Markup Language code to prevent line-break where a space appears)		no code blue
		NCBI	National Center for Biotechnology Information (NIH)
NBT	nitroblue tetrazolium reduction (tests)	NCC	neurocysticercosis
			no concentrated carbohydrates
	normal breast tissue		nursing care card
NBTE	nonbacterial thrombotic endocarditis		Nursing Care Center Accreditation Program (The Joint Commission)

N

NCCAH	nonclassical congenital adrenal hyperplasia	NCGS	noncebiac gluten sensitivity
NCCAM	National Center for Complementary and Alternative Medicine (NIH)	NCHCT	noncontrast head computed tomography
		NCHGR	National Center for Human Genome Research (NIH)
NCCDPHP	National Center for Chronic Disease and Prevention and Health Promotion (CDC)	NCHS	National Center for Health Statistics
		NCI	National Cancer Institute
NCCI	National Correct Coding Initiative		neurocognitive impairment
NCCLS	National Committee for Clinical Laboratory Standards	NCIC	National Cancer Institute of Canada
NCCM	noncompaction cardiomyopathy	NCICB	National Cancer Institute Center for Bioinformatics
NCC MERP	National Coordinating Council for Medication Error Reporting and Prevention (Index)	NCIC-CTG	National Cancer Institute of Canada Clinical Trials Group
NCCN	National Comprehensive Cancer Network	NCI-CTC	National Cancer Institute Common Toxicity Criteria
	National Comprehensive Cancer Network (guidelines)	NCI-CTCAE	National Cancer Institute Common Toxicity Criteria Adverse Event
NCCP	noncardiac chest pain		
NCCT	noncontrast computed tomography	NCID	National Center for Infectious Diseases (CDC)
NCCTG	North Central Cancer Treatment Group	NCIE	nonbullous congenital icthyosiform erythroderma
NCCU	neurosurgical continuous care unit	NCI-EDRN-BRL	National Cancer Institute - Early Detection Research Network-Biomarker Reference Laboratory
NCD	National Coverage Determination (Manual)		
	neck-capsule distance	NCIM	National Collection of Industrial Microorganisms (India)
	neurocognitive disorder		
	no congenital deformities		
	normal childhood diseases		
	not considered disabling	NCIPC	National Center for Injury Prevention and Control (CDC)
	not considered disqualifying		
	Nursing-Care Dependency (scale)		
NCDB	National Cancer Data Base	NCIS	Naional Coroners Information System (Australia)
NCDR	new case-detection rate		
NCDs	national coverage determinations		nursing care information sheet
		NCIT	Nursing Care Intervention Tool
	noncommunicable diseases		
NCE	new chemical entity	NCJ	needle catheter jejunostomy
NCEH	National Center for Environmental Health (CDC)	NCKX	sodium-calcium-potassium exchanger
NCEP	National Cholesterol Education Program	NCL	neuronal ceroid lipofuscinosis
			nidopallium caudolaterale
NCEZID	National Center for Emerging and Zoonotic Infectious Diseases (CDC)		no cautionary labels
			nuclear cardiology laboratory
		NCLC	nonsmall cell lung carcinoma
NCF	neurocognitive function	NCLD	neonatal chronic lung disease
	neutrophilic chemotactic factor	NCM	caudomedial nidopallium
	no cold fluids		nailfold capillary microscope
NC=F	non-completer=failure		neurocutaneous melanocytosis
NCFM	North Carolina Food Microbiology of the North Carolina State University where the probiotic strain, Lactobacillus acidophilus NCFM, was first discovered		nonclinical manager
		Ncm	Newton centimeter
			Newton centimeters (measurement of torque)
		n-cm	Newton centimeters (torque measurement)

NCMP	National Child Measurement Programme (United Kingdom)	noncontact supervision not clinically significant nurse controlled sedation
NCNC	normochromic, normocytic	Nutcracker syndrome
NC/NC anemia	normocytic-normochromic anemia	zinostatin (neocarzinostatin)
		NCSCs	neural crest stem cells
NCNR	National Center for Nursing Research (NIH)	NCSE	nonconvulsive status epilepticus
		NCS/EMG	nerve conduction studies/ electromyography
NCNS	no complications, no sequelae		
NCO	no complaints offered noncommissioned officer	NCSLC	may have meant NSCLC (nonsmall cell lung cancer)
NCOA	National Council on Aging	NCSME	nonclinically significant macular edema
NCOG	North California Oncology Group	NCSN	National Certified School Nurse
NCORP	NCI (National Cancer Institute) Community Oncology Research Program ((National Institutes of Health; National Cancer Institute)	NCT	Clinical Trial Registry Number neoadjuvant chemotherapy neutron capture therapy noncontact tonometry noncontrast computed tomography number connection test Nursing Care Technician
NCOS	Neurogenic Claudication Outcome Score		
NCOs	noncommissioned officers	NCTD	norcantharidin (synthetic small molecule derivative of naturally occurring cantharidin from the medicinal insect blister beetle; capable of chemoprevention and tumor inhibition)
NCP	no caffeine or pepper noncalcified plaque noncancer patients nursing care plan nutrition care plan		
nCPAP	nasal continuous positive airway pressure		
NCPB	neurolytic celiac plexus block	NCTR	National Center for Toxicological Research
NCPDP	National Council for Prescription Drug Programs	NCU	neonatal care unit
NCPE	non-cardiogenic pulmonary edema	NCV	nerve conduction velocity nuclear venogram
NCPH	noncirrhotic portal hypertension	NCVHS	National Committee on Vital and Health Statistics
NcpPCu	nonceruloplasmin plasma copper	NCVT	neonatal cerebral venous thrombosis
NCPR	no cardiopulmonary resuscitation	NCX	sodium-calcium exchanger
NCQA	National Commission for Quality Assurance	ND	Doctor of Naturopathy (Naturopathic Physician) nasal deformity nasal discharge nasoduodenal natural death neck dissection neonatal death neurological development neurotic depression Newcastle disease no data no defects no disease nondisabling nondistended none detectable normal delivery normal development
nCR	nodular complete response		
NCRA	National Cancer Registrars Association		
NCRAD	National Cell Repository for Alzheimer Disease		
NCRC	nonchild-resistant container		
NCRI	National Cancer Research Institute (United Kingdom)		
NCRP	National Council on Radiation Protection and Measurements		
NCRR	National Center for Research Resources (NIH)		
NCRT	neoadjuvant chemoradiation therapy		
NCS	nerve conduction studies neurocardiogenic syncope no concentrated sweets		

	normal diet	NDIR	nondispersive infrared
	North Dakota	NDIRS	nondispersive infrared
	nose drops		spectrometer
	not detected	ndkA	nucleoside diphosphate kinase A;
	not diagnosed		see gene website www.ncbi
	not done		.nlm.nih.gov/gene
	nothing done	NDL	non-dioxin-like
	Nursing Doctorate	ndl	nudel; see gene website www.ncbi
Nd	neodymium		.nlm.nih.gov/gene
N&D	nodular and diffuse	NDL-PCBs	non-dioxin-like polychlorinated
N/D	see ND		biphenyls
ND3	NADH dehydrogenase	NDM	neonatal diabetes mellitus
	(nicotinamide adenine	NDM-1	New Delhi metallo-beta-
	dinucleotide/reduced)		lactamase 1
	subunit 3; see gene website	NDMA	N-nitrosodimethylamine
	www.ncbi.nlm.nih.gov/gene		(a potential carcinogenic
NDA	New Drug Application		nitrosamine found in drinking
	no data available		water)
	no demonstrable antibodies	NDMG	The German National Disease
	no detectable activity		Management Guideline
NDB	Nursing Data Base	NDMM	newly diagnosed multiple
NDBE	nondysplastic Barrett esophagus		myeloma
NDC	National Drug Code	NDMS	National Disaster Medical System
	Nicotine Dependence Center	NDNQI	National Database of Nursing
	nondigestible carbohydrates		Quality Indicators
NDCCB	nondihydropyridine calcium	Nd/NT	nondistended, nontender
	channel blocker	NDO	neurogenic detrusor overactivity
ND-CKD	nondialysis chronic kidney	NDOC	newly diagnosed human
	disease		immunodeficiency virus-
NDCM	nonischemic dilated		positive and out-of-care
	cardiomyopathy	NDP	nedaplatin
NDD	National Dysphagia Diet		net dietary protein
	neurological determination of		Nurse Discharge Planner
	death	NDPH	new daily persistent headache
	no dialysis days	NDPs	nondesignated preliminary
NDD1	National Dysphagia Diet 1		(residents)
NDD2	National Dysphagia Diet 2	NDR	neurotic depressive reaction
NDD3	National Dysphagia Diet 3		normal detrusor reflex
	(dysphagia advanced)	NDRD	nondiabetic renal disease
NDD-CKD	nondialysis dependent-chronic	NDRDs	nondiabetic renal diseases
	kidney disease	NDRF	nondialysis-dependent renal
NDDI-E	Neurological Disorders Depres-		failure
	sion Inventory for Epilepsy	NDRI	norepinephrine and dopamine
NDDM	newly detected diabetes mellitus		reuptake inhibitor
NDDR	Nursing Daily Documentation	NDS	Neurologic Disability Score
	Records		neuropathy disability score
NDE	near-death experience		New Drug Submission
NDEA	no deviation of electrical axis	NDSC	nasal dermoid sinus cyst
NDF	neutral density filter (test)	NDSO	nasolacrimal drainage system
	no disease found		obstruction
NDFF	nondermatophyte filamentous	NDST	neurodevelopmental screening
	fungi		test
NDGA	nordihydroguaiaretic acid	NDT	nasal duodenostomy tube
ndh	see gene website, www.ncbi.nlm		Neurocognitive Driving Test
	.nih.gov/gene		neurodevelopmental techniques
NDI	National Death Index		neurodevelopmental treatment
	Neck Disability Index		noise detection threshold
	nephrogenic diabetes insipidus	NDTL	nondominant temporal lobe

ND tube	nasoduodenal tube	necroinflam	necroinflammation
NDV	Newcastle disease virus	NECT	nonenhanced computed
NDVI	normalized difference		tomography scan
	vegetation index	NED	neuroendocrine differentiation
Nd:YAG	neodymium:yttrium-aluminum-		no evidence of disease
	garnet (laser)	NEDA	no evidence of disease activity
Nd:YLF	neodymium: yttrium-lithium-	NEDSS	National Electronic Disease
	fluoride (laser)		Surveillance System
NE	nasoenteric	NEE	neonatal epileptic
	nausea and emesis		encephalopathy
	Nebraska	NEEG	normal electroencephalogram
	neonatal encephalopathy	NEEP	negative end-expiratory pressure
	nephropathica epidemica	Ne/ERN	error negativity/error-related
	neurological examination		negativity
	never exposed	Neer test	a single dose of pegfilgrastim
	no effect		and a single-use On-body
	no enlargement		Injector, applied to the skin
	norepinephrine		during the chemotherapy
	norethindrone		appointment. It is designed
	Northeast		to automatically administer
	not elevated		pegfilgrastim the next day
	not estimable	NEF	negative expiratory force
	not examined	NEFA	nonesterified fatty acids
Ne	neon	NEFAs	nonesterified fatty acids
NEAA	nonessential amino acids	Neff	effective sample size
NEA-BC	Nurse Executive, Advanced	NEFG	normal external female genitalia
	Certification- Board Certified	NEFL	neurofilament, light polypeptide
NEAC	norethindrone acetate		(gene)
NEAD	nonepileptic attack disorder	NEFT	nasoenteric feeding tube
NEAMD	nonexudative age-related	NEG	negative
	macular degeneration		neglect
NEAT	nonexercise activity	NEG-LEE	negative lower extremity
	thermogenesis		edema
	not evaluated at triage	negot	negotiation(s)
NEB	hand-held nebulizer	NEH	neutrophilic eccrine hidradenitis
NE-BC	Nurse Executive-Board	NEHI	neuroendocrine cell hyperplasia
	Certified Credential		of infancy
NEBs	neuroepithelial bodies	NEI	National Eye Institute (NIH)
nebs	nebulizer treatments	NEI-RQL-42	National Eye Institute Refrac-
NEC	necrotizing enterocolitis		tive Error Quality of Life
	noise equivalent counts		Instrument
	nonejection click	NEISS-AIP	National Electronic Injury
	nonesterified cholesterol		Surveillance System-All
	not elsewhere classified		Injury Program (Database,
NECC	negative emotional cues and		CDC)
	concerns	NEI VFQ	National Eye Institute Visual
	neuroendocrine carcinoma of		Functioning Questionnaire
	the cervix	NEJM	*New England Journal of*
	New England Case-Control		*Medicine*
	(study)	NEK	NEver in mitosis Kinase
	New England Center for		NIMA (never in mitosis A)-
	Children (Southborough, MA)		related protein kinase NIMA1
	New England Compounding		(gene)
	Center	NELT	neuroendocrine lung tumor
nec fas	necrotizing fasciitis	NEM	neurotrophic enhancing
nec fasc	necrotizing fasciitis		molecule
NECR	noise-equivalent count rate		no evidence of malignancy
	(radiology)		nucleoside excision mutation

NEMB	Notice of Exclusion from Medicare Benefits
NEMD	nonexudative macular degeneration
	nonspecific esophageal motility disorder
NEMO	nuclear factor-kappa-B (NF-κB) essential modulator
NEMS	nanoelectromechanical systems
	National Elder Mistreatment Study
	Nine Equivalents of Nursing Manpower Use Score
	nursing manpower use score
	Nutrition Environment Measures Survey
NEMS-P	Nutrition Environment Measures Survey-Perceived
NEMS-R	Nutrition Environment Measures Survey for Restaurants
NEMS-S	Nutrition Environment Measures Survey in Stores
NEMU	direct distance from nose-ear-mid-umbilicus
NENs	neuroendocrine neoplasms
NENT	nasal endotracheal tube
NEO	necrotizing external otitis
NEOD	neonatal death
NEO-FFI	NEO-Five Factor Inventory (neuroticism, extraversion, openness, agreeableness, and conscientiousness)
NEOH	neonatal high risk
NEOM	neonatal medium risk
	normal extraocular muscles
NEOP	neopterin
neo-SCJ	neosquamocolumnar junction
NEP	needle-exchange program
	neutral endopeptidase
	no evidence of pathology
NEPA	netupitant and palonosetron
NEPD	no evidence of pulmonary disease
NEPHRO	nephrogram
NEPPK	nonepidermolytic palmoplantar keratoderma
NEPS	nonepileptic psychogenic status
NEPs	needle exchange programs
NEQ	noise equivalent quanta (radiology)
NEQAS	National External Quality Assurance Scheme (United Kingdom)
NER	no evidence of recurrence
	nucleotide excision repair
nERCP	transnasal endoscopic retrograde cholangiopancreatography
NERD	no evidence of recurrent disease
	nonerosive reflux disease

NERDS	nodules, eosinophilia, rheumatism, dermatitis, and swelling
NERP-1	neuroendocrine regulatory peptide-1
NERT	natural endogenous reverse transcription
Nervo	Nervo (Nervo Corporation) Senza Spinal Cord (implanted) Stimulation System (for the treatment of chronic pain)
NES	Night eating syndrome
	nonepileptic seizure
	nonstandard electrolyte solution
	not elsewhere specified
NESP	novel erythropoiesis stimulating protein darbepoetin [Aranesp])
NESS	National Enterovirus Surveillance System (CDC)
NESSCA	Neurological Examination Score for Spinocerebellar Ataxia
NESTT	nonhazardous explosives for security training and testing
NET	choroidal or subretinal neovascularization
	Internet
	naso-endotracheal tube
	neoadjuvant endocrine therapy
	neuroectodermal tumor
	neuroendocrine tumors
NETA	norethindrone acetate (Aygestin)
NETs	neuroendocrine tumors
NETSS	National Electronic Telecommunications System for Surveillance
NETT	nasal endotracheal tube
NETZ	needle (diathermy) excision of the transformation zone
NEURO	neurologic
	neurological
Neuro	Neurologist
	neurology
neuropsych	neuropsychiatric
neuro re-ed	neuromuscular re-education
neut	neutrophilic white blood cell
neutro	neutroneutropenia
	neutrophils
neuts	neutrophils
NEVA	nocturnal electrobioimpedance volumetric assessment (penile measurement)
NEX	nose-to-ear-to-xiphoid
	number of excitations (radiology)
NextGen study	focuses on carrier status and medically actionable secondary findings in a population of women planning a pregnancy

NEXUS	National Emergency X-Radiography Utilization Study (criteria)	NFL	nerve fiber layer nerve fibers length (corneal nerve) novantrone (mitoxantrone), fluorouracil, and leucovorin
NF	National Formulary necrotizing fasciitis Negro female neurofibromatosis night float (work rotation) night frequency (of voiding) none found nonfasting nonformulary normal flora not found nursed fair nursing facility	NfL	neurofilament light chain protein (a biomarker for neurodegen-erative dementia diseases)
		NF-L	neurofilament light polypeptide
		NFLD	nerve fiber layer defect (corneal nerve) nerve fibers length density (corneal nerve)
		NFLE	nocturnal frontal lobe epilepsy
Nf	*Naegleria fowleri*	NFLX	norfloxacin (Noroxin)
NF1	neurofibromatosis type 1	NFM	neurofilament medium
NF2	neurofibromatosis type 2 neurofibromin 2 (gene)	NFNC	no lung fibrosis nor lung cancer
		NFNs	notch-filtered noises
NF90	nuclear factor 90	NFP	natural family planning no family physician not for publication not-for-profit
NF-κB	nuclear factor-kappa B (a protein complex that controls transcription of DNA [deoxyribonucleic acid], cytokine production, and cell survival)		
		NFPA	National Fire Protection Agency nonfluent progressive aphasia nonfunctioning pituitary adenoma nutrition-focused physical assessment
NFA	Nerve Fiber Analyzer®		
NFALD	may have meant NAFLD (nonalcoholic fatty liver disease)	NFPAs	nonfunctioning pituitary adenomas
		NFPE	nutrition-focused physical examination
NFALO	Nerve Fiber Analyzer laser oththalmoscope	NFPF	nutrition-focused physical findings
NFAP	nursing facility-acquired pneumonia	NF-pNET	nonfunctioning pancreatic neuroendocrine tumors
NFAR	no further action required	NFR	nociceptive flexion reflex not for resuscitation
NFBG	natural flour baked goods		
NFC	nailfold capillaroscopy	NFRT	Nociceptive Flexion Reflex Threshold
NFCE	nonfatal cardiac events		
NFCS	Neonatal Facial Coding System	NFS	cysteine desulfurase, putative (gene)
NFD	nephrogenic fibrosing dermopathy no family doctor		
		NFs	neurofilaments normal fibroblasts
NFFD	not fit for duty	NFST	National Food Safety and Toxicology Center, Michigan State University, East Lansing, MI, USA
NFGNB	nonfermenting gram-negative bacilli		
NFH	neurofilament heavy		
NFI	nerve-function impairment no further information no-fault insurance normal female infant	NFT	no further treatment
		NFTD	normal full-term delivery
		NFTE	not found this examination
		NFTs	neurofibrillary tangles neurologic function tests
NFIB	nuclear factor I/B; see gene website; www.ncbi.nlm.nih .gov		
		NFTSD	normal full-term spontaneous delivery
NFIP	National Flood Insurance Program	NFTT	nonorganic failure to thrive
		NFV	nelfinavir (Viracept)
NF-kB	nuclear factor kappa-light-chain-enhancer of activated B cells	NFW	nursed fairly well

N

NG	nasogastric	NGT	nasogastric tube
	night guard		normal glucose tolerance
	nitroglycerin	NGTD	no growth to date
	no growth	NgTD	negative to date
	norgestrel	NGTP	nitroglycerin paste (proper name
ng	nanogram (10-9 gram)		is nitroglycerin ointment)
N/G	see NG	NGTT	normal glucose tolerance test
NGAL	neutrophil gelatinase-associated	ng × h/mL	nanograms times hours per
	lipocalin		milliliter (area under the
NGAU	nongranulomatous anterior uveitis		curve [AUC] values)
NGB	neurogenic bladder	NG tube	nasogastric tube
NGCH	neonatal giant cell hepatitis	NGU	nongonococcal urethritis
NGCs	nerve guidance conduits	NGUS	National Guard of the United
NGD	neuronopathic Gaucher disease		States
	no-go decay	NGV	not getting vaccinated
ng/dL	nanograms (10-9 gram) per	NH	neonatal hyperbilirubinemia
	deciliter (100 milliliters)		New Hampshire
NGDT	National Gamete Donation Trust		non-Hispanic
	(United Kingdom)		normal-hearing
NGF	nerve growth factor		nursing home
NGGCT	nongerminomatous germ cell	Nh	nihonium
	tumor	$-NH_2$	amine
ngh/mL	nanograms times hours per	NH_3	ammonia
	milliliter (area under the	$NH_{(4)}+$	ammonium
	curve [AUC] values)	NHA	no histologic abnormalities
n giv	not given	NHANES III	third National Health and
NGJ	nasogastro-jejunostomy		Nutrition Examination Survey
ng/kg	nanogram/kilogram	NHAP	nursing home-acquired
ng/kg/min	nanogram/kilogram/minute		pneumonia
NGL	neoglycolipid	nHAp	hydroxyapatite nanocrystals
ng/L	nanograms per liter	NHB	Naval Hospital Bremerton
ng/mL	nanograms per milliliter		nonheart beating (donor)
N(glom)	glomerular number	nHB	non-Hispanic blacks
NGM	norgestimate	NHBCL	non-Hodgkin B-cell
NGMA	Non-Grant Medical Assistance		lymphomas
NG-MAST	*Neisseria gonorrhoeae* multi-	NHBD	nonheart-beating donors
	antigen sequesnce typing	NHBPEP	National High Blood Pressure
NGN	necrotizing glomerulonephritis		Education Program
ngn	see gene website www.ncbi.nlm		(recommendations)
	.nih.gov/gene	NHC	neighborhood health center
ngn-3	neurogenin-3 (a pancreatic		neonatal hypocalcemia
	marker)		nursing home care
N9-GP	nonacog beta pegol inj	NH_4Cl	ammonium chloride
	(Rebinyn; recombinant	NHCU	nursing home care unit
	glycoPEGylated factor IX)	NHD	nocturnal hemodialysis
NG/OG	nasogastric/orogastric (tube)		normal hair distribution
NGOs	nongovernmental organizations	NHE	sodium/hydrogen exchanger
NGR	nasogastric tube replacement	NHEJ	nonhomologous end-joining
NGRI	not guilty by reason of insanity	NHGRI	National Human Genome
NgRs	Nogo receptors (a family of		Research Institute (NIH)
	cell surface receptors that	NHIS	National Health Interview
	are broadly expressed in the		Survey
	mammalian brain)	NHK	normal human keratinocytes
NGS	next generation sequencing (for	NHL	nodular histiocytic lymphoma
	viral detection)		non-Hodgkin lymphomas
NGSF	nothing grown so far	nHL	normalized hearing level
NGSP	National Glycohemoglobin	NHLBI	National Heart, Lung, and
	Standardization Program		Blood Institute (NIH)

NHLPP	hereditary neuropathy with liability for pressure palsy		not isolated
			nutritional insufficiency
NHM	no heroic measures	Ni	nickel
NHND	nonhemorrhagic neurological deficit	N/I	see NI
		NIA	National Institute on Aging (NIH)
NHO	notify house officer		no information available
NHOPI	Native Hawaiians and other Pacific Islanders	NIAAA	National Institute on Alcohol Abuse and Alcoholism (NIH)
NHP	Naval Hospital Pensacola	NIACHO	National Integrated
	nonhuman primate		Accreditation for Healthcare
	Nottingham Health Profile		Organizations
	nursing home placement	NIADDK	National Institute of Arthritis,
NHPCO	National Hospice and Palliative Care Organization (position statement)		Diabetes, and Digestive and Kidney Diseases (NIH)
		NIAID	National Institute of Allergy and Infectious Diseases
NHPs	natural health products		
NHPT	nine-hole peg test		National Institute of Allergy and Infectious Diseases (NIH)
	Nine-Hole Peg Test		
NHR	noise-to-harmonic ratio	NIAL	not in active labor
	N-terminal heptad repeat	NIAMS	National Institute of Arthritis and Musculoskeletal and Skin Diseases (NIH)
NHRC	Naval Health Research Center		
NHRs	nuclear hormone receptors		
NHS	Nance-Horan syndrome	NIA-RI	National Institute on Aging– Reagan Institute
	National Health Service (UK)		
	Newborn Hearing Screening (Program)	NIBP	noninvasive blood pressure
		NIBPM	noninvasive blood pressure measurement
NHSBT	National Health Service Blood and Transplant		
		NIBS	noninvasive brain stimulation
NHSN	National Healthcare Safety Network	NIBSC	National Institute for Biological Standards and Control (United Kingdom)
NHSP	Newborn Hearing Screening Program		
		NIBUT	noninvasive (tear) breakup time
NHSS	National Health Service Survey (China)	NIC	neonatal intensive care
			non-invasive cardiology
	National HIV (human immunodeficiency virus) Surveillance System (CDC)		Nursing Intervention Classification
		NICC	neonatal intensive care center
	Spanish National Health Surveys		noninfectious chronic cystitis
		NICCM	National Institute of Child Care Management
NHSs	neurological hard signs		
	nocturnal hypermotor seizures	NICD	National Institute for Communicable Diseases (National Health Laboratory Services, Johannesburg, South Africa)
NHSW	nonhealing surgical wound		
NHT	neoadjuvant hormonal therapy		
	nursing home transfer		
NHTR	nonhemolytic transfusion reaction		
NHTSA	National Highway Traffic Safety Administration		nonspecific intraventricular conduction delay
NHU	nonhealing ulcer		nonspecific intraventricular conduction disturbance
NHW	nonhealing wound		
NHYA	may have meant NYHA (New York Heart Association [classification of heart disease])		Notch1 Intracellular Domain (the transcription factor which controls cell fate and differentiation in embryonic and tumor cells)
NI	neurological improvement	NICE	National Institute for Clinical Excellence (United Kingdom)
	no improvement		
	no information		new, interesting, and challenging experiences
	none indicated		
	not identified		

NICH	noninvoluting congenital hemangioma	NIDU	noninjection drug use
NICHD	National Institute of Child Health and Human Development (NIH)	nidus	a word meaning a place in which something is formed or deposited; a site of origin
NICHs	noninvoluting congenital hemangiomas	NIEHS	National Institute of Environmental Health Sciences (NIH)
NICM	nonischemic cardiomyopathy	NIEPs	noninfectious enveloped particles
NICMO	nonischemic cardiomyopathy	NIF	negative inspiratory force
NICMP	nonischemic cardiomyopathy		neutrophil inhibitory factor
NICMY	nonischaemic cardiomyopathy		not in file
NICO	neuralgia-inducing cavitational osteonecrosis	NiFe	nickel–iron alloy
		nifF	flavodoxin; see gene website www.ncbi.nlm.nih.gov/gene
	noninvasive cardiac output (monitor)	NIFS	noninvasive flow studies
NicoE	National Intrepid Center of Excellence	NIFTP	noninvasive follicular thyroid neoplasm with papillary-like nuclear features
NICOM	noninvasive cardiac output monitor	NIG	NSAIA (nonsteroidal anti-inflamatory agent) induced gastropathy
NICP	nonischemic chest pain		
nICP	noninvasive intracranial pressure	night	nocte
		NIGMS	National Institute of General Medical Sciences (NIH)
NICS	noninvasive carotid studies		
NICU	neonatal intensive care unit	NIH	National Institutes of Health
	neurosurgical intensive care unit	NIHD	noise-induced hearing damage
	new infant care unit	NIHL	noise-induced hearing loss
NID	no identifiable disease	NIHSS	National Institutes of Health Stroke Scale
	not in distress		
NIDA	National Institute of Drug Abuse (NIH)	NIID	neuronal intranuclear inclusion disease
NIDA five	National Institute on Drug Abuse screen for cannabinoids, cocaine metabolite, amphetamine/methamphetamine, opiates, and phencyclidine	NIL	not in labor
		nil	nothing; zero
		N-ILM	negative for intraepithelial lesion or malignancy
		nil per os	nothing orally (nothing per mouth)
NIDCAP	Newborn Individualized Developmental Care and Assessment Program	NIM	nerve integrity monitor
		NIMAs	noninherited maternal antigens
NIDCD	National Institute of Deafness and other Communication Disorders (NIH)	NIMH	National Institute of Mental Health (NIH)
		NIMHDIS	National Institute for Mental Health Diagnostic Interview Schedule (NIH)
NIDCM	nonischemic dilated cardiomyopathy		
NIDCR	National Institute of Dental and Craniofacial Research (NIH)	NIMM	neuroimmunophilin
		NIMR	National Institute of Medical Research (United Kingdom)
NIDD	noninsulin-dependent diabetes	NIMS	National Incident Management System (a division of the Federal Emergency Management Agency [FEMA])
NIDDK	National Institute of Diabetes and Digestive and Kidney Diseases (NIH)		
NIDDM	noninsulin-dependent diabetes mellitus		nerve integrity monitoring system
NIDDM2	noninsulin-dependent type 2 diabetes mellitus	NIMV	nasal intermittent mandatory ventilation
NIDM	noninsulin-dependent diabetes mellitus		noninvasive mechanical ventilation
NIDR	National Institute of Dental Research (NIH)	NINDS	National Institute of Neurological Disorders and Stroke (NIH)

N

NINDS-SPSP	National Institute of Neurological Disorders and Stroke and Society for Progressive Supranuclear Palsy (criteria)	NISCMP	nonischemic secondary cardiomyopathy
NiNP	nickel nanoparticles	NISH	nonradioactive *in situ* hybridization
NINR	National Institute for Nursing Research (NIH)	NISP	Nurse Independent and Supplementary Prescribers (United Kingdom)
NINU	neuro intermediate nursing unit	NISS	New Injury Severity Score
NINVS	noninvasive neurovascular studies	NISs	no-impact sports
NIOPCs	no intraoperative complications	Nissen fundoplication	a surgical procedure to treat gastroesophageal reflux disease (GERD) and hiatal hernia
NIOSH	National Institute of Occupational Safety and Health (Centers for Disease Control and Prevention)	NIST	National Institute of Standards and Technology
NiOx	nickel oxide	NISV	nonionic surfactant vesicle
NIOX MINO	a point-of-care medical device for measuring fractional exhaled nitric oxide	NIT	Nit-Occlude® PDA-R device (device for percutaneous closure of osmium secundumatrial septal defects)
NiOx NPs	nickel oxide nanoparticles		
NIOX VERO	a point-of-care medical device for measuring fractional exhaled nitric oxide	NITD	neuroleptic-induced tardive dyskinesia
NIP	catnip National Immunization Program no infection present no inflammation present	NITE	National Institute of Technology and Evaluation (Tokyo, Japan)
		Nitrazine test	a diagnostic for preterm premature rupture of membranes
NIPAs	noninherited paternal antigens		
NIPD	nocturnal intermittent peritoneal dialysis noninvasive prenatal diagnosis	Nitro	nitroglycerin (this is a dangerous abbreviation) sodium nitroprusside (this is a dangerous abbreviation)
NIPHS	noninsulinoma pancreatogenous hypoglycemia syndrome (adults-onset nesidioblastosis)	NITS	non-intubated thoracic surgery
NIPPV	noninvasive positive-pressure ventilation	NIV	noninvasive vascular assessment noninvasive ventilation
NIPS	Neonatal Infant Pain Scale non-invasive pacing study noninvasive prenatal screening	NIVA	Norwegian Institute for Water Research
NIP/S	noninvasive programming stimulation	NIVAS	non-intubated video abscessoscopy
NIPSV	noninvasive pressure-support ventilation	NIVCB	no intraventricular conduction block
NIPT	noninvasive prenatal testing	NIVCD	nonspecific intraventricular disturbance
NIPV	noninvasive pulmonary ventilation	NIVD	normalized interhemispheric volume difference
NIR	near infrared nitroprusside-induced relaxation	NIVLS	noninvasive vascular laboratory studies
NIRCA	nonisotopic RNase cleavage assay	NIVM	noninvasive monitoring
		NIVs	nutrient intake values
NIRDM	noninsulin-requiring diabetes mellitus	NIVTS	non-intubated video thoracoscopy
NIRS	near infrared spectroscopy	NIXRs	nurse initiated X-rays
NIS	Nationwide Inpatient Sample nutrition intake study sodium iodide symporter (protein)	NIZ	no interruption zone
		NJ	nasojejunal New Jersey
NISCM	nonischemic secondary cardiomyopathy	NJH	National Jewish Health
		NJT	nasojejunal tube

N

NJ tube	nasojejunal tube
NK	natural killer (cells)
	not known
NK_1	neurokinin 1
NKA	no known allergies
NKAS	National Kidney Allocation Scheme (United Kingdom)
nkat	nanokatal (nanomole/sec)
NKB	neurokinin B
	no known basis
	not keeping baby
NKC	nonketotic coma
NKD	no known diseases
NKDA	no known drug allergies
NKFA	no known food allergies
NKF/K-DOQ	National Kidney Foundation Kidney Disease Outcomes Quality Initiative (guidelines)
NKF-K/DOQI	National Kidney Foundation Kidney Disease Outcomes Quality Initiative
NKH	nonketotic hyperglycemia
NKHA	nonketotic hyperosmolar acidosis
NKHHC	nonketotic hyperglycemic-hyperosmolar coma
NKHOC	nonketotic hyperosmolar coma
NKHS	nonketotic hyperosmolar syndrome
NKI	Netherlands Cancer Institute
	no known injury
NKLA	No-Kill Los Angeles (pet adoption centers)
NKMA	no known medication (medical) allergies
NKR	National Kidney Registry NK (natural killer)-cell receptor; see gene website www.ncbi .nlm.nih.gov/gene
NK-1R	neurokinin 1 receptors
NKSi	needle knife sinusotomy
NKSt	needle knife stricturotomy
NKT	natural-killer T (cells)
NK/T-cell	natural killer T cell
NL	nasolacrimal
	needle localization
	nonlatex
	normal
	normal libido
	normal limits
nL	nanoliter (if nL was used in the clinical setting it would be dangerous as it could be seen or heard as mL)
NLA	no latex allergy
NLB	needle liver biopsy
nLBP	nonspecific low back pain

NLC	nocturnal leg cramps
NLC & C	normal libido, coitus, and climax
NLD	nasolacrimal duct
	necrobiosis lipoidica diabeticorum
	no local doctor
	nonverbal learning disabilities
NLDO	nasolacrimal duct obstruction
NLDS	nasolacrimal duct stenosis
NLDs	nasolacrimal ducts
NLE	neonatal lupus erythematosus
	nursing late entry
NLEA	Nutrition Labeling and Education Act of 1990
Nl EF	normal ejection fraction
NLF	nasolabial fold
	nelfinavir (Viracept)
	neonatal liver failure
NLFGNR	nonlactose fermenting gram-negative rod
NLG	natural language generation
	neuroligin
	N-linked glycosylation
NLM	National Library of Medicine
	no limitation of motion
NLMC	nocturnal leg muscle cramp
NLN	National League of Nursing
	National Lymphedema Network
	no longer needed
	Nordic Council on Medicines (Nordiska Lakemedelsnamnden)
NLNAC	National League for Nursing Accrediting Commission
NLNW	no-lyse-no-wash
NLO	nasolacrimal occlusion
NLP	natural language processing
	no light perception
	nodular liquifying panniculitis
NLPHL	nodular lymphocyte-predominant Hodgkin lymphoma
NLR	negative-likelihood ratio
	neutrophil-to-lymphocyte ratio
NLRs	NOD (nucleotide-binding oligimerization domain)-like receptors
NLS	neonatal lupus syndrome
NLs	neuroimmunophilin ligands
NLST	National Lung Screening Trial
NLT	not later than
	not less than
NLV	nelfinavir (Viracept)
NLX	naloxone
NM	nanometer (nm) (10^{-9} meters)
	Negro male
	neoplastic meningitis
	neurodynamic mobilization

N

	neuromuscular	NMIBC	nonmuscle-invasive bladder cancer
	neuronal microdysgenesis		
	New Mexico	NMJ	neuromuscular junction
	nodular melanoma	NMKB	not married, keeping baby
	nonmalignant	NML	normal
	normal metabolizer	NMM	neuromuscular manipulative medicine
	not measurable		
	not measured		nodular malignant melanoma
	not mentioned	NMN	nicotinamide mononucleotide
	nuclear medicine		no middle name
	nurse manager	NMNKB	not married, not keeping baby
N & M	nerves and muscles	NMO	neuromyelitis optica (Devic syndrome)
	night and morning		
N0M0	no (positive) nodes, no metastases		neuromyelitis optics
		NMOH	no medical ocular history
NMA	National Medical Association	nmol	nanomole (one billionth $[10^{-9}]$ of a mole)
	nonmyeloablative		
	nuclear material accountancy	nmol/L	nanomoles/liter (one billionth of a mole per liter)
NMB	neuromuscular blockade		
NMBA	neuromuscular blocking agent	NMOSDs	neuromyelitis optica spectrum disorders
NMBs	neuromuscular blockers		
NMC	no malignant cells	NMP	normal menstrual period
nmCRPC	nonmetastatic castration-resistant prostate cancer	NMPPAS	nonresonant multiphoton photoacoustic spectroscopy
NMD	Doctor of Naturopathic Medicine	NMR	nuclear magnetic resonance (same as magnetic resonance imaging)
	neuromaturational delay		
	neuromuscular disorders	NMRA	nuclear magnetic resonance angiography
	neuronal migration disorders		
	Normosol M and 5% Dextrose®	nmrA	see gene website, www.ncbi.nlm.nih.gov/gene
	progressive neuromuscular disease		
		N-MRA	Native-MR (magnetic resonance) angiography
NMDA	N-methyl-D-aspartate		
NMDARs	N-methyl-D-aspartate receptors	NMRC	National Medical Research Council (Singapore Ministry of Health)
NMDC	nonmammographically detected cancer		
			Naval Medical Research Center
NMDP	National Marrow Donor Pool		non-mydriatic retinal camera
	National Marrow Donor Program®	NMRE	neuromuscular re-education
		NMRG	no murmur, rub, or gallop
NMDR	nonmonotonic dose-response (curve)	NMRS	nuclear magnetic resonance spectroscopy
NME	new molecular entity	NMRT®	Nuclear Medicine Radiologic Technologist (Registered)
NMES	neuromuscular electrical stimulation		
		NMS	neonatal morphine solution
NMF	neuromuscular facilitation		neuroleptic malignant syndrome
NMFP	nonmydriatic fundus photography		non-motor symptoms
		NMSC	nonmelanoma skin cancer
	nonmydriatic multifield fundus photography	NMSCs	nonmelanoma skin cancers
		NMSE	normalized mean square error
NMG	normal mammary glands	NMSIDS	near-miss sudden infant death syndrome
NMH	neurally mediated hypotension		
NMHH	no medical health history	NMSS	NonMotor Symptoms Scale
NMI	no manifest improvement	NMSs	non-motor symptoms
	no mental illness	NMST	nonmyeloablative allogeneic stem cell transplantation
	no middle initial		
	no more information	NMT	nebulized mist treatment
	normal male infant		no more than

NMT®	Nuclear Medicine Technologist Registered
NMTB	neuromuscular transmission blockade
NMTCB	Nuclear Medicine Technology Certification Board
NMU	nitrosomethylurea
NMW	nominal molecular weight
	nurse-midwife
NN	narrative notes
	Navajo neuropathy
	neonatal
	neural network
	newborn nursery
	normal nursery
	nurses' notes
N-N	normal to normal (intervals)
N/N	negative/negative
NNA	N omega-nitro-L-arginine
NNB	normal newborn
	number-needed-to-benefit
NNBC	node-negative breast cancer
NNC	noticeable negative change(s)
	nurse-nurse collaboration
NND	neonatal death
	New Nordic Diet
	number needed to detain
NNDSS	National Notifiable Diseases Surveillance System
NNE	neonatal necrotizing enterocolitis
NNH	number needed to harm
NNIS	National Nosocomial Infections Surveillance
NNL	no new laboratory (test orders)
NNM	Nicolle-Novy-MacNeal (media)
NNN	normal newborn nursery
NNNB	non-neurogenic neurogenic bladder
NNNS	NICU (neonatal intensive care unit) Network Neurobehavioral Scale
NNO	no new orders
NNP	National Naloxone Programme (Scotland)
	Neonatal Nurse Practitioner
	non-nociceptive pain
N:NPK	grams of nitrogen to non-protein kilocalories
NNR	not necessary to return
NNRTI	non-nucleoside reverse transcriptase inhibitor
NNS	neonatal screen (hematocrit, total bilirubin, and total protein)
	nicotine nasal spray
	non-nutritive sucking
	non-nutritive sweetener(s)
	number needed to screen

NNSS	NPC (Niemann-Pick disease type C) Neurological Severity Score(s)
NNSSTI	non-nutritive suck spatiotemporal index
NNS STI	non-nutritive suck spatiotemporal index
NNT	number needed to treat
NNTB/NNTH	number needed to treat benefit-to-harm ratio
NNTH	number needed to treat to harm
NNU	net nitrogen utilization
NNVAMD	non-neovascular age-related macular degeneration
NNWT	noncontact normothermic wound therapy
NO	nasal obstruction
	nasal oxygen
	nitric oxide
	nitroglycerin ointment
	none obtained
	nonobese
	number (no.)
	nursing office
No	nobelium
N/O	see NO
no	number
N₂O	nitrous oxide
NO₂	nitrogen dioxide
NOA	non-obstructive azoospermia
NOAA	National Oceanic and Atmospheric Administration
NOAC	novel (new or non-vitamin K antagonist) oral anticoagulant(s) (rivaroxaban [Xarelto], dabigatran [Pradaxa], edoxaban[Savaysa], and apixaban [Eliquis]). This is a dangerous abbreviation as it has been read as no oral anticoagulant(s) or no anticoagulant(s). If it is necessary to abbreviate this term use DOAC (direct oral anticoagulant[s])
NOAC ICH	non-vitamin K oral anticoagulant-associated intracerebral hemorrhage
NOACs	novel (new or non-vitamin K antagonist) oral anticoagulant(s) (See NOAC)
NOAE	nonoccupational asbestos exposures
NOAEL	no observed adverse effect level
NOAF	new-onset atrial fibrillation

NOAg	silver hyponitrite	NOGM	nonoxidative glucose
NOAK	non-vitamin K antagonists		metabolism
	(also known as NOAC; novel	NOH	neurogenic orthostatic
	[new] oral anticoagulant[s];		hypotension
	rivaroxaban [Xarelto],	NOHCM	non-obstructive hypertrophic
	dabigatran [Pradaxa],		cardiomyopathy
	edoxaban [Savaysa], and	NOI	nature of illness
	apixaban [Eliquis])	NOK	next of kin
Nob	see gene website, www.ncbi.nlm	NOL	not on label
	.nih.gov/gene	NOM	nonoperative management
NOBN	nonocclusive bowel necrosis		nonsuppurative otitis media
NOC	nonorgan-confined	NOMAC	nomegestrol acetate
	Nursing Outcome Classification	NOMAC/E2	nomegestrol acetate/17beta-
noc.	night		estradiol
NOCAD	nonobstructive coronary artery	NOMe-seq	Nucleosome Occupancy and
	disease		Methylome-sequencing
NOCD	new-onset autoimmune disease	NOMI	nonocclusive mesenteric
nocebo effect	when the expectation of a		infarction
	negative outcome precipitates	NOMID	neonatal-onset multisystem
	the corresponding symptom		inflammatory disease
	or leads to its exacerbation	NOMNC	Notice of Medicare Noncoverage
noche	night	NOMO	Nodal modulator
NOCs	N-Nitroso compounds		not homosexual (slang)
noct	nocturnal		nuclear orbital plus molecular
nocte	night; at night		orbital (theory)
	at bedtime	NOMS	National Outcomes
NOD	nonobese diabetic		Measurement System
	notice of disagreement		(American Speech-Language
	notify of death		Hearing Association)
NOD1	nucleotide binding oligomerization		not on my shift
	domain containing 1 (gene)	NON	non-optic neuritis
NOD2	nucleotide binding oligomerization	NO/N₂	nitric oxide; nitrogen
	domain containing 2 (gene)	Non-24	non-24-hour sleep-wake
NODAT	new-onset diabetes after		disorder is a circadian rhythm
	transplantation		disorder causing nighttime
NODM	new-onset diabetes mellitus		sleep problems including an
nodM	glucosamine--fructose-6-		urge to sleep during the day
	phosphate aminotransferase;		It effects 70% of people who
	see gene website www.ncbi		are totally blind
	.nlm.nih.gov/gene	noncom	noncommissioned officer
NOE	naso-orbitoethmoid		(US military)
	naturally occurring endotoxin	noncon	noncontact
NOED	no observed effect dose	Noncon Robo	noncontact specular microscope
NOEL	no observable effect level	NONMEM	nonlinear mixed-effects model
NOF	National Osteoporosis Founda-		(modeling)
	tion (treatment criteria)	nonOp	non-operation
	nonossifying fibroma	nonpal	not palpable
NOFA	Notice of Funds Availability	NonPARs	Nonparticipating Physicians
NOFT	nonorganic failure to thrive		(Medicare)
NOFTT	nonorganic failure to thrive	NonPharmacy	nonpharmacologic
NOGA	non-fluoroscopic mapping	nonprod	nonproductive
	system that simultaneously	non-REM	nonrapid eye movement (sleep)
	registers the electrical and	non rep	do not repeat
	mechanical activities of the	non-res	non-resident
	left ventricle, enabling online	NONSTEMI	non-ST-segment elevation
	assessment of myocardial		myocardial infarction
	viability (Johnson & Johnson	non-STEMI	non-ST-segment elevation
	Company, Irwindale, CA)		myocardial infarction

N

non-TBLs	non-true bifurcation lesions	NOV L	human insulin zinc suspension (Novolin L)
NON-TC	non-tunneled catheter		
NONVIZ	not visualized	NOV N	human insulin isophane suspension (Novolin N)
N₂O:O₂	nitrous oxide to oxygen ratio		
NOOB	not out of bed	NOV R	human insulin regular (Novolin R)
NOP	not on patient		
NOPP	nature of presenting problems	NoVs	noroviruses
NOPR	National Oncology PET (positron emission tomography) Registry	NP	nasal polyps nasal prongs nasopharyngeal
			near point
NOPr	nociceptin receptor		neck pain
NOR	norethynodrel normal nortriptyline		neuropathic pain
			neurophysin
			neuropsychiatric
NORA	Nationwide Organ Recovery Transport Alliance		neutrogenic precautions
			newly presented
NOR-EPI	norepinephrine (Levophed)		no pain
norm	normal		nonpalpable
NORs	nucleolar organizer regions		nonpitting (as in nonpitting edema)
NORSE	new-onset refractory status epilepticus		
			not performed
NOS	neonatal opium solution (diluted deodorized tincture of opium)		not pregnant
			not present
	new-onset seizures		nuclear pharmacist
	nitric oxide synthase		nuclear pharmacy
	no organisms seen		nurse practitioner
	not on staff		nursed poorly
	not otherwise specified	Np	neptunium
	number of services rendered (Medicare)	N/P	see NP
		NPA	nasal pharyngeal airway
NoS	no show		nasopharyngeal aspirate
NOS3	nitric oxide synthase, type 3		near point of accommodation
NOSI	nitric oxide synthase inhibitors		no previous admission
NOSIE	Nurse's Observation Scale (Schedule) for Inpatient Evaluation	NPAC	nasopharyngeal adenocarcinoma
		NPAF	nonparoxysmal atrial fibrillation
NOSPECS	categories for classifying eye changes in Graves' ophthalmopathy: no signs or symptoms, only signs, soft tissue involvement with symptoms and signs, proptosis, extraocular muscle involvement, corneal involvement, and sight loss (visual acuity)	npAIR	nonparaneoplastic autoimmune retinopathy
		N-PASS	Neonatal Pain, Agitation, and Sedation Scale
		NPAT	nonparoxysmal atrial tachycardia
		NPBC	node-positive breast cancer
		NPBCC	nonpigmented basal cell carcinoma
		NPC	nasopharyngeal carcinoma
NOSs	nitric oxide synthases		near-point convergence
NOT	nocturnal oxygen therapy		Niemann-Pick disease Type C (sphingomyelin lipidosis)
NOTA Study	Non Operative Treatment for Acute Appendicitis study		
			no prenatal care
NOTES	natural orifice transluminal endoscopic surgery		no previous complaint(s)
			nodal premature contractions
NOTT	nocturnal oxygen therapy trial		nonpatient contact
NOU	not on unit		nonproductive cough
NOV	Novartis		nonprotein calorie
NoV	norovirus	NP-C	Nurse Practitioner, Certified
Nov	November	NPCa	nasopharynx cancer
November	Phonetic Alphabet for N; pronounced NO-VEM-BER	NPCC	nonprotein carbohydrate calories

N

NPCPAP	nasopharyngeal continuous positive airway pressure	NPIF	nasal peak inspiratory flow
		NPIS	Numeric Pain Intensity Scale
NPCR	National Program of Cancer Registries (CDC)	NPIT	nonpalpable intraabdominal testis
NPD	narcissistic personality disorder	NPJT	nonparoxysmal junctional tachycardia
	Niemann-Pick disease		
	no pathological diagnosis	NPK	nonprotein kilocalories
	nonpolarized contact dermoscopy	NPL	nasopalatine line
			nasopharyngolaryngoscopic
	nonprescription drugs		neural protamine lispro (an insulin)
NPDB	National Practitioner Data Bank		
	Niemann-Pick disease type B	NPL component	insulin lispro protamine suspension
NPD-B	Niemann-Pick disease, type B		
NPDL	nodular poorly differentiated lymphocytic	NPLD	nonpegylated liposomal doxorubicin (Myocet [United Kingdom and other countries])
NPDMR	nonproliferative diabetes mellitus retinopathy		
NPDR	nonproliferative diabetic retinopathy	NPLSM	neoplasm
		NPM	nothing per mouth
NPDS	National Poison Data System (American Association of Poison Control Centers)	Npm1	nucleophosmin; see gene website www.ncbi.nlm.nih .gov/gene
	Neck Pain and Disability Scale	NPN	nonprotein nitrogen
	nonpenetrating deep sclerectomy	nPNA	normalized protein equivalent of nitrogen appearance
NPE	neurogenic pulmonary edema		
	neuropsychologic examination	NPNC	no prenatal care
	no palpable enlargement	NPNT	nonpalpable, nontender
	normal pelvic examination	NPO	new patient orientation (this is a dangerous abbreviation as it will be read as nothing by mouth)
NPEC	nasopharyngeal epithelial cells		
	nonpathogenic Escherichia coli		
NPEM	nocturnal penile erection monitoring		
			nothing by mouth
NPEP	nonoccupational (human immunodeficiency virus) postexposure prophylaxis	NPOA	neurogenic paraosteoarthropathy
		NPOC	nonpurgeable organic carbon
			nursing plan of care
NPEV	new patient evaluation program	NPOD	Neuropsychiatric Officer of the Day
NPF	nasopharyngeal fiberscope		
	no predisposing factor	NP/OP	nasopharyngeal/oropharyngeal
NPFE	negative pressure-driven forced expiration	NPOS	number of positive nodes
		NPP	nonphysician practitioner
NPFL	nurse practitioner fracture liaison		normal postpartum
N-PFMSO₄	nebulized preservative-free morphine sulfate		Nurse Practitione, Psychiatric
		NPPA	nonprimary pancreatic adenocarcinoma
NPFS	nonpenetrating filtering surgery		
NPG	nonpregnant	NP/PA	nurse practitioners/physician assistants
	normal-pressure glaucoma		
NPGN	nonproliferative glomerulonephritis	Nppa	natriuretic peptide precursor A; see gene website www.ncbi .nlm.nih.gov/gene
	nonpseudomonas gram-negative		
NPH	isophane insulin (neutral protamine Hagedorn)	NPPE	negative-pressure pulmonary edema
		NPPI	nonpeptidic protease inhibitor
	no previous history	NPPNG	nonpenicillinase-producing Neisseria gonorrhoeae
	normal-pressure hydrocephalus		
NPhx	nasopharynx	NPPV	noninvasive positive-pressure ventilation
NPI	National Provider Identifier		
	Neuropsychiatric Inventory	NPQ	Northwick Park Neck Pain Questionnaire
	no present illness		
	Nottingham Prognostic Index		

NPR	normal pulse rate	NR	do not repeat
	nothing per rectum		newly reformulated
	nursing progress record		no refills
NP ref	new patient referral		no report
NPRL	normal pupillary reaction to light		no response
			no return
NPRM	Notice of Proposed Rulemaking		none reported
NPRS	numerical pain rating scale		nonreactive
NPS	nasopharyngoscopy		nonrebreathing
	National Pharmaceutical Stockpile		nonresponder
			normal range
	neuropsychiatric symptoms		normal reaction
	new patient set-up		not reached
	novel psychoactive substances		not reacting
NPs	nurse practitioners		not remarkable
NPSA	nonphysician surgical assistant		not resolved
NPSD	nonpotassium-sparing diuretics		number
NPSF	National Patient Safety Foundation		nursing referral
		NRAEMT	Nationally Registered Advanced Emergency Medical Technician
NPSG	National Patient Safety Goal		
	nocturnal polysomnography		
NPSLE	neuropsychiatric systemic lupus erythematosus	NRAF	nonrheumatic atrial fibrillation
		NRAS	neuroblastoma RAS viral (v-ras) oncogene homolog
NPT	near-patient tests		
	neopyrithiamin hydrochloride		NRAS (neuroblastoma ras) proto-oncogene, GTPase
	no prior tracings		
	nocturnal penile tumescence	nr-axSpA	nonradiographic axial spondyloarthritis
	normal pressure and temperature		
NPTA	National Pharmacy Technician Association	NRB	Noninstitutional Review Board
			nonrebreather (oxygen mask)
NPU	net protein utilization	NRBC	normal red blood cell
NPUAP	National Pressure Ulcer Advisory Panel (guidelines/staging)		nucleated red blood cell
		NRBM	negative regression binomial model
NPV	negative predictive value		
	nothing per vagina		nonrebreathing mask
NPWT	negative-pressure wound therapy	NRBO	nonreversible bronchial obstruction
NPX	naproxen	NRBR	not read by radiologist
NPx	nasopharynx	NRBS	nonrebreathing system
	nephrectomy	NRC	National Research Council
	neurological physical examination		normal retinal correspondence
			Nuclear Regulatory Commission
NPY	neuropeptide Y		
NPZ	neuropsychologic text z	NRCT	National Registry of Childhood Tumours (UK)
NQECN	nonqueratinizing epidermoid carcinoma		
		NRD	nephropathy requiring dialysis
NQF	National Quality Forum		neural respiratory drive
NQMI	non-Q wave myocardial infarction		neuroretinal disorder
NQMWI	may have meant NQWMI (non-Q wave myocardial infarction)	NRDS	neonatal respiratory distress syndrome
		NREH	normal renin essential hypertension
NQR	not quite right (slang)	NREM	nonrapid eye movement
NQT	narrow QRS complex tachycardia	NREMR	Nationally Registered Emergency Medical Responder
NQW	non-Q-wave	NREMS	nonrapid eye movement sleep
NQWMI	non-Q wave myocardial infarction	NREMT	Nationally Registered Emergency Medical Technician

NREMT-P	National Registry of Emergency Medical Technicians– Paramedic level	NRPR	nonbreathing pressure relieving
		NRR	net reproduction rate
		NRRT	neutral red retention time
NREVSS	National Respiratory and Enteric Virus Surveillance System (CDC)	NRS	Neurobehavioral Rating Scale
			noninvasive respiratory support
			Numeric Rating Scale
NRF	National Research Foundation of Korea		nutrition risk screening
		NRSA	National Research Service Awards (National Institutes of Health)
	normal renal function		
nrfA	nitrite reductase, formate-dependent, cytochrome (gene)	nrsg	nursing
		NRSs	nonrandomized studies
		NRSTS	non-rhabdomyosarcoma soft tissue sarcoma
NRFHR	nonreassuring fetal heart rate		
NRFHRs	nonreassuring fetal heart rate patterns	NRT	Neural response telemetry (audiology testing)
NRFHRT	nonreassuring fetal heart rate tracings		neuromuscular reeducation techniques
NRFHT	nonreassuring fetal heart (rate) tracing		nicotine-replacement therapy
		nRT	reticular thalamic nucleus
	nonreassuring fetal heart tones	NRTC	National Research and Training Center (University of Illinois at Chicago)
NRFHTs	nonreassuring fetal heart tones		
NRFM	nonrebreathing face mask		
NRFS	nonreassuring fetal status	NRTI	nucleoside reverse transcriptase inhibitor
NRFWB	nonreassuring fetal well-being		
NRG	a national clinical trials network group; NRG is an acronym derived from names of its parental groups; National Surgical Adjuvant Breast and Bowel Project (NSABP), the Radiation Therapy Oncology Group (RTOG), and the Gynecologic Oncology Group (GOG)	NRTL	nonrandom two-liquid (model)
		NRTs	nitron radical traps
		NRV	Nutrient Reference Values (Australia)
		NRXN3	neurexin 3 (gene/protein)
		NS	nephrotic syndrome
			neurological signs
			neurosarcoidosis
			neurosurgery
	energy		never-smokers
	neuregulin		nipple stimulation
nrgA	ammonium transporter (gene)		no sample
NRH	nodular regenerative hyperplasia		nodular sclerosis
NRI	nerve root involvement		nonsmoker
	nerve root irritation		nonspecific
	no recent illnesses		normal saline solution (0.9% sodium chloride solution)
	norepinephrine reuptake inhibitor		normospermic
NRL	natural rubber latex		no-show
N-RLX	nonrelaxed		not seen
NRM	no regular medicines		not significant
	nonrebreathing mask		nuclear sclerosis
	normal range of motion		nursing service
	normal retinal movement		NuStep
NRN	no return necessary		nutrition support
NRNST	nonreassuring-nonstress test		nutritive sucking
NRO	neurology		nylon suture
NROM	normal range of motion	Ns	Newton second
NRP	Nationally Registered Paramedic	N/S	see NS
		NS1	nonstructural protein 1 (gene/ protein)
	neonatal resuscitation program		
	nonreassuring patterns		nonstructural protein (gene/ protein)
NRP1	neuropilin-1		

421

N

NSA	National Security Agency	NSCH	National Survey of Children's
	neck-shaft angle		Health
	no salt added	NSCHO	nonstructural carbohydrates
	no significant abnormalities	NSCIC	may have meant NSCLC
	nonstandard appearance (slang)		(nonsmall cell lung cancer)
	normal serum albumin	NSCID	National Spinal Cord Injury
	(albumin, human)		Database
	number of signals averaged	NSCIDRC	National Spinal Cord Injury
	(radiology)		Data Research Center
NS5A	nonstructural 5A protein (of the	NSCIs	neoplastic spinal cord injuries
	hepatic C virus)	NSCJ	neosquamocolumnar junction
NSAA	nonsteroidal antiandrogen	NSCLA	nonsmall cell lung
NSABP	National Surgical Adjuvant		adenocarcinoma
	Breast Project	NSCLC	nonsmall cell lung cancer
NSAD	no signs of acute disease	NSCLCa	nonsmall cell lung cancer
NSAE	neonatal systemic air	NSCLL	may have meant NSCLC
	embolism		(nonsmall cell lung
	neurological sequelae due to		carcinoma)
	acute encephalopathy	NSCL/P	nonsyndromic cleft lip with/
	neurosensory adverse events		without cleft palate
	nonserious adverse event	NSCLS	may have meant NSCLC
NSAIA	nonsteroidal anti-inflammatory		(nonsmall-cell lung cancer)
	agent	NSCST	nipple stimulation contraction
NSAID	nonsteroidal anti-inflammatory		stress test
	drug(s) (celecoxib, ibupro-	NS-CST	nipple stimulation-contraction
	fen, meloxicam, naproxen,		stress test
	etc.)	NSCT	nonsubsampled contourlet
NSAIDs	nonsteroidal anti-inflammatory		transform
	drugs (celecoxib, ibuprofen,	NSCU	neonatal special care unit
	meloxicam, naproxen, etc.)		neurosurgical care unit
NSAP	nonspecific abdominal pain	NSD	nasal septal deviation
NSAR	nonsteroidal anti-rheumatics		no significant disease
	(also known as NSAIDS		(difference, defect, deviation)
	[nonsteroidal anti-		nominal standard dose
	inflammatory drugs])		nonstructural deterioration
NSAT	nonsustained atrial tachycardia		normal spontaneous delivery
NSB	nonspecific binding	NSDA	nonsteroid dependent asthmatic
NS5B	nonstructural 5B protein of the	NSDU	neonatal stepdown unit
	hepatitis C virus	NSE	neuron-specific enolase
NSBB	nonselective beta-blockers		normal saline enema (0.9%
NSBGP	nonspecific bowel gas pattern		sodium chloride)
NSC	National Security Council	N s̄ E	nausea without emesis
	neural stem cells	NSEACS	non-ST-elevation acute coronary
	no significant change		syndromes
	nonservice connected	NSET	nested stromal-epithelial tumor
	nuclear sclerotic cataract	NSETMI	may have meant NSTEMI
NSCC	nonsmall cell carcinoma		(Non ST-segment elevated
NSCCa	nonsmall cell carcinoma		myocardial infarction)
NSCCC	neuroendocrine small cell	NSF	nephrogenic systemic fibrosis
	colorectal carcinoma		no significant findings
NSCCL	nonsmall cell carcinoma of the	NSFTD	normal spontaneous full-term
	lung		delivery
NSCD	nonservice-connected disability	NSG	nursing
NSCE	may have meant NCSE	NSGCT	nonseminomatous germ cell
	(nonconvulsive status		tumor
	epilepticus)	NSGCTT	nonseminomatous germ-cell
NSCFPT	no significant change from		tumor of the testis
	previous tracing	NSGI	nonspecific genital infection

N

NSGSV	nursing supervisor
NSGT	nonseminomatous germ-cell tumor
NSGY	neurosurgery
NSHC	no-self-harm contract
NSHD	nodular sclerosing Hodgkin disease
NSHL	nonsyndromic hearing loss
NSI	needlestick injury
	negative self-image
	no signs of infection
	no signs of inflammation
NSIAD	may have meant NSAID (nonsteroidal anti-inflammatory drug)
NSIADs	may have meant NSAIDs (nonsteroidal anti-inflammatory drugs)
NSICU	neurosurgery intensive care unit
NSID	nonsyndromal intellectual disability
NSILA	nonsuppressible insulin-like activity
nSIMV	nasal synchronized intermittent mandatory ventilation
NSIP	nonspecific interstitial pneumonia
NSIT	needle-less single-incision technique
	no-signaling in time
	Novel Sequence Identification Tool (software)
NSIVCD	nonspecific intraventricular conduction defect
NSL	normal saline (0.9% sodium chloride inj) lock
NSLBP	nonspecific low back pain
NSLC	nonsmall cell lung cancer
NSLP	National School Lunch Program
NSLRP	nerve-sparing laparoscopic radical prostatectomy
NSlRr	neutral, sidebent left, rotated right
NSM	negative surgical margin
	neurogenic stunned myocardium
NSMC	may have meant NMSC (nonmelanoma skin cancer)
NSMMVT	nonsustained monomorphic ventricular tachycardia
NSN	Neo-Synephrine
	nephrotoxic serum nephritis
	nonsentinel nodes
NSNSAIDs	nonselective nonsteroidal anti-inflammatory drugs
NSO	Neosporin® ointment
NSOH	normal state of health
NSOM	near field scanning optical microscope
NSOP	no soft organs palpable

NSP	neck and shoulder pain
NSPC	neural stem/progenitor cell
NSPCs	neural stem/progenitor cells
NSPDR	National Screening Programme for Diabetic Retinopathy
NSPL	National Suicide Prevention Lifeline
NSPs	needle and syringe exchange programs
	nonstarch polysaccharides
NSPVT	nonsustained polymorphic ventricular tachycardia
NSQ	nighttime sleep quality
NSQIP	National Surgical Quality Improvement Program (American College of Surgeons)
NSR	nasoseptal repair
	nonspecific reaction
	normal sinus rhythm
	not seen regularly
NSRI	National Sodium Reduction Initiative (targets)
	National Stroke Research Institute, (Victoria, Australia)
	norepinephrine selective reuptake inhibitor
	Noxious Stimulation Response Index
NSRP	nerve-sparing radical prostatectomy
NSrRl	neutral, sidebend right, rotated left
NSRRP	nerve-sparing radical retropubic prostatectomy
NSS	nephron-sparing surgery
	neurological signs stable
	neurological soft signs
	neuropathy symptom score
	normal size and shape
	not statistically significant
	nutritional support service
	sodium chloride 0.9% (normal saline solution)
NSS-2 Bridge	NeuroStim System 2 (a brain-stimulating device (electro auricular device) for patients suffering from debilitating withdrawal symptoms caused addiction to heroin and other opioids
NSSA	normalized singular spectrum area
NSSC	normal size, shape and consistency (uterus)
NSSI	nonsuicidal self-injury
NSSIB	nonsuicidal self-injurious behavior

N

NSSIs	needlestick and sharps injuries	NSV	nonspecific vaginitis
	nonsuicidal self-injuries	NSVB	normal spontaneous vaginal birth
NSSL	normal size, shape, and location	NSVD	nonstructural valve deterioration
NSSNTFM	normal size shape nontender freely moveable (uterus)		nonstructural valve dysfunction normal spontaneous vaginal
NSSP	normal size, shape, and position		delivery
NSSs	neurological soft signs	NSVT	nonsustained ventricular
NSSTT	nonspecific ST and T-wave		tachycardia
NS-STT	nonspecific ST-segment and T-wave	NSX NSY	neurosurgical examination nursery
NS-STTA	nonspecific ST-segment and T-wave abnormalities	NT	nasotracheal next time
NSSTTW	nonspecific ST-segment and T-wave		Nordic Track® normal temperature
NSSTTWA	nonspecific ST-segment and T-wave abnormalities		normotensive nortriptyline
NSSTW	nonspecific ST segment wave		not tender
NSST-TWCs	nonspecific ST-T-wave changes		not tested
NSSVT	nonsustained supraventricular tachycardia		nourishment taken nuchal translucency (the
NST	no special type		sonographic appearance of
	nonmyeloablative stem-cell		a collection of fluid under
	transplant		the skin behind the fetal
	Nonsense Syllable Test		neck in the first-trimester of
	nonstress test		pregnancy)
	normal sphincter tone		numbness and tingling
	not sooner than		nursing technician
	nutritional support team	N&T	nose and throat
NSTACS	non-ST elevation acute coronary		numbness and tingling
	syndrome	N/T	see NT
NSTD	nonsexually transmitted disease	N Tachy	nodal tachycardia
NSTE	non-ST segment elevation	NT-ANP	N-terminal atrial natriuretic
nSTE-ACS	non-ST-elevation acute coronary		peptide
	syndrome	NTAP	New Technology Add-on
N-STEMI	non-ST-segment elevation		Payment
	myocardial infarction	NTBD	neural-tube birth defect
NSTGCT	nonseminomatous testicular	NTBI	nontransferrin-bound iron
	germ cell tumor	NTBM	nontubercular meningitis
NSTI	necrotizing soft-tissue infection	ntBNP	amino-terminal pro-B-type brain
NSTMI	non-ST-segment elevation		natriuretic peptide
	myocardial infarction	NT-BNP	N-terminal probrain natriuretic
	(N-STEMI)		peptide
NSTs	nerve sheath tumors	NTBR	not to be resuscitated
	nutrition support teams	NTBS	National Transfusion Blood
NSTT	nonseminomatous testicular		Service
	tumors	NTC	neurotrauma center
NSTW	nonbeneficiary status through		non-tunneled catheter
	suspension or termination	NTCC	non-tunneled cuffed catheter
	of disability cash payments	NTCP	normal tissue complication
	due to work (Social Security		probability
	Administration)		normal tissue complication
NSU	neurosurgical unit		probability (radiation therapy)
	nonspecific urethritis	NTCS	no tumor cells seen
NSUD	nonsubstance use dependent	NTD	negative to date
NSURG	NeuroSpine Surgery Research		neural-tube defects
	Group (Prince of Wales		nitroblue tetrazolium dye (test)
	Private Hospital, Sydney,	NTDB	National Trauma Databank
	Australia)	NTDC	nontraumatic dental condition

NTDCs	nontraumatic dental conditions	NT&P	numbness, tingling, and pain
NTDLC	non-tunneled double lumen catheters	N/T/P	numbness, tingling, and pain
		NT-pBNP	N-terminal fragment protein precursor brain natriuretic peptide
NTDs	neglected tropical diseases		
NTE	neutral thermal environment	NTPD	nocturnal tidal peritoneal dialysis
	not to exceed	NTPR	National Transplantation Pregnancy Registry
NTEC	neonatal transient eosinophilic colitis		
		NT-proBNP	N-terminal probrain natriuretic peptide
NTED	neonatal toxic-shock-syndrome-like exanthematous disease		
		NTR	Netherlands Trial Register
NTF	neurotropic factor	NTS	nasotracheal suction
	normal throat flora		nicotine transdermal system
NTG	nitroglycerin		nontyphoidal salmonellae
	nontoxic goiter		nucleus tractus solitarii
	nontreatment group	NTSCI	nontraumatic spinal cord injury
	normal tension glaucoma		
NTGO	nitroglycerin ointment	NTSIP	National Toxic Substance Incidents Program (Centers for Disease Control and Prevention)
NTH	noninsulin-treated hypoglycemia		
	nonteaching hospital		
NTHC	non-tunneled hemodialysis catheter		
		NTSV	nulliparous, term and singleton pregnancies with vertex presentation
nth degree	to the maximum amount		
NTHFR	may have meant MTHFR (methylenetetrahydrofolate reductase)		
		NTT	nasotracheal tube
			near-total thyroidectomy
NTHs	nonteaching hospitals		nonthrombocytopenic term (infant)
NTI	narrow therapeutic index		
	nasotracheal intubation		nonteponemal test
	no treatment indicated	NTTP	no tenderness to palpation
NTICU	neurotrauma intensive care unit	NTTS	nitroglycerin transdermal therapeutic system (patches)
NTIS	National Technical Information Service (U.S. Department of Commerce)		
		NTU	nephelometric turbidity units
		NTUs	nephelometric turbidity units
NTL	nectar-thick liquid (diet consistency)	NTV	nontarget vessel
			nontransvenous
	no time limit	NTW	negative T waves
	nortriptyline (Aventyl; Pamelor)		numbness/tingling/weakness
NTLE	neocortical temporal-lobe epilepsy	N/T/W	numbness, tingling, weakness
		NTWs	negative T waves
NTM	nocturnal tumescence monitor	NTX	naltrexone (ReVia)
	nontuberculous mycobacterium		neurotoxicity
NTMB	nontuberculous myobacteria	Ntx	N-telopeptide
NTMI	nontransmural myocardial infarction	NTZ	natalizumab (Tysabri)
			nitazoxanide (Alinia)
			nitrazine paper
NTND	not tender, not distended	NTZ Long-acting®	oxymetazoline nasal spray
NT/ND	not tender, not distended		
NTO	nonthrombotic occlusion	NU	name unknown
NTOS	neurogenic thoracic outlet syndrome	NuA4	nucleosome acetyltransferase of H4 (histone acetyltransferase complex)
NTP	narcotic treatment program		
	National Toxicology Program		
	non-ThinPrep (slides)	NUB	see gene website, www.ncbi.nlm.nih.gov/gene
	nonthrombocytopenic preterm (infant)		
		NUC	see gene website, www.ncbi.nlm.nih.gov/gene
	normal temperature and pressure		
	numbness, tingling, and pain	Nuc Med	Nuclear Medicine Department
	sodium nitroprusside	NUCOG	neuropsychiatry unit cognitive assessment tool

N

NUD	nonulcer dyspepsia	NVCD	non-VWD (von Willebrand disease) coagulation defect
NuDESC	Nursing Delirium Screening Scale		
Nu-DESC	Nursing Delirium Screening Scale	N/V/C/D	nausea, vomiting, constipation, and diarrhea
nuets%	per cent of white blood cells that are neutrophils	nvCJD	new-variant Creutzfeldt-Jakob disease
NUG	necrotizing ulcerative gingivitis		
nullip	nullipara	NVD	nausea, vomiting, and diarrhea
num	number		neck vein distention
NUN	nonurea nitrogen		neovascularization of the (optic) disc
NURF	nonuremic renal failure		
	nucleosome remodeling factor		neurovesicle dysfunction
	see gene website, www.ncbi.nlm .nih.gov/gene		no venereal disease
			no venous distention
Nuss	as in the Nuss Procedure, a minimally-invasive procedure, invented by Dr. Donald Nuss for treating pectus excavatum		nonvalvular disease
			normal vaginal delivery
		N/V/D	nausea, vomiting, diarrhea
		NVDC	nausea, vomiting, diarrhea, and constipation
NUSS	Non-Union Scoring System (long bones)	N/V/D/C	nausea, vomiting, diarrhea, and constipation
nutr	nutrition	NVDRS	National Violent Death Reporting System
NUTRIC score	NUTrition RIsk in Critically Ill		
NUTS	Nomenclature of Territorial Units for Statistics (Nomenclature of Territorial Units for Statistics [European Union])	NVE	native
			native valve endocarditis
			neovascularization elsewhere
		NVF	nonvertebral fracture
		N/V/F/C	nausea, vomiting, fever, and chills
Nux	part of the name, Nux Vomica, a homeopath remedy	N/V/F/C/SOB	nausea, vomiting, fever, chills, or shortness of breath
NV	naked vision	NVG	neovascular glaucoma
	nausea and vomiting		neoviridogrisein
	near vision	NVI	neovascularization of the iris
	negative variation	NVID	neurovascular intact distally
	neovascularization	NVIE	native valve infective endocarditis
	neurovascular		
	Nevada	NVIU	neurovascular Intermediate unit
	new vessel	NVL	neurovascular laboratory
	next visit	NVLD	nonverbal learning disability
	nonvenereal	NVM	neovascular membrane
	nonveteran		noncompaction of the ventricular myocardium
	normal value		
	Noroviruses	NV-MSVT	Nonverbal Medical Symptom Validity Test
	not vaccinated		
	not verified	NVN	Netherlands Society of Neurology
N&V	nausea and vomiting		
N/V	nausea and vomiting	nVNS	noninvasive vagal nerve stimulator
N+V	nausea and vomiting		
NVA	near visual acuity	NVO	near vision only (glasses prescription)
NVAF	nonvalvular atrial fibrillation		
NVAS	numeric visual analog scale	NVOP	neurovascular orofacial pain (facial migraine)
NVB	Navelbine (vinorelbine tartrate)		
	neurovascular bundle	NVP	nausea and vomiting of pregnancy
NVBo	oral vinorelbine		nevirapine (Viramune)
NVC	nailfold video capillaroscopy	NVR	nonviolent restraint
	neurovascular checks	NVS	neurological vital signs
	neurovascular compression		neurovascular status
NVCC	non-VA (Veterans Administration) Care Consultant	NVSCs	nonverbal social cues

NVSD	may have meant NSVD (normal spontaneous vaginal delivery	NYB	New York Blood Center
NVSI	National Vaccine and Serum Institute (China)	NYC	New York City, New York, USA
		NYD	not yet diagnosed
NVSS	normal variant short stature	NY-ESO-1	New York esophageal squamous cell carcinoma 1
NVST	neurovascular spastic torticollis		
NVT	nonvaccine types (serotypes)	NYHA	New York Heart Association (classification of heart disease)
NVUGIB	nonvariceal upper gastrointestinal bleeding		
NW	naked weight	NYHA 1	New York Heart Association Class 1 (classification of heart disease- Patients with cardiac disease but without result- ing in limitation of physical activity. Ordinary physical activity does not cause undue fatigue, palpitation, dyspnea, or anginal pain)
	nasal wash		
	nasal width		
	no worse		
	normal weight		
	Northwest		
	not weighed		
NWB	nonweight bearing	NYHA 2	New York Heart Association Class 2 (classification of heart disease- Patients with cardiac disease resulting in slight limitation of physical activity. They are comfortable at rest. Ordinary physical activity results in fatigue, palpitation, dyspnea, or anginal pain.)
NWBing	nonweight bearing		
NWBL	nonweight bearing, left		
NWB LLE	nonweight bearing, left lower extremity		
NWBR	nonweight bearing, right		
NWB RLE	nonweight bearing, right lower extremity		
NWC	number of words chosen		
NWD	neuroleptic withdrawal	NYHA 3	New York Heart Association Class 3 (classification of heart disease- Patients with cardiac disease resulting in marked limitation of physical activity. They are comfortable at rest. Less than ordinary activity causes fatigue, palpitation, dyspnea, or anginal pain.)
	normal well developed		
NWI	normalized wall index		
	notch width index		
	Nursing Work Index		
NWI-R	Nursing Work Index-Revised		
NWL	needle-wire localization		
	nonweight losers		
NWPT	negative wound pressure therapy		
NWR	nociceptive withdrawal reflex	NYHA 4	New York Heart Association Class 4 (classification of heart disease- Patients with cardiac disease resulting in the inabil- ity to carry on any physical activity without discomfort. Symptoms of heart failure or the anginal syndrome may be present even at rest. If any physical activity is undertaken, discomfort is increased)
	nonword repetition (test;score)		
NWS	New World screwworm (*Cochliomyia hominivorax* [Coquerel])		
NWTS	National Wilms Tumor Study (rating scale)		
NWTSG	National Wilms Tumor Study Group		
Nx	nephrectomy		
	next		
NX211	liposomal lurtotecan	NYHA class	see NYHA
NXG	necrobiotic xanthrogranuloma	NYPD	New York Police Department
NXT	Naoxintong Capsule (a traditional Chinese medicine for the treatment of cardiovascular and cerebrovascular diseases)	NYRFE	not yet ready for extubation
		NYSDOH	New York State Department of Health
		nyst	nystagmus
NXY-059	disufenton sodium (Cerovive)	NYU	New York University
NY	New York	NZ	enzyme
NYAH	New York Heart Association (classification of heart disease) (Romance languages; see NYHA)	nZVI	nanoscale zerovalent iron

N

O

O	eye
	objective findings
	obvious
	occlusal
	often
	open
	oral
	ortho
	Oscar (Phonetic Alphabet for O; pronounced OSS-CAH)
	other
	output
	oxygen
	pint
	pyrrolysine
	zero
°	degrees (as in 40° C; 40 degrees centigrade)
	hours (as in every 4°). This is a dangerous abbreviation as it is read as a zero.
"	ditto
	foot
	hour
	inch
	inch (inches)
	second
ō	negative
	no
	none
	pint
	without
O+	blood type O positive (O positive is preferred)
O +	blood type O positive (O positive is preferred)
O−	blood type O negative (O negative is preferred)
O −	blood type O negative (O negative is preferred)
O×1	oriented to time
O×2	oriented to time and place
O×3	oriented to time, place, and person
O×4	oriented to time, place, person, and objects (watch, pen, book)
Ⓞ	orally (by mouth)
O157	Escherichia coli O157
O2	both eyes
	oxygen
O2−	superoxide
O3	ozone
OA	occipital artery
	occipitoatlantal

	occiput anterior
	old age
	on admission
	on arrival
	open abdomen (procedure)
	ophthalmic artery
	optic atrophy
	oral airway
	oral alimentation
	osteoarthritis
	Other Adjustments (Medicare code)
	ovarian ablation
	Overeaters Anonymous
O & A	observation and assessment
	odontectomy and alveoloplasty
O/A	on or about
OAA	Old Age Assistance
	oral anticancer agent(s)
OAA/S	Observer's Assessment of Alertness/Sedation
OAAs	oral anticancer agents
OAB	overactive bladder
OAB-q	Overactive Bladder Questionnaire
OABSS	overactive bladder symptoms score
OAC	occipital artery catheterization
	oesophageal adenocarcinoma (UK and other countries)
	omeprazole, amoxicillin, and clarithromycin
	oral anticoagulant(s)
	overaction
OACA	oral anticancer agent
OACD	occupational allergic contact dermatitis
	oral anticancer drug
OACDs	oral anticancer drugs
OACIS	Osaka Acute Coronary Insufficiency Study
OAD	obliterative airway disease
	occlusive arterial disease
	overall diameter
OAE	otoacoustic emissions
OAEs	otoacoustic emissions
OAF	oral anal fistula
	osteoclast activating factor
OAG	open angle glaucoma
OAGB	one-anastomosis gastric bypass
OAH	obesity-associated hypoventilation
	osteoarthritis of the hip
oah	see gene website, www.ncbi .nlm.nih.gov/gene
OAHI	obstructive apnea-hypopnea index
OAI	Osteoarthritis Initiative (database)
OAL	ocular adnexal lymphoma

OALT	orthotopic autologous liver transplantation	OATH	obstruction due to adenotonsillar hypertrophy
OAM	omeprazole, amoxicillin, and metronidazole	OATP	organic anion transporting polypeptide
OAMER	over-active milk ejection reflex	OATS procedure	Osteochondral Autograft Transfer System (a procedure for transplantation of hyaline cartilage)
OAN	oncocytic adrenocortical neoplasm(s)		
O and P	ova and parasites (stool examination)	OAV	oculoauriculovertebral (dysplasia)
OA/OS	ovarian ablation/suppression	OAVS	oculoauriculovertebral spectrum
OAP	old age pension	OAW	oral airway
OAR	off-access ratio	OB	obese
	organ at risk (from radiation therapy)		obesity
			obliterative bronchiolitis
	Ottawa Ankle Rules		obstetrics
O-arm	Intraoperative registration and ver-		occult blood
	ification of anatomic landmarks		oceanic boundlessness
	performed with a 3-dimensional		osteoblast
	mobile computed tomography-	OBA	Office of Biotechnology
	guided system (Medtronic,		Activities (NIH)
	Minneapolis MN)		office-based anesthesia
OARRS	Automated Rx (prescription)	OB-A	obstetrics-aborted
	Reporting System (Ohio)	OBB	office-based biopsy
OARs	organs at risk		open breast biopsy
	organs at risk (from radiation		optical bidirectional beacon
	therapy)	OBC	objectified body consciousness
OARSI	Osteoarthritis Research		oral birth control
	Society International	OBD	obscure digestive bleeding
	(recommendations)		opioid-induced bowel
OARSS	may have meant OARRS		dysfunction
	(Ohio Automated Rx		optimal biologic dose
	Reporting System)	OB-Del	obstetrics-delivered
	may have meant OARS (organs at	OBE	objective binge eating
	risk (from radiation therapy))		out-of-body experience
OAS	Older Adult Services	OBE-CALP	placebo capsule or tablet
	oral allergy syndrome	OBER	Office of Biological and
	organic anxiety syndrome		Environmental Research
	outpatient assessment service		(Department of Energy)
	overall survival	OBERD	Outcomes Based Electronic
	Overt Aggression Scale		Research Database
OAs	oral anticancer agents		www.oberd.com
OASDHI	Old Age, Survivors, Disability,	obes	obesity
	and Health Insurance	OBF	ocular blood flow
OASDI	Old-Age, Survivors, and		orbital blowout fracture(s)
	Disability Insurance	Ob-Gyn	obstetrics and gynecology
	(Social Security Program)	OBI	occult hepatitis B infection
OASI	Old Age and Survivors Insurance	obits	obituary
OASIS	Outcomes and Assessment	OBJ	objective function
	Information Set	Obj	objective
OASO	overactive superior oblique	ObjN	Object Naming
OASR	overactive superior rectus	OBL	osteoblasts
OASS	Overt Agitation Severity Scale	obl	oblique
OAT	oligoasthenoteratozoospermia	OBmarg	obtuse marginal
	opioid agonist treatments	OBMT	omeprazole, bismuth salt, metro-
	oral anticoagulant therapy		nidazole, and tetracycline
	ornithine aminotransferase		Outpatient Based Medical Team
	osteochondral autologous	OB-ND	obstetrics-not delivered
	transplantation	OBOC	one-bead one-compound

OBOR	obstetric operating room	OCC	occasionally
OBP	office blood pressure		occipital
OBPP	obstetric brachial plexus palsy		occlusal
OBR	optimized background regimen		occlusion
OBRA	Omnibus Budget		old chart called
	Reconciliation Act	OCCAs	ovarian clear cell adenocarcinomas
OBRR	obstetric recovery room	occas	occasional
OBS	obstetrical service	OCCC	open chest cardiac compression
	Office-Based Surgery		ovarian clear cell carcinoma
	organic brain syndrome	occl	occlusion
obs	observed (observation)	OCCM	open chest cardiac massage
Obst	obstetrician	OCC PR	open chest cardiopulmonary
	obstetrics		resuscitation
obstr	obstruction	OCC Th	occupational therapy
obsv	observation(s)	Occup Rx	occupational therapy
	observed	OCD	obsessive-compulsive disorder
OBT	obtained		osteochondritis dissecans
	optimized background therapy	OCE	oral cannabis extract
OBTC	on-bead two-color		outpatient code editor
OBTM	omeprazole, bismuth subcitrate,	OCF	osteopathy in the cranial field
	tetracycline, and metronidazole	OCFAs	odd-chain fatty acids
	(for eradicating Helicobacter	OCFD	obsessive-compulsive Facebook
	pylori infections)		disorder
OBUS	obstetrical ultrasound	OCG	oral cholecystogram
OBV	Oblique view (mode)	OCH	orbital cavernous hemangioma
	olfactory bulb ventricle	OCHA	Office for the Coordination
OBW	open bed warmer		of Humanitarian Affairs
OBx	open biopsy		(United Nations)
OC	observed cases	OCHIN	Oregon Community Health
	obstetrical conjugate		Information Network
	occlusal curvature (dental)	OCHS	Oculocerebral Hypopigmentation
	off cord		Syndrome (Cross Syndrome)
	office call	OcHTN	ocular hypertension
	on call	OCI	Obsessive-Compulsive Inventory
	only child		optic canal involvement
	open cholecystectomy	OCIS	Orthogonal Cultural
	open colectomy		Identification Scale
	open crib	OCIs	occipitocervical injuries
	optical chromatography	OCJ	osteochondral junction
	oral care	OCK	Ockelbo virus
	oral contraceptive	OCL	occlusion
	osteocalcin		Orthopedic Casting Laboratory
	osteoclast		(splint)
	ovarian cancer		osteoclasts
	OxyContin (oxycodone)	OCL®	oral colonic lavage
	oxygen concentrator	o-CLAD	obstructive chronic lung allograft
O & C	onset and course		dysfunction
O/C	off cord	OCM	Oncology Care Model (Centers
OCA	obeticholic acid (Ocaliva)		for Medicare and Medicaid)
	oculocutaneous albinism		one-carbon metabolism
	open care area		optical coherence microscopy
	oral contraceptive agent		other-cause of mortality
	osteochondral allograft	OCME	Office of the Chief Medical
OCAD	obstructive coronary artery		Examiner
	disease	OCN	obsessive-compulsive neurosis
OCAs	osteochondral allografts		Oncology Certified Nurse
OCB	obstructive chronic bronchitis	OCNS	Obsessive-Compulsive
OCBZ	oxcarbazepine (Trileptal)		Neurosis Scale

O-CNV	occult choroidal neovascularization	
OC/OP	oral cavity and oropharynx	
OCOPs	online communities of practice	
OCOR	on-call to operating room	
OCP	ocular cicatricial pemphigoid	
	Onchocerciasis Control Program	
	oral contraceptive pills	
	ova, cysts, parasites	
OCPD	obsessive-compulsive personality disorder	
OCPs	oral contraceptive pills	
	organochlorine pesticides	
OCR	oculocephalic reflex	
	optical character recognition	
OCS	Obsessive-Compulsive Scale	
	obsessive-compulsive symptoms	
	Office of Child Services (government agency)	
	oral cancer screening	
11-OCS	11-oxycorticosteroid	
OCT	octreotide (Sandostatin)	
	optical coherence tomograph (tomography)	
	oral cavity tumors	
	ornithine carbamyl transferase	
	oxytocin challenge test	
Oct	October	
OCTA	optical coherence tomography angiography	
OCTD	open carpal tunnel decompression	
OCTOR	software that analyzes optical coherence tomography images	
OCTR	open carpal tunnel release	
OCU	observation care unit	
OCVD	other cardiovascular disease	
OCVM	occult cerebrovascular malformations	
OCX	oral cancer examination	
OCy	osteocyte	
OD	Doctor of Optometry	
	Officer-of-the-Day	
	oligodendroglial	
	on duty	
	once daily (This is a DANGEROUS abbreviation that should NOT be used. It appears on the medabbrev. com and other Do Not Use Lists, as this is commonly understood to mean right eye; spell out "once daily")	
	open discectomy	
	optic disc	
	optical density	
	optical density (radiology)	
	oral-duodenal	

	oropharyngeal dysphagia	
	outdoor	
	outside diameter	
	ovarian dysgerminoma	
	overdose	
	right eye	
ODA	occipitodextra anterior	
	once-daily aminoglycoside	
	osmotic driving agent	
ODAC	Oncologic Drugs Advisory Committee (of the US Food and Drug Administration)	
	on-demand analgesia computer	
ODAT	one day at a time	
ODB	outpatient database	
ODC	oral disease control	
	ornithine decarboxylase	
	outpatient diagnostic center	
ODCH	ordinary diseases of childhood	
ODCs	ozone-depleting chemicals	
ODD	oculodentodigital (dysplasia)	
	opposition defiance disorder	
OD'd	overdosed	
ODDs	orally disintegration dosage (forms)	
ODE	optic disc edema	
ODECL	open-door expansile cervical laminoplasty	
ODed	overdosed	
ODF	orally disintegrating film	
ODF1	outer dense fiber of sperm tails 1 (gene)	
ODG	oligodendroglioma	
	open distal gastrectomy	
ODH	obstructed diaphragmatic hernia	
	optic disc hemorrhage(s)	
	oxidative dehydrogenation	
ODI	Oswestry Disability Index	
	oxygen desaturation index	
ODM	occlusion dose monitor	
	Operational Data Model	
	ophthalmodynamometry	
ODMP	on-going date management plan	
ODN	optokinetic nystagmus	
ODO	osteotomy distraction osteogenesis	
ODP	occipitodextra posterior	
	offspring of diabetic parents	
OD/P	right eye patched	
ODQ	on direct questioning	
ODS	obstructed defecation syndrome	
	Office of Drug Safety (FDA)	
	organized delivery system	
	osmotic demyelination syndrome	
ODSH	2-O, 3-O-desulfated heparin	
ODSS	Office of Disability Support Services	
ODSU	oncology day stay unit	
	One-Day Surgery Unit	

O

ODT	occipitodextra transerve	O₂ER	oxygen extraction ratio
	optical Doppler tomography	OERR	order entry/results-reports
	orally disintegrating tablet		(Veterans Administration's
ODTS	organic dust toxic syndrome		physician computer order
ODU	optical density units		entry system)
ODVs	occlusion-derived viruses	OES	optical emission spectroscopy
ODX	Oncotype Dx ™ (an assay	OET	oral esophageal tube
	for breast cancer treatment	OETT	oral endotracheal tube
	planning by exploring the	OF	occipital-frontal
	expression of 21 genes)		optic fundi
odx	oxaloacetate decarboxylase;		osteitis fibrosa
	see gene website www.ncbi		outlet forceps (delivery)
	.nlm.nih.gov/gene		ovarian function
OE	oblique external (muscles)	O/F	oral facial
	on examination	OFA	occipital face area
	on exertion		Occlusal Fingerprint Analyser
	orthopedic examination		ofatumumab (Arzerra)
	otitis externa	OFAR	oxaliplatin, fludarabine, cytarabine
O&E	observation and examination		(ara-C), and rituximab
O-E	standard observed minus	OFC	occipital-frontal circumference
	expected		orbitofacial cleft
OEA	oleoylethanolamide		osteitis fibrosa cystica
OEC	Orthopedic Equipment Company	OFD	occipitofrontal diameter
	outer ear canal		open-flap debridement
	oxygen-evolving complex	OFDI	optical frequency domain
OECD	Organization for Economic		imaging
	Cooperation and Development	OFDS	orofaciodigital syndrome(s)
OECs	olfactory ensheathing cells	OFF	shoes off during weighing
OED	optimal experiment design	OFFD	organ-failure-free days
	oral epithelial dysplasia	OFG	orofacial granulomatosis
	organ-equivalent doses	OFH	osteonecrosis of the
OEF	Operation Enduring Freedom		femoral head
	(Afghanistan)	OFI	other febrile illness
	oxygen extraction fraction	OFLOX	ofloxacin (Floxin)
OEF/OIF/OND	Operation Enduring Freedom	OFLX	ofloxacin (Floxin)
	and Operation Iraqi Freedom/	OFM	open-face mask
	Operation New Dawn		oral focal mucinosis
OEI	opioid escalation index	OFMs	oral-facial movements
O₂EI	oxygen extraction index	OFNE	oxygenated fluorocarbon
OEIS complex	a combination of defects		nutrient emulsion
	consisting in omphalocele,	OFPF	optic fundi and peripheral fields
	bladder exstrophy,	OFR	oxygen-free radicals
	imperforate anus and	OFRs	ocular following responses
	spinal defects	OFS	osteoplastic frontal sinusotomy
OEL	occupational exposure level	OFTT	organic failure to thrive
OEM	Occupational and Environmental	OFV	objective function value
	Medicine	OG	Obstetrics-Gynecology
	original equipment manufacturer		orogastric (feeding)
	ovarian endometriosis		outcome goal (long-term goal)
OENT	oral endotracheal tube	Og	oganesson
OEP	Office of Emergency	OGA	O-GlcNAcase; see gene website
	Preparedness		www.ncbi.nlm.nih.gov/gene
	oil of evening primrose	Ogap	optical gap
	(evening primrose oil)	OGC	oculogyric crisis
OEPA	vincristine (Oncovin), etoposide,	OGCT	ovarian germ cell tumor
	prednisone, and doxorubicin	OGD	oesophagogastroduodenoscopy
	(Adriamycin)		(United Kingdom and
OER	oxygen extraction ratios		other countries)

	Office of Generic Drugs (of the Food and Drug Administration)	OHFT	overhead frame and trapeze
		OHG	oral hypoglycemic
		OHHs	Oncological-Hospitals-at-Home
OGF	opioid growth factor	OHI	oral hygiene instructions
OGFr	opioid growth factor receptor	OHIAA	hydroxyindolacetic acid
OGGT	see OGTT	OHL	oral hairy leukoplakia
OGIB	obscure gastrointestinal bleeding	ohm	the electrical resistance between
OGM	olfactory groove meningioma		two points of a conductor
	overgeneral (autobiographical)		when a constant potential
	memory		difference of 1 volt, applied
OGNP	Obstetric-Gynecology Nurse		to these points, produces
	Practitioner		in the conductor a current
OGPA	oxygen generating portable		of 1 ampere
	equipment	7-OHMTX	7-hydroxymethotrexate
OGS	Observational Gait Scale	OHNBS	may have meant OHNS
	osteogenic sarcoma		(otolaryngology-head
OGT	orogastric tube		and neck surgery)
	Oxford Gene Technology	OHNS	oncologic head and neck surgery
	(Oxford UK)		Otolaryngology, Head, and
OGTT	oral glucose tolerance test		Neck Surgery (Dept.)
OG tube	orogastric tube	OHP	obese hypertensive patient
OH	occupational history		oxygen under hyperbaric pressure
	ocular history	OHPC	hydroxyprogesterone caproate
	ocular hypertension		inj (Makena)
	Ohio	OHPG	17-hydroxyprogesterone
	on hand	OHQOL	oral health-related quality of life
	open-heart	OHR	open hernia repair
	oral hygiene	OHRP	Office for Human Research
	orthostatic hypotension		Protections (Department of
	outside hospital		Health Human Services)
	over head		open-heart rehabilitation
−OH	hydroxyl		program
17-OH	17-hydroxycorticosteroids	OHR-QOL	oral health-related quality of life
O/H	see OH	OHRR	open-heart recovery room
OHA	oral hypoglycemic agents	OHS	obesity hypoventilation
OHB	occult hepatitis B		syndrome
	oral hygiene behavior		occupational health service
O₂Hb	oxyhemoglobin		ocular histoplasmosis syndrome
OHC	outer hair cell (in cochlea)		ocular hypoperfusion syndrome
OHCA	out-of-hospital cardiac arrest		open-heart surgery
OHCbl	hydroxycobalamine		Oxford hip score
OHCM	obstructive hypertrophic	OHSS	ovarian hyperstimulation
	cardiomyopathy		syndrome
	Ossabaw (a swine model) high	oHSV	oncolytic herpes simplex virus
	cholesterol with metformin	OHT	ocular hypertension
OHCP	4-hydroxycyclophosphamide		overhead trapeze
	oral health care professional	OHTN	ocular hypertension
	oral health care provider	OHTx	orthotopic heart transplantation
17-OHCS	17-hydroxycorticosteroids	OHU	Occupational Health Unit
25(OH)D₃	25-hydroxy vitamin D		(United Kingdom)
	(calcifediol, Calderol)		open heart unit
OHD	hydroxy vitamin D	OHV	oral health visit
	organic heart disease	OHV-2	ovine herpesvirus-2
OHE	overt hepatic encephalopathy	OHVIRA	obstructed hemivagina and
OHF	old healed fracture		ipsilateral renal anomaly
	Omsk hemorrhagic fever		(a rare syndrome charac-
	overhead frame		terized by Müllerian duct
OHFA	hydroxy fatty acid		and renal anomalies)

O

OHVS	Obesity Hypoventilation Syndrome	OJD	Objective Judgement Discrepancy
OI	obesity index		Ovine Johne's Disease
	opportunistic infection	OJI	on the job injury
	orthostatic intolerance	OJT	on-the-job training
	osteogenesis imperfecta		orojejunal tube
	otitis interna	OK	all right
	ovulation induction		approved
	oxygen index		correct
OIC	opioid-induced constipation		Ok; an International Society
OICA	ophthalmic segment of the		of Blood Transfusion (ISBT)
	internal carotid artery		blood group
OICD	occupational irritant contact		Oklahoma
	dermatitis		orthokeratology contact lens
OICU	obstetric intensive care unit	Ok-a	a blood group antigen
OID	orbital inflammatory disease	Ok(a)	a blood group antigen
OIE	Office International des	OK'd	approved; agreed
	Epizooties (now known	OKAN	optokinetic after nystagmus
	as the World Organization	OKC	odontogenic keratocyst
	for Animal Health)		open kinetic chain (exercises)
	World Organization for Animal	OKd	approved; agreed
	Health	OKN	optokinetic nystagmus
OIF	oil-immersion field	OKS	Oxford Knee Score
	Operation Iraqi Freedom	OKT	Ortho Kung T-cell, designation
OIG	Office of the Inspector General		for a series of antigens
OIH	opioid-induced hyperalgesia	OL	left eye
	orthoiodohippurate		open label (study)
OIHA	orthoiodohippuric acid		open-loop
OI&I	occupational injury and illness	OLA	occipitolaevoanterior
OIM	optical immunoassay		occiput left anterior
OIN	oxaliplatin (Eloxatin)-induced	oLAD	ostial left anterior descending
	neurotoxicity		(coronary artery)
OINT	ointment	OLAP	online analytical processing
OIP	opioid-induced pruritus	OLB	open-liver biopsy
	opportunistic intestinal	OLBPQ	Oswestry Low Back Pain
	parasites		Questionnaire
	other indicated procedures	OLBx	open-lung biopsy
	outpatient individual	OLC	ouabain-like compound
	psychotherapy	OLD	obstructive lung disease
OIR	oxygen-indyced retinopathy	OLE	olive leaf extract
OIRDA	occipital intermittent rhythmical		open-label extension
	delta activity	OLED	optimal long exposure dose
OIS	ocular ischemic syndrome		organic light emitting diode
	optical intrinsic signal	OLF	ouabain-like factor
	(imaging)	OLGB	omega-loop gastric bypass
	optimum information size	OLH	open left hepatectomy
Ois	opportunitisic infections	OLHD	One Leg Hop for Distance test
OIT	ovarian immature teratoma	OLIF	oblique lumbar interbody fusion
OIU	optical internal urethrotomy	oligo	oligohydramnios
OJ	orange juice. This is a	OLINDA/EXM	personal computer code per-
	DANGEROUS abbreviation		forms dose calculations and
	that should **NOT** be used.		kinetic modeling for radio-
	It appears on the MedAbbrev		pharmaceuticals (Organ Level
	and other "Do Not Use		INternal Dose Assessment/
	Lists," as it has been read as		EXponential Modeling)
	left or right eye (OS or OD).	OLL	oral lichenoid lesions
	Use "orange juice."	OLLO	Oldenburg Logatome Corpus
	orthoplast jacket		(a speech database)

O

OLM	ocular larva migrans		oral motor exercise
	ophthalmic laser microendoscope		otitis media with effusion
OLNM	occult lymph node metastases	OMED	oral morphine equivalent dose
OLP	oral lichen planus	7-OMEN	menogaril
OLR	optic labyrinthine righting	OMERACT-	Outcome measures in
	otology, laryngology, and	OARSI	Rheumatology Clinical
	rhinology		Trials-Osteoarthritis
OLRM	ordinary linear regression model		Research Society
OLS	ordinary least squares		International
	ouabain-like substance	OMEs	oral morphine equivalents
OLT	occipitolaevoposterior	OM3-FFA	omega-3 free fatty acid
	orthotopic liver transplantation	OMFS	oral and maxillofacial surgery
OLTP	online transaction processing	OMG	ocular myasthenia gravis
OLTx	orthotopic liver transplantation	OMH	Office of Mental Health
OLV	one-lung ventilation		(New York State)
OLZ	olanzapine (Zyprexa)	OMI	old myocardial infarct
OM	every morning (this is a	OMIEI	oral medication induced
	dangerous abbreviation)		esophageal injury
	obtuse marginal	OMIF	oral maxillofacial
	ocular melanoma	OMIN	Online Mendelian Inheritance
	oral motor		in Man
	oral mucositis	OMJ	oral moisturizing jelly
	organomegaly		osteomyelitis of the jaw
	osteomalacia	OML	oral mucosal lesion(s)
	osteomyelitis	OMM	optimized medical management
	otitis media		oral mucosal melanoma
O_2M	oxygen mask		osteopathic manipulative
OM_1	first obtuse marginal branch of		medicine
	the circumflex coronary artery		outer mitochondrial membrane
OM1/2	obtuse marginal branches 1/2	OMN	oligomeganephronia
	(coronary artery)	OMP	oculomotor (third nerve) palsy
OM1/2/3	obtuse marginal branches 1/2/3		open mediastinal biopsy
	(coronary artery)	OMPA	otitis media, purulent, acute
OM_2	second obtuse marginal	OMPC	otitis media, purulent, chronic
	branch of the circumflex	OMR	operative mortality rate
	coronary artery	OMS	oral morphine sulfate
OM3	omega-3 fatty acids		organic mental syndrome
OM4	obtuse marginal 4 branch		organic mood syndrome
	(coronary artery)		Ostomy Management Specialist
OMA	older maternal age	OMSA	otitis media secretory
OMAAV	otitis media with ANCA		(or suppurative) acute
	(anti-neutrophil cytoplasm	OMSC	otitis media secretory
	antibody)-associated vasculitis		(or suppurative) chronic
OMAC	otitis media, acute, catarrhal	OMSS	order management scanning
OMAS	Olerud-Molander Ankle Score		system
	otitis media, acute, suppurating	OMT	omentectomy
OMB	obtuse marginal branch		opiate maintenance treatments
	Office of Management and		oral mucosal transudate
	Budget		Osteopathic manipulative
OMB_1	first obtuse marginal branch		treatment
OMB_2	second obtuse marginal branch	OMU-CT	ostiomeatal unit-computed
OMC	open mitral commissuortomy		tomography
	ostiomeatal complex	OMVC	open mitral valve
OMCA	otitis media, catarrhalis, acute		commissurotomy
OMCC	otitis media, catarrhalis, chronic	OMVD	optimized microvessel density
OMD	organic mental disorder		(analysis)
OME	Office of Medical Examiner	OMVI	operating motor vehicle
	oral morphine equivalent		intoxicated

OMW	one-minute walk	ONH	older normal-hearing
OMX	omentectomy		optic nerve head
	optical microscopy experimental		optic nerve hypoplasia
ON	every night (this is a dangerous	ONJ	osteonecrosis of the jaw
	abbreviation)	ONL	out of normal limits
	optic nerve	ONM	ocular neuromyotonia
	optic neuritis	ONO	Otoneuroophthalmology
	optic neurophathy	ONP	oculomotor nerve palsy
	oronasal	ONPO$_2$	optic nerve oxygen tension
	Ortho-Novum®	ONPS	oronasopharyngeal suction
	osteonecrosis	ON-Q®	an automatic-continuous
	overnight		delivery local anesthetic
O/N	oxygen-to-nitrogen ratio		pump and catheter
ONA	optic nerve aplasia	ONQI	Overall Nutritional Quality
	optic nerve avulsion		Index
ONAP	other nonaffective psychoses	ONRR	overnight recovery room
ONB	occipital nerve block	ONS	Office for National Statistics
	olfactory neuroblastoma		(United Kingdom)
	orthotopic neobladder		Oncology Nursing Society
ONBs	occipital nerve blocks		oral nutritional supplement
	olfactory neuroblastomas	ONSD	optic nerve sheath decompression
ONC	Office of the National	ONSF	optic nerve sheath fenestration
	Coordinator (for Health	ONSI	Observation-based Nocturnal
	Information Technology		Sleep Inventory
	oncology	ONSR	overnight swelling response
	Orthopedic Nurse, Certified		(corneal)
	over-the-needle catheter	ONTD	open neural tube defect(s)
	vincristine (Oncovin)	ONTR	orders not to resuscitate
	(note: for intraVENOUS	OO	olive oil
	administration only)		ophthalmic ointment
once a day	see once daily		oral order
once a month	There is no widely acceptable,		osteoid osteoma
	recognized abbreviation for		out of
	monthly or once a month,	O&O	off and on
	write it out.	o/o	on account of
once a week	There is no widely acceptable,	O2O3	oxygen-ozone (therapy)
	recognized abbreviation	OOA	Office of Aging
	for weekly or once a week,		Old Order Amish
	write it out.	OOB	out of bed
once daily	there is no safe abbreviation	OOBA	4-octyldecyloxybenzoic acid
	as OD also means right	OOBBRP	out of bed with bathroom
	eye and handwriten QD		privileges
	has been mistaken for	OOBL	out of bilirubin light
	four times daily (QID);	OOBTC	out of bed to chair
	use- once daily	OOBTT	out of bed to toilet
once per day	there is no safe abbreviation	OOC	onset of contractions
	as OD also means right eye		out of cast
	and handwriten QD has been		out of control
	mistaken for four times daily	OO Con	out of control
	(QID); use- once daily	OOCS	opioid and other controlled
OND	Office of New Drugs (FDA)		substances
	ondansetron (Zofran)	OOD	out of doors
	other neurologic disorder(s)		outer orbital diameter
ONDCP	Office of the National Drug	OO-EMG	electromyographic recording of
	Control Policy (US President's		the orbicularis oculi muscles
	Commission)	OOF	out of facility
ONF	oronasal fistula	OOH	out of hospital
ONFH	osteonecrosis of the femoral head	OOHA	out of hospital (cardiac) arrest

OOHCA	out-of-hospital cardiac arrest	OPAD	older people with advanced dementia
OOH-GP	out-of-hours general practitioner		Orofacial Pain Assessment Device
OOH&NS	ophthalmology, otorhinolaryngology, and head and neck surgery	oPAD	origami paper analytical device
OOH-PC	out-of-hours primary care	oPAP	Online Personal Action Plan
OOI	out of isolette	OPAT	outpatient parenteral antibiotic therapy
OOL	onset of labor		
OOLR	ophthalmology, otology, laryngology, and rhinology	OPB	outpatient basis
		OPC	operable pancreatic carcinoma
OOM	onset of menarche		oropharyngeal candidiasis
OON	out of network (health insurance)		oropharynx cancer
OOO	of obscure origin		outpatient care
	on our own (slang)		outpatient catheterization
	one on one		outpatient clinic
	out of office	OPCA	olivopontocerebellar atrophy
	out of the ordinary	OPCAB	off-pump coronary artery bypass (grafting)
OOP	out of pelvis		
	out of plaster	OPCABG	off-pump coronary artery bypass grafting
	out on pass		
	out-of-pocket	OPCD	olivopontocerebellar degeneration
OOPD	Office of Orphan Product Development (FDA)	op cit	in the work cited
		OPCR	outpatient cardiac rehabilitation
Ooph	oophorectomized	OPCs	oligodendrocyte cells
OOPS	out of program status		oligodendrocyte precursor cells
	out-of-pocket spending		oligodendrocyte progenitor cells
OOR	out of room	OPCS-4	Classification of Surgical Operations and Procedures (4th revision)
	out-of-range (values)		
OORW	out of radiant warmer		
OOS	out of sequence	OPCx	oligodendrocyte progenitor cells
	out of specification (deviation from standard)	OPD	oropharyngeal dysphagia
			Orphan Products Development (office of)
	out of splint		
	out of stock		outpatient department
OOT	out of town	O'p'-DDD	mitotane (Lysodren)
OOU	orthopedics observation unit		
OOV	out-of-vocabulary	OPDRA	Office of Postmarketing Drug Risk Assessment (FDA)
OOW	out of wedlock		
	out of work	OPDs	outpatient departments
OP	oblique presentation		ovulation prediction devices
	occiput posterior	OPDUR	on-line prospective drug utilization review
	open		
	open prostatectomy	OPE	oral peripheral examination
	operation		outpatient evaluation
	organophosphorous	OPEC	Organization of the Petroleum Exporting Countries
	oropharyngeal		
	oropharynx	OPEN	vincristine (Oncovin), prednisone, etoposide, and mitoxantrone (Novantrone)
	oscillatory potentials		
	osteoporosis		
	outpatient	open appy	open appendectomy
	overpressure	open chole	open cholecystectomy
O&P	ova and parasites (stool examination)	OPEP	occupational post-exposure prophylaxis
O/P	see OP		oscillating positive expiratory pressure
OPA	Office of the Public Advocate (guardians)		
		OPERA	outpatient endometrial resection/ablation
	oral pharyngeal airway		
	outpatient anesthesia	OPET	optical positron emission tomography
OPAC	opacity (opacification)		

O

OPF	Oligo Polyethylene glycol Fumarate	OPPR	outpatient pulmonary rehabilitation
	omental pedicle flap	OPPS	Outpatient Prospective Payment System
	osteoplastic flaps		
OPG	ocular plethysmography	OPPT	Office of Pollution Prevention and Toxics (of the United States Environmental Protection Agency)
	optic pathway glioma		
	orthopantomogram (dental)		
	osteoprotegerin		
OPGs	optic pathway gliomas	OPQ	Office on Pharmaceutical Quality (US Food and Drug Administration)
OPHL	open partial horizontal laryngectomy		
Ophth	ophthalmic	OPQRST	onset, provocation, quality, radiation, severity, and time (an EMT mnemonic used in initial patient questioning)
	Ophthalmology		
ophthy	Ophthalmology		
OPI	opiates		
OPIAD	opioid associated androgen deficiency	OPR	outpatient rehabilitation
		OPRDU	outpatient renal dialysis unit
OPIDP	organophosphate-induced delayed polyneuropathy	OPRT	orotate phosphoribosyl transferase
		OPS	Objective Pain Scores
OPIM	optical phase interference microscopy		operations
			orange palpebral spots
	other potentially infectious material		Orpington prognostic scale
			orthogonal polarizarion spectral (imaging)
OPK	ovulation predictor kit		
OPKA	opsonophagocytic killing assay		outpatient surgery
OPL	oral premalignant lesion		overnight polysomnography
	other party liability	OPSCC	oropharyngeal squamous cell carcinoma
OPLC	optimum performance liquid chromatography		
		OPSI	overwhelming postsplenectomy infection
	Outpatient laparoscopic cholecystectomy		
		OPSS	overwhelming post-splenectomy sepsis syndrome
OPLL	ossification of posterior longitudinal ligament		
		OPSU	oblique partial sit-up
OPLS	Orthogonal Projections to Latent Structures		outpatient surgical unit
		OPSY	open psychiatry
OPM	occult primary malignancy	OPT	optimal pharmacological therapy
	Office of Personnel Management		optimum
	oral and pharyngeal mucositis		outpatient treatment
OPMD	oculopharyngeal muscular dystrophy	OPT c CA	Ohio pediatric tent with compressed air
OPMs	occult primary malignancies	OPT c O$_2$	Ohio pediatric tent with oxygen
OPN	osteopontin	optho	ophthalmology
OP/NP	oropharyngeal/ nasopharyngeal	OpTME	open total mesorectal excision
OPO	organ procurement organization(s)	OPTN	Organ Procurement and Transplantation Network
	outpatient observation	OPT-NSC	outpatient treatment, nonservice-connected
	overnight pulse oximetry		
OPOC	oral pharynx, oral cavity	OPT-SC	outpatient treatment, service-connected
OPOs	optical parametric oscillators		
	organ procurement organization representatives	OPTX	occult pneumothorax
		OPU	oocyte pick-up
OPP	opposite		ovum pick-up
	osteopathic principles and practice	OPUS	Outcomes Following Vaginal Prolapse Repair and Mid Urethral Sling (trial)
OPPE	Ongoing Professional Practice Evaluation		
		opus	a word meaning any artistic work, especially one on a large scale
OPPG	oculopneumoplethysmography		
OPPOS	opposition		

O

OPUS-1	a clinical trial to assess the efficacy and safety of lifitegrast ophthalmic solution 5% (Xiidra) compared with placebo in subjects with dry eye disease
OPUS-2	a clinical trial to assess the efficacy and safety of lifitegrast ophthalmic solution 5% (Xiidra) compared with placebo in subjects with dry eye disease
OPUS-3	a clinical trial to assess the efficacy and safety of lifitegrast ophthalmic solution 5% (Xiidra) compared with placebo in subjects with dry eye disease
OPV	oral polio vaccine (no longer available)
	outpatient visit
OPWDD	Office for People With Developmental Disabilities (New York)
OPx	oropharynx
OR	odds ratio
	oil retention
	oocyte retrievals
	open reduction
	operating room
	Oregon
	Orthodox
	own recognizance
ORA	occiput right anterior
ORADEs	opioid-related adverse drug events
oral prep	oral preparatory
ORB	order read back (orders taken verbally or by telephone from a physician)
Orbeye®	a small video microscope that provides high-resolution 3-dimensional imaging of the structure of tissue, blood vessels and other features by displaying the progress of surgical procedures on a 55-inch monitor
ORC	outpatient rehabilitation centers
ORCH	orchiectomy
ORD	ordering
	orderly
OREF	open reduction, external fixation
ORF	open reading frame
OR&F	open reduction and fixation
ORG	obesity-related glomerulopathy
ORH	Office of Rural Health (Veterans Administration)
	open radical hysterectomy

	open right hemicolectomy
	University of Oxford, John Radcliffe Hospital (UK)
orientedX1	oriented to person
orientedX2	oriented to person and place
orientedX3	oriented to person, place, and time
orientedX4	oriented to person, place, time, and date
ORIF	open reduction internal fixation
oris	Latin word meaning mouth
ORL	oblique retinacular ligament
	otorhinolaryngology (otology, rhinology and laryngology)
ORM	ormeloxifene
ORMF	open reduction metallic fixation
ORN	operating room nurse
	osteoradionecrosis
Orn	ornithine
ORO	olfactory recess opacity
oroph	oropharyngeal
OROS	ostomotic release oral system
OROS-MPH	osmotic release oral system-methylphenidate
ORP	occiput right posterior
	odds ratio product
	open radical prostatectomy
	ossicular replacement prosthesis
ORPP	open reduction and percutaneous pinning
ORQ	Occupational Role Questionnaire
ORR	objective response rate
	overall response rate
ORRP	open radical retropubic prostatectomy
ORS	oculorespiratory syndrome
	olfactory reference syndrome
	oral rehydration salts
ORSA	oxacillin-resistant *Staphylococcus aureus*
ORT	oestrogen (estrogen)-replacement therapy
	operating room technician
	oral rehydration therapy
	Registered Occupational Therapist
orth	orthopedics
ORTHO	Orthopedics
ortho-k	orthokeratology
ORV	oral rabies vaccination (vaccine)
	outbreak response vaccination
OR X1	oriented to time
OR X2	oriented to time and place
OR X3	oriented to time, place, and person
OR X4	oriented to time, place, person, and objects (watch, pen, book)

O

ORYX	The Joint Commission's mandatory national hospital quality reporting system
OS	left eye
	mouth (this is a dangerous abbreviation as it is read as left eye)
	occipitosacral
	oligospermic
	open surgery
	opening snap
	opening speed
	ophthalmic solution (this is a dangerous abbreviation as it is read as left eye)
	oral surgery
	orthopedic shoes
	Osgood-Schlatter (disease)
	osmium
	osteosarcoma
	overall survival
O/S	oil to surfactant ratio
OSA	obstructive sleep apnea
	off-site anesthesia
	online sexual activities
	osteosarcoma
OSA/HS	obstructive sleep apnea/ hypopnea syndrome
OSAP	ovary-specific acidic protein (gene/protein)
OSAS	obstructive sleep apnea syndrome
O2 sat	oxygen saturation (the fraction of oxygen-saturated hemoglobin relative to total hemoglobin (unsaturated + saturated) in the blood)
OSB	Office of Surveillance and Biometrics (FDA)
	open spina bifida
OSBS	obstructive sleep breathing disorders
OSC	oral self-care
Osc	oscillator
OSCAR	On-line Survey Certification and Reporting
Oscar	Phonetic Alphabet for O; pronounced OSS-CAH
OSCC	oral squamous cell carcinoma
	oropharyngeal squamous cell carcinoma
OSCE	Objective Structured Clinical Examination
OSD	one-stop dispensing (United Kingdom)
	oral solid dose
	Osgood-Schlatter disease (a condition in which the patellar tendon insertion

	on the tibial tuberosity becomes inflamed)
	overseas duty
	overside drainage
OSDI	Ocular Surface Disease Index Questionnaire
OSE	Office of Surveillance and Epidemiology (FDA)
	ovarian surface epithelium
OSESC	opening snap ejection systolic click
OSFE	osteotome sinus floor elevation (procedure)
OSFED	other specified feeding and eating disorders
OSFM	oral saliva fertility monitoring
OSFT	outstretched fingertips
OSG	osteosonogram (osteosonogrammetry)
OSH	occupational safety and health
	open saphenous (vein) harvest
	optical scanning holography
	outside hospital
	outside hospital(s)
OSHA	Occupational Safety and Health Administration
OSHT	Occupational Safety and Health Technologist
OSI	oscillatory shear index
	osseointegration speed index
	overall stability index
	oxidative stress index
O sign	a patient whose mouth is open when unconscious (slang)
	abdominal radiograph showing an O-shaped configuration of the gastric band
OSIS	Oxford Shoulder Instability Score
OSL	optically stimulated luminescent
OSLD	optically stimulated luminescent dosimeter
osm	osmolality
OSMF	oral submucous fibrosis
OSMO	osmolality
osmol gap	measured osmolality minus calculated osmolarity
OSM S	osmolarity serum
OSM U	osmolarity urine
OSN	off-service note
OSOM	outer stripe of the outer medulla
OSOM® Card Pregnancy Test	a qualitative test for determination of human chorionic gonadotropin in urine for the early detection of pregnancy
OSOM® Trichomonas Rapid Test	rapid test for Trichomonas vaginalis vaginal infections

O

OSOTC	Ohio Solid Organ Transplant Consortium		on-treatment
			oral transmucosal
OSP	outside pass		orotracheal
OS/P	left eye patched		outlier threshold
OSR	open septorhinoplasty		oxytocin (Pitocin)
	open sigmoid resection	O/T	oral temperature
	open surgical repair	OTA	Occupational Therapy Assistant
	outside records		open to air
oSRP	open septorhinoplasty	otalgia	a word meaning pain in the ear
OSS	open-source software	OTB	ochratoxin B
	osseous		ocular tuberculosis
	over-shoulder strap		orbital tuberculosis
OSSA	oxacillian-susceptible *Staphylococcus aureus*	OTC	occult tumor cells ornithine transcarbamoylase
OSSI	orthognathic surgery simulating instrument		Orthopedic Technician, Certified over-the-counter (sold without
OSSN	ocular surface squamos neoplasia		prescription) oxytetracycline
OSSP	objective structured self-assessment and	OTCD	ornithine transcarbamylase deficiency
	peer-feedback	OTD	onset-to-door (time)
OST	occipitosubtemporal		optimal therapeutic dose
	optimal sampling theory		organ tolerance dose
	osteogenic sarcoma		out-the-door
osteo	a combining form denoting relationship to bone, as in	OTE	(McMaster) Overall Treatment Evaluation
	osteo-degenerative diseases		over-the-ear
OSTP	Office of Science and Technology	OTF	off the floor
	Policy	OTFC	oral transmucosal fentanyl
os trigonum Syndrome	A small, extra bone found at the back of the ankle when		citrate (Fentanyl Oralet; Actiq))
	subjected to ankle injury or	OTG	outflow-tract gradient
	in athletes who sports require	OTH	other
	frequent ankle flexion, causes	OTHS	occupational therapy home
	pain and stiffness at the ankle		service
	which tends to be worse when	OTIS	Organization of Teratology
	pointing your toes. There is		Information Services
	often swelling and a small	OTJ	on-the-job (injury)
	lump behind the ankle which	OTL	otolaryngologist
	is often tender to touch.	OTLIF	open transforaminal lumbar
OSU	occasional stimulant user(s)		interbody fusion
OSV	objective sleep variables	OTLx	orthotropic liver transplantation
	online signature verification	OTM	oligodendrocyte transmembrane
	open subinguinal		protein; see gene website
	varicocelectomy		www.ncbi.nlm.nih.gov/gene
	Orbis-Sigma valve		Olive tail moment
	oseltamivir (Tamiflu)		orthodontic tooth movement
	oxygen saturation variability	OTO	one-time only
OSW	open surgical wound		otolaryngology
OSX	osterix (an essential transcrip-		otology
	tion factor in osteoblast	Otol	Otolaryngology
	differentiation and osteocyte	OTP	Opioid Treatment Program
	function)		(Substance Abuse and
OT	occiput transverse		Mental Health Services
	Occupational Therapist		Administration)
	occupational therapy	OTPs	opioid treatment programs
	old tuberculin	OTPT	oral triphasic tablets
	one time		(contraceptive)

OTR	Occupational Therapist, Registered	OVA1®	a qualitative serum test that combines the results of five immunoassays (CA 125, apolipoprotein A1, beta-2 microglobulin, transferrin, and pre-albumin) into a single numerical result (range 0-10). It is an aid to further assess the likelihood that a primary epithelial ovarian malignancy is present.
OTRL	Occupational Therapist, Registered Licensed		
OT/RT	occupational therapy/recreational therapy		
OTS	occupational therapy student		
	orotracheal suction		
	Orthopedic Trauma Service		
OTSC	over-the-scope clip		
OTSCC	oral tongue squamous cell carcinoma	OVAL	ovalocytes
OTSS	open tracheal suction system	OvCa	ovarian cancer
OTT	oral transmit time	OVCF	osteoporotic vertebral compressive fracture(s)
	orotracheal tube		
	overall treatment time	OVD	occlusal vertical dimension
OTTs	onset-to-treatment times		ophthalmic viscosurgical device
OTU	operational taxonomic unit		
OTUs	operational taxonomic units	oVEMPs	ocular vestibular-evoked myogenic potential(s)
OTV	occipitotemporal vein		
	oseltamivir phosphate (Tamiflu)	OVERACT	Outcome Measurement in Rheumatology Clinical Trials
OTW	off-the-wall		
	over-the-wire (stent)	overwt	over weight
OTX	omental tumor xenograft (model)	OVF	Octopus® visual field
		OVH	open vein harvesting
otx	orthodenticle-related protein; see gene website; www.ncbi.nlm.nih.gov/gene		oral verrucous hyperplasia
			ovariohysterectomy
			overlap volume histogram
OTX2	orthodenticle homeobox 2 [Homo sapiens (human)]; see gene website; www.ncbi.nlm.nih.gov/gene	OVLT	organum vasculosum of lamina terminalis
		OVN	sodium orthovanadate
		OVP	open visitation policy
OTZ	L-2-oxothiazolidine-r-carboxylate (a cysteine precursor; procysteine)	OVPP	optimal viewing position
		OVR	occupational and vocational rehabilitation
OU	each eye (both eyes)		Office of Vocational Rehabilitation
	observation unit		
OUA	ouabain	OVS	obstructive voiding symptoms (syndrome)
OUD	opioid use disorder		
OUES	oxygen uptake efficiency slope	OVSS	oblique vaginal septum syndrome
OUI	overflow urinary incontinence		
OULQ	outer upper left quadrant	OVT	oncolytic virus therapy
OUP	Oxford University Press		ovarian vein thrombosis
OU/P	both eyes patched	OVX	ovariectomized
OURQ	outer upper right quadrant		ovariectomy
OUS	obstetric ultrasound	OW	once weekly (this is a dangerous abbreviation)
outcm	outcome		
outp	outpatient		open wound
OUTPT	outpatient		oral warts
out pt	outpatient (a patient whose treatment does not require an overnight stay in the hospital)		out of wedlock
			outer wall
			ova weight
			overground walking
OV	office visit		overweight
	ovary	O/W	oil-in-water (emulsion)
	ovum		otherwise
OVA-1	see OVA1®	OWA	ordered weighted averaging

OWCP	Office of Workers' Compensation Programs (Department of Labor)
OWH	Office of Women's Health
OWI	operating (a vehicle) while impaired
OWL	out of wedlock
OWNK	out of wedlock, not keeping (baby)
OWP	oral white patches
OWR	open wedge resection Osler-Weber-Rendu (disease)
OWT	zero work tolerance
OX	oximeter
OXA	oxacillinase oxaliplatin (Eloxatin)
OXC	oxcarbazepine (Trileptal)
Oxi	oximeter (oximetry)
Ox-LDL	oxidized low-density lipoprotein
OXLIPN	oxaliplatin-induced peripheral neuropathy
OXM	pulse oximeter
OXPHOS	oxidative phosphorylation
OxPt	oxaliplatin (Eloxatin)
OXT	oxytocin (Oxytocin)
OXY	oxycodone
Oxy-5®	benzoyl peroxide
Oxy®IR	oxycodone immediate release capsules
OXZ	oxazepam (Serax)
OZ	optical zone
oz	ounce (1 ounce equals approximately 30 mL) ounce (28.35 grams)
OZS	oral zinc supplementation
OZs	optical zones ounces

P	after (P with a line above) Lasix (furosemide) as in vitamin P (slang) Papa (Phonetic Alphabet for P; pronounced PAH-PAH) para pending peripheral phosphorus pint plan *Plasmodium* poor probability (as in P = 0.05) proline (also referred to as Pro) protein Protestant pulse pupil produce
p	post posterior
/P	partial lower denture
P	statistical probability value
P/	partial upper denture
P02	may have meant PO2 (partial pressure of oxygen [reflects the amount of oxygen gas dissolved in the blood])
P04	see PO4
P1	pilocarpine 1% ophthalmic solution postnatal day 1 proximal phalanx
P16	see gene website, www.ncbi.nlm.nih.gov/gene
P2	middle phalanx postnatal day 2
P₂	pulmonic second heart sound
P-2	pulmonic second sound
P20	Ocusert® P20
P3	distal phalanx postnatal day 3
32ₚ	radioactive phosphorus
P40	Ocusert® P40
P53	tumor suppressive gene
p63	tumor protein 63, also known as transformation-related protein 63; It is used in immunohistochemistry. Also known as transformation-related protein 63 and TP63

p-63	tumor protein 63, also known as transformation-related protein 63; It is used in immunohistochemistry. Also known as transformation-related protein 63 and TP63	PA arrest	prolonged apnea arrest
		PAAS	post-ablationv atrial scar
		PAAs	popliteal artery aneurysms
		PAB	posterior axillary boost
			prealbumin
			prealbumin (transthyretin)
			premature atrial beat
PA	panic attack		pulmonary artery banding
	paranoid	PAb	polyclonal antibody (antibodies that are secreted by different B cell lineages within the body)
	peanut allergy		
	Pennsylvania		
	periapical (x-ray)		
	pernicious anemia		
	personal alarm	PABA	aminobenzoic acid (para-aminobenzoic acid)
	pharyngeal airway		
	phenol alcohol	PABC	pregnancy-associated breast cancer
	physical activity		
	Physician Assistant	PABD	preoperative autologous blood donation
	pineapple		
	placental abruption	PABIR	postacute brain injury rehabilitation
	placental abruption (the early separation of a placenta from the lining of the uterus before completion of the second stage of labor)		
		PAbs	polyclonal antibodies
		PAC	cisplatin (Platinol), doxorubicin (Adriamycin), and cylcophosphamide
	platelet aggregometry		perennial allergic conjunctivitis
	posterior-anterior (posteroanterior) (x-ray)		pharmacist-run anticoagulant clinic
	prealbumin		phenacemide
	premature adrenarche		Physical Assessment Center
	presents again		Physician Assistant, Certified
	primary aldosteronism		picture archiving communication (system)
	prior approval		
	prior authorization		Port-a-cath®
	professional association (similar to a corporation)		post-acute care
			Preadmission Clinic
	Pseudomonas aeruginosa		premature atrial contraction
	psychiatric aide		prophylactic anticonvulsants
	psychoanalysis		pulmonary artery catheter
	pulmonary artery	PA-C	Physician Assistant, Certified
Pa	pascal	PA Cath	pulmonary artery catheter (Swan-Ganz catheter)
	protactinium		
P&A	percussion and auscultation	PACCM	Pulmonary, Allergy, and Critical Care Medicine
	position and alignment		
	phenol and alcohol	PACD	photoallergic contact dermatitis
$P_2 > A_2$	pulmonic second heart sound greater than aortic second heart sound	PACE	physical activity calorie equivalents
			Physician Assessment and Clinical Education
P/A	see PA		population-adjusted clinical epidemiology
PA02	see PAO2		
PAA	popliteal artery aneurysm		Programs of All-Inclusive Care for the Elderly
	pulmonary artery aneurysm		
PAAA	para-anastomotic aneurysm of the aorta	PACG	primary angle-closure glaucoma
PAAD	persistently and acutely disabled	PACH	pipers to after coming head
PAAF	pancreatitis-associated ascitic fluid	pachy	pachymetry (a device to measure the thickness of the cornea)
PaAF	paroxysmal atrial fibrillation		
	enoyl-CoA hydratase-isomerase	PACI	partial anterior cerebral infarct
PAAPs	personal asthma action plans	P acnes	Propionibacterium acnes

P

PACNS — primary angiitis of the central nervous system

PaCO$_2$ — partial pressure (tension) of carbon dioxide, artery

PAcP — prostatic acid phosphatase

PACS — picture archiving and communication system

PACT — Metastatic Pancreatic Adenocarcinoma Clinical Trial
Patient Aligned Care Team (Veterans Administration)
Pediatric Advanced Care Team
Planning, Access, Care, and Treatment
prism and alternate cover test
Program of Assertive Community Treatment
Psychosocial Assessment of Candidates for Transplantation

PACU — post-acute care unit
postanesthesia care unit

PAD — pain, agitation, and delirium
pelvic adhesive disease
periampullary diverticula
peripheral artery disease
persistently and acutely disabled
pharmacologic atrial defibrillator
physician-assisted death
preliminary anatomic diagnosis
preoperative autologous donation
primary affective disorder
pulmonary artery diastolic
pulsed amperometric detection

pAD — prodromal Alzheimer disease

PADA — percentage of applied dose absorbed
platelet adhesion assay

PADB — Proteomic Analysis DataBase

padB — phenylacetyl-CoA:acceptor oxidoreductase; see gene website www.ncbi.nlm.nih.gov/gene

PADC — pancreatic ductal adenocarcinoma

PADCAB — perfusion-assisted direct coronary artery bypass

PADLs — physical activities of daily living

PADP — pulmonary artery diastolic pressure

PadR — phenolic acid decarboxylase regulator

pADRs — preventable adverse drug reactions

PADS — Post Anesthesia Discharge Scoring System

PADT — primary androgen deprivation therapy

Padua Inventory — a self-report measure of obsessive and compulsive symptoms

Padua Score — prediction score to determine anticoagulation need for venous thromboembolism patients

PAE — percutaneous angiographic embolization
postanoxic encephalopathy
postantibiotic effect
pre-admission evaluation
pre-anesthesia evaluation
progressive assistive exercise

PAEDP — pulmonary artery and end-diastole pressure

PAEE — physical activity energy expenditure

PAEF — primary aortoenteric fistula

PAEs — phthalate acid esters
postoperative adverse events

PAF — paroxysmal atrial fibrillation
platelet-activating factor
population attributable fraction
pure autonomic failure

PA&F — percussion, auscultation, and fremitus

PAFE — postantifungal effect

PAFI — plasmon-assisted fluoro-immunoassay

PA Fib — paroxysmal atrial fibrillation

P Afib — paroxysmal atrial fibrillation

PAFL — pneumothorax-associated fibroblastic lesion

PAFO — Plastic ankle-foot orthosis

PAFs — population-attributable fractions

PAG — periaqueductal gray (also known as central gray)

PAGA — premature appropriate for gestational age

PAGCL — postarthroscopic glenohumeral chondrolysis

PAGE — polyacrylamide gel electrophoresis

PAGN — phenylacetylglutamine

PA-gram — pulmonary arteriogram

PAH — para-aminohippurate
partial abdominal hysterectomy
phenylalanine hydroxylase
polycyclic aromatic hydrocarbons
polynuclear aromatic hydrocarbon
predicted adult height
primary adrenal hyperplasia
pulmonary arterial hypertension

PAHC — physician-assistant home care
Psychosocial Aspects of Hereditary Cancer (questionnaire)

pAHI — PAT (peripheral arterial tone) apnea hypopnea index

PAHO	Pan American Health Organization
PAHTN	pulmonary arterial hypertension
PA Htn	pulmonary arterial hypertension
PAI	penetrating abdominal injury
	plasminogen activator inhibitor
	platelet accumulation index
PAI-1	plasminogen activator inhibitor-1
PAIDS	pediatric acquired immunodeficiency syndrome
PAIgG	platelet-associated immunoglobulin G
PAINAD	Pain Assessment (Tool) in Advanced Dementia
PA-INJ	popliteal artery injury
PAIR	Puncture, Aspiration, Injection, Respiration (technique)
PAIS	Psychological Adjustment to Illness Scale
PAIVMs	passive accessory intervertebral movements
PA-IVS	pulmonary atresia with an intact ventricular septum
PAK	p21-activated kinase
	pancreas and kidney
PAL	peripheral arterial line
	physical activity levels
	posterior axillary line
	posteroanterior and lateral
	power-assisted lipoplasty
	progressive-addition lenses
	pyothorax-associated lymphoma
pal	paleolithic
PALA	N-phosphoacetate-L aspartate
PA/Lat	posteroanterior/lateral (view)
PALB2	partner and localizer of BRCA2 gene
PALB	see gene website; www.ncbi.nlm.nih.gov
PAlb	prealbumin
PalB	Pseudozyma (formerly Candida) antarctica lipase B
paleo	paleolithic
Pa Line	pulmonary artery line
PALISI	Pediatric Acute Lung Injury, and Sepsis Investigators
PALIVE	Pediatric Acute Lung Injury Mechanical Ventilation (study)
PALM	photoactivated light microscopy
	primary adult-type lactose malabsorption
PALM-COEIN	the classification system for abnormal uterine bleeding (AUB) approved by the International Federation of Gynecology and Obstetrics ([structural- endometrial polyps, adenomyosis, leiomyoma, malignancy and hyperplasia] [functional- coagulopathy, ovulatory dysfunction, endo- metrial, Iatrogenic, and not yet classified]) (see AUB)
PALN	para-aortic lymph node
PALND	para-aortic lymphadenectomy
PALP	palpation
palps	Palpitations
PALS	pediatric advanced life support
	periarterial lymphatic sheath
PAM	partial allosteric modulators
	Payment Accuracy Measurement
	potential acuity meter
	primary acquired melanosis
	primary amebic meningoencephalitis
	protein A mimetic
	pulmonary artery mean
2-PAM	pralidoxime (Protopam)
PA/MAPCAs	pulmonary atresia and major aortopulmonary collateral arteries
PAME	pre-anesthesia medical examination
PAMG-1	placental alpha-microglobulin-1 (a diagnostic for preterm premature rupture of membranes)
PAMI	Primary Angioplasty in Myocardial Infarction (study)
PAML	Phylogenetic Analysis by Maximum Likelihood (program package)
	pre-admission medication list
PAMM	paracentral acute middle maculopathy
PAMORA	peripherally-acting mu-opioid receptor antagonist (class of drugs)
PAMP	pulmonary arterial (artery) mean pressure
PAMPs	pathogen-associated molecular patterns
pAMR	pathologic antibody-mediated rejection
PAMs	porcine alveolar macrophages
	positive allosteric modulators
PAN	pancreas
	pancreatic
	pancuronium (Pavulon)
	panobinostat
	panoral x-ray examination
	periodic alternating nystagmus
	polyacrylonitrile (filter)
	polyarteritis nodosa
	polyomavirus-associated nephropathy

pANCA	perinuclear antineutrophil cytoplasmic antibody		prostatic acid phosphatase
			pulmonary alveolar proteinosis
pancx	pancreatectomized		pulmonary artery pressure
PANDAS	pediatric autoimmune neuropsychiatric disorders associated with streptococcal infections	PAPA	PACE (Physician Assessment and Clinical Education) Aging Physician Assessment
P and D	possibly misheard, see PND prepped and draped		pyoderma gangrenosum with pyogenic sterile arthritis and cystic acne
PANENDO	panendoscopy		pyogenic arthritis, Pyoderma
PANESS	physical and neurological examination for soft signs		gangrenosum, and acne pyogenic sterile arthritis,
pan-HER	pan-human EGF (epidermal growth factor) receptor		pyoderma gangrenosum, and acne
panhypopit	panhypopituitarism	Papa	Phonetic Alphabet for P;
PanIN-1	pancreatic intraepithelial neoplasm (low grade); there is a 1A and 1B	PAPASH	pronounced PAH-PAH pyoderma gangrenosum with pyogenic sterile arthri-
PanIN-2	pancreatic intraepithelial neoplasm (moderate grade)		tis, acne, and hidradenitis suppurativa
PanIN-3	pancreatic intraepithelial neoplasm (high grade)	PAPAW	pushrim-activated power-assisted wheelchair
PANN	paraconsistent artificial neural network	PAPE	post-admission physician evaluation
PANP	pelvic autonomic nerve preservation	PAPi	pulmonary artery pulsatility index
PANSS	Positive and Negative Syndrome Scale	PAPm	mean pumonary artery pressure
PANSS-EC	Positive and Negative Symptoms of Schizophrenia-Excited Component	PAPNAP	a daytime study for patients who have anxiety about starting positive airway pressure therapy
PAO$_2$	alveolar oxygen pressure (tension)	PAP Nap	a daytime study for patients who have anxiety about starting
PaO$_2$	arterial oxygen pressure (tension)		positive airway pressure therapy
PAO	peak acid output periacetabular osteotomy peripheral arterial occlusion pregnancy-associated osteoporosis pustulotic arthro-osteitis	PAPPA	pregnancy-associated plasma protein-A; see gene website www.ncbi.nlm.nih.gov/gene
		PAPP-A	pregnancy-associated plasma protein A
PAOD	peripheral arterial occlusive disease	PAPR	powered-air purifying respirator
		PA pressure	pulmonary artery pressure
PAOP	pulmonary artery occlusion pressure	PAP-RIA	prostatic acid phosphatase radioimmunoassay
PAP	Papanicolaou test (smear) (a method of screening by collecting cells; it is used to detect potentially pre-cancerous and cancerous processes in the cervix)	PAPS	primary antiphospholid syndrome
		PA/PS	pulmonary atresia/pulmonary stenosis
		PAP smear	Papanicolaou test (smear) (a method of screening by collecting cells; it is used to detect potentially pre-cancerous and cancerous processes in the cervix)
	partial atretic plate passive-aggressive personality Patient Assistance Program peroxidase-anti-peroxidase pokeweed antiviral protein positive airway pressure potential acuity pinhole primary atypical pneumonia		
		PAPVC	partial anomalous pulmonary venous connection
		PAPVR	partial anomalous pulmonary venous return

P

PAQ	Persistence and Adherence Questionnaire
PAQ-A	Physical Activity Questionnaire for Adolescents
PAQ-C	Physical Activity Questionnaire for Children
PAQLQ	Pediatric Asthma Quality of Life Questionnaire
PAR	parafin
	parainfluenza (paramyxovirus) vaccine
	parallel
	participating (physician)
	Patient Access Representative
	perennial allergic rhinitis
	platelet aggregate ratio
	population attributable risks
	possible allergic reaction
	postanesthetic recovery
	procedures, alternatives, and risks
	pulmonary arteriolar resistance
PAR1	pseudoautosomal region 1
PARA	number of pregnancies producing viable offspring
	paraplegic
	parathyroid
PARA 1	having borne one child
Paraflu	Parainfluenza
PARAGON-HF trial	Prospective Comparison of Angiotensin Receptor Neprilysin Inhibitor With Angiotensin Receptor Blocker Global Outcomes in HFpEF [heart failure with preserved ejection fraction]; comparing sacubitril/valsartan to valsartan in reducing morbidity and mortality)
PARC	perennial allergic rhinoconjunctivitis
	pulmonary and activation-regulated chemokine
PARDS	pediatric acute respiratory distress syndrome
pA/REDV	persistent absent or reversed end diastolic velocity
PARF	pediatric acute renal failure
PARL	presenilins-associated rhomboid-like protein
PAROM	passive assistance range of motion
parox	paroxysmal
PARP-1	poly(adenosine 5′-diphosphate-ribose) polymerase-1
PARQ	procedures, risks, alternatives and questions

PARR	plasma aldosterone/renin activity ratio
	postanesthesia recovery room
PARS	postanesthesia recovery score
PARs	participating physicians (Medicare)
PART	para-aortic radiotherapy
Part D	Medicare Prescription Drug Plan
parto	a Spanish word meaning childbirth, delivery, or labor
PARU	postanesthetic recovery unit
PAS	aminosalicylic acid (para-aminosalicylic acid)
	perinatal arterial stroke
	periodic acid-Schiff (reagent)
	peripheral anterior synechia
	pharyngeal airway space
	physician-assisted suicide
	pneumatic antiembolic stocking
	postanesthesia score
	postanesthetic shivering
	premature auricular systole
	Professional Activities Study
	pulmonary artery stenosis
	pulmonary artery systolic
	pulsatile antiembolism system (stockings)
PA-S	Physician Assistant, Student
PASA	aminosalicylic acid (para-aminosalicylic acid)
	posterior sector acetabular angle
	proximal articular set angle
PAS-ADD	Psychiatric Assessment Schedule for Adults with Developmental Disability
PASARR	Preadmission Screening Assessment and Annual Resident Review
PASAT	Paced Auditory Serial Addition Test
PA/S/D	pulmonary artery systolic/diastolic
PASE	pacing atrial stress echocardiography
	Physical Activity Scale for the Elderly
PASEF	parallel accumulation-serial fragmentation
Pas Ex	passive exercise
PASG	pneumatic antishock garment
PASH	pseudoangiomatous stromal hyperplasia
	Pyoderma gangrenosum, acne, and suppurative hidradenitis
PASI 75	at least 75% improvement in psoriasis area and severity index
PASI	Psoriasis Area and Severity Index

PASIPD	Physical Activity Scale for Individuals with a Physical Disability
PASK	peripheral anterior stromal keratopathy
PASP	pulmonary artery systolic pressure
PASRR	Preadmission Screening and Resident Review
PASS	Pain Anxiety Symptoms Scale
passr	probabilistic air segmentation and sparse regression
PAST	Pain Assessment Skills Tool
	penicillin allergy skin testing
PASTA	partial articular supraspinatus tendon avulsion
PASV	pressure-activated safety-valve
PAT	over-anxious patient
	Paddington alcohol test
	paroxysmal atrial tachycardia
	passive alloimmune thrombocytopenia
	patella
	patient
	percent acceleration time
	peripheral arterial tone
	peripheral artery tonometry
	perivascular adipose tissue
	platelet aggregation test
	preadmission testing
	pregnancy at term
	process analytical technology
	Psychosocial Assessment Tool
PATB	pes anserinus tendonitis/bursitis
PATC	Preoperative Assessment Testing Clinic
PATH	pathology
	Physicians at Teaching Hospitals (medicare audit)
	pituitary adrenotropic hormone
patho	a prefix meaning: disease, causing disease
Patio repair	preserve the tract and turn it inside out (for repairing urethrocutaneous fistulae)
PATOS	Pan Asian Trauma Outcomes Study
PATP	preadmission testing program
PATS	payment at time of service
PATSS	postablation tubal sterilization syndrome
PATT	partial activated thromboplastin time
PAU	penetrating aortic ulcer
paunt	paternal aunt
PAUs	penetrating aortic ulcers
	penetrating atherosclerotic ulcers

PAV	paced atrioventricular delay
	Pavulon (pancuronium bromide)
	pre-admission visit (hospice care initial home visit)
	proportional assist ventilation
p3AVB	persistent third-degree atrioventricular block
PAVC	partial atrioventricular canal defect
	pulmonary artery vascular conductance
PAVD	peripheral arterial vascular disease
PAVe	procarbazine, melphalan (Alkeran), and vinblastine (Velban)
PAVF	pulmonary arteriovenous fistula
PAVI	percutaneous aortic valve implantation
PAVK-86	a quality of life in peripheral arterial occlusive disease questionnaire
pAVK	peripheral arterial occlusive disease (Germany)
PAVM	pancreatic arteriovenous malformation
	pulmonary arteriovenous malformation
PAVNRT	paroxysmal atrial ventricular nodal re-entrant tachycardia
PAVR	percutaneous aortic valve replacement
PAVSD	pulmonary atresia and ventricular septal defect
pAVSD	partial atrioventricular septal defect
PAWP	pulmonary artery wedge pressure
PAWS	Pediatric Acute Wound Service
	post-acute-withdrawal syndrome
PAX	periapical x-ray
PB	barometric pressure
	British Pharmacopeia
	parafin bath
	peanut butter
	Pepto-Bismol
	peribulbar
	peripheral blood
	phenylbutyrate
	piggyback
	powder board
	power building
	premature beat
	Presbyterian
	protein-bound
	Prussian Blue
	pudendal block
	pusher behavior
	pyridostigmine bromide (Mestinon)

P

Pb	lead	PBJ	pancreaticobiliary ductal
	phenobarbital		junction
P&B	pain and burning		peanut butter and jelly
	Papanicolaou and breast		(sandwich)
	(examinations)		probation before judgment
	phenobarbital and belladonna	PB&J	peanut butter and jelly
p/b	postburn		(sandwich)
PBA	percutaneous bladder aspiration	PBK	pseudophakic bullous
	pseudobulbar affect		keratopathy
PBAC	Pharmaceutical Benefits Advisory	PBL	peripheral blood lymphocyte
	Committee		positive beam limitation
PBAL	protected bronchoalveolar		(radiology)
	lavage		primary brain lymphoma
P bars	parallel bars		primary breast lymphoma
P-bars	parallel bars		problem-based learning
PBAV	percutaneous balloon aortic	PBLAC	pictorial blood loss assessment
	valvuloplasty		chart
PbB	whole blood lead	PBLC	premature birth live child
PbBP	lead-binding protein(s)	PB-LC-EI-MS	particle beam liquid
PBC	point of basal convergence		chromatography-electron
	prebed care		impact-mass spectrometry
	primary biliary cirrhosis	PBLD	phenazine biosynthesis-like pro-
PBCC	pigmented basal cell carcinoma		tein domain; see gene website
PBCM	Preventive Basic Care		www.ncbi.nlm.nih.gov/gene
	Management (program)		Problem-Based Learning Dis-
PBD	percutaneous biliary drainage		cussion (American Society of
	pneumatic balloon dilatation		Anesthesiologists)
	postburn day	PBM	pancreaticobilliary maljunction
	proliferative breast disease		peroneus brevis muscle
PBDE	polybrominated diphenyl ether		pharmacy benefit management
	(flame retardant)		(manager)
pBDL	partial bile duct ligation		photobiomodulatio
PBDs	peroxisomal biogenesis disorders		porcelain bonded to metal
	psychotic and behavioral		crown
	disturbances	PBMC	peripheral blood mononuclear
PBE	partial breech extraction		cell
	population bioequivalence	PBMNC	peripheral blood mononuclear
	power building exercise		cell
PBED	percutaneous biportal endoscopic	PBMs	peripheral blood monocytes
	decompression		preference-based measures
PBF	peripheral blood film		protein-binding microarrays
	placental blood flow	PBMT	Perioperative Blood
	pulmonary blood flow		Management Technologist
PBFS	penile blood flow study	PBMV	percutaneous balloon mitral
PBG	porphobilinogen		valvuloplasty
	pressure breathing for	PBN	polymyxin B sulfate, bacitracin,
	G protection		and neomycin
	pupillary block glaucoma	PB:ND	problem: nursing diagnosis
PBGD	porphobilinogen deaminase	PBNP	Poisson-Boltzmann and Nernst-
PBH	persistent black hole (magnetic		Planck (equations and models)
	resonance imaging indicator	PbNP	lead nitroprusside
	of neuronal loss)	PBNS	percutaneous bladder neck
PbH	hair lead		stabilization
PBHs	persistent black holes (magnetic	PBO	placebo
	resonance imaging indicator	PBP	penicillin-binding protein
	of neuronal loss)		phantom breast pain
PBI	partial breast irradiation		pharmacy bulk package
	protein-bound iodine		protein-bound polysaccharide

PBPC	peripheral blood progenitor cell
PBPCT	peripheral blood progenitor cell transplantation
PBPI	penile-brachial pulse index
	perinatal brachial plexus injury
PBPK	physiologically based pharmokinetic
PBPs	penicillin-binding proteins
PBR	Patient's Bill of Rights
	peripheral benzodiazepine receptor
	peripheral benzodiazepine receptor (gene/protein; also known as translocator protein [TSPO])
	positive BOLD (blood oxygen level-dependent signal) response
PbR	Payment by Results (United Kingdom)
PBRs	photobioreactors
PBRSAs	performances-based risk-sharing arrangements (payment models based on paying for positive healthcare outcomes)
PBS	Pharmaceutical Benefit Scheme (lists all of the medicines available at the Australian's Government-subsidized price)
	phosphate-buffered saline
	prune-belly syndrome
PBSC	peripheral blood stem cells
PBSCT	peripheral blood stem-cell transplantation
PBSO	prophylactic bilateral salpingo-oophorectomy
PBST	phosphate-buffered saline plus 0.1% Tween-20
PBSt	posterior-biceps-semitendinosus
PBT	primary brain tumor
	proton beam therapy
PBT$_4$	protein-bound thyroxine
PbtO2	partial pressure of oxygen in brain tissue (normal range, 25 to 50 millimeters of mercury)
PbtO$_2$	brain tissue partial pressure of oxygen
PBU	power base unit
PBV	percutaneous balloon valvuloplasty
PBW	postbronchiolitic wheezing
	predicted body weight
PBx	prostatic biopsy
PBZ	phenoxybenzamine (Dibenzyline)
	pyribenzamine
ΦBZ	phenylbutazone

PC	after meals
	cisplatin (Platinol) and cyclophosphamide
	packed cells
	paclitaxel; carboplatin
	palliative care
	pancreatic cancer
	pathologic consultation
	patient condition
	percutaneous cholecystostomy
	perinatal care
	pheochromocytoma
	photocoagulation
	placebo-controlled (study)
	platelet concentrate
	platform cane
	Pneumocystis carinii
	point convergence
	politically correct
	poor condition
	popliteal cyst
	posterior canals (vestibular)
	posterior chamber
	prednicarbate
	premature contractions
	present complaint
	present correction (eyeglasses)
	pressure control
	productive cough
	professional corporation
	prostate cancer
	psychiatric counselor
	pubococcygeus (muscle)
	pulmonary contusion
P/C	see PC
PCA	passive cutaneous anaphylaxis
	patient care assistant (aide)
	patient-controlled analgesia
	penicillamine (Cuprimine)
	pill count adherence
	polychromatic angiography
	porous coated anatomic (joint replacement)
	portacaval anastomosis
	postcardiac arrest
	postciliary artery
	postconceptional age
	posterior cerebral artery
	posterior communicating artery
	posterior cricoarytenoid (muscles)
	principal components analysis
	procainamide
	procoagulation activity
	prostate cancer
PCa	prostate cancer
PCA-1	prostate cancer antigen-1
	Purkinje cell cytoplasmic antibody-1

PCA3	prostate cancer associated 3 (gene/protein)		prothrombin complex concentrate; a concentrate of human coagulation factors II, VII, IX, and X as well as the anti-thrombotic proteins C and S (Kcentra)
PCAC	Physical Care Assessment Center		
	preparative continuous annular chromatography		
P-CAC	preparative continuous annular chromatography	PCC3	3-factor prothrombin complex concentrate (factors II, IX and X) (Profilnine SD)
PCAD	posterior circulation arterial dissections	PCC4	4-factor prothrombin complex concentrate (Factors II, VII, IX, X) (found in Kcentra)
PCAM	patient-controlled analgesia morphine	PCCA	propionyl CoA carboxylase, alpha polypeptide (gene)
PCaM	metastatic prostate cancer		
PCAP	predisposing for prostate cancer; see gene website www.ncbi .nlm.nih.gov/gene	PCCC	pediatric critical care center
		PCCI	penetrating craniocerebral injuries
PCaP	North Carolina-Louisiana Prostate Cancer Project	PCCM	primary care case management pulmonary and critical care medicine
pCAP	phosphocoumaryl aminopropionic acid		
PCA pump	patient-controlled analgesia pump	PCCN	Primary Community Care Network
			Primary Community Care Nurse
PCARP	posterior column ataxia and retinitis pigmentosa	PCCP	percutaneous compression plate
		PCCS	Palliative Care Consultation Service
PCASSO	patient-centered access to secure systems online	PCCs	prothrombin complex concentrates
PCAST	President's Council of Advisors on Science and Technology	PCCT	palliative care consult team peritoneal contrast computed tomography phase-contrast computer tomography postcontrast computer tomography
PCAT	pericoronary adipose tissue		
pcaU	see gene website www.ncbi.nlm .nih.gov/gene		
PCB	pancuronium bromide para cervical block placebo postcoital bleeding prepared childbirth procarbazine (Matulane) *Pseudomonas cepacia bacteremia*		
		PCCU	postcoronary care unit progressive coronary care unit
		PCD	pacer-cardioverter-defibrillator paraneoplastic cerebellar degeneration paroxysmal cerebral dysrhythmia plasma cell dyscrasias polarized contact dermoscopy pomalidomide, cyclophosphamide, and dexamethasone postmortem cesarean delivery primary ciliary dyskinesia programmed cell death pyruvate carboxylase deficiency
PCBH	personal care boarding home		
PCBMN	palmar cutaneous branch of the median nerve		
PC-BPPV	posterior canal benign paroxysmal positional vertigo		
PCBs	polychlorinated biphenyls		
PCBUN	palmar cutaneous branch of the ulnar nerve		
PCC	patient care coordinator patient-centered care petrous carotid canal pheochromocytoma pneumatosis cystoides coli poison control center post coital contraception posterior cervical cage(s) precipitated calcium carbonate progressive cardiac care	PCDAI	Pediatric Crohn Disease Activity Index
		PCDDs	polychlorinated dibenzo-p-dioxins (agricultural pesticides)
		PCDFs	polychlorinated dibenzofurans (agricultural pesticides)
		PCE	physical capacities evaluation potentially compensable event pseudophakic corneal edema

PCE®	erythromycin particles in tablets
PCEA	patient-controlled epidural analgesia
PCEAO	postcarotid endarterectomy airway obstruction
PCEC	purified chick embryo cell (culture)
PCECV	purified chick embryo cell vaccine
PCET	Penn Conditional Exclusion Test
PCF	pharyngeal conjunctival fever
	post-cancer fatigue
	posterior cervical fusion
PCFL	primary cutaneous folicular lymphoma
PCFT	platelet complement fixation test
PCG	phonocardiogram
	plasma cell granuloma
	primary care giver
	primary congenital glaucoma
	pubococcygeus (muscle)
PCGG	percutaneous coagulation of gasserian ganglion
PCGL	pubococcygeal line
PCGLV	poorly contractile globular left ventricle
PCG/Ts	Primary Care Groups and Trusts
PCH	paroxysmal cold hemoglobinuria
	periocular capillary hemangioma
	personal care home
PChE	pseudocholinesterase
PchE	plasma cholinesterase
pchG	see gene website; www.ncbi.nlm .nih.gov
PCHI	permanent childhood hearing impairment
PCHL	permanent childhood hearing loss
PCHP	Palliative Care Homebound Program (Mayo Clinic)
PC&HS	after meals and at bedtime
PC/HS	after meals and at bedtime
PChTh	polychemotherapy
PCI	percutaneous coronary intervention
	peritoneal cancer index
	pneumatosis cystoides intestinalis
	prophylactic cranial irradiation
PCIM	patient-controlled intravenous morphine
	phase contrast inverted microscopy
pCIMT	pediatric constraint-induced movement therapy
PCINA	patient-controlled intranasal analgesia
PC IOL	posterior chamber intraocular lens

PC IOLs	posterior chamber intraocular lens
PCIP	Pre-Existing Conditions Insurance Plan
PC-IPAA	proctocolectomy and ileal pouch-anal anastomosis
PC-IRV	pressure-controlled inverse-ratio ventilation
PCI-S	percutaneous coronary intervention with stenting
PCIs	percutaneous coronary interventions
P300-CIT	P300-Concealed Information Test
PCIT	Parent-Child Interaction Therapy
PCJ	pneumocystis jiroveci
PCKD	polycystic kidney disease
PCKLD	polycystic kidney and liver disease
PCL	pacing cycle length
	percutaneous litholapaxy
	plasma cell leukemia
	posterior chamber lens
	posterior cruciate ligament
	proximal collateral ligament
PCLD	polycystic liver disease
pCLE	probe-based confocal laser endomicroscopy
PCLI	plasma cell labeling index
PCLM	pancreatic cancer with liver metastases
PCLN	psychiatric consultation liaison nurse
PCLR	paid claims loss ratio
PCLS	precision-cut lung slices
PCM	paracoccidiodomycosis
	petroclival meningioma
	pharmaceutical case management
	primary cutaneous melanoma
	protein-calorie malnutrition
	pubococcygeal muscle
PCMD	power of combinatorial molecular discrimination
PCMH	patient-centered medical home
	Primary Care Medical Home (certification)
PCMHI	Primary Care Mental Health Integration (Veterans Affairs)
PCMHs	patient-centered medical homes
PCMM	primary cutaneous malignant melanoma
PCMN	palmar cutaneous branch of the median nerve
PCMR	phase-contrast magnetic resonance (imaging)
	proportional cancer mortality ratio

P

PC-MRI	phase-contrast magnetic resonance imaging
PCMX	chloroxylenol
PCMZL	primary cutaneous marginal zone B-cell lymphoma
PCN	penicillin
	percutaneous nephrostomy
	peroneal communicating nerve
	primary care nursing
PCNA	patient care nursing assistant
	proliferating cell nuclear antigen
PCNB	percutaneous core-needle biopsy
PCNE	Pharmaceutical Care Network Europe
PCNIs	patient-centered nursing interventions
PCNL	percutaneous nephrolithotomy
PCNR	contrast-to-noise-ratio
PCNs	posterior cervical nodes
PCNSL	primary central nervous system lymphoma
PCNT	percutaneous nephrostomy tube
PCNU	polycarbonate-urethane
PCO	patient complains of
	polycystic ovary
	posterior capsular opacification
PCO$_2$	partial pressure (tension) of carbon dioxide, artery
PCOA	patient controlled oral analgesia
PCoA	posterior communicating artery
	principal coordinate analysis
pcoA	copper resistance protein; see gene website www.ncbi.nlm .nih.gov/gene
PCOC	Palliative Care Outcomes Collaboration
	palliative care outpatient clinic
	pregnancy and obstetrical complication
	prenatal cocaine exposure
PCOD	polycystic ovarian disease
PCOE	prescriber (physician) computer order entry
PCOF	peripheral cemento-ossifying fibroma
	polycystic ovarian follicle (syndrome)
P COMM	posterior communicating (artery)
P COMMA	posterior communicating artery
PCON	pial circulation of the optic nerve
PCORI	Patient-Centered Outcomes Research Institute
PCOS	polycystic ovary syndrome
PcoS	copper resistant sensor kinase; see gene website; www.ncbi .nlm.nih.gov/gene
pCOT	plasma cotinine

PCP	Palliative Care Program
	pancytopenia
	patient care plan
	phencyclidine (phenylcyclohexyl piperidine)
	pneumocystis jiroveci pneumonia (formerly known as pneumocystis carinii pneumonia)
	posterior capsular plication
	primary care person
	primary care physician
	primary care provider
	prochlorperazine (Compazine)
	pulmonary capillary pressure
PcpA	Pneumococcal choline binding protein A
PCPC	Pediatric Cerebral Performance Category (scale)
pcPO2	percutaneous oxygen partial pressure
PCP pneumonia	pneumocystis jiroveci pneumonia (formerly known as pneumocystis carinii pneumonia)
PCP prophylaxis	pneumocystis jiroveci pneumonia (formerly known as pneumocystis carinii pneumonia) prophylaxis
PCPs	personal care products
PCPT	Prostate Cancer Prevention Trial
PCPT-RC	Prostate Cancer Prevention Trial Risk Calculator
PCR	patient care report
	pentostatin, cyclophosphamide, and rituximab
	percutaneous coronary revascularization
	polymerase chain reaction
	posterior capsule rupture
	protein catabolic rate
pCR	pathological complete response
PCr	plasma creatinine
PCRA	pure red-cell aplasia
PCrb	paclitaxel and carboplatin
PCRB	perchlorate-reducing bacteria
pCRB	pathologic complete response in the breast
PCRIs	peripheral cornea relaxing incisions
PCR/PSA	polymerase chain reaction analysis of prostate-specific antigen
PCRs	polymerase chain reactions
PCR-SSCP	polymerase chain reaction – single strand conformational polymorphism
PCRYO	pooled cryoprecipitate

P

PCS	paraspinal compartment syndrome	pCTL	precursor cytotoxic T lymphocytes
	patient care system	pCTR	partial cricotracheal resection
	patient-controlled sedation	pCTRs	partial cricotracheal resections
	pedicle signal change	PCTS	patient-controlled transdermal system
	pelvic congestion syndrome		
	personal care service	PCTU	pediatric cardiothoracic intensive care unit
	photon correlation spectroscopy		
	physical component summary	PCU	palliative care unit
	portable cervical spine		patient care unit
	portacaval shunt		primary care unit
	post cholecystectomy syndrome		progressive care unit
	postconcussion syndrome		protective care unit
P c/s	primary cesarean section	PCUN	palmar cutaneous branch of the ulnar nerve
PCSA	physiological cross-sectional area (the area of the cross section of a muscle perpendicular to its fibers, generally at its largest point. It is typically used to describe the contraction properties of pennate muscles)		
		PCV	packed cell volume
			polycythemia vera
			polypoidal choroidal vasculopathy
			pressure-controlled ventilation
			procarbazine, lomustine (CCNU [Cee Nu]), and vincristine
PCSK9	proprotein convertase subtilisin/ kexin type 9 (gene/protein)	PCV7	pneumococcal conjugate vaccine (7-valent) (no longer available)
PCSM	prostate cancer-specific mortality		
PCSO	partial coronary sinus occlusion	PCV13	Pneumococcal 13-Valent Conjugate Vaccine (Prevnar 13)
PC-SPES	an herbal refined powder preparation of eight medicinal plants		
		PCV 23	pneumococcal vaccine polyvalent (Pneumovax 23)
PCSS	Post-Concussion Symptom Scale	PCVC	percutaneous central venous catheter
PCSs	postconcussive symptoms		
PCST	Portal color sort test	PCVG	pressure controlled, volume guaranteed (ventilators)
PCSW	palliative care social work		
PCSWs	photonic crystal surface waves		principal component variable grouping
PCT	parasite-clearance time		
	Patient Care Technician	PCW	postconceptional weeks
	percent	PCWP	pulmonary capillary wedge pressure
	perfusion computed tomography		
	person-centered therapy	PCX	paclitaxel (Taxol)
	photochemical treatment		paracervical
	poker chip tool (for pain rating)		podocalyxin
	porphyria cutanea tarda	Pcx	pyruvate carboxylase;see gene website www.ncbi.nlm.nih .gov/gene
	postcoital test		
	posterior chest tube		
	Primary Care Trust	PCXR	portable chest radiograph
	primary care trust (United Kingdom)	PCZ	procarbazine (Matulane)
			prochlorperazine (Compazine)
	primary chemotherapy	PD	interpupillary distance
	prism and cover test		Paget disease
	procalcitonin		pancreaticoduodenectomy
	progesterone challenge test		panic disorder
	pseudochylothorax		Parkinson disease
PCTA	percutaneous transluminal angioplasty		patient detected
			percutaneous drain
PCTc	procalcitonin clearance rate		periodontitis
PCT-IDS	primary chemotherapy and interval debulking surgery		peritoneal dialysis
			personality disorder
PCTL	percentile		Peyronie disease

P

	pharmacodynamics	PDAP	peritoneal dialysis-associated peritonitis
	pleurectomy/decortication		
	pocket depth (dental)	PDAT	phospholipid:diacylglycerol acyltransferase (gene)
	poorly differentiated		
	post dates	PDB	preperitoneal distention balloon
	postnatal day	PDBP	Parkinson Disease Biomarker Program (National Institute of Neurological Disorders and Stroke)
	postural drainage		
	power Doppler		
	pressure dressing		
	primary dysmenorrhea	PDC	patient denies complaints
	prism diopter(s)		Perinatal Diagnostic Center
	probing depth (dental)		poorly differentiated carcinoma
	progressive disease		private diagnostic clinic
	psychotic disorder		property damage collision (crash)
	pulmonary disease		proportion of days covered
	pupillary distance		pyruvate dehydrogenase complex
Pd	palladiumå	PD&C	postural drainage and clapping
P&D	possibly misheard, see PND	PDCA	Plan-Do-Check-Act (process improvement)
	prepped and draped		
P/D	packs per day (cigarettes)	PD catheter	peritoneal dialysis catheter
	pleurectomy/decortication	PDD	cisplatin (Platinol)
	poorly differentiated		pachydermodactyly
PD1	programmed cell death 1 (gene)		Parkinson disease dementia
PD-1	programmed-cell death protein 1 (gene/protein)		percentage depth dose
			pervasive developmental disorder
¹⁰³Pd	palladium 103		premenstrual dysphoric disorder
Pd125	palladium 125		prescribed daily dose
2-PD	two point discriminatory test		primary degenerative dementia
P3D	persistent postural-perceptual dizziness		pulsed discharge detection
		PDDA	poly(diallyldimethylammonium chloride)
PD5	post-natal day 5		
PDA	pancreatic ductal adenocarcinoma	p-DDAP	p-dodecylaminophenol
	parenteral drug abuser	PDD NOS	pervasive development disorder not otherwise specified
	patent ductus arteriosus		
	pathological demand avoidance (syndrome)	PDDs	pervasive developmental disorders
	personal digital assistant	PDE	paroxysmal dyspnea on exertion
	photodiode array		pulsed Doppler echocardiography
	polymorphic delta activity (electroencephalograph)		
		PDE3	phosphodiesterase type 3
	poorly differentiated adenocarcinoma	PDE4	phosphodiesterase type 4
		PDE10A	phosphodiesterase type 10A
	post discharge assessment	PDEGF	platelet-derived epidermal growth factor
	Post Discharge Assistant		
	posterior descending (coronary) artery	PDEIs	phosphodiesterase inhibitors (Viagra, Levitra, and Cialis)
	Preliminary Denial of Accreditation (The Joint Commission)	PDET	pancreaticoduodenal endocrine tumor
	property damage accident	Pdet	detrusor pressure
PDAC	pancreatic ductal adenocarcinoma	Pdet.Qmax	detrusor pressure at maximum flow
PDAD	photodiode array detector		
P/D Ad Ca	poorly differentiated adenocarcinoma	PDF	Portable Document Format
			probability distribution function
PD-ADSA	pendant drop-axisymmetric drop shape analysis	PDFC	premature dead female child
		PDFF	proton-density fat fraction
PDAF	platelet-derived angiogenesis factor	PDFI	peptide deformylase inhibitor
		Pd3G	pregnanediol 3-glucuronide
PDA ligation	patent ductus arteriosus ligation	PdG	pregnanediol-3-glucuronide

P

PDGF	platelet-derived growth factor
PDGFR	platelet-derived growth factor receptor
PDGFRA	platelet derived growth factor receptor alpha (gene/protein)
PDGFR-beta	platelet derived growth factor receptor beta (gene/protein)
PDGT	percutaneous decompression gastrostomy tube
PDGXT	predischarge graded exercise test
PDH	past dental history
	pyruvate dehydrogenase
PDHM	pasteurized donor human milk
PDI	Pain Disability Index
	phasic detrusor instability
	psychomotor developmental index
PD-IDC	invasive ductal carcinoma patients with Paget disease
PDIGC	patient dismissed in good condition
Pdiol	pregnanediol
PDIP	proximodistal interphalangeal
PDIS	Personal Disability Identity Scale
PDIs	perylene diimide derivatives (organic semiconductors)
	potential drug interactions
	protein disulfide isomerases
PDK	pyruvate dehydrogenase kinase
PDK-1	phosphoinositide-dependent kinase 1
PDL	periodontal ligament
	poorly differentiated lymphocytic
	postures of daily living
	preferred drug list
	progressively diffused leukoencephalopathy
	pulsed-dye laser
PDL-1	programmed cell death protein-ligand 1
PD-L1	programmed death ligand 1 (gene/protein)
PDLA	poly(D-lactide) also known as poly (D-lactic acid)
PDL-D	poorly differentiated lymphocytic-diffuse
PDL-N	poorly differentiated lymphocytic-nodular
PDM	pain during movement
	pregestational diabetes mellitus
	prepuce-degloving method
	primary dermal melanoma
PDMC	premature dead male child
PDMP	prescription drug monitoring program
PDMS	polydimethylsiloxane

PD-MSCs	placenta-derived mesenchymal stem cells
PDN	Paget disease of the nipple
	painful diabetic neuropathy
	prednisolone (this is a dangerous abbreviation as it also has been used for prednisone)
	prednisone (this is a dangerous abbreviation as it also has been used for prednisolone)
	private duty nurse
	prosthetic disk nucleus
PDNE	poorly differentiated neuroendocrine (carcinoma)
PDNOS	personality disorder not otherwise specified
PdNPs	palladium nanoparticles
PDNV	postdischarge nausea and vomiting
PDOC	previously diagnosed human immunodeficiency virus-positive and out-of-care
	primary drug of concern
	prolonged disorders of consciousness
PDOX	pegylated doxorubicin
PDP	pachydermoperiostosis
	Parkinson disease psychosis
	peak diastolic pressure
	prescription drug plan
PD & P	postural drainage and percussion
PDPH	postdural puncture headache
PDPHA	postdural puncture headache
PDPM	peripapillary detachment in pathologic myopia
PDPN	podoplanin; see gene website www.ncbi.nlm.nih.gov/gene
pDPN	painful diabetic peripheral neuropathy
PDPT	patient-delivered partner therapy
PD/PV	postural drainage/percussion/ vibration
PDQ	Pain Disability Questionnaire
	Peyronie Disease Questionnaire
	pretty damn quick (at once)
PDQ-39	Parkinson's Disease Questionnaire
PDQ-R	Personality Diagnostic Questionnaire-Revised
PDR	pancreaticoduodenal resection
	patients' dining room
	Physicians' Desk Reference
	point of decreasing response
	postdelivery room
	proliferative diabetic retinopathy
	prospective drug review
	pulsed-dose rate
PDRcVH	proliferative diabetic retinopathy with vitreous hemorrhage

P

PDRM	preventable drug-related morbidity	PDWHF	platelet-derived wound healing factors
PDRN	polydeoxyribomucleotide	PDWI	proton-density-weighted image(s)
PDRP	proliferative diabetic retinopathy		
PDRUL	palmar distal radioulnar ligament	PDX	patient derived xenografts pyridoxine
PDS	pain dysfunction syndrome	PDx	principal diagnosis
	pancreatic duct stones	pDXA	peripheral dual energy x-ray absorptiometry
	persistent developmental stuttering	PE	cisplatin (Platinol) and etoposide
	Pharmaceutical Development Section (NIH)		pedal edema
	pigment dispersion syndrome		pelvic examination
	polydioxanone suture		pericardial effusion
	power Doppler sonography		pharyngoesophageal
	primary debulking surgery		phenytoin equivalent (150 mg of
	Progressive Deterioration Scale		fosphenytoin sodium is equiv-
PDSA	Plan, Do, Study, Act (a quality		alent to 100 mg of phenytoin
	improvement technique:		sodium)
	Plan - the change to be tested		physical education (gym)
	or implemented; Do - carry		physical examination
	out the test or change;		physical exercise
	Study - data before and after		plasma exchange
	the change and reflect on		pleural effusion
	what was learned; Act - plan		pneumatic equalization
	the next change cycle or full		polyethylene
	implementation)		preeclampsia
	pulmonary digital subtraction		premature ejaculation
	angiography		pressure equalization
PDSCC	poorly differentiated squamous		prolonged exposure (therapy)
	cell carcinoma		protein equivalent
PDSD	Pesquisa Dimensões Sociais das		pulmonary edema
	Desigualdades (Social Dimen-		pulmonary embolism
	sions of Inequalities [study])	P&E	prep (patient preparation for
	proton driven spin diffusion		surgery) and enema
PDSS	Postpartum Depression	P/E	progesterone to estradiol ratio
	Screening Scale		protein energy to total energy
PDT	percutaneous dilatational		(ratio)
	tracheostomy	P_1E_1®	epinephrine 1%, pilocarpine
	photodynamic therapy		1% ophthalmic solution
	postdisaster trauma	PE24	Preemie Enfamil 24
PDTC	pyrrolidine dithiocarbamate	PE20	see gene website www.ncbi.nlm
PDU	PCR (polymerase chain		.nih.gov/gene
	reaction) - detectable units	PEA	palmitoyelethanolamide
	pulsed Doppler ultrasonography		pelvic examination under
PDUFA	Prescription Drug User Fee Act		anesthesia
	(1992)		phenylethylamine
PDUR	postdialysis urea rebound		pre-emptive analgesia
	prospective drug utilization		pulmonary endarterectomy
	review		pulseless electrical activity
PDUS	power Doppler ultrasonography	PEA arrest	pulseless electrical activity
PD-US7	power Doppler seven-joint		(cardiac) arrest
	ultrasound score	peAF	persistent atrial fibrillation
PDV	peak diastolic flow velocity	Peanut	primitive neuroectodermal
	preventive dental visit		tumor (PNET) (slang)
PDVI	power Doppler vascular index	PEARL	physiologic endometrial ablation/
PDW	passive death wish		resection loop
	platelet distribution width		pupils equal and reactive to light

P

458

PEARLA	pupils equal and react to light and accommodation	PEDF	pigment epithelial-derived factor
PEARS	personalized external aortic root support	PEDI	pediatric evaluation of disability inventory
PEAS	proximal extracranial artery stenosis	pedi	pediatrics
PEAs	performance-enhancing agents	PEDI-DEG	pediatric deglycerolized red blood cells
PEAT	pediatric emergency assessment tool	PEDro	Physiotherapy Evidence Database (Scale/score)
PEB	cisplatin, etoposide, and bleomycin	PEDS	Pedestrian Environment Data Scan
PEC	pectoralis		pediatrics
	Physician Emergency Certificate (the 15 day hold certificate used in psychiatric hospitals)	PEDs	performance-enhancing drugs
			periodic epileptiform discharges
			personal electronic devices
	posterior exterior chain (of muscles)	Peds	pediatrics
	preeclampsia	PedsQL 4.0	Pediatric Quality of Life Inventory, version 4.0
	Psychiatric Emergency Clinic	Peds-SOPA	Pediatric Survey of Pain Attitudes
	pulmonary ejection click	PEDT	Premature Ejaculation Diagnostic Tool
PECARN	Pediatric Emergency Care Applied Research Network	PE/DVT	pulmonary embolism/deep vein thrombosis
PECCE	planned extracapsular cataract extraction	PEE	punctate epithelial erosion
PECD	percutaneous endoscopic cervical discectomy	PEEK	polyetheretherketone
		PEEP	position, environment, elimination, and pain
PECHO	prostatic echogram		
PECHR	peripheral exudative choroidal hemorrhagic retinopathy		positive end-expiratory pressure
		PEEPhi	positive end-expiratory pressure high
PECO$_2$	mixed expired carbon dioxide tension	PEERLA	see PEARLA
PEComas	Perivascular epithelioid cell neoplasms	PEF	cisplatin (Platinol), epirubicin, and fluorouracil
			peak expiratory flow
PECOS	Provider Enrollment, Chain and Ownership System (an electronic Medicare enroll-ment system through which providers and suppliers can: submit Medicare enrollment applications; view and update enrollment information; com-plete the revalidation process; withdraw from the Medicare Program; and track the status of a submitted Medicare enrollment application)	PEFR	peak expiratory flow rate
		PEFSR	partial expiratory flow static recoil curve
		PEG	pegylated
			percutaneous endoscopic gastrostomy
			pneumoencephalogram
			polyethylene glycol
		PEG-ELS	polyethylene glycol and iso-osmolar electrolyte solution
		PEGG	Parent Education and Guidance Group
PECS	Picture Exchange Communica-tion System	PEG-J	percutaneous endoscopic gastrojejunostomy
PeCT	perioperative chemotherapy	PEG-JET	percutaneous endoscopic gastrostomy with jejunal extension tube
PED	paroxysmal exertion-induced dyskinesia		
	pediatric emergency department	PEG-LD	pegylated liposomal doxorubicin (Doxil)
	pediatrics	PEG-PLGA	poly(ethylene glycol)-b-poly (lactic-co-glycolic acid)
	performance-enhancing drug		
	pigment epithelial detachments	PEG-SOD	polyethylene glycol-conjugated superoxide dismutase (pegorgotein)
	Pipeline Embolization Device (Covidien, Mansfield, MA)		
PEDD	proton-electron dipole-dipole		

P

PEG tube	percutaneous endoscopic gastrostomy tube	pend	pending laboratory results; pending decision
PEH	paraesophageal hernia postexercise hypotension	pen g	penicillin G (this is a dangerous abbreviation that could be five different drug formulations having different routes of administration)
PEHR	personal electronic health record portable electronic health record		
PEI	cisplatin (Platinol), etoposide, and ifosfamide		
	percutaneous ethanol injection	PENIA	particle-enhanced nephelometric immunoassay
	phosphate excretion index physical efficiency index	PENS	percutaneous electrical nerve stimulation
	polyethylenimine	Pen Vee K	may have meant penicillin V potassium
PeIN	penile intraepithelial neoplasia		
PE/IOL	phacoemulsification with intra-ocular lens (implantation)	Pen VK	penicillin V potassium
		PEO	Paroxysmal Event Observer progressive external ophthalmoplegia
PEIT	percutaneous ethanol injection therapy		
PEITC	phenethyl isothiocyanate	PEOMS	may have meant POEMS
PEJ	percutaneous endoscopic jejunostomy	syndrome	syndrome, a rare, chronic, disabling paraneoplastic disorder characterized by Peripheral-neuropathy, Organomegaly, Endocrinopathy, Monoclonal plasma cells disorder and Skin changes
	pharyngoesophageal junction		
PEK	punctate epithelial keratopathy		
PEL	pelvis		
	permissible exposure limits		
	primary effusion lymphomas		
	protein electrophoresis	PEP	Paroxysmal Event Profile
PELCA	percutaneous endoscopic laser coronary angioplasty		patient education program
			pharmacologic erection program
PELD	percutaneous endoscopic lumbar diskectomy		positive expiratory pressure
			post-ERCP (endoscopic retrograde cholangiopancreatography) pancreatitis
PELE	postextubation laryngeal edema		
PELF	cisPlatin, epirubicin, levoleu-covorin (or leucovorin), and fluorouracil		postexposure prophylaxis
			preejection period
PELOD	pediatric logistic organ dysfunction (score)		primary endpoint
			primer extension
PELV	pelvimetry		preamplification
PEM	pediatric emergency		protein electrophoresis
	positron emission mammography	PEPD	paroxysmal extreme pain disorder
	postexertional malaise	PEP/ET	pre-ejection period/ejection time
	prescription event monitoring	PEPFAR	President's Emergency Plan for AIDS (Acquired Immune Deficiency Syndrome) Relief
	protein-energy malnutrition		
PEMA	phenylethylmalonamide		
P_{emax}	maximum expiratory pressures	PEPI	preejection period index
PEMS	Palatable Eating Motives Scale	PEPM	per enrollee per month
	physical, emotional, mental, and safety	PEPP	payment error prevention program
		PEP-R	Psychoeducational Profile-Revised
	post-exercise muscle soreness	PEPS	psychoeducation with problem-solving (therapy)
PEMU	polyelectrolyte multilayers (ultrathin membranes made by alternating adsorption of oppositely charged polyelectrolytes on substrates)		
		pepS	aminopeptidase (gene)
		PEQ	patient experience questionnaire
		PER	by
PEN	pancreatic endocrine neoplasm		pediatric emergency room
	parenteral and enteral nutrition		pertussis (whooping cough) vaccine, antigens not otherwise unspecified
	penicillin		
	perineal		
	Pharmacy Equivalent Name		protein efficiency ratio

P

PER$_a$	pertussis, acellular antigen(s), vaccine
perAF	persistent atrial fibrillation
PERC	perceptual
	perchloroethylene
	percutaneous
PERCIST	PET (positron emission tomography) Response Criteria in Solid Tumors
Perc Neph	percutaneous nephrolithotomy
percut	percutaneous
PERDS	peri-engraftment respiratory distress syndrome
PERDs	personal emergency radiation detectors
perf	perforation
PERG	pattern electroretinograph
peri	a prefix for around, about, or near
	a prefix meaning around or surrounding
Peri Care	perineum care
PERIO	periodontal disease
	periodontitis
Periop	perioperative
peri-pads	perineal pads
periph	peripherally
perit	peritoneal
PERK	PRKR (interferon-induced double-stranded RNA [ribonucleic acid]-activated protein kinase)-like endoplasmic reticulum kinase
pERK	phosphorylated extracellular-regulated kinase
PERL	pupils equal, reactive to light
PERLA	pupils equally reactive to light and accommodation
PERLLA	see PEARLA
PERM	Parker Personality Measure
	progressive encephalomyelitis with rigidity and myoclonus
perM	see gene website www.ncbi.nlm.nih.gov/gene
Permacath	a long-term central venous catheter placed just below the neck. It consists of 2 lumens so that blood can flow in and out at the same time during the hemodialysis treatment
Perma Cath	see Permacath
Permcath	a long-term central venous catheter placed just below the neck. It consists of 2 lumens so that blood can flow in and out at the same time during the hemodialysis treatment.

per os	by mouth (This is a DANGEROUS abbreviation that should NOT be used. It appears on the medabbrev.com and other Do Not Use Lists, as the OS has been understood as left eye; use "PO" or spell out "by mouth")
PERR	pattern evoked retinal response
PERRAs	post-embolization residual or recurrent aneurysms
PERRL	pupils equal, round, and reactive to light
PERRLA	pupils equal, round, reactive to light and accommodation
PERRLADC	pupils equal, round, reactive to light and accommodation directly and consensually
PERRRLA	pupils equal, round, regular, react to light and accommodation
PeRRT	predicting early rapid response team (score)
PERS	personal emergency response systems
PERT	pancreatic enzyme replacement therapy
	program evaluation and review technique
	Pulmonary Embolism Response Team
PERTL	pupils equal and reactive to light
PERV	porcine endogenous retroviruses
PER$_w$	pertussis, whole-cell antigens, vaccine
PES	paclitaxel-eluting stent
	pediatric emergency service(s)
	pharyngoesophageal segment
	polyethersulfone
	postextubation stridor
	Practice Environment Scale
	preexcitation syndrome
	programmed electrical stimulation
	proximal esophageal sphincter
	pseudoexfoliation syndrome
	Psychiatric Emergency Services
PESA	percutaneous epididymal sperm aspiration
PESI	Pulmonary Embolism Severity Index (score)
PESI-MS	probe electrospray ionization-mass spectrometry
PESIT	Perception of Social Inference Test
PES-NWI	Practice Environment Scale of the Nursing Work Index
peSPL	peak equivalent sound pressure level
PEST	parameter estimation by sequential testing

P

PET	penetrating extrimity trauma		Pontiac fever
	poor exercise tolerance		port film
	positron-emission tomography		power factor
	post-exposure treatment		preservative free
	preeclamptic toxemia		Problem Focused
	pressure equalizing tubes		proctalgia fugax
	problem elicitation technique		prostatic fluid
PETCO$_2$	partial pressure of end-tidal		pulmonary fibrosis
	carbon dioxide		push fluids
PET CT	positron emission tomography	Pf	*Plasmodium falciparum*
	and computed tomography	P/F	arterial partial oxygen pressure
PETE	physical education teacher		to the fraction of inspired
	education		oxygen (ratio)
PEth	phosphatidylethanol	PF3	platelet factor 3
PETHEMA	Programa Español de	PF4	platelet factor 4
	Tratamientos en Hematología	16PF	The Sixteen Personality
	(Group of the Spanish Society		Factors test
	of Hematology)	PFA	foscarnet (phosphonoformatic
PETMRI	positron-emission tomography		acid) (Foscavir)
	and magnetic resonance		patellofemoral arthritis
	imaging		platelet function analysis
PETN	pentaerythritol tetranitrate		psychological first aid
PETO2	end-tidal partial pressure of		pure free acid
	oxygen	P-03FA	prescription form of omeg-3
PET-PiB	positron emission tomograpy		fatty acids (Omacor)
	using the imaging tracer,	PFAA	profunda femoris artery
	Pittsburgh Compound B, a		aneurysm
	derivative of the dye used to	PFAC	Patient and Family Advisory
	identify amyloid at autopsy		Council
PETS	Patient Experience of the		posterior fossa arachnoid cysts
	Trauma System	PFAPA	periodic fever, aphthous stoma-
PET/TAC	positron emission tomography		titis, pharyngitis and cervical
	and tomografia assiale com-		adenitis (syndrome)
	puterizzata (*Italian*: computed	PFAT	preservative-free artificial tears
	axial tomography)	PFat	percentage of body fat
PE tubes	pressure-equalization tubes	PFB	potential for breakdown
PEU	pediatric emergency units		pseudofolliculitis barbae
	psychiatric emergency units	PFC	Partners for Children (a California
PEVAR	percutaneous endovascular		pediatric palliative care pilot
	repair		program offering hospice-like
PEW	protein-energy wasting		services)
PEWS	Pediatric Early Warning System		patellofemoral chondromalacia
	(Score)		patient-focused care
PEX	plasma exchange		perfluorochemical
	pseudoexfoliation (glaucoma)		permanent flexure contracture
PEx	physical examination		persistent fetal circulation
PEX# 3	plasma exchange number three		prefrontal cortex
pexy	a word termination meaning		preserved functional capacity
	fixation (putting together)		prolonged febrile convulsions
PEY	patient exposure years	PFCC	patient and family-centered care
PF	pancreatic fistula	PFCM	patellofemoral chondromalacia
	patellofemoral	PF	patellofemoral compartments
	peak flow	compartments	
	pemphigus foliaceus	PFCs	perfluorinated compounds
	peripheral fields	PFD	pelvic floor dysfunction
	Pharmacopeia Forum	PFDF	plantarflexion/dorsiflexion
	plantar fasciitis	PF/DF	plantarflexion/dorsiflexion
	plantarflexion	P̄ FEEDS	after feedings

P

PFFD	proximal femoral focal deficiency (defect)	PFO	paradoxical embolism
PFFFP	Pall filtered fresh frozen plasma		patent foramen ovale
PFFS	Private Fee-for-Service		persistent foramen ovale
PFG	patellofemoral grind		pissed, fell over (slang for drunk patient)
	percutaneous fluoroscopic gastrostomy	PFOA	perfluorooctanoic acid
	proximal femur geometry	PFO closure	patent foramen ovale closure
	pulsed-field gradient		persistent foramen ovale closure
PFGE	pulsed field gel electrophoresis	PFOS	perfluorooctane sulfonate
PFH	progressive facial hemiatrophy (Parry-Romberg syndrome)	PFP	probability of obtaining a false positive
PF4/heparin IgG	platelet factor 4/heparin immunoglobulin G		progression free probability
			proinsulin fusion protein
PfHRP-2	*Plasmodium falciparum* histidine-rich protein 2	PFPC	Pall filtered packed cells
		PFPS	patellofemoral pain syndrome
PFHx	positive family history	PFPT	pelvic floor physical therapy
PFI	pill-free intervals	PFR	parotid flow rate
	platinum-free interval		peak flow rate
	present for intubation		pelvic floor relaxation
	progression-free interval	P/F ratio	arterial partial oxygen pressure to the fraction of inspired oxygen (ratio)
PFIC	progressive familial intrahepatic cholestasis		
PFIC1	progressive familial intrahepatic cholestasis type 1	PFRC	plasma-free red cells
		P-free diet	phosphorus-free diet
PFIC2	progressive familial intrahepatic cholestasis type 2	pfrmd	performed
		PFROM	pain-free range of motion
PFIC3	progressive familial intrahepatic cholestasis type 3	PFS	patellar femoral syndrome
			patient financial services
PFIF	People Finder Information Format		Physician Fee Schedule
			Piper Fatigue Scale
PFIs	Plans For Improvement (The Joint Commission)		post-finasteride syndrome (sexual side effects [erectile dysfunction], depression, anxiety and cognitive complaints)
PFJ	patellofemoral joint		
PFJS	patellofemoral joint syndrome		
PFL	cisplatin (Platinol), fluorouracil, and leucovorin		prefilled syringe
			preservative-free solution (system)
	recently, standing for patellofemoral ligament		primary fibromyalgia syndrome
			progression-free survival
PFL+IFN	cisplatin (Platinol), fluorouracil, leucovorin, and interferon alfa 2b		prolonged febrile seizure
			pulmonary function studies (study)
PFLX	pefloxacin (not available in the US)	PFS1	first progression-free survival
		PFS2	second progression-free survival
PFM	peak flow meter	PFSH	past, family, social history (histories)
	pelvic-floor muscle		
	permanent first molars	PfSPZ	Plasmodium falciparum sporozoite
	porcelain fused to metal		
	primary fibromyalgia	PFT	parafascicular thalamotomy
PFMC	pelvic floor muscle contraction		per feeding tube
PFME	pelvic floor muscle exercise		peritoneal fat tissue
PFN	probability of obtaining a false negative		pulmonary function test
		PFTA	perfluorotetradecanoic acid
	proximal femoral nail		preservative-free triamcinolone acetone ophth inj(Triesence)
PFNA	perfluorononanoic acid		
	proximal femoral nail antirotation	PFT's	pulmonary function tests
PFNs	perifissural nodules	PFTC	primary fallopian tube carcinoma

P

PFTE	may have meant PTFE (polytetrafluoroethylene)		primary generalized dystonia
PFTM	pelvic-floor tension myalgia		primary graft disfunction
PFTs	pulmonary function tests		prolonged grief disorder
PFU	plaque-forming unit	3-PGDH	3-phosphoglyerate-dehydrogenase
PFUD	pelvic fracture urethral defect(s)	PGE	partial generalized epilepsy
PFUI	pelvic fracture urethral injury		posterior gastroenterostomy
PFV	prototype foamy virus		prostaglandin E
PFW	pHisoHex® face wash		proximal gastric exclusion
PFWB	Pall filtered whole blood	PGE₁	alprostadil (prostaglandin E1)
	Psychological General Well-Being (index)	PGE₂	dinoprostone (prostaglandin E2)
PFWT	pain-free walking time	PGED	Practice Guideline for Eating Disorders
PFWW	platform front-wheel walker	P. gel	Prostin gel
PFX	Perfexion (Leksell Gamma Knife; a precise radiosurgery device)	PGESM	Patient's Global Evaluation of Study Medication
		PGF	paternal grandfather
PG	paclitaxel and gemcitabine	PGF₂α	dinoprost (prostaglandin F₂α)
	paged in hospital	pgf	paternal grandfather
	paregoric	PGGF	paternal great-grandfather
	pathological gambling	PGGM	paternal great-grandmother
	performance goal (short-term goal)	PGH	pituitary growth hormones
		PGI	potassium, glucose, and insulin
	phosphatidylglycerol	PGI₂	epoprostenol (Prostacyclin)
	pigmentary glaucoma	PGIC	Patient Global Impression of Change
	placental grade (biophysical profile)	PGIS	Patient Global Improvement Scale
	polygalacturonate		Personal Growth Initiative Scale
	practice guidelines	PGIs	Patient Global Impressions
	pregnant	PGI-S	Patient Global Impression of Severity
	propylene glycol		
	prostaglandin	PGI-SI	Patient Global Impression of Severity and Improvement
	pyoderma gangrenosum		
pg	picogram (one trillionth of a gram [10-12 gram])	PGJ	pomegranate juice
		PGL	persistent generalized lymph-adenopathy
PGA	prothrombin time, gamma-glutamyl transpeptidase activity, and serum apolipoprotein AI concentration		primary gastric lymphoma
		PGL-1	phosphoglycerate kinase-1
		PGM	paternal grandmother
			phosphoglucomutase
	prostaglandin A	PGME	postgraduate medical education
PGAD	persistent genital arousal disorder	pg/mL	picograms/milliliter
PGAP	Progressive Goal Attainment Program	PGN	peptidoglycan
			progress note
PGAs	prostaglandin analogs		proliferative glomerulonephritis
pgaunt	paternal great aunt	PGNMID	proliferative glomerulonephritis with monoclonal immuno-globulin G deposits
PGB	pregabalin (Lyrica)		
PGBD	polyglucosan body disease		
PGBH	post-gastric bypass (surgery) hypoglycemia	PGO	ponto-geniculo-occipital
		PGP	paternal grandparent
PGCA	gutta-percha-filled canal area(s)	Pgp	P-glycoprotein
PGCG	peripheral giant cell granuloma	P-gp	P-glycoprotein
PGCH	postinfantile giant cell hepatitis	PGR	pulse-generated runoff
PGCR	pharyngoglottal closure reflex	PgR	progesterone receptor
PGCs	primordial germ cells	P-graph	penile plethysmograph
PGD	patient-generated data	PGRN	Pharmacogenomics Research Network
	pelvic girdle dysfunction		
	preimplantation genetic diagnosis		progranulin

PGRT	percutaneous ganglion radiofrequency thermocoagulation
	presence of gross residual tumor
PGS	Persian Gulf syndrome
	posterior glottic stenosis
	postgastrectomy syndrome
	purple glove syndrome
PGT	play-group therapy
PGt	pharmacogenetics
PGT-A	preimplantation genetic testing for aneuploidy
PGTb	primary gastric tuberculosis
PGTC	primary generalized tonic-clonic (seizures)
P±GTC	partial seizures with or without generalized tonic-clonic seizures
pGTD	persistent gestational trophoblastic disease
PGT-M	preimplantation genetic testing for a monogenic disorder
PGTP	for primary glaucoma triple procedure
pgtP	phosphoglycerate transporter protein; see gene website, www.ncbi.nlm.nih.gov/gene
PGT-SR	preimplantation genetic testing for chromosomal structural rearrangements
PG-TXL	poly (L-glutamic acid)-paclitaxel
PGU	postgonococcal urethritis
pguncle	paternal great uncle
PGV	posterior gastric vein
PGW	person gametocyte week
PGx	pharmacogenomics
PGY1	postgraduate year one (first year resident)
PGY3	postgraduate year three (third year resident)
PGY2	postgraduate year two (second year resident)
PH	past history
	personal history
	pinhole
	poor health
	procedure history
	profound hypothermia
	pubic hair
	public health
	pulmonary hypertension
	putaminal hemorrhage
pH	hydrogen ion concentration
P&H	physical and history
P/H	see PH
Ph+	Philadelphia chromosome positive
Ph−	Philadelphia chromosome-negative

PH1	primary hyperoxaluria type 1
PH3	Primary hyperoxaluria type 3
Ph1	Phase I clinical trial (studies assess the safety of a drug or device)
Ph2	Phase II clinical trial (studies test efficacy of a drug or device)
Ph3	Phase III clinical trial (studies involve randomized and blind testing in several hundred to several thousand patients)
Ph4	Phase IV (post marketing surveillance trials)
Ph¹	Philadelphia chromosome
PHA	arterial pH
	passive hemagglutinating
	paternal history of alcoholism
	peripheral hyperalimentation
	phenylalanine
	phytohemagglutinin antigen
	postoperative holding area
	prone horizontal abduction
PHAC	Public Health Agency of Canada
PhAc	pharmaceutically active compound
PHACE	posterior fossa malformation, facial cavernous hemangioma, arterial anomalies, coarctation of the aorta/cardiac defects and eye abnormalities (syndrome)
PHACES	Posterior fossa malformations, Hemangiomas, Arterial malformations, Coarctation of the aorta/Cardiac defects, Eye abnormalities, and Sternal defects (syndrome)
PHACO	phacoemulsification
PHACO OD	phacoemulsification of the right eye
PHACO OS	phacoemulsification of the left eye
PHAL	peripheral hyperalimentation
PHAR	pharmacist
	pharmacy
	pharynx
Pharm	Pharmacy
PharmD	Doctor of Pharmacy
PharmGKB	Pharmacogenomics Knowledgebase (pharmgkb.org)
PHAT	pleomorphic hyalinizing angiectatic tumor
P4HB	poly-4-hydroxybutyrate
	prolyl 4-hydroxylase subunit beta (gene)
PHb	pyridoxylated hemoglobin

P

PHC	permissive hypercapnia	Phi	pressure high
	posthospital care	Phigh	initial ventilator high setting
	primary health care	P-High	pressure high
	primary hepatocellular carcinoma	PhIII	Phase 3 clinical trail
PHCA	profound hypothermic cardiac arrest	PHIS	pharmacy home infusion services
PHCC	Primary Health Care Center		posthead injury syndrome
PHCFs	primary health care facilities	PHL	permanent hearing loss
Ph+CML	Philadelphia chromosome positive chronic myeloid leukemia		Philadelphia (chromosome)
		phleb	phlebectomy
			phlebitis
PHCP	pharyngeal constrictor paresis	PHLF	posthepatectomy liver failure
PHCPs	primary healthcare practitioners	PHLIS	Public Health Laboratory Information System
PHCs	primary health centers		
PHD	paroxysmal hypnogenic dyskinesia	PHLMS	Philadelphia Mindfulness Scale
		PHLS	Public Health Laboratory Service (United Kingdom)
	Public Health Department		
PhD	Doctor of Philosophy	PHM	partial hydatidiform mole
	phospholipase D		pasteurized human milk
PHE	periodic health examination		population health management
	Public Health England		preventive health maintenance
	(an executive agency of the	PHMB	polyhexamethylene biguanine
	Department of Health in the	PHMD	polyhexamethylene (Baquacil, a pool cleaner)
	United Kingdom; mission-		
	to protect and improve the	PHMM	posterior horn of the medial meniscus
	nation's health and to address		
	inequalities)	PHMMs	product hidden Markov models
Phe	phenylalanine (also referred to as F)	PHN	postherpetic neuralgia
			Public Health Nurse
pHealth	Personalized Health (wearable micro and nano technologies)		Puritan® heated nebulizer
		PHNC	public health nurse coordinator
PHEIC	Public Health Emergency of International Concern	PHNI	pinhole no improvement
		PHO	Physician/Hospital Organization
PHEN-FEN	phentermine and fenfluramine	PHOB	phobic anxiety
phenobarb	phenobarbital (slang)	PHOD	Pediatric Hematology Oncology Department
PHEO	pheochromocytoma		
PHEP	progressive home exercise program	PhoD	a family of extracytoplasmic phosphodiesterases (gene/ protein)
PHER	passive hip external rotation		
	Public Health Emergency Re-	PHONO	phonophoresis
	sponse (Centers for Disease	PHOS	phosphatase phosphate
	Control and Prevention)		Phosphorous
Ph Eur	European Pharmacopoeia	photo-CIDNP	photochemically-induced
Ph Eur BRP	The European Pharmacopoeia		dynamic nuclear polarization
	Biological Reference	PHP	plantar heel pain
	Preparation		pooled human plasma
PHF	paired helical filament		postheparin plasma
PHG	portal hypertensive gastropathy		prepaid health plan
PHH	paraesophageal hiatus hernia		primary hyperparathyroidism
	posthemorrhagic hydrocephalus		pseudohypoparathy-roidism
PHHI	persistent hyperinsulinemic		pyridoxalated hemoglobin
	hypoglycemia of infancy		polyoxyethylene conjugate
PHI	patient health information	PHPBT	pediatric Helicobacter pylori breath test
	personal health information		
	phosphohexose isomerase	PHPPO	Public Health Practice Program Office
	prehospital index		
	Prostate Health Index	PHPT	primary hyperparathyroidism
	protected health information	P-HPTH	primary hyperparathyroidism

PHPV	persistent hyperplastic primary vitreous
PHQ2	two-item Patient Health Questionnaire (a screen for depression)
PHQ-2	2-item Patient Health Questionnaire (a screening tool for depression)
PHQ 8	Patient Health Questionnaire-8 (8-item screen for depression)
PHQ 9	Patient Health Questionnaire-9 (9-item screen for depression)
PHQ-9-M	Patient Health Questionnaire-9-item screen for depression modified for teens)
PHR	peak heart rate
	personal health record
PhRMA	Pharmaceutical Research and Manufacturers of America (Formerly the Pharmaceutical Manufacturers Association)
PHRN	Pre-Hospital Registered Nurse
PHRs	personal health records
PHS	partial hospitalization program
	polygenic hazard score (to predict clinical cognitive decline in Alzheimer disease)
	prolene hernia system
	US Public Health Service
PHS-IR	The United States Public Health Service defined 12 criteria of Increased-Risk for transmissible hepatitis B, C, and human immunodeficiency virus infections in potential organ donors where clinicians are required to document informed consent
PHT	phenytoin (Dilantin)
	portal hypertension
	posterior hyaloidal traction
	postmenopausal hormone therapy
	primary hyperthyroidism
	pulmonary hypertension
PHTC	pulmonary hypertensive crises
PHTG	postprandial hypertriglyceridemia
PHTN	portal hypertension
	prehypertension
	pulmonary hypertension
PHTR	Prehospital Trauma Registry
PHV	peak height velocity
	pediatric health visit
PHVA	pinhole visual acuity
pHVA	plasma homovanillic acid
PHVD	posthemorrhagic ventricular dilatation
PHVO	partially hydrogenated vegetable oil(s)

PHx	partial hepatectomy
	past history
Phx	pharynx
PHY	physician
phy ed	physical education
Phyll	Phyllomedusa, a genus of tree frogs
PhyO	physician's orders
Phy Rx	physical therapy
PHYS	physical
	physician
	physiology
phys ed	physical education
PI	package insert
	pallidal index
	pancreatic insufficiency
	Pearl Index
	pelvic incidence
	performance improvement
	peripheral iridectomy
	persistent illness
	physically impaired
	plaque index (dental)
	pneumatosis intestinalis
	poison ivy
	Ponderal index
	postincident
	postinfection
	postinjury
	premature infant
	present illness
	pressure injury
	primary immunodeficiency
	principal investigator
	protease inhibitor
	pulmonary infarction
	pulmonic insufficiency
	pulsatility index
Pi	infusion pressure (ultrafiltration circuit line pressure)
PI-3	parainfluenza 3 virus
P & I	probe and irrigation
PIA	pain in the ass (slang)
	personal injury accident
	polysaccharide intercellular adhesin
PIAF	platinol, recombinant interferon alpha 2B, doxorubicin (Adriamycin), and fluorouracil
PIAGN	postinfectious acute glomerulonephritis
PIAT	Peabody Individual Achievement Test
PIB	partial ileal bypass
	professional information brochure
PiB	Pittsburgh compound B
PIBD	paucity of interlobular bile ducts

P

PIBF	progesterone-induced blocking factor
PIC	intracochlear pressure
	penicillin-inhibitor combinations
	peripherally inserted catheter
	personal injury collision (crash)
	polysaccharide-iron complex
	postintercourse
PICA	Porch Index of Communicative Ability
	posterior inferior cerebellar artery
	posterior inferior communicating artery
Pica	a disorder characterized by an appetite for substances largely non-nutritive (e.g., metal, clay, dirt, paper, etc.
PICC	peripherally inserted central catheter
	purple in color catheter (purple urine bag syndrome)
PICC line	peripherally inserted central catheter line
PiCCO	Pulse index Continuous Cardiac Output (hemodynamic monitoring device)
PICD	paracentesis-induced circulatory dysfunction
PICHI	pulse-inversion contrast harmonic imaging
PIC line	peripherally inserted catheter line
Pico	a prefix in the metric system denoting a factor of 10^{-12} or 0.000,000,000,001
PICS	postintensive care syndrome
	pelvic inclination correction system
	poison-induced cardiogenic shock
PICs	Pacific Islands countries
	Poisons Information Centers
	postoperative infectious complications
pics	pictures
PICT	pancreatic islet cell transplantation
PiCT	prothrombinase-induced clotting time
PICTS	Polish Interventional Cardiology TAVI (transcatheter aortic valve implantation) Survey
	Psychological Inventory of Criminal Thinking Styles
PICTs	Pacific island countries and territories

PICU	pediatric intensive care unit
	psychiatric intensive care unit
PICVA	percutaneous *in situ* coronary venous arterialization
PICVC	peripherally inserted central venous catheter
PID	pelvic inflammatory disease
	pocket-sized (ultrasound) imaging device
	post injury days
	primary immunodeficiency
	prolapsed intervertebral disk
	proportional-integral-derivative (controller)
PIDC	Pediatric Infectious Disease Clinic
	post-ischemic dilated cardiomyopathy
PIDD	primary immunodeficiency disease
PIE	pulmonary infiltration with eosinophilia
	pulmonary interstitial emphysema
PIEE	pulsed irrigation for enhanced evacuation
PIF	peak inspiratory flow
	powdered infant formula
PIFG	poor intrauterine fetal growth
PIFP	persistent idiopathic facial pain
PIFR	peak inspiratory flow rate
PIG	pertussis immune globulin
PIGD	postural instability and gait difficulty (disorder)
PIGF	placental growth factor
PIGI	pregnancy-induced glucose intolerance
PIGN	postinfectious glomerulonephritis
PIGO	phenytoin-induced gingival overgrowth
PIH	postinflammatory hyperpigmentation
	pregnancy-induced hypertension
	preventricular intraventricular hemorrhage
	prolactin-inhibiting hormone
PIIID	peripheral indwelling intermediate infusion device
PIIS	posterior inferior iliac spine
PIJ	proximal interphalangeal joint
PIK3CA	phosphatidylinositol-4,5-bisphosphate 3-kinase catalytic subunit alpha (gene)
PIL	patient information leaflet
	purpose of life
PILC	pillared interlayered clay(s)
	pleomorphic invasive lobular carcinoma

PILO	pilocarpine	PIPAC	pressurized intraperitoneal
PIM	potentially inappropriate		aerosol chemotherapy
	medication	PIPB	performance index phonetic
	Program Integrity Manual		balance
	pulse-inversion mode	PI-PB	performance
	(ultrasound)		intensity-phonemically
P_{imax}	maximum inspiratory pressures		balanced
PIMI	perioperative ischaemic	PIPG	peak instantaneous pressure
	myocardial injury (score)		gradient
PIMIA	potentiometric ionophore		periictal pseudoprogression
	mediated immunoassay	PIPIDA	N-para-isopropyl-acetanilide-
PIMS	programmable implantable		iminodiacetic acid
	medication system	PIPJ	proximal interphalangeal joint
PIMs	potentially inappropriate medi-	PIP joint	proximal interphalangeal joint
	cations (see Beers Criteria)	PIPP	Premature Infant Pain Profile
PIN	pain in the neck (no place for	PIPP-R	Premature Infant Pain Profile –
	such a term in a written		Revised
	document)	PIPS	photon-induced photoacoustic
	personal identification number		streaming
	population impact number	PIPs	potentially inappropriate
	posterior interosseous nerve		prescriptions
	prostatic intraepithelial	PIP/TAZ	piperacillin sodium; tazobactam
	neoplasia		sodium (Zosyn)
	provider identification number	PIP/TAZO	piperacillin sodium; tazobactam
PIN 3	prostatic intraepitheal neoplasia,		sodium inj (Zosyn)
	Grade III	PIP/TZ	piperacillin-tazobactam (Zosyn)
PINC	pregnancy-induced noncoding	PIQ	Performance Intelligence
	RNA (ribonucleic acid)		Quotient (part of Wechsler
PIND	progressive intellectual and		tests)
	neurological deterioration		posterior-inferior quadrant
pINN	proposed International	PIR	pirarubicin
	Nonproprietary Name	PI-RADS	Prostate Imaging and Reporting
PINP	N-terminal propeptide of type I		and Data System
	collagen	PIRBA	*Pirellula baltica*
PINS	persons in need of supervision	PIRRT	prolonged intermittent renal
	progressive inhibition of		replacement therapy
	neuromuscular structures	PIRS	percutaneous internal ring
	(technique)		suturing
PIO	pemoline (Cylert)	PIS	pregnancy interruption service
PIO_2	partial pressure of inspired	PIs	principle Investigators
	oxygen		propofol infusion syndrome
PIOK	poikilocytosis	PISA	phase invariant signature
PIOL	phakic intraocular lens		algorithm
	primary intraocular lymphoma		proximal isovelocity surface
PION	posterior ischemic optic		area
	neuropathy	PISD	paracentral inferior-superior
PIOP	patient informed of policy		difference
PIP	peak inspiratory pressure		postirradiated sudden deafness
	Performance in Practice		psychotropic-induced sexual
	postictal psychosis		dysfunction
	postinfusion phlebitis	PISF	peri-implant sulcus fluid (dental)
	proximal interphalangeal (joint)	PIT	pancreatic islet transplantation
	pulmonary immaturity of		patellar inhibition test
	prematurity		peak isometric torque
	pulmonary insufficiency of the		Pitocin (oxytocin)
	premature		Pitressin (vasopressin) (this is a
PIPA	postinflammatory pigment		dangerous abbreviation)
	alteration		pituitary

P

	psychodynamic interpersonal therapy	PJD	peak joint displacement
	pulsed-inotrope therapy		physical job demands
PITA	pain in the ass (slang)		posterior juxtascleral depot
	powered intracapsular tonsillectomy and adenoidectomy	PJI	periprosthetic joint infection
pitC	phosphatidylinositol transfer protein; see gene website; www.ncbi.nlm.nih.gov/gene		prosthetic Joint Infection
		PJIF	prosthetic joint implant failure
		PJK	proximal junctional kyphosis
		PJP	*pneumocystis jirovecii* pneumonia
PITEF	post-intubation tracheoesophageal fistula	PJRT	permanent junctional reciprocating tachycardia
PITFL	posterior inferior tibiofibular ligament	PJS	peritoneojugular shunt
			Peutz-Jeghers syndrome
PITP	pseudo-idiopathic thrombocytopenic purpura	PJT	paroxysmal junctional tachycardia
		PJVT	paroxysmal junctional-ventricular tachycardia
PITR	plasma iron turnover rate	PK	penetrating keratoplasty
PITS	pulled in two syndrome (a serious complication of strabismus surgery that occurs when an extraocular muscle ruptures under tension)		pharmacokinetics
			plasma potassium
			pyruvate kinase
		PKA	proteins kinase A
		PKAN	pantothenate kinase 2 ; see gene website www.ncbi.nlm.nih.gov /gene
PIU	probelamtic (pathological) Internet use		pantothenate-kinase-associated neurodegeneration
PIV	parainfluenza virus		
	patient identified the vial (allergens)	PKB	prone knee bend
		PKC	protein kinase C
	peripheral intravenous	PKCd	protein kinase C delta; see gene website www.ncbi.nlm.nih.gov /gene
PIV-3	parainfluenza virus type 3		
PIV-5	parainfluenza virus 5		
PIVD	protruded intervertebral disk	PKD	Parkinson disease
PIVF	pacing-induced ventricular fibrillation		paroxysmal kinesigenic dyskinesia
			pharmacodynamics
PIVH	periventricular-intraventricular hemorrhage		polycystic kidney disease
		PKDL	post-kala-azar dermal leishmaniasis
PIVKA	proteins induced in vitamin K absence		
		PKE	paired kidney exchange
PIVM	passive intervertebral motion		passive knee extension (test)
PIVs	parainfluenza viruses	PKG	protein kinase G; see gene website, www.ncbi.nlm.nih .gov/gene
	peripheral intravenous (catheters; accesses; lines)		
PIWT	partially impacted wisdom teeth		
PIXE	particle-induced X-ray emission	PKH2	Paul Karl Horan 2 (green fluorescent vital dye)
	proton-induced X-ray emission		
PIXI	Peripheral Instantaneous X-ray Imaging (dual-energy x-ray absorptiometry system)	PKH26	Paul Karl Horan 26 (red fluorescent vital dye for
		PKH67	Paul Karl Horan 67 (green fluorescent vital dye)
PIZZ	protease inhibitor phenotype ZZ (results in ?(1)-Antitrypsin deficiency)	PKI	public key infrastructure
		PKN	Parkinson disease
PiZZ	homozygosity for the Z mutant allele	PKND	paroxysmal nonkinesigenic dyskinesia
			pyknodysostosis
PJ	pickle juice	PKO	palm kernel oil
	procelin jacket (crown)	PKP	penetrating keratoplasty
PJA	pancreaticojejunoanastomosis		percutaneous kyphoplasty
	proximal junctional angle	PK/PD	pharmacokinetic/ pharmacodynamic
PJB	premature junctional beat		
PJC	premature junctional contractions	PKR	phased knee rehabilitation

P

PKS	Pallister Killian syndrome
pkt	packet
PK Test	Prausnitz-Knstner transfer test
PKTY	patient known to you
PKU	phenylketonuria
pk yrs	pack-years (smoking one pack of cigarettes a day for one year is termed 1 pack-year of smoking, thus 2 packs a day for 20 years would be 40 pack-years)
PL	light perception
	palmaris longus
	peroneus longus (muscle)
	pharyngolaryngectomy
	place
	placebo
	plantar
	plasma
	plethoric (infant color)
	plethysmography
	posterolateral
	problem list
	project leader
	prone lying
	transpulmonary pressure
PLA	placebo
	Plasma-Lyte A
	polyactide
	poly-L-lactic acid (Sculptra)
	posterolateral (coronary) artery
	potentially lethal arrhythmia
	Product License Application
	pulpolinguoaxial
PLAC	placenta
Plac	placebo
PLAC test	quantitative determination of lipoprotein-associated phospholipase A2 (PLAC is copyrighted marketing logo for plaque)
PLAD	proximal left anterior descending (artery)
Plan B®	levonorgestrel (a progestogen emergency contraceptive)
PLA2R1	phospholipase A2 receptor 1 (gene)
PLAP	placental alkaline phosphatase
PLATC	platelet concentration
PLATP	platelet pheresis
PLAX	parasternal long axis
PLB	percutaneous liver biopsy
	percutaneous lung biopsy
	phospholamban
	placebo
	posterolateral branch
	posterolateral branch (coronary artery)
	pursed-lip breathing

PLBF	posterolateral bone fusion
PLBO	placebo
PLC	peripheral lymphocyte count
	permanent legal custodianship
	phospholipase C
	pityriasis lichenoides chronica
PLCH	pulmonary Langerhans cell histiocytosis
plcmnt	placement
P-LCR	platelet larger cell ratio
PLCS	posterior lamina cribrosa surface
pLCX	proximal left circumflex artery
PLD	partial lower denture
	Pegylated liposomal doxorubicin (Doxil)
	percutaneous laser diskectomy
	polycystic liver disease
PLDD	percutaneous laser disk decompression
PLDF	posterior lumbar decompression and fusion
PLE	polymorphic light eruption
	polypodium leucotomos extract (natural fern extract)
	protein-losing enteropathy
PlE	pleural effusions
PLED	periodic lateralizing epileptiform discharge
PLEDs	periodic lateralized epileptiform discharges
PlEf	pleural effusion
PLEK	posterior lamellar endothelial keratoplasty
PLEs	psychosis-like experiences
PLETH	plethysmography
PleurX®	a home-management catheter drainage system for pleural effusions or malignant ascites
PLEVA	pityriasis lichenoides et varioliformis acuta
PLEX	plasma exchange
PLF	posterolateral fusion
	prior level of function
PLFC	premature living female child
PLG	plague (*Yersinia pestis*) (*la Peste*) vaccine
PLGA	pediatric low-grade astrocytomas
	poly(lactic-co-glycolic acid)
PLGG	pediatric low-grade glioma
PLH	paroxysmal localized hyperhidrosis
PLHIV	people living with human immunodeficiency virus
plica	a fold or ridge
PLIE	Preventing Loss of Independence through Exercise
PLIF	posterior lumbar interbody fusion

P

PLIG	posterior lumbar interbody graft	PLQ	plaque(s)
PLIL	partial laryngectomy with inbrication laryngoplasty		Poisson Linear-Quadratic (model for estimating the tumor control probability and normal tissue complication probability)
Plimit	maximal pressure that the vessel could generate to open the output valve		
PLIS	pooled local index of significance	PLR	pupillary light reflex
		PLRs	positive likelihood ratios
PLK	posterior lamellar keratoplasty	PLRT	passive leg raise test
PLKD	polycystic liver and kidney disease		postlumpectomy radiotherapy
		PLS	Papillon-Lefèvre syndrome
PLL	posterior longitudinal ligament		partial least squares
	prolymphocytic leukemia		phantom limb syndrome
PLLA	poly-l-lactic acid		plastic surgery
PLLCI	posterior locked lateral compression injury		point locator stimulator
			Preschool Language Scale
PLLs	posterior longitudinal ligaments		primary lateral sclerosis
	preferred listening levels	PLs	premalignant lesions
	prolymphocytic leukemias	PLSD	protected least significant difference (statistical test)
PLM	partial lateral meniscectomy		
	periodic leg movement	PLSO	posterior leafspring orthosis
	Plasma-Lyte M	PLSR	partial least squares regression
	polarized-light microscope	PLST	progressively lowered stress threshold
	precise lesion measuring (device)		
	product-line manager	PLSURG	plastic surgery
PLMC	premature living male child	PLT	platelet
PLMD	periodic limb movement disorders	PLTC	platelet count
			posterior-lateral-temporal cortex
PLMI	periodic limb movement index (total number of leg movements per hour of sleep)	PLTCCS	primary low transverse cervical cesarean section
		PLTCD	primary low transverse cesarean delivery
PLMS	periodic limb movements during sleep	PLTCS	primary Low-Transverse Cesarean Section
PLMT	painful legs and moving toes (syndrome)		primary low-transverse cesarean section
	partial lateral meniscal tear	PLTCs	possible life-threatening obstetric conditions
PLN	pelvic lymph node		
	phospholamban	pLTD	long-term depression of the phrenic nerve
	popliteal lymph node		
PLND	pelvic lymph node dissection	PLT EST	platelet estimate
PLO	pluronic lecithin organogel	P-LTEC	pediatric long term extended care facilities
PLOF	previous level of functioning		
PLOS	postoperative length of stay	PLTF	plaintiff
	Public Library of Science	PLTs	platelets
PLOSA	physiologic low stress angioplasty	PLUG	plug the lung until it grows
		PLV	partial left ventriculectomy
PLOT	porous layer open tubular (columns)		posterior left ventricular
		PLVAD	percutaneous left ventricular assist device
Plow	low ventilator settings		
P-Low	pressure low	PLVAs	potentially lethal ventricular arrhythmias
PLP	partial laryngopharyngectomy		
	phantom limb pain	PLVB	posterolateral ventricular branch
	protolipid protein	PLVD	persistent left ventricular dysfunction
PLPH	postlumbar puncture headache		
PLPs	padlock probes	PLWH	people living with HIV (human immunodeficiency virus)
	platelet-like particles		
		PLX	plexus

P

PLYO	plyometric	PMBV	percutaneous mitral balloon valvuloplasty
PLZF	promyelocytic leukemia zinc finger	PMC	papillary microcarcinoma
PM	afternoon or evening (p.m.)		posterior medial cortex
	evening		premature mitral closure
	pacemaker		pseudomembranous colitis
	papillary muscles	PMCP	para-monochlorophenol
	paraspinal mapping		perinatal mortality counseling
	partial mastectomy		program
	particulate matter	PMCT	perinatal mortality counseling team
	perceptual motor		postmortem computed
	Performance Measure (The Joint Commission)		tomography
	periodontal maintenance	PMCWR	post-mastectomy chest wall relapse
	petit mal	PMD	Pelizaeus-Merzbacher disease
	physical medicine		pellucid marginal degeneration
	physical mixture		perceptual motor development
	pilomatricoma		persistent microvascular damage
	pneumomediastinum		primary medical doctor
	poliomyelitis		primary myocardial disease
	polymyositis		primidone (Mysoline)
	poor metabolizers		private medical doctor
	posteromedial		progressive muscular dystrophy
	postmenopausal	PMDA	Pharmaceuticals and Medical Devices Agency (Japan)
	postmortem	PMDD	premenstrual dysphoric disorder
	presents mainly	pMDI	pressurized metered-dose inhaler
	pretibial myxedema	PM/DM	polymyositis and
	primary motivation		dermatomyositis
	project manager	PMDS	persistent Mullerian duct syndrome
	prostatic massage		Phelan-McDermid syndrome
	pulpomesial	PMDs	potentially malignant disorders
Pm	*Plasmodium malariae*		psychogenic movement disorders
	promethium	PME	pelvic muscle exercise
PM$_{10}$	particulate matter less than 10 micrometers diameter		phosphomonoester(s)
PMA	pneumatic muscle actuation		polymorphonuclear esosinophil (leukocytes)
	positive mental attitude		postmenopausal estrogen
	post-menstrual age		progressive myoclonus epilepsy
	premarket approval (application) (for medical devices)	PMEALS	after meals
	premenstrual asthma	PMEC	pseudomembranous enterocolitis
	primary meninococcal arthritis	PMED	particle mediated epidermal delivery (vaccination)
	Prinzmetal angina	PMET	pediatric medical emergency team
	progress myoclonic ataxia		plasma membrane electron transport
PMAA	Premarket Approval Application (medical devices)	PMF	peptide mass fingerprinting
Pmab	panitumumab (Vectibix)		posterior malleolar fracture
PMAD	postpartum mood and anxiety disorders		premacular fibrosis
PM and R	physical medicine and rehabilitation		primary myelofibrosis
PMB	polymorphonuclear basophil (leukocytes)		progressive massive fibrosis
	polymyxin B		pupils mid-position, fixed
	postmenopausal bleeding	PMFF	paramedian forehead flap
PMBC	pure mucinous breast carcinoma	PMF/U	prostate message fluid/urine
PMBCL	primary mediastinal large B-cell lymphoma	PMG	Permanente Medical Group

P

PMGCT	primary mediastinal germ cell tumor	PMNS	postmalarial neurological syndrome
pMGN	primary membranous glomerulonephritis	PMO	postmenopausal osteoporosis probable medication overuse
PMH	past medical history	pmol	picomole
PMHCNS-BC	Adult Psychiatric-Mental Health Clinical Nurse Specialist-Board Certified	PMOP	postmenopausal osteoporosis
		PMP	pain management program Prescription Monitoring Program
PMHNP	Psychiatric Mental Health Nurse Practitioner		previous menstrual period
PMHR	predicted maximal heart rate		pseudomyxoma peritonei
PMHS	postmortem human surrogates		psychotropic medication plan
PMHx	past medical history	PMP22	peripheral myelin protein-22 gene
PMI	pacemaker implantation Pain Management Index	PMPA	tenofovir (Viread)
	past medical illness	PMPB	postmenopausal bleeding
	patient medication instructions		premature male pattern baldness
	perioperative myocardial injury	pmpB	polymorphic outer membrane protein; see gene website www.ncbi.nlm.nih.gov/gene
	plea of mental incompetence		
	point of maximal impulse		
	posterior myocardial infarction	PMPC	placenta-mediated pregnancy complication
PMID	PubMed Unique Identifier (National Library of Medicine)	PMPM	per member, per month
PMJ	Purkinje-muscle junction	PMPO	postmenopausal palpable ovary
PMK	phosphomevalonate kinase	PMPY	per member, per year
PML	polymorphonuclear leukocytes	PMQR	plasmid-mediated quinolone-resistant
	posterior mitral leaflet		
	premature labor	PMR	pacemaker rhythm
	progressive multifocal leukoencephalopathy		percutaneous revascularization polymorphic reticulosis
	promyelocytic leukemia		polymyalgia rheumatica
PMLCL	primary mediastinal large-cell lymphoma		premedication regimen prior medical record
PMLD	Pelizaeus-Merzbacher-like disease		progressive muscle relaxation
PMLE	polymorphous light eruption		proportional mortality ratios
PML-RARA	promyelocytic leukemia / retinoic acid receptor alpha (fusion protein)	PM&R	physical medicine and rehabilitation
		PMRs	postmarketing requirements
PMM	partial medial meniscectomy		proportional morbidity ratios
	perioperative medication management	PMRT	postmastectomy radiotherapy
		PMS	performance measurement system
	probe mic measurement		periodic movements of sleep
PMMA	polymethyl methacrylate		Phelan-McDermid Syndrome
PMMF	pectoralis major myocutaneous flap		piriformis muscle syndrome poor miserable soul (slang)
PMMR	postmortem magnetic resonance (imaging)		postmarketing surveillance postmenopausal syndrome
PMMT	partial medial meniscal tear		premenstrual syndrome
PMMTB	precision medical molecular tumor board		psammomatous melanotic schwannoma
PMN	polymodal nociceptors		pulse, motor, and sensory
	polymorphonuclear leukocyte	PMS1	postmeiotic segregation increased 1; see gene website www.ncbi.nlm.nih.gov/gene
	Premarket Notification (medical devices)		
PMNL	polymorphonuclear leukocyte	PMS2	postmeiotic segregation increased 2; see gene website www.ncbi.nlm.nih.gov/gene
PMNN	polymorphonuclear neutrophil		
PMnR	Pain Management and Rehabilitation		

PM/Scl ab	polymyositis/scleroderma antibodies		positional nystagmus
PMSE	polyhydramnios, megalenceph-aly, and symptomatic epilepsy (syndrome)		postnasal
			postnatal
			practical nurse
			premie nipple
PMSF	phenylmethylsulfonyl fluoride		primary nurse
PMSV	perceived message sensation value		progress note
			pyelonephritis
PMT	pacemaker-mediated tachycardia	PN0	pathologically node-negative
		PN1	postnatal day 1
	percutaneous mechanical thrombectomy	PN$_2$	partial pressure of nitrogen
		P & N	pins and needles
	pharmacomechanical thrombectomy		psychiatry and neurology
		PNA	Pediatric Nurse Associate
	photomultiplier tube (radiology)		peptide nucleic acid
	point of maximum tenderness		pneumonia
	posteromedial thigh (flap)		polynitroxyl albumin
	premenstrual tension	PNa	plasma sodium
PMTA	Premarket Tobacco Application (US Food and Drug Administration)	PNAB	percutaneous needle aspiration biopsy
		PNAC	parenteral nutrition associated cholestasis
PMTCT	prevention of mother-to-child transmission	PNA FISH	peptide nucleic acid fluores-cence in situ hybridization
pMTD	population-based maximum tolerated dose	PNALD	parenteral nutrition–associated liver disease
PMTS	premenstrual tension syndrome	pNAP	pyramidal nine-accelerometer package
PMU	permanent make-up	PNAR	perennial nonallergic rhinitis
PMV	Passy-Muir (speaking) Valve	PNAS	prudent no added salt
	percutaneous mitral (balloon) valvuloplasty	PNB	percutaneous needle biopsy
			perineal biopsy
	prolapse of mitral valve		popliteal nerve block
PMVL	posterior mitral valve leaflet		premature newborn
PMVR	percutaneous mitral valve repair		premature nodal beat
PmVSD	perimembranous ventricular septal defects		prostate needle biopsy
PMVT	polymorphic ventricular tachycardia	PNBx	prostate needle biopsy
		PNC	penicillin
	portomesenteric venous thrombosis		peripheral nerve conduction
PMW	pacemaker wires		postnecrotic cirrhosis
	postmenopausal woman (women)		premature nodal contraction
PMX-B	polymyxin-B sulfate		prenatal care
PMX-HP	polymyxin-B hemoperfusion		prenatal course
PMZ	postmenopausal zest		Psychiatric Nurse Clinician
PN	pain	PNCA	parent/nurse-controlled analgesia
	parenteral nutrition	PNC-A	postnecrotic cirrhosis class A of the Child Pugh Classification for Severity of Liver Disease
	peanut (when testing for an allergy)		
	percussion note	PNC-B	postnecrotic cirrhosis due to hepatitis B
	percutaneous nephrosonogram		
	percutaneous nephrostomy	PNCC	Prenatal Care Coordination
	percutaneous nucleotomy	PNC-C	postnecrotic cirrhosis class C of the Child Pugh Classification for Severity of Liver Disease
	periarteritis nodosa		
	peripheral neuropathy		
	plexiform neurofibroma		postnecrotic cirrhosis due to hepatitis C
	pneumonia		
	polyarteritis nodosa	PNC-E	postnecrotic cirrhosis due to ethanol
	poorly nourished		

P

PNCV7	pneumococcal 7-valent conjugate vaccine (Prevnar)		PNLD	pallido-nigro-luysian degeneration
PND	paraneoplastic disorder		PNLT	percutaneous nephrolithotripsy
	paroxysmal nocturnal dyspnea		PNM	primary nodular melanoma
	pelvic node dissection		PNMA	paraneoplastic Ma Family
	postnasal drip		PNMG	persistent neonatal myasthenia gravis
	postnatal depression			
	pregnancy, not delivered		PNMS	phrenic nerve magnetic stimulation
PNDS	Perioperative Nursing Data Set			
	postnasal drip syndrome			prenatal maternal stress
PNE	percutaneous nerve evaluation		PNMT	phenylethanolamine-N-methyltransferase
	peripheral nerve evaluation			
	peripheral neuroepithelioma		PNNP	Perinatal Nurse Practitioner
	primary nocturnal enuresis		PNO	percutaneous nocturnal oximetry
PNEA	psychogenic nonepileptic attacks			potentially nonoperative (patient)
PNECs	predicted no effect concentrations		PNOS	psychosis, not otherwise specified
PNED	Progetto Nazionale Emorragia Digestiva (Italian registry on upper gastrointestinal bleeding)		PNP	peak negative pressure
				Pediatric Nurse Practitioner
				pneumoperitoneum
PNEE	paroxysmal nonepileptic event(s)			progressive nuclear palsy
	prenatal ethanol exposure			Public Health Nurse
	psychogenic non epileptic event(s)			purine nucleoside phosphorylase
PNES	psychogenic nonepileptic seizures		P1NP	procollagen type 1 amino-terminal propeptide (a bone turnover marker)
	primitive neuroectodermal tumors		PNQ	pyranonaphthoquinone
pNET	pancreatic neuroendocrine tumor		PNR	person needed ride (minor ailment but called ambulance instead of taxi)(slang)
PNET-MB	primitive neuroectodermal tumors-medulloblastoma			physician's nutritional recommendation
pneum	pneumonia			
PNEUMO	pneumothorax		PNRB	partial non-rebreather (oxygen mask)
PNF	primary nonfunction			
	proprioceptive neuromuscular fasciculation (reaction)		PNRS	Pain Numeric Rating Scale
			PNS	paraneoplastic neurological syndromes
P/N/F	pooling/nitrazine/ferning			partial nonprogressing stroke
PNFA	progressive nonfluent aphasia			peripheral nerve stimulator
pNF-H	phosphorylated neurofilament heavy subunit			peripheral nervous system
				posterior nasal spine (cephalometric landmark)
PNFS	peripheral nerve field stimulation			practical nursing student
PNFs	plexiform neurofibromas			Pump N' Style (breast pump machine)
PNG	Papua New Guinea			
PNGD	palisaded neutrophilic and granulomatous dermatitis		PNSD	peripheral nervous system disorders
PNH	paroxysmal nocturnal hemoglobinuria		PNSF	pedicled nasoseptal flap
	polynitroxyl-hemoglobin		PNSP	penicillin-nonsusceptible Streptococcus pneumoniae
	progressive nodular hyperplasia			
PNI	perineural invasion		PNST	peripheral nerve sheath tumors(s)
	peripheral nerve injury		PNT	percutaneous nephrostomy tube
	Prognostic Nutrition Index			percutaneous neuromodulatory therapy
PNKD	paroxysmal nonkinesigenic dyskinesia			pneumatic trabeculoplasty
PNL	percutaneous nephrolithotomy		pnthx	pneumothorax
	prenatal labs		PNTM	pulmonary nontuberculous mycobacterial (disease)
	preterm no labor			

P

PNTML	pudenal-nerve terminal motor latency	POAF	postoperative atrial fibrillation
PNTX	pneumothorax	POAG	primary open-angle glaucoma
pNTP	para-nitrothiophenol	POAHC	power of attorney for health care
PNU	pneumococcal (*Streptococcus pneumoniae*) vaccine, not otherwise specified	POAL	primary ocular adnexal lymphoma
	protein nitrogen units	POARisk	Present-On-Admission Risk
PNUcn-7	pneumococcal (*Streptococcus pneumoniae*)conjugate	POAS	pee on a stick (slang-pregnancy test)
	vaccine, 7-valent	POB	phenoxybenzamine (Dibenzyline)
PNUps23	pneumococcal (*Streptococcus pneumoniae*) polysaccharide, 23-valent vaccine		place of birth
		POBA	plain old balloon angioplasty
		POBC	primary operable breast cancer
PNUS	perineal ultrasound	PObHx	past obstetrical history
	peripheral nerve ultrasound	POC	peri-operative chemotherapy
	prenatal ultrasound		plans of care
PNUs	pneumonia		point-of-care
PNV	postoperative nausea and vomiting		position of comfort
			postoperative care
	prenatal vitamins		product of conception
Pnx	pneumonectomy		proof of concept
	pneumothorax	POC-BG	point-of-care blood glucose
PO	by mouth (*per os*)	POCC	postoperative cognitive change
	phone order	POCD	postoperative cognitive dysfunction
	postoperative		
	preoperative	PoCG	postcentral gyrus
	probation officer	POCgluc	point-of-care glucometer
	prophylactic oophorectomy	POC glucose	point-of-care glucose monitoring
	pulse oximetry		
	punctual occlusion	POCGMD	point-of-care glucose monitoring device
Po	*Plasmodium ovale*		
	polonium	POCS	peroral cholangioscopy
P&O	parasites and ova		point of care summary
	prosthetics and orthotics		projection onto convex sets (radiology)
PO2	partial pressure of oxygen (reflects the amount of		
		POCs	portable oxygen concentrators
	oxygen gas dissolved in the blood)		progestin-only contraceptives
		POCT	point-of-care testing (test)
PO₄	phosphate		point-of-care therapy
POA	pancreatic oncofetal antigen	POCUS	point-of-care ultrasonography
	plan of action	POD	pacing on demand
	power of attorney		place of death
	present on admission		Podiatry
	present on arrival		point-of-dispensing
	Present-on-Admission (indicator)		polycystic ovarian disease
			postoperative delirium
	primary optic atrophy		prevention of disability
PoAb	polyclonal antibody (antibodies that are secreted by different B cell lineages within the body)		probability of detection
			progression of disease
		POD0	day of surgery (postoperative day zero)
		POD 0	day of surgery (postoperative day zero)
POACH	prednisone, vincristine (Oncovin), doxorubicin (Adriamycin), cyclophosphamide, and cytarabine		
		POD1	postoperative day 1
		POD2	postoperative day 2
		POD3	postoperative day 3
POAD	peripheral obstructive arterial disease	POD4	postoperative day 4
		POD5	postoperative day 5

POD#1	postoperative day one	*POHS*	by mouth, at bedtime
PODCI	Pediatric Outcomes Data Collection Instrument	POHx	oral history
		POI	Personal Orientation Inventory
podo	podocytes		point of interest
	podophyllotoxin		postoperative ileus
PODs	patient's own drugs		postoperative instructions
PODx	preoperative diagnosis	POIB	place outpatient in inpatient bed
POE	patient-oriented evidence		
	point (portal, port) of entry	POID	prevention of impairments and disabilities
	position of ease		
	prone on elbows	POIK	poikilocytosis
	provider order entry	POIs	points of interest
POEM	Patient-Oriented Eczema Measure	POK	post-obstructed kidney
	Patient-Oriented Evidence That Matters	POKs	primary oral keratinocytes
		POL	physician's office laboratory
	peroral endoscopic myotomy		poliovirus vaccine, not otherwise specified
POEMS syndrome	a rare, chronic, disabling paraneoplastic disorder characterized by **P**eripheral neuropathy, **O**rganomegaly, **E**ndocrinopathy, **M**onoclonal plasma cells disorder and **S**kin changes		premature onset of labor
		POLD	pigmentary orthochromatic leukodystrophy
			polymerase delta
			postoperative liver dysfunction
		POLF	postoperative liver failure
POET	peroral endoscopic tumor (resection)	POLG	polymerase (DNA directed), gamma; see gene website, www.ncbi.nlm.nih.gov/gene
	post offer evaluation test		
	PreOperative therapy in Esophagogastric adenocarcinoma Trial	polio	poliomyelitis
		POLS	postoperative length of stay
POEx	postoperative exercise	POLST	Physician Orders for Life-Sustaining Treatment (Paradigm)
POF	physician's order form		
	position of function		
	premature ovarian failure	POLT	partial orthotopic liver transplantation
PO3FA	prescription form of omeg-3 fatty acids (Omacor)		
		POLY	polychromic erythrocytes
P of I	proof of illness		polymorphonuclear leukocyte
POG	Pediatric Oncology Group	POLY-CHR	polychromatophilia
	Penthrane,® oxygen, and gas (nitrous oxide)	polypill	such as a fixed combination dosage form containing aspirin 100 mg, simvastatin 40 mg and ramipril 2.5, 5, or 10 mg
	period of gestation		
	positions of gaze (for extraocular muscle)		
		polys	polymorphonuclencytes
	products of gestation	POM	pain on motion
POGO	percentage of glottic opening		polyoximethylene
POH	past ocular history		postoperative morbidity
	perillyl alcohol		prescription-only medication
	personal oral hygiene	P-OM3	prescription-grade omega-3 fatty acids (Lovaza)
	poor oral health		
	presumed ocular histoplasmosis	POMA	Performance-Oriented Mobility Assessment
	progressive osseous heteroplasia		
	prone on hands	POMAF	preoperative medical assessment form
POHA	preoperative holding area		
POHCA	pediatric out-of-hospital cardiac arrest	POMC	pro-opiomelanocortin
		POME	preoperative medical evaluation
POHI	physically or otherwise health impaired		pulmonary oil micro-embolism (syndrome)
POHS	presumed ocular histoplasmosis syndrome	POMH-UK	Prescribing Observatory of Mental Health-United Kingdom

P

POMP	prednisone, vincristine (Oncovin), methotrexate, and mercaptopurine (Purinthol)
POMR	perioperative mortality rate problem-oriented medical record
POMS	Profile of Mood States
POMS-FI	Fatigue-Inertia Subscale of the Profile of Mood States
PON	paraoxonase (genes) postoperative note
PONI	postoperative narcotic infusion
PONV	postoperative nausea and vomiting
POOH	postoperative open heart (surgery)
POOL	premature onset of labor
poop	feces (slang)
POP	pain on palpation pelvic organ prolapse persistent occipitoposterior persistent organic pollutants plaster of paris popiliteal posterior oral pharynx
POp	postoperative
POPC	Pediatric Overall Performance Category (scale)
POPE study	phenotypes of chronic obstructive pulmonary disease
POPF	postoperative pancreatic fistula
PoPH	portopulmonary hypertension
poplit	popliteal
POPQ	Pelvic Organ Prolapse Quantification
POP-Q	Pelvic Organ Prolapse Quantification
PO/PR	orally or rectally
POPRAS	Problem-Oriented Perinatal Risk Assessment System
POPS	postoperative pain service
POPs	persistent organic pollutants progesterone-only pills
POPTA	passed out prior to arrival
POPV	popliteal vein
POQ	Patient Outcome Questionnaire
POQD	once daily by mouth (this is a dangerous abbreviations as it read as four times daily by mouth)
POR	physician of record prevalence odds ratios problem-oriented record
porB	protochlorophyllide oxidoreductase B; see gene website www.ncbi.nlm.nih .gov/gene
PORC	post operative recovery after the use of neuromuscular blockers (curarization)

PORN	pornography progressive outer retinal necrosis
PORP	partial ossicular replacement prosthesis
PORR	postoperative recovery room
PORT	perioperative respiratory therapy portable portal film postoperative radiotherapy postoperative respiratory therapy prostate-only radiotherapy
PORT-A-CATH	an implanted device designed to permit repeated access to the venous system for the parenteral delivery of medications, fluids, and nutrition
POS	Palliative Outcome Scale parosteal osteosarcoma partial-onset seizures physician's order sheet place of service (Medicare) point-of-service point-of-service (plan) positive
PoS	plane of surgery
POSHPATE	Problem, Onset, associated Symptoms, previous History, Precipitating factors, Alleviating/aggravation factors, Timing, an Etiology
POSL	pulse optically stimulated luminescence dosimeter (radiology)
pOsm	plasma osmolality (the plasma concentration of a solution expressed as the total number of solute particles per kilogram)
POSS	Pasero Opioid-Induced Sedation Scale
poss	possible
POSSUM	Physiological and Operative Severity Score for the enUmeration of Mortality and Morbidity (score)
POST	postoperative sore throat
post	posterior postmortem examination (autopsy)
PostC	posterior chamber
PostCap	posterior capsule
POST form	Physicians Order for Scope of Treatment form (patient's wishes about the use of cardiopulmonary resuscitation, medical intervention, antibiotics, and artificially administered nutrition)

Post-M	urine specimen after prostate massage		paradoxical pulse
post op	postoperative		partial upper and lower dentures
Post Sag D	posterior sagittal diameter		pedal pulse
post tib	posterial tibial		per protocol
PostVD	posterior vitreous detachment		periodontal pockets
POSYC	Pain Observation Scale for Young Children		peripheral pulses
			pin prick
			pink puffer (emphysema)
POT	peak occupancy time		placenta previa
	plans of treatment		Planned Parenthood
	potassium		plasmapheresis
	potential		plaster of paris
	primary orthoscopic tremor		poor person
potC	polyamine transporter subunit (gene)		posterior pituitary
			postpartum
POTS	postural orthostatic tachycardia syndrome		postprandial
			prescribing practitioners
POTs	pop-over transfers (refers to methods body position/ location transferring of disabled patients)		presenting part
			private patient
			prophylactics
			protoporphyria
Pott disease	tuberculous spondylitis		proximal phalanx
Potts shunt	an anastomosis between the descending aorta and the left pulmonary artery (named after Dr. Willis J. Potts)		psychogenic polydipsia
			pulse pressure
			push pills
		P2P	peer-to-peer
POTUS	President of the United States		phenyl-2-propanone (also known as phenylacetone; used in clandestine laboratories to illicitly manufacture the schedule II controlled substances)
POTUs	phage operational taxonomic units		
POU	placenta, ovaries, and uterus		
	point-of-use		
	prescription opioid use		pyrimidinergic receptor P2Y4 (gene)
POUR	postoperative urinary retention		
POV	postoperative vomiting	P4P	pay-for-performance
	primary outcome variable	P5P	pyridoxal-5-phosphate (an active form of vitamin B6 [pyridoxine])
	privately owned vehicle		
POVA	postoperative ventricular arrhythmia		
		P-P	probability-probability (plots)
	Protection of Vulnerable Adults (United Kingdom)	P&P	pins and plaster
pOVA	ovalbumin peptide	P/P	positive/positive
POVD	peripheral occlusive vascular disease		proline homozygous see PP
POVH	postoperative ventral hernia	PPA	palpation, percussion, and auscultation
POW	Powassan (virus)		
	prisoner of war		peripapillary atrophy
POW1	postoperative week 1		phenylpropanolamine
POWD	prevention of worsening disability		phenylpyruvic acid
			postpartum amenorrhea
POWs	postoperative weeks		Prescription Pricing Authority (United Kingdom)
POWSBP	pulse oximetry waveform systolic blood pressure		
			primary progressive aphasia
POX	proline oxidase	PP&A	palpation, percussion, and auscultation
	pulse oximeter (reading)		
P OX	pulse oximetry	PPACA	Patient Protection and Affordable Care Act (called the Affordable Care Act (ACA) or "ObamaCare")
POY	postoperative year		
PP	near point of accommodation		
	pancreatic pseudocyst		

PPAH	primary pulmonary (arterial) hypertension
PPALND	pelvic and para-aortic lymph node dissection
PPAOS	primary progressive apraxia of speech
PPAR	peroxisome proliferator-activated receptor
PPAR$_g$	peroxisome-proliferator-activated receptor gamma
PPARs	peroxisome proliferator-activated receptors
PPAS	postpolio atrophy syndrome
PPB	parts per billion
	pleuropulmonary blastoma
	positive pressure breathing
	prostate puncture biopsy
PPBC	Patient Perception of Bladder Condition (diary/scale)
	post-partum birth control
PPBE	postpartum breast engorgment
PPBS	postprandial blood sugar
PPBTL	postpartum bilateral tubal ligation
ppbv	parts per billion by volume
PPC	pediatric palliative care
	plaster of paris cast
	positive product control
	posterior parietal cortex
	primary peritoneal carcinoma
	progressive patient care
PPCA	postpartum cerebral angiitis
	primary peritoneal carcinoma
	probabilistic principal component analysis
	protective protein/cathepsin A
ppcA	phosphoenolpyruvate carboxylase; see gene website www .ncbi.nlm.nih.gov/gene
PPCD	posterior polymorphous corneal dystrophy
	Preschool Program for Children with Disabilities
PPCF	plasma prothrombin conversion factor
PPCG	pedicled partial-thickness clavicular graft
PPCI	primary percutaneous coronary intervention
PPCL	primary plasma cell leukemia
PPCM	peripartum cardiomyopathy
PPCP	pharmacists' patient care process
+PPD	positive purified protein derivative (test)
PPD	packs per day
	para-phenylenediamine (a dye)
	permanent partial disability (rating)
	pinch point density (histologic)

	posterior polymorphous dystrophy
	postpartum day
	postpartum depression
	probing pocket depth (dental)
	purified protein derivative (of tuberculin)
	pylorus-sparing pancreaticoduodenectomy
P&PD	percussion and postural drainage
PPD1	postpartum day 1
PPD2	postpartum day 2
	preaxial polydactyly type 2
	pyruvate phosphate dikinase (gene)
PPD3	postpartum day 3
PPD-B	purified protein derivative, Battey
PPDH	peritoneopericardial diaphragmatic hernia (veterinary)
PPDR	preproliferative diabetic retinopathy
PPD-S	purified protein derivative, standard
PPE	palmar-plantar erythrodysesthesia (syndrome)
	papilledema
	parapneumonic pleural effusion
	personal protective equipment
	preparticipation physical evaluation
	professional performance evaluation
	pruritic papular eruption
Ppeak	peak airway pressure (ventilator parameter)
PPED	personal protective eye device
	postprostatectomy erectile dysfunction
PPES	palmar-plantar erythrodysesthesia syndrome
	pedal pulses equal and strong
PPF	pellagra preventive factor
	plasma protein fraction
	propofol (Diprivan)
PPFC	peripancreatic fluid collection
PPFE	pleuroparenchymal fibroelastosis
PPFT	peak plantar flexion torque
	postpyloric feeding tube
PPG	penile plethysmography
	permanent pacemaker generator
	photoplethysmography
	portal pressure gradients
	postprandial glucose
	pylorus-preserving gastrectomy
PPGI	psychophysiologic gastrointestinal (reaction)

P

PPGSS	papular-purpuric "glove and socks" syndrome	PPLOV	painless progressive loss of vision
PPH	postpartum hemorrhage	PPLV	percentage of predicted lung volume
	primary postpartum hemorrhage		
	primary pulmonary hypertension	PPM	parts per million
	procedure for prolapse and hemorrhoids		permanent pacemaker
			persistent pupillary membrane
PPHN	persistent pulmonary hypertension of the newborn		physician practice management
			polypropylene mesh
PPHP	pseudo-pseudohypoparathyroidism	PPMA	postpoliomyelitis muscular atrophy
PPHTN	portopulmonary hypertnesion	PPM/AICD	permanent pacemaker / automatic implantable
PPHx	previous psychiatric history		
PPI	patient package insert	PPMD	posterior papillary muscle distances
	permanent pacemaker insertion		
	prepulse inhibition		posterior polymorphous dystrophy
	Present Pain Intensity		postpartum major depression
	proton-pump inhibitor (e.g. omeprazole [Prilosec], lansoprazole [Prevacid])		postpartum mood disorder
		PPMI	Parkinson's Progression Markers Initiative
	Psychopathic Personality Inventory		permanent pacemaker implantation
PPIA	parental presence during induction of anesthesia	PPMP	persistent postmastectomy pain (syndrome)
PPIC	Patient Perception of Integrated Care (survey)	PPMS	primary-progressive multiple sclerosis
	peptidylprolyl isomerase C (gene)		psychophysiologic musculo-skeletal (reaction)
PPID	peptidylprolyl isomerase D; see gene website www.ncbi.nlm.nih.gov/gene	PPMs	potentially pathogenic microorganisms
	pituitary pars intermedia dysfunction (veterinary)	PPMT	see gene website, www.ncbi.nlm.nih.gov/gene
PPIs	protein-protein interactions	PPMV	proprietary and patent medicine vendor
	proton-pump inhibitors (e.g. omeprazole [Prilosec], lansoprazole [Prevacid])	PPN	peripheral parenteral nutrition
			peripheral polyneuropathy
PPIUS	Patient Perception of Intensity of Urgency Scale	PPNAD	primary pigmented nodular adrenocortical disease
PPIVMs	passive physiological intervertebral movements	PPNG	penicillinase producing Neisseria gonorrhoeae
PPIX	protoporphyrin nine	PPO	permanent punctual occlusion
PpIX	photosensitizer protoporphyrin IX		prefered provider organization
PPJ	pure pancreatic juice		pump-prime only
PPK	population pharmacokinetics	PPOB	postpartum obstetrics
P1PK	P1PK; an International Society of Blood Transfusion (ISBT) blood group	PPOC	preferred place of care
		PPOD	preferred place of death
		PPP	palmoplantar pustulosis
PPL	pars plana lensectomy		patient portable profile
	posterior parietal lobe		patient prepped and positioned
Ppl	pleural pressure		pearly penile papules
Pplat	plateau pressure (the pressure applied to small airways and alveoli during positive-pressure mechanical ventilation)		pedal pulse present
			peripheral pulses palpable (present)
			persistent postpartum pain
			plaque-type palmoplantar psoriasis
PPLND	pelvic and para-aortic lymph node dissection		platelet-poor plasma
PPLO	pleuropneumonia-like organisms		postpartum psychosis

	preferred practice patterns	
	preoperative progressive	
	pneumoperitoneum	
	primary periodic paralysis	
	proportional pulse pressure	
	(SBP minus DBP)/SBP	
	protamine paracoagulation	
	phenomenon	
PPPBL	peripheral pulses palpable both	
	legs	
PPPD	persistent postural-perceptual	
	dizziness (formerly known as	
	'phobic postural vertigo' or	
	'chronic subjective dizziness')	
	pylorus-preserving	
	pancreatoduodenectomy	
PPPG	postprandial plasma glucose	
PPPM	Parents' Postoperative Pain	
	Measure	
	per patient, per month	
PPPROM	previable preterm premature	
	rupture of membranes	
	prolonged preterm premature	
	rupture of membranes	
PPPV	per patient per visit	
	polyvalent pneumococcal	
	polysaccharide vaccination	
	prepancreatic postduodenal	
	portal vein	
PPPY	per patient, per year	
PPQ	Postoperative Pain	
	Questionnaire	
ppqv	parts per quadrillion by volume	
PPR	patient progress record	
	proportion of patients relapsed	
PPr	periodontal prophylactics	
PPRC	Physician Payment Review	
	Commission	
PPRD	progressive pseudorheumatoid	
	dysplasia	
PPRF	paramedic pontine reticular	
	formation	
	posterior pelvic ring fixation	
P-PROM	preterm premature rupture of	
	membranes	
PPS	Palliative Performance Scale	
	pentosan polysulfate (Elmiron)	
	per protocol set	
	percent of peristaltic swallows	
	peripheral pulmonary stenosis	
	point-prevalence-survey	
	postpartum sterilization	
	postperfusion syndrome	
	postpericardiotomy syndrome	
	postpoliomyelitis syndrome	
	postpump syndrome	
	prospective payment system	
	pulses per second	

ppsD	phenolpthiocerol synthesis	
	type-I polyketide synthase;	
	see gene website www.ncbi	
	.nlm.nih.gov/gene	
PPSE	postprandial symptom	
	exacerbation	
PPSS	peripheral protein sparing	
	solution	
PPSV23	pneumococcal polysaccharide	
	vaccine 23 valent version	
	(Pneumovax 23)	
PPT	pacemaker parameter test	
	partially porous titanium	
	parts per trillion	
	person, place, and time	
	Physical Performance Test	
	posterior pelvic tilt	
	postpartum thyroiditis	
	Pott puffy tumor	
	pressure pain threshold	
ppt	percent precipitate	
PPTD	pancreas-preserving total	
	duodenectomy	
	postpartum thyroid dysfunction	
	Psychological Predictors of	
	Therapeutic success in	
	Diabetes (questionnaire)	
PPTF	propentofylline	
PPTg	pedunculopontine tegmental	
	nucleus	
PPTL	postpartum tubal ligation	
PPTR	pulsed photothermal	
	radiometry	
PPTs	pediatric physical therapists	
PPTTN	painful posttraumatic trigeminal	
	neuropathy	
pptv	parts per trillion by volume	
PPU	perforated peptic ulcer	
	postpartum unit	
	prone press-ups	
PPV	pars plana vitrectomy	
	patent processus vaginalum	
	percutaneous polymethylmeth-	
	acrylate vertebroplasty	
	phakomatosis	
	pigmentovascularis	
	pneumococcal polysaccharide	
	vaccine	
	porcine parvovirus	
	positive predictive value	
	positive-pressure ventilation	
PPV23	pneumococcal polysaccharide	
	vaccine, 23 valent version	
	(Pneumovax 23)	
PPVD	partial posterior vitreous	
	detachment	
	perifoveal posterior vitreous	
	detachments	

P

	persistent primary visual disturbance		progesterone receptor
	postpartum voiding dysfunction		progressive resistance
PPVI	percutaneous pulmonary valve implantation		prolonged remission
			prone
PPVT	Peabody Picture Vocabulary Test		Protestant
			pubic rams
PPVV	peak portal vein velocity		Puerto Rican
PPW	plantar puncture wound		Puerto Rico
	posterior pharyngeal wall		pulmonic regurgitation
	premature P-wave		pulse rate
	prepregnant weight	PR-2	Bennett pressure ventilator
PPWK	paperwork	PR3	proteinase 3 (gene/protein)
PPX	paclitaxel poliglumex	P & R	pelvic and rectal
	pramipexole dihydrochloride (Mirapex)		pulse and respiration
		P=R	pupils equal in size and reaction
	prophylaxis	PR+	progesterone receptor positive
	propoxyphene	PR−	progesterone receptor negative
PPY	packs per year (cigarettes)	PRA	panel reactive antibodies (organ transplants)
PPYLL	potentially productive years of life lost		panel-reactive antibody
PQ	Paraquat poisoning		percent reactive antibody
	pronator quadratus		plasma renin activity
pQCT	peripheral quantitative computed tomography		prerenal azotemia
		PRAFO	pressure relief ankle-foot orthosis
PQI	Practice Quality Improvement (radiology)	PRAM	Pediatric Respiratory Assessment Measure
PQIs	Prevention Quality Indicators	PRAMS	Pregnancy Risk Assessment Monitoring System
PQOCN	Psychiatric Questionnaire Obsessive-Compulsive Neurosis	PRAP	Prostate Cancer Risk Assessment Program
PQoL	perceived quality of life		Psychosocial Risk Assessment in Pediatrics
PQP	piperaquine phosphate		
PQQ	pyrroloquinoline quinone	PRAT	platelet radioactive antiglobulin test
PQRI	Physician Quality Reporting Initiative (Medicare)	PRB	partial rebreathing mask
	Product Quality Research Initiative		post-radiotherapy biopsy
PQRS	Physician Quality Reporting System	PRBB	combined peribulbar and retrobulbar block
PQRST	Provokes/Palliates; Quality/ Quantity; Region/Radiates; Severity; Timing (chest pain evaluation)	PRBC	packed red blood cells
			parasitized red blood cells
		PRBCs	packed red blood cells
		PRBPR	may have meant BRBPR (bright red blood per rectum)
PR	far point of accommodation	PRBS	pseudo-random binary sequence
	pack removal	PRBs	permeable reactive barriers
	panoramic radiography (dental)	PRC	packed red cells
	partial remission		Pain Rehabilitation Center
	partial response		peer review committee
	patient relations		People's Republic of China
	Patient Responsibility (Medicare code)		perirhinal cortex
			perirolandic cortex
	per rectum		proximal row carpectomy
	perennial rhinitis	PRC2	polycomb repressive complex 2
	pityriasis rosea	PRCA	pure red cell aplasia
	praseodymium	PrCa	prostate cancer
	preferred route	prcB	proteasome subunit beta (gene)
	premature	PRCC	papillary renal cell carcinoma
	profile		

P

PRCD	parkinsonism-related cervical dystonia	PREFS	post-relapse-event-free-survival
	progressive rod-cone degeneration	PREG	Pregestimil® (infant formula) pregnancy
PrCG	precentral gyrus	prelim	preliminary
PRCI	per radiologist clinical indication	prem	premature
		Pre-M	urine specimen before prostate massage
PRCP	prolylcarboxypeptidase; see gene website www.ncbi.nlm .nih.gov/gene	premed	before medical school (curriculum, education, student, etc)
PRCT	partial rotator cuff tear	PREMIE	premature infant
	prospective randomized controlled trial	Pre-O₂	preoxygenation
		pre op	before surgery
PRD	paired reflex depression	PREP	Pain Relieving Exercise Program
	polycystic renal disease	PrEP	pre-exposure prophylaxis
	pseudophakic retinal detachment	prep	prepare for surgery preposition
PrdGP	predominant Gleason pattern		see gene website www.ncbi.nlm .nih.gov/gene
PRDI	patient-reported dosing information	PRERLA	pupils round, equal, react to light and accommodation
PRDI 1	positive regulatory domain I element	PRES	posterior reversible encephalopathy syndrome
PRDR	pulsed-reduced dose-rate radiotherapy	PRE-SAT	presaturation (radiology)
Prdx6	peroxiredoxin 6	press	pressure
PRE	passive resistance exercises	pressor	a word meaning tending to elevate blood pressure
	progressive resistive exercise	prev	prevent
	proton relaxation enhancement		previous
PRE3-ANCA	proteinase 3 antineutrophil cytoplasmic antibodies	previa	a word meaning - appearing before or in front of
PREA	Pediatric Research Equity Act (2003)	PREV PD	Previous paid amount on this claim. (Medicare)
Pre-AD	preclinical Alzheimer disease	PRFA	percutaneous radiofrequency ablation
prealb	prealbumin		
Pre-B ALL	precursor-B-cell acute lymphoblastic leukemia	prfA	peptide chain release factor 1; see gene website, www.ncbi .nlm.nih.gov/gene
PrEC	prostate epithelial cell line		
precert	precertification; precertified; precertify	PRFD	percutaneous radio-frequency denervation
pre-cert	precertification precertified	PRFNB	percutaneous radio-frequency facet nerve block
PRED	prednisolone (this is a dangerous abbreviation as it also has been used for prednisone)	PrFP	pre-exposure prophylaxis
		PRFs	psychosocial risk factors
		PRG	phleborheogram
	prednisone (this is a dangerous abbreviation as it also has been used for prednisolone)	PRGN	progranulin
		PRH	past relevant history
preDM	prediabetes mellitus		postocclusive reactive hyperemia
PREE	partial reinforcement extinction effect		preretinal hemorrhage
		PRHO	preregistration house officer
	Patient-Rated Elbow Evaluation (score)	PRI	Pain Rating Index
			Patient Review Instrument
pREE	predicted resting energy expenditure	PRICE	protection (of affected area), rest, ice, compression, and elevation
preE	preeclampsia		
preemie	premature baby (a birth that takes place more than three weeks before the baby is due)	PRID	progesterone-releasing intravaginal device

prils	angiotensin-converting enzyme inhibitor class of drugs (ACE inhibitors)		protein
			prothrombin
			protrusion
prim	primary	Pro	proline (also referred to as P)
PRIMIP	primipara (1st pregnancy)	prob	probable
PRINCE	protection with brace, rest, ice, NSAIDs (nonsteroidal anti-inflammatory drugs), compression, and elevation (initial treatment of ankle sprains)		problem
		proBNP	pro-brain natriuretic peptide
		PROC	procedure
		PROCAL	high-protein and high-calcium preload
PRIND	prolonged ischemic neurological deficit	PRO-CTCAE	Patient-Reported Outcomes version of the Common Terminology Criteria for Adverse Events
P-R interval	the period from the beginning of the P wave to the beginning of the QRS electrocardiography complex		
		PROCTO	procotoscopic
			proctology
		PROD	pentoxyresorufin O-dealkylase
PRIS	propofol-related infusion syndrome		production
		ProD	paritaprevir, ritonavr, ombitasvir, and dasabuvir (Viekira Pak)
PRISM	Pediatric Risk of Mortality Score		
		prod	produce
PRISMA	Preferred Reporting Items for Systematic Reviews and Meta-Analyses (guidelines)	ProF	Profile of Fatigue
		ProFaNE	Prevention of Falls Network Europe
PRIT®	pretargeted radioimmunotherapy	PROG	prognathism
pRJ	protease-treated royal jelly		prognosis
PRK	photorefractive keratectomy		program
PRL	prolactin		progressive
PRLA	pupils react to light and accommodation	PROM	passive range of motion
			premature rupture of membranes
PRLL	percutaneous remodeling of ligamentum flavum and lamina (surgery)	ProMACE	prednisone, methotrexate, calcium leucovorin, doxorubicin (Adriamycin), cyclophosphamide, and etoposide
PRM	partial rebreathing mask		
	passive range of motion	PROMIS	Patient Reported Outcomes Measurement Information System (survey)
	phosphoribomutase		
	photoreceptor membrane		
	prematurely ruptured membrane	PROMM	passive range of motion machine
	primidone (Mysoline)		
PRMF	preretinal macular fibrosis	PROMPT	Patient-Reported Outcome Mortality Prediction Tool
PRMS	progressive relapsing multiple sclerosis		
			Prompts for Restructuring Oral Muscular Phonetic Targets
PRM-SDX	pyrimethamine; sulfadoxine (Fansidar)		
		PROMs	Patient Reported Outcome Measures
PRMT6	protein arginine methyltransferase 6 (gene/protein)		
		Promy	promyelocyte
PRN	as the occasion arises (as needed)	PROMYELO	promyelocytes
	plaque reduction neutralization	PRON	pronation
PRNS	phrenic repetitive nerve stimulation	PROP	physiologic reduced oxygen protocol
PRNs	proximal femoral nails	PROPH	prophylaxis
PRNT	plaque-reduction neutralization test	prophy	prophylaxis
		ProQOL	Professional Quality of Life
PRO	patient-reported outcomes	PROS	prostate
	proagility shuttle run		prosthesis
	Professional Review Organization	PROs	patient-reported outcomes
	proline	PROS AG	prostate-specific antigen (more commonly expressed as PSA)
	pronation		

PROSPERO	international prospective register of systematic reviews	PRRS	porcine Reproductive and Respiratory Syndrome
PROSPR	Population-based Research Optimizing Screening through Personalized Regimens (National Institutes of Health; National Cancer Institute)	PRRs	proportional reporting ratios
		PRRT	peptide receptor radioligand therapy
			peptide receptor radionuclide therapy
Protein C Concentrate (Human)	Ceprotin	PRRTP	Psychosocial Residential Rehabilitation Treatment Program (Veterans Health Administration)
protime	prothrombin time		
pro time	prothrombin time	PRS	Pain Rating Scale
PROT REL	protrusive relationship		photon radiosurgery system
prov	provisional		Pierre Robin syndrome
PROVIMI	proteins, vitamins, and minerals		polygenic risk score
PROX	proximal		postradiation sarcoma
PRP	panretinal photocoagulation		pressure redistribution surface
	patient recovery plan		prolonged respiratory support
	penicillin-resistant pneumococci	PRSA	paradoxical respiratory sinus arrhythmia
	penicllinase-resistant penicillin		
	pityriasis rubra pilaris		phase-rectified signal averaging
	platelet-rich plasma		
	polyribose ribitol phosphate	PRSL	potential renal solute load
	poor progression of R wave in precordial leads	PRSP	penicillinase-resistant synthetic penicillins
	progressive rubella panencephalitis		penicillin-resistant *Streptococcus pneumoniae*
PrP	prion protein	prsP	see gene website www.ncbi.nlm .nih.gov/gene
PrPc	cellular prion protein		
PRP-D	*Haemophilus influenzae*, type b diphtheria conjugate vaccine	PRSs	positive rolandic spikes
		PRSS1	protease, serine, 1 (trypsin 1); see gene website www.ncbi .nlm.nih.gov/gene
PRP-OMP	polyribosylribitol phosphate-outer membrane protein conjugate (Hib) Vaccine		
		PRST	Blood Pressure, Heart Rate, Sweating, and Tears (scale to assess analgesic needs)
PRPP	5-phosphoribosyl-1-pyrophosphate		
	percutaneous reduction and percutaneous pinning	PRT	pelvic radiation therapy
			protamine response test
PRPT	partial response of the primary tumor		Proton radiotherapy
		PRTCA	percutaneous rotational transluminal coronary angioplasty
PRQ	Partner Relationship Questionnaire		
	Personal Resource Questionnaire	PRTE	post-radiation treatment effect
		PRTEE	Patient-Rated Tennis Elbow Evaluation
	pressure rate quotient		
PRQ-a	Personal Resource Questionnaire-adapted	prtF	see gene website www.ncbi.nlm .nih.gov/gene
PRRC	platelet rich red cells	PRTH-C	prothrombin time control
prrC	see gene website www.ncbi.nlm .nih.gov/gene	PRTN3	proteinase 3 (gene/protein)
		PRU	Plavix reaction units
PRRE	pupils round, regular, and equal	PrU	pressure ulcer
PRRERLA	pupils round, regular, equal; react to light and accommodation	PRUJ	proximal radioulnar joints
		PrUs	pressure ulcers
		PRUV	persistent right umbilical vein
PRRL	pupil(s) round, reactive to light	PRV	pentavalent rotavirus vaccine (iRotaTeq) (replaced by the term ROTA, then by RV5)
PRRLA	pupils, round, reactive to light and accommodation		
PrRP	prolactin-releasing peptide		polycythemia rubra vera

P

PRVC	pressure regulated volume control
	pressure-regulated, volume-control (ventilation)
PRVEP	pattern reversal visual evoked potentials
PRW	past relevant work
	platform rolling walker
	polymerized ragweed
PRWP	poor R-wave progression
PRX	panoramic facial x-ray
PRZF	pyrazofurin
PS	paradoxic sleep
	paranoid schizophrenia
	pathologic stage
	patient satisfaction
	patient's serum
	peak systolic
	pedicle screw
	performance status
	peripheral smear
	phosphatidylserine
	physical status
	piriformis (muscle) syndrome
	plastic surgery (surgeon)
	pluripotent stem (cells)
	polysulfone (filter)
	posterior subscapsular (cataract type)
	posterior synechiae
	posterior synechiotomy
	posterior-stabilized
	pressure sore
	pressure support
	protective services
	Proteus syndrome
	pulmonary stenosis
	pyloric stenosis
	pyrimethamine; sulfadoxine (Fansidar)
	serum from pregnant women
P&S	pain and suffering
	paracentesis and suction
	permanent and stationary
P/S	polyunsaturated to saturated fatty acids ratio
PS1	presenilins-1, see gene website, www.ncbi.nlm.nih.gov/gene
PS2	presenilins-2, see gene website, www.ncbi.nlm.nih.gov/gene
PS I	healthy patient with localized pathological process
PS II	a patient with mild to moderate systemic disease
PS III	a patient with severe systemic disease limiting activity but not incapacitating
PS IV	a patient with incapacitating systemic disease

PS V	moribund patient not expected to live (These are American Society of Anesthesiologists' physical status patient classifications. Emergency operations are designated by E after the classification.)
PSA	distal tingling on percussion ×Tinels sign)
	Patient Safety Attendant
	polysubstance abuse
	power spectral analysis
	procedural sedation analgesic
	product selection allowed
	Program Support Assistant
	prostate-specific antigen
PsA	psoriatic arthritis
PSAB	pretreatment prostate-specific antigen
PSAC	plasmodial surface anion channel
	preschool-age children
pSac	peak systolic acceleration
PSAD	prostate-specific antigen density
PSADT	prostate-specific antigen doubling time
PSAE	proximal splenic artery embolization
PSAG	*Pseudomonas aeruginosa*
PSAMD	prostate-specific antigen mass density
PSAP	prostate specific acid phosphatase
PSAPs	personal sound amplification products
PsAQoL	Psoriatic Arthritis Quality of Life
PSAR	prostate-specific antigen recurrence
PSARP	posterior sagittal anorectoplasty
PSAs	prostate-specific antigen (tests)
	pseudoaneurysms
	public service announcements
PSAT	phosphoserine aminotransferase; see gene website www.ncbi.nlm.nih.gov/gene
	Preliminary Scholastic Aptitude Test
PSAt	prostate specific antigen total
PSAV	prostate-specific antigen velocity
PSB	patient specific bin (a bin in an automated medication dispensing cabinet)
	problem sexualized behaviors
PSBO	partial small bowel obstruction
PSBP	peak systolic blood pressure
psbP	oxygen evolving enhancer 2 of Photosystem II (gene)

P

PSC	Pediatric Symptom Checklist	PSFS	Patient Specific Functional Scale
	percutaneous suprapubic cystostomy	PSFs	point-spread functions (radiology)
	posterior semicircular canal	PSFV	providing a smoke-free vehicle
	posterior subcapsular cataract	PSG	peak systolic gradient
	primary sclerosing cholangitis		polysomnogram
	Primary Stroke Center		portosystemic gradient
	pronation spring control	PSGN	poststreptococcal
	pubosacrococcygeal (diameter)		glomerulonephritis
	pulmonary sclerosing cholangitis	PSH	parastomal hernias
			paroxysmal sympathetic hyperactivity
PSCA	prostate stem cell antigen		partial stapled hemorrhoidopexy
PSCC	penile squamous cell carcinoma		past surgical history
	posterior subcapsular cataract		postspinal headache
PSC Cat	posterior subcapsular cataract	pSHF	posterior second heart field
PSC cirrhosis	primary sclerosing cholangitis cirrhosis	PSHx	past surgical history
PSCH	peripheral stem cell harvest	PSI	passenger space intrusion (motor vehicle accident)
PSCI	post-stroke cognitive impairment		Patient Safety Indicator
	Primary Self-Concept Inventory		Physiologic Stability Index
PSCO	posterior scleral canal opening		pounds per square inch
	presacral canalicular obstruction		prostate seed implant
PSCP	papillary serous carcinoma of the peritoneum		punctate subepithelial infiltrate
	posterior subcapsular precipitates	Psi	psilocybin
PSCT	peripheral stem cell transplant	PSIC	pediatric surgical intensive care
PSCU	pediatric special care unit	PSID	pocket-size (ultrasound) imaging device
PSD	partial sleep deprivation	PSIF	posterior spinal instrumentation and fusion
	pattern standard deviation		
	peritoneal surface disease		reversed fast imaging with steady-state precession
	pilonidal sinus disease		
	poststroke delirium	PSIG	pounds per square inch gauge
	poststroke depression	PSIMV	pressure synchronized intermittent mandatory ventilation
	power spectral density		
	psychosomatic disease	PSIP	post-surgical inguinal pain
PSDA	Patient Self-Determination Act	PSIR	phase-sensitive inversion-recovery (radiology)
PSDC	postsynaptic dorsal column		
PSDS	palmar surface desensitization	PSIS	posterior superior iliac spine
PSDT	patient-specific drill template	psitt	psittacosis
PSE	photosensitive epilepsy	PSJ	Pharmaceutical Society of Japan
	portal systemic encephalopathy		pubic symphysis joint
	pseudoephedrine		pulmonary sinus junction
PSE2003b	Penn State Equation 2003 b (used to calculate calorie needs in the intensive care unit)	PSK	protein-bound polysaccharide K (kureha)
			see gene website, www.ncbi.nlm .nih.gov/gene
PSED	posterior segment eye diseases	PSL	pigmented skin lesions
PSEN1	presenilin 1 (gene)		prednisolone
PSEN2	presenilin 2 (gene)	PSM	pansystolic murmur
PSF	percutaneous screw fixation		patient self-management
	percutaneous skeletal fixation		positive surgical margin
	point-spread function (radiology)		presystolic murmur
	posterior spinal fusion		propensity score matching
PSFH	past medical, family and social history	PSMA	personal self-maintenance activities
	providing a smoke-free home		progressive spinal muscular atrophy
PSFI	posterior spinal fusion with instrumentation		

P

	prostate-specific membrane antigen	PSRA	pressure sore risk assessment
PSMF	protein-sparing modified fasting (Blackburn diet)	PSRBOW	premature spontaneous rupture of bag of waters
PSM-R	Optimism-Pessimism Scale, revised	PSReA	poststreptococcal reactive arthritis
PSMS	Physical Self Maintenance Scale	PSRF	pedicle screw and rod fixation
PSMV	portal-superior mesenteric vein	PSRFs	psychosocial risk factors
	pressure-support mechanical ventilation	PsrP	Pneumococcal serine-rich repeat protein
PSN	peripheral sensory neuropathy	PSRT	photostress recovery test
PSNP	progressive supranuclear palsy	PSS	painful shoulder syndrome
PSO	Patient Safety Officer		pediatric surgical service
	Patient Safety Organization		personal social services
	pedicle subtraction osteotomy		Phenotypic-sensitivity scores
	pelvic stabilization orthosis		physiologic saline solution
	physician supplemental order		(0.9% sodium chloride)
	Polysporin ointment		portosystemic shunts
	proximal subungual		post-stroke seizure
	onychomycosis		primary Sjögren syndrome
PsO	psoriasis		progressive systemic sclerosis
pSO2	arterial oxygen saturation	PSSA	Psychosocial Structured
psoas	a muscle/tendon in the lumbar area		Activities (program)
		pssA	phosphatidylserine synthase;
			see gene website www.ncbi
PsOb	pseudo-onion bulbs		.nlm.nih.gov/gene
PSOC	papillary serous ovarian carcinoma	PSSIF	posterior segmental spinal instrumentation and fusion
	Puget Sound Oncology Consortium	PSSP	penicillin-sensitive *Streptococcus pneumoniae*
P/sore	pressure sore	PSSV	Pre-Study Site Visit
PSOs	pedicle subtraction osteotomies	PST	palliative sedation therapy
	principal secondary outcomes		paroxysmal supraventricular
PSOT	peripheral squamous odontogenic tumor		tachycardia patient self-testing
PSP	pancreatic spasmolytic peptide		Patient Service Technician
	Personal and Social Performance (scale)		penicillin skin testing platelet survival time
	phenolsulfonphthalein		posterior shoulder tightness
	photostimulable phosphor		posterior sub-Tenon (Capsule)
	primary spontaneous pneumothorax		postural stress test preoperative systemic therapy
	progressive supranuclear palsy		pulsed stimulation treatment
PsP	pseudoprogression	pSTAT3	phosphorylated signal
PSPC	papillary serous peritoneal carcinoma		transducer and activator of transcription 3
PSPDV	posterior superior pancreaticoduodenal vein	PSTC	Predictive Safety Testing Consortium
PSPH	phosphoserine phosphatase;see gene website www.ncbi.nlm .nih.gov/gene	PSTD	see PTSD
		pstD	see gene website www.ncbi.nlm .nih.gov/gene
	postspinal puncture headache	PSTIM	Pulse Stimulation Treatment
PSPP	Physical Self Perception Profile	PSTJ	posterior subtalar joint
PSQ	posterior-superior quadrant	PSTK	phosphoseryl-tRNA (transfer
PSQI	Pittsburgh Sleep Quality Index	gene/protein	ribonucleic acid) kinase)
PSR	per surgeon's request	PSTP	Physician Scientist Training
	posthumous sperm retrieval		Program
	post-stroke recrudescence	PSTS	prevertebral soft tissue swelling
	Psychiatric Status Rating (scale)	PSTs	paralytic shellfish toxins

P

pSTS	posterior superior temporal sulcus		posterior tibial
			Preferred Term
PSTT	placental site trophoblastic tumor		preterm
			pronator teres
PSU	pseudomonas (*P. aeruginosa*) vaccine	Pt	prothrombin time
			pint (1 pint US = 473 mL; 1pint UK = 568 mL)
PSUC	preterm spontaneous uterine contractions		platinum
			point
PSUD	psychoactive substance use disorder	pT	pathologic tumor (various lettered and numbered stages, such as pT1)
pSup	after supper (it is doubtful that this would be understood)		
		pt	patient
PSUR	Periodic Safety Update Report	pT0	no tumor
	periodic safety update reporting	PT2	inorganic phosphate transporter; see gene website www.ncbi .nlm.nih.gov/gene
PSV	peak systolic velocity		
	persistent sciatic vein(s)		
	pressure supported ventilation		
	Pre-Study (Site) Visit	P&T	Pharmacy and Therapeutics (Committee)
PSVC	portosystemic venous connections		
	premature supraventricular contraction		paracentesis and tubing (of ears)
			peak and trough
			permanent and total
PsVNA	pseudovirion neutralization assay	P/T	pain and tenderness
			piperacillin/tazobactam (Zosyn®)
PSVT	paroxysmal supraventricular tachycardia		
		p/t	prior to
PSW	psychiatric social worker	P1/2T	pressure one-half time
PSWC	periodic sharp wave complexes (electroencephalograph)	pT1	size and/or extension of the primary tumor given by pathologic examination of a surgical specimen
PSWF	positive sharp wave fibrillations (electromyograph)		
PSWL	placebo-subtracted weight loss	pT2	size and/or extension of the primary tumor given by pathologic examination of a surgical specimen
	plasma shock wave lithotripsy		
PSWQ	Penn State Worry Questionnaire		
PSX	pseudoexfoliation		
PSY	presexual youth	pT3	size and/or extension of the primary tumor given by pathologic examination of a surgical specimen
psych	psychiatry		
	psychologic		
	psychology		
PsyD	Doctor of Psychology		
	pyschological distress	pT4	size and/or extension of the primary tumor given by pathologic examination of a surgical specimen
PSZ	pseudoseizures		
PT	cisplatin (Platinol)		
	parathormone		
	parathyroid	PTA	pancreas transplant alone
	paroxysmal tachycardia		patellar tendon autograft
	partial thickness		percutaneous transluminal angioplasty
	patch test		
	patellar tendon		peritonsillar abscess
	patient (pt is preferred)		Physical Therapist Assistant
	pelvic tilt		plasma thromboplastin antecedent
	phacotrabeculectomy		posterior tibial artery
	phage type		post-traumatic amnesia
	Pharmacy Technician		pretreatment anxiety
	phenytoin (Dilantin)		prior to admission
	phototoxicity		prior to appointment
	Physical Therapist		prior to arrival
	physical therapy		pure-tone average
	pine tar	PTAB	popliteal-tibial artery bypass

P

PTAC	pulmonary transit of agitated contrast(bubbles)	PTCDLM	pregnancy, term, complicated delivered, living male
pTAC	plasma time-activity curve	PTCH	see gene website; www.ncbi.nlm.nih.gov/gene
PtaC	see gene website; www.ncbi.nlm.nih.gov/gene	PTCI	post-traumatic cerebral infarction
PT's	see PT		post-traumatic cognitions inventory
PTAF	pressure transducer airflow		
PTAL	percutaneous tendo-Achilles lengthening	PTCL	peripheral T-cell lymphoma
PTAN	Provider Transaction Access Number	PTCM	post-translational modification
		PTCR	percutaneous transluminal coronary recanalization
PTAS	percutaneous transluminal angioplasty with stent placement	PTCRA	percutaneous transluminal coronary rotational atherectomy
ptau	phosphorylated tau (tua is a protein found in the plaque observed in patients with Alzheimer disease)	PTCS	percutaneous transhepatic cholangioscopy
			pseudotumor cerebri syndrome
		PTCs	pain treatment centers
p-Tau	phosphorylated Tau protein		papillary thyroid carcinomas
PTB	patellar tendon bearing		post-treatment controllers
	potassium taurine bicarbonate		premature termination codons
	preterm birth		product technical complaints
	pulmonary tuberculosis	PTCT	parent to child transmission
pTB	peritoneal tuberculosis		percutaneous transcatheter thermotherapy
PTBA	percutaneous transluminal balloon angioplasty		
		PtCu	platinum-copper nanoparticles
PTBD	percutaneous transhepatic biliary drain (drainage)	PTCU	Psychiatric TeleConsultation Unit
PTBD-EF	percutaneous transhepatic biliary drainage–enteric feeding	PTD	percutaneous transhepatic drainage
pTBI	pediatric traumatic brain injury		percutaneous transpedicular diskectomy
	penetrating traumatic brain injury		period to discharge
PTBS	post-traumatic brain syndrome		permanent and total disability
PTB-SC-SP	patellar tendon bearing-supracondylar-suprapatellar		persistent trophoblastic disease
			pharmacy to dose
PTC	papillary thyroid carcinoma		pharyngotracheal duct
	participant		preterm delivery
	Patient Testing Center		prior to delivery
	patient to call	PTDM	post-transplant diabetes mellitus
	pediatric trauma center	PTDP	permanent transvenous demand pacemaker
	percutaneous transhepatic cholangiography		
	phenylthiocarbamide	PTDs	protein-transduction domains
	plasma thromboplastin components	PTE	post-traumatic epilepsy
			pretibial edema
	plasma-sprayed titanium coating		proximal tibial epiphysis
	post-tetanic count		pulmonary thromboembolectomy
	premature tricuspid closure		pulmonary thromboembolism
	preterm contractions	PTE-4®	trace metal elements injection (there is also a #5 and #6)
	prior to conception		
	pseudotumor cerebri	PTEA	percutaneous trans-tracheal endoscopic approach
PT-C	prothrombin time control		
PTCA	percutaneous transluminal coronary angioplasty	PTED	pulmonary thromboembolic disease
PtCA	Patient Care Assistant	PTEE	pediatric (multiplane) transe-sophageal echocardiographic (probe)
PTCDLF	pregnancy, term, complicated delivered, living female		
		PTEF	peak tidal expiratory flow

PTEG	percutaneous transesophageal gastrotubing		pudding-thick liquid (diet consistency)
PTEN	phosphatase and tensin homolog		Sodium Pentothal
PTER	percutaneous transluminal endomyocardial revascularization	PTLA	percutaneous transluminal laser angioplasty
PTF	patient transfer form	PTLC	preoperative total lymphocyte count
	Patient Treatment File		preparative thin-layer chromatography
	pentoxifylline (Trental)		
	post-tetanic facilitation	pTLC	predicted total lung capacity
PTFE	polytetrafluoroethylene	PTLCs	preoperative total lymphocyte counts
PTFE graft	expanded polytetrafluoroethylene graft	PTLD	post-transplant lymphoproliferative disease
PTFJ	proximal tibiofibular joint		post-transplant lymphoproliferative disorder
PTFL	posterior talofibular ligament		
PTFs	product technical failures	PTLDS	post-treatment Lyme disease syndrome
PTG	parathyroid gland		
	photoplethysmogram	PTLF	post-transplant liver function (score)
PTGBD	percutaneous transhepatic gallbladder drainage		
PTH	parathyroid hormone (also called parathormone)	PTLR	percutaneous transmyocardial laser revascularization
	post-toilet hygiene	PTLS	post-tubal ligation syndrome
	post-transfusion hepatitis	PTLV-1	primate T-lymphotropic virus type 1
	prior to hospitalization		
PTHA	post-traumatic headache	PTLV-2	primate T-lymphotropic virus type 2
PTHC	percutaneous transhepatic cholangiography		
		PTLV-3	primate T-lymphotropic virus type 3
	pseudotumoral hemicerebellitis		
PTHi	intact parathyroid hormone	PTLV-4	primate T-lymphotropic virus type 4
PTHrP	parathyroid hormone-related protein	Pt LWBS	patient left without being seen (This implies the patient was registered but not triaged or assessed. Check to see if this conforms to your facility's definition)
PTHS	post-traumatic hyperirritability syndrome		
PTHx	parathyroidectomy		
	past trauma history		
PThx	pneumothorax		
PTI	pressure-time integral		
	prior to induction	PTM	patient monitored
ptime	prothrombin time		posterior trabecular meshwork
PTINR	prothrombin time/international normalization ratio		post-translational modification
			pretibial myxedema
PT INR	international normalized ratio of prothrombin time	PTMC	papillary thyroid microcarcinoma
PT-INR	international normalized ratio of prothrombin time		percutaneous transvenous mitral commissurotomy
pTis	the staging category, carcinoma in situ	PTMDF	pupils, tension, media, disc, and fundus
PTJV	percutaneous transtracheal jet ventilation	PTMR	percutaneous transmyocardial revascularization
PTK	pancreas-after-kidney (transplantation)	PTMS	parathymosin; see gene website, www.ncbi.nlm.nih.gov/gene
	phototherapeutic keratectomy	PTMs	post-translational modifications
	protein tyrosine kinase		post-traumatic migraines
PTL	parthenolide	PTN	proximal tibia nails
	platelet	PT-NANB	post-transfusion non-A, non-B (hepatitis C)
	premature tooth loss		
	preterm labor	PTNB	preterm newborn
	primary testicular lymphoma	PTNIL	preterm not-in-labor

pTNM	postsurgical resection-pathologic staging of cancer	PTRA	percutaneous transluminal renal angioplasty
PTNS	percutaneous tibial nerve stimulation	PtRDS	patient-reported level of respiratory distress
PTO	part-time occlusion (eye patch) please turn over proximal tubal obstruction	PTR-MS	proton transfer reaction mass spectrometry
PTOA	posttraumatic osteoarthritis prior to our arrival	PTS	patellar tendon suspension Pediatric Trauma Score permanent threshold shift post-thrombotic syndrome post-traumatic seizure(s) prior to surgery
PTOC	part time on call percent time-off cardioplegia		
PTOD	post-traumatic olfactory dysfunction post-traumatic oromandibular dystonia		
		pts	patients
P to P	point to point	PTSA	percutaneous testicular sperm aspiration
PTOS	Pennsylvania Trauma Outcome Study	PTSD	post-traumatic stress disorder
Ptot	total power	PTSD-T	post-traumatic stress disorder related to the transplant
PT/OT	physical therapy and occupational therapy	ptsH	phosphohistidinoprotein-hexose phosphotransferase component of the phospho-transferase system; see gene website www.ncbi.nlm.nih .gov/gene
PTP	patient teaching protocol phonation threshold pressure planned treatment period posterior tibial pulse post-transfusion purpura pretest clinical probability (score) preventative training program		
		PTSS	post-traumatic stress symptom
		PTST	persistently negative tuberculin skin test
PTPA	percutaneous transluminal pulmonary angioplasty phosphotyrosyl phosphatase activator	PTT	partial thromboplastin time penile traction therapy pharyngeal transit time platelet transfusion therapy posterior tibial tendon protein truncation testing pulse transit time
ptpe	protein-tyrosine phosphatase e; see gene website www.ncbi .nlm.nih.gov/gene		
		PTTA	pure tone threshold audiometrics
PTPI	protein tyrosine phosphatase inhibitor	PTTAC	may have meant PTAC (pulmonary transit of agitated contras [bubbles])
Ptpi	triose-phosphate isomerase (gene)	PTT-C	partial thromboplastin time control
PTPM	post-traumatic progressive myelopathy	PTTD	posterior tibial tendonitis dysfunction
PTPN	peripheral (vein) total parenteral nutrition	PTTG	pituitary tumor transforming gene
PTPS	6- pyruvoyltetrahydropterin synthase (gene/protein)	PTTI	posterior tibial tendon insufficiency provisional total tolerable intake
PTPs	protein tyrosine phosphatases		
PTPTT	prothrombin time and partial thromboplastin time	PTTK	partial thromboplastin time with kaolin
PT/PTT	prothrombin time and partial thromboplastin time	PTTW	patient tolerated traction well
PT pulse	polarization transfer pulse	PTU	pain treatment unit pregnancy, term, uncomplicated propylthiouracil
PTR	paratesticular rhabdomyosarcoma patella tendon reflex patient test results patient to return prothrombin time ratio		
		PTUCA	percutaneous transluminal ultra-sonic coronary angioplasty
		PTUDLF	pregnancy, term, uncomplicated delivered, living female
PT-R	prothrombin time ratio	PTUDLM	pregnancy, term, uncomplicated delivered, living male

P

PTV	patient-triggered ventilation	PUGSI	periumbilical ultrasound-guided
	periotest value		saline infusion
	planning target volume	PUH	peptic ulcer hemorrhage
	(radiation therapy)		posterior urethral hemangioma
	posterior tibial vein	PUI	passive ultrasonic irrigation
PTVA	percutaneous transseptal		(dental)
	ventricular assist		person under investigation
PTVP	percutaneous transluminal		postoperative unplanned
	valvuloplasty		intubation
PTVs	planning target volumes		problematic use of the Internet
	(radiation therapy)	PUJ	pelviu
PTWC	Permit to Work Certificate		pelviureteral junction
PTWI	provisionally tolerable weekly	PUK	peripheral ulcerative keratitis
	intake	pul.	pulmonary
PTWTKG	patient's weight in kilograms	pulm	pulmonary
PTX	paclitaxel (Taxol)	pulmn	pulmonary; lungs
	parathyroidectomy	pulmon	pulmonary
	pelvic traction	PULP	pulpotomy
	pentoxifylline (Trental)	PulseA	pulse apical
	phototherapy	PULSE OX	pulse oximetry
	pneumothorax	PulseR	pulse radial
PTX3	pentraxin 3	PULSES	(physical profile) physical con-
PTZ	pentylenetetrazol		dition, upper limb functions,
	phenothiazine		lower limb functions, sensory
P-Tz	piperacillin sodium; tazobactam		components, and excretory func-
	sodium (Zosyn)		tions, and support factors
PU	paws up (dead) (Veterinary	pulv	pulvinar
	slang)	PUM	Positive Urgency Measure
	pelvic-ureteric	PUN	papillary urothelial neoplasm
	pelviureteral		plasma urea nitrogen
	peptic ulcer	puncle	paternal uncle
	pick up	PUND	pregnancy, uterine, not delivered
	pregnancy urine	PUNL	percutaneous ultrasonic
	pressure ulcer		nephrolithotripsy
	push-ups	PUNLMP	papillary urothelial neoplasm of
Pu	plutonium		low malignant potential
	ultrafiltrate pressure (ultrafiltra-	PUO	pruritus of unknown origin
	tion circuit line pressure)		pyrexia of unknown origin
P & U	Pharmacia & Upjohn Company	PUP	percutaneous ultrasonic
PUA	pelvic (examination) under		pyelolithotomy
	anesthesia		previously untreated patient
PUAB	periurethral adjustable balloon	P/UP	paired verses unpaired group
PUB	peptic ulcer bleeding	PUPD	polyuria and polydipsia
	pubic	pUPD	paternal uniparental disomy
PUBS	percutaneous umbilical blood	PU/PD	polyuria and polydipsia
	sampling	PU/PL	partial upper and lower dentures
	purple urine bag syndrome	PUPPP	pruritic urticarial papules and
PUC	pediatric urine collector		plaques of pregnancy
PUCAI	pediatric ulcerative colitis	PUPPS	pruritic urticarial papules and
	activity index		plaques (of pregnancy)
PUD	partial upper denture	PUPS	see PUPPS
	peptic ulcer disease	PUR	postoperative urinary retention
	percutaneous ureteral dilatation	Pur	purine
PUE	pyrexia of unknown etiology	PURA	pressure-ulcer risk assessment
PUF	pure ultrafiltration	PurD	purging disorder
PUFA	polyunsaturated fatty acids	PUS	percutaneous ureteral stent
PUFFA	polyunsaturated free fatty acids		preoperative ultrasound
PUG	protective undergarment	PUU	Puumala hantavirus

PUUV	Puumala virus	PVC	paclitaxel, vinblastine, and cisplatin
PUV	posterior urethral valves		peripheral venous catheter
	pregnancy of uncertain viability		polyethylene vacuum cup
PUVA	psoralen (methoxsalen)		polyvinyl chloride
	plus ultraviolet light of A wavelength (treatment)		porcelain veneer crown
			postvoiding cystogram
PUVB	psoralen ultraviolet B radiation		premature ventricular contraction
PUW	pick-up walker		pulmonary venous congestion
PV	papillomavirus	PVC ablation	premature ventricular contraction ablation
	Parvovirus		
	pemphigus vulgaris	PVCD	percutaneous vascular closure device
	per vagina		
	percutaneous vertebroplasty	PVCM	paradoxical vocal cord motion
	pharmacovigilance	Pvco$_2$	partial pressure (tension) of carbon dioxide, vein
	physical violence		
	plasma volume	PVCR	posterior vertebral column resection
	polio vaccine		
	polycythemia vera	PVCs	premature ventricular contractions
	popliteal vein	PVC's	premature ventricular contractions
	portal vein		
	postoperative vomiting	PVD	patient very disturbed
	postvoiding		peripheral vascular disease
	predicted value		posterior vitreous detachment
	prenatal vitamins		premature ventricular depolarization
	projectile vomiting		
	pulmonary vein		provoked vestibulodynia
Pv	*Plasmodium vivax*	PVDA	prednisone, vincristine, daunorubicin, and asparaginase
P & V	peak and valley		
	pyloroplasty and vagotomy	PvDBP	Plasmodium vivid Duffy binding protein
PVA	polyvinyl alcohol		
	Prinzmetal's variant angina	pvdD	pyoverdine synthetase D (gene)
	pulmonary valve annulus	PVDF	polyvinylidene difluoride
	pulmonic valve area	P(VDF-TrFE)	poly (vinylidene fluoride-trifluoroethylene)
PVAD	paracorporeal ventricular assist device		
		PVDO	posterior (cranial) vault distraction osteogenesis
	pediatric left ventricular assist device		
		pVDZ	a Dunning's correlation consistent basis set
	pneumatic left ventricular assist device		
		pvdZ	siderophore biosynthesis protein (gene)
	prolonged venous access devices		
		PVE	partial volume effect
pVAD	percutaneous left ventricular assist device		perivenous encephalomyelitis
			portal vein embolization
PVAI	pulmonary vein antrum isolation		premature ventricular extrasystole
			prosthetic value endocarditis
Pval	probability value		
PVAM	potential visual acuity meter	P vera	Pistacia vera
PVAN	polyomavirus-associated nephropathy		polycythemia vera
		PVES	popliteal vascular entrapment syndrome
PVAR	pulmonary vein atrial reversal		
PVARP	postventricular atrial refractory period	PVEs	partial volume effects
		Pves	intravesical pressure
PVAT	perivascular adipose tissue	PVF	peripheral visual field
PVB	cisplatin, (Platinol) vinblastine, and bleomycin	PVFM	paradoxical vocal fold motion
		PVFMD	paradoxic vocal fold movement disorder
	paravertebral block		
	porcelain veneer bridge		paradoxical vocal fold movement disorder
	premature ventricular beat		

P

PVFS	postviral fatigue syndrome		polyvinylpyrrolidone
pVFSE	pulsed videofluoroscopic swallowing examination		portal venous pressure posteroventral pallidotomy
PVGM	perifoveolar vitreoglial membrane	P-VP-B	cisplatin (Platinol), etoposide (VP-16), and bleomycin
PVGT	Problem Video Game Playing Test	PVR	peripheral vascular resistance perspective volume rendering
PVH	periventricular hemorrhage periventricular hyperintensity pulmonary vascular hypertension		portal vein reconstruction postvoiding residual proliferative vitreoretinopathy pulmonary valve replacement
pVHI	Pediatric Voice Handicap Index		pulmonary vascular resistance
PVI	pelvic venous incompetence penile-vaginal intercourse		pulse volume recording
	peripheral vascular insufficiency peritumoral vascular invasion	PVRI	pulmonary vascular resistance index
	Pleth variability index	PVRQOL	Pediatric Voice-Related Quality-of-Life
	portal-vein infusion protracted venous infusion	PVRs	postvoid residual (volumes)
	pulmonary valve insufficiency pulmonary vein isolation	PVS	percussion, vibration and suction
PVID	people with visual impairment and diabetes		peripheral vascular surgery peritoneovenous shunt
PVIE	prosthetic valve infective endocarditis		persistent vegetative state Plummer-Vinson syndrome
PVK	penicillin V potassium		programmed ventricular
PVL	peripheral vascular laboratory periventricular leukomalacia		stimulation pubovaginal sling
	Phanton-Valentine leukocidin portal vein ligation		pulmonic valve stenosis
	prosthesis paravalvular leak	PVSC	pediatric variable-stiffness colonoscope
PVM	paraverteabral muscle proteins, vitamins, and minerals	PVST	portal venous system thrombosis postvaccination serologic testing
PVMD	pubovisceral muscle defects		prevertebral soft tissue
PVMS	paravertebral muscle spasms	PVT	paroxysmal ventricular
PVN	peripheral venous nutrition		tachycardia
PVNH	periventricular nodular heterotopia		Physical Volume Test portal vein thrombosis
PVNS	pigmented villonodular synovitis		previous trouble
PVO	peripheral vascular occlusion		private
	portal vein occlusion pulmonary venous occlusion	PVTT	proximal vein thrombosis tumor thrombus in the
PVo	pulmonary valve opening		portal vein
Pvo₂	partial pressure (tension) of oxygen, vein	PVU	patient verbalized understanding
	peripheral vascular occlusive	PVUR	primary vesicoureteral reflux
	disease	PVV	persistent varicose veins
PVOD	postviral olfactory dysfunction	PVWMD	periventricular white matter
	pulmonary vascular obstructive disease	PW	disease pacing wires
	pulmonary veno-occlusive disease		palatal width
PVOS	Pediatric Voice Outcome Survey		patient waiting
PVP	cisplatin (Platinol) and etoposide (VePesid)		plantar wart posterior wall
	penicillin V potassium		presents with
	percutaneous vertebroplasty		pulse width
	peripheral venous pressure		puncture wound
	Photoselective Vaporization of the Prostate	Pw	withdrawal pressure (ultrafiltration circuit line pressure)
		P&W	pressures and waves

P

P/W	presented with		plagiocephaly without synostosis
	presents with		port-wine stain
PWA	persons with AIDS		Prader-Willi syndrome
	P-wave axis	PWT	pad weight test(s)
PWACR	Prader-Willi/Angleman critical		posterior wall thickness
	region		primary writing tremor
P wave	part of the electrocardio-graphic	PWTd	posterior wall thickness at
	cycle representing atrial		end-diastole
	depolarization	PWV	polistes wasp venom
PWB	partial weight bearing		pulse-wave velocity
	physical well being	PWVL	powder vial (pharmaceutical
	Positive Well-being (scale)		dosage form)
	psychological well-being	Px	physical exam
PWB20	partial weight-bearing at 20%		pneumothorax
PWB30	partial weight-bearing at 30%		prognosis
PWB40	partial weight-bearing at 40%		prophylaxis
PWB70	partial weight-bearing at 70%	PXA	pleomorphic xanthoastrocytoma
PWBAT	partial-weight bearing as	PXAT	paroxysmal atrial tachycardia
	tolerated	PXE	pseudoxanthoma elasticum
PWBL	partial weight bearing, left	PXF	pseudoexfoliation
PWBR	partial weight bearing, right	PXFG	pseudoexfoliation glaucoma
PWC	personal watercraft	PXFS	pseudoexfoliation syndrome
	physical working capacity	PXG	pseudoexfoliation glaucoma
	powered wheelchair	PXL	paclitaxel (Taxol)
PWCA	personal watercraft accident	PXN	paxillin (gene; focal adhesion
PWCT	perfusion-weighted computed		adaptor protein)
	tomography	PXR	pregnane x receptor; see gene
PWD	patients with diabetes		website www.ncbi.nlm.nih
	person(s) with a disability		.gov/gene
	pink, warm, and dry	PXRD	power X-ray diffraction
	powder	PXS	dental prophylaxis (cleaning)
PwD	people with dementia	PXT	paroxetine (Paxil)
PWE	people with epilepsy	Pxt	peroxinectin-like; see gene
PWH	patients with hemophilia		website, www.ncbi.nlm.nih
PWI	pediatric walk-in clinic		.gov/gene
	perfusion-weighted (magnetic	PY	pack years (see pk yrs)
	resonance) imaging		person-year
	posterior wall infarct		Purely Yours (breast pump
	posterior wall isolation		machine)
PWID	people who inject drugs	P2Y12	a protein found mainly, but not
	Possession with Intent to		only on the surface of blood
	Distribute		platelet cells
PWK	paperwork		see gene website, www.ncbi.nlm
PWLV	posterior wall of left ventricle		.nih.gov/gene
PWM	pokeweed mitogens	PYAR	person years at risk
PWMI	posterior wall myocardial	PYE	person-years of exposure
	infarction	pyelo	a combining form denoting
PwMS	persons (people) with multiple		relationship to the renal
	sclerosis		pelvis, as in pyelo-ureteral
PWO	per written order		necrosis
	persistent withdrawal occlusion		pyelonephritis
PWP	pulmonary wedge pressure	PYHx	packs per year history
PWR	Parkinson Wellness Recovery	Pyl	pyrrolysine
	(gym)	PYLL	potential years of life lost
	platelet-to-white blood cell ratio	PYO	person-years of observation
	postnatal weight retention	PYP	pyrophosphate
PWS	partial-wave spectroscopy	PYP®	technetium Tc 99m
	perceived wellness survey		pyrophosphate kit

P

PYR	pyrazinamide
	pyruvate
Pyr	person-years
	pyrene
Pyxis	a semi-automated drug dispensing system
PYY	peptide YY
PZ	peripheral zone
PZA	pyrazinamide
	pyrazoloacridine (a drug class of sedative/hyponotics)
PZD	partial zona drilling
	partial zonal dissection
PZI	protamine zinc insulin
PZR	posterior zygomatic root

Q

Q	glutamine
	quadrant
	quadriceps
	Quebec
	quickening
q	every (care must be taken to make sure that the handwritten q is not seen as a 9)
Q1	first quartile
	first quintile
q1	every hour
Q2	second quartile
	second quintile
q2	every 2 hours
Q3	third quartile
	third quintile
Q4	fourth quartile
	fourth quintile
q4	every 4 hours
Q5	fifth quintile
q6	every 6 hours
q8	every 8 hours
q12	every 12 hours
Q15	histocompatibility 2, Q region locus 15 (gene)
q24	every 24 hours
q48	every 48 hours (every other day)
QA	quality assurance
	quinolinic acid
QAC	before each meal
	before every meal (this is a dangerous abbreviation)
qac	quaternary ammonium compound-resistance protein; see gene website www.ncbi.nlm.nih.gov/gene
q AC	before each meal
QACHS	before meals and at bedtime
QAC&HS	before meals and at bedtime
QACs	quaternary ammonium compounds
QAD	quadriceps
	questionable Alzheimer disease (dementia)
qADAM	quantitative Androgen Deficiency in the Aging Male (questionnaire/report)
QALE	quality-adjusted life expectancy
QALYs	quality-adjusted life years
QAM	every morning
QAMA	quantitative analysis of methylated alleles
QAMAC	this could mean, every morning before breakfast

QAPI	quality assessment and performance improvement		The International Conference on Harmonization specifications on both daily doses and concentration limits of metallic impurities in pharmaceutical final products and in active pharmaceutical ingredients and excipients.
QA/QC	quality assurance/quality control		
QART	Quality Assurance in Radiotherapy		
QAS	quality-adjusted survival		
QATTP	quality-adjusted time to progression		
QB	blood flow	**Q4D**	every four days (this a dangerous abbreviation; spellout- every 4 days)
	blood pump speed (renal dialysis)		
QbD	Quality by Design (a systematic approach to drug development)	**q7d**	every 7 days (this is a dangerous abbreviation as it can be misread as four times daily (qid)
QBL	quantitative blood loss		
	questionable bone loss	**QDA**	quality data code
QBR	quality-based reimbursement	**q daily**	every day (this is a dangerous abbreviation as it could be read as 9 daily; use every day)
QC	quad cane		
	quality checks		
	quality control	**QDAM**	once daily in the morning
	quick catheter	**QDAY**	everyday (every day)
	quick charge	**q day**	everyday (every day) (care must be taken to make sure that the handwritten q is not seen as a 9)
QCA	quantitative coronary angiography		
QCC	quality control circles		
	quaternary cation compound(s)	**QDB**	query-dependent banded
QCCG	QuikClot® Combat Gauze®	**QD-LFIAS**	quantum dot-based lateral flow immunoassay system
QCM	quartz crystal microbalance		
QCM-D	quartz crystal microbalance with dissipation (monitoring)	**QDNs**	quantum dot nanocrystals
		Qdots	quantum dots
Qcompound	Chinese cucumber	**QDPM**	once daily in the evening
QCP	quantum critical points	*QDS*	United Kingdom abbreviation for four times a day
	Quick Chaser *H. pylori* (an antigen detection kit for Helicobacter pylori)		
		QDs	quantum dots
QCSW	Qualified Clinical Social Worker	**QE**	quinidine effect
QCT	quantitative computed tomography	**QEC**	quantum error correction
			Quick Exposure Check
QD	dialysate flow	**QED**	every even day (this is a dangerous abbreviation as it will be read as four times daily-QID)
	once daily. This is a DANGEROUS abbreviation that should NOT be used. It appears on the MedAbbrev and other "Do Not Use Lists," as it has been misread as four times daily (QID). Use "once daily," "every day" or "once per day."		
			quick and early diagnosis
		QEE	quadriceps extension exercise
		qEEG	quantitative electroencephalography
		QEMG	quantitative electromyography
Q1D	once daily (this a dangerous abbreviation as it can be read as four times a day (QID) spell out- once daily)	**QF**	quadriceps femoris (muscle)
			queso fresco (Mexican-style soft cheese)
Q2D	every two days (this a dangerous abbreviation; spellout- every 2 days)	**QFB**	Químico Farmacéutico Biólogo (Chemist Pharmacist Biologist; Pharmacist in Mexico)
		Q fever	an infection caused by the bacterium Coxiella burnetii ("Q" stands for "query" and was applied at a time when the causative agent was unknown)
Q3D	every three days (this a dangerous abbreviation; spell out- every 3 days)		
	quasi-three-dimensional	**QFG**	QuantiFERON-TB Gold In-Tube test (to diagnose latent tuberculosis infection)

QFN	QuantiFERON®-TB Gold In-Tube [tuberculosis diagnostic agent)
QFN-G-IT	QuantiFERON®-TB Gold In-Tube (tuberculosis diagnostic agent)
QF-PCR	quantitative fluorescence polymerase chain reaction
QFT-G	QuantiFERON®-TB Gold In-Tube [tuberculosis diagnostic agent)
QFT-IT	QuantiFERON-TB Gold In-Tube (tuberculosis test)
QFV	Q fever (*Coxiella burnetii*) vaccine
QGS	quantitative gate SPECT (single-photon emission computed tomography)
qh	every hour
q1h	every hour
q2h	every 2 hours
q3h	every 3 hours
q4h	every 4 hours
q 4h	every 4 hours
q6h	every 6 hours
q8h	every 8 hours
q 8 h	every 8 hours
q12h	every 12 hours
q24h	every 24 hours (once daily)
q48h	every 48 hours (every other day)
QHC	questionable hematopoietic cells
QHD	Qushi Huayu Decoction (a traditional Chinese herbal medicine)
QHPs	Qualified Health Plans (Affordable Care Act)
qhr	every hour (this is a dangerous abbreviations as it can be ready as qhs [every bedtime] use "every hour.")
q4hrs	every four hours
q6hrs	every six hours
q8hrs	every eight hours
q12hrs	every 12 hours
q HS	every night
qhsmx1	every night, may repeat one time
QIAD	Quantitative Inventory of Alcohol Disorders
QIB	quantitative imaging biomarker
QIC	qualified independent contractor
QID	four times daily (four times a day)
QID AC/HS	four times daily, before meals and at bedtime
QIDM	four times daily with meals and at bedtime
QIDP	Qualified Infectious Disease Product (US Food and Drug Administration)

QID PC/HS	four times daily, after meals and at bedtime
QIDS	Quick Inventory of Depressive Symptomatology
QIDS-C	Quick Inventory of Depressive Symptoms-Clinician
QIDS-SR	Quick Inventory of Depressive Symptomatology-Self-Rated
QIDS-SR-16	Quick Inventory of Depressive Symptomatology' self-rated 16 items
QIF	quantitative immunofluorescence
QIG	quantitative immunoglobulins
QIMT	quantitative intima media thickness
QIO	Quality Improvement Organization
QIP	Quality Incentive Program
QIS	Quality Indicator Survey (Center for Medicare and Medicaid Services)
Qis	quality indicators
QIT	Quality Improvement Team
QIW	four times a week (this is a dangerous abbreviation)
QJ	quadriceps jerk
QKD	Korotkoff sounds interval
QL	quadratus lumborum quality of life
QLC	quad-lumen catheter
QLF	quantitative light-induced fluorescence
QLFT	qualitative fit test (respirator-related)
QLI	Quality of Life Index
QLQ-C30	Quality of Life Questionnaire Quality of Life Questionnaire (30 questions) (European Organization for Research and Treatment of Cancer)
QLS	quality of life score
QM	every morning (this is a dangerous abbreviation as it will not be understood)
Q3M	every 3 months (this is a dangerous abbreviations as it may be misinterpreted)
Q6M	every 6 months (this is a dangerous abbreviations as it may be misinterpreted; write it out)
QM1	Quartermaster-First-Class- (Naval-Rating)
QM2	Quartermaster-Second-Class- (Naval-Rating)
QM3	Quartermaster-Third-Class- (Naval-Rating)

Q-MAC	quantitative microarray antibody capture
Qmax	maximal flow rate
QMB	qualified Medicare beneficiary
QM2c	Quartermaster 2nd Class
QME	quantum master equation
	Questionnaire of Memory Efficiency
QMGS	Quantitative Myasthenia Graves Score
QMHP	qualified mental health provider
QMI	Q-wave myocardial infarction
QMLT	quadriceps muscle layer thickness
q mo	every month: do not abbreviate this unusual direction, spell out- every month (this is a dangerous abbreviation as it might not be understood or interpreted as every Monday)
QMP	qualified medical personnel (to provide appropriate medical screening)
	quality monitoring program
QMR	Quality Measurement and Reporting
QMRA	quantitative microbial risk assessment
QMRP	qualified mental retardation professional
QMs	quality measures
qMS	quadrupole mass spectrometry
QMT	quantitative muscle testing
qn	every night. This is a **DANGEROUS** abbreviation that should **NOT** be used. It appears on the MedAbbrev and other "Do Not Use Lists," as it has been read as every hour (qh). Use "every night."
QNA	quinacrine (formally marketed in the US as Atabrine)
QNFT	quantitative fit test (respirator-related)
QNOC	every night
QNS	quantity not sufficient
QOC	quality of care
QOD	every other day (This is a DANGEROUS abbreviation that should NOT be used. It appears on the medabbrev. com and other Do Not Use Lists, as it is not commonly understood or understood as every once daily; spell out "every other day")
Q OD	see QOD
Q O D	see QOD

QOF	Quality and Outcomes Framework (pay-for-performance system in UK)
qoh	every other hour (this is a dangerous abbreviation as it is read as every day or four times a day-QID)
qohs	every other day at bedtime (this is a dangerous abbreviation as it is not recognized)
QOL	quality of life
QOLIE-31	quality of life in epilepsy
QOM	quality of motion
QON	every other night (this is a dangerous abbreviation)
QOPI	Quality Oncology Practice Initiative (of the American Society of Clinical Oncology)
QOW	every other week (this is a dangerous abbreviation as it may be misread or not understood)
qPCR	quantitative polymerase chain reaction
QPIC	Questionnaire of Personal Illness Causes
QPM	every afternoon; every evening (this is an ambiguous abbreviation which should not be used; check with prescriber/facility for the intended meaning)
qpm	every evening (this is a dangerous abbreviation as it can be read as 9 PM)
q PM	every afternoon; every evening (this is an ambiguous abbreviation which should not be used; check with prescriber/facility for the intended meaning)
QPOS	Quality Point of Service
QP/QS	ratio of pulmonary blood to systemic blood flow
QPS	quadripulse (transcranial) magnetic stimulation
	Quantitative Perfusion SPECT (single photon emission computed tomography) (software)
QQH	every four hours (United Kingdom)
QqQ	triple-quadrupole mass spectrometer
qqs	every four hours (United Kingdom)
QR	quiet room
QRA	quantitative risk assessment

QRC	qualified rehabilitation consultant
	qualitative radiocardiography
QRDR	quinolone resistance-determining region(s)
QRE	quality-related event
QREADS	a system for clinical digital radiologic image display developed at the Mayo Clinic
QRG	quick reference guide
QRM	Quality Risk Management
QRN	quinolone resistance
QRNG	quinolone-resistant *N. gonorrhoeae*
QRS	part of electrocardio-graphic wave representing ventricular depolarization
QRSd	QRS (part of the electrocardio-graphic wave representing ventricular repolarization) duration
qRT-PCR	quantitative reverse transcription polymerase chain reaction
QS	every shift
	quadriceps set
	quadrilateral socket
	Quality Services (Department)
	sufficient quantity
qs ad	a sufficient quantity to make
QSAR	quantitative structure-activity relationship
QSART	quantitative sudomotor axon reflex test
QSEN	Quality and Safety Education for Nurses (six competencies, along with innovative curricular guides to better prepare nurses to improve the health care systems)
q shift	every shift
QSI	quorum sensing inhibitory
Q sign	a patient whose mouth is open with their tongue hanging out when unconscious (slang)
QSL	quarters, subsistence, and laundry
qSOFA	quick Sepsis-related Organ Failure Assessment
QSP	physiological shunt fraction
Qs/Qt	intrapulmonary shunt fraction
QSRL	Q-switched ruby laser
QSS	quadrilateral space syndrome
	quantified smoking status
QST	quantitative sensory testing
Q-Sweat	a commercial quantitative sweat measurement system
QT	quart
	the time between the beginning of the QRS complex and the end of the T-wave

QTB	quadriceps tendon bearing
QTC	quantitative tip cultures
QTc	the QTc interval is the length of time it takes the electrical system in the heart to repolarize, adjusted for heart rate (normal 350-440 milliseconds)
QTc 505	a 505 millisecond interval for the electrical system in the heart to repolarize, adjusted for heart rate (normal 350-440 milliseconds)
QTcB	Bazett heart-rate corrected QT intervals
QTcF	QT interval corrected for heart rate using Fridericia's formula
QTF	QOLIBRI (Quality of Life after Brain Injury) Task Force
	quartz tuning fork
QTI	QT interval (measurement of the time between the start of the Q wave and the end of the T wave)
Q-T interval	a measure of the time between the start of the Q wave and the end of the T wave
QTL	quantitative trait locus
QTOF	quadrupole time-of-flight
QTP	quetiapine fumarate (Seroquel)
QTPPs	quality target product profiles
QTR	quadriceps tendon rupture
QTT	quantitative thermal testing
	Queensland tick typhus
QTTs	quantitative trait transcripts
Qtts	may have meant gtts (Latin for drops)
QTV	QT interval variability (electrocardiogram)
Q-TWiST	quality-adjusted time without symptoms (of disease) and toxicity
QTY	quantity
QU	quiet
QUAD	quadrant
	quadriceps
	quadriplegic
quadgem	quadgeminal; quadgeminy
QUADS	quadriceps muscles
	quadriplegics
	quintuplets
quads	quadrants
qual	qualitative
	quality
QUAL/QUAN	qualitative and quantitative
quan	quantitative
quant	quantitative
	quantity

QUART	quadrantectomy, axillary dissection, and radiotherapy
QUD	Question Under Discussion
Quebec	Phonetic Alphabet for Q; pronounced KEH-BECK
QuEChERS	Quick, Easy, Cheap, Effective, Rugged, and Safe; a method of analysis to examine pesticide residues in food
QUEST	Quality of Upper Extremity Skills Test
QuickDASH	Quick Disabilities of the Arm, Shoulder, and hand
QUICKI	Quantitative Insulin-Sensitivity Check Index
quid	a word meaning a cut or wad of something chewable
Quid pro quo	I want something, you want something. You give me what I want, I'll give you what you want; something for something (Latin)
QUIGs	quality indicator groups
QUIN	quinolinic acid
QUM	Quality Use of Medicines (Australia)
QuMA	quantitative microsatellite analysis
QUS	quantitative (bone) ultrasound
q.v.	on this matter, go see . . .
q-value	the q-value of a test measures the proportion of false positives incurred (called the false discovery rate) when that particular test is called significant
q visit	every visit
QW	every week (this is a dangerous abbreviation)
	Q-wave
q2w	every 2 weeks (this is a dangerous abbreviation)
q3w	every 3 weeks (this is a dangerous abbreviations)
q4w	every four weeks (this is a dangerous abbreviation)
QWB	Quality of Well-Being (scale)
QWBA	quantitative whole body autoradiography
QWE	every weekend (this is a dangerous abbreviation)
q week	every week
QWK	once a week (this is a dangerous abbreviation)
q4wk	every four weeks (this is a dangerous abbreviation
QWMI	Q-wave myocardial infarction

R

R	arginine
	radial
	Ragweed (allergies)
	rate
	ratio
	reacting
	recombinant
	recording personnel (Cardiology)
	rectal
	rectum
	regular
	regular insulin (it is dangerous to use abbreviations for insulin therapy)
	resistant
	respiration
	reticulocyte
	retinoscopy
	rifampicin [part of tuberculosis regimen as in RHZ (E/S)/HR]
	right (this is a dangerous abbreviation; spell out "right" to avoid surgical, treatment, and diagnosis-related errors)
	Ritalin (methylphenidate; as in Vitamin R)
	roentgen
	Romeo (Phonetic Alphabet for R; pronounced ROW-ME-OH)
	rub
®	rectal; rectally; rectum Registered Trademark
+R	Rinne test, positive
−R	Rinne test, negative
(R)	ratio
	right (this is a dangerous abbreviation; spell out "right" to avoid surgical errors)
R#	Blood Bank specimen identification number
R>L	right greater then left
R/0	may have meant R/O (rule out or ruled out)
R0	no residual disease
R1	microscopic residual tumor
R10	non-stress (fetal well-being) test score reactive by 10 score
R15	non-stress (fetal well-being) test score reactive by 15 score

R2	spin density projection-assisted R2-magnetic resonance imaging (R2-MRI; FerriScan scan); for measurement of liver iron concentration; R2 stands for proton transverse relaxation rates
R-2	rohypnol (Roofies) (slang)
RA	radial artery
	radiographic absorptiometry
	rales
	readmission
	Regulatory Affairs
	renal artery
	repeat action
	retinoic acid
	rheumatoid arthritis
	right arm
	right atrial
	right atrium
	right auricle
	robotic-assisted
	room air
	rotational atherectomy
Ra	radium
R/A	see RA
RAA	renin-angiotensin-aldosterone
	right atrial abnormality
	right atrial appendage
RA A	right atrial pressure, a wave
rAAA	ruptured abdominal aortic aneurysm
RAAS	renin-angiotensin-aldosterone system
RAB	rabies vaccine, not otherwise specified
	rice (rice cereal), applesauce, and banana (diet)
RABBIT	Rheumatoid Arthritis Observation of Biologic Therapy (risk scores)
RAB$_{DEV}$	rabies vaccine, duck embryo culture
rabdo	may have meant rhabdo
RAB$_{FRhL-2}$	rabies vaccine, diploid fetal-rhesus-lung-2 cell line
RABG	room air blood gas
RAB$_{DCV}$	rabies vaccine, human diploid cell culture
RABig	rabies immune globulin
RAB$_{PCEC}$	rabies vaccine, purified chick embryo cell culture
RABSO	robotic-assisted bilateral salpingo-oophorectomy

RAC	Recombinant DNA Advisory Committee
	Recovery Audit Contractor
	residential aged care (tube)
	right antecubital
	right atrial catheter
	robotic-assisted cholecystectomy
RACA	right anterior cerebral artery
RACCO	right anterior caudocranial oblique
RACE	rapid amplification of cDNA (complementary deoxyribonucleic acid) ends
RACP	Royal Australasian College of Physicians
RACs	Recovery Audit Contractors
RaCT	randomized active control trial
	recalcified whole-blood activated clotting time
	Risk Assessment Categorization Tool
RACZ	a procedure of dissolving lumbar scar tissue (epidurolysis) (Dr. Gabor Racz)
RAD	ionizing radiation unit
	radical
	radiology
	rapid antigen detection
	reactive airway disease
	reactive attachment disorder
	renal (tubule) assist device
	right axis deviation
rad	radiation
RADAC	Regional Alcohol and Drug Assessment Center
RADARS	Researched Abuse, Diversion, and Addiction-Related Surveillance (data collection system)
RADCA	right anterior descending coronary artery
RADE	reactive airway disease exacerbation
radic	radical
Rad Imp	radium implant
RADISH	rheumatoid arthritis diffuse idiopathic skeletal hyperostosis
RADONC	
Rad Onc	radiation oncology
RADS	ionizing radiation units
	rapid assay delivery systems
	reactive airway disease syndrome
RADT	rapid antigen detection testing

RAE	relative age effect
	renal arterial embolization
	right atrial enlargement
	Ring Adair Elvin (tube)
RAEB	refractory anemia, erythroblastic
RAEB2	refractory anemia with excess blasts, type 2
RAEB-T	refractory anemia with excess blasts in transition
RAF	rapid atrial fibrillation
RAFF	rectus abdominis free flap
RAFN	retrograde/antegrade femoral nail
RAFT	Rehabilitative Addicted Family Treatment
RAG	room air gas
RAGE	receptor of advanced glycation endproducts
RA-GPEHR	robotic-assisted giant paraesophageal hernia repair
RAH	right atrial hypertrophy
RAHB	right anterior hemiblock
rAHF	antihemophilic factor (recombinant)
RAI	radioactive iodine
	Resident Assessment Instrument
RAIA	radioiodine-avid
	rapid-acting insulin analogue
rAIA	ruptured aortoiliac aneurysms
RAID	radioimmunodetection
	Rheumatoid Arthritis Impact of Disease
RAIL	robotic-assisted Ivor-Lewis (esophagectomy)
RA-ILD	rheumatoid arthritis interstitial lung disease
	rheumatoid arthritis-associated interstitial lung disease
RAILE	robot-assisted Ivor-Lewis esophagectomy
RAINBOW Trial	ramucirumab plus paclitaxel versus placebo plus paclitaxel in patients with previously treated advanced gastric or gastroesophageal junction adenocarcinoma
RAIR	rectoanal inhibitory reflex
RaISS	response-adjusted international scoring system (predictor of transplant outcomes)
RAIT	radioimmunotherapy
RAIU	radioactive iodine uptake
RAK	reference air karma
RAKT	robotic-assisted kidney transplantation
RAL	raltegravir (Isentress)
RALA	v-ral simian leukemia viral oncogene homolog A; see gene website www.ncbi.nlm.nih.gov/gene
RALC	right-angle linear cutter (stapling device)
RA lead	right atrium pacemaker lead
RALH	robotic-assisted laparoscopic hysterectomy
RALIS	a mathematical algorithm for early detection of neonate late onset sepsis incorporating six vital signs measured every 2 hours
RALMA	robotic-assisted laparoscopic Mitrofanoff appendicovesicostomy
RALN	radiotracer-assisted localization of lung nodules
RALP	robotic-assisted laparoscopic prostatectomy
	robotic-assisted laparoscopic pyeloplasty
RALPN	robot-assisted laparoscopic partial nephrectomy
RALRP	robot-assisted laparoscopic radical prostatectomy
RALS	robotic assisted laparoscopic surgery
RALT	routine admission laboratory tests
RAM	radioactive material
	rapid alternating movements
	rectus abdominis myocutaneous
RA/MAC	regional anesthesia with monitored anesthesia care
RAMBAs	retinoic acid metabolism blocking agents
RAM CPAP	RAM® cannula (features soft, gently curved prongs designed for patient comfort, flexible design, and available in seven sizes) with bubble continuous positive airway pressure
rami	plural of ramus (a branch)
RAMP®	Rapid Analyte Measurement Platform
RAMRIS	Rheumatoid Arthritis MRI Scoring System
RAMs	radiation-associated meningiomas
	resistance-associated mutations
	risk-assessment models
ramus	a word meaning branch
RAN	resident's admission notes
R2AN	second year resident's admission notes

Rand 36　health-related quality of life questionnaire/score (The RAND Corporation, nonprofit institution; the RAND name originated as a contraction of research and development)

Ranger®　a pressure infusion device used in to warm large volumes of fluid over a short period of time

RANKL　receptor activator of nuclear factor kB ligand

RANTES　regulated upon activation, normal T cell expressed and secreted

RANZCOG　Fellows of the Royal Australian and New Zealand College of Obstetricians and Gynaecologists

RANZCP　Fellows of the Royal Australian and New Zealand College of Psychiatrists

RAO　radial artery occlusion
recurrent airway obstruction
retinal artery occlusion
right anterior oblique

R AOM　recurrent Acute Otitis Media

RAOOD　renal artery ostial occlusive disease

RAP　recurrent abdominal pain
renal artery pseudoaneurysm
request for advance payment
request for anticipated payment
Resident Assessment Protocol
resident assessment protocol (long-term care)
right abdominal pain
right atrial pressure

RAPA　radial artery pseudoaneurysm

RAPD　random amplified polymorphic DNA
relative afferent pupillary defect

RAPH　Raph; an International Society of Blood Transfusion (ISBT) blood group

RAPID　Routine Assessment of Patient Index Data

RAPN　robot-assisted partial nephrectomy

RAPs　Resident Assessment Protocols

RAPT　Risk Assessment and Predictor Tool

RAQ　right anterior quadrant

RAR　right arm, reclining

RARA　retinoic acid receptor alpha; see gene website www.ncbi.nlm.nih.gov/gene

R/A ratio　ratio of peak velocity of retrograde flow (R) to peak velocity of antegrade flow (A)

RARC　robot-assisted radical cystectomy

RARCs　Remittance Advice Remark Codes (Medicare)

RARP　robot-assisted (laparoscopic) radical prostatectomy

RARS　refractory anemia with ring sideroblasts
see gene website; www.ncbi.nlm.nih.gov/gene

RARs　retinoic acid receptors

RARS-T　refractory anemia with ring sideroblasts associated with marked thrombocytosis

RAS　recurrent aphthous stomatitis
renal artery stenosis
renal artery stenting
renin-angiotensin system
restrictive allograft syndrome
reticular activating system
retinoic acid syndrome
right arm, sitting

RASC　robotic-assisted sacrocolpopexy

RASE　rapid-acquisition spin echo

RASL　reduction-association scapholunate (procedure)

RASO　right anterior superior oblique

RASP　radiographical adjacent segment pathology

rASRM score　Revised American Society for Reproductive Medicine (score/staging) (Infertility with endometriosis staging)

RASS　Richmond Agitation-Sedation Scale

RAST　radioallergosorbent test

RAT　right anterior thigh

RA test　test for rheumatoid factor

RATG　rabbit antithymocyte globulin

RA-TLH　robot-assisted total laparoscopic hysterectomy

RATS　robotic-assisted thoracoscopic surgery

RATx　radiation therapy

RAU　recurrent aphthous ulcers

RA-UIP　rheumatoid arthritis-associated usual interstitial pneumonia

RAV　repeated and verified (refers to telephone orders)

RA V　right atrial pressure, v wave

Rave　a large party or festival featuring electronic dance music, mostly known for the excessive use of psychedelic drugs

R

RAVLT	Rey Auditory Verbal Learning Test	RBD	REM (rapid eye movement sleep) behavior disorder
RAVs	resistance-associated variants		right border of dullness
R(AW)	airway resistance		right brain-damaged
RAWD	racecadotril (available in France as Acetorphan) for the treatment of acute watery diarrhea (in children)	RbDe	residue-based diagram editor
		RBE	relative biologic effectiveness
		RBF	renal blood flow
		RBG	random blood glucose
RA Z	right atrial pressure, z point	RBH	regular bowel habit
RB	recumbent bike		residual bone height
	relieved by		retrobulbar hemorrhage
	retinoblastoma		roughness, breathiness, and
	retrobulbar		hoarseness (perceptual voice
	right breast		quality evaluation)
	right buttock	RBHOMS	Royal Brisbane Hospital
	Rose Bengal		Outcome Measure for
Rb	rubidium		Swallowing
R&B	right and below	RBI	Robust Process Improvement
R/B	risk verses benefit	RB-ILD	respiratory bronchiolitis-
	risks and benefits		associated interstitial lung
RBA	right basilar artery		disease
	right brachial artery	R BKA	right below-knee amputation
	risk-benefit assessment	RBL	Roche Biomedical Laboratory
	risks, benefits, and alternatives (discussion with patient)	RBM	restricted Boltzmann machine
			risk-based monitoring
R/B/A	see RBA	RBO	read back order (orders taken
RBAC	Role Based Access Control (electronic medical records)		verbally or by telephone from a physician)
RBAE	radiographic bone aluminum equivalency	RBON	retrobulbar optic neuritis
		RBOs	risks, benefits, and options
RBAI	right brachial-ankle index	RBOW	rupture bag of water
RBANS	Repeatable Battery for the Assessment of Neuropsychological Status	RBP	Rarebit perimetry
			recurrent bacterial pneumonia
			retinol-binding protein
RbAp	retinoblastoma-associated protein	RBR	read by radiologist
		RBRVS	Medicare resource-based
rbAPC	may have meant rhAPC (recombinant human activated protein C)		relative-value scale
		RBS	random blood sugar
			redback spider
RBAV	read back and verified	RBSE	role breadth self-efficacy
RBB	retrobulbar block		(employees' perceived
	right breast biopsy		capability of carrying out a
	right bundle branch		broader and more proactive
RBBB	right bundle branch block		set of work tasks that extend
RBBBB	may have meant RBBB (right bundle branch block)		beyond prescribed technical requirements)
		rbST	recombinant bovine
RBBX	right breast biopsy examination		somatotropin
RBC	ranitidine bismuth citrate	RBT	rational behavior therapy
	red blood cell (count)		rose bengal test
RBCD	right border cardiac dullness	RBTO	reliability based topology
RBCDW	red blood cell distribution width		optimization
		RBU	rehabilitation bed-unit
rBCG	recombinant Bacillus Calmette-Guerin (vaccine)		rifabutin (Mycobutin)
		RBUS	renal and bladder ultrasonogram
RBCM	red blood cell mass	RBV	read back verbal (order)
RBCs	red blood cells		ribavirin (Rebetol; Virazole)
RBC s/f	red blood cells spun filtration		right brachial vein
RBCV	red blood cell volume		

RBVO	read back verbal order		resectable colon cancer
	retinal branch vein occlusion		right cranial-caudal
RBW	recipient body weight		(mammogram view)
	rectilinear biphasic waveform		Roman Catholic Church
RBX	ruboxistaurin	RCCA	right common carotid artery
RC	race	RCCS	Registered Congenital Cardiac
	radiocarpal (joint)		Monographer
	rate control; rate controlled	RCCT	randomized controlled clinical
	rectal cancer		trial
	Red Cross	RCD	refractory coeliac disease
	report called		relative cardiac dullness
	Respiratory Care	RCDAD	recurrent *Clostridium difficile-*
	retention catheter		*associated* diarrhea
	retrograde cystogram	RCDH	right-sided congenital
	retruded contact (position)		diaphragmatic hernia
	right coronary	rCDI	recurrent Clostridium difficile
	Roman Catholic		infection
	root canal	RCDM	remote clinical decision-making
	rotator cuff	RCDP1	rhizomelic chondrodysplasia
R&C	reasonable and customary		punctata type 1
	(charges)	RCDs	respiratory chain disorders
R+C	reasonable and customary	RCE	right carotid endarterectomy
	(charges)	RCEA	right carotid endarterectomy
R/C	reclining chair	rCEA	reoperative carotid
RCA	radiographic contrast agent		endarterectomy
	radionuclide cerebral	R-CEOP	rituximab, cyclophosphamide,
	angiogram		epirubicin, Oncovin
	regional citrate anticoagulation		(vincristine), and
	Respiratory Care Assistant		prednisolone
	right carotid artery	RCEP	Registered Clinical Exercise
	right coronary artery		Physiologist
	rolling circle amplification	RCES	Recurrent Corneal Erosion
	root cause analysis		Syndrome
RCAB	right coronary artery branch	RCF	Reiter complement fixation
RCA CTO	right coronary artery, chronic	RCF®	enteral nutrition product
	total occlusion	RCFA	right common femoral
RC/AL	residential care, assisted living		angioplasty
rCARD	real-time Clinical Abbreviation		right common femoral artery
	Recognition and	RCFE	residential care facility for the
	Disambiguation		elderly
RCAT	Rhinitis Control Assessment	RCFV	right common femoral vein
	Test	RCH	residential care home
RCAVF	radiocephalic arteriovenous	RCHF	right-sided congestive heart
	fistula		failure
RCB	residual cancer burden	R-CHOP	rituximab plus
RCBA	Reading Comprehension Battery		cyclophosphamide,
	for Aphasia		doxorubicin
RCBF	regional cerebral blood flow		(hydroxydaunorubicin),
RCBS	random capillary blood sugar		vincristine (Oncovin),
RCBs	may have meant RBCs (red		and prednisone
	blood cells)	R2-CHOP	rituximab and lenalidomide
rCBV	regional cerebral blood volume		(Revlimid) plus
	relative cerebral blood volume		cyclophosphamide,
RCC	rape crisis center		doxorubicin
	Rathke cleft cyst		(hydroxydaunorubicin),
	Rathke cleft cysts		vincristine (Oncovin),
	relative cell counts		and prednisone
	renal cell carcinoma	RChT	radiochemotherapy

RCIA	red (blood) cell immune adherence	RCRI	revised cardiac risk index
	right common iliac artery	RCS	Raynaud Condition Score
RC/IC	Roofer Cholim Cancer Society (an organization dedicated to funding insurance policies for cancer-stricken patients)		reduced concentrated sweets
			refractory cardiogenic shock
			Registered Cardiac Sonographer
			repeat cesarean section
RCIN	radiographic-contrast-media-induced nephropathy		reticulum cell sarcoma
			retrosternal clear space
RCIP	rape crisis intervention program		Royal College of Surgeons
RCIs	Reliable Change Indices	RCT	randomized clinical trial
RCIV	right common iliac vein		Registered Care Technologist
RCJ	radiocapitellar joint		relational-cultural therapy
RCJs	retrospective confidence judgments		root canal therapy
			Rorschach Content Test
RCL	radial collateral ligament		rotator cuff tear
	range of comfortable loudness	RCTA	rotator cuff tear arthroplasty
RCM	radiographic contrast media	rctA	transcriptional regulator protein; see gene website www.ncbi .nlm.nih.gov/gene
	reflectance confocal microscopy		
	restricted cardiomyopathy		
	retinal capillary microaneurysm	RCTh	radiochemotherapy
	right costal margin	RCTRs	resolvin conjugates in tissue regeneration
RCMAR	Resource Centers for Minority Aging Research (NIH)		
		RCTs	randomized controlled trials
RCMD	refractory cytopenia with multilineage dysplasia	RCU	respiratory care unit
		RCV	red cell volume
RCN	radiocontrast-agent-induced nephrotoxicity		right colic vein
		RCVA	right-hemispheric cerebrovascular accident
R-CNN	region-based convolutional neural network		
			rotational coronary venous angiography
RCO	revoked court order		
RCo	ristocetin cofactor	RCVAT	right costovertebral angle tenderness
RCOF	required coefficient of friction		
RcoF	ristocetin cofactor activity (von Willebrand ristocetin cofactor activity)	RCVD	received
		RCVP	retrograde coronary vein perfusion
RCOG	Royal College of Obstetricians and Gynaecologists		rituximab, cyclophosphamide, vincristine, and prednisolone
RCOT	revoked court-ordered treatment	R-CVP	rituximab, cyclophosphamide, vincristine, and prednisone
RCP	respiratory care plan	RCVS	reversible cerebral vasoconstriction syndrome
	Respiratory Care Practitioner		
	retrograde cerebral perfusion	RCVT	Registered Cardiovascular Technologist
	right chest port		
	Royal College of Physicians	RCW	reduced capacity to work
RCPM	raven-colored progressive matrices		removable-cast walker
		RCX	ramus circumflexus
RCPSC	Royal College of Physicians and Surgeons of Canada	RD	radial deviation
			Raynaud disease
RCPT	Registered Cardiopulmonary Technician		reaction of degeneration
			reading disability
RCR	replication-competent retrovirus (assay)		recommended dose
			reflex decay
	responsible conduct of research		Registered Dietitian
	rotator cuff repair		renal disease
RCRA	Resource Conservation Recovery Act (U.S. Environmental Protection Agency)		respiratory disease
			respiratory distress
			restricted duty

	retinal detachment	RDOD	retinal detachment, right eye
	Reye disease	RDOS	retinal detachment, left eye
	rhabdomyosarcoma	RDP	random donor platelets
	right deltoid		rapid-onset dystonia
	risk difference		parkinsonism
	ruptured disk		right dorsoposterior
R&D	research and development	RDPE	reticular degeneration of the
R/D	recipient/donor		pigment epithelium
	recruitment (airway subsequent	RDQ	Roland Disability Questionnaire
	re-opening) and derecruitment	RDR	recombination-dependent
	(repetitive closure)		replication
	research and development		relative dose response
RDA	recommended daily allowance		response-dose-ratio
	Registered Dental Assistant	RDS	research diagnostic criteria
	representational difference		respiratory distress syndrome
	analysis	RDT	rapid diagnostic test
RDAVC	right-dominant atrioventricular		regular dialysis (hemodialysis)
	canal		treatment
RDAVR	rapid deployment aortic valve	RDTD	referral, diagnosis, treatment,
	replacement		and discharge
RDB	randomized double-blind (trial)	RDTs	rapid diagnostic tests
RDCS	Registered Diagnostic Cardiac	RDU	recreational drug use
	Sonographer		renal dialysis unit
RDC/TMD	research diagnostic criteria	RDVT	recurrent deep vein thrombosis
	for temporomandibular	RDW	red (cell) distribution width
	disorders	RDWCV	coefficient of variation of the
RDD	renal dose dopamine		red (blood cell) distribution
	Rosai-Dorfman disease		width
RDE	remote data entry	RDW-CV	red cell distribution width
	respiratory disturbance events		coefficient of variation
RDEA	right deviation of electrical	RDW-SD	standard deviation of the red
	axis		(blood cell) distribution width
RDEB	recessive dystrophic	RDX	radixin; see gene website www
	epidermolysis bullosa		.ncbi.nlm.nih.gov/gene
RDF	radial distribution function	RE	concerning
	recombination directionality		radiation exposure
	factor		Rasmussen's encephalitis
	refuse-derived fuel		rectal examination
	Resource Description		reflux esophagitis
	Framework		regarding
	right dorsal frontal		regional enteritis
RDG	right dorsogluteal		reticuloendothelial
RDH	Registered Dental Hygienist		retinol equivalents
RDHAP	rituximab, dexamethasone,		right ear (this is a dangerous
	high-dose cytarabine (ara-C),		abbreviation as it can be read
	and cisplatin (Platinol)		as right eye)
RDI	recommended dietary intake		right eye (this is a dangerous
	respiratory distress index		abbreviation as it can be read
	respiratory disturbance (distress)		as right ear)
	index		rowing ergometer
RDIH	right direct inguinal hernia	Re	rhenium
RDLBBB	rate-dependent left bundle	186Re	rhenium 186
	branch block	R & E	rest and exercise
RDM	right deltoid muscle		round and equal
RDMS	Registered Diagnostic Medical	Re:	regarding
	Sonographer	R↑E	right upper extremity
RDMs	reactive drug metabolites	R↓E	right lower extremity
RDN	Registered Dietitian Nutritionist	RE✓	recheck

REACH	Registration, Evaluation, Authorization and restriction of Chemicals (European Union)
	Resources for Enhancing Alzheimer's Caregiver Health (a multisite research program sponsored by the National Institute on Aging and the National Institute on Nursing Research)
react	reactivity
READM	readmission
REAH	respiratory epithelial adenomatoid hamartoma
RE-AIM	reach, effectiveness, adoption, implementation, maintenance
REAL	Revised European American Lymphoma (classification)
REALM	Rapid Estimation of Adult Literacy in Medicine
REALM-SF	Rapid Estimate of Adult Literacy in Medicine short-form
Rebbet	Rational Emotion Behavior Therapy (REBT)
REBOA	resuscitative endovascular balloon occlusion of the aorta
REBT	Rational Emotive Behavior Therapy
REC	gingival recession
	rear end collision
	recommend
	recommendation(s)
	reconciliation
	record
	recovery
	recreation
	recur
	research ethics committee
RECA	right external carotid artery
RECC	RNA (ribonucleic acid) editing core complex
recC	see gene website www.ncbi.nlm .nih.gov/gene
RECD	real-ear-to-coupler differences
recD	see gene website, www.ncbi.nlm .nih.gov/gene
rec'd	received
	recommended
	recorded
	recovered
recert	recertification
recip	reciprocating
recirc	recirculation

RECIST	Response Evaluation Criteria in Solid Tumors (guidelines)
	CR = complete response
	PR = partial response
	PD = progressive disease
	SD = stable disease
RECK	reversion-inducing-cystein-rich protein with kazal motifs; see gene website www.ncbi .nlm.nih.gov/gene
RE-CK	re-check
RECON	reconstruction
RECOS	a prospective multicenter registry of consecutive patients undergoing shoulder surgery recruited in nine hospitals in Italy which estimated venous thromboembolic complications and thromboprophylaxis use after shoulder surgery
RECPs	relativistic effective core potentials
Rec Rel	record release
RECs	respiratory epithelial cells
recs	recommendations; recommends
RECT	rectum
Rec Th	Recreation Therapy
REDA	Registered Eating Disorders Associate
REDF	reversed end-diastolic flow (umbilical-artery Doppler ultrasonography)
redo	a word meaning to do over again
REDs	reproductive endocrine diseases
Reds	red blood cells
RED SUBS	reducing substances
redux	reduction
REDV	reversed end-diastolic flow velocity
REE	resting energy expenditure
RE-ED	re-education
REEDA	redness, edema, ecchymosis, discharge and approximation (a scale to assess healing of episiotomies)
R-EEG	resting electroencephalogram
REEGT	Registered Electroencephalogram Technologist
re-eval	reevaluation
REF	refused
	renal erythropoietic factor
ref	refer; referred; referring
ref→	refer to
refs	references

REG	radioencephalogram	REP CK	rapid electrophoresis creatine kinase
	regression analysis		
	regular	REPL	recurrent early pregnancy loss
	requested		
Reg	regenerating gene	R-EPOCH	rituximab and etoposide, prednisone, vincristine (oncovin), cyclophosphamide, and doxorubicin (hydroxydaunorubicin)
Reg block	regional block anesthesia		
regurg	regurgitation		
rehab	rehabilitation		
REI	Reproductive Endocrinology and Infertility		
REIA	right external iliac artery	repol	repolarization
rEIA	recombinant enzyme immune assay	REPS	repetitions
		REP SGIS	repeated side-glide in standing
REIL	repeated extension in lying	REPT	Registered Evoked Potential Technologist
REILD	radioembolization-induced liver disease	REQ	required
		reqd	required
REIS	repeated extension in standing	req'd	required
REJ	receptor for egg jelly (domain)	REQS	requirements
		RER	renal excretion rate
rej	rejection		respiratory exchange ratio
REL	relative	RER+	replication error positive
	religion	RERA	respiratory effort-related arousal
REL%	relative per cent		
RELE	resistive exercise, lower extremities	RERAs	respiratory effort-related arousals
REM	rapid eye movement	RERIC	Region Emilia Romagna Cardiac Surgery registry (database)
	real ear measure		
	recent event memory		
	remarried	ReRT	reirradiation
	remission	RES	recurrent erosion syndrome
Rem	roentgen equivalent in man (a unit of radiation dosage)		resection
			resident
REMA	resazurin microtiter assay (A method for detecting multidrug-resistant Mycobacterium tuberculosis by using a reduction of resazurin)		reticuloendothelial system
			reversible encephalopathic syndrome
		RESC	resuscitation
		resch	reschedule
		ReSCU	Respiratory Special Care Unit
REMEDI	Regenstrief National Center for Medical Device Informatics (Infusion Pump Collaborative)	resec	resection
		RESP	respirations
			respiratory
REMI	remifentanil (Ultiva)	resps	respirations (as in resps/minute)
REMS	rapid eye movement sleep	REST	RE1 (Repressor Element-1)-silencing transcription factor (gene/protein) (also known as neuron-restrictive silencer factor)
	Risk Evaluation and Mitigation Strategies		
ReMV	Rehmannia mosaic virus		
remv	removal		
rent	a word meaning a slit or opening made by tearing, rending, cutting, or ripping		restoration
			restriction of environmental stimulation therapy
REO	respiratory and enteric orphan (viruses)	REST/NRSF	repressor element-1 (re1) silencing transcription factor/neuron-restrictive silencer factor
REP	rapid electrophoresis		
	repair		
	repeat	RESUS	resuscitation
	repeated	RESVH	right endoscopic saphenous vein harvest
	report		

rESWT	radial extracorporeal shock wave therapy		rheumatic fever
			rheumatoid factor
RET	resistance exercise training		right foot
	retention		ring finger
	reticulocyte		risk factor
	retina	Rf	rutherfordium
	retired	R/F	retroflexed
	retraction	RF6	rejection-free survival at
	return		6 months
	right esotropia	RFA	radiofrequency ablation
ret detach	retinal detachment		resonance frequency analysis
retic	reticulocyte		right femoral artery
retics	reticulocytes		right forearm
RETN	resistin; see gene website		right frontoanterior
	www.ncbi.nlm.nih.gov/gene	RF ablation	radiofrequency ablation
RETRO	retrograde	RFAs	radiofrequency ablations
RETRX	retractions	RFB	radial flow chromatography
RETs	reticulocytes		residual functional capacity
Rett Syndrome	an X-linked dominant disorder		retained foreign body
	caused frequently by muta-	RFBOT	radiofrequency to the
	tions in the methyl-CpG-		base-of-tongue
	finding protein 2 gene	RFC	reduced folate carrier
	(MECP2). Patients show a	RFCA	radiofrequency catheter ablation
	short period of developmen-	RFD	residue-free diet
	tal stagnation followed by a	RFDT	Reach in Four Directions Test
	rapid regression in language	RFE	return flow enema
	and motor development.	RFEM	right femoral
REUA	retropubic extraurethral	RFET	reverse frozen elephant trunk
	adenomectomy	RFFF	radial forearm free flap
REUE	resistive exercise, upper		(reconstruction of pharyngeal
	extremities		defect)
REUR	real ear unaided response	RFFIT	rapid fluorescent focus
REV	reticuloendotheliosis virus		inhibition test
	reverse	RFg	visual fields by Goldmann-type
	review		perimeter
	revolutions	rFGF-2	recombinant fibroblast growth
	room eye view		factor-2
revasc	revascularization	RFH	radiofrequency hyperthermia
REVASC Trial	Does percutaneous coronary		reactive follicular hyperplasia
	intervention (PCI) of chronic	RfH	refractory hypertension
	total occlusions (CTOs), also	RFI	request for information
	known as CTO-PCI, improve		Requirement for Improvement
	left ventricular function in		(The Joint Commission)
	addition to PCI of relevant	RFID	radio frequency identification
	coexisting non-CTO vessels	RFIL	repeated flexion in lying
	(No-CTO-PCI)?	RFIPC	Rating Form of IBD
Revd	Reverend		(inflammatory bowel disease)
Rex	routine exercise		Patient Concerns
RF	radiofrequency	RFIS	repeated flexion in standing
	radiographic and fluoroscopic	RFIs	Requirements For Improvement
	rectus femurs		(The Joint Commission)
	reduction fixation	RFISit	repeated flexion in sitting
	refill; refilled (prescriptions)	RFISS	repeated flexion in step-standing
	regurgitant fraction (cardiology)		radionuclide functional
	renal failure		lymphoscintigraphy
	respiratory failure	RFL	right frontolateral
	restricted fluids	rfl	refil
	retroflexed	RFLF	retained fetal lung fluid

RFLP	restriction fragment length polymorphism
	restriction fragment length polymorphism (patterns)
RFM	rifampin (Rifadin)
RFMP-4	a 4-month regimen of daily rifampicin (for prevention of latent tuberculosis infection progression to active disease)
RFNA	radiofrequency nerve ablation
rFNA	random fine-needle aspiration
	repeat fine-needle aspiration
RFOV	reconstruction field of view (radiology)
RFP	red fluorescent protein
	Renal function panel (see Laboratory Panels)
	request for payment
	request for proposal
	right frontoposterior
RFR	reason for referral
RFS	rapid frozen section
	recurrence-free
	recurrence-free survival
	refeeding syndrome
	Reflux Finding Score
	relapse-free survival
RFT	radiofrequency treatment
	renal function test(s)
	respiratory function test
	right frontotemporal
	right frontotransverse
	routine fever therapy
RFTA	radiofrequency thermal ablation
RFTC	radiofrequency thermocoagulation
RFTVR	radio frequency tissue volume reduction (Somnoplasty®)
RFU	relative fluorescence units
	routine follow-up
RFUT	radioactive fibrinogen uptake
RFV	reason for visit
	right femoral vein
RFVA	reversal of flow in the vertebral artery
rFVIIa	recombinant activated coagulation factor VII NovoSeven
	recombinant activated factor VIIa
	recombinant factor VIIa
rFVIII FS	antihemophilic factor (recombinant), formulated with sucrose (Kogenate)
RFVTA	radiofrequency volumetric thermal ablation
RFVTR	radiofrequency volumetric tissue reduction
RFW	radiofrequency wave
RFx	regulatory factor X; see gene website www.ncbi.nlm.nih.gov/gene
RG	regurgitated (infant feeding)
	right (upper outer) gluteus
Rg	roentgenium
R/G	rebound/guarding
	red/green
RGA	right gastroepiploic artery
rGBM	recurrent glioblastoma
RGC	retinal ganglion cell
RGCL	retinal ganglion cell layer
RGCSE	refractory generalized convulsive status epilepticus
R-GCVP	rituximab, gemcitabine, cyclophosphamide, vincristine, and prednisolone
RGDP	Regional Gross Domestic Product
RGEA	right gastroepiploic artery
RGI	rhamnogalacturonan I
RGL	retinal ganglion (cell) layer
RGM	rapidly growing *Mycobacteria*
	recurrent glioblastoma multiforme
	right gluteus medius
RGO	reciprocating gait orthosis
RGP	retrograde pyelogram (also RPG)
	rigid gas permeable (contact lenses)
RgPg	retrograde pyelogram
RGR	relative growth rate
	retinal G protein coupled gene
rGSV	right great saphenous vein
RGT	response-guided therapy
RGVT	retrograde (fill) voiding trial
RH	racial harassment
	radical hysterectomy
	reduced haloperidol
	relative humidity
	rest home
	retinal hemorrhage
	Rh; an International Society of Blood Transfusion (ISBT) blood group
	right hand
	right handed
	right hemisphere
	right hyperphoria
	room humidifier
Rh	Rhesus factor in blood
	rhodium
Rh+	Rhesus factor positive
	Rhesus positive
Rh−	Rhesus negative

RHA	rheumatoid arthritis (therapeutic) vaccine	r-hGH(m)	mammalian-cell–derived recombinant human growth hormone (Serostim)
	right hepatic artery		
rHA	recombinant human albumin	RHH	right homonymous hemianopsia
RHAA	hypogastric artery aneurysm	RHI	regular human insulin (it is dangerous to use abbreviations for insulin therapy)
rhaA	L-rhamnose isomerase (gene)		
RHABDO	rhabdomyolysis		
RH/AG	Rh-associated glycoprotein; an International Society of Blood Transfusion (ISBT) blood group	RHIA	Registered Health Information Administrator
		RhIG	Rh immune globulin
		RHINO	rhinoplasty
rhAPC	recombinant human activated protein C	RHIO	regional health information organization
RHB	raise head of bed	RHIOs	regional health information organizations
	right heart border		
RHb	reduced hemoglobin	RHIs	repeated head impacts
rhBMP-2	recombinant human bone morphogenetic protein 2	RHIT	Registered Health Information Technician
rhBMP-7	recombinant human bone morphogenetic protein 7	RHK	rotating hinge knee (prosthesis)
		RHL	right hemisphere lesions
RH/BSO	radial hysterectomy and bilateral salpingo-oophorectomy		right heptic lobe
		Rhlg	Rhesus (blood factor) immune globulin (RhoGAM)
RHC	respiration has ceased		
	right heart catheterization	rhm	roentgens per hour at one meter
	right hemicolectomy	RHO	right heel off
	routine health care	Rho(D)	immune globulin to an Rh-negative woman
	rural health clinic		
rhCG	recombinant human chorionic gonadotropin	RhoGAM®	Rho (D) immune globulin
		RHP	resting head pressure
rhCRP	recombinant human C-reactive protein	rhPDGF	recombinant human platelet-derived growth factor
RHD	radial head dislocation	RHR	resting heart rate
	relative hepatic dullness	RHS	right-hand side
	reverse homodigital dorsoradial (flap)	RHT	regional hyperthermia
			right hypertropia
	rheumatic heart disease	rhTSH	recombinant human thyroid-stimulating hormone
	right-hand dominant		
rh-DNase	dornase alfa (Pulmozyme)	rHuEPO	recombinant human erythropoietin
RHDS	Registered Healthcare Documentation Specialist		
		rHuKGF	recombinant human keratinocyte growth factor (Palifermin)
rhEPO	recombniant human erythropoietin		
rheum	rheumatism	rhupua	coexistence of rheumatoid arthritis and systemic lupus erythematosus
	rheumatoid; rheumatic		
	rheumatologic		
	rheumatology	RHV	right hepatic vein
RHF	restricted Hartree-Fock	RHW	radiant heat warmer
	rheumatic fever vaccine	Rhy-1	see gene website, www.ncbi.nlm.nih.gov/gene
	right heart failure		
Rh factor	Rhesus factor (an inherited protein found on the surface of red blood cells)	R-HyperCVAD	rituximab with hyperfractionated cyclophosphamide, vincristine, Adriamycin (doxorubicin), and dexamethasone
RHG	right-hand grip		
Rh/G	RhoGAM	RHZ(E/S)/HR	a tuberculosis treatment regimen consisting of rifampicin, isoniazid, pyrazinamide, ethambutol, streptomycin, and isoniazid
rhGAA	recombinant human lysosomal acid alpha-glucosidase		
rhGH	recombinant human growth hormone		

RI	ramus intermedius (coronary artery)	RIDT	rapid influenza diagnostic test(s)
	refractive index	RIE	radiation induced emesis
	Registered Indian (Canada)		reactive ion etching
	regular insulin (it is dangerous to use abbreviations for insulin therapy)		rocket immunoelectrophoresis
		RIETE	Register Informatizado de Enfermedad TromboEmbólica (Computerized Registry of Patients with Venous Thromboembolism)
	relapse incidence		
	renal insufficiency		
	resistive Index		
	respiratory illness	RIF	rifampin
	respiratory index		right iliac fossa
	response inhibition		right index finger
	retroillumination		rigid internal fixation
	Rhode Island	RIFLE	Risk, Injury, Failure, Loss of kidney function, End-stage kidney disease (classification)
	rooming in		
R/I	reperfusion injury	R IF MP	right index finger metacarpal joint
	see RI	RIG	rabies immune globulin
RIA	radioimmunoassay	RIGH	rabies immune globulin human inj (HyperRAB S/D; Imogam Rabies-HT; Kedrab)
	reversible ischemic attack		
RIAC	rapid inflation, asymmetrical compression (device)		
RIAO	right inferior anterior oblique	RIGS	radioimmunoguided surgery
RIAS	Reynolds Intellectual Assessment Scales	RIH	right inguinal hernia
		RIHD	right intrahepatic (bile) duct
	Roter Interaction Analysis System	RIHP	renal interstitial hydrostatic pressure
RIAT	radioimmune antiglobulin test	RIHR	Registered in Human Relations (Canadian Examining Board of Health Care Practitioners)
RIBA	recombinant immunoblot assay		
RIBC	residual infiltrating breast cancer		
RIBE	radiation-induced bystander effect		right inguinal hernia repair
RIC	receiver-in-canal	RIIA	right internal iliac artery
	reduced intensity conditioning	RIJ	right internal jugular
	right iliac crest	RIJV	right internal jugular vein
	right internal carotid (artery)	RILD	radiation-induced liver disease
R-ICA	right internal carotid artery	RILF	radiation-induced lung fibrosis
RICC	radioimmunocytochemistry	RIM	Reference Information Model (www.hl7.org)
	relative increase in cell count(s)		
ricc	revealed intra-observer reliability	RIMA	reversible inhibitor of monoamine oxidase-type A
RICE	rest, ice, compression, and elevation		right internal mammary anastamosis
R-ICE	rituximab, ifosfamide, carboplatin, and etoposide		right internal mammary artery
RICM	right intercostal margin	RIMP	rectal internal mucosal prolapse
RICS	right intercostal space		RV (right ventricular) index of myocardial performance
RICU	respiratory intensive care unit		
RID	radial immunodiffusion	RIN	radiocontrast-induced nephropathy
	ruptured intervertebral disk		
RIDL	Release of Insects with a Dominant Lethal	RIND	reversible ischemic neurologic defect
RIDP	Remote Identity Proofing (the process of validating sufficient information that uniquely identifies a person; e.g., credit history, personal demographic information and other indicators [Centers for Medicare & Medicaid Services])	rINN	recommended International Nonproprietary Name
		Rint	airway resistance measured by the interrupter technique
		RINV	radiation-induced nausea and vomiting
		RIO	right inferior oblique (muscle)
		RIOJ	recurrent intrahepatic obstructive jaundice

RIOL	remove intraocular lens
R-IOL	remove intraocular lens
RIP	radioimmunoprecipitin test
	rapid infusion pump
	respiratory inductance plethysmograph
	rhythmic inhibitory pattern
RIPA	ristocetin-induced platelet agglutination
RIPE	rifampin, isoniazid, pyrazinamide, and ethambutol (treatment for tuberculous)
R-IPI	revised International Prognostic Index (used for risk stratification of patients with lymphomas)
RIPSS	Revised International Prognostic Scoring System
RIPV	right inferior pulmonary vein
RIR	right inferior rectus
RIRM	Rusk Institute of Rehabilitation Medicine
RIS	radioimmunoscintigraphy
	Radiologically Isolated Syndrome
	responding to internal stimuli
	risperidone (Risperdal)
	RNA (ribonucleic acid)-induced silencing complex
RISA	radioactive iodinated serum albumin
RiskMAP	Risk Minimization Action Plan (FDA)
RISO	right inferior superior oblique
RISS	regular insulin sliding scale
	rituximab (Rituxan)-induced serum sickness
R-ISS	revised International Staging System (for risk stratification in patients with multiple myeloma)
RIST	radioimmunosorbent test
RIT	radioactive iodine therapy
	radioimmunotherapy
	reduced-intensity transplant
	ritonavir (Norvir)
	Rorschach Inkblot Test
RITA	right internal thoracic artery
RITE	receiver-in-the-ear
RiUP	topical monoxide (a Japanese hair growth import)
RIV3	recombinant influenza vaccine, Trivalent (Flublok)
RIVCF	removable inferior vena cava filter
RIVD	ruptured intervertebral disk
RIX	radiation-induced xerostomia

RJ	radial jerk (reflex)
	right jugular
RK	radial keratotomy
	right kidney
RKA	range of knee angle
RKO	robotic knee orthosis
RKS	renal kidney stone
RKT	Registered Kinesiotherapist
RKW	right kidney weight
RL	right lateral
	right leg
	right lower
	right lung
	Ringer's lactate
	Ringer's lactate inj, a mixture of sodium chloride, sodium lactate, potassium chloride, and calcium chloride in water; also known as Hartman's solution
	rotation left
R → L	right to left
R/L	see RL
RLA	Rancho Los Amigos Level of Cognitive Functioning Scale (Levels 1-8) http://www.tbims.org/combi/lcfs/lcfs.pdf
	right lower arm
RLB	right lateral bending
	right lateral border
RLBCD	right lower border of cardiac dullness
RLC	Registered Lactation Consultant
	residual lung capacity
RLD	Referenced Listed Drug (FDA)
	related living donor
	remaining life expectancy
	restrictive lung disease
	right lateral decubitus
	ruptured lumbar disk
RLDP	right lateral decubitus (sleeping) position
RLDSP	right lateral decubitus sleeping position
RLE	refractive lens exchange (cataract surgery)
	right lower extremity
RLF	retrolental fibroplasia
	right lateral femoral
RLFP	Remaining Lifetime Fracture Probability
RLG	right lateral gaze
RLGS	restriction landmark genomic scanning
RLH	reactive lymphoid hyperplasia
RLHC	right, left heart catheterization
R&LHC	right and left heart congestion
R+LHC	right and left heart congestion
R/LHC	right and left heart congestion

RLL	radiolucent line
	right liver lobe
	right lower leg
	right lower lid
	right lower lobe
RLL PNA	right lower lobe (of lung) pneumonia
RLN	recurrent laryngeal nerve
	regional lymph node(s)
RLND	regional lymph node dissection
RLNM	regional lymph node metastasis
RLO	rectal lumen obliteration
	Rickettsia-like organism
RLP	referred leg pain
RLPV	right lower pulmonary vein
RLQ	right lower quadrant
RLQD	right lower quadrant defect
RLR	right lateral rectus
R/L ratio	right ventricle to left ventricle end-diastolic diameter ratio
RLRP	right lateral recumbent position
RLRS	Rosenbaum Learned Resourcefulness Scale
RLRTD	recurrent lower respiratory tract disease
RLS	radial line scans
	resonance light scattering
	restless legs syndrome
	Ringer's lactate solution
	stammerer who has difficulty in enunciating R, L, and S
RLSB	right lower scapular border
	right lower sternal border
RLSh	right-to-left shunt
rISS	revised International Staging System (for risk stratification in patients with multiple myeloma)
RLT	right lateral thigh
RLTCS	repeat low transverse cesarean section
RLUs	relative light units
RLV	Residual Lung Volume
	round ligament varicosities
RLV/BWR	remnant liver volume to donor body weight ratio
RLWD	rat lungworm disease
	routine laboratory work done
RLX	raloxifene (Evista)
	right lower extremity
RM	radical mastectomy
	rapid metabolizer
	reduction mammoplasty
	remote monitoring
	repetitions maximum
	respiratory movement
	risk manager (management)
	risk model
	roller massage

	room
	rowing machine
R&M	routine and microscopic
1RM	single repetition maximum lift
RMA	reduction in metabolic activity
	refused medical assistance
	Registered Medical Assistant
	right mentoanterior
	Rivermead motor assessment
R-MAT	Risk-Based Microbial Assessment Tool
RMB	right main bronchus
RMBPC	Revise Memory and Behavior Problems Checklist
RMC	reasonable medical certainty
RMCA	right main coronary artery
	right middle cerebral artery
RMCAT	right middle cerebral artery thrombosis
RMCL	right midclavicular line
RMCT	Regenerative Medicine and Cell Therapy
RMD	recommended maintenance dose
	restrictive myocardial disease
	rippling muscle disease
	risk management database
RMDQ	Roland and Morris disability questionnaire
RME	rapid maxillary expansion
	reasonable maximum exposure
	relative measurement error
	resting metabolic expenditure
	right mediolateral episiotomy
RMEE	right middle ear exploration
rMET	recombinant methioninase
RMF	right middle finger
RMG	recurrent malignant glioma
	Retinal Müller glial (cells)
R/M/G	rubs, murmurs, and gallops
RMGIC	resin-modified glass ionomer cement (dental)
RMGs	recurrent malignant gliomas
	retinal Mueller glial cells
RMH	rhabdomyomatous mesenchymal hamartoma
RMI	Risk of Malignancy Index
	Rivermead Mobility Index
RMIS	robotic minimally invasive surgery
RMK #1	remark number 1
RML	right mediolateral
	right middle lobe
RMLE	right mediolateral episiotomy
RMLO	right medial-lateral oblique (mammogram view)
RMMA	rhythmic masticatory muscle activity

RMN	remote magnetic (catheter) navigation		ribonucleic acid
			routine nursing assistance
RMO	responsible medical officer	RNAi	ribonucleic acid interference
rMOG	recombinant myelin oligodendrocyte glycoprotein	RNBC	Registered Nurse Board Certified
		RNC	Registered Nurse, Certified
RMP	right mentoposterior	RNCA	registered nurse controlled analgesia
RMPs	risk management program		
RMPV	right middle pulmonary vein	RNCC	registered nurse care coordinator
RMQ	Roland-Morris (disability) Questionnaire	RNCD	Registered Nurse, Chemical Dependency
RMR	resting metabolic rate	RNCM	registered nurse case manager
	right medial rectus	RNCNA	Registered Nurse, Certified in Nursing Administration
	root mean square residue		
RMRM	right modified radical mastectomy	RNCNAA	Registered Nurse, Certified in Nursing Administration Advanced
RMS	ready-made spectacles		
	red-man syndrome	RNCS	Registered Nurse, Certified Specialist
	Rehabilitation Medicine Service		
	relapsing form of multiple sclerosis	RND	radical neck dissection
			reflex neurovascular dystrophy
	repetitive motion syndrome	RNEF	resting (radio-) nuclide ejection fraction
	rhabdomyosarcoma		
	robotic mesh sacrocolpopexy	RNF	regular nursing floor
	Rocky Mountain spotted fever vaccine	RNFA	registered nurse first assistant
		RNFL	retinal nerve fiber layer
	root-mean-square	RNFLT	retinal nerve fiber layer thickness
RMS®	rectal morphine sulfate (suppository)	RNG	random number generation (generator)
RMSB	right middle sternal border	rng	ribonuclease G; see gene website www.ncbi.nlm.nih.gov/gene
RMSE	root-mean-square error		
RMSEA	root mean square error of approximation	RNHCIs	religious nonmedical health care institutions
RMSEC	root mean square errors for calibration	RNI	reactive nitrogen intermediates
			rubella nonimmune
RMSECV	root mean square errors for cross validation	RNLP	Registered Nurse, license pending
RMSF	Rocky Mountain spotted fever	RNM	resultant net moment
RMSs	rhabdomyosarcomas	RNMS	reactive nitrogen metabolites
RMS stent	right mainstem bronchus stent	RNP	Registered Nurse Practitioner
RMT	Registered Music Therapist		restorative nursing program
	right mentotransverse		ribonucleoprotein
RMTD	rate of the margin-tumor distance	RNPL	ratio between negative and positive lymph nodes
	rhythmic midtemporal discharge	RNR	ribonucleotide reductase
rmtD	rDNA (recombinant ribonucleic acid) methyltransferase D	RNS	recurrent nephrotic syndrome
			repetitive nerve stimulation
rMTT	relative mean transit time		replacement normal saline (0.9% sodium chloride)
RMV	respiratory minute volume		
RMW	respiratory musce weakness	RNST	reactive nonstress test
RN	radiation necrosis	RNT	Registered Nurse Teacher
	radical nephrectomy	RNU	radical nephroureterectomy
	Registered Nurse	RNUD	recurrent nonulcer dyspepsia
	right nostril (nare)	RNV	radionucleotide ventriculogram
Rn	radon	RNx	valve-sparing (aortic) root replacement
R/N	renew		
RNA	radionuclide angiography	RNY	Roux-en-Y (gastric bypass surgery)
	restorative nursing assistant		

RNY-GB	Roux-en-Y gastric bypass		rests and related pressure
RO	reality orientation		measuring devices
	relative odds	ROI	region of interest (radiology)
	report of		release of information
	reset osmostat		request old information
	reverse osmosis	ROIDS	hemorrhoids
	routine order(s)	ROIH	right oblique inguinal hernia
	rule out	ROJM	range of joint motion
	ruled out	ROL	right occipitolateral
	Russian Orthodox	ROLC	roentgenologically occult lung
R/O	rule out		cancer
	ruled out	ROLL	Radioguided Occult Lesion
ROA	radiographic osteoarthritis		Localization
	right occiput anterior	ROM	range of motion
ROAC	repeated oral doses of activated		rifampicin 600 mg,
	charcoal		ofloxacin 400 mg, and
ROAD	reversible obstructive airway		minocycline 100 mg
	disease		right otitis media
ROAM	range of ankle motion		rolling-over maneuver
ROB	routine obstetrical(visit)		rupture of membranes
RoB	risk of bias	ROM+	a test kit that detects both
ROBE	routine operative breast		alpha-fetoprotein and Insulin-
	endoscopy		like growth factor-binding
ROBF	return of bowel function		protein 1 using a monoclonal/
ROBO	run over by owner (Veterinary		polyclonal antibody approach
	slang)		to diagnose premature rupture
ROC	receiver operating characteristic		of membranes
	record of contact	ROMA	representative oliogonucleotide
	resident on call		microarray analysis
	residual organic carbon	RoMAT	Role Model Apperception Tool
	resumption of care		(an instrument to assess
	rocuronium bromide (Zemuron)		clinical trainers as role models)
ROCF	Rey-Osterrieth complex figure	Romb	Romberg
ROCM	rhino-Orbits-Cerebral	ROMCP	range of motion complete and
	mucormycosis		painfree
ROCs	receiver operating	ROME	range of motion exercise(s)
	characteristics	Romeo	Phonetic Alphabet for R;
ROD	rapid opioid detoxification		pronounced ROW-ME-OH
	relaparotomy on demand	ROMI	rule out myocardial infarction
	renal osteodystrophy	ROM Plus®	a test kit that detects both
RODA	rapid opiate detoxification under		alpha-fetoprotein and Insulin-
	anesthesia		like growth factor-binding
ROE	report of event		protein 1 using a monoclonal/
	right otitis externa		polyclonal antibody approach
ROES	remover order enter service		to diagnose premature rupture
ROF	recovery of function		of membranes
	review of outside films	ROMSA	right otitis media, suppurative,
ROG	rogletimide		acute
ROH	removal of hardware	ROMSC	right otitis media, suppurative,
	renal oligohydramnion		chronic
	rubbing alcohol	ROMWNL	range of motion within normal
ROHHAD	rapid-onset obesity with		limits
	hypothalamic dysfunction,	RON	radiation optic neuropathy
	hypoventilation, and	R on T	a ventricular stimulus causes
	autonomic dysregulation		premature depolarization of
	(a pediatric disorder)		cells that have not completely
ROHO	a manufacturer of seat cushions,		repolarized
	head rests, heel rests, back	RONTD	risk of neural tube defect

ROOF	retro-orbicularis oculi fat	resting position
ROP	retinopathy of prematurity	restorative proctocolectomy
	right occiput posterior	retinitis pigmentosa
ROPE	pulse-rate over pressure	retrograde pyelogram
	evaluation (index)	retroperitoneal
RoPE	The Risk of Paradoxical	retropubic prostatectomy
	Embolism (study)	root plane
Ropi	ropivacaine (Naropin)	R&P research and planning
ROPS	roll-over protection structures	risk and prevention
ROR	reporting odds ratio	R/P recurrence or progression
	retinoid-related orphan receptor	RPA radial photon absorptiometry
	the French acronym for	recursive partitioning analysis
	measles-mumps-rubella	Registered Physician's Assistant
	vaccine	renoportal anastomosis
R or L	right or left	repolarization alternans
RoRx	radiation therapy	restenosis postangioplasty
ROS	reactive oxygen species	retinitis punctata albescans
	review of systems	retroillumination photography
	rod outer segments	analysis
	rule out sepsis	ribonuclease protection assay
ROS1	ROS porto-oncogene 1, receptor	right pulmonary artery
	tyrosine kinase (gene/protein)	RPAC Registered Physician's Assistant
ROSA	rank-order stability analysis	Certified
ROSC	restoration of spontaneous	RPANs recombinant pseudoadenoviral
	circulation	nanoparticles
	return of spontaneous	RPB Radiation Protection Bureau
	circulation	(Canada)
ROSE	rapid on-site evaluation	rating of perceived breathlessness
ROSS	review of signs and symptoms	retroperitoneal bleeding
ROT	remedial occupational therapy	revenue-per-bed
	right occiput transverse	rotating packed bed
	rotation	RPC recurrent pyogenic cholangitis
	rotator	root planing and curettage
ROTA	Rotavirus Vaccine (replaced by	RPCA right posterior communicating
	the terms RV1 and RV5)	artery
ROTC	Reserve Officer Training Corps	Robust Principle Component
ROTEM®	rotation thromboelastometry	Analysis
	(provides information on	R-PCA right posterior cerebral artery
	hyperfibrinolysis; require-	RPCDBM randomized, placebo-controlled,
	ment for factor, fibrinogen or	double-blind, multinational
	platelet substitution; extent of	(study)
	dilutional coagulopathy; and	RPCF Reiter protein complement
	heparin and protamine dosage	fixation
	monitoring	RPCT randomized, placebo-controlled
ROU	recurrent oral ulcer	trial
ROUB	Registered Ophthalmic	RPCUS Reformed Presbyterian Church
	Ultrasound Biometrist	in the United States
ROUL	rouleaux (rouleau)	RPD rate of perceived dyspnea
Roux en Y	double loop gastric bypass	relative population doublings
ROV	return office visit	removable partial denture
ROW	rest of (the) week	reported progression date
RP	radial pulse	reticular pseudodrusen
	radical prostatectomy	rib-pelvis distance
	radiopharmaceutical	RPDA right posterior descending artery
	Raynaud phenomenon	RPDB Registered Persons Database
	rectal pressure	(Canada)
	Registered Pharmacist	RPDL reduced protein diet with 2% of
	responsible party	leucine

RPE	rating of perceived exertion	rplV	see gene website www.ncbi.nlm .nih.gov/gene
	recurrent pleural effusion		
	retina pigment epithelial	RPM	respirations per minute
	retina pigment epithelium		revolutions per minute
	reward prediction error	RPMI	Roswell Park Memorial Institute
RPED	retina pigment epithelium detachment	RPMI-1640	Roswell Park Memorial Institute number 1640, a media utilizing
RPEP	rabies postexposure prophylaxis		a bicarbonate buffering system, amino acids, and vitamins,
	right pre-ejection period		used to culture human normal
RPF	regional progression-free		and neoplastic leukocytes
	relaxed pelvic floor	RPM/L	respirations per minute per liter
	renal plasma flow	RPMS	repetitive peripheral magnetic
	retroperitoneal fibrosis		stimulation
RPFNA	random periareolar fine-needle aspiration	RPMs	red pulp macrophages
		RPMs	Return-to-the-Problem Markers
rPFS	radiographic progression-free survival		risk prediction models
		RPN	renal papillary necrosis
RPFT	Registered Pulmonary Function Therapist		resident's progress notes
			robotic partial nephrectomy
RPG	retrograde percutaneous gastrostomy	R₂PN	second year resident's progress notes
	retrograde pyelogram	RpnA	recombination-promoting
RPGN	rapidly progressive glomerulonephritis		nuclease A
		RPNI	regenerative peripheral nerve
RPH	retroperitoneal hemorrhage		interface
RPh	Registered Pharmacist	RpnI	ribophorin I (gene/protein)
RPHA	reverse passive hemagglutination	RPNIs	regenerative peripheral nerve
RPI	regional perfusion index (transcutaneous oxygen pressure measurement)		interfaces
		RPO	right posterior oblique
		RPOC	retained products of conception
	resting pressure index		routine post-op care
	reticulocyte production index	RPP	radical perineal prostatectomy
RPICA	right posterior internal carotid artery		rate-pressure product
			retropubic prostatectomy
RPICCE	round pupil intracapsular cataract extraction	RPPC	routine post-partum care
		rPPC	right posterior parietal cortex
RPL	recurrent pregnancy loss	RPPS	retropatellar pain syndrome
	retroperitoneal lymphadenectomy	RPQ	Rivermead Post-Concussion Symptoms Questionnaire
	retroperitoneal lymphocele	RPR	rapid plasma reagin (test for
RPLA	reversed passive latex agglutination		syphilis)
			Reiter protein reagin
RPLAD	may have meant RPLND (retroperitoneal lymph node dissection)	RPRNR	rapid plasma reagin nonreactive
		RPS	Repositioning
			retroperitoneal sarcoma
rplB	ribosomal protein L2; see gene website; www.ncbi.nlm.nih.gov		rhabdoid predisposition syndrome
RPLC	reversed-phase liquid chromatography	rPS	residual pluripotent stem (cells)
		RPSGT	Registered Polysomnography
RPLD	radiophotoluminescence dosemeter		Technologist
		RPSO	right posterior superior oblique
	retroperitoneal lymph-node dissection	RPT	Registered Physical Therapist
		rpt	repeat
RPLND	retroperitoneal lymph node dissection	RPTA	Registered Physical Therapist Assistant
RPLS	reversible posterior leukoencephalopathy syndrome	RPTs	renal proximal tubules
		RPU	retropubic urethropexy

RPUS	radiologist-performed ultrasound
RPV	right portal vein
	right pulmonary vein
	rilpivirine (Edurant)
RPVI	Registered Physician in Vascular Interpretation
RPVL	recombinant Panton-Valentine leukocidin
	right portal vein ligation
RQ	respiratory quotient
RQI	Risk Quantification Index
	RNA (ribonucleic acid) Quality Index
RQLQ	Respiratory Quality of Life Questionnaire
RR	rate ratio (s)
	recovery room
	red reflex (normal eye reflex)
	regular rate
	regular respirations
	relative risk
	respiratory rate
	response rate
	retinal reflex
	rotation right
R&R	rate and rhythm
	recent and remote
	recession and resection
	remove and replace
	resect and recess (muscle surgery)
	rest and recuperation
R/R	rales-rhonchi
	relapsed or refractory
RRA	radioiodine remnant ablation
	radioreceptor assay
	Registered Radiologist Assistant
	Registered Record Administrator (for newer title, see RHIA)
	right radial artery
	right renal artery
RRAM	rapid rhythmic alternating movements
R/R AML	refractory or recurrent acute myeloid leukemia
RRB	Railroad Retirement Board
	restricted and repetitive behavior (scale)
RRBs	restricted repetitive behaviors
RRC	cohort relative risk
	respiratory rate corrected (for ventilated patient)
RRCT	registry-based randomized clinical trials
RRCT,no(m)	regular rate, clear tones, no murmurs

RRD	removable rigid dressing
	rhegmatogenous retinal detachment
RRDR	rifampicin resistance-determining region
RRE	round, regular, and equal (pupils)
RRED®	Rapid Rare Event Detection
RREF	resting radionuclide ejection fraction
R3 Report	provides the Requirements, Rationale and References that The Joint Commission employs in the development of new requirements
RRF	residual renal function
	ribosome recycling factor
rrf	see gene website, www.ncbi.nlm.nih.gov/gene
RRHI-24	Revised Health Hardiness Inventory
RRI	renal resistive index
RR-IOL	remove and replace intraocular lens
RRL	rabbit reticulocyte lysate
	Reduced Representation Library
rrl	see gene website www.ncbi.nlm.nih.gov/gene
RRM	reduced renal mass
	right radial mastectomy
	risk-reducing mastectomy
RRMM	relapsed or relapsed and refractory multiple myeloma
RRMS	relapsing-remitting multiple sclerosis
RRNA	Resident Registered Nurse Anesthetist
rRNA	ribosomal ribonucleic acid
RRND	right radical neck dissection
RROM	resistive range of motion
R rot	right rotation
RRP	radical retropubic prostatectomy
	recurrent respiratory papillomatosis
RRR	recovery room routine
	reduced rank regression
	regular rhythm and rate
	relative risk reduction
RRRN	round, regular, and react normally
RRRP	Rapid Response Radiotherapy Program
RRRmacron sM	regular rate and rhythm without murmur
RRS	rapid response system
	resonance Rayleigh scattering
RRSO	risk-reducing salpingo-oophorectomy

RRT	Rapid Response Team	RSCS	respiratory system compliance
	Registered Respiratory		score
	Therapist	rscu-PA	recombinant, single-chain,
	renal replacement therapy		urokinase-type plasminogen
RRTP	relative risk, target population		activator
RRTx	renal retransplantation	RSCV	right subclavian vein
RRU	rapid reintegration unit		right superior caval vein
RRVO	repair relaxed vaginal outlet	RSD	reflex sympathetic dystrophy
RRVS	recovery room vital signs		relative standard deviation
RRV-TV	live, tetravalent rotavirus	%RSD	percent relative standard
	vaccine (RotaShield)		deviation
	(no longer available)	RSDS	reflex-sympathetic dystrophy
	rhesus rotavirus tetravalent		syndrome
	(vaccine)	RSE	rattlesnake envenomation
RRW	rales, rhonchi or wheezes		reactive subdural effusion
R/R/W	rales, rhonchi, or wheezes		refractory status epilepticus
RS	Raynaud syndrome		right sternal edge
	rectal swab	RSF	remodeling and spacing factor
	Recurrence Score		(complex)
	recurrent seizures		rheumatoid synovial fibroblasts
	Reed-Sternberg (cell)	RsF	risk factors
	Reiters syndrome	RSF1	remodeling and spacing factor 1;
	remote sensing		see gene website, www.ncbi
	reschedule		.nlm.nih.gov/gene
	respiratory score	RSFA	resting-state fluctuation of
	restart		amplitude
	Rett syndrome	rsfA	prespore-specific transcriptional
	Reye syndrome		regulator; see gene website
	rhythm strip		www.ncbi.nlm.nih.gov/gene
	Richter syndrome	rs-fc	resting-state functional
	right side		connectivity
	Ringer solution	rs-fcMRI	resting-state functional-
	rumination syndrome		connectivity magnetic
$^{rs}O_2$	regional oxygen saturation		resonance imaging
R & S	restraint and seclusion	RSG	rosiglitazone (Avandia)
R/S	reschedule	RSH	relative sub-hazards
	rest stress		renal subcapsular hemorrhage
	rupture spontaneous		reproductive and sexual health
	see RS	R&SH	reproductive and sexual health
RSA	radiostereometric	RSHF	right sided heart failure
	recurrent spontaneous abortion	RSI	rapid sequence induction
	reverse shoulder arthroplasty		rapid-sequence intubation
	right sacrum anterior		Reflux Symptom Index
	right subclavian artery		repetitive strain (stress) injury
	Roentgen stereometric analysis	R/S I	resuscitation status one
	root cause analysis		(full resuscitative effort)
RSAB	recurrent spontaneous abortion	R/S II	resuscitation status two (no code,
RSAPE	remitting seronegative arthritis		therapeutic measures only)
	with pitting edema	R/S III	resuscitation status three (no
RSB	right sternal border		code, comfort measures only)
RSBI	rapid shallow breathing index	R-SICU	respiratory-surgical intensive
RSBP	resting systolic blood pressure		care unit
RSBQ	Rett Syndrome Behavior	RSIs	retained surgical items
	Questionnaire	RSL	Radioactive Seed Localization
RSC	right subclavian (artery) (vein)		radioscapholunate
RScA	right scapuloanterior		renal solute load
RSCL	Rotterdam Symptom Check List	RSLR	reverse straight leg raise
RScP	right scapuloposterior	RSLT	reduced-size liver transplantation

RSM	remote study monitoring	RSWA	REM (rapid eye movement) sleep without atonia
RSMR	risk-standardized mortality rates		
RSNI	round spermatid nuclear injection	RSxN	resection
		RT	radiation therapy
RSO	right salpingooophorectomy		Radiologic Technologist
	right superior oblique		reaction time
RSOC	regular source of care		recreational therapy
RSOP	right superior oblique palsy		rectal temperature
RSP	rapid straight pacing		renal transplant
	respirable suspended particles		repetition time
	restriction site polymorphism		resistance training
	right sacroposterior		Respiratory Therapist
RS3PE	remitting seronegative symmetrical synovitis with pitting edema		respiratory therapy
			return
			reverse transcriptase
RSPV	right superior pulmonary vein		Richter transformation
RSR	regular sinus rhythm		right
	relative survival rate		right thigh
	right superior rectus		Romberg Test (a test used in an examination of neurological function for balance, and also as a test for driving under the influence of an intoxicant; a positive test is when the patient stands with their feet together (touching each other) and patient is asked to close their eyes and the patient begins to sway or fall)
RSRI	renal:systemic renin index		
RSS	Ramsey Sedation Scale		
	reduced space symbologies		
	rehabilitation swallow study		
	representative sample sectioned		
	Rich Site Summary or Really Simple Syndication, is a method of distributing news headlines and other content on the Web		
			room temperature
	Russell-Silver syndrome	R/T	related to
RSSE	Russian spring-summer encephalitis	RTA	ready to administer
			renal tubular acidosis
RST	rapid simple tests		road traffic accident
	rapid Streptococcal test	RTA1	renal tubular acidosis type 1
	right sacrum transverse	RTA2	renal tubular acidosis type 2
RSTL	relaxation skin tension line	RTA3	renal tubular acidosis type 3
RSTs	Rodney Smith tubes	RTA4	renal tubular acidosis type 4
RSU	radiation-induced skin ulceration	RTA I	renal tubular acidosis type 1
RSV	respiratory syncytial virus	RTA IV	renal tubular acidosis type 4
	respiratory syncytial virus vaccine	RTAE	right atrial enlargement
		RTAH	right anterior hemiblock
	right subclavian vein	RTAT	right anterior thigh
RSVA	respiratory syncytial virus subtype A	RTB	red TheraBand
			resting tidal breathing
RSV A	respiratory syncytial virus subtype A		return to baseline
			return to bed
RSV B	respiratory syncytial virus subtype B	RTBD	retrograde transhepatic biliary drainage
RSVC	right superior vena cava	RT(BD)	Registered Technologist, Bone Densitometry
rSVG	reversed saphenous vein graft		
RSV$_{IGIV}$	respiratory syncytial virus immune globulin, intravenous	RT(BS)	Registered Technologist, Breast Sonography
RSV$_{mab}$	respiratory syncytial virus monoclonal antibody, intramuscular (palivizumab; Synagis)	RTC	ratio-to-target concentrations
			Readiness to Change (questionnaire)
			return to clinic
RSVP	rapid serial visual presentation		rotator cuff
RSVT	respiratory systolic variation test		round the clock
RSW	right-sided weakness		

RT(CI)	Registered Technologist, Cardiac-Interventional Radiography	RT(M)	Registered Technologist, Mammography
RTCR	rotator tear cuff repair	RTMC1	real-time myocardial contrast perfusion imaging
RTCT	radiotherapy and chemotherapy	RTMD	right mid-deltoid
RT(CT)	Registered Technologist, Computed Tomography	RT(MR)	Registered Technologist, Magnetic Resonance Imaging
RTCV	reaction time coefficient of variation	rtMRI	real-time magnetic resonance imaging
RT(CV)	Registered Technologist, Cardiovascular-Interventional Radiography	rTMS	repetitive transcranial magnetic stimulation
RTD	return to doctor	RTN	renal tubular necrosis
RT3D	real-time three-dimensional (echocardiography)	RT(N)	Registered Technologist, Nuclear Medicine Technology
RTED	recurrent thromboembolic disease	RTNM	retreatment staging of cancer
rTEG	rapid thrombelastography	RTO	return to office
RTER	return to emergency room	RTOG	Radiation Therapy Oncology Group
rt.↑ext.	right upper extremity	RTOR	return to the operating room
RTF	ready-to-feed	RTP	renal transplant patient
	return to flow		return to pharmacy
rTFA	ruminant trans fatty acids		return-to-play (guidelines)
RTFS	return to flying status	rtPA	alteplase (recombinant tissue-type plasminogen activator) (Activase)
RTG	retigabine (ezogabine; Potiga)		
RTH	ready to hang		
	right total hip (arthroplasty)	RT-PCR	reverse transcriptase-polymerase chain reaction
RTHA	resurfacing total hip arthroplasty	rt-PCR	real-time polymerase chain reaction
R-THA	right total hip arthroplasty		
RTHR	revision total hip replacement	RT-PEPC	rituximab and thalidomide and prednisone, etoposide, procarbazine, and cyclophosphamide
	right total hip replacement (it is safer to spell out "right")		
R THR	right total hip replacement (it is safer to spell out "right")	RTPJ	right temporoparietal junction
RTI	reproductive tract infection	RT(QM)	Registered Technologist, Quality Management
	respiratory tract infection		
	reverse transcriptase inhibitor	RT-qPCR	reverse transcription-quan-titative polymerase chain reaction
	road traffic injuries		
RTIS	response to internal stimuli		
RTK	rhabdoid tumor of the kidney	RTR	Registered Technologist of Radiography
	right total knee (arthroplasty)		
RTKA	revision total knee arthroplasty		renal transplant recipient(s)
	right total knee arthroplasty		return to room
R TKR	right total knee replacement (it is safer to spell out "right")	RT(R)	Registered Technologist, Radiography
RTL	reactive to light	RTRR	return to recovery room
	return-to-learn	RTS	radial tunnel syndrome
	right temporal lobectomy		raised toilet seat
			real-time scan
RTLC	reduced total lung capacity		Resolve Through Sharing
RTLF	respiratory-tract lining fluids		return to school
RTLH	robotic (or robotic-assisted) total laparoscopic hysterectomy		return to sender
			return-to-sport
RTLS	real-time location system		Revised Trauma Score
	right-to-left shunt		Rothmund-Thomson syndrome
RTLSs	real-time location systems		Rubinstein-Taybi syndrome
RTM	regression to the mean	RT(S)	Registered Technologist, Sonography
	routine medical care		

RTSA	reversed total shoulder arthroplasty	RUDI	revision using distal inflow
RTSp	return to sport	RUDS	reactive upper airways dysfunction syndrome
RTSR	reverse total shoulder replacement	RUE	right upper extremity
RTST	return-to-sports-time	RUF	Ready-to-Use Food
RTT	Respiratory Therapy Technician		recto-urethral fistula
	Rett syndrome		rufinamide (Benzel)
RT(T)	Registered Technologist, Radiation Therapy	RUG	resource utilization group retrograde urethrogram
RTTP	radiotherapy treatment planning	RUI	recurring urinary infections
rTTP	relative time to peak		reflex urinary incontinence
RTU	ready to use	RUJ	radioulnar joint
RT₃U	resin triiodothyronine uptake	RUL	radioulnar ligament
RTUS	realtime ultrasound		right upper lid
RTV	ritonavir (Norvir)		right upper lobe
	rotavirus vaccine, not otherwise specified	Rumi	O-glucosyltransferase
		rumi	see gene website, www.ncbi.nlm.nih.gov/gene
RT(VI)	Registered Technologist, Vascular-Interventional Radiography	RUOQ	right upper outer quadrant
		RUPERT	robotic upper-extremity repetitive trainer
RTVrr	rotavirus vaccine, rhesus reassortant	RUPG	retrograde ureteropyelography
RT(VS)	Registered Technologist, Vascular Sonography	rupt	ruptured
		RUPV	right upper pulmonary vein
RTW	return to ward	RUQ	right upper quadrant
	return to work	RUQD	right upper quadrant defect
	Richard Turner Warwick (urethroplasty)	RUQUS	right upper quadrant ultrasound
		RURTI	recurrent upper respiratory tract infection
RTWD	return to work determination		
RTX	resiniferatoxin	RUS	resonant ultrasound spectroscopy
	rituximab (Rituxin)		
RTx	radiation therapy	RUSB	right upper scapular border
	renal transplantation		right upper sternal border
RU	relative units	Rusk	Howard A. Rusk, a pioneer in the rehabilitation of the physically disabled in the United States
	residual urine		
	resin uptake		
	retrograde ureterogram		
	returns demonstration (patient demonstrates an understanding)	rusk	a sweet raised bread dried and browned in an oven
	right upper	RUT	rapid urease test
	routine urinalysis	RUTF	ready-to-use therapeutic food
Ru	ruthenium	RUTI	recurring urinary tract infections
R&U	radius and ulna	RUTIs	recurrent urinary tract infections
R/U	see RU	RUV	residual urine volume
RU 486	mifepristone (Mifeprex)	RUX	right upper extremity
RUA	right upper arm	RV	rectovaginal
	routine urine analysis		regurgant volume (cardiology)
RUB	rubella virus vaccine		residual volume
RUC	RVS (Relative Value Scale) Update Committee (American Medical Association)		respiratory volume
			retinal vasculitis
			return visit
			rhinovirus
RUCs	regular uterine contractions		right ventricle
RUD	radial-ulnar deviation		rubella vaccine
Rud	Resource Utilization in Dementia (questionnaire)	R&V	repeat and verify (physician's orders)
RUDE	Risky, Unrealistic, Difficult, or Expensive (treatments)	R & V	read-back and verified
		R/V	record and verify system

RV1	rotavirus vaccine live (Rotarix; monovalent rotavirus vaccine live)
RV5	rotavirus vaccine live (Rota Teq; pentavalent rotavirus vaccine live)
	rotavirus vaccine (pentavalent)
	rotavirus vaccine, pentavalent (RotaTeq) (formerly called ROTA)
RVA	rabies vaccine, adsorbed
	right ventricular angiography
	right ventricular apex
	right vertebral artery
	rotavirus group A
RVAD	right ventricular assist device
RVAO	rotational vertebral artery occlusion (Bow-hunter syndrome)
RVAT	Risk and Vulnerability Assessment Tool
RVATS	robotic video-assisted thoracoscopic surgery
RVATs	rare variant association tests
R-VATS	robot-assisted video-assisted thoracoscopic surgery
RVB	resonating valence bond
	rotavirus group B
RVC	rotavirus group C
RVCD	right ventricular conduction deficit
RVCP	Rural Veterans Coordination Pilot (Department of Veterans Affairs)
RVCs	remote voluntary contractions
RVCT	rapid valve closing time
RVD	reference vessel diameter
	regulatory volume decrease
	relative vertebral density
	renal vascular disease
	right ventricular dysfunction
RVDCC	right ventricle-dependent coronary circulation
RVDD	right ventricular diastolic diameter
RVDP	right ventricular diastolic pressure
RVE	rectovaginal examination
	right ventricular enlargement
RVEDD	right ventricle end-diastolic diameter
RVEDP	right ventricular end-diastolic pressure
RVEDV	right ventricular end-diastolic volume
RVEF	right ventricular ejection fraction
RVET	right ventricular ejection time

RVF	residual volume fraction
	Rift Valley fever
	right ventricular function
	right visual field
RVFP	right ventricular filling pressure
RVG	Radio VisioGraphy
	radionuclide ventriculography
	right ventrogluteal
RVH	renovascular hypertension
	right ventricular hypertrophy
RVHT	renovascular hypertension
RVI	right ventricle infarction
RVID	right ventricular internal dimension
RVIDd	right ventricle internal dimension diastole
RVL	right vastus lateralis
RV lead	right ventricle pacemaker lead
RVLM	rostral ventrolateral medulla
RVLP	Retrovirus-like particles
RVM	relevance vector machine
	respiratory volume monitoring
	rostral ventromedial medulla
RVMB	rectal and vaginal microbicides
RVMI	right ventricular myocardial infarction
RVO	relaxed vaginal outlet
	retinal vein occlusion
	right ventricular outflow
	right ventricular overactivity
RVOT	rapid valve opening time
	right ventricular outflow tract
RVOTH	right ventricular outflow tract hypertrophy
RVOTO	right ventricular outflow tract obstruction
RVOTVT	right ventricular outflow tract-ventricular tachycardia
RVP	respiratory virus panel
	right ventricular pacing
	right ventricular pressure
RV-PA	right ventricle to pulmonary artery (pressure gradient, shunt)
RV-pacing	right ventricular pacing
RVPan	respiratory virus panel
RV-PCR	rapid-viability-polymerase chain reaction
RVPT	right ventricular pacing threshold
RVR	rapid ventricular response
	rapid virological response
	renal vascular resistance
	right ventricular rhythm
RVRMS	robotic vitreous retinal microsurgery system
RVRT	recognition visual reaction time
RVS	right ventricular size
	routine vital signs

RVSB	single-breath residual volume
RVSD	residual ventricular septal defect
	right ventricular systolic diameter
RVSF	right ventricular shortening fraction
	right ventricular systolic function
RVSP	right ventricular systolic pressure
RVST	right cervical vagosympathetic trunk
RVSV	right ventricular stroke volume
rVSV	recombinant vesicular stomatitis virus
RVSW	right ventricular stroke work
RVSWI	right ventricular stroke work index
RVT	recurrent ventricular tachycardia
	registered vascular technologist
	Registered Vascular Technologist
	Registered Veterinary Technician
	renal vein thrombosis
RV/TLC	residual volume to total lung capacity ratio
RVU	relative-value units
RVV	rubella vaccine virus
RVVC	recurrent vulvovaginal candidiasis
RVvO	right ventricle volume overload
RVVT	right ventricle (originated) ventricular tachycardia
	Russell viper venom time
RVWD	right ventricular wall device
RW	radiant warmer
	ragweed
	red welt
	respite worker
	rolling walker
R/W	return to work
RWB	refined wheat bread
	religious well-being
RWD domain	three major RWD-containing proteins: RING finger-containing proteins, WD-repeat-containing proteins, and yeast DEAD (DEXD)-like helicases
RWE	real-world evidence (clinical evidence about benefits or risks of medical products derived from analyzing real world data)
RWIs	recreational water illnesses
RWL	rapid weight loss
	recommended weight limit
	respiratory water loss
RWM	regional wall motion
RWMA	regional wall motion abnormalities

RWMI	wall motion abnormality score index
RWP	ragweed pollen
RWR	retention-weighted recall
RWS	ragweed sensitivity
	rhythmic weight shift
RWT	relative wall thickness
RWW	raw wastewater
	reclaimed wastewater
Rx	drug
	medication
	pharmacy
	prescribing
	prescription
	radiation-induced xerostomia
	radiotherapy
	reaction
	recommend
	take
	therapy
	treatment
Rxd	treated; prescribed
Rx'd	treated
	treated; prescribed
RXed	treated; prescribed
RXN	reaction(s)
RXRs	retinoid X receptors
RXS	resonance x-ray scattering
Rxs	prescriptions
RXT	radiation therapy
	right exotropia
RYBG	Roux-en-Y gastric bypass (Romance languages)
RYGB	Roux-en-Y gastric bypass (surgery)
RYGBP	Roux-en-Y gastric bypass (surgery)
RYGP	may have meant or from non-English language, RYGB (Roux-en-Y gastric bypass)
RYHJ	Roux-en-Y hepaticojejunostomy
RYO	roll-your-own (cigarettes)
RYP	Rate Your Plate (questionnaire/ score)
	red yeast rice
	Roux-en-Y reconstruction with pouch
RYR	red yeast rice
	ryanodine receptor; see gene website www.ncbi.nlm.nih .gov/gene
RYR1	ryanodine receptor 1 (gene)
RYR2	ryanodine receptor 2 (gene)
Rz	ribozyme
RZV	recombinant zoster vaccine (Zoster Vaccine Recombinant, Adjuvanted; Shingrix)
RZ Z	right atrial pressure, z point

R

S

S	sacral
	scrub
	second (s)
	sensitive
	serine
	serum
	Sierra (Phonetic Alphabet for S; pronounced SEE-AIR-RAH)
	single
	sister
	soft
	son
	South (as in the location 2S would be second floor, South wing)
	sponge
	Staphylococcus
	streptomycin [part of tuberculosis regimen as in RHZ (E/S) /HR
	subjective findings
	suction
	suicide
	sulfur
	supervision
	surgery
	susceptible
s	without (see symbols)
/S	without (an S with a line above)
/S/	signature
s̄	without (sin in Latin; this is a dangerous abbreviation)
S'	shoulder
S₁	first heart sound
S₂	second heart sound
S₃	third heart sound (ventricular filling gallop)
S₄	fourth heart sound (atrial gallop)
s< >S	sit-to-stand and stand-to-sit (therapeutic exercise)
S1	first sacral nerve root
	first sacral vertebrae
S2	second sacral nerve root
	second sacral vertebrae
S3	third sacral nerve root
	third sacral vertebrae
S4	fourth sacral nerve root
	fourth sacral vertebrae
S5	fifth sacral nerve root
	fifth sacral vertebrae
S100	A protein family composed of 21 members that exhibit a high degree of structural similarity but are not functionally interchangeable. Dysregulated expression of multiple members of the S100 family is a common feature of human cancers, with each type of cancer showing a unique S100 protein profile or signature.
SI..SIV	symbols for the first to fourth heart sounds
SA	sacroanterior
	salicylic acid
	semen analysis
	serratus anterior (muscle)
	Sexoholics Anonymous
	sexual activity
	short axis
	sinoatrial
	sinus arrhythmia
	skeletal abnormalities
	skeletal age
	sleep apnea
	slow acetylator
	sock aid (occupational therapy)
	Spanish American
	spinal anesthesia
	Staphylococcus aureus
	status asthmaticus
	subarachnoid
	substance abuse
	suicide alert
	suicide attempt
	surface area
	surgical ablation
	surgical assistant
	sustained action
Sa	Saturday
S&A	sugar and acetone
S/A	same as
	stature to age (ratio)
	sugar and acetone
SA02	may have meant SaO2 (arterial oxygen percent saturation)
SAA	same as above
	serum amyloid A
	severe aplastic anemia
	splenic artery aneurysm
	Stokes-Adams attacks
	synthetic amino acids
SAAF	Strong African American Families (program)
SAAG	serum-ascites albumin gradient
SAAM	statin-associated autoimmune myopathy
SAAM II	Simulation, Analysis, and Modeling Software II (kinetic analysis and integrated systems modeling in order

	to understand the physiology		single-ascending dose
	and pathophysiology of		social anxiety disorder
	metabolic systems and the		source-axis distance
	distribution and clearance		standard axillary dissection
	of drugs)		subacromial decompression
SAANDs	selective apoptotic antineoplastic		subacute dialysis
	drugs		sugar and acetone determination
SAARDs	slow-acting antirheumatic drugs		sugar, acetone, and diacetic acid
SAB	serum albumin		superior axis deviation
	sinoatrial block	SADBE	squaric acid dibutyl ester
	Spanish-American Black	SADD	Students Against Drunk Driving
	spontaneous abortion	SADE	serious adverse device effects
	Staphylococcus aureus	SADH	secondary alcohol dehydrogenase
	bacteremia		(gene fragment)
	subarachnoid bleed	SADL	simulated activities of daily living
	subarachnoid block	SADNI	selective antibody deficiency
SAb0	no spontaneous abortions		with normal immunoglobulins
SABA	short-acting beta-2 agonist	SA D/O	schizoaffective disorder
SAbd	shoulder abduction	SADQ	Severity of Alcohol Dependence
SABER	single-allele base extension		Questionnaire
	reaction	SADRs	suspected adverse drug reactions
SABG	secondary alveolar bone grafting	SADS	Schedule for Affective Disorders
SABO	may have meant SAb0-no		and Schizophrenia
	spontaneous abortions		sudden arrhythmic death
SABR	screening auditory brainstem		syndrome
	response	SADs	severe autoimmune diseases
	spontaneous abortion rate	SADS-C	Schedule for Affective Disorders
	stereotactic ablative radiotherapy		And Schizophrenia – Change
SABs	side air bags		Version
SAC	safe abortion care	SAE	selective splenic
	school-age children		angioembolization
	seasonal allergic conjunctivitis		sepsis-associated encephalopathy
	segmental antigen challenge		serious adverse event
	serial abdominal closure		short above elbow (cast)
	serum aminoglycoside	SAECG	signal-averaged electrocardiogram
	concentration	SAEI	small artery elasticity index
	short arm cast	SAESU	Substance Abuse valuating
	spinal arachnoid cysts		Screen Unit
	Standardized Assessment of	SAF	Self-Analysis Form
	Concussion		self-articulating femoral
	substance abuse counselor		Spanish-American female
SACC	short arm cylinder cast		subcutaneous abdominal fat
SACD	subacute combined degeneration	SAFA	surgical atrial fibrillation ablation
sACE	serum angiotensin-converting	SAFARI	Sarcopenia And Function in
	enzyme activity		Aging Rehabilitation (study)
s-ACE	serum angiotensin-converting		Substandard and Falsified
	enzyme activity		Antimalarial Research
SACH	solid ankle, cushioned heel		Impact (mode)
SACP	selective antegrade cerebral	SAFE	surgery, antibiotics, facial
	perfusion		cleanliness, and environ-
SACS	sacsin molecular chaperone		mental change (a trachoma
	(gene)		control program)
SACT	sinoatrial conduction time	SAFER	Survey Analysis for Evaluating
	systemic anti-cancer therapy		Risk (The Joint Commission)
SAD	schizoaffective disorder	SAFHS	sonic accelerated fracture
	seasonal affective disorder		healing system
	Self-Assessment Depression	SAFT	synthetic aperture focusing
	(scale)		technique

SAG	sodium antimony gluconate	SAMHSA	Substance Abuse and Mental Health Services Administration (U.S. Department of Health and Human Services)
SAGAM	Scientific Advisory Group on Antimicrobials (EMEA)		
Sag D	sagittal diameter		
SAGE	serial analysis of gene expression	SAMI	Substance Abuse, Mental Illness (program)
SAH	selective amygdalohippocampectomy	sAML	secondary acute myeloid leukemia
	subarachnoid hemorrhage		
	systemic arterial hypertension	SAMMPRIS	Stenting Aggressive Medical Management for Prevention of Recurrent Stroke in Intracranial Stenosis (clinical trial)
SAHA	suberoylanilide hydroxamic acid (Vorinostat [Zolinza])		
SAHM	Society for Adolescent Health and Medicine		
SAHS	sleep apnea/hypopnea (hypersomnolence) syndrome	SAMPLE	symptoms/signs, allergies, medications, past medical history, last oral intake, and events prior to arrival (an EMT mnemonic used in initial patient questioning)
SAI	self-administered injectable		
	Sodium Amytal® interview		
SAID	systemic autoinflammatory disease		
SAIDH	see SIADH	SAMR	subclinical antibody mediated rejection
SAIO	subacute intestinal obstruction		
SAIS	subacromial impingement syndrome	SAMS	spinal arteriovenous metameric syndrome (Cobb syndrome; juvenile type spinal arteriovenous malformation)
SAL	salicylate		
	salmeterol (Serevent)		
	Salmonella		statin-associated muscle symptoms
	sensory acuity level		
	sterility assurance level	SAMS-CI	statin-Associated Muscle Symptom Clinical Index
	suction-assisted lipoplasty	SAMU	Service d'Aide Médicale Urgente (French prehospital emergency system)
SALAC	subacute lack of asthma control		
SALAD	sound-alike, look-alike drug(s) (names)		
sALCL	systemic anaplastic large-cell lymphoma	SAN	side-arm nebulizer
			sinoatrial node
			slept all night
SALK	surgical arthroscopy, left knee	SANA	Sexual Assault Nurse Examiner
SALP	serum alkaline phosphatase	SAna	sinoatrial nodal artery
SALR	serratus anterior-latissimus-rib (composite flap)	SANC	short arm navicular cast
			sinoatrial-node cell(s)
SALS	sporadic amyotrophic lateral sclerosis	S and I	see S&I
		SANDO	sensory ataxic neuropathy, dysarthria, and ophthalmoparesis
SAM	methylprednisolone sodium succinate (Solu-Medrol), aminophylline, and metaproterenol (Metaprel)		
		S1 and S2	sacral vertebrae 1 and 2
		S2 AND S3	sacral vertebrae 2 and 3
		S3 and S4	sacral vertebrae 3 and 4
	S-adenosylmethionine	S4 and S5	sacral vertebrae 4 and 5
	selective antimicrobial modulation	S and T	science and technology
		S and W	soap and water
	self-administered medication	SANE	Sexual Assault Nurse Examiner
	severe acute malnutrition		Single Assessment Numeric Evaluation (measure of function, orthopedics)
	short arc motion		
	sleep apnea monitor		
	Spanish-American male	sang	sanguinous
	statin-associated myalgia	SANK	Sankyo Company,(a pharmaceutical company)
	systolic anterior motion		
SAMe	S-adenosylmethionine (ademetionine)		reference number
		SA node	sinoatrial node
SAME	syndrome of arthralgias, myalgias, and edema	SANS	Schedule (Scale) for the Assessment of Negative Symptoms

	sympathetic autonomic nervous system
SA-NVIE	Staphylococcus aureus native valve infective endocarditis
SAO	small airway obstruction
	Southeast Asian ovalocytosis
	superior anterior oblique
SaO$_2$	arterial oxygen percent saturation
SAOD	smoking aortic occlusive disease
SAP	Sample Accountability Program
	serum alkaline phosphate
	serum amyloid P
	severe acute pancreatitis
	sporadic adenomatous polyps
	stable angina pectoris
	standard automated perimetry
	statistical analysis plan
	superior articular process
	systolic arterial pressure
SAPAS	Standardized Assessment of Personality – Abbreviated Scale
SAPD	self-administration of psychotropic drugs
SAPH	saphenous
SAPHO	synovitis, acne, pustulosis, hyperostosis, and osteomyelitis (syndrome)
S-APHOS	serum alkaline phosphatase
SAPS	Scale for the Assessment of Positive Symptoms
	short arm plaster splint
	Simplified Acute Physiology Score
SAPs	shock-absorbing pylons
SAPS II	Simplified Acute Physiology Score version II
SAPTA	stent-assisted percutaneous transluminal angioplasty
SAQ	saquinavir (Invirase)
	Seattle Angina Questionnaire
	Sexual Adjustment Questionnaire
	short-arc quadriceps
	Spinal Appearance Questionnaire
SAQ/r	saquinavir; ritonavir
SAR	seasonal allergic rhinitis
	Senior Assistant Resident
	sexual attitudes reassessment
	specific absorption rate (radiology)
	structural activity relationships
	subacute rehabilitation (center)
	suspected adverse reaction
SARA	Scale for the Assessment of Ataxia
	sexually acquired reactive arthritis
	SQUID (superconducting quantum interference device) array for reproductive assessment

SARAN	senior admitting resident's admission note
SARC	seasonal allergic rhinoconjunctivitis
SARDs	systemic autoimmune rheumatic diseases
SARI	severe acute respiratory infection
SARK	surgical arthroscopy, right knee
SARM	Staphylococcus aureus resistant methicillin (French)
SARME	surgically-assisted rapid maxillary expansion
SARMs	selective androgen receptor modulators
SARP	see gene website www.ncbi.nlm.nih.gov/gene
	several ankyrin repeat protein
	severe acute radiation pneumonitis
	Severe Asthma Research Program (database)
	Streptomyces antibiotic regulatory protein
SARPE	surgically-assisted rapid palatal expansion
S Arrh	sinus arrhythmia
SARRTP	Substance Abuse Residential Rehabilitation Treatment Program (Veterans Administration)
SARS	severe acute respiratory syndrome
SARS-CoV	severe acute respiratory syndrome-associated coronavirus
SART	sexual assault response team
	Society for Assisted Reproductive Technology
	standard acid reflux test
SARTCORS	Society for Assisted Reproductive Technology Clinic Outcomes Reporting System
SAS	saline, agent, and saline
	scalenus anticus syndrome
	Sedation-Agitation Scale
	see assessment sheet
	Self-rating Anxiety Scale
	short arm splint
	Simpson-Angus Scale
	sleep apnea syndrome
	Social Adjustment Scale
	Specific Activity Scale
	statistical applications software
	subarachnoid space
	subaxial subluxation
	sulfasalazine (Azulfidine)
	Surgical Apgar Score
	synthetic absorbable sutures

SASA	Sex Abuse Survivors Anonymous	SAVI®	strut-adjusted volume implant (radiation therapy delivery for breast cancer)
SASD	State Ambulatory Surgery Databases		
	subacromial-subdeltoid (bursa)	SAVR	specific anti-viral response
	symptomatic adult spinal deformity		surgical aortic valve replacement
SASH	saline, agent, saline, and heparin	SAX	short axis
SASP	sulfasalazine (salicylazo-sulfapyridine; Azulfidine)	SAXS	small-angle X-ray scattering
		SB	safety belt
SASS	Social Adaptation Self-Evaluation Scale		sandbag
			scleral buckling
SASSAD	six area, six sign atopis dermitis (severity score)		seat belt
			sedentary behaviors
SASSI	A Short and Sweet Screening Instrument for Cognitive Impairment		seen by
			Sengstaken-Blakemore (tube)
			shave biopsy
	Substance Abuse Subtle Screening Inventory		sick boy
			side bend
SAST	slide agglutination serotyping		side bending
SAT	methylprednisolone sodium succinate (Solu-Medrol), aminophylline, and terbutaline		sinus bradycardia
			sleep bruxism
			slide board
			small bowel
	saturated		sodium bicarbonate
	saturation		spina bifida
	self-administered therapy		sponge bath
	Senior Apperception Test		stand-by
	speech awareness threshold		Stanford-Binet (test)
	spontaneous awakening trial		sternal border
	subacute thyroiditis		stillbirth
	subcutaneous adipose tissue		stillborn
Sat	Saturday		stone basketing
SATC	substance abuse treatment clinic		Swiss ball
sating	a word meaning to provide someone with more than enough; glut	Sb	antimony
		SB +	wearing seat belt
		SB −	not wearing seat belt
SATL	surgical Achilles tendon lengthening	S/B	see SB
		SBA	serum bactericidal activity
SATP	substance abuse treatment program		standby angioplasty
			standby assist
SATS	refers to oxygen saturation levels		standby assistant (assistance)
SAT/SBT	spontaneous awakening trials and spontaneous breathing trials		Summary Basis of Approval
		SBAC	small bowel adenocarcinoma
satting	saturating	SB-ACL	single-bundle (hamstring autograft) anterior cruciate ligament (reconstruction)
SATU	substance abuse treatment unit		
SAUD	severe alcohol use disorder(s)		
S aureus	*Staphylococcus aureus*	SBAR	Situation, Background, Assessment, Recommendation (a technique for communicating patient information)
SAV	select a vent (diameter; hearing aid-related)		
	sensed atrioventricular (delay)		
	Supra-Annular valve	SBARQ	Situation, Background, Assessment, Recommendation, Questions (a technique for communicating patient information)
SaV	sapovirus		
SAVD	spontaneous assisted vaginal delivery		
save shot	opioid-overdose-reversal medication naloxone(slang)		
		SBA/SBG	stand-by assist/stand-by guard
SAVI	STING (stimulators of interferon genes)-associated vasculopathy of infancy	SBB	stereotactic breast biopsy
		SBBO	small-bowel bacterial overgrowth
		SBBx	small bowel mucosal biopsy

SBC	sensory binocular cooperation	SBIRT	screening, brief intervention,
	single base cane		and referral to treatment
	small-bore Connector (initiative)	SBJ	skin, bones, and joints
	standard bicarbonate	SBK	spinnbarkeit
	strict bed confinement	SBL	side-bend left
	summary of benefits and coverage		sparse Bayesian learning
	superficial bladder cancer		sponge blood loss
S1BC	Stage 1, Bleeding Concern	sBLA	supplemental Biologics License
SBCAD	short branched chain amino		Application
	acid deficiency	SBLEO	suicide by law enforcement
sBCC	superficial basal cell carcinoma		officer (pronounced S-B-Leo)
SBCE	small-bowel capsule endoscopy	SB-LM	Stanford-Binet Intelligence
SBCT	Brazilian Society of Thoracic		Test-Form LM
	Surgery	SBM	stone basket manipulation
	severe blunt chest trauma	SBMA	spinobulbar muscular atrophy
	single breath count test		(Kennedy disease)
SBD	sleep-related breathing disorder	SBMD	sensory-based motor disorder
	straight bag drainage	SBMs	spontaneous bowel movements
SBE	saturated base excess	SBO	small bowel obstruction
	self-breast examination		specified bovine offals
	short below-elbow (cast)	SBOD	scleral buckle, right eye
	shortness of breath on exertion	SBOE	surgical blood order equation
	simulation-based education	SBOH	State Board of Health
	single-balloon enteroscope	SBOM	soybean oil meal
	standardized base excess	SBOS	scleral buckle, left eye
	subacute bacterial endocarditis	SBOT	serous borderline ovarian tumour
	subjective binge eating	SBP	school breakfast program
SBEBs	sensory-based exploratory		scleral buckling procedure
	behaviors (smelling, licking,		small bowel phytobezoars
	spitting, manipulating		spontaneous bacterial peritonitis
	and/or swallowing)		systolic blood pressure
SBEM	small breast epithelial mucin	SBPT	specific bronchial provocation tests
	spontaneous bacterial empyema		subchondral bone plate thickness
SBEP	somatosensory brainstem	sBPT	synchronous balneophototherapy
	evoked potentials	SBQ	Sedentary Behavior Questionnaire
SBF	splanchnic blood flow		Snoring, Tired, Observed,
SBFI	serial block face imaging		blood Pressure, BMI (body
SBFT	small bowel feeding tube		mass index), Age, Neck
	small bowel follow through		circumference, and Gender
SBG	small baby guidelines		(STOP BANG Questionnaire,
	stand-by guard		a tool to screen patients for
SBGM	self blood-glucose monitoring		obstructive sleep apnea)
SBH	State Board of Health	SBQC	small based quad cane
SBI	Screening and Brief Intervention	SBR	side-bend right
	silicone (gel-containing) breast		sluggish blood return
	implants		strict bed rest
	something bad inside	SBRAD	Small Business Research and
	(undiagnosed cancer, etc.		Demonstration (Centers
	discovered during surgery)		for Medicare and Medicaid
	(Veterinary slang)		Services)
	sulcular bleeding index (dental)	SBRN	superficial branch radial nerve
	systemic bacterial infection	SBRT	stereotactic body radiation
SBID	small bowel intussusception		therapy
	disease	SBS	serum blood sugar
S-bil	serum bilirubin		shaken baby syndrome
SB-IPMN	side branch (pancreatic duct-		short (small) bowel syndrome
	involved) intraductal papillary		sick-building syndrome
	mucinous neoplasm		side-by-side

	small bowel series		synthetic cannabinoid
	sphenobasilar synchondrosis		systolic click
	State Behavioral Scale (a method	Sc	scandium
	to monitor sedation in critically	sc	without correction (without
	ill pediatric patients)		glasses)
SBSA	Self-Beliefs Related to Social	S&C	sclerae and conjunctivae
	Anxiety (Scale)	S/C	sugar-coated (tablets)
SBT	serum bactericidal titers	SCA	sickle cell anemia
	single blastocyst transfer		spinocerebellar ataxia
	small bowel transplantation		standard clinical assessment
	special baby Travesol		subclavian artery
	spontaneous breathing trial		subcommissural annuloplasty
SBTB	sinus breakthrough beat		subcutaneous abdominal (block)
SBTKA	simultaneous bilateral total		sudden cardiac arrest
	knee arthroplasty		superior cerebellar artery
SBTs	spontaneous breathing trials	ScA	*Scedosporium apiospermum*
SBTT	small bowel transit time	Sca	serum calcium
SBTx	small bowel transplantation	SCA1	spinocerebellar ataxia type 1
SBU	secondary building unit	SCA2	spinocerebellar ataxia type 2
	Swedish Council on Health	SCA7	spinocerebellar ataxia type 7
	Technology Assessment	SCAD	segment colitis associated with
SBV	sindbis Virus		diverticula
	single binocular vision		short chain acyl-coenzyme A
SBW	seat belts worn		dehydrogenase
SBX	symphysis, buttocks, and xiphoid		spontaneous coronary artery
SC	scaphocapitate		dissection
	schizophrenia		stable coronary artery disease
	Schwann cell	sCAD	spontaneous cervical artery
	Scianna; an International Society		dissection
	of Blood Transfusion (ISBT)	SCADD	short-chain acyl-CoA (acyl
	blood group		coenzyme A) dehydrogenase
	screening colonoscopy		deficiency
	secure core (used in psychiatric	SCAFI	Spinocerebellar Ataxia
	emergency services)		Functional Index
	self-care	SCAIF	supraclavicular artery island flap
	serum creatinine	SCAMP	Standardized Clinical Assessment
	service connected		and Management Plan
	shower chair		Standardized, Concentrated
	sick call		With Added Macronutrients
	sickle cell		Parenteral (nutrition regimen)
	small (blood pressure) cuff	SCAN	suspected child abuse and neglect
	Snellen chart	SCAP	scapula; scapulae; scapular
	South Carolina		Severe Community Acquired
	spinal cord		Pneumonia (prognostic scores
	sport cord		for influenza pneumonia
	standard cane		patients)
	sternoclavicular		stem cell apheresis
	straight cane		stem cells of the apical papilla
	subclavian	SCAPE	sympathetic crashing acute
	subclavian catheter		pulmonary edema
	subcutaneous (this is a dangerous	SCAR	spectral gradient acoustic
	abrevation as it can be read as		reflectometry
	SL, sublingual. Use subcut or	SCARD	Skin Cancer Audit Research
	spell it out.		Database (Skin Cancer
	succinylcholine		College of Australia and
	sulfur colloid		New Zealand)
	supportive care		Society of Chairs of Academic
	surveillance cultures		Radiology Departments

S

SCARED	Screen for Child Anxiety Related Emotional Disorders
Scarf osteotomy	a corrective bunion surgical procedure
SCARMD	severe childhood autosomal recessive muscular dystrophy
SCARs	severe cutaneous adverse reactions
SCAT	sheep cell agglutination titer
	sickle cell anemia test
	spectrogram correlation and transformation
	Sport Concussion Assessment Tool
	subcutaneous adipose tissue
SCAT2	Sports ConcussionAssessment Tool-Second Edition
SCATBI	Scales of Cognitive Ability for Traumatic Brain Injury
SCA type 1	spinocerebellar ataxias, type I
SCB	Standard Code Book
	strictly confined to bed
SCBA	self-contained breathing apparatus
SCBC	small cell bronchogenic carcinoma
SCBE	single-contrast barium enema
SCBF	spinal cord blood flow
SCBMs	spontaneous, complete bowel movements
SCBs	synthetic cannabinoids
SCC	semicircular canals
	short course chemotherapy (for tuberculosis)
	sickle cell crisis
	small cell carcinoma
	spinal cord compression
	squamous cell carcinoma
	subcallosal cingulate cortex
SCCA	semi-closed circle absorber
	squamous cell carcinoma antigen
SCCa	squamous cell carcinoma
SCCB	small cell cancer of the bladder
SCCC	squamous-cell carcinoma of the conjunctiva
SCCD	semicircular canal dehiscence
	spontaneous cervicocranial dissection
	subclinical cobalamin deficiency
SCCE	squamous cell carcinoma of the esophagus
sCCF	spontaneous carotid-cavernous fistula
SCCHN	squamous cell carcinoma of the head and neck
SCCI	subcutaneous continuous infusion
SCCIS	squamous cell carcinoma in situ
SCCL	solitary cerebral cysticercal lesion
	squamous cell cancer-like

	squamous cell carcinoma of the larynx
	Squamous cell carcinoma of the lip
	squamous cell carcinoma of the lung
ScCL	scleral contact lens
SCCM	Society of Critical Care Medicine
SCCOT	squamous cell carcinoma of the oral tongue
SCCP	small cell carcinoma of the prostate
	squamous cell carcinoma of the penis
SCCS	self-controlled case-series
SCCs	squamous cell carcinomas
SCC/T	squamous cell carcinoma of the oral tongue
SCD	semicircular canal dehiscence
	sequential compression device
	service connected disability
	sickle cell disease
	specific carbohydrate diet
	spinal cord disease
	spondylo-costal dysostosis
	subacute combined degeneration
	sudden cardiac death
ScDA	scapulodextra anterior
sCDAI	short Crohn's Disease Activity Index
SCDD	symptomatic cervical disk disease
SCD-HeFT	Sudden Cardiac Death in Heart Failure Trial
SCDM	soybean-casein digest medium
ScDP	scapulodextra posterior
SCDs	sudden cardiac deaths
SCD's	see SCD
SCDS-TEDS	sequential compression devices and thromboembolism deterrent stockings
SCE	saline contrast echocardiography
	sister chromatid exchange
	soft cooked egg
	specialized columnar epithelium
	spinal cord ependymoma
SCEMIA	self-contained enzymatic membrane immunoassay
SCEP	somatosensory cortical evoked potential
SCF	slow coronary flow
	special care formula
	staged columnar fixation
	stem cell factor
	supra ciliochoroidal fluid
SCFA	short-chain fatty acid
SCFE	slipped capital femoral epiphysis
SCFGT	Southern California Figure Ground Test

SCFN	subcutaneous fat necrosis	SCIPP	sacrococcygeal to inferior pubic point
SCG	seismocardiography	SCIPs	spinal cord injury patients
	serum Chemogram	sci-RNA-seq	single-cell combinatorial
	sodium cromoglycate		indexing ribonucleic acid
	substitute care giver		sequencing (a combinatorial
SCH	schistosomiasis (*Schistosoma* sp.) vaccine		indexing strategy to profile
	Sports concussion headache		the transcriptomes of
	subclinical hypothyroidism		single cells or nuclei)
	supracervical hysterectomy	SCIs	spinal cord injuries
SCh	succinylcholine chloride	SCIT	single-chain immunotoxin
sched	schedule; scheduled		social cognition and interaction
SCHF	subcondylar humerus fracture		training
sCHF	systolic congestive heart failure		subcutaneous immunotherapy
SCHIP	State Children's Health Insurance Program	SCIU	spinal cord injury unit
		SCIV	subclavian intravenous
SCHISTO	schistocytes	SCIWORA	spinal cord injury without
schiz	schizophrenia		radiographic abnormalities
schizo	schizophrenia	SCJ	squamocolumnar junction
SCHLP	supracricord hemilaryngopharyngectomy		sternoclavicular joint
		sCJD	sporadic Creutzfeldt-Jakob disease
SCHNC	squamous cell head and neck cancer	SC joint	sternoclavicular joint
SCHO	structural carbohydrate	SCK	subclinical ketosis
SCHT	subclinical hypothyroidism	sCK	serum creatine kinase
SchT	Schirmer test	SCL	Sedation consciousness level
SCI	silent cerebral infarct		sinus cycle length
	specific COX-2 inhibitor		skin conductance level
	spinal cord injury		symptom checklist
	spinal cord ischemia	Scl70	topoisomerase I
	subcoma insulin	Scl-70	a specific antibody marker of systemic sclerosis
SCIC	sickle cell intrahepatic cholestasis		
	spinal cord injury center	SCL-90	Symptoms Checklist–90 items
SC-ICD	single-chamber implantable cardioverter defibrillator	ScLA	scapulolaeva anterior
		SCLAX	subcostal long axis
SCID	severe combined immunodefi- ciency disorders (disease)	SCLC	small cell lung cancer
		SCLCa	small cell lung cancer
	structured clinical interview for DSM-III-R	SCLD	sickle cell lung disease
		SCLE	subacute cutaneous lupus erythematosis
SCIDs	severe combined immunodefi- ciency disorders (diseases)		
		SCLL	stem cell leukaemia-lymphoma (syndrome)
SciELO	Scientific Electronic Library Online		
		SCLN	supraclavicular lymph node
SCIF	supraclavicular island flap	ScLP	scapulolaeva posterior
SCIG	subcutaneous immunoglobulin	SCLS	systemic capillary leak syndrome (Clarkson Disease)
SCII	Strong-Campbell Interest Inventory		
		SCLs	soft contact lenses
SCIM	Spinal Cord Independence Measure		synthetic combinatorial libraries
		SCLV	supraclavicular
SCIM-III	Spinal Cord Independence Measure version III	SCM	scalene muscle
			scanning capacitance microscopy
SCIM-SR	Spinal Cord Independence Measure - Self Report		sensation, circulation, and motion
			split cord malformation
SCIP	Screening and Crisis Intervention Program		spondylitic caudal myelopathy
			sternocleidomastoid
	Surgical Care Improvement Project (The Count Commission)		supraclavicular muscle
		Scm	see gene website www.ncbi.nlm .nih.gov/gene

SDUE	somatic dysfunction upper extremity		single-end cane
SDV	single-dose vial		size exclusion chromatography
	sleeping disease virus (salmonid alpha virus 2)		spontaneous echo contrast
			steric exclusion chromatography
	source document verification	SECG	scalp electrocardiogram
SDVT	symptomatic deep venous thrombosis	SEC HPT	secondary hyperparathyroidism
		SECL	seclusion
SDwe	within-experiment standard deviation	SECPR	standard external cardiopulmonary resuscitation
SDX/PYR	sulfadoxine-pyrimethamine (Fansidar)	SE-CPT	single-electrode current perception threshold
SE	saline enema (0.9% sodium chloride)	SECS	Safe, Easy, Cheap, and Sensible (treatments)
	self-employed		self-expanding covered stent
	self-examination	SECs	sinusoidal endothelial cells
	Shannon entropy		squamous epithelial cells
	side effect	secs	seconds
	sleep efficiency	SED	sedation nurse
	soft exudates		sedimentation
	southeast		serious emotional disturbances
	special education		skin erythema dose
	spherical equivalent		socially and emotionally disturbed
	spin echo		spondyloepiphyseal dysplasia
	staff escort	S/ED	systolic/end diastolic
	standard error	SeDBP	seated diastolic blood pressure
	Starr-Edwards (valve, pacemaker)	SEDDS	self-emulsifying drug-delivery system
	status epilepticus	SED-NET	severely emotional disturbed - network
	stress echocardiography		
	surgical excision	sed rate	(erythrocyte) sedimentation rate
Se	selenium	sed rt	sedimentation rate
S&E	seen and examined	SEDS	socio-economic and demographic status
	suicidal and eloper		
S/E	suicidal and eloper		solution-enhanced dispersion by supercritical fluids
SEA	sheep erythrocyte agglutination (test)		
	side-entry (venous) access	SEDs	skin entrance doses (radiology)
	Southeast Asia		standard erythemal doses
	Staphylococcal enterotoxin A	SEDT	spondylo-epiphyseal dysplasia tarda
	subdural electrode array		
	synaptic electronic activation	SEE	standard error of estimate
SEAC	spinal epidural arachnoid cyst	SEEDs	Support, Education, Empowerment, and Directions
SEAL	subcutaneous endoscopically assisted ligation		
		SEEG	stereoelectroencephalographic
SEAR	Self-Esteem and Relationship	sEEG	spot electroencephalography
	Southeast Asia refugee	SEER	Surveillance, Epidemiology, and End Results (program)
SEB	Staphylococcus enterotoxin B		
	surrogate end-point biomarker	SEERS	Synthetic Environments for Emergency Response Simulation
SebK	seborrheic keratoses		
SEB K	seborrheic keratosis	SEF	spectral edge frequency (anesthesia-depth monitor)
seb ker	seborrheic keratosis		
sebo	seborrheic	SEG	segment
SEBT	Star Excursion Balance Test		sonoencephalogram
SEC	second		surveillance error grid
	secondary	SEGA	subependymal giant-cell astrocytoma
	secretary		
	section	SEGRA	selective glucocorticoid-receptor agonist
	selenocysteine	segs	segmented neutrophils

SEH	spinal epidural hematomas
	subependymal hemorrhage
SEI	Self-Esteem Inventory
	subepithelial (comeal) infiltrate
SEID	systemic exertion intolerance
	disease
seipin-nKO	neuronal seipin-knockout (mice)
SEJ	Staphylococcus (aureus)
	enterotoxin gene J
SEL	spinal epidural lipomatosis
SELDI	surface enhanced laser
	desorption/ionization
SELDI-TOF MS	surface enhanced laser
	desorption/ionization-time of
	flight mass spectrometry
SELEX	systematic evolution of ligands
	by exponential enrichment
SELFVD	sterile elective low forceps
	vaginal delivery
SEM	scanning electron microscopy
	semen
	slow eye movement
	standard error of mean
	structural equation modeling
	systolic ejection murmur
Sema4D	semaphorin 4D
S-EMBU-A	a shorten, self-report based on
	the Egna Minnen Beträffande
	Uppfostran-Adolescent
	questionnaire, (Swedish
	acronym for "Own Memories
	of Parental Rearing"), that
	assesses perceived parental
	rearing style in adolescents
SEMD	spondyloepimetaphyseal
	dysplasias
sEMG	surface electromyography
SEMI	subendocardial myocardial
	infarction
semi	a combining form meaning half,
	partial, informal, or somewhat
SEMS	self-expanding metallic stent
SeMV	Sesbania mosaic virus
sem ves	seminal vesicles
SEN	spray each nostril
senA	senofilcon A (Vistakon; a soft
	contact lens)
SENC	Spanish Society of Community
	Nutrition (Sociedad Espanola
	de Nutricion Comunitaria)
SENC-MRI	strain-encoded magnetic
	resonance imaging
Senna	is a natural medicine derived from
	the senna plant; senna contains
	sennosides which acts as a
	stimulant laxative (Senokot)
SENS	sensitivity
	sensorium

SEOC	serous epithelial ovarian
	carcinoma
SEP	multiple sclerosis (French)
	separate
	separation
	serum electrophoresis
	solitary extramedullary
	plasmacytoma
	somatosensory evoked potential
	syringe exchange program
	systolic ejection period
Sep	September
SEPS	subdural evacuation port system
	subfascial endoscopic perforator
	surgery
SEPs	supervised exercise programs
septo	a relationship to the septum
SEQ	sequela
SEQS	sequences
SER	scanning equalization
	radiography
	sertraline (Zoloft)
	side effects records
	signal enhancement ratio
	surgical emergency room
Ser	serine
SERA-TEK	technetium-99m hexametazime
SERD	selective estrogen receptor
	down-regulator (e.g
	fulvestrant [Faslodex])
	supraesophageal manifestations
	of reflux disease
Serial 7's	a mental status examination
	(starting with a 100, count
	backward by 7s)
SER-IV	supination external rotation,
	type 4 fracture
SERM	selective estrogen-receptor
	modulator
SERMs	selective estrogen receptor
	modulators
SEROSANG	serosanguineous
SERP-ACWA	Skin Exposure Reduction
	Paste Against Chemical
	Warfare Agents
SERS	surface-enhanced Raman
	spectroscopy
SERs	somatosensory evoked responses
serv	service
SES	sick euthyroid syndrome
	sirolimus-eluting stents
	socioeconomic status
	standard electrolyte solution
SeSBP	seated systolic blood pressure
sessile	a word meaning fixed in one
	place; immobile; attached
	directly by its base without
	a stalk or peduncle

S

SET	signal extraction technology	SFARI	Simon Foundation Autism
	single embryo transfer		Research Iniatitive (database)
	skin-end-point titration	SFA/UFA	saturated/unsaturated fatty
	social environmental therapy		acids ratio
	systolic ejection time	SFB	single frequency bioimpedance
sETOH	serum ethanol (alcohol)	SF3B1	splicing factor 3b subunit 1
seton	a piece of surgical thread or		(gene)
	rubber band that is left in an	SFC	spinal fluid count
	anal fistula for several weeks		subarachnoid fluid collection
	to keep it open. This allows		supercritical fluid
	it to drain and helps it heal,		chromatography
	while avoiding the need to		superior frontal cortex
	cut the sphincter muscles	SFCNVM	subfoveal choroidal neovascular
SEV	sevoflurane (Ultane)		membranes
SEVI	semen-derived enhancer of	SFD	scaphoid fossa depression
	Virus Infection		small for dates
	slow electron velocity-map	SFDA	State Food and Drug
	imaging		Administration (China)
SEVO	sevoflurane	SFE	supercritical fluid extraction
SEWB	social and emotional well-being	SFED	single-fraction equivalent dose
SEWHO	shoulder-elbow-wrist-hand		(radiation therapy)
	orthosis		six-food elimination diet (treat-
SF	safflower oil		ment approach for eosinophilic
	salt-free		esophagitis where dairy, wheat,
	saturated fat		eggs, soy, nuts, and seafood
	scarlet fever		are avoided)
	seizure frequency		Société Française d'Endoscopie
	seminal fluid		Digestive (French Society of
	skull fracture		Digestive Endoscopy)
	small finger		sugar-free energy drink
	soft feces	sfEMG	single-fiber electromyography
	sound field	SFF	solid freeform fabrication
	spinal fluid		supracondylar femoral fracture
	standard fractionation	SFG	suboptimal fetal growth
	(radiation therapy)		sum frequency generation
	starch-free		superior frontal gyrus
	stock (standard) formula (iron-	SFGS	Sunnybrook Facial Grading
	fortified term infant formula)		Scale
	stone-free	SFGs	susceptibility-induced magnetic
	sugar-free		field gradients
	symptom-free	SFH	schizophrenia family history
	synovial fluid		Smoke-Free Homes (Program)
S-F	structure-function (claims)		subfoveal hemorrhage
S&F	slip and fall		symphysis-fundal height
	soft and flat	SFHM	Senior Fellow in Hospital
	store and forward		Medicine
S/F	see SF	SFHN	San Francisco Health Network
SF-6	sulfahexafluoride	SFI	sciatic functional index
SF-12	a 12 question health survey to		Shenqi Fuzheng injection
	measure functional health and	SFJ	saphenofemoral junction
	well-being from the patient's	SFL	sitting forward lean
	point of view	sFLC	serum free light chain (component
SF-36	Short Form-36 Health Survey		of immunoglobulins)
SFA	French Society for Arthroscopy		serum free light chain(s)
	saturated fatty acids	SFM	scanning force microscopy
	superficial femoral artery		simple facemask
	visceral fat area (VFA) and	SFMA	Selective Functional Movement
	subcutaneous fat area		Assessment

S

SFMC	sagittal fractures of the mandibular condyle
	soluble fibrin monomer complex
	synovial fluid mononuclear cells
SF-MPQ	Short-Form McGill Pain questionnaire
SFN	small fiber neuropathy
	sulforaphane
SFNM	subfoveal neovascular membranes
SFO	safflower oil
SFOB	sleep-related falling out of bed
SFOV	scan field of view (radiology)
SFP	simulated fluorescence process
	simultaneous foveal perception
	spinal fluid pressure
SFPN	small-fiber polyneuropathy
SFPT	standard fixation preference test
SFRT	stereotactic fractionated radiotherapy
SFS	split function studies
	Standards Flow Sheets
SFT	solitary fibrous tumor
	subcutaneous fat tissue
SFTP	solitary fibrous tumor of the pleura
SFTR	sagittal, frontal, transverse, rotation
SFTS	stenosing flexor tenosynovitis
SFTs	solitary fibrous tumors
SFU	Society for Fetal Urology
SFUP	surgical follow-up
SFV	Semliki Forest virus
	simian foamy viruses
	superficial femoral vein
SFW	shell fragment wound
SFWB	social/family well-being
SFWD	symptom-free walking distance
SFX	serial femtosecond crystallography
SFx	stress fracture
SG	salivary gland
	scrotography
	serum glucose
	side glide
	skin graft
	specific gravity
	Swan-Ganz (catheter)
Sg	seaborgium
S-G	Swan-Ganz (catheter)
S/G	swallow/gag
SGA	small for gestational age
	subjective global assessment (dietary history and physical examination)
	substantial gainful activity (employment)
	symptomatic gastric amyloidosis

SG-ACLr	semitendinosus-gracilis anterior cruciate ligament reconstruction
SGAP	superior gluteal artery perforator (flap)
SGAPs	second-generation antipsychotics
SGAs	second-generation antihistamines
	second-generation antipsychotics
	somatic genomic abnormalities
sGaw	specific airway conductance
SGB	stellate ganglion block
	Swiss gym ball
SGC	Swan-Ganz catheter
SGCNB	stereotactic guided core-needle biopsy
SGCT2	sodium-glucose cotransporter 2
SGCT2I	sodium-glucose cotransporter 2 inhibitor
SGD	salivary gland dysfunction
	specific granule deficiency
	specific growth delay
	speech generating device (related to AAC devices used in speech therapy)
	straight gravity drainage
	sweat gland density
SGE	significant glandular enlargement
	subdural grid electrodes
SGF	simulated gastric fluid
	slow graft function
SGGT	serum gamma-glutamyl transpeptidase
SGGTs	solution-gated graphene transistors
SGHL	superior glenohumeral ligament
SGI	suppurative granulomatous inflammation
SGIS	side-glide in standing
s̄ gl	without correction (without glasses)
SGLT2	sodium/glucose cotransporter member 2; see gene website www.ncbi.nlm.nih.gov/gene
SGLT2i	sodium-glucose co-transporter-2 inhibitors
SGLT2 inhibitor	sodium/glucose cotransporter 2 inhibitor (e.g. Invokana [canagliflozin], Farxiga [dapagliflozin propanediol], Jardiance [empagliflozin])
SGM	serum glucose monitoring
SGN-35	brentuximab vedotin (Adcetris)
SGNA	stellate ganglion nerve activity (veterinary)
	Subjective Global Nutrition Assessment
SGNFD	sweat gland nerve fiber density
SGO	Society of Gynecologic Oncologists

SGOT	serum glutamic oxalo-acetic transaminase (same as AST)	SHARE	Survey of Health, Ageing and Retirement in Europe
SGP	Schering-Plough Corporation	SHAS	supravalvular hypertrophic aortic stenosis
SGPA	supra glandular pituitary adenoma		
SGPG	sulfated glucuronic paragloboside	S Hb	sickle hemoglobin screen
SGPT	serum glutamate pyruvate transaminase (same as ALT)	SHBG	sex hormone-binding globulin
		sHBO$_2$T	systemic hyperbaric oxygen therapy
SGR	sustainable growth rate Sustainable Growth Rate Sustainable Growth Rate (Medicare formula)	SHBRV	silver-haired bat rabies virus
		SHC	subsequent hospital care
		SHCN	special healthcare needs
sgRNA	single-guided ribonucleic acid	SHCP	spastic hemiparetic cerebral palsy
SGRQ	St George's Respiratory Questionnaire	SHD	Sago hemolytic disease standard hemodialysis structural heart disease survival to hospital discharge
SGRQ-A	St. Georges Respiratory Questionnaire translated into American English		
		SHE	sexual health education
SGS	second-generation sulfonylurea short gut syndrome subglottic stenosis	SHEA	Society for Hospital Epidemiology of America (guidelines)
		SHEENT	skin, head, eyes, ears, nose, and throat
sGS	surgical Gleason score	SHEP	Systolic Hypertension in the Elderly Program (trial)
sGST	soluble glutathione-S-transferases		
SGTCS	secondarily generalized tonic-clonic seizures	SHF	systolic heart failure
		SHG	shigellosis (*Shigella* sp.) vaccine sonohysterography
SGV	short gastric vein		
SGW	straight-tipped guide wire Surgeon General's Warning	SHGT	somatic-cell human gene therapy
SH	sclerosing hemangioma self-help serum hepatitis sexual harassment short shoulder shower social history stapled hemorrhoidopexy sulfhydryl (group) surgical history systemic hypertension thiol (−SH)	SHH	sonic hedgehog (signaling pathways); see gene website; www.ncbi.nlm.nih.gov/gene
		SHHF	spontaneously hypertensive heart failure
		SHI	Self-Harm Inventory standard heparin infusion
		Shig	*Shigella*
		SHIM	Sexual Health Inventory for Males (questionnaire)
		SHINE	Serving Health Insurance Needs of Elders (Florida)
−SH	thiol	SHIP	Sexual Health in Practice (UK study) State Health Insurance Assistance Program Study of Health in Pomerania (Germany)
S&H	speech and hearing suicidal and homicidal		
S/H	suicidal/homicidal ideation		
SH2	sarc homology region 2		
SHA	super-heated aerosol survival to hospital admission	SHIV	simian-human immunodefi- ciency virus
SHAFT	Shopping, Housework, Account- ing (bills), Food preparation, and Transportation (driving); (instrumental activities of daily living)	SHL	sudden hearing loss supraglottic horizontal laryngectomy
		SHLD	shoulder
SHAL	standard hyperalimentation	shldr	shoulder
sham	a word meaning a thing that is not what it is purported to be	SHMB	severe hypersensitivity to mosquito bites
SHAP	Southampton Hand Assessment Procedure (score)	SHMF	Similac human milk fortifier
		SHNL	see SNHL
SHAPS	Snaith-Hamilton Pleasure Scale	SHO	Senior House Officer

ShOB	shortness of breath	SIADs	systemic inflammatory and autoimmune diseases
SHOP	Small Business Health Options Program	SIAHD	May have intended SIADH (syndrome of inappropriate antidiuretic hormone[secretion])
SHOT	Serious Hazards of Transfusion (United Kingdom's hemovigilance program)		
SHOX	Short stature <u>HO</u>mebo<u>X</u> (gene)	SIAS	Social Interaction Anxiety Scale
SHP	secondary hypertension, pulmonary	SIAT	supervised intermittent ambulatory treatment
SHPT	secondary hyperparathyroidism	SIB	self-inflating bulb
SHPTH	secondary hyperparathyroidism		self-injurious behavior
SHR	scapulohumeral rhythm		simultaneous integrated boost (external beam radiotherapy)
SHRC	shortened, held, resisted contraction		
		SIBC	serum iron-binding capacity
S-HRV	short-term heart rate variability	sIBM	sporadic-inclusion body myositis
SHS	second hand (tobacco) smoke	s-IBM	sporadic inclusion-body myositis
	Self History Sheet	SIBO	small intestinal bacterial overgrowth
	sliding hip screw		
	student health service	sibs	siblings
sHT	subclinical hypothyroidism	SIC	self-intermittent catherization
S-HTP	Synthetic House-Tree-Person (drawing test)		squamous intraepithelial cells
			Standard Industrial Classification
SHUTi	Sleep Healthy Using The internet		
SHV	short hepatic vein	SICA	surgically induced corneal astigmatism
	sulfhydryl variant		
SHx	social history	Sicca	dry, as in Sicca Syndrome, an autoimmune disease that destroys the exocrine glands that produce tears and saliva (same as Sjögren Syndrome)
SI	International System of Units		
	sacroiliac		
	sacroiliitis		
	sagittal index		
	sector iridectomy		subcutaneous implantable cardioverter-defibrillator
	self-inflicted		
	sensory integration	SICD	sudden infant crib death
	seriously ill	S-ICD	subcutaneous implantable cardioverter-defibrillator
	sexual intercourse		
	signal intensity	SICH	supratentorial intracerebral hematoma
	small intestine		
	stiffness index	sICH	spontaneous intracerebral hemorrhage
	stress incontinence		
	strict isolation		symptomatic intracranial hemorrhage
	stroke index		
	suicidal ideation	SICI	short-interval intracortical inhibition
	superimposed		
Si	silicon	SICK scapula syndrome	scapular malposition, inferomedial border prominence, coracoid pain and malposition, and dyskinesis of scapular movement
S&I	suction and irrigation		
	support and interpretation		
S/I	see SI		
SIA	small intestinal atresia		
	surgically-induced astigmatism	SICOG	Southern Italy Cooperative Oncology Group
	systemic immune activation		
SIAARTI	Italian Society of Anesthesia, Analgesia, Resuscitation and Intensive Care	SICT	selective intracoronary thrombolysis
		SICU	surgical intensive care unit
SIAD	syndrome of inappropriate antidiuresis	SID	once daily (used in veterinary medicine)
SIADH	syndrome of inappropriate antidiuretic hormone hypersecretion	SID	source to image distance (radiology)
			strong ion difference

548

SIDA	French and Spanish abbreviation for AIDS
	stable isotope dilution assay
SIDAH	may have meant SIADH (syndrome of inappropriate antidiuretic hormone hypersecretion)
SIDAM	structured interview for the diagnosis of dementia of Alzheimer type
SIDAM-A	structured interview for the diagnosis of dementia of the Alzheimer type, multi-infarct dementia, and dementias of other etiology according to ICD-10 and DSM-III-R
SIDD	syndrome of isolated diastolic dysfunction
SIDERO	siderocyte
SIDFF	superimposed dorsiflexion of foot
sidH	see gene website; www.ncbi .nlm.nih.gov/gene
SIDM	steroid-inducted diabetes mellitus
SIDP	Society of Infectious Diseases Pharmacists
SIDP-IV	structured interview for DSM-IV (Diagnostic and Statistical Manual of Mental Disorders 4th Edition) personality disorders
SIDS	sudden infant death syndrome
SIEA	superficial inferior epigastric artery
SIEDY	Structured Interview on Erectile Dysfunction
SIEP	serum immunoelectrophoresis
Sierra	Phonetic Alphabet for S; pronounced SEE-AIR-RAH
SIEV	superficial inferior epigastric vein
SIFE	serum immunofixation electrophoresis
SIFO	small intestinal fungal overgrowth
SIG	sigmoidoscopy
	significant
	Standards Interpretation Group (The Joint Commission)
Sig	patient's directions to appear on medication label (Latin for, let it be marked)
SIGECAPS	Sleep changes, Interest (loss), Guilt (worthlessness), Energy (lack), Concentration (difficulty), Appetite (weight loss) Psychomotor (anxiety or lethargic), Suicidal (death pre-occupation); (SIG-E-CAPS, a mnemonic for depression indicators)

sigM	ribonucleic acid polymerase ECF (extracytoplasmic function)-type sigma factor [sigma(M)]) gene
sIgM	surface immunoglobulin M
SIGN	Scottish Intercollegiate Guidelines Network
signal 12	12-lead electrocardiograms
Signal 99	patient in cardiac or respiratory distress
SIH	spontaneous intracranial hypotension
SIHD	stable ischemic heart disease
SI/HI	suicidal ideation/homicidal ideation
SII	self-inflicted injury
	Social Insurance Institution of Finland
	Speech Intelligibility Index
SIJ	sacroiliac joint
SIJD	sacroiliac joint dysfunction
SIJF	sacroiliac joint fusion
SI joint	sacroiliac joint
SIJS	sacroiliac joint syndrome
SIL	seriously ill list
	sister-in-law
	son-in-law
	squamous intraepithelial lesion
SILC	single-incision laparoscopic cholecystectomy
	Stroke Interventional Laboratory Consensus (Society of Vascular and Interventional Neurology)
SILFVD	sterile indicated low forceps vaginal delivery
SILS	single-incision laparoscopic surgery
SILT	sensation intact to light touch
SILV	simultaneous independent lung ventilation
SIM	selective ion monitoring
	Similac®
	simulation
	structured illumination microscopy
	surface-induced mineralization
Sim c Fe	Similac with iron®
SIMCU	surgical intermediate care unit
SIMD	Scottish Index of Multiple Deprivation
	substance-induced major depression
	substance-induced mood disorder
SIMS	Secondary-ion mass spectroscopy
SIMV	synchronized intermittent mandatory ventilation
SIN	salpingitis isthmica nodose

SINAN	National Information System for Notifiable Diseases (Brazil)	SIRVA	shoulder injury related to vaccine administration
SiNC	silicon nanocrystal	SIS	saline infusion sonohysterography
SiNCs	silicon nanocrystals		segment involvement score
sinus tach	sinus tachycardia		sister
SIOD	Schimke immuno-osseous dysplasia		small intestinal submucosa
			Stroke Impact Scale
SIP	Sickness Impact Profile		subacromial impingement syndrome
	spontaneous intestinal perforation		Surgical Infection Stratification (system)
	stroke in progression		
	subcutaneously implanted ports	SISCOM	subtraction ictal SPECT (single-photon emission computed tomography) coregistered to MRI (magnetic resonance imaging); a diagnostic tool to localize the seizure-onset zone in nonlesional and extratemporal epilepsies
	sympathetically independent pain		
SIPAP	a classification designed for MRI, to characterize pituitary adenomas with emphasis on extrasellar extensions and impact on adjacent structures		
SiPAP™	a continuous positive airway pressure (CPAP) delivery device	SISI	Short Increment Sensitivity Index
		SISS	severe invasion streptococcal syndrome
SIPAT	Stanford Integrated Psychosocial Assessment for Transplantation	SISW	self-inflicted stab wound
		SIT	self-instructional training
SIPC	settlement-inducing protein complex		serum inhibitory titers
			silicon-intensified target
sipC	pathogenicity island 1 effector protein; see gene website www.ncbi.nlm.nih.gov/gene		Slossen Intelligence Test
			specific immunotherapy (allergy)
			sperm immobilization test
SIPD	substance-induced psychotic disorder		structured interrupted therapy
			supraspinatus, infraspinatus, teres (insertions)
SIPE	superimposed preeclampsia		surgical intensive therapy
SI-PEC	superimposed preeclampsia	SITA	standard infertility treatment algorithm
SIPES	single-incision pediatric endosurgery		Swedish Interactive Thresholding Algorithm
SiPM	silicon photomultiplier		
SIPS	Structured Interview for Prodromal Syndromes (Symptoms)	SITA-SAP	Swedish Interactive Threshold Algorithm-standard automated perimetry
SIQ	sick in quarters		
SIQ-JR	Suicidal Ideation Questionnaire-Junior	SIT BAL	sitting balance
		SITS	single-incision thoracoscopic surgery
SIR	standardized incidence rate (ratio)		
SIRAS	Rapid Influenza Testing in Ambulatory Settings	SITS-ISTR	Safe Implementation of Thrombolysis in Stroke-International Stroke Thrombolysis Register
SIRF	severely impaired renal function		
SIRFA	standard information reporting form for ambulance	SITS-MOST	Safe Implementation of Thrombolysis in Stroke-Monitoring Study
SIRGE	A drug-waste collection and recycling system used in the European Union		
		SIT TOL	sitting tolerance
		Situ	position or site, as in "in situ"
siRNA	small interfering ribonucleic acid	SIUP	single intrauterine pregnancy
SIRPIDs	stimulus-induced rhythmic, periodic, or ictal discharges	SIV	self-inflicted violence
			simian immunodeficiency virus
SIRS	solvent infrared spectroscopy	SIVB	self-inflected violent behavior
	systemic inflammatory response syndrome	SIVD	subcortical ischemic vascular dementia (disease)
SIRT	selective internal radiation therapy	SIVP	slow intravenous push

SIW	self-inflicted wound	Skid Row	an impoverished area, typically
	slow-intermittent-walking		urban, inhabited by the poor,
SIWA	sit-to-walk (movement pattern)		the homeless, or others
SJ	surgical jejunostomy		considered disreputable or
SJC	swollen joint count		forgotten by society.
SJCRH	St. Jude Children's Research	SKINT	skinfold thickness
	Hospital (preferred	SKIP	Shal K(potassium)-channel inter-
	abbreviation "St. Jude")		acting protein; see gene website
SJHST	Shu-Jing-Hwo-Shiee-Tang		www.ncbi.nlm.nih.gov/gene
	(a Chinese herbal formula	skn-1	protein skinhead-1 (gene)
	used for osteoarthritis)	SKP	scanning Kelvin probe
sJIA	systemic juvenile idiopathic		(microscopy)
	arthritis	skp	periplasmic chaperone; see gene
SJM	St. Jude Medical (heart valve		website www.ncbi.nlm.nih
	prosthesis)		.gov/gene
SJP	solitary juvenile polyps	SKPM	scanning Kelvin probe
S-JRA	systemic juvenile rheumatoid		microscopy
	arthritis	SKPT	simultaneous kidney-pancreas
SJS	Schwartz-Jampel syndrome		transplantation
	Stevens-Johnson syndrome	SKRBT	Saiko-ka-ryukotsu-borei-To
	Swyer-James syndrome		(Japanese herbal medicine)
SJS/TEN	Stevens-Johnson syndrome	SKS	simultaneous kissing stents
	and toxic epidermal	SKs	seborrheic keratoses
	necrolysis (severe cutaneous	Sks	skeletal fusions with sterility;
	adverse reactions)		see gene website www.ncbi
SJT	SAM (SAM is the name of		.nlm.nih.gov/gene
	the company) junctional	SK-SD	streptokinase streptodornase
	tourniquet	SKTC	single-knee to chest (stretch)
S$_{jvO2}$	jugular venous oxygen saturation	SKU	stock keeping unit (related to
SJW	St. John's wort		product identification)
SK	Scheuermann kyphosis	SKY	spectral karyotyping
	seborrheic keratosis	SL	saline lock (intravenous catheter
	senile keratosis		that is threaded into a peripheral
	solar keratosis		vein, flushed with 0.9% sodium
	streptokinase		chloride injection)
S & K	single and keeping (baby)		scapholunate
SKAO	supracondylar knee-ankle orthosis		secondary leukemia
SKAs	skills, knowledge, and		sensation level
	abilities (ratings)		sentinel lymphadenectomy
SKB	SmithKline Beecham		serious list
SKC	single knee to chest		shortleg
SKD	severe keratinocyte dysplasia		side-lying
SkD	skeletal dysplasias		single-leg
skd	skuld; see gene website www		slight
	ncbi.nlm.nih.gov/gene		staging laparoscopy
SKE	sitting knee extension		sublingual
SKE-BKE	signal-known-exactly,	S-L	Silberstein and Lipton
	background-known-exactly		(headache-related criteria)
	(radiology)	S/L	see SL
SKID I	Structured Clinical Interview		slit lamp (examination)
	for DSM-IV (Strukturierte		speech/language
	Klinische Interview for	SLA	sacrolaeva anterior
	DSM-IV)		sex and love addictions
SKID II	Structured Clinical Interview for		slide latex agglutination
	DSM-IV Axis II Personality		The Satisfaction with Life Areas
	Disorders (Strukturierte	SLAA	Sex and Love Addicts
	Klinische Interview for		Anonymous
	DSM-IV)	SLAC	scapholunate advanced collapse

S

SLADH	may have meant SIADH (syndrome of inappropriate antidiuretic hormone hypersecretion)	SLE-ITP	systemic lupus erythematosus-associated immune thrombo-cytopenia purpura
SLAD-R	Selective laryngeal adductor denervation-reinnervation (surgery)	SLEP	Shelf Life Extension Program
		SLEV	St. Louis encephalitis virus
		SLEX	slit-lamp examination (biomicroscopy)
SLAM	Systemic Lupus Activity Measure	SLex	sialyl Lewis x (antigen)
SLAMF7	SLAM (signaling lymphocyte activation molecule) family member 7 (gene/protein)	SLFVD	sterile low forceps vaginal delivery
		SLGXT	symptom-limited graded exercise test
SLAM-R	SLE (systemic lupus erythematosus) Activity Measure, revised	SLH	sclerosing lobular hyperplasia single-leg hop
		SLHs	sober living houses
SLAP	serum leucine amino-peptidase superior labral anteroposterior (shoulder lesion)	SLI	severe limb ischemia specific language impairment
		SLIC	Sub axial Cervical (Spine) Injury Classification
Slat	time to onset of sleep	SLIL	scapholunate interosseous ligament
SLATE II	Simplified Algorithm for Treat-ment Eligibility II (an individ-ually randomized evaluation of a clinical algorithm to reliably determine a patient's eligibility for immediate antiretroviral treatment initiation without waiting for laboratory results or additional clinic visits	SLIP TRIAL	Greenwich Lumbar Stenosis SLIP Study: A Multi-center, Ran-domized, Prospective Clinical Trial Comparing Spinal Lami-nectomy to Laminectomy With Instrumented Pedicle Screw Fusion for Lumbar Stenosis With Grade I Spondylolisthesis
SLB	short leg brace surgical lung biopsy	SLIs	specific language impairments
		SLIS	subcutaneous lateral internal sphincterotomy
SLBB	single living baby boy	SLIT	sublingual immunotherapy
SLBG	single living baby girl	SLIUP	single live intrauterine pregnancy
SLC	short leg cast symptomatic lymphocele	SLIV	Stem-Loop IV
SLCC	short leg cylinder cast	SLJ	Sinding-Larsen-Johansson (disease) standing long jump
SLCG	sulfolithocholyglycine		
SLCT	Sertoli-Leydig cell tumor	SLK	superior limbic keratoconjunctivitis
SLD	scapholunate dissociation seizure-line discharges semantic linked data specific language disorder stealth liposomal doxorubicin straight-line distance sum of longest diameters	SLKT	simultaneous liver-kidney transplant
		SLL	second-look laparotomy small lymphocytic lymphoma
		SLL/CLL	small lymphocytic lymphoma/chronic lymphocytic leukemia
SLDD	skipped-level disk degeneration	SLLT	Semantic List Learning Task) cued recall with semantic cues and recognition memory are assessed; internal reliability, convergent, and discriminant validity are evaluated)
SLDs	second-line drugs (anti-tuberculosis)		
SLE	slit-lamp examination speech language evaluation St. Louis encephalitis subjective life expectancy systemic lupus erythematosus		
		SLMFVD	sterile low midforceps vaginal delivery
SLeA	sialyl Lewis a (antigen)	SLMMS	slightly more marked since
SLED	sustained low-efficiency dialysis	SLMP	since last menstrual period
SLEDAI	Systemic Lupus Erythematosus Disease Activity Index	SLN	sentinel lymph node(s) superior laryngeal nerve
SLEDD	sustained low-efficiency daily dialysis	SLNB	sentinel lymph node biopsy

SLNBx	sentinel lymph node biopsy	SLUD	salivation, lacrimation, urination, and defecation
SLND	sentinel lymph node detection		
SL NG	sublingual nitroglycerin	SLUDGE	salivation, lacrimation, urination,
SLNM	sentinel lymph node mapping		diarrhea, gastrointestinal
SLNP	superior laryngeal nerve paresis		upset, and emesis (signs and
SLNTG	sublingual nitroglycerin		symptoms of cholinergic
SL NTG	sublingual nitroglycerin		excess)
SLNWBC	short leg nonweight-bearing cast	SLUMS	Saint Louis University Mental
SLNWC	short leg nonwalking cast		Status (a 30-point screening
SLO	scanning laser ophthalmoscope		questionnaire for cognitive
	(ophthalmoscopy)		impairment)
	second-look operation	SLV	since last visit
	shark liver oil	SLVD	systolic left ventricular
	Smith-Lemli-Opitz (syndrome)		dysfunction
	streptolysin O	SLWB	severely low birth weight
SLOA	short leave of absence	SLWC	short leg walking cast
Slob	Slowpoke (Slo) channel-binding	SM	sadomasochism
	protein		service mark (such as The Pause
SLOM	serious left otitis media		that Refreshes)
SLONM	sporadic late-onset nemaline		setup margin (for radiotherapy)
	myopathy		skim milk
SLOS	Smith-Lemli-Opitz syndrome		small
slovn	may have meant slow		splenomegaly
SLP	scanning laser polarimeter		sports medicine
	single-limb progression		Stairmaster®
	Speech Language Pathologist		streptomycin
	speech language pathology		syringomyelia
	superficial lamina propria		systolic motion
SLPI	secretory leukocyte protease		systolic murmur
	inhibitor	Sm	samarium
SLPMS	short-leg posterior-molded splint	153Sm	samarium 153
SLR	straight-leg raising	SMA	severe malarial anemia
SLRE	symptomatic localization-related		skilled meal assessment
	epilepsy		smallpox vaccine, not otherwise
SLRS	stereotactic linac radiosurgery		specified
SLRT	straight-leg raising tenderness		smooth muscle actin
	straight-leg raising test		smooth muscle antibody
SLS	second-look sonography		spinal muscular atrophy
	short leg splint		superior mesenteric artery
	shrinking lungs syndrome		supplemental motor area
	single leg stance	SMA 1	spinal muscular atrophy type 1
	single-limb support	SMA 2	spinal muscular atrophy type 2
SLT	sacrolaeva transversa	SMA 3	spinal muscular atrophy type 3
	scanning laser tomography	SMA7	laboratory test panel for sodium,
	selective laser trabeculoplasty		potassium, bicarbonate or
	single lung transplantation		carbon dioxide, blood urea,
	smokeless tobacco		nitrogen, creatinine, and
	speech and language therapy		glucose
	Speech Language Therapist	Sm ab	Smith antigen antibodies
	spontaneous labor at term	SMAC	second mitochondria -derived
	swing light test		activator of caspases
SLTA	severe life-threatening asthma		sequential multiple analyzer
	standard language test for aphasia		and computer
SLTEC	Shiga-like toxin-producing	Smad	proteins homologs of mothers
	Escherichia coli		against decapentaplegic gene
SLT-I	Shiga-like toxin I	SMAD3	SMAD family member 3
sl. tr.	slight trace		gene (mothers against
SLTx	single-lung transplantation		decapentaplegic homolog 3)

S

SMAE	spontaneous movement in all extremities	
SMA-II	spinal muscular atrophy type II	
SMAO	superior mesenteric artery occlusion	
SMAR	self-medication administration record	
SMART syndrome	stroke-like migraine attacks after radiation therapy (syndrome)	
SMAS	superficial musculoaponeurotic system (graft; flat)	
	superior mesenteric artery syndrome	
	supplemental motor area syndrome	
SMAST	Short Michigan Alcohol-ism Screening Test	
SMA syndrome	superior mesenteric artery syndrome	
SMAT	see me about this (slang)	
	superior mesenteric artery thromboembolism	
	surface mechanical attrition treatment	
SMAvac	smallpox (vaccinia virus) vaccine	
SM AVM	Spetzler-Martin; arteriovenous malformation	
SMB	simulated moving bed (chromatography)	
SMBG	self-monitoring blood glucose	
SMBP	self-measured blood pressure	
SMBT	seated medicine ball throw	
SMC	skeletal myxoid chondrosarcoma	
	special mouth care	
SMCA	sorbitol MacConkey agar	
SMCD	senile macular chorio-retinal degeneration	
SMCP	submucous cleft palate	
SMCs	smooth muscle cells	
SMD	senile macular degeneration	
	sensory modulation disorder	
	sexual masochism disorder	
	standardized mean difference	
SMDA	Safe Medical Defice Act	
SMDK	spondylometaphyseal dysplasia Kozlowski (a type of skeletal dysplasias)	
SME	significant medical event	
	subject-matter expert	
	surgical mediastinal exploration	
SMEDDS	self-microemulsifying drug-delivery system	
SMEI	severe myoclonic epilepsy in infancy	
SMF	streptozocin, mitomycin, and fluorouracil	
SMFA	Selective Functional Movement Assessment	

	Short Musculoskeletal Functional Assessment
	sodium monofluoroacetate
SMFM	Society for Maternal Fetal Medicine
SMFP	sodium monofluorophosphate
SMFR	self-myofascial release
SMFT	surgical margins free of tumor
SMFVD	sterile midforceps vaginal delivery
SMG	submachine gun
	submandibular gland
SMH	state mental hospital
SMI	sensory motor integration (group)
	serious mental illness
	service mix index
	severely mentally impaired
	small volume infusion
	suggested minimum increment
	sustained maximal inspiration
SMID	severe motor and intellectual disabilities
SMIDS	suppertime mixed insulin and daytime sulfonylureas
SMILE	safety, monitoring, intervention, length of stay and evaluation
	Small Incision Lenticule Extraction
	submucosal minimally invasive lingual excision
	sustained maximal inspiratory lung exercises
s-MIPI	simplified MCL (mantle cell lymphoma) International Prognostic Index
SMIs	self-management interventions
SMIT	standard mycological identification techniques
SMK1	see gene website, www .genenames.org
SMK	smoker
	suppurative microbial keratitis
SML	surface microlayer
SMLM	single-molecule localization microscopy
SMM	smoldering multiple myeloma
sMMVT	sustained monomorphic ventricular tachycardia
SMN	second malignant neoplasia
	survival of motor neuron; see gene website; www.ncbi .nlm.nih.gov/gene
SMN1	survival of motor neuron 1; see gene website www.ncbi .nlm.nih.gov/gene
SMN2	survival of motor neuron 2, centromeric; see gene website www.ncbi.nlm.nih.gov/gene

SMO	Senior Medical Officer		standard medical therapy
	site management organization(s)		study management team
	slip made out	SMU	safe medicine use
	supramalleolar orthosis (orthotic)		seizure monitoring unit
SMOF	Soy oil, MCT (mid-chain triglycerides), Olive oil, and Fish oil (lipid emulsion)	smu	see gene website www.ncbi.nlm .nih.gov/gene
SMOG	saline (0.9% sodium chloride solution), mineral oil, and glycerin enema)	SMV	simeprevir (Olysio) stentless mitral valve submentovertical superior mesenteric vein
	Simple Measure of Gobbledygook (score; a readability measure of patient information)	SMVT	superior mesenteric vein thrombosis sustained monomorphic ventricular tachycardia
SMON	subacute myelo-opticoneuropathy		
SMOP	Saint Marys Outpatient Clinic	SMX-TMP	sulfamethoxazole and
SMORs	standardized mortality odds ratios		trimethoprim (SMZ-TMP)
SMP	safety management plan	SMZBCL	splenic marginal zone B-cell
	safety monitoring plan		lymphoma
	self-management program	SMZL	splenic marginal-zone
	sympathetically maintained pain		lymphoma
SmPC	Summary of Product Character-	SMZ/TMP	sulfamethoxazole and
	istics (European Union)		trimethoprim (also SMX-TMP)
SMPN	sensorimotor polyneuropathy	SMZ-TMP	sulfamethoxazole and
SMQs	Standardized MedDRA (Medical		trimethoprim (also SMX-TMP)
	Dictionary for Regulatory	SN	scapular notching
	Activities) Queries		sciatic notch
SMR	self-myofascial release		see note
	senior medical resident		serial number
	skeletal muscle relaxant		silver nitrate
	sleeping metabolic rate		sinus node
	standardized mortality ratio		skilled nurse
	submucous resection		staff nurse
SMRC	Supplemental Medical		student nurse
	Review/Contractor		superior nasal
sMRI	structural magnetic resonance		suprasternal notch
	imaging	Sn	tin
SMRR	submucous resection and	S/N	signal to noise ratio
	rhinoplasty	SNA	specimen not available
SMRs	standardized mortality ratios		Student Nursing Assistant
SMRT	silencing mediator of retinoid and		sympathetic nerve activity
	thyroid (hormone receptors)	SNa	serum sodium
SMRT-CO	Systolic blood pressure, Multilobar infiltrates, Respiration rate, Tachycardia, Confusion, Oxygen (prognostic scores for influenza pneumonia patients)	SNA angle	an angle measuring the antero-posterior relationship of the maxillary basal arch on the an-terior cranial base (dentistry; oral maxillofacial surgery)
		SNAC	scaphoid nonunion advanced collapse
SMS	scalded mouth syndrome	SNAE	Sustained pain-free and No
	senior medical student		Adverse Events
	Smith-Magenis syndrome	Snafu	situation normal, all fouled up
	somatostatin (Zecnil)		(slang; polite form)
	stiff-man syndrome	SNAGs	sustained natural apophyseal
SMSA	standard metropolitan statistical		glides
	area	SNAP	scheduled nursing activities
SMSF	Scale for Mood and Sense of		program
	Fatigue (score)		Score for Neonatal Acute
SMT	smooth muscle tumors		Physiology
	sputum methylation testing		

	sensory nerve action potential	SNFM	subfoveal neovascular membranes
	Supplemental Nutrition Assistance Program (US Dept of Agriculture-Food Stamps program)	SNF/MR	skilled nursing facility for the mentally retarded
	Swanson, Nolan, and Pelham (rating scale)	SNGFR	single nephron glomerular filtration rate
SNAP-25	synaptosome-associated protein 25 kDa	SNGP	supranuclear gaze palsy
		SNHL	sensorineural hearing loss
SNAP-PE	Score for Neonatal Acute Physiology-Perinatal Extension	SNIB	saphenous nerve infrapatellar branches
SNAPs	sensory nerve action potentials		Section of Neuroendocrine Immunology and Behaviour (National Institute of Mental Health)
SNAQ	Short Nutritional Assessment Questionnaire		
	Simplified Nutritional Appetite Questionnaire	SNID	sinonasal inflammatory disease
SnaQ	Snake Anxiety Questionnaire	Sniff Test	a fluoroscopic examination used to check how the diaphragm moves during activities such as breathing normally and inhaling rapidly
SNARC	Spatial-Numerical Association of Response Codes		
SNaRI	serotonin noradrenergic reuptake inhibitor	SNIF NMR	site-specific natural isotope fractionation studied by nuclear magnetic resonance
SNASA	Salford Needs Assessment Schedule for Adolescents		
SNAT	suspected nonaccidental trauma	SNIIRAM	French national healthcare system database (système national d'information interrégimes de l'Assurance Maladie)
SNB	scalene node biopsy sciatic nerve block sentinel (lymph) node biopsy splanchnic nerve blockade	SNIP	silver nitrate immunoperoxidase strict no information in paper
SNB angle	an angle showing the anterior limit of the mandibular basal arch in relation to the anterior cranial base (dentistry; oral maxillofacial surgery)	SNIPPV	synchronized nasal intermittent positive-pressure ventilation
		SNIPS	single nucleotide polymorphism (SNP)
		SNK	Student-Newman-Keuls (test)
SNBx	sentinel node biopsy	SNL	spinal nerve ligation
SNC	skilled nursing care	SNLB	may have meant SLNB (sentinel lymph node biopsy)
SNc	substantia nigra compacta		
SNCA	synuclein alpha (gene/protein [a presynaptic protein that is associated with the pathophysiology of synucleinopathies, including Parkinson disease])	SNM	sacral neuromodulation sentinel (lymph) node mapping serotoninergic neuroenteric modulators student nurse midwife
SNCV	sensory nerve conduction velocity	SNMMI	Society of Nuclear Medicine and Molecular Imaging
SND	selective neck dissection single needle device sinus node dysfunction striatonigral degeneration sympathetic nerve discharge	SnMp	tin-mesoporphyrin
		SNMT	sinonasal malignant tumor
		SNN	sensory neuronopathy spiking neural network stannin; see gene website www.ncbi.nlm.nih.gov/gene
SNDA	Supplemental New Drug Application		
SNE	subacute necrotizing encephalomyelopathy	SNOMED	Systematized Nomenclature of Medicine
SNEP	student nurse extern program	SNOMED CT	Systematized Nomenclature of Medicine Clinical Terms
SnET2	tin ethyl etiopurpurin	SNOMED RT	Systematized Nomenclature of Medicine Reference Terminology
SNF	Simon nitinol filter skilled nursing facility		
SnF$_2$	stannous fluoride	SNOOP	Systematic Nursing Observation of Psychopathology
SNFABN	Skilled Nursing Facility Advance Beneficiary Notice		

SNOs	S-nitrosothiols		significant other
SNOT-20	Sino-Nasal Outcome Test, 20-item		silicone oil
SNOT-22	Sino-Nasal Outcome Test, 22-item		special observation
SNP	simple neonatal procedure		sphincter of Oddi
	single nucleotide polymorphism		standing orders
	sodium nitroprusside		suboccipital
SNPD	stereotactic neurosurgery for		suggestive of
	psychiatric disorders		superior oblique
SNP-LP	single nucleotide		supraoptic
	polymorphisms –		supraorbital
	linkage disequilibrium		sutures out
SNPs	single nucleotide		sympathetic ophthalmia
	polymorphisms	SO_2	sulfur dioxide
SN-PSG	split-night polysomnograms	SO_3	sulfite
SNR	signal-to-noise ratio	SO_4	sulfate
SNr	substantia nigra reticularis	S&O	salpingo-oophorectomy
SNRB	selective nerve root block	S-O	salpingo-oophorectomy
SNRI	selective noradrenergic reuptake	S/O	see SO
	inhibitor		suggestive of
	serotonin norepinephrine	SOA	serum opsonic activity
	reuptake inhibitor		shortness of air
SNRT	sinus node recovery time		spinal opioid analgesia
SNRv	signal-to-noise ratio velocity		stimulus onset asynchrony
SNS	sacral nerve stimulation		supraorbital artery
	social networking site(s)		swelling of ankles
	specialized nutrition support	SOAA	signed out against advice
	sterile normal saline (0.9% sodium	SOAM	sutures out in the morning
	chloride, sterile)	SOAMA	signed out against medical advice
	Strategic National Stockpile	SOAP	subjective, objective, assessment,
	Supplemental Nursing System		and plans
	(for nursing mothers)	SOAPIE	subjective, objective, assessment,
	Swiss Narcolepsy Scale		plan, implementation, (inter-
	sympathetic nervous system		vention), and evaluation
SNs	Schmorl nodes	SOAPIER	subjective, objective, assessment,
SNSA	sympathetic nervous system		plan, intervention, evaluation,
	activity		and revision
SNSs	social networking sites	SOAPP®-R	Screener and Opioid
SNT	sinuses, nose, and throat		Assessment for Patients
	soft, non-tender		with Pain-Revised
	suppan nail technique	SOAR	SSI/SSDI (Supplemental Security
SNTND	soft, nontender, nondistended		Income/Social Security Dis-
S/NT/ND	soft, nontender, nondistended		ability Insurance) Outreach,
SNU	skilled nursing unit		Access and Recovery
SNUC	sinonasal undifferentiated	SOAS	South Asia
	carcinoma	SOAs	semiconductor optical amplifiers
SNV	Sin Nombre virus		stimulus onset asynchronies
	skilled nursing visit	SOAT	Standardized Orthopedic
	spleen necrosis virus		Assessment Tool
SNVs	single-nucleotide variants	SOAT1	sterol O-acyltransferase 1;
SNX	see gene website, www.ncbi.nlm		see gene website www.ncbi
	.nih.gov/gene		.nlm.nih.gov/gene
	sorting nexin(s)	SOB	see order book
	subtotal nephrectomy (rats)		shortness of breath (this abbre-
	suction		viation has caused problems)
SO	second opinion		side of bed
	Service Officer	SOBAR	short of breath at rest
	sex offender	SOBE	short of breath on exertion
	shoulder orthosis	SOBOE	short of breath on exertion

SOBT	salivary occult blood test	SOGI	sexual orientation and gender identity
	stool occult blood test	SOGS	South Oaks Gambling Screen
SOC	see old chart	SOH	sexually oriented hallucinations
	sense of control	SOH	state of health
	slouch overcorrect (exercise)	SOHND	supraomohyoid neck dissection
	socialization	SoHx	social history
	standard of care	SOI	signs of infection
	start of care		slipped on ice
	state of consciousness		sudden overwhelming infection
	Statement of Conditions (The Joint Commission)		surgical orthotopic implantation (implant)
	states of change		syrup of ipecac
	suboccipital craniectomy	SOIV	swine-origin influenza A virus
	synovial osteochondromatosis		(also known as H1N1)
	system organ class	S-OIV	swine-origin influenza A virus
S & OC	signed and on chart (e.g. permit)		(also known as H1N1)
SOCC	sexual offender civil commitment	SOL	sleep onset latency
SocHx	social history		solution
SOCMOB	standing on corner minding own business (when inexplicably injured) (slang)		space occupying lesion
		SOL I	special observations level one (there are also SOL II and SOL III)
SOCS2	suppressor of cytokine signaling 2 (gene/protein)	soln	solution
SOCs	System Organ Classes	SOLT	single orthotopic lung transplantation
SOD	septo-optic dysplasia (de Morsier syndrome)	SOM	secretory otitis media
	sinovenous occlusive disease		serous otitis media
	sphincter of Oddi dysfunction		somatization
	superoxide dismutase		sphincter of Oddi manometry
	surgical officer of the day	SOMA	self-orienting millimeter-scale applicator (an ingestible self-orienting system for oral delivery of macromolecules)
SOD1	superoxide dismutase 1, soluble (gene)		
SODA	Severity of Dyspepsia Assessment	SOMI	sterno-occipital mandibular immobilizer
SODAS	spheriodal oral drug absorption system	SONICC	second-order nonlinear (optical) imaging of chiral crystals
sodium bicarb	sodium bicarbonate	SONK	spontaneous osteonecrosis of the knee
SOE	source of embolism		
	symptomatic occipital epilepsy	Sono	sonogram
SoE	strength of evidence	sonohyst	sonohysterography
SOF	sofosbuvir (Sovaldi)	SONP	solid organs not palpable
	Special Operations Forces	SOO	site of origin
	synthetic oviductal fluid (culture media)	SOOB	sit out of bed
		SOOC	skin-orbicularis oculi complex
SoF	summary of findings	SOOF	standing-on-one-foot
SOFA	sepsis-related organ failure assessment		suborbicularis oculi fat
		SOOL	spontaneous onset of labor
	Sequential Organ Failure Assessment (score)	SOP	standard operating procedure
		SOPA	Survey of Pain Attitudes
SOFAS	Social and Occupational Functioning Assessment Scale	sopA	secreted effector protein; see gene website; www.ncbi .nlm.nih.gov/gene
SOF-BE1	synthetic oviductal fluid-bovine embryo 1 (culture media)		
SOF CPRE	French Society of Plastic Reconstructive and Aesthetic Surgery	SopD	secreted protein in the Sop family; transferred to eukaryotic cells (Salmonella outer protein D) (gene/protein)
SOG	suggestive of good		
	superior occipital gyrus		

SOPM	sutures out in afternoon (or evening)
sOPN	secreted osteopontin
SOR	sensory overresponsivity
	sign own release
	strength of recommendation
	sub-occipital release
SORA	stable on room air
SOREM	sleep-onset rapid eye movement
SORL1	sortilin-related receptor 1 (gene)
SORL	spiral oblique retinacular ligament
SORO-ESRD	syndrome of rapid-onset end-stage renal disease
SORT	surgical operating room time
SOS	if there is need
	may be repeated once if urgently required (Latin: si opus sit)
	sacrament of the sick
	self-obtained smear
	Signs of Suicide (prevention program)
	sinusoidal obstruction syndrome
	speed of sound
	sudden onset of sleep
	suicidal observation status
SOSOB	sit on side of bed
SOSs	standardized order sets
Sost	sclerotin
SOT	Sensory Organization Test
	solid organ transplant
	something other than
	stream of thought
SOTP	Sex Offender Treatment Provider
	solid organ transplanted patients
SOU	sense of urgency
SOV	signs of vitality
SOVs	self-obtained vaginal swabs
SOW	Scope of Work
SOX2	SRY (sex determining region Y)-box 2; see gene website www.ncbi.nlm.nih.gov/gene
SOX9	see gene website www.ncbi.nlm.nih.gov/gene; one of the main genetic factors of mammalian sex determination
SOZ	seizure onset zone
SOZT	superior oblique Z-tenotomy
SP	sacrum to pubis
	sequential pulse
	serum protein
	shoulder press
	silent period (related to electromyographic responses)
	spastic dysphonia
	speech
	Speech Pathologist
	spinal

	spinous process
	spouse
	stand and pivot
	stand pivot
	standard procedure
	standardized procedures
	status post
	sternal precautions
	Streptococcus pneumoniae
	sulfadoxine-pyrimethamine (Fansidar)
	supplementary prescribing
	suprapubic catheter
	systolic pressure
sp	species
S1P	site-1 protease; see gene website www.ncbi.nlm.nih.gov/gene
	stage 1 palliations
S2P	site-2 protease; see gene website www.ncbi.nlm.nih.gov/gene
	stage 2 palliations
SP02	see SPO2
SP 1	suicide precautions number 1
SP 2	suicide precautions number 2
S&P	Standard & Poor's Financial Services
S/P	see SP
	status post
	suprapubic
SPA	albumin human (formerly known as salt-poor albumin)
	scintillation proximity assay
	serum prothrombin activity
	sheep pulmonary adenomatosis
	single photon absorptiometry
	single port access (laparoscopic surgery)
	special protocol assessment
	Speech Pathology and Audiology
	spontaneous platelet aggregation
	stimulation produced analgesia
	student physicians assistant
	subperiosteal abscess
	suprapubic aspiration
SpA	spondylarthritis
	spondyloarthritis
SP-A	surfactant-specific protein A
SPAC	satisfactory postanesthesia course
SPAD	single-photon avalanche diode
SPADI	Shoulder Pain and Disability Index
SPAG	small-particle aerosol generator
SPAMM	spatial modulation of magnetization
SPAP	State Pharmacy Assistance Program
SPAR	spine-associated Rap GTPase activating protein

S

SPARCC	Spondyloarthritis Research Consortium of Canada (index)
SPB	solitary plasmacytoma of bone
	spindle pole body (bodies)
	spontaneous preterm birth
	Streptococcus pneumoniae bacteremia
SPBD	spontaneous perforation of the bile duct
SPBE	saw palmetto berry extract
SPBI	serum protein bound iodine
SPBT	suprapubic bladder tap
SPBx	saturation prostate biopsy
SPC	saturated phosphatidylcholine
	sclerosing pancreatocholangitis
	single-point cane
	statistical process control
	Summary of Product Characteristics
	suprapubic catheter
SPCA	serum prothrombin conversion accelerator (factor VII)
	short posterior ciliary artery
SP cath	suprapubic catheter
SPCM	scanning photocurrent microscopy
	Seated Postural Control Measure
	severe protein-calorie malnutrition
	spectinomycin
	superior pharyngeal constrictor muscle
SPCT	simultaneous prism and cover test
SPCU	Specialist Palliative Care Inpatient Unit
	specialist palliative care unit
	surgical progressive care unit
SPD	schizotypal personality disorder
	Sterile Processing Distribution
	subcorneal pustular dermatosis
	Supply, Processing, and Distribution (department)
	suprapubic drainage
SP-D	surfactant protein D
SPDA	superior pancreaticoduodenal artery
	symptomatic patent ductus arteriosus
SPDP	spleen-preserving distal pancreatectomy
SPDs	sexual pain disorders
SPE	saw palmetto extract
	septic pulmonary embolism
	serum protein electrophoresis
	Skill Performance Evaluation program of the Federal Motor Carrier Safety Administration
	solid-phase extraction

	stomach preserving esophagectomy
	superficial punctate erosions
	superimposed preeclampsia
sPE	severe preeclampsia
SPEB	streptococcal pyrogenic exotoxins B
SPEC	streptococcal pyrogenic exotoxins C
	specimen
sPEC	severe preeclampsia
spec	specimen
Spec Ed	special education
spec grav	specific gravity
SPECT	single-photon emission computed tomography
SPECT/CT	single-photon emission computed tomography/computed tomography
SPED	serous pigment epithelium detachment
speD	S-adenosylmethionine decarboxylase; see gene website www.ncbi.nlm.nih.gov/gene
speed	methamphetamine (slang)
SPEED2	Standard Patient Evaluation of Eye Dryness 2
SPEEP	spontaneous positive end-expiratory pressure
SPEN	spatiotemporally encoded (radiology)
SPEP	serum protein electrophoresis
SPET	single-photon emission tomography
SPF	semipermeable film
	S-phase fraction
	split products of fibrin
	sun protective factor
sp fl	spinal fluid
SPG	scrotopenogram
	sphenopalatine ganglion
SpG	specific gravity
SPGES	solid-phase gastric emptying studies
SPGEs	screen-printed gold electrodes
SPGR	spoiled gradient recalled echo
SP GR	specific gravity
SPGT	see SGPT, serum glutamate-pyruvate transaminase
SPH	severely and profoundly handicapped
	sighs per hour
	sphere (ophthalmology)
	spherocytes
SpHb™ monitoring	multi-wavelength spectrophotometric method for noninvasive and continuous hemoglobin monitoring

SPHERO	spherocytes	sPMA	supplemental premarket approval application (FDA)
SPHM	Safe Patient Handling and Movement	SPMD	scapuloperoneal muscular dystrophy
SPHPS	Smarter Public Health Prevention System (provides real-time reporting of public health threats to public health leaders)	SPMDs	semipermiable membrane devices
		SPME	solid-phase microextraction
		SPMI	severely and persistently mentally ill
SPI	speech processor interface surgical peripheral iridectomy	SPMS	secondary progressing multiple sclerosis
SPIA	solid phase immunoabsor-bent assay	SPMs	second primary malignancies
		SPMSD	Sanofi-Pasteur Merck Sharp & Dohme (pharmaceutical firm)
Spice	A mixture containing the psychoactive drug methylenedioxypyrovalerone (MDPV)	SPMSQ	Short Portable Mental Status Questionnaire
		SPN	solitary pulmonary nodule student practical nurse superficial peroneal nerve
SPID	sum of pain intensity difference		
SPIDER	steady-state projection imaging with dynamic echotrain readout	SPn	*Streptococcus pneumoniae*
		S pneumoniae	Streptococcus pneumoniae
		SPNK	single parent not keeping (baby)
SPIDER®	single port instrument delivery extended reach (surgical system)	SPNP	solid pseudopapillary neoplasm of the pancreas
SPIE	significant postradiosurgery injury expression	SPO	status postoperative superior posterior oblique
SPIF	spontaneous peak inspiratory force	SpO2	oxygen saturation by pulse oximeter
SPIFE	serum protein and immunofixation electrophoresis (system)	spondylo	a word denoting a relationship to a vertebra
SPIM	selective plane illumination microscopy	SPONK	spontaneous osteonecrosis of the knee
S-PIN	Steinmann pin	spont	spontaneous
SPINK1	serine protease inhibitor Kazal type 1	SponVe	spontaneous ventilation
		SPOREs	Specialized Programs of Research Excellence (National Cancer Institute)
SPIO	superparamagnetic iron oxide		
SPJ	Structured Professional Judgement	SPP	Sexuality Preference Profile single presentation phenotype skin perfusion pressure species (specus) super packed platelets suprapubic prostatectomy
SPK	simultaneous pancreas-kidney (transplant) single parent keeping (baby) superficial punctate keratitis	
SPKT	simultaneous pancreas-kidney transplantation	Sp Path	Speech Pathology
SPL	sound pressure level superior parietal lobule	SPPB	Short Physical Performance Battery
SPL®	Staphylococcal Phage Lysate	SPPI	Standardized Polyvalent Psychiatric Interview
SPLATTT	split anterior tibial tendon transfer	
SPLC	single-port laparoscopic cholecystectomy	SPQ	Schizotypal Personality Questionnaire
SPLK	simultaneus cadaver-pancreas and living-donor kidney transplant	SPR	scan projection radiograph (radiology) Society of Pediatric Radiology surface plasmon resonance symptomatic pelvic relaxation
SPM	scanning probe microscopy second primary malignancy spontaneous pneumomediastinum	
		SPRAS	Sheehan Patient Rated Anxiety Scale
SPM96	statistical parametric mapping 96	SPRi	Surface Plasmon Resonance Imaging
SPMA	spinal progressive muscle atrophy	

561

SP-RIA	solid-phase radioimmunoassay	SPUS	surgeon-performed ultrasound
SPRINT	Systolic Blood Pressure Intervention Trial	SPV	slow-phase velocity superior petrosal vein systolic pressure variation
SPR-MS	surface plasmon resonance mass spectrometry	SPVC	Shelhigh procine pulmonic value conduits
SPRN	shadow of prion protein (gene)	SPVR	systemic peripheral vascular resistance
SPROM	spontaneous premature rupture of membrane	SPX	smallpox vaccine, not otherwise specified
SPRT	sequential probability ratio test	SPx	spontaneous pneumothorax
SPS	shoulder pain and stiffness	SPX$_v$	smallpox vaccine (vaccinia virus)
	simple partial seizure	SPY	*Streptococcus pyogenes*
	Social Phobia Scale		sulfapyridine
	sodium polyethanol sulfonate	SPY Elite™	intraoperative microsurgery
	sodium polystyrene sulfonate (Kayexalate; SPS®)		tissue perfusion mapping with laser-assisted indocyanine
	status post surgery		green imaging
	Stiff-Person Syndrome	SQ	sleep quality
	systemic progressive sclerosis		status quo
SPSA	simultaneous perturbation stochastic approximation	sq	subcutaneous (This is a DANGEROUS abbreviation
sPSA	serum prostate-specific antigen		that should NOT be used.
SPSP	short-term psychodynamic		It appears on the medabbrev
	supportive psychotherapy		.com and other Do Not Use
	Society for Progressive Supranuclear Palsy		Lists, as the q has been read as every; use subcut or spell
	spectral-spatial (pulses)		out subcutaneous)
SPSS	various statistics and related		square
	software programs (originally,	s/q	a ratio of the incidence frequency
	Statistical Package for the		among first-degree relatives
	Social Sciences)		(e.g. siblings) to the incident
SPSU	straight partial sit-up		frequency among general
SPT	second primary tumors		population
	skin prick test	SqCa	squamous cell carcinoma
	standing pivot transfer	SqCC	squamous cell carcinomas
	supportive periodontal therapy	Sq Cca	squamous cell carcinoma
	suprapubic tenderness	Sq cell CA	squamous cell carcinoma
	surgical preparation time (start	sqcm	square centimeters
	surgical preparation to incision)		(929 sq cm = 1 sq foot)
SPTAN1	spectrin alpha, non-erythrocytic 1		square centimeter(s)
	(gene; mutations cause early	SQE	subcutaneous emphysema
	infantile epileptic encephalopa-	SqEP	squamous epithelial cells
	thy type 5, also associated with	SQH	subcutaneous heparin (this is a
	severe West syndrome with		dangerous abbreviation)
	hypomyelination and pontocer-	SQI	Signal Quality Index
	ebellar atrophy)	SQICD	subcutaneous implantable
SP TAP	spinal tap		cardioverter-defibrillator
SPTB	spontaneous preterm birth	SQLS	Schizophrenia Quality of
SPTCL	subcutaneous panniculitis-like		Life Scale
	T-cell lymphoma	SQM	square meter(s)
sPTH	serum parathyroid hormone	sq m	see sqm
SPTL	spontaneous preterm labor	sqPCR	semiquantitative polymerase
	subcutaneous panniculitis-like		chain reaction
	T-cell lymphoma	SQPT	may have meant SGPT (serum
SPTs	second primary tumors		glutamate pyruvate transami-
	single-patient trials		nase ([also known as alanine
SP TUBE	suprapubic tube		aminotransferase- ALT])
SPTX	static pelvic traction		
SPU	short procedure unit		

SQS	subcutaneous nerve stimulation		superior rectal artery
SQT	sequential therapy for the eradication of Helicobacter pylori (H. pylori); 5 days of treatment with esomeprazole and amoxicillin, followed by 5 days of esomeprazole, clarithromycin, and tinidazole		surface replacement arthroplasty
		SRAC	Scarce Resource Allocation Committee
		SRAN	surgical resident admission note
		SRB	Saiko-ka-ryukotsu-borei-To (Japanese herbal medicine)
	short QT (interval)	SRBAs	selective relaxant binding agents
S1Q3T3	a prominent S wave in lead I, a Q wave and inverted T wave in lead III (an electrocardiogram pattern; a sign of acute cor pulmonale [McGinn-White sign])	SRBC	sheep red blood cells
			sickle red blood cells
		SRBD	seizure-related brain damage
			sleep-related breathing disorders
		SRBOW	spontaneous rupture of bag of waters
SQ-T	standardized quality tablet	sRBP	serum retinol binding protein
SQTS	short QT Syndrome	SRBPs	sleep-related breathing problems
squam	squamous	SRBT	Saiko-ka-ryukotsu-borei-To (Japanese herbal medicine)
squames	a word meaning scales or scalelike substances	SRC	scleroderma renal crisis
			sport-related concussion
		src	source
SQUID	superconducting quantum interference device	SRCC	sarcomatoid renal cell carcinoma
SQV	saquinavir (Fortovose; Invirase) Site Qualification Visit	SRCS	Division of Surveillance, Research and Communication Support (FDA)
SR	screen	SRCT	small round cell tumors
	sedimentation rate	SRD	service-related disability
	see report		smallest real difference
	senior resident		sodium-restricted diet
	service record	SRE	sex and relationships education
	side rails		skeletal related event
	sinus rhythm	SREAT	steroid-responsive encephalopathy associated with autoimmune thyroiditis
	sit and reach		
	slow release		
	smooth-rough	SREC	Sharpened Romberg, eyes closed
	social recreation	SREDA	subclinical rhythmic electrographic discharge of adults
	speech recognition		
	standard risks	SREO	Sharpened Romberg, eyes open
	stimulus response	SREs	skeletal related events
	stretch reflex	SRF	somatotropin releasing factor
	superior rectus		subretinal fluid
	suppression ratio	SRFA	slow-releasing factor of anaphylaxis
	sustained release		
	sustained release tablets or capsules (and other forms of extended release)	SR-FTIR	synchrotron radiation Fourier transform infrared (microspectroscopy)
	sustained response	SRGVHD	steroid-resistant graft-versus-host disease
	suture removal		
	system review	SRH	self-rated health
	systemic reaction		sexual and reproductive health
Sr	senior		signs of recent hemorrhage
	strontium		subretinal hemorrhage
89Sr	strontium 89	SR-HVCD	stroma-rich variant of hyaline-vascular type of Castleman's disease
S&R	seclusion and restraint		
	smooth and rough		
S/R	strong/regular (pulse)	SRI	serotonin reuptake inhibitor
SRA	serotonin release assay	SRIB	severe recurrent intestinal bleeding
	steroid-resistant asthma		

SRICU	surgical respiratory intensive care unit	SRS	Silver-Russell syndrome
			somatostatin receptor scintigraphy
SRIF	somatotropin-release inhibiting factor (somatostatin; Zecnil)		stereotactic radiosurgery
SRIS	Self Reflection and Insight Scale	macron s RS	without redness or swelling
SRIs	serotonin reuptake inhibitors (Zoloft, Paxil, Prozac, Lexapro, etc.)	SRS-A	slow-reacting substance of anaphylaxis
		SRSE	super-refractory status epilepticus
SRK	smooth-rod Kaneda (implant)		
SRL	sirolimus (Rapamune)	SRSP	short-range surface plasmon
SRM	spontaneous rupture of membranes (also SROM)	SRSS	screw rack stored screws
			self-reported severity score
SRMD	stress-related mucosal damage	SRSs	speech recognition scores
SRMH	self-rated mental health		spontaneous recurrent seizures
SRMS	sustained-release morphine sulfate		spontaneous reporting systems
			stent-related symptoms
SRMs	specified risk materials		stress-related symptoms
SRNA	Student Registered Nurse Anesthetist	SRSV	small round structured viruses
		SRT	salvage radiotherapy
sRNA	small ribonucleic acids		sedimentation rate test
SR-NE	sinus rhythm, no ectopy		sleep-related tumescence
SRNS	steroid-resistant nephrotic syndrome		speech reception threshold
			speech recognition technology
SRNV	subretinal neovascularization		speech recognition testing
SRNVM	subretinal neovascular membrane		speech recognition threshold
			stereotactic radiotherapy
SRO	sagittal ramus osteotomy		surfactant replacement therapy
	single room occupancy		sustained release theophylline
	smallest region of overlap		swallow reaction time
	Steele-Richardson-Olszewski (syndrome)	SRTR	Scientific Registry of Transplant Recipients
	sustained-release oral	SRU	side rails up
SROA	sports-related osteoarthritis	SRUA	suture removal under Anesthesia
SROCPI	Self-Rating Obsessive-Compulsive Personality Inventory	SRUS	solitary rectal ulcer syndrome
		SRVC	subcutaneous reservoir and ventricular catheter
SROM	self range of motion	srvg	serving (as in serving size)
	serous right otitis media	SR ↑ X2	both siderails up
	spontaneous rupture of membrane	SRx	spectacle refraction
		SRY	see gene website www.ncbi.nlm .nih.gov/gene; one of the main genetic factors of mammalian sex determination
S-ROM®	Sivash-range of motion femoral modular stem prosthesis (DePuy Companies)		
SROS	Steele-Richardson-Olszewski syndrome	SS	sacral slope
			sacral sulcus
SROs	suicide-related outcomes		sacrosciatic
SRP	scaling and root planing (dental)		saline (sodium chloride 0.9%) soak
	septorhinoplasty		saline solution (0.9% sodium chloride)
	short-rib polydactyly		
	somatostatin receptor-positive		saliva sample
	stapes replacement prosthesis		salt sensitivity (sensitive)
SRPH	self-rated physical health		salt substitute
SRQ-20	self-reporting questionnaire fo 20 questions (mental health)		serotonin syndrome
			serum sickness
SRR	surgical recovery room		short stay
SRRIAT	surgical repair with right infra-axillary thoracotomy		sickle cell
SRRS	social readjustment rating scale		signs and symptoms

	single-session (treatment)
	single-strength (as compared
	to double-strength)
	Sjögren syndrome
	skin score
	slip sent
	Social Security
	social service
	social support
	somatostatin (Zecnil)
	Sostre score
	sprain/strain
	stainless steel
	static stretching
	steady state
	step stool
	subaortic stenosis
	summation sound
	suprasciatic (notch)
	susceptible
	Sweet syndrome
	symmetrical strength
	Sézary syndrome
ss	sliding scale or 1/2. This is a **DANGEROUS** abbreviation that should **NOT** be used. It appears on the MedAbbrev and other "Do Not Use Lists," as it has been read as numbers 55 and 1/2. Use "sliding scale" or "1/2."
S⁻¹...⁻⁴	suicide risk classifications
S1S2	first and second heart sounds
	sacral vertebrae 1 and 2
S1-S2	sacral vertebrae 1 and 2
S1/S2	sacral vertebrae 1 and 2
S2S	skin to skin (infant and mother)
S2S3	sacral vertebrae 2 and 3
S2-S3	sacral vertebrae 2 and 3
S3S4	sacral vertebrae 3 and 4
S3-S4	sacral vertebrae 3 and 4
S4S5	sacral vertebrae 4 and 5
S4-S5	sacral vertebrae 4 and 5
S&S	shower and shampoo
	signs and symptoms
	sitting and supine
	sling and swathe
	soft and smooth (prostate)
	support and stimulation
	swish and spit
	swish and swallow
S/S	Saturday and Sunday
	signs and symptoms
	sprain/strain
SS#	Social Security number
SSA	sagittal split advancement
	salicylsalicylic acid (salsalate)
	second-stage arrest (obstetrics)

	sessile serrated adenoma
	Sjögren syndrome type A antigen
	Sjögrens syndrome antigen A
	Social Security Administration
	specific surface area
	Subjective Symptoms Assessment (profile)
	sub-Saharan Africa
	sulfasalicylic acid (test)
SS-A	Sjögren syndrome type A antigen
SSADH	succinic semialdehyde dehydrogenase
SSAP	sequence-specific amplification polymorphism
SSAR	suspected serious adverse event
SSAs	standard sedative agents
sSAT	superficial subcutaneous adipose tissue
SSB	Sjögren syndrome type B antigen
	Sjögren's syndrome B
	standard spine board
	sucking, swallowing, breathing (suck, swallow, breathe) (problems in any one of these processes or lack of coordination among these processes can have a profound effect on the infant's feeding abilities)
SS-B	Sjögren syndrome antigen B
SSBE	short-segment Barrett esophagus
SSBP	sitting systolic blood pressure
SSBs	single-strand breaks
	sugar-sweetened beverages
SSC	sign symptom complex
	silver sulfadiazine and chlorhexidine
	Similac® and special care
	skin-to-skin contact
	sliding scale coverage
	Special Services for Children
	spermatogonial stem cell
	stainless steel crown
	standard straight cane
	state-spanning coactivity
	Surgical Safety Checklist
SSc	systemic sclerosis (scleroderma)
SSCA	single shoulder contrast arthrography
SSc-APAH	systemic sclerosis-associated pulmonary arterial hypertension
SSCBs	sugar-sweetened carbonated beverages
SSCC	superior semicircular canal supraglottic squamous cell carcinoma

S

SSCD	superior semicircular canal dehiscence		subacute spongiform encephalopathy
SSCE	stretch-shortening cycle efficiency		systemic side effects
SSCE-MRI	steady-state contrast-enhanced magnetic resonance imaging	SSED	Summary of Safety and Effectiveness Data (Food and Drug Administration)
SSCIs	substrate-selective COX-2 (cyclo-oxygenase-2) inhibitors (selective type of non-steroidal anti-inflammatory drug [rofecoxib, celecoxib])	SSEH	spontaneous spinal epidural hematoma
		SSEP	somatosensory-evoked potentials
		SSEPs	somatosensory evoked potentials
		SSET	Sniffin' Sticks Extended test (for olfactory testing)
SSCL-30	30-item Somatic Symptoms Checklist		Supporting Students Exposed to Trauma
SSCM	Society of Critical Care Medicine (quidelines for the sustained use of sedatives and analgesics)	SSF	subscapular skinfold
		SSFP	steady state free precession
		SSG	sodium stibogluconate
SSCP	single-stranded conformational polymorphism		sublabial salivary gland
		sSGA	suspected small for gestational age fetus
	substernal chest pain		symmetrical small for gestational age
SSCr	stainless steel crown		
SSc-RP	systemic sclerosis-related vasculopathy, as manifested by Raynaud Phenomenon	SSGs	small-sided games
			split skin grafts
SSCs	permatogonial stem cells	SSH	single-story house
SSCU	surgical special care unit	SSHL	sudden sensorial hearing loss
SSCVD	sterile spontaneous controlled vaginal delivery	SSI	septic sacroiliitis
			sliding scale insulin
SSD	Hounsfield units		Snore Symptom Inventory
	schizophrenia-spectrum disorders		Social Skills Inventory
	serosanguineous drainage		sub-shock insulin
	sickle cell disease		superior sector iridectomy
	silver sulfadiazine (Silvadene)		Supplemental Security Income
	skin-to-stone distance		surgical site infection
	Social Security disability	SSI-3	Stuttering Severity Instrument
	somatic symptom disorder	SSI-CCM	synthetic sentence indentification with contralateral competing message
	source to skin distance		
	subsyndromal delirium		
	surface shaded display (radiology)	SSIGN	stage, size, grade and necrosis (criteria score for high risk of clear cell renal cell carcinoma recurrence postoperatively)
SSDD	sigmoid sinus diverticulum and/or dehiscence		
	steady-state daily dosing		
SSDEs	size-specific dose estimates (radiology)	SSI-ICM	synthetic sentence identification with ipsilateral competing message
SSDH	spinal subdural hematoma		
SSDI	Social Security death index	SSIOAC	super-selective intra-ophthalmic artery chemotherapy
	Social Security disability income		
	Social Security disability insurance	SSIP	solvent-separated ion pairs
ss DNA	single-stranded deoxyribonucleic acid	SSIs	surgical site infections
		SSKI	saturated solution of potassium iodide
SSDs	schizophrenia spectrum disorders		
SSDU	surgical step-down unit	SSL	sacro-spinous ligament
SSE	saline solution enema (0.9% sodium chloride)		second stage of labor
			selective sentinel lymphadenectomy
	skin self-examination		subtotal supraglottic laryngectomy
	soapsuds enema		
	sterile speculum exam		

S

SSLC	superficial sentinel lymphatic channel
SSLF	sacrospinous ligament fixation
SSLPs	Sure Start Local Programmes (UK)
SSLR	seated straight leg raise
	serum sickness-like reaction
SSLS	Satisfaction with Simulated Learning Scale
	single-site laparoscopic surgery
SSLs	Staphylococcal superantigen-like proteins
SSM	short stay medical
	skin surface microscopy
	skin-sparing mastectomy
	Spinal Stenosis Measure (symptoms)
	superficial spreading melanoma
SSMA	supplementary sensorimotor area
SSN	severely subnormal
	Social Security number
SSNA	skin sympathetic nerve activity
	splanchnic sympathetic nerve activity
ssnA	see gene website www.ncbi.nlm.nih.gov/gene
SSNB	suprascapular nerve block
SSNHL	sudden sensorineural hearing loss
SSNMR	solid-state nuclear magnetic resonance spectroscopy
SSNRI	selective serotonin and norepinephrine reuptake inhibitor
SSNS	steroid-sensitive nephrotic syndrome
SSO	second surgical opinion
	sequence-specific oligonucleotide
	short stay observation (unit)
	Spanish speaking only
SSOP	Second Surgical Opinion Program
	sequence-specific oligonucleotide probe
SSP	sequence-specific primer
	short stay procedure (unit)
	superior spermatic plexus
	supragingival scaling and prophylaxis (dental)
	supraspinatus
SSPA	staphylococcal slime polysaccharide antigens
SSPC	salivary stem/progenitor cells
	serous surface papillary carcinoma (adenocarcinoma)
SSPE	subacute sclerosing panencephalitis
SSPG	steady-state plasma glucose
SSPH	System of Social Protection in Health (Mexico)
SSPL	saturation sound pressure level

SSPU	surgical short procedure unit
SSQ	Sleepiness Symptoms Questionnaire
	Social Support Questionnaire
	Speech, Spatial and Qualities of Hearing Scale questionnaire
	Spiegel Sleep Questionnaire
	subjective sleep quality
	Sydney Swallow Questionnaire
SSq	skin and subcutaneous (level of debridement)
SSqM	skin, subcutaneous, and muscle (level of debridement)
SSqMB	skin, subcutaneous, muscle, and bone (level of debridement)
SSR	Sleep Self-Reporting
	substernal retractions
	sympathetic skin response
SSRDs	single-subject research designs
SSRFC	surrounding subretinal fluid cuff
SSRIs	selective serotonin reuptake inhibitors (citalopram [Celexa], escitalopram [Lexapro], fluoxetine [Prozac], fluvoxamine [Luvox], paroxetine [Paxil], and sertraline [Zoloft])
ssRNA	single-stranded deoxyribonucleic acid
SSRO	sagittal split ramus osteotomy (dental)
SSRP	subgingival scaling and root planing (dental)
SSRs	simple sequence repeats
SSS	layer upon layer
	scalded skin syndrome
	Scandinavian Stroke Scale
	segment stenosis score
	Sepsis Severity Score
	Severity Scoring System (Darts Snakebite)
	short stay service (unit)
	sick sinus syndrome
	skin and skin structures
	Spanish-speaking sometimes
	sphincter-saving surgery
	spontaneous saliva swallowing
	Stanford Sleepiness Scale
	Steiner silver stain
	sterile saline soak
	subclavian steal syndrome
	superior sagittal sinus
SSSB	sagittal split setback
SSSDW	significant sharp, spike, or delta waves
SSSE	self-sustained status epilepticus
SSSIs	skin and skin structure infections
SSSPD	subtotal stomach-preserving pancreatoduodenectomy

S

s/s/sp/dp/tp	sural, saphenous, superficial peroneal, deep peroneal, and tibial nerves		split thickness
SSSS	staphylococcal scalded skin syndrome		spondee threshold
			station (obstetrics)
SSSs	small short spikes (encephalography)		stent thrombosis
			stomach
SST	sagittal sinus thrombosis		straight
	Simple Shoulder Test		straight-top (bifocals)
	somatostatin (Zecnil)		strength training
SSTI	skin and soft tissue infection(s)		stress testing
SSTS	sufentanil sublingual tablet system		stretcher
			subtotal
SSU	short stay unit		Surgical Technologist
SSUS	sacrospinous uterine suspension		survival time
SSUs	short-stay units		synapse time
SSV	simian sarcoma virus	st	stone (1 stone = 6.35 Kg or 14 pounds)
SSVF	Supportive Services for Veteran Families (Department of Veterans Affairs program)	S&T	science and technology
			sulfamethoxazole and trimethoprim (SMZ-TMP or SMX-TMP)
SSVS	stochastic search variable selection	S/T	short term
SSVs	small saphenous veins	ST2	suppression of tumorigenicity 2 (gene)
SSW	slow spike and wave (electroencephalogram)	STA	Schirmer tests with anesthesia
	Staggered Spondaic Word Test (audiology test)		second trimester abortion
			spike-triggered averaging
	stimulated skin wrinkling		staphylococcus vaccine, not otherwise specified
SSwB	sucking-swallowing-breathing		station of fetus
SSX	sulfisoxazole acetyl		superficial temporal artery
S/SX	signs/symptoms	STAAMP	Study of Tranexamic Acid during Air Medical Prehospital transport (trial)
S/Sx	signs and symptoms		
SSYC	Salmonella, Shigella, Yersinia and Campylobacter species. (the classic bacterial enteric pathogens)	STAaur	Staphylococcus aureus vaccine
		stab.	polymorphonuclear leukocytes (white blood cells, in nonmature form)
SSZ	sulfasalazine (Azulfidine)	STABS	Social Thoughts and Beliefs Scale
ST	esotropic	STACH	short-term acute care hospital
	sacrum transverse	STAD	short-term androgen deprivation
	Schiotzs tonometry	STAF	Score for the Targeting of Atrial Fibrillation
	Schirmer Test (dry-eye test)		
	scleral thickness	STAG	see gene website, www.ncbi .nlm.nih.gov/gene
	semitendinosus (muscle)		
	shock therapy	STAg	soluble tachyzoite antigen
	short term	STAI	State-Trait Anxiety Inventory
	sinus tachycardia	STAI-I	State-Trait-Anxiety Index–I
	skin tear	STALIF	STand Alone Lumbar Interbody Fusion
	skin test		
	slight trace	STA-MCA	superficial temporary artery-middle cerebral artery (anastomosis; bypass)
	slow-twitch		
	smokeless tobacco		
	soft tissue	Stamm	Laparoscopic Stamm Gastrostomy
	soft tissue (technique)		
	sore throat	STAPES	stapedectomy
	spasmodic torticollis	staph	Staphylococcus aureus
	speech therapist	Staph aureus	Staphylococcus aureus
	speech therapy	Staph epi	Staphylococcus epidermis
	sphincter tone		

STARI — southern-tick-associated rash illness

STARR — stapled transanal rectal resection

STA_{SPL} — staphylococcus vaccine, bacteriophage lysate

STAT — immediately
signal transducers and activators of transcription

STATE — State Tobacco Activities Tracking and Evaluation (an interactive web-based application and data tool providing up-to-date state-level information related to tobacco use; Centers for Disease Control and Prevention's Office on Smoking and Health)

Statins — a class of drugs that lowers cholesterol blood levels (such as atorvastatin [Lipitor], rosuvastatin [Crestor], simvastatin [Zocor], etc)

STATs — signal transducers and activators of transcription

status quo — the current state of things; present customs, practices, and power relations

STAXI — State-Trait Anger Expression Inventory

STAXI-2 — State-Trait Anger Expression Inventory-2

STB — solutab (a tablet that dissolves in the mouth for quicker absorption)
stillborn

STBAL — standing balance

sTBI — severe traumatic brain injury

StBx — stereotactic biopsy

ST BY — stand by

STC — serum theophylline concentration
shock and trauma center
soft tissue calcification
special treatment center
stimulate to cry
stroke treatment center
subtotal colectomy
sugar-tong cast

St Cath — straight catheter

Stch — see gene website www.ncbi.nlm.nih.gov/gene

ST CLK — station clerk

STD — sexually transmitted disease(s)
short-term disability (this intended meaning will create problems as the well-known meaning of STD is sexually transmitted disease[s])

— skin test dose
— skin to tumor distance
— sodium tetradecyl sulfate

STDIs — sexually transmitted diseases and infections

STDL — short-term disability leave

STDs — sexually transmitted diseases

STD TF — standard tube feeding

STE — steps to enter
ST-segment elevation

STEACS — ST-segment elevation acute coronary syndromes

STEADI — Stopping Elderly Accidents, Deaths, and Injuries (Centers for Disease Control and Prevention)

STEAM — stimulated-echo acquisition mode

STEC — shiga toxin-producing *Escherichia coli*

STEC-HUS — hemolytic uremic syndrome caused by Shiga toxin-producing Escherichia coli

STED — stimulated emission depletion (microscopy)

ST elevation — ST-segment elevation of an electrocardiogram

STEM — scanning transmission electron microscope

STEMI — ST-segment elevation myocardial infarction

Stemmi — may have meant STEMI (ST-segment elevation myocardial infarction)

STEMO — Stroke Emergency Mobile (vehicle service)

Stemy — may have meant STEMI (ST-segment elevation myocardial infarction)

STEPS — System for Thalidomide Educating and Prescribing Safety

STER — submucosal tunneling endoscopic resection

Stereo — steropsis

STET — single photon emission tomography
submaximal treadmill exercise test

STETH — stethoscope

ST eval — speech therapy evaluation

STF — slip, trip, and fall (injuries)
special tube feeding
standard tube feeding

STFA — slip, trip and fall accidents
subcutaneous transposition of the femoral artery
Surgical Technologist First Assistant

569

sTfR	soluble transferrin receptor	stnA	stoned A; see gene website www.ncbi.nlm.nih.gov/gene
STFU	short-term follow-up		
STG	short term goal(s) split-thickness graft superior temporal gyri	STNBG	split-thickness nail bed graft
		STN-DBS	subthalamic nucleus deep brain stimulation
stg	stage	STNI	subtotal nodal irradiation
STGV	short-term glycemic variability	STNM	surgical evaluative staging of cancer
STH	soft tissue hemorrhage soil-transmitted helminths somatotrophic hormone subtotal hysterectomy supplemental thyroid hormone		
		STNR	symmetrical tonic neck reflex
		STNT	troponin T1, slow skeletal type (gene)
		sTnT	skeletal muscle-specific troponin T
STHB	said to have been		
STI	sexually transmitted infection signal transduction inhibitor(s) soft tissue injury structured treatment interruptions sum total impression systolic time interval	S to	sensitive to
		StO2	tissue oxygen saturation
		STOB	STop to OBesty (course)
		S-TOFHLA	Short version of the Test of Functional Health Literacy in Adults
STI 571	imatinib mesylate (Gleevec)	STOPBANG	Snoring, Tired, Observed, blood Pressure, BMI (body mass index), Age, Neck circumference, and Gender (a tool to screen patients for obstructive sleep apnea)
STICU	surgical and trauma intensive care unit		
STILLB	stillborn		
stim	stimulation		
STIMI	see STEMI		
STING	endoscopic subureteral injection of collagen (procedure)		
		STORCH	syphilis, toxoplasmosis, other agents, rubella, cytomegalo- virus, and herpes (maternal infections)
STIPs	spatio-temporal interest points		
STIR	short TI (tau) inversion recovery		
STIs	sexually transmitted infections systolic time intervals		
		STORM	stochastic optical reconstruction microscopy
STJ	scapulothoracic joint subtalar joint		
		STP	short-term plans sodium thiopental step training progression
STJN	subtalar joint neutral		
STK	streptokinase		
STL	sent to laboratory serum theophylline level	STPD	standard temperature and pressure–dry
STLE	St. Louis encephalitis	STPF	stabilized temperature platform furnace
STLI	subtotal lymphoid irradiation		
STLOM	swelling, tenderness, and limitation of motion	STPI	single-time-point imaging State-Trait Personality Inventory
STLT	subthreshold laser treatment	STPS	Short-Term Performance Status
STLV	simian T-lymphotrophic viruses	STPT	second-trimester pregnancy termination
STM	scanning tunneling microscope short-term memory soft tissue mobilization sternocleidomastoideus streptomycin		
		STR	scotopic threshold response short tandem repeat short-term rehabilitation signs of a stroke (ask patient to- smile; talk [speak a simple sentence]; raise both arms) single-tablet regimen sister small tandem repeat strength stretcher systolic time ratio
ST-MCL	ST segment monitoring at the midclavicular line		
STMI	ST-elevation myocardial infarction		
STML	short-term memory loss		
STMS	Short Test of Mental Status		
STMT	Seat Movement		
STN	station subtalar neutral subthalamic nucleus		
		Strab	strabismus

STRAFI — stray-field imaging

STRAFI-MAS — stray-field imaging with magic-angle spinning

sTRAIL — soluble tumor-necrosis-factor-related apoptosis-inducing ligand

STRAWB — strawberry

strep — streptococcus; streptomycin

Strep pneumonia — Streptococcus pneumoniae

STRICU — shock/trauma/respiratory intensive care unit

stridor — a word meaning a harsh high-pitched respiratory sound such as the inspiratory sound often heard in acute laryngeal obstruction

STRN — soft tissue radionecrosis

Str Post MI — strictly posterior myocardial infarction

STS — serologic test for syphilis
short-term survivors
sit-to-stand
skin to skin
slide thin slab
Society of Thoracic Surgeons (guidelines)
sodium tetradecyl sulfate
sodium thiosulfate
soft tissue sarcoma
soft tissue swelling
somatostatin (Zecnil)
standard threshold shift (audiology)
staurosporine
superior temporal sulcus
Surgical Technology Student

STs — sequence types

ST-SDDI — short-term sequential digital dermoscopy imaging

ST segment — The flat, isoelectric section of the electrocardiogram between the end of the S wave and the beginning of the T wave. It represents the interval between ventricular depolarization and repolarization.

STSG — split thickness skin graft

sTSH — sensitive thyroid stimulating hormone
serum thyroid-stimulating hormone

STSS — streptococcal-induced toxic shock syndrome

STS score — Society of Thoracic Surgeons score (risk models predict the risk of operative mortality and morbidity after adult cardiac surgery on the basis of patient demographic and clinical variables; the models are primarily used to adjust for case mix when comparing outcomes across institutions with different patient populations)

STS-SPT — simple two-step swallowing provocation test

STST — sit-to-stand test

sTST — subjective total sleep time

STT — scaphotrapeziotrapezoid (scaphoid-trapezium-trapezoid) (joint of the thumb)
serial thrombin time
skin temperature test
soft tissue tumor
standard triple therapy for the eradication of Helicobacter pylori (H. pylori); 10 days of treatment with esomeprazole, amoxicillin, and clarithromycin
subtotal thyroidectomy

ST-T — a segment of the electrocardiogram wave

STT#1 — Schirmer tear test one

STT#2 — Schirmer tear test two

STTA — sub-Tenon triamcinolone acetonide (injection)

STTb — basal Schirmer tear test

STT joint — scaphotrapeziotrapezoid (scaphoid-trapezium-trapezoid; joint of the thumb)

STTOL — standing tolerance

STTs — soft tissue tumors

STTW — ST-T wave (a segment of the electrocardiogram wave)

STU — shock trauma unit
surgical trauma unit

STUMP — smooth muscle tumor of uncertain malignant potential

Stupp regimen — concomitant and adjuvant temozolomide (Temodar) along with radiotherapy following surgery

STV — short-term variability

STV 0 — short-term variability-absent

STV+ — short-term variability-present

STV inter — short-term variability-intermittent

STW — handrail-supported treadmill walking
sewage treatment works
sex-trade worker
sitting to walking
sludge treatment wetlands
Spot-the-Word (test)

STW 5	a liquid herbal formulation of nine herbs (Iberogast-manufactured by Steigerwald [STeigerWald])
STX	stricture
Stx DIA	Shiga toxin enzyme immunoassay
STZ	streptozocin (Zanosar)
SU	sensory urgency
	set up
	sit-ups
	Somogyi units
	stasis ulcer
	stroke unit
	sulfonylurea
	supine
Su	Sunday
S&U	supine and upright
S/U	shoulder/umbilicus
	set up
SUA	serum uric acid
	single umbilical artery
SUB	single-use bioreactor
	Skenes urethra and Bartholin's glands
	subcutaneous ureteral bypass
subcm	subcentimeter (having dimensions less than a centimeter)
subconj	subconjunctiva
	subconjunctival
Subcu	subcutaneous
SUBCUT	subcutaneous
Subepi M Inj	subepicardial myocardial injury
SUB-I	sub-investigator
SUBL	sublingual
subling	sublingual (under the tongue)
SUBMAND	submandibular
subq	subcutaneous
subqu	subcutaneous
subs	substances
subscapularis	subscap
subtract	subtrochanteric
sUCBT	single-unit unrelated (umbilical) cord blood transplantation
SUCC	succinylcholine
SUCRA	surface under the cumulative ranking curve
SUCT	suction
SUD	substance use dependent
	substance use disorder(s)
	sudden unexpected death
SuDBP	supine diastolic blood pressure
SUDD	symptomatic uncomplicated diverticular disease
SUDEP	sudden unexpected (unexplained) death in epilepsy
SUDI	sudden unexpected death in infancy

SUDS	Single-Use Diagnostic System (for detection of exposure to human immunodeficiency virus)
	Subjective Unit of Distress (Disturbance) (Discomfort) Scale
	sudden unexplained death syndrome
SUDs	substance use disorders
SUE	spontaneous urinary extravasation
	stroke of other undetermined etiology
SUF	symptomatic uterine fibroids
SUG	sonourethrography
SUI	stress urinary incontinence
	suicide
SUID	sudden unexplained infant death
SUIOS	Simplified Urinary Incontinence Outcome Score
SULFPRIM	sulfamethoxazole and trimethoprim
SUMO	small ubiquitin-like modifier
sump	a word meaning a low-lying place, such as a pit, that receives drainage
SUN	serum urea nitrogen
SUNA	short-lasting unilateral neuralgiform headache attacks with cranial autonomic symptoms
SUNCT	short-lasting unilateral neuralgiform headache attacks with conjunctival injection and tearing
SUNDS	sudden unexplained nocturnal death syndrome
SUO	syncope of unknown origin
SUP	stress ulcer prophylaxis
	superior
	supervise(r)
	supervision
	supination
	supinator
	symptomatic uterine prolapse
sup	supine
SUPAC	Scale-Up and Post Approval Change
superv	supervisor
supp	suppository
suppl	supplementation
supps	supplements
SUPPS-P	Swedish version of the 20-item UPPS-P (Urgency, Premeditation, Perseverance, Sensation seeking, and Positive urgency) Impulsive Behavior Scale

S

supra	a prefix meaning above or over
supraclav	supraclavicular
SUPRV	supervision
supv	supervisor; supervise; supervision
SUR	suramin (Metaret)
	surgery
	surgical
surg	surgeon
	surgery
	surgical
Surgi	Surgigator
SURs	standardized uptake ratios
	sulfonylurea receptors
Surv	surviving
surv	survival
SUS	single-use system
SUSAR	Suspected Unexpected Serious Adverse Reactions
SUSARs	suspected and unsuspected serious adverse reactions
Su Sa SP DP T	sural, saphenous, superficial peroneal, deep peroneal, and tibial nerves
Su/Sa/SP/DP/T	sural, saphenous, superficial peroneal, deep peroneal, and tibial nerves
SUSP	suspension
sust	sustained
SUT	safe use time
sut	see gene website www.ncbi.nlm .nih.gov/gene
SUTs	single-unit technologies
SUUD	sudden unexpected, unexplained death
SUV	standard uptake variable
	standardized uptake volume
SUVmax	maximum standardized uptake value (the ratio of the image derived radioactivity concentration and the whole body concentration of the injected radioactivity was seen in a positron-emission tomography scan)
SUVs	standard uptake valves
SUX	succinylcholine
	suction
SUZI	subzonal insertion
SV	scimitar vein
	seminal vesical
	severe
	sick visit
	sievert (radiation unit)
	sigmoid volvulus
	single ventricle
	single vessel
	snake venom
	splenic vein

	stroke volume
	subclavian vein
S/V	surface area to volume ratio
	stent-to-vessel diameter ratio
SV40	simian virus 40
SVA	small volume admixture
	supraventricular arrhythmia
SVAB	stereotactic vacuum-assisted biopsy
SVAR	structural vector autoregression
SVAS	supravalvular aortic stenosis
SVB	saphenous vein bypass
SVBG	saphenous vein bypass graft
SVC	service connected
	slow vital capacity
	subclavian vein compression
	superior vena cava
SVCO	superior vena cava obstruction
SVC-RPA	superior vena cava and right pulmonary artery (shunt)
SVCS	superior vena cava syndrome
SVC syndrome	superior vena cava syndrome
SVD	single-vessel disease
	singular value decomposition
	small vessel disease
	spontaneous vaginal delivery
	structural valve deterioration (dysfunction)
SVDPV	Saint Vincent de Paul Village
SVE	sterile vaginal examination
	Streptococcus viridans endocarditis
	subcortical vascular encephalopathy
	supraventricular ectopy
SV&E	suicidal, violent, and eloper
SVES	supraventricular extrasystoles
SVET	single-volume exchange transfusion
SVF	sleep videofluoroscopy
	splenic vein flow
	stromal vascular fraction
SVG	saphenous vein graft
SVG-OM	saphenous vein graft to obtuse marginal (artery)
SVG-PDA	saphenous vein graft to the posterior descending artery
SVG-RCA	saphenous vein graft to the right coronary artery
SVH	subjective visual horizontal (test)
SVI	seminal vesicle invasion
	severe visual impairment
	stroke volume index
SVID	small vessel ischemic disease
S VISC	serum viscosity
SVL	severe visual loss
SVLR	stroke volume during leg raise
SVM	support vector machines

SVN	small volume nebulizer		sandwich
SVO	small vessel occlusion		sea water
SVO$_2$	mixed venous oxygen saturation		seriously wounded
SVOO	systemic ventricular outflow obstruction		shallow walk (aquatic therapy)
			short wave
SVP	sexually violent person/predator		Social Work
	small-volume parenteral		Social Worker
	splenic vessel preservation		Southwest
	spontaneous venous pulse		stab wound
	synovial volar phalangeal		standard walker
SVPB	supraventricular premature beat		sterile water
SVPC	supraventricular premature complexes	S&W	swallowing reflex Smith and Wesson
	supraventricular premature contraction	S/W	soap and water somewhat
SV/PP	stroke volume to pulse pressure ratio	SWA	spoke with slow-wave activity
svPPA	semantic variant primary progressive aphasia		(electroencephalographic) Social Work Associate
SVPS	supravalvular pulmonary stenosis		stroke while awake
SVPs	sexually violent persons/ predators	SWAL-QOL	swallow quality-of-life (questionnaire to asses
	small-volume parenterals		difficulty in swallowing)
	subviral particles	SWAN	statewide adoption network
SVR	superficial venous reflux	SWAP	short-wavelength automated
	supraventricular rhythm		perimetry
	sustained virological response	SWAT	skin wound assessment and
	systemic vascular resistance		treatment
SVR4	sustained virological response at 4 weeks	sWAT	subcutaneous white adipose tissue
SVR12	sustained virological response at week 12	SWB	social well being spiritual well-being
SVR24	sustained virological response at week 24		subjective well-being swing bed
SVR72	sustained virological response at week 72	SWC	sleep-wake cycle
SVRI	systemic vascular resistance index	SWCNT	single-walled carbon nanotube
SVRT	simple visual reaction time	SWD	short wave diathermy
SVS	The Society for Vascular Surgery	SWE	shear wave elastography
SVSR	supervisor	Sweet Milk	propofol (Diprivan) (slang)
SVT	splanchnic vein thrombosis	Swer	Social Worker
	splenic vein thrombosis	SWFI	sterile water for injection
	superficial vein thrombosis	SWG	standard wire gauge
	superficial venous thrombophlebitis	SWI	sterile water for injection surgical wound infection
	supraventricular tachycardia		susceptibility-weighted imaging
	symptom validity test(s)	S&WI	skin and wound isolation
SVTs	supraventricular tachycardias	SWJs	square wave jerks
SVV	stroke volume variance	SWL	Satisfaction With Life (scale)
SVVD	spontaneous vertex vaginal delivery		shock wave lithotripsy
SVX	seminal vesicle-excised	SWLS	Satisfaction With Life Scale
SVZ	subventricular zone	SWMA	segmental wall-motion abnormalities
SW	saline well (intravenous catheter that is threaded into a peripheral	SWME	Semmes-Weinstein monofilament examination
	vein, flushed with 0.9% sodium chloride injection; also known	SWMF	Semmes-Weinstein monofilament (peripheral
	as a saline lock)		neuropathy test)
		SWO	superficial white onychomycosis

SWOG	Southwest Oncology Group	sync	synchronize(d)
SWOP	symptoms worsen or persist		synchronous
SWOT	strengths, weaknesses, opportunities, threats (analysis)	Synd	Syndapin; see gene website www.ncbi.nlm.nih.gov/gene
		synd	syndrome
SWP	small whirlpool	SYN-D	synthadotin
	southwest Pacific	synd-1	syndecan-1
	systematic weaning process	SYN Fl	synovial fluid
SWR	soft wrist restraints	SYP	synaptophysin; see gene website www.ncbi.nlm.nih .gov/gene
	surface wrinkling retinopathy		
	surgical waiting room		
SWS	sheltered workshop	SYPH	syphilis
	slow wave sleep	SYR	syrup
	social work service	SYS	system
	student ward secretary		systemic
	Sturge-Weber syndrome		systolic
SWSD	Shift-work sleep disorder	SyS	syndromic surveillance
SWT	shuttle-walk test		synovial sarcoma
	stab wound of the throat	SYS BP	systolic blood pressure
SWTSI	systolic wall thickening score index	SYST	system
			systemic
SWU	septic work-up		systole
SWW	static wall walk (aquatic therapy)		systolic
SWYC	Survey of Wellbeing of Young Children (screens for social-emotional, motor, cognitive and language delays, as well as autism and family risk (including parent mental health concerns, substance use, food insecurity, and family violence)	SYX	syntaxin(s)(a family of membrane integrated Q-SNARE proteins participating in exocytosis)
		SZ	schizophrenic
			seizure
			suction
		SZD	severely zinc deficient
		SZN	streptozocin (Zanosar)
		SZP	schizophrenia
Sx	signs	S/Z ratio	used in Speech Pathology as an indicator of laryngeal pathology (measures the length of time a person can sustain the sound 's', divided by the length of time they can sustain the sound 'z')
	suction		
	surgery		
	symptom(s)		
SXA	single-energy x-ray absorptiometry		
Sx's	symptoms	SZs	schizophrenics
SXN	suction	SzS	Sézary syndrome
SXR	skull x-ray	SZU	chronic undifferentiated schizophrenics
Sxs	symptoms		
SXT	sulfamethoxazole and trimethoprim (Bactrim; co-trimoxazole)		
sycE	see gene website www.ncbi.nlm .nih.gov/gene		
SYK	spleen tyrosine kinase		
syl	syllables		
SYM	symmetrical		
	symptom		
symp	sympathetic		
	symptom		
SYMPAQ	Symptom Management, Pain and Quality of Life (a palliative care clinic; Mayo Clinic)		
SYN	synovial		

S

T

T	inverted T wave
	tablespoon (15 mL) (this is a dangerous abbreviation)
	Tango (Phonetic Alphabet for T; pronounced TANG-GO)
	teach (taught)
	temperature
	tender
	tension
	tesla (unit of magnetic flux density in radiology)
	testicles
	testosterone
	thoracic
	threonine
	thymidine
	trace
	transcribed
	tricep
	Tuesday
	tympanic
t	teaspoon (5 mL) (this is a dangerous abbreviation)
T	*taenia*
	Toxoplasma
T°	temperature
T+	increased intraocular tension
T−	decreased intraocular tension
T0	time zero
T1/2	half-live
	half life
T 1/2	half life
$T_{1/2}$	half-life
T1	first thoracic nerve root
	first thoracic vertebrae
	first trimester
T_1	tricuspid first sound
T1a	a term used in cancer stage tumor-size findings. Its meaning varies as it is cancer-type-dependent.
T2	second thoracic nerve root
	second thoracic vertebrae
	second trimester
T_2	tricuspid second sound
T-2	dactinomycin, doxorubicin, vincristine, and cyclophosphamide
T2a	a tumor stage (see cancarstaging.org)
2,4,5-T	2,4,5-trichlorophenoxyacetic acid
T3	third thoracic nerve root
	third thoracic vertebrae
	third trimester
	transurethral thermo-ablation therapy (Targis)
	Tylenol with codeine 30 mg (this is a dangerous abbreviation)
T_3	triiodothyronine (liothyronine; Cytomel)
T4	CD4 (helper-inducer cells)
	fourth thoracic nerve root
	fourth thoracic vertebrae
T_4	levothyroxine sodium (Synthroid)
	thyroxine
T5	fifth thoracic nerve root
	fifth thoracic vertebrae
T6	sixth thoracic nerve root
	sixth thoracic vertebrae
T7	seventh thoracic nerve root
	seventh thoracic vertebrae
T-7	free thyroxine factor
T8	eighth thoracic nerve root
	eighth thoracic vertebrae
T9	ninth thoracic nerve root
	ninth thoracic vertebrae
T10	tenth thoracic nerve root
T-10	methotrexate, calcium leucovorin rescue, doxorubicin, cisplatin, bleomycin, cyclophosphamide, and dactinomycin
T11	eleventh thoracic nerve root
	eleventh thoracic vertebrae
T12	twelfth thoracic nerve root
	twelfth thoracic vertebrae
T13	trisomy 13 (a congenital chromosomal disorder)
T-20	enfuvirtide (Fuzeon)
T21	an extra copy of the genes located on chromosome 21 (trisomy 21; causative of Down syndrome)
TA	Takayasus arteritis
	teaching assistant
	temperature axillary
	temporal arteritis
	temporal artery
	tendon Achilles
	tension applanation
	therapeutic abortion
	therapeutic activity
	tibialis anterior (muscle)
	tracheal aspirate
	traffic accident
	transapical (approach)
	transport aide
	transversus abdominus (muscle)
	tricuspid atresia
	truncus arteriosus
	tubular adenoma

Ta	tantalum		total abdominal colectomy
	tonometry applanation		total allergen content
T(A)	axillary temperature		total arterial compliance
T&A	tonsillectomy and adenoidectomy		triamcinolone
	tonsils and adenoids		triamcinolone cream
TA1	thymosin alpha-1		trigeminal automatic cephalgias
TA-55	stapling device	TACC	thoracic aortic cross-clamping
TAA	Therapeutic Activities Aide	TACE	transarterial chemoembolization
	thoracic aortic aneurysm	tachy	tachycardic
	total ankle arthroplasty	tachy-brady	a cardiac rhythm disturbance
	transverse aortic arch	syndrome	resulting in alternating
	triamcinolone acetonide		episodes of bradycardia and
	tumor-associated antigen		tachycardia
	(antibodies)	TACI	total anterior cerebral infarct
TAAA	thoracoabdominal aortic		transcatheter arterial
	aneursym		chemotherapy infusion
TAAD	thoracic aortic aneurysm and		transmembrane activator
	dissection		and calcium-modulating
	type A aortic dissection		cyclophilin ligand interactor
TAAR1	trace amine-associated receptor 1	TACL	Therapeutic Advances in
TAB	tablet		Childhood Leukemia and
	temporal artery biopsy		Lymphoma (consortium/trial)
	therapeutic abortion		transarterial
	threatened abortion		chemo-lipiodolization
	total androgen blockade	tac-MRA	timed arterial compression mag-
	triple antibiotic (bacitracin,		netic resonance angiography
	neomycin, and polymyxin–this	TACO	transfusion-associated circulatory
	is a dangerous abbreviation)		overload
TABE	tumor-associated blood	TACS	thoracic aorta calcium score
	eosinophilia	TACs	trigeminal autonomic
TABHSO	may have meant TAHBSO		cephalalgias
	(total abdominal	tACS	transcranial alternating current
	hysterectomy, bilateral		stimulation
	salpingo-oophorectomy)	TACT	total atrial conduction time
TABI	transfusion-associated bacterial		tuned aperture computed
	infection(s)		tomography
tablespoon	a liquid unit of measure equiv-	TAD	take as directed (for safety rea-
	alent to 15 mL (1/2 ounce)		sons this should not be used;
	(write 15 mL as it should not		explicit directions should be
	be abbreviated)		used for prescriptions and
Tablo	a home hemodialysis system		medical records)
tablo	Turkish word for table (as in		thoracic asphyxiant dystrophy
	Tablo 1)		tobacco, alcohol, intravenous
TABO	triple antibiotic ointment		drug use
	(bacitracin, neomycin, and		transverse abdominal diameter
	polymyxin)	T/A/D	tobacco, alcohol, intravenous
TABR	thanks, and best regards (slang)		drug use
TABS	Test of Adaptive Behavior in	TADAC	therapeutic abortion, dilation,
	Schizophrenia		aspiration, and curettage
	transfusion-associated	TADC	tumor-associated dendritic cells
	bacteremia/sepsis	TAE	transcatheter arterial embolization
TAC	docetaxel (Taxotere)	TAF	tenofovir alafenamide fumarate
	doxorubicin, (Adriamycin)		(Viread)
	and cyclophosphamide		thoracoabdominal flap
	tacrolimus (Prograf, also TRL)		tissue angiogenesis factor
	tetracaine, Adrenalin® and		Total Active Flexion (score)
	cocaine	TAFI	thrombin-activatable fibrinolysis
	tibial artery catheter		inhibitor

TAFRO syndrome	Thrombocytopenia, Anasarca, myeloFibrosis, Renal dysfunction, and Organomegaly (an atypical manifestation of multicentric Castleman's disease)	TAMIS-II	Tokai Acute Myocardial Infarction Study II
TAG	triacylglycerol(s)	t-AML	therapy-related acute myeloid leukemia
	tumor-associated glycoprotein	TAMOF	thrombocytopenia-associated multiple-organ failure
TAGA	term average gestational age	TAMR	transversus abdominis muscle release
	term, appropriate for gestational age	TAN	Treatment Authorization Number
TAGs	triacylglycerols		treatment-as-needed
TA-GVHD	transfusion-associated graft-versus-host disease		tropical ataxic neuropathy
TAH	total abdominal hysterectomy	T and A	see T&A
	total artificial heart	T and L	thunder and lightning
TAH-BSO	total abdominal hysterectomy, bilateral salpingo-oophorectomy	T and S	type and screen
		TANF	Temporary Assistance for Needy Families
TAHL	thick ascending limb of Henles loop	Tango	Phonetic Alphabet for T; pronounced TANG-GO
TAHLSO	total abdominal hysterectomy, left salpingo-oophorectomy	TANGO2	transport and golgi organization 2 homolog (gene)
TAH-LSO	total abdominal hysterectomy, left salpingo-oophorectomy	TANI	total axial (lymph) node irradiation
TAHRSO	total abdominal hysterectomy, right salpingo-oophorectomy	TAO	thromboangitis obliterans
			thyroid-associated opthalmopathy
TAH-RSO	total abdominal hysterectomy, right salpingo-oophorectomy		triple antibiotic ointment (neomycin, polymyxin b
TAHUSO	total abdominal hysterectomy and unilateral salpingo-oophorectomy		sulfates, and bacitracin zinc [Neosporin ointment])
			troleandomycin
TAI	tau aggregation inhibitor	TAP	tone and positioning
	thoracic aortic injury		tonometry by applanation
T Air	air puff tonometry		transabdominal preperitoneal (laparoscopic hernia repair)
TAKE	Targeting Abnormal Kinetic Effects (scale)		transesophageal atrial paced
TAL	tendon Achilles lengthening		transversus abdominis plane (block)
	total arm length		trypsinogen activation peptide
TA-LCA	thyroarytenoid-lateral cricoarytenoid muscle complex		tumor-activated prodrug
		TAPB	Transversus abdominis plane block
T ALCON	Alcon® tonometry	TAP block	transversus-abdominis-plane block
TALEN	transcription activator–like effector nuclease	TAPES	Trinity Amputation and Prosthesis Experience Scales
talgd	talgdrüese (German for sebaceous gland)	TAPP	transabdominal preperitoneal (hernia repair)
T-ALL	T-cell acute lymphoblastic leukemia		transabdominal preperitoneal polypropylene (mesh-plasty)
TALP	total alkaline phosphatase	T APPL	applanation tonometry
TAM	tamoxifen (Novaldex)	taps	draining of fluids
	technology acceptance model		quick, light blows
	teenage mother	TAPS	Test of Auditory Processing Skills
	terminology asset management		twin anemia-polycythemia sequence
	thyroarytenoid (muscle) myectomy	TAPSE	tricuspid annular plane systolic excursion
	total active motion		
	tumor-associated macrophages	TAPVC	total anomalous pulmonary venous connection
TAMIS	transanal minimally invasive surgery		

T

TAPVD   total anomalous pulmonary venous drainage

TAPVR   total anomalous pulmonary venous return

TAR   thoracic aortic rupture
thrombocytopenia with absent radius
tissue-air ratio
total ankle replacement
total anorectal reconstruction
transverses abdominis (muscle) release
treatment administration record
treatment authorization request

TARA   total articular replacement arthroplasty

TARE   transarterial radioembolization

TARP   transoral atlantoaxial reduction plate

TARP syndrome   Talipes equinovarus, Atrial septal defect, Robin sequence, and Persistent left superior vena cava

TArr   time of arrival

TARS   threonyl-tRNA (transfer ribonucleic acid) synthetase
transaxillary robotic surgery

TARs   total ankle replacements
trait-associated regions

TART   tenderness, asymmetry, restricted motion, and tissue texture changes
tumorectomy and radiotherapy

TARV   may have meant TAVR, (transcatheter aortic valve replacement)

TAS   therapeutic activities specialist
Thrombolytic Assessment System
transabdominal sutures
transarticular screw(s)
turning against self
typical absence seizures

TASC   Trans-Atlantic Inter-Society Consensus (guidelines)

TASE   template-assisted selective epitaxy
transabdominal specimen extraction

TASH score   Trauma-Associated Severe Hemorrhage (score; to estimate the risk for the need of massive blood transfusions to prevent lethal exsanguination)

TASP   Transcription Application Service Provider
Transit Authority Suicide Prevention (US Department of Veterans Affairs)

TasP   treatment as prevention (antiretroviral therapies for HIV [human immunodeficiency virus] treatment

TASS   toxic anterior segment syndrome

TAT   tandem autotransplants
tell a tale
temporal artery temperature
tetanus antitoxin
thematic apperception test
thrombin-antithrombin III complex
'til all taken
tired all the time
total adipose tissue
transactivator of transcription
transfusion-associated transmission
transplant-associated thrombocytopenia
triple antiplatelet therapy (aspirin, clopidogrel, and cilostazol)
turnaround time(s)
tyrosine aminotransferase

TA-TAVR   transapical transcatherter aortic valve replacement

TATE   tumor-associated tissue eosinophilia

TATFAR   Trans-Atlantic Taskforce on Antimicrobial Resistance

TaTME   transanal total mesorectal excision

TATT   tired all the time

TAU   treatment as usual
tumescence activity units

TAUC   target area under the curve
time-averaged urea concentration

tauR   taurine transcriptional regulator; see gene website www.ncbi.nlm.nih.gov/gene

TAUSA   thrombolysis and angioplasty in unstable angina

TAV   tricuspid aortic valve

TAVAR   may have meant TAVR (transcatheter aortic valve replacement)

TAVI   transcatheter aortic valve implantation

TAVPR   may have meant TAPVR (total anomalous pulmonary venous return)

TAVR   transcatheter aortic valve replacement

TAWR   total airway resistance

TAX   cefotaxime (Claforan)
paclitaxel (Taxol)
thiafentanil-azaperone-xylazine (veterinary)

TAZ	transcriptional co-activator with PDZ-binding motif (oncogene)	TBDP	total-body digital photography
TB	Tapes for the Blind	TBE	tick-borne encephalitis
	teach-back		time to bacterial eradication
	term birth		timed barium esophagogram
	terrible burning		to be evaluated
	Thera-Band® (stretch straps for	TBEC	tracheobronchial epithelial cells
	progressive exercise)	TBE_e	tick-borne encephalitis, eastern
	thought broadcasting		subtype (Far eastern encephali-
	toothbrush		tis, Russian spring-summer e.,
	total base		Taiga e.) vaccine
	total bilirubin	T-berg	Trendelenburg (position)
	total body	TBEV	tick-borne encephalitis virus
	tracheobronchial	TBE_w	tick-bone encephalitis, western
	tub bath		subtype (Central European
	tuberculosis		encephalitis) vaccine
Tb	terbium	TBF	time between failures
T&B	tendonitis and bursitis		total blood flow
TBA	thyroid biochemical abnormalities		total-body fat
	to be absorbed		tubularized bladder flap
	to be added	TBFO	total body fluid overload
	to be administered	TBG	thyroxine-binding globulin
	to be admitted	TBH	Turbuhaler (multi-dose dry
	to be announced		powder inhaler)
	to be arranged	tBH	tert-butyl hydroperoxide
	to be assessed	TBI	tick-borne illness(es)
	total bile acid		to be infused
	total body (surface) area		toothbrushing instruction
	traditional birth attendant		total-body irradiation
TBAD	type B aortic dissection		traumatic brain injury
TBAGA	term birth appropriate for	TBII	thyrotropin-binding inhibitor
	gestational age		immunoglobulin
T-band	Theraband (a flexible exercise	TBIL	total bilirubin
	device used to improve grip	T-bil	total bilirubin
	strength)	T bili	total bilirubin
	therapeutic band	T-bili	total bilirubin
T-bar	tracheotomy bar (a device used	TBIs	traumatic brain injuries
	in respiratory therapy)	TBK	total-body potassium
TBARS	thiobarbituric acid reactive	tbl	tablespoon (15 mL) this is
	substances		a dangerous abbreviation
			use 15 mL
TBB	transbronchial biopsy	TBLB	transbronchial lung biopsy
TBBL	transblepharoplasty brow lift	TBLBx	transbronchial lung biopsy
TBBx	transbronchial biopsy	TBLC	term birth, living child
TBC	to be cancelled	TBLF	term birth, living female
	total-blood cholesterol	TBLI	term birth, living infant
	total-body clearance	TBLM	term birth, living male
	tuberculosis	TBLN	tuberculous lymphadenitis
	tuberculosis culture	TBLs	true bifurcation lesions
TBCR	Tsurumai Biologics Commu-	TBM	tracheobronchomalacia
	nication Registry (the study		tuberculous meningitis
	compared the long-term safety		tubule basement membrane
	of biologics [infliximab,	TBMg	total-body magnesium
	etanercept, adalimumab, and	TBMN	thin basement membrane
	tocilizumab] by initiation year		nephropathy
	of treatment in patients with	TBN	total-body nitrogen
	rheumatoid arthritis in Japan)	TBNA	transbronchial needle aspiration
TBD	to be determined		treated but not admitted
tBDL	total bile duct ligation	TBNa	total-body sodium

TBNK reagent	contains the antibodies to identify and enumerate the T-lymphocytes, T-helper cells, cytotoxic T-cells, total B-lymphocytes and Natural Killer lymphocytes	TBx	targeted (prostate) biopsy
		TBZ	tetrabenazine (Xenazine)
			thiabendazole (Mintezol)
		TC	docetaxel (Taxotere) and cisplatin
			docetaxel (Taxotere) plus cyclophosphamide
TBO	toludine blue O		paclitaxel (Taxol) and carboplatin
TBOCS	Tale-Brown Obsessive-Compulsive Scale		paclitaxel (Taxol) and cisplatin
			tactile cues
TBP	thyroxine-binding protein		tai chi (exercise program)
	time before being seen by physician		talocrural (joint)
			team conference
	toe blood pressure		telephone call
	total-body phosphorus		temperature current
	total-body protein		terminal cancer
	tuberculous peritonitis		testicular cancer
TBPA	thyroxine-binding prealbumin		thioguanine and cytarabine
TBPM	time-based prospective memory		thoracic circumference
TBR	total-bed rest		throat culture
TBRF	tick-bone relapsing fever		tinea capitis
TBS	tablespoon (15 mL) (this is a dangerous abbreviation, use 15 mL)		tissue culture
			to (the) chest
			Tobacco Counseling
	tachycardia bradycardia syndrome		tolonium chloride
			tonic-clonic
	The Bethesda System (reporting cervical and vagina cytology)		tonsillar coblation
			tooth clenching
	thick blood smear		total cholesterol
	timed barium swallow		total communication
	total-serum bilirubin		tracheal collar
	Townes-Brocks Syndrome		trauma center
	trabecular bone score (an analytical tool that performs grey-level texture measurements on lumbar spine dual X-ray absorptiometry images, and thereby captures information relating to trabecular microarchitecture)		true conjugate
			tubocurarine
			tunneled catheter
		Tc	technetium
		T&C	turn and cough
			type and crossmatch
		T/C	telephone call
			ticarcillin-clavulanic acid (Timentin)
TBSA	total-body surface area		to consider
	total-burn surface area		tumor tissue-to-normal cerebellum tissue (uptake ratio)
TBSE	total-body skin examination		
tbsp	tablespoon (15 mL) this is a dangerous abbreviation use 15 mL	T1c	the prostate cancer stage defined as nonpalpable disease diagnosed by needle biopsy
TBST	Tris-buffered saline and Tween 20		
TBT	time before triage	T&C#3	Tylenol with 30 mg codeine
	tolbutamide test	Tc99	technetium-99
	tracheal bronchial toilet	TCA	thioguanine and cytarabine
	transbronchoscopic balloon tipped		tissue concentrations of antibiotic(s)
TBTO	tributylin oxide		trichloroacetic acid
TBUT	tear break-up time (dry-eye test)		tricuspid atresia
TBV	thiotepa, bleomycin, and vinblastine		tricyclic antidepressant
	total-blood volume		tumor chemosensitivity assay
	transluminal balloon valvuloplasty		tumor clonogenic assays
TBW	total body weight	tCa	total calcium
	total-body water	TCABG	triple coronary artery bypass graft

T

TCAD	transplant-related coronary-artery disease	TCE-MEP	transcranial electrical motor-evoked potential(s)
	tricyclic antidepressant	TCES	transcranial electrical stimulation
TCAR	tiazofurin	TCF	docetaxel, (Taxotere) cisplatin,
	transcarotid artery revascularization		and fluorouracil
TCB	to call back	TCFA	thin cap fibroatheroma
	tumor cell burden	TCGA	The Cancer Genome Atlas (database)
TcB	transcutaneous bilirubin	99mTcGHA	technetium Tc 99m glucceptate
TCBD	tetracyanobutadiene	TCGS	tonic-clonic generalized seizures
TcBili	transcutaneous bilirubin	TCH	paclitaxel (Taxol), carboplatin,
TCBL	T cell binding ligand		and trastuzumab (Herceptin)
TCBS	thiosulfate, citrate, bile, and		thunderclap headache
	sucrose [medium]		total cost of hospitalization
TCC	2,3,5-triphenyl tetrazolium		turn, cough, hyperventilate
	chloride	T-CH	total serum cholesterol
	Tai Chi Chuan	99mTc-HAS	technetium Tc-99m-labeled
	tobacco cessation counseling		human serum albumin
	total contact cast	TC/HDL-C	total cholesterol to high-density
	total cost of care		lipoprotein cholesterol (ratio)
	transient care center	T-Chol	total cholesterol
	transitional cell carcinoma	TCHP	docetaxel, carboplatin,
	tunneled cuffed catheter		trastuzumab, and pertuzumab
TCCa	transitional cell carcinoma		Traditional Chinese herbal
TCCB	transitional cell carcinoma of		products
	bladder	TCHRs	traditional Chinese herbal
TCCC	Tactical Combat Casualty Care		remedies
	(guidelines)	TCI	target-control infusion
TC/CL	ticarcillin-clavulanate		Temperament and Character
	(Timentin)		Inventory
TcCO2	transcutaneous carbon dioxide		to come in
TCD	T-cell depleted		transcutaneous immunization
	transcerebellar diameter	TCID	tissue culture infective dose
	transcranial Doppler	TCIE	transient cerebral ischemic
	(ultrasonography)		episode
	transcystic duct	TCIs	topical calcineurin inhibitors
	transverse cardiac diameter		(tacrolimus [Protopic];
	tunneled catheter drainage		pimecrolimus [Elidel])
TcdA	*Clostridium difficile* toxin A	TCIT	therapeutic crisis intervention
TCDB	turn, cough, and deep breath		training
TcdB	*Clostridium difficile* toxin B	TC joint	talocrural joint
TC&DB	turn cough and deep breath	Tck	cytokine-activated T cells
TCDD	tetrachlorodibenzo-p-dioxin	TCL	tibial collateral ligament
	(dioxin)		transverse carpal ligament
	threshold contrast detail	TCM	tissue culture media
	detectability (radiology)		traditional Chinese medicine
TCDS	transcranial color duplex		transcutaneous (oxygen)
	sonography		monitor
99mTc DTPA	technetium Tc 99m pentetate		Transitional Care Management
TCE	total-colon examination	99mTcMAA	technetium Tc 99m albumin
	toxicity composite endpoint		microaggregated
	transcatheter embolotherapy	tcMEP	transcranial motor-evoked
	trichloroethylene		potential
T-cell	a lymphocyte of a type produced	TCMH	tumor-direct cell-mediated
	or processed by the Thymus		hypersensitivity
	(hence the name) gland and	t-CMML	therapy-related chronic
	actively participating in the		myelomonocytic leukemia
	immune response	TCMR	T cell-mediated rejection

TCMS	transcranial cortical magnetic stimulation		TCU	transitional care unit
TCMZ	trichlormethiazide (Naqua)		Tcurrent	current temperature
TCN	tetracycline			current time
	triciribine phosphate (tricyclic nucleoside)		TCVA	thromboembolic cerebral vascular accident
TCNS	transcutaneous nerve stimulator		TCVC	tunneled central venous catheter
TCNU	tauromustine		TCVL	tunneled central venous line
TCO	taken care of		TCVs	thimerosal-containing vaccines
TCO₂	total carbon dioxide		TCW	telephone caseworker
TcO₂	transcutaneous oxygen pressure		TCZ	tocilizumab (Actemra injection)
TcO₄⁻	pertechnetate		TD	Takayasus disease
TCOC	Total Cost of Care			tardive dyskinesia
TCOM	transcutaneous oxygen monitor			tegmen dehiscence
TCOMs	transcutaneous oxygen measurements			temporary disability
				terminal device
T Con	temporary conservatorship			test dose
TCOs	thalamocortical oscillations			tetanus-diphtheria toxoids (pediatric use)
	total coronary occlusions			tidal volume
	transparent conducting oxides			tolerance dose
TCP	thrombocytopenia			tone decay
	transcutaneous pacing			total disability
	tranylcypromine (Parnate)			transdermal (this is a dangerous abbreviation as it has been seen as TID (three times daily)
	tricalcium phosphate			
	tumor control probability			
TCP02	may have meant transcutaneous oxygen pressure (TcPO2)			transverse diameter
				travelers' diarrhea
TCPC	total cavopulmonary connection			treatment discontinued
TcPCO₂	transcutaneous carbon dioxide		Td	tetanus-diphtheria toxoids (adult type)
TCPL	time-cycled, pressure-limited (ventilation)			
TcPO2	transcutaneous oxygen pressure		T'd	could mean treated, transcribed, transplanted, transferred, etc.
⁹⁹ᵐTcPYP	technetium Tc 99m pyrophosphate			
TCR	T-cell receptor		T&D	test and diagnostic
	transcription-coupled repair		T/D	treatment discontinued
TCRE	transcervical resection of the endometrium		T1D	type 1 diabetes (mellitus). This is a **DANGEROUS** abbreviation that should **NOT** be used. It appears on the MedAbbrev and other "Do Not Use Lists," as it has been read as three times daily (TID). Use "DM-1" or "type 1 diabetes."
	tripolar concentric ring electrodes			
TCRF	radiofrequency volumetric reduction			
TCRFTA	temperature-controlled radiofrequency tissue ablation			
TCS	testicular cancer survivors		T2D	type 2 diabetes mellitus
	tethered-cord syndrome		TDAC	tumor-derived activated cell (cultures)
	tonic-clonic seizure			
	topical corticosteroid		TDB	total daily basal (insulin dose)
	transcranial sonography		TDC	test drug concentrations
	Treacher Collins syndrome			thyroglossal duct cyst
	triclosan			tunneled dialysis catheter
⁹⁹ᵐTcSC	technetium Tc 99m sulfur colloid			twist drill craniotomy
TCT	technician-check-technician		Tde	see gene website; www.ncbi.nlm.nih.gov
	thyrocalcitonin			
	tincture		tDCS	transcranial direct current stimulation
	transcatheter therapy			
	triple combination tablet (abacavir, lamivudine, and zidovudine)		TDD	telephone device for the deaf
				thoracic duct drainage
tctB	see gene website; see gene website www.ncbi.nlm.nih.gov/gene			total daily dose
			TDDDS	transdermal drug delivery system

TDE	tobacco dependence education	TDPs	transdermal drug products
	total daily energy (requirement)	TDPWB	touchdown partial weight-bearing
TDEC	tumor-derived endothelial cells	TDR	total disk replacement
TDF	tenofovir disoproxil fumarate (Viread)		transmitted drug resistance
	testis determining factor		transmural dispersion of repolarization
	total-dietary fiber		traumatic diaphragmatic rupture
	tumor dose fractionation	TdR	thymidine
TDF/FTC	tenofovir disoproxil fumarate (Viread) and emtricitabine (Emtriva)	TDS	Teacher Drool Scale
			technically difficult study
			total dissolved solids
TDGA	thiodiglycolic acid		traveler's diarrhea syndrome
TDH	L-theronine dehydrogenase; see gene website www.ncbi .nlm.nih.gov/gene	*TDS*	three times a day (United Kingdom)
		TD's	delirium tremens
	traumatic diaphragmatic hernia	TDT	tentative discharge tomorrow
TDI	time-delay integration (radiology)		transmission disequilibrium test
	tissue Doppler imaging		Trieger Dot Test
	tolerable daily intake		tumor doubling time
	toluene diisocyanate	TdT	terminal deoxynucleotidyl transferase
	total daily insulin		
	traumatic dental injury(ies)	TDW	target dry weight
TDIs	therapist-directed interventions	TDWB	touch down weight bearing
	traumatic dental injuries	TDx®	fluorescence polarization immunoassay
TDK	tardive diskinesia		
TDL	thoracic duct lymph	T1DX	United States Type 1 Diabetes Exchange (registry)
TDLN	tumor-draining lymph nodes		
TDM	therapeutic drug monitoring	TDY	sex determining region Y; see gene website www.ncbi.nlm .nih.gov/gene
T1DM	type 1 diabetes mellitus. This is a **DANGEROUS** abbreviation that should **NOT** be used. It appears on the MedAbbrev and other "Do Not Use Lists," as it has been read as three times daily with meals (TIDM). Use "DM-1" or "type 1 diabetes."		
			temporary duty (US military)
			typically developing youth
		TE	echo time
			tennis elbow
			terminal extension
			therapeutic equivalence
T2DM	type 2 diabetes mellitus		therapeutic exercise
T3DM	three times daily with meals		tissue engineering
TDM1	ado-trastuzumab emtansine (Kadcyla)		tissue expander
			tooth extraction
TDMAC	tridodecylmethyl ammonium chloride		toxoplasmic encephalitis
			trace elements (chromium, copper, iodine, manganese, selenium, molybdenum and zinc)
TD-MALS	time-dependent, multiangle (static) light scattering		
TDN	totally digestible nutrients		tracheoesophageal
	transdermal nitroglycerin		transesophageal echocardiography
TDNTG	transdermal nitroglycerin		transrectal electroejaculation
TDNWB	touchdown nonweightbearing	Te	tellurium
TDO	tricho-dento-osseous (syndrome)	*t*E	total expiratory time
	tryptophan 2,3-dioxgenase; see gene website, www.ncbi.nlm .nih.gov/gene	T&E	testing and evaluation
			training and evaluation
			trial and error
TDP43	TAR (transactive response) DNA (deoxyribonucleic acid)-binding protein 43	T/E	testosterone to epitestosterone ratio
			testosterone/estrogen (ratio)
TdP	torsades de pointes		trunk-to-extremity skinfold thickness (index)
TDPDS	temporomandibular disorder pain dysfunction syndrome		

T

TEA	thoracic epidural analgesia	TEDs/SCDs	thromboembolic stockings and
	thromboendarterectomy		sequential compression devices
	Time and Extent Application	TEE	total energy expended
	(FDA)		transesophageal
	total elbow arthroplasty		echocardiography
	tranexamic acid (Cyklokapron;		transnasal endoscopic
	Lysteda)		ethmoidectomy
	transluminal extraction	TEED	total electrical energy delivered
	atherectomy	TEEP	transesophageal echo probe
TEAE	treatment-emergent adverse event		transesophageal
TEAEs	treatment-emergent adverse events		echocardiography with pacing
TEAP	transesophageal atrial pacing	TEEPS	transesophageal
teaspoon	a liquid unit of measure equiva-		electrophysiological study
	lent to 5 mL (write 5 mL as it	TEER	transepithelial electrical
	should not be abbreviated)		resistance
TEAVR	totally endoscopic aortic valve	TEET	triplet excitation energy transfer
	replacement	TEEU	transesophageal endoscopic
TEB	thoracic electrical bioimpedance		ultrasound
TEBG	testosterone-estradiol binding	TEF	toxic equivalency factor
	globulin		tracheoesophageal fistula
TeBG	testeosterone binding globulin	TE fistula	tracheoesophageal fistula
TeBIDA	technetium 99m trimethyl	TEFRA	The United States' 1982
	1-bromo-imono diacetic acid		Tax Equity and Fiscal
TE biopsy	trophectoderm biopsy		Responsibility Act
TEC	thromboembolic complication	TEG	thromboelastogram
	thymic epithelial cancer(s)		(thromboelastography)
	total eosinophil count	TEGS	Test for the Effect of a Gene Set
	toxic *Escherichia coli*	TEGs	thromboelastographs
	transient erythroblastopenia of	TEH	theophylline, ephedrine, and
	childhood		hydroxyzine
	transluminal extraction-		thrombosed external hemorrhoids
	endarterectomy catheter	TEI	therapeutic equivalence
	transpapillary endoscopic		interchange
	cholecystostomy		total episode of illness
	triethyl citrate		transesophageal imaging
T&EC	trauma and emergency center	TEL	telemetry
TECA	titrated extract of *Centella asiatica*		telephone
TECAB	totally endoscopic (off-pump)	tele	telemetry
	coronary artery bypass grafting	TEM	temozolomide (Temodar)
Tech	technician		thromboelastometry
	technique		transanal endoscopic
	technologist		microsurgery
TED	therapeutic effective dose		transmission electron microscopy
	thromboembolic disease	TeM	tenomodulin
	thyroid eye disease	TEMI	transient episodes of myocardial
	tobacco, EtOH (alcohol), and		ischemia
	drugs	TEMIS	Trauma and Emergency
t/e/d	tobacco, etoh (alcohol), and		Medicine Information System
	drugs		(Los Angeles County)
TEDDY study	The Environmental Determinants	TEMLA	transcervical extended mediastinal
	of Diabetes in the Young		lymphadenectomy
TED hose	thromboembolic disease support	TEMP	temporal
	stockings		temporary
TEDS	thromboembolic disease	temp	temperature
	stockings	temps	temperatures
	transesophageal echo-Doppler	TEMPS-A	Temperament Evaluation of
	system		Memphis, Paris and San
	Treatment Episode Data Set		Diego Auto-questionnaire

T

TEMS	tactical emergency medical support	TESA	testicular sperm aspiration
	transanal endoscopic microsurgery	TESE	testicular sperm extraction
TEMs	technical errors of measurement	TESI	thoracic epidural steroid injection
	tetraspanin-enriched microdomains	Tesio	tunneled hemodialysis catheters
TEN	tension (intraocular pressure)	TESS	Toronto Extremity Salvage Score
	toxic epidermal necrolysis		Total Evolutive Shoulder System
TEN®	Total Enteral Nutrition		Toxic Exposure Surveillance System
TenC	tenascin C (gene/protein)		treatment emergent signs and symptoms
tend	tenderness		Treatment Emergent Symptom Scale
TENS	Toxic Epidermal Necrolysis Syndrome (Stevens-Johnson Syndrome)	TEST	testosterone
	transcutaneous electrical nerve stimulation	TET2	tet methylcytosine dioxygenase 2 (gene)
TENs	titanium elastic nails	TET	total ejection time
TENT	total evidence nucleotide tree	TEU	token economy unit
TeNT	tetanus neurotoxin		transesophageal ulttrasound
TEOAE	transient evoked otoacoustic emission (test)	TEV	talipes equinovarus (deformity)
			venous thromboembolism (French and Spanish abbreviation)
TEP	total endoprosthesis		
	total extraperitoneal (laparoscopic hernia repair)	TEVAP	transurethral electrovaporization of the prostate
	tracheoesophageal prosthesis		thoracic endovascular aneurysm repair
	tracheoesophageal puncture		
	tubal ectopic pregnancy		thoracic endovascular aortic repair
TEPP	testis, prostate and placenta-expressed protein; see gene website; www.ncbi .nlm.nih.gov	TEVR	thoracic endovascular aortic repair
		TEWL	transepidermal water loss
		TEX	tumor-derived exosome
		TEx	time to exhaustion
	tetraethyl pyrophosphate	Tex	Texas (current postal abbreviation for Texas is TX)
	totally extraperitoneal prosthetic repair		
TEPPS	Tiffany-Eckenrode Program Participation Scale	tex	texture
		TEX cells	exhausted T cells
TEQ	toxic equivalents	TF	tactile fremitus
TER	terlipressin		tail flick (reflex)
	total elbow replacement		tetralogy of Fallot
	total energy requirement		Thomsen-Friedenreich (antigen)
	transnasal endoscopic resection		tibiofemoral
	transurethral electroresection		tissue factor
TERB	terbutaline		to follow
TERC	Test of Early Reading Comprehension		transfeminine
			transfemoral (approach)
TERM	full-term		trial frame
	terminal		trigger finger
			tube feeding
TERP	transanal endorectal pull-through	Tf	transferring
TERT	human telomerase reverse transcriptase (also hTRT)	t/f	to follow
			transfer (patient)
	tertiary	TFA	thigh-foot angle
	total end-range time		topical fluoride application
TES	therapeutic electrical stimulation		trans fatty acids
	thoracic endometriosis syndrome		transfemoral access (interventional cardiology)
	thoracic endoscopic sympathectomy		transfemoral amputee
	transcorneal electrical stimulation		trifluoroacetic acid
	treatment emergent symptoms	TFAV	Thiafora virus

TFB	trifascicular block	TF-TAVR	transfemoral transcatheter aortic valve replacement
TFBC	The Family Birthing Center		
TFC	thoracic fluid content	TFTD	transcervical falloposcopy tubal dilatation
	time to following commands		
	triangular fibrocartilage	TFTs	thyroid function tests
TF-CBT	trauma focused cognitive behavioral therapy	TFU	telephone follow-up
		TFV	tenofir (Viread)
TFCC	triangular fibrocartilage complex	T25FW	timed 25-foot Walk
tfdA	see gene website www.ncbi.nlm.nih.gov/gene	TG	thioguanine
			Total Gym (exercise device)
TFE3	transcription factor E3		transplant glomerulopathy
TFEI	transforaminal epidural injection		triglycerides
TFESI	transforaminal epidural steroid injection	Tg	thyroglobulin
		6-TG	thioguanine
TFF	tangential flow filtration	TGA	Therapeutic Goods Administration (Australia)
	trefoil factor family (peptides)		
TFFC	Total flavonoids of Flos Chrysanthemi		thermal gravimetric analyses
			third-generation antidepressant
TF-Fe	transferrin-bound iron		thrombin generation assay
TFG	TRK (tropomyosin-receptor kinase)-fused gene; see gene website www.ncbi.nlm.nih.gov/gene		transient global amnesia
			transposition of the great arteries
		TGAR	total graft area rejected
		TGB	tiagabine (Gabatril)
Tfh	T follicular helper (cells)	TGC	tight glucose control
TFI	total fluid intake		tight glycemic control
	treatment free interval	TGCE	temparature gradient capillary electrophoresis
TFL	tensor fasciae latae		
	transnasal fiberoptic laryngoscopy	TGCT	tenosynovial giant-cell tumor
	trimetrexate, fluorouracil, and leucovorin		testicular germ cell tumor(s)
		TGD	thyroglossal duct
	trunk forward lean		tumor growth delay
TFLS	Texas Functional Living Scale	TGDC	thyroglossal duct cyst
TFLs	tail flick latencies	TGE	targeted genomic enrichment
TFM	transverse friction massage		tendon gliding exercises
TFMA	talo-first metatarsal angles		transient gene expression
TFME	thin-film micro extraction		transmissible gastroenteritis
TFMR	termination (abortion) for medical reason(s)	TGEV	transmissible gastroenteritis virus
		TGF	transforming growth factor
TFN	trochanteric fixation nail	TGF-β	transforming growth factor-beta
TFNA	testicular Fine Needle Aspiration	TGFA	triglyceride fatty acid
	thyroid fine-needle aspiration	TG-GCMS	thermogravimetric analysis coupled to gas chromatography/mass spectroscopy
	transbronchial fine-needle aspiration		
TFO	triplex-forming oligonucleotide	TGGE	temperature-gradient gel electrophoresis
TFOs	triplex-forming oligonucleotides		
TFP	trifluoperazine (formerly available as Stelazine)	TGH	triacylglycerol hydrolase
		TGI	tracheal gas insufflation
	trifunctional protein deficiency	TGJ tube	transgastrostomal jejunal tube
TFPI	tissue-factor pathway inhibitor	TGL	triglyceride level
TFR	total fertility rate	TGLP	total glossectomy with laryngeal preservation
TFS	focal electrical stimulation		
TFs	tube feedings	TGMs	transglutaminases
TFSI	transforaminal (epidural) steroid injection	TGN	trans-Golgi network
			trochanteric gamma nail
TFT	thin film transistor	TGNC	transgender and nonconforming
	Thought Field Therapy	TGO	transposition of the greater omentum
	thumb-finding test		
	trifluridine (trifluorothymidine)	T gondii	Toxoplasma gondii

TGP	total glucosides of paeony	THE	total-head excursion
TGR	tenderness, guarding, and rigidity		transhepatic embolization
TGS	tactile guidance system	Ther	therapeutic
	tincture of green soap	Thera Band®	A progressive exercise system
TGs	triglycerides		utilizing synthetic and natural
TG-SPAD	time-gated single-photon		rubber tubing, cord, and
	avalanche diode		sheeting to provide resistance
TGT	thromboplastin generation test	ther act	therapeutic activities
TGTL	total glottic transverse	Ther Ex	therapeutic exercise
	laryngectomy	thera ex	therapeutic exercise
TGV	thoracic gas volume	THES	trichohepatoenteric syndrome
	transposition of great vessels	THF	thymic humoral factor
TGXT	thallium-graded exercise test	THG	tetrahydrogestrinone
TGZ	troglitazone (Rezulin)		The Heart Group
TH	teaching hospital		third-harmonic generation
	therapeutic hypothermia	THg	total mercury
	thrill	THH	Tripterygium hypoglaucum
	thyroid hormone		Hutch (a Chinese herbal
	total hysterectomy		medicine)
	type and hold	THI	transient hypogammaglobulin-
Th	thick		emia of infancy
	thorium	Thi	time high
	Thursday	TH-ICH	thalamic intracerebral hemorrhage
Th1	T helper cell, type 1	T-High	time high
Th2	T helper cell, type 2	THKAFO	trunk-hip-knee-ankle-foot
THA	tacrine (tetrahydroacridine;		orthosis
	Cognex)	THKAFO-LU	lockable joints using trunk-hip-
	total hip arthroplasty		knee-ankle-foot orthosis
	transient hemispheric attack	THKR-1	Total Hip and Total Knee Replace-
THAA	thyroid hormone autoantibodies		ment, Regional Anesthesia (The
	tubular hypoplasia aortic arch		Joint Commission advanced
THABSO	see TAHBSO		certification program)
THAD	transient hepatic attenuation	THKR-2	Total Hip and Total Knee Replace-
	differentiation		ment, Postoperative Ambula-
THAL	thalassemia		tion on the Day of Surgery (The
	thalidomide (Thalomid)		Joint Commission advanced
	therapeutic lifestyle changes		certification program)
THAM®	tromethamine	THKR-3	Total Hip and Total Knee
T-hand	Theraband		Replacement, Discharged to
THAT	Toronto Hospital Alertness Test		Home (The Joint Commission
THb	total hemoglobin		advanced certification program)
THBI	thyroid hormone binding index	THKR-4	Total Hip and Total Knee Replace-
THBO₂	topical hyperbaric oxygen		ment, Preoperative Functional/
THBR	thyroid hormone-binding ratio		Health Status Assessment (The
THBSO	total abdominal		Joint Commission advanced
	hysterectomy and bilateral		certification program)
	salpingo-oophorectomy	THL	transvaginal hydrolaparoscopy
THC	cannabinoids	ThL	thin liquids
	tetrahydrocannabinol (dronabinol)	THLAA	tubular hypoplasia left aortic
	transhepatic cholangiogram		arch
ThC	thigh circumference	THM	take-home methadone
THCT	triple-phase helical computer	THMs	trihalomethanes
	tomography	THN	take-home naloxone
TH-CULT	throat culture		(kits; Scotland)
tHcy	total homocysteine		tetrahydronaphthalene
THD	transanal hemorrhoidal	THOR	thoracentesis
	dearterialization		thoracic
THDC	tunnelled hemodialysis catheter		thorax

$THBO_2$

thou	thousand	TIA TLKW	transient ischemic attack, time last known well (the length of time since a patient was last known to be well before a transient ischemic attack)
THP	take home packs		
	Tamm-Horsfall protein		
	topical hemostatic powder		
	total hip precautions		
	total hip prosthesis	TIB	tibia
	transhepatic portography		tibial (nerve)
	trihexyphenidyl (Artane)		time in bed
THR	target heart rate		time in bed (polysomnography related)
	thrombin receptor		
	total hip replacement	TIBANT	tibialis anterior tendon
	total hip resurfacing	tib-ant	tibialis anterior
	training heart rate	TIBC	total iron-binding capacity
Thr	threonine	TIBFIB	tibula and fibula
THRA	total hip replacement arthroplasty	tib-fib	tibia and fibula
THRev	total hip revision	TIBI-CaP	Total Illness Burden Index for Prostate Cancer
THRL	total hip replacement, left		
thromb	thrombosis	TIB	a scientific apparatus manufacturer
thrombo	a prefix or combining form denoting a relationship to a clot	MOLBIOL	
		TIBS	transillumination breast spectroscopy
THRR	total hip replacement, right		
	transient hyperemic response ratio	TIC	paclitaxel (Taxol), ifosfamide, and cisplain
THS	Tolosa-Hunt syndrome		
THs	teaching hospitals		tachycardia-induced cardiomyopathy
THTV	therapeutic home trial visit		
THU	tetrahydrouridine		total ion chromatograms
Thu	Thursday		trypsin-inhibitor capacity
Thurs	Thursday (Thu is preferred)		tubal intraepithelial carcinoma
	Thursday	TICA	tensorial-independent component analysis
THV	therapeutic home visit		
	transcatheter heart valve		terminal internal carotid artery
THx	thyroidectomy		traumatic intracranial aneurysm
THY	thymectomy	TICI	Thrombolysis in Cerebral Infarction (score [the association between clot characteristics and successful recanalization])
	thymine		
	thymus		
THz	terahertz (a unit of electromagnetic wave frequency equal to one trillion hertz [10^{12} hertz])		
		TICM	tachycardia-induced cardiomyopathy
TI	inversion time (radiology)		
	terminal ileus	TICOSMO	trauma, infection, chemical/drug exposure, organ systems, stress, musculoskeletal, and other (prompts used during history taking for possible etiologies of problems)
	thallium imaging		
	therapeutic index		
	thought insertion		
	time following inversion pulse (radiology)		
		TICS	diverticulosis
	tortuosity index	TICU	thoracic intensive care unit
	transischial		transplant intensive care unit
	transverse diameter of inlet		trauma intensive care unit
	treponema immobilization	TID	three times daily (three times a day)
	tricuspid incompetence		
	tricuspid insufficiency		transillumination defect
Ti	titanium	t.i.d.	three times daily (TID is preferred as periods are unnecessary and in some cases there is a character limitation where computer orders are to be entered)
TI4	therapeutic interchange for . . .		
TIA	trabecular-iris angle		
	transient ischemic attack		
TIA-1	T-cell restricted intracellular antigen-1		
TIAs	transient ischemic attacks	TIDAC	three times daily, before meals

TIDCC	three times daily with food	TIP	toxic interstitial pneumonitis
TIDCs	tumor-infiltrating dendritic cells		tube in place
tidhol	may have meant tidal		tubularized incised plate
TIDM	May be T1DM which is type I		(urethroplasty)
	diabetes mellitus (see T1DM)	TIP & P	tube in place and patent
TIDPC	three times daily, after meals	TIPPS	threshold ion-pair production
TIDs	transillumination defects		spectroscopy
TIDWM	three times daily, with meals	TIPS	transjugular intrahepatic
TIE	transient ischemic episode		portosystemic shunt
	tracheal intubation fiberscope	Tipsitis	infection of transjugular
	transoral incisionless		intrahepatic portosystemic
	fundoplication		stent shunt (TIPSS)
TIG	tetanus immune globulin	TIPSS	transjugular intrahepatic
TIH	trans-iliac herniation		portosystemic stent shunt
	tumor-inducing hypercalcemia	TIPU	tubularized-incised plate
TIIDM	type II diabetes mellitus		urethroplasty
TIL	term pregnancies in spontaneous	TIR	technician in the room
	labor	TIRDA	temporal intermittent
	tumor-infiltrating lymphocytes		rhythmic delta activity
TILC	time interval from last		(electroencephalograph)
	chemotherapy	TIRF	transmucosal immediate-release
	totally intracorporeal laparo-		fentanyl
	scopic colectomy	TIRFM	total-internal reflection
%tile	percentile		fluorescence microscopy
TILF	may have meant TLIF (trans-	TIS	transverse iliosacral
	foraminal lumbar interbody		tumor *in situ*
	fusion)	TISCC	tethering in situ click chemistry
TILs	tumor infiltrating lymphocytes	TISS	Therapeutic Intervention
TIMI	Thrombolysis in Myocardial		Scoring System
	Infarction (trial)	TISS-28	Therapeutic Intervention Scoring
TIMP	Test of Infant Motor Performance		System based on the 28 items
	tissue inhibitor of	TIT	*Treponema* (*pallidum*)
	metalloproteinase		immobilization test
TIMP-2	Tissue inhibitors of		triiodothyronine (liothyronine)
	metalloproteinase 2	titer test	Concentration of a substance
TIMPs	tissue-inhibitors to		in solution or the strength of
	metalloproteinases		such a substance determined
TIMS	trapped ion mobility		by titration
	spectrometry	TIUP	term intrauterine pregnancy
TIMV	Torque-tenominivirus	TIV	tracheostomy-invasive ventilation
TIN	Taxpayer Identification Number		trivalent inactivated influenza
	testicular intraepithelial		vaccine
	neoplasia	TIVA	total intravenous anethesia
	three times a night (this is a	TIVAD	totally implantable venous
	dangerous abbreviation)		access device
	tubulointerstitial nephritis	TIVC	thoracic inferior vena cava
tinct	tincture	+tive	positive
TIND	Treatment Investigational	TIVS	temporary intravascular shunt
	New Drug (application)	TIW	three times a week. This is a
T₃/ind	triiodothyronine to thyroxine		DANGEROUS abbreviation
	index		that should NOT be used. It
TINEM	there is no evidence of		appears on the MedAbbrev
	malignancy		and other "Do Not Use Lists,"
TINU	tubulointerstitial nephritis and		as it has been read as Tuesday
	uveitis (syndrome)		and Wednesday (T/W), twice
TiO₂	titanium dioxide		a week, and three times daily
TiO₂-NPs	titanium dioxide nanoparticles		(TID). Use "three times a
tIOL	toric intraocular lenses		week."

590

Ti-Zr	titanium-zirconium (alloy)		thoracolumbar
TJ	tendon jerk		total laryngectomy
	tight junction		transverse line
	triceps jerk		trial leave
TJ-54	Yokukansan (a Japanese herbal		tubal ligation
	medicine)	Tl	thallium
TJA	total joint arthroplasty	T&L	thunder and lightning
TJC	tender joint count	T/L	terminal latency
	The Joint Commission	TL BLT	tubal ligation, bilateral
	(formerly JCAHO, the Joint	TLA	translumbar arteriogram
	Commission on Accreditation		(aortogram)
	Healthcare Organizations)		transverse ligament of atlas
TJLB	transjugular liver biopsy	TLA1	transparent leaf area peptide
TJLBx	transjugular liver biopsy		(gene/protein)
TJM	thrust joint manipulation	TLAC	triple lumen Arrow catheter
	tremulous jaw movement	TLC	tender loving care
TJN	tongue jaw neck (dissection)		therapeutic lifestyle changes
	twin-jet nebulizer		thin layer chromatography
TJP	tight junction proteins		titanium linear cutter
TJR	total joint replacement		T-lymphocyte choriocarcinoma
TK	thoracic kyphosis		total lift chair
	thymidine kinase		total lung capacity
	toxicokinetics		total lymphocyte count
TKA	total knee arthroplasty		total-lift chair
	tyrosine kinase activity		transitional living center
TKD	tokodynamometer		triple lumen catheter
TKE	terminal knee extension	TlCl	thallium chloride
TKI	tyrosine kinase inhibitor	TLCO	carbon monoxide lung transfer
TKIC	true knot in cord		Total Life Cycle Cost of
TKIs	tyrosine kinase inhibitors		Ownership
TkL	thickened liquids	TLD	thermoluminescent dosimeter
TKNO	to keep needle open	TLDA	temporal lobe delta activity
TKO	to keep (vein; intravenous line)		(electroencephalograph)
	open	TLE	temporal lobe epilepsy
TKP	thermokeratoplasty		transvenous lead extraction
	total knee prosthesis	TLE-HS	temporal lope
TKR	total knee replacement		epilepsy-hippocampal
	total knee revision		sclerosis
TKRA	total knee replacement	TLESI	transforaminal lumbar epidural
	arthroplasty		steriod injection
TKRev	total knee revision	TLESR	transient lower esophageal
TKRL	total knee replacement, left		sphincter relaxation
TKRR	total knee replacement, right	TLFB	timeline follow back (interview)
TKs	achykinins	TlFP(6)	thallium(I) hexafluorophosphate
	tyrosine kinases	TLGA	liver-type glutaminase
TKTL1	transketolase-like protein 1		transfected cells
TKV	total kidney volume (an imaging	TLGLL	T-cell large granular lymphocyte
	biomarker for tracking and		leukemia
	predicting the natural history	T-LGLL	T-cell large granular
	of patients with autosomal		lymphocytic leukemia
	dominant polycystic kidney	TLH	total laparoscopic hysterectomy
	disease)	TLHBSO	total laparoscopic
TKVO	to keep vein open		hysterectomy bilateral
TL	labor at term		salpingo-oophorectomy
	tandem-leg	TLH/BSO/LND	total laparoscopic hysterectomy
	team leader		with bilateral salpingo-
	thermoluminescence		ophorectomy and pelvic/
	thickened liquids		aortic lymph node dissection

TLI	total lymphoid irradiation
	translaryngeal intubation
	Tucker-Lewis index
TLICS	Thoracolumbar Injury Classification and Severity (score)
TLIF	transforaminal lumbar interbody fusion
TLIS	total lung Injury Score
TLISS	thoracolumbar Injury Severity Score
TLJ	thoracolumbar junction
TLJA	thoracolumbar junction alignment
TLK	thermal laser keratoplasty
TLKW	time last known well (the amount of time since the patient was last known to be well before a transient ischemic attack or stroke)
TLL	Thermomyces lanuginosus lipase
Tll	tailless; see gene website www.ncbi.nlm.nih.gov/gene
T-LLy	T-cell lymphoblastic lymphoma
TLM	thalidomide (Thalomid)
	torn lateral meniscus
	transoral laser microsurgery
TLNB	term living newborn
TLO	thoracolumbar orthosis
Tlo	time low
TLOA	temporary leave of absence
TLOC	transient loss of consciousness
TLOVR	time-to-loss of virologic response [algorithm]
T-Low	time low
TLP	total laparoscopic prostatectomy
	transitional living program
TLPD	T-cell lymphoproliferative disease
	total laparoscopic pancreaticoduodenectomy
TLR	target-lesion revascularization
	tonic labyrinthine reflex
TLR3	toll-like receptor 3
TLR4	toll-like receptor 4
TLRs	toll-like receptors
TLS	threshold-based level set
	total length of stay
	tumor lysis syndrome
TLSO	thoracolumbosacral orthosis
TLSO brace	thoracolumbosacral orthosis brace
TLSP	trypsin-like serine protease
TLSSO	thoracolumbosacral spinal orthosis
TLST	thoracolumbar spine trauma
TLSW	time last seen well
TLT	threshold laser treatment
	tonsillectomy
TLTBI	treatment of latent tuberculosis infection

TLUS	the time elapsed from ingestion of the first dose of medication to passage of the last unformaed stool
TLUSG	transcutaneous laryngeal ultrasonography
TLV	total liquid ventilation
	total lung volume
	two-lung ventilation
TL V	threshold limit value
TLVAB	transient left-ventricular apical ballooning
TM	tarsometatarsal (joint)
	temperature by mouth
	tetrathiomolybdate
	thalassemia major
	Thayer-Martin (culture)
	thyromegaly
	Tibetan Medicine
	total mastectomy
	trabecular meshwork
	trach (tracheostomy) mask
	tracheomalacia
	trademark (unregistered)
	transcendental meditation
	transmasculine
	transmetatarsal
	transverse myelitis
	treadmill
	tropical medicine
	tumor
	tympanic membrane
Tm	thulium
T & M	type and crossmatch
T/M	tumor-to-muscle (ratio)
TMA	thermomechanical analysis
	thrombotic microangiopathy
	tissue microarray
	trained medication aid
	transcription mediated amplification
	transmetatarsal amputation
	trimethylamine
T/MA	tracheostomy mask
T1MA	talar 1 meta-tarsal angle
Tmab	trastuzumab (Herceptin)
TMAO	trimethylamine-N-oxide
TMAS	Taylor Manifest Anxiety Scale
TMAs	tissue microarrays
TMA-uria	trimethylaminuria
Tmax	the time after administration of a drug when the maximum plasma concentration is reached
TMB	tetramethylberizidine
	therapeutic back massage
	transient monocular blindness
	trimethoxybenzoates
	tumor mutation burden

TMC	transmural colitis		TMLR	transmyocardial laser revascularization
	Transtheoretical Model of Change		TMM	torn medial meniscus
	trapeziometacarpal			total muscle mass
	triamcinolone		Tmm	McKay-Marg tension
TM2c	Torpedoman's Mate 2nd Class		t-MN	therapy-related myeloid neoplasms
TMCA	trimethylcolchicinic acid			
TMCC	temoral mandibular cervical chain (of muscles)		TMNB	transcarinal mediastinal needle biopsy
TMCN	triamcinolone		TMNG	toxic multinodular goiter
TMD	temporomandibular dysfunction (disorder)		TMO	transcaruncular medial orbitotomy
	terrien marginal degeneration		TMP	thallium myocardial perfusion
	thyromental distance			transmembrane pressure
	transient myeloproliferative disorder			trimethoprim
	treating physician			tympanic membrane perforation
t-MD	therapy-related myelodysplastic syndromes		TMP-SMX	trimethoprim and sulfamethoxazole (correct name is sulfamethoxazole and trimethoprim [SMZ-TMP])
TMDD	target-mediated drug disposition			
t-MDS	therapy-related myelodysplastic syndrome		TMP-SMZ	trimethoprim and sulfamethoxazole (correct name is sulfamethoxazole and trimethoprim [SMZ-TMP]
TME	thermolysin-like metalloendopeptidase			
	total mesorectal excision		TMPT	may have meant TPMT (thiopurine S-methyltransferase)
	toxic-metabolic encephalopathy			
	tumor microenvironment		TMR	targeted motor reinnervation
TMEP	telangiectasis macularis eruptive perstans			targeted muscle reinnervation
				temporary medication refill
TMET	treadmill exercise test			tissue-maximum ratio
TMEV	Theilers murine encephalomyelitis virus			trainable mentally retarded
				transmyocardial revascularization
TMF	Tecnis Multifocal Acrylic (lens)			transverse digital microradiography
TMG	tensiomyography			
	transverse musculocutaneous gracilis (flap)		TMRW	tomorrow
			TMS	Toronto Mindfulness Scale
	trimegestone			transcranial magnetic stimulation
	trimethylguanosine		TMs	tympanic membranes
TMH	tear meniscus height		TM's	tympanic membranes
	trainable mentally handicapped		TMSBP	Targeted Medication Safety Best Practices
TMI	threatened myocardial infarction			
	transmandibular implant		TMSI	Task Management Strategy Index
	transmural infarct		TMST	treadmill stress test
T>MIC	time above minimum inhibitory concentration		TMT	tarsometatarsal
				tarsometatarsal (joint)
TMID	temporomandibular (joint) intracapsular disease			teratoma with malignant transformation
TMJ	temporomandibular joint			treadmill test
TMJD	temporomandibular joint dysfunction			tympanic membrane thermometer
			TMTC	too many to count
TMJS	temporomandibular joint syndrome		TMTJ	tarsometatarsal joint
			TMT joint	tarsometatarsal joint
TMK	transmembrane kinase		TMTX	trimetrexate (Neutrexin)
Tmk	thymidylate kinase (gene)		TMUGS	Tumor Marker Utility Grading Scale
TML	tongue midline			
	treadmill		TMVIV	transcatheter mitral valve-in-valve (replacement)
TMLP	transumbilical multi-stab laparoscopic pyeloplasty			
			TMVL	transient monocular visual loss

TMVR	transcatheter mitral valve repair	TNG	nitroglycerin
	transcatheter mitral valve		toxic nodular goiter
	replacement	TnH	troponin H
TMVR/r	transcatheter mitral valve repair	TNI	total nodal irradiation
	and replacement	TnI	troponin I
TMW	ten-meter walk	TNIL	term not-in-labor
TMX	tamoxifen (Novaldex)	TNJ	Tahitian Noni Juice
	temperature maximum		talonavicular joint
TMZ	temazepam (Restoril)	TN joint	talonavicular joint
	temozolomide (Temodar)	TNK	tenecteplase (TNKase®)
TN	normal intraocular tension	TNKase®	tenecteplase
	talonavicular (joint)	TNL	term no labor
	team nursing	Tnl	troponin l
	temperature normal	TNM	primary tumor, regional lymph
	Tennessee		nodes, and distant metastasis
	tree nut		(used with subscripts for the
	trigemial neuralgia		staging of cancer)
	triple negative	t-NNT	threshold number needed to
Tn	troponin		treat
T&N	tension and nervousness	TNO	Nederlandse Organisatie voor
	tingling and numbness		toegepast-Natuurwetenschap-
T/N	tumor tissue-to-normal brain		pelijk Onderzoek (Dutch for
	tissue (uptake ratio)		the Netherlands Organisa-
TMZF®	beta titanium alloy (titanium,		tion for Applied Scientific
	molybdenum, zirconium,		Research)
	and iron)	TNP	test not performed
TNA	total nutrient admixture		time to neurologic progression
TNAB	transthoracic needle biopsy		transdermal nicotine patch
TNAs	transient neurological attacks	TNPM	transient neonatal pustular
TNB	term newborn		melanosis
	transnasal butorphanol	TnpM	transposition modulator protein
	transrectal needle biopsy		(gene)
	(of the prostate)	TNR	tonic neck reflex
	Tru-Cut® needle biopsy	TNS	transcutaneous nerve stimulation
TNBC	triple-negative breast cancer(s)		(stimulator)
TNBL	thoracic neuroblastoma		transient neurologic symptoms
	triple-negative basal-like		Trauma Nurse Specialist
	(breast cancer cell)		trigeminal nerve stimulation
TNBP	transurethral needle biopsy of		Tullie-Niebörg syndrome
	prostate	TNSS	total nasal symptom score
TNc	troponin C	TNT	thiotepa, mitoxantrone (Novan-
TNCC	Trauma Nursing Course Certified		trone), and paclitaxel (Taxol)
TND	term, normal delivery		transnasal tracheoscopy
TNDM	transient neonatal diabetes		treating to new targets
	mellitus		triage and treatment
TNE	transnasal endoscopy		triamcinolone and nystatin
	transnasal esophagoscopy	TnT	troponin T
	true nonenhanced (radiology)	TNTC	too numerous to count
TN-EGD	transnasal	TNTS	transnasal, transsphenoidal
	esophagogastroduodenoscopy	TNTs	titanate nanotubes
TNF	tumor necrosis factor		tunneling nanotubes
TNFA	tumor necrosis factor alpha	TNU	tobacco nonuser
TNF-bp	tumor necrosis factor binding		Trauma Neurosurgical
	protein		(Intensive Care) Unit
TNFi	tumor necrosis factor inhibitors	TNV	tobacco necrosis virus
	(e.g. etanercept [Enbrel],		total nas cima al volume
	infliximab [Remicade],	TNV-D	tobacco necrosis virus, strain D
	adalimumab [Humira])	TNW	total number of words

TNWB	terminal noncardioplegic warm blood (perfusion)	TODs	target organ damages
TNY	trichomonas and yeast	TOE	transoesophageal echocardiography (United Kingdom and other countries)
TO	old tuberculin		
	telephone order	TO-EGD	transoral esophagogastroduodenoscopy
	temperature, oral		
	time off	TOETVA	transoral endoscopic thyroidectomy-vestibular approach
	tincture of opium (warning: this is NOT paregoric)		
	total obstruction	TOF	tetralogy of Fallot
	transfer out		time of flight (radiology)
	turbulence onset		total of four
T&O	tandem and ovoid insertion		train-of-four
	tubes and ovaries	TOFMS	time-of-flight mass spectrometry
T(O)	oral temperature	TOGV	transposition of the great vessels
T/O	see TO	TOH	throughout hospitalization
	throughout		transient osteoporosis of the hip
	time out	TOI	Trial Outcome Index
TO4	train of 4	TOL	tolerated
TOA	time of arrival		trial of labor
	transverse occiput anterior	TOLAC	trial of labor after cesarean section
	tubo-ovarian abscess	TOLD	Test of Language Development
TOAA	to affected areas	TOM	therapeutic outcomes monitoring
TOAST	Trial of Org 10172 (Danaparoid Sodium) in Acute Stroke Treatment (criteria for non-postoperative strokes)		therapy outcome measure
			tomorrow
			transcutaneous oxygen monitor
		ToM	theory-of-mind
TOAT	triple oral antithrombotic therapy (warfarin, clopidogrel [Plavix], and aspirin)	TOMM	Test of Memory Malingering
		Tomo	tomography
		TOMS	transobturator male sling
TOB	tobacco	tomy	a suffix meaning a "surgical incision"
	tobramycin		
TOBI®	tobramycin inhalation solution	TON	tonight
tobra	tobramycin		traumatic optic neuropathy
TOBY	Moderate Hypothermia to Treat Perinatal Asphyxial Encephalopathy (TOtal BodY hypothermia; a multi-center, prospective, randomized study)	TOP	termination of pregnancy
			Topografov (virus)
			topotecan (Hycamtin)
		TOP-8	Treatment Outcome PTSD (post-traumatic stress disorder) (scale)
TOC	table of contents		
	test-of-cure (post-therapy visit)	tophi	a word meaning chalky deposits of sodium urate occurring in gout
	total occlusal convergence		
	total organic carbon	TOPJ	temporo-occipito-parietal junction
	transfer of care	TOPL	Test of Pragmatic Language
	transition of care	TOPO	topotecan (Hycamtin)
TO₂c	tissue oxygen consumption	Topo I	topoisomerase I
TOCE	transcatheter oily chemoembolization	TOPPS	trans-obturator polypropylene sling
TOCO	tocodynamometer	TOPS	Take Off Pounds Sensibly
TOCU	transoral carotid ultrasonography	TOPV	trivalent oral polio vaccine
TOD	intraocular pressure of the right eye	TOR	termination of resuscitation
			toremifene (Faneston)
	target organ damage	Tor	torsades
	target-organ disease	TORB	telephone order read back
	time of day	Tor BSST	Toronto Bedside Swallowing Screening Test
	time of death		
	time of departure	TOR-BSST	Toronto Bedside Swallowing Screening Test
	tubal occlusion device		

TORC	Test of Reading Comprehension
TORCH	toxoplasmosis, others (other viruses known to attack the fetus), rubella, cytomegalovirus, and herpes simplex (maternal viral infections)
TORP	total ossicular replacement prosthesis
Torr	a unit of pressure
	Torricelli (unit of pressure equal to 1/760 atmosphere; approximately equal to one millimeter of mercury)
TORS	transoral robotic surgery
TORT	total operating room time
	transoral robotic thyroidectomy
TORV	telephone order that is repeated back and verified as correct
TOS	intraocular pressure of the left eye
	thoracic outlet syndrome
	Type of Service
TOSH	The Orthopedic Specialty Hospital, Murray, Utah
TOT	tip-of-the-tongue
	transobturator tape
	triple oral therapy (metformin, glyburide, and pioglitazone)
total A	total albumin
TOT BILI	total bilirubin
TOTM	trioctyltrimellitate
toto	a word meaning, as a whole
TOT sling	transobturator sling
TOUA	transient occlusion of uterine arteries
TOV	telephone order verified
	trial of void
TOW	time off work
TOWL	Test of Written Language
TOX	toxoplasmosis (*Toxoplasma gondii*) vaccine
Tox	Botox Cosmetic (onabotulinumtoxinA) for injection
tox	toxicology
TOXO	toxoplasmosis
ToxRefDB	Toxicity Reference Database (US Environmental Protection Agency)
TP	"T" piece
	talc pleurodesis
	teaching physician
	temperature and pressure
	temporoparietal
	tender point
	tensor palatini
	therapeutic pass
	ThinPrep Pap (test)
	thiopental (Pentothal)
	thought process

	thrombophlebitis
	thymidine phosphorylase
	tibial-peroneal
	time to progression
	Todds paralysis
	toe pressure
	toilet paper
	total protein
	transverse process
	transverse processes
	trastuzumab and paclitaxel
	treating physician
	treatment plan
	trigger point
	true positive
T:P	trough-to-peak ratio
T&P	temperature and pulse
	turn and position
T/P	template/primer
TP1	treatment phase one
TP2	treatment phase two
TP3	treatment phase three
TP53	tumor protein p53 (gene)
TPA	temporary portacaval anastomosis
	third-party administrator
	tissue polypeptide antigen
	total parenteral alimentation
tPA	alteplase, recombinant (tissue plasminogen activator; Activase)
T-PA	alteplase, recombinant (tissue plasminogen activator) (Activase)
T PACE	temporary pacemaker
TPAD	tethered pelvic assist device
TPAIT	total pancreatectomy with autologous islet transplantation
TP/AIT	total pancreatectomy with autologous islet (cell) transplantation
TPAL	term infant(s), premature infant(s), abortion(s), living children
TPB	Theory of Planned Behavior
TPC	target plasma concentration
	tender-point count
	total patient care
	total plate count
	total proctocolectomy
	touch preparation cytology
	treatment of physician's choice
	tunneled pleural catheter
TPC + IPAA	total proctocolectomy with ileal J-pouch with pouch-anal anastomosis
TPD	threshold pyrogenic dose
	total perfusion deficit
	treatable protocol depth

	tropical pancreatic diabetes	TPLSM	two-photon laser-scanning microscope
	typhoid vaccine, not otherwise specified	TPM	temporary pacemaker
TPD$_a$	typhoid vaccine, attenuated live (oral Ty21a strain)		topiramate (Topamax)
			total passive motion
TPD$_{AKD}$	typhoid vaccine, acetone-killed and dried (U.S. military)	t-PMET	trans-plasma membrane electron transport
TPD$_{HP}$	typhoid vaccine, heat and phenol inactivated, dried	TPMP	See [^{11}C]TPMP (search for 11CTPMP)
TPD$_{VI}$	typhoid vaccine, *Vi* capsular polysaccharide	tPMPs	thrombin-induced platelet microbicidal proteins
TPE	therapeutic plasma exchange	TPM SMX	see TMP/SMZ
	total placental estrogens	TPMT	thiopurine methyltransferase
	total protective environment		thiopurine S-methyltransferase,
T-penia	thrombocytopenia		gene (polymorphic enzyme
TPF	docetaxel, (Taxotere) cisplatin (Platinol), and fluorouracil		variant responsible for the metabolism of a wide range
	trained participating father		of clinical drugs [azathi-
TP fracture	transverse process fracture		oprine, mercaptopurine,
TPG	translesion pressure gradients		thioguanine, etc.,])
	transplumonary gradient	TPN	total parenteral nutrition
TPH	the patient has...	TPN/IL	total parenteral nutrition and
	thromboembolic pulmonary hypertension		Intralipid (fat emulsion, intravenous)
	trained participating husband	TpnT	troponin T
TPHA	*Treponema pallidum* hemagglutination	tpnT	cointegrate resolution protein T; see gene website www.ncbi
T PHOS	triple phosphate crystals		.nlm.nih.gov/gene
TPI	treatment phase one	TPO	see gene website; www.ncbi
	Treponema pallidum immobilization		.nlm.nih.gov/gene
	triose phosphate isomerase		thrombopoietin
TPIAT	total pancreatectomy with islet		thyroid peroxidase
	autotransplantation		thyroperoxidase
T-piece	a T shaped endotracheal tube	TPOAb	thyroid peroxidase antibodies
	attachment using a flow of	TPOD	trauma pelvic orthotic device
	oxygen-air and no ventilatory	TPOra	thrombopoietin receptor agonists
	assistance to facilitate	TPO RA	thrombopoietin receptor agonists
	weaning	TPP	thiamine pyrophosphate
TPII	treatment phase two		Translational Pharmacogenetics
TPIII	treatment phase three		Program (of the National In-
TPIT	trigger point injection therapy		stitutes of Health Pharmacog-
TPJ	temporo-parietal junction		enomics Research Network)
t$_{pk}$	time to peak	TpP	thrombus precursor protein
TPL	thromboplastin	TP & P	time, place, and person
TPLA	three-port laparoscopic	TPP1	tripeptidyl peptidase 1
	appendectomy	TP-PA	*Treponema pallidum* particle
T plasty	tympanoplasty		agglutination (for syphilis
TPLC	three-port laparoscopic		screening)
	cholecystectomy	TPPL	trans pars plana lensectomy
TPLIF	two-photon laser-induced	TPPM	temporary-permanent pacemaker
	fluorescence		(externally placed permanent
TPLL	three-port laparoscopic ligation		generators attached to active
T-PLL	T-cell prolymphocytic leukemia		fixation transvenous leads)
TPLO	tibial plateau leveling osteotomy (Veterinary)		Tongji prognostic predictor model (for hepatitis B-related
			acute-on-chronic liver failure)
TPLSG	three-port laparoscopic sleeve gastrectomy	TPPN	total peripheral parenteral nutrition

T

TPPS	Toddler-Preschooler Postoperative Pain Scale	TR	repetition time (radiology)
			telephone report
TPPV	trans pars plana vitrectomy		test results
TPQ	tridimensional personality questionnaire		therapeutic recreation
			time to repeat
TPR	temperature		time to repetition (radiology)
	temperature, pulse, and respiration		to return
			trace
	termination of parental rights		transfusion reaction
	tissue-phantom ratio		transplant recipients
	total peripheral resistance		trapezius
T/P ratio	testosterone-to-progesterone ratio		treatment
			tremor
	trough-to-peak ratio		tricuspid regurgitation
TPRI	total peripheral resistance index		tumor recurrence
T-PRO	total protein		tumor registry
TPROM	prelabour rupture of membranes at term	Tr	rectal temperature
			tincture
T PROT	total protein		training
TPR QID	temperature, pulse, and respiration rate to be taken 4 times a day	T&R	taking and retaining
			tenderness and rebound
			treated and released
TPR TID	temperature, pulse, and respiration rate to be taken 3 times a day		turn and reposition
		T/R	see TR
			test-to-reference (ratio)
TPS	tender point score	T®	rectal temperature
	transperineal sonography	TRA	therapeutic recreation associate
	typhus (*rickettsiae* sp.) vaccine		thyroid remnant ablation
tPSA	total prostate-specific antigen		to run at
TPT	thermal perception threshold		transradial access (interventional cardiology)
	tibial-peroneal trunk		
	time to peak tension		transradial approach (for angioplasty procedures)
	topotecan (Hycamtin)		
	transpyloric tube		trastuzumab (Herceptin)
	treadmill performance test		traumatic rupture of the aorta
TpT	troponin T		tumor regression antigen
TPT2	Tactical Pneumatic Tourniquet 2-inch	TrA	transverses abdominis
		t-RA	tretinoin (*trans*-retinoic acid)
TPT3	Tactical Pneumatic Tourniquet 3-inch	TRAb	thyrotropin-receptor antibody
		TRAbs	TSH (thyroid-stimulating hormone) receptor antibodies
tPTEF	time to peak tidal expiratory flow		
TPTL	threatened preterm labor	TRAC	traction
TP trunk	tibial-peroneal trunk	TRACE	time-resolved amplified cryptate emission
tPTX	tension pneumothorax		
TPU	tropical phagedenic ulcer	TRACH	tracheal
TPUs	target pressure ulcers		tracheostomy
T-putty	Theraputty	trache	tracheostomy
TPV	tenofir (Aptivus)	trached	tracheostomy preformed
TPVA	tibioperoneal vessel angioplasty	TRACS	Transfusion Requirements After Cardiac Surgery (study)
TPV/r	tipranavir; ritonavir		
TPVR	total peripheral vascular resistance	TRADD	TNF (tumor necrosis factor) receptor type 1 associated death domain (protein)
TPW	temporary pacemaker wire		
TPX	thromboprophylaxis	TRAEs	treatment-related adverse events
Tpx	thioredoxin peroxidase	TRAFO	tone-reducing ankle/foot orthosis
TPZ	tirapazamine		
TQD	target quit date	TRAIL	tumor-necrosis-factor-related apoptosis-inducing ligand
TQM	total quality management		

TRALI	transfusion-related acute lung injury
TRAM	transverse rectus abdominis myocutaneous (flap)
	transverse rectus abdominum muscle
	Treatment Rating Assessment Matrix
	Treatment Response Assessment Method
TRAMP	transversus and rectus abdominis musculo-peritoneal (flap)
TRANCE	tumor necrosis factor–related activation-induced cytokine
TRANS	transfers
trans	transsexual
Trans D	transverse diameter
transmet	transmetatarsal
transporter	XPORTER
TRANS Rx	transfusion reaction
TRAP	tartrate-resistant (leukocyte) acid phophatase
	Telomeric Repeat Amplification Protocol
	thrombospondin-related anonymous protein
	total radical-trapping antioxidant parameter
	translating ribosomal affinity purification
	trapezium
	trapezius muscle
	twin-reversed arterial perfusion
TRAPS	TFN (tumor necrosis factor) receptor-associated periodic syndrome
TRAS	transplant renal artery stenosis
	trastuzumab (Herceptin)
TRAs	trastuzumab (Herceptin)
TRB	return to baseline
TR BandTM	a dual compression balloons provide precise compression of the radial artery to ensure blood return-without compromising local nerve structure
TRBC	total red blood cells
TRBF	total renal blood flow
TRBT	transurethral resection of bladder tumor
TRC	tanned red cells
TRCB	transretinal choroidal biopsy
TRCC	transradial cardiac catheterization
TRCHA	Tax Relief and Health Care Act of 2006
TRD	tongue-retaining device
	total-retinal detachment
	traction retinal detachment

	treatment-related death
	treatment-resistant depression
TRD=F	treatment-related discontinuation=failure
TRDN	transient respiratory distress of the newborn
TRE	treatment-resistant epilepsy
TREC	T-cell receptor-rearrangement excision circles
Treg	regulatory T cells
Tregs	regulatory T-cells
Tren	Trendelenberg (position)
Trend	Trendelenberg (position)
Trep	Treponema palladium (syphilis pathogen)
TRF	terminal restriction fragment
TRFIA	time-resolved fluorescence immunoassay
TRF-NOMO	translation- and rotation-free nuclear orbital plus molecular orbital
TrgEMG	triggered electromyographic (stimulation)
TRH	protirelin (thyrotropin-releasing hormone) (Relefact TRH®; Thypinone®)
TRHR	thyrotropin-releasing hormone receptor
TRI	teleretinal imaging
	transient radicular irritation
	transradial intervention
	trimester
TriA	tricuspid atresia
T₃RIA	triiodothyronine level by radioimmunoassay
TRIAC	triiodothyroacetic acid
TRIAM	triamcinolone
TRIB	tribbles (proteins)
TRIC	trachoma inclusion conjunctivitis
Tricare	healthcare program for active-duty service members and their families
TRICH	*Trichomonas*
TRICKS	time-resolved imaging contrast kinetics
TRIG	triglycerides
trigem	trigeminal; trigeminy
trigly	triglycerides
TRIGs	triglycerides
triple A	see AAA
triple-H therapy	hypervolemia, hemodialysis, and hypertension
triptans	a class of drugs for migraine therapy such as zolmitriptan (Zomig), almotriptan malate (Axert), eletriptan HBr (Relpax), naratriptan HCl (Amerge), etc.

TRISS	Trauma Injury Severity Score	TRS	the real symptom
Tri-V	triangle ventricular (pacing)		Therapeutic Recreation Specialist
Trk	tropomyosin-related kinase		time-resolved spectroscopy
TRL	tacolimus (Prograf, also TAC)		transmission Raman spectroscopy
TRLO	Tasmanian Rickettsia-like organism		tremor rating scale
TR-LSC	time-resolved liquid scintillation counting	TRSE	transrectal specimen extraction
		TRT	tangential radiation therapy
TRM	treatment-related mortality		testosterone replacement therapy
TR-MNs	therapy-related myeloid neoplasms		thermoradiotherapy
			thoracic radiation therapy
			tinnitus retraining therapy
TRM-SMX	trimethoprim-sulfamethoxazole (correct name is sulfame-thoxazole and trimethoprin; SMZ-TMP; SMX-TMP)		treatment-related toxicity
		TR/TE	time to repetition and time to echo in spin (echo sequence of magnetic resonance imaging)
TRMT	treatment	TRU	trauma resuscitation unit
tRNA	transfer ribonucleic acid	T₃RU	triiodothyronine resin uptake
TRNBP	transrectal needle biopsy prostate	TRUBT	may have meant TURBT (transurethral resection of bladder tumor)
TRNBxPr	transrectal needle biopsy of the prostate		
TRND	Trendelenburg (position)	Tru-D	an automated room disin-fection device that uses ultraviolet-C radiation to sekill micro-organisms (total room ultraviolet disinfection) (see tru-d.com)
TRNG	tetracycline-resistant *Neisseria gonorrhoeae*		
Trng	training		
TRO	thyroid-related orbitopathy		
	to return to office	TRUP	could be referring to transure-thral resection of the prostate (TURP)
	triple rule-out(computed tomo-graphic angiography to diag-nose pulmonary embolism, coronary artery stenosis, and aortic dissection)		
			thyroid hormone receptor uncou-pling protein; see gene website www.ncbi.nlm.nih.gov/gene
	troponin	TRUS	transrectal ultrasonography
TROC	N-2,2,2-trichloroethoxycarbonyl	TRUSP	transrectal ultrasonography of the prostate
troc	trochanter		
troch	trochanter	TRUST	toluidine red unheated serum test
TROFO	trofosfamide	TRV	total renal volume
TROM	torque range of motion		tricuspid regurgitation jet velocity
	total range of motion	TRX	see gene website, www.gene names.org
TrOOP	true out-of-pocket (costs)		
TROP	troponin	Trx	thioredoxin
trops	troponins	TRZ	triazolam (Halcion)
TRP	tubular reabsorption of phosphate	TS	Tay-Sachs (disease)
Trp	tryptophan (also referred to as W)		telomerase
T&RP	temperature, respiratory rate, and pulse rate		temperature sensitive
			test solution
TRP-1	tyrosine-related protein-1		thoracic spine
TRPI	traffic-related pedestrian injuries		throat swab
TRPS	trichorhinophalangeal syndrome (types I, II, and III)		thymidylate synthase
			timed samplings
TrPs	trigger points		toe signs
TRPT	transplant		Tourette syndrome
trpT	troponin T; see gene website, www.ncbi.nlm.nih.gov/gene		Transplant Safety (standard)
			transsexual
TRPV1	transient receptor potential cation channel subfamily V member 1		Trauma Score
			tricuspid stenosis
			triple strength
TRR	tumor response rate		tuberous sclerosis

	turbulence slope
	Turners syndrome
Ts	Schiotz tension
	T suppressor cell
	tennessine
T&S	type and screen
T/S	thoracic spine
	trimethoprim/sulfamethoxazole
	(correct name is sulfamethox-
	azole and trimethoprin)
	tumor tissue- to-normal striatum
	tissue (uptake ratio)
T+S	type and screen
TSA	toluenesulfonic acid
	total shoulder arthroplasty
	total surface area
	trichostatin A
	tryptone soya (blood) agar
	tumor-specific antigen
	type-specific antibody
	tyramine signal amplification
TSAb	thyroid stimulating antibodies
tSAH	traumatic subarachnoid
	hemorrhage
TSApl	tryptic soy agar with
	polysorbate 80 and lecithin
TSAR®	tape surrounded Appli-rulers
TSAS	Total Severity Assessment Score
T sat	transferrin saturation
TSB	total serum bilirubin
	trypticase soy broth
TSBA	total serum bile acid
	tryptic soy broth agar
TSBB	transtracheal selective bronchial
	brushing
TSC	technetium sulfur colloid
	theophylline serum concentration
	total symptom complex
	tuberous sclerosis complex
TSC1	tuberous sclerosis complex 1;
	see gene website www.ncbi
	.nlm.nih.gov/gene
TSC2	tuberous sclerosis complex 2;
	see gene website www.ncbi
	.nlm.nih.gov/gene
TSCA	Toxic Substance Control Act
TSCC	thymic squamous cell carcinoma
	tongue squamous cell carcinoma
	tonsillar squamous cell carcinoma
	Trauma Symptom Checklist for
	Children (ages 11-16 years)
TSCg	transitional structural
	chemogenomics
TSCI	traumatic spinal cord injury
T-score	number of standard devia-
	tions from the average bone
	mineral density (BMD) of a
	25-30 year old woman

TSCp	transitional structural
	chemoproteomics
TSCr	tubular secretion of creatinine
TSCs	trophoblast stem cells
TSCYC	Trauma Symptom Check-
	list for Young Children
	(ages 3-10 years)
TSD	target to skin distance
	Tay-Sachs disease
	total sleep deprivation
	T-(tumor) stage downstaging
TSDH	traumatic subdural hematoma
TSDO	transsutural distraction
	osteogenesis
TSDP	tapered steroid dosing package
TSE	targeted systemic exposure
	testicular self-examination
	total skin examination
	transanal specimen extraction
	transmissible spongiform
	encephalopathy
	turbo spin-echo (magnetic
	resonance imaging)
TSEBT	total skin electron beam therapy
T set	tracheotomy set
TSF	Taylor spatial frame
	tricep skin fold (thickness)
TSFT	tricep skin fold thickness
TSGA	term small gestational age
TSGs	tumor suppressor genes
TSH	thyroid-stimulating hormone
	trocar site hernia
TSH-RH	thyroid-stimulating hormone
	(thyrotropin)-releasing
	hormone
TSI	thyroid stimulating
	immunoglobulin
	tobramycin solution for
	inhalation (TOBI®)
	Toscana in Italia (from HapMap
	[A catalog of common genetic
	variants that occur in human
	beings])
	thymidylate synthase inhibitors
TSJS	transverse/sigmoid junction sinus
TSK	Tampa Scale for Kinesiophobia
	(Questionnaire)
T-skull	trauma skull
TSL	tooth surface loss
	total stent length
TSLO	tracking scanning laser
	ophthalmoscope
TSM	two-spotted spider mite
T-SMBP	telemetric data transmission
	self-measured blood pressure
TSNAs	tobacco-specific nitrosamines
TSOAC	target-specific oral anticoagu-
	lant(s) (rivaroxaban [Xarelto],

	dabigatran [Pradaxa], edoxaban [Savaysa], and apixaban [Eliquis]		total sleep time
TSP	thrombospondin		trans-scrotal testosterone
	total serum protein		treadmill stress test
	tropical spastic paraparesis		tuberculin skin test(s)
tsp	teaspoon (5 mL) (this is a dangerous abbreviation) use 5 mL	TSTA	tumor-specific transplantation antigens
T-SP	thoracic spine	T-STEP	tissue-specific tagging of endogenous proteins
TSPA	thiotepa	TSTM	too small to measure
TSPE	thymidylate synthetase protein expression	TSTs	tuberculin skin tests
TSperm	total number of sperm per ejaculate	TSVD	truncated singular-value decomposition
TSPg	transitional structural pharmacogenomics	TSVT	Taipan snake venom time (assay)
T-spine	thoracic spine	TT	targeted therapy
TSPO	translocator protein (gene/protein; also known as the peripheral benzodiazepine receptor [PBR])		Test Tape®
			testicular torsion
			tetanus toxoid (no longer available)
			thiotepa (Thioplex)
T SPOT.TB®	an in vitro diagnostic test that measures T cells specific to Mycobacterium tuberculosis antigens		thoracostomy tube
			thrombin time
			thrombolytic therapy
			thymol turbidity
TSPp	transitional structural pharmacoproteomics		tilt table
			tilt testing
TSPR	transmission surface plasmon resonance (spectroscopy)		toe-touch (test)
			tonometry
TSR	total shoulder replacement		total testosterone
	transsphenoidal resection		total thyroidectomy
TSRH®	a spinal System to help provide immobilization and stabilization of spinal segments as an adjunct to fusion of the thoracic, lumbar, and/or sacral spine		tourniquet test
			transit time
			transtracheal
			treponemal test
			triceps thickness
			trichorionic triplets
TSRPT	transsphenoidal resection of pituitary tumor		true trough
			tuberculin tested
TSS	therapeutic staff support		twitch tension
	thumb spica splint		tympanic temperature
	total serum solids		tympanostomy tube
	total symptom scores	Tt	temporal artery temperature
	toxic shock syndrome	T-T	time-to-time
	transsphenoidal surgery	T&T	tobramycin and ticarcillin
	treatment-satisfaction status (score)		touch and tone
			tympantomy and tube (insertion)
	tumor score system	T/T	T tube
TSSA	trypomastigote small surface antigen		trace of ____ /trace of ____
		$T_1...T_{12}$	thoracic nerve 1 through 12
TSSH	trans-sphenoidal hypophysectomy (also TSH)	$T_1...T_{12}$	thoracic vertebra 1 through 12
		T6-T7	thoracic vertebrae levels 6 and 7
TSSR	total spinal segment replacement	TT3	total triiodothyronine
TSST	toxic shock syndrome toxin	TT4	total thyroxine
	Trier Social stress Test	TTA	total toe arthroplasty
TST	Targeted Solutions Tool®		transtibial amputee
	titmus stereocuity test		transtracheal aspiration
	total serum testosterone		trauma team activation

T

TTAS	telephone triage and advice services		in the normal development of embryonic epithelial cells of the thyroid and lung)
TTAT	toe touch as tolerated		
	traumatic thoracic aortic transaction	TTFC	time to first cigarette (of the day after waking
T-Tau	Total tau (tau is a microtubule-stabilizing protein primarily localized in central nervous system neurons, but also expressed at low levels in astrocytes and oligodendrocytes. Total tau assay uses a combination of monoclonal antibodies that react with both normal and phosphorylated tau)	TTFields	tumor-treatment fields
		TTFM	transit-time flow measurement
		TTFN	time to first NRT (nicotine replacement therapy)
		TTG	total triglyceride
		tTg	tissue transglutaminase
		tTGA	tissue-transglutaminase antibody
		TTGE	temporal temperature (gradient) gel electrophoresis
			timed-temperature gradient electrophoresis
TTB	time to benefit (the time point at which patients are expected to derived benefit from treatment)	tTg-IgA	tissue transglutaminase immunoglobulin A
		ttgS	see gene website, www.ncbi.nlm .nih.gov/gene
	tub transfer bench (occupational therapy)	TTH	table-top height
TTC	2,3,5- triphenyltetrazolium chloride (stain to distinguish different myocardial injury areas and cerebral ischemia)		tension-type headache
		TTHs	tension-type headaches
		TThSa	Tuesday, Thursday, and Saturday (this is a dangerous abbreviation)
	Takotsubo cardiomyopathy		
	transtracheal catheter	T-Th-Sa	Tuesday, Thursday, and Saturday (this is a dangerous abbreviation)
	trying to conceive		
TTCAR	trying to conceive after reversal		
TTD	tarsal tunnel decompression	TTI	Teflon tube insertion
	temporary total disability		total time to intubate
	total tumor dose		transfer to intermediate
	transverse thoracic diameter		triangular titanium implants
	trichothiodystrophy		tympanostomy tube insertion
TTDC	transthoracic device closure (technology for the repair of ventricular septal defects)	TTII	thyrotropin-binding inhibitory immunoglobulins
TTDE	touch-tone data entry	TTIs	transfusion-transmitted infections
	transthoracic color Doppler echocardiography	TTJV	transtracheal jet ventilation
TTDM	thallim threadmill	ttk	tramtrack; see gene website www.ncbi.nlm.nih.gov/gene
TTDP	time-to-disease progression	TTKG	transtubular potassium gradient
TTDPM	threshold to detection of passive motion	TTL	tensor tympani ligament
TTE	time-to-event	TTM	targeted temperature management (cooling patient to 36 for 24 hours, slowly warming to 37 over 8 hours, and then maintenance at normothermia for 72 hours)
	time-to-exhaustion		
	transthoracic echocardiography		
	trial terminated early		
t-test	Student's t-test		total tumor mass
TTF	time to treatment failure		transtelephonic monitoring
	treatment with a device which delivers alternating low-intensity fields to disrupt cell division in cancer cells (NovoTTF-100A)		transtheoretical model
			trichotillomania
		TTMP	tibial tunnel middle point
	tumor treatment fields	TTN	time to normalization
TTF-1	thyroid transcription factor-1 (a tissue-specific transcription factor that plays a critical role		transient tachypnea of the newborn
		TTNA	transthoracic needle aspiration

T

TTNB	transient tachypnea of the newborn	TT-TG	tibial tuberosity to trochlear groove (distance)
TTND	time to nondetectable	TTTS	twin-twin transfusion syndrome
TTO	tea tree oil	T-tube	a narrow flexible tube in the form of a T
	time trade-off		
	to take out	TTUTD	tetanus toxoid up-to-date
	transfer to open	TTV	Torque-tenovirus
	transtracheal oxygen		total tumor volume
TTOC	transtracheal oxygen catheter		transfusion-transmitted virus
TTOD	tetanus toxoid outdated		TT virus
TTOP	time to objective progression	TTVIs	transfusion-transmitted viral infections
TTOT	transtracheal oxygen therapy		
TTP	tender to palpation	TTVP	temporary transvenous pacemaker
	tender to pressure	TTVPM	temporary transvenous pacemaker
	thrombotic thrombocytopenic purpura	TTVR	transcatheter tricuspid valve replacement
	time to pregnancy	TTW	Ticket to Work
	time to tumor progression	TTWB	touch-toe weight bearing
	time-to-progression	TTX	tetrodotoxin
	Tobacco Treatment Program	TTx	thrombolytic therapy
	total talar prosthesis	TTxB	tub transfer bench
TTPA	tocopherol (alpha) transfer protein; see gene website www.ncbi.nlm.nih.gov/gene	TTY	telephone typewriters
		Tty	tympanic thermometry (temperature)
		tty	see gene website www.ncbi.nlm .nih.gov/gene
TTP-HUS	thrombotic thrombocytopenic purpura and hemolytic uremic syndrome	TTYL	talk (text) to you later (slang)
		TU	Todd units
TTPP	time to PSA (prostate-specific antigen) progression		transrectal ultrasound
			transurethral
TTR	time to therapeutic range		tuberculin units
	transthyretin		tumor
	triceps tendon reflex	Tu	Tuesday
TTR amyloidosis	transthyretin amyloidosis	250-TU	250 tuberculin units
TTR-FAP	transthyretin familial amyloid polyneuropathy	TUB	tuberculosis vaccine, not BCG
		tubal	tubal litigation
TTS	Tako-Tsubo syndrome		tubal pregnancy
	tarsal tunnel syndrome	TUBB3	class III beta-tubulin
	temporary threshold shift	TUBRT	may have meant TURBT (transurethral resection of the bladder tumor)
	testing-induced syncope		
	through the skin		
	transdermal therapeutic system	TUBS	traumatic, unidirectional insta- bility and Bankart lesion
	transfusion therapy service		
	transtympanic steroids	TUD	take as directed (this is a dan- gerous abbreviation as it may be read as TID [three times daily or not understood)
	Tuesday, Thursday, and Saturday		
TTs	tympanostomy tubes		
T-T-S	Tuesday, Thursday, and Saturday		
T/T/S	Tuesday, Thursday, and Saturday		tobacco use disorder
TTS HD	hemodialysis Tuesday, Thursday, and Saturday	TUDCA	tauroursodeoxycholic acid
		TUDS	temporary ureteral drainage system
TTT	tilt-table test		
	time to treatment termination	TUE	transurethral extraction
	tolbutamide tolerance test	Tue	Tuesday
	total tourniquet time	TUEB	transurethral enucleation with bipolar
	transpupillary thermotherapy		
	turn-to-turn transfusion	TUES	transumbilical endoscopic surgery
TTTF	time to treatment failure	TUEs	therapeutic use exemptions
TTTG	tibial tuberosity to trochlear groove (distance)	TUF	total ultrafiltration

TUG	timed Up and Go (test)	turn q2h	turn patient every 2 hours
	total urinary gonadotropin	TURP	transurethral resection of
TUG1	taurine-upregulated gene 1		prostate
TUGT	timed-up-and-go test	TURPT	transurethral resection of
TUH	Temple University Hospital		prostate tumor
	(Philadelphia PA)	TURS	transurethral resection syndrome
TUIBN	transurethral incision of	TURs	temporary use recommendations
	bladder neck		transurethral resections
TUIBNC	transurethral incision of the	TURT	transurethral resection of tumor
	bladder neck contracture	TURV	transurethral resection valves
TUIP	transurethral incision of the	TURVN	transurethral resection of vesical
	prostate		neck
TUL	transureteral lithotripsy	TUTL	transuterine tubal lavage
	tularemia (*Francisella*	TUU	transureteroureterostomy
	tularensis) vaccine	TUUL	transurethral ureterolithotripsy
TULIA	test for upper limb apraxia	TUV	transurethral valve
TULIP®	transurethral ultrasound-guided	TUVis	transurethral vaporization in
	laser-induced prostatectomy		saline (0.9% sodium chloride
	(system)		soln)
TULIPS	touch-up and loop incorporated	TUVP	transurethral vaporization of the
	primers (an alternative PCR		prostate
	technique)	TV	television
TUMP	tumor(s) of uncertain malignant		temporary visit
	potential		testicular volume
TUMT	transurethral microwave		thyroid volume
	thermotherapy		tidal volume
TUN	total urinary nitrogen		tonic vergence
TUNA	transurethral needle ablation		transvenous
TUNEL	terminal deoxynucleotidyl		trial visit
	transferase-mediated dUTP-		*Trichomonas vaginalis*
	biotin nick-end labeling		tricuspid valve
TUPAC	tobacco use prevention and		tulane virus
	cessation	tv	tidal volumn
TUPR	transurethral prostatic resection	T&V	transverse and vertical
TUR	transurethral resection	T/V	touch-verbal
T_3UR	triiodothyronine uptake ratio	TVA	total vascular area
TURB	transurethral resection of the		tricuspid valve area
	bladder		tubulovillous adenoma
	turbidity		tumor virus receptor A
TURBN	transurethral resection bladder	TVAC	thrombus vacuum aspiration
	neck		catheter
TURBNC	may have meant TUIBNC		time-varying acceleration
	(transurethral incision of		coefficient
	bladder neck contracture)	TVAD	turbodynamic ventricular assist
TURBP	transurethral resection biopsy of		device
	the prostate	TVAR	time-varying autoregressive
TURBS	may have meant TURPs		(model/analysis)
	(transurethral resections of	Tvar	T-wave variability
	the prostate)	TVC	total vascular conductance
	termination upstream ribosome		total viable count
	binding site		triple voiding cystogram
TURBT	transurethral resection of the		true vocal cord
	bladder tumor	TVc	tricuspid valve closure
TURis	transurethral resection in saline	TVCL	typical value of clearance
	(0.9% sodium chloride soln)	TVCs	true vocal cords
	(Olympus, Tokyo, Japan	TVD	triple vessel disease
	[system])	TVDALV	triple vessel disease with an
turn q2	turn patient every 2 hours		abnormal left ventricle

TVE	total vascular exclusion
	transvenous embolization
	tricuspid valve endocarditis
TVEC	Talimogene laherparepvec (an
	oncolytic virus approved in
	the therapy of metastatic mel-
	anoma) (Imlygic injection)
	transvenous electrical
	cardioversion
TVF	tactile vocal fremitus
	target vessel failure
	true vocal fold
TVH	total vaginal hysterectomy
TVHBSO	total vaginal hysterectomy bilat-
	eral salpingo-oophorectomy
TVI	time velocity integral
TVIE	tricuspid valve infective
	endocarditis
TV IE	tricuspid valve infective
	endocarditis
TVL	total vaginal length
	tunica vasculosa lentis
TVLB	transvaginal luteal biopsy
TVM	transvaginal mesh
TVN	tonic vibration response
TVO	total vascular occlusion
	transtrochanteric valgus
	osteotomy
	tuberculous vertebral
	osteomyelitis
TVOB	transvaginal ovarian biopsy
TVOCs	total volatile organic compounds
TVOR	translational vestibulo-ocular
	reflex
	transvaginal oocyte retrieval
TVP	deep vein thrombosis (French
	and Spanish abbreviation)
	tensor veli palatini (muscle)
	transvenous pacemaker
	transvesicle prostatectomy
TVPM	tensor veli palatini muscle
	transvenous pacemaker
TVPS-R	Test of Visual Perceptual Skills –
	Revised
TVR	target vessel revascularization
	(rate)
	Telaprevir
	tricuspid valve replacement
TVRSS	total vasomotor rhinitis symp-
	tom score
TVS	temporary vascular shunt
	transvaginal sonography
	transvenous system
	trigemino-vascular system
TVSC	transvaginal sector scan
TVT	tension-free vaginal tape
	total vaginal thickness
	transvaginal taping

TVTO	tension-free vaginal tape,
	obturator route
TVT O	tension-free vaginal tape,
	obturator route
TVT-O	tension-free vaginal
	tape-obturator
TVT sling	tension-free vaginal tape sling
TVU	total volume of urine
	transvaginal ultrasonography
TVUS	transvaginal ultrasonography
TVW	total vaginal width
TW	talked with
	tapwater
	test weight
	thought withdrawal
	Trophermyma whippleii
	T-wave
T/W	see TW
	thickness-to-width (ratio)
	tumor tissue-to-white matter
	tissue (uptake ratio)
5-TW	five times a week (this is a
	dangerous abbreviation)
TW2	Tanner-Whitehouse mark 2
	(bone-age assessment)
TWA	time-weighted average
	total wrist arthroplasty
	T-wave alternans
TWAR	Chlamoydophila (Chlamydia)
	pneumoniae
T-wave	part of the electrocardio-
	graphic cycle, representing
	a portion of ventricular
	repolarization
TWB	total weight bearing
TWBC	terminal warm blood
	cardioplegia (perfusion)
	total white blood cell (count)
TWD	total white and differential count
TWE	tapwater enema
TWEAK	tumor necrosis factor-like weak
	inducer of apoptosis
TWETC	tapwater enema 'til clear
TWF	total-wrist fusion
TWG	total weight gain
TWH	transitional wall hyperplasia
TWHW ok	toe walking and heel walking all
	right
TWI	tooth-wear index
	T-wave inversion
T1WI	T1 weighted image (magnetic
	resonance imaging term for
	short repetition time and short
	echo time)
T2WI	T2 weighted image (magnetic
	resonance imaging term for
	long repetition time and long
	echo time)

TWiST	time without symptoms of progression or toxicity	TYCO #3	Tylenol with 30 mg of codeine (#1 = 7.5 mg, #2 = 15 mg and #4 = 60 mg of codeine present)
TWL	thermal withdrawal latency		
	total weight lifted	TyG-BMI	triglyceride and glucose index combined with body mass index (a favorable marker of insulin resistance)
	total weight loss		
TWOC	trial without catheter		
TWP	twin pregnancy		
TWR	total wrist replacement two-week rule (referrals)	Tyl	Tylenol (acetaminophen) tyloma (callus)
TWSTRS	Toronto Western Spasmodic Torticollis Rating Scale	TYMP	tympanogram
		tymps	tympanic membranes
TWT	timed walking test	TYR	tyrosinase
TWWD	tap water wet dressing		tyrosine
TX	Texas	TYRX	a fully absorbable antibacterial
Tx	therapist	envelope	envelope (contains minocy-
	therapy		cline and rifampin) available
	traction		for cardiac implantable
	transcription		electronic devices including
	transfer		implantable cardioverter
	transfuse		defibrillators and pacemakers
	transplant		(TyRx Pharma, a subsidiary
	transplantation		of Medtronics, was the origi-
	treatment		nator of product)
	tympanostomy	TYVM	thank you very much (slang)
tx	therapeutic	TZ	target zone
T & X	type and crossmatch		temozolomide (Temodar)
Tx'd	treated		transition zone
TXA	tranexamic acid (Cyklokapron; Lysteda)	TZCS	time-zone change syndrome
		TZD	thiazolidinedione
TXA_2	thromboxane A_2	TZDM	may be T2DM, type 2 diabetes mellitus
TXB2	thromboxane B2		
TXE	Timoptic-XE®	TZDs	thiazolidinediones
Txed	treated	TZM	temozolomide (Temodar)
Tx'ed	treated		
TXER	troxerutin		
TXF	tamoxifen		
Txf	transfer		
txfer	transfer		
TXFR	transfer		
Tx'g	treating		
TXL	paclitaxel (Taxol) (this is a dangerous abbreviation as it can be read as TXT)		
TXM	type and crossmatch		
TxM Guide	Translational Medicine Guide		
TXMT	treatment		
TXN	troxerutin		
TxNA	treatment-naïve alcoholics		
TXP	transplant		
TXR	targeted x-ray		
TXS	type and screen		
TXT	docetaxel (Taxotere) (this is a dangerous abbreviation as it can be read as TXL)		
TY	thank you (slang) tympanic		
T & Y	trichomonas and yeast		
Ty21a	live oral typhoid vaccine		

T

U

U	selenocysteine
	Ultralente Insulin® (it is dangerous to use abbreviations for insulin therapy)
	umbilicus
	umbilicus (as in fundus at U)
	Uniform (Phonetic Alphabet for U; pronounced (YOU-NEE-FORM) or (OO-NEE-FORM)
	unilateral
	unit(s) (This is a MOST DANGEROUS abbreviation when written poorly, therefore should NOT be used. It appears on the medabbrev. com and other Do Not Use Lists, as it has been read as 0, 4 ,6, or cc causing life-threatening overdoses; spell out "unit or units")
	unknown
	upper
	uranium
	uridine (also referred to as Urd)
	urine
Ⓤ	Kosher
U/	at umbilicus
U/1	1 finger breadth below umbilicus
1/U	1 finger over umbilicus
U100	100 units per milliliters
24U	24-hour urine (collection)
μ	micro
UA	umbilical artery
	unable
	unauthorized absence
	uncertain about
	unstable angina
	upper airway
	upper arm
	uric acid
	urinalysis
	uterine activity
U/A	see UA
UAA	uncomplicated acute appendicitis
	unnatural amino acids
UABD	upper airway bronchodilation
UAC	umbilical artery catheter
	under active
	upper airway congestion
UA/C	uric acid to creatinine (ratio)
UACEs	unplanned acute care encounters
UACR	urinary albumin/creatinine ratio

UACS	upper airway cough syndrome
UA C&S	urine analysis, culture and sensitivity
UAD	upper airway disease
	use as directed (for safety reasons this should not be used; explicit directions should be used for prescriptions and medical records)
	uterine artery Doppler
UADE	unanticipated adverse device event
UADT	upper aerodigestive tract
UAE	unexpected adverse event
	United Arab Emirates
	urinary albumin excretion
	uterine artery embolization
UAER	urinary albumin excretion rate
UAF	ureteroarterial fistula
UAG	unacylated ghrelin
UAI	unprotected anal intercourse
UAL	umbilical artery line
	up as desired (ad lib)
UAM	urinalysis with microscope
UA&M	urinalysis and microscopy
UANC	uncomplicated antenatal confinement
UA/NSTEMI	unstable angina and non-ST-segment elevation myocardial infarction
UAO	upper airway obstruction
UAOM	unilateral acute otitis media
UAP	unlicensed assistive personnel
	unstable angina pectoris
	upper abdominal pain
UAPD	Union of American Physicians and Dentists
UAPF	upon arrival patient found
UAPI	umbilical artery pulsatility index
UARI	umbilical artery resistance index
U-ARM	upper arm
UARS	upper airway resistance syndrome
UAS	upstream activating sequence
UASA	upper airway sleep apnea
UAT	up as tolerated
UATC	upper aerodigestive tract (oral cavity, pharynx, larynx) cancer
UA/UC	urinary albumin to urinary creatinine ratio
UAV	unicuspid aortic valve
UAVC	univentricular atrioventricular connection
uAVG	upper arm arteriovenous graft
UAVM	uterine arteriovenous malformation

uAVM	unruptured brain arteriovenous malformation	U/C	see UC
		UCABG	urgent coronary artery bypass graft (surgery)
UAW	ultrasound-assisted wound (treatment)	UCAD	unstable coronary artery disease
	upper airways	UCAF	uncontrolled atrial fibrillation
UB	upper-body	UCB	umbilical cord blood
UBAs	urethral bulking agents		unconjugated bilirubin (indirect)
UBB	ubiquitin B (gene)		Unicorn Campbell Boy (orthotics)
	underbody blast (as in Improvised explosive devices under the vehicle)	UCBL	University California Berkeley Laboratory (orthosis)
		UCBT	umbilical cord-blood transplantation
UBC	unicameral bone cyst	UCCL	ulnocarpal collateral ligament
	University of British Columbia (brace)	UCCs	urgent care centers
		UCD	urine collection device
	upper body cycle		usual childhood diseases
UBD	universal blood donor	UCd	urine cadmium level
	upper body dressing	UCDAI	Ulcerative Colitis Disease Activity Index (Also Known As: Sutherland Index, Modified Ulcerative Colitis Disease Activity Index)
UBE	upper body ergometer		
UBF	unknown black female		
	uterine blood flow		
UBG	urobilinogen		
Ubg	ultimobranchial glands; see gene website, www.ncbi.nlm.nih.gov/gene	UCDVA	uncorrected distance visual acuity
		UCE	urea cycle enzymopathy
			unexplained chronic fatigue
UBH	ubiquitin homology (domain)		urethrocutaneous fistula
UBI	ultraviolet blood irradiation	UCG	urinary chorionic gonadotropins
UBM	ultrasound biomicroscopy	UCHD	usual childhood diseases
	unknown black male	UCHI	usual childhood illnesses
UBO	unidentified bright object	UCH-LI	ubiquitin C-terminal hydrolase LI
UBP	ubiquitin specific peptidase 3; see gene website www.ncbi.nlm.nih.gov/gene	UCHS	uncontrolled hemorrhagic shock
		UCI	urethral catheter in
			usual childhood illnesses
	university-based practice	UCL	ulnar collateral ligament
	unspecified bronchiolitis/ pneumonia		uncomfortable loudness level
			unilateral cleft lip
	upper back pain	UCLA	University of California, Los Angeles (activity score)
UBS	Basic Units of Health (Brazil)		
	upper body strength	UCLC	ulnocarpal ligamentous complex
UBT	^{13}C-urea breath test	UCLP	unilateral cleft lip and palate
	Unit Based Technician	UCN-01	7-hydroxystaurosporin
	upper-body (ergometer) test	UCN	urocortin
	uterine balloon therapy	UCO	urethral catheter out
UBW	usual body weight	UCP	umbilical cord prolapse
UC	ulcerative colitis		uncommon compensatory pattern
	umbilical cord		uncoupling protein
	unchanged		United Cerebral Palsy
	unconscious		urethral closure pressure
	Unit clerk	UCP-3	uncoupling protein −3
	United Church of Christ	UCPPE	uncomplicated parapneumonic effusion
	urea clearance		
	urgent care	UCPs	urine collection pads
	urinary catheter	UCR	unconditioned reflex
	urine culture		unconditioned response
	urothelial carcinoma		usual, customary, and reasonable (fees)
	usual care		
	uterine contraction	UCr	urinary creatinine excretion
U&C	urethral and cervical	UCRE	urine creatinine
	usual and customary		

U

UCRP	universal coagulation reference plasma
UCS	unconscious
	unilateral coronal synostosis
UC&S	urine culture and sensitivity
UCSD	University of California, San Diego
UCSF-CaPRA	University of California, San Francisco Cancer of the Prostate Risk Assessment
UCTD	undifferentiated connective tissue disease
uCTX-II	urinary C-telopeptide of type II collagen
UCu	urine copper level
UCVA	uncorrected visual acuity
UCX	urine culture
UD	take as directed (for safety reasons this should not be used; explicit directions should be used for prescriptions and medical records; this Latin-origin abbreviation appears on the MedAbbrev and other "Do Not Use Lists," as it has been read as once daily (OD) or not understood)
	ugly duckling (sign) (pigmented moles)
	ulnar deviation
	ultrasonic dissection
	unit dose
	urethral dilatation
	urethral discharge
	urodynamics
	uterine distension
U/d	units per day (this is a dangerous abbreviation as the handwritten U can easily look like a zero; use units/day)
UDA	undifferentiated arthritis
	Unit of Dental Activity
UDAP	undifferentiated abdominal pain
UDAS	Urine Drug Analysis System
UDC	uninhibited detrusor (muscle) capacity
	usual diseases of childhood
UDCA	ursodeoxycholic acid (Ursodiol)
UDCTD	undifferentiated connective tissue dysplasia
UDE	undetermined etiology
UDF	ultrapure dialysis fluid
	undifferentiated type
UDH	unobstructed diaphragmatic hernia
UDI	Urogenital Distress Inventory
Udip	dipstick urinalysis

UDM	uncontrolled diabetes
	undiagnosed diabetes mellitus
	undocumented migrants
	urine drug monitoring
	use-dilution method
UDN	ulnar digital nerve
	updraft nebulizer
UDO	undetermined origin
UDP	unassisted diastolic pressure
UDPGT	uridinediphospho-glucuronyl transferase
UDS	uncomplicated diverticulitis of the sigmoid
	unconditioned stimulus
	Uniform Data Set
	urine drug screen
	urodynamic study(ies)
UDST	unilateral dermatomal superficial telangiectasia
UDS-UPDRS	Movement Disorder Society-United Parkinson's Disease Rating Scale
UDT	undescended testicle(s)
	urine drug test
UDU	uniformity of dosage units
UDVA	uncorrected distance visual acuity
UE	ultrasound elastography
	under elbow
	undetermined etiology
	upper extremity
uE3	unconjugated estriol
U & E	urea and electrolytes (see Laboratory Panels)
U+E	urea and electrolytes
U/E	see UE
UEA	upper extremity amputations
UEBW	ultrasound estimated bladder weight
UEC	uterine endometrial carcinoma
UEDs	unilateral epileptiform discharges
UEDVT	upper extremities deep venous thrombosis
UEF	upper extremity fracture
UEFI	Upper Extremity Functional Index
UEFI-15	Upper Extremity Functional Index,15-item version
UEFI-20	Upper Extremity Functional Index, 20-item version
UEP	Unequal Error Protection
	upper-extremity performance
UES	undifferentiated embryonal sarcoma
	upper esophageal sphincter
UE's	upper extremities
UESEP	upper extremity somatosensory evoked potential

UESP	upper esophageal sphincter pressure	UGFS	ultrasound-guided foam sclerotherapy
uEtG	urinary ethyl glucuronide	UGH	uveitis, glaucoma, and hyphema (syndrome)
uETOH	urinary ethanol		
UF	ultrafiltration	UGI	upper gastrointestinal series
	until finished	UGI w/SBFT	upper gastrointestinal (series) with small bowel follow through
UFA	unsaturated fatty acid(s)		
UFC	urinary free cortisol		
UFCT	ultrafast computed tomography	UGIB	upper gastrointestinal bleeding
UFD	ubiquitin fusion degradation	UGID	upper gastrointestinal disease
ufd	ubiquitin fusion degradation protein; see gene website www.ncbi.nlm.nih.gov/gene	UGIE	upper gastrointestinal endoscopy
		UGIH	upper gastrointestinal (tract) hemorrhage
		UGIM	upper gastrointestinal malignancies
UFE	uterine fibroid embolization		
UFF	unusual facial features		
UFFI	urea formaldehyde foam insulation	UGIS	upper gastrointestinal series
		UGIT	upper gastrointestinal tract
UFG	ultrafine-grained	UGK	urine, glucose, and ketones
	Universidade Federal de Goiás (Federal University of Goias; Brazil)	ug/L	micrograms per liter (the correct symbol for micro may not be available)
UFH	unfractionated heparin	UGME	undergraduate medical education
UFM	unaccompanied foreign minors		
	uroflowmetry	ug/mL	micrograms per milliliter (the correct symbol for micro may not also be available)
UFN	until further notice		
UFO	unflagged order		
	unidentified foreign object	UGP	urinary gonadotropin peptide
UFOV	useful field of view	UGR	urethrogenital reflex
UFR	ultrafiltration rate	UGS	urogenital sinus
UFS	urofacial syndrome		usual gait speed
UFT	uracil and tegafur	UGT	upper genital tract
UFT-UMP	follicular tumor of uncertain malignant potential		urudine glucuronosyltransferase, see gene website www.ncbi .nlm.nih.gov/gene
UFV	ultrafiltration volume		
UG	until gone	UGT1A1	uridine diphosphate glucoronosyltransferase, uridine diphosphate glucosyl-transferase
	urinary glucose		
	urogenital		
ug	microgram (the correct symbol for micro may not also be available)		
		UGTI	ultrasound-guided thrombin injection
∤g	microgram. This is a **DANGEROUS** abbreviation that should **NOT** be used. It appears on the MedAbbrev and other "Do Not Use Lists," as when it is handwritten it has been read as milligram (mg). Use "mcg."	UGVA	ultrasound-guided vascular access
		uGy	microgray (1 gray equals 1,000,000 micrograys; a gray is defined as the absorption of one joule of radiation energy per kilogram of matter)
		UH	umbilical hernia
UGA	under general anesthesia		unfavorable history
	urogenital atrophy		University Hospital
UGB	upper-gastrointestinal-tract bleeding	UHBI	upper hemibody irradiation
		uhCG	urinary human chorionic gonadotrophin
UGCR	ultrasound-guided compression repair		
		UHDDS	Uniform Hospital Discharge Data Set
UGDP	University Group Diabetes Project		
		UHDRS	Unified Huntington Disease Rating Scale
UGET	ultrasound-guided embryo transfer	UHDs	ulcer-healing drugs

UHF	ultrahigh field		urine potassium
	ultrahigh frequency		urokinase
	United Hospital Fund	UKA	unicompartmental knee
	unrestricted Hartree-Fock		arthroplasty
UHMW-PE	ultra-high molecular-weight	uka	unicondylar knee anthroplasty
	polyethylene		urinary kallikrein activity
UHP	University Health Plan	UKCCLG	United Kingdom Children's
UHPLC	ultra-high-performance liquid		Cancer and Leukaemia Group
	chromatography	UKE	unknown etiology
UHR	ultra-high risk	UK IC	urokinase intracoronary
	ultra-high-resolution	UKM form	an application form for
u/hr	units per hour (it is safer to use		registration as a British citizen
	units/hr as the handwritten U		by a person born before 1983
	has been mistaken for a zero		to a British mother
	causing a ten-fold overdoses)	UKNDS	United Kingdom neurological
UHR-OCT	ultrahigh-resolution optical		disability score
	coherence tomography	UKO	unknown origin
UHS	ultracision harmonic scalpel	UKOSS	United Kingdom Obstetric
	Ultrapro® Hernia System		Surveillance System
UI	urinary incontinence	UKR	unicompartmental knee
UIA	unruptured intracranial		replacement
	aneurysms	UL	Unit Leader
	uretero-intestinal anastomotic		upper left
UIB	Unemployment Insurance		upper lid
	Benefits		upper limb
UIBC	unbound iron binding capacity		upper lobe
	unsaturated iron binding	U & L	upper and lower
	capacity	U/L	unilateral
UIC	ultrasound-indicated cerclage		units per liter (this is a
	urinary iodine concentration		dangerous abbreviation
UID	once daily (this is a dangerous		since a handwritten U can be
	abbreviation, spell out "once		mistaken for a zero)
	daily")		upper and lower
UIEP	urine (urinary)	ULA	upper limb amputees
	immunoelectrophoresis		upper limb amyoplasia
UIF	umbilico-inguinal fistula		upper limits of agreement
	ureteral-iliac fistula	ULAb	used lead acid battery
UIFE	urine immunofixation	ULA-OP	ultrasound advanced
	electrophoresis		open-platform
UIP	usual interstitial pneumonitis	ULBW	ultra low birth weight (between
	(pneumonia)		501 and 750 g)
UIQ	upper inner quadrant	ULC	ultrasound lung comet-tail
UIR	unfavorable intermediate risk		(artifacts)
	unidentified infrared (emission		upper lateral cartilage (nasal)
	bands)	ULD	Unverricht-Lundborg disease
UIs	uncertainty intervals	ULDT	ultra low-dose therapy
UITN	Urinary Incontinence Traetment	ULE	unilateral laterothoracic
	Network		upper limb exercises
uIU	micro-international units (μIU)	ULL	ulnolunate ligament
UIV	undetermined isolated vertigo	ULLE	upper lid, left eye
	upper instrumented vertebra	ULLS	unilateral lower limb suspension
UJ	universal joint (syndrome)	ULM	unilateral mastectomy
UJP	may have meant UPJ (uretero-		unprotected left main (coronary
	pelvic junction)		artery disease)
	ungapped joint probability	ULMCA	unprotected left main coronary
	unrecognized joint penetration		artery
UK	United Kingdom	ULMS	uterine leiomyosarcomas
	unknown	ULN	upper limits of normal

ULOD	ultra-late-onset disease	UNC	uncrossed
ULPA	ultra-low particulate air		ureteroneocystostomy
ULQ	upper left quadrant	uncal	a word meaning a hook-shaped
ULRE	upper lid, right eye		process or structure
ULS	uterosacral ligament suspension	UNDEL	undelivered
ULSB	upper left sternal border	underwt	under weight
ULT	ultralow temperature	UNDP	United Nations Development
	urate (uric acid) lowering		Program
	therapy	UNE	ulnar neuropathy at the elbow
ultra-MIS	ultra-minimally invasive		urinary norepinephrine
ULTT1	upper limb tension test 1	*UNG*	ointment
	(median nerve)	uNGAL	urinary neutrophil gelatinase-
ULTT2a	upper limb tension test 2a		associated lipocalin
	(medial nerve)	ungt	ointment
ULTT2b	upper limb tension test 2b	UNHS	universal newborn hearing
	(radial nerve)		screening
ULTT3	upper limb tension test 3 (ulnar	UNI	unilateral
	nerve)	Uniform	Phonetic Alphabet for U; pro-
ULYTES	electrolytes, urine		nounced YOU-NEE-FORM
UM	ultrarapid metabolizer		or OO-NEE-FORM
	unmarried	unilat	unilateral
	utilization management	UNIT	Universal Nonverbal Intelligence
	uveal melanoma		Test
UMA	unmeasured anions	UNK	unknown
UMA/CR	urine microalbumin to creatinine	UNL	upper normal levels
	ratio	UNNA	Unna Boot; 4 inches by 10 yards
Umb	umbilical		gauze impregnated zinc oxide
Umb A Line	umbilical artery line		and calamine, used toys
umb ven	umbilical vein		wrap to treat venous ulcers
Umb V Line	umbilical venous line		or as a supportive wrap for
UMCD	uremic medullary cystic disease		foot sprains. Named after a
UMD	unipolar mood disorder		German dermatologist, Paul
U-MDD	unipolar major depressive		Gerson Unna)
	disorder	UNOS	United Network for Organ
umec	umeclidinium		Sharing
UMI	unrecognized myocardial	UN/P	unpatched eye
	infarction	UN/P OD	unpatched right eye
u/mL	units per milliliter (this is a	UN/P OS	unpatched left eye
	dangerous abbreviation; use	UNS	universal neonatal screening
	units/mL)		unsatisfactory
UMLBP	undiagnosed mechanical low	UNSAT	unsatisfactory
	back pain	unsp	unspecified
UMLS	Unified Medical Language	unspe	unspecified
	System	unspec	unspecified
UMN	upper motor neuron (disease)	uNTx	urinary N-telopeptide
UMn	urine manganese level	UNVA	uncorrected near visual acuity
umol	micromole	U/O	see UO
UMP	uncertain malignant potential	UO	under observation
	uridine 5'-monophosphate		undetermined origin
UMRS	Unified Myoclonus Rating Scale		ureteral orifice
UMSS	University of Michigan Sedation		urinary output
	Scale	UOA	undifferentiated oligoarthritis
UN	ulnar nerve		unicondylar osteoarticular
	undernourished		allografts
	urinary nitrogen		unobstructive azoospermia
UNA	urinary nitrogen appearance	UOb	upper-body obese
UNa	urine sodium	UOD	ultrasound osmotic dehydration
unacc	unaccompanied		unplanned operative delivery

UOM	ulcerative oral mucositis	UPO	metastatic carcinoma of
	units of measure		unknown primary origin
UONx	unilateral optic nerve transection	UPOR	usual place of residence
UOP	urinary output	UPP	urethral pressure profile
UOQ	upper outer quadrant		urethral pressure profilometry
UORBC	uncrossmatched type-O packed		uvulopalatoplasty
	red blood cells	UPPE	uncomplicated parapneumonic
UOS	unknown onset stroke (unclear		effusion
	symptom onset time)	UPPP	uvulopalatopharyngoplasty
	upper oesophageal sphincter	UPPPP	uvula-preserving
	(United Kingdom and other		palatopharyngoplasty
	countries)	U/P ratio	urine to plasma ratio
Uosm	urinary osmolality	uPRBC	units packed red blood cells
uOsm	urine osmolality (the urine con-		transfused
	centration of a solution ex-	U-PRO	urine protein
	pressed as the total number of	UPS	ubiquitin-proteasome system
	solute particles per kilogram)		uninterrupted power source
UOT	ultrasound-mediated optical		Urgency Perception Scale
	tomography	UPSC	uterine papillary serous
UP	unipolar		carcinoma
	universal precautions	UPSIT	University of Pennsylvania
	ureteropelvic		Smell Identification Test
✓ up	check up	UPT	uptake
U/P	urine to plasma (creatinine)		urine pregnancy test
UP3	uvulopalatopharyngoplasty	UPVC	uteroplacental vascular
uPA	urokinase-type plasminogen		compromise
	activator	UQ	upper quartile
Up Ad Lib	out of bed as desired (check	UR	unrelated
	with facility's meaning)		upper respiratory
UPb	urine lead level		upper right
UPC	Universal Product Code		urinary retention
	unknown primary carcinoma		utilization review
UPCI	University of Pittsburgh Cancer	URA	unilateral renal agenesis
	Institute	Ura	uracil
uPCI	urine protein creatinine index	URAC	Utilization Review
UPCR	urine protein to creatinine ratio		Accreditation Commission
UPD	uniparental disomy	UR AC	uric acid
UPDRS	Unified Parkinson Disease Rat-	URAS	unilateral renal artery stenosis
	ing Scale	URC	unlicensed relative care (foster
UPEP	urine protein electrophoresis		care homes)
UPF	ultraviolet protection factor		upper rectal cancer
	uvulopalatal flap	UrC	urachal carcinoma
UPG	uroporphyrinogen	URD	undifferentiated respiratory
UPI	universal patience identifier		disease
UPIN	unique physician (provided)		unrelated donor
	identification number		upper respiratory disease
UPJ	ureteropelvic junction	Urd	uridine
UPJO	ureteropelvic junction		uridine (also referred to as U)
	obstruction	URE	Uniform Rules of Evidence
UPLC-MS/MS	ultra-high performance liquid	URF	unique recombinant forms
	chromatography/tandem mass		urethrorectal fistula
	spectrometry	URFOs	unintended retained foreign
UPLIF	unilateral posterior lumbar		objects
	interbody fusion	URG	urgent
UPMC	University of Pittsburgh	URI	upper respiratory infection
	Medical Center	URIC A	uric acid
UPN	unique patient number	url	unrelated
UPNC	uncomplicated post natal course	UR&M	urinalysis, routine and microscopic

U

urn randomization	a system for assigning patients to treatment groups in clinical trials in an attempt to eliminate experimental bias (involves placing balls in an urn [vasel])	USAT	ultrasound-assisted thrombolysis
		USB	upper sternal border
		USC	uterine serous carcinoma
		USCB	ultrasound guided-core biopsy
		U-SCOPE	ureteroscopy
		US CVC	ultrasound central venous catheter (placement)
URO	urology	USCVD	unsterile controlled vaginal delivery
UROB	urobilinogen		
UroCa	urothelial cancer	USDA	United States Department of Agriculture
UROD	ultra-rapid opiate detoxification [under anesthesia]		
UROGYN	urogynecology	usec	microseconds (= sec)
UROL	Urologist urology	USEDCARP	ureterosigmoidostomy, small bowel fistula, extra chloride, diarrhea, carbonic anhydrase inhibitors, adrenal insuffi- ciency, renal tubular acidosis, and pancreatic fistula (com- mon causes of nonanion gap metabolic acidosis)
UroLift	a minimally invasive system to treat an enlarged prostate or benign prostatic hyperplasia that lifts or holds the enlarged prostate tissue out of the way so it no longer blocks the urethra		
		USEIR	United States Eye Injury Registry
URP	urotensin II-related peptide	USEMSs	uncovered self-expandable metal stents
URQ	upper right quadrant		
URR	urea reduction ratio	USEPA	United States Environmental Protection Agency
URS	ureterorenoscopy		
URSB	upper right sternal border	USF2	upstream stimulatory factor 2
URS/LL	ureteroscopy with laser lithotripsy	USG	ultrasmall gold (particles) ultrasonography ultrasound-guided urine specific gravity
URT	upper respiratory tract uterine resting tone		
URTI	upper respiratory tract infection		
URTS	upper respiratory tract symptoms	USGA	ultra sound-guided access
US	ultrasonography ultrasound unit secretary United States of America	USH	United Services for Handicapped Usher syndrome usual state of health
		USH1	Usher syndrome type 1
U/S	see US ultrasound	USH2	Usher syndrome type 2
		USH3	Usher syndrome type 3
US7	7-joint ultrasound score	USI	urinary stress incontinence
USA	unit services assistant United States Army United States of America unstable angina	USL	uterosacral ligament
		USLF	uterosacral ligament fixation
		USLS	uterosacral ligament suspension
		USLs	uterosacral ligaments
USAF	United States Air Force	USM	ultrasonic mist
USAISR	United States Army Institute of Surgical Research	USMB	ultrasound-stimulated microbub- bles (USMB pretreatment has enabled higher-dose radiation effects with conventional radiation dosing)
USAMRIID	United States Army Medical Re- search Institute of Infectious Diseases		
		USMC	United States Marine Corps
USAN	United States Adopted Names	USMLE	United States Medical Licensing Examination
USA/NSTEMI	unstable angina and non-ST segment elevation myocardial infarction		
		USN	ultrasonic nebulizer United States Navy
USAP	unstable angina pectoris	USO	unilateral salpingo-oophorectomy
USAQ	Unstable Angina Symptoms Questionnaire		
		USOGH	usual state of good health
USAR	unexpected suspected adverse reaction	USOH	usual state of health

USP	unassisted systolic pressure	uTDA	urinary toluenediamine
	United States Pharmacopeia	*ut dict*	as directed
	(a nonprofit organization	UTE	ultrashort echo time
	that sets standards for drugs;	UTF	usual throat flora
	drugs designated USP or	UTG	ultimate treatment goal
	contained in their compendia,		uninodular toxic goiter
	meet their standards for purity	UTH	upward transtentorial herniation
	and potency)	UTI	urinary tract infection
USP44	ubiquitin specific peptidase	UTIs	urinary tract infections
	44 (gene)	UTL	ulnotriquetral ligament
uSpA	undifferentiated spondyloarthritis		unable to locate
USPC	uterine serous papillary		useful therapeutic life
	carcinoma	UTM	urinary-tract malformations
USPDC	United States Pharmacopeia	UTMD	ultrasound-targeted microbubble
	Drug Classification		destruction
USPHS	United States Public Health	UTMDACC	University of Texas M.D.
	Service		Anderson Cancer Center
USPI	ulnar styloid process index	UTN	unmet treatment needs (index)
	United Surgical Partners		unreamed tibial nails
	International	UTO	unable to obtain
USPSTF	United States Preventive		upper tibial osteotomy
	Services Task Force		uterus, tubes, and ovaries
	United States Preventive	Utox	urine toxicology screening
	Services Task Force (an inde-	U Tox	urinary toxicology screening
	pendent panel of non-Federal	UTP	uridine triphosphate
	health care experts that	UTR	untranslated region
	evaluates the latest scientif-	UTRI	may have meant URTI (upper
	ic evidence on clinical and		respiratory tract infection)
	preventive services)	UTrIs	unscheduled treatment
USS	Upshaw-Schulman syndrome		interruptions
USUCVD	unsterile uncontrolled vaginal	UTS	ulnar tunnel syndrome
	delivery		ultrasound
USVMD	urine specimen volume measur-	UTT	urinary tract tumor(s)
	ing device	UTTCC	upper tract transitional-cell
USVs	ultrasonic vocalizations		carcinoma
USW	US white (population)	UTUC	upper-tract urothelial carcinoma
USWS	unihemispheric slow-wave sleep	UTV	ultrasound transmission velocity
USWs	ultra-slow waves	UTW	unsupported treadmill walking
	ultrasonic standing waves	UTWB	unable to weight bear
UT	upper thoracic	UTx	uterine transplantation
	upper trapezius (muscle)	Utx	see gene website www.ncbi.nlm
	ureteral catheter		.nih.gov/gene
	Utah	UTZ	ultrasound
UT60	60 decree of upper trunk	UU	ureteroureterostomy
	inclination	U/U+	uterine fundus at umbilicus
UTA	unable to assess		(usually modified as number
	urinary tract anomaly		of finger breadths above)
UTC	unable to calculate	U/U−	uterine fundus at umbilicus
	undifferentiated thyroid carcinoma		(usually modified as number
	urinary tract calculi		of finger breadths below)
UtCa	uterine cancer	UUD	uncontrolled unsterile delivery
UTCD	may have meant,	UUE	unused, unwanted, or expired
	undifferentiated connective		(medications)
	tissue disease (UCTD)		urinary urea excretion
UTD	unable to determine	UUI	urge urinary incontinence
	up to date	UUMN	unilateral upper motor neuron
	Urinary Tract Dilation Classifi-	UUN	urinary urea nitrogen
	cation System	UUO	Unilateral ureteral obstruction

UUT	upper urinary tract
UUTI	uncomplicated urinary tract infections
UV	ultraviolet
	umbilical vein
	ureterovesical
	urine volume
UVA	ultraviolet A light
	ureterovesical angle
UVA1	ultraviolet A1 (phototherapy; 350-400 nanometers)
UVATS	uniportal video-assisted thoracoscopic surgery
UVB	ultraviolet B light
UVBI	ultraviolet blood irradiation
UVC	ultraviolet C light
	umbilical vein catheter
UVCP	unilateral vocal cord paralysis
UVEB	unifocal ventricular ectopic beat
UVF	ureterovaginal fistula
UVGI	ultraviolet germicidal irradiation
UVH	univentricular heart
UVIB	ultraviolet irradiation of blood
UVJ	ureterovesical junction
UVL	ultraviolet light
	umbilical venous line
UVP	utero-vaginal prolapse
UVPP	uvulopalatopharyngoplasty
UVR	ultraviolet radiation
UVS	unprotected vaginal sex
UVs	unclassified variants
UVT	unsustained ventricular tachycardia
UV-VIS	ultraviolet-visible (spectrometer)
UW	unilateral weakness
U/WB	unit of whole blood
uWBC	urine white blood cells
UWF	ultrawide field
	unknown white female
UWFI	ultrawide field imaging
UWHC	Wisconsin Hospital and Clinics
UWL	unexplained weight loss
	unstirred water layer
UWM	unknown white male
	unwed mother
UW-QOLv4	University of Washington Quality of Life Questionnaire, version 4
UXO	unexploded ordnance
UZn	urine zinc level

V

V	five
	gas volume
	minute volume
	vaccinated
	vagina
	valine
	Valium (diazepam); as in vitamin V (slang)
	vanadium
	vein
	ventilation (L/min)
	ventricular
	verb
	verbal
	vertebral
	very
	veteran
	Viagra (sildenafil citrate) as in "vitamin V" (slang)
	Victor (Phonetic Alphabet for V; pronounced (VIK-TAH)
	viral
	vision
	vitamin
	voided
	volt
	volume (with any number, such as V20)
	vomiting
v	versus
+V	positive vertical divergence
V1	cortical visual area 1
	fifth cranial nerve, ophthalmic division
V2	cortical visual area 2
	fifth cranial nerve, maxillary division
V3	fifth cranial nerve, mandibular division
V4	cortical visual area 4
V_1 to V_6	precordial chest leads
3-V	3-vessel (cord)
VA	alveolar gas volume
	vacuum aspiration
	valproic acid
	venous access
	venous aneurysms
	ventriculoatrial
	verbal abuse
	verbal autopsy
	vertebral artery
	Veterans Administration
	Virginia
	visual acuity
V&A	vagotomy and antrectomy

V/A	see VA	VACTER	vertebral defects, imperforate
	violence and abuse		anus, cardiac anomalies,
VAAESS	Vaccine-Associated Adverse		tracheoesophageal fistula,
	Events Surveillance System		and renal anomalies
	(Canada)	VACTERL	vertebral defects, imperforate
VAB	vacuum-assisted biopsy		anus, cardiac anomalies,
	variable atrial blockage		tracheoesophageal fistula,
	vinblastine, dactinomycin		renal anomalies, and limb
	(actinomycin D),		anomalies
	bleomycin	VACTREL	may have meant VACTERL
VABB	vacuum-assisted breast biopsy	VACTRL	vertebral defects, imperforate
VABC	Vascular Access-Board		anus, cardiac anomalies,
	Certified		tracheoesophageal fistula,
VABG	vitalized allogeneic bone		renal anomalies, and limb
	grafting		anomalies
VABP	ventilator-associated bacterial	VAD	vascular access dysfunction
	pneumonia		vascular (venous) access device
VABS	Vineland Adaptive Behavior		ventricular assist device
	Scales		vertebral artery dissection
VAC	etoposide (VePesid),		Veterans Administration
	cytarabine (ara-C),		Domiciliary
	and carboplatin		vincristine, doxorubicin
	vacuum-assisted closure		(Adriamycin), and
	(dressings)		dexamethasone
	ventilator-associated condition	VaD	vascular dementia
	ventriculoarterial conduction	VADCS	ventricular atrial distal coronary
	vincristine, doxorubicin		sinus
	(Adriamycin), and	VaDe	vas deferens
	cyclophosphamide	VADRIAC	vincristine, doxorubicin
VAC'd	the use of vacuum-assisted		(Adriamycin), and
	closure		cyclophosphamide
VAC'ed	the use of vacuum-assisted	VADs	ventricular assist devices
	closure	VAE	venous air embolism
VA cc	distance visual acuity with		ventilator-associated event
	correction	VA-ECMO	venous-arterial extracorporeal
VA ccl	near visual acuity with		membrane oxygenation
	correction	VAERS	Vaccine Adverse Events
VACD	vincristine, actinomycin D,		Reporting System
	cyclophosphamide, and	VAEs	ventilator-associated events
	doxorubicin	VAFD	vascular access flush device
VACE	*Vitex agnus-castus* extract	VAG	vagina
	(Chaste tree berry extract)	vag	vaginal
VAC EXT	vacuum extractor	VAG HYST	vaginal hysterectomy
Vac Extrac	vacuum extractor	VAH	Veterans Administration
VAC/IE	vincristine, doxorubicin		Hospital
	(Adriamycin), cyclophos-	VAHBE	ventricular atrial His bundle
	phamide, ifosfamide and		electrocardiogram
	etoposide	VAHRA	ventricular atrial height
VAC$_{ig}$	vaccinia immune globulin		right atrium
VACIME	vincristine, doxorubicin	VAHS	virus-associated hemophagocytic
	(Adriamycin), cyclophos-		syndrome
	phamide, ifosfamide, mesna,	VAI	vertebral artery injury
	and etoposide		Voluntary Action Indicated
VACO	Veterans Administration		(FDA)
	Central Office	VaIN 1	vaginal intraepithelial neoplasia
VACS	Veterans Aging Cohort Study		grade 1
VACs	ventilator-associated	VaIN 2	vaginal intraepithelial neoplasia
	conditions		grade 2

V

VaIN 2/3	vaginal intraepithelial neoplasia grade 2/3	varn	street name for cocaine
VaIN 3	vaginal intraepithelial neoplasia grade 3	VARS	valyl (aminoacy)-tRNA (transfer ribonucleic acid) synthetase (gene/protein)
Val	valine	VAS	vas deferens
VALE	visual acuity, left eye		vascular
VALI	ventilator-associated lung injury		vasectomy vibroacoustic stimulator (stimulation)
VAM	video-assisted mediastinoscopy		Visual Analogue Scale (Score)
VAMC	Veterans Affairs Medical Center	VASC	Visual-Auditory Screen Test
VAMLA	video-assisted mediastinoscopic lymphadenectomy		for Children
VAMP®	venous-arterial manage-ment protection system	VA sc	distance visual acuity without correction
VAMS	Visual Analogue Mood Scale	vascath	vascular (left) internal jugular catheter
VAN	vancomycin	Vas cath	a temporary catheter used
	vanilla		for hemodialysis until a
vanco	vancomycin		more permanent access has
VANCO/P	vancomycin-peak		time to mature or when a
VANCO/T	vancomycin-trough		fistula or graft access cannot
VAOD	visual acuity, right eye		be obtained; it is usually
VAOS	visual acuity, left eye		inserted via the subclavian
VA OS LP with P	visual acuity, left eye, left perception with projection		or jugular vessels
VAP	venous access port	VA scl	near visual acuity without correction
	ventilator-associated pneumonia Vertical Auto Profile (compre-	VASH	Veterans Affairs Supportive Housing
	hensive cholesterol-related testing technology/device)	vasH	see gene website www.ncbi .nlm.nih.gov/gene
	video-assisted parathyroidectomy	VA shunt	ventriculoatrial shunt
	vincristine, asparaginase, and prednisone	VASO	Veteran's Administration Service Officer
VAPCS	ventricular atrial proximal coronary sinus	VASPI	Visual Analogue Self Assessment Scales For
Vapotherm	a high-velocity nasal cannula insufflation device		Pain Intensity
VAPP	vaccine-associated paralytic poliomyelitis	VAS RAD	vascular radiology
		VASs	visual analog scales
VAPR	venous access pressure ratio	VASST	Vasopressin and Septic
VAPS	visual analogue pain scale		Shock Trial
VAPs	ventilator-associated pneumonias	VAST	Vibro-acoustic Stimulator
		vast	a word meaning very great in
VAR	variant		scope or size; enormous
	varicella (chickenpox) (*varicella zoster* virus) (Varivax) vaccine	VAT	Vascular Access Team ventilatory anaerobic threshold ventricular activation time
VARD	video-assisted retroperitoneal debridement		vertebral artery test video-assisted thoracoscopy
	videoscopic-assisted retroperito-neal debridement		visceral adipose tissue
Vard	vardenafil HCL (Levitra)	VATER	a set of birth defects which
VARE	visual acuity, right eye		often occur together
VARig	varicella-zoster immune glonulin		[vertebral defects (V), anorectal malformations (A), cardiac defects (C),
varix	a word meaning an abnormally dilated and lengthened vein, artery, or lymph vessel; especially a varicose vein		tracheoesophageal fistula with or without esophageal atresia (TE), and renal malformations (R)]

VATERL	a set of birth defects which often occur together [vertebral defects (V), anorectal malformations (A), cardiac defects (C), tracheoesophageal fistula with or without esophageal atresia (TE), renal malformations (R), and limb defects (L)]
VATH	vinblastine, doxorubicin (Adriamycin), thiotepa, and fluoxymesterone (Halotestin)
VATS	video assisted thoracic surgery
VAVD	vacuum-assisted vaginal delivery
	vacuum-assisted venous drainage
VAWCM	vacuum-assisted wound closure and mesh-mediated fascial traction
VAX-D	vertebral axial decompression
VB	vaginal bleeding
	Van Buren (catheter)
	venous blood
	vertebral body
	vinblastine and bleomycin
	vinblastine (Velban)
	virtual bronchoscopy
VB_1	first voided bladder specimen
VB_2	second midstream bladder specimen
VB_3	third voided urine specimen
VBAC	vaginal birth after cesarean
VBAI	vertebrobasilar artery insufficiency
VBAP	vincristine, carmustine (BiCNU), doxorubicin (Adriamycin), and prednisone
VBC	vinblastine, bleomycin, and cisplatin
VBD	vertebrobasilar dolichoectasia
VBDS	vanishing bile duct syndrome
VBeam	vascular beam (a pulsed dye laser used to treat dilated blood vessels, such as in rosacea)
VBG	venous blood gas
	vertical banded gastroplasty
VBGP	vertical banded gastroplasty
VBI	vertebrobasilar insufficiency
VBICAD	vertebrobasilar intracranial atheromatous disease
VBID	value-based insurance designs
V Big	ventricular bigeminy
VBL	vinblastine (Velban)
vBloc	vagal nerve blockade

vBLoc®	vagal blocking therapy; a treatment for obesity (EnteroMedics)
VBM	vinblastine, bleomycin, and methotrexate
	voxel-based morphometry
VBMCP	vincristine, carmustine (BiCNU), melphalan, cyclophosphamide, and prednisone
vBMD	volumetric bone mineral density
VBP	vinblastine, bleomycin, and cisplatin
VBR	ventricular brain ratio
VBS	vertebral-basilar system
	videofluoroscopic barium swallow (evaluation)
VB-SCCD	variation-based sparse cortical current density
VBSS	video barium swallow study
VBT	vascular brachytherapy
VBX	VIABAHN balloon expandable (endoprosthesis; goremedical.com/products /viabahn)
VbX	vibration exercise (a warm-up modality to enhance athletic performance)
VBZ	valbenazine (ingrezza)
VC	color vision
	etoposide (VePesid) and carboplatin
	pulmonary capillary blood volume
	varicocele
	vena cava
	verbal cueing
	verbal cues
	vincristine (note: for intra-VENOUS administration only)
	virtual colonoscopy
	vital capacity
	vitamin C
	vocal cords
	volume control
	volumetric capnography
	voluntary cough
Vc	bortezomib (Velcade)
V&C	vertical and centric (a bite)
V/C	see VC
	voriconazole and caspofungin
VC's	see VC
VCA	vasoconstrictor assay
VCAC	ventriculocoronary arterial communications
VCAM	vascular cell adhesion molecule

VCAP	vincristine, cyclophosphamide, doxorubicin (Adriamycin), and prednisone
Vcc	vision with correction
VCCA	velocity common carotid artery
VCD	vascular closure device
	vocal cord dysfunction
VCDR	vertical cup-to-disc ratio
VCE	vaginal cervical endocervical (smear)
	video capsule endoscopy
VCF	Vaginal Contraception Film™
	vertebral compression fracture (s)
VCFS	velo-cardio-facial syndrome
VCFs	vertebral compression fractures
VCG	vectorcardiography
	voiding cystogram
VCI	vascular cognitive impairment
	vocal cord injuries
	volume contrast imaging
vCJD	variant Creutzfeldt-Jakob disease
VCL	curvilinear velocity
	Veterans Crisis Line
VCM	vancomycin
VCO	ventilator CPAP oxyhood
VCO2	ventilator-derived carbon dioxide production
VCP	vocal cord palsy
VCPR	veterinarian-client-patient relationship
VCR	video cassette recorder
	vincristine sulfate (Oncovin) (note: for intraVENOUS administration only)
VCs	verbal cues
VCSEL	vertical cavity surface emitting laser
VCSS	Venous Clinical Severity Score
VCT	vascular choroidal thickness
	venous clotting time
	volumetric computed tomography
	voluntary counselling and testing
VCTE	vibration-controlled transient elastography (measures liver stiffness)
VCTS	vitreal corneal touch syndrome
VCU	voiding cystourethrogram
VCUG	vesicoureterogram
	voiding cystourethrogram
VCV	varicella virus
	volume-control ventilation
VCW	vena contracta width
	vertebral canal width
VCZ	voriconazole (Vfend)

VD	vaginal delivery
	venereal disease
	vessel disease
	viral diarrhea
	voided
	voiding diary
	volume dose
	volume of distribution
+VD	positive vertical divergence
V_D	deadspace volume
V_d	volume of distribution
V&D	vomiting and diarrhea
V/D	See VD or V&D
1-VD	one-vessel disease
VDA	vascular disrupting agent
	venous digital angiogram
	visual discriminatory acuity
VDAC	vaginal delivery after cesarean
VDAC1	voltage dependent anion channel type 1
VDBP	vitamin D-binding protein
VDC	Veteran Directed Care Program (Veterans administration)
	vincristine, doxorubicin, and cyclophosphamide
VDC-IE	vincristine, doxorubicin, cyclophosphamide, ifosfamide and etoposide
VDD	atrial synchronous ventricular inhibited pacing
	vitamin D deficiency
VDDR I	vitamin D dependency rickets type I
VDDR II	vitamin D dependency rickets type II
VDE	vasodilatory edema
VDEPT	virus-directed enzyme prodrug therapy
VDF	vardenafil (Levitra)
	vinylidene fluoride
VDG	venereal disease–gonorrhea
Vdg	voiding
VDH	valvular disease of the heart
VDI	Vasculitis Damage Index
	Ventilatory Demand Index
	vitamin D insufficiency
VDIP	vasoactive drug infusion pump
VDJ	variable diversity joining
VDL	vasodepressor lipid
	visual detection level
VDO	varus derotational osteotomy
VD or M	venous distention or masses
VDP	vinblastine, dacarbazine, and cisplatin (Platinol)
VD-PACE	bortezomib (Velcade), dexamethasone, cisplatin (Platinol), doxorubicin (Adriamycin), and Etoposide

VDPCA	variable-dose patient-controlled analgesia
VDR	vitamin D receptor (gene)
VDRA	vitamin D receptor activation
	vitamin D receptor activator
vdra	vitamin D (1,25- dihydroxyvitamin D3) receptor a (gene)
VDRAs	vitamin D receptor agonists
VDRE	vitamin D responsive element(s)
VDRF	ventilator dependent respiratory failure
VDRL	Venereal Disease Research Laboratory (test for syphilis)
VDRO	varus derotation osteotomy
	varus derotational osteotomy
VDRR	vitamin D-resistant rickets
VDRS	Verdun Depression Rating Scale
VDS	vasodepressor syncope
	venereal disease—syphilis
	Verbal Descriptor Scale
	vindesine (Eldisine)
	volume of dead-space
VDT	vibration detection threshold
	video display terminal
	visual display terminal
	volume doubling time
VDT-PACE	bortezomib, (Velcade), dexamethasone, thalidomide, cisplatin (Platinol), doxorubicin (Adriamycin), cyclophosphamide, and etoposide
VD/VT	dead space to tidal volume ratio
VD/VT phy	dead space physiologic to tidal volume
VDZ	vedolizumab (Entyvio)
VE	minute volume (expired)
	vacuum extraction
	vaginal examination
	ventricular ectopy
	vertex
	Vietnam era
	virtual endoscopy
	visual examination
	vitamin E
	vocational evaluation
Ve	minute ventilation
+VE	positive
−VE	negative
V/E	violence and eloper
VEA	ventricular ectopic activity
	viscoelastic agent
VEB	ventricular ectopic beat
VEC	vecuronium (Norcuron)
	velocity-encoded cine
VECG	vector electrocardiogram
VE/CO2	quotient between ventilation and volume of exhaled carbon dioxide

VED	vacuum erection device
	vacuum extraction delivery
	ventricular ectopic depolarization
	vitamin E deficiency
	voluntary eye donation
VEE	Venezuelan equine encephalitis
VEE$_a$	Venezuelan equine encephalitis vaccine, attenuated live
VEE$_I$	Venezuelan equine encephalitis vaccine, inactivated
VEEG	video-electroencephalography
VEEV	Venezuelan equine encephalitis virus
VEF	visually evoked field
VEG	vegetation (bacterial)
	videoesophagram
VEGF	vascular endothelial growth factor
VEGF-A	vascular endothelial growth factor A
veggies	vegetables
VEH	visual eye height
veh	vehicle
VeIP	vinblastine (Velban), ifosfamide, and cisplatin (Platinol)
VEL	Vel; an International Society of Blood Transfusion (ISBT) blood group
Vel	Velcade (bortezomib)
vel	velocity
VEMP	vestibular evoked myogenic potentials
VEMPs	vestibular evoked myogenic potentials
VE-MRI	velocity-encoded magnetic resonance imaging
VEN	verrucous epidermal nevus
ven	venous
VENC	velocity encoding value (radiology)
VENT	ventilation
	ventilator
	ventral
	ventricular
VEO-IBD	very early onset inflammatory bowel disease
VEP	visual evoked potential
VEPTR	vertical expandable prosthetic titanium rib (instrumentation)
VER	ventricular escape rhythm
	visual evoked responses
VERDICT	Veterans Evidence-based Research Dissemination Implementation Center
VERP	ventricular effective refractory period
VERT	velocity-enhanced resistance training

vert	vertical	VFs	visual fields
veru	veru montanum	VFSE	videofluoroscopic swallowing examination
VES	ventricular extrasystoles		
	video-endoscopic surgery	VFSS	videofluoroscopic swallowing study
	vitamin E succinate		
	Vulnerable Elders Survey (UK)	VFT	venous filling time
VESS	video endoscopic swallowing study		ventricular fibrillation threshold
			visceral fat tissue
vest	vestibular	VFVT	very fast ventricular tachycardia
VET	veteran	VFW	Veterans of Foreign Wars
	Veterinarian	VG	vein graft
	veterinary		ventricular gallop
VEV	varicose esophageal veins		ventrogluteal
VF	left leg (electrode)		very good
	ventricular fibrillation		vitellogenin (gene)
	vertebral fracture	V&G	vagotomy and gastroenterotomy
	vertical float (aquatic therapy)	VGAD	vein of Galen aneurysmal dilatation
	videofluoroscopic		
	visual field	VGAM	vein of Galen aneurysmal malformation
	vocal fold		
	vocal fremitus	VGB	vigabatrin (Sabril)
VFA	vertebral fracture assessment	VGCC	voltage-gated calcium channel(s)
	vertebrobasilar fusiform aneurysm		
		VGCV	valganciclovir (Valcyte)
VF arrest	ventricular fibrillation arrest	VGE	venous gas emboli
VFC	Vaccines for Children (Program)		viral gastroenteritis
VFCB	vertical flow clean bench	VGF	vein graft failure
VFD	ventilator-free days	VGH	very good health
	visual fields	VGI	Cryptococcus gatti isolate
VFFC	visual fields full to confrontation	VGKC	voltage-gated potassium channel
VFFS	videofluoroscopic feeding studies	V(glom)	glomerular volume
		VGM	vein graft myringoplasty
VFFs	vocal fold fibroblasts	VGPO	volume-guaranteed pressure option
VFFTC	visual fields full to confrontation		
VFI	viable female infant	VGPR	very good partial response (remission)
	visual fields intact		
	Visual Functioning index	VGRF	vertical component of ground reaction force
VFib	ventricular fibrillation		
V fib	ventricular fibrillation	VGS	viridans-group streptococci
VFL	vinflunine	VGs	virulence genes
VFM	vector flow mapping	VH	vaginal hysterectomy
VFMI	vocal fold motion impairment		variceal hemorrhage
VFO	very fast oscillations		vertical heterophoria
	visceral fat obesity		Veterans Hospital
VFP	vertical float progression (aquatic therapy)		viral hepatitis
			visual hallucinations
	vitreous fluorophotometry		vitreous hemorrhage
	vocal fold paralysis		von Herrick (grading system)
VFPN	Volu-feed premie nipple	VH I	very narrow anterior chamber angles
VFPs	venous foot pumps		
VFQ-25	National Eye Institute 25-item Visual Function Questionnaire	VH II	moderately narrow anterior chamber angles
		VH III	moderately wide open anterior chamber angles
VFR	visiting friends and relatives (possible contacts for communicable diseases)		
		VH IV	wide open anterior chamber angles
VFRN	Volu-feed regular nipple	VHA	Veterans Health Administration
VFRs	visiting friends and relatives		Voluntary Hospitals of America

V

VHbs	Vitreoscilla hemoglobins	Vici syndrome	a progressive neurodevelopment multisystem disorder characterized by failure to develop the corpus callosum, cataracts, hypopigmentation of the eyes and hair, cardiomyopathy, and combined immunodeficiency
VHC	valved holding chamber		
VHD	valvular heart disease		
	vascular hemostatis device		
VHDL	very-high-density lipoprotein		
VHDL-R	very-high-density lipoprotein receptor		
VHE	valproate (VPA)-induced hyperammonemic encephalopathy		
		VICP	Vaccine Injury Compensation Program
	very-high-energy		
	viral hepatitis E	Vi CPs	typhoid Vi (capsular) polysaccharide vaccine (Typhim Vi)
VHF	viral hemorrhagic fever		
VHI	The Voice Handicap Index		
VHI10	voice handicap index 10 (voice quality measure)	VICs	valvular interstitial cells
		Victor	Phonetic Alphabet for V; pronounced VIK-TAH
VHI 10	voice handicap index 10 (voice quality measure)		
		VID	videodensitometry
vHIT	video head impulse test	VIDD	ventilator-induced diaphragmatic dysfunction
VHL	von Hippel-Lindau disease (complex)		
		VIE	virtual intravascular endoscopy
VHP	vaporized hydrogen peroxide	VIG	vaccinia immune globulin
			vinblastine, ifosfamide, and gallium nitrate
	very high protein (enteral nutrition)	VIGRT	volumetrically image-guided radiotherapy
VHR	vagal hyperreactivity	VIH	Spanish and French abbreviation for human immunodeficiency virus
	ventral hernia repair		
	very high risk		
VHR-ALL	very high risk subtype of acute lymphoblastic leukemia		ventral incisional hernia
			ventral incisional herniorrhaphy
		VIHR	ventral incisional hernia repair
VHS	viral hemorrhagic septicemia	vii	seven
	virion host shutoff	viii	eight
VHs	vertebral hemangiomas	VILI	ventilator-induced lung injury
	visual hallucinations	VIM	ventralis intermedius
VHSV	viral hemorrhagic septicemia virus	VIM-DBS	ventralis intermedius thalamic nucleus deep brain stimulation
VI	six		
	velocity index	VIMS	visually induced motion sickness
	vests intermedius	VIN	vibration-induced nystagmus
	vilanterol		vulvar intraepithelial neoplasm
	volume index	VIN 1	vulvar intraepithelial neoplasia grade 1
VIA	visual inspection with 4% acetic acid	VIN 2	vulvar intraepithelial neoplasia grade 2
via	by way of		
vib	vibration	VIN 3	vulvar intraepithelial neoplasia grade 3
VIBS	Victim's Information Bureau Service	VIN I	vulvar intraepithelial neoplasia grade I
VICA	velocity internal carotid artery	VIN II	vulvar intraepithelial neoplasia grade II
VICD	virus-induced CNS (central nervous system) dysfunction	VIN III	vulvar intraepithelial neoplasia grade III
VICH	International Cooperation on Harmonization of Technical Requirements for Registration of Veterinary Products	VIP	etopside (VePesid), ifosfamide, and cisplatin (Platinol)
			vasoactive intestinal peptide
			vasoactive intracorporeal pharmacotherapy

	Vattikuti Institute prostatectomy	*VIZ*	namely
	very important patient	VJ	vertical jump
	vinblastine, ifosfamide, and cisplatin (Platinol)	V-J	ventriculo-jugular (shunt)
	voluntary interruption of pregnancy	VJH	vertical jump height
VIPN	vincristine-induced peripheral neuropathy	VKA	vitamin K antagonist
		VKAs	vitamin K antagonists
VIPomas	vasoactive intestinal peptide-secreting tumors	VKC	vernal keratoconjunctivitis
		VKCFD	vitamin K-dependent coagulation factors deficiency
VIQ	Verbal Intelligence Quotient (part of Wechsler tests)	VKDB	vitamin K deficiency bleeding
		VKH	Vogt-Koyanagi-Harada disease
VIR	Vascular Interventional Radiology	VKOR	vitamin K epoxide reductase
	viral	VKORC1	vitamin K epoxide reductase complex, subunit 1 (gene/ a highly polymorphic enzyme variant responsible for the metabolism of warfarin)
	virulent		
	virus		
VIS	Vaccine Information Statement		
	Visual Impairment Service	VKS	vitamin K supplement
VISA	vancomycin-intermediate-resistant *Staphylococcus aureus*		von Kármán-sodium (dynamo)
		Vks	K vitamins
		VL	left arm (electrode)
VISC	vitreous infusion suction cutter		vastus lateralis
VISI	Vaccine Identification Standards Initiative		vial
			viral load
	volar intercalated segmental instability		visceral leishmaniasis (kala-azar)
		VLA	vertical long-axis
VISN	Veterans Integrated Service Networks		very-late antigen
		VLAD	variable life-adjusted display
vis perc	visual perception (perceptual)	VLAP	vaporization laser ablation of the prostate
VISs	Vaccine Information Statements		
		VLBW	very low birth weight (less than 1500 g)
VIST	Vascular Intervention System Trainer		
		VLBWPN	very low birth weight preterm neonate
VistA	Veterans Health Information Systems and Technology Architecture		
		VLC	visible light communications
		VLCAD	very-long-chain acyl coenzyme A dehydrogenase
VIT	venom immunotherapy		
	vital	VLCADD	very long chain acyl coenzyme A dehydrogenase deficiency
	vitamin		
	vitreous	VLCD	very low calorie diet
Vital Signs	The taking and recording of body temperature, pulse rate, blood pressure, and respiratory rate (adults)	VLCFA	very-long-chain fatty acids
		VLCHP	very low carbohydrate, high protein (diet)
		VLDL	very-low-density lipoprotein
		VLE	vision left eye
		VLED	very-low-energy diet
Vitamin	see individual letters such as B, D, G, H, K, P, R, V, etc.	VLF	very-low-frequency
		VLH	ventrolateral nucleus of the hypothalamus
Vitamin D2	ergocalciferol		
Vitamin D3	cholecalciferol	VLK	vascularized limbal keratitis
Vit C	vitamin C (ascorbic acid)	VLL	vastus lateralis longus
VIT CAP	vital capacity	VLM	visceral larva migrans
vit D	vitamin D	VLNT	vascularized lymph node transfer
Vit D2	vitamin D2 (ergocalciferol)	VLO	vastus lateralis oblique (muscle)
Vit D3	vitamin D3 (cholecalciferol)	Vlo	viral load
Vitoss®	a synthetic bone graft substitute	VLP	virus-like particle
Vits	vitamins	VLPFC	ventrolateral prefrontal cortex
VIU	visual internal urethrotomy	VLPP	Valsalva leak point pressure

VLR	vastus lateralis release
VLS	vanishing lung syndrome
	vapor-liquid-solid
	vascular leak syndrome
	vulvar lichen sclerosus
VLs	viral loads
VLST	very late stent thrombosis (beyond 1 year after implantation)
VLUs	venous leg ulcers
VM	venous malformation
	ventilated mask
	ventimask
	Venturi mask
	vestibular membrane
	voice mail
VM 26	teniposide (Vumon)
VMA	vanillylmandelic acid
	vitreomacular adhesion
Vmail	voicemail
VMAT	Veterinary Medical Assistance Team
	volumetric-modulated arc therapy
VMAT-2	vesicular monoamine transporter-2
Vmax	maximal velocity
	peak flow velocity
VMCP	vincristine, melphalan, cyclophosphamide, and prednisone
VMD	Doctor of Veterinary Medicine (DVM)
	vertical maxillary deficiency
VME	vertical maxillary excess
VMF	vibration-induced white finger (syndrome)
VMG	vibromyography
VMH	ventromedial hypothalamus
VMI	vendor-managed inventory
	viable male infant
	visual motor integration
VML	vastus medialis lateralis
	vastus medialis longus
VMM	voicemail message
VMMC	voluntary male medical circumcision
VMMR	voicemail message received
VMMS	voicemail message sent
VMN	ventromedial (hypothalamic) nucleus
VMO	vaccinia melanoma oncolysate
	vastus medialis oblique
VMOVM	left message on voicemail
VMP	bortezomib (Velcade) melphalan, and prednisone
vmPFC	ventromedial prefrontal cortex
VMR	vasomotor rhinitis

VMS	vanilla milkshake
	variable muscle stimulator
VMT	vehicle miles traveled
	vitreomacular traction
VMTS	vitreomacular traction syndrome
VMU	vertebral motion unit
VN	vasculitic neuropathy
	visiting nurse
VNI	Cryptococcus neoformans isolate molecular type I
VNII	Cryptococcus neoformans isolate molecular type 2
VNIII	Cryptococcus neoformans isolate molecular type 3
VNIV	Cryptococcus neoformans isolate molecular type 4
VNA	Visiting Nurses' Association
VNB	vinorelbine (Navelbine)
VNC	vesicle neck contracture
VNE	virtual nonenhanced (radiology)
VNG	videonystagmograph videonystagmography
VNP	ventilated nosocomial pneumonia
	videonasopharyngoscopy
	virus-like nanoparticles
VNPs	virus-like nanoparticles
VNS	vagal nerve stimulator
	vagus nerve stimulation
VNTR	variable number of tandem repeats
VNUS	a patented system using a percutaneous endovascular approach with a segmental radiofrequency abolition system to treat superficial venous insufficiency and varicose veins (VNUS Closure procedure)
VO	verbal order
	visual observation
V₂O₅ / V_2O_5	vanadium pentoxide
V/O	see VO
VO2	an index of the body's efficiency at producing work. It is expressed in milliliters of oxygen consumed per minute, and adjusted for body weight in kilograms: mL/kg/min
VOA	ventralis oralis anterior
	volume of activation
VOC	vaso-occlusive crisis
VOCA	voice-output communication aid
VOCAB	vocabulary
VocD	vocabulary diversity
VOCOR	vaso-occlusive crisis
	void on-call to operating room
VOCs	volatile organic compounds

VOCTOR	void on-call to operating room	V & P	vagotomy and pyloroplasty
VOD	veno-occlusive disease		ventilation and perfusion
	vision right eye	V/P	See VP and V & P
VOE	vascular occlusive episode	VP-16	etoposide (VePesid)
VOG	video-oculography	VPA	valproic acid
vog	volcanic smog		ventricular premature activation
VOGM	vein of Galen malformation		vigorous physical activity
VO₂I	oxygen consumption index	vpaced	ventricular-paced
VOI	value of information	V-Pad	sanitary napkin
VOL	Valuation of Life	VPAP	variable positive airway pressure
	volume	vPAT	virally-encoded polyamine
	voluntary		acetyltransferase
VOM	vomited	VPB	ventricular premature beat
VOMS	vestibular/ocular motor	VPBs	ventricular premature beats
	screening	VPC	velopharyngeal closure
VOMs	volatile organic metabolites		ventricular premature complexes
VOO	continuous ventricular		ventricular premature contractions
	asynchronous pacing		virtual private cloud
	virgin olive oil		vulval precursor cell
VOOD	vesico-outlet obstructive disease	VPCs	ventricular premature complexes
VOP	venous occlusion		ventricular premature contractions
	plethysmography		vulval precursor cells
	ventralis oralis posterior	VPD	ventricular premature
	ventricular overdrive pacing		depolarization
VOR	vestibulo-ocular reflex	VPDC	ventricular premature depolar-
VORB	verbal order read back		ization contraction
VORC	vestibulo-ocular reflex	VPDF	vegetable protein diet plus fiber
	cancellation	VPDs	ventricular premature
vorC	see gene website, www.ncbi		depolarizations
	.nlm.nih.gov/gene	VPE	vacuolar-processing enzyme;
VORI	voriconazole (Vfend)		see gene website www.ncbi
VORTEC	Viabahn Open Revascularization		.nlm.nih.gov/gene
	Technique	VPEP	visceral pain-evoked potentials
VORV	verbal order that is repeated	VPF	vascular permeability factor
	back and verified as correct		velopharyngeal function
VOR/VSR	vestibulo-ocular and	VPG	vocal process granuloma
	vestibulospinal reflexes	VPg	viral genome-linked protein
VOS	vision left eye	VPH	veterinary public health
VOSS	visual observation shivering		Virtual Physiological Human; a
	score		major European e-Science ini-
VOT	Visual Organization Test		tiative intended to support the
VOU	vision both eyes		development of patient-specific
VOV	repeat Black Verification of		computer models and their
	oral orders		application in personalized and
	verbal order verified		predictive healthcare
VP	etoposide (VePesid) and		visceral pain hypersensitivity
	cisplatin (Platinol)	VPI	velopharyngeal incompetence
	vagal paraganglioma		velopharyngeal insufficiency
	variegate porphyria	VPL	ventro-posterolateral
	velopharyngeal	Vplasty	consists in designing a v-shaped
	venipuncture		flap on the wall of the large
	venous pressure		vessel and a longitudinal
	ventricular pacing		incision on the small one.
	ventriculoperitoneal (shunt)		The V-flap is then introduced
	vertebroplasty		into the V-defect of the small
	vestibular paroxysm		vessel, creating a smooth
	visual perception		transition of the diameters
	voiding pressure		between the two vessels

V

VPLN	vaccine-primed lymph node (cells)
VPLS	ventilation-perfusion lung scan
VPM	venous pressure module
	visual perceptual motor
VPN	virtual private network
VPO	velopharyngeal opening
VPP	vertex positive potential
Vpr	viral protein R
VPR	virtual patient record
	volume pressure response
VPRS	Verbal Pain Rating Scale
VPS	valvular pulmonic stenosis
	ventriculoperitoneal shunt
VP shunt	ventriculoperitoneal shunt
VPT	vascularized patellar tendon
	vibration perception threshold
VPTs	vibratory perception thresholds
VPV	ventilatory pattern variability
VQ	vector quantization
	ventilation perfusion (scan)
V/Q	ventilation perfusion (ratio)
	ventilation perfusion (scan)
VQI	Vascular Quality Initiative (The Society for Vascular Surgery initiative designed to improve the quality, safety, effectiveness, and cost of vascular health care)
VQM	voice quality measurements
VQS	ventilation perfusion scintigraphy
VQ scan	ventilation perfusion lung scintigraphy
VR	right arm (electrode) valve replacement
	valve replacement
	venous resistance
	ventricular rhythm
	verbal reprimand
	violent restraint
	virtual reality
	visionary restructuralization
	vocational rehabilitation
	volume rendered (radiology)
VRA	visual reinforcement audiometry
	visual response audiometry
VRAD	virus removal and eradication by DFPP (double filtration plasmapheresis)
VRAM	vertical rectus abdominis myocutaneous (flap)
VRAM flap	vertical rectus abdominis myocutaneous flap
VRB	vinorelbine (Navelbine)
VRBPAC	Vaccines and Related Biological Products Advisory Committee (Food and Drug Administration)

VRC	vocational rehabilitation counselor
VRD	bortezomib (Velcade), lenalidomide (Revlimid), and dexamethasone
	vascular remodeling diseases
	von Recklinghausen disease
VRDF	may have meant VDRF (ventilator-dependent respiratory failure)
VRDL	Viral and Rickettsial Disease Laboratories (California State Department of Public Health)
VRDL-CF	Viral and Rickettsial Disease Laboratory (California State Department of Public Health) complement fixation test
VRDs	vascular remodeling diseases
	very rare (birth) defects
VRE	vancomycin-resistant enterococci
	vision right eye
VREF	vancomycin-resistant *Enterococcus faecium*
VRE UTI	vancomycin-resistant enterococci urinary tract infection
VRI	viral respiratory infection
VRL	ventral root, lumbar
	vinorelbine (Navelbine)
VRO	vertical ramus osteotomy (dental)
VRP	vascular rehab program
	vocational rehabilitation program
VR-QoL	vision-related quality of life
VRR	volume reduction ratio
VRS	viral rhinosinusitis
VRSA	vancomycin-resistant *Staphylococcus aureus*
VRT	variance of resident time
	ventral root, thoracic
	vertical radiation topography
	visual restoration therapy
	Visual Retention Test
	vocational rehabilitation therapy
VRTA	Vocational Rehabilitation Therapy Assistant
VRU	ventilator rehabilitation unit
VRV	vacuum relief valve
$V_3R\cdot\cdot V_6R$	right sided precordial leads
VS	vagal stimulation
	vegetative state
	ventricular stimulation
	versus (*vs*)
	very sensitive
	vestibular schwannoma
	viscerosomatic
	visit

visited

vital signs, (primary four: body temperature, pulse rate, blood pressure, and respiratory rate)

volume support

V/S   vital signs (temperature, pulse, and respiration)

volts per second

VSA   variant surface antigens

VSADP   vocational skills assessment and development program

VSBE   very short below elbow (cast)

VSBR   vertical scar breast reduction

VSC   rectovaginal screening culture
vertical semicircular canal

VSCC   vulvar squamous cell carcinoma

VSD   Vaccine Safety Datalink
ventricular septal defect
vesico-sphincter dyssynergia

VSE   vancomycin-sensitive Enterococcus
vasopressin, steroids, and epinephrine
vibration sonoelastography
videofluoroscopic swallow evaluation

VSED   voluntarily stopping eating and drinking

VSF   vascular signal fraction

VSF-36   Veterans Short-Form 36

VSFS   vibrational sum frequency spectroscopy

VSFs   vascular surgery fellows

VSG   vertical sleeve gastrectomy

VSGP   vertical supranuclear gaze palsy

VSGS   ventriculosubgaleal shunt

VSGs   variant surface glycoproteins

VSH   Verran-Snyder-Halpern sleep scale score)

VSI   visual motor integration

Vsim   similar velocities

vSIM   simulations of real scenarios to allow students to interact with virtual patients in an online environment

VSLI   vincristine sulfate liposomal injection
vincristine sulfate liposome inj

VSMC   vascular smooth muscle cell

VSN   visuospatial neglect
vital signs normal

VSO   vertical subcondylar oblique

VSOK   vital signs normal

VSP   vertical stabilization program
virtual surgical planning

VSQOL   vision-specific quality of life
Vital Signs Quality of Life

VSR   venous stasis retinopathy
ventricular septal rupture
vestibulospinal reflex

vsrD   see gene website www.ncbi.nlm.nih.gov/gene

VSRR   valve sparing root reimplantation

VSS   apparent volume of distribution
Vancouver Scar Scale
variable spot scanning
videofluoroscopic swallow studies
visual sexual stimulation
visual snow syndrome
vital signs stable

VSSAF   vital signs stable, afebrile

VST   visual search task

Vstap   stapes velocity

V-stim   ventricular stimulation

VSTM   visual short-term memory

VSULA   vaccination scar, upper left arm

VSV   vesicular stomatitis virus

VSVT   Victoria Symptom Validity Test (a computerized test that uses a forced-choice, two-alternative model to assess possible exaggeration or feigning of cognitive impairments)

VT   validation therapy
ventilatory threshold
ventricular tachycardia
Vermont
voiding trial

V$_t$ tidal volume

VTA   vascular trageting agents
ventral tegmental area

VT ablation   ventricular tachycardia ablation

VTACH   ventricular tachycardia

V Tach   ventricular tachycardia

VTB   vascular tumor burden

VTBD   volume to be determine

VTBI   volume to be infused

VTC   video teleconferencing

VTCs   venous thrombotic complications

VTD   bortezomib (Velcade), thialido-mide and dexamethasone

VTD-PACE   bortezomib (Velcade), tha-lidomide, dexamethasone, cisplatin (Platinol-AQ), adriamycin, cyclophospha-mide, and etoposide

VTE   venous thromboembolism

Vte   tidal volume exhaled

VTEC   verotoxin-producing Escherichia coli

VTED   venous thromboembolic disease

Vteff/kg   tidal volume effective/kilogram

VTEP   venous thromboembolism prophylaxis

V

VTF	vibrotactile feedback	V-V	ventriculovenous (shunt)
	Vogel-Tammann-Fulcher	V&V	vulva and vagina
	(behavior; equation [used for	V/V	volume to volume ratio
	the description of temperature		Vulva/Vagina
	dependence of viscosity])	VVA	vulvovaginal atrophy
VTG	vertigo	VVB	venovenous bypass
Vti	tidal volume inhaled	VVC	vulvovaginal candidiasis
VTL	vocal-tract length	VVD	vaginal vertex delivery
VTM	ventral tuberomammillary	VVDL	dual-lumen venovenous catheter
	video-telemedicine	VV-ECMO	venovenous extracorporeal
	vitamin and trace mineral		membrane oxygenation
VT-NS	ventricular tachycardia	VVETP	Vietnam Veterans Evaluation
	nonsustained		and Treatment Program
VTOL	vaginal trial of labor	VVFR	vesicovaginal fistula repair
	vertical takeoff and landing	VVG	Verhoeff van Gieson (stain)
VTOP	voluntary termination of	VVI	vector velocity imaging
	pregnancy	V/VI	grade 5 on a 6 grade basis
VTOS	venous thoracic outlet syndrome		venous valvular insufficiency
VTP	voluntary termination of		ventricular demand pacing
	pregnancy	VVI-40	ventricular backup pacing
VTPC	volume target pressure control		at 40/minute
	(ventilation)	VVIR	ventricular demand inhibited
VTR	velocity of tricuspid regurgitation		pacemaker
	vertical transmission rate	VVL	varicose veins ligation
VTS	Volunteer Transport Service		verruca vulgaris of the larynx
VTs	ventricular tachyarrhythmias	VVLST	very-very late stent throm-
VT-S	ventricular tachycardia sustained		bosis (beyond 5 year after
VTSRS	Verdun Target Symptom		implantation)
	Rating Scale	VVOR	visual-vestibulo-ocular-reflex
VTT	venous tumor thrombus	VVP	varicose veins of pelvic
VT/VF	ventricular tachycardia and/or		Vibrio vulnificus protease
	ventricular fibrillation	VVR	ventricular response rate
	ventricular tachycardia/fibrillation	VVS	vasovagal syncope
VTX	vertex		vulvar vestibulitis syndrome
VU	venous ulcer	VVs	varicose veins
	verbalizes understanding	VVT	ventricular synchronous pacing
	vesicoureteral (reflux)	VVV	a cardiac pacing mode
V/U	verbalize understanding		visit-to-visit variability
v/u	verbalizes understanding	VW	vessel wall
VUA	vesicourethal anastomosis	VWB	venous whole blood
VUC	voided-urine cytology		von Willebrand factor
VUDBMT	volunteer unrelated-donor bone	VWD	ventral wall defect
	marrow transplantation	vWD	von Willebrand disease
VUDS	videourodynamic study (studies)	vWD 2	von Willebrand disease type 2
VUF	vesicouterine fistula	vWD type 2	von Willebrand disease type 2
VUJ	vesico ureteral junction	vWF	von Willebrand factor
VUJO	vesico-ureteric junction	vWF:RCo	von Willebrand factor: ristocetin
	obstruction		cofactor
VUR	vesicoureteric reflux	vWF:RCof	von Willebrand factor: ristocetin
VURD	posterior urethral valves, unilat-		cofactor
	eral vesicoureteral reflux, and	VWFS	visual word-form system
	renal dysplasia (syndrome)	VWING	a single-piece titanium device
VUS	video ultrasonography		that allows repeated access
VUV	vacuum ultraviolet		of an arteriovenous fistulas
VV	vaccina virus		through a single puncture site
	variable (mechanical) ventilation		(buttonhole technique)
	varicose veins	VWM	ventricular wall motion
	vulvar vestibulitis		visual working memory

VW-MRI	vessel wall magnetic resonance imaging		
vWS	van der Woude syndrome		
vWS2	van der Woude syndrome 2		
vW type 2	von Willebrand (disease) type 2		
Vx	vaccination		
Vx	vitrectomy		
V-XT	V-pattern exotropia		
V-Y flap	A flap in which the incision is shaped like a V and after closure like a Y, to lengthen a localized area of tissue		
V-Y plasty	a technique in which a flap is incised in the shape of a V but advanced and inset so that the resulting suture line has the shape of a Y; used to gain additional length of tissue		
VZ	varicella zoster		
VZIG	varicella zoster immune globulin		
VZV	varicella zoster virus (Varivax)		
VZV PCR	varicella zoster virus diagnosis aided by polymerase chain reaction amplification		

W	tryptophan (also referred to as Trp)
	tungsten
	wash
	watt; is a derived unit of power, defined as a joule per second
	watts
	wearing glasses
	Wednesday
	week
	weight
	well
	West (as in the location e.g. 2W, is second floor, West wing)
	Whiskey (Phonetic Alphabet for W; pronounced (WIS-KEY)
	white
	whoop
	widowed
	wife
	with
	work
	worse
W-1	insignificant (allergies)
W-3	minimal (allergies)
W-5	moderate (allergies)
W-7	moderate-severe (allergies)
W-9	severe (allergies)
W-10	Interagency Transfer Form
W18	a synthetic fentanyl-type opioid which is 10,000 times more powerful than morphine resulting in street-drug-overdose deaths
W 22	Central Institute for the Deaf 22 Word List
w/	with
WA	Washington
	when awake
	while awake
	White American
	wide awake
	with assistance
W-A	Wyeth-Ayerst Laboratories
W & A	weakness and atrophy
W/A	see WA
	weight to age (ratio)
WAB	Western Aphasia Battery
WAB-AQ	Western Aphasia Battery Aphasia Quotient
WAC	well adult comprehensive (examination)
	wholesale acquisition cost
WACA	wide area circumferential ablation

WACDD	Western Australian Children Diabetes Database (registry)	WATs	wearable activity trackers
WACH	wedge adjustable cushioned heel	watt	is a derived unit of power, defined as a joule per second (symbol is W)
WAD	whiplash-associated disorder(s)		
WADA	World Anti-Doping Agency	watts	is a derived unit of power, defined as a joule per second (symbol is W)
WAF	weakness, atrophy, and fasciculation		
	white adult female	WAW	wait and watch
WAGR	Wilm tumor, aniridia, genitourinary malformations, and mental retardation (syndrome)	WAWOC	with and without contrast
		WAZ	weight-for-age Z scores
		WB	waist belt
WAHA	warm autoimmune hemolytic anemia		weight bearing
			weightbearing
WAI	wideband acoustic immittance (test)		well baby
			Western blot
WAICH	warfarin-associated intracerebral hemorrhage		whole blood
		Wb	Wuchereria bancrofti (a parasitic nematode)
WAIHA	warm autoimmune hemolytic anemia		
		W/B	see WB
WAIS	Wechsler Adult Intelligence Scale	WBA	whole-blood aggregometry
			whole-blood assay
WAIS-R	Wechsler Adult Intelligence Scale-Revised	WBACT	whole-blood activated clotting time
WAL	water-assisted lipoplasty	WBAN	wireless body area network
	within acceptable limits	WBAT	weight bearing as tolerated
	Wyeth-Ayerst Laboratories	WBBS	whole body bone scintigraphy (scan)
WALANT	wide awake, local anesthesia, no tourniquet (an anesthesia technique for minor hand, wrist, and other surgeries.		
		WBC	weight bearing with crutches
			well baby clinic
			white blood cell (count)
WALK	weight-activated locking knee (prosthesis)	WBCC	white blood cell count
		WBCs	white blood cells
WAM	white adult male	WBCT	whole-blood clotting time
	wrist-worn activity monitor	WB CVMR	whole body cardiovascular magnetic resonance (imaging)
WAP	wandering atrial pacemaker		
WAPRT	whole abdominopelvic radiation therapy		
		WBD	weeks by dates (for gestational age)
WARF	warfarin sodium (this is a dangerous abbreviation; use Warfarin)		
		WBDOs	waterborne disease and outbreaks
WARI	wheezing associated respiratory infection	WB-DWI	whole body diffusion-weighted MRI
WAS	whiplash-associated disorders	WBE	weeks by examination (for gestational age)
	Wiskott-Aldrich syndrome		
WASI	walk-to-sit (movement pattern)		whole-body extract
	Wechsler Abbreviated Scale of Intelligence	WBGD	whole-body glucose disposal
		WBH	weight-based heparin (dosing)
WASO	wake time after sleep onset		whole-body hyperthermia
WASp	Wiskott-Aldrich syndrome protein		Women and Babies Hospital
WASS	Wasserman test	WBI	weight bias internalization
WAT	word association test		whole-bowel irrigation
Watchman Device	a permanent implant designed to close the left atrial appendage in the heart to reduce the risk of stroke in people with atrial fibrillation not caused by a heart valve problem (Boston Scientific)		whole-brain irradiation
			whole-breast irradiation
		WBing	weight bearing
		W Bld	whole blood
		WB-MRI	whole-body magnetic resonance imaging
		WBN	wellborn nursery

W

WBNAA	whole-brain *N*-acetylaspartate	WCH	white coat hypertension
WBOS	wide base of support	WCHE	well child health exam
WBP	whole body plethysmography	WCHF	worsening chronic heart failure
WBPTT	whole-blood partial thrombo- plastin time	WCI	Ways of Coping Inventory
		WC/LC	warm compresses and lid scrubs
WBQ	web-based questionnaires	WCM	waist circumference in men
WBQC	wide-base quad cane		whole cow's milk
WBR	whole-body radiation	W/cm²	watts per square centimeter
WBRT	whole-brain radiotherapy	WCN	widespread cutaneous necrosis
WBS	weeks by size (for		World Congress of Nephrology
	gestational age)	WCON	Certified Wound Ostomy Nurse
	weight-bearing surface	WCP	whole chromosome painting
	whole-body scan		(a term used to describe the
	whole-body scintigraphy		direct visualization using in
	Williams-Beuren syndrome		situ hybridization of specific
WBTF	Waring Blender tube feeding		chromosomes in metaphase
WBTT	weight bearing to tolerance		spreads and in interphase
WBUS	weeks by ultrasound		nuclei)
WBV	whole blood volume	WCR	waist-to-chest ratio
	whole-body vibration	WCS	white-collar sign
WBW	whole-body washdown		work capacity specialist
WBXRT	whole-brain radiotherapy	WCST	Wisconsin Card Sorting Test
WC	waist circumference	WCT	wide-complex tachycardia
	ward clerk	WCTM	will continue to monitor
	ward confinement	WCV	within-subject coefficient of
	warm compress		variation
	wet compresses	WCVs	well-child visits
	wheel chair	WCW	Warr-Cook-Wall (job satisfac-
	wheelchair		tion rating scale)
	white count		wet cell weight
	whooping cough		white-collar workers
	will call	WD	ward
	with contrast (media)		well developed
	woman's Condom		well differentiated
	workers' compensation		wet dressing
W/C	See WC		Whipple disease
WCA	work capacity assessment		Wilson disease
WCB	will call back		word
	Workers' Compensation Board		working distance
WCBP	women of child-bearing		wound
	potential	W&D	warm and dry
WCC	well child check	W/D	warm and dry
	well-child care		wet-dry ratio (lungs)
	white cell count		withdrawal
	Wound Care Certification		withdrawn
WCCT	weighted change of concentra-	W4D	Worth four-dot (test for fusion)
	tion in time	WDCC	well-developed collateral
WCD	wearable cardioverter		circulation
	defibrillator	WDEIA	wheat-dependent,
W-CDMA	wideband code division multiple		exercise-induced anaphlaxis
	access	WDF	white divorced female
WCE	white coat effect	WDHA	watery diarrhea, hypokalemia,
	wireless capsule endoscopy		and achlorhydria
	work capacity evaluation	WDHH	watery diarrhea, hypokalemia,
WCEI	Wound Care Education Institute		and hypochlorhydria
WCF	waist circumference in women	WDI	warm, dry, and intact (skin)
WCFS	Workplace Cognitive Failure		weight distribution index
	Scale		World Drug Index

W

WD&I	warm, dry, and intact (skin)	WEL	water-equivalent pathlength (charged-particle lung therapy)
W/D/I	warm, dry, and intact (skin)		
WDL	within defined limits		
WDLL	well-differentiated lymphocytic lymphoma		Weight Efficacy Lifestyle (questionnaire)
WDLS	well-differentiated liposarcoma	WEMINO	wall-eyed monocular internuclear ophthalmoplegia
WDM	white divorced male		
WDMA	Waking-day Motor Assessment	wen	sebaceous cyst
WDP	within defined parameters	wens	sebaceous cysts
WDQ	Whiplash Disability Questionnaire	WEP	weekend pass
		WES	whole exome sequencing
WDS	word discrimination score	WESR	Westergren erythrocyte sedimentation rate
WDTC	well-differentiated thyroid cancer		
		WEUP	willful exposure to unwanted pregnancy
WDT-UMP	well-differentiated tumors of uncertain malignant potential		
		WF	well flexed
			wet film
WDWF	well-developed, white-female		white female
WDWG	well dressed, well groomed		wound fluid
WDWM	well-developed, white-male	W&F	weakness and fatigue
WDWN	well-developed, well-nourished	W/F	weakness and fatigue
WD/WN	well-developed well-nourished	WFB	wooden foreign body
WDWNAAF	well-developed, well-nourished African-American female	WFC	work-to-family conflict
		WFD	Water Framework Directive (European Union)
WDWNAAM	well-developed, well-nourished African-American male		
		WFE	wavefront error
WDWNBM	well-developed, well-nourished black male		Williams flexion exercises
		W FEEDS	with feedings
WDWNMAF	well-developed, well-nourished, Mexican-American female	WFH	white-faced hornet
		WFI	water for injection
WDWNMAM	well-developed, well-nourished, Mexican-American male	WFL	within full limits
			within functional limits
WDWNWF	well-developed, well-nourished white female	WFLC	white female living child
		WFM	wide-field fluorescence microscopy
WDWNWM	well-developed, well-nourished white male		
		WFNS	World Federation of Neuro-surgeons (grading system of subarachnoid hemorrhage)
WDXRF	wavelength-dispersive x-ray fluorescence		
WE	weekend	WF-O	will follow in office
	wide excision	WFR	wheel-and-flare reaction
	wrist extenders	WFS	Wolfram syndrome
W/E	weekend	WFSBP	World Federation of Societies of Biological Psychiatry (guidelines)
WEBINO	wall-eyed bilateral internuclear ophthalmoplegia		
WED	withdrawal-emergent dyskinesia	WG	Wegener granulomatosis
		WGA	week gestational age
Wed	Wednesday		wheat germ agglutinin
WE-DESS	water excitation double-echo steady state (magnetic resonance imaging)		whole genome amplification
		WGL	wire-guide localization
		WGS	whole-genome sequencing
WEDI	Workgroup for Electronic Data Interchange	wgt	weight
		WGTS	whole-gut transit scintigraphy
WEE	Western equine encephalitis	WGTT	whole gut transit time
weekly	There is no widely acceptable, recognized abbreviation for weekly or once a week, write it out.	WH	walking heel (cast)
			well healed
			well hydrated
			work hardening
wEGA	weeks' estimated gestational age	WHA	warmed humidified air

WHAS	Women's Health Assessment Scale
WHC	water-holding capacity; see gene website www.ncbi.nlm.nih.gov/gene
WHCs	wound-healing complications
WHF	World Heart Federation
	worsening heart failure
WHFO	wrist-hand-finger orthosis
WHI	Women's Health Initiative
whiff test	several drops of potassium hydroxide are added to a microscopic slide containing the vaginal discharge; a characteristic fishy odor is considered a positive test and is suggestive of bacterial vaginosis
WHIM	Worts, Hypogammaglobulinamia, Infections, and Mylelokathexis (syndrome)
Whipple procedure	pancreaticoduodenectomy
WHIS	War Head-Injury Score
Whiskey	Phonetic Alphabet for W; pronounced WIS-KEY
Whites	white blood cells
WHL	width, height and length
WHNP	Women's Healthcare Nurse Practitioner
WHNR	well-healed, no residuals
WHNS	well-healed, no sequelae
	well-healed, nonsymptomatic
WHO	waste handling option (renal dialysis)
	World Health Organization
	wrist-hand orthosis
WHOART	World Health Organization Adverse Reaction Terms (Terminology)
WHO DDE	World Health Organization Drug Dictionary Enhanced (a dictionary/coding system of medicinal product information, used to identify drug names and provides information about a drug's active ingredients and its therapeutic use[s])
WHOL	worst headache of (his/her) life (describes the common characteristic of subarachnoid hemorrhage)
WHOQOL-100	World Health Organization Quality of Life 100-Item (instrument)
WHOQOL-BREF	brief version of the World Health Organization Quality of Life
WHP	whirlpool
WHPB	whirlpool bath

WHpR	waist-to-hip ratio
WHR	waist circumference/hip circumference ratio
WHS	Wolf-Hirschhorn syndrome
WHSS	well-healed surgical scar
WHtR	waist to height ratio
WHV	woodchuck hepatitis virus
WHVP	wedged hepatic venous pressure
WH/WD	withholding/withdrawal (of life support)
WHZ	wheezes
WI	ventricular demand pacing
	walk-in
	Wisconsin
	within
W+I	work and interest
w/i	within
WIA	wounded in action
WIB	Well-being and Ill-being (score; a method for evaluating quality of life)
	Western immunoblot
WIC	Women, Infants, and Children (program)
WiCON	with contrast
WID	widow
	widower
WIED	walk-in emergency department
WIFi	Wound Ischemia and Foot infection (scoring system)
WiFi	Wireless Fidelity (a technology that allows electronic devices to connect to a wireless local area network)
wiht	may have meant with
WIN	well-infant nursery
	wick-in-needle
w/in	within
WIP	work in progess
WIQ	Walking Impairment Questionnaire
WIR	with in reach (call light)
WIS	walk-in shower
	Ward Incapacity Scale
	Wister Institute
WISC	Wechsler Intelligence Scale for Children
WISC-III	Wechsler Intelligence Scale for Children-Third Edition
WISC-IV	Wechsler Intelligence Scale for Children-Fourth Edition
WISC-R	Wechsler Intelligence Scale for Children-Revised
WISN	warfarin-induced skin necrosis
WISQARS	Web-based Injury Statistics Query and Reporting System
WIT	warm ischemia time
	water-induced thermotherapy

W

with	with has been abbreviated as c with a dash above and as w	
WJMSCs	Wharton's jelly multipotent mesenchymal stromal cells	
WK	work	
wk	week(s)	
3×/WK	three times a week	
WKHL	Weck hem-o-lock (suture clip)	
WKI	Wakefield Inventory	
wkly	weekly	
WKND	weekend days	
WKO	weighted kypho-orthosis (kypho-orthosis is a combination of kyphosis and scoliosis)	
wk o	week old	
WKR	Wistar-Kyoto rats	
WKS	Wernicke-Korsakoff Syndrome	
wks	weeks	
WL	waiting list	
	Warning Letter (FDA)	
	wave length	
	weight loss	
W:L	wall-to-lumen thickness ratio	
W/L	see WL	
	wall-to-lumen thickness ratio	
	width to length ratio	
WLCS	well leg compartment syndrome	
WLD	white line disease (Veterinary)	
	written-language disorder	
Wld	wallerian degeneration; see gene website www.ncbi.nlm.nih .gov/gene	
Wld(S)	Wallerian degeneration slow	
WLE	white light endoscopy	
	wide local excision	
WLF	whole lung field (radiology)	
WLI	weight-length index	
WLK	walking	
WLL	whole-lung lavage	
WLM	working level months	
WLMI	weekly loading-maintenance infusion	
WLN	Wallersterin Laboratory nutrient (agar)	
WLQ	Work Limitation Questionnaire	
WLS	weighted least squares	
	weight-loss surgery	
	wet lung syndrome	
WLST	withdrawal of life-sustaining therapy	
WLT	waterload test	
WLW	Wei-Lin-Weissfeld (marginal proportional hazards model)	
	women-loving women	
WM	Waldenstrom macrogloulinemia	
	wall motion	
	warm, moist	
	weight maintenance	

	Western medicine	
	wet mount	
	white male	
	white matter	
	whole milk	
	with meals	
	working memory	
W/M	see WM	
W/m2	Watt per square meter	
WMA	wall motion abnormality	
WMB	wholemeal bread	
WMC	white-matter change(s)	
	wireless motility capsule	
	working memory capacity	
WMD	warm moist dressings (sterile)	
	weapons of mass destruction	
	weighted mean differences	
WME	well-male examination	
WMF	white married female	
WMFT	Wolf Motor Function Test	
WMH	white matter hyperintensities	
WMH-CIDI	World Mental Health Composite International Diagnostic Interview	
WMHs	white matter hyperintensities	
WMI	wall motion index	
	weighted mean index	
WMIS	World Molecular Imaging Society	
WML	white matter lesions (cerebral)	
WMLC	white male living child	
WMM	white married male	
WMP	warm moist packs (unsterile)	
	weight management program	
	wound management program	
WMS	watermelon stomach (gastric antral vascular ectasia)	
	Wechsler Memory Scale	
	Wilson-Mikity syndrome	
WMSDs	work-related musculoskeletal disorders	
WMSI	wall-motion score index	
WMT	Word Memory Test	
WMTs	wireless medical telemetry service	
WMX	whirlpool, massage, and exercise	
WN	well nourished	
W/N	well nourished	
	within	
WNC	well-nourished child (children)	
	well-nourished controls	
WND	wound	
WNE	West Nile encephalitis	
WNF	well-nourished female	
	West Nile fever	
WNL	within normal limits	
WNL × 4	upper and lower extremities within normal limits	

WNLS	weighted nonlinear least squares
WNM	well-nourished male
WNND	West Nile neuroinvasive disease
WNR	within normal range
WNt^{50}	Wagner-Nelson time 50 hours
WNV	West Nile virus
WNWD	well-nourished, well-developed
WO	wean off
	week of
	weeks old
	wide open
	Withholding (Medicare code)
	without
	wrist orthosis
	written order
W/O	water-in-oil (emulsion)
	without
WOA	weeks of age
	without assistance
WOB	work of breathing
WOBS	left without being seen
WOC	wound, ostomy, and continence
WoCBP	women of childbearing potential
WOCF	worst observation carried forward
WOCN	Wound, Ostomy and Continence Nurses (Society)-formerly known as the International Association for Enterostomal Therapy (IEAT)
WOCON	without contrast
WOD	wall-occiput distance
WOF	Wheel of Fortune (a computerized two-choice, probabilistic monetary reward task)
	work of flexion
WOI	window of (embryo) implantation
WoI	window of interest
WoK	Web of Knowledge (database)
WOL	weeks of lactation
WOLS	weighted ordinary least squares
	withdrawal of life support
WOLST	withdrawal of life-sustaining treatment
WOMAC	Western Ontario and McMaster Universities Osteoarthritis Index
WON	walled-off (pancreatic) necrosis
Wood units	an expression pulmonary vascular resistance; measurement is made by subtracting pulmonary capillary wedge pressure from the mean pulmonary arterial pressure and dividing by cardiac output in liters per minute (1 Wood unit = 1 mm[Hg] per L/min
WOP	without pain
WOPN	walled-off pancreatic necrosis

W or A	weakness or atrophy
WORD	Wechsler objective reading dimensions
work comp	workers' compensation
WORLD/ DLROW	a test used in mental status examinations (patient is asked to spell WORLD backwards)
WOS	white opaque substance
	Wound Ostomy Services
WoS	Web of Science (an online academic citation index provided by Thomson Reuters)
wound-vac	vacuum-assisted closure
W/out	without
WOW	Wonders of Walking (program)
WoW	World of Warcraft (online game)
W/OW	wall/outer-wall ratio
WOWN	Work Only When Needed (seasonal/temporary work)
WP	wall pulleys
	wedge pressure
	whirlpool
W/P	See WP
WPAI	Work Productivity and Activity Impairment (Questionnaire)
WPATH	World Professional Association for Transgender Health
WPATH SOC	World Professional Association for Transgender Health Standards of Care
WPBs	Weibel-Palade bodies
WPBT	whirlpool, body temperature
WPCs	washed packed cells
WPD	Whipple pancreatoduodenectomy
	White Plague Disease
WPFM	Wright peak flow meter
WPI	whey protein isolate
	Work Preference Inventory
WPIC	Western Psychiatric Institute and Clinic (University of Pittsburgh Medical Center)
wpm	words per minute
WPN	without previous neoplasia
WPNS	wireless peripheral nerve stimulation
WPOA	wearing patch on arrival
WPP	Wechsler Preschool and Primary Scale of Intelligence
WPPSI	Wechsler Preschool and Primary Scale of Intelligence
WPPSI-R	Wechsler Preschool and Primary Scale of Intelligence, Revised
WPR	written progress report
WPRT	whole-pelvic radiotherapy
WPS	water-pipe smoking
	words per sentence
	Worker Protection Standard

W

WPS-RA	Work Productivity Survey-Rheumatoid Arthritis
WPT	wavelet packet transform
WPV	wild poliovirus
	within-person variability
	workplace violence
WPV1	type 1 wild poliovirus
WPW	Wolff-Parkinson-White (syndrome)
WPWS	Wolff-Parkinson-White syndrome
WQ	water quality
WR	waiting room
	Wassermann reaction
	word recognition
	wrist
WRA	with-the-rule astigmatism
WRAIR	Walter Reed Army Institute of Research
WRAMC	Walter Reed Army Medical Center
WRAP	Wisconsin Registry for Alzheimer Prevention
WRARU	Walter Reed AFRIMS (Armed Forces Research Institute of Medical Sciences) Research Unit
WRAT	Wide Range Achievement Test
WRAT-R	The Wide Range Achievement Test, Revised
WRBC	washed red blood cells
WRC	total worm count
	warfarin-related coagulopathy
	washed red (blood) cells
WRCR	total worm count reduction
WRF	worsening renal function
W/Rh	tungsten/rhodium (anode target/ filter combinations used in mammography)
WRICH	warfarin related intracerebral hemorrhage
WRIOT	Wide Range Interest-Opinion Test (for career planning)
WRL	World Reference Laboratory for Foot-and-Mouth Disease (Institute for Animal Health, Survey United Kingdom)
WRN	Werner syndrome protein
WRR	wheezes, rales, and rhonchi
W/R/R	wheezes, rales, and rhonchi
WRRR	wheezes, rales, rhonchi, or rubs
W/R/R/R	wheezes, rales, rhonchi, or rubs
WRS	Wiedemann-Rautenstrauch syndrome
	Wolcott-Rallison syndrome
	word recognition score
	work-related stress
WRT	weekly radiation therapy
	with respect (regards) to

W/R/T	see WRT
WRTC	Washington Regional Transplant Consortium
	Western Regional Training Centre for Health Services Research (Canada)
WRUED	work-related upper-extremity disorder
WRULD	work-related upper-limb disorders
wRVUs	work relative value units
WS	Waardenburg syndrome (classified into four subtypes, WS1-WS4)
	walking speed
	ward secretary
	watt seconds
	Werner syndrome
	West syndrome
	Williams syndrome
	Withering Syndrome
	work simplification
	work simulation
	work status
W&S	wound and skin
W/S	see WS
	weight to stature (ratio)
WSCE	water-soluble contrast enemas
WSCP	Williams Syndrome Cognitive Profile
WSD	Western-style diet
	white spot disease
	word sense disambiguation
WSEP	Williams syndrome, early puberty
WSepF	white separated female
WSepM	white separated male
WSF	white single female
WSIs	whole slide images
WSL	white-spot lesions
WSLP	Williams syndrome, late puberty
WSM	white single male
WSMDs	wheeled and seated mobility devices
WSN	wireless sensor network
WSO	white superficial onychomycosis
WSOC	water-soluble organic compounds
WSOW	women who have sex with only women
WSP	wearable speech processor
	white without pressure (retina)
	Wolbachia surface protein
WSR	waist-to-stature ratio
	wall shear rate
WS-RLO	Withering Syndrome-Rickettsia-like organism
WSSV	White spot syndrome virus

WST	water swallow test	WW	watchful waiting
	Wheelchair Skills Test		Weight Watchers
	Wheelchair Skills Training		wheeled walker
WSTP	Wheelchair Skills Training	WW1	World War I
	Program	WW2	World War 2 (WWII)
WSW	women who have sex with	WWI	World War I
	women		World War One
WT	wait times	WWII	World War Two
	waived testing	W/W	weight-to-weight ratio
	walking tank	W → W	wet-to-wet
	walking training	WWAC	walk with aid of cane
	Warshaw Technique	WWB	wholegrain wheat bread
	(splenic vessel preservation)	WW Brd	whole wheat bread
	weight (wt)	WWC	What Works Clearinghouse
	wild-type		(procedures/standards)
	Wilms tumor		Women's Wellness Center(s)
	wisdom teeth	WWE	well-woman examination
	work therapy	WWidF	white widowed female
wt	weight	WWidM	white widowed male
W/T	see WT	WWO	we will obtain
	wet/dry weight ratio	W/WO	with and without
w/t	wild type	WWOP	white without pressure
0WT	zero work tolerance	WWP	warm and well perfused
WT1	Wilms tumor 1 (gene)		white-on-white perimetry
WTC	World Trade Center	WWT	willingness to trade-off
WtCM	wild-type littermates cultures		(life expectancy)
W-T-D	wet to dry	WWTP	wastewater treatment plant
WTE	waste-to-energy (plant)	WWW	World Wide Web
	white tea extract	wx	waxy (gene)
WTF	wedge transmission factor(s)	WY	Wyoming
WTP	willingness to pay	WYOU	women years of usage
WTQ	work to quota	WZ	Wyner-Ziv
WTR	willingness to return	WZC	Wyner-Ziv coding
WTS	whole tomography slice	WZVC	Wyner-Ziv video coding
WTT	work to tolerance		
WTW	white-to-white		
	(distance [ophthalmology])		
WtW	welfare-to-work		
WU	Wood unit(s)		
	work-up		
	Wunsch units		
W/U	warm up (as in before exercise)		
	work-up		
WUP	warming-up period		
	warm-up		
W/up	work-up		
WUS	wake-up stroke (symptoms first		
	noted on waking)		
WV	West Virginia		
	whispered voice		
	wound vacuum		
W/V	weight-to-volume ratio		
WVAC	World Veterinary Association		
	Conference		
WVC	warm vertical compaction		
	(dental)		
	wildlife-vehicle collision(s)		
WVD	Wigner-Ville distribution		

W

X

X	break
	capecitabine (Xeloda) This is a dangerous abbreviation
	cross
	crossmatch
	Ecstasy (methylenedioxymeth-amphetamine; MDMA)
	exophoria for distance
	extra
	female sex chromosome
	for (as in- Augmentin $\times$ 2 weeks)
	start of anesthesia
	ten
	times
	X-Ray (Phonetic Alphabet for X; pronounced ECKS-RAY)
	xylocaine
$\bar{x}$	except
	sample mean
X'	exophoria at 33 cm
X1	repeat one time
X^2	chi-square
X+2	xyphoid plus 2 fingerbreadths
X+#	xyphoid plus number of fingerbreadths
X3	orientation as to time, place and person
Xa anti-Xa	anti- (blood clotting factor) Xa
X-ALD	X-linked adrenoleukodystrophy
XANES	X-ray absorption near-edge structure
XBRT	external beam radiation therapy
XBT	xylose breath test
XC	excretory cystogram
	time critical (medications which have a 30 minute plus or minus time window in which to be administered)
XCCL	crossed-coupled-cavity-laser
	exaggerated craniocaudal lateral
XCF	aortic cross clamp off
XCI	X-chromosome inactivation
XCO	aortic cross clamp on
XD	times daily
X2d	for 2 days (e.g., take diphenhydr-amine 25 mg at bedtime x2d)
X3d	for 3 days (e.g., take diphen-hydramine 25 mg at bedtime x3d)
X4d	for 4 days (e.g., take diphenhydr-amine 25 mg at bedtime x4d)
X&D	examination and diagnosis
XDP	xeroderma pigmentosum
XDR	extensively (extremely) drug-resistant
XDR-TB	extensively (extremely) drug-resistant tuberculosis
XE	capecitabine (Xeloda)
Xe	xenon
^{133}Xe	xenon, isotope of mass 133
XeCl	xenon chloride
XeCT	xenon-enhanced computed tomography
X-ed	crossed
XELIRI	capecitabine (Xeloda) and irino-tecan; also known a Capiri
XELOXIRI-Bev	capecitabine (Xeloda), leucovo-rin, oxaliplatin, and irinotecan plus bevacizumab
XEM	xonics electron mammography
XENCs	extraembryonic endoderm cells
XES	x-ray energy spectrometer
XFELs	X-ray free-electron lasers
XFER	transfer
XFERS	transfers
X-Fix	external bone fixation device
XFM	x-ray fused with magnetic resonance imaging
X-friction	To soften and break down scar tissue by placing finger tips over a scar and moving back and forth with mild pressure.
XFS	exfoliation syndrome
XFSWD	Xiang-Fu-Si-Wu Decoction (used to treat gynecology diseases in China)
XG	Xg; an International Society of Blood Transfusion (ISBT) blood group
XGA	xanthogranulomatous appendicitis
XGP	xanthogranulomatous pyelonephritis
XGS	xanthogranulomatous salpingitis
XI	eleven
XII	twelve
XIAP	X-linked inhibitor of apoptosis
XIP	xiphoid process
	x-ray in plaster
XK	Kx; an International Society of Blood Transfusion (ISBT) blood group
XKO	not knocked out
XL	extended release (once a day oral solid dosage form)
	extra large
	forty
XLA	X-linked agammaglobulinemia
XLAG	X-linked acrogigantism
XLAP	exploratory laparotomy
X-leg	cross leg
XLFDP	cross-linked fibrin degradation products

XLH	X-linked hypophosphatemic rickets	X STOP	an interspinous process decompression system
XLHED	X-linked hypohidrotic ectodermal dysplasia	XT	exotropia
			extract
XLIF®	extreme lateral interbody fusion		extracted
XLJR	X-linked juvenile retinoschisis	X(T')	intermittent exotropia at 33 cm
XLMR	X-linked mental retardation	X(T)	intermittent exotropia
XLOA	X-linked optic atrophy	xTAG RVP	a respiratory virus panel fast assay
XLP	X-linked lymphoproliferative (syndrome)	XTLE	extratemporal-lobe epilepsy
	X-linked proliferative (syndrome)	xtrndl	extranodal
XLPE	crosslinked polyethylene	XU	excretory urogram
XLRS	X-linked retinoschisis	XULN	times upper limit of normal
XLT	X-linked thrombocytopenia	XV	fifteen
XM	crossmatch	XX	normal female sex chromosome type
X-mat.	crossmatch		twenty
XMG	mammogram	XXX	neutral stance
XML	extensible markup language		thirty
XMM	xeromammography	XX/XY	sex karyotypes
XMR	magnetic resonance and x-rays	XY	normal male sex chromosome type
XMRV	xenotropic murine leukemia virus-related virus	XYL	lidocaine (Xylocaine®)
XMT	cross matched		xylose
XNA	xenoreactive natural antibodies	XYLO	Lidocaine (Xylocaine)
xol-1	see gene website (sex switch gene); see gene website www .ncbi.nlm.nih.gov/gene	XYZ	three-dimensional positioning based on X, Y, and Z axes
XOM	extraocular movements	XZT	zolazepam and tiletamine
XOP	x-ray out of plaster		
XP	xanthelasma palpebrarum		
	xeroderma pigmentosum		
X-P	X-ray photography		
XPLANT	may have meant explant (tissue taken from the body and grown in an artificial medium)		
XPN	xanthogranulomatous pyelonephritis		
xport	Transport		
XPS	X-ray photoelectron spectroscopy		
XR	extended release		
	x-ray		
X-Ray	Phonetic Alphabet for X; pronounced ECKS-RAY		
XRD	X-ray diffraction		
	x-ray diffraction		
XRF	x-ray fluorescence		
XRII	x-ray image intensifier		
XRIP	x-ray image processing		
XRNT	extended-release naltrexone		
XR-NTX	extended-released naltrexone		
XRs	radiographs (X-rays)		
Xrs	respiratory system reactance		
XRT	radiation therapy		
XS	excessive		
x's	exudates		
X-SCID	X-linked severe combined immunodeficiency disease		
XS-LIM	exceeds limits of procedure		

		YIP1	second-year intern physician
		YIP2	second-year intern physician
		YJV	yellow jacket venom
		Y2K	year 2,000
Y	male sex chromosome	YLC	youngest living child
	tyrosine	YLD	years of life with disability
	Yankee (Phonetic Alphabet for Y; pronounced YANG-KEY)	YLL	years of life lost
		YLS	years of life saved
	year	YMA	yeast-malt extract agar (media)
	year old		young to middle-aged
	yellow	YMC	young male Caucasian
	Yes	YMRS	Young Mania Rating Scale
	yttrium	Y/N	yes/no
Y90	yttrium 90	YNH	younger normal-hearing
Y-90	yttrium-90	YNS	yellow nail syndrome
YA	young adult	YO	years old
YAC	yeast artificial chromosome	Y/O	years old
YACs	yeast artificial chromosomes	YOA	years of age
YACP	young adult chronic patient	YOAAF	year-old African-American female
YACSs	young adult cancer survivors		
YADH	yeast alcohol dehydrogenase	YOAAM	year-old African-American male
YAG	yttrium aluminum garnet (laser)	YOB	year of birth
Yankee	Phonetic Alphabet for Y; pronounced YANG-KEY	YOD	year of death
		YOF	year-old female
YAP	yttrium-aluminum-perovskite laser	YOGV	Yogue virus
		YOM	year-old male
YAS	youth action section (police)	YOPD	young-onset Parkinson disease
yay	a word to express triumph, approval, or encouragement	YORA	younger-onset rheumatoid arthritis
YAZ®	ethinylestradiol and drospire-none, an oral contraceptive	YOWF	year-old white female
		YOWM	year-old white male
Yb	ytterbium	YPC	YAG (yttrium aluminum garnet) posterior capsulotomy
YBOCS	Yale-Brown Obsessive-Compulsive Scale		
		YPLL	years of potential life lost before age 65
Y-BOCS	Yale-Brown Obsessive Compulsive Scale		
		YPT	Yersinia pseudotuberculosis
YD	young diabetic	yr	year
yd	yard (36 inches; 0.9144 meters)	YRBSS	Youth Risk Behavior Surveil-lance System
Y/D	yesterday		
yday	yesterday	YRI	Yoruba in Ibadan, Nigeria (from HapMap [A catalog of common genetic variants that occur in human beings])
y'day	yesterday		
Yel	yellow		
YEM	yeast mannitol extract		
	Yemanuclein	YR/O	year old
	Young's elastic modulus	Yrs	years
YEPQ	Yale Eating Patterns Questionnaire	YSC	yolk sac carcinoma
		YT	Yt; an International Society of Blood Transfusion (ISBT) blood group
yesT	see gene website www.ncbi.nlm.nih.gov/gene		
yest	yesterday	YTB	yellow TheraBand
YF	yellow fever	YTD	year to date
YFH	yellow-faced hornet	YTDY	yesterday
YFI	yellow fever immunization	YW	young women
YFV	yellow-fever virus	YYYY	4-digit designation for the year
yGT	gamma-glutamyltransferase		
YGTSS	Yale Global Tic Severity Scale		
YHL	years of healthy life		
YIAT	Young Internet Addiction Test		

Z

Z   impedance
pyrazinamide [part of tuberculosis regimen as in RHZ (E/S)/HR]
Zulu (Phonetic Alphabet for Z; pronounced ZOO-LOO)

ZA   zoledronic acid injection (Zometa; Reclast)

ZAL   zaleplon (Sonata)

ZAP   zoster-associated pain

ZB   zinc-blende (Zinc sulfide [ZnS])

ZCQ   Zurich Claudication Questionnaire

ZD   Zenker diverticulum
zinc-deficient

Z-drugs   the bedtime sedatives zaleplon (Sonata), zolpidem (Ambien), and zopiclone

ZDV   zidovudine (Retrovir)

ZE   Zollinger-Ellison (syndrome)

Z-E   Zollinger-Ellison (syndrome)

ZEBOV   Zaire species of Ebola virus

ZEEP   zero end-expiratory pressure

ZEM   Zemuron (rocuronium bromide)

ZES   Zollinger-Ellison syndrome

ZESR   zeta erythrocyte sedimentation rate

ZF   zinc finger (proteins)

ZFN   zinc-finger nuclease

ZFP   zinc finger protein

ZIFT   zygote intrafallopian (tube) transfer

ZIG   zoster serum immune globulin

Zika   the Zika virus was identified in Rhesus monkeys in 1947 and named after the Zika Forest in Uganda

ZIKV   Zika virus

ZINB   zero-inflated negative binomial (model)

ZIO patch   single-use, and water-resistant 14-day continuous cardiac rhythm monitor patch (ZIO® XT Patch, iRhythm Technologies, Inc)

ZIP   zero-inflated Poisson (model)
zoster immune plasma

ziv aflibercept inj   Zaltrap

z-joint   zygapophysial joint

Z-line   the gastroesophageal junction that joins the esophagus to the stomach

ZLR   likelihood ratio Z-scores

ZMC   zygomatic
zygomatic maxillary compound (complex)

Zn   zinc

ZnO   zinc oxide

ZnOE   zinc oxide and eugenol

ZnPc   zinc phthalocyanine

ZnPP   zinc protoporphyrin

ZnPT   zinc pyrithione

ZNS   zolmitriptan (Zomig) nasal spray
zonisamide (Zonegran)

$ZnSO_4$ zinc sulfate

ZnT8   solute carrier family 30 (zinc transporter), member 8 gene

ZnT-8   solute carrier family 30 (zinc transporter), member 8 gene

ZnT8Ab   zinc transporter 8 autoantibody

ZOE   zinc oxide and eugenol (dental)

ZOI   zone of inhibition

ZOL   zoledronic acid (Zometa, Relcast)

ZOOM   Guarana

ZOS   zoster (shingles) vaccine (replaced by the term HZV)

ZOT   zonula occludens toxin

Z-Pack   see Z-Pak

Z-Pak   a 6-tablet pack of azithromycin (Zithromax) 250 mg

ZPC   zero point of charge
zopiclone

ZPE   zero-point (vibrational) energy

ZPIV   Zika purified inactivated vaccine

Z-plasty   a plastic surgery technique that is used to improve the functional and cosmetic appearance of scars using a Z-shaped incision

ZPO   zinc peroxide

ZPP   zinc protoporphyrin

ZPPP   Z-palatopharyngoplasty

ZPS   Zubrod performance status

ZPT   zinc pyrithione

ZPTO   zinc pyrithione

Zr   zirconium

ZS   Zellweger syndrome

ZS9   sodium zirconium cyclosilicate

ZSB   zero stools since birth

Z-Score   indicates by how many standard deviations an observation or datum is above or below the mean (also known as standard score)

ZSR   zeta sedimentation rate

ZSRDS   Zung Self-Rating Depression Scale

ZT   zeitgeber time

Zulu   Phonetic Alphabet for Z; pronounced ZOO-LOO

ZV   Zika virus

ZVL   zoster vaccine live (Zostavax)

ZVZ   may have meant VZV (varicella-zoster virus)
zero valent zinc

Additions, Corrections, and Suggestions are Welcomed

Please send them via any means shown below:

Neil M Davis
605 Louis Drive, Suite 508B
Warminster PA 18974-2830

FAX 215 442 7432
Email neil@medabbrev.com
Secure website www.medabbrev.com

Thank you for your help in the past.

Have You Used the medabbrev.com website Version of This Book?

- It is instantaneously searchable for the meanings of abbreviations
- It is reverse searchable (search for all the abbreviations containing a particular word)
- Each week, about 30 new entries are added

See the preface (page vii) for access instructions. A one-year, single-user access is included in the purchase price of the book. Also one-year subscriptions (no book) are available for purchase.

Multi-User Site Licenses for medabbrev.com are Available for Your Intranet

Medical facilities can substitute their own "Do Not Use" list of dangerous abbreviations for the one present. The ability also exists to list abbreviations that are unique to your region and/or organization which would normally not appear in any national list. These lists would be controlled by the facility or company. A no-cost, 3-week trial and pricing information are available by calling 215 442 7430 or via an e-mail request to ev@medabbrev.com

Chapter 5
Symbols and Greek Letters

Symbols

↑	above	↑↑	extensor
	alive		extensor response (positive
	elevated		Babinsky)
	greater than		testes undescended
	high		
	improved	‖	parallel
	increase		parallel bars
	rising		
	up	√	check
	upper		flexion
↑g	increasing	√'d	checked
↓	dead	√'ing	checking
	decrease		
	depressed	#	fracture
	diminished		number
	down		pound
	falling		weight
	lower		
	lowered		
	normal plantar reflex	∴	therefore
	restricted	∵	because
↓g	decreasing	Δ scan	delta scan (computed tomography scan)
→	causes to		
	greater than		
	progressing	+	plus
	results in		positive
	showed		present
	to		
	to the right	−	absent
	transfer to		minus
	yields		negative
←	less than	/	extend
	resulted from		extended
	to the left		slash mark signifying per, and, over, as a blood pressure of 160 over 100, or with (this is a dangerous symbol as it is mistaken for a one)
↔	same as		
	stable		
	to and from		
	unchanging	±	either positive or negative
↓↓	flexor		no definite cause
	plantar response (Babinski)		plus or minus
	testes descended		very slight trace

>	greater than (can be confused with <, use "greater than")		zero
	left ear-bone conduction threshold	⊙	start of an operation
		⊗	end of anesthesia
≥	greater than or equal to		
		@	at
<	caused by	†	one
	less than (can be confused with >, use "less than")	††	two
	right ear-bone conduction threshold	♂	male
		♀	female
≤	less than or equal to	♂♂	gay
≮	not less than	♀♀	lesbian
≯	not more than		
	above	■	deceased male
∨	diastolic blood pressure	●	deceased female
	increased	□	living male
			left ear-masked air conduction threshold
	below	○	living female
	systolic blood pressure		respiration
≠	not equal to		right ear-air conduction threshold
≅	approximately equal to	◇	sex unknown
=	equal		
	equal to	(□)	adopted living male
		*	birth
'	feet	†	dead
	minutes (as in 30')		death
"	inches	♀	standing
	seconds		
		○—<	recumbent position
~	about		
	approximately	♀	sitting position
	difference		
≈	approximately equal to	♥	heart
≡	identical		

Greek Letters

×	left ear-air conduction threshold	
	ten	A α	alpha
		β B	beta
]	left ear-masked bone conduction threshold	Γ γ	gamma
[	right ear-masked	Δ δ	anion gap
	bone conduction		change
			delta
△	right ear-masked air conduction threshold		delta gap
			prism diopter
	change		temperature
			trimester
○	threshold		
	reversible	E ε	epsilon
?	question	Z ζ	zeta
	questionable	H η	eta
–	not tested	Θ θ	negative
Ø	no		theta
	none	I ι	iota
	without	K κ	kappa

Λ λ	lambda	T τ	tau
M μ	micro	Υ υ	upsilon
	mu	Φ φ	phenyl
			phi
N ν	nu		thyroid
Ξ ξ	xi	X χ	chi
O o	omicron	Ψ ψ	psi
Π π	pi		psychiatric
P ρ	rho	Ω ω	omega
Σ σ	sigma		ohm
	sum of		
	summary		

Additions, Corrections, and Suggestions are Welcomed

Please send them via any means shown below:

Neil M Davis
605 Louis Drive, Suite 508B
Warminster PA 18974-2830

FAX 215 442 7432
Email neil@medabbrev.com
Secure website www.medabbrev.com

Thank you for your help in the past.

Have You Used the medabbrev.com website Version of This Book?

- It is instantaneously searchable for the meanings of abbreviations
- It is reverse searchable (search for all the abbreviations containing a particular word)
- Each week, about 30 new entries are added

See the preface (page vii) for access instructions. A one-year, single-user access is included in the purchase price of the book. Also one-year subscriptions (no book) are available for purchase.

Multi-User Site Licenses for medabbrev.com are Available for Your Intranet

Medical facilities can substitute their own "Do Not Use" list of dangerous abbreviations for the one present. The ability also exists to list abbreviations that are unique to your region and/or organization which would normally not appear in any national list. These lists would be controlled by the facility or company. A no-cost, 3-week trial and pricing information are available by calling 215 442 7430 or via an e-mail request to ev@medabbrev.com

Chapter 6

Tables, Lists, and Conversions

Numbers and letters for teeth

Two adult numbering systems and a deciduous system are shown. The adult systems are shown as numbers, whereas deciduous teeth are lettered. The system commonly used in the U.S. is 1 to 32 (shown in bold face type).

1 (18)	upper right 3rd molar		**17** (38)	lower left 3rd molar
2 (17) (A)	upper right 2nd molar		**18** (37) (K)	lower left 2nd molar
3 (16) (B)	upper right 1st molar		**19** (36) (L)	lower left 1st molar
4 (15)	upper right 2nd bicuspid		**20** (35)	lower left 2nd bicuspid
5 (14)	upper right 1st bicuspid		**21** (34)	lower left 1st bicuspid
6 (13) (C)	upper right canine (eyetooth)		**22** (33) (M)	lower left canine
7 (12) (D)	upper right lateral incisor		**23** (32) (N)	lower left lateral incisor
8 (11) (E)	upper right central incisor		**24** (31) (O)	lower left central incisor
9 (21) (F)	upper left central incisor		**25** (41) (P)	lower right central incisor
10 (22) (G)	upper left lateral incisor		**26** (42) (Q)	lower right lateral incisor
11 (23) (H)	upper left canine		**27** (43) (R)	lower right canine
12 (24)	upper left 1st bicuspid		**28** (44)	lower right 1st bicuspid
13 (25)	upper left 2nd bicuspid		**29** (45)	lower right 2nd bicuspid
14 (26) (I)	upper left 1st molar		**30** (46) (S)	lower right 1st molar
15 (27) (J)	upper left 2nd molar		**31** (47) (T)	lower right 2nd molar
16 (28)	upper left 3rd molar		**32** (48)	lower right 3rd molar

UPPER   UPPER

	1	**2**	**3**	**4**	**5**	**6**	**7**	**8**	**9**	**10**	**11**	**12**	**13**	**14**	**15**	**16**	
	18	17	16	15	14	13	12	11	21	22	23	24	25	26	27	28	
		A	B			C	D	E	F	G	H			I	J		
Right																	**Left**
		T	S			R	Q	P	O	N	M			L	K		
	48	47	46	45	44	43	42	41	31	32	33	34	35	36	37	38	
	32	**31**	**30**	**29**	**28**	**27**	**26**	**25**	**24**	**23**	**22**	**21**	**20**	**19**	**18**	**17**	

LOWER   LOWER

Laboratory Test Panels*

	Cl CO₂ K Na	BUN Ca Creat Gluc	Alb Alk P AST(SGOT) ALT(SGPT) T Bili TP	ANA ESR RF Ur Ac	Calc LDL HDL T Chol Trig VLDL	Alb Phos	HAAb, IgM Ab HbcAb, IgM Ab HbsAG HCAb
Lytes (electrolyte panel)	X						
BMP (basic metabolic panel) or MBP, MPB	X	X					
CMP (comprehensive metabolic panel)	X	X	X				
HFP (hepatic function panel)			X plus D Bili				
AP (arthritis panel)				X			
LP (lipid Panel)					X		
RFP (renal function panel)	X	X				X	
AHP (acute hepatitis panel)							X

*These can vary from institution to institution and from year to year

Abbreviation Key

Ab-antibody
Alb-albumin
Alk P-alkaline phosphate
ALT (SGPT)-alanine aminotransferase (serum glutamate pyruvate)
ANA-antinuclear antibody
AST (SGOT)-aspartate-aminotransferase (serum glutamate oxaloacetic transaminase)
BUN-blood urea nitrogen
Ca-calcium
Calc LDL-calculated low-density lipoprotein
LDL-low density lipoprotein

Cl-chloride
CO₂-carbon dioxide
Creat-creatinine
D Bili-direct bilirubin
ESR-erythrocyte sedimentation rate
Gluc-glucose
HAAb-hepatitis A antibody
HBcAb-hepatitis B core antibody
HBsAg-hepatitis B surface antigen
HCAb-hepatitis C antibody
HDL-high-density lipoprotein

IgM-immunoglobulin M
K-potassium
Na-sodium
Phos-phosphate
RF-rheumatoid factor
T Bili-total bilirubin
T Chol-total cholesterol
TP-total protein
Trig-triglycerides
Ur Ac-uric acid
VLDl-very low-density lipoprotein

See text for meaning of the abbreviations shown

Complete Blood Count

$$10,000 \Big\rangle \begin{array}{c} 11.7 \\ 36.5 \end{array} \Big\langle \begin{array}{l} 50S,\ 25B,\ 35L,\ 5M\ 2N,\ 3E \\ 83/29/30 \\ 290,00 \end{array}$$

$$WBC \Big\rangle \begin{array}{c} HgB \\ HCT \end{array} \Big\langle \begin{array}{l} Segs/Bands/Lymphs/Monos/Basos/Eos \\ MCV\text{-}MCH\text{-}MCHC \\ platelet\ count \end{array}$$

Electrolyte Panel

142	99	sodium	chloride
4.7	25	potassium	carbon dioxide

Blood Gases

7.4/80/48/98/25   pH/PO$_2$/PCO$_2$/% O$_2$ saturation/bicarbonate

Obstetrical shorthand

$$\frac{2\ cm | 80\%}{-2\ Vtx} \quad 2\ cm = \text{dilation of cervix}$$

80% = degree of cer-   Vtx = vertex; presen-
    vix effacement   tation of fetus,
                               (breech = Br)

−2 = station; distance
    above (+) or
    below (−) the
    spine of the ischium measured in cm

Reflexes

Reflexes are usually graded on a 0 to 4+ scale. The designations +, ++, +++, and ++++ should not be used.

4+ may indicate disease often associated with clonus
    very brisk, hyperactive
3+ brisker than average
    possibly but not necessarily indicative of disease
2+ average
    normal
1+ low normal
    somewhat diminished
0   may indicate neuropathy
    no response

Muscle strength[1]

0—No muscular contraction detected
1—A barely detectable flicker or trace of contraction
2—Active movement of the body part with gravity eliminated
3—Active movement against gravity
4—Active movement against gravity and some resistance
5—Active movement against full resistance without evident fatigue. This is normal muscle strength

Pulse[1]

0	completely absent
+1	markedly impaired (or 1+)
+2	modererately impaired (or 2+)
+3	slightly impaired (or 3+)
+4	normal (or 4+)

Gradation of intensity of heart murmurs[1]

1/6 or I/VI   may not be heard in all positions
very faint, heard only after the listener has "tuned in"
2/6 or II/VI   quiet, but heard immediately upon placing the stethoscope on the chest
3/6 or III/VI   moderately loud
4/6 or IV/VI   loud
5/6 orV/VI   very loud, may be heard with a stethoscope partly off the chest (thrills are associated)
6/6 or VI/VI   may be heard with the stethoscope entirely off the chest (thrills are associated)

Tonsil Size

0	no tonsils
1	less than normal
2	normal
3	greater than normal
4	touching

Grades of Severity of Knee Arthritis *(arthroscopic)*

Grade 1:   Early changes show *fissuring* (breaks) in the cartilage
Grade 2:   More extensive full thickness breaks in the cartilage
Grade 3:   Intermittent loss of cartilage with breaks
Grade 4:   Exposed *subchondral* (below the cartilage) bone

Metric Prefixes and Symbols

Prefix	Symbol	
tera-	T	1,000,000,000,000 or (10^{12}) one trillion
giga-	G	1,000,000,000 or (10^{9}) one billion
mega-	M	1,000,000 or (10^{6}) one million
kilo-	k	1,000 or (10^{3}) one thousand
hecto-	h	100 or (10^{2}) one hundred
deka-	da	10 or (10^{1}) ten
deci-	d	0.1 or (10^{-1}) one-tenth
centi-	c	0.01 or (10^{-2}) one-hundredth
milli-	m	0.001 or (10^{-3}) one-thousandth
micro-	μ	0.000,001 or (10^{-6}) one-millionth
nano-	n	0.000,000,001 or (10^{-9}) one-billionth
pico-	p	0.000,000,000,000,001 or (10^{-12}) one-trillionth
femto-	f	0.000,000,000,000,001 or (10^{-15}) one-quadrillionth
atto-	a	0.000,000,000,000,000,001 or (10^{-18}) one-quintillionth

Kilograms/Pounds Conversions
To convert pounds to kilograms, divide by 2.2
To convert kilograms to pounds, multiply by 2.2
After carrying out a calculation, always make sure your answer is reasonable by checking with the table below.

kilograms	pounds
0.5	1.1
1	2.2
5	11
10	22
25	55
50	110
75	165
100	220

Fahrenheit/Centigrade Conversions
To convert Centigrade to Fahrenheit

°F = 32 plus (9/5 times °C)   or   °F = 32 plus (1.8 times °C)

To convert Fahrenheit to Centigrade

°C = 5/9 times (°F minus 32)   or   °C ≈ 0.556 times (°F minus 32)

After carrying out a calculation, always make sure your answer is reasonable by checking with the table below.

°Centigrade	°Fahrenheit
0	32
2	36
8	46
15	59
20	68
25	77
30	86
36	96.8
37	98.6
38	100.4
39	102.2
40	104
41	105.8
50	122
100	212

Apothecary symbols (Should never be used)

The symbols presented below are for informational use. The apothecary system should **not** be used. Only the metric system should be used. The methods of expressing the symbols, the meanings, and the equivalence are not the classic ones, nor are they precise, but reflect the usual intended meanings when used by some older physicians in writing prescription directions.

Symbol	Meaning	Symbol	Meaning
ℨ or ℨ ͨ	dram, teaspoonful, (5 mL)	℥ or ℥ ͨ	ounce, (30 mL)
		gr	grain (approximately 65 mg)
ℨ ͭͭ	two drams, 2 tea-spoonfuls, (10 mL)	ℳ	minim (approximately 0.06 mL)
ℨ͞s͞s	half ounce, table-spoonful, (15 mL)	gtt	drop

Reference

1. Adopted from Bates, B., *Bates' Guide to Physical Examinations and History Taking*, 11th ed. Philadelphia: Wolters Kluwer Lippincott Williams and Wilkins; 2018.

Chapter 7

Cross-Referenced List of Generic and Brand Drug Names

Listed below is a cross-referenced index of generic and brand drug names. Generic names begin with a lower case letter while brand names begin with a capital letter. This partial list consists of frequently prescribed drugs, new drugs, and recently discontinued drugs.

In the web version of this book (see page vii), when the drug name is clicked, you are connected to its Wikipedia monograph. The web version is updated weekly.

The meanings of abbreviated and coded drug names can be found in Chapter 4 (Lettered Abbreviations and Acronyms).

This listing is intended to allow readers to reference generic and trade drug names. Since products are added and taken off the market daily, this listing can not be relied on for accuracy of availability. See warning in Chapter 1.

Complete indices of United States drug names can be found in current editions of Drug Facts and Comparisons[1]. A complete list of world-wide names may be found in Martindales.[2] These and other references should be used to determine the equivalence of products, strengths, and dosage forms. Although several products may be listed under one generic name they may differ in strength, dosage form, or concentration available, as is the case with estradiol transdermal (Climara, Estraderm, and Vivelle).

When a product is often prescribed and/or labeled generically, the generic name is shown in italics. Some products are marketed without a brand name, as in the case of thioguanine. In such cases only the generic name is listed.

The following abbreviations are used in this listing:

EC	enteric coated	SR	sustained release tablets or capsules, and other
HCl	hydrochloride		designations for extended release dosage forms such as CR, LX, SA, LA, CC, XR, SR, CD, XT, etc.
IM	intramuscular	susp	suspension
IV	intravenous	(W)	withdrawn or discontinued from US market
inj	injection	(WA)	withdrawn or discontinued from U.S. Market but
oint	ointment		available under it's generic name and/or another brand name from another manufacturer(s)
ophth	ophthalmic		
soln	solution		

A

abacavir sulfate	Ziagen	abciximab	ReoPro
abaloparatide inj	Tymlos	Abelcet	amphotericin B lipid complex
abarelix	Plenaxis		
abatacept	Orencia	Abilify	aripiprazole
Abbokinase	urokinase	Abilify Maintena	aripiprazole SR susp inj

abiraterone	Zytiga
Ablavar	gadofosveset trisodium inj
abobotulinumtoxin A inj	Dysport
Abraxane	*paclitaxel-albumin inj*
Abreva	docosanol cream (over-the-counter)
Abthrax	raxibacumab
acalabrutinib	Calquence
ACAM 2000 (W)	smallpox (vaccinia) (W)
acamprosate calcium	Campral
acarbose	Precose
Accolate	zafirlukast
AccuNeb	albuterol inhalation soln
Accupril	*quinapril HCl*
Accuretic	*quinapril; hydrochlorothizide*
Accutane (W)	isotretinoin (W)
Accuzyme	papain; urea oint
acebutolol HCl	Sectral
Aceon	perindopril erbumine
acetaminophen	paracetamol / Tylenol
acetaminophen 300 mg with Codeine Phosphate (15, 30, and 60 mg)	Phenaphen with Codeine (#2, 3, and 4) (WA) / Tylenol with Codeine (#2, 3, and 4)
acetaminophen inj	Ofirmev
acetazolamide	Diamox
acetazolamide SR	Diamox Sequels
acetohydroxamic acid	Lithostat
acetominophen	may have meant acetaminophen (Tylenol)
acetylcysteine	Mucomyst
acetylcysteine effervescent tablet	Cetylev
Achromycin (WA)	*tetracycline HCl*
Aciphex	rabeprazole sodium
acitretin	Soriatane
aclidinium bromide and formoterol fumarate inhaler	Duaklir
aclidinium bromide inhalation	Trudorza Pressair
Actemra	tocilizumab
Acthar PH	corticotropin repository inj
ActHIB/Tripedia	*Haemophilus b* conjugate vaccine reconstituted with diphtheria and tetanus toxoids and acellular pertussis vaccine adsorbed
Acthrel	corticorelin ovine triflutate
Actifed	*triprolidine HCl; pseudoephedrine HCl*
Actigall	*ursodiol*
Actimmune	interferon gamma 1-b
Actiq	fentanyl citrate buccal lozenge / *fentanyl oral transmucosal*
Activase	alteplase, recombinant
Activella (W)	norethindrone acetate; estradiol
Actonel	risedronate sodium
Actos	pioglitazone HCl
Acular	ketorolac tromethamine ophth
acyclovir	Zovirax
Adacel	*diphtheria, tetanus, and acellular pertussis (TdaP) vaccine (adult type)*
Adalat	nifedipine
Adalat CC	*nifedipine SR*
adalimumab inj	Humira
adalimumab-adaz inj	Hyrimoz
adalimumab-adbm inj	Cyltezo
adalimumab-atto inj	Amjevita
adapalene	Differin
Adapin (WA)	*doxepin HCl*
Adcetris	*brentuximab vedotin* / brentuximab vedotin inj
Adderall	amphetamine; dextroamphetamine mixed salts
Adderol	may have meant Adderall (amphetamine and dextroamphetamine)
Addium	an over-the-counter product sold as a brain enhancer [L-tyrosine, GABA (gamma-aminobutyric acid), Bacopa Monnieri, Alpha GPC (alpha glycerylphosphoryl-choline), Vinpocetine, Huperzine A]
Addyi	flibanserin
adefovir dipivoxil	Hepsera / Preveon
Adempas	riociguat
Adenocard	adenosine
adenosine	Adenocard
Aderall	may have meant Adderall (amphetamine and dextroamphetamine)
Adipex-P	*phentermine HCl*
Adivan	may be referring to Ativan (lorazepam)
Adlyxin	lixisenatide inj
Admelog	insulin lispro inj

ado-trastuzumab emtansine inj	Kadcyla
Adrenalin	epinephrine
Adriamycin	*doxorubicin HCl*
Advair Diskus	fluticasone propionate; salmeterol inhalation powder
Advicor	lovastatin; niacin
Advil	ibuprofen
Adynovate	antihemophilic factor [recombinant] pegylated inj
Adzenys ER	amphetamine SR oral susp
AeroBid	flunisolide
afatinib	Gilotrif
Afinitor	*everolimus*
aflibercept intravitreal inj	Eylea
Afluria	influenza vaccine
Afrezza	insulin human, inhalation powder
Afrin nasal spray	*oxymetazoline HCl*
Afstyla	anti-hemophilic factor (recombinant), single chain inj
agalsidase beta	Fabrazyme
Agenerase (W)	amprenavir (W)
Aggrastat	tirofiban HCl
Aggrenox	aspirin; extended-release dipyridamole
Agriflu	influenza virus vaccine type A and B inj
Agrylin (WA)	*anagrelide HCl*
Aimovig	erenumab aooe inj
Ajovy	fremanezumab-vfrm inj
Akineton (W)	biperiden (W)
Akovaz	ephedrine sulfate inj
Alamast	pemirolast potassium ophth soln
alatrofloxacin mesylate IV (W)	Trovan inj (W)
albendazole	Albenza
Albenza	albendazole
albiglutide inj	Tanzeum
albumin (human), sonicated	Albunex
albumin human	Albuminar
	Albutein
	Buminate
	Plasbumin
Albuminar	*albumin human*
Albunex	*albumin (human), sonicated*
Albutein	*albumin human*
Albuteral	may have meant Albuterol
albuterol	Proventil
	salbutamol
	Ventolin
albuterol inhalation soln	AccuNeb
albuterol SR	Proventil Repetabs
	Volmax
albuterol sulfate inhalation aerosol	Proventil HFA
	ProAir HFA
albuterol sulfate inhalation powder	ProAir RespiClick
Aldactazide	*spironolactone; hydrochlorothiazide*
Aldactone	spironolactone
Aldara	imiquimod cream
aldesleukin	Proleukin
Aldomet	*methyldopa*
Aldoril	*methyldopa; hydrochlorothiazide*
Aldurazyme	laronidase
Alecensa	alectinib
alectinib	Verzenio
	Alecensa
alefacept	Amevive
alemtuzumab inj	Campath
	Lemtrada
alendronate sodium	Fosamax
Alesse	*levonorgestrel; ethinyl estradiol*
Aleve	naproxen sodium
Alfenta	alfentanil HCl
alfentanil HCl	Alfenta
Alferon	interferon alfa-n3 (human leukocyte derived)
Alfuria	Quadrivalent influenza vaccine inj
alfuzosin	UroXatral
alglucerase	Ceredase
Alimta	pemetrexed disodium
Alinia	nitazoxanide
Aliqopa	copanlisib inj
alirocumab inj	Praluent
aliskiren hemifumarate	Tekturna
alitretinoin	Panretin
Alkeran	melphalan
Allegra	*fexofenadine HCl*
allopurinol	Zyloprim
allopurinol and lesinurad	Duzallo
almotriptan malate	Axert
Alocril	nedocromil ophth soln
alogliptin	Nesina
alogliptin; metformin	Kazano
alogliptin; pioglitazone	Oseni
Alomide	lodoxamide tromethamine ophth soln
Alora	*estradiol transdermal*
Alosetron (W)	Lotronex (W)
Aloxi	palonosetron HCl

alpelisib	Piqray	Amerge	naratriptan HCl
alpha₁-proteinase inhibitor (human)	Prolastin	Amevive	alefacept
		Amicar	*aminocaproic acid*
Alphagan (W)	brimonidine tartrate ophth (W)	Amidate	*etomidate*
		amifampridine phosphate	Firdapse
Alphanate	antihemophilic factor/ von willebrand factor complex (human) inj	amifostine	Ethyol
		amikacin liposome inhal susp	Arikayce
Alphanate/VWF Complex/Human	Antihemophilic Factor/ Von Willebrand Factor Complex Inj	amikacin sulfate	Amikin
		Amikin	*amikacin sulfate*
alprazolam	Xanax	amiloride HCl	Midamor
Alprolix	coagulation factor IX (recombinant) inj	amiloride; hydro- chlorothiazide	Moduretic
alprostadil	Caverject Edex Prostin VR	*amino acid inj*	Aminosyn Travasol TrophAmine
alprostadil urethral suppository	Muse	amino acid with electrolytes in dextrose with calcium inj (various concentrations)	Clinimix E (W)
Alrex	loteprednol etabonate ophth susp		
Alsuma	sumatriptan inj		
Altabax	retapamulin oint.		
Altace	*ramipril*	amino acids. electrolytes, dextrose and lipid inj (for IV infusion into a central vein	Kabiven
alteplase (for catheter occlusions)	Cathflo Activase		
alteplase, recombinant	Activase		
Altreno	tretinoin lotion	amino acids. electrolytes, dextrose and lipid inj (for IV infusion into a peripheral or central vein	Perikabiven
altretamine	Hexalen		
aluminum acetate	Domeboro		
aluminum carbonate (W)	Basaljel (W)		
aluminum hydroxide	Amphojel	aminocaproic acid	Amicar
aluminum hydroxide, magnesium hydroxide, and simethicone	Mylanta	aminocaproic acid gel	Caprogel
		aminoglutethimide (W)	Cytadren (W)
aluminum hydroxide; magnesium hydroxide	Maalox	aminolevulinic acid HCl topical soln	Levulan Kerastick
Alunbrig	brigatinib	aminolevulinic HCl acid tablets (a fluorescing optical imaging agent)	Gleolan
Alupent (W)	*metaproterenol sulfate*		
Alustra (W)	hydroquinone topical susp (W)		
Alvesco	circlesonide inhalation	aminophylline	aminophylline
alvimopan	Entereg	aminosalicylic acid	Paser
amantadine HCl	Symmetrel	Aminosyn	*amino acid inj*
amantadine SR	Gocovri	amiodarone	amiodarone
Amaryl	*glimepiride*	*amiodarone HCl*	*amiodarone HCl*
Ambian	may have meant Ambien (*zolpidem tartrate*)	amiodorone	may have meant amiodarone
		Amitiza	lubiprostone
Ambien	*zolpidem tartrate*	*amitriptyline HCl*	Elavil (WA)
Ambien CR	zolpidem tartrate sustained release tab		*amitriptyline HCl*
		Amjevita	adalimumab-atto inj
AmBisome	liposomal amphotericin B	AmLactin	ammonium lactate lotion
ambrisentan	Letairis	amlexanox oral paste	Aphthasol
amcinonide (W)	Cyclocort (W)		

658

amlodipine and olmesartan	Azor	Anafranil	clomipramine HCl
amlodipine besylate	Norvasc	anagrelide HCl (W)	Agrylin (W)
amlodipine besylate; atorvastatin calcium	Caduet	anakinra	Kineret
		anastrozole	Arimidex
amlodipine besylate; benazepril HCl	Lotrel	Anbesol	benzocaine
		Ancef (WA)	cefazolin sodium
amlodipine; valsartan	Exforge	Ancobon	flucytosine
ammonium lactate lotion	AmLactin	Androderm	testosterone transdermal system
Ammonul	sodium phenylacetate and sodium benzoate inj 10%	AndroGel	testosterone gel
		Androgel-DHT	dihydro-testosterone transdermal
amobarbital sodium	Amytal	Anectine	succinylcholine chloride
amoxapine	amoxapine	Anexsia	hydrocodone bitartrate; acetaminophen
amoxicillian	may have meant amoxicillin	Angiomax	bivalirudin
amoxicillin	Amoxil Trimox Wymox	angiotensin II acetate inj	GiaPreza
		anidulafungin IV	Eraxis
amoxicillin/ clavulanate potassium SR	Augmentin XR	Annovera	segesterone acetate and ethinyl estradiol vaginal system
amoxicillin; clavulanic acid	Augmentin	Anoro Ellipta	umeclidinium and vilanterol inhalation powder
Amoxil	amoxicillin		
Amphadase	hyaluronidase inj (bovine)	Ansaid (WA)	flurbiprofen
		Antabuse	disulfiram
amphetamine resins (W)	Biphetamine (W)	Antagon	ganirelix acetate
		Anthem	obiltoxaximab inj
amphetamine SR oral susp	Adzenys ER Dyanavel XR	anti hemophilic factor inj (recombinant)	Kovaltry
amphetamine; dextroamphetamine mixed salts	Adderall	antihemophilic factor (recombinant)	ReFacto
		antihemophilic factor (recombinant) inj	Novoeight
Amphojel (WA)	aluminum hydroxide		
Amphotec	amphotericin B cholesteryl sulfate	antihemophilic factor (recombinant) porcine sequence	Obizur
amphotericin B (W)	Fungizone (W)		
amphotericin B cholesteryl sulfate	Amphotec	anti-hemophilic factor (recombinant), single chain inj	Afstyla
amphotericin B lipid complex	Abelcet	antihemophilic factor [recombinant] pegylated inj	Adynovate
ampicillin	Principen		
ampicillin sodium; sulbactam sodium	Unasyn	anti-inhibitor coagulant complex inj	Feiba
amprenavir (W)	Agenerase (W)	Antilirium	physostigmine salicylate
Ampyra	dalfampridine	antipyrine otic (W)	Auralgan (W)
amrinone (former name)	inamrinone (new name)	antithrombin III (human)	Thrombate III
Amrix	cyclobenzaprine SR		
amsacrine	Amsidyl	antithrombin, recombinant inj	ATryn
Amsidyl	amsacrine		
Amvisc	sodium hyaluronate	antithymocyte globulin, (rabbit)	Thymoglobulin
Amytal	amobarbital sodium inj		
Amyvid	florbetapir F18 inj		
Anadrol-50	oxymetholone		

Antivert	*meclizine*
Antizol	fomepizole
Anturane (W)	sulfinpyrazone (W)
Anusol HC	hydrocortisone cream
	hydrocortisone suppositories
Anzemet	dolasetron mesylate
Apadaz	benzhydrocodone and acetaminophen
apalutamide	Erleada
Aphthasol	amlexanox oral paste
Apidra	insulin glulisine [rDNA origin]
apixaban	Eliquis
Apixiban	may have meant apixaban (Eliquis)
Aplisol	tuberculin skin test
Apokyn	apomorphine HCl inj
apomorphine HCl	Uprima
apomorphine HCl inj	Apokyn
Aposyn	exisulind
apremilast	Otezla
aprepitant	Emend capsules
aprepitant inj	Cinvanti
Apresazide (W)	hydralazine HCl; hydrochloro-thiazide (W)
Apresoline (WA)	*hydralazine HCl*
Apriso	mesalamine SR capsules
aprotinin	Trasylol
Aptiom	eslicarbazepine
Aptivus	tipranavir
Aptosyn (W)	exisulind (W)
aquaMephyton (WA)	*phytonadione inj*
Aralen	*chloroquine phosphate*
Aramine	metaraminol bitartrate
Aranesp	darbepoetin alfa
Arava	leflunomide
Arcalyst	rilonacept
Arcapta Neohaler	indacaterol inhalation powder
arcitumomab	CEA-Scan
ardeparin sodium (W)	Normiflo (W)
Arduan (W)	pipecuronium bromide (W)
Aredia	*pamidronate disodium*
Arestin	minocycline HCl dental microspheres
arformoterol tartrate inhalation	Brovana
argatroban	argatroban
arginine HCl	R-Gene
Aricept	donepezil HCl
Arimidex	*anastrozole*
aripiprazole	Abilify
aripiprazole SR susp inj	Abilify Maintena Aristada
Aristada	aripiprazole SR susp inj
Aristocort	triamcinolone acetonide
Arixtra	fondaparinux sodium
armodafinil	Nuvigil
Arnuity Ellipta	fluticasone furoate inhalation powder
Aromasin	exemestane
Arranon	nelarabine
arsenic trioxide	Trisenox
artemether/ lumafentrine combination	Coartem
Arthrotec	diclofenac; misoprostol
articaine; epinephrine	Septocaine
Artiss	fibrin sealant, human, topical
Arymo ER	morphine sulfate SR tablet
Arzerra	ofatumumab
Asacol	mesalamine
Asceniv	immune globulin intravenous, human-slra
asenapine maleate	Saphris
asfotase alfa inc	Strensiq
asparaginase	Elspar
Asparlas	calaspargase pegol-mknl inj
aspirin 325 mg with codeine phosphate (30 and 60 mg)	Empirin with codeine #3 and #4
aspirin and omeprazole	Yosprala
aspirin buffered	Bufferin
aspirin EC	Ecotrin
aspirin; extended-release dipyridamole	Aggrenox
Astagraf XL	tacrolimus SR
Astelin	azelastine HCl nasal spray
astemizole (W)	Hismanal (W)
Atacand	candesartan cilexetil
Atacand HCT	candesartan cilexetil; hydrochlorothiazide
Atarax (WA)	*hydroxyzine HCl*
atazanavir and cobicistat	Evotaz
atenolol	Tenormin
atenolol; chlorthalidone	Tenoretic
atezolizumab inj	Tecentriq
Atgam	lymphocyte immune globulin
Ativan	*lorazepam*
Atomoxetine HCl	Strattera
atorvastatin	may have meant atorvastatin (Lipitor)
atorvastatin and ezetimibe	Liptruzet

atorvastatin calcium	Lipitor
atovaquone	Mepron
atovaquone; proguanil HCl	Malarone
atracurium besylate	Tracrium
Atridox	doxycycline hyclate gel
Atripla	efavirenz, emtricitabine, and tenofovir
Atromid-S	clofibrate
atropine sulfate tablets	Sal-Tropine
Atrovent	*ipratropium bromide*
ATryn	antithrombin, recombinant inj
Aubagio	*teriflunomide*
Augmentin	*amoxicillin; clavulanic acid*
Augmentin XR	*amoxicillin; clavulanate potassium SR*
auranofin	Ridaura
Aurolate	gold sodium thiomalate
aurothioglucose (W)	Solganal (W)
Auryxia	ferric citrate
Austedo	deutetrabenazine
Auvi Q	epinephrine HCl (auto-injector) inj
Avalide	irbesartan; hydrochlorothiazide
avanafil	Stendra
Avandamet	rosigitazone maleate; metformin HCl
Avandia	Rosiglitazone maleate
Avapro	irbesartan
Avastin	bevacizumab
avatrombopag	Doptelet
AVC Vaginal	sulfanilamide vaginal cream
Aveed	testosterone undecanoate inj
Avelox	moxifloxacin HCl
avelumab inj	Bavencio
Aventyl	*nortriptyline HCl*
Avinza	*morphine sulfate tab SR*
Avita	*tretinoin cream 0.025%*
Avitene	collagen hemostat
Avodart	dutasteride
Avonex	interferon beta-la
Avycaz	ceftazidime and avibactam inj
Axert	almotriptan malate
axicabtagene ciloleucel inj	Yescarta
Axid	*nizatidine*
Axiron	*testosterone topical soln*
Axitinib	Inlyta
azacitidine	Vidaza
Azactam	*aztreonam*
AzaSite	azithromycin ophth soln

azatadine maleate	Optimine
azathioprine	Imuran
Azedra	iobenguane I 131 inj
azelaic acid cream	Azelex
azelaic acid topical foam	Finacea
azelaic cream	Finevin
azelastine HCl and fluticasone proprionate nasal spray	Dymista
azelastine HCl nasal spray	Astelin
azelastine HCl ophth soln	Optivar
Azelex	azelaic acid cream
Azilect	rasagiline mesylate
azilsartan medioxomil	Edarbi
azithromycin	Zithromax
azithromycin ophth soln	AzaSite
Azmacort	triamcinolone acetonide aerosol
Azopt	brinzolamide ophth susp
Azor	amlodipine and olmesartan
aztreonam	Azactam
Azulfidine	*sulfasalazine*
Azurette	*desogestrel and ethinyl estradiol*

B

B & O Suprettes	opium; belladonna suppositories
baby aspirin	aspirin tablets 81 mg
Bacid	a probiotic tablet *(L. acidophilus, L. bulgaricus, B. bifidum, and S. thermopiles)*
bacitracin inj	*bacitracin inj*
bacitracin ophth oint	*bacitracin ophth oint*
bacitracin Zinc external Oint	*bacitracin Zinc external Oint*
baclofen	Lioresal
Bactraban	see Bactroban
Bactrim	*sulfamethoxazole; trimethoprim*
Bactrim DS	sulfamethoxazole and trimethoprim double strength
Bactroban	mupirocin nasal ointment
BAL in Oil	dimercaprol

baloxavir marboxil	Xofluza
balsalazide disodium	Colazal
Banzel	rufinamide
Baraclude	entecavir
barbituates	may have meant barbiturates (a class of anti-epileptic, sedative, sleep-inducing drugs derived from barbituric acid; e.g. phenobarbital, pentobarbital, Amytal, etc)
baricitinib	Olumiant
Basaglar	insulin glargine
Basaljel	aluminum carbonate
basiliximab	Simulect
Bavencio	avelumab inj
Baxdela	delafloxacin
Baycol (W)	cerivastatin sodium (W)
Baza Protect Cream	zinc oxide and dimethicone with petrolatum; and vitamins A, D & E
BCG intravesical	Pacis TheraCys TICE BCG
becaplermin gel	Regranex
beclomethasone dipropionate	Qvar
bedaquiline	Sirturo
belatacept inj	Nulojix
Belbuca	buprenorphine film Hal buccal film patch
Beleodaq	belinostat inj
belimumab	Benlysta
belinostat inj	Beleodaq
belladonna	belladonna tincture (a homoeopathic medication; it's active ingredients include atropine, scopolamine and hyoscyamine)
Bellergal-S (W)	*phenobarbital; ergotamine; belladonna (W)*
Belsomra	suvorexant
Belviq	lorcaserin
Benadryl	*diphenhydramine HCl*
benazepril HCl	Lotensin
bendamustine HCl inj	Bendeka Treanda
Bendeka	bendamustine HCl inj
Benedryl	may have mean Benadryl (diphenhydramine HCl)
BeneFix	factor IX, (recombinant)
Benicar	olmesartan medoxomil
Benicar HCT	olmesartan medoxomil; hydrochlorothiazide
Benlysta	*belimumab*
benralizumab inj	Fasenra
bentoquatam	IvyBlock
Bentyl	*dicyclomine HCl*
BenzaClin	clindamycin; benzoyl peroxide gel
Benzamycin	erythromycin; benzoyl peroxide topical gel
benzhydrocodone and acetaminophen	Apadaz
benzocaine	Anbesol Hurricaine Orabase Orajel
benzocaine soln	Hurricaine One
benzocaine; tetracaine HCl	Cetacaine
benzodiazepines	a class of antianxiety, anticonvulsant, and sedative drugs such as diazepam, chlordiazepoxide, carbamezapine, etc.
benzonatate	Tessalon
benztropine mesylate	Cogentin
benzyl alcohol lotion	Ulesfia
bepotastine besilate ophth soln	Bepreve
Bepreve	bepotastine besilate ophth soln
beractant	Survanta
Berroca	*vitamin B complex; folic acid; vitamin C*
besifloxacin HCl ophth soln	Besivance
Besivance	besifloxacin HCl ophth soln
Besponsa	inotuzumab ozogamicin inj
Betadine	povidone iodine
Betagan	levobunolol HCl
betaine anhydrous	Cystadane
betamethasone	Celestone
Betamethasone diproprionate	Diprosone (WA)
betamethasone valerate (foam)	Luxiq
betamethasone; clotrimazole cream	Lotrisone
Betapace	*sotalol*
Betaseron	interferon beta-1b
betaxolol	Kerlone
betaxolol HCl ophth soln	Betoptic
betaxolol HCl ophth susp	Betoptic S
bethanechol chloride	Urecholine

Betoptic	betaxolol HCl ophth soln
Betoptic S	betaxolol HCl ophth suspension
betrixaban	BevyxXa
bevacizumab	Avastin
bevacizumab-bvzr inj	Zirabev
Bevespi Aerosphere	glycopyrrolate and formoterol fumarate inhalation aerosol
BevyxXa	betrixaban
bexarotene gel	Targretin
Bextra (W)	valdecoxib (W)
Bexxar	tositumomab and I-131 tositumomab
bezlotoxumab inj	Zinplava
Biaxin	*clarithromycin*
Biaxin XL	*clarithromycin SR*
bicalutamide	Casodex
Bicillin C-R	penicillin G benzathine; penicillin G procaine (for IM use only)
Bicillin L-A	penicillin G benzathine (for IM use only)
Bicitra (WA)	*sodium citrate; citric acid*
BiCNU	carmustine
BiDil	isosorbide dinitrate; hydralazine
Biktarvy	bictegravir, emtricitabine, and tenofovir alafenamide
BIO-HPF	a capsule containing medicinal herbs and minerals to treat gastric and duodenal ulcers and inflammation
Biperiden (W)	Akineton (W)
Biphetamine (W)	amphetamine resins (W)
bisacodyl	Dulcolax
bismuth subsalicylate; metronidazole; tetracycline HCl	Helidac
bisoprolol fumarate; hydrochlorothiazide	Ziac
bitolterol mesylate (W)	Tornalate (W)
bleomycin sulfate	*bleomycin sulfate*
blinatumomab inj	Blincyto
Blincyto	blinatumomab inj
Blocadren	*timolol maleate*
Bloxiverz	neostigmine methylsulfate inj
boceprevir (w)	Victrelis
Boniva	ibandronate
Bonjesta	doxylamine succinate and pyridoxine HCl

bortezomib	Velcade
bosentan	Tracleer
Bosulif	*bosutinib*
bosutinib	Bosulif
Botox	onabotulinumtoxinA inj
Botox Cosmetic	onabotulinumtoxinA inj
Bravelle	urofollitropin
bremelanotide inj	Vyleesi
brentuximab vedotin inj	Adcetris
Breo Ellipta	fluticasone furoate and vilanterol inhalation powder
Brethaire	terbutaline sulfate aerosol
Brethine	*terbutaline sulfate tablets and inj*
bretylium tosylate	Bretylol
Bretylol	bretylium tosylate
Brevibloc	esmolol HCl
Brevital Sodium	methohexital sodium
brexanolone inj	Zulresso
Bridion	sugammadex inj
brigatinib	Alunbrig
Brilinta	*ticagrelor*
brimonidine gel	Mirvaso
brimonidine/timolol ophth soln	Combigan
Brineura	cerliponase alfa intraventricular inj
Brintellix	vortioxetine (name changed to Trintellix)
brinzolamide and brimonidine tartrate ophth susp	Simbrinza
brinzolamide ophth suspension	Azopt
Brisdelle	paroxetine
Briton	sugammadex inj
brivaracetam	Briviact
Briviact	brivaracetam
brodalumab inj	Siliq
bromfenac ophth sol	Xibrom
bromocriptine mesylate	Parlodel
brompheniramine maleate	*brompheniramine maleate*
brompheniramine maleate; phenylpropano- lamime	Dimetapp Extentabs
Brovana	arformoterol tartrate inhalation
Bryhali	halobetasol propionate lotion
Bucladin-S (W)	buclizine HCl (W)
buclizine HCl (W)	Bucladin-S (W)
budesonide capsule	Entocort EC

budesonide inhalation powder (W) — Pulmicort Turbuhaler (W)
budesonide intranasal suspension — Rhinocort Aqua Nasal Suspension
budesonide SR tablet — Uceris
budesonide/ and formoterol fumarate inhalation — Symbicort
Bufferin — *aspirin buffered*
bumetanide — Bumex
Bumex — *bumetanide*
Buminate — albumin human
Bunavail — buprenorphine; naloxone buccal film
Buphenyl — phenylbutyrate sodium
bupivacaine — see bupivacaine
bupivacaine HCl — Marcaine HCl / Sensorcaine
bupivacaine Liposome inj — Exparel
buprenorphine and naloxone — Zubsolv
buprenorphine extended-release inj — Suboxone
buprenorphine film Hal buccal film patch — Belbuca
buprenorphine HCl — Subutex
buprenorphine HCl; naloxone HCl — Suboxone
buprenorphine implant — Probuphine
buprenorphine transdermal system — Butrans
buprenorphine; naloxone buccal film — Bunavail
bupropion HCl — Wellbutrin
bupropion HCl SR — Wellbutrin SR / Zyban
burosumab-twza inj — Crysvita
BuSpar — *buspirone HCl*
buspirone HCl — BuSpar
busulfan — Myleran
busulfan inj — Busulfex
Busulfex — busulfan inj
butabarbital sodium — Butisol
butalbital; acetaminophen; caffeine — Fioricet
butalbital; aspirin; caffeine — Fiorinal
butenafine HCl — Mentax
Butisol — *butabarbital sodium*
butoconazole nitrate vaginal cream — Gynazole

butorphanol tartrate inj — Stadol
butorphanol tartrate nasal spray (W) — Stadol NS (W)
Butrans — buprenorphine transdermal system
Bydureon — exenatide inj
Byetta — exenatide inj
Bystolic — nebivolol
Byvalson — nebivolol and valsartan

C

C1 esterase inhibitor (Human) — Cinryze
C1 esterase inhibitor [recombinant] inj — Ruconest
C1 esterase inhibitor inj — Haegarda
cabazitaxel inj — Jevtana
cabergoline (W) — Dostinex (W)
Cabliv — caplacizumab inj
Cabometyx — cabozantinib
cabonzantinib — Cometriq
cabozantinib — Cabometyx
Ca-DTPA — pentetate calcium trisodium (trisodium calcium diethylenetriamine-pentaacetate)
Caduet — amlodipine besylate; atorvastatin calcium
Cafcit — *caffeine citrate inj*
Cafergot — ergotaminetar-trate; caffeine
caffeine citrate inj — Cafcit
Calan SR — *verapamil HCl SR*
calaspargase pegol-mknl inj — Asparlas
Calciferol — *ergocalciferol*
Calcimar — calcitonin
calcipotriene cream — Dovonex
calcipotriene foam — Sorilux
calcitonin — Calcimar
calcitonin-salmon — Miacalcin
calcitriol — Rocaltrol
calcium carbonate — Os-Cal 500 / Tums
calcium carbonate and calcitriol — Corcal
calcium carbonate; vitamin D and K chewable — Viactiv
Caldolor — *ibuprofen*
calfactant intratracheal susp — Infasurf

664

Calmoseptine oint	zinc oxide, menthol, glycerin, and lanolin oint
Calquence	acalabrutinib
Cambia	diclofenac potassium for oral soln
Campath	alemtuzumab
camphorated tincture of opium	paregoric (this is NOT tincture of opium; Paregoric has just 0.4 mg/mL of morphine, whereas tincture of opium contains 10 mg/mL, a 25-fold difference)
Campral	acamprosate calcium
Camptosar	*irinotecan HCl*
canagliflozin	Invokana
canagliflozin and metformin HCl	Invokamet XR
canakinumab inj	Ilaris
Cancidas	caspofungin acetate
candesartan cilexetil	Atacand
candesartan cilexetil; hydrochlorothiazide	Atacand HCT
cangrelor inj	Kengreal
cannabidiol oral soln	Epidiolex
Capastat Sulfate	capreomycin sulfate
capecitabine	Xeloda
Capital w/ Codeine Suspension	codeine phosphate; acetaminophen suspension
Capitrol (W)	chloroxine (W)
caplacizumab inj	Cablivi
Capoten	*captopril*
Caprelsa	vandetanib
capreomycin sulfate	Capastat Sulfate
Caprogel	aminocaproic acid gel
capromab pendetide	ProstaScint
capsaicin patch	Qutenza
captopril	Capoten
Carac	flourouracil cream
Carafate	sucralfate
Carbaglu	carglumic acid carglumic acid oral
carbamazepine	Tegretol
carbamazepine SR	Carbatrol Tegretol-XR
carbamide peroxide otic	Debrox
Carbatrol	carbamazepine SR
carbenicillin (W)	Geocillin (W)
Carbex (WA)	*selegiline*
carbidopa, levodopa, and entacapone	Stalevo
carbidopa/levodopa enteral susp	Duopa
Carbo Taxol	carboplatin inj and paclitaxel inj (Taxol)
Carbocaine	*mepivacaine HCl*
carboplatin	carboplatin
carboprost tromethamine Inj	Hemabate
Carbotaxol	carboplatin inj and paclitaxel inj (Taxol)
Cardene	*nicardipine HCl*
Cardiolite	technetium Tc-99m sestamibi
Cardiotec	technetium Tc-99m teboroxime kit
Cardizem	*diltiazem HCl*
Cardizem CD	*diltiazem HCl SR*
Cardura	*doxazosin mesylate*
carfilzomib inj	Kyprolis
carglumic acid oral	Carbaglu
cariprazine	Vraylar
carisoprodol	Soma
carmustine	BiCNU
carmustine implantable wafer	Gliadel
Carnitor	*levocarnitine*
CaroSpir	spironolactone oral susp
carvedilol	Coreg
Casodex	*bicalutamide*
caspofungin acetate	Cancidas
Cataflam	*diclofenac potassium*
Catapres	*clonidine HCl*
Cathflo Activase	alteplase (for catheter occlusions)
Caverject	alprostadil
CEA-SCAN	arcitumomab
Ceclor (WA)	*cefaclor*
Cedax	ceftibuten
CeeNu (WA)	lomustine
cefaclor	Ceclor
cefadroxil	Duricef
Cefadyl (WA)	cephapirin sodium
cefalexin	see cephalexin
cefamandole nafate (W)	Mandol (W)
cefamandole sodium (W)	Mandol (W)
cefazolin sodium	cefazolin sodium
cefdinir	Omnicef
cefditoren pivoxil	Spectracef
cefepime HCl	Maxipime
cefixime (W)	Suprax (W)
Cefizox (W)	*ceftizoxime sodium* (W)
Cefobid (W)	cefoperazone sodium (W)
cefoperazone sodium (W)	Cefobid (W)
Cefotan (WA)	cefotetan
cefotaxime sodium	Claforan
cefotetan	*cefotetan*
cefoxitin sodium	Mefoxin

665

cefpodoxime proxetil	Vantin
cefprozil	Cefzil
ceftaroline fosamil inj	Teflaro
ceftazidime	Ceptaz
	Fortaz
	Tazicef
	Tazidime
ceftazidime and avibactam inj	Avycaz
ceftibuten	Cedax
Ceftin	*cefuroxime axetil*
ceftizoxime sodium	Cefizox
ceftolozane and tazobactam inj	Zerbaxa
ceftriaxone sodium	Rocephin
cefuroxime axetil	Ceftin
cefuroxime sodium	Zinacef
cefuroxime sodium (W)	Kefurox (W)
Cefzil	*cefprozil*
Celebrex	celecoxib
celecoxib	Celebrex
Celestone	betamethasone
Celexa	*citalopram hydrobromide*
CellCept	*mycophenolate mofetil*
cellulose and citric acid	Plenity
cemiplimab-rwlc inj	Libtayo
cenegermin-bkbj ophth soln	Oxervate
Cenestin	synthetic conjugated estrogens, A
Centrum	vitamins; minerals
cephalexin	Keflex
cephalexin HCl	*cephalexin HCl*
cephalothin sodium (W)	Keflin (W)
cephradine	Velosef (WA)
Cephulac	lactulose
Ceprotin	Protein C Concentrate (Human) inj
Ceptaz	ceftazidime
Cequa	cyclosporin ophth soln
Cerdelga	eliglustat
Cerebyx	fosphenytoin sodium
Ceredase	alglucerase
Cerefolin NAC	L-methylfolate calcium, Algae-S powder, methylcobalamin, and N-acetylcysteine
Cerezyme	imiglucerase
ceritinib	Zykadia
cerivastatin sodium (W)	Baycol (W)
cerliponase alfa intraventricular inj	Brineura
Cernevit-12	multivitamins for infusion
certolizumab pegol	Cimzia
Cerubidine	daunorubicin HCl
Cervarlx	human papillomavirus bivalent vaccine, recombinant, susp inj
Cervidil	dinoprostone vaginal insert
Cervitec Plus	chlorhexidine-thymol varnish
Cetacaine	benzocaine; tetracaine HCl
cetirizine HCl	Zyrtec
cetirizine HCl; pseudoephedrine HCl SR	Zyrtec-D
cetirizine ophth soln	Zerviate
cetrorelix	Cetrotide
Cetrotide	cetrorelix
cetuximab	Erbitux
Cetylev	acetylcysteine effervescent tablet
cevimeline HCl	Evoxac
Chantix	*varenicline tartrate*
Chenodal	chenodiol
chenodiol	Chenodal
chloral hydrate	chloral hydrate
chlorambucil	Leukeran
chloramphenicol	Chloromycetin
chloramphenicol ophth	Chloroptic ophth
ChloraPrep	chlorhexidine gluconate 2% and Isopropyl alcohol 70% swabstick applicator skin antiseptic
chlordiazepoxide HCl	Librium
chlordiazepoxide HCl; amitriptyline HCl	Limbitrol
chlorhexidine gluconate	Hibiclens PerioChip
chlorhexidine gluconate mouth rinse	Peridex
Chloromycetin inj	chloramphenicol sodium succinate
chloroprocaine HCl	Nesacaine
Chloroptic ophth (W)	chloramphenicol ophth (W)
chloroquine phosphate	Aralen
chlorothiazide	Diuril
chloroxine (W)	Capitrol (W)
chlorpheniramine maleate	Chlor-Trimeton
chlorpheniramine maleate SR	*chlorpheniramine maleate SR*
chlorpromazine	Thorazine (WA)
chlorpropamide	Diabinese

chlorthalidone	Hygroton
Chlor-Trimeton	chlorpheniramine maleate
chlorzoxazone 250 mg	Paraflex
chlorzoxazone 500 mg	Parafon Forte DSC
Cholebrine	iocetamic acid
cholecalciferol	*cholecalciferol* Vitamin D3
cholestyramine resin	Questran; Prevalite
choline chloride inj	Intrachol
choline magnesium trisalicylate (W)	Trilisate (W)
Choloxin (W)	dextrothyroxine sodium (W)
choriogonadotropin alfa	Ovidrel
chorionic gonadotropin	*chorionic gonadotropin* HCL
Chronulac	lactulose
Chymodiactin	chymopapain
chymopapain	Chymodiactin
Cialis	tadalafil
ciclesonide nasal aerosol	Zetonna
ciclesonide nasal susp	Omnaris
ciclopirox cream and lotion	Loprox
ciclopirox soln	Penlac Nail Lacquer
cidofovir	Vistide
cilostazol	Pletal
Ciloxan	*ciprofloxacin ophth soln*
cimetidine HCl	Tagamet
Cimzia	certolizumab pegol
cinacalcet	Sensipar
cinacalet HCl	Senispar
Cinqair	reslizumab inj
Cinryze	C1 esterase inhibitor (Human)
Cinvanti	aprepitant inj
Cipro	*ciprofloxacin HCl*
Cipro HC Otic	ciprofloxacin; hydrocortisone otic
ciprofloxacin HCl	Cipro
ciprofloxacin ophth soln	Ciloxan
ciprofloxacin otic soln	Otiprio
ciprofloxacin; hydrocortisone otic	Cipro HC Otic
circlesonide inhalation	Alvesco
cisapride (W)	Propulsid (W)
cisatracurium besylate	Nimbex
cisplatin	cisplatin
citalopram hydrobromide	Celexa

cladribine	Leustatin (WA) Mavenclad
Claforan	cefotaxime sodium
Clarinex	desloratadine
clarithromycin	Biaxin
clarithromycin SR	Biaxin XL
Claritin	*loratadine*
Claritin D	*loratadine; pseudoephedrine sulfate*
clemastine fumarate	Tavist
Cleocin	clindamycin HCl
clevidipine inj emulsion	Cleviprex
Cleviprex	clevidipine inj emulsion
Climara	estradiol transdermal
clindamycin and benzoyl peroxide gel	Onexton
clindamycin HCl	Cleocin
clindamycin phosphate pledgets	Clindets
clindamycin; benzoyl peroxide gel	BenzaClin
Clindets	clindamycin phosphate pledgets
Clinoril	*sulindac*
clobazam	Onfi
clobazam oral film	Sympazan
clobetasol foam	Olux
clofarabine	Clolar
clofibrate	Atromid-S
Clolar	clofarabine
Clomid	*clomiphene citrate*
clomiphene citrate	Clomid
clomipramine HCl	Anafranil
clonazepam	Klonopin
clonidine HCl	Catapres
clonidine HCl inj	Duraclon
clopidogrel bisulfate	Plavix
clorazepate dipotassium	Tranxene
Clorpactin WCS-90	oxychlorosene sodium
clotrimazole	Gyne-Lotrimin Lotrimin Mycelex
clozapine	Clozaril
Clozaril	*clozapine*
Co Q-10	Coenzyme Q-10
coagulation factor IX (recombinant)	BeneFix
coagulation factor IX (recombinant) inj	Alprolix
coagulation factor IX inj	Ixinity
coagulation factor VII [recombinant] Fc fusion protein inj	Eloctate

coagulation factor VII a (recombinant) — NovoSeven

coagulation factor XIII A-subunit (recombinant) inj — Tretten

coal tar product — Zetar

Coartem — artemether/lumafentrine combination

cobimetinib — Cotellic

codeine phosphate; acetaminophen suspension — Capital w/ Codeine Suspension

codeine sulfate — *codeine sulfate*

codiene — see codeine

codiene sulfate — may have meant codeine sulfate

coenzyme Q10 — UbiQGel

Cogentin — benztropine mesylate

Cognex (W) — *tacrine HCL (W)*

Colace — *docusate sodium*

Colazal — *balsalazide disodium*

ColBENEMID (W) — *probenecid; colchicine (W)*

colchicine tablets — Colcrys

colchinine inj (W) — colchicine inj (W)

Colcrys — colchicine tablets

colesevelam HCl — Welchol

Colestid — colestipol HCl

colestipol HCl — Colestid

colistimethate sodium — Coly-Mycin M

colistin sulfate; hydrocortisone, and neomycin otic soln — Coly-Mycin S

collagen hemostat — Avitene

collagenase — Santyl

collagenase clostridium histolyticum inj — Xiaflex

Collyrium — tetrahydrozoline HCl ophth

Colomed — short chain fatty acids enema

Coly-Mycin M (WA) — *colistimethate sodium*

Coly-Mycin S — colistin sulfate; hydrocortisone, and neomycin otic soln

CoLyte — *polyethylene glycol-electrolyte soln*

CoLyte powder — polyethylene glycol 3350 and electrolytes

Combigan — brimonidine/timolol ophth soln

CombiPatch — norethindrone acetate; estradiol transdermal

Combivent — *ipratropium bromide; albuterol sulfate*

Combivir — lamivudine; zidovudine

Combunox — oxycodone HCl, ibuprofen

Cometriq — cabonzantinib

Compazine (WA) — *prochlorperazine*

Complera — emtricitabine, rilpivirine, and tenofovir disoproxil fumarate

Comtan — entacapone

Comvax — *Haemophilus b* conjugate; Hepatitis B vaccine

Concerta — *methylphenidate HCl SR*

Condylox — *podofilox gel*

conivaptan — Vaprisol

conjugated estrogens and bazedoxifene — Duavee

Consensi — amlodipine and celecoxib

Contrave — naltrexone and bupropion

ConZip — tramadol HCL SR

copanlisib inj — Aliqopa

Copaxone — glatiramer acetate Inj

Copiktra — duvelisib

CoQ10 — Coenzyme Q-10

Corcal — calcium carbonate and calcitriol

Cordarone — *amiodarone HCl*

Coreg — *carvedilol*

Corgard — *nadolol*

Corlanor — ivabradine

Corlopam — fenoldopam mesylate

Cortef — *hydrocortisone*

corticorellin ovine triflutate — Acthrel

corticotropin repository inj — Acthar PH

cortisone acetate — Cortone Acetate

Cortone Acetate — cortisone acetate

Cortrosyn — cosyntropin

Corvert — ibutilide fumarate

Cosentyx — secukinumab inj

Cosmegen — dactinomycin

Cosopt — *dorzolamide HCl; timolol maleate ophth soln*

cosyntropin — Cortrosyn

Cotellic — cobimetinib

Cotempla XR-ODT — methylphenidate extended-release orally disintegrating

Cotrim — sulfamethoxazole; trimethoprim

co-trimoxazole — Bactrim
Cotrim
Septra
sulfamethoxazole; trimethoprim

Coumadin — *warfarin sodium*

Covera HS — *verapamil HCl SR bedtime formulation*

Cozaar	losartan potassium	cyproheptadine HCl	cyproheptadine HCl
Cozar	may have meant Cozaar (losartan potassium)	Cyramza	ramucirumab inj
		Cystadane	betaine anhydrous
Creon	pancrelipase	Cystagon	cysteamine bitartrate
Cresemba	isavuconazonium sulfate tablets and inj	cysteamine bitartrate	Cystagon
		cysteamine bitartrate SR tablet	Procysbi
Crestor	rosuvastatin calcium		
Crinone	progesterone gel	Cystospaz-M	hyoscyamine sulfate SR
crisaborole oint	Eucrisa	Cytadren (W)	aminoglutethimide (W)
Crixivan	indinavir	cytarabine	cytarabine
crizotinib	Xalkori	cytarabine and daunorubicin liposome inj	Vixens
CroFab	crotalidae polyvalent immune fab (ovine)		
	rattlesnake anti-venom	cytarabine, liposomal inj	DepoCyt
crofelemer	Fulyzaq		
cromolyn sodium	Gastrocrom	Cytomel	liothyronine sodium
	Nasalcrom	Cytosar-U (WA)	cytarabine
	Opticrom	Cytotec	misoprostol
crotalidae polyvalent immune fab (ovine)	CroFab	Cytovene	ganciclovir
		Cytoxan	cyclophosphamide
crotamiton	Eurax		
Crysvita	burosumab-twza inj		
Cubicin	daptomycin		
Cumadin	may have meant Coumadin (warfarin sodium)		
			D
Cuprimine	penicillamine		
Curosurf	poractant alpha intratracheal susp	D.H.E. 45	dihydroergot-amine mesylate inj
Cutivate	fluticasone propionate cream & ointment	dabigatran etexilate	Pradaxa
		dabrafenib	Tafinlar
Cuvitru	Immune Globulin Subcutaneous (Human) inj	dacarbazine	DTIC-Dome
		daclatasvir	Daklinza
		daclizumab	Zenapax
Cuvposa	glycopyrrolate oral soln	daclizumab inj	Zinbryta
cyanocobalamin nasal gel	Nascobal	Dacogen	decitabine inj
		dacomitinib	Vizimpro
cyclobenzaprine HCl	Flexeril	dactinomycin	Cosmegen
cyclobenzaprine SR	Amrix	Daklinza	daclatasvir
Cyclogyl	cyclopentolate HCl	dalbavancin inj	Dalvance
cyclopentolate HCl	Cyclogyl	dalfampridine	Ampyra
cyclophosphamide	Cytoxan	Daliresp	roflumilast
	Neosar	dalteparin sodium	Fragmin
cycloserine	Seromycin	Dalvance	dalbavancin inj
cyclosporin ophth soln	Cequa	danaparoid sodium	Orgaran
cyclosporine	Sandimmune	danazol (W)	Danocrine (W)
cyclosporine capsules (modified) and oral soln	Neoral	Danocrine (WA)	danazol
		Dantrium	dantrolene sodium
		dantrolene sodium	Dantrium
cyclosporine capsules, (modified)	Gengraf	dantrolene sodium inj	Ryanodex
		dapagliflozin	Farxiga
cyclosporine ophth emulsion	Restasis	dapsone	dapsone
		daptomycin	Cubicin
Cyklokapron	tranexamic acid inj	Daranide (W)	Dichlorphenamide (W)
Cylert (W)	pemoline (W)	Daraprim	pyrimethamine
Cyltezo	adalimumab-adbm inj	daratumumab inj	Darzalex
Cymbalta	duloxetine	darbepoetin alfa	Aranesp
Cypher Stent	sirolimus-eluting stent	darifenacin	Enablex
		darunavir	Prezista

darunavir and cobicistat	Prezcobix
Darvocet-N 100 (W)	*propoxyphene napsylate acetaminophen (W)*
Darvon (W)	*propoxyphene HCl (W)*
Darvon Compound 65 (W)	*propoxyphene HCl; aspirin; caffeine (W)*
Darzalex	daratumumab inj
dasabuvir, ombitasvir, paritaprevir, and ritonavir SR tablets	Viekira XR
dasatinib	Sprycel
daunorubicin citrate liposomal	DaunoXome
daunorubicin HCl	Cerubidine
DaunoXome	daunorubicin citrate liposomal
dAVP	deamino-vasopressin
Daypro	oxaprozin
DDAVP	desmopressin acetate (1-deamino-8-D-arginine vasopressin) (injection, nasal spray, and tablet)
Debrox	carbamide peroxide otic
Decadron	*dexamethasone*
Deca-Durabolin (W)	nandrolone decanoate (W)
decitabine inj	Dacogen
Declomycin	demeclocycline HCl
deferasirox	Exjade
deferoxamine mesylate	Desferal
defibrotide sodium inj	Defitelio
Defitelio	defibrotide sodium inj
degarelix acetate inj	Firmagon
delafloxacin	Baxdela
delavirdine mesylate	Rescriptor
Delestrogen	*estradiol valerate*
Delstrigo	doravirine, lamivudine, and tenofovir disoproxil fumarate
Demadex	*toresmide*
demecarium bromide (W)	Humorsol (W)
demeclocycline HCl	Declomycin
Demerol	*meperidine HCl*
Demser	metyrosine
Denavir	penciclovir cream
dengue tetravalent vaccine, live inj	Dengvaxia
Dengvaxia	dengue tetravalent vaccine, live inj
denileukin diftitox	Ontak
denosumab inj	Prolia Xgeva

deoxycholic acid inj	Kybella
Depacon	*valproate sodium inj*
Depakene	*valproic acid*
Depakote	*divalproex sodium*
Depakote ER	*divalproex sodium SR*
Deplin	a medical food capsule containing L-methylfolate
Depo Medrol	methylprednisolone acetate SR inj
Depo Provera	medroxyprogesterone acetate SR inj
DepoCyt	cytarabine, liposomal inj
DepoDur	morphine sulfate extended-release liposome inj
depomedral	may have meant Depo-Medrol (*methylprednisolone acetate SR inj*)
depomedrol	may have meant Depo-Medrol (*methylprednisolone acetate SR inj*)
Depo-Medrol	methylprednisolone acetate SR inj
Depo-Provera	medroxyprogesterone acetate SR inj
Depo-Testosterone	testosterone cypionate SR inj
Descovy	emtricitabine and tenofovir alafenamide
Desferal	*deferoxamine mesylate*
desflurane	Suprane
desipramine HCl	Norpramin
Desirudin	iprivask
desloratadine	Clarinex
desmopressin acetate	DDAVP
desmopressin acetate nasal spray	Noctiva
desogestrel and ethinyl estradiol	Azurette Kariva Mircette
desogestrel; ethinyl estradiol	Desogen Ortho-Cept
desonide	Tridesilon
desoximetasone	Topicort
Desoxyn	*methamphetamine HCl*
desvenlafaxine succinate	Pristiq
Desyrel (WA)	*trazodone HCl*
Detrol	tolterodine tartrate
Detrol LA	tolterodine tartrate (SR)
deutetrabenazine	Austedo
Dexamet stent	dexamethasone-eluting stent
dexamethasone	Decadron Hexadrol

dexamethasone intravitreal implant	Ozurdex
dexamethasone-eluting stent	Dexamet stent
dexchlorpheniramine maleate SR	*dexchlorpheniramine maleate SR*
Dexedrine (WA)	dextroamphetamine sulfate
dexfenfluramine HCl (W)	Redux (W)
Dexferrum	*iron dextran inj*
dexlansoprazole	Kapidex
Dexilant	*dexlansoprazole*
dexmedetomidine HCl inj	Precedex
dexrazoxane	Zinecard
dextroamphetamine sulfate	Dexedrine (WA)
dextromethorphan HBr; quinidine sulfate	Nuedexta
dextrothyroxine sodium (W)	Choloxin (W)
DiaBeta	*glyburide*
Diabinese	*chlorpropamide*
Diamox (WA)	acetazolamide
Diamox Sequels	acetazolamide SR
Diapid (W)	lypressin (W)
Diastat	diazepam rectal gel
diatrizoate meglumine and diatrizoate sodium oral soln	Gastrografin
diazepam	Valium
diazepam emulsified inj	Dizac
diazepam rectal gel	Diastat
diazoxide	Hyperstat
Dibenzyline	phenoxybenz-amine HCl
dibucaine	Nupercainal
dichlorphenamide	Keveyis
dichlorphenamide (W)	Daranide
Diclegis	doxylamine succinate and pyridoxine HCl
diclofenac epolamine topical system	Licart
diclofenac gel	Solaraze
diclofenac potassium	Cataflam
diclofenac potassium for oral soln	Cambia
diclofenac sodium	Voltaren
diclofenac sodium inj	Dyloject
diclofenac sodium SR	Voltaren-XR
diclofenac sodium topical soln	Pennsaid
diclofenac sodium; misoprostol	Arthrotec

dicloxacillin sodium	*dicloxacillin sodium*
dicyclomine HCl	Bentyl
didanosine	Videx
didanosine SR	Videx EC
Didronel	*etidronate disodium*
diethylcarbamazine citrate	Hetrazan
diethylpropion HCl	*diethylpropion HCl*
Differin	adapalene
Dificid	*fidaxomicin*
diflorasone diacetate	Florone
Diflucan	fluconazole
diflunisal	*diflunisal*
difluprednate ophth emulsion	Durezol
Digibind	digoxin immune fab
digoxin	Lanoxin
digoxin capsules (W)	Lanoxicaps (W)
digoxin immune fab	Digibind
dihydroergotamine mesylate inj	D.H.E. 45
dihydroergotamine mesylate nasal spray	Migranal
dihydrotestosterone transdermal	Androgel-DHT
Dilacor XR	*diltiazem HCl SR*
Dilantin	*phenytoin*
Dilaudid	*hydromorphone HCl*
diltiazem HCl	Cardizem
diltiazem HCl SR	Cardizem CD
diltiazem HCl SR	*diltiazem HCl SR*
	Dilacor XR
	Tiazac
diltiazem maleate SR	Tiamate
dimenhydrinate	Dramamine
dimercaprol	BAL in Oil
dimethyl fumarate	Tecfidera
dinoprostone gel	Prepidil
dinoprostone vaginal insert	Cervidil
dinoprostone vaginal suppositories	Prostin E2
dinutuximab inj	Unituxin
Diovan	valsartan
Diovan HCT	valsartan; hydrochlorothiazide
Dipentum	olsalazine sodium
diphenhydramine HCl	Benadryl
diphenoxylate HCl; atropine sulfate	Lomotil
diphtheria and tetanus toxoids and acellular pertussis adsorbed and inactivated poliovirus vaccine	Kinrix

diphtheria and tetanus toxoids and acellular pertussis adsorbed, inactivated poliovirus and Haemophilus b conjugate	Pentacel
diphtheria and tetanus toxoids and pertussis vaccine, adsorbed	DTwP
diphtheria, tetanus, and acellular pertussis vaccine (adult type) (TdaP)	Adacel
dipivefrin	Propine
Diprivan	propofol
Diprosone (WA)	*betamethasone dipropionate*
dipyridamole	Persantine
dirithromycin	Dynabac
Disalcid	salsalate
disopyramide phosphate	Norpace
disulfiram	Antabuse
Ditropan	*oxybutynin chloride*
Diulo (WA)	*metolazone*
Diuril	*chlorothiazide*
divalproex sodium	Depakote
divalproex sodium SR	Depakote ER
Dizac	*diazepam emulsified ing*
DMHA	dimethylhexylamine (Octodrine) (over-the-counter)
dobutamine HCl	Dobutrex
Dobutrex (WA)	*dobutamine HCl*
docetaxel	Taxotere
docusate calcium	Surfak
docusate sodium	Colace
dofetilide	Tikosyn
dolasetron mesylate	Anzemet
Dolophine	*methadone HCl*
dolutegravir	Tivicay
dolutegravir and lamivudine	Dovato
dolutegravir and rilpivirine	Juluca
Domeboro	aluminum acetate
donepezil HCl	Aricept
dopamine HCl	Intropin (WA)
Dopar (W)	*levodopa (W)*
Dopram	doxapram HCl
Doptelet	avatrombopag
doravirine	Pifeltro
Doribax	doripenem
doripenem	Doribax
dornase alpha	Pulmozyme

Doryx	*doxycycline hyclate SR*
dorzolamide HCl	Trusopt
dorzolamide HCl; timolol maleate ophth soln	Cosopt
Dostinex (WA)	*cabergoline*
Dovato	dolutegravir and lamivudine
Dovonex	calcipotriene cream
doxacurium chloride (W)	Nuromax (W)
doxapram HCl	Dopram
doxazosin mesylate	Cardura
doxepin HCl	*doxepin HCl* Sinequan
doxepin HCl cream	Prudoxin
doxercalciferol	Hectorol
Doxil	doxorubicin, liposomal
doxorubicin HCl	Adriamycin Rubex
doxorubicin, liposomal	Doxil
doxycycline hycate SR	Doryx
doxycycline hyclate	Vibramycin
doxycycline hyclate gel	Atridox
doxylamine succinate and pyridoxine HCl	Bonjesta Diclegis
Dramamine	*dimenhydrinate*
Drisdol	*ergocalciferol*
Dristan Long Lasting	*oxymetazoline HCl*
Drixoral Syrup	pseudoephedrine HCl; bromphiramine maleate
dronabinol	Marinol
dronabinol oral soln	Syndros
dronedarone	Multaq
droperidol (W)	Inapsine (W)
drospireno	Slynd
drospirenone; ethinyl estradiol	Gianvi Yasmin
Droxia	*hydroxyurea*
droxidopa	Northera
Dsuvia	sufentanil sublingual tablet
DTIC-Dome (WA)	*dacarbazine*
Duaklir	aclidinium bromide and formoterol fumarate inhaler
Duavee	conjugated estrogens and bazedoxifene
Ducolax	may have meant Dulcolax (Bisacodyl)
Duetact	pioglitazone HCl and glimepiride
Duexis	*ibuprofen and famotidine*

dulaglutide inj	Trulicity
Dulcolax	*bisacodyl*
Dulera	*mometasone furoate and formoterol fumarate inhalation*
duloxetine	Cymbalta
Duobrii	halobetasol propionate and tazarotene lotion
DuoNeb	ipratropium bromide and albuterol sulfate inhalation soln
Duopa	carbidopa/levodopa enteral susp
dupilumab inj	Dupixent
Dupixent	dupilumab inj
Durabolin (W)	nandrolone phenpropionate (W)
Duraclon	clonidine HCl epidural inj
Duragesic	*fentanyl transdermal*
Duramorph	morphine sulfate inj
Durezol	difluprednate ophth emulsion
Duricef (WA)	*cefadroxil*
Durolane	hyaluronic acid cosmetic Inj
	hyaluronic acid inj
durvalumab inj	Imfinzi
dutasteride	Avodart
Dutrebis	lamivudine and raltegravir
duvelisib	Copiktra
Duzallo	allopurinol and lesinurad
Dyanavel XR	amphetamine SR oral susp
Dyazide	*triamterene 37.5 mg; hydrochlorothiazide 25 mg*
Dyloject	diclofenac sodium inj
Dymista	azelastine HCl and fluticasone proprionate nasal spray
Dynabac	dirithromycin
DynaCirc	*isradipine*
dyphylline	Lufyllin
Dyrenium	triamterene
Dysport	abobotulinumtoxin A inj

E

E.E.S. 400	erythromycin ethylsuccinate
ecallantine inj	Kalbitor
EchoGen	perflenapent emulsion
echothiophate iodide	Phospholine Iodide
Ecotrin	*aspirin EC*

eculizumab	Soliris
edaravone inj	Radicava
Edarbi	*azilsartan medoxomil*
Edecrin	ethacrynic acid
edetate disodium	Endrate
Edex	alprostadil inj
edoxaban inj	Savaysa
edrophonium chloride	Tensilon
efalizumab	Raptiva
efavirenz	Sustiva
efavirenz, emtricitabine, and tenofovir	Atripla
Efexor	see Effexor XR (venlafaxine HCl SR)
Effexor (WA)	*venlafaxine HCl*
Effexor XR	*venlafaxine HCl SR*
Effient	prasugrel
efinaconazole topical solution	Jublia
eflornithine HCl cream	Vaniqa
Efudex	fluorouracil cream
Egrifta	tesamorelin acetate inj
elagolix	Orilissa
elapegademase-lvlr inj	Revcovi
Elaprase	idursulfase
Elara (1:1) hybrid	blended of CBD and THC strains of Cannabis (content ratio 1:1, CBD [cannabidiol] to THC [tetrahydrocannabinol]) (a medical marijuana product by Knox Medical)
Elavil (WA)	*amitriptyline HCl*
elbasvir and grazoprevir	Zepatier
Eldepryl	selegiline HCl
Eldisine (W)	vindesine sulfate (W)
Elelyso	taliglucerase alfa
Elepsia XR	levetiracetam SR
Elestat	epinastine
eletriptan HBr	Relpax
Elidel	pimecrolimus cream
Eligard	*leuprolide acetate*
eliglustat	Cerdelga
Eliquis	apixaban
Elitek	rasburicase
Elivil	may have meant Elavil (amitriptyline HCl)
Elixophyllin	theophylline
Ellence	*epirubicin HCl*
Ellipta	umeclidinium
Elmiron	pentosan polysulfate sodium

Elocon	mometasone furoate topical
Eloctate	coagulation factor VII [recombinant] Fc fusion protein inj
Eloquis	may have meant Eliquis (apixaban)
elosulfase alfa	Vimizim
elotuzumab inj	Explicit
Eloxatin	oxaliplatin
Elspar	asparaginase
eltrombopag	Promacta
eluxadoline	Viberzi
elvitegravir, cobicistat, emtricitabine, and tenofovir	Stribild
elvitegravir, cobicistat, emtricitabine, and tenofovir alafenamide	Genvoya
elvitegravir, cobicistat, emtricitabine, and tenofovir disoproxil fumarate (also known as E/C/F/ TDF) (single-tablet regimen)	Stribild
Elzonris	tagraxofusp-erzs inj
Emadine	emedastine difumarate opthth soln
emapalumab-lzsg inj	Gamifant
Embeda	morphine sulfate and naltrexone HCl SR
Emcyt	estramustine phosphate sodium
emedastine difumarate opthth soln	Emadine
Emend capsules	aprepitant
Emend inj	Fosaprepitant
Emflaza	defrazacort
Emgality	galcanezumab-gnlm inj
emicizumab-kxwh inj	Hemlibra
EMLA Cream	lidocaine; prilocaine cream
empagliflozin	Jardiance
empagliflozin and linagliptin	Glyxambi
empagliflozin and metformin HCl SR	Synjardy SR
Empirin with codeine #3 and #4	*aspirin 325 mg with codeine phosphate (30 and 60 mg)*
Empliciti	elotuzumab inj
emtricitabine	Emtriva
emtricitabine and tenofovir alafenamide	Descovy

emtricitabine and tenofovir disoproxil fumarate	Truvada
emtricitabine, efavirenz, and tenofovir	Atripla
emtricitabine, rilpivirine, and tenofovir disoproxil fumarate	Complera
Emtriva	emitricitabine
E-Mycin	erythromycin
Enablex	darifenacin
enalapril maleate	Vasotec
enalapril maleate; felodipine SR (W)	Lexxel (W)
enalapril maleate; hydrochlorothiazide	Vaseretic
enasidenib	Idhifa
Enbrel	etanercept
Endari	L-glutamine oral powder
Endocet	oxycodone HCl; acetaminophen
Endrate	edetate disodium
Enduron	*methyclothiazide*
enflurane	Ethrane
enfuvirtide	Fuzeon
Engerix-B	*hepatitis B vaccine*
Enkaid	encainide HCl
enoxaparin sodium	Lovenox
entacapone	Comtan
entecavir	Baraclude
Entereg	alvimopan
Entex LA	phenylpropanolamine HCl; guaifenesin SR
Entocort	budesonide
Entocort EC	budesonide capsule
Entresto	valsartan and sacubitril
Entyvio	vedolizumab inj
Envarsus XR	tacrolimus SR
enzalutamide	Xtandi
Eovist	gadoxetate disodium inj
Epanova	omega-3-caboxylic acids
Epclusa	sofosbuvir and velpatasvir
ephedrine sulfate inj	Akovaz
Epidiolex	cannabidiol cannabidiol oral soln
epinastine	Elestat
epinephrine	Adrenalin
epinephrine HCl (auto-injector) inj	Auvi Q
epirubicin HCl	Ellence
Epivir	lamivudine
Epivir HBV	lamivudine
eplerenone	Inspra

epoetin alfa	Epogen
	Procrit
epoetin alfa-epbx inj	Retacrit
Epogen	epoetin alfa
epoprostenol sodium	Flolan
eprosartan mesylate	Teveten
eprosartan mesylate;	Teveten HCT
hydrochloro-	
thiazide	
eptifibatide	Integrilin
Equanil (WA)	*meprobamate*
eRapa	rapamycin
eravacycline inj	Xerava
Eraxis	anidulafungin IV
Erbitux	cetuximab
Erelzi	etanercept-szzs
erenumab aooe inj	Aimovig
Ergamisol (W)	levamisole HCl (W)
ergocalciferol	Calciferol
	Drisdol
ergoloid mesylates	Hydergine
ergotamine tartrate	Ergostat
ergotamine tartrate;	Cafergot
caffeine	
Ergotrate	ergonovine maleate
eribulin mesylate inj	Halaven
Erivedge	vismodegib
Erleada	apalutamide
erlotinib	Tarceva
Ertaczo	sertaconazole
ertapenem sodium	Invanz
ertugliflozin	Steglatro
ertugliflozin and	Segluromet
metformin HCl	
ertugliflozin and	Steglujan
sitagliptin	
Ery-Tab	erythromycin EC
Erythrocin Stearate	erythromycin stearate
erythromycin	*erythromycin*
	E-Mycin
erythromycin base	PCE Dispertab
coated particles	
erythromycin EC	Ery-Tab
erythromycin	E.E.S. 400
ethylsuccinate	
erythromycin	Pediazole
ethylsuccinate;	
sulfisoxazole	
erythromycin stearate	Erythrocin Stearate
erythromycin;	Benzamycin
benzoyl peroxide	
topical gel	
Esbriet	pirfenidone
Escherichia coli	E. coli
escitalopram oxalate	Lexapro
Esclim	*estradiol transdermal*
Eserine Sulfate	physostigmine ophth
	ointment

Esgic	butalbital, acetaminophen,
	and caffeine
Esidrix (WA)	hydrochlorothiazide
Eskata	hydrogen peroxide
	topical soln
esketamine nasal	Spravato
spray	
eslicarbazepine	Aptiom
esmolol HCl	Brevibloc
esomeprazole	Nexium
magnesium	
Esperoct	turoctocog alfa pegol inj
estazolam	*estazolam*
Estrace	*estradiol*
Estraderm	*estradiol transdermal*
estradiol	Estrace
	may have meant
	estradiol
estradiol hemihydrate	Vagifem
vaginal tab	
estradiol transdermal	Alora
	Climara
	Esclim
	Estraderm
	Vivelle
estradiol transdermal	Menostar
system	
estradiol vaginal	Imvexxy
insert	
estradiol vaginal ring	Estring
estradiol valerate	Delestrogen
estradiol valerate	Natazia
and dienogest	
estramustine	Emcyt
phosphate sodium	
Estratest	estrogens, esterified;
	methyltestosterone
Estring	estradiol vaginal ring
estrogens conjugate,	Cenestin
A synthetic	
estrogens, conjugated	Premarin
estrogens,	Premphase
conjugated;	Prempro
medroxypro-	
gesterone acetate	
estrogens, esterified	Estratest H.S.
methyltestosterone,	
half strength	
estrogens, esterified;	Estratest
methyltestosterone	
estropipate	Ogen
Estrostep	norethindrone acetate;
	ethinyl estradiol
eszopiclone	Lunesta
etanercept	Enbrel
etanercept-szzs	Erelzi
etanercept-ykro	Eticovo
etelcalcetide inj	Parsabiv

E
R

675

eteplirsen inj   Exondys 51
ethacrynic acid   Edecrin
ethambutol HCl   Myambutol
ethchlorvynol (W)   Placidyl (W)
Ethezyme   papain; urea oint
ethinyl estradiol;   Seasonale
  (91 day cycle)
ethionamide   Trecator-SC
Ethmozine   moricizine
ethosuximide   Zarontin
Ethrane   enflurane
ethyl chloride   ethyl chloride
Ethyol   amifostine
Eticovo   etanercept-ykro
etidronate disodium   Didronel
etodolac   *etodolac*
etomidate   Amidate
etonogestrel implant   Nexplano
  Nexplanon?
etonogestrel; ethinyl   NuvaRing
  estrodial vagina
  ring
Etopophos   etoposide phosphate
  diethanolate
etoposide   VePesid
etoposide phosphate   Etopophos
  diethanolate
Etrafon   *perphenazine;*
  amitriptyline HCl
etravirine   Intelence
Eucrisa   crisaborole oint
Euflexxa   sodium Hyaluronate
  Intra-articular Inj
Eulexin (WA)   *flutamide*
Eurax   crotamiton
Euthroid (WA)   liotrix
Eutonyl   pargyline HCl
Evenity   romosozumab inj
everolimus   Zortress
everolimus-eluting   Promus
  coronary stent   Xience V
  system
Evista   raloxifene HCl
Evithrom   thrombin, topical
  (human)
evolocumab inj   Repatha
Evotaz   atazanavir and cobicistat
Evoxac   cevimeline HCl
Exelon   *rivastigmine tartrate*
exemestane   Aromasin
exenatide inj   Bydureon
  Byetta
Exforge   amlodipine; valsartan
Exjade   deferasirox
Ex-Lax   *sennosides*
Exondys 51   eteplirsen inj
Exparel   bupivacaine Liposome
  inj

Extavia   interferon beta-1b
Extraneal   icodextrin 7.5% with
  electrolyte peritoneal
  dialysis solution
Eylea   aflibercept intravitreal inj
ezetimibe   Zetia
ezetimibe and   Liptruzet
  atorvastatin
ezetimibe; simvastin   Vytorin
ezogabine   Potiga

F

Fabrazyme   agalsidase beta
Factive   gemifloxacin mesylate
factor IX complex inj   Profilnine SD
factor IX, concentrate   BeneFix
Factrel (W)   gonadorelin HCl (W)
famciclovir   Famvir
famotidine   Pepcid
famotidine, oral   Pepcid RPD
  disintegrating
  tablet
Famvir   *famciclovir*
Fanapt   iloperidone
Fansidar   sulfadoxine;
  pyrimethamine
Fareston   toremifene citrate
Farxiga   dapagliflozin
Farydak   panobinostat
Fasenra   benralizumab inj
Faslodex   fulvestrant
Fastin   *phentermine HCl*
fat emulsion   Intralipid
  Liposyn II and III
FDgard   over-the-counter
  capsule for function
  dyspepsia containing
  coated microspheres
  of caraway oil and
  l-Menthol, along with
  fiber and amino acids
  (from gelatin protein)
febuxostat   Uloric
Feiba   anti-inhibitor coagulant
  complex inj (Factor
  VIII inhibitor
  bypassing activity)
felbamate   Felbatol
Felbatol   felbamate
Feldene   *piroxicam*
felodipine   Plendil
Femara   letrozole
Femhrt   norethindrone acetate;
  ethinyl estradiol

FemPatch (WA)	*estradiol transdermal*	fingolimod	Gilenya
fenfluramine HCl (W)	Pondimin (W)	Fioricet	butalbital, acetaminophen, and caffeine
fenofibrate	Triglide	Fiorinal	*butalbital; aspirin;*
fenofibric acid	TriLipix		*caffeine*
fenoldopam mesylate	Corlopam	Firazyr	*icatibant*
fenoprofen calcium	Nalfon	Firdapse	amifampridine phosphate
fentanyl base sublingual liquid	Subsys	Firmagon	*degarelix acetate inj*
fentanyl citrate buccal lozenge	Actiq	Firvanq	vancomycin HCl for oral soln
fentanyl citrate inj (W)	Sublimaze (W)	Flagyl	*metronidazole*
		Flagyl ER	*metronidazole SR*
fentanyl iontophoretic transdermal	Ionsys	flavocoxid	Limbrel
		flavoxate HCl	Urispas
Fentanyl Oralet (WA)	*fentanyl transmucosal*	Flaxedil (W)	gallamine triethiodide (W)
fentanyl transdermal	Duragesic	flecainide acetate	Tambocor
Fentnyl	may have meant Fentanyl	Flexeril	*cyclobenzaprine HCl*
Feosol	*ferrous sulfate*	flibanserin	Addyi
Ferahemme	ferumoxytol inj	Flolan	epoprostenol sodium
Fergon	*ferrous gluconate*	Flomax	*tamsulosin HCl*
Feridex	ferumoxide HCl	Flonase	fluticasone propionate spray
Fer-In-Sol	*ferrous sulfate*	Florastor Kids	a probiotic (S. boulardii)
ferric carboxymaltose	Injectafer	florbetapir F18 inj	Amyvid
ferric citrate	Auryxia	Florinef (WA)	*fludrocortisone acetate*
	ferric citrate	Florone	diflorasone diacetate
ferric pyrophosphate citrate soln	Triferic	Floropryl	isoflurophate
		Flovent (W)	fluticasone propionate spray (W)
Ferriprox	deferiprone		
Ferrlecit	sodium ferric gluconate complex in sucrose inj	Flowtuss	hydrocodone bitartrate and guaifenesin soln
ferrous gluconate	Fergon	Floxin	*ofloxacin*
ferrous sulfate	Feosol	Floxin Otic	*ofloxacin otic soln*
	Fer-In-Sol	floxuridine	FUDR
ferrous sulfate SR	SlowFe	Fluad	influenza vaccine, adjuvanted inj
Fertinex	urofollitropin for inj		
ferumoxide HCl	Feridex	Flublok	influenza vaccine inj
ferumoxytol inj	Feraheme	fluconazole	Diflucan
fesoterodine fumarate	Toviaz	flucytosine	Ancobon
		Fludara	*fludarabine phosphate*
Fetzima	levomilnacipran	fludarabine phosphate	Fludara
fexofenadine HCl	Allegra	fludrocortisone acetate	Florinef
Fiasp	insulin aspart inj		
fibrin sealant, human, topical	Artiss	Flumadine	rimantadine
		flumazenil	Romazicon
fibrinogen concentrate, human inj	Riastap	flunisolide	Aero Bid
		fluocinolone acetonide	Synalar
fidaxomicin	Dificid	fluocinolone acetonide intravitreal implant	Iluvien
filgrastim	Neupogen		
filgrastim-sndz inj	Zarxio	fluocinonide	Lidex
Finacea	azelaic acid topical foam	fluorescein sodium soln	Fluorescite
finafloxacin otic susp	Xtoro		
finasteride	Propecia 1 mg tablet	fluorescein sodium strips	Fluor-I-Strip
	Proscar 5 mg tablet		
Finevin	azelaic cream		

F R

Fluorescite	fluorescein sodium soln
Fluor-I-Strip	fluorescein sodium strips
fluorometholone	FML
Fluoroplex	fluorouracil cream
fluorouracil cream	Carac
	Efudex
	Fluoroplex
fluorouracil inj	fluorouracil inj
Fluothane	halothane
fluoxetine HCl	Prozac
	Sarafem
fluphenazine	*fluphenazine*
flurbiprofen	Ansaid
flutamide (W)	Eulexin (W)
fluticasone furoate and vilanterol inhalation powder	Breo Ellipta
fluticasone furoate inhalation powder	Arnuity Ellipta
fluticasone propionate cream & ointment	Cutivate
fluticasone propionate spray	Flonase
fluticasone propionate spray (W)	Flovent (W)
fluticasone propionate; salmeterol inhalation powder	Advair Diskus
fluvastatin sodium	Lescol
FML	fluorometholone
Focalin	dexmethylphenidate HCl
Folex PFS (WA)	*methotrexate inj*
folic acid	Folvite
Follistim	follitropin beta
follitropin alfa	Gonal-F
follitropin beta	Follistim
Folotyn	pralatrexate inj
Folvite	*folic acid*
fomepizole	Antizol
fondaparinux sodium	Arixtra
Foradil	formoterol fumarate
Forane	*isoflurane*
formoterol fumarate	Foradil
Fortaz	*ceftazidime*
Forteo	teriparatide
Fosamax	*alendronate sodium*
fosamprenavir calcium	Lexiva
Fosaprepitant	Emend inj
foscarnet (W)	Foscavir (W)
Foscavir (W)	foscarnet (W)
fosfomycin tromethamine	Monurol
fosinopril sodium	Monopril
fosphenytoin sodium	Cerebyx
fospropofol disodium inj	Lusedra

Fosrenol	lanthanum carbonate
fostamatinib disodium hexahydrate	Tavalisse
Fragmin	dalteparin sodium
fremanezumab-vfrm inj	Ajovy
Fresenius	tigecycline inj
Frova	frovatriptan succinate
frovatriptan succinate	Frova
FUDR	*floxuridine*
Fulphila	pegfilgrastim-jmdb inj
fulvestrant	Faslodex
Fulyzaq	crofelemer
Furacin (W)	nitrofurazone (W)
furosemide	Lasix
Fusilev	levoleucovorin for injection
Fuzeon	enfuvirtide
Fycompa	perampanel

G

gabapentin	Neurontin
gabapentin enacarbil	Horizant
gabapentin enacarbil SR	Horizant
Gabitril	tiagabine HCl
gadobenate dimeglumine	MultiHance
gadofosveset trisodium inj	Ablavar Vasovist
gadopentetate dimeglumine	Magnevist
gadoteridol	ProHance
gadoversetamide	OptiMark
gadoxetate disodium inj	Eovist
Galafold	migalastat
galantamine HBr (hydrobromide)	Razadyne (formerly called Reminyl)
galcanezumab-gnlm inj	Emgality
gallium nitrate	Ganite
galsulfase	Naglazyme
Galvus	vildagliptin
Galzin	zinc acetate
GAMASTAN	immune globulin [human]
Gamifant	emapalumab-lzsg inj
Gamimune N	*immune globulin intravenous*
Gammagard S/D	*immune globulin intravenous*
Gammaplex	immune globulin, IV, human inj

Gamunex-C	immune globulin (human) inj
ganciclovir	Cytovene
ganciclovir ophthalmic implant (W)	Vitrasert (W)
ganirelix acetate	Antagon
Ganite	gallium nitrate
Gantanol (W)	sulfamethoxazole (W)
Garamycin	*gentamicin sulfate*
Gardasil	papillomavirus recombinant vaccine quadrivalent (types 6, 11, 16, 18) human
Gardasil 9	papillomavirus 9-valent (types 6, 11, 16,18, 31, 33, 45, 52, and 58) vaccine, recombinant, human
Gastrocrom	cromolyn sodium
Gastrografin	diatrizoate meglumine and diatrizoate sodium oral soln
gatifloxacin (W)	Tequin (W)
gatifloxacin ophth soln	Zymar
Gattex	teduglutide
Gazyva	obinutuzumab
gefitinib	Iressa
gemcitabine HCl	Gemzar
gemfibrozil	Lopid
gemifloxacin	Factive
Gemma hybrid	is a hybrid Cannabis product with a high THC content (content ratio 40:1,THC [tetrahydrocannabinol] to CBD [cannabidiol])
gemtuzumab ozogamicin	Mylotarg
Gemzar	gemcitabine HCl
Gengraf	*cyclosporine capsules, (modified)*
Genitor	nitroglycerin powder for sublingual use
Genotropin	*somatropin for inj*
gentamicin sulfate	Garamycin
gentamycin	see gentamicin (correct spelling)
Genvoya	elvitegravir, cobicistat, emtricitabine, and tenofovir alafenamide
Geocillin (W)	carbenicillin (W)
Geodon	ziprasidone HCl
Geref	sermorelin acetate
Gianvi	drospirenone; ethinyl estradiol
GiaPreza	angiotensin II acetate inj

Gilenya	fingolimod
Gilotrif	afatinib
gilteritinib	Xospata
glatiramer acetate Inj	Copaxone Glatopa
Glatopa	glatiramer acetate Inj
glecaprevir and pibrentasvir	Mavyret
Gleevac	may have meant Gleevec (imatinib mesylate)
	imatinib mesylate
Gleolan	aminolevulinic HCl acid tablets (a fluorescing optical imaging agent)
Gleostine	lomustine
Gliadel	carmustine implantable wafer
glimepiride	Amaryl
glipizide	Glucotrol
glipizide SR	Glucotrol XL
glipside; metformin	Metaglip
GlucaGen	glucagon (rDNA origin)
glucagon	glucagon
glucagon (rDNA origin)	GlucaGen
glucarpidase inj	Voraxaze
Glucola (W)	glucose polymer solution, 50 grams (screening for gestational diabetes, the 50 g, 1-hour glucose challenge test)
Glucophage	*metformin HCl*
Glucophage XR	*metformin HCl SR*
Glucotrol	*glipizide*
Glucotrol XL	*glipizide SR*
Glucovance	*glyburide; metformin HCl*
glyburide	DiaBeta Micronase
glyburide micronized	Glynase
glyburide; metformin HCl	Glucovance
glycerin ophth soln	Ophthalgan
GlycoLax	polyethylene glycol 3350
glycopyrrolate	Robinul
glycopyrrolate and formoterol fumarate inhalation aerosol	Bevespi Aerosphere
glycopyrronium cloth	Qbrexza
Glydo	lidocaine HCl jelly
Glynase	*glyburide micronized*
Glyset	miglitol
Glyxambi	empagliflozin and linagliptin
Gocovri	amantadine SR

G
R

golimumab	Simponi	*Haemophilus b*	ActHIB/Tripedia
GoLYTELY	*polyethylene*	conjugate vaccine	
	glycolectrolyte soln	reconstituted with	
Golytely	sodium sulfate, sodium	diphtheria and	
	bicarbonate, sodium	tetanus toxoids and	
	chloride, and	acellular pertussis	
	potassium chloride	vaccine adsorbed	
	(for bowel cleansing	*Haemophilus b* con-	Comvax
	prior to gastrointestinal	jugate; Hepatitis B	
	examination)	vaccine	
GoLYTELY powder	polyethylene glycol 3350	haemophilus b vaccine	HibTITER
	and electrolytes		PedvaxHIB
gonadorelin HCl	Factrel (W)	halcinonide	Halog
(W)		Halcion	*triazolam*
Gonal-F	follitropin alfa	Haldol	*haloperidol*
goserelin acetate	Zoladex	Halfan	halofantrine HCl
implant		halobetasol	Duobrii
Gralise	*gabapentin ER*	propionate and	
granisetron HCl	Kytril	tazarotene lotion	
granisetron inj SR	Sustol	halobetasol	Bryhali
granisetron	Sancuso	propionate lotion	
transdermal		halofantrine HCl	Halfan
system		Halog	halcinonide
Granix	tbo-filgrastim inj	haloperidol (W)	Haldol
Grass Pollen	GRASTEK	haloprogin (W)	Halotex (W)
Allergen Extract		Halotestin (W)	fluoxymesterone (W)
GRASTEK	Grass Pollen Allergen	Halotex (W)	haloprogin (W)
	Extract	halothane	Fluothane
grepafloxacin HCl	Raxar (W)	Hartmann's solution	a mixture of sodium
(W)			chloride, sodium
Grifulvin V	*griseofulvin microsize*		lactate, potassium
guaifenesin	Organidin NR		chloride, and calcium
	Mucinex		chloride in water; also
	Robitussin		known as Ringer's
guaifenesin; codeine	Robitussin A-C		lactate inj and RL
phosphate	Tussi-Organidin NR	Harvoni	ledipasvir and sofosbuvir
guaifenesin;	Robitussin-DM	Havrix	*hepatitis A vaccine,*
dextromethor			*inactivated*
phan		Healon	*sodium hyaluronate*
guanabenz acetate	Wytensin	Hectorol	doxercalciferol
guanadrel (W)	sulfate Hylorel (W)	Helidac	bismuth subsalicylate;
guanfacine	Intuniv		metronidazole;
guanfacine HCl	Tenex		tetracycline HCl
guselkumab Inj	Tremfya	Hemabate	carboprost tromethamine
Gynazole	butoconazole nitrate		Inj
	vaginal cream	Hemlibra	emicizumab-kxwh inj
Gyne-Lotrimin	clotrimazole	*heparin sodium*	*heparin sodium*
		hepatitis A	Twinrix
		inactivated;	
		hepatitis B	
H		(recombinant)	
		vaccine	
		hepatitis A vaccine,	Havrix
Habitrol	nicotine transdermal	inactivated	Vaqta
	system	hepatitis B immune	NABI-HB
Haegarda	C1 esterase inhibitor inj	globulin (human)	
haemophilus b conju-	Hiberix	hepatitis B vaccine	Engerix-B
gate vaccine inj			Recombivax HB

Hepsera	adefovir dipivoxil
Herceptin	trastuzumab
heroin	an opioid drug made from morphine, a natural substance taken from the seed pod of the various opium poppy plants grown in Southeast and Southwest Asia, Mexico, and Colombia (not commercially available)
herpes zoster subunit vaccine inj	Shingrix
Herplex	idoxuridine
Herzuma	trastuzumab-Pkrb inj
Hespan	*hetastarch*
hetastarch	Hespan
hetastarch in lactated electrolyte inj (W)	Hextend (W)
Hetlioz	tasimelteon
Hetrazan	diethylcarbam-azine citrate
Hexadrol (WA)	*dexamethasone*
Hexalen	altretamine
Hextend (W)	hetastarch in lactated electrolyte inj (W)
Hiberix	haemophilus b conjugate vaccine inj
Hibiclens	*chlorhexidine gluconate*
Hib-Immune (W)	haemophilus b vaccine
HibTITER	haemophilus b vaccine
Hiprex	*methenamine hippurate*
Hismanal (W)	astemizole (W)
histrelin acetate inj	Supprelin LA; Vantas
Hivid (W)	zalcitabine (W)
homatropine hydrobromide ophth	Isopto Homatropine
Horizant	gabapentin enacarbil SR
Humalog	insulin, lispro (human) lispro insulin, human, inj
Humalog Mix75/25	insulin lispro protamine susp 75%; insulin lispro inj 25% [rDNA origin]
human immunoglobulin 10% with recombinant human hyaluronidase	HyQvia
human papillomavirus bivalent vaccine, recombinant, susp inj	Cervarlx
Humatin	paromomycin sulfate
Humatrope	somatropin

Humira	adalimimab
Humor	adalimumab inj
Humorsol (W)	demecarium bromide (W)
Humulin 70/30	isophane insulin suspension 70%, insulin inj 30% (human)
Humulin L (W)	insulin zinc suspension (Lente) (human) (W)
Humulin N	isophane insulin suspension (NPH) (human)
Humulin R	insulin inj (human)
Humulin U Ultralente (W)	insulin zinc suspension, extended, (human) (W)
Hurricaine One	benzocaine soln
Hurricane	benzocaine
Hyalgan	sodium hyaluronate
hyaluronic acid inj	Durolane
hyaluronidase inj	Amphadase (bovine); Hylenex (human); Vitrase (ovine)
Hycamtin	topotecan HCl
Hycet	hydrocodone bitartrate and acetaminophen oral soln (discontinued in the US; may be available as a generic product)
Hydergine	ergoloid mesylates
Hydra	is a Cannabis Sativa product with a high THC content (content ratio 30:1, THC [tetrahydro-cannabinol] to CBD [cannabidiol])
hydralazine HCl	Apresoline
hydralazine HCl; hydrochlorothiazide	Apresazide
hydralazine; hydro-chlorothiazide; reserpine (W)	Ser-Ap-Es (W)
Hydrea	*hydroxyurea*
hydrochlorothiazide	Esidrix (WA) HydroDIURIL Microzide Oretic (WA)
hydrocodone bitartrate extended release	Hysingla ER
hydrocodone bitartrate 7.5 mg; ibuprofen 200 mg	Vicoprofen
hydrocodone bitartrate and guaifenesin soln	Flowtuss

hydrocodone bitartrate SR	Hysingla ER
hydrocodone bitartrate; acetaminophen	Anexsia 5/500 Anexsia 7.5/650 Lorcet 10/650 Lorcet-HD (5/500) Lorcet plus (7.5/650) Lortab 2.5/500; 5/500; 7.5/500; 10/500 Norco Vicodin Vicodin ES Zydone 5/400, 7.5/400, 10/400
hydrocodone polistirex; chlorpheniramine	Tussionex
hydrocortisone	Cortef *hydrocortisone*
hydrocortisone buteprate cream	Pandel
hydrocortisone sodium succinate	Solu-Cortef
HydroDIURIL	*hydrochlorothiazide*
hydroflumethiazide (W)	Saluron (W)
hydrogen peroxide topical soln	Eskata
hydromorphone HCl	Dilaudid
Hydromox (W)	quinethazone (W)
hydroquinone topical susp (W)	Alustra (W)
hydroquinone; tretinoin; flucinolone cream	Tri-Luma
hydroxychloroquine sulfate	Plaquenil
hydroxyprogesterone caproate inj	Makena
hydroxyurea	Droxia Hydrea
hydroxyzine HCl	Atarax
hydroxyzine pamoate	Vistaril
Hygroton	chlorthalidone
hylan G-F 20 inj (a derivative of hyaluronan [sodium hyaluronate])	Synvisc
Hylorel (W)	guanadrel sulfate (W)
hyoscyamine sulfate orally disintegrating tab	NuLev
hyoscyamine sulfate SR	Cystospaz-M Levbid
hyoscyamine sulfate tablet	Levsin
hyoscyamine sulfate tablet dispersible	Anaspaz

Hyperab (W)	rabies immune globulin, human
HyperRAB S/D	rabies immune globulin (human) solvent/detergent treated
Hyperstat (WA)	*diazoxide*
Hyper-Tet (W)	tetanus immune globulin (human) (W)
HyQvia	human immunoglobulin 10% with recombinant human hyaluronidase
Hyrimoz	adalimumab-adaz inj
Hytrin	*terazosin HCl*
Hyzaar	*losartan potassium; hydrochlorothiazide*

I

Iansoprazole; amoxicillin; clarithromycin	Prevpac
ibandronate	Boniva
ibilizumab-uiyk inj	Trogarzo
Ibrance	palbociclib
ibritumomab tiuxetan	Zevalin
ibrutinib	Imbruvica
ibuprofen	Advil Motrin
ibuprofen and famotidine	Duexis
Ibuprophen	see ibupropen (Motrin)
ibutilide fumarate	Corvert
IC NTG	intracoronary nitroglycerin
icatibant	Firazyr
Iclusig	*ponatinib*
icodextrin 7.5% with electrolyte peritoneal dialysis solution	Extraneal
icosapent ethyl	Vascepa
Idamycin	*idarubicin*
idarubicin	Idamycin
idarucizumab inj	Praxbind
idelalisib	Zydelig
Idhifa	enasidenib
idoxuridine	Herplex
idursulfase	Elaprase
IFEX	ifosfamide
ifosfamide	IFEX
Ilaris	canakinumab inj
iloperidone	Fanapt
iloprost	Ventavis
Ilosone (W)	erythromycin estolate (W)
Ilumya	tildrakizumab-asmn inj

Iluvien — fluocinolone acetonide intravitreal implant
Imagent GI — perflubron
imatinib mesylate — Gleevec
Imbruvica — ibrutinib
imciromab pentetate — Myoscint
Imdur — *isosorbide mononitrate SR*
Imfinzi — durvalumab inj
imiglucerase — Cerezyme
imipenem-cilastatin sodium — Primaxin
imipramine HCl — Tofranil
imiquimod cream — Aldara
Imitrex — *sumatriptan*
Imlygic — talimogene laherparepvec inj
immune globulin (human) inj — Gamunex-C
immune globulin [human] — GAMASTAN
immune globulin intravenous — Gamimune N / Gammagard S/D
immune globulin intravenous (human) — Octagam
immune globulin intravenous, human - ifas inj — PANZYGA
immune globulin intravenous, human-slra — Asceniv
Immune Globulin Subcutaneous (Human) inj — Cuvitru
immune globulin, I, v., human inj — Gammaplex
Imodium — *loperamide HCl*
Imogam — rabies immune globulin, human
Impavido — miltefosine
Imuran — *azathioprine*
Imvexxy — estradiol vaginal insert
Inapsine (WA) — *droperidol*
Inbrija — levodopa powder for inhalation
Incivek (W) — telaprevir (W)
incobotulinumtoxin A inj — Xeomin
Increlex — mecasermin
Incruse Ellipta — umeclidinium inhalation powder
indacaterol inhalation powder — Arcapta Neohaler
indapamide — Lozol
Inderal (WA) — *propranolol HCl*
Inderide (WA) — *propranolol HCl; hydrochlorothiazide*

Indica — Cannabis indica, formally known as Cannabis sativa forma indica, is an annual plant in the Cannabaceae family
indinavir — Crixivan
indium In-111 pentetreotide — OctreoScan
Indocin — *indomethacin*
indomethacin — Indocin
Infasurf — calfactant intratracheal susp
INFeD — *iron dextran inj*
Infergen — interferon alfacon-1
Inflectra — infliximab-dyyb inj
infliximab — Remicade
infliximab abda inj — Renflexis
infliximab-dyyb inj — Inflectra
infliximab-qbtx inj — Ixifi
influenza vaccine — Afluria
influenza vaccine inj — Flublok
influenza vaccine, adjuvanted inj — Fluad
influenza virus vaccine type A and B inj — Agriflu
ingenol mebutate gel — Picato
Ingrezza — valbenazine
Injectafer — ferric carboxymaltose inj
Inlyta — axitinib
Innohep — tinzaparin sodium
Innovar (W) — fentanyl citrate; droperidol (W)
Inocor (W) — *inamrinone lactate*
INOmax — nitric oxide for inhalation
inotersen inj — Tegsedi
inotuzumab ozogamicin inj — Besponsa
Inspra — eplerenone
insulin aspart (rDNA origin) — NovoLog
insulin aspart inj — Fiasp
Insulin degludec inj — Tresiba
insulin degludec inj / liraglutide inj — Xultophy
insulin detemir [rDNA origin] — Levemir
insulin glargine — Basaglar
insulin glargine & lixisenatide inj — Soliqua 100/33
insulin glargine (rDNA origin) — Lantus
insulin glarine inj — Toujeo
insulin glulisine [rDNA origin] — Apidra
insulin human, inhalation powder — Afrezza

I
Rx

insulin inj (human)	Humulin R	Ionamin	phentermine resin
	Novolin R	Ionsys	fentanyl iontophoretic
	Velosulin Human		transdermal
insulin lispro (human)	Humalog	iopamidol	Isovue
insulin lispro inj	Admelog	iopanoic acid (W)	Telepaque (W)
insulin lispro	Humalog Mix75/25	iopromide	Ultravist
protamine susp		iotrolan	Osmovist
75%; insulin lispro		ioversol	Optiray
inj 25% [rDNA		ioxilan (W)	Oxilan (W)
origin]		*ipilimumab*	Yervoy
insulin zinc	Humulin L (W)	Iplex	mecasermin rinfabate
suspension (Lente)	Novolin L (W)	Ipol	poliovirus vaccine
(human) (W)			inactivated
insulin zinc	Ultralente U (W)	ipratropium bromide	Atrovent
suspension,		ipratropium bromide	DuoNeb
extended (beef) (W)		and albuterol sulfate	
insulin zinc	Humulin U Ultralente	inhalation soln	
suspension,	(W)	ipratropium bromide;	Combivent
extended, (human)		albuterol sulfate	
(W)		iprivask	Desirudin
Integrilin	eptifibatide	irbesartan	Avapro
Intelence	etravirine	irbesartan;	Avalide
interferon alfa-2a (W)	Roferon-A (W)	hydrochlorothiazide	
interferon alfa-2b	Intron A	Iressa	gefitinib
interferon alfacon-1	Infergen	irinotecan HCl	Camptosar
interferon alfa-n¹	Wellferon	irinotecan liposome inj	Onivyde
lymphoblastoid		iron dextran inj	Dexferrum
interferon alfa-n3	Alferon		INFeD
(human leukocyte		iron sucrose inj	Venofer
derived)		isavuconazonium	Cresemba
interferon beta-1a	Rebif	sulfate tablets	
interferon beta-1b	Betaseron	and inj	
	Extavia	Isentress	raltegravir
interferon beta-la	Avonex	Ismelin (W)	guanethidine
interferon gamma 1-b	Actimmune		monosulfate (W)
Intrachol	choline chloride inj	ISMO	*isosorbide mononitrate*
Intralipid	*fat emulsion*	isocarboxazid	Marplan
Intron A	interferon alfa-2b	isoetharine HCl soln	Bronkosol
Intropin (WA)	*dopamine HCl*	isoflurane	Forane
Intuniv	guanfacine	isoflurophate	Floropryl
Invanz	ertapenem sodium	*isoniazid*	Nydrazid
Invega	paliperidone ER	isoniazid; rifampin	Rifamate
Invega Sustenna	paliperidone palmitate inj	isophane insulin	Humulin 70/30
	(given every month)	suspension (NPH)	Novolin 70/30
Invega Trinza	paliperidone palmitate inj	70%, insulin inj	
	(given every 3 months)	30% (human)	
Inveltys	loteprednol etabonate	isophane insulin	Humulin N
	ophth susp	suspension(NPH)	Novolin N
Inversine (W)	mecamylamine HCl (W)	(human)	
Invirase	saquinavir mesylate	isoproterenoc HCl inj	Isuprel
Invokamet XR	canagliflozin and	Isoptin	*verapamil HCl*
	metformin HCl	Isopto Carbachol (W)	carbachol (W)
Invokana	canagliflozin	Isopto Carpine	pilocarpine HCl ophth
iobenguane I 131 inj	Azedra	Isopto Homatropine	homatropine
iocetamic acid	Cholebrine		hydrobromide ophth
iodamide meglumine	Renovue 65	Isopto Hyoscine	scopolamine
iodixanol	Visipaque		hydrobromide ophth
iohexol	Omnipaque	Isordil (WA)	*isosorbide dinitrate*

Isordil Titradose	isosorbide dinitrate
isosorbide dinitrate	Isordil
	Isordil Titradose
	isosorbide dinitrate
isosorbide dinitrate;	BiDil
hydralazine	
isosorbide mononitrate	ISMO
isosorbide mononitrate	Imdur
SR	
isotretinoin (W)	Accutane (W)
Isovue	iopamidol
isoxsuprine HCl	Vasodilan
isradipine	DynaCirc
Istodax	romidepsin inj
Isuprel	isoproterenoc HCl inj
Isuprel (WA)	isoproterenol HCl
itraconazole	Sporanox
ivabradine	Corlanor
ivacaftor	kalydeco
ivermectin	Stromectol
ivermectin lotion	Sklice
ivermectin topical	Soolantra
cream	
ivosidenib	Tibsovo
IvyBlock	bentoquatam
ixabepilone	Ixempra
ixazomib	Ninlaro
ixekizumab	Taltz
Ixempra	ixabepilone
Ixiaro	Japanese encephalitis
	vaccine, inactivated
	adsorbed susp inj
Ixifi	infliximab-qbtx inj
Ixinity	coagulation factor IX inj

J

Jakafi	ruxolitinib
Jalyn	dutasteride and
	tamsulosin
Jantoven	warfarin sodium
Janumet XR	*sitagliptin and metformin*
	HCl SR
Januvia	sitagliptin
Japanese encephalitis	Ixiaro
vaccine,	
inactivated	
adsorbed susp inj	
Jardiance	empagliflozin
Jarra Loca	a mixture of alcoholic
	beverages and medicines
	(psychotropic and
	hypoglycemic drugs)
Jentadueto XR	linagliptin and metformin
	HCl

Jetrea	*ocriplasmin*
Jevtana	cabazitaxel inj
Jivi	antihemophilic factor
	recombinant,
	PEGylated-aucl inj
Jublia	efinaconazole topical
	solution
Juluca	dolutegravir and
	rilpivirine
Juvederm	hyaluronic acid cosmetic
	Inj
Juxtapid	lomitapide
Jynarque	tolvaptan

K

Kabiven	amino acids.electrolytes,
	dextrose and lipid inj
	(for IV infusion into a
	central vein
Kadcyla	ado-trastuzumab
	emtansine inj
Kadian	*morphine sulfate SR*
Kalbitor	ecallantine inj
Kaletra	Lopinavir; ritonavir
kalydeco	ivacaftor
kanamycin sulfate	Kantrex
Kantrex	*kanamycin sulfate*
Kanuma	sebelipase alfa inj
Kaon	*potassium gluconate*
Kaon-Cl	*potassium chloride SR*
Kapidex	dexiansoprazole
Kappra	may have meant Keppra
	(levetiracetam)
Kariva	*desogestrel and ethinyl*
	estradiol
Kayexalate	*polystyrene sulfonate*
	sodium
Kazano	alogliptin; metformin
Kcentra	prothrombin complex
	concentrate, human
Kdur	see K-Dur (potassium
	chloride tablets)
K-Dur	*potassium chloride SR*
Kedrab	rabies immune globulin,
	human inj
Keflex	*cephalexin*
Keflin	*cephalothin sodium*
Keftab (WA)	*cephalexin HCl*
Kefurox (WA)	*cefuroxime sodium*
Kefzol (W)	cefazolin sodium
Kemadrin (W)	*procyclidine HCl (W)*
Kenalog	triamcinolone
	acetonide
Kengreal	cangrelor inj

Kepivance	palifermin	Kynamro	mipomersen sodium inj
Keppra	*levetiracetam*	Kyprolis	carfilzomib inj
Kerlone	*betaxolol*	Kytril	*granisetron HCl*
Kerydin	tavaborole topical soln		
Ketalar	ketamine HCl		
ketamine HCl	Ketalar		
Ketek	telithromycin		
ketoconazole	Nizoral		
Ketofol	various combinations		
	of ketamine and	labetalol HCl	Normodyne
	propofol injections		Trandate
	(not commercially	labetolol	may have meant labetalol
	available)	Lac-Hydrin	lactic acid; ammonium
ketoprofen SR	Oruvail		lactate lotion
ketorolac	Toradol (W)	lacosamide	Vimpat
tromethamine (W)		lactaid Ringers	may have meant
ketorolac	Acular		Ringer's lactate inj,
tromethamine			a mixture of sodium
ophth			chloride, sodium
ketotifen fumarate	Zaditor		lactate, potassium
ophth soln			chloride, and calcium
Keveyis	dichlorphenamide		chloride in water; also
Kevzara	sarilumab inj		known as Hartman's
Keytruda	pembrolizumab inj		solution and RL
Kineret	anakinra	lactic acid;	Lac-Hydrin
Kinrix	diphtheria and tetanus	ammonium	
	toxoids and acellular	lactate lotion	
	pertussis adsorbed and	lactulose	Cephulac
	inactivated poliovirus		Chronulac
	vaccine	Lamictal	*lamotrigine*
Kisqali	ribociclib	Lamisil	*terbinafine HCl*
Klaron	sodium sulfacetamide	lamivudine	Epivir
	lotion		Epivir HBV
Klonopin	*clonazepam*	lamivudine and	Dutrebis
Klor-Con 10	*potassium chloride SR*	raltegravir	
K-Lyte	*potassium bicarbonate;*	lamivudine;	Combivir
	potassium citrate	zidovudine	
	effervescent	lamivudine;	Trizivir
K-Lyte/Cl	*potassium chloride*	zidovudine;	
	potassium	abacavir sulfate	
	bicarbonate	lamotrigine	Lamictal
	effervescent	lanadelumab inj	Takhzyro
Kolyum	*potassium chloride;*	Lanoxicaps (W)	digoxin capsules (W)
	potassium gluconate	Lanoxin	*digoxin*
Kombiglyze XR	saxagliptin HCl and	lanreotide	Somatuline
	metformin HCl	lansoprazole	Prevacid
Konsyl-D	*psyllium*	lanthanum carbonate	Fosrenol
Korlym	mifepristone	Lantus	insulin glargine (rDNA
Kovaltry	anti hemophilic factor inj		origin)
	(recombinant)	lapatinib	Tykerb
K-Phos	potassium phosphate	Lariam	mefloquine HCl
	monobasic	Larodopa (W)	levodopa (W)
Krintafel	tafenoquine	laronidase	Aldurazyme
Krystexxa	pegloticase	larotrectinib	Vitrakvi
Kuvan	sapropterin	Lartruvo	olaratumab inj
	dihydrochloride	Lartruvo (W)	olaratumab inj (W)
Kybella	deoxycholic acid inj	Lasix	furosemide
Kymriah	tisagenlecleucel inj	latanoprost	Xalatan

latanoprost and netarsudil ophth soln — Rocklatan

latanoprostene bunod ophth soln — Vyzulta

Latuda — lurasidone HCl

Lazanda — *fentanyl nasal spray*

ledipasvir and sofosbuvir; simeprevir and sofosbuvir (2 tablets) — Viekira

ledipasvir and sofosbuvir — Harvoni

leflunomide — Arava

Lemtrada — alemtuzumab inj

lenalidomide — Revlimid

L-enantiomer — Tyzeka

lenvatinib — Lenvima

Lenvima — lenvatinib

lepirudin — Refludan

Lescol — fluvastatin sodium

lesinurad — Zurampic

Letairis — ambrisentan

letermovir — Prevymis

letrozole — Femara

leucovorin calcium — *leucovorin calcium*

Leukeran — chlorambucil

Leukine — sargramostim

leuprolide acetate — Eligard
Lupron

leuprolide acetate implant — Viadur (W)

Leustatin (WA) — cladribine

levalbuterol HCl inhalation soln — Xopenex

levamisole HCl (W) — Ergamisol (W)

Levaquin — levofloxacin

Levbid — *hyoscyamine sulfate SR*

Levemir — insulin detemir [rDNA origin]

levetiracetam — Keppra
Spritam

levetiracetam SR — Elepsia XR

Levimir — see Levemir

Levitra — vardenafil HCl

Levlite — *levonorgestrel; ethinyl estradiol*

levobunolol HCl — Betagan

levobupivacaine (W) — Chirocaine (W)

levocabastine HCl ophth susp (W) — Livostin (W)

levocarnitine — Carnitor

levocetirizine — Xylzal

levocetirizine dihydrochloride — Xyzal

levodopa (W) — Dopar (W)
Larodopa (W)

levodopa powder for inhalation — Inbrija

levodopa; carbidopa — Parcopa
Sinemet

levodopa; carbidopa SR — Sinemet CR

Levo-Dromoran — levorphanol tartrate

levofloxacin — Levaquin

levofloxacin ophth soln — Quixin

levoleucovorin for injection — Fusilev

levomethadyl acetate HCl (W) — Orlaam (W)

levomilnacipran — Fetzima

levonorgestrel — Plan B

levonorgestrel implant (W) — Norplant (W)

levonorgestrel uterine system — Skyla

levonorgestrel, ethinyl estradiol tablets and ethinyl estradiol tablets — Quartette

levonorgestrel; ethinyl estradiol — Alesse
Levlite
Nordette
Preven Emergency Contraceptive Kit
Tri-Levlen
Triphasil

levonorgestrel-releasing intrauterine system — Mirena

Levophed — norepinephrine bitartrate

Levoquin — may have meant Levaquin (levofloxacin)

levorphanol tartrate — Levo-Dromoran

levothyroxine sodium — Levoxyl
Synthroid

Levoxyl — *levothyroxine sodium*

Levsin — hyoscyamine sulfate tablet

Levulan Kerastick — aminolevulinic acid HCl topical soln

Lexapro — escitalopram oxalate

Lexiscan — regadenoson inj

Lexiva — fosamprenavir calcium

Lexxel (W) — enalapril maleate; felodipine SR (W)

L-glutamine oral powder — Endari

Lialda — mesalamine multimatrix tablets

Librax (W) — clidinium; chlordiazepoxide (W)

LOTEMAX SM	loteprednol etabonate ophth gel
Lotensin	*benazepril HCl*
loteprednol etabonate ophth gel	LOTEMAX SM
loteprednol etabonate ophth susp	Alrex
	Inveltys
Lotrel	*amlodipine besylate; benazepril HCl*
Lotrimin	clotrimazole
Lotrisone	betamethasone; clotrimazole cream
Lotronex (W)	alosetron (W)
lovastatin	Mevacor
lovastatin; niacin	Advicor
Lovaza	omega-3-acid ethyl esters
Lovenox	*enoxaparin sodium*
loxapine succinate	Loxitane
Loxitane	*loxapine succinate*
Lozol	indapamide
lubiprostone	Amitiza
Lucemyra	lofexidine
Lucentis	ranibizumab inj
lucinactant intratracheal susp	Surfaxin
Ludiomil (WA)	*maprotiline HCl*
Lufyllin	dyphylline
lumacaftor and ivacaftor	Orkambi
LumenHance	manganese chloride
Lumigan (W)	bimatoprost ophth soln (W)
Lumoxiti	moxetumomab pasudotox-tdfk inj
Lunelle (W)	medroxy-progesterone acetate; estradiol cypionate inj (W)
Lunesta	eszopiclone
Lupron	leuprolide acetate
lurasidone HCl	Latuda
Lusedra	fospropofol disodium inj
lusutrombopag	Mulpleta
Lutathera	lutetium Lu 177 dotatate inj (a Lu-177-labeled somatostatin analogue peptide)
lutropin alfa	Luveris
Luveris	lutropin alfa
Luvox CR	*fluvoxamine maleate SR*
Luxiq	betamethasone valerate (foam)
Luxturna	voretigene-neparvovec-rzyl subretnal inj
Lyme disease vaccine (W)	LYMErix (W)
LYMErix (W)	Lyme disease vaccine (W)
lymphocyte immune globulin	Atgam

Lymphoseek	technetium Tc 99m tilmanocept inj
Lynparza	olaparib
lypressin (W)	Diapid (W)
Lyrica	pregabalin
Lysodren	mitotane

M

M.V.I.-12	*vitamin, multiple inj*
Maalox	*aluminum hydroxide; magnesium hydroxide*
macitentan	Opsumit
Macrobid	*nitrofurantoin macrocrystals and monohydrate*
Macrodantin	*nitrofurantoin macrocrystals*
Macugen	pegaptanib
magaldrate	Riopan
Magnacet	oxycodone; acetaminophen
magnesium chloride SR	Slow-Mag
magnesium oxide	MAG-OX 400
magnesium sulfate	*magnesium sulfate*
Magnevist	gadopentetate dimeglumine
MagOx	magnesium oxide
	magnesium oxide (over-the counter)
MAG-OX 400	magnesium oxide
Makena	hydroxyprogesterone caproate inj
Malarone	atovaquone; proguanil HCl
Mandol (W)	cefamandole nafate (W)
	cefamandole sodium (W)
mangafodipir trisodium	Teslascan
manganese chloride	LumenHance
maraviroc	Selzentry
Marcaine HCl	*bupivacaine HCl*
Marinol	*dronabinol*
Marplan	isocarboxazid
Marqibo	vincristine sulfate liposome inj
Matulane	procarbazine HCl
Mavenclad	cladribine
Mavik	*trandolapril*
Mavyret	glecaprevir and pibrentasvir
Maxalt	rizatriptan benzoate
Maxalt-MLT	rizatriptan oral disintegrating tablet
Maxaquin	lomefloxacin

Maxface	cross-linked hyaluronic acid inj (a filler for correction of scars and augmentation of cheeks and chins)	medroxyprogesterone acetate (W)	Cycrin (W)
		medroxyprogesterone acetate SR	Depo-Provera
Maxide	may have meant Maxzide (*triamterene 75 mg; hydrochlorothiazide 50 mg*)	medroxy-progesterone acetate; estradiol cypionate inj	Lunelle
		mefenamic acid	Ponstel
		mefloquine HCl	Lariam
Maxipime	cefepime HCl	Mefoxin (WA)	*cefoxitin sodium*
Maxzide	*triamterene 75 mg; hydrochlorothiazide 50 mg*	Megace	*megestrol acetate*
		megestrol acetate	Megace
Maxzide-25MG	*triamterene 37.5 mg; hydrochlorothiazide 25 mg*	Mekinist	trametenib
		melatonin	melatonin
		Mellaril (WA)	*thioridazine HCl*
may have meant metoprolol	metaprolol	melphalan	Alkeran
		memantine HCl	Namenda
may have meant opioid (a class of narcotic drugs [morphine, codeine, heroin, oxycodone, meperidine, Diluadid, fentanyl, etc.])	opiod	memantine HCl extended-release and donepezil HCl	Namzaric
		Menactra	meningococcal vaccine
		menadiol sodium diphosphate (W)	Synkayvite (W)
		meningococcal (groups A, C, Y, and W-135) oligosaccharide diphtheria CRM197 conjugate vaccine	Menveo
Mayzent	siponimod		
mazindol	Sanorex		
MCT oil	medium chain triglycerides oil (fats that are naturally found in coconut and palm kernel oil; over-the-counter)	meningococcal group B vaccine	Trumenba
		meningococcal vaccine	Menactra Menomune
		Menomune	meningococcal vaccine
measles, mumps, rubella vaccines, combined	M-M-R II	Menostar	*estradiol transdermal system*
		menotropins	Pergonal (WA) Repronex
Mebaral	*mephobarbital*		
mebendazole	Vermox	Mentax	butenafine HCl
mecamylamine HCl (W)	Inversine (W)	Menveo	meningococcal (groups A, C, Y, and W-135) W-135) oligosaccharide diphtheria CRM197 conjugate vaccine
mecasermin	Increlex		
mecasermin rinfabate	Iplex		
mechlorethamine gel	Valchlor Gel		
mechlorethamine HCl	Mustargen	*meperidine HCl*	Demerol
mechlorethamine HCl inj	Valchlor	mephentermine sulfate (W)	Wyamine (W)
Meclan (W)	*meclocycline sulfosalicylate*	mephenytoin (W)	Mesantoin (W)
meclizine	Antivert	mephobarbital	Mebaral
meclocycline sulfosalicylate (W)	Meclan (W)	Mephyton	*Phytonadione*
		mepivacaine HCl	Carbocaine
Meclomen	*meclofenamate sodium*	mepolizumab inj	Nacala
Medrol	*methylprednisolone*	meprobamate	Equanil Miltown
Medrol Dosepak	a package of Medrol (methylprednisolone)	Mepron	atovaquone
		Mepsevil	vestronidase alfa-vjbk inj
medroxyprogesterone acetate	Provera	mequinol; tretinoin	Solage

mercaptopurine	Purinethol
Meridia (W)	*sibutramine HCl monohydrate (W)*
meropenem	Merrem
meropenem and vaborbactam inj	Vabomere
Merrem	meropenem
Meruvax II	rubella virus vaccine live attenuated
mesalamine	Asacol
	Rowasa
mesalamine multimatrix tablets	Lialda
mesalamine SR capsules	Apriso
Mesantoin (W)	mephenytoin (W)
mesna	Mesnex
Mesnex	mesna
mesoridazine besylate (W)	Serentil (W)
Mestinon	pyridostigmine bromide
Metadate ER	*methylphenidate HCl SR*
metaformin	may have meant metformin (Glucophage)
Metaglip	*glipizide; metformin*
Metamucil	*psyllium*
Metaprel	metaproterenol sulfate
metaproterenol sulfate	Alupent (W) Metaprel
metaraminol bitartrate	Aramine
Metaret	suramin
Metastron	strontium-89 chloride inj
metaxalone	Skelaxin
metformin and dapagliflozin SR	Xigduo XR
metformin HCl	Glucophage
metformin HCl SR	Glucophage XR
methadone HCl	Dolophine
methamphetamine HCl	Desoxyn
methazolamide	Neptazane
methenamine combination	Urised
methenamine hippurate	Hiprex
Methergine (WA)	*methylergonovine maleate*
methicillin sodium (W)	Staphcillin (W)
methimazole	Tapazole
methocarbamol	Robaxin
methohexital sodium	Brevital Sodium
methotrexate oral soln	Xatmep
methotrexate sodium preservative-free inj	Folex PFS (WA)

methotrexate tablets	Rheumatrex
methoxsalen	Oxsoralen
methoxsalen extracorporeal administration	Uvadex
methoxy polyethylene glycol-epoetin beta	Mircera
methscopolamine bromide	Pamine
methyclothiazide	Enduron
methyldopa	Aldomet
methyldopa; hydrochlorothiazide	Aldoril
methylergonovine maleate	Methergine
Methylin	*methylphenidate HCl*
Methylin ER	*methylphenidate HCl SR*
methylnaltrexone bromide	Resistor
methylnaltrexone bromide inj	Relistor
methylphenidate HCl	Methylin Ritalin
methylphenidate SR	Concerta Metadate ER Methylin ER Ritalin SR
methylprednisolone	Medrol
methylprednisolone acetateSR inj	Depo-Medrol
methylprednisolone sodium succinate inj	Solu-Medrol
methylprednisone	may have meant methylprednisolone (Medrol)
methysergide maleate (W)	Sansert (W)
Meticorten (WA)	*prednisone*
metoclopramide HCl	Reglan
metolazone	Zaroxolyn
Metopirone	metyrapone
metoprolol succinate SR	Toprol XL
metoprolol tartrate	Lopressor
MetroGel-Vaginal	*metronidazole vaginal gel*
metronidazole	Flagyl
metronidazole SR	Flagyl ER
metronidazole vaginal gel	MetroGel- Vaginal
metropolol	may have meant metoprolol
metroprol	may have mean metoprolol succinate SR (Toprol XL) or metoprolol tartrate (Lopressor)
metyrapone	Metopirone

M R

691

metyrosine	Demser	Mircette	desogestrel and ethinyl
Mevacor	lovastatin		estradiol
Mexate (WA)	methotrexate	Mirena	levonorgestrel-releasing
mexiletine HCl	Mexitil		intrauterine system
Mexitil	mexiletine HCl	mirtazapine	Remeron
Miacalcin	calcitonin-salmon	mirtazapine orally	Remeron SolTab
mibefradil	Posicor (W)	disintegrating tab	
dihydrochloride(W)		Mirvaso	brimonidine gel
micafungin sodium	Mycamine	misoprostol	Cytotec
Micardis	telmisartan	Mithracin (W)	plicamycin (W)
miconazole nitrate	Monistat	mitomycin	Mutamycin
Micro K	potassium chloride SR	mitotane	Lysodren
Microgestin	norethindrone acetate;	mitoxantrone HCl	Novantrone
	ethinyl estradiol	mitragynine	the main alkaloid of
Microgestin Fe	norethindrone acetate;		Kratom, a Southeast
	ethinyl estradiol;		Asian psychoactive
	ferrous fumerate		substance derived from
Micronase	glyburide		the plant Mitragyna
Micronor	norethindrone		speciosal
Microzide	hydrochlorothiazide	Mivacron (W)	mivacurium chloride (W)
Midamor	amiloride HCl	mivacurium	Mivacron (W)
midazolam HCl	Versed (WA)	chloride (W)	
midazolam nasal	Nayzilam	M-M-R II	measles, mumps, rubella
spray			vaccines, combined
midodrine HCl	ProAmatine	Moban	molindone HCl
midostaurin	Rydapt	Mobic	meloxicam
Mifeprex	mifepristone	modafinil	Provigil
mifepristone	Korlym	Moduretic	amiloride HCl;
	Mifeprex		hydrochlorothiazide
migalastat	Galafold	moexipril HCl	Univasc
miglitol	Glyset	moexipril HCl;	Uniretic
miglustat	Zavesca	hydrochlorothiazide	
Migranal	dihydroergotamine	mogamulizumab-	Poteligeo
	mesylate nasal spray	kpkc inj	
milnacipran	Savella	molindone HCl	Moban
milrinone lactate	Primacor	mometasone furoate	Dulera
miltefosine	Impavido	and formoterol	
Miltown	meprobamate	fumarate inhalation	
minimally invasive	deferiprone	Mometasone furoate	Nasonex
skin tightening		monohydrate nasal	
Minipress	prazosin HCl	spray	
Minocin	minocycline HCl	mometasone furoate	Elocon
minocycline HCl	Minocin	topical	
minocycline HCl	Arestin	Monistat	miconazole nitrate
dental micospheres		Monopril	fosinopril sodium
minoxidil tablets (W)	Loniten (W)	montelukast sodium	Singulair
minoxidil topical	Rogaine	Monurol	fosfomycin tromethamine
Mintezol (W)	thiabendazole (W)	moricizine	Ethmozine
Miochol E	acetylcholine ophth	morphine sulfate	there is no safe
mipomersen sodium	Kynamro		abbreviation for
inj			morphine sulfate
mirabegron	Myrbetriq		(this could be
MiraLax	polyethylene glycol		said for most
	3350		other drugs)
Mirapex	pramipexole		Roxanol
	dihydrochloride	morphine sulfate	Embeda
Mircera	methoxy polyethylene	and naltrexone	
	glycol-epoetin beta	HCl SR	

morphine sulfate extended-release liposome inj	DepoDur
morphine sulfate inj	Duramorph
morphine sulfate SR	Kadian
	MS Contin
	Oramorph SR
	Roxanol SR
morphine sulfate SR tablet	Arymo ER
morphine sulfate tab SR	Avinza
morphine sulfate, immediate release concentrated oral soln	Roxanol-T
Motegrity	prucalopride
Motrin	ibuprofen
Movantik	naloxegol oxalate
MoviPrep powder	polyethylene glycol 3350 and electrolytes
moxetumomab pasudotox-tdfk inj	Lumoxiti
moxidectin	moxidectin
moxifloxacin HCl	Avelox
Mozobil	plerixafor inj
MS Contin	*morphine sulfate SR*
Mucinex	*guaifenesin*
Mucomyst	*acetylcysteine*
Mulpleta	lusutrombopag
Multaq	dronedarone
Multi-12 (vial 1 and vial 2)	multiple vitamins for infusion
MultiHance	gadobenate dimeglumine
multiple vitamins for infusion	Multi-12 (vial 1 and vial 2)
multivitamins for infusion	Cernevit-12
mupirocin nasal ointment	Bactroban
muromonab-CD3	Orthoclone OKT3
Muse	alprostadil urethral suppository
Mustargen	mechlorethamine HCl
Mutamycin	mitomycin
Myambutol	ethambutol HCl
Mycamine	micafungin sodium
Mycelex (WA)	*clotrimazole*
Mycifradin Sulfate	neomycin sulfate oral soln
Myciguent (W)	neomycin sulfate ointment and cream (W)
Mycolog Cream	*nystatin; triamcinolone cream*
mycophenolate mofetil	CellCept
mycophenolic acid	Myfortic

Mycostatin (WA)	*nystatin*
Mydriacyl	*tropicamide*
Myfortic	mycophenolic acid
Mykrox (WA)	*metolazone*
Mylanta	aluminum hydroxide, magnesium hydroxide, and simethicone
Myleran	busulfan
Mylicon	*simethicone*
Mylotarg	gemtuzumab ozogamicin
Myobloc	rimabotulinumtoxinB inj
Myochrysine (WA)	gold sodium thiomalate
Myoscint	imciromab pentetate
Myrbetriq	mirabegron
Mysoline	*primidone*

N

NABI-HB	hepatitis B immune globulin (human)
nab-paclitaxel	albumin-bound paclitaxel (Abraxane)
nabumetone	Relafen
Nacala	mepolizumab inj
nadolol	Corgard
nafcillin	nafcillin
Naglazyme	galsulfase
nalbuphine HCl	Nubain
naldemedine tosylate	Symproic
Nalfon	*fenoprofen calcium*
nalidixic acid	NegGram
nalmefene HCl	Revex
naloxegol oxalate	Movantik
naloxone HCl	Narcan (WA)
naltrexone	ReVia
naltrexone and bupropion	Contrave
Namenda	memantine HCl
Namzaric	memantine HCl extended-release and donepezil HCl
nandrolone decanoate (W)	Deca-Durabolin (W)
nandrolone phenpropionate (W)	Durabolin (W)
naphazoline ophth soln	Vasocon
Naprelan	*naproxen sodium SR*
naproxen	Naprosyn
naproxen sodium	Anaprox
naproxen sodium SR	Naprelan
naratriptan HCl	Amerge
Narcam	may have meant Narcan (naloxone HCl inj)

N
R

Narcan (WA)	naloxone HCl	Neo-Synephrine	phenylephrine HCl inj
Nardil	phenelzine sulfate	Neptazane	methazolamide
Naropin	ropivacaine HCl inj	Nesacaine	chloroprocaine HCl
Nasacort AQ	triamcinolone acetonide nasal inhaler	Nesina	alogliptin
		nesiritide	Natrecor
Nasalcrom	cromolyn sodium	netarsudil ophth soln	Rhopressa
Nascobal	cyanocobalamin nasal gel	netilmicin sulfate (W)	Netromycin (W)
Nasonex	Mometasone furoate monohydrate nasal spray	Netromycin (W)	netilmicin sulfate (W)
		netupitant and palonosetron	Akynzeo
natalizumab	Tysabri		
Natazia	estradiol valerate and dienogest	Neulasta	pegfilgrastim inj
		Neumega	oprelvekin
nateglinide	Starlix	Neupogen	filgrastim
Natesto	testosterone nasal gel	Neupro	rotigotine transdermal system
Natpara	parathyroid hormone, recombinant human inj		
		Neurolite	technetium Tc-99m bicisate kit
Natrecor	nesiritide		
Natroba	spinosad topical	Neurontin	gabapentin
Navane	thiothixene	Neutrexin	trimetrexate glucuronate
Navelbine	vinorelbine tartrate	nevirapine	Viramune
Nayzilam	midazolam nasal spray	Nexavar	sorafenib tosylate
nebivolol	Bystolic	Nexium	esomeprazole magnesium
nebivolol and valsartan	Byvalson	Nexplanon	etonogestrel implant
		Nexterone	amiodarone HCl Inj
NebuPent	pentamidine isethionate aerosol	Niaspan	niacin SR
		nicardipine HCl	Cardene
necitumumab inj	Portrazza	Niclocide (W)	niclosamide (W)
nedocromil inhalation	Tilade	niclosamide (W)	Niclocide (W)
		Nicobid (W)	niacin SR
nedocromil ophth soln	Alocril	NicoDerm CQ	nicotine transdermal
		Nicorette	nicotine polacrilex
nefazodone HCl	Serzone (W)	nicotine nasal spray	Nicotrol NS
NegGram (W)	nalidixic acid (W)	nicotine polacrilex	Nicorette
nelarabine	Arranon	nicotine transdermal	Habitrol
nelfinavir mesylate	Viracept		Nicotrol
Nembutal	pentobarbital sodium inj		Prostep
neomycin sulfate ointment and cream (W)	Myciguent (W)	Nicotrol	nicotine transdermal
		Nicotrol NS	nicotine nasal spray
		nifedipine	Adalat
neomycin sulfate oral soln	Mycifradin Sulfate		Procardia
		nifedipine SR	Adalat CC
Neoral	cyclosporine capsules (modified) and oral soln		Procardia XL
		Nilandron	nilutamide
		nilotinib	Tasigna
Neosar (WA)	cyclophosphamide	nilutamide	Nilandron
Neosporin Ointment	polymyxin; neomycin; bacitracin	Nimbex	cisatracurium besylate
		nimodipine (W)	Nimotop (W)
Neosporin ophth Ointment	polymyxin; neomycin; bacitracin	Nimotop (W)	nimodipine (W)
		Ninlaro	ixazomib
Neosporin ophth soln	polymyxin; neomycin	nintedanib	Ofev
Neosproin Cream	polymyxin; neomycin	Nipent	pentostatin inj
neostigmine methylsulfate	Prostigmin	Nipride	nitroprusside sodium
		niraparib tosylate	Zejula
		nisoldipine SR	Sular
neostigmine methylsulfate inj	Bloxiverz	nitazoxanide	Alinia
		nitisinone	Orfadin
NeoSure	premature infant enriched (feeding) formula	nitric oxide for inhalation	INOmax

Nitro-Bid	*nitroglycerin oint*
Nitro-Dur	*nitroglycerin transdermal*
nitrofurantoin macrocrystals	Macrodantin
nitrofurantoin macrocrystals and monohydrate	Macrobid
nitrofurazone (W)	Furacin (W)
nitroglycerin	Nitro-Bid
nitroglycerin oint (W)	Nitropaste (W)
nitroglycerin ointment	Nitro-Bid
nitroglycerin powder for sublingual use	Genitor
nitroglycerin sublingual tablets	Nitrostat
nitroglycerin transdermal	Nitrek Nitro-Dur Transderm-Nitro
nitroglycerine	nitroglycerin
Nitropaste (W)	nitroglycerin oint (W)
Nitrostat	*introglycerin sublingual tablets*
nivolumab inj	Opdivo
Nix	permethrin
nizatidine	Axid
Nizoral	*ketoconazole*
Noctiva	desmopressin acetate nasal spray
nofetumomab (W)	Verluna (W)
nolatrexed dihydrochloride (W)	Thymitaq (W)
Nolvadex (W)	*tamoxifen citrate*
nonacog beta pegol inj	Rebinyn
Norco	*hydrocodone bitartrate; acetaminophen*
Norcuron	*vecuronium bromide*
Nordette	*levonorgestrel; ethinyl estradiol*
Norditropin	*somatropin inj*
norelgestromin; ethinyl estradiol transdermal	Ortho Evra
norepinephrine bitartrate	Levophed
norethindrone	Micronor
norethindrone acetate, ethinyl estradiol, and ferrous fumarate	LO Minastrin FE
norethindrone acetate; estradiol transdermal	CombiPatch
norethindrone acetate; ethinyl estradiol	Estrostep Loestrin

norethindrone; ethinyl estradiol (or mestranol)	Activella (W) Femhrt Ortho-Novum (products)
Norflex	orphenadrine citrate
norfloxacin	Noroxin
Norgesic (W)	orphenadrine citrate; aspirin; caffeine (W)
norgestimate and ethinyl estradiol	Sprinterc
norgestimate; ethinyl estradiol	Ortho Tri-Cyclen
norgestrel; ethinyl estradiol	Lo/Ovral Ovral
Normiflo (W)	ardeparin sodium (W)
Normodyne	*labetalol HCl*
Noroxin	norfloxacin
Norpace	*disopyramide phosphate*
Norplant (W)	levonorgestrel implant (W)
Norpramin	*desipramine HCl*
Northera	droxidopa
nortriptyline HCl	Aventyl Pamelor
Norvasc	*amlodipine besylate*
Norvir	ritonavir
Novantrone	*mitoxantrone HCl*
Novocain HCl	*procaine HCl*
Novoeight	antihemophilic factor (recombinant) inj
Novolin 70/30	isophane insulin suspension (NPH) 70%, insulin inj 30% (human)
Novolin L (W)	insulin zinc suspension (Lente)(Human) (W)
Novolin N	isophane insulin suspension (NPH) (human)
Novolin R	insulin inj (human)
NovoLog	insulin aspart (rDNA origin)
NovoSeven	coagulation factor VII a (recombinant)
Noxafil	posaconazole
Nplate	romiplostim inj
Nubain	nalbuphine HCl
Nucynta	tapentadol
Nuedexta	dextromethorphan hydrobromide and quinidine sulfate
Nulecit	*sodium ferric gluconate complex in sucrose inj*
NuLev	hyoscyamine sulfate orally disintegrating tab

N R

Nulojix	belatacept
	belatacept inj
Numorphan	oxymorphone HCl
Nupercainal	dibucaine
Nuplazid	pimavanzserin
Nuromax (W)	doxacurium chloride (W)
nusinersen intrathecal inj	Spinraza
Nutropin AQ	somatropin inj
Nuvail	poly-ureaurethane topical soln
NuvaRing	etonogestrel; ethinyl estrodial vagina ring
Nuvigil	armodafinil
Nuzyra	omadacycline
Nydrazid	isoniazid
NyQuil	acetaminophen, dextromethorphan, and doxylamine succinate (over-the-counter; for cold and flu relief)
nystatin	Mycostatin
	Mycostatin (WA)
nystatin topical powder	Nystop
nystatin; triamcinolone cream	Mycolog Cream
Nystop	hystatin topical powder

O

obeticholic acid	Ocaliva
obiltoxaximab inj	Anthem
obinutuzumab	Gazyva
Obizur	antihemophilic factor (recombinant) porcine sequence
Ocaliva	obeticholic acid
OCL soln	polyethylene glycol 3350 and electrolytes
ocrelizumab inj	Ocrevus
Ocrevus	ocrelizumab inj
ocriplasmin	Jetrea
Octagam	immune globulin intravenous (human)
Octodrine	mimethylhexylamine (DMHA) (over-the-counter)
OctreoScan	indium In-111 pentetreotide
octreotide acetate	Sandostatin
octreotide acetate susp for inj	Sandostatin LAR Depot

Odactra	house dust mite (Dermatophagoides farinae and Dermatophagoides pteronyssinus) allergenic extract for sublingual use
Odomzo	sonidegib
Odrahybrid	a hybrid Cannabis product with a high THC content (content ratio 60:1, THC [tetrahydrocannabinol] to CBD [cannabidiol])
ofatumumab	Arzerra
Ofev	nintedanib
Ofirmev	acetaminophen inj
ofloxacin	Floxin
ofloxacin otic soln	Floxin Otic
Ogen	estropipate
olanzapine	Zyprexa
olanzapine; fluoxetine	Symbyax
olaparib	Lynparza
olaratumab inj	Lartruvo
olaratumab inj (W)	Lartruvo (W)
olmesartan medoxomil	Benicar
olmesartan medoxomil; hydrochlorothiazide	Benicar HCT
olodatero inhalation	Striverdi Respimat
olopatadine HCl ophth soln	Pazeo
olopatadine HCl ophth soln 0.1%	Patanol
olopatadine HCl ophth soln 0.2%	Pataday
olsalazine sodium	Dipentum
Olumiant	baricitinib
Olux	clobetasol foam
Olysio	simeprevir
Omacor	name changed to Lovaza
omadacycline	Nuzyra
omalizumab	Xolair
omega-3-acid ethyl esters	Lovaza (formerly called Omacor)
omega-3-caboxylic acids	Epanova
omeprazole	Prilosec
Omidria	phenylephrine and ketorolac ophth soln
Omnaris	ciclesonide nasal susp
Omnicef	cefdinir
Omnipaque	iohexol
onabotulinumtoxinA inj	Botox Botox Cosmetic

onasemnogene abeparvovec-xioi inj — Zolgensma

Oncaspar — pegaspargase

OncoScint — satumomab pendetide

Oncovin — vincristine sulfate (note: for intraVENOUS administration only)

ondansetron — Zofran

ondansetron orally disintegrating tab — Zofran ODT

Onexton — clindamycin and benzoyl peroxide gel

Onfi — *clobazam*

Onglyza — saxagliptin

Onivyde — irinotecan liposome inj

Onpattro — patisiran inj

Ontak — denileukin diftitox

Ontruzant — trastuzumab-dttb inj

Onxol — *paclitaxel inj*

Onzetra Xsail — sumatriptan nasal powder

Opana — oxymorphone HCl

Opdivo — nivolumab inj

Ophthaine (WA) — *proparacaine*

Ophthalgan — glycerin ophth soln

Ophthetic — proparacaine HCl

opioids — a class of narcotic drugs (morphine, codeine, heroin, oxycodone, meperidine, Diluadid, fentanyl, etc.)

opium; belladonna suppositories — B & O Supprettes

oprelvekin — Neumega

Opsumit — macitentan

Opticrom — cromolyn sodium

OptiMark — gadoversetamide

Optimine — azatadine maleate

Optiray — ioversol

Optivar — azelastine HCl ophth soln

Ora Verse — *phentolamine mesylate inj*

Orabase — benzocaine

Orajel — benzocaine

Oramorph SR — morphine sulfate SR

Orap — pimozide

Orapred — *prednisolone sodium phosphate*

Orbactiv — oritavancin inj

Orencia — abatacept

Oretic (WA) — *hydrochlorothiaxide*

Oreton Methyl (WA) — *methyltestosterone*

Orfadin — nitisinone

Organidin NR — *guaifenesin*

Orgaran — danaparoid sodium

Orilissa — elagolix

Orinase (WA) — *tolbutamide*

oritavancin inj — Orbactiv

Orkambi — lumacaftor and ivacaftor

Orlaam (W) — levomethadyl acetate HCl (W)

orlistat — Xenical

Ornade Spansules (W) — phenylpropanolamine HCl; chlorpheniramine maleate SR (W)

orphenadrine citrate — Norflex

Ortho Evra — norelgestromin; ethinyl estradiol transdermal

Ortho Tri-Cyclen — norgestimate; ethinyl estradiol (combinations)

Ortho-Cept — desogestrel; ethinyl estradiol

Orthoclone OKT3 — muromonab-CD3

Ortho-Novum (products) — norethindrone; ethinyl estradiol (or mestranol)

Ortho-Prefest — 17β-estradiol; norgestimate

Oruvail — ketoprofen SR

Oscal — calcium supplement with vitamin D

Os-Cal 500 — *calcium carbonate*

oseltamivir phosphate — Tamiflu

Oseni — alogliptin; pioglitazone

osimertinib mesylate inj — Tagrisso

Osmovist — iotrolan

ospemifene — Osphena

Ospen — phenoxymethylpenicillin (this brand is not marketed in the US) (also known as penicillin V and penicillin VK)

Osphena — ospemifene

Otezla — apremilast

Otiprio — ciprofloxacin otic soln

Otrivin — xylometazoline

Ovidrel — choriogonadotropin alfa

ovine hyaluronidase (W) — Vitrase (W)

Ovral — norgestrel; ethinyl estradiol

oxaliplatin — Eloxatin

Oxandrin — oxandrolone

oxandrolone — Oxandrin

oxaprozin — Daypro

oxazepam — *oxazepam*

oxcarbazepine — Trileptal

oxcarbazepine extended release tablets — Oxtellar XR

Oxervate — cenegermin-bkbj ophth soln

oxiconazole nitrate cream	Oxistat
Oxilan (W)	ioxilan (W)
Oxistat	oxiconazole nitrate cream
Oxsoralen	methoxsalen
Oxtellar XR	oxcarbazepine extended release tablets
oxybutun	may have meant oxybutynin chloride (Ditropan)
oxybutynin chloride	Ditropan
oxychlorosene sodium	Clorpactin WCS-90
oxycodone and naloxone SR	Targiniq ER
oxycodone HC; acetaminophen	Tylox (WA)
oxycodone HCl	Percolone (W) Roxicodone
oxycodone HCl and naltrexone HC	Troxyca
oxycodone HCl SR	OxyContin
oxycodone HCl, ibuprofen	Combunox
oxycodone HCl; acetaminophen	Endocet Percocet 5/325; 7.5/500; 10/650 Roxicet
oxycodone HCl; aspirin	Percodan
oxycodone; acetaminophen	Magnacet
OxyContin	*oxycodone HCl SR*
oxymetazoline HCl	Afrin nasal spray Dristan Long Lasting
oxymetazoline HCl cream	Rhofade
oxymetholone	Anadrol-50
oxymorphone HCl	Numorphan Opana
oxymorphone HCl extended release tablets	Opana ER
oxytocin	Pitocin
Ozempic	semaglutide inj
Ozurdex	dexamethasone intravitreal implant

P

Pacerone	amiodarone HCl
pacilitaxel-eluting stent	Taxus Express2 stent V-Flex plus PTX stent
Pacis	BCG intravesical
paclitaxel	Taxol

paclitaxel inj	Onxol
paclitaxel-eluting coronary stent system	Taxus
PainBloc24	capsaicin 0.25% topical analgesic (over-the-counter)
PainBlock24	see PainBloc24
palbociclib	Ibrance
palifermin	Kepivance
paliperidone ER	Invega
paliperidone palmitate inj (given every month)	Invega Sustenna
paliperidone palmitate inj (given every 3 months)	Invega Trinza
palivizumab	Synagis
Palladone XL (WA)	*hydromorphone HCl SR*
palonosetron HCl	Aloxi
Palynziq	pegvaliase pqpz inj
Pamelor	*nortriptyline HCl*
pamidronate disodium	Aredia
Pamine	*methscopolamine bromide*
Panadol	acetaminophen
Pancrease	pancrelipase EC
pancrelipase	Creon Zenpep
pancrelipase EC	Pancrease
pancuronium bromide	Pavulon
Pandel	hydrocortisone buteprate cream
panitumumab inj	Vectibix
panitumumob	Vectibix
panobinostat	Farydak
Panretin	alitretinoin
pantoprazole	Protonix
PANZYGA	immune globulin intravenous, human - ifas inj
papain; urea oint	Accuzyme Ethezyme
papaverine HCl SR	Pavabid (WA)
papillomavirus recombinant vaccine quadrivalent (types 6, 11, 16, 18) human	Gardasil
papillomavirus 9-valent (types 6, 11, 16,18, 31, 33, 45, 52, and 58) vaccine, recombinant, human	Gardasil 9

Paracetamol	acetaminophen (Tylenol) (available in the European Union)
paracetamol	*acetaminophen*
Paradione	paramethadione (W)
Paraflex	*chlorzoxazone 250 mg*
Parafon Forte DSC	*chlorzoxazone 500 mg*
paramethadione (W)	Paradione (W)
Parathar	teriparatide acetate
parathyroid hormone, recombinant human inj	Natpara
Parcopa	*levodopa; carbidopa*
paregoric	camphorated tincture of opium (this is NOT tincture of opium; Paregoric has just 0.4 mg/mL of morphine, whereas tincture of opium contains 10 mg/mL, a 25-fold difference)
pargyline HCl	Eutonyl
paricalcitol	Zemplar
Parlodel	*bromocriptine mesylate*
Parnate	*tranylcypromine sulfate*
paromomycin sulfate	Humatin
paroxetine	Brisdelle
paroxetine HCl	Paxil
Parsabiv	etelcalcetide inj
Paser	aminosalicylic acid
pasireotide diaspartate inj	Signifor
pasireotide diaspartate inj susp long-acting release	Signifor LAR
Pataday	olopatadine HCl ophth soln 0.2%
Patanol	olopatadine HCl ophth soln 0.1%
patiromer sorbitex calcium	Veltassa
patisiran inj	Onpattro
Pavabid (W)	papaverine HCl SR
Pavulon (WA)	*pancuronium bromide*
Paxil	*paroxetine HCl*
Pazeo	olopatadine HCl ophth soln
pazopanib	Votrient
PBZ (W)	tripelennamine HCl
PCE Dispertab	erythromycin base coated particles
Pediazole (WA)	*erythromycin ethylsuccinate; sulfisoxazole*
Pedmark	sodium thiosulfate inj
PedvaxHIB	haemophilus b vaccine

pegaptanib	Macugen
pegaspargase	Oncaspar
Pegasys	peginterferon alfa-2a
pegfilgrastim cbqv inj	Udenyca
pegfilgrastim inj	Neulasta
pegfilgrastim-jmdb inj	Fulphila
peginterferon alfa-2a	Pegasys
peginterferon alfa-2b inj (recombinant)	Peg-Intron
peginterferon beta-1a inj	Plegridy
Peg-Intron	peginterferon alfa-2b inj (recombinant)
pegloticase	Krystexxa
pegvaliase-pqpz inj	Palynziq
pegvisomant	Somavert
pembrolizumab inj	Keytruda
pemetrexed disodium	Alimta
pemirolast potassium ophth soln	Alamast
pemoline	Cylert (WA)
penciclovir cream	Denavir
penicillamine	Cuprimine
penicillin G benzathine	Bicillin L-A (for IM use only)
	Permapen (for IM use only)
penicillin G benzathine; penicillin G procaine	Bicillin C-R (for IM use only)
penicillin G procaine	Wycillin (for IM use only)
Penicillin VK	penicillin V potassium
Penlac Nail Lacquer	ciclopirox soln
pennicillin	see penicillin
Pennsaid	diclofenac sodium topical soln
Pentacel	diphtheria and tetanus toxoids and acellular pertussis adsorbed, inactivated poliovirus and Haemophilus b conjugate
pentaerythritol tetranitrate (W)	Peritrate (W)
pentagastrin (W)	Peptavlon (W)
Pentam 300	pentamidine isethionate inj
pentamidine isethionate aerosol	NebuPent
pentamidine isethionate inj	Pentam 300
Pentaspan	pentastarch
pentastarch	Pentaspan
pentazocine HCl	Talwin

pentazocine HCl; naloxone HCl	Talwin Nx	Peritrate (W)	pentaerythritol tetranitrate (W)
pentetate calcium trisodium (trisodium calcium diethylenetriamine-pentaacetate)	Ca-DTPA	Perjeta	pertuzumab
		Permapen	penicillin G benzathine (for IM use only)
		permethrin	Nix
		Permitil (WA)	*fluphenazine HCl*
pentetate zinc trisodium (trisodium zinc diethylenetriamine-pentaacetate)	ZN-DTPA	perphenazine; amitriptyline HCl	Etrafon
			Triavil (W)
		Persantine	*dipyridamole*
		pertuzumab	Perjeta
pentobarbital sodium	Nembutal	petrolatum, white	Vaseline
pentosan polysulfate sodium	Elmiron	Phenaphen with Codeine (#2, 3, and 4) (WA)	*acetaminophen 300 mg with Codeine Phosphate (15, 30, and 60 mg)*
pentostatin inj	Nipent		
Pentothal	thiopental sodium		
pentoxifylline	Trental	phenazopyridine HCl	Pyridium
PENVK	Pen VK (penicillin V potassium)	phendimetrazine tartrate	Plegine
Pepcid	*famotidine*	phenelzine sulfate	Nardil
Pepcid RPD	*famotidine, oral disintegrating tablet*	Phenergan	*promethazine HCl*
		phenobarbital	*phenobarbital*
Peptavlon	Pentagastrin	phenobarbital, ergotamine; belladonna	Bellergal-S
Pepto	Pepto-Bismol (active ingredient, bismuth subsalicylate)		
		phenoxybenzamine HCl	Dibenzyline
Pepto-Bismol	an over-the-counter product; active ingredient, bismuth subsalicylate	phentermine and topiramate SR	Qsymia
		phentermine HCl	Adipex-P
			Fastin
peramivir inj	Rapivab		Lomaira
perampanel	Fycompa	phentermine resin	Ionamin
Percocet 5/325; 7.5/500; 10/650	*oxycodone HCl; acetaminophen*	*phentolamine mesylate inj*	Ora Verse
Percodan	*oxycodone HCl; aspirin*	phenylbutyrate sodium	Buphenyl
Percolone (WA)	*oxycodone HCl*		
perflenapent emulsion	EchoGen	phenylephrine and ketorolac ophth soln	Omidria
perflubron	Imagent GI		
Pergonal (WA)	*menotropins*	phenylephrine HCl	Neo-Synephrine
Periactin(WA)	*cyproheptadine HCl*	phenylephrine HCl inj	Vazculep
Peri-Colace	*docusate sodium; senna concentrate*	phenylpro-panolamine HCl; chlorpheniramine maleate SR (W)	Ornade Spansules (W)
Peridex	chlorhexidine gluconate mouth rinse		
Perikabiven	amino acids.electrolytes, dextrose and lipid inj (for IV infusion into a peripheral or central vein	phenylpro-panolamine HCl; guaifenesin SR	Entex LA
		Phenytek	phenytoin sodium, extended
perindopril arginine and amlodipine besylate	Prestalia	phenytoin	Dilantin
		PhosLo	*calcium acetate*
perindopril erbumine	Aceon	Phospholine Iodide	echothiophate iodide
Perinethol	*mercaptopurine*	Photofrin	porfimer sodium
Periostat	*doxycycline hyclate 20 mg tab & cap*	physostigmine ophth ointment	Eserine Sulfate

physostigmine salicylate	Antilirium
phytonadione	Mephyton
phytonadione inj	aquaMephyton (WA)
Picato	ingenol mebutate gel
Pifeltro	doravirine
pilocarpine HCl ophth	Isopto Carpine
pilocarpine HCl tablet	Salagen
pilodocanol injectable foam	Varithena
pimavanzserin	Nuplazid
pimecrolimus cream	Elidel
pimozide	Orap
pindolol	Visken
Pink Lady	xylocaine viscous and a liquid antacid such as Maalox for treating emergency room patients to help determine if the chest pains are either heart or digestive related (slang)
pioglitazone HCl	Actos
pioglitazone HCl and glimepiride	Duetact
pipecuronium bromide (W)	Arduan (W)
piperacillin sodium; tazobactam sodium	Zosyn
Pipracil (WA)	*piperacillin sodium*
Piqray	alpelisib
pirfenidone	Esbriet
piroxicam	Feldene
pitavastatin calcium	Livalo
Pitocin	*oxytocin*
Pitressin	*vasopressin*
Placidyl (W)	ethchlorvynol (W)
Plan B	levonorgestrel
Plaquenil	*hydroxychloroquine sulfate*
Plasbumin	*albumin human*
plasma protein fraction	Plasma-Plex Plasmanate Plasmatein Protenate
Plasmanate	plasma protein fraction
Plasma-Plex (WA)	plasma protein fraction
Plasmatein (WA)	plasma protein fraction
Platinol (WA)	*cisplatin*
Platinol AQ (WA)	*cisplatin*
Plavix	clopidogrel bisulfate
plazomicin inj	Zemdri
plecanatide	Trulance
Plegine	phendimetrazine tartrate

Plegridy	peginterferon beta-1a inj
Plenaxis	abarelix
Plendil	*felodipine*
Plenity	cellulose and citric acid
Plenvu	bowel prep (polyethylene glycol 3350, sodium ascorbate, sodium sulfate, ascorbic acid, sodium chloride, and potassium chloride oral soln)
plerixafor inj	Mozobil
Pletal	*cilostazol*
Plexion	sulfacetamide sodium and sulfur lotion
plicamycin (W)	Mithracin (W)
pneumococcal 13-valent conjugate vaccine	Prevnar 13
pneumococcal 7-valent conjugate vaccine	Prevnar Prevnar 7
pneumococcalvaccine	Pneumovax
Pneumovax	pneumococcal vaccine
podofilox gel	Condylox
Polaramine Repetabs (W)	*dexchlorpheniramine maleate SR*
polatuzumab vedotin-piiq inj	Polivy
polidocanol injectable foam	Varithena
poliovirus vaccine inactivated	Ipol
Polivy	polatuzumab vedotin-piiq inj
polyethylene glycol 3350	GlycoLax; MiraLax
polyethylene glycol 3350 and electrolytes	OCL; MoviPrep; CoLyte; GoLYTELY
poly-l-lactic acid	Sculptra
polymyxin B sulfate; trimethoprim ophth soln	Polytrim
polymyxin; neomycin	Neosporin Cream Neosporin ophth soln
polymyxin; neomycin; bacitracin	Neosporin Ointment Neosporin ophth Ointment
polymyxin-B sulfate inj	*polymyxin-B sulfate inj*
polystyrene sulfonate sodium	Kayexalate
Polytrim	polymyxin B sulfate; trimethoprim ophth soln
poly-ureaurethane topical soln	Nuvail

pomalidomide	Pomalyst
Pomalyst	pomalidomide
ponatinib	Iclusig
Pondimin (W)	fenfluramine HCl (W)
Ponstel	mefenamic acid
Pontocaine	*tetracaine HCl*
poractant alpha intratracheal susp	Curosurf
porfimer sodium	Photofrin
Portrazza	necitumumab inj
posaconazole	Noxafil
Posicor (W)	mibefradil dihydro-chloride (W)
potassium phosphate monobasic	K-Phos
potassium bicarbonate; potassium citrate effervescent	K-Lyte
potassium chloride SR	Kaon-Cl
	K-Dur
	Klor-Con 10
	Slow-K (WA)
	Micro K
potassium chloride; potassium bicarbonate effervescent	K-Lyte/Cl
potassium chloride; potassium gluconate	Kolyum
potassium citrate tab	Urocit-K
potassium gluconate	Kaon
Poteligeo	mogamulizumab-kpkc inj
Potiga	*ezogabine*
povidone iodine	Betadine
Pradaxa	dabigatran etexilate
pralatrexate inj	Folotyn
pralidoxime chloride	Protopam
Praluent	alirocumab inj
pramipexole dihydrochloride	Mirapex
pramlintide	Symlin
pramlintide acetate	Symlin
pramoxine HCl	Tronothane HCl
Prandin	repaglinide
prasterone (W)	Aslera (W)
prasugrel	Effient
Pravachol	*pravastatin sodium*
pravastatin sodium	Pravachol
Praxbind	idarucizumab inj
prazosin HCl	Minipress
Precedex	dexmedetomidine HCl inj
Precose	acarbose
Pred Forte	prednisolone acetate ophth susp
prednisolone acetate ophth susp	Pred Forte
prednisolone sodium phosphate	Orapred
prednisolone syrup	Prelone
prednisone	*prednisone*
pregabalin	Lyrica
Prelone	*prednisolone syrup*
Premarin	estrogens, conjugated
Premphase	estrogens, conjugated; medroxyprogesterone acetate
Prempro	estrogens, conjugated; medroxyprogesterone acetate
Prepidil	dinoprostone gel
preservative-free triamcinolone acetone ophth inj	Triesence
Prestalia	perindopril arginine and amlodipine besylate
Prevacid	*lansoprazole*
Prevalite	cholestyramine resin
Preven Emergency Contraceptive Kit	levonorgestrel; ethinyl estradiol
Preveon	adefovir dipivoxil
Prevnar 7	pneumococcal 7-valent conjugate vaccine
Prevnar 13	pneumococcal 13-valent conjugate vaccine
Prevpac	lansoprazole; amoxicillin; clarithromycin
Prevymis	letermovir
Prezcobix	darunavir and cobicistat
Prezista	darunavir
Prialt	ziconotide
Priftin	rifapentine
Prilosec	*omeprazole*
Primacor	milrinone lactate
primaquine phosphate	*primaquine phosphate*
Primaxin	imipenemcila-statin sodium
primidone	Mysoline
Primsol	trimethoprim
Principen	*ampicillin*
Prinivil	*lisinopril*
Priscoline (W)	tolazoline (W)
Pristiq	desvenlafaxine succinate
ProAir HFA	albuterol sulfate inhalation aerosol
ProAir RespiClick	albuterol sulfate inhalation powder
ProAmatine	*midodrine HCl*
Pro-Banthine (WA)	*propantheline bromide*
probenecid; colchicine	ColBENEMID (W)

ProbioSlim	an over-the-counter weight-loss product containing LactoSpore probiotics, green tea leaf extract, and fig, kiwi, and papaya extracts
Probuphine	buprenorphine implant
procainamide	Pronestyl
procaine HCl	Novocain HCl
Procan SR (W)	*procainamide HCl SR*
Procanbid	procainamide HCl SR
procarbazine HCl	Matulane
Procardia	*nifedipine*
Procardia XL	*nifedipine SR*
Prochieve	progesterone gel
prochlorperazine	Compazine (WA)
Procrit	epoetin alfa
procyclidine HCl	Kemadrin
Procysbi	cysteamine bitartrate SR tablet
Profilnine SD	factor IX complex inj
Profraf	*tacrolimus*
progesterone gel	Crinone Prochieve
progesterone micronized	Prometrium
Prograf	*tacrolimus*
ProHance	gadoteridol
ProHIBiT	haemophilus b vaccine
Prokine (WA)	sargramostim
Prolastin	alpha1-proteinase inhibitor (human)
Proleukin	aldesleukin
Prolia	*denosumab*
Prolixin (W)	*fluphenazine HCl*
Proloid (W)	thyroglobulin (W)
Promacta	Eltrombopag
promethazine HCl	Phenergan
Prometrium	progesterone micronized
Promus	everolimus-eluting coronary stent system
Pronestyl	procainamide
Propacet-100 (W)	propoxyphene napsylate; acetaminophen (W)
propafenone HCl	Rythmol
propantheline bromide	Pro-Banthine
proparacaine HCl	Ophthaine (WA) Ophthetic
Propecia	finasteride tablets 1 mg
Propine	dipivefrin
propofol	Diprivan
propoxyphene HCl (W)	Darvon (W)
propoxyphene HCl; acetaminophen (W)	*propoxyphene HCl; acetaminophen (W)*

propoxyphene HCl; aspirin; caffeine (W)	Darvon Compound 65 (W)
propoxyphene napsylate; acetaminophen (W)	Darvocet-N 100 (W) Propacet-100 (W)
propranolol	propranolol
propranolol HCl; hydrochlorothiazide (W)	Inderide (W)
Propulsid (W)	cisapride (W)
Proscar	*finasteride tablets 5 mg*
ProSom (WA)	*estazolam*
ProstaScint	capromab pendetide
Prostep	*nicotine transdermal system*
Prostigmin	*neostigmine methylsulfate*
Prostin E$_2$	dinoprostone vaginal suppositories
Prostin VR	alprostadil
protamine sulfate	*protamine sulfate*
protein C	Ceprotin
Protenate	plasma protein fraction
prothrombin complex concentrate, human	Kcentra
Protonix	*pantoprazole*
Protopam	pralidoxime chloride
Protopic	tacrolimus oint
Protropin	somatrem
Protropin II	*somatropin for inj*
Provasil	an over-the-counter product sold as a brain enhancer [vitamin C, folic acid, vitamin B12, resveratrol, and N-acetyl-L-carnitine, biotin, choline bitartrate, phosphatidylcholine, phosphatidylserine, docosahexaenoic acid (DHA), Bacopa monnieri, ginkgo extract, and ginseng]
Provenge	sipuleucel-T inj
Proventil	*albuterol*
Proventil HFA	*albuterol sulfate inhalation aerosol*
Proventil Repetabs	*albuterol SR*
Provera	*medroxyprogesterone acetate*
Provigil	modafinil
Prozac	*fluoxetine HCl*
prucalopride	Motegrity
Prudoxin	doxepin HCl cream
Prussian Blue	Radiogardase

pseudoephedrine HCl	Sudafed
pseudoephedrine HCl; bromphiramine maleate	Drixoral Syrup
psyllium	Konsyl-D Metamucil
Pulmicort Turbuhaler (W)	budesonide inhalation powder (W)
Pulmozyme	dornase alfa
Purinethol	*mercaptopurine*
Pyridium	*phenazopyridine HCl*
pyridostigmine bromide	Mestinon
pyrimethamine	Daraprim
pyrimethamine; sulfadoxine	Fansidar

Q

Q-10	Coenzyme Q-10
Qbrexza	glycopyrronium cloth
Qsymia	phentermine and topiramate SR
Qtern	saxagliptin and dapagliflozin
Quadramet	samarium SM 153 lexidronam
Quadrivalent influenza vaccine inj	Alfuria
Qualaquin	quinine sulfate
Quartette	levonorgestrel, ethinyl estradiol tablets and ethinyl estradiol tablets
Quarzan (W)	clidinium bromide (W)
Qudexy XR	topiramate SR
Questran	cholestyramine resin
Questran (W)	cholestyramine (W)
quetiapine fumerate	Seroquel
Quinaglute (WA)	*quinidine gluconate SR*
quinapril HCl	Accupril
quinapril; hydrochlorothiazide	Accuretic
quinethazone (W)	Hydromox (W)
Quinidex Extentabs (WA)	*quinidine sulfate SR*
quinidine sulfate SR	Quinidex Extentabs
quinine sulfate	Qualaquin
quinupristin; dalfopristin	Synercid
Quixin	levofloxacin ophth soln
Qutenza	*capsaicin patch*

Qvar	beclomethasone diproprionate inhalation aerosol

R

RabAvert	rabies vaccine for human use
rabeprazole sodium	Aciphex
rabies immune globulin (human) solvent/detergent treated	HyperRAB S/D
rabies immune globulin, human	Hyperab (W) Imogam
rabies immune globulin, human inj	Kedrab
rabies vaccine for human use	RabAvert
rabies vaccine, adsorbed	rabies vaccine, adsorbed
Radicava	edaravone inj
Radiogardase	Prussian Blue
Radium Ra 223 dichloride inj	Xofigo
raloxifene HCl	Evista
raltegravir	Isentress
ramelteon	Rozerem
ramipril	Altace
ramucirumab inj	Cyramza
Ranexa	ranolazine
ranibizumab inj	Lucentis
ranitidine bismuth citrate (W)	Tritec (W)
ranitidine HCl	Zantac
ranolazine	Ranexa
rapacuronium bromide (W)	Raplon (W)
Rapaflo	silodosin
Rapamune	sirolimus
rapamycin	eRapa
Rapivab	peramivir inj
Raplon (W)	rapacuronium bromide (W)
Raptiva	efalizumab
rasagiline mesylate	Azilect
rasburicase	Elitek
rattlesnake anti-venom	CroFab
ravulizumab-cwvc inj	Ultomiris
Raxar (W)	grepafloxacin HCl (W)
raxibacumab	Abthrax
Razadyne	*galanthamine HBr*
Rebetol	*ribavirin*
Rebetron (W)	ribavirin; interferon alfa-2b (W)

Rebif	interferon beta-1a
Rebinyn	nonacog beta pegol inj
reboxetine mesylate	Vestra
Reclast inj	zoledronic acid inj
recombinant coagula- tion factor IX inj	Rixubis
Recombivax HB	*hepatitis B vaccine*
Recothrom	thrombin, topical (recombinant)
Redux (W)	dexfenfluramine HCl (W)
Refacto	antihemophilic factor (recombinant)
Refludan	lepirudin
regadenoson inj	Lexiscan
Regitine (WA)	*phentolamine mesylate*
Reglan	*metoclopramide HCl*
Regor	an indica-dominant cross between Cannatonic and Afghan Skunk Cannabis strains; (content ratio 45:1, CBD [cannabidiol] to THC [tetrahydrocannabinol])
regorafenib	Stivarga
Regranex	becaplermin gel
Regroton (W)	chlorthalidone; reserpine (W)
Relafen	nabumetone
Relenza	zanamivir for inhalation
Relistor	methylnaltrexone bromide inj
Relpax	eletriptan HBr
Remeron	*mirtazapine*
Remeron SolTab	mirtazapine orally disintegrating tab
Remicade	infliximab
remifentanil HCl	Ultiva
Reminyl (now called Razadyne)	galantamine HBr (hydrobromide)
Remodulin	treprostinil sodium
Renagel	sevelamer HCl
Renflexis	infliximab abda inj
Renova	*tretinion topical*
Renovue 65	iodamide meglumine
Renvela	sevelamer HCl
ReoPro	abciximab
repaglinide	Prandin
Repatha	evolocumab inj
Repronex	*menotropins*
Requip	*ropinirole HCl*
Rescriptor	delavirdine mesylate
Rescula (W)	unoprostone isopropyl ophth soln (W)
reserpine	Serpasil
Resistor	methylnaltrexone bromide
reslizumab inj	Cinqair
RespiGam	respiratory syncytial virus immune globulin intravenous (human)
respiratory syncytial virus immune globulin intra- venous (human)	RespiGam
Restasis	cyclosporine ophth emulsion
Restoril	*temazepam*
Restylane	hyaluronic acid cosmetic Inj
Retacrit	epoetin alfa-epbx inj
retapamulin oint.	Altabax
Retavase	reteplase
reteplase	Retavase
Retin-A	*tretinoin topical*
Retin-A Micro	*tretinoin gel*
Retrovir	*zidovudine*
Revcovi	elapegademase-lvlr inj
revefenacin for inhalation	Yupelri
Revex (W)	nalmefene HCl
ReVia	*naltrexone*
Revlimid	lenalidomide
Reyataz	atazanavir sulfate atazanavir sulfate (W)
Rezulin (W)	troglitazone (W)
R-Gene	arginine HCl
Rheumatrex	*methotrexate tablets*
Rhinocort Aqua Nasal Suspension	budesonide intranasal suspension
RH$_O$ (D) immune globulin	RhoGAM
RH$_O$ immune globulin IV (human)	WinRho SD
Rhofade	oxymetazoline HCl cream
RhoGAM	RH$_O$ (D) immune globulin
Rhopressa	netarsudil ophth soln
Riastap	fibrinogen concentrate, human inj
ribavirin	Rebetol Virazole
ribavirin; interferon alfa-2b (W)	Rebetron (W)
ribociclib	Kisqali
Ridaura	auranofin
Rifadin	*rifampin*
Rifamate	isoniazid; rifampin
rifampin	Rifadin Rimactane
rifapentine	Priftin
rifaximin	Xifaxan
rilonacept	Arcalyst
Rilutek	riluzole
riluzole	Rilutek
rimabotulinumtoxinB inj	Myobloc

Rimactane	*rifampin*
rimantadine	Flumadine
rimexolone	Vexol
Ringer's lactate inj	a mixture of sodium chloride, sodium lactate, potassium chloride, and calcium chloride in water; also known as Hartman's solution and RL
Ringers lactaid	may have meant Ringer's lactate inj
riociguat	Adempas
Riopan	magaldrate
risankizumab-rzaa inj	Skyrizi
risedronate sodium	Actonel
Risperdal	*risperidone*
risperidone	Risperdal
Ritalin	*methylphenidate HCl*
Ritalin SR	*methylphenidate SR*
ritonavir	Norvir
Rituxan	rituximab
Rituxan Hycela	rituximab/hyaluronidase human inj
rituximab	Rituxan
rituximab/ hyaluronidase human inj	Rituxan Hycela
rituximab-abbs inj	Truxima
RiUP	topical monoxidil (a Japanese hair growth import)
rivaroxaban	Xarelto
rivastigmine tartrate	Exelon
Rixubis	recombinant coagulation factor IX inj
rizatriptan benzoate	Maxalt
rizatriptan oral disintegrating tablet	Maxalt-MLT
Robaxin	*methocarbamol*
Robinul	*glycopyrrolate*
Robitussin	*guaifenesin*
Robitussin A-C	*guaifenesin; codeine phosphate*
Robitussin-DM	*guaifenesin; dextromethorphan*
Rocaltrol	calcitriol
Rocephin	*ceftriaxone sodium*
Rocklatan	latanoprost and netarsudil ophth soln
rocuronium bromide	Zemuron
rocuronium bromide inj	Zemuron
rofecoxib	Vioxx
Roferon-A (W)	interferon alfa-2a (W)
roflumilast	Daliresp
Rogaine	*minoxidil topical*
rolapitant	Varubi

Romazicon	flumazenil
romidepsin inj	Istodax
romiplostim inj	Nplate
romosozumab inj	Evenity
ropinirole HCl	Requip
ropivacaine HCl inj	Naropin
rosigitazone maleate; metformin HCl	Avandamet
Rosiglitazone maleate	Avandia
rosuvastatin calcium	Crestor
Rotarix	rotavirus vaccine, live, oral
Rotashield (W)	rotavirus (W) vaccine, live, oral, tetravalent
rotavirus vaccine, live, oral	Rotarix
rotavirusvaccine, live, oral, (W) tetravalent	Rotashield (W)
rotigotine transdermal system	Neupro
Rowasa	mesalamine
Roxanol	*morphine sulfate*
Roxanol SR	*morphine sulfate SR*
Roxanol-T	*morphine sulfate, immediate release concentrated oral soln*
Roxicet	*oxycodone HCl; acetaminophen*
Roxicodone	*oxycodone HCl*
Roxycodone	may have meant Roxicodone (oxycodone HCl)
Rozerem	ramelteon
rubella virus vaccine live attenuated	Meruvax II
Rubex (WA)	*doxorubicin HCl*
Rubraca	rucaparib
rucaparib	Rubraca
Ruconest	C1 esterase inhibitor [recombinant] ink
rufinamide	Banzel
ruxolitinib	Jakafi
Ryanodex	dantrolene sodium inj
Rydapt	midostaurin
Rythmol	*propafenone HCl*

S

Sabril	vigabatrin
sacrosidase	Sucraid
safinamide	Xadago
Saizen	*somatropin*
Salagen	*pilocarpine HCl tablet*
salbutamol sulfate	*albuterol sulfate*

salmeterol xinafoate inhalation powder	Serevent Diskus
salsalate	Disalcid
Sal-Tropine	atropine sulfate tablets
samarium SM 153 lexidronam	Quadramet
Samsca	tolvaptan oral
Sanctura	trospium chloride
Sancuso	granisetron transdermal system
Sandimmune	*cyclosporine*
Sandoglobulin (W)	*immune globulin intravenous*
Sandostatin	*octreotide acetate*
Sandostatin LAR Depot	octreotide acetate susp for inj
Sanorex	mazindol
Sansert (W)	methysergide maleate (W)
Santyl	collagenase
Saphris	asenapine maleate
sapropterin dihydrochloride	Kuvan
saquinavir mesylate	Invirase
saquinavir soft gel capsule (W)	Fortovase (W)
Sarafem	*fluoxetine*
sarecycline	Seysara
sargramostim	Leukine Prokine (WA)
sarilumab inj	Kevzara
satumomab pendetide	OncoScint
Savaysa	edoxaban inj
Savella	milnacipran
saxagliptin	Onglyza
saxagliptin and dapagliflozin	Qtern
saxagliptin HCl and metformin HCl	Kombiglyze XR
Saxenda	liraglutide inj
Sclerosol	talc, sterile aerosol
Scopace	scopolamine hydrobro-mide, soluble tab
scopolamine hydrobromide ophth	Isopto Hyoscine
scopolamine hydrobromide, soluble tab	Scopace
scopolamine transdermal	Transderm Scop
Sculptra	poly-l-lactic acid
Seasonale	ethinyl estradiol; (91 day cycle)
sebelipase alfa inj	Kanuma
secnidazole	Solosec
secukinumab inj	Cosentyx

Segluromet	ertugliflozin and metformin HCl
Seldane (W)	terfenadine (W)
Seldane D (W)	terfenadine; pseudo-ephedrine HCl (W)
selegiline HCl	Eldepryl
selenium sulfide	Selsun Blue
selexipag	Uptravi
Selsun Blue	selenium sulfide
Selzentry	maraviroc
semaglutide inj	Ozempic
Senispar	cinacalcet HCl
sennosides	Ex Lax Senokot
sennosides; docusate sodium	Senokot-S
Senokot	*senna concentrates*
Senokot-S	*sennosides; docusate sodium*
Sensipar	cinacalcet
Sensorcaine; Marcaine	bupivacaine HCl
Septocaine	articaine; epinephrine
Septra	*sulfamethoxazoletri-methoprim*
Ser-Ap-Es (W)	hydralazine; hydrochlorothiazide; reserpine (W)
Serax (WA)	*oxazepam*
Serentil (W)	mesoridazine besylate (W)
Serevent Diskus	salmeterol xinafoate inhalation powder
Serlect	sertindole
sermorelin acetate	Geref
Seromycin	*cycloserine*
Seroquel	quetiapine fumerate
Seroquil	may have meant Seroquel (quetiapine fumarate)
Serostim	somatropin (rDNA origin) for inj
Serpasil	*reserpine*
sertaconazole	Ertaczo
sertindole	Serlect
sertraline HCl	Zoloft
Serzone (W)	nefazodone HCl
sevelamer HCl	Renagel; Renvela
sevoflurane	Ultane
Seysara	sarecycline
Shingrix	zoster vaccine recombi-nant, adjuvanted inj
short chain fatty acids enema	Colomed
sibutramine HCl monohydrate	Meridia
Signifor	pasireotide diaspartate inj
Signifor LAR	pasireotide diaspartate inj susp long-acting release
sildenafil citrate	Viagra

S
R

Siliq	brodalumab inj
silodosin	Rapaflo
siltuximab inj	Sylvant
Silvadene	*silver sulfadiazine*
silver sulfadiazine	Silvadene
Simbrinza	brinzolamide and brimonidine tartrate ophth susp
simeprevir	Olysio
simethicone	Mylicon
Simponi	golimumab
Simulect	basiliximab
simvastatin	Zocor
sinecatechins oint	Veregen
Sinemet	*levodopa; carbidopa*
Sinemet CR	*levodopa; carbidopa SR*
Sinequan (WA)	*doxepin HCl*
Singulair	montelukast sodium
siponimod	Mayzent
sipuleucel-T inj	Provenge
sirolimus	Rapamune
sirolimus-eluting stent	Cypher Stent
Sirturo	bedaquiline
sitagliptin	Januvia
sitagliptin and metformin HCl SR	Janumet XR
Sivextro	tedizolid phosphate
Skelaxin	*metaxalone*
Skelid	tiludronate disodium
Sklice	ivermectin lotion
Skyla	levonorgestrel uterine system
Skyrizi	risankizumab-rzaa inj
Slo-bid	*theophylline SR*
Slo-Phyllin	*theophylline*
Slow Fe	*ferrous sulfate SR*
Slow-K (WA)	*potassium chloride SR*
Slow-Mag	magnesium chloride SR
Slynd	drospireno
smallpox (vaccine) (W)	ACAM 2000 (W)
sodium citrate; citric acid	Bicitra (WA)
sodium ferric gluconate complex in sucrose inj	Ferrlecit
sodium hyaluronate	Amvisc
	Healon
	Hyalgan
sodium Hyaluronate Intra-articular Inj	Euflexxa
sodium oxybate oral soln	Xyrem
sodium phenylacetate and sodium benzoate inj 10%	Ammonul
sodium phenylbutyrate	Buphenyl
sodium phosphate tab	Visicol

sodium sulfacetamide lotion	Klaron
sodium tetradecyl sulfate	Sotradecol
sodium thiosulfate inj	Pedmark
sodium zirconium cyclosilicate for oral suspension	Lokelma
sofosbuvir	Sovaldi
sofosbuvir and velpatasvir	Epclusa
Solage	mequinol; tretinoin
Solaraze	diclofenac gel
Solganal (W)	aurothioglucose (W)
solifenacin succinate	Vesicare
Soliqua 100/33	insulin glargine & lixisenatide inj
Soliris	eculizumab
Solosec	secnidazole
Solu-Cortef	hydrocortisone sodium succinate
Solumedrol	see Solu-Medrol
Solu-Medrol	*methylprednisolone sodium succinate*
Soma	*carisoprodol*
somatostatin	Zecnil
somatrem	Protropin
somatropin (rDNA origin) for inj	Serostim
somatropin for inj	Genotropin
	Humatrope
	Norditropin
	Nutropin
	Protropin II
	Saizen
somatropin inj	Nutropin AQ
Somatuline	lanreotide
Somavert	pegvisomant
Sonata	*zaleplon*
sonidegib	Odomzo
Soolantra	ivermectin topical cream
sorafenib tosylate	Nexavar
Soriatane	acitretin
Sorilux	calcipotriene foam
sotalol	Betapace
Sotradecol	sodium tetradecyl sulfate
Sovaldi	sofosbuvir
SpaceOAR Hydrogel	for men who undergo radiation treatment for prostate cancer. It acts as a spacer providing space between the rectum and the prostate, making it much less likely that the rectum is exposed to radiation.
sparfloxacin (W)	Zagam (W)
spectinomycin HCl	Trobicin

Spectracef	*cefditoren pivoxil*
Spinraza	nusinersen intrathecal inj
Spiriva HandiHaler	tiotropium bromide inhalation powder
spironolactone	Aldactone
spironolactone oral susp	CaroSpir
spironolactone; hydrochlorothiazide	Aldactazide
Sporanox	itraconazole
Spravato	esketamine nasal spray
Sprinterc	norgestimate and ethinyl estradiol
Spritam	levetiracetam
Sprycel	dasatinib
Stadol	butorphanol tartrate inj
Stadol NS (WA)	*butorphanol tartrate nasal spray*
Stalevo	carbidopa, levodopa, and entacapone
stanozolol (W)	Winstrol (W)
Staphcillin (W)	methicillin sodium (W)
Starlix	nateglinide
stavudine SR	Zerit XR
Steglatro	ertugliflozin
Steglujan	ertugliflozin and sitagliptin
Stelara	ustekinumab
Stelazine (W)	*trifluoperazinex HCl* (W)
Stendra	avanafil
Stiolto Respimat	tiotropium bromide and olodeterol inhalation spray
Stivarga	*regorafenib*
Strattera	Atomoxetine HCl
Strensiq	asfotase alfa inc
Streptase (W)	Streptokinase (W)
streptokinase (W)	Streptase (W)
streptomycin sulfate	streptomycin sulfate
streptozocin	Zanosar
Striant	testosterone buccal
Stribild	elvitegravir, cobicistat, emtricitabine, and tenofovir disoproxil fumarate (also known as E/C/F/TDF) (single-tablet regimen)
Striverdi Respimat	olodatero inhalation
Stromectol	ivermectin
strontium-89 chloride inj	Metastron
Sublimaze (W)	fentanyl citrate inj (W)
Suboxone	buprenorphine extended-release inj buprenorphine HCl; naloxone HCl
Subsys	fentanyl base sublingual liquid

Subutex	buprenorphine HCl
succinylcholine chloride	Anectine
Sucraid	sacrosidase
sucralfate	Carafate
sucroferric oxyhyroxide	Velphoro
Sudafed	pseudoephedrine HCl
Sufenta	sufentanil citrate
sufentanil citrate	Sufenta
sufentanil sublingual tablet	Dsuvia
sugammadex inj	Bridion Briton
Sulamyd sodium (W)	*sulfacetamide sodium ophth*
Sular (WA)	*nisoldipine SR*
sulfacetamide sodium and sulfur lotion	Plexion
sulfacetamide sodium ophth	*sulfacetamide sodium ophth*
sulfadoxine; pyrimethamine	Fansidar
sulfamethoxazole (W)	Gantanol (W)
sulfamethoxazole and trimethoprim	Bactrim DS
sulfamethoxazole-trimethoprim	Bactrim Cotrim co-trimoxazole Septra
sulfanilamide vaginal cream	AVC Vaginal
sulfasalazine	Azulfidine
sulfinpyrazone (W)	Anturane (W)
sulindac	Clinoril
Sultrin (W)	triple sulfa vaginal cream (W)
sumatriptan	Imitrex
sumatriptan inj	Alsuma Zembrace SymTouch
sumatriptan nasal powder	Onzetra Xsail
sumatriptan nasal spray	Tosymra
sumatriptan patch	Zecuity
sumatriptan; naproxen sodium	Treximet
Sumycin (WA)	*tetracycline HCl*
sunitinib malate	Sutent
Supprelin LA	histrelin acetate inj
Suprane	desflurane
Suprax (W)	cefixime (W)
Suprep	bowel prep kit oral solution (sodium sulfate/potassium sulfate/magnesium sulfates soln)
suramin	Metaret

Surfak	docusate calcium	talc, sterile aerosol	Sclerosol
Surfaxin	lucinactant intratracheal susp	taliglucerase alfa	Elelyso
Surmontil	*trimipramine maleate*	talimogene laherparepvec inj	Imlygic
Survanta	beractant	Taltz	ixekizumab
Sustiva	Efavirenz	Talwin	*pentazocine HCl*
Sustol	granisetron inj SR	Talwin Nx	*pentazocine HCl;*
Sutent	sunitinib malate		*naloxone HCl*
suvorexant	Belsomra	Talzenna	talazoparib
Sylvant	siltuximab inj	Tambocor	flecainide acetate
Symbicort	budesonide/ and	Tamiflu	oseltamivir phosphate
	formoterol fumarate	tamoxifen citrate	*tamoxifen citrate*
	inhalation	tamsulosin HCl	Flomax
Symbyax	olanzapine; fluoxetine	Tanzeum	albiglutide inj
Symdeko	tezacaftor and ivacaftor	Tapazole	*methimazole*
Symlin	pramlintide	tapentadol	Nucynta
	pramlintide acetate	Tarceva	erlotinib
Symmetrel	*amantadine HCl*	Targiniq ER	oxycodone and naloxone
Sympazan	clobazam oral film		SR
Symproic	naldemedine tosylate	Targretin	bexarotene gel
Symtuza	darunavir, cobicistat,	Tarka	trandolapril; verapamil SR
	emtricitabine, and	tarzarotene gel	Tazorac
	tenofovir alafenamide	Tasigna	nilotinib
Synagis	palivizumab	tasimelteon	Hetlioz
Synalar	*fluocinolone acetonide*	Tasmar	tolcapone
Syndros	dronabinol oral soln	tasosartan (W)	Verdia (W)
Synercid	quinupristin; dalfopristin	tavaborole topical soln	Kerydin
Synjardy SR	empagliflozin and	Tavalisse	fostamatinib disodium
	metformin HCl SR		hexahydrate
Synkayvite (W)	menadiol sodium	Tavist	*clemastine fumarate*
	diphosphate (W)	Taxol	*paclitaxel*
synopinine (W)	Florotag (W)	Taxotere	docetaxel
synthetic conjugated	Cenestin	Taxus	paclitaxel-eluting stent
estrogens, A		Tazicef	*ceftazidime*
Synthroid	*levothyroxine sodium*	Tazidime (WA)	*ceftazidime*
Synvisc	hylan G-F 20 inj	Tazorac	tarzarotene gel
	(a derivative of	tbo-filgrastim inj	Granix
	hyaluronan [sodium	TBS	tablespoon (15 mL)
	hyaluronate])		(this is a dangerous
			abbreviation)
		Tdap	tetanus toxoid, reduced
			diphtheria toxoid and
	T		acellular pertussis
			vaccine (adults and
			children 7 years and
tacrine HCl (W)	Cognex (W)		older; Adacel)
tacrolimus	Prograf	Tecentriq	atezolizumab inj
tacrolimus oint	Protopic	Tecfidera	dimethyl fumarate
tacrolimus SR	Astagraf XL	technetium Tc 99m	Lymphoseek
	Envarsus XR	tilmanocept inj	
tadalafil	Cialis	technetium Tc-99m	Cardiotec
tafenoquine	Krintafel	technetium Tc-99m	Neurolite
Tafinlar	dabrafenib	bicisate kit	
Tagamet	*cimetidine HCl*	technetium Tc-99m	Ultratag
tagraxofusp-erzs inj	Elzonris	red blood cell kit	
Tagrisso	osimertinib mesylate inj	technetium Tc-99m	Cardiolite
Takhzyro	lanadelumab inj	sestamibi	
talazoparib	Talzenna	teboroxime kit	

Technivie	ombitasvir, paritaprevir, and ritonavir
tecovirimat	Tpoxx
Teczem (W)	enalapril maleate; diltiazem malate (W)
tedizolid phosphate	Sivextro
teduglutide	Gattex
Teflaro	*ceftaroline fosamil inj*
tegaserod maleate	Zelnorm
Tegretol	carbamazepine
Tegsedi	inotersen inj
Tekturna	aliskiren aliskiren hemifumarate
telaprevir (W)	Incivek (W)
telavancin HCl	Vibativ
telbivudine	Tyzeka
Teldrin (WA)	*chlorpheniramine maleate SR*
Telepaque (W)	*iopanoic acid (W)*
telithromycin	Ketek
telmisartan	Micardis
telotristat epirate	Xermmelo
telotristat ethyl	Xermelo
temazepam	Restoril
Temodar	temozolomide
temozolomide	Temodar
temsirolimus	Torisel
tenecteplase	TNKase
Tenex	*guanfacine HCl*
teniposide	Vumon
tenofovir disoproxil fumarate	Truvada Viread
tenofovir, efavirenz and emtricitabine	Atripla
Tenoretic	*atenolol; chlorthalidone*
Tenormin	atenolol
Tensilon (WA)	*edrophonium chloride*
Tenuate (WA)	*diethylpropion HCl*
Tequin	gatifloxacin
Tequin (W)	gatifloxacin (W)
Terazol	*terconazole*
terazosin HCl	Hytrin
terbinafine HCl	Lamisil
terbutaline sulfate	terbutaline sulfate
terbutaline sulfate aerosol	Brethaire
terbutaline sulfate tablets and inj	Brethine
terbutaline sulfate tablets and inj (W)	Bricanyl (W)
terconazole	Terazol
terfenadine (W)	Seldane (W)
terfenadine; pseudoephedrine HCl (W)	Seldane D (W)
teriflunomide	Aubagio
teriparatide	Forteo
teriparatide acetate	Parathar

tesamorelin acetate inj	Egrifta
Teslac (W)	testolactone (W)
Teslascan	mangofodipir trisodium
Tessalon	benzonatate
Testim	testosterone gel
Testoderm (WA)	*testosterone transdermal*
Testoderm TTS (WA)	*testosterone transdermal*
testolactone (W)	Teslac (W)
testosterone buccal	Striant
testosterone cypionate SR	DEPO- Testosterone
testosterone enanthate inj	Xyosted
testosterone gel	AndroGel Testim
testosterone nasal gel	Natesto
testosterone transdermal	Androderm Testoderm (W) Testoderm TTS (W)
testosterone undecanoate inj	Aveed
tetanus immune globulin (human) (W)	Hyper-Tet (W)
tetanus toxoid, reduced diphtheria toxoid and acellular pertussis vaccine (Adults and children 10 years and older; Adacel)	Tdap
tetrabenazine	Xenazine
tetracaine HCl	Pontocaine
tetracycline HCl	Achromycin (WA) Sumycin
tetrahydrozoline HCl ophth	Collyrium Visine Extra
Teveten HCT	eprosartan mesylate; hydrochlorothiazide
thalidomide	Thalomid
Thalomid	thalidomide
Tham	tromethamine
Theo-Dur (WA)	*theophylline SR*
theophylline	Elixophyllin Slo-Phyllin
theophylline SR	Slo-bid Theo-Dur (WA) Uniphyl
TheraCys	BCG intravesical
Theragran	*vitamins*
thiabendazole (W)	Mintezol (W)
thiethylperazine maleate	Torecan
thioguanine	thioguanine
thiopental sodium	Pentothal
Thioplex	thiotepa
thioridazine HCl	Mellaril
thiotepa	Thioplex

711

thiothixene	Navane	Timoptic-XE	*timolol maleate ophth soln, gel forming*
Thorazine (WA)	chlorpromazine	Tinactin	tolnaftate
Thrombate III	antithrombin III (human)	Tindamax	tinidazole
thrombin, topical (human)	Evithrom	tinidazole	Tindamax
thrombin, topical (recombinant)	Recothrom	tinzaparin sodium	Innohep
		tioconazole	Vagistat-1
thymalfasin	Zadaxin	tiotropium bromide and olodeterol inhalation spray	Stiolto Respimat
Thymitaq (W)	nolatrexed dihydrochloride (W)		
Thymoglobulin	anti-thymocyte globulin, (rabbit)	tiotropium bromide inhalation powder	Spiriva HandiHaler
Thyrogen	thyrotropin alpha	tipranavir	Aptivus
thyroglobulin (W)	Proloid (W)	tirofiban HCl	Aggrastat
thyroid	*thyroid*	tisagenlecleucel inj	Kymriah
Thyrolar	liotrix	Tivicay	dolutegravir
thyrotropin (W)	Thytropar (W)	tizanidine HCl	Zanaflex
thyrotropin alpha	Thyrogen	TKM Ebola	an investigational systemically delivered ribonucleic acid interference (RNAi) therapeutic that utilizes lipid nanoparticle delivery technology for the treatment of Ebola virus infection (Tekmira Pharmaceuticals, Canada)
Thytropar (W)	thyrotropin (W)		
tiagabine HCl	Gabitril		
Tiamate	*diltiazem maleate SR*		
tianeptine Sulfate	an atypical antidepressant over-the-counter drug in the US, marketed for its anti-anxiety and antidepressant properties. Marketed outside the US as Coaxil, Stablon, and Tatinol		
		TNKase	tenecteplase
Tiazac	*diltiazem HCl SR*	TOBI	tobramycin soln for inhalation
Tibsovo	ivosidenib		
ticagrelor	Brilinta	TobraDex	tobramycin; dexamethasone oint and susp
Ticar (W)	ticarcillin disodium (W)		
ticarcillin disodium (W)	Ticar (W)		
ticarcillin; clavulanic acid	Timentin	tobramycin soln for inhalation	TOBI
TICE BCG	BCG intravesical	tobramycin sulfate ophth	Tobrex
Ticlid (WA)	*ticlopidine*		
ticlopidine	Ticlid	tobramycin; dexamethasone oint and susp	TobraDex
Tigan	*trimethobenzamide HCl*		
tigecycline inj	Fresenius	Tobrex	tobramycin sulfate ophth
	Tygacil	tocainide HCl	Tonocard
Tikosyn	dofetilide	tocilizumab	Actemra
Tilade	nedocromil inhalation	tofacitinib citrate	Xeljanz
tiludronate disodium	Skelid	Tofranil	*imipramine HCl*
Timentin	*ticarcillin; clavulanic acid*	tolazamide	Tolinase (WA)
timolol maleate	Blocadren	tolazoline (W)	Priscoline (W)
timolol maleate ophth soln	Timoptic	tolbutamide	Orinase
		tolcapone	Tasmar
timolol maleate ophth soln, gel forming	Timoptic-XE	Tolectin	*tolmetin sodium*
		Tolinase (WA)	*tolazamide*
timolol maleate; dorzolamide HCl	Cosopt	tolmetin sodium	Tolectin
		tolnaftate	Tinactin
Timoptic	timolol maleate ophth soln	tolterodine tartrate	Detrol
		tolterodine tartrate (SR)	Detrol LA

tolvaptan	Jynarque
	Samsca
tolvaptan oral	Samsca
Tonocard	tocainide HCl
Topamax	*topiramate*
Topicort	desoximetasone
topiramate	Topamax
topiramate SR	Qudexy XR
	Trokendi XR
Topomax	may have meant
	Topamax (topiramate)
Toporol	may have meant Toprol
	XL (metoprolol
	succinate SR)
topotecan HCl	Hycamtin
Toprol XL	*metoprolol succinate SR*
Toradol	*ketorolac tromethamine*
Toradol (WA)	*ketorolac tromethamine*
Torecan	thiethylperazine maleate
toremifene citrate	Fareston
Torisel	temsirolimus
Tornalate (W)	*bitolterol mesylate (W)*
torsemide	Demadex
tositumomab and	Bexxar
I-131 tositumomab	
Tosymra	sumatriptan nasal spray
Totacillin-N	ampicillin sodium
Toujeo	insulin glarine inj
Toviaz	fesoterodine fumarate
Tpoxx	tecovirimat
trabectedin inj	Yondelis
Tracleer	bosentan
Tracrium	atracurium besylate
Tradjenta	*linagliptin*
tramadol	may have meant
	tramadol (Ultram)
tramadol HCl	Ultram
tramadol HCL SR	Ultram ER; ConZip
tramadol;	Ultracet
acetaminophen	
trametenib	Mekinist
Tramodol	may have meant tramadol
	(Ultram)
Trandate	*labetalol HCl*
trandolapril	Mavik
trandolapril;	Tarka
verapamil SR	
tranexamic acid inj	Cyklokapron
tranexamic acid oral	*tranexamic acid oral*
Transderm Scop	*scopolamine transdermal*
Transderm-Nitro	*nitroglycerin transdermal*
Tranxene	*clorazepate dipotassium*
tranylcypromine	Parnate
sulfate	
trastuzumab	Herceptin
trastuzumab-dttb inj	Ontruzant
trastuzumab-Pkrb inj	Herzuma
trastuzumab-qyyp inj	Trazimera

Trasylol	aprotinin
Travasol	*amino acid inj*
Travatan Z	travoprost ophth soln
travoprost ophth soln	Travatan Z
Trazadone	may have meant
	Trazodone (Deseryl)
Trazimera	trastuzumab-qyyp inj
trazodone	Desyrel
Treanda	bendamustine HCl inj
Trecator-SC	ethionamide
Trelegy Ellipta	fluticasone furoate,
	umeclidinium, and
	vilanterol dry powder
	inhaler
Trelstar Depot	triptorelin pamoate
Trelstar LA	triptorelin pamoate
	(3 month inj)
Tremfya	guselkumab Inj
Trental	*pentoxifylline*
treprostinil sodium	Remodulin
Tresiba	Insulin degludec inj
tretinion topical	Renova
	Retin-A
tretinoin lotion	Altreno
tretinoin cream	Avita
0.025%	
tretinoin gel	Retin-A Micro
Tretten	coagulation factor
	XIII A-subunit
	(recombinant) inj
Trexall	*methotrexate tablets*
Treximet	sumatriptan; naproxen
	sodium
triamcinolone	Aristocort
triamcinolone	Kenalog
acetonide	
triamcinolone	Azmacort
acetonide aerosol	
triamcinolone	Nasacort
acetonide nasal	
inhaler	
triamcinolone	Tri-Nasal
acetonide nasal	
spray	
triamcinolone	Trivaris
acetonide ophth inj	
triamcinolone	Triesence
acetonide susp	
intraocular inj	
triamterene	Dyrenium
triamterene 37.5 mg;	Maxzide -25MG
hydrochlorothiazide	
25 mg	
triamterene 75 mg;	Maxzide
hydrochlorothiazide	
50 mg	
Triavil (WA)	*perphenazine;*
	amitriptyline HCl

T
R

triazolam	Halcion	Trobicin (W)	spectinomycin HCl (W)
Tricor	*fenofibrate*	Trogarzo	ibilizumab-uiyk inj
Tri-Cyclen	norgestimate; ethinyl estradiol	troglitazone (W)	Rezulin (W)
		Trokendi XR	topiramate SR
Tridesilon	desonide	tromethamine	Tham
Tridil (WA)	*nitroglycerin inj*	Tronothane HCl	pramoxine HCl
Tridione (W)	trimethadione (W)	TrophAmine	*amino acid inj*
Triesence	preservative-free triamcinolone acetone ophth inj	Tropicacyl (WA)	*tropicamide*
		tropicamide	Mydriacyl
			Tropicacyl
Triferic	ferric pyrophosphate citrate soln	trospium chloride	Sanctura
		trovafloxacin mesylate (W)	Trovan tablets (W)
trifluridine	Viroptic		
trifluridine and tipiracil	Lonsurf	Trovan inj (W)	alatrofloxacin mesylate IV (W)
Triglide	fenofibrate		
trihexyphenidyl HCl	Artane (W)	Trovan tablet (W)	trovafloxacin mesylate (W)
Trilafon (W)	*perphenazine*		
Trileptal	*oxcarbazepine*	Troxyca	oxycodone HCl and naltrexone HCl
Tri-Levlen	*levonorgestrel; ethinyl estradiol*		
		Trudorza Pressair	aclidinium bromide inhalation
TriLipix	fenofibric acid		
Trilisate (W)	choline magnesium trisalicylate (W)	Trulance	plecanatide
		Trulicity	dulaglutide inj
Tri-Luma	hydroquinone; tretinoin; flucinolone cream	Trumenba	meningococcal group B vaccine
trimetazidine	Livantra	Trusopt	dorzolamide HCl
trimethadione (W)	Tridione (W)	Truvada	emtricitabine and tenofovir disoproxil fumarate
trimethobenzamide HCl (D)	Tigan (D)		
trimethoprim	Primsol	Truxima	rituximab-abbs inj
trimetrexate glucuronate	Neutrexin	trypan blue ophth soln	Vision Blue
		tuberculin skin test	Aplisol
trimipramine maleate	Surmontil	*tubocurarine*	*tubocurarine*
Trimox	*amoxicillin*	tubocurarine	tubocurarine
Tri-Nasal (WA)	*triamcinolone acetonide nasal spray*	Tucks	witch hazel pads
		Tudorza Pressair	*aclidinium bromide inhalation*
Trintellix	vortioxetine (name changed from Brintellix)		
		Tums	*calcium carbonate*
		turoctocog alfa pegol inj	Esperoct
Triostat	liothyronine sodium inj		
Triphasil	*levonorgestrel; ethinyl estradiol*	Tussionex	hydrocodone polistirex; chlorphenir-amine
triple sulfa vaginal cream	Sultrin	Tussi-Organidin NR	guaifenesin; codeine phosphate
triprolidine HCl; pseudoephedrine HCl	Actifed	Twinrix	hepatitis A inactivated; hepatitis B (recombinant) vaccine
triptorelin pamoate	Trelstar Depot		
triptorelin pamoate (3 month inj)	Trelstar LA	Tygacil	tigecycline inj
		Tykerb	lapatinib
Trisenox	arsenic trioxide	Tylenol	*acetaminophen*
Tritec (W)	ranitidine bismuth citrate (W)	Tylenol #2	Tylenol with Codeine #2 (acetaminophen 300 mg with Codeine Phosphate 15 mg)
Trivaris	triamcinolone acetonide ophth inj		
Tri-Vi-Flor	vitamins A, D, & C; fluoride	Tylenol #3	Tylenol with Codeine #3 (acetaminophen 300 mg with Codeine Phosphate 30 mg)
Trizivir	lamivudine; zidovudine; abacavir sulfate		

T
Rx

Tylenol #4	Tylenol with Codeine #4 (acetaminophen 300 mg with Codeine Phosphate 60 mg
Tylenol with Codeine (#2, 3, and 4)	*acetaminophen 300 mg with Codeine Phosphate (15, 30, and 60 mg)*
Tylonal	may have meant Tylenol (acetaminophen)
Tylox (WA)	oxycodone HC; acetaminophen
Tymlos	abaloparatide inj
Typhim Vi	typhoid vaccine
typhoid vaccine	Typhim Vi
tyropanoate sodium (W)	Bilopaque (W)
Tysabri	natalizumab
Tyzeka	L-enantiomer telbivudine

U

UbiQGel	coenzyme Q10
Uceris	budesonide SR tablet
Udenyca	pegfilgrastim cbqv inj
Ulesfia	benzyl alcohol lotion
Uloric	febuxostat
Ultane	*sevoflurane*
Ultiva	remifentanil HCl
Ultomiris	ravulizumab-cwvc inj
Ultracet	*tramadol HCl; acetaminophen*
Ultralente U (W)	insulin zinc suspension, extended (beef) (W)
Ultram	*tramadol HCl*
Ultram ER	tramadol HCL SR
Ultratag	technetium Tc-99m red blood cell kit
Ultravist	iopromide
umeclidinium and vilanterol inhalation powder	Anoro Ellipta
umeclidinium inhalation powder	Incruse Ellipta
Unasyn	*ampicillin sodium; sulbactam sodium*
Unipen (WA)	*nafcillin sodium*
Uniphyl	*theophylline SR*
Uniretic	*moexipril HCl; hydrochlorothiazide*
Unisom	diphenhydramine HCl; over-the-counter sleep-aid tablets, capsules, and liquidUnisom

Unituxin	dinutuximab inj
Univasc	*moexipril HCl*
unoprostone isopropyl ophth soln (W)	Rescula (W)
Uprima (WA)	*apomorphine HCl*
Uptravi	selexipag
Urecholine	*bethanechol chloride*
uridine triacecate	Vistogard
urine protein	U-PRO
Urised (WA)	*methenamine combination*
Urispas	flavoxate HCl
urofollitropin	Bravelle
urofollitropin for inj	Fertinex
urokinase	Abbokinase
UroXatral	alfuzosin
URSO	*ursodiol*
ursodiol	Actigall
	URSO
ustekinumab	Stelara
Uvadex	methoxsalen extracorporeal administration

V

Vabomere	meropenem and vaborbactam inj
Vagifem	estradiol hemihydrate vaginal tab
Vagistat-1	tioconazole
valacyclovir	Valtrex
valbenazine	Ingrezza
Valchlor	mechlorethamine HCl inj
Valchlor Gel	mechlorethamine gel
Valcyte	valganciclovir
valdecoxib (W)	Bextra (W)
valganciclovir	Valcyte
Valium	*diazepam*
valproate sodium inj	Depacon
valproic acid	Depakene
valrubicin, (for intravesical use)	Valstar
valsartan	Diovan
valsartan; hydrochlorothiazide	Diovan HCT
Valstar	valrubicin, (for intravesical use)
Valtrex	*valacyclovir*
Vanceril (W)	beclomethasone dipropionate (W)
Vancocin	*vancomycin HCl*
vancomycin HCl	Vancocin
vancomycin HCl for oral soln	Firvanq
vandetanib	Caprelsa

Vaniqa	eflornithine HCl cream	verapamil HCl SR	Calan SR
Vantas	histrelin acetate inj		Verelan
Vantin	cefpodoxime proxetil	verapamil HCl SR	Covera HS
Vaponefrin (W)	epinephrine racemic (W)	bedtime formulation	Verelan PM
Vaprisol	conivaptan	Verdia (W)	tasosartan (W)
	conivpatan HCl	Veregen	sinecatechins oint
Vaqta	*hepatitis A vaccine*	Verelan	*verapamil HCl SR*
	inactivated	Verelan PM	*verapamil HCl SR*
vardenafil HCl	Levitra		*bedtime formulation*
varenicline tartrate	Chantix	Verluna (W)	nofetumomab (W)
varicella virus	Varivax	Vermox	mebendazole
vaccine		Versed (WA)	midazolam HCl
Varithena	polidocanol injectable	verteporfin inj	Visudyne
	foam	Verzenio	alectinib
Varivax	varicella virus vaccine	Vesanoid (WA)	*tretinoin capsules*
Varubi	rolapitant	Vesicare	solifenacin succinate
Vascepa	icosapent ethyl	Vestra	reboxetine mesylate
Vaseline	petrolatum, white	vestronidase	Mepsevil
Vaseretic	*enalapril maleate;*	alfa-vjbk inj	
	hydrochlorothiazide	Vexol	rimexolone
Vasocon	naphazoline ophth soln	Vfend	voriconazole
Vasodilan	*isoxsuprine HCl*	Viactiv	calcium carbonate;
vasopressin	Pitressin		vitamin D and K
vasopressin inj	Vasostrict		chewable
Vasostrict	vasopressin inj	Viadur (W)	leuprolide acetate
Vasotec	*enalapril maleate*		implant
Vasovist	gadofosveset trisodium inj	Viagra	sildenafil citrate
VAXELIS	Diphtheria and Tetanus	Vibativ	telavancin HCl
	Toxoids and Acellular	Viberzi	eluxadoline
	Pertussis Adsorbed,	Vibramycin	*doxycycline hyclate*
	Inactivated Poliovirus,	Vicoden	see Vicodin
	Haemophilus b	Vicodin	*hydrocodone bitartrate;*
	Conjugate		*acetaminophen*
	[Meningococcal	Vicoprofen	*hydrocodone bitartrate*
	Protein Conjugate]		*7.5 mg; ibuprofen*
	and Hepatitis B		*200 mg*
	[Recombinant]	Victoza	*liraglutide* (rDNA
	Vaccine		origin) *inj*
Vazculep	*iphenylephrine HCl inj*		liraglutide inj
Vectibix	panitumumab inj	Victrelis	*boceprevir (w)*
vecuronium bromide	Norcuron	vidarabine	Vira-A (W)
vedolizumab inj	Entyvio	monohydrate (W)	
velaglucerase alfa inj	Vpriv	Vidaza	azacitidine
Velban	vinblastine sulfate	Videx	didanosine
Velcade	bortezomib	Videx EC	*didanosine SR*
Velosef (WA)	cephradine	Viekira	ledipasvir and
Velosulin Human	insulin inj (human)		sofosbuvir; simeprevir
Velphoro	sucroferric oxyhyroxide		and sofosbuvir
vemurafenib	Zelboraf		(2 tablets)
Venclexta	venetoclax	Viekira XR	dasabuvir, ombitasvir,
venetoclax	Venclexta		paritaprevir, and
venlafaxine HCl	Effexor (WA)		ritonavir SR tablets
venlafaxine HCl SR	Effexor XR	vigabatrin	Sabril
Venofer	*iron sucrose inj*	Vigadrone	vigabatrin for soln
Ventavis	iloprost	Viibryd	*vilazodone HCl*
Ventolin	albuterol	vilazodone HCl	Viibryd
VePesid	*etoposide*	vildagliptin	Galvus
verapamil HCl	Isoptin	Vimizim	elosulfase alfa

Vimpat	lacosamide
vinblastine sulfate	Velban
vincristine sulfate	Oncovin
vincristine sulfate note: for intra-VENOUS administration only)	Oncovin
vincristine sulfate liposome inj	Marqibo
vindesine sulfate	Eldisine
vinorelbine tartrate	Navelbine
Vioform (W)	clioquinol (W)
Vioxx	rofecoxib
Vira-A	vidarabine monohydrate (W)
Viracept	nelfinavir mesylate
Viramune	nevirapine
Virazole	ribavirin
Viread	tenofovir disoproxil fumarate
Viroptic	trifluridine
Visicol	sodium phosphate tab
Visine Extra	tetrahydrozoline HCl ophth
Vision Blue	trypan blue ophth soln
Visipaque	iodixanol
Visken	*pindolol*
vismodegib	Erivedge
Vistaril	*hydroxyzine pamoate*
Vistide	cidofovir
Vistogard	uridine triacecate
Visudyne	verteporfin inj
Vit D	cholecalciferol
Vitamin D	cholecalciferol
Vitamin D3	cholecalciferol
Vitrakvi	larotrectinib
Vitrase	hyaluronidase inj (ovine)
Vitrase (W)	ovine hyaluronidase (W)
Vitrasert (W)	ganciclovir ophthalmic implant (W)
Vitravene (W)	fomivirsen sodium inj (W)
Vitrelis	*boceprevir*
Vivactil	*protriptyline HCL*
Vivelle	*estradiol transdermal system*
Vizimpro	dacomitinib
Volmax	albuterol SR
Voltaren	*diclofenac sodium*
Voltaren-XR	*diclofenac sodium SR*
von Willebrand factor [recombinant] inj	Vonvendi
Vonvendi	von Willebrand factor [recombinant] inj
vorapaxar	Zontivity
Voraxaze	glucarpidase inj
voretigene-neparvovec-rzyl subretnal inj	Luxturna

voriconazole	Vfend
vorinostat	Zolinza
vortioxetine	Brintellix
	Trintellix (name changed from Brintellix)
Vosevi	sofosbuvir, velpatasvir, and voxilaprevir
Vosol	2% acetic acid nonaqueous otic soln
Votrient	pazopanib
Vpriv	velaglucerase alfa inj
Vraylar	cariprazine
VSL#3®	a concentrated probiotic, containing 8 different strains of beneficial bacteria (the initials VSL have no meaning)
Vumon	teniposide
Vyleesi	bremelanotide inj
Vytorin	ezetimibe; simvastin
Vyvanse	lisdexamfetamine dimesylate
VYXEOS	daunorubicin and cytarabine liposome inj
Vyzulta	latanoprostene bunod ophth soln

W

warfarin sodium	Coumadin Jantoven
warfin	may have meant warfarin sodium (Coumadin)
Welbutin	may have meant Wellbutrin (bupropion HCl)
Welchol	colesevelam HCl
Wellbutrin	bupropion HCl
Wellbutrin SR	bupropion HCl SR
Wellferon	interferon ALFA-n[1] lymphoblastoid
WinRho SD	RH₀ (D) immune globulin IV (human)
Winstrol (W)	stanozolol (W)
witch hazel pads	Tucks
Wyamine (W)	mephentermine sulfate (W)
Wycillin (for IM use only)	penicillin G procaine (for IM use only)
Wygesic (W)	*propoxyphene HCl; acetaminophen (W)*
Wymox (WA)	*amoxicillin*
Wytensin (WA)	*guanabenz acetate*

X

Xadago	safinamide
Xalatan	latanoprost
Xalkori	crizotinib
Xanax	*alprazolam*
Xarelto	*rivaroxaban*
Xatmep	methotrexate oral soln
Xefo; available outside the United states	lornoxicam
Xeljanz	tofacitinib citrate
Xeloda	capecitabine
XELOX	capecitabine (Xeloda) and oxaliplatin (Eloxatin)
Xenaderm	trypsin, balsam peru, and castor oil ointment
Xenazine	tetrabenazine
Xenical	orlistat
Xeomin	incobotulinumtoxin A inj
Xepi	ozenoxacin cream
Xeralto	may have meant Xarelto (rivaroxaban)
Xerava	eravacycline inj
Xermelo	telotristat ethyl
Xermmelo	telotristat epirate
Xgeva	*denosumab inj*
Xiaflex	collagenase clostridium histolyticum inj
Xibrom	bromfenac ophth sol
Xience V	everolimus-eluting coronary stent system
Xifaxan	rifaximin
Xigduo XR	metformin and dapagliflozin SR
Xigris (W)	*drotrecogin alfa* (W)
Xiidra	lifitegrast ophth soln
Xofigo	Radium Ra 223 dichloride inj
Xofluza	baloxavir marboxil
Xolair	omalizumab
Xopenex	levalbuterol HCl inhalation soln
Xospata	gilteritinib
Xtampza ER	oxycodone SR
Xtandi	*enzalutamide*
Xtoro	finafloxacin otic susp
Xultophy	insulin degludec inj / liraglutide inj
Xylocaine HCl	*lidocaine HCl*
xylometazoline	Otrivin
Xyosted	testosterone enanthate inj
Xyrem	sodium oxybate oral soln
Xyzal	levocetirizine dihydrochloride (over-the-counter)

Y

Yasmin	drospirenone; ethinyl estradiol
Yervoy	*ipilimumab inj*
Yescarta	axicabtagene ciloleucel inj
Yondelis	trabectedin inj
Yosprala	aspirin and omeprazole
Yupelri	revefenacin for inhalation

Z

Zadaxin	thymalfasin
Zaditor	ketotifen fumarate ophth soln
zafirlukast	Accolate
Zagam (W)	Sparfloxacin (W)
zalcitabine (W)	Hivid (W)
zaleplon	Sonata
Zaltrap	ziv-aflibercept inj
Zanaflex	*tizanidine HCl*
zanamivir for inhalation	Relenza
Zanax	May have meant Xanax (alprazolam)
Zanosar	streptozocin
Zantac	*ranitidine HCl*
Zarontin	*ethosuximide*
Zaroxolyn	*metolazone*
Zarxio	filgrastim-sndz inj
Zavesca	miglustat
Zecuity	sumatriptan patch
Zejula	niraparib tosylate
Zelboraf	vemurafenib
Zelnorm	tegaserod maleate
Zembrace SymTouch	sumatriptan inj
Zemdri	plazomicin inj
Zemplar	paricalcitol
Zenapax	daclizumab
Zenpep	*pancrelipase*
Zepatier	elbasvir and grazoprevir
Zerbaxa	ceftolozane and tazobactam inj
Zerit XR	*stavudine SR*
Zerviate	cetirizine ophth soln
Zestoretic	*lisinopril; hydrochlorothiazide*
Zestril	*lisinopril*
Zetar	coal tar product
Zetia	ezetimibe
Zetonna	ciclesonide nasal aerosol
Zeuterin	zinc gluconate injection, neutralized by arginine (veterinary)

Order Form and Prices for the 16th Edition of
Medical Abbreviations: 55,000 Conveniences at the
Expense of Communication and Safety
Authored by Neil M Davis
ISBN 978-0-931431-00-5

THE BOOK (prices shown include a 1-year single-user access license to the Internet version of the book (a $20 value) which is updated with 30 new entries per week)

1–11 copies (book and Internet version)	$39.95 each plus S & H
12 or more copies (book and Internet version)	$26.65 each plus S & H

Shipping and handling charges to the 48 contiguous US states shown below

Number of books ordered	For the 48 contiguous US states
1 Book	add $8 to the cost of the book
2–6 Books	add $16 to the cost of the books
7–10 Books	add $22 to the cost of the books
12 Books	add $28 to the cost of the books

For larger orders, contact us for pricing.

For S & H costs to Hawaii, Alaska, Puerto Rico, or countries other than the USA, contact one of the sites shown below.
- Orders shipped to Pennsylvania, add 6% sales tax.
- No sales tax for other US states (subject to change)
- Purchase orders are accepted

1-YEAR, SINGLE-USER ACCESS LICENSE TO THE INTERNET VERSION OF THE BOOK (medabbrev.com is updated with over 30 new entries each week [no book, just the ever-growing Internet version])

1-year, Single-User Access License (Internet version only—no book) For computers and/or WiFi-enabled devices	$19.95

- Orders from Pennsylvania, add 6% sales tax.
- No sales tax for other US states (subject to change)
- No S & H charges
- Credit Cards or other forms of prepayment only (secure web site)

PAYABLE BY–

Visa	MasterCard	Discover
American Exp.	Check	Money Order

ORDER FROM AND MAKE CHECK PAYABLE TO–

Neil M Davis Associates
605 Louis Drive, Suite 508B
Warminster PA 18974-2830

(continued)

721

Order and Price Information—continued

ORDERS MAY BE MAILED TO THE ADDRESS ON PREVIOUS PAGE OR

Phone 215 442 7430
Fax 215 442 7432
Secure Web site www.medabbrev.com
E-mail ev@neilmdavis.com

Where applicable, please have ready your credit card number, expiration date, security code number, phone number, and mailing address.

COUNTRIES OTHER THAN THE UNITED STATES

- Pay by credit card or in US dollars through corresponding US bank or an International Money Order in US currency.
- Book Prices shown on previous page
- To obtain shipping costs or provide shipping instructions call 215 442 7430, FAX 215 442 7432 or E-mail to ev@neilmdavis.com

Information Needed on Order Form

PLEASE PRINT OR TYPE

Name

Address

City   State   Zip Code

Phone (   )

Attention (If Applicable)

Number of **books** ordered (**includes** a 1-year, single-user Internet access license) _____

Number of 1-year, single-user Internet access licenses (No book wanted) _____

PO # (If applicable) _____

Method of payment:

_____ Check or money order enclosed

_____ Visa   _____ MasterCard

_____ Discover   _____ American Express

Card Number _____

Exp. Date _____ Security Code _____

Cardholder's Name _____

Phone Number _____

Signature _____

CONCURRENT MULTI-USER ACCESS LICENSES TO THE INTERNET VERSION are available. The ability exists for you to add and control a list on abbreviations which are unique to your locale and/or organization, that would not normally appear in a national list. Hospitals and other healthcare facilities have the ability to add and control their own list of dangerous abbreviations which should not be used. To obtain a price list, a copy of the license agreement, and a no obligation, 3-week free trial call 215 442 7430, FAX 215 442 7432 or E-mail ev@medabbrev.com

Zevalin	ibritumomab tiuxetan
Ziac	*bisoprolol fumarate; hydrochlorothiazide*
Ziagen	abacavir sulfate
ziconotide	Prialt
zidovudine	Retrovir
zidovudine; lamivudine	Combivir
zileuton	Zyflo
Zinacef	*cefuroxime sodium*
Zinbryta	daclizumab inj
zinc acetate	Galzin
zinc oxide, menthol, glycerin, and lanolin oint	Calmoseptine oint
Zinecard	dexrazoxane
Zinplava	bezlotoxumab inj
Zioptan	tafluprost ophth soln
ziprasidone HCl	Geodon
Zirabev	bevacizumab-bvzr inj
Zithromax	*azithromycin*
ziv-aflibercept inj	Zaltrap
ZMAPP	an experimental serum mixture of 3 humanized monoclonal antibodies for immunological protection against the Ebola virus (Mapp Biopharmaceutical) (From Wikipedia)
ZN-DTPA	pentetate zinc trisodium (trisodium zinc diethylenetriamine-pentaacetate)
Zocor	*simvastatin*
Zofran	*ondansetron*
Zofran ODT	*ondansetron orally disintegrating tab*
Zoladex	goserelin acetate implant
zoledronic acid for inj	Zometa
zoledronic acid inj	Reclast inj
Zolgensma	onasemnogene abeparvovec-xioi inj
Zolinza	vorinostat
zolmitriptan	Zomig
zolmitriptan orally disintegrating tablet	Zomig-ZMT
Zoloft	*sertraline HCl*
zolpidem tartrate	Ambien

zolpidem tartrate sustained release tab	
Zometa	zo
Zomig	zo
Zomig-ZMT	zol dis
Zonegram	zonisam
zonisamide	Zonegram
Zontivity	vorapaxar
Zortress	*everolimus*
Zostavax	zoster vaccine l
zoster vaccine live inj	Zostavax
zoster vaccine recombinant, adjuvanted inj	Shingrix
Zosyn	*piperacillin sodium; tazobactam sodium*
Zotran	may have meant Zofran (ondansetron) or a drug marketed outside the US (Zotran [alprazolam])
Zovirax	*acyclovir*
Zubsolv	buprenorphine and naloxone
Zulresso	brexanolone inj
Zurampic	lesinurad
Zyban	bupropion HCl SR
Zydelig	idelalisib
Zydone 5/400, 7.5/400, 10/400	*hydrocodone bitartrate; acetaminophen*
Zyflo	zileuton
Zykadia	ceritinib
Zyloprim	*allopurinol*
Zymar	gatifloxacin ophth soln
Zyprexa	olanzapine
Zyrtec	*cetirizine HCl*
Zyrtec-D	cetirizine HCl; pseudoephedrine HCl SR
Zytiga	*abiraterone*
Zyvox	linezolid

References

1. Facts and Comparisons. St. Louis, MO: Wolters Kluwer Health; Facts and Comparisons, Inc. (published monthly and online)

2. Sweetman SC. Ed. Martindale: 36th edition. The Pharmaceutical Press. London, 2009 (and online).

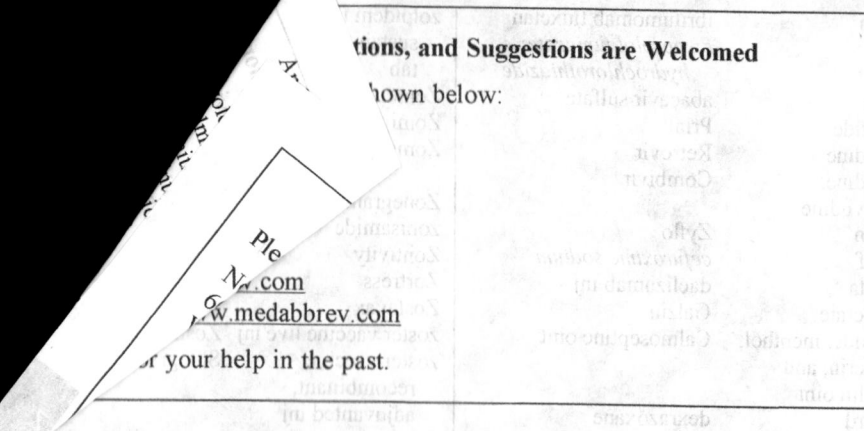

tions, and Suggestions are Welcomed

hown below:

Ple

N..com

.w.medabbrev.com

r your help in the past.

Have You Used the medabbrev.com website Version of This Book?

- It is instantaneously searchable for the meanings of abbreviations
- It is reverse searchable (search for all the abbreviations containing a particular word)
- Each week, about 30 new entries are added

See the preface (page vii) for access instructions. A one-year, single-user access is included in the purchase price of the book. Also one-year subscriptions (no book) are available for purchase.

Multi-User Site Licenses are Available

Medical facilities can substitute their own "Do Not Use" list of dangerous abbreviations for the one present. The ability also exists to list abbreviations that are unique to your region and/or organization which would normally not appear in any national list. These lists would be controlled by the facility or company. A no-cost, 3-week trial and pricing information are available by calling 215 442 7430 or via an e-mail request to ev@medabbrev.com